J. M. and M. J. Cohen

The Penguin Dictionary of

Twentieth-century Quotations

VIKING

VIKING

Published by the Penguin Group
Penguin Books Ltd, 27 Wrights Lane, London W8 5TZ, England
Penguin Books USA Inc., 375 Hudson Street, New York, New York 10014, USA
Penguin Books Australia Ltd, Ringwood, Victoria, Australia
Penguin Books Canada Ltd, 10 Alcorn Avenue, Toronto, Ontario, Canada M4V 3B2
Penguin Books (NZ) Ltd, 182–190 Wairau Road, Auckland 10, New Zealand

Penguin Books Ltd, Registered Offices: Harmondsworth, Middlesex, England

The Penguin Dictionary of Modern Quotations first published in Penguin 1971
This revised and expanded edition first published 1993
10 9 8 7 6 5 4 3 2 1

The Penguin Dictionary of Modern Quotations copyright © J. M. and M. J. Cohen, 1971, 1980
The Penguin Dictionary of Twentieth-century Quotations copyright © M. J. Cohen and
the Estate of the late J. M. Cohen, 1993

Typeset by Datix International Limited, Bungay, Suffolk
Set in 8½/10½ pt Monophoto Photina
Printed in England by Clays Ltd, St Ives plc

A CIP catalogue record for this book is available from the British Library

ISBN 0–670–82165–9

It needs no dictionary of quotations to remind me that the eyes are the windows of the soul.

MAX BEERBOHM, *Zuleika Dobson*

So writing is largely quotation, quotation newly energized, as a cyclotron augments the energies of common particles circulating.

HUGH KENNER, *The Pound Era*

I have a predilection for plays that don't depend on lines you can quote.

TOM STOPPARD, in the *Guardian*,
18 March 1988

It's a showy habit I've got . . . To be always quoting poetry and stuff. Some of us use our brains, and some of us our memories.

BARBARA TRAPIDO,
Brother of the More Famous Jack

What a good thing Adam had. When he said a good thing he knew nobody had said it before.

MARK TWAIN, *Notebooks*

Foreword

This new edition is very different from its predecessors – when it was first published over twenty years ago, its latest quotation was Richard Nixon's celebration of the first moon landing as 'the greatest week in the history of the world since the creation'. Our book was conceived as a complement to the original *Penguin Dictionary of Quotations*, a collection of twentieth-century lines that were either remembered, memorable or deserved to be recalled. But where the original dictionary of quotations was (and still is) a reference book containing thousands of classic entries that cannot be left out, from the Bible to Byron, from Shakespeare to Shaw, a modern dictionary is far more subjective, an anthology of the treasurable, drawn from the page and the screen, from songs and advertisements, from graffiti and Graham Greene. Some entries have proved ephemeral and have lost their place, but we have kept the words of First World War songs and Second World War radio catchphrases; though they may stir no memories in our younger readers, they will be recollected by older ones. We have also added large numbers from the last decade. Selection remains personal, however, and the quotation gatherer like the historian finds it easier to be judicious over the significance of his or her material when it is no longer quite contemporary.

This third edition sees a major change in policy. When the book was first published, we avoided any overlap with *The Penguin Dictionary of Quotations* itself. Since Churchill's unforgettable eulogy to the pilots of the Battle of Britain, 'Never in the field of human conflict was so much owed by so many to so few', had deserved its place in our first dictionary, we felt it should not reappear in its twentieth-century companion volume. Yet his put-down of Montgomery, 'in defeat unbeatable, in victory unbearable', appeared in *Modern Quotations*. The output of many other writers was split somewhat arbitrarily between the volumes, and readers were surprised by what seemed like glaring omissions. We have now corrected this confusing division. The greatly expanded *New Penguin Dictionary of Quotations* reaches far deeper into the twentieth century and contains all the classic lines from Churchill and Chesterton, from Auden and Orwell, while this third edition of its contemporary cousin, *The Penguin Dictionary of Modern Quotations*, now renamed *The Penguin Dictionary of Twentieth-century Quotations*, contains all these inescapable entries plus many more: a deeper trawl of Stoppard, say, with forty-four entries as opposed to the eight in the senior book. Churchill's contribution of fifty-one in *The New Penguin Dictionary of Quotations* swells to twice that number in this dictionary, allowing for such delightful descriptions as that of Foster Dulles as the 'only case I know of a bull who carries his own china shop around with him'. So *The New Penguin Dictionary of Quotations* remains the dictionary of necessary quotations extended into the 1990s, and this volume, we hope, retains its mix of the indispensable and the unfamiliar – a combination of 'I always wondered who said that' with 'I wish I had said that'.

As hunter-gatherers from more than nine decades, we have been immensely helped by the many friends and correspondents who over the years have answered our appeals for suggestions in a number of newspapers and magazines. They have raided their memories, opened their commonplace-books to us and greatly enriched our harvesting. Among those who have provided such valuable help are: Sally Adams, Brian W. Aldiss, Ian Angus, John Armatys, Sydney D. Bailey, Guy Bellamy, Philippa Bignell, Henry Blyth, Ronald Blythe, Edward Booth-Clibborn of the Design and Art Directors Association of London, Ivan Brown, John Brunner, Dr and Mrs O. Buchan, Margaret Busby, G. M. Byrne, D. Campbell, Victor Cappaert, Patrick Carey, J. L. Carr, Martin Childs, Gerald Cinamon, Charlotte Cohen, Colin Cohen, Margaret Coombs, Ian Crofton, Helena Cronin, John Dacey, Dr Peter Davison, Silvana Dean, Eilís Dillon, Vince Dowd, Wanda Ealing, T. Eldridge, Quentin Falk, Ron Farquhar, Valerie Ferguson, Peter Ford, M. Fores, John Fulford, Charles Fyffe, Michael Gilkes, Anna Girvan of USIS Reference Center, John Gloag, Jonathon Green, Colin Greenland, Frank Hancock, G. V. Hardyman, J. R. Hart, Jim Heath of the Performing Rights Society, Donald Hickling, Emma Hickman, Pat Hickman, R. D. Hill, Sunil Hiranandani, Simon Hoggart, Eric Hutton, Philip Kemp, Jim Knowlson, Arthur Koestler, Tony Lacey, Phyllis M. Lee, J. Leeman, Claire L'Enfant, Roselle Le Sauteur, Ellie Ling, K. A. Llewellyn, Cathy Ludbrook, T. J. Lustig, Kevin McDermott, Malcolm McEachran, Donald McFarlan, Peter Madgwick, John Major, Jonathan Marwil, Peter Matthews, G. Miller, Ken Mullen, Christopher Murphy, Lt.-Col. N. T. P. Murphy, Neville Osmond, Eric Partridge, H. M. Paton, R. D. Pearce, Jeremy Perkins, Frank Pike, Ben Pimlott, Nigel Price, B. Ramsay, James Reeves, B. Rochester, John M. Ross, Andrew Salkey, Ronald Searle, Dennis Sinclair, J. Sinclair, Per Skjaeveland, Finbarr Slattery, Geoffrey Smith, Godfrey Smith, R. Stanton, Stephen Stirling, Geoffrey Strachan, Melvyn Strong, Andrew Tems of the Enfield Central Library, W. J. Thaxter, Vera Thomas, Stanley Thomas, Ann Thorp, E. Trehern, Glenn Trueman, Richard Usborne, Paul Vaughan, Anne Walmsley, Richard Walters, D. Wilson, Anthony Wilttome, Edward Winter, Jon Wynne-Tyson, Igor Zaitsev.

Especial thanks are due to Ingrid von Essen, Brian Thompson and Elizabeth Teague, to Helen Jeffrey who edited this third edition with such skill, and to David Bowron who has prepared its index.

We have not always been able to trace years of birth and death and would be grateful to our readers for making good any such omissions. We gain immeasurably, as the roll call of acknowledgements above testifies, from your help and suggestions for entries. Please write to the editors c/o Penguin Books, 27 Wrights Lane, London W8 5TZ.

A

DANNIE ABSE 1923–

1 So in the simple blessing of a rainbow, / in the bevelled edge of a sunlit mirror, / I have seen, visible, Death's artifact / like a soldier's ribbon on a tunic tacked. [*The Pathology of Colours*]

GOODMAN ACE 1899–1982

2 TV – a clever contraction derived from the words Terrible Vaudeville. However, it is our latest medium – we call it a medium because nothing's well done. [Letter to Groucho Marx, *The Groucho Letters*, n.d.]

3 I would have answered your letter sooner, but you didn't send one. ['Sunday 1950']

4 All I can say is that if you read these routines and you like them, then you're the easiest guy to write for since Moses wrote the Ten Commandments after that Short Story Conference with God. [23 June 1953]

CHINUA ACHEBE 1930–

5 He was full of cliché, but then a cliché is not a cliché if you have never heard it before; and our ordinary reader clearly had not and so was ready to greet each one with the same ecstasy it must have produced when it was first coined. For Cliché is but pauperized Ecstacy. [*Anthills of the Savannah*, 1]

6 Does the blind man own his escort? No, neither do we the story; rather it is the story that owns us and directs us. It is the thing that makes us different from cattle; it is the

mark on the face that sets one people apart from their neighbours. [9]

7 Writers don't give prescriptions . . . They give head-aches! [12]

DEAN ACHESON 1893–1971

8 Great Britain has lost an Empire and not yet found a role. [Speech at West Point Military Academy, 5 Dec. 1962]

9 A memorandum is written not to inform the reader but to protect the writer. [In the *Wall Street Journal*, 8 Sept. 1977]

10 It is worse than immoral, it's a mistake. [Of USA's involvement in Vietnam. Quoted by Alistair Cooke in radio broadcast *Letter from America*]

DOUGLAS ADAMS 1952–

11 The Hitch-hiker's Guide to the Galaxy. [Title of BBC radio series and book, 1979]

12 Don't panic. [*The Hitch-hiker's Guide to the Galaxy*, preface]

13 The Answer to the Great Question of . . . Life, the Universe and Everything . . . Is . . . Forty-two. [Ch. 27]

14 It can hardly be a coincidence that no language on Earth has ever produced the expression 'as pretty as an airport'. [*The Long Dark Tea-time of the Soul*, opening words]

15 Kate's spirits sank to the very bottom of her being and began to prowl around there making a low growling noise. [Ch. 1]

16 The first ten million years were the worst . . . and the second ten million years, they were the worst too. The third ten million

years I didn't enjoy at all. After that I went into a bit of a decline. [*The Restaurant at the End of the Universe*, Ch. 18]

FRANKLIN P. ADAMS 1881–1960

1 The rich man has his motor car, / His country and his town estate. / He smokes a fifty-cent cigar / And jeers at Pate. [*The Rich Man*]

2 Yet though my lamp burns low and dim, / Though I must slave for livelihood – / Think you that I would change with him? / You bet I would!

3 The trouble with this country is that there are too many politicians who believe, with a conviction based on experience, that you can fool all of the people all of the time. [Disagreeing with Abraham Lincoln's dictum. *Nods and Becks*]

FRANK R. ADAMS 1884–1963 and WILL H. HOUGH 1882–1962

4 I Wonder Who's Kissing Her Now. [Title of song in musical *Prince of Tonight*, 1909, music by Harold Orlob]

RICHARD ADAMS 1920–

5 Many human beings say that they enjoy the winter, but what they really enjoy is feeling proof against it. [*Watership Down*, Ch. 50]

HAROLD ADAMSON 1906–1980

6 Comin' in on a Wing and a Prayer. [Title of song]

JOY ADAMSON 1910–1985

7 If there must be a lion in the household, then let it be as small as possible. [*Born Free*, Ch. 1]

CHARLES ADDAMS 1912–1988

8 What's got your back up, Quasimodo? [Cartoon caption]

RICHARD ADDINSELL 1904–1977

9 How Now, Brown Cow! [Title of number from revue *RSVP*]

GEORGE ADE 1866–1944

10 Anybody can Win unless there Happens to be a Second Entry. [*Thirty Fables in Slang*, 'The Fable of the Brash Drummer']

11 The music teacher came twice each week to bridge the awful gap between Dorothy and Chopin. [In *Dictionary of Humorous Quotations*, ed. Evan Esar]

HOMER ADKINS

12 Basic research is like shooting an arrow into the air and, where it lands, painting a target. [From *Nature*, 1984, 312.212, in *Dictionary of Scientific Quotations*, ed. A. L. Mackay]

ALFRED ADLER 1870–1937

13 [When he heard that an egocentric had fallen in love] Against whom? [In J. Bishop, *Some of My Best Friends*, 'Exponent of the Soul']

LARRY ADLER 1914–

14 Vasectomy means not ever having to say you're sorry. [Parody of line from E. Segal, *Love Story*; see 340:12. Contributed to BBC programme *Quote . . . Unquote* and recorded in book of selections from the programme, ed. N. Rees]

POLLY ADLER [US madam] 1900–1962

15 A House is Not a Home. [Title of book]

THEODOR ADORNO 1903–1969

16 In the nineteenth century the Germans painted their dream and the outcome was invariably vegetable. The French needed only to paint a vegetable and it was already a dream. [*Minima Memoralia*, Pt 1, 29]

17 In psycho-analysis nothing is true except the exaggerations.

18 The splinter in your eye is the best magnifying-glass.

19 A German is someone who cannot tell a lie without believing it himself. [2, 70]

20 True thoughts are those alone which do not understand themselves. [3, 122]

ADVERTISEMENTS

1 Beanz Meanz Heinz. [For Heinz baked beans, late 1960s. Ascr. to Ruth Watson of Young and Rubicam agency]

2 Body Odour. [B.O. For Lifebuoy soap, c. 1930]

3 Born 1820 – Still Going Strong. [For Johnnie Walker whisky, c. 1910]

4 Clunk, click, every trip. [For car safety belts, early 1970s. Ascr. to Chris Sharpe]

5 Drinka pinta milka day. [Late 1950s. Ascr. to B. Whitehead of National Milk Publicity Council]

6 Dr Williams' pink pills for pale people. [c. 1900]

7 Even your best friends won't tell you. [For Listerine mouthwash, 1920s]

8 Every picture tells a story. [For Sloane's Backache and Kidney Pills, c. 1907]

9 Finger-lickin' good. [For Kentucky Fried Chicken, 1970s]

10 Full of eastern promise. [For Fry's Turkish Delight, late 1950s]

11 Go to work on an egg. [British Egg Marketing Board, from 1957. Ascr. to Fay Weldon of Mather and Crowther agency]

12 Guinness is Good for You. [For Guinness beer. Ascr. to O. Greene of S. H. Benson agency, 1929]

13 Heineken. Refreshes the parts other beers cannot reach. [From 1975. Ascr. to Terry Lovelock *et al.* of Collett, Dickenson, Pearce and Partners in *Design and Art Direction '78*, ed. E. Booth-Clibborn]

14 I dreamed I was Cleopatra [and variants] in my Maidenform bra. [Late 1940s. Ascr. to Norman Craig and Kummel agency]

15 I'm only here for the beer. [For Double Diamond beer, 1971. Ascr. to Ros Levenstein]

16 Is your journey really necessary? [Railway poster of 1939–45 War]

17 The man from the Pru. [Used from late 1940s, but phrase of 19 cent. origin]

18 A Mars a day helps you work, rest and play. [For Mars bars, from 1960s. Ascr. to Norman Gaff]

19 My Goodness, My Guinness. [For Guinness beer. Ascr. to John Gilroy of S. H. Benson agency, 1935]

20 Penny plain, twopence coloured. [For Pollock's Toy Theatres]

21 Put a Tiger in Your Tank. [For Esso petrol, from 1964]

22 Stop me and buy one. [For Walls ice-cream, 1920s. Ascr. to Cecil Rodd]

23 That's Shell, that was. [For Shell petrol, from late 1930s]

24 *Vorsprung durch Technik.* – Advance through Technology. [For Audi cars, from late 1980s. Ascr. to Stephen Hooper of Bartle, Bogle, Hegarty agency]

25 We're number two. We try harder. [For Avis car rental, 1960s. Ascr. to Doyle, Dane and Bernbach agency]

26 What did you do in the Great War, daddy? [Recruiting poster, 1914–18 War]

27 Whiter than white. [Detergent advertisement]

28 Worth a guinea a box. [For Beecham's Pills]

29 Wot a lot I got. [For Smarties sweets, from late 1950s. Ascr. to A. Pugh of J. Walter Thompson]

30 You can take a White Horse anywhere. [For White Horse whisky, from late 1960s. Ascr. to L. Heath at KMP partnership in Nigel Rees, *Slogans*]

ADVERTISING COPYWRITER

31 *The Times* is read by the people who run the country.

The *Guardian* is read by the people who would like to run the country.

The *Financial Times* is read by the people who own the country.

The *Daily Telegraph* is read by the people who remember the country as it used to be.

The *Daily Express* is read by the people who think the country is still like that.

The *Daily Mail* is read by the wives of the men who run the country.

The *Daily Mirror* (which once tried to run the country) is read by the people who think they run the country.

The *Morning Star* is read by people who would like another country to run the country.

The *Sun* – well, Murdoch has found a gap in the market – the oldest gap in the world. [F. Hirsch and D. Gordon, *Newspaper Money*, Ch. 4, epigraph]

Æ *see* RUSSELL, GEORGE

PROFESSOR ABEL AGANBEGYAN 1932–

1 You only find complete unanimity in a cemetery. [On Russian economic reforms. In the *Guardian*, 27 June 1987]

HERBERT AGAR 1897–1980

2 The truth that makes men free is for the most part the truth which men prefer not to hear. [*A Time for Greatness*, Ch. 7]

JAMES AGATE 1877–1947

3 The leader-writer in a great Northern daily said on the morning after King Edward died that if he had not been a king he would have been the best type of sporting publican. [*Ego 1*, 1935]

4 Is the Pathetic Fallacy less fallacious than we think? [*Ego 4*, 10 June 1940]

5 Long experience has taught me that in England nobody goes to the theatre unless he or she has bronchitis. [*Ego 6*. See also 338:14]

6 I like listening to it [Tchaikovsky's Fifth] just as I like looking at a fuchsia drenched with rain. [*Ego 8*, 1947]

JAMES AGEE 1909–1955

7 If music be the breakfast food of love, kindly do not disturb until lunch time. [On Hollywood musicals. In *Age of Film*]

VICE-PRESIDENT SPIRO T. AGNEW 1918–

8 To some extent, if you've seen one city slum you've seen them all. [Speech during election campaign at Detroit, 18 Oct. 1968]

JONATHAN AITKEN, MP 1942–

9 If you asked her [Margaret Thatcher] about Sinai, she would probably think it was the plural for sinus. [In James Prior, *The Balance of Power*, p. 107]

ANNA AKHMATOVA 1889–1966

10 Only the dusty flowers, / the clank of censers, and tracks / leading from somewhere to nowhere. [*Requiem 1935–1940*, v, trans. Richard McKane]

11 But in the room of the banished poet / Fear and the Muse stand watch by turn, and the night falls, / without the hope of dawn. [*Voronezh* (written after her visit to the banished Osip Mandelstam there), trans. S. Kunitz and M. Hayward]

12 [When asked what Robert Frost looked like] He's a grandfather turned into a grandmother. [Quoted by Joseph Brodsky in interview with D. M. Thomas in *Quarto*, Dec. 1981]

ZOË AKINS 1886–1958

13 The Greeks Had a Word for It. [Title of play]

ALAIN [ÉMILE AUGUSTE CHARTIER] 1868–1951

14 Nothing is more dangerous than an idea when that's the only one you have got. [*Propos sur la religion*, 74]

15 What is fictitious in a novel is not so much the story but the method by which thought develops into action, a method which never occurs in daily life. [In E. M. Forster, *Aspects of the Novel*, 3]

EDWARD ALBEE 1928–

16 Who's Afraid of Virginia Woolf? [Title of play]

17 Musical beds is the faculty sport around here. [*Who's Afraid of Virginia Woolf?*, Act I]

18 I have a fine sense of the ridiculous, but no sense of humour.

19 Until you start ploughing pertinent wives, you really aren't working. The way to a man's heart is through his wife's belly and don't you forget it. [II]

1 You gotta have a swine to show you where the truffles are.

RICHARD ALDINGTON 1892–1962

2 Wearily the sentry moves / Muttering the one word: 'Peace.' [*Picket*]

3 Kill winter with your cannon / Hold back Orion with your bayonets / And crush the spring leaf with your armies. [*In the Trenches*]

BRIAN ALDISS 1925–

4 Hubris clobbered by Nemesis. [Shortest definition of science fiction. *Science Fiction Art*, Introduction]

5 Science fiction is no more written for scientists than ghost stories are written for ghosts. [*Penguin Science Fiction*, Editor's Introduction]

6 Keep violence in the mind / Where it belongs. [*Barefoot in the Head*]

VICENTE ALEIXANDRE 1898–1984

7 Poetry must be human. If it is not human, it is not poetry. [Interview on receiving the Nobel Prize. In the *Observer*, 'Sayings of the Week', 9 Oct. 1977]

SAMUEL ALEXANDER

8 Evil is not . . . wholly evil; it is misplaced good. [*Space, Time and Deity*]

NELSON ALGREN 1909–1981

9 He [Algren] shunts aside all rules, regulations, and dicta, except for three laws he says a nice old Negro lady once taught him: Never play cards with any man named 'Doc'. Never eat at any place called 'Mom's'. And never, ever, no matter what else you do in your whole life, *never* sleep with anyone whose troubles are worse than your own. [H. E. F. Donohue, *Conversations with Nelson Algren*, Foreword]

MUHAMMAD ALI [CASSIUS CLAY] 1942–

10 I am the greatest. [Slogan first used in Nov. 1962]

11 Float like a butterfly, sting like a bee. [Career slogan. Ascr. to Drew 'Bundini' Brown in the *New York Herald Tribune*, 26 Feb. 1964]

FRED ALLEN [JOHN F. SULLIVAN] 1894–1956

12 A celebrity is a person who works hard all his life to become known, then wears dark glasses to avoid being recognized. [*Treadmill to Oblivion*]

13 A conference is a gathering of important people who singly can do nothing, but together can decide that nothing can be done. [In Jonathon Green, *Cynic's Lexicon*]

14 A gentleman is any man who wouldn't hit a woman with his hat on. [In Laurence J. Peter, *Peter's Quotations*]

HERVEY ALLEN 1889–1949

15 Religions change: beer and wine remain. [*Anthony Adverse*, Pt. 1, Ch. 3, sect. xx]

WOODY ALLEN 1935–

16 Is sex dirty? Only if it's done right. [In film *All You've Ever Wanted to Know about Sex*]

17 The food in this place is really terrible. Yes, and such small portions. That's essentially how I feel about life. [In film *Annie Hall*, scripted with Marshall Brickman]

18 Fun? that was the most fun I've ever had without laughing. [Of sex]

19 I was thrown out of NYU my freshman year . . . for cheating on my metaphysics final. You know I looked within the soul of the boy sitting next to me.

20 I would have killed myself but I was in analysis with a strict Freudian and if you kill yourself . . . they make you pay for the sessions you miss.

21 Hey, don't knock masturbation! It's sex with someone I love.

22 You can't ride two horses with one behind. [In film, *Broadway Danny Rose*]

23 If it bends, it's funny; if it breaks, it's not funny. [In film *Crimes and Misdemeanours*]

24 Showbusiness is worse than dog eat dog, it's dog doesn't return other dog's phone calls.

1 Catholicism – that's die now and pay later. [In film *Hannah and Her Sisters*]

2 And if it turns out that there is a God, I don't believe that he is evil. The worst that can be said is that he's an under-achiever. [In film *Love and Death*]

3 Well, I'm old-fashioned. I don't believe in extramarital relationships. I think people should mate for life, like pigeons or Catholics. [In film *Manhattan*, scripted with Marshall Brickman]

4 I'm short enough and ugly enough to succeed on my own. [In film *Play It Again Sam*]

5 I'm married. I-I-I just met a wonderful new man. He's fictional, but you can't have everything. [In film *The Purple Rose of Cairo*]

6 I'm really a timid person – I was beaten up by Quakers. [In film *Sleeper*, scripted with Marshall Brickman]

7 My brain: it's my second favourite organ.

8 I worked with Freud in Vienna. Um yes, we, we broke over the concept of penis envy. Freud felt that it should be limited to women. [In film *Zelig*]

9 Eternal nothingness is OK if you're dressed for it. [*Getting Even*, 'My Philosophy']

10 Not only is there no God, but try getting a plumber on weekends.

11 Then Job fell to his knees and cried to the Lord, 'Thine is the kingdom and the power and the glory. Thou hast a good job. Don't blow it.' [*Without Feathers*, 'The Scrolls']

12 The lion and the calf shall lie down together but the calf won't get much sleep.

13 It's not that I'm afraid to die. I just don't want to be there when it happens. ['Death (A Play)']

14 Money is better than poverty, if only for financial reasons. ['The Early Essays']

15 It was partially my fault we got divorced . . . I had a tendency to place my wife under a pedestal. [In Chicago nightclub, Mar. 1964]

16 For a while we pondered whether to take a vacation or get a divorce. We decided that a trip to Bermuda is over in two weeks but a divorce is something you always have. [In *Time* magazine, 3 July 1972]

17 I do not believe in the afterlife, although I am bringing a change of underwear.

18 All that sun and the streets are so clean. Have you ever considered why? All the garbage is on television. [On Hollywood. In *New Woman*, Mar. 1989, variant in film *Annie Hall*]

19 My parents were very old world. They come from Brooklyn which is the heart of the Old World. Their values in life are God and carpeting. [In Adler and Feinman, *Woody Allen: Clown Price of American Humor*, Ch. 2]

20 I am an only child. I have one sister.

21 I want to tell you a terrific story about oral contraception. I asked this girl to sleep with me and she said 'no'.

22 I am at two with nature. [3]

23 Some guy hit my fender the other day, and I said unto him. 'Be fruitful, and multiply.' But not in those words.

24 I asked the girl if she could bring a sister for me. She did. Sister Maria Teresa. It was a very slow evening. We discussed the New Testament. We agreed that He was very well adjusted for an only child.

25 And my parents finally realize that I'm kidnapped and they snap into action immediately: they rent out my room. [In E. Lax, *Woody Allen and His Comedy*]

26 My one regret in life is that I am not someone else. [Epigraph]

27 Death is an acquired trait. [Ch. 11]

28 I don't want to achieve immortality through my work . . . I want to achieve it through not dying. [12]

29 There have been times when I've thought about suicide – but with my luck it would probably turn out to be only a temporary solution. [In *Apt and Amusing Quotations*, ed. G. F. Lamb, 'Death']

30 Basically my wife was immature. I'd be at home in the bath and she'd come in and sink my boats. [In *Nudge Nudge, Wink Wink*, ed. Nigel Rees, 12]

31 My wife got the house, the car, the bank account, and if I marry again and have children, she gets them too. [In *Was It Good for You Too?*, ed. Bob Chieger]

LINCOLN ALLISON 1946–

1 I rarely drink alone where I'm known; they always think you've quarrelled with your wife. [In *New Society*, 20 Mar. 1980]

LISA ALTHER 1944–

2 If this was adulthood, the only improvement she could detect in her situation was that now she could eat dessert without eating her vegetables. [*Kinflicks*, Ch. 2]

3 People knew a man by the company he kept, but they generally knew a woman by the man who kept her.

4 There was nothing wrong with her that a vasectomy of the vocal cords wouldn't fix. [4]

5 He picked her up out of the dirt and turned her into the clod she was today. [*Original Sins*, Pt 4, Ch. 1]

ROBERT ALTMAN 1922–

6 After all, what's a cult? It just means not enough people to make a minority. [Interview in the *Guardian*, 11 Apr. 1981]

LEO AMERY 1873–1955

7 Speak for England. [To Arthur Greenwood, spokesman for the Labour Party, in House of Commons, 2 Sept. 1939, but Harold Nicolson, in his diary, attr. the words to Robert Boothby]

8 You have sat too long here for any good you have been doing. Depart, I say, and let us have done with you. In the name of God, *go!* [Speech, repeating Cromwell's words, addressed to Neville Chamberlain's government, House of Commons, 7 May 1940]

SIR KINGSLEY AMIS 1922–

9 The point about white burgundies is that I hate them myself . . . so closely resembling a cold chalk soap and alum cordial with an additive or two to bring it to the colour of children's pee. [*The Green Man*, 'The Red-haired Woman']

10 I have never understood why anybody agreed to go on being a rustic after about 1400. ['Dr Thomas Underhill']

11 If there's one word which sums up everything that's gone wrong since the war, it's 'workshop'. [*Jake's Thing*]

12 Lucky Jim. [Title of novel]

13 He thought what a pity it was that all his faces were designed to express rage or loathing. Now that something had happened that really deserved a face, he'd none to celebrate it with. As a kind of token, he made his Sex Life in Ancient Rome face. [*Lucky Jim*, Ch. 25]

14 Outside every fat man there is an even fatter man trying to close in. [*One Fat Englishman*, Ch. 3. See also 88:24, 286:14, 392:25, 401:20]

15 He was of the faith chiefly in the sense that the church he currently did not attend was Catholic. [8]

16 It was no wonder that people were so horrible when they started life as children. [14]

17 The rewards for being sane may not be very many but knowing what's funny is one of them. [*Stanley and the Women*, Pt 2]

18 Work was like cats were supposed to be: if you disliked and feared it and tried to keep out of its way, it knew at once and sought you out and jumped on your lap and climbed all over you to show how much it loved you. Please God, he thought, don't let me die in harness. [*Take A Girl Like You*, Ch. 5]

19 Feeling a tremendous rakehell, and not liking myself much for it, and feeling rather a good chap for not liking myself much for it, and not liking myself at all for feeling rather a good chap. [*That Uncertain Feeling*, Ch. 7]

20 More will mean worse. [Of expansion of higher education. In *Encounter*, July 1960]

21 Tapped untalent. [On *Robbins Report on Higher Education*, which suggested that higher education should cater for 'the untapped talent']

22 She [Margaret Thatcher] doesn't sound compassionate, I agree. And she hasn't got compassionate hair. If you want compassionate hair you have to go to Shirley Williams. [Interview with John Mortimer in the *Sunday Times Books*, 18 Sept. 1988]

MARTIN AMIS 1949–

1 Someone watches over us when we write. Mother. Teacher. Shakespeare. God. [*London Fields*]

2 The middle-management of Manhattan stared on, their faces as thin as credit cards. [*Money*, p. 32]

3 Martina is not a woman of the world. She is a woman of somewhere else. [134]

4 We don't really go that far into other people, even when we think we do. We hardly ever go in and bring them out. We just stand at the jaws of the cave, and strike a match, and ask quickly if anybody's there. [310]

5 Spielberg, the most popular, is bright and articulate, but his idea of intellection is to skip an hour's TV. [On cinema directors. *The Moronic Inferno*, 'Brian De Palma']

6 When success happens to an English writer, he acquires a new typewriter. When success happens to an American writer, he acquires a new life. ['Kurt Vonnegut']

7 Prohibition came too late and stopped too early for the good of American prose. ['The Great American Mix', *Observer*, 16 Feb. 1986]

8 Most writers need a wound, either physical or spiritual. [Interview with John Updike in the *Observer*, 30 Aug. 1987]

CLIVE ANDERSON 1952–

9 Is there no beginning to your talents? [To Jeffrey Archer in Channel 4 TV series *Clive Anderson Talks Back*, and in the *Independent on Sunday*, 1 Dec. 1991]

HARRY ANDERSON

10 Beer, beer, glorious beer, / Fill yourself right up to here. [*Beer*, written by Steve Leggett and Will Godwin]

MAXWELL ANDERSON 1888–1959 and LAURENCE STALLINGS 1894–1968

11 What Price Glory? [Title of play]

ROBERT ANDERSON 1917–

12 All you're supposed to do is every once in a while give the boys a little tea and sympathy. [*Tea and Sympathy*, Act I]

SHERWOOD ANDERSON 1876–1941

13 The beaten, ignorant, Bible-ridden, white South. [In Arthur M. Schlesinger Jr, *The Politics of Upheaval*, Pt. I, Ch. 4, sect. v]

TERRY ANDERSON [Hostage in Beirut] 1947–

14 People are capable of doing an awful lot when they have no choice and I had no choice. Courage is when you have choices. [In the *Observer*, 'Sayings of the Week', 10 May 1992]

GIULIO ANDREOTTI 1919–

15 [When asked how his party, the Christian Democrats, had remained in government in Italy for over 35 years almost continuously without being worn out] Political power wears out those who have not got it. [In the *New Statesman*, 19 July 1985]

SIR NORMAN ANGELL 1872–1967

16 The Great Illusion. [Title of book, 1910, which proved that war could not pay]

MAYA ANGELOU 1928–

17 Life loves the liver of it. [In *Conversations with M.A.*, ed. Jeffrey M. Elliot]

ANNA

18 The diffrense from a person and an angel is easy: Most of an angel is in the inside and most of a person on the outside. [Fynn, *Mister God, This Is Anna*, Ch. 1]

ANNE, PRINCESS ROYAL 1950–

19 When I appear in public people expect me to neigh, grind my teeth, paw the ground and swish my tail – none of which is easy. [In the *Observer*, 'Sayings of the Week', 22 May 1977]

ANONYMOUS

Epigrams

20 An actuary is someone who finds accountancy too exciting. [Definition quoted by Richard Boston in the *Guardian*, 20 July 1987]

1 Bigamy is having one husband too many. Monogamy is the same. [A woman. Epigraph to Erica Jong, *Fear of Flying*, Ch. 1]

2 Black is beautiful. [Black Power slogan]

3 Blessed are the cracked, for they shall let in the light. [In David Weeks with Kate Ward, *Eccentrics: The Scientific Investigation*, Ch. 3]

4 A camel is a horse designed by a committee.

5 The future is not what it was. [Attr. to an anonymous professor of economics by Bernard Levin in the *Sunday Times*, 22 May 1977]

6 Half of Christendom worships a Jew, and the other half a Jewess. [In H. L. Mencken, *New Dictionary of Quotations*]

7 He is a real pessimist – he could look at a doughnut and only see the hole in it. [In P. and J. Holton, *Quote and Unquote*]

8 An intellectual – one educated beyond the bounds of common sense.

9 A liberal is a conservative who has been arrested. [In Tom Wolfe, *The Bonfire of the Vanities*, Ch. 24]

10 Living in the past has one thing in its favour – it's cheaper. [In *Dramatists' Guild Bulletin*, 1963]

11 The local definition [in South Africa] of a patriot is a man who cannot sell his house. [Quoted by Denis Healey in the *Observer*, 6 July 1986]

12 Logic is the art of going wrong with confidence. [In W. H. Auden, *A Certain World*]

13 Marriage is an attempt to change a night owl into a homing pigeon.

14 Military justice is to justice as military music is to music. [In Max Ophuls's film *The Memory of Justice*]

15 The new definition of psychiatry is the care of the id by the odd. [In M. B. Strauss, *Familiar Medical Quotations*]

16 A pessimist is a man who is never happy unless he is miserable; even then he is not pleased. [In C. Hunt, *The Best Howlers*]

17 A pessimist is just a well-informed optimist. [Quoted by Robert Mackenzie in the BBC TV programme *24 Hours*, 18 Mar. 1968, as current Czech aphorism on Dubček's government]

18 A politician is an animal who can sit on a fence and yet keep both ears to the ground. [In H. L. Mencken, *New Dictionary of Quotations*]

Poems

19 And not / to spot / the purer / Führer. [Continuation of W. N. Ewer's: 'How odd / Of God / To choose / The Jews'. See 121:17 for original lines]

20 Clean-limbed American boys are not like any others. / Only clean-limbed American boys have mothers. [An American. In review in *The Times Literary Supplement*, 1964]

21 Dear Sir, your astonishment's odd, / I am always about in the quad, / And that's why the tree / Continues to be / As observed by yours faithfully, God. [Limerick riposte to earlier limerick by Ronald Knox; see 215:16]

22 The god-men say when die go sky / Through Pearly Gates where river flow, / The god-men say when die we fly / Just like eagle-hawk and crow – / Might be, might be; but I don't know. [North Australian aborigine version of Christianity]

23 *Heaven* is where / the police are British / the cooks are French / the engineers are German / the administrators are Swiss / and the lovers are Italian.
Hell is where / the police are German / the cooks are British / the engineers are Italian / the administrators are French / and the lovers are Swiss. [Letter in the *Independent*, 2 June 1990]

24 I don't like the family Stein! / There is Gert, there is Ep, there is Ein. / Gert's writings are punk, / Ep's statues are junk, / Nor can anyone understand Ein. [In Robert Graves and Alan Hodge, *The Long Weekend*, Ch. 12]

25 If she were cast as Lady Godiva the horse would steal the act. [Of a certain actress]

26 I'm sixty-one today, / A year beyond the barrier, / And what was once a Magic Flute / Is now a Water Carrier.

27 Little nips of whisky, little drops of gin, / Make a lady wonder where on earth she's bin.

Anonymous

Sayings

1 American women like quiet men: they think they're listening.

2 The best contraceptive is a glass of cold water: not before or after, but instead. [Pakistan delegate at International Planned Parenthood Federation Conference]

3 [A Bloomingdale executive, when asked by Rupert Murdoch why that famous store was not advertising in Murdoch's loss-making *New York Post*] But Rupert, Rupert, your readers are my shop-lifters! [In review of Michael Leapman's *Barefaced Cheek* in the *Guardian*, 7 July 1983]

4 Delightfully simple. It is refreshing to meet a man who has played the piano for twenty years in a brothel. [On Attlee and the Lynskey Inquiry. In O. Brown, *The Extended Tongue*]

5 The Eagle has landed. [NASA announcement of landing of moon module, 21 July 1969. See also 171:21]

6 The eternal triangle. [Book review in the *Daily Chronicle*, 5 Dec. 1907]

7 God don't come when you want Him but He's right on time. [Jazz historian. In Tennessee Williams, *Memoirs*]

8 He [W. H. Auden] didn't love God, he just fancied him. [In *Dictionary of Twentieth Century Quotations*, ed. Nigel Rees]

9 He [H. G. Wells] sold his birthright for a pot of message. [Quoted by George Lyttelton in letter, 24 Jan. 1962, *Lyttelton–Hart-Davis Letters*, ed. Rupert Hart-Davis, Vol. 3]

10 The Irish don't know what they want and won't be happy till they get it. [Infantry officer, 1975]

11 It isn't the wild ecstatic leap across I deplore. It's the weary trudge home. [On double beds versus single beds]

12 [When asked what working for Robert Maxwell was like] It's most exciting. He always has 10 balls in the air at the same time, and two of them are mine.

13 It's not the bullet with my name on it that worries me. It's the one that says 'to whom it may concern'. [A Belfast resident. In the *Observer*, 'Sayings of the Week', 20 Oct. 1991]

14 It was said that he [Ernest Bevin] never ceased to regard the Soviet Union as a breakaway organization from the Transport and General Workers' Union. [Quoted by Michael Foot in the *Observer*, 19 Oct. 1980]

15 A king is a thing men have made for their own sakes, for quietness' sake, just as in a family one man is appointed to buy meat. [A Spaniard in justification of the monarchy. In Richard Hoggart and Douglas Johnson, *An Idea of Europe*]

16 Montezuma's revenge. [Proverbial nickname for digestive complaint suffered by European visitors to Mexico]

17 Mrs Thatcher may be a woman but she isn't a sister. [Feminist writer at the time of 1979 general election. In the *Observer*, 7 Oct. 1979]

18 ADMIRING FRIEND: My, that's a beautiful baby you have there!
MOTHER: Oh, that's nothing – you should see his photograph! [In Daniel Boorstin, *The Image*, Ch. 1]

19 The Navy's here! [Call on boarding German commerce destroyer *Altmark* carrying British prisoners. In Winston S. Churchill, *The Gathering Storm*, Ch. 31]

20 Never put a hot baby on a cold slab.

21 The only man who could bend over backwards and forwards at the same time. [Of Kurt Waldheim. In the *Sunday Times*, 17 Nov. 1985]

22 The only reason so many people attended his funeral was they wanted to make sure he was dead. [Of Louis B. Mayer, the movie mogul. In Leslie Halliwell, *Filmgoer's Book of Quotes*, Some attr. to Samuel Goldwyn]

23 Only the other evening I picked up Bertrand Russell, and I said to him: 'Well, Lord Russell, what's it all about?' and, do you know, he couldn't tell me. [A taxi-driver to T. S. Eliot. In *The First Cuckoo*, ed. Kenneth Gregory]

24 Regret cannot come today: have not yet got home yesterday. [Telegram attr. to employee during traffic crisis]

25 She makes you think you married too soon. [A New York taxi-driver on Deborah Kerr's arrival there. In the *Sunday Times*, 8 Mar. 1987]

1 She's a well-balanced girl. She has a chip on each shoulder. [See also 310:1]

2 Sitting in a cloud of wasps eating an ant sandwich. [Definition of an English picnic. See also 390:2]

3 Talent is what a man possesses and genius what possesses man. [Isaac Stern quoting 'a famous English writer' in BBC TV Levin interview. In the *Listener*, 9 June 1983]

4 *Teppichfresser!* – Animal that chews the carpet! [German editor of Adolf Hitler. In W. L. Shirer, *The Rise and Fall of the Third Reich*, Ch. 12]

5 There are only four problems with Soviet agriculture: spring, summer, autumn and winter. [In the *Sunday Times*, 17 Nov. 1985]

6 [An Italian immigrant, when asked to say what 40 years of American life had taught him] There is no free lunch. [In Alistair Cooke, *America*, Epilogue]

7 These are my principles and if you don't like them, I have others.

8 The trains run to time. [Common remark in praise of Italian Fascism]

9 The trouble with self-made men is that they're working with inferior materials. [In *Picking on Men*, comp. Judy Allen]

10 Two anarchists talking: 'What time is it by your bomb?' [In *Geoffrey Madan's Notebooks*, ed. J. A. Gere and John Sparrow, 'Humorous and Memorable']

11 Walk out backwards so I'll think you're coming home. [Attr. to country and western lyric writer]

12 We are Upper Volta, but with missiles. [A Soviet member of Politburo. Political joke current 1988–9]

13 We'd rather eat grass standing up than eat beef on our knees. [Nicaraguan saying quoted by Charlotte Cornwell in *Time Out*, 22–8 Mar. 1984]

14 We pretend to work and they pretend to pay us. [Russian workers' joke. In the *Listener*, 16 June 1988]

15 We're like mushrooms: we're kept in the dark all the time, and every now and again someone opens a door and throws a heap of manure all over us. [Of the ignorance of the Cabinet in the Callaghan government. In S. Hoggart, *On the House*, p. 100]

16 What is the difference between Capitalism and Communism? Capitalism is the exploitation of man by man; Communism is the reverse. [Polish joke. In R. T. Tripp, *International Thesaurus of Quotations*]

17 When I [an old Oklahoma farmer] was a young man we had ten cows and we did very well. When I was thirty we had twenty cows and we did no better. When I was forty we had forty cows and we were barely making it. Now I'm seventy and we have seventy cows, we are not making it at all, and it's all the fault of the Agricultural Extension Service. [In D. A. Schon, *Change and Industrial Society*]

18 While he [Tolstoy] lived no man needed to feel an orphan. [In the *Sunday Times*, 31 Dec. 1989]

19 You could walk through Ronald Reagan's deepest thoughts without getting your ankles wet. [A US senator in BBC TV documentary on presidential election, 27 Oct. 1980]

20 You had to stand in line to hate him. [Of Harry Cohn of Columbia Pictures. In Barry Norman, *The Hollywood Greats*, Preface]

Slogans

21 A bayonet is a weapon with a worker at each end. [British pacifist slogan, 1940]

22 Be like Dad, keep Mum. [Ministry of Information slogan, 1941]

23 Be Realistic: Demand the Impossible. [Slogan of 1968. In the *Listener*, 20 Apr. 1988]

24 Careless talk costs lives. [British slogan, 1940; US version: 'Loose talk costs lives']

25 *Deutschmark über Alles.* [Placard at rally for German reunification in Dresden. In the *Independent*, 'Quote Unquote', 16 Dec. 1989]

26 Every government carries a health warning. [Badge slogan, 1976]

27 I Like Ike. [Button slogan, 1947, encouraging Eisenhower to run as president. Ascr. to Henry D. Spalding in *Oxford Dictionary of Modern Quotations*, ed. Tony Augarde]

28 *Ils ne passeront pas.* – They shall not pass. [Watchword during defence of Verdun, 1916; see 295:14. The phrase was used again

during the defence of Madrid by the government, 1936–8, in the Spanish form of *¡no pasarán!*; see 185:2]

1 I'm backing Britain. [Slogan of 1968]

2 Join the Army, see the world, meet interesting people and kill them. [Pacifist slogan, 1970s]

3 Keep on trucking.

4 Lousy but loyal. [East End slogan at King George V's Jubilee, 1935]

5 Make love, not war. [Hippie slogan, 1960s]

6 Old lawyers never die – they just lose their appeal. [On a mug of John Mortimer, in the *Observer*, 20 Feb. 1983]

7 Say it loud, we're gay and we're proud ... Two, four six, eight, gay is just as good as straight ... Three, five, seven, nine, lesbians are mighty fine. [Gay Liberation Front slogans. In Jeffrey Weeks, *Coming Out, Homosexual Politics in Britain from the Nineteenth Century to the Present*]

8 Think globally, act locally. [Ecological slogan quoted by Fritjof Capra]

9 Why does free love cost so much? [Button slogan. In Robert Reisner, *Graffiti*, 'Love']

Songs

10 The bells of hell go ting-a-ling-a-ling / For you but not for me. [Song of 1914–18 War]

11 Casey Jones, he mounted to the cabin, / Casey Jones, with his orders in his hand! / Casey Jones, he mounted to the cabin, / Took his farewell trip into the promised land. [*Casey Jones*, c. 1905]

12 If the sergeant steals your rum, / Never mind! [Soldier's song of 1914–18 War]

13 My brother's a slum missionary / Saving young virgins from sin: / He'll save you a blonde for a shilling – / By God, how the money rolls in. [Song. In T. R. Ritchie, *The Singing Street*]

14 Nice one, Cyril. / Nice one, son! / Nice one, Cyril. / Let's have another one! [Advertising slogan, became football chant, prompted by Cyril Knowles]

15 A poor aviator lay dying / At the end of a bright summer's day; / And his comrades were gathered around him / To carry his fragments away. [*A Poor Aviator*, sung in Korea, 1954, but dates from 1914–18 War. In Alan Lomax, *Folk Songs of North America*, No. 234]

16 Take the manifolds out of my larynx / And the cylinders out of my brain, / Take the piston rods out of my kidneys, / And assemble the engine again.

17 She was poor but she was honest, / Victim of the squire's whim: / First he loved her, then he left her, / And she lost her honest name. [Song of 1914–18 War, of which there are many versions]

18 Wash me in the water / Where you wash your dirty daughter / And I shall be whiter / Than the whitewash on the wall. [Song of 1914–18 War: *The Top of the Dixie Lid*]

19 We are Fred Karno's Army, / The ragtime infantry; / We cannot fight, we cannot shoot, / What bloody good are we! [Song of 1914–18 War, sung to hymn tune]

20 We're here because we're here because we're here because we're here. [US song of 1914–18 War]

JEAN ANOUILH 1910–1987

21 Love is, above all, the gift of oneself. [*Ardèle*, Act II]

22 Everybody's honest in one way or another. The trouble is, there's only one official way. [*Dinner with the Family*, Act III]

23 The object of art is to give life a shape. [*The Rehearsal*, Act I, sc. ii]

24 Apart from my amnesia, my memory's very good. [*Traveller without Luggage*, Act II, sc. i]

25 Man dies when he wants, as he wants, of what he chooses. [Attr.]

GUILLAUME APOLLINAIRE 1880–1918

26 *Ah Dieu! que la guerre est jolie / Avec ses chants ses longs loisirs* – Ah God, how pretty war is with its songs, its long rests! [*L'adieu du cavalier*]

1 *Voie lactée ô sœur lumineuse / Des blancs ruisseaux de Chanaan / Et des corps blancs des amoureuses / Nageurs morts suivrons-nous d'ahan / Ton cours vers d'autres nébuleuses –* Milky Way, O shining sister of the white streams of Canaan and the white bodies of women in love, shall we follow your track towards other nebulae, panting like dead swimmers? [*La chanson du mal-aimé*]

2 *Les souvenirs sont cors de chasse / Dont meurt le bruit parmi le vent –* Memories are hunting-horns, whose noise dies away in the wind. [*Cors de chasse*]

3 *Bergère ô tour Eiffel troupeau des ponts bêle ce matin. –* Shepherdess O Eiffel Tower the herd of bridges is bleating this morning. [*Zone*]

SIR EDWARD APPLETON 1892–1965

4 I do not mind what language an opera is sung in so long as it is a language I don't understand. [In the *Observer*, 'Sayings of the Week', 28 Aug. 1955]

YASSER ARAFAT 1930–

5 I am challenging Israel to peace. [On Palestine Liberation Organization initiative. Interview in *Vanity Fair*, Feb. 1989]

LOUIS ARAGON 1897–1982

6 *Ô mois des floraisons mois des métamorphoses / Mai qui fut sans nuage et Juin poignardé / Je n'oublierai jamais les lilas ni les roses / Ni ceux que le printemps dans ses plis a gardés. –* O month of flowerings, month of metamorphoses, May without cloud and June that was stabbed, I shall never forget the lilac and the roses, nor those whom the spring has kept in its folds. [*Les lilas et les roses*]

7 *Le démenti des fleurs au vent de la panique / Aux soldats qui passaient sur l'aile de la peur / Aux vélos délirants aux canons ironiques / Au pitoyable accoutrement des faux campeurs. –* The flowers, contradiction of the wind of panic, of the soldiers who passed on the wings of fear, of the delirious bicycles, of the ironic guns, of the pitiable equipment of the bogus campers.

8 *Fuyez les bois et les fontaines / Taisez-vous oiseaux querelleurs / Vos chants sont mis en quarantaine / C'est le règne de l'oiseleur / Je reste roi de mes douleurs. –* Flee the woods and the springs. Be silent, wrangling birds. Your songs are sent to Coventry. It is the reign of the bird-catcher. I remain king of my griefs. [*Richard II quarante*]

9 *J'ai bu l'été comme un vin doux. –* I drank summer like a sweet wine. [*Zone libre*]

ROBERT ARDREY 1908–1980

10 But we were born of risen apes, not fallen angels, and the apes were armed killers besides. And so what shall we wonder at? Our murders and massacres and missiles, and our irreconcilable regiments? Or our treaties whatever they may be worth; our symphonies, however seldom they may be played; our peaceful acres, however frequently they may be converted into battlefields; our dreams, however rarely they may be accomplished. The miracle of man is not how far he has sunk but how magnificently he has risen. We are known among the stars by our poems, not our corpses. [*African Genesis*, quoted by John Julius Norwich in *Christmas Crackers*, '1972']

LORD ARDWICK [JOHN BEAVAN, former editor of the *Manchester Evening News* and *Daily Herald*] 1910–

11 The wages of sin are increased circulation. [In the *Independent*, 'Quote Unquote', 29 Apr. 1989]

HANNAH ARENDT 1906–1975

12 The fearsome word-and-thought-defying banality of evil. [Referring to revelations of the Eichmann trial in Jerusalem, 1961. *Eichmann in Jerusalem*, Ch. 15]

13 Under conditions of tyranny, it is far easier to act than to think. [In W. H. Auden, *A Certain World*, 'Tyranny']

14 Revolutionaries don't make revolutions. The revolutionaries are those who know when power is lying in the street and then they can pick it up. Armed uprising by itself has never yet led to a revolution. [In *Woman Talk 2*, comp. Michèle Brown and Ann O'Connor, 'Politics']

MICHAEL ARLEN 1895–1956

1 It is a sorry business to inquire into what men think, when we are every day only too uncomfortably confronted with what they do. [*The Three Cornered Moon*]

2 She not only expects the worst, but makes the worst of it when it happens. [In A. Andrews, *Quotations for Speakers and Writers*]

AYI KWEI ARMAH 1939–

3 Even those who have not been anywhere know that the black man who has spent his life fleeing from himself into whiteness has no power if the white master gives him none. [*The Beautyful Ones are Not Yet Born*, Ch. 6]

ANNE ARMSTRONG 1927–

4 In the space age the most important space is between the ears. [In the *Guardian*, 30 Jan. 1974]

NEIL ARMSTRONG 1930–

5 That's one small step for [a] man. One giant leap for mankind. [On landing on the moon, 21 July 1969. In the transcript the word 'a' is inaudible]

SIR ROBERT [later LORD] ARMSTRONG 1927–

6 It contains a misleading impression, not a lie. It was being economical with the truth. [Of his evidence at the Peter Wright–MI5 trial in Melbourne. In the *Observer*, 'Sayings of the Year', 28 Dec. 1986. The phrase dates back to Edmund Burke, *Letters on a Regicide Peace*. See also 209:1, 379:22]

PETER ARNO 1904–1968

7 I consider your conduct unethical and lousy. [Cartoon caption]

8 Well, back to the old drawing board. [Cartoon caption, as designer walks away from crashed plane]

BEATRICE ARTHUR 1926–

9 [When asked by Lucille Ball, 'Could you be persuaded to have a drink, dear?'] Well, maybe just a tiny triple. [From film *Auntie Mame*, screenplay by Paul Zindel, in *Movie Quote Book*, ed. Harry Haun]

GEORGE ASAF [GEORGE H. POWELL] 1880–1951

10 What's the use of worrying? / It never was worth while, / So, pack up your troubles in your old kit-bag, / And smile, smile, smile. [*Pack up your Troubles in Your Old Kit-bag*]

NEAL ASCHERSON 1932–

11 The trouble about a free market economy is that it requires so many policemen to make it work. [*Games with Shadows*, 'Policing the Marketplace']

12 He [Willy Brandt] was taller than those around him, seeing always beyond them into places where human beings went hungry and into prisons where decent men and women rotted for their opinions. [In the *Observer*, 29 Mar. 1987]

13 Franz-Josef Strauss was an example of a rare but very distinct species of politician: those who understand democracy but can't do it. [9 Oct. 1988]

JOHN ASH 1948–

14 We see the envelope they are / but the soul of things stays shut, / like a library on Sundays. [*Disbelief*, 'Unsentimental Journey']

JOHN ASHBERY 1927–

15 My name has gotten to be a household word – at least in certain households. I think there are now people who know my name, but don't know what I do. I'm famous for being famous. [Interview in *PN Review*, No. 46, 1985]

16 There is the view that poetry should improve your life. I think people confuse it with the Salvation Army. [In the *Observer*, 'Sayings of the Week', 8 Oct. 1989]

PADDY ASHDOWN, MP 1941–

17 You no longer speak for Britain, you speak for the past. [To Margaret Thatcher on

her opposition to the single European currency. In the *Independent*, 'Quote Unquote', 3 Nov. 1990]

DAISY ASHFORD 1881–1972

1 Mr Salteena was an elderly man of 42 and was fond of asking people to stay with him. [*The Young Visiters*, Ch. 1]

2 I am parshial to ladies if they are nice I suppose it is my nature. I am not quite a gentleman but you would hardly notice it but cant be helped anyhow.

3 I am very pale owing to the drains in this house. [2]

4 What I say is what dose it matter we cant all be of the Blood royal can we. [5]

5 My own idear is that these things are as piffle before the wind.

6 I am very fond of fresh air and royalties.

7 Here I am tied down to this life he said . . . being royal has many painful drawbacks. [6]

8 My life will be sour grapes and ashes without you. [8]

9 Oh Bernard muttered Ethel this is so sudden. No no cried Bernard and taking the bull by both horns he kissed her violently on her dainty face. My bride to be he murmered several times. [9]

10 She had very nice feet and plenty of money. [12]

ISAAC ASIMOV 1920–1992

11 The Laws of Robotics:

(1) A robot may not injure a human being, or through inaction allow a human being to come to harm.

(2) A robot must obey the orders given it by human beings, except where such orders would conflict with the First Law.

(3) A robot must protect its own existence as long as such protection does not conflict with the First and Second Laws. [*I, Robot*, 'Runaround']

ARTHUR ASKEY 1900–1982

12 Hello playmates! [Catchphrase in BBC radio comedy programme, from 1938 onwards]

13 Ay thang you!

14 Have you read any good books lately?

H. H. ASQUITH, EARL OF OXFORD 1852–1928

15 We must wait and see. [Speech in House of Commons, 3 Apr. 1910, referring to the Budget. Later interpreted as referring to the war]

16 One to mislead the public, another to mislead the Cabinet, and the third to mislead itself. [On the War Office's keeping three sets of figures. In Alistair Horne, *The Price of Glory*, Ch. 2]

17 Youth would be an ideal state if it came a little later in life. [In the *Observer*, 15 Apr. 1923]

18 It is fitting that we should have buried the Unknown Prime Minister by the side of the Unknown Soldier. [Attr., at the funeral of Bonar Law, 5 Nov. 1923]

19 Our two rhetoricians [Churchill and Lloyd George] . . . have good brains of different types. But they can only think talking, just as some people can only think writing. Only the salt of the earth can think inside, and the bulk of mankind cannot think at all! [In *The Wit of the Asquiths*, comp. Mary Tester, 'The Imperialists']

MARGOT ASQUITH, COUNTESS OF OXFORD 1865–1945

20 He [Lloyd George] could not see a belt without hitting below it. [From *Autobiography*, in the *Listener*, 11 June 1953]

21 Lord Birkenhead is very clever, but sometimes his brains go to his head.

22 If not a great soldier he is at least a great poster. [Of the 'Kitchener Needs You' campaign. In *The Wit of the Asquiths*, comp. Mary Tester]

23 Ettie is so strong; she will be made into Bovril when she dies. [Of Lady Desborough's unflagging vitality. Quoted by Lord David Cecil in the *Observer Review*, 20 Dec. 1981]

24 Ettie [Lady Desborough] tells enough white lies to ice a cake.

25 You know the kind of thing – the salad was decorated with the Lord's Prayer in

beetroot. [Of Lady Desborough's 'fussy and over-elaborate food']

1 We mean to live very quietly, only seeing the King and a few friends. [On her husband's fall from power]

2 Lord Dawson was not a good doctor: King George V himself told me that he would never have died, had he had another doctor!

3 I have no face, only two profiles clapped together. [In *Hammer and Tongues*, ed. Michèle Brown and Ann O'Connor, 'Appearance']

4 Jean Harlow [Hollywood's sexy actress] kept calling Margot Asquith by her first name, or kept trying to: she pronounced it Mar*g*ot. Finally Margot set her right. 'No, no, Jean. The *t* is silent as in Harlow.' [T. S. Matthews, *Great Tom*, Ch. 7]

FRED ASTAIRE 1899–1987

5 [Astaire] Can't act. Can't sing. Slightly bald. Can dance a little. [Anon. Goldwyn talent scout. In Leslie Halliwell, *Filmgoer's Book of Quotes*]

JOHN JACOB ASTOR IV 1864–1912

6 I asked for ice, but this is ridiculous. [Just before the *Titanic* was sunk by an iceberg. In D. Sinclair, *Dynasty: The Astors and Their Times*]

NANCY, VISCOUNTESS ASTOR 1879–1964

7 [To Churchill]: Winston, if I were married to you, I'd put poison in your coffee.
CHURCHILL: Nancy, if you were my wife, I'd drink it. [At Blenheim Palace, *c.* 1912. In E. Langthorne, *Nancy Astor and Her Friends*]

8 Grass is growing on the Front Bench. [In the *Observer*, 'Sayings of the Week', 17 Mar. 1940]

9 I married beneath me. All women do. [Speech at Oldham, 1951]

P. W. ATKINS 1940–

10 There is no need to look for a purpose behind it all: energy has just gone on spreading, and the spreading has happened to generate elephants and enthralling opinions. [*The Creation*, 'Why Things Change']

E. L. ATKINSON 1882–1929 and APSLEY CHERRY-GARRARD 1866–1959

11 A very gallant gentleman. [Inscription on the burial-place of Captain Oates in the Antarctic, 1912]

CHARLES ATLAS [ANGELO SICILIANO] 1894–1972

12 You too can have a body like mine. [Body-building advertising slogan. Ascr. to Charles Roman in Jonathon Green, *Says Who?*]

CLEMENT [later EARL] ATTLEE 1883–1967

13 Democracy means government by discussion but it is only effective if you can stop people talking. [Speech at Oxford, 14 June 1957]

14 The House of Lords is like a glass of champagne which has stood for five days. [In *The Fine Art of Political Wit*, ed. Leon A. Harris]

15 Few thought he was even a starter / There were many who thought themselves smarter / But he ended PM / CH and OM / An earl and a knight of the garter. [On himself in letter to Tom Attlee, 8 Apr. 1956]

ROGER ATTRILL [Governor of Winson Green Prison, Birmingham]

16 Prison is an effective deterrent to those who walk past the gate, not through it. [In the *New Statesman*, Sept. 1980]

MARGARET ATWOOD 1939–

17 Gardening is not a rational act. What matters is the immersion of the hands in the earth, that ancient ceremony of which the Pope kissing the tarmac is merely a pallid vestigial remnant. [*Bluebeard's Egg*, 'Unearthing Suite']

18 I was a good typist; ... at my high school typing was regarded as a female

secondary sex characteristic, like breasts. [*Lady Oracle*, Ch. 4]

1 I was quite fat by this time and all fat women look the same, they all look forty-two.

2 You can have a men's novel with no women in it except possibly the landlady / or the horse, but you can't have a women's novel with no men in it. / Sometimes men put women in men's novels / but they leave out some of the parts; / the heads, for instance. [From *Poem*, in Resa Dudovitz, *The Myth of Superwoman*]

3 You fit into me / like a hook into an eye / a fish hook / an open eye. [*Power Politics*, 'You fit into me']

4 If the national mental illness of the United States is megalomania, that of Canada is paranoid schizophrenia. [In *Barnes and Noble Book of Quotations*, ed. Robert I. Fitzhenry, 'Canada']

W. H. AUDEN 1907–1973

5 Yet no one hears his own remarks as prose. [*At a Party*]

6 August for the people and their favourite islands. / Daily the steamers sidle up to meet / The effusive welcome of the pier. [*August for the people*]

7 Hinting at the forbidden like a wicked uncle, / Night after night to the farmer's children you beckon. [*The Capital*]

8 Speechless Evil / Borrowed the language of Good / And reduced it to noise. [*The Cave of Making*, Postscript]

9 Within these breakwaters English is spoken: without / Is the immense, improbable atlas. [*Dover*]

10 Let us honour if we can / The vertical man / Though we value none / But the horizontal one. [*Epigraph*]

11 He knew human folly like the back of his hand, / And was greatly interested in armies and fleets; / When he laughed, respectable senators burst with laughter, / And when he cried the little children died in the streets. [*Epitaph on a Tyrant*]

12 One tapped my shoulder and asked me 'How did you fall, sir?' / Whereat I awakened. [*1st January 1931*]

13 Alone, alone, about the dreadful wood / Of conscious evil runs a lost mankind, / Dreading to find its Father. [*For the Time Being*, 'Chorus']

14 When the Sex War ended with the slaughter of the Grandmothers, / They found a bachelor's baby suffocating under them; / Somebody called him George and that was the end of it: / They hitched him up to the Army. ['Soldiers']

15 To us he is no more a person. / Now but a whole climate of opinion / Under whom we conduct our differing lives. [*In Memory of Sigmund Freud*]

16 In the nightmare of the dark / All the dogs of Europe bark, / And the living nations wait, / Each sequestered in its hate. [*In Memory of W. B. Yeats*]

17 Intellectual disgrace / Stares from every human face, / And the seas of pity lie / Locked and frozen in each eye.

18 When I try to imagine a faultless love / Or the life to come, what I hear is the murmur / Of underground streams, what I see is a limestone landscape. [*In Praise of Limestone*]

19 And on the issue of their charm depended / A land laid waste, with all its young men slain, / The women weeping, and its towns in terror. [*In Time of War*, xix]

20 It is time for the destruction of error. / The chairs are being brought in from the garden, / The summer talk stopped on that savage coast / Before the storms. [*It is time*]

21 To throw away the key and walk away, / Not abrupt exile, the neighbours asking why, / But following a line with left and right, / An altered gradient at another rate. [*The Journey*]

22 Lay your sleeping head, my love, / Human on my faithless arm. [*Lay your sleeping head*]

23 Look, stranger, at this island now / The leaping light for your delight discovers. [*Look Stranger*]

24 Private faces in public places / Are wiser

and nicer / Than public faces in private places. [*Marginalia*]

1 Five minutes on even the nicest mountain / Is awfully long. [*Mountains*]

2 About suffering they were never wrong, / The Old Masters. [*Musée des Beaux Arts*]

3 Even the dreadful martyrdom must run its course / Anyhow in a corner, some untidy spot / Where the dogs go on with their doggy life.

4 O Unicorn among the cedars, / To whom no magic charm can lead us, / White childhood moving like a sigh / Through the green woods. [*New Year Letter*, Pt III]

5 The glacier knocks in the cupboard. / The desert sighs in the bed, / And the crack in the tea-cup opens / A lane to the land of the dead. [*One Evening*]

6 God bless the USA, so large, / So friendly, and so rich. [*On the Circuit*]

7 To the man-in-the-street, who, I'm sorry to say, / Is a keen observer of life, / The word 'Intellectual' suggests straight away / A man who's untrue to his wife. [*The Orators*, epigraph]

8 Attractions for their coming week / Are Masters Wet, Dim, Drip and Bleak. [Ode, 'Roar Gloucestershire']

9 The Oxford Don: 'I don't feel quite happy about pleasure.' ['Journal of an Airman']

10 Only those in the last stage of disease could believe that children are true judges of character.

11 To ask the hard question is simple. [*The Question*]

12 Verse was a special illness of the ear; / Integrity was not enough. [*Rimbaud*]

13 His truth acceptable to lying men.

14 Over the heather the west wind blows, / I've lice in my tunic and a cold in my nose. / The rain comes pattering out of the sky, / I'm a Wall soldier and I don't know why. [*Roman Wall Blues*]

15 Embrace me, belly, like a bride. [*The Sea and the Mirror*, II, 'Stephano's Song']

16 At Dirty Dick's and Sloppy Joe's / We drank our liquor straight, / Some went upstairs with Margery, / And some, alas, with Kate. ['Song of the Master and the Boatswain']

17 The nightingales are sobbing in / The orchards of our mothers, / And hearts that we broke long ago / Have long been breaking others.

18 My Dear One is mine as mirrors are lonely.

19 There is no such thing as the State / And no one exists alone; / Hunger allows no choice / To the citizen or the police; / We must love one another or die. [*September 1, 1939*]

20 Out of the air a voice without a face / Proved by statistics that some cause was just. [*The Shield of Achilles*]

21 No hero is mortal till he dies. [*A Short Ode to a Philologist*]

22 Their fate must always be the same as yours, / To suffer the loss they were afraid of, yes, / Holders of one position, wrong for years. [*Since you are going to begin today*]

23 Harrow the house of the dead; look shining at / New styles of architecture, a change of heart. [Sonnet: *Sir, no man's enemy*]

24 O for doors to be open and an invite with gilded edges / To dine with Lord Lobcock and Count Asthma. [*Song*]

25 So take your proper share man, of / Dope and drink: / Aren't you the Chairman of / Ego, Inc? [*Song of the Devil*]

26 The stars are dead; the animals will not look: / We are left alone with our day, and the time is short and / History to the defeated / May say Alas but cannot help or pardon. [*Spain 1937*]

27 Noises at dawn will bring / Freedom for some, but not this peace / No bird can contradict. [*Taller Today*]

28 A shilling life will give you all the facts. [*Who's Who*]

29 This great society is going smash; / They cannot fool us with how fast they go, / How much they cost each other and the gods! / A culture is no better than its woods. [*Winds*]

30 Be clean, be tidy, oil the clock, / Weed the garden, wind the clock; / Remember the Two. [*The Witnesses*]

1 Of course, Behaviourism 'works'. So does torture. Give me a no-nonsense, down-to-earth behaviourist, a few drugs, and simple electrical appliances, and in six months I will have him reciting the Athanasian creed in public. [*A Certain World*, 'Behaviourism']

2 Good can imagine Evil, but Evil cannot imagine Good. ['Imagination']

3 All sin tends to be addictive, and the terminal point of addiction is what is called damnation. ['Hell']

4 Some books are undeservedly forgotten; none are undeservedly remembered. [*The Dyer's Hand*, Pt 1, 'Reading']

5 No poet or novelist wishes he were the only one who ever lived, but most of them wish they were the only one alive, and quite a number fondly believe their wish has been granted. ['Writing']

6 The greatest writer cannot see through a brick wall but unlike the rest of us he does not build one.

7 When I find myself in the company of scientists, I feel like a shabby curate who has strayed by mistake into a drawing room full of dukes. [2, 'The Poet and the City']

8 If men were as much lizards as lizards / They'd be worth looking at. [5, 'D. H. Lawrence', epigraph]

9 Man is a history-making creature who can neither repeat his past nor leave it behind.

10 A verbal art like poetry is reflective; it stops to think. Music is immediate; it goes on to become. [8, 'Notes on Music']

11 If music in general is an imitation of history, opera in particular is an imitation of human wilfulness.

12 Geniuses are the luckiest of mortals because what they must do is the same as what they most wanted to do. [Foreword to Dag Hammarskjöld, *Markings*]

13 Art is our chief means of breaking bread with the dead. [In *The New York Times*, 7 Aug. 1971]

14 Music is the best means we have of digesting time. [In Robert Craft, *Stravinsky: Chronicle of a Friendship*]

15 We are all here on earth to help others; what on earth the others are here for I don't know. [In *Barnes and Noble Book of Quotations*, ed. Robert I. Fitzhenry, 'Goodness']

16 He [Tennyson] had the finest ear, perhaps, of any English poet; he was also undoubtedly the stupidest. [Introduction to his selection of Tennyson's poetry. In Humphrey Carpenter, *Auden: A Biography*, Pt 2, Ch. 4. T. S. Eliot countered that if Auden had been a better scholar, he would have known many stupider]

17 My face looks like a wedding-cake left out in the rain. [In Ch. 6]

18 Writers are usually in the unfortunate predicament of having to speak the truth without the authority to speak it. [In Charles Osborne, *W. H. Auden: The Life of a Poet*, Ch. 13]

19 People who attend chamber music concerts are like Englishmen who go to church when abroad.

20 A professor is one who talks in someone else's sleep.

21 The best prose writer in the US. [Of M. F. K. Fisher. In the *Guardian* at her death, 27 June 1992]

W. H. AUDEN and J. GARRETT
1902–1966

22 Poetry, in fact, bears the same kind of relation to Prose, using prose simply in the sense of all those uses of words that are not poetry, that algebra bears to arithmetic. [*The Poet's Tongue*, Introduction]

W. H. AUDEN and CHRISTOPHER ISHERWOOD 1904–1986

23 Acts of injustice done / Between the setting and the rising sun / In history lie like bones, each one. [*The Ascent of F6*, Act II, sc. v]

AUSCHWITZ 1940–1945

24 *Arbeit macht frei.* – Work Sets You Free. [Slogan above concentration camp's main gate]

GEORGE AXELROD 1922–

25 The Seven Year Itch. [Title of play and subsequently film, giving existing term a new meaning]

ALAN AYCKBOURN 1939–

1 If S-E-X ever rears its ugly head, close your eyes before you see the rest of it. [*Bedroom Farce*, Act III]

2 If you're very good in this life, you might just come back in the next as a shoe-cleaning kit. [*Henceforward*, Act III]

3 If you gave Ruth a rose, she'd peel all the petals off to make sure there weren't any greenfly. And when she'd done that, she'd turn round and say, do you call that a rose? Look at it, it's all in bits. [*The Norman Conquests: Table Manners*, Act I, sc. ii]

4 Comedy is tragedy interrupted. [Interview]

A. J. [later **SIR FREDDIE**] AYER 1910–1989

5 No morality can be founded on authority, even if the authority were divine. [*Essay on Humanism*]

6 The principles of logic and metaphysics are true simply because we never allow them to be anything else. [*Language, Truth and Logic*]

PAM AYRES 1947–

7 And when at last I'm seated by / The great typewriter in the sky, / Let me type the letters right, / In the morning and at night, / Let the Snopake grow on trees, / Let man's hands stay off me knees, / Let it be a place harmonic, / With no need for gin and tonic, / Thank you in anticipation / Of a favourable reply, / Craving your indulgence, / Yours sincerely. / Goodbye. [*Some More of Me Poetry*, 'The Secretary's Song']

8 I might have been a farmyard hen, / Scratchin' in the sun, / There might have been a crowd of chicks, / After me to run, / There might have been a cockerel fine, / To pay us his respects, / Instead of sittin' here, / Till someone comes and wrings our necks. [*Some of Me Poetry*, 'The Battery Hen']

9 I see the Time and Motion clock, / Is sayin' nearly noon, / I 'spec me squirt of water / Will come flyin' at me soon, / And then me spray of pellets / Will nearly break me leg, / And I'll bite the wire nettin' / And lay one more bloody egg.

10 Oh, I wish I'd looked after me teeth, / And spotted the perils beneath, / All the toffees I chewed, / And the sweet sticky food, / Oh, I wish I'd looked after me teeth. ['Oh, I Wish I'd Looked After Me Teeth']

11 Medicinal discovery, / It moves in mighty leaps, / It leapt straight past the common cold / And gave it us for keeps. ['Oh, No, I Got a Cold']

B

ISAAC BABEL 1894–?1939

1 No iron can stab the heart with such force as a full stop put just at the right place. [*Guy de Maupassant*]

LAUREN BACALL 1924–

2 You know how to whistle, don't you, Steve? You just put your lips together and blow. [To Humphrey Bogart in film *To Have and Have Not*, script by Jules Furthman and William Faulkner]

3 He [Humphrey Bogart] cried at all his own weddings – and with reason. [In Nathaniel Benchley, *Humphrey Bogart*]

SIR FRANCIS BACON 1909–1992

4 How can I take an interest in my work when I don't like it? [Quoted by Sir John Rothenstein in *Francis Bacon*, Introduction]

5 Painting is its own language, and when you try to talk about it, it's like an inferior translation. [Profile in the *Observer*, 19 May 1985]

6 I am an old man, but I am profoundly optimistic about nothing. [Interview on LWT programme *The South Bank show*, 1985. In *Dictionary of Art Quotations*, comp. Ian Crofton]

LORD BADEN-POWELL 1857–1941

7 The scouts' motto is founded on my initials, it is: Be Prepared. [*Scouting for Boys*, Pt 1]

8 Dyb - dyb - dyb. [Wolf cub call, derived from 'Do your best']

ARTHUR 'BUGS' BAER 1897–1975

9 It was as helpful as throwing a drowning man both ends of a rope. [In A. Andrews, *Quotations for Speakers and Writers*]

10 There is no such thing as a little garlic. [In Frank Muir, *Frank Muir Book*]

11 Alimony is like buying oats for a dead horse. [From *New York American*, in Jonathon Green, *Cynic's Lexicon*]

ENID BAGNOLD 1889–1981

12 It's not the party of life in the end that's important. It's the comment in the bedroom. [*The Loved and the Envied*]

S. D. BAILEY 1916–

13 It has been said that this Minister [the Lord Privy Seal] is neither a Lord, nor a privy, nor a seal. [*British Parliamentary Democracy*]

14 [The party system] is merely a convenient device to enable the majority to have their way and the minority to have their say. [*The British Party System*]

BERYL BAINBRIDGE 1934–

15 I haven't the humility to find anything beneath me. [*An Awfully Big Adventure*, 3]

16 He was worrying needlessly seeing he was a Methodist, a belief which favoured an artificial rather than a natural classification of guilt. [8]

17 Being constantly with children was like wearing a pair of shoes that were expensive

and too small. She couldn't bear to throw them out, but they gave her blisters. [*Injury Time*, Ch. 4]

1 It amazed Ann that Mrs Kershaw, who held such strong views, should send her children to a Parochial school with a vicar coming in twice a week to take morning prayers. You'd have thought she might have preferred one of those progressive places where the teachers were called by their christian names and told to shut up. [*Sweet William*, Ch. 1]

2 Old soldiers, she knew, never died; in her father's case she felt it was not so much that he was fading away, as he had never been there in the first place.

3 He is, after all, the reflection of the tenderness I bear for myself. It is always ourselves we love. [*A Weekend with Claud*, 'Maggie']

4 We are essentially fragile. We don't have to wait for the sword or some other equally sensational weapon to strike us down. One may go just as easily with the measles or diphtheria, meningitis, colic, influenza or mere hunger. There are so many ways of us dying it's astonishing any of us choose old age. [*Young Adolf*, Ch. 12]

5 A man is two people, himself and his cock. A man always takes his friend to the party. Of the two, the friend is the nicer, being more able to show his feelings. [In *Picking on Men*, comp. Judy Allen, variant in the *Observer*, 17 Oct. 1982]

6 He [Reggie Smith, Olivia Manning's husband] was the kind of man who would pop out for a packet of fags, and not come back for a couple of months. [In the *Guardian*, 18 Sept. 1987]

7 The vital accessories to my work are my reference books, such as the complete Shakespeare and a prayer book, and a large refuse bin. [Interview in the *Guardian*, 8 Aug. 1991]

KENNETH BAINBRIDGE 1904–

8 Now we are all sons of bitches. [After first atomic test, of which he was in charge. *The Decision to Drop the Bomb*]

BRUCE BAIRNSFATHER 1888–1959

9 Well, if you knows of a better 'ole, go to it. [*Fragments from France*, 1, 1915]

VADIM BAKATIN [First candidate in Russian presidential election] 1937–

10 Making capitalism out of socialism is like making eggs out of an omelette. [Said in May 1991. In *Hutchinson Gallup Info 92*]

HYLDA BAKER 1908–1986

11 She knows, you know! [Of her silent partner, Cynthia. Catchphrase in comedy act]

JOSEPHINE BAKER 1906–1975

12 It's far easier to become a star again than become one. [In Bruce Chatwin, *What am I Doing Here*, 'André Malraux']

KENNETH BAKER, MP 1934–

13 The Labour Party has just been led by Dixon of Dock Green. Now it's being led by Worzel Gummidge. [On Michael Foot's replacing James Callaghan as leader. In S. Hoggart, *On the House*, p. 120]

GEORGES BALANDIER 1920–

14 *Le tiers monde* – The Third World. [Title of book, 1956, but he attr. term to Alfred Sauvy in *Le nouvel observateur*, 14 Aug. 1952]

JAMES BALDWIN 1924–1987

15 The white man discovered the Cross by way of the Bible, but the black man discovered the Bible by way of the Cross. [*Evidence of Things Not Seen*]

16 The Fire Next Time. [Title of book derived from lines in Negro spiritual *Home in That Rock*: 'God gave Noah the rainbow sign, / No more water, the fire next time!']

17 If the concept of God has any validity or use, it can only be to make us larger, freer, and more loving. If God cannot do this, then it is time we got rid of Him. [*The Fire Next Time*, 'Down at the Cross']

1 Consider the history of labour in a country [USA] in which, spiritually speaking, there are no workers, only candidates for the hand of the boss's daughter.

2 Anyone who has ever struggled with poverty knows how extremely expensive it is to be poor. [*Nobody Knows My Name*, 'Fifth Avenue, Uptown']

3 If they take you in the morning, they will be coming for us that night. [Epigraph to Angela Davis, *If They Come in the Morning*]

4 It is a great shock at the age of five or six to find that in a world of Gary Coopers you are the Indian. [Speech at Cambridge Union, 17 Feb. 1965]

STANLEY [later EARL] BALDWIN
1867–1947

5 A lot of hard-faced men who look as if they had done well out of the war. [Of the House of Commons returned in the 1918 election. In J. M. Keynes, *Economic Consequences of the Peace*, Ch. 5]

6 What the proprietorship of these papers [referring to Beaverbrook and Rothermere] is aiming at is power, and power without responsibility – the prerogative of the harlot through the ages. [By-election speech, 18 Mar. 1931. Lord Birkenhead claims in *Rudyard Kipling*, Ch. 20, that the phrase originated with Kipling and was borrowed by his cousin, Stanley Baldwin. See also 104:9, 214:27, 361:12, 401:19]

7 The only defence is in offence, which means that you have to kill more women and children more quickly than the enemy if you want to save yourselves. [Speech in House of Commons, 10 Nov. 1932]

8 When you think about the defence of England, you no longer think of the chalk cliffs of Dover. You think of the Rhine. That is where our frontier lies today. [Speech in House of Commons, 30 July 1934]

9 My lips are not yet unsealed. Were these troubles over I would make a case, and I guarantee that not a man would go into the Lobby against us. [Speech in House of Commons on the Abyssinia crisis, 10 Dec. 1935]

10 Supposing I had gone to the country and said that Germany was rearming and we must rearm ... I cannot think of anything that would have made the loss of the election from my point of view more certain. [Speech in House of Commons, 12 Nov. 1936]

11 Then comes Winston with his hundred-horse-power mind and what can I do? [In G. M. Young, *Stanley Baldwin*, Ch. 11]

12 The intelligent are to the intelligentsia what a gentleman is to a gent. [In 13]

13 There are three groups that no British Prime Minister should provoke: the Vatican, the Treasury and the miners. [Attr. There are variants from other politicians. R. A. Butler's version of Baldwin's 'Do not run up your nose dead against the Pope and the NUM [National Union of Mineworkers]' in his *The Art of Memory*, p. 110]

14 I met Curzon in Downing Street, from whom I got the sort of greeting a corpse would give to an undertaker. [Attr. In 1933 on Baldwin's becoming Prime Minister, a job coveted by Curzon. In J. Wintle and R. Kenin, *Dictionary of Biographical Quotation*]

15 I would rather be an opportunist and float than go to the bottom with my principles round my neck. [Attr.]

A. J. BALFOUR 1848–1930

16 Defence of philosophic doubt. [Article in *Mind*, 1878]

17 The energies of our system will decay, the glory of the sun will be dimmed, and the earth, tideless and inert, will no longer tolerate the race which has for a moment disturbed its solitude. Man will go down into the pit, and all his thoughts will perish. [*The Foundations of Belief*, 1895, Pt I, Ch. 1]

18 It is unfortunate, considering that enthusiasm moves the world, that so few enthusiasts can be trusted to speak the truth. [Letter to Mrs Drew, 19 May 1891]

19 His Majesty's Government views with favour the establishment in Palestine of a national home for the Jewish people, and will use its best endeavours to facilitate the achievement of this object, it being clearly understood that nothing shall be done that

may prejudice the civil and religious rights of non-Jewish communities in Palestine. [Letter to Lord Rothschild, 2 Nov. 1917, the so-called Balfour Declaration]

1 Christianity naturally, but why journalism? [To Frank Harris, who claimed that the two greatest curses of civilization were Christianity and journalism. In Margot Asquith, *Autobiography*, Ch. 10]

2 Nothing matters very much, and very few things matter at all. [Attr.]

J. G. BALLARD 1930–

3 Later, as he sat on his balcony eating the dog, Dr Robert Laing reflected on the unusual events. [*High-rise*, opening words]

PIERRE BALMAIN 1914–1982

4 The trick of wearing mink is to look as though you are wearing a cloth coat. The trick of wearing a cloth coat is to look as though you are wearing a mink. [In the *Observer*, 'Sayings of the Week', 13 Feb. 1955]

ALBERT BAND 1924–

5 'The music isn't right,' he says. 'It's a picture about France,' he said, 'so I want a lot of French horns.' [In Lillian Ross, *Picture*, 'Throw the Little Old Lady Down the Stairs!']

TALLULAH BANKHEAD 1903–1968

6 Cocaine isn't habit-forming. I should know – I've been using it for years. [In Lillian Hellman, *Pentimento*, 'Theatre']

7 There is less of this than meets the eye. [Of the revival of a Maeterlinck play. In Alexander Woollcott, *Shouts and Murmurs*, 'Capsule Criticism']

8 I'm as pure as the driven slush. [In the *Observer*, 'Sayings of the Week', 24 Feb. 1957]

9 The only thing I regret about my past is the length of it. If I had to live my life again I'd make all the same mistakes – only sooner. [In L. and M. Cowan, *The Wit of Women*]

10 They used to photograph Shirley Temple through gauze. They should photograph me through linoleum. [In Leslie Halliwell, *Filmgoer's Book of Quotes*]

11 [When a man greeted her with the words 'I haven't seen you for forty-one years!'] I thought I told you to wait in the car. [In *Quote . . . Unquote Book of Love, Death and the Universe*]

NANCY BANKS-SMITH 1929–

12 The most formidable headmaster I ever knew was a headmistress . . . She had X-ray pince-nez and that undivided bust popularized by Queen Mary. I think she was God in drag. [In the *Guardian*, 8 Jan. 1977]

13 In my experience, if you have to keep the lavatory door shut by extending your left leg, it's modern architecture. [20 Feb. 1979]

14 The reason saints wear haloes is so, when they pass the hat round, they don't keep anything for themselves. [5 Feb. 1986]

15 Who said 'If you can remember the sixties you weren't really there'? I can't remember. [2 June 1987]

16 Northerners . . . don't live in the north, because the north already lives in them. Penny Lane is in their ears and in their eyes. [On the death of Russell Harty, 9 June 1988]

17 Charles Robertson is an accountant. If they come any greyer than that they're squirrels. [12 Apr. 1989]

18 The philosophical attitude of a flamingo I once saw standing in a crocodile pool on one leg. Because it only had one leg. One more bite and it would be a duck. [8 Feb. 1990]

19 It is not possible to look and listen with equal attention and, in any competition, the eyes have it. [23 Mar.]

20 It is not the job of the general to be winning. It is his job to win. [Of General Eisenhower and his relationship with General Montgomery, 9 May]

21 Wearing his slept-in face . . . [Of comedian Frankie Howerd, 2 June]

22 The cab driver took her to Times Square, which is like hell without the hygiene. [8 Dec.]

1 You carry forever the fingerprint that comes from being under someone's thumb. [30 Jan. 1991]

2 In my view, a nation which eats cheese for breakfast has little room for criticism. [6 Feb. 1992]

JOHN BANVILLE 1945–

3 Where do you think you are living, eh? This is the world, look around you, look at it! You want certainty, order, all that? Then invent it! [*Mefisto*, p. 193]

LYNN BARBER 1944–

4 Her [Fiona Pitt-Kethley's] father's particular hobby was getting ordained. [In the *Independent on Sunday*, 2 June 1991]

5 It seems so *lazy* to have an affair with your secretary, like always going to the nearest restaurant instead of the best. [9 Feb. 1992]

MAURICE BARING 1874–1945

6 We see the contrast between the genius which does what it must and the talent which does what it can. [On Pushkin's *Mozart and Salieri. Outline of Russian Literature*, Ch. 3]

7 If you would know what the Lord God thinks of money, you have only to look at those to whom He gives it. [Quoted by Dorothy Parker in *Writers at Work*, ed. Malcolm Cowley, First Series]

GEORGE BARKER 1916–1991

8 When the guns begin to rattle / And the men to die / Does the Goddess of the Battle / Smile or sigh? [*Battle Hymn of the New Republic*]

H. GRANVILLE BARKER 1877–1946

9 What is the prose for God? [*Waste*, Act II]

10 MOORE: The fame of the actress is transitory.
BARKER: Not so transitory as the fame of the authors she represents; their works remain to decry them. The actress is more fortunate: she leaves only a name and a legend. [In George Moore, *Conversations in Ebury Street*, Ch. 18]

HOWARD BARKER 1946–

11 The theatre must start to take its audience seriously. It must stop telling them stories they can understand. [In the *Guardian*, 10 Feb. 1986]

RONNIE BARKER 1929–

12 The marvellous thing about a joke with a double meaning is that it can only mean one thing. [*Sauce*, 'Daddie's Sauce']

RONNIE BARKER and RONNIE CORBETT 1930–

13 CORBETT: It's goodnight from me . . .
BARKER: And it's goodnight from him. [Catchphrase closing lines to TV comedy series *The Two Ronnies*, from 1970s]

BINNIE BARNES 1905–

14 He's the kind of bore who's here today and here tomorrow. [In *Hammer and Tongues*, ed. Michèle Brown and Ann O'Connor, 'Pessimism']

JULIAN BARNES 1946–

15 You *can* have your cake and eat it; the only trouble is you get fat. [*Flaubert's Parrot*, Ch. 7]

16 It is easy, after all, not to be a writer. Most people aren't writers, and very little harm comes to them. [9]

17 We'd both been to the country and found it disappointingly empty. [*Metroland*, Pt 1, 4]

18 Women were brought up to believe that men were the answer. They weren't. They weren't even one of the questions. [*Staring at the Sun*, Pt 2]

19 I've always thought you are what you are and you shouldn't pretend to be anyone else. But Oliver used to correct me and explain that you are whoever it is you're pretending to be. [*Talking It Over*, 2]

20 I've always said, if you want to outwit an Englishman, touch him when he doesn't want to be touched. [7]

1 That fetid compartment of the local bookshop which ought to be called Self-Pity but instead is mysteriously labelled Self-Help. [12]

ANN BARR 1929– and PETER YORK 1947–

2 Anyone who has read Proust is not a Sloane Ranger. [*Official Sloane Ranger Handbook*]

SIR JAMES BARRIE 1860–1937

3 His lordship may compel us to be equal upstairs, but there will never be equality in the servants' hall. [*The Admirable Crichton*, I]

4 They say that in the wood you get what nearly everybody here is longing for – a second chance. [*Dear Brutus*, Act I]

5 Fame is rot; daughters are the thing. [II]

6 The same kind, beaming smile that children could warm their hands at. [III]

7 If it's heaven for climate, it's hell for company. [*The Little Minister*, Ch. 3]

8 It's grand, and ye canna expect to be baith grand and comfortable. [10]

9 I do loathe explanations. [*My Lady Nicotine*, Ch. 14]

10 When the first baby laughed for the first time, the laugh broke into a thousand pieces and they all went skipping about, and that was the beginning of fairies. [*Peter Pan*, I]

11 Everytime a child says, 'I don't believe in fairies,' there's a little fairy somewhere that falls down dead.

12 To die will be an awfully big adventure. [III]

13 That is ever the way. 'Tis all jealousy to the bride and good wishes to the corpse. [*Quality Street*, Act I]

14 What is algebra exactly; is it those three-cornered things? [II]

15 But the gladness of her gladness / And the sadness of her sadness / Are as nothing, Charles, / To the badness of her badness when she's bad. [*Rosalind*]

16 'It's a kid or a coffin,' he said sharply, knowing that only birth or death brought a doctor here. [*Sentimental Tommy*, Ch. 1]

17 A boy does not put his hand into his pocket until every other means of gaining his end has failed.

18 It might be said of these two boys that Shovel knew everything but Tommy knew other things. [3]

19 One's religion is whatever he is most interested in, and yours is Success. [*The Twelve-pound Look*, I]

20 It's a sort of bloom on a woman. If you have it [charm], you don't need to have anything else; and if you don't have it, it doesn't much matter what else you have. [*What Every Woman Knows*, I]

21 A young Scotsman of your ability let loose upon the world with £300, what could he not do? It's almost appalling to think of; especially if he went among the English.

22 You've forgotten the greatest moral attribute of a Scotsman, Maggie, that he'll do nothing which might damage his career. [II]

23 There are few more impressive sights in the world than a Scotsman on the make.

24 He had the most atrocious bow-wow public park manner. [III]

25 I have always found that the man whose second thoughts are good is worth watching.

26 Every man who is high up likes to feel that he has done it all himself; and the wife smiles, and lets it go at that. It's our only joke. Every woman knows that. [IV]

27 Never ascribe to an opponent motives meaner than your own. ['Courage', rectorial address, St Andrews University, 3 May 1922]

KARL BARTH 1886–1968

28 Men have never been good, they are not good, they never will be good. [*Christian Community*, p. 36]

29 Whether the angels play only Bach in praising God I am not quite sure: I am sure, however, that en famille they play Mozart. [In obituary in *The New York Times*, 11 Dec. 1968]

DONALD BARTHELMÉ 1931–1989

30 The first problem in finding a lost father is to lose him decisively. [*The Dead Father*]

ROLAND BARTHES 1915–1980

1 What I claim is to live to the full the contradiction of my time, which may well make sarcasm the condition of truth. [*Mythologies*, Preface]

2 I think that cars today are almost the exact equivalent of the great Gothic cathedrals: I mean the supreme creation of an era, conceived with passion by unknown artists, and consumed in image if not in usage by a whole population which appropriates them as a purely magical object. ['The New Citroën']

3 *Myth is a type of speech* . . . Innumerable other meanings of the word 'myth' can be cited against this. But I have tried to define things not words. ['Myth Today']

4 The human subject has changed: intimacy and solitude have lost their value, the individual has become increasingly gregarious, he wants collective, massive, often paroxysmal music, the expression of US rather than ME. [In David Dubal, *Evenings with Horowitz*, Afterword]

BERNARD M. BARUCH 1870–1965

5 The cold war. [Speech, 16 Apr. 1947, Columbia, South Carolina. In the *Boston Globe*, 1 Apr. 1949. In fact Baruch gave credit for the phrase to his speech-writer, H. B. Swope]

6 I will never be an old man. To me, old age is always fifteen years older than I am. [In the *Observer*, 'Sayings of the Week', 21 Aug. 1955]

7 A political leader must keep looking over his shoulder all the time to see if the boys are still there. If they aren't still there, he's no longer a political leader. [In obituary in *The New York Times*, 21 June 1965]

JACQUES BARZUN 1907–

8 Intellect deteriorates after every surrender as folly, unless we consciously resist, the nonsense does not pass by but into us. [*The House of Intellect*]

'COUNT' BASIE 1904–1984

9 I just sit, wink and play. [Describing his musical ability. In obituary in the *Sunday Times*, 29 Apr. 1984]

EDGAR BATEMAN and GEORGE LE BRUNN

10 Wiv a ladder and some glasses, / You can see to 'Ackney Marshes, / If it wasn't for the 'ouses in between. [Song: *If it wasn't for the 'ouses in between*, 1900]

L. FRANK BAUM 1856–1919

11 The road to the City of Emeralds is paved with yellow brick. [*The Wonderful Wizard of Oz*, Ch. 2. This became 'Follow the yellow brick road' in the musical version]

SIR ARNOLD BAX 1883–1953

12 You should make a point of trying every experience once, except incest and folk-dancing. [Quoting 'sympathetic Scot'. *Farewell to My Youth*, 'Cecil Sharp']

GEORGE BAXT 1923–

13 I never get invited to orgies. It's just as well. I wouldn't know which way to turn. [From *The Dorothy Parker Murder Case*, in the *Sunday Times*, 13 Oct. 1985]

SIR BEVERLEY BAXTER 1891–1964

14 Beaverbrook is so pleased to be in the Government that he is like the town tart who has finally married the Mayor! [In Sir Henry Channon, *Chips: The Diaries*, 12 June 1940]

RABBI ANTHONY BAYFIELD 1946–

15 As everyone knows, where there are two Jews there are three opinions. [In the *Guardian*, 31 Dec. 1987]

STEPHEN BAYLEY 1951–

16 Civilizations are remembered by their artefacts, not their bank-rates. [In the *Observer*, 9 Mar. 1986]

LILIAN BAYLIS 1874–1937

17 I can't see anything but hands and we can't pay you for that. [On turning down Michael Redgrave at a Shakespeare audition. In his obituary in the *Guardian*, 22 Mar. 1985]

1 Dear God, send me good actors and send them cheap. [Of 1932 season at the Old Vic, London. In Dame Peggy Ashcroft's obituary in the *Guardian*, 15 June 1991]

'BEACHCOMBER' *see* MORTON, J. B.

DITTA BEARD

2 I don't put anything in writing. If it's important enough, you shouldn't, and if it is not important enough, why bother? [In Anthony Sampson, *The Sovereign State*, Ch. 9]

VICE-ADMIRAL EARL BEATTY
1871–1936

3 Chatfield, there seems to be something wrong with our bloody ships today. [Attr., on sinking of battle-cruisers at Battle of Jutland, 30 May 1916, according to Winston Churchill, *The World Crisis*, Ch. 41]

WARREN BEATTY 1937–

4 I'm not going to make the same mistake once. (Of marriage. In *Was It Good for You Too?*, ed. Bob Chieger]

5 The difference between directing yourself and being directed is the difference between masturbating and making love. [From *Premiere*, in the *Independent on Sunday*, 5 Jan. 1992]

GEORGE BEAUCHAMP

6 She was one of the early birds, / And I was one of the worms. [Song: *She was a Sweet Little Dickie Bird*, sung by Beauchamp]

SIMONE DE BEAUVOIR 1908–1986

7 One is not born a woman, one becomes one. [*The Second Sex*, Ch. 2]

8 For years I thought my work was in front of me, and now it is behind me: at no moment was it with me. [In obituary in the *Observer*, 20 Apr. 1986]

LORD BEAVERBROOK 1879–1964

9 With the publication of his [Earl Haig's] Private Papers in 1952, he committed suicide twenty-five years after his death. [*Men of Power*, p. xviii]

10 He [Lloyd George] did not seem to care which way he travelled provided he was in the driver's seat. [*The Decline and Fall of Lloyd George*, Ch. 7]

11 This is my final word. It is time for me to become an apprentice once more. I have not settled in which direction. But somewhere, sometime, soon. [Speech at Dorchester Hotel, London, on 25 May 1964, his 85th birthday; his last public statement]

12 If you can walk over a man once, you can walk over him as often as you like. [Quoted by Sir John Junor in interview in the *Sunday Times*, 3 Sept. 1989]

SAMUEL BECKETT 1906–1989

13 It is suicide to be abroad. But what is it to be at home . . . what is it to be at home? A lingering dissolution. [*All That Fall*]

14 We could have saved sixpence. We have saved fivepence. (*Pause*) But at what cost?

15 That's what hell must be like, small chat to the babbling of Lethe about the good old days when we wished we were dead. [*Embers*]

16 But we breathe, we change! We lose our hair, our teeth! Our bloom! Our ideas! [*Endgame*]

17 CLOV: Do you believe in the life to come?
HAMM: Mine was always that.

18 After all I'm your father. It's true if it hadn't been me it would have been someone else. But that's no excuse.

19 Personally I have no bone to pick with graveyards. [*First Love*]

20 No better, no worse, no change. [*Happy Days*, Act I]

21 For why be discouraged, one of the thieves was saved, that is a generous percentage. [*Malone Dies*, slight variant in *Waiting for Godot*, Act I]

22 Death must take me for someone else.

23 The sun shone, having no alternative, on the nothing new. [*Murphy*, opening words]

24 There is no return game between a man and his stars.

1 Ever tried. Ever failed. No matter. Try again. Fail again. Fail better. [*Nohow On*, '*Worstward Ho*']

2 Where I am, I don't know, I'll never know, in the silence you don't know, you must go on, I can't go on, I'll go on. [*The Unnamable*, last words]

3 Nothing to be done. [*Waiting for Godot*, Act I, opening words]

4 ESTRAGON: . . . Let's go.
VLADIMIR: We can't.
ESTRAGON: Why not?
VLADIMIR: We're waiting for Godot.

5 He can't think without his hat.

6 VLADIMIR: That passed the time.
ESTRAGON: It would have passed in any case.
VLADIMIR: Yes, but not so rapidly.

7 We all are born mad. Some remain so. [II]

8 They give birth astride of a grave, the light gleams an instant, then it's night once more.

9 [James] Joyce was a synthesizer, trying to bring in as much as he could. I am an analyser, trying to leave out as much as I can. [In *The New York Times*, 'Beckett at 75', 19 Apr. 1981]

10 I suppose that I'm a spoiled hermit. [Quoted at his death by John Montague in the *Observer*, 27 Dec. 1989]

11 All art is the same – an attempt to fill an empty space. [Interview with Peter Lennon in the *Guardian*, 25 Jan. 1990]

GERALDINE BEDELL 1956–

12 Feminism is an insurrection, not a coffee morning. [In the *Independent*, 14 Nov. 1988]

WILLIAM BEEBE 1877–1962

13 The isness of things is well worth studying; but it is their whyness that makes life worth living. [In Konrad Lorenz, *On Aggression*, Ch. 2]

SIR THOMAS BEECHAM 1879–1961

14 Musicians did not like the piece [Strauss's *Elektra*] at all. One eminent British composer on leaving the theatre was asked what he thought of it. 'Words fail me,' he replied, 'and I'm going home at once to play the chord of C major twenty times over to satisfy myself that it still exists.' [*A Mingled Chime*, Ch. 18]

15 The plain fact is that music *per se* means nothing; it is sheer sound, and the interpreter can do no more with it than his own capacities, mental and spiritual, will allow, and the same applies to the listener. [33]

16 A musicologist is a man who can read music but can't hear it. [In H. Proctor-Gregg, *Beecham Remembered*, 'Beecham's Obiter Dicta']

17 There are two golden rules for an orchestra: start together and finish together. The public doesn't give a damn what goes on in between. [In H. Atkins and A. Newman, *Beecham Stories*]

18 A kind of musical Malcolm Sargent. [Of Herbert von Karajan]

19 The English may not like music – but they absolutely love the noise it makes.

20 Why do we have to have all these third-rate foreign conductors around – when we have so many second-rate ones of our own?

21 You have between your legs the most sensitive instrument known to man, and all you can do is to sit there and scratch it. [To woman cellist. Attr. in *Dictionary of Musical Quotations*, comp. I. Crofton and D. Fraser]

22 The sound of the harpsichord resembles that of a bird-cage played with toasting forks. [Attr.]

'CAPTAIN BEEFHEART' 1941–

23 Everybody's coloured or else you wouldn't be able to see them. [In *Dictionary of Outrageous Quotations*, comp. C. R. S. Marsden]

PATRICIA BEER 1924–

24 He considered it essential to believe in the existence of hell but unnecessary to believe that there was anybody in it. [*Moon's Ottery*, Ch. 6]

MAX BEERBOHM 1872–1956

25 He [G. Bernard Shaw] cannot see beyond

his own nose. Even the fingers he outstretches from it to the world are (as I shall suggest) often invisible to him. [*Around Theatres*, 'A Conspectus of G.B.S.']

1 I believe the twenty-four hour day has come to stay. [*A Christmas Garland*, 'Perkins and Mankind']

2 It is doubtful whether the people of southern England have even yet realized how much introspection there is going on all the time in the Five Towns. ['Scruts']

3 Most women are not so young as they are painted. [*A Defence of Cosmetics*]

4 There is always something rather absurd about the past. [*1880*]

5 To give an accurate and exhaustive account of that period would need a far less brilliant pen than mine.

6 A swear-word in a rustic slum / A simple swear-word is to some, / To Masefield something more. [*Fifty Caricatures*, caption; parody of W. Wordsworth]

7 Undergraduates owe their happiness chiefly to the consciousness that they are no longer at school. The nonsense which was knocked out of them at school is all put gently back at Oxford or Cambridge. [*Going Back to School*]

8 None, it is said, of all who revelled with the Regent, was half so wicked as Lord George Hell. [*The Happy Hypocrite*, Ch. 1]

9 No Roman ever was able to say, 'I dined last night with the Borgias'. [*Hosts and Guests*]

10 Fate wrote her [Queen Caroline] a most tremendous tragedy, and she played it in tights. [*King George the Fourth*]

11 'After all,' as a pretty girl once said to me, 'women are a sex by themselves, so to speak.' [*The Pervasion of Rouge*]

12 I looked out for what the metropolitan reviewers would have to say. They seemed to fall into two classes: those who had little to say and those who had nothing. [*Seven Men*, 'Enoch Soames']

13 O the disgrace of it! – / The scandal, the incredible come-down! ['Savonarola Brown']

14 A hundred eyes were fixed on her, and half as many hearts lost to her. [*Zuleika Dobson*, Ch. 1]

15 She had the air of a born unpacker – swift and firm, yet withal tender . . . She was one of those born to make chaos cosmic. [2]

16 Zuleika, on a desert island, would have spent most of her time in looking for a man's footprint. [2]

17 She was hardly more affable than a cameo. [3]

18 The dullard's envy of brilliant men is always assuaged by the suspicion that they will come to a bad end. [4]

19 Women who love the same man have a kind of bitter freemasonry.

20 You will find that the woman who is really kind to dogs is always one who has failed to inspire sympathy in men. [6]

21 Beauty and the lust for learning have yet to be allied. [7]

22 You will think me lamentably crude: my experience of life has been drawn from life itself.

23 You cannot make a man by standing a sheep on its hind legs. But by standing a flock of sheep in that position you can make a crowd of men. [9]

24 She had the sensitiveness, though no other quality whatsoever, of the true artist. [10]

25 There he adjusted his hat with care, and regarded himself very seriously, very sternly, from various angles, like a man invited to paint his own portrait for the Uffizi. [14]

26 The Socratic manner is not a game at which two can play. [15]

27 'Ah, say that again,' she murmured. 'Your voice is music.'
He repeated his question.
'Music,' she said, dreamily; and such is the force of habit that 'I don't,' she added, 'know anything about music, really. But I know what I like.' [16]

28 And love levels all, doesn't it? Love and the Board school. [17]

29 Byron! – he would be all forgotten today if he had lived to be a florid old gentleman with iron-grey whiskers, writing very long, very able letters to *The Times* about the Repeal of the Corn Laws. [18]

30 What were they going to do with the

Grail when they found it, Mr Rossetti? [Cartoon caption]

1 Of course we all know that [William] Morris was a wonderful all-round man, but the act of walking round him has always tired me. [In S. N. Behrman, *Conversations with Max*, Ch. 2]

2 It's not in support of cricket but as an earnest protest against golf. [On subscribing a shilling to W. G. Grace's Testimonial. In *Carr's Dictionary of Extraordinary English Cricketers*]

BRENDAN BEHAN 1923–1964

3 He was born an Englishman and remained one for years. [*The Hostage*, Act I]

4 PAT: He was an Anglo-Irishman.
MEG: In the blessed name of God, what's that?
PAT: A Protestant with a horse.

5 Meanwhile I'll sing that famous old song, 'The Hound that caught the Pubic Hare'.

6 When I came back to Dublin, I was courtmartialled in my absence and sentenced to death in my absence, so I said they could shoot me in my absence.

7 I wish I'd been a mixed infant. [II]

8 I am a sociable worker.

9 Go on, abuse me – your own husband that took you off the streets on a Sunday morning, when there wasn't a pub open in the city. [III]

10 We're here because we're queer / Because we're queer because we're here.

11 Other people have a nationality. The Irish and the Jews have a psychosis. [*Richard's Cork Leg*, Act I]

BRIAN BEHAN 1927–

12 Brighton is Dublin without priests. Brighton is tolerance by the sea. Dublin is intolerance by the sea. [Interview in the *Sunday Times*, 18 Sept. 1988]

EDWARD BEHR 1926–

13 Anyone Here Been Raped and Speaks English? [Title of book, reputedly based on question British TV reporter asked Belgian refugees in the Congo]

CLIVE BELL 1881–1964

14 It would follow that 'significant form' was form behind which we catch a sense of ultimate reality. [*Art*, Pt 1, Ch. 3]

15 One account ... given me by a good artist, is that what he tries to express in a picture is 'a passionate apprehension of form'.

16 Art and Religion are, then, two roads by which men escape from circumstance to ecstasy. [II. 1]

17 I will try to account for the degree of my aesthetic emotion. That, I conceive, is the function of the critic. [II. 3]

18 Let the artist have just enough to eat, and the tools of his trade: ask nothing of him. Materially make the life of the artist sufficiently miserable to be unattractive, and no one will take to art save those in whom the divine daemon is absolute. [V. 1]

19 Comfort came in with the middle classes. [*Civilization*, Ch. 4]

20 Only reason can convince us of those three fundamental truths without a recognition of which there can be no effective liberty: that what we believe is not necessarily true; that what we like is not necessarily good; and that all questions are open. [5]

H. E. BELL

21 Parents are the very last people who ought to be allowed to have children. [Speech at University of Reading, Mar. 1977]

JAMES WARNER BELLAH 1899–1976
and WILLIS GOLDBECK 1899–1979

22 When the legend becomes fact, print the legend. [In film *Who Shot Liberty Valance?*]

GUY BELLAMY 1935–

23 A French five minutes is ten minutes shorter than a Spanish five minutes, but slightly longer than an English five minutes which is usually ten minutes. [*Comedy Hotel*, Ch. 12]

24 If this paper had covered the crucifixion, Fred thought, it would have had a graph on the front page showing the rising cost of timber. [*I Have a Complaint to Make*, Ch. 5]

1 Did you know that hamsters mate one day in three and fight two days in three? Just like human beings. [7]

2 Either we've got bats or the mice have taken up hang-gliding. [*The Nudists*, Ch. 4]

3 I'm in the last eight of the world celibacy championships. Meet the Pope in the quarter finals. [*The Secret Lemonade Drinker*, Ch. 1]

4 THE WORLD ENDED YESTERDAY. TODAY IS AN ACTION REPLAY.

5 If all Englishmen were like him we wouldn't have colonized the Isle of Wight. [2]

6 The world beats a path past his door. [*The Sinner's Congregation*, Ch. 7]

7 Reporters don't believe in anything, vicar. It's an article of faith. [*A Village Called Sin*, Ch. 15]

HILAIRE BELLOC 1870–1953

8 When people call this beast to mind, / They marvel more and more / At such a little tail behind, / So large a trunk before. [*The Bad Child's Book of Beasts*, 'The Elephant']

9 I shoot the Hippopotamus / With bullets made of platinum, / Because if I use leaden ones / His hide is sure to flatten 'em. ['The Hippopotamus']

10 The nicest child I ever knew / Was Charles Augustus Fortescue. [*Cautionary Tales*, 'Charles Augustus Fortescue']

11 Alas! That such affected tricks / Should flourish in a child of six! ['Godolphin Horne']

12 The chief defect of Henry King / Was chewing little bits of string. ['Henry King']

13 They answered, as they took their fees, / 'There is no cure for this disease'.

14 There was a boy whose name was Jim; / His friends were very good to him. ['Jim']

15 'Ponto!' he cried, with angry frown, / 'Let go, Sir! Down, Sir! Put it down!'

16 And always keep a hold of Nurse / For fear of finding something worse.

17 Lord Lundy from his earliest years / Was far too freely moved to tears. ['Lord Lundy']

18 In my opinion butlers ought / To know their place, and not to play / The Old Retainer night and day.

19 We had intended you to be / The next Prime Minister but three.

20 My language fails! / Go out and govern New South Wales!

21 Matilda told such dreadful lies, / It made one gasp and stretch one's eyes; / Her aunt, who, from her earliest youth, / Had kept a strict regard for truth, / Attempted to believe Matilda: / The effort very nearly killed her. ['Matilda']

22 And summoned the immediate aid / Of London's noble Fire Brigade.

23 Her aunt was off to the theatre / To see that interesting play / *The Second Mrs Tanqueray*.

24 For every time she shouted 'Fire!' / They only answered 'Little liar!'

25 A trick that everyone abhors / In little girls is slamming doors. ['Rebecca']

26 Child! do not throw this book about! / Refrain from the unholy pleasure / Of cutting all the pictures out! [*Dedication on the Gift of a Book to a Child*]

27 From quiet homes and first beginning, / Out to the undiscovered ends, / There's nothing worth the wear of winning, / But laughter and the love of friends. [*Dedicatory Ode*]

28 They died to save their country and they only saved the world. [*The English Graves*]

29 I said to Heart, 'How goes it?' Heart replied: / 'Right as a Ribstone Pippin!' But it lied. [*Epigrams*, 'The False Heart']

30 I'm tired of Love: I'm still more tired of Rhyme. / But Money gives me pleasure all the time. ['Fatigue']

31 Of this bad world the loveliest and best / Has smiled and said 'Good Night', and gone to rest. ['On a Dead Hostess']

32 The accursed power which stands on Privilege / (And goes with Women, and Champagne, and Bridge) / Broke – and Democracy resumed her reign: / (Which goes with Bridge, and Women, and Champagne). ['On a General Election']

33 When I am dead, I hope it may be said: / 'His sins were scarlet, but his books were read'. ['On His Books']

34 The Devil, having nothing else to do, /

Went off to tempt my Lady Poltagrue. / My Lady, tempted by a private whim, / To his extreme annoyance, tempted him. ['On Lady Poltagrue']

1 Pale Ebenezer thought it wrong to fight, / But Roaring Bill (who killed him) thought it right. ['The Pacifist']

2 Sally is gone that was so kindly, / Sally is gone from Ha'nacker Hill. [*Ha'nacker Mill*]

3 Remote and ineffectual Don / That dared attack my Chesterton. [*Lines to a Don*]

4 Dons admirable! Dons of might! / Uprising on my inward sight / Compact of ancient tales, and port, / And sleep – and learning of a sort.

5 Lord Finchley tried to mend the Electric Light / Himself. It struck him dead: And serve him right! / It is the business of the wealthy man / To give employment to the artisan. [*Lord Finchley*]

6 Oh! let us never, never doubt / What nobody is sure about! [*More Beasts for Worse Children*, 'The Microbe']

7 I had an aunt in Yucatan / Who bought a python from a man / And kept it for a pet. / She died, because she never knew / These simple little rules and few: – / The snake is living yet. ['The Python']

8 Birds in their little nests agree with Chinamen, but not with me. [*New Cautionary Tales*, 'On Food']

9 The Moral is (I think, at least) / That Man is an UNGRATEFUL BEAST. ['A Reproof of Gluttony']

10 When I am living in the Midlands / That are sodden and unkind. [*The South Country*]

11 I will hold my house in the high wood / Within a walk of the sea, / And the men that were boys when I was a boy / Shall sit and drink with me.

12 Do you remember an inn, / Miranda? [*Tarantella*]

13 The fleas that tease in the high Pyrenees.

14 You find when you are giving up the ghost, / That those who loved you best despised you most. [In Sagittarius and D. George, *The Perpetual Pessimist*]

15 It is the best of all trades, to make songs, and the second best to sing them. [*On Everything*, 'On Song']

16 The Servile State. [Title of book]

17 When you have lost your inns drown your empty selves, for you will have lost the last of England. [*This and That*, 'On Inns']

18 I always like to associate with a lot of priests because it makes me understand anti-clerical things so well. [Letter to E. S. P. Haynes, 9 Nov. 1909. In Robert Speaight, *Life of Hilaire Belloc*, Ch. 17]

19 The poor darlings [the Jews], I'm awfully fond of them and I'm awfully sorry for them, but it's their own silly fault – they ought to have let God alone. [Letter to the author. In Ch. 19]

SAUL BELLOW 1915–

20 Everyone knows there is no fineness or accuracy of suppression. If you hold down one thing you hold down the adjoining. [*The Adventures of Augie March*, quoted by Salman Rushdie in lecture 'Is Nothing Sacred?', 6 Feb. 1990]

21 A first-class man subsists on the matter he destroys, just as the stars do. [*The Bellarosa Connection*]

22 The word 'colleague' had far more weight here [Romania]. Americans now said 'associate', as in 'Ali Baba and the Forty Associates'. [*The Dean's December*, Ch. 4]

23 There's the big advantage of backwardness. By the time the latest ideas reach Chicago, they're worn thin and easy to see through. You don't have to bother with them and it saves lots of trouble. [6]

24 Tears may be intellectual, but they can never be political. They save no man from being shot, no child from being thrown alive into the furnace. [12]

25 As a rule Corde avoided cemeteries and never went near the graves of his parents. He said it was just as easy for your dead to visit you, only by now he would have to hire a hall. [15]

26 America is so big, and everyone is working, making, digging, bulldozing, trucking, loading, and so on, and I guess the sufferers suffer at the same rate. [*Henderson the Rain King*, Ch. 3]

1 A man may say, 'From now on I'm going to speak the truth.' But the truth hears him and runs away and hides before he's even done speaking. [*Herzog*, p. 271]

2 History had created something new in the USA, namely crookedness with self-respect or duplicity with honour. [*Humboldt's Gift*, p. 217]

3 The only real distinction at this dangerous moment in human history and cosmic development has nothing to do with medals and ribbons. Not to fall asleep is distinguished. Everything else is mere popcorn. [277]

4 The secret motive of the absent-minded is to be innocent while guilty. Absent-mindedness is spurious innocence. [*More Die of Heartbreak*, p. 155]

5 Erotic practices have become diversified. Sex used to be single-crop farming, like cotton or wheat; now people raise all kinds of things. [317]

6 Was it my sister or was it you who said I was a phoenix who runs with arsonists? [334]

7 I am more stupid about some things than about others; not equally stupid in all directions; I am not a well-rounded person. [*Mr Sammler's Planet*, Ch. 2]

8 Conquered people tend to be witty.

9 Mr Sammler with his screwy visions! He saw the increasing triumph of Enlightenment – Liberty, Equality, Adultery! [3]

10 There is much to be said for exotic marriages. If your husband is a bore, it takes years longer to discover it. [6]

11 I think that New York is not the cultural centre of America, but the business and administrative centre of American culture. [Radio interview. In the *Listener*, 22 May 1969]

12 After all these years wallowing in low seriousness – low seriousness, you understand, is high seriousness that's failed. [Interview in the *Sunday Times*, 12 Jan. 1975]

13 Bellow says he spent the first third of his life absorbing material, the second third trying to make himself famous, and the last third trying to avoid fame. [Edward Hoagland, *Learning to Eat Soup*]

14 In expressing love we belong among the undeveloped countries. [In *Lover's Quotation Book*, ed. Helen Handley]

15 One cannot touch a fig-leaf without it turning into a price tag. [Attr.]

LUDWIG BEMELMANS 1898–1982

16 An American woman, a tourist, a refugee from a conducted tour of the Châteaux de la Loire. She dismissed the historic safari with the words: 'Nothing but thick walls and running comment.' [*How to Travel Incognito*, Ch. 1]

ROBERT BENCHLEY 1889–1945

17 Even nowadays a man can't step up and kill a woman without feeling just a bit unchivalrous. [*Chips off the Old Benchley*, 'Down in Front']

18 I had just dozed off into a stupor when I heard what I thought was myself talking to myself. I didn't pay much attention to it, as I knew practically everything I would have to say to myself, and wasn't particularly interested. ['The First Pigeon of Spring']

19 My only solution for the problem of habitual accidents . . . is for everybody to stay in bed all day. Even then, there is always the chance that you will fall out. ['Good Luck']

20 A great many people have come up to me and asked how I manage to get so much work done and still keep looking so dissipated. ['How to Get Things Done']

21 The biggest obstacle to professional writing today is the necessity for changing a typewriter ribbon. ['Learn to Write']

22 I have been told by hospital authorities that more copies of my works are left behind by departing patients than those of any other author. ['Why Does Nobody Collect Me?']

23 Often Daddy sat up very late working on a case of Scotch. [*Editha's Christmas Burglar*]

24 I haven't been abroad in so long that I almost speak English without an accent. [*Inside Benchley*, 'The Old Sea Rover Speaks']

25 The wise man thinks once before he speaks twice. [*Maxims from the Chinese*]

26 In America there are two classes of travel – first class, and with children. [*Pluck and Luck*]

1 The surest way to make a monkey of a man is to quote him. [*Quick Quotations*]

2 Show me a Sunday paper which has been left in a condition fit only for kite flying, and I will show you an antisocial and dangerous character who has left it that way. [*The Wreck of the Sunday Paper*]

3 Streets full of water. Please advise. [Telegram on arriving in Venice]

4 [When asked by Scott Fitzgerald, 'Don't you know drinking is a slow death?'] So who's in a hurry? [In review of Sheilah Graham's *The Garden of Allah* in the *Sunday Times*, 20 June 1971]

5 I do most of my work sitting down; that's where I shine. [In R. E. Drennan, *Wit's End*]

6 As for me, except for an occasional heart attack – I feel as young as I ever did. [In Groucho Marx, *The Groucho Letters*]

7 One who gets paid per word, per piece, or perhaps. [Definition of a freelance writer. Quoted by James Thurber in letter to Frances Glennon, 24 June 1959, *Selected Letters*, ed. Helen Thurber and Edward Weeks]

8 Only a humorist could take humour apart, and he has too much humour to do it.

9 She sleeps alone at last. [Suggested epitaph on a certain actress. In *Dictionary of Twentieth Century Quotations*, ed. Nigel Rees]

JULIEN BENDA 1867–1956

10 *La trahison des clercs*. – The treason of the intellectuals. [Title of book, 1927]

EDUARD BENES 1884–1948

11 *Sécurité collective*. – Collective security. [Words written on a typed draft put before the League of Nations, 1932. A French delegate is said to have protested, '*Impossible; ce n'est pas français.*' – 'Impossible; it's not French.' In G. M. Young, *Stanley Baldwin*, Ch. 17]

STEPHEN VINCENT BENÉT 1898–1943

12 Bury my heart at Wounded Knee. [*American Names*]

WALTER BENJAMIN 1892–1940

13 All the decisive blows are struck left-handed. [*One-way Street*]

14 The art of the critic in a nutshell: to coin slogans without betraying ideas.

15 Technology is not the mastery of nature but of the relationship between nature and humanity. [In the *New Statesman*, 30 Jan. 1987]

TONY BENN, MP 1925–

16 I am on the right wing of the middle of the road with a strong radical bias. [Said in 1950s. In *Dictionary of Twentieth Century Quotations*, ed. Nigel Rees]

17 The British House of Lords is the British Outer Mongolia for retired politicians. [On renouncing his peerage. In the *Observer*, 4 Feb. 1962. Also ascr. to Molotov; see 267:7]

18 Britain today is suffering from galloping obsolescence. [In the *Observer*, 'Sayings of the Week', 2 Feb. 1963]

19 Whereas 25 years ago we were an empire, now we are a colony, with the IMF running our financial affairs, the Common Market Commission running our legislation and NATO running our armed forces. [To the Queen. In his diaries, *Conflicts of Interest*, 8 May 1979]

20 A faith is something you die for; a doctrine is something you kill for: there is all the difference in the world. [In the *Observer*, 'Sayings of the Week', 16 Apr. 1989]

21 Most things in life are moments of pleasure and a lifetime of embarrassment; photography is a moment of embarrassment and a lifetime of pleasure. [In the *Sunday Times*, 31 Dec.]

RICHARD BENNER

22 Canada is a country so square that even the female impersonators are women. [From film *Outrageous*, in the *Guardian*, /21 Sept. 1978]

ALAN BENNETT 1934–

23 Life is rather like a tin of sardines – we're all of us looking for the key. [*Beyond the Fringe*]

24 We roll back the lid of the sardine tin of life, we reveal the sardines, the riches of life

therein, and we get them out, we enjoy them. But, you know, there's always a little piece in the corner you can't get out. I wonder – I wonder, is there a little piece in the corner of your life? I know there is in mine.

1 Mr Craven's always been on the side of progress: he had false teeth when he was twenty-seven. [*Enjoy*, Act I]

2 If you've got tits you don't work for the council; you get yourself into the private sector.

3 I have never understood this liking for war. It panders to instincts already catered for within the scope of any respectable domestic establishment. [*Forty Years On*, Act I]

4 [BERTRAND] RUSSELL: But then I have led a very sheltered life. I had no contact with my own body until the spring of 1887, when I suddenly found my feet. I deduced the rest logically.

5 Were we closer to the ground as children or is the grass emptier now?

6 Sidney and Beatrice Webb – two nice people if ever there was one. [Not in published text]

7 It's the one species I wouldn't mind seeing vanish from the face of the earth. I wish they were like the White Rhino – six of them left in the Serengeti National Park, and all males. [Of dogs. *Getting On*, Act I]

8 I had a good education but it never went to my head, somehow. It should be a journey ending up with you at a different place. It didn't take with me. My degree was a kind of inoculation. I got just enough education to make me immune from it for the rest of my life.

9 I thought life was going to be like Brahms, do you know? Instead it's well it's been Eric Coates. And very nice, too. But not Brahms. [II]

10 Classics – and in particular modern classics – are the books one thinks one ought to read, thinks one has read. [*Kafka's Dick*, Introduction]

11 The theory these days (or one of them) is that the reader brings as much to the book as the author. So how much more do readers bring who have never managed to get

through the book at all? It follows that the books one remembers best are the books one has never read.

12 All modesty is false, otherwise it's not modesty. [Act I]

13 The only son who ever told the truth about his father was Jesus Christ – and there are doubts about him. [II]

14 Quite candidly I've never seen the point of the sea. Except where it meets the land. The shore has point, the sea none. Of course when you say you miss the sea that's what you mean: you miss the shore. [*The Old Country*, Act I]

15 They are the most embarrassed people in the world, the English. You cannot look each other in the face ... Is there anyone not embarrassed in England? The Queen perhaps. She is not embarrassed. With the rest it's 'I won't make you feel bad as long as you don't make me feel bad'. That is the social contract. Society is making each other feel better.

16 One of the few lessons I have learned in life is that there is invariably something odd about women who wear ankle socks.

17 The good is better than the best, else what does society mean? [II]

18 We were put to Dickens as children but it never quite took. That unremitting humanity soon had me cheesed off.

19 My trouble is I lack what the English call character. By which they mean the power to refrain. [*Single Spies*, 'An Englishman Abroad']

20 The trouble is, whenever I meet anybody they're always on their best behaviour. And when one is on one's best behaviour one isn't always at one's best. ['A Question of Attribution']

21 If you think squash is a competitive activity try flower-arranging. [*Talking Heads*, 'Bed among the Lentils']

22 'But he's so silly,' pompous people would tell you, not understanding that was why one loved him, that to be silly is not to be foolish. [Of Russell Harty at his funeral, 1988]

23 [When asked whether he was homo-

sexual, at an Aids benefit concert] That was a bit like asking a man crawling across the Sahara whether he would prefer Perrier or Malvern water. [In the *Observer*, 12 June 1988]

1 A book chooses its readers as a play chooses its audience. [In *With Great Pleasure*, ed. Alec Reid]

ARNOLD BENNETT 1867–1931

2 'Ye can call it influenza if ye like,' said Mrs Machin. 'There was no influenza in my young days. We called a cold a cold.' [*The Card*, Ch. 8]

3 'What great cause is he identified with?'
  'He's identified . . . with the great cause of cheering us all up.' [Last words of the book]

4 A man accustomed to think in millions – other people's millions. [*Journal*, June 1929]

5 Every Briton is at heart a Tory – especially every British Liberal. [Dec. 1929]

6 Mr Lloyd George . . . spoke for a hundred and seventeen minutes, in which period he was detected only once in the use of an argument. [*Things That Have Interested Me*, 'After the March Offensive']

7 Pessimism, when you get used to it, is just as agreeable as optimism. ['The Slump in Pessimism']

8 Being a husband is a whole-time job. That is why so many husbands fail. They cannot give their entire attention to it. [*The Title*, Act I]

9 Journalists say a thing that they know isn't true, in the hope that if they keep on saying it long enough it *will* be true. [II]

10 Between thirty and forty a man may have reached the height of discretion without having tumbled over the top into the feather-bed of correctitude. [In *Evening Standard Years*, 29 May 1930]

11 Good taste is better than bad taste, but bad taste is better than no taste. [In the *Observer*, 'Sayings of the Week', 24 Aug. 1930]

JACK BENNY 1894–1974

12 Cannibal – A guy who goes into a restaur-

ant and orders the waiter. [In A. K. Adams, *Cassell's Book of Humorous Quotations*]

13 I don't deserve this, but I have arthritis, and I don't deserve that either. [On accepting an award. In P. and J. Holton, *Quote and Unquote*]

A. C. BENSON 1862–1925

14 Land of Hope and Glory, Mother of the Free, / How shall we extol thee, who are born of thee? / Wider still and wider shall thy bounds be set; / God who made thee mighty, make thee mightier yet. [Song, set to music by Sir Edward Elgar in *Pomp and Circumstance*]

E. C. BENTLEY 1875–1956

15 I cannot think of any repartee, / I simply wag my great, long, furry ears. [*Ballade of Plain Common Sense*]

16 Geography is about maps, / But Biography is about chaps. [*Biography for Beginners*]

17 What I like about Clive / Is that he is no longer alive. / There is a great deal to be said / For being dead. ['Clive']

18 George the Third / Ought never to have occurred. / One can only wonder / At so grotesque a blunder. ['George III']

19 Sir Christopher Wren / Said, 'I am going to dine with some men, / If anybody calls / Say I am designing St Paul's.' ['Sir Christopher Wren']

ERIC BENTLEY 1916–

20 Farce . . . is the theatre of the surrealist body. [*The Life of Drama*, Ch. 7]

NICOLAS BENTLEY 1908–1978

21 He who enjoys a good neighbour, said the Greeks, has a precious possession. Same goes for the neighbour's wife. [In *Treasury of Humorous Quotations*, ed. Evan Esar and Nicolas Bentley]

22 His was the sort of career that made the Recording Angel think seriously about taking up shorthand.

LLOYD BENTSEN [Unsuccessful US vice-presidential candidate] 1921–

23 Oh, what if I am a textual deviant. [On

departing from his written speeches. In the *Independent*, 'Quote Unquote', 5 Nov. 1988]

BERNARD BERENSON 1865–1959

1 In figure painting, the type of all painting, I have endeavoured to set forth that the principal if not sole source of life enchantments are Tactile Values, Movement and Space Composition. [*The Decline of Art*]

2 We define genius as the capacity for productive reaction against one's training.

3 History is an art which must not neglect the known facts. [Attr.]

ELISABETH BERESFORD

4 Make Good Use of Bad Rubbish. [*The Wombles*, Ch. 1]

5 Human Beings are an untidy lot. They'd lose their arms and legs if they weren't joined on right.

JOHN BERGER 1926–

6 The dead are the imagination of the living. [*And Our Faces, My Heart, Brief as Photos*]

7 The five senses within whose pentagon each man is alone. [*G*, III. 5]

8 If we could all live a thousand years . . . we would each, at least once during that period, be considered a genius. Not because of our great age, but because one of our gifts or aptitudes, however slight in itself, would coincide with what people at that particular moment took to be the mark of genius. [6]

9 It is not usually possible in a poem or a story to make the relationship between particular and universal fully explicit. Those who try to do so end up writing parables. [*Pig Earth*, 'Historical Afterword']

10 All stories, before they are narrated, begin with the end. [*Story for Aesop*]

11 All weddings are similar but every marriage is different. Death comes to everyone but one mourns alone. [*The White Bird*, 'The Storyteller']

12 The spectacle creates an eternal present of immediate expectation; memory ceases to be necessary or desirable. With the loss of memory the continuities of meaning and judgement are also lost to us. The camera relieves us of the burden of memory. [In *New Society*, 17 Aug. 1978]

13 Peasants are the most observant class in the world. They notice and read more coded signs every day than an intelligence agent does in a week. This makes them brilliant tacticians. But they have seldom been in a position to be strategists, and their philosophy has been opposed to it. [17 May 1979]

14 Photography, because it stops the flow of life, is always flirting with death. [22/29 Dec. 1983]

15 Every city has a sex and age which have nothing to do with demography. Rome is feminine . . . London is a teen-ager and urchin, and, in this, hasn't changed since the time of Dickens. Paris, I believe, is a man in his twenties in love with an older woman. [In the *Guardian*, 27 Mar. 1987]

16 Every painted image of something is also about the absence of the real thing. All painting is about the presence of absence. This is why man paints. The broken pictorial space confesses the art's wishfulness. [In *New Statesman and Society*, 15 July 1988]

17 Post-modernism has cut off the present from all futures. The daily media add to this by cutting off the past. [In the *Guardian*, 21 Sept. 1989]

JOHN BERGER *et al.*

18 The social presence of a woman is different in kind from that of a man . . . A man's presence suggests what he is capable of doing to you or for you . . . A woman's presence . . . defines what can and cannot be done to her. [*Ways of Seeing*]

19 To be naked is to be oneself. To be nude is to be seen naked by others, and yet not recognized for oneself . . . Nudity is a form of dress.

INGRID BERGMAN 1915–1982

20 Play it, Sam. Play 'As Time Goes By'. [In film *Casablanca*, script by Julius J. Epstein, Philip G. Epstein and Howard Koch. Usually misquoted as 'Play it again, Sam' and falsely attr. to Humphrey Bogart in that film]

1 A gentleman farmer who raises goose-flesh. [Of Alfred Hitchcock at his 80th birthday dinner, 1979. In *Woman Talk 2*, comp. Michèle Brown and Ann O'Connor]

IRVING BERLIN 1888–1989

2 Come on and hear, come on and hear, Alexander's Ragtime Band. [Song: *Alexander's Ragtime Band*]

3 Doin' What Comes Natur'lly. [Title of song in musical *Annie Get Your Gun*, Act I]

4 There's No Business Like Show Business. [Title of song]

5 They say that falling in love is wonderful, / It's wonderful, so they say. [Song: *Falling in Love*]

6 Anything You Can Do, I Can Do Better. [Title of song, II]

7 The Hostess with the Mostes' on the Ball. [Title of song in musical *Call Me Madam*, Act I]

8 We joined the Navy to see the world, / And what did we see? We saw the sea. [Song: *We Saw the Sea*, in musical *Follow the Fleet*]

9 God Bless America. [Title of song]

10 I'm dreaming of a white Christmas, / Just like the ones I used to know. [Song: *White Christmas*, in musical *Holiday Inn*]

11 This is the army, Mr Jones, / No private rooms or telephones. [Song: *This is the Army*]

12 Oh, How I Hate to Get Up in the Morning. [Title of song in musical *Yip, Yip Yaphank*]

13 The song is ended / But the melody lingers on. [Song: *The Song is Ended*, in musical *Ziegfeld Follies*]

SIR ISAIAH BERLIN 1909–

14 Rousseau was the first militant lowbrow. [In the *Observer*, 'Sayings of the Week', 9 Nov. 1952]

15 Society moves by some degree of parricide, by which the children, on the whole, kill, if not their fathers, at least the beliefs of their fathers, and arrive at new beliefs. This is what progress is. [In BBC TV programme *Men of Ideas*, 19 Jan. 1978]

CHAIM BERMANT 1929–

16 Although he [David Ben-Gurion] did not believe in God himself, he somehow gave the impression that God believed in him. [In the *Observer*, 4 Sept. 1983]

GEORGES BERNANOS 1888–1948

17 The wish to pray is a prayer in itself. [*The Diary of a Country Priest*, Ch. 4]

JEFFREY BERNARD 1932–

18 I often think of making a geographical change but in my experience it just does not work. If you went to the South Pole the first person you would meet there would be yourself. [*More Low Life*, 'Dead End']

19 [It was] Fred Astaire who made envy legitimate. You wouldn't have minded being in his shoes, so to speak. ['Who's Coming to Dinner?']

20 The libel laws ... have always made it virtually impossible to write a really good racing book about anything but the horses. [In the *Spectator*, 29 Mar. 1986]

See also under WATERHOUSE, KEITH

ERIC BERNE 1910–1970

21 Human life is mainly a process of filling in time until the arrival of death, or Santa Claus, with very little choice, if any, of what kind of business one is going to transact during the long wait. [*Games People Play*, Ch. 18]

CARL BERNSTEIN 1944–

22 We are in the process of creating what deserves to be called the idiot culture. Not an idiot sub-culture, which every society has bubbling beneath the surface and which can provide harmless fun; but the culture itself. For the first time, the weird and the stupid and the coarse are becoming our cultural norm, even our cultural ideal. [In the *Guardian*, 3 June 1992]

CHUCK BERRY 1926–

23 Roll Over, Beethoven! [Title of song]

JOHN BERRYMAN 1914–1972

1 Blossomed Sarah, and I / blossom. Is that thing alive? I hear a famisht / howl. [*Homage to Mistress Bradstreet*, 21]

2 The moon came up late and the night was cold, / Many men died – although we know the fate / Of none, nor of anyone, and the war / Goes on, and the moon in the breast of man is cold. [*The Moon and the Night and the Men*]

3 I see the dragon of years is almost done, / Its claws loosen, its eyes / Crust now with tears, lust and a scale of lies. [*New Year's Eve*]

4 The statue, tolerant through years of weather, / Spares the untidy Sunday throng its look. [*The Statue*]

5 News of one day, one afternoon, one time. / If it were possible to take these things / Quite seriously, I believe they might / Curry disorders in the strongest brain, / Immobilize the most resilient will, / Stop trains, break up the city's food supply, / And perfectly demoralize the nation. [*World-Telegram*]

6 The artist is extremely lucky who is presented with the worst possible ordeal which will not actually kill him. [Interview in *Paris Review*, Winter 1972]

VALDIS BERZINS [Latvian journalist]

7 We praise the Russian army that liberated us from fascism. But why did they stay so long? [In the *Independent*, 'Quote Unquote', 12 May 1990]

THEOBALD VON BETHMANN HOLLWEG 1856–1921

8 Just for a word – 'neutrality', a word which in wartime has so often been disregarded, just for a scrap of paper – Great Britain is going to make war. [To Sir Edward Goschen, 4 Aug. 1914]

SIR JOHN BETJEMAN 1906–1984

9 And is it true? And is it true, / This most tremendous tale of all, / Seen in a stained-glass window's hue, / A Baby in an ox's stall? [*Christmas*]

10 Spirits of well-shot woodcock, partridge, snipe / Flutter and bear him up the Norfolk sky. [*Death of King George V*]

11 As beefy ATS / Without their hats / Come shooting through the bridge, / And 'cheerioh' and 'cheeri-bye' / Across the waste of waters die. [*Henley-on-Thames*]

12 Phone for the fish-knives, Norman, / As Cook is a little unnerved; / You kiddies have crumpled the serviettes / And I must have things daintily served. [*How to Get on in Society*]

13 The Church's Restoration / In eighteen-eighty-three / Has left for contemplation / Not what there used to be. [*Hymn*]

14 In the licorice fields at Pontefract / My love and I did meet ... / Her sturdy legs were flannel-slack'd, / The strongest legs in Pontefract. [*The Licorice Fields at Pontefract*]

15 Rumbling under blackened girders, Midland, bound for Cricklewood, / Puffed its sulphur to the sunset where that Land of Laundries stood. [*Parliament Hill Fields*]

16 Pam, I adore you, Pam, you great big mountainous sports girl / Whizzing them over the net, full of the strength of five. [*Pot Pourri from a Surrey Garden*]

17 The gas was on in the Institute, / The flare was up in the gym. [*A Shropshire Lad*]

18 Come, friendly bombs, and fall on Slough. / It isn't fit for humans now. [*Slough*]

19 Miss J. Hunter Dunn, Miss J. Hunter Dunn, / Furnish'd and burnish'd by Aldershot sun. [*A Subaltern's Love-song*]

20 As I struggle with double-end evening tie, / For we dance at the Golf Club, my victor and I.

21 Childhood is measured out by sounds and smells / And sights, before the dark of reason grows. [*Summoned by Bells*, Ch. 4]

22 The dread of beatings! Dread of being late! / And, greatest dread of all, the dread of games! [7]

23 Aunt Elsie, aunt of normal Scottish boys. / Adopted aunt of lone abnormal me. [8]

24 Spiritually I was at Eton, John. [9]

25 For, while we ate Virginia hams / Contemporaries passed exams.

1 But I'm dying now and done for, / What on earth was all the fun for? / For I'm old and ill and terrified and tight. [*Sun and Fun*]

2 Broad of Church and broad of mind, / Broad before and broad behind, / A keen ecclesiologist, / A rather dirty Wykehamist. [*The Wykehamist*]

3 Bournemouth is one of the few English towns that one can safely call 'her'. [*First and Last Loves*]

4 History must not be written with bias, and both sides must be given, even if there is only one side.

5 Ghastly Good Taste or, a Depressing Story of the Rise and Fall of English Architecture. [Title and subtitle of book]

6 I can speak only for myself, I would like to be a stationmaster on a small country branch line (single track). [When asked to name 'a most suitable second employment' by *Horizon* questionnaire, 1946]

7 Foot and note disease. [Attr.]

BRUNO BETTELHEIM 1903–1990

8 No longer can we be satisfied with a life where the heart has its reasons which reason cannot know. Our hearts must know the world of reason, and must be guided by an informed heart. [In the *Guardian* at his death, 15 Mar. 1990]

ANEURIN BEVAN 1897–1960

9 This island is almost made of coal and surrounded by fish. Only an organizing genius could produce a shortage of coal and fish in Great Britain at the same time. [Speech at Blackpool, 18 May 1945]

10 No attempt at ethical or social seduction can eradicate from my heart a deep burning hatred for the Tory Party ... So far as I am concerned they are lower than vermin. [Speech at Manchester, 4 July 1948]

11 I know that the right kind of political leader for the Labour Party is a desiccated calculating machine. [Always assumed, though Bevan denied it, to refer to Hugh Gaitskell. At Labour Party Conference, 29 Sept. 1954]

12 There is no reason to attack the monkey [Selwyn Lloyd] when the organ-grinder [Harold Macmillan] is present. [Speech in House of Commons, 16 May 1957]

13 If you carry this resolution and follow out all its implications and do not run away from it, you will send a Foreign Secretary, whoever he was, naked into the conference chamber. [On unilateral disarmament. At Labour Party Conference, 3 Oct.]

14 He [Churchill] is a man suffering from petrified adolescence. [In Vincent Brome, *Aneurin Bevan*, Ch. 11]

15 Damn it all, you can't have the crown of thorns and the thirty pieces of silver. [In Michael Foot, *Aneurin Bevan*, Vol. 2, Ch. 1]

16 We know what happens to people who stay in the middle of the road. They get run over. [In the *Observer*, 'Sayings of the Week', 6 Dec. 1953]

17 I read the newspaper avidly. It is my one form of continuous fiction. [3 Apr. 1960]

18 Fascism is not in itself a new order of society. It is the future refusing to be born. [In A. Andrews, *Quotations for Speakers and Writers*]

19 Aneurin Bevan used to say there were two ways to get into government – one was to crawl into a government and the other was to kick your way in. [In BBC radio programme *The Week in Westminster*, 15 July 1989]

EDWYN BEVAN 1870–1943

20 Argument, generally speaking in religion, can do no more than clear the track; it cannot make the engine move. [*Hellenism and Christianity*]

LORD BEVERIDGE 1879–1963

21 The trouble in modern democracy is that men do not approach to leadership until they have lost the desire to lead anyone. [In the *Observer*, 'Sayings of the Week', 15 Apr. 1934]

22 Scratch a pessimist, and you find often a defender of privilege. [17 Dec. 1943]

ERNEST BEVIN 1881–1951

1 I didn't ought never to have done it. It was you, Willie, what put me up to it. [To Lord Strang, after recognizing communist China. In C. Parrott, *The Serpent and the Nightingale*, Ch. 3]

2 My policy is to be able to take a ticket at Victoria Station and go anywhere I damn well please. [In the *Spectator*, 20 Apr. 1951]

3 [When told a Labour colleague was his own worst enemy] Not while I'm alive, he ain't! [There are various candidates for the insult. In Michael Foot, *Aneurin Bevan*, Vol. 2, Ch. 1]

4 [When asked his opinion of Anthony Eden's speeches] Clitch, clitch, clitch. [Attr. See also 82:11]

GEORGES BIDAULT 1899–1983

5 The weak have one weapon: the errors of those who think they are strong. [In the *Observer*, 'Sayings of the Week', 15 July 1962]

AMBROSE BIERCE 1842–1914

6 When Eve saw her reflection in a pool, she sought Adam and accused him of infidelity. [*The Devil's Dictionary*]

7 *Applause*, n. The echo of a platitude.

8 *Bore*, n. A person who talks when you wish him to listen.

9 *Brain*, n. An apparatus with which we think that we think.

10 *Calamity*, n. Calamities are of two kinds: misfortune to ourselves, and good fortune to others.

11 *Cannon*, n. An instrument employed in the rectification of national boundaries.

12 *Debauchee*, n. One who has so earnestly pursued pleasure that he has had the misfortune to overtake it.

13 *Egotist*, n. A person of low taste, more interested in himself than in me.

14 While your friend holds you affectionately by both your hands you are safe, because you can watch both his. [Entry under *Epigram*]

15 *Faith*, n. Belief without evidence in what is told by one who speaks without knowledge, of things without parallel.

16 *Future*, n. That period of time in which our affairs prosper, our friends are true and our happiness is assured.

17 *Garter*, n. An elastic band intended to keep a woman from coming out of her stockings and desolating the country.

18 *Hand*, n. A singular instrument worn at the end of a human arm and commonly thrust into somebody's pocket.

19 *Marriage*, n. The state or condition of a community consisting of a master, a mistress and two slaves, making in all two.

20 *Patience*, n. A minor form of despair, disguised as a virtue.

21 *Peace*, n. In international affairs, a period of cheating between two periods of fighting.

22 *Prejudice*, n. A vagrant opinion without visible means of support.

23 *Riot*, n. A popular entertainment given to the military by innocent bystanders.

STEVE BIKO 1946–1977

24 The most potent weapon in the hands of the oppressor is the mind of the oppressed. [Address to Cape Town Conference, 1971. In *Penguin Dictionary of Political Quotations*, comp. Robert Stewart]

MICHAEL BILLINGTON 1939–

25 Thomas Mann, forever viewing life as if someone has sent it him to review. [Review of Christopher Hampton's play *Tales of Hollywood*, in which Mann is one of the characters, in the *Guardian*, 2 Sept. 1983]

26 All drama is a form of anthropology. [In the *Guardian*, 30 Nov. 1987]

MAEVE BINCHY 1940–

27 The starring role of Housewife – a woman who married a house. [In the *Guardian*, 5 Feb. 1985]

28 They used to say that if you lost your virginity in Cork someone would be sure to find it before teatime and bring it back to your mother. [16 Apr.]

LAURENCE BINYON 1869–1943

29 Now is the time for the burning of the leaves. [*The Burning of the Leaves*]

1 With proud thanksgiving, a mother for her children, / England mourns for her dead across the sea. [*For the Fallen*]

2 They shall grow not old, as we that are left grow old: / Age shall not weary them, nor the years condemn. / At the going down of the sun and in the morning / We will remember them.

F. E. SMITH, EARL OF BIRKENHEAD 1872–1930

3 JUDGE: I have read your case, Mr Smith, and I am no wiser now than I was when I started.

SMITH: Possibly not, My Lord, but far better informed. [In *Life of F. E. Smith* by his son, the second Earl of Birkenhead, Ch. 9]

4 JUDGE: You are offensive, sir.

SMITH: We both are; the difference is that I'm trying to be and you can't help it. [In C. E. Bechofer Roberts ('Ephesian'), *Lord Birkenhead*, Ch. 3]

5 MR JUSTICE DARLING: And who is George Robey?

SMITH: Mr George Robey is the Darling of the music-halls, m'lud. [In A. Wilson, *The Prime Minister of Mirth*, Ch. 1]

LORD BIRKETT 1883–1962

6 I do not object to people looking at their watches when I am speaking. But I strongly object when they start shaking them to make sure they are still going. [In the *Observer*, 30 Oct. 1960]

ELIZABETH BISHOP 1911–1979

7 [Bishop] said of art that it makes us feel that 'life is all right for the time being'. [In *New Society*, 22/29 Dec. 1983]

MORRIS BISHOP 1893–1973

8 'I cannot hear a single word; / Yell if you like,' said Dr Slade. / He patted his Unhearing Aid. [*Free from Speech*]

9 There I stood and humbly scanned / The miracle that sense appals, / And I watched the tourists stand / Spitting in Niagara Falls. [*Public Aid for Niagara Falls*]

10 The lights burn low in the barber-shop / And the shades are drawn with care / To hide the haughty barbers / Cutting each other's hair. [*The Tales the Barbers Tell*]

11 We all know Mumsy was vague and clumsy, / Dithering, drunken and dumb. [*There's Money in Mother and Father*]

TERENCE BLACKER 1948–

12 They liked celebrity in those days; they thought it was catching. [*Fixx*, p. 107]

13 Dullness, I now realize, is like halitosis; the sufferer is always the last to know. [In the *Independent on Sunday*, 4 Aug. 1991]

ERIC BLAIR *see* ORWELL, GEORGE

EUBIE BLAKE 1883–1983

14 If I'd known I was going to live this long, I'd have taken better care of myself. [On his 100th birthday, five days before his death. In the *Observer*, 20 Feb. 1983]

COLIN BLAKEMORE 1944–

15 If the cells and fibre in one human brain were all stretched out end to end, they would certainly reach to the moon and back. Yet the fact that they are not arranged end to end enabled man to go there himself. The astonishing tangle within our heads makes us what we are. [From BBC Reith Lectures, in the *Listener*, 25 Nov. 1976]

16 The biological (if not the aesthetic) value of remembering is not that it allows one to reminisce about the past but that it permits one to calculate coldly about the unknown future. [2 Dec.]

LESLEY BLANCH 1907–

17 Her [Jane Digby El Mezrab's] whole life was spent riding at breakneck speed towards the wilder shores of love. [*The Wilder Shores of Love*, 2. 1]

ALAN BLEASDALE 1946–

18 Gizza job, go on, gizzit! [Yosser Hughes in *Boys from the Blackstuff*, 'Jobs for the Boys' and *passim*]

19 I know I'm a nobody, but I'm nobody else's nobody. [In film *No Surrender*]

EDWARD BLISHEN 1920–

1 Around his part of town even original sin is secondhand. [Quoting a backstreet teacher. From *A Nest of Teachers*, in the *Guardian*, 31 Jan. 1980]

KAREN BLIXEN see DINESEN, ISAK

ALEXANDER BLOK 1880–1921

2 The right words in the right order. [Of poetry. In D. Burg and G. Feifer, *Solzhenitsyn*]

ROY BLOUNT JR 1941–

3 Any given generation gives the next generation advice that the given generation should have been given by the previous one but now it's too late. [From *Don't Anybody Steal These*, in *Antaeus: Journals, Notebooks and Diaries*, ed. D. Halpern, p. 50]

4 It's nothing I can take credit for. It's just something in my jeans. [53]

EDMUND BLUNDEN 1896–1974

5 Old farm-houses with their white faces / Fly, and their ghosts have taken their places; / Even the signposts like grim liars / Point to trapping brakes and briars. [*Evening Mystery*]

6 Can she who shines so calm be fear? / What poison pours she in slumber's ear?

7 I am for the woods against the world, / But are the woods for me? [*The Kiss*]

8 Dance on this ball-floor thin and wan, / Use him as though you love him; / Court him, elude him, reel and pass, / And let him hate you through the glass. [*Midnight Skaters*]

9 And nigh this toppling reed, still as the dead / The great pike lies, the murderous patriarch, / Watching the water-pit shelving and dark / Where through the plash his lithe bright vassals tread. [*The Pike*]

10 I have been young, and now am not too old; / And I have seen the righteous forsaken, / His health, his honour and his quality taken, / This is not what we were formerly told. [*Report on Experience*]

11 The field and wood, all bone-fed loam, / Shot up a roaring harvest-home. [*Rural Economy*]

12 I saw the sunlit vale, and the pastoral fairy-tale; / The sweet and bitter scent of the may drifted by; / But it looked like a lie, / Like a kindly meant lie. [*The Sunlit Vale*]

DAVID BLUNKETT, MP 1947–

13 Nothing has changed except the smile. [Comparing the governments of Margaret Thatcher and John Major. In the *Independent*, 'Quote Unquote', 9 Nov. 1991]

WILFRID SCAWEN BLUNT 1840–1922

14 I like the hunting of the hare / Better than that of the fox. [*The Old Squire*]

15 The drawing is on the level of that of an untaught child of seven or eight years old, the sense of colour that of a tea-tray painter, the method that of a schoolboy who wipes his fingers on a slate after spitting on them. [Of the Post-Impressionist Exhibition. Diary, 15 Nov. 1910]

RONALD BLYTHE 1922–

16 As for the British churchman, he goes to church as he goes to the bathroom, with the minimum of fuss and no explanation if he can help it. [*The Age of Illusion*, Ch. 12]

17 An industrial worker would sooner have a £5 note but a countryman must have praise. [*Akenfield*, Ch. 5, 'Christopher Falconer']

18 Suffolk used to worship Sunday, not God . . . Bugger Sunday, I say, and praise God when you can. [6, 'Gregory Gladwell']

19 A man telling one how he makes a wheel – or a fortune – will inadvertently tell one much more. [*From the Headlands*, 'The Writer as Listener']

20 One of the reasons why old people make so many journeys into the past is to satisfy themselves that it is still there. [*The View in Winter*, Introduction]

21 All streets are theatres. [Ch. 7]

HUMPHREY BOGART 1899–1957

22 Here's looking at you, kid. [In film *Casa-*

blanca, script by Julius J. Epstein, Philip G. Epstein and Howard Koch. See 38:20 for the line usually attr. – falsely – to him]

1 The trouble with the world is that everybody in it is three drinks behind. [From *Esquire* magazine, 1964, in Jonathon Green, *Consuming Passions*]

NIELS BOHR 1885–1962

2 Two sorts of truth: trivialities, where opposites are obviously absurd, and profound truths, recognized by the fact that the opposite is also a profound truth. [In *Nelis Bohr: His Life and Work*, ed. S. Rozental, p. 328. See also 249:20]

3 An expert is a man who has made all the mistakes, which can be made, in a very narrow field. [To Edward Teller, 10 Oct. 1972. In *Dictionary of Scientific Quotations*, ed. A. L. Mackay]

ROBERT BOLT 1924–

4 ROPER: I'd cut down every law in England to do that.
MORE: Oh? And when the last law was down, and the Devil turned round on you – where would you hide, Roper, the laws being flat? This country's planted thick with laws from coast to coast – Man's laws, not God's – and if you cut them down – and you're just the man to do it – d'you really think you could stand upright in the winds that would blow then? [*A Man for All Seasons*, Act I]

5 The nobility of England, my lord, would have snored through the Sermon on the Mount. [II]

6 I think Lenin was an admirable man, possessed by a terribly wrong idea. It was terribly wrong because it was only partly right. And it was so absolutely punitive that it needed to be absolutely right. [*State of Revolution*, Introduction]

ERMA BOMBECK 1927–

7 Never go to a doctor whose office plants have died. [In *Hammer and Tongues*, ed. Michèle Brown and Ann O'Connor, 'Medicine']

8 The only reason I would take up jogging is so that I could hear heavy breathing again. [In *The 637 Best Things Anybody Ever Said*, comp. Robert Byrne]

MARGARET BONANNO 1950–

9 It is only possible to live happily ever after on a day to day basis. [*A Certain Slant of Light*]

ANDREW BONAR LAW 1858–1923

10 If I am a great man, then a good many of the great men of history are frauds. [To the author, in Lord Beaverbrook, *Politicians and the War*, Vol. 2, Ch. 4]

11 We have heard of people being thrown to the wolves, but never before have we heard of a man being thrown to the wolves with a bargain on the part of the wolves that they would not eat him. [Speech in House of Commons on Colonel Seely's proffered resignation as War Minister, Mar. 1914]

12 Look at that man's eyes. You will hear more of him later. [Of Mussolini. To a secretary, 1922]

13 I must follow them; I am their leader. [In E. T. Raymond, *Mr Balfour*, Ch. 15]

14 He [Lord Birkenhead] would sooner keep hot coals in his mouth than a witticism. [Attr.]

EDWARD BOND 1934–

15 I write about violence as naturally as Jane Austen wrote about manners. Violence shapes and obsesses our society, and if we do not stop being violent we have no future. [*Lear*, Author's Preface]

16 Of course, that's only a symbol, but we need symbols to protect us from ourselves. [*Narrow Road to the Deep North*, Pt I, sc. iv]

17 The English sent all their bores abroad, and acquired the empire as a punishment. [II. i]

SIR DAVID BONE 1874–1959

18 It's 'Damn you, Jack – I'm all right!' with you chaps. [*The Brassbounder*, Ch. 3]

JAMES BONE 1872–1962

19 He made righteousness readable. [Of C. P. Scott of the *Manchester Guardian*]

KYRIL BONFIGLIOLI 1928–1985

1 But in the Lower Sixth we all got either religion or Communism – it goes with acne you know. Vanishes as soon as you have proper sexual intercourse. [*Don't Point That Thing at Me*, Ch. 6]

2 Ornithology used to be an arcane hobby for embittered schoolmasters, dotty spinsters and lonely little boys but now it is as normal a weekend occupation as rug-making or wife-swapping. [18]

VIOLET BONHAM CARTER [later LADY ASQUITH] 1887–1969

3 My father [H. H. Asquith] liked thinking alone – Winston Churchill liked thinking aloud. [In *The Wit of the Asquiths*, comp. Mary Tester]

4 Sir Stafford Cripps has a brilliant mind – until he makes it up!

5 Tories are not always wrong, but they are always wrong at the right moment. [In the *Observer*, 'Sayings of the Week', 26 Apr. 1964]

DIETRICH BONHOEFFER 1906–1945

6 Man has learned to cope with all questions of importance without recourse to God as a working hypothesis. [*Letters and Papers from Prison*, Letter, 8 June 1944]

7 Now that it has come of age, the world is more godless, and perhaps it is for that very reason nearer to God than ever before. [18 July 1944]

8 It is the characteristic excellence of the strong man that he can bring momentous issues to the fore and make a decision about them. The weak are always forced to decide between alternatives they have not chosen themselves. ['Miscellaneous Thoughts']

9 A God who let us prove his existence would be an idol. [*No Rusty Swords*]

10 The man for others. [Of Jesus Christ. In John A. T. Robinson, *Honest to God*, Ch. 4]

EDWARD DE BONO 1933–

11 A memory is what is left when something happens and does not completely unhappen. [*The Mechanism of Mind*]

12 A myth is a fixed way of looking at the world which cannot be destroyed because, looked at through the myth, all evidence supports that myth. [*PO, Beyond Yes and No*]

13 Unhappiness is best defined as the difference between our talents and our expectations. [In the *Observer*, 'Sayings of the Week', 12 June 1977]

JOHN BOORMAN 1933–

14 It [film making] is the business of turning money into light and then back into money again. [Quoted by Tom Stoppard in the *Sunday Times*, 20 Jan. 1980; later used as title of book]

15 All movie-making is seeing with a child's eye. [At Montreal Festival opening of his film *Hope and Glory*. In the *Guardian*, 3 Sept. 1987]

DANIEL BOORSTIN 1914–

16 The celebrity is a person who is known for his well-knownness. [*The Image*, Ch. 2]

17 In the twentieth century our highest praise is to call the Bible 'the World's Best-Seller'. And it has come to be more and more difficult to say whether we think it is a best-seller because it is great, or vice versa. [4]

18 A best-seller was a book which somehow sold well simply because it was selling well.

ROBERT [later LORD] BOOTHBY 1900–1986

19 Of all the political pygmies, he [Sir Samuel Hoare] was the pygmiest. [*Reflections of a Rebel*, Ch. 10]

J. BASIL BOOTHROYD 1910–1988

20 I've always thought the worst thing about drowning was having to call 'Help!' You must look such a fool. It's put me against drowning. [In *Apt and Amusing Quotations*, ed. G. F. Lamb, 'Eating']

JORGE LUIS BORGES 1899–1986

21 Writing is nothing more than a guided dream. [*Doctor Brodie's Report*, Preface]

22 I have known uncertainty: a state unknown to the Greeks. [*Ficciones*, 'The Babylonian Lottery']

1 The visible universe was an illusion or, more precisely, a sophism. Mirrors and fatherhood are abominable because they multiply it and extend it. ['Tlön, Uqbar, Orbis, Tertius']

2 Like every writer, he measured the virtues of other writers by their performances, and asked that they measure him by what he conjectured or planned. [*The Secret Miracle*]

3 The Falklands thing [war of 1982] was a fight between two bald men over a comb. [In *Time* magazine, 14 Feb. 1983]

4 We have stopped believing in progress. What progress that is! [In Ibarra, *Borges et Borges*]

5 A good reader is rarer than a good writer. [In Robert Robinson, *Dog Chairman*, 'Arm in Arm with Borges']

6 The advantage of having imitators is that at last they cure you of yourself. [Quoted by Philip Roth in interview in the *Independent*, 2 Sept. 1990]

JORGE LUIS BORGES and ADOLFO BIOY CASARES 1914–

7 A good actor does not make his entry before the theatre is built. [*Seis problemas para don Isidro Parodi*, written under the pseudonym H. Bustos Domecq]

J. C. BOSSIDY 1860–1928

8 And this is good old Boston, / The home of the bean and the cod, / Where the Lowells talk to the Cabots, / And the Cabots talk only to God. [Toast proposed at Holy Cross Alumni dinner, Boston, Massachusetts, 1910]

PRESIDENT P. W. BOTHA 1916–

9 After all, Moses had a mixed marriage. [Speech, 4 Sept. 1980]

10 We do not force people in South Africa to move to new homes, we coerce them. [Freudian slip? Was 'convince' intended? At press conference in Switzerland, June 1984]

HORATIO BOTTOMLEY 1860–1933

11 I haven't made a study of the question, but I certainly think it is high time Brighton was relieved. [When questioned on the Jewish National Home, Dec. 1918. In Julian Symons, *Horatio Bottomley*, Ch. 15]

12 VISITOR: Ah, Bottomley, sewing?
BOTTOMLEY: No, reaping. [When discovered sewing mail bags by a prison visitor. In 19]

13 I HAVE PAID, BUT – [Headline to his story of his life in prison, printed in *Weekly Dispatch* after his release]

NADIA BOULANGER 1887–1979

14 [When asked by Leonard Bernstein on her deathbed if she was hearing music in her skull and, if so, which composer] One music . . . with no beginning, no end. [In Bruno Monsaingeon, *Mademoiselle*]

PIERRE BOULEZ 1925–

15 Suddenly, we have this mentality now, that if we destroy a building the past will be destroyed, and we will have no roots any more. A strong civilization is one that can replace things. [Interview in the *Guardian*, 13 Jan. 1989]

16 Revolutions are celebrated when they are no longer dangerous.

17 I prefer people who chop off heads to people who celebrate people who chop off heads. [Of the bicentenary of the French Revolution]

18 For me that is the definition of a great work – a landscape painted so well that the artist disappears in it. [In Joan Peyser, *Boulez*]

SIR H. E. BOULTON 1859–1935

19 When Adam and Eve were dispossessed / Of the garden hard by Heaven, / They planted another one down in the west, / 'Twas Devon, glorious Devon! [*Glorious Devon*]

20 Speed, bonny boat, like a bird on the wing; / 'Onward', the sailors cry; / Carry the lad that's born to be king / Over the sea to Skye. [*Skye Boat Song*]

PHILIPPE BOUVARD 1929–

1 Why does frugality only count as a virtue when it is practised by people with no money? [*Un oursin dans le caviar*, p. 306.]

ELIZABETH BOWEN 1899–1973

2 Experience isn't interesting till it begins to repeat itself – in fact, till it does that, it hardly *is* experience. [*The Death of the Heart*, Pt I, Ch. 1]

3 The heart may think it knows better: the senses know that absence blots people out. We have really no absent friends. [II. 2]

4 She had to confess inexperience; her personality was still too much for her, like a punt-pole. [*Friends and Relations*, Pt I, Ch. 1]

5 I suppose art is the only thing that can go on mattering once it has stopped hurting. [*The Heat of the Day*, Ch. 16]

6 She was anxious to be someone, and, no one ever having voiced a prejudice in her hearing without impressing her, had come to associate prejudice with identity. You could not be a someone without disliking things. [*The House in Paris*, Pt I, Ch. 1]

7 Meetings that do not come off keep a character of their own. They stay as they were projected. [II. 2]

8 Jealousy is no more than feeling alone among smiling enemies. [8]

9 When you're young, you think of marriage as a train you simply have to catch. You run and run until you've caught it, and then you sit back and look out of the window and realize you're bored. [In conversation will Molly Keane, recalled in interview in the *Sunday Times*, 11 Sept. 1988]

DAVID BOWIE 1947–

10 The worst joke God can play is to make you an artist, but only a mediocre artist. [In *Wit and Wisdom of Rock and Roll*, ed. Maxim Jakubowski]

PAUL BOWLES 1910–

11 The only effort worth making is the one it takes to learn the geography of one's own nature. [In the *Sunday Times Books*, 23 July 1989]

SIR MAURICE BOWRA 1898–1971

12 I'm a man / More dined against than dining. [Attr. by J. Betjeman in *Summoned by Bells*, Ch. 9]

ANDREW BOYLE 1919–1991

13 'Au contraire,' as the Frenchman once said on the storm-tossed ship when asked if he had dined. [*Punch*, 27 Nov. 1974]

GENERAL BRABAZON

14 Of the stationmaster at Aldershot he [Brabazon] inquired on one occasion in later years: 'Where is the London twain?' 'It has gone, Colonel.' 'Gone! Bwing another!' [In Winston Churchill, *My Early Life*, Ch. 5]

LORD BRABAZON 1884–1964

15 I take the view, and always have done, that if you cannot say what you have to say in twenty minutes, you should go away and write a book about it. [Speech in House of Lords, 21 June 1955]

CHARLES BRACKETT 1892–1969 and BILLY WILDER 1906–

16 He was five foot three! I went to a judge. A woman needs a man not a radiator cap. [In film *Hold Back the Dawn*]

MALCOLM BRADBURY 1932–

17 There were moments when Henry was glad he was a writer, for writers could live in their own minds and didn't have to go out at all. [*Cuts*, 5]

18 It had always seemed to Louis that a fundamental desire to take postal courses was being sublimated by other people into sexual activity. [*Eating People is Wrong*, Ch. 5]

19 I like the English. They have the most rigid code of immorality in the world.

20 It amuses me, you know, the way you seem to see women. You think of them as sort of loose-fitting men. [6]

21 'Are you married, Mr Willoughby?' asked the wife of the Vice-Chancellor ... 'I don't suppose he believes in it,' said the Vice-Chancellor in disgruntled tones. 'Well, why buy

the cow,' asked Willoughby reasonably, 'when you can steal milk through the fence?' [8]

1 'We stay together, but we distrust one another.' 'Ah, yes ... but isn't that a definition of marriage?' [*The History Man*, Ch. 3]

2 Of course, as Henry James says, the house of fiction has many windows. Your trouble is you seem to have stood in front of most of them. [12]

3 Sex you can get anywhere in the world. But class, I mean, real class, you can only get in Britain. [TV play *Love on a Gunboat*]

4 In Slaka, sex is just politics with the clothes off. [*Rates of Exchange*, 4. III]

5 Here we have a saying: a good friend is someone who visits you when you are in prison. But a *really* good friend is someone who comes to hear your lectures.

6 Conversation is never easy for the British, who are never keen to express themselves to strangers or, for that matter, anyone, even themselves. [5. III]

7 You probably know, the better class of Briton likes to send his children away to school until they're old and intelligent enough to come home again. Then they're too old and intelligent to want to.

8 Reading someone else's newspaper is like sleeping with someone else's wife. Nothing seems to be precisely in the right place, and when you find what you are looking for, it is not clear then how to respond to it. [*Stepping Westward*, Bk I, Ch. 1]

9 My experience of ships is that on them one makes an interesting discovery about the world. One finds one can do without it completely. [2]

10 There was something craggy and hard about their personalities that discouraged access ... They don't spend themselves in relationships until they know what the odds are; long hours spent as babies lying in the rain outside greengrocers' shops have made them tough. [Of the English. II. 4]

11 English history is all about men liking their fathers, and American history is all about men hating their fathers and trying to burn down everything they ever did. [5]

12 The English are polite by telling lies. The Americans are polite by telling the truth.

13 A good writer, in my experience, is a good writer who does not write a large number of books but works back over the first one and gets it more or less right. [*Unsent Letters*]

14 If God had meant us to have group sex, I guess he'd have given us all more organs. [*Who Do You Think You Are?*, 'A Very Hospitable Person']

15 The British have long had a taste for bad books, but they like them well written. [On the award of the Booker Prize. In the *Observer*, 25 Oct. 1981]

16 A county, as the locals say, cut off on three sides by the sea, and on the fourth by British Rail. [Of Norfolk. From BBC radio programme *In the Air*, in the *Listener*, 28 Oct. 1982]

MALCOLM BRADBURY and CHRISTOPHER BIGSBY 1941–

17 You Liberals think that goats are just sheep from broken homes. [TV play *After Dinner Game*]

18 A typical historian. You people raise hindsight to the status of a profession.

19 I simply happen to believe in change through Marx and Engels, not through Marks and Spencers.

20 If God had been a Liberal there wouldn't have been ten commandments, there would have been ten suggestions.

RAY BRADBURY 1920–

21 The Day It Rained Forever. [Title of book]

F. H. BRADLEY 1846–1924

22 Metaphysics is the finding of bad reasons for what we believe upon instinct; but to find these reasons is no less an instinct. [*Appearance and Reality*, Preface]

23 An unearthly ballet of bloodless categories. [*The Principles of Logic*, Bk 3, Pt 2, Ch. 4]

24 His mind is open; yes, it is so open that nothing is retained: ideas simply pass

through him. [In *Treasury of Humorous Quotations*, ed. Evan Esar and Nicolas Bentley]

GENERAL OMAR BRADLEY
1893–1981

1 The wrong war, at the wrong place, at the wrong time, and with the wrong enemy. [At the Senate inquiry over General MacArthur's proposal to carry the Korean conflict into China, 15 May 1951]

2 The way to win an atomic war is to make certain it never starts. [In the *Observer*, 'Sayings of the Week', 20 Apr. 1952]

CARYL BRAHMS 1901–1982 and
S. J. SIMON 1904–1948

3 Downstairs a billiard saloon, upstairs a brothel – what more can a villain want? [*Don't Mr Disraeli*, Ch. 1]

4 The suffragettes were triumphant. Woman's place was in the gaol. [*No Nightingales*, Ch. 37]

5 If there are cat-calls ... you are sure at least that the audience is still there. [*Six Curtains for Stroganova*, Ch. 13]

H. N. BRAILSFORD 1873–1958

6 One knows what a war is about only when it is over. [*The Levellers and the English Revolution*, Ch. 1]

JOHN BRAINE 1922–1986

7 Room at the Top. [Title of book]

ERNEST BRAMAH [E. B. SMITH]
1868–1942

8 When struck by a thunderbolt it is unnecessary to consult the Book of Dates as to the precise meaning of the omen. [*The Wallet of Kai Lung*, 'Transmutation of Ling']

9 An expression of no-encouragement. ['Confession of Kai Lung']

10 The whole narrative is permeated with the odour of joss-sticks and honourable high-mindedness. ['Ill-regulated Destiny of Kin Yen']

CONSTANTIN BRANCUSI 1876–1957

11 Sculpture is not for young men. [In Ezra Pound, *ABC of Reading*, 'Treatise on Reading', III]

MARLON BRANDO 1924–

12 He's the kind of guy that when he dies, he gives God a bad time for making him bald. [Of Frank Sinatra. In the *Daily Mail*, 30 Mar. 1977]

13 I'll make him an offer he can't refuse. [In film *The Godfather*, script by Mario Puzo and Francis Ford Coppola]

14 I coulda had class! I coulda been a contender! I coulda been somebody! Instead of a bum, which is what I am! [In film *On the Waterfront*, screenplay by Budd Schulberg, echoed by Robert de Niro in film *Raging Bull*]

G. W. BRANDT ?1920–

15 Surrounded on all sides, I won the war single-handed. [In *Cassell's Encyclopaedia of Literature*, 'Plot']

GEORGES BRAQUE 1882–1963

16 Art is meant to disturb. Science reassures. [*Pensées sur l'art*]

17 Truth exists; only lies are invented.

18 I do not believe in things: I believe in relationships. [In J. Culler, *Saussure*, Ch. 4]

WERNHER VON BRAUN 1912–1977

19 It was very successful, but it fell on the wrong planet. [Of the first V2 to fall on London during 1939–45 War. On BBC radio at his death, 17 June 1977]

20 Basic research is when I'm doing what I don't know I'm doing. [In W. H. Auden and L. Kronenberger, *Faber Book of Aphorisms*]

BERTOLT BRECHT 1898–1956

21 I love the people with their simple straightforward minds. It's only that their smell brings on my migraine. [*The Caucasian Chalk Circle*, V, trans. Eric Bentley]

22 You want justice, but do you want to pay for it, hm? When you go to a butcher you know you have to pay, but you people

go to a judge as if you were off to a funeral supper.

1 Take note of what men of old concluded: / That what there is shall go to those who are good for it, / Children to the motherly, that they prosper, / Carts to good drivers, that they be driven well, / The valley to the waterers, that it yield fruit.

2 It was never decreed that a god mustn't pay hotel bills. [*The Good Woman of Setzuan*, Prologue, trans. Eric Bentley]

3 It isn't important to come out on top, what matters is to be the one who comes out alive. [*In the Jungle of the Cities*, sc. 10, trans. Gerhard Nellhaus]

4 Unhappy the land that has no heroes . . . No. Unhappy the land that is in need of heroes. [*The Life of Galileo*, 13, trans. Desmond I. Vesey]

5 Science knows only one commandment: contribute to science. [14]

6 What they could do with round here is a good war. What else can you expect with peace running wild all over the place. You know what the trouble with peace is? No organization. [*Mother Courage*, 1, trans. Eric Bentley]

7 I don't trust him. We're friends. [3]

8 When a soldier sees a clean face, there's one more whore in the world.

9 THE CHAPLAIN: We're in God's hands now!
MOTHER C.: I hope we're not as desperate as that, but it *is* hard to sleep at night.

10 What happens to the hole when the cheese is gone? [6]

11 War is like love, it always finds a way.

12 She's not so pretty anyone would want to ruin her.

13 Don't tell me peace has broken out. [8]

14 THE COOK [*to the Chaplain*]: As a grown man, you should know better than to go round advising people.

15 As the old Czech proverb has it, 'Sweaty feet seldom come singly.' [*Schweyk in the Second World War*, II, trans. William Rowlinson]

16 A man who sees another man on the street corner with only a stump for an arm will be so shocked the first time he'll give him sixpence. But the second time it'll only be a threepenny bit. And if he sees him a third time, he'll have him cold-bloodedly handed over to the police. [*The Threepenny Opera*, I. i, trans. Desmond I. Vesey and Eric Bentley]

17 The wickedness of the world is so great you have to run your legs off to avoid having them stolen from under you. [I. iii]

18 Grub first, then ethics. [II. i]

19 What is robbing a bank compared to founding one? [III. i]

20 Oh the shark has pretty teeth, dear, / And he shows them pearly white. / Just a jack-knife has Macheath / And he keeps it out of sight.

21 The question: Is he then living?
Answer: He is lived. [*Diaries 1920–1922*, ed. H. Ramthun, trans. J. Willett]

22 The people / Had forfeited the confidence of the government / And could win it back only / By redoubled efforts. Would it not be easier / In that case for the government / To dissolve the people / And elect another? [*The Solution*]

GERALD BRENAN 1894–1987

23 Intellectuals are people who believe that ideas are of more importance than values. That is to say, their own ideas and other people's values. [*Thoughts in a Dry Season*, 'Life']

24 Everyone is a bore to someone. That is unimportant. The thing to avoid is being a bore to oneself.

25 Old age takes away from us what we have inherited and gives us what we have earned.

26 In a happy marriage it is the wife who provides the climate, the husband the landscape. ['Marriage']

27 When we attend the funerals of our friends we grieve for them, but when we go to those of other people it is chiefly our own deaths that we mourn for. ['Death']

28 Religions are kept alive by heresies, which are really sudden explosions of faith. Dead religions do not produce them. ['Religion']

1 For Gothic, which is Germanic in spirit although modified by French order and clarity, is all revolt and aspiration. ['Art and Architecture']

2 The cliché is dead poetry. English, being the language of an imaginative race, abounds in clichés, so that English literature is always in danger of being poisoned by its own secretions. ['Literature']

3 [Henry] Miller is not really a writer but a non-stop talker to whom someone has given a typewriter.

4 When I write a page that reads badly I know that it is myself who has written it. When it reads well it has come through from somewhere else. ['Writing']

5 Poets and painters are outside the class system, or rather they constitute a special class of their own, like the circus people and the gipsies. For the sake of their moral health they should be relatively poor and should mix mainly with their own kind. When they are short of money it is better for them to practise shop-lifting than to give lectures.

6 Every Spaniard is like a man-of-war, armed cap-à-pie to defend himself. That is why so much restraint and good manners are necessary. One man-of-war must reassure the other man-of-war that its guns will not be wanted. ['People and Places']

7 You can't get at the truth by writing history; only the novelist can do that. [When invited to write the Spanish volume in the Oxford History of Europe. In The Times Literary Supplement, 28 Nov. 1986]

ALFRED BRENDEL 1931–

8 Silence is the essence of music. It is really the basis. [Interview in the Observer, 6 Dec. 1987]

HOWARD BRENTON 1942– and
DAVID HARE 1947–

9 What on earth is all this stuff about the truth? Truth? Why, when everywhere you go people tell lies. In pubs. To each other. To their husbands. To the children. To the dying – and thank God they do. No one tells the truth. Why single out newspapers? [Pravda, Act II, sc. 4]

JIMMY BRESLIN 1930–

10 [President] Nixon is a purposeless man, but I have great faith in his cowardice. [In the Observer, 16 Nov. 1969]

ARISTIDE BRIAND 1862–1932

11 People think too historically. They are always living half in a cemetery. [In H. L. Mencken, New Dictionary of Quotations]

MARSHALL BRICKMAN 1941–

12 After a week at Claridges, one has the conviction that one died in the 17th century. Under very good circumstances. [Interview in the Guardian, 13 Sept. 1980]

13 The director of a film is treated by his staff the way a group of passengers would treat a psychotic ship's captain during a typhoon; namely, with respect and apprehension.

See also under ALLEN, WOODY

ALAN BRIEN 1925–

14 My theory is that mature woman is physically polygamous but emotionally monogamous, while mature man is emotionally polygamous but physically monogamous. [In the New Statesman, 6 Dec. 1968]

15 I have done almost every human activity inside a taxi which does not require main drainage. [In Punch, 5 July 1972]

16 I once met a man who claimed to have elevated his status, without perpetrating a falsehood, by entering in the profession or title space 'Elector of Marylebone', after the fashion of 'Elector of Hanover'. [9 Oct. 1974]

RAYMOND BRIGGS 1934–

17 Fungus inspects his trousers which have been marinading overnight. [Fungus the Bogeyman]

18 Bogeys are, by nature, libidinous (lusting after books) and almost all are libertines – (those who habitually disregard the law and borrow more books than they have tickets for).

ASHLEIGH BRILLIANT

1 Right now would be a good time to postpone everything. [Quoted by Eric Korn in *The Times Literary Supplement*, 20 Mar. 1987]

2 I can face anything except the future, and parts of the past and present.

3 All I Want is a Warm Bed and a Kind Word and Unlimited Power. [Title of book]

MATTHEW BRODERICK 1962–

4 Cameron's so tight, if you stuck a piece of coal up his ass in two weeks you'd have a diamond. [In film *Ferris Bueller's Day Off*, script by John Hughes]

JOSEPH BRODSKY 1940–

5 For some reason, the past doesn't radiate such immense monotony as the future does. Because of its plenitude, the future is propaganda. So is grass. [*Less Than One*, title essay]

6 Ambivalence, I think, is the chief characteristic of my nation [Russia].

7 In the country [Russia] where I spent thirty-two years, adultery and movie-going are the only forms of free enterprise. Plus Art.

8 In the business of writing what one accumulates is not expertise but uncertainties.

9 The formula for prison is lack of space counterbalanced by a surplus of time.

10 The army is a peasant's idea of order.

11 Art does not imitate life if only for fear of clichés. ['Keening Muse']

12 No poem is ever written for its story line's sake only, just as no life is lived for the sake of an obituary.

13 Prosody, which is simply a repository of time within language.

14 Separation is a more lasting experience than being together.

15 Winter is an abstract season; it is low on colours ... and big on the imperatives of cold and brief daylight ... beauty at low temperatures *is* beauty. [*Watermark*, p. 27]

16 It's a habit with prophets to be unhealthy. / Most seers are cripples. [*Adieu, Mademoiselle Véronique*, V, trans. George L. Kline]

17 In our past there is greatness – but prose in our future. [VIII]

18 Who needs a whole girl if you've got her knee? [One-line poem. In interview in *Poetry Review*, Spring 1988]

19 When you looked at her [Anna Akhmatova] you could understand instantly how it was possible for Russia to be run by empresses. [Interview in *Quarto*, Dec. 1981]

20 The philosophy of the state, its ethics – not to mention its aesthetics – are always 'yesterday'; language, literature are always 'today', and often – particularly in the case where a political system is orthodox – they may even constitute 'tomorrow'. [Acceptance speech of the 1987 Nobel Prize for Literature, trans. Barry Rubin]

21 Lenin was literate, Stalin was literate, so was Hitler. As for Mao Zedong, he even wrote verse. What all these men had in common, though, was that their hit list was longer than their reading list.

HUGH BRODY 1943–

22 Dependence entails vulnerability. The relationship between the hunter and the hunted, therefore, has a certain equality. Ultimately, no-one can be superior to that upon which he depends. [*Living Arctic*, Ch. 5]

23 The easiest place in which to carry technology is in the mind. [6]

24 We cannot see, and find it very hard to believe in, jurisdictions which exist in the minds of a people. We need some form of political tourism; we need to be able to visit an office, to watch a debate, to make a journey that is guided by the language of hierarchical authority. We need to ask questions. [7]

COLM BROGAN 1902–1977

25 There is only one word for aid that is genuinely without strings, and that word is blackmail. [Attr.]

SIR DENIS BROGAN 1900–1974

26 The combination of a profound hatred of war and militarism with an innocent delight

in playing soldiers is one of these apparent contradictions of American life that one has to accept. [*The American Character*, Pt 1, Ch. 5]

J. BRONOWSKI 1908–1974

1 Among the multitude of animals which scamper, fly, burrow and swim around us, man is the only one who is not locked into his environment. His imagination, his reason, his emotional subtlety and toughness, make it possible for him not to accept the environment but to change it. And that series of inventions, by which man from age to age has remade his environment, is a different kind of evolution – not biological, but cultural evolution. I call that brilliant sequence of cultural peaks *The Ascent of Man*. [*The Ascent of Man*, Ch. 1]

2 We have to understand the world can only be grasped by action, not by contemplation. The hand is more important than the eye ... The hand is the cutting edge of the mind. [3]

3 That is the essence of science: ask an impertinent question, and you are on the way to the pertinent answer. [4]

4 And he [John von Neumann] was a genius, in the sense that a genius is a man who has *two* great ideas. [13]

5 The wish to hurt, the momentary intoxication with pain, is the loophole through which the pervert climbs into the minds of ordinary men. [*The Face of Violence*, Ch. 5]

6 The world is made of people who never quite get into the first team and who just miss the prizes at the flower show. [6]

7 Therapy has become what I think of as the tenth American muse. [In *Radio Times*]

PETER BROOK 1925–

8 I don't particularly mind waste, but I think it's a pity not to know what one is wasting. Some old ladies use pound notes as bookmarks: this is silly only if it is absentminded. [*The Empty Space*, Ch. 1]

9 It is not the fault of the holy that it has become a middle-class weapon to keep children good. [2]

RUPERT BROOKE 1887–1915

10 Blow out, you bugles, over the rich Dead! / There's none of these so lonely and poor of old, / But, dying, has made us rarer gifts than gold. / These laid the world away: poured out the red / Sweet wine of youth; gave up the years to be / Of work and joy, and that unhoped serene, / That men call age; and those who would have been, / Their sons, they gave, their immortality. [*The Dead*]

11 Honour has come back, as a king, to earth, / And paid his subjects with a royal wage; / And Nobleness walks in our ways again; / And we have come into our heritage.

12 The cool kindliness of sheets, that soon / Smooth away trouble; and the rough male kiss / Of blankets. [*The Great Lover*]

13 Unfading moths, immortal flies, / And the worm that never dies. / And in that Heaven of all their wish, / There shall be no more land, say fish. [*Heaven*]

14 Breathless, we flung us on the windy hill, / Laughed in the sun, and kissed the lovely grass. [*The Hill*]

15 And then you suddenly cried and turned away.

16 Here tulips bloom as they are told; / Unkempt about those hedges blows / An English unofficial rose; / And there the unregulated sun / Slopes down to rest when day is done, / And wakes a vague unpunctual star, / A slippered Hesper. [*The Old Vicarage, Grantchester*]

17 And spectral dance, before the dawn, / A hundred Vicars down the lawn; / Curates, long dust, will come and go / On lissom, clerical, printless toe; / And oft between the boughs is seen / The sly shade of a Rural Dean.

18 For England's the one land, I know, / Where men with Splendid Hearts may go; / And Cambridgeshire, of all England, / The shire for Men who Understand.

19 For Cambridge people rarely smile, / Being urban, squat, and packed with guile.

20 They love the Good; they worship Truth; / They laugh uproariously in youth; / (And

when they get to feeling old, / They up and shoot themselves, I'm told).

1 Stands the Church clock at ten to three? / And is there honey still for tea?

2 Now, God be thanked who has matched us with His hour, / And caught our youth, and wakened us from sleeping. [*Peace*]

3 And the worst friend and enemy is but Death.

4 War knows no power. Safe shall be my going, / Secretly armed against all death's endeavour; / Safe though all safety's lost; safe where men fall; / And if these poor limbs die, safest of all. [*Safety*]

5 If I should die, think only this of me: / That there's some corner of a foreign field / That is for ever England. There shall be / In that rich earth a richer dust concealed. [*The Soldier*]

6 And think, this heart, all evil shed away, / A pulse in the eternal mind, no less / Gives somewhere back the thoughts by England given.

7 In hearts at peace, under an English heaven.

8 Spend in pure converse our eternal day; / Think each in each, immediately wise; / Learn all we lacked before; hear, know, and say / What this tumultuous body now denies; / And feel, who have laid our groping hands away; / And see, no longer blinded by our eyes. [Sonnet: *Not with Vain Tears*]

9 Oh! Death will find me long before I tire / Of watching you; and swing me suddenly / Into the shade and loneliness and mire / Of the last land! [Sonnet: *Oh! Death will find me*]

GARY BROOKER 1945– and **KEITH REID** 1946–

10 A Whiter Shade of Pale. [Title of song performed by Procol Harum, 1967]

ANITA BROOKNER 1938–

11 Eventually he asked her to marry him. In this he showed sense; it is best to marry for purely selfish reasons. [*A Start in Life*, 22]

12 I think you always feel braver in another language. [In the *Observer*, 7 Aug. 1988]

13 Satire is dependent on strong beliefs, and on strong beliefs wounded. [In the *Spectator*, 23 Mar. 1989]

LOUISE BROOKS 1908–1985

14 I can't once remember him [Charlie Chaplin] still. He was always standing up as he sat down and going out as he came in. [In Kenneth Tynan, *Show People*]

15 The great art of films does not consist of descriptive movement of face and body but in the movements of thought and soul, transmitted in a kind of intense isolation.

16 I never gave away anything without wishing I had kept it; nor kept anything without wishing I had given it away. [Suggesting her own epitaph]

MEL BROOKS 1926–

17 That's it, baby, if you've got it, flaunt it. [In film *The Producers*]

18 We were so poor, my mother couldn't afford to have me. The lady next door gave birth to me. [In *Playboy*, Dec. 1974]

19 Never shoot a film in Belgrade Yugoslavia! The whole town is illuminated by a 20-watt night light and there's nothing to do. You can't even go for a drive. Tito is always using the car. [In *Newsweek*, 17 Feb. 1975, variant in Kenneth Tynan, *Show People*]

20 Usually, when a lot of men get together it's called a war. [From the *Listener*, 1978, and in Jonathon Green, *Cynic's Lexicon*]

21 Tragedy is if I cut my finger . . . Comedy is if you walk into an open sewer and die. [In Kenneth Tynan, *Show People*]

VAN WYCK BROOKS 1886–1963

22 His wife not only edited his works but edited him. [*The Ordeal of Mark Twain*, Ch. 5]

'BIG BILL' BROONZY 1893–1958

23 I guess all songs is folk songs. I never heard no horse sing 'em. [In C. Keil, *Urban Blues*]

BRIGID BROPHY 1929–

24 History is in the shit sense. You have left

it behind you. Fiction is piss: a stream of past events but not behind you, because they never really happened. [*In Transit*, sect. I, 1]

1 An airport is a free-range womb. [4]

2 We Irish had the right word on the tip of our tongue, but the imperialist got at that. What should trip off it we trip over. [6]

3 The thriller is the cardinal twentieth-century form. All it, like the twentieth century, wants to know is: Who's Guilty? [11]

HEYWOOD BROUN 1888–1939

4 Free speech is about as good a cause as the world has ever known ... Everybody favours free speech in the slack moments when no axes are being ground. [In *New York World*, 23 Oct. 1926]

5 Just as every conviction begins as a whim so does every emancipator serve his apprenticeship as a crank. A fanatic is a great leader who is just entering the room. [6 Feb. 1928]

6 The best newspaperman who has ever been President of the United States. [Of Franklin D. Roosevelt. In D. Boorstin, *The Image*, Ch. 1]

7 The man who has cured himself of B.O. and halitosis, has learned French to surprise the waiter, and the saxophone to amuse the company, may find that people still avoid him because they do not like him. [In D. W. Brogan, *The American Character*, Pt I, sect. 6]

CRAIG BROWN 1957–

8 Journalism could be described as turning one's enemies into money. [In the *Observer*, 'Sayings of the Week', 30 Sept. 1990. See also 64:12]

H. RAP BROWN 1943–

9 Violence is American as apple pie. [Speech in Washington, 27 July 1967]

IVOR BROWN 1891–1974

10 Mr Gielgud has the most meaningless legs imaginable. [Review of performance of *Romeo and Juliet*, 1924. In *No Turn Unstoned*, 1, comp. Diana Rigg]

JOHN MASON BROWN 1900–1969

11 To many people dramatic criticism must seem like an attempt to tattoo soap bubbles. [In Frank Muir, *Frank Muir Book*]

12 Some television programmes are so much chewing gum for the eyes. [Interview, 28 July 1955]

LEW BROWN 1893–1958

13 Climb upon my knee, Sonny Boy; / Though you're only three, Sonny Boy. [Song: *Sonny Boy*, sung by Al Jolson]

14 Life is Just a Bowl of Cherries. [Title of song in musical *Scandals*, music by Ray Henderson, sung by Ethel Merman]

See also 'BUDDY' DE-SYLVA and LEW BROWN

LEW BROWN, CHARLES TOBIAS 1898–1970 and SAM H. STEPT

15 Don't Sit Under the Apple Tree with Anyone Else but Me. [Title of song, 1942]

OLIVER BROWN

16 A shiver ran through the Scottish MPs, frantically looking for a spine to run up. [*The Extended Tongue*]

PETE BROWN 1940–

17 I support the left, though I'm leaning to the right. [Song: *The Politician*]

RITA MAE BROWN 1944–

18 I think the reward for conformity is that everyone likes you except yourself. [*Bingo*, Ch. 35]

SEYMOUR BROWN 1885–1947

19 O You Beautiful Doll! [Title of song, music by Nat Ayer]

W. J. BROWN, MP 1917–1960

20 We have not yet lost this war, but we are overdrawn on the Bank of Miracles. [In the *Observer*, 'Sayings of the Week', 16 Aug. 1942]

LENNY BRUCE 1923–1966

1 People should be taught what is, not what should be. All my humour is based on destruction and despair. If the whole world were tranquil, without disease and violence, I'd be standing in the breadline – right back of J. Edgar Hoover. [Epigraph to *The Essential Lenny Bruce*, ed. J. Cohen]

2 Every day people are straying away from the church and going back to God. Really. ['Religions Inc.']

3 That fact is that you and I have had such bad early toilet training, that the worst sound in the world to all of us is when that toilet-flush noise finishes before you do. ['The Dirty Word Concept']

4 Because I'm Jewish, a lot of people ask why I killed Christ. What can I say? It was an accident. It was one of those parties that got out of hand.

5 I'll die young, but it's like kissing God. [Of his drug-taking. In R. Neville, *Playpower*]

THE BRUNDTLAND REPORT 1987

6 The Earth is one, but the world is not. [World Commission on Environment and Development, *Our Common Future*, opening words]

JOHN BRUNNER 1934–

7 POPULATION EXPLOSION Unique in human experience, an event which happened yesterday but which everyone swears won't happen until tomorrow. [*Stand on Zanzibar*, 'The Hipcrime Vocab']

FRANK BRUNO 1961–

8 Boxing's just show business with blood. [In the *Observer*, 'Sayings of the Week', 24 Nov. 1991]

9 Know what I mean, 'Arry? [Catchphrase. In profile in the *Sunday Times*, 8 Jan. 1989]

DAVID BRYER 1944–

10 The poor are not just living off the crumbs from the rich man's table, they are being asked to put the crumbs back. [At 50th anniversary press conference of Oxfam, London, 5 Oct. 1992]

MARTIN BUBER 1878–1965

11 I and Thou. [Title of book]

12 The real struggle is not between East and West, or capitalism and communism, but between education and propaganda. [In A. Hodes, *Encounter with Martin Buber*]

JOHN BUCHAN [LORD TWEEDSMUIR] 1875–1940

13 But for the bold experiment of Fascism the decade has not been fruitful in constructive statesmanship. [In the *Morning Post*, 31 Dec. 1929]

14 An atheist is a man who has no invisible means of support. [In H. E. Fosdick, *On Being a Real Person*, Ch. 10]

FRANK BUCHMAN 1878–1961

15 Suppose everybody cared enough, everybody shared enough? There is enough in the world for everyone's need but not for everyone's greed. [*Remaking the World*]

16 I thank heaven for a man like Adolf Hitler, who built a front line of defence against the anti-Christ of Communism. [Interview in *New York World-Telegram*, 25 Aug. 1936]

ART BUCHWALD 1925–

17 Ascot is so exclusive that it is the only racecourse in the world where the horses own the people. [*I Choose Caviar*, 'Ordeal at Ascot']

18 I explained to him I had simple tastes and didn't want anything ostentatious, no matter what it cost me. ['A New Lease on Texas']

19 I always wanted to get into politics, but I was never light enough to make the team. [From 'Fan Letter to Nixon', in H. Thompson, *Fear and Loathing on the Campaign Trail, '72*]

MICHAEL BUERK 1946–

20 He's got to wrap up a quarter of a lifetime, hasn't he, and move out into the open world? [On Nelson Mandela's release after 27 years in gaol. On BBC TV, 11 Feb. 1990]

NIKOLAI A. BUKHARIN 1888–1938

1 We might have a two-party system, but one of the two parties would be in office and the other in prison. [Attr. in Isaac Deutscher, *The Prophet Armed, Trotsky: 1879–1921*]

VLADIMIR BUKOVSKY 1942–

2 Society already understands that the criminal is not he who washes our dirty linen in public, but he who dirties the linen. [Said on 5 Jan. 1972. In *Radio Times*, 19 Sept. 1977]

3 The pessimist is the man who believes things couldn't possibly be worse, to which the optimist replies: 'Oh yes they could!' [In the *Guardian Weekly*, 10 July 1977]

ALAN [later LORD] BULLOCK 1914–

4 The people Hitler never understood, and whose actions continued to exasperate him to the end of his life, were the British. [*Hitler*, Pt VIII, 5]

5 Hitler showed surprising loyalty to Mussolini, but it never extended to trusting him. [XI. 3]

IVOR BULMER-THOMAS, MP 1905–

6 If ever he [Harold Wilson] went to school without any boots it was because he was too big for them. [At Conservative Party Conference, Blackpool, 12 Oct. 1949. See also 405:15]

H. C. BUNNER 1855–1896

7 Shake was a dramatist of note; / He lived by writing things to quote. [*Shake, Mulleary and Go-ethe*]

'BUGS BUNNY'

8 What's up Doc? [Catchphrase from film cartoon 1937–1963, attr. to 'Tex' Fred Avery, became title of film, 1972]

BASIL BUNTING 1900–1985

9 Name and date / split in soft slate / a few months obliterate. [*Briggflatts*, 1]

10 It looks well enough on the page, but never / well enough. [2]

11 It is time to consider how Domenico Scarlatti / condensed so much music into so few bars. [4]

12 Who / swinging his axe / to fell kings, guesses / where we go? ['Coda']

LUIS BUÑUEL 1900–1983

13 If someone were to tell me I had twenty years left, and ask me how I'd like to spend them, I'd reply: 'Give me two hours a day of activity, and I'll take the other 22 in dreams ... provided I can remember them.' [*My Last Breath*, Ch. 9]

14 I am an atheist still, thank God. [In Ado Kyrou, *Luis Buñuel: An Introduction*]

15 I would give my life for a man who is looking for the truth. But I would gladly kill a man who thinks that he has found the truth. [Quoted by Carlos Fuentes in the *Guardian*, 24 Feb. 1989]

LUTHER BURBANK 1849–1926

16 Heredity is just environment stored. [In *Dictionary of Scientific Quotations*, ed. A. L. Mackay]

JULIE BURCHILL 1960–

17 Sex without using someone is as difficult as eating without chewing. [In the *Observer*, 2 Mar. 1986]

ANTHONY BURGESS 1917–

18 O my brothers ... [*A Clockwork Orange, passim*]

19 Who ever heard of a clockwork orange? ... The attempt to impose upon man, a creature of growth and capable of sweetness, to ooze juicily at the last round the bearded lips of God, to attempt to impose, I say, laws and conditions appropriate to a mechanical creation, against this I raise my sword-pen. [Ch. 2]

20 It was the afternoon of my eighty-first birthday, and I was in bed with my catamite when Ali announced that the archbishop had come to see me. [*Earthly Powers*, opening sentence]

1 God was still ... the best of the dramatic poets, though shapeless and uneconomical. A bit like Charles Dickens. God was good on the physical and emotional sides and a great one for hate. He generously spilled his own hate into his dearest creation. [*Enderby's Dark Lady*, 7]

2 He said it was artificial respiration, but now I find I am to have his child. [*Inside Mr Enderby*, Pt I, Ch. 4, ii]

3 Bath twice a day to be really clean, once a day to be passably clean, once a week to avoid being a public menace. [2. i]

4 *Pax Romana*. Where they made a desolation they called it a peace. What absolute nonsense! It was a nasty, vulgar sort of civilization, only dignified by being hidden and under a lot of declensions.

5 Would you try it for, say, six months, a poem every week? Preferably set in the form of prose, so as not to offend anyone. [3. ii]

6 Rome's just a city like anywhere else. A vastly overrated city, I'd say. It trades on belief just as Stratford trades on Shakespeare. [II. 2. i]

7 A sure sign of an amateur is too much detail to compensate for too little life. [In *The Times Literary Supplement*, 18 June 1971]

8 You never know why God singles people out for special treatment. Take Lazarus – pissed every night, screwed everyone, slain in a tavern. [Interview with Martin Amis in the *Observer*, 12 Oct. 1980]

9 Reality is what I see, not what you see. [In the *Sunday Times Magazine*, 18 Dec. 1983]

10 Perhaps psychoanalysis could only come about in a Vienna of stiff collars and whale-bone corsets. If Freud had worn a kilt in the prescribed Highland manner he might have had a different attitude to genitals. [In the *Observer*, 24 Aug. 1986]

11 The trouble began with Forster. After him it was considered ungentlemanly to write more than five or six [novels]. [Interview in the *Guardian*, 24 Feb. 1989]

12 Music says nothing to the reason: it is a kind of closely structured nonsense. [In the *Observer*, 23 July]

GELETT BURGESS 1866–1951

13 I never saw a Purple Cow, / I never hope to see one; / But I can tell you, anyhow, / I'd rather see than be one! [*Burgess Nonsense Book*, 'The Purple Cow']

14 Ah, yes! I wrote the 'Purple Cow' – / I'm sorry, now, I wrote it! / But I can tell you anyhow, / I'll kill you if you quote it! ['*Cinq ans après*']

JOHNNY BURKE 1908–1964

15 Don't you know each cloud contains / Pennies from Heaven? [Song: *Pennies from Heaven*, music by A. Johnston]

16 Or would you like to swing on a star, / Carry moonbeams home in a jar, / And be better off than you are, / Or would you rather be a fish? [Song: *Swinging on a Star*]

See also under **BING CROSBY** *and* **BOB HOPE**

CAROL BURNETT 1933–

17 The first time someone said, 'What are your measurements?' I answered, 'Thirty-seven, twenty-four, thirty-eight – but not necessarily in that order. [In US film. In *Was It Good for You Too?*, ed. Bob Chieger]

ERNIE BURNETT and GERALD GRIFFIN

18 We'll meet again, don't know where, / Don't know when, / But I know we'll meet again some sunny day. [Song: *We'll Meet Again*, 1939]

W. R. BURNETT 1899–1982

19 The Asphalt Jungle. [Title of book]

GEORGE BURNS 1896–

20 Too bad all the people who know how to run the country are busy driving taxi cabs and cutting hair. [In Michael Shea, *Influence*, Ch. 27]

JOHN BURNS 1858–1943

21 Every drop of the Thames is liquid 'istory. [To transatlantic visitors, attr. by Sir Frederick Whyte. In the *Daily Mail*, 25 Jan. 1943]

WILLIAM S. BURROUGHS 1914–

1 No one owns life, but anyone who can pick up a frying pan owns death. [In Adrian Henri, *Adrian Henri's Last Will and Testament*]

2 No problem can be solved. When a situation becomes a problem, it becomes insoluble. Problems are by definition insoluble. No problems can be solved, and all solutions lead to more problems. [To Allen Ginsberg over the telephone. In Barry Miles, *Ginsberg*, Ch. 17]

B. H. BURT 1880–1950

3 'You can tell a man who boozes from the company he chooses.' / And the pig got up and slowly walked away. [Song: *The Pig Got Up . . .*]

4 When you're all dressed up and no place to go. [Title of song, 1913, music by Silvio Hein]

NAT BURTON

5 There'll be blue birds over / The white cliffs of Dover. [Song: *The White Cliffs of Dover*, 1942, music by Walter Kent]

RICHARD BURTON 1925–1984

6 [When buttonholed in an hotel lobby by an American with Welsh forebears who said, 'You and I ought to get on well, Mr Burton. We're both Selts.'] I am a Selt. *You* are a sunt. [In Philip Norman, *Your Walrus Hurt the One You Love*]

7 The Welsh are all actors. It's only the bad ones who become professionals. [In the *Listener*, 9 Jan. 1986]

8 [When asked by Gabriel Byrne why he had made so many films, instead of going back to the theatre] Because I couldn't bear not to have somewhere to go in the mornings. [Interview in the *Observer Magazine*, 6 Mar. 1988]

DR DOUGLAS BUSCH

9 Behavioural psychology is the science of pulling habits out of rats. [In Laurence J. Peter, *Peter's Quotations*]

BARBARA BUSH 1925–

10 I am going to tell you the honest truth, the President is never going to eat broccoli. [In the *Independent*, 'Quote Unquote', 31 Mar. 1990]

PRESIDENT GEORGE BUSH 1924–

11 Read my lips: no new taxes. [Speech accepting Republican nomination in presidential election, Aug. 1988. Coined by Pat Noonan]

12 A thousand points of light. [Referring to private initiative in charity work]

13 America is never wholly herself unless she is engaged in high moral principle. We as a people have such a purpose today. It is: to make kinder the face of the nation, and gentler the face of the world. [Inaugural presidential address, Washington, 20 Jan. 1989]

14 Our funds are low. We have a deficit to bring down. We have more will than wallet.

15 A line has been drawn in the sand. [At press conference on movement of US forces into Saudi Arabia in Iraq crisis, 9 Aug. 1990]

ALDO BUSI 1948–

16 [A good salesman must have] the quality of saying with ten thousand words arousing enthusiasm what others said with ten words causing people to yawn. [*The Standard Life of a Temporary Pantyhose Salesman*]

KOFI BUSIA

17 Diplomacy . . . means the art of nearly deceiving all your friends, but not quite deceiving all your enemies. [Interview, 2 Feb. 1970. In *Simpson's Contemporary Quotations*]

NICHOLAS MURRAY BUTLER 1862–1947

18 An expert is one who knows more and more about less and less. [Commencement address, Columbia University]

R. A. [later LORD] BUTLER 1902–1982

19 Q: Mr Butler, would you say that this is

the best Prime Minister we have? A: Yes. [Interview about Anthony Eden's premiership, London Airport, 8 Jan. 1956]

1 [On being told that Anthony Eden was the son of a mad baronet and a beautiful woman] That's the trouble with Anthony – half mad baronet, half beautiful woman. [In S. Hoggart, *Back in the House*]

2 Politics is the art of the possible. [Epigraph to his memoirs, *The Art of the Possible*, derived from Bismarck. See also 139:7]

3 You know it's the best machine in the world, but you're not quite sure what to do with it. [Comparing Whitehall to a Rolls-Royce. In the *Sunday Times*, 8 Jan. 1989]

SAMUEL BUTLER 1835–1902

4 Some who had received a liberal education at the Colleges of Unreason, and taken the highest degrees in hypothetics, which are their principal study. [*Erewhon*, Ch. 9]

5 Straighteners, managers and cashiers of the Musical Banks.

6 While to deny the existence of an unseen kingdom is bad, to pretend that we know more about it than its bare existence is no better. [15]

7 The wish to spread those opinions that we hold conducive to our own welfare is so deeply rooted in the English character that few of us can escape its influence. [20]

8 It has been said that the love of money is the root of all evil. The want of money is so quite as truly.

9 Spontaneity is only a term for man's ignorance of the gods. [25]

10 It has, I believe, been often remarked that a hen is only an egg's way of making another egg. [*Life and Habit*, Ch. 8]

11 Life is one long process of getting tired. [*Notebooks*, Ch. 1, 'Life', 7]

12 Life is the art of drawing sufficient conclusions from insufficient premises. [9]

13 All progress is based upon a universal innate desire on the part of every organism to live beyond its income. [16]

14 The healthy stomach is nothing if not

conservative. Few radicals have good digestions. [Ch. 6, 'Indigestion']

15 Though analogy is often misleading, it is the least misleading thing we have. [Ch. 7, 'Thought and Word', 2]

16 When a man is in doubt about this or that in his writing, it will often guide him if he asks himself how it will tell a hundred years hence. [Final note]

17 If Bach wriggles, Wagner writhes. [Ch. 8, 'Musical Criticism']

18 The history of art is the history of revivals. ['Anachronism']

19 The phrase 'unconscious humour' is the one contribution I have made to the current literature of the day. ['*Homo Unius Libri*: Myself and "Unconscious Humour"']

20 I am the *enfant terrible* of literature and science. [Ch. 12, 'Myself']

21 Virgil was no good because Tennyson ran him, and as for Tennyson – well, Tennyson goes without saying. ['Blake, Dante, etc.']

22 An apology for the Devil – it must be remembered that we have only heard one side of the case. God has written all the books. [Ch. 14, 'An Apology for the Devil']

23 God is Love – I dare say. But what a mischievous devil Love is! ['God is Love']

24 To live is like to love – all the reason is against it, and all healthy instinct for it. ['Life and Love']

25 The public buys its opinions as it buys its meat, or takes in its milk, on the principle that it is cheaper to do this than to keep a cow. So it is, but the milk is more likely to be watered. [Ch. 17, 'Public Opinion']

26 To be at all is to be religious more or less. [Ch. 22, 'Religion']

27 An honest God's the noblest work of man. [*Further Extracts*, Vol. i, 'An Honest God' (reversing Pope)]

28 Brigands demand money or your life, whereas women require both. [Vol. iv, 'Women and Brigands']

29 Taking numbers into account, I should think more mental suffering had been undergone in the streets leading from St George's,

Hanover Square, than in the condemned cells of Newgate. [*The Way of All Flesh*, Ch. 13]

1 Every man's work, whether it be literature or music or pictures or architecture or anything else, is always a portrait of himself. [14]

2 That vice pays homage to virtue is notorious; we call it hypocrisy. [19]

3 Pleasure after all is a safer guide than either right or duty.

4 The advantage of doing one's praising for oneself is that one can lay it on so thick and exactly in the right places. [34]

5 There's many a good tune played on an old fiddle. [61]

6 'Tis better to have loved and lost than never to have lost at all. [77]

7 Stowed away in a Montreal lumber room / The Discobolus standeth and turneth his face to the wall; / Dusty, cobweb-covered, maimed and set at naught, / Beauty crieth in an attic and no man regardeth: / O God! O Montreal! [*Psalm of Montreal*]

RONALD BUTT 1920–

8 The path of politicians is bestrewn by banana skins, sometimes on ice. [In *The Times*, 16 Feb. 1989]

A. S. BYATT 1936–

9 He's one of those men who argues by increments of noise – so that as you open your mouth he says another, cleverer, louder thing. [*Possession*, Ch. 15]

10 Autobiographies tell more lies than all but the most self-indulgent fiction. [*Sugar*, 'The Day That E. M. Forster Died']

MAX BYGRAVES 1922–

11 Good idea – son! [Catchphrase in variety act, late 1950s and early 1960s]

12 I've arrived – and to prove it, I'm here. [Catchphrase in BBC radio comedy series *Educating Archie*, 1950–53]

DOUGLAS BYNG 1893–1987

13 I'm Millie, a messy old mermaid. [Song]

14 I'm one of the Queens of England / But I can't remember which. [Song: *I'm One of the Queens of England*]

15 No wonder they call me the Virgin Queen. / I was never off the verge. [In obituary in the *Guardian*, 26 Aug. 1987]

C

JAMES BRANCH CABELL 1879–1958

1 I am willing to taste any drink once. [*Jurgen*, Ch. 1]

2 I shall marry in haste and repeat at leisure. [16]

3 Why is the King of Hearts the only one that hasn't a moustache? [*The Rivet in Grandfather's Neck*]

4 The optimist proclaims that we live in the best of all possible worlds; and the pessimist fears this is so. [*The Silver Stallion*, Bk iv, Ch. 26]

IRVING CAESAR 1895–

5 Tea for Two, and Two for Tea. [Title of song in musical *No, No, Nanette*, Act II, music by Vincent Youmans]

JOHN CAGE 1912–1992

6   I have nothing to say
/   and I am saying it   and that is /
poetry. [*Lecture on Nothing*]

SAMMY CAHN 1913–1993

7 Give me five minutes more, / Only five minutes more, / Let me stay, / Let me stay in your arms. [Song: *Five Minutes More*]

8 Love and marriage, love and marriage, / Go together like a horse and carriage. [Song: *Love and Marriage*, in musical *Our Town*]

MICHAEL CAINE 1933–

9 [Film acting] is not so much acting as reacting, doing nothing with tremendous skill. [In *City Limits*, 28 Feb.–6 Mar. 1986]

10 Theatre is like operating with a scalpel. Film is operating with a laser. [In BBC TV programme *Acting*, 28 Aug. 1987]

11 Not many people know that. [Catchphrase used as title of his book]

JAMES [later LORD] CALLAGHAN 1912–

12 A lie can be half-way round the world before the truth has got its boots on. [Speech, 1 Nov. 1976]

13 If Labour is dead in Scotland then, from now on, I shall believe in life in the hereafter. [At a Glasgow rally. In the *Guardian*, 6 Sept. 1977]

14 Either back us or sack us. [Speech at Labour Party Conference, Brighton, 5 Oct.]

15 I see no signs of mounting crisis. [When returning on 10 Jan. 1979 from Guadeloupe Summit Conference to find his government in ruins. In S. Hoggart, *On the House*, p. 151. Usually misquoted as 'Crisis? What crisis?']

MARIA CALLAS 1923–1977

16 That is the difference between good teachers and great teachers: good teachers make the best of a pupil's means: great teachers foresee a pupil's ends. [Kenneth Harris, *Kenneth Harris Talking to*: 'Maria Callas']

MEL CALMAN 1931–

17 Doctor – I keep getting these pains in my wallet. [Cartoon caption in *But It's My Turn to Leave You...*]

18 Please don't interrupt me when I'm interrupting.

1 I like Maggie [Thatcher]; she knows my own mind. [*Help*]

2 One man's meat is another woman's Sunday gone. [Cartoon caption in the *Guardian*, 15 Oct. 1986]

3 I have seen the Future – and it was being Repaired. [Cartoon caption in *The Times*, 30 Dec. See also 357:2, 376:6]

STEPHANIE CALMAN

4 The types who make passes at girls who wear glasses – so they can see themselves in the reflection. [From *Gentlemen Prefer My Sister*, in *Picking on Men*, comp. Judy Allen. See also 291:4]

ITALO CALVINO 1923–1985

5 I may have had to make some effort myself, at first, to learn not to read, but now it comes quite naturally to me. The secret is not refusing to look at the written words. On the contrary, you must look at them, intensely, until they disappear. [*If on a Winter's Night a Traveller*, Ch. 3]

6 Everything has already begun before, the first line of the first page of every novel refers to something that has already happened outside the book. [7]

7 Because writing always means hiding something in such a way that it then is discovered. [8]

8 The things that the novel does not say are necessarily more numerous than those it does say and only a special halo around what is written can give the illusion that you are reading also what is not written. [10]

9 But perhaps it is this same distrust of our senses that prevents us from feeling comfortable in the universe. [*Mr Palomar*, 'the eye and the planets']

JAMES CAMERON 1911–1985

10 If you want to make a fortune, don't work on a newspaper: own it. There is absolutely no obligation to read it, even if you can. [*Cameron in the Guardian*, 'Thanks a Million']

11 It's like asking a patient, 'Would you like your appendix put back in?' [On the Common Market Referendum in Britain, June 1975. In the *Sunday Times*, 15 June 1975]

12 The making of evanescent bricks with ephemeral straw. [Definition of journalism. In the *Independent*, 28 July 1991. See also 56:8]

NORMAN CAMERON 1905–1953

13 Forgive me, Sire, for cheating your intent, / That I, who should command a regiment, / Do amble amiably here, O God, / One of the neat ones in your awkward squad. [*Forgive Me Sire*]

14 When you confess your sins before a parson, / You find it no great effort to disclose / Your crimes of murder, bigamy and arson, / But can you tell him that you pick your nose? [*Punishment Enough*]

15 These two hated each other at half sight. [*Rimbaud and Verlaine*]

JOSEPH CAMPBELL 1879–1944

16 As a white candle / In a holy place, / So is the beauty / Of an aged face. [*The Old Woman*]

17 Her brood gone from her / And her thoughts as still / As the water / Under a ruined mill.

PATRICK CAMPBELL 1913–1980

18 The word 'charade' is derived from the Spanish *charrada*, the chatter of clowns. Beyond that, charades have no connection with any kind of entertainment, living or dead. [*A Short Trot with a Cultured Mind*, 'The Chatter of Clowns']

19 Magda was foreign – so foreign, indeed, that it was only possible to place her low down in the Balkans. ['The Crime in the Cloakroom']

MRS PATRICK CAMPBELL 1865–1940

20 It doesn't matter what you do in the bedroom as long as you don't do it in the street and frighten the horses. [In Daphne Fielding, *The Duchess of Jermyn Street*, Ch. 2]

1 The deep, deep peace of the double-bed after the hurly-burly of the chaise-longue. [Of her marriage. In Alexander Woollcott, *While Rome Burns*, 'The First Mrs Tanqueray']

ROY CAMPBELL 1902–1957

2 Or like a poet woo the moon, / Riding an arm-chair for my steed, / And with a flashing pen harpoon / Terrific metaphors of speed. [*The Festivals of Flight*]

3 You praise the firm restraint with which they write – / I'm with you there, of course: / They use the snaffle and the bit all right, / But where's the bloody horse? [*On Some South African Novelists*]

4 Burn, with Athens and with Rome, / A sacred city of the mind. [*Toledo, July 1936*]

5 I hate 'Humanity' and all such abstracts: but I love *people*. Lovers of 'Humanity' generally hate *people and children*, and keep parrots or puppy dogs. [*Light on a Dark Horse*, Ch. 13]

6 Translations (like wives) are seldom faithful if they are in the least attractive. [In *Poetry Review*, June/July 1949]

ALBERT CAMUS 1913–1960

7 I am well aware that an addiction to silk underwear does not necessarily imply that one's feet are dirty. None the less, style, like sheer silk, too often hides eczema. [*The Fall*]

8 A single sentence will suffice for modern man: he fornicated and read the papers.

9 How many crimes committed merely because their authors could not endure being wrong!

10 You know what charm is: a way of getting the answer yes without having asked any clear question.

11 Alas, after a certain age every man is responsible for his face.

12 It hurts me to confess it, but I'd have given ten conversations with Einstein for a first meeting with a pretty chorus-girl.

13 Don't wait for the Last Judgement. It takes place every day.

14 Too many people have decided to do without generosity in order to practise charity.

15 A person I knew used to divide human beings into three categories: those who prefer having nothing to hide rather than being obliged to lie, those who prefer lying to having nothing to hide, and finally those who like both lying and the hidden.

16 The absurd is born of this confrontation between the human need and the unreasonable silence of the world. [*The Myth of Sisyphus*, 'Absurd Walls', trans. J. O'Brien]

17 The absurd has meaning only in so far as it is not agreed to. ['Philosophical Suicide']

18 The absurd is sin without God.

19 The struggle itself towards the heights is enough to fill a man's heart. One must imagine Sisyphus happy. [Title essay]

20 The secret of my universe: just imagine God without man's immortality. [*Notebooks*]

21 Every fulfilment is slavery. It drives us to a higher fulfilment.

22 An intellectual is someone whose mind watches itself. [*Notebooks, 1935–42*]

23 I know of only one duty, and that is to love.

24 Mother died today. Or, maybe, yesterday: I can't be sure. [*The Outsider*, Pt 1, Ch. 1, trans. Stuart Gilbert]

25 I laid my heart open to the benign indifference of the universe. [II. 5]

26 All I maintain is that . . . there are pestilences and there are victims; no more than that. If, by making that statement, I, too, become a carrier of the plague-germ, at least I don't do it wilfully. I try, in short, to be an innocent murderer. [*The Plague*, Pt IV, Ch. 6, trans. Stuart Gilbert]

27 If one denies that there are grounds for suicide one cannot claim them for murder. One cannot be a part-time nihilist. [*The Rebel*, Introduction]

28 What is a rebel? A man who says no. [Ch. 1]

29 Martyrs do not build churches: they are the mortar, or the alibi. They are followed by the priests and bigots. [2]

1 All modern revolutions have ended in a reinforcement of the power of the state.

2 To lose the touch of flowers and women's hands is the supreme separation. [In the *Guardian*, 30 Sept. 1974]

3 It is from the moment when I shall no longer be more than a writer that I shall cease to write. [Quoted by Nadine Gordimer in the *Guardian*, 4 Oct. 1991]

ELIAS CANETTI 1905–

4 If a mother could be content to be nothing but a mother; but where would you find one who would be satisfied with that part alone? [*Auto da Fé*, Pt I, Ch. 1]

5 Among the most sinister phenomena in intellectual history is the avoidance of the concrete. [*Conscience of Words*, 'Power and Survival']

6 The Englishman likes to imagine himself at sea, the German in a forest. It is impossible to express the difference of their national identity more concisely. [*Crowds and Power*, 'The Crowd in History']

7 To circumvent death, to evade it, is one of the oldest and strongest desires of rulers.

8 The various languages you ought to have: one for your mother, which you will subsequently never speak again; one which you only read but never dare to write; one in which you pray but without understanding a single word; one in which you do arithmetic and to which all money matters belong; one in which you write (but no letters); one in which you travel, and in this you can also write your letters. [*The Human Province*, '1942']

9 Whenever you observe an animal closely, you feel as if a human being sitting inside were making fun of you.

10 People are thankful to their forebears because they never knew them. ['1943']

11 Of all the words in all languages I know, the greatest concentration is in the English word I.

12 We are never sad enough to improve the world. We are hungry again too soon.

13 How much one has to say in order to be heard when silent.

14 We have laid hands on everything and then believe that it is everything. ['1944']

15 The unity of a nation consists mainly in its being able to act, when necessary, like a single paranoic. ['1945']

16 One invention still lacking: how to reverse explosions.

17 True writers encounter their characters only *after* they've created them. ['1946']

18 God was a mistake. But it is hard to decide whether too early or too late. ['1948']

19 Perhaps every breath you take is someone else's last. ['1950']

20 He kept turning the other cheek until they stuck a medal on it. ['1955']

21 The finest statue of a man would be a horse that has thrown him off.

22 Perhaps, of all people, only Klee treated dreams with the proper awe, as the most inviolable thing to occur in a human being. ['1960']

23 Everything he knows is always present to him. He knocks on all doors and enters nowhere. Having knocked, he thinks he has been there. ['1962']

24 He would like to start from scratch. Where is scratch? ['1965']

25 In history, there seems to be only a negative learning. One notes what one has done to others in order to hold it against them. ['1969']

26 Dialectics, a kind of false teeth. ['1970']

DAVID CANNADINE 1950–

27 Of necessity, the more contemporary history becomes the more it becomes contemporary hearsay. [In *New Society*, 6 Dec. 1984]

28 In the Britain of the 1980s, there are only three people who really matter, and all of them are women. But before their pre-eminence is hailed as embodying the long-overdue triumph of the feminist movement, it is worth remembering precisely how unusual they are: Dame Edna Everidge, Mrs Margaret Thatcher, and Queen Elizabeth II. [In *New Statesman and Society*, 10 June 1988]

29 In our rampantly secular world, biogra-

phy is now the only certain form of life after death. [In the *Observer*, 21 Apr. 1991]

HUGHIE CANNON 1877–1912

1 Won't you come home, Bill Bailey, won't you come home? [Song: *Won't You Come Home, Bill Bailey?*, 1902]

MORTIMER CAPLAN 1916–

2 There is one difference between a tax collector and a taxidermist – the taxidermist leaves the hide. [In *Time* magazine, 1 Feb. 1963]

JOHN CAPLES 1900–1990

3 They laughed when I sat down at the piano. But when I started to play! [Advertisement for US school of music]

AL CAPONE 1899–1947

4 I've been accused of every death except the casualty list of the World War. [In Kenneth Allsop, *The Bootleggers*, Ch. 11]

5 This [suburban Chicago] is virgin territory for whorehouses. [16]

TRUMAN CAPOTE 1924–1984

6 None of them [the Beat novelists] can write, not even Mr Kerouac. What they do . . . isn't writing at all – it's typing. [On US TV, Feb. 1959]

7 Other Voices, Other Rooms. [Title of book]

8 Venice is like eating an entire box of chocolate liqueurs at one go. [In the *Observer*, 'Sayings of the Week', 26 Nov. 1961]

9 Dry and draughty, like an abandoned temple. [Of Greta Garbo. From *Answered Prayers*, in *The Times Literary Supplement*, 5 Dec. 1986]

FRANK CAPRA 1897–1991

10 I made mistakes in drama. I thought drama was when actors cried. But drama is when the audience cries. [On French TV, Feb. 1983. In *Chambers Film Quotes*, comp. Tony Crawley]

FRITJOF CAPRA 1939–

11 Scientists, therefore, are responsible for their research not only intellectually but also morally . . . the results of quantum mechanics and relativity theory have opened up two very different paths for physics to pursue. They may lead us – to put it in extreme terms – to the Buddha or to the bomb, and it is up to each of us to decide which path to take. [*The Turning Point*, II. 3]

ERNESTO CARDENAL 1925–

12 *Señor quienquiera que haya sido el que ella iba a llamar / y no llamó (y tal vez no era nadie / o era Alguién cuyo número no está en el Directorio de Los Ángeles) / contesta Tú el teléfono!* – Lord, whoever it was that she was going to call up, she did not call (perhaps it was no one, perhaps it was Somebody whose name is not in the Los Angeles telephone directory) answer Thou the telephone! [*Oración por Marilyn Monroe*]

SIR NEVILLE CARDUS 1889–1975

13 He [Yehudi Menuhin] never *performs*; he communicates to us, through his fiddle, often in spite of his fiddle, the divinely given best of him. [*Full Score*, 'Menuhin']

14 At Trent Bridge it is always four o'clock in the afternoon and 300 for 2. [In untraced cricket article]

15 Here was art greater than life and not, as with nearly all the art of today, as small as life. [Of Jacob Epstein's sculpture. In the *Guardian*, 1961, reprinted 11 Sept. 1986 on 25th anniversary of paper's first being printed in London]

JOHN CAREY 1934–

16 Her [Lady Diana Cooper's] capacity for abstract thought seems to have been roughly that of a strawberry mousse. [In the *Sunday Times*, 20 Sept. 1981]

17 It [Beatrice Webb's diary] could just as well have been composed by an intelligent cockroach. [From *Original Copy*, in review in *The Times Literary Supplement*, 24 July 1987]

18 His achievement has been to take the sex out of glamour. [Of Danny La Rue. Review of his autobiography *From Drag to Riches* in the *Sunday Times*, 25 Oct.]

PETER CAREY 1943–

1 She understood, as women often do more easily than men, that the declared meaning of a spoken sentence is only its overcoat, and the real meaning lies underneath its scarves and buttons. [*Oscar and Lucinda*, 43]

2 But I'm such a bad scholar, I feel like a man with a white cane knocking into knowledge. [Interview in the *Sunday Times*, 20 Mar. 1988]

DALE CARNEGIE 1888–1955

3 How to Win Friends and Influence People. [Title of book]

J. L. CARR 1912–

4 You must understand, James, that their English God is not so dominant a business institution as ours [the American God]. [*The Battle of Pollocks Crossing*, p. 155]

5 *You* have not had thirty years' experience ... *You* have had one year's experience ... *You* have had one year's experience 30 times. [*The Harpole Report*, Ch. 21. See also 267:6]

6 In rural England, people live wrapped tight in a cocoon; only their eyes move to make sure that nobody gets more than themselves. [*How Steeple Sinderby Wanderers Won the FA Cup*, Pt 2]

ALEXIS CARREL 1873–1944

7 Intelligence is almost useless to someone who has no other quality. [From *Man the Unknown*, Ch. 4, 6, in *Dictionary of Scientific Quotations*, ed. A. L. Mackay]

SANTIAGO CARRILLO 1915–

8 For years, Moscow ... was our Rome. We spoke of the Great October Socialist Revolution as if it were our Christmas. That was the period of our infancy. Today we have grown up. [Speech at East Berlin Conference of European Communist and Workers' Parties, 29 June 1976]

JASPER CARROTT 1945–

9 There's Tory childbirth – abolishes all Labour. Then there's SDP childbirth – you have it in the middle of the road. And then there's Militant Tendency childbirth – in Labour for years, then suddenly expelled. [From TV series *Carrott's Lib*, in the *Listener*, 28 Oct. 1982]

10 I am cursed with a right leg that arouses the desire of any male dog that happens to be passing. I used to think that this only happened to me but I've discovered that many people have the same problem. They have a *femme fatale* limb. [*Sweet and Sour Carrott*, p. 44]

ANTHONY CARSON

11 The civil guard are a secret hard-hatted race like ghosts with rifles who are really longing to be human. [*On to Timbuctoo*, Ch. 2]

12 Pigeons, those dull, unmysterious city unemployables, dressed in their grey, second-hand suits. [12]

13 She was a blonde nearly-young American woman of such dynamism that the tideless waves struggled to get farther up the beach. [*A Rose by Any Other Name*, Ch. 10]

14 The apples fell and the swallows crossed off the days. [21]

15 There is never any doubt, then, that one has arrived in Spain ... There is a faint sound of drums, a smell of crude olive-oil, and current of strong, leaking electricity. [*A Train to Tarragona*, Pt I, Ch. 2]

SIR EDWARD [later LORD] CARSON 1854–1935

16 [Cross-examining an Irish witness]
CARSON: Are ye a teetotaller?
WITNESS: No, I'm not.
CARSON: Are ye a modtherate dhrinker?
No answer.
CARSON: Should I be roite if I called ye a heavy dhrinker?
WITNESS: That's my business.
CARSON: Have ye any *other* business?
[H. Montgomery Hyde, *Carson*, Ch. 7 sect. ii]

17 My only great qualification for being put in charge of the Navy is that I am very much at sea. [Said to senior Admiralty staff on formation of Coalition, 1916. In 2. i]

JOHNNY CARSON 1925–

1 If it weren't for Philo T. Farnsworth, inventor of television, we'd still be eating frozen radio dinners. [In *The 637 Best Things Anybody Ever Said*, comp. Robert Byrne]

MARCO CARSON

2 And by my grave you'd pray to have me back, / So I could see how well you looked in black. [*To Any Woman*]

RACHEL CARSON 1907–1964

3 For all at last return to the sea – to Oceanus, the ocean river, like the ever-flowing stream of time, the beginning and the end. [*The Sea around Us*, last words]

JOHN CARSWELL 1918–

4 She was dealt a high card in life, but it was the wrong suit. [*The Exile: A Life of Ivy Litvinov*, last para.]

ANGELA CARTER 1940–1992

5 What is marriage but prostitution to one man instead of many? [*Nights at the Circus*, 'London 2']

6 A gee-string of very respectable dimensions, more of a gee-gee string, would have kept a horse decent. [*Wise Children*, 2]

7 He was a man with a great future behind him, already. [3]

8 She looked a million dollars, I must admit, even if in well-used notes. [5]

PRESIDENT JIMMY CARTER 1924–

9 I've looked on a lot of women with lust. I've committed adultery in my heart many times. This is something God recognizes I will do – and I have done it – and God forgives me for it. [Interview in *Playboy*, Nov. 1976]

'MIZ' LILLIAN CARTER [Mother of President Jimmy Carter] 1898–1983

10 I love all my children, but some of them I don't like. [In *Woman*, 9 Apr. 1977]

SYDNEY CARTER 1915–

11 Dance, then, wherever you may be; / I am the Lord of the Dance, said he, / And I'll lead you all, wherever you may be, / And I'll lead you all in the Dance, said he. [Gospel song: *Lord of the Dance*, music adapted from Shaker hymn tune, *The Gift to be Simple*]

DAME BARBARA CARTLAND 1904–

12 At fifty you have the choice of keeping your face or your figure and it's *much* better to keep your face. [Interview in the *Daily Mail*, 10 July 1981]

13 It was I who introduced bottled water into India. [In the *Independent*, 'Quote Unquote', 18 Mar. 1989]

JOYCE CARY 1888–1957

14 She had a mannish manner of mind and face, able to feel hot and think cold. [*Herself Surprised*, Ch. 7]

15 To abuse a man is a lover-like thing and gives him rights. [35]

16 Sara could commit adultery at one end and weep for her sins at the other, and enjoy both operations at once. [*The Horse's Mouth*, Ch. 8]

17 He has a face like what Cardinal Newman's would have been if he had gone into the army instead of the Church, grown an Old Bill moustache, lost most of his teeth, and only shaved on Saturdays, before preaching. [11]

18 Remember I'm an artist. And you know what that means in a court of law. Next worst to an actress. [14]

19 Anarchists who love God always fall for Spinoza because he tells them that God doesn't love them. This is just what they need. A poke in the eye. To a real anarchist a poke in the eye is better than a bunch of flowers. It makes him see stars. [16]

20 Hell is paved with good intentions, but heaven goes in for something more dependable. Solid gold. [22]

21 The only good government . . . is a bad one in a hell of a fright. [32]

22 It was as dark as the inside of a Cabinet Minister. [33]

1 Of course, I always liked big women. I suppose I was meant to be a sculptor or architect. [38]

2 I ain't complaining – it's a duty laid down upon us by God – but the Pax Britannia takes a bit of keeping up – with 'arf the world full of savages and 'arf the other 'arf just getting in the way. [*Mister Johnson*]

3 It is the misfortune of an old man that though he can put things out of his head he can't put them out of his feelings. [*To be a Pilgrim*, Ch. 8]

4 The will is never free – it is always attached to an object, a purpose. It is simply the engine in the car – it can't steer. [In *Writers at Work*, ed. Malcolm Cowley, First Series]

RICHARD CASEMENT 1942–1982

5 Somebody not prepared to use induction would have to drink all the water in the sea before being prepared to admit that the sea is salty. [*Man Suddenly Sees to the Edge of the Universe*]

'CASSANDRA' [SIR WILLIAM CONNOR] 1909–1967

6 What a genius the Labour Party has for cutting itself in half and letting the two parts writhe in public. [In the *Daily Mirror*]

7 To have been alive with him [Winston Churchill] was to have dined at the table of history.

8 I suppose nobody has ever been struck a direct blow by a rabbit. At least, not deliberately.

SIR HUGH CASSON 1910–

9 The British love permanence more than they love beauty. [In the *Observer*, 'Sayings of the Week', 14 June 1964]

BARBARA [later LADY] CASTLE 1911–

10 She is so clearly the best man among them. [On Margaret Thatcher's becoming Conservative Party leader. *Diaries*, 11 Feb. 1975]

TED [later LORD] CASTLE 1907–1979

11 In Place of Strife. [Title of Labour Government White Paper, 17 Jan. 1969, suggested to his wife, Barbara Castle, then Secretary of State for Employment]

HARRY CASTLING

12 Let's All Go down the Strand. [Title of song, 1908, sung by Charles Whittle, to which refrain became 'Have a banana!']

FIDEL CASTRO 1926–

13 *La Historia me absolverá.* – History will absolve me. [Of the unsuccessful assault on the Moncada Barracks. Said on 26 July 1953]

WILLA CATHER 1873–1947

14 Oh the Germans classify, but the French arrange. [*Death Comes to the Archbishop*, 'Prologue']

15 Most of the basic material a writer works with is acquired before the age of fifteen. [In *Writer's Quotation Book*, ed. James Charlton]

WYNN CATLIN 1930–

16 Diplomacy is the art of saying 'Nice Doggie!' till you can find a rock. [In *Kiss Me Hardy*, ed. Roger Kilroy]

PATRICK SKENE CATLING 1925–

17 Of course you can get a quart into a pint pot – you can get a couple of gallons into it, if you stay till closing time. [Review of J. A. Simpson's *Concise Oxford Dictionary of Proverbs* in the *Spectator*, 8 Jan. 1983]

CHARLES CAUSLEY 1917–

18 Who is the smiling stranger / With hair as white as gin, / What is he doing with the children / And who could have let him in? [*Innocent's Song*]

19 You must take off your clothes for the doctor / And stand as straight as a pin, / His hand of stone on your white breastbone / Where the bullets all go in. [*Recruiting Drive*]

20 Ears like bombs and teeth like splinters: / A blitz of a boy is Timothy Winters. [*Timothy Winters*]

CONSTANTINE CAVAFY 1863–1933

1 And now, what will become of us without barbarians? Those people were a kind of solution. [*Waiting for the Barbarians*]

EDITH CAVELL 1865–1915

2 I realize that patriotism is not enough. I must have no hatred or bitterness towards anyone. [Last words, 12 Oct. 1915]

MADISON JULIUS CAWEIN 1865–1914

3 An old Spanish saying is that 'a kiss without a moustache is like an egg without salt'. [*Nature-notes*]

ELENA CEAUŞESCU 1919–1989

4 We [she and her husband President Nicolae Ceauşescu of Romania] want to die together, we do not want mercy. [Just before their execution, 25 Dec. 1989]

LORD DAVID CECIL 1902–1986

5 It does not matter that Dickens' world is not life-like; it is alive. [*Early Victorian Novelists*]

AIMÉ CÉSAIRE 1913–

6 *ma négritude n'est pas une pierre, sa surdité ruée contre la clameur du jour / ma négritude n'est pas une taie d'eau morte sur l'oeil mort de la terre / ma négritude n'est ni une tour ni une cathédrale.* – my Negritude is not a stone, its deafness thrown against the clamour of the day / my Negritude is not a speck of dead water on the dead eye of earth / my Negritude is neither a tower nor a cathedral. [*Cahier d'un retour au pays natal* (*Return to My Native Land*), trans. Emile Snyders]

7 There are two ways of losing oneself: by insulation in the particular or by dilution in the 'universal'. [*Letter to Maurice Thorez*, 1956]

MARC CHAGALL 1889–1985

8 What a genius, that Picasso ... It's a pity he doesn't paint. [In François Gilot and Carlton Lake, *Life with Picasso*, Pt 6]

9 When I am finishing a picture I hold some God-made object up to it – a rock, a flower, the branch of a tree or my hand – as a kind of final test. If the painting stands up beside a thing man cannot make, the painting is authentic. If there's a clash between the two, it is bad art. [In Laurence J. Peter, *Peter's Quotations*]

10 One cannot be precise and still be pure. [In the *Observer*, 'Sayings of the Week', 3 May 1964]

11 The fingers must be educated, the thumb is born knowing. [In *Barnes and Noble Book of Quotations*, ed. Robert I. Fitzhenry, 'Painters']

PATRICK CHALMERS 1872–1942

12 What's lost upon the roundabouts we pulls up on the swings. [*Roundabouts and Swings*, 2]

JOSEPH CHAMBERLAIN 1836–1914

13 Provided that the City of London remains as it is at present, the clearing-house of the world. [Speech at Guildhall, London, 19 Jan. 1904]

14 Learn to think Imperially.

15 The day of small nations has long passed away. The day of Empires has come. [Speech at Birmingham, 12 May]

NEVILLE CHAMBERLAIN 1869–1940

16 What a day! Two salmon this morning, and the offer of the Exchequer this afternoon. [Letter declining office, May 1923. In K. Feiling, *Life of Neville Chamberlain*, 7]

17 In war, whichever side may call itself the victor, there are no winners, but all are losers. [Speech at Kettering, 3 July 1938]

18 How horrible, fantastic, incredible it is that we should be digging trenches and trying on gas-masks here because of a quarrel in a faraway country between people of whom we know nothing! [Radio broadcast, 27 Sept.]

19 I believe it is peace for our time ... peace with honour. [Speech after Munich Agreement, 30 Sept. Echoes Disraeli]

1 This morning the British Ambassador in Berlin handed the German Government a final note stating that, unless we heard from them by eleven o'clock that they were prepared at once to withdraw their troops from Poland, a state of war would exist between us. I have to tell you that no such undertaking has been received, and that consequently this country is at war with Germany. [BBC radio broadcast, 3 Sept. 1939]

2 Whatever may be the reason – whether it was that Hitler thought he might get away with what he had got without fighting for it, or whether it was that after all the preparations were not sufficiently complete – however, one thing is certain: he missed the bus. [Speech to Conservative and Unionist Associations, 4 Apr. 1940]

3 The peace offensive. [Attr. Winston S. Churchill, *The Gathering Storm*, Ch. 24]

ANDRÉ CHAMSON 1900–1983

4 One should never place one's trust in the future. It doesn't deserve it. [*On ne voit pas les coeurs*, Act II, sc. 1]

RAYMOND CHANDLER 1888–1959

5 The General spoke again, slowly, using his strength as carefully as an out-of-work showgirl uses her last good pair of stockings. [*The Big Sleep*, Ch. 2]

6 It was a blonde. A blonde to make a bishop kick a hole in a stained-glass window. [*Farewell, My Lovely*, Ch. 13]

7 She gave me a smile I could feel in my hip pocket. [18]

8 California, the department-store state. The most of everything and the best of nothing. [*The Little Sister*, Ch. 13]

9 A big hard-boiled city with no more personality than a paper cup. [Of Los Angeles. 26]

10 Real cities have something else, some bony structure under the muck. Los Angeles has Hollywood – and hates it. It ought to consider itself damn lucky. Without Hollywood it would be a mail order city. Everything in the catalogue you could get better somewhere else.

11 Down these mean streets a man must go who is not himself mean. [*Pearls are a Nuisance*, 'The Simple Art of Murder']

12 If my books had been any worse, I should not have been invited to Hollywood, and if they had been any better, I should not have come. [Letter to Charles Morton, assoc. ed. of the *Atlantic Monthly*, 12 Dec. 1945]

13 Would you convey my compliments to the purist who reads your proofs and tell him or her that I write in a sort of broken-down patois which is something like the way a Swiss waiter talks, and that when I split an infinitive, God damn it, I split it so it will stay split. [Letter to Edward Weeks, ed. of the *Atlantic Monthly*, 18 Jan. 1947]

14 The Bible . . . is a lesson in how not to write for the movies. [Letter to Edgar Carter, 28 Mar.]

15 It is not enough for a critic to be right, since he will occasionally be wrong. It is not enough for him to give colourable reasons. He must create a reasonable world into which his reader may enter blindfold and feel his way to the chair by the fire without barking his shins on the unexpected dust mop. [Letter to Frederick Lewis Allen, 7 May 1948]

16 The great critics, of whom there are piteously few, build a home for the truth.

17 After all the public is entitled to what it wants, isn't it? The Romans knew that and even they lasted four hundred years after they started to putrefy. [Of TV. Letter to Carl Brandt, 15 Nov. 1951]

18 By his standards anyone who noticed how many walls the room had would be observant. [Of an interviewer who got things wrong. From *Selected Letters*, ed. F. MacShane, in the *Sunday Times*, 29 Nov. 1981]

19 I guess God made Boston on a wet Sunday. [Quoted by George Higgins on the centenary of Chandler's birth, in the *Guardian*, 17 June 1988]

SIR CHARLES CHAPLIN 1889–1977

20 All I need to make a comedy is a park, a policeman and a pretty girl. [*My Autobiography*, Ch. 10]

1 I remain just one thing and one thing only – and that is a clown. It places me on a far higher plane than any politician. [In the *Observer*, 'Sayings of the Week', 17 June 1960]

2 Life is a tragedy when seen in close-up, but a comedy in long-shot. [In obituary in the *Guardian*, 28 Dec. 1977]

SID CHAPLIN 1916–1986

3 Education is a sieve as well as a lift. [*The Day of the Sardine*, Ch. 2]

ARTHUR CHAPMAN 1873–1935

4 Out where the smile dwells a little longer, / That's where the West begins. [*Out Where the West Begins*]

PRINCE CHARLES 1948–

5 What is proposed is like a monstrous carbuncle on the face of a much-loved and elegant friend. [Of a planned extension to the National Gallery, London. Speech to Royal Institute of British Architects, Hampton Court, 30 May 1984]

6 If science has taught us anything, it is that the environment is full of uncertainties. It makes no sense to test it to destruction. While we wait for the doctor's diagnosis, the patient may easily die. [Speech at North Sea Summit, Nov. 1987]

7 You have to give this much to the Luftwaffe: when it knocked down our buildings, it didn't replace them with anything more offensive than rubble. *We* did that. [Of redevelopment around St Paul's. Speech at Mansion House, London, 1 Dec.]

8 It is a clever way of building a nuclear power station in the middle of London without anyone objecting. [Of the National Theatre. In BBC TV programme *Omnibus*, 28 Oct. 1988]

9 If we can stop the sky turning into a microwave oven, we still face the prospect of living in a garbage dump. [In the *Independent*, 'Quote Unquote', 11 Mar. 1989]

10 In fact, I'm about as useful as Linda Lovelace with lockjaw. [At a private dinner, confessing his ignorance of the subject under discussion. In S. Hoggart, *On the House*, p. 96]

ALEXANDER CHASE, 1926–

11 Psychiatry's chief contribution to philosophy is the discovery that the toilet is the seat of the soul. [*Perspectives*]

DAVE CHASEN 1899–1973

12 Bogart's a helluva nice guy till 11.30 p.m. After that he thinks he's Bogart. [In Leslie Halliwell, *Filmgoer's Book of Quotes*]

BRUCE CHATWIN 1940–1989

13 Being lost in Australia gives you a lovely feeling of security. [*Songlines*, 10]

14 Tyranny sets up its own echo-chamber; a void where confused signals buzz about at random; where a murmur or innuendo causes panic: so, in the end, the machinery is more likely to vanish, not with war or revolution, but with a puff, or the voice of falling leaves. [*Utz*, p. 120]

15 And like all self-possessed people he was prey to doubt. [*What am I Doing Here*, 'Heavenly Horses']

JOHN CHEEVER 1912–1982

16 We travel by plane, oftener than not, and yet the spirit of our country seems to have remained a country of railroads. [*Bullet Park*, Pt I, Ch. 1]

17 He loved to quote the axiom, 'Trust your editor, and you'll sleep on straw.' [In Susan Cheever, *Home before Dark*, Ch. 11]

CHER 1946–

18 The trouble with some women is they get all excited about nothing – and then marry him. [In *Hammer and Tongues*, ed. Michèle Brown and Ann O'Connor, 'Husbands']

APSLEY CHERRY-GARRARD 1882–1959

19 Polar exploration is at once the cleanest and most isolated way of having a bad time which has been devised. [*The Worst Journey in the World*, Introduction]

20 Take it all in all, I do not believe anybody on earth has a worse time than an Emperor penguin.

See also E. L. **ATKINSON** and **APSLEY CHERRY-GARRARD**

CHARLIE CHESTER 1914–

1 Down in the jungle / Living in a tent, / Better than a prefab – / No rent! [In BBC radio comedy series *Stand Easy*]

G. K. CHESTERTON 1874–1936

2 Are they clinging to their crosses, / F. E. Smith? [*Antichrist*]

3 But the souls of Christian peoples ... / Chuck it, Smith!

4 No psychoanalyst has knocked / The bottom out of Bottom's dream. [*The Apology of Bottom the Weaver*]

5 I rose politely in the club / And said, 'I feel a little bored: / Will someone take me to a pub?' [*A Ballade of an Anti-Puritan*]

6 The gallows in my garden, people say, / Is new and neat and adequately tall. [*A Ballade of Suicide*]

7 After all / I think I will not hang myself today.

8 Before the gods that made the gods / Had seen their sunrise pass, / The White Horse of the White Horse Vale / Was cut out of the grass. [*The Ballad of the White Horse, 1*]

9 I tell you naught for your comfort, / Yea, naught for your desire, / Save that the sky grows darker yet / And the sea rises higher.

10 For the great Gaels of Ireland / Are the men that God made mad, / For all their wars are merry, / And all their songs are sad. [2]

11 When all philosophies shall fail, / This word alone shall fit; / That a sage feels too small for life, / And a fool too large for it. [8]

12 The wine they drink in Paradise / They make in Haute Lorraine. [*A Cider Song*]

13 The road from heaven to Hereford / Where the apple wood of Hereford / Goes all the way to Wales.

14 With monstrous head and sickening cry / And ears like errant wings, / The devil's walking parody / On all four-footed things. [*The Donkey*]

15 Fools! for I also had my hour; / One far fierce hour and sweet: / There was a shout about my ears, / And palms before my feet.

16 The men that worked for England / They have their graves at home. [*Elegy in a Country Churchyard*]

17 And they that rule in England, / In stately conclave met, / Alas, alas for England / They have no graves as yet.

18 St George he was for England, / And before he killed the dragon / He drank a pint of English ale / Out of an English flagon. [*The Englishman*]

19 Merrily taking twopenny ale and cheese with a pocket knife; / But these were luxuries not for him who went for the Simple Life. [*The Good Rich Man*]

20 White founts falling in the courts of the sun, / And the Soldan of Byzantium is smiling as they run. [*Lepanto*]

21 Strong gongs groaning as the guns boom far, / Don John of Austria is going to the war.

22 You will find me drinking gin / In the lowest kind of inn, / Because I am a rigid Vegetarian. [*The Logical Vegetarian*]

23 The folk that live in Liverpool, their heart is in their boots; / They go to hell like lambs, they do, because the hooter hoots. [*Me Heart*]

24 From all that terror teaches, / From lies of tongue and pen, / From all the easy speeches / That comfort cruel men, / From sale and profanation / Of honour and the sword, / Deliver us, good Lord! [*O God of Earth and Altar*]

25 You have weighed the stars in the balance, and grasped the skies in a span: / Take, if you must have answer, the word of a common man. [*The Pessimist*]

26 'What of vile dust?' the preacher said. / Methought the whole world woke. [*The Praise of Dust*]

27 Before the Roman came to Rye or out to Severn strode, / The rolling English drunkard made the rolling English road. [*The Rolling English Road*]

28 That night we went to Birmingham by way of Beachy Head.

29 For there is good news yet to hear and

fine things to be seen, / Before we go to Paradise by way of Kensal Green.

1 Smile at us, pay us, pass us; but do not quite forget. / For we are the people of England, that never have spoken yet. [*The Secret People*]

2 God made the wicked Grocer / For a mystery and a sign, / That men might shun the awful shop / And go to inns to dine. [*The Song against Grocers*]

3 He crams with cans of poisoned meat / The subjects of the King, / And when they die by thousands / Why, he laughs like anything.

4 Earth will grow worse till men redeem it, / And wars more evil, ere all wars cease. [*A Song of Defeat*]

5 For the men no lords can buy or sell, / They sit not easy when all goes well.

6 The Nothing scrawled on a five-foot page.

7 They haven't got no noses, / The fallen sons of Eve. [*The Song of Quoodle*]

8 And goodness only knowses / The Noselessness of Man.

9 If an angel out of heaven / Brings you other things to drink, / Thank him for his kind attentions, / Go and pour them down the sink. [*The Song of Right and Wrong*]

10 Tea, although an Oriental, / Is a gentleman at least; / Cocoa is a cad and coward, / Cocoa is a vulgar beast.

11 But Higgins is a Heathen, / And to lecture rooms is forced, / Where his aunts, who are not married, / Demand to be divorced. [*The Song of the Strange Ascetic*]

12 I remember my mother, the day that we met, / A thing I shall never entirely forget; / And I toy with the fancy that, young as I am, / I should know her again if we met in a tram. [*Songs of Education*, 3, 'For the Crêche']

13 Invoke the philologic pen / To show you that a Citizen / Means Something in the City. [4, 'Citizenship']

14 And Noah he often said to his wife when he sat down to dine, / 'I don't care where the water goes if it doesn't get into the wine'. [*Wine and Water*]

15 The villas and the chapels where / I learned with little labour / The way to love my fellow-man / And hate my next-door neighbour. [*The World State*]

16 I am afraid of the Patchwork Peril, which is all colours and none; I am afraid of bits of Bolshevism and bits of insane individualism and bits of independence in the wrong place, floating hither and thither and colliding with they know not what. [*All I Survey*, 'On Dependence and Independence']

17 It is arguable that we ought to put the State in order before there can really be such a thing as a State school. ['On Education']

18 A great deal of contemporary criticism reads to me like a man saying: 'Of course I do not like green cheese: I am very fond of brown sherry.' ['On Jonathan Swift']

19 The modern world seems to have no notion of preserving different things side by side, of allowing its proper and proportionate place to each, of saving the whole varied heritage of culture. It has no notion except that of simplifying something by destroying nearly everything. ['On Love']

20 He set out seriously to describe the indescribable. That is the whole business of literature, and it is a hard row to hoe. ['On Literary Cliques']

21 No animal ever invented anything so bad as drunkenness – or so good as drink. [*All Things Considered*, 'Wine When It is Red']

22 The man who does not look at his change is no true poet. [*The Apostle and the Wild Ducks*, ed. Dorothy E. Collins]

23 At the back of our mind [exists] . . . a forgotten blaze or burst of astonishment at our own existence. The object of the artistic and spiritual life is to dig for this submerged sunrise of wonder. [From *Autobiography*, in Denis Healey, *The Time of My Life*, Pt 1, Ch. I]

24 There is a great man who makes every man feel small. But the real great man is the man who makes every man feel great. [*Charles Dickens*, Ch. 1]

25 Circumstances break men's bones; it has never been shown that they break men's optimism. [2]

1 America has a new delicacy, a coarse, rank refinement. [6]

2 A sober man may become a drunkard through being a coward. A brave man may become a coward through being a drunkard. [8]

3 A man looking at a hippopotamus may sometimes be tempted to regard a hippopotamus as an enormous mistake; but he is also bound to confess that a fortunate inferiority prevents him personally from making such mistakes. [10]

4 Either criticism is no good at all (a very defensible position) or else criticism means saying about an author the very things that would have made him jump out of his boots.

5 All slang is metaphor and all metaphor is poetry. [*The Defendant*, 'Defence of Slang']

6 'My country, right or wrong', is a thing that no patriot would think of saying except in a desperate case. It is like saying, 'My mother, drunk or sober'. ['Defence of Patriotism']

7 The rich are the scum of the earth in every country. [*The Flying Inn*, Ch. 15]

8 The word 'orthodoxy' not only no longer means being right; it practically means being wrong. [*Heretics*, Ch. 1]

9 A man's opinion on tramcars matters; his opinion on Botticelli matters; his opinion on all things does not matter.

10 As enunciated today, 'progress' is simply a comparative of which we have not settled the superlative. [2]

11 There is no such thing on earth as an uninteresting subject; the only thing that can exist is an uninterested person. [3]

12 We ought to see far enough into a hypocrite to see even his sincerity. [5]

13 Every man speaks of public opinion, and means by public opinion, public opinion minus his opinion. [8]

14 Charity is the power of defending that which we know to be indefensible. Hope is the power of being cheerful in circumstances which we know to be desperate. [12]

15 Honour is a luxury for aristocrats, but it is a necessity for hall-porters. [13]

16 To be born into this earth is to be born into uncongenial surroundings, hence to be born into a romance. [14]

17 A good novel tells us the truth about its hero; but a bad novel tells us the truth about its author. [15]

18 The oligarchic character of the modern English commonwealth does not rest, like many oligarchies, on the cruelty of the rich to the poor. It does not even rest on the kindness of the rich to the poor. It rests on the perennial and unfailing kindness of the poor to the rich.

19 The artistic temperament is a disease that afflicts amateurs. [17]

20 The old are always fond of new things. Young men read chronicles, but old men read newspapers. [18]

21 Bigotry may be roughly defined as the anger of men who have no opinions.

22 An artist will betray himself by some sort of sincerity. [*The Incredulity of Father Brown*, 'The Dagger with Wings']

23 Where does a wise man kick a pebble? On the beach. Where does a wise man hide a leaf? In the forest. [*The Innocence of Father Brown*, 'The Broken Sword']

24 Every work of art has one indispensable mark ... the centre of it is simple, however much the fulfilment may be complicated. ['The Queer Feet']

25 The human race, to which so many of my readers belong, has been playing at children's games from the beginning, and will probably do it till the end, which is a nuisance for the few people who grow up. [*The Napoleon of Notting Hill*, Bk I, Ch. 1]

26 When the chord of monotony is stretched most tight, then it breaks with a sound like a song.

27 I never in my life said anything merely because I thought it funny; though, of course, I have an ordinary human vainglory, and may have thought it funny because I had said it. [*Orthodoxy*, Ch. 1]

28 The men who really believe in themselves are all in lunatic asylums. [2]

29 Poets do not go mad; but chess-players do.

30 The madman is not the man who has lost his reason. The madman is the man who has lost everything except his reason.

1 The cosmos is about the smallest hole that a man can hide his head in.

2 Reason is itself a matter of faith. It is an act of faith to assert that our thoughts have any relation to reality at all. [3]

3 Mr Shaw is (I suspect) the only man on earth who has never written any poetry.

4 Every man who will not have softening of the heart must at last have softening of the brain.

5 I came to the conclusion that the optimist thought everything good except the pessimist, and that the pessimist thought everything bad, except himself. [5]

6 A man's friend likes him but leaves him as he is: his wife loves him and is always trying to turn him into somebody else.

7 All conservatism is based upon the idea that if you leave things alone you leave them as they are. But you do not. If you leave a thing alone you leave it to a torrent of change. [7]

8 Angels can fly because they take themselves lightly.

9 The *rules* of a club are occasionally in favour of the poor member. The drift of a club is always in favour of the rich one. [9]

10 When we apply it, you call it anarchy; and when you apply it, I call it exploitation. [*The Scandal of Father Brown*, 'The Crime of the Communist']

11 It isn't that they can't see the solution. It is that they can't see the problem. ['The Point of a Pin']

12 Every politician is emphatically a promising politician. ['The Red Moon of Meru']

13 Lying in bed would be an altogether perfect and supreme experience if only one had a coloured pencil long enough to draw on the ceiling. [*Tremendous Trifles*]

14 Hardy went down to botanize in the swamp, while Meredith climbed towards the sun. Meredith became, at his best, a sort of daintily dressed Walt Whitman: Hardy became a sort of village atheist brooding and blaspheming over the village idiot. [*The Victorian Age in Literature*, Ch. 2]

15 If a thing is worth doing it is worth doing badly. [*What's Wrong with the World*, 'Folly and Female Education']

16 'The Christian ideal,' it is said, 'has not been tried and found wanting; it has been found difficult and left untried.' ['The Unfinished Temple']

17 The English statesman is bribed not to be bribed. He is born with a silver spoon in his mouth, so that he may never afterwards be found with the silver spoons in his pocket.

18 The machinery of science must be individualistic and isolated. A mob can shout round a palace; but a mob cannot shout down a telephone. The specialist appears, and democracy is half spoilt at a stroke.

19 To be clever enough to get all that money, one must be stupid enough to want it. [*The Wisdom of Father Brown*, 'Paradise of Thieves']

20 Journalism largely consists in saying 'Lord Jones Dead' to people who never knew Lord Jones was alive. ['The Purple Wig']

21 Blasphemy itself could not survive religion; if anyone doubts that, let him try to blaspheme Odin. [In the *Daily News*, 24 June 1904]

22 When you break the big laws, you do not get liberty; you do not even get anarchy. You get the small laws. [29 July 1905]

23 Mankind is not a tribe of animals to which we owe compassion. Mankind is a club to which we owe our subscription. [10 Apr. 1906]

24 A dying monarchy is always one that has too much power, not too little; a dying religion always interferes more than it ought, not less. [11 Mar. 1911]

25 Democracy means government by the uneducated, while aristocracy means government by the badly educated. [In *The New York Times*, 1 Feb. 1931]

26 [The Victorians] were lame giants; the strongest of them walked on one leg a little shorter than the other. [In W. H. Auden and L. Kronenberger, *Faber Book of Aphorisms*]

27 Tradition may be defined as an extension of the franchise. Tradition means giving votes to the most obscure of all classes, our ancestors. It is the democracy of the dead.

[Quoted by D. J. Boorstin in the *Listener*, 11 Dec. 1975]

1 Education is simply the soul of a society as it passes from one generation to another. [In the *Observer*, 'Sayings of the Week', 6 July 1924]

2 Hitlerism is almost entirely of Jewish origin. [23 July 1933]

3 The object of opening the mind, as of opening the mouth, is to shut it again on something solid. [Quoted by Katharine Whitehorn in the *Observer*, 28 Dec. 1986]

4 A puritan's a person who pours righteous indignation into the wrong things. [Attr.]

5 New roads: new ruts. [Attr.]

ALBERT CHEVALIER 1861–1923

6 Wot's the good of Hanyfink? – Why – Nuffink! [Music-hall refrain]

7 There ain't a lady livin' in the land / As I'd swop for my dear old Dutch! [*My Old Dutch*, 1901, in collab. Charles Ingle]

8 Laugh! I thought I should 'ave died, / Knocked 'em in the Old Kent Road. [*Wot Cher*, or *Knocked 'em in the Old Kent Road*, music by Charles Ingle]

MAURICE CHEVALIER 1888–1972

9 Considering the alternative ... it's not too bad at all. [Of old age. In M. Freedland, *Maurice Chevalier*, Ch. 20]

10 Many a man has fallen in love with a girl in a light so dim he would not have chosen a suit by it. [*News Summaries*, 17 July 1955]

G. F. CHEW 1924–

11 A physicist who is able to view any number of partially successful models without favouritism is a bootstrapper. [In Fritjof Capra, *The Turning Point*, II. 3]

NOAM CHOMSKY 1928–

12 Colourless green ideas sleep furiously. [Sentence to illustrate grammatical structure as independent of meaning. *Syntactic Structures*, 2. 3]

CHOU EN-LAI *see* ZHOU ENLAI

ERIC CHRISTIANSEN

13 It is still a puzzle how the natives of this island [Britain] mime almost any form of political barbarism of which geography spares them the immediate experience. [In the *Independent*, 5 Nov. 1988]

DAME AGATHA CHRISTIE 1890–1976

14 The happy people are failures because they are on such good terms with themselves that they don't give a damn. [*Sparkling Cyanide*]

15 An archaeologist is the best husband any woman can have: the older she gets, the more interested he is in her. [Ascr. in news report, 9 Mar. 1954]

RANDOLPH CHURCHILL 1911–1968

16 I should never be allowed out in private. [Letter to his hostess, apologizing for rudeness. In B. Roberts, *Randolph*]

SIR WINSTON CHURCHILL 1874–1965

17 The wars of the peoples will be more terrible than those of kings. [Speech in House of Commons on Army Estimates, 1901. In *Maxims and Reflections*, sect. V]

18 It cannot in the opinion of His Majesty's Government be classified as slavery in the extreme acceptance of the word without some risk of terminological inexactitude. [Speech in House of Commons, 22 Feb. 1906]

19 *The Times* is speechless [over Irish Home Rule] and takes three columns to express its speechlessness. [Speech at Dundee, 14 May 1908]

20 He [Lord Charles Beresford] is one of those orators of whom it was well said, 'Before they get up they do not know what they are going to say; when they are speaking, they do not know what they are saying; and when they sit down they do not know what they have said.' [Speech in House of Commons, 20 Dec. 1912]

21 The maxim of the British people is 'Business as usual'. [Speech at Guildhall, London, 9 Nov. 1914]

1 The grass grows green on the battlefield, but never on the scaffold. [On Irish Rebellion, 1916. Attr.]

2 Labour is not fit to govern. [Speech at 1920 election]

3 Frightfulness is not a remedy known to the British pharmacopoeia. [Speech in House of Commons, 8 July 1920]

4 I decline to be impartial as between the fire brigade and the fire. [Of General Strike, 7 July 1926]

5 You cannot ask us to take sides against arithmetic. You cannot ask us to take sides against the obvious facts of the situation. [31 Aug.]

6 A hopeful disposition is not the sole qualification to be a prophet. [30 Apr. 1927]

7 I have waited fifty years to see the Boneless Wonder [Ramsay MacDonald] sitting on the Treasury Bench. [28 Jan. 1931]

8 India is a geographical term. It is no more a united nation than the Equator. [Speech in Royal Albert Hall, 18 Mar.]

9 We know that he [Ramsay MacDonald] has, more than any other man, the gift of compressing the largest amount of words into the smallest amount of thought. [23 Mar. 1933]

10 So they [the Government] go on in strange paradox, decided only to be undecided, resolved to be irresolute, adamant for drift, solid for fluidity, all-powerful for impotence. [Speech in House of Commons, 12 Nov. 1936]

11 We have sustained a defeat without a war. [Describing Munich, 5 Oct. 1938]

12 I cannot forecast to you the action of Russia. It is a riddle wrapped in a mystery inside an enigma; but perhaps there is a key. That key is Russian national interest. [BBC radio broadcast, 1 Oct. 1939]

13 I would say to the House, as I said to those who have joined this Government, 'I have nothing to offer but blood, toil, tears and sweat.' [First speech in House of Commons as Prime Minister, 13 May 1940]

14 You ask: 'What is our aim?' I can answer in one word: 'Victory!' Victory at all costs, victory in spite of all terror, victory however long and hard the road may be: for without victory there is no survival.

15 We shall defend our island, whatever the cost may be, we shall fight on the beaches, we shall fight on the landing grounds, we shall fight in the fields and in the streets, we shall fight in the hills; we shall never surrender. [4 June]

16 What General Weygand called the 'Battle of France' is over. I expect the Battle of Britain is about to begin . . . [Speech in House of Commons, 18 June]

17 Let us therefore brace ourselves to our duties, and so bear ourselves that, if the British Empire and its Commonwealth last for a thousand years, men will still say: 'This was their finest hour.'

18 Learn to get used to it [bombing]. Eels get used to skinning. [Notes for speech, 20 June]

19 Never in the field of human conflict was so much owed by so many to so few. [Of Battle of Britain. Speech in House of Commons, 20 Aug.]

20 We are waiting for the long-promised invasion. So are the fishes. [BBC radio broadcast to the French people, 21 Oct.]

21 Give us the tools, and we will finish the job. [BBC radio broadcast, addressed to President Roosevelt, 9 Feb. 1941. See also 158:7]

22 They [the British] are the only people who like to be told how bad things are – who like to be told the worst. [Speech in House of Commons, 10 June]

23 You [Hitler] do your worst, and we will do our best. [Speech at Civil Defence Services' Luncheon, 14 July]

24 It becomes still more difficult to reconcile Japanese action with prudence or even sanity. What kind of people do they think we are? [Speech to US Congress, 24 Dec.]

25 'In three weeks England will have her neck wrung like a chicken.' Some chicken; some neck! [Speech to Canadian Senate, 30 Dec. See also 399:10]

26 This is not the end. It is not even the beginning of the end. But it is, perhaps, the end of the beginning. [Of the victory in Egypt. Speech at Mansion House, London, 10 Nov. 1942]

1 I have not become the King's First Minister in order to preside over the liquidation of the British Empire.

2 The Almighty in His infinite wisdom did not see fit to create Frenchmen in the image of Englishmen. [Speech in House of Commons, 10 Dec.]

3 There is no finer investment for any community than putting milk into babies. [BBC radio broadcast, 21 Mar. 1943]

4 The empires of the future are the empires of the mind. [Speech at Harvard University, 16 Sept.]

5 A splendid moment in our great history and in our small lives. [On the unconditional surrender of Germany, 1945]

6 There are few virtues which the Poles do not possess and there are few errors they have ever avoided. [Speech in House of Commons after Potsdam Conference, 16 Aug.]

7 An iron curtain has descended across the Continent. [Address at Westminster College, Fulton, USA, 5 Mar. 1946. See also 145:18, 352:4]

8 We must build a kind of United States of Europe. [Speech in Zürich, 19 Sept.]

9 No one pretends that democracy is perfect or all-wise. Indeed, it has been said that democracy is the worst form of government except all those other forms that have been tried from time to time. [Speech in House of Commons, 11 Nov. 1947]

10 The English never draw a line without blurring it. [16 Nov. 1948]

11 The whole prospect and outlook of mankind grew immeasurably larger, and the multiplication of ideas also proceeded at an incredible rate. This vast expansion was unhappily not accompanied by any noticeable advance in the stature of man either in his mental faculties or his moral character. His brain got no better; but it buzzed more. [Address in Massachusetts, 31 Mar. 1949]

12 Perhaps it is better to be irresponsible and right than to be responsible and wrong. [Party Political Broadcast, London, 26 Aug. 1950]

13 Mr Attlee combines a limited outlook with strong qualities of resistance. [Speech in Royal Albert Hall, 27 Apr. 1951]

14 Personally I like short words and vulgar fractions. [Speech in Margate, 10 Oct. 1953]

15 Talking jaw-jaw is always better than war-war. [Speech in White House, Washington, 26 June 1954. See also 245:9]

16 It was a nation and race dwelling all around the globe that had the lion's heart. I had the luck to be called upon to give the roar. [Speech at Palace of Westminster on his 80th birthday, 30 Nov.]

17 This bright, nimble, fierce, and comprehending being – Jack Frost dancing bespangled in the sunshine. [Of G. Bernard Shaw. *Great Contemporaries*]

18 I wrote my name at the top of the page, I wrote down the number of the question '1'. After much reflection, I put a bracket round it thus '(1)'. But thereafter I could not think of anything connected with it that was either relevant or true ... It was from these slender indications of scholarship that Mr Weldon drew the conclusion that I was worthy to pass into Harrow. It is very much to his credit. [*My Early Life*, Ch. 2]

19 Thus I got into my bones the essential structure of the ordinary British sentence – which is a noble thing.

20 So they told me how Mr Gladstone read Homer for fun, which I thought served him right.

21 Headmasters have powers at their disposal with which Prime Ministers have never yet been invested.

22 Certainly the prolonged education indispensable to the progress of society is not natural to mankind. [3]

23 And here I say to parents, especially wealthy parents, 'Don't give your son money. As far as you can afford it, give him horses.' [4]

24 I was never tired of listening to his wisdom or imparting my own. [7]

25 It is a good thing for an uneducated man to read books of quotations. [Of himself. 9]

26 One voyage to India is enough; the others are merely repletion. [10]

27 Everyone threw the blame on me. I have noticed that they nearly always do. I suppose

it is because they think I shall be able to bear it best. [17]

1 Buller was a characteristic British personality. He looked stolid. He said little, and what he said was obscure. [18]

2 I have always been against the Pacifists during the quarrel, and against the Jingoes at its close. [26]

3 Those who can win a war well can rarely make a good peace and those who could make a good peace would never have won the war.

4 Moral of the Work. In war: resolution. In defeat: defiance. In victory: magnanimity. In peace: goodwill. [*The Second World War*, Vol. 1, epigraph, but originally used to describe 1914–18 War]

5 One day President Roosevelt told me that he was asking publicly for suggestions about what the war should be called. I said at once 'the Unnecessary War'. [Preface]

6 I have never seen a human being who more perfectly represented the modern conception of a robot. [Of Molotov. 20]

7 'Winston is back.' [Signal of Board of Admiralty to the Fleet on his return to the Admiralty, 1939. 22]

8 I felt as if I were walking with destiny, and that all my past life had been but a preparation for this hour and this trial . . . My warnings over the last six years had been so numerous, so detailed, and were now so terribly vindicated, that no one could gainsay me . . . I was sure I should not fail. Therefore, although impatient for the morning, I slept soundly and had no need for cheering dreams. Facts are better than dreams. [Closing words, 38]

9 The Mosquito Armada as a whole was unsinkable. In the midst of our defeat glory came to the Island people, united and unconquerable; and the tale of the Dunkirk beaches will shine in whatever records are preserved of our affairs. [Vol. 2, 5]

10 We must be very careful not to assign to this deliverance [Dunkirk] the attributes of a victory. Wars are not won by evacuations.

11 Any chortling by officials who have been slothful in pushing this bomb, over the fact that at present it has not succeeded, will be viewed with great disfavour by me. [To General Ismay. 8]

12 When I look back on all these worries I remember the story of the old man who said on his deathbed that he had had a lot of trouble in his life, most of which had never happened. [23]

13 No one can guarantee success in war, but only deserve it. [27]

14 The Battle of Britain was won. The Battle of the Atlantic had now to be fought. [31]

15 In my experience . . . officers with high athletic qualifications are not usually successful in the higher ranks. [Appendix C, 4 Feb. 1941]

16 I have only one purpose, the destruction of Hitler, and my life is much simplified thereby. If Hitler invaded Hell I would make at least a favourable reference to the Devil in the House of Commons. [3. 20]

17 Before Alamein we never had a victory. After Alamein we never had a defeat. [4. 33]

18 Tell them from me they are unloading history. [Telegram to the Port Commandant at Tripoli. 40]

19 [When asked whether the Niagara Falls looked the same as when he first saw them] Well, the principle seems the same. The water still keeps falling over. [5. 5]

20 I said that the world must be made safe for at least fifty years. If it was only for fifteen to twenty years then we should have betrayed our soldiers. [20]

21 I then demonstrated with the help of three matches my idea of Poland moving westwards.

22 Peace with Germany and Japan on our terms will not bring much rest . . . As I observed last time, when the war of the giants is over the wars of the pygmies will begin. [25]

23 In Franklin Roosevelt there died the greatest American friend we have ever known and the greatest champion of freedom who has ever brought help and comfort from the New World to the Old. [28]

24 Dictators ride to and fro upon tigers which they dare not dismount. And the

tigers are getting hungry. [*While England Slept*]

1 He [Lenin] alone could have led Russia into the enchanted quagmire; he alone could have found the way back to the causeway. He saw; he turned; he perished . . . The Russian people were left floundering in the bog. Their worst misfortune was his birth, their next worst – his death. [*The World Crisis*, Ch. 4, 'Aftermath']

2 Jellicoe was the only man on either side who could lose the war in an afternoon.

3 We should have the art [of making atomic bombs] rather than the article [the bombs themselves]. [Secret memo to Lord Cherwell, Nov. 1951]

4 It is always wise to look ahead, but difficult to look farther than you can see. [In the *Observer*, 'Sayings of the Week', 27 July 1952]

5 The difference between him [Mr Asquith] and Arthur [Balfour] is that Arthur is wicked and moral, Asquith is good and immoral. [In E. T. Raymond, *Mr Balfour*, Ch. 13]

6 He's a modest little man with much to be modest about. [On Clement Attlee's becoming Prime Minister. Attr. in Michael Foot, *Aneurin Bevan*]

7 He is a sheep in wolf's clothing. [Usually assumed to be of Clement Attlee, though Churchill told Denis Brogan he had been referring to Ramsay MacDonald]

8 Feed a grub on royal jelly and it may become a queen. [On Clement Attlee. Attr.]

9 It is a fine thing to be honest but it is also very important to be right. [Of Stanley Baldwin. Attr.]

10 There, but for the grace of God, goes God. [Of Sir Stafford Cripps. In L. Kronenberger, *The Cutting Edge*, but also ascr. to H. J. Mankiewicz on Orson Welles]

11 The only case I know of a bull who carries his own china shop around with him. [Of John Foster Dulles. In *The Times Higher Education Supplement*, 31 Dec. 1982]

12 They consist entirely of clichés – clichés old and new – everything from 'God is Love' to 'Please adjust your dress before leaving'. [Of Anthony Eden's speeches. Attr. in *Life*, 9

Dec. 1940, but Churchill disclaimed. See also 42:4]

13 [General de Gaulle is] like a female llama surprised in her bath. [In Nigel Rees, *Quotable Trivia*]

14 At every crisis he [the Kaiser] crumpled. In defeat, he fled; in revolution, he abdicated; in exile, he remarried. [In *Geoffrey Madan's Notebooks*, ed. J. A. Gere and John Sparrow, 'Livres sans nom']

15 It was a case of dislike before first sight. [Describing Kitchener's reaction to him. Attr.]

16 In defeat unbeatable; in victory unbearable. [Of Viscount Montgomery. In Edward Marsh, *Ambrosia and Small Beer*, Ch. 5, sect. ii]

17 EDWARD MARSH: I'm in favour of kissing him [Roosevelt] on both cheeks. CHURCHILL: Yes, but not on all four. [Attr.]

18 This is the sort of English up with which I will not put. [Marginal comment on state document. In Sir Ernest Gowers, *Plain Words*]

19 An appeaser is one who feeds a crocodile – hoping that it will eat him last. [Said in 1954. In Jonathon Green, *Cynic's Lexicon*]

20 Don't talk to me about naval tradition. It's nothing but rum, sodomy and the lash. [In P. Gretton, *Former Naval Person*, Ch. 1]

21 You and I must take care not to lose the next war. [To Lord Ismay, apropos the Nuremberg trials. Quoted by A. J. P. Taylor in BBC TV programme *The Warlords*, 6 Sept. 1976]

22 [In reply to G. Bernard Shaw's offer of tickets for the first night of *St Joan* 'for yourself and a friend, if you have one', he answered that he could not make the first night, but asked instead for tickets] for the second night, if there is one. [Attr.]

COUNT GALEAZZO CIANO 1903–1944

23 As always, victory finds a hundred fathers, but defeat is an orphan. [Diary entry, 9 Sept. 1942]

JOHN CIARDI 1916–1986

24 One look at the rush-hour jam in the subway and you know why no one rides it

any more. [In *Saturday Review*, 'Manner of Speaking', 8 Aug. 1964]

1 You don't have to suffer to be a poet. Adolescence is enough suffering for anyone. [In *Writer's Quotation Book*, ed. James Charlton]

E. M. CIORAN 1911–

2 Without the possibility of suicide, I would have killed myself long ago. [In the *Independent*, 'Quote Unquote', 2 Dec. 1989]

ERIC CLAPTON 1945–

3 I've felt that the only way to survive was with dignity, pride and courage. I heard that in certain forms of music, and I heard it most of all in the blues, because it was always an individual. It was one man and his guitar against the world. [In ITV programme *The South Bank Show*, 1987]

KENNETH [later LORD] CLARK 1903–1983

4 Medieval marriages were entirely a matter of property, and, as everyone knows, marriage without love means love without marriage. [*Civilization*, Ch. 3]

5 It's a curious fact that the all-male religions have produced no religious imagery – in most cases have positively forbidden it. The great religious art of the world is deeply involved with the female principle. [7]

6 I wonder if a single thought that has helped forward the human spirit has ever been conceived or written down in an enormous room: except, perhaps, in the reading room of the British Museum.

7 Opera, next to Gothic architecture, is one of the strangest inventions of Western man. It could not have been foreseen by any logical process. [9]

8 This gives French Classical architecture a certain inhumanity. It was the work not of craftsmen, but of wonderfully gifted civil servants.

9 Rococo even spread to England, although the native good sense of a fox-hunting society prevented its more extravagant flights.

10 Television is a form of soliloquy. [In the *Guardian*, 26 Nov. 1977]

MANNING CLARK 1915–1991

11 All those who have something to say are deeply divided, and therefore tormented men or women – that is, they are both innocent children and devils. [*A Discovery of Australia*, 'Being an Historian']

WILLIAM CLARK

12 [Today's world is] like a ship in which the steerage passengers report the stern is sinking, to receive the reply from those in the first class lounge that they'll consider helping, but first they must deal with the rise in the price of fillet steak. [In B. Whittaker, *A Bridge of People*]

ARTHUR C. CLARKE 1917–

13 Overhead without any fuss the stars were going out. [*Nine Billion Names of God*, last words]

14 Any sufficiently advanced technology is indistinguishable from magic. [*Profiles of the Future*]

15 It is three thousand light years from the Vatican. [*The Star*, first line]

16 Open the pod door, Hal. [In film *2001: A Space Odyssey*, scripted with Stanley Kubrick]

17 If an elderly but distinguished scientist says that something is possible, he is almost certainly right, but if he says that it is impossible he is very probably wrong. [In the *New Yorker*, 9 Aug. 1969]

GRANT CLARKE 1891–1931 and EDGAR LESLIE 1885–1976

18 And then he'd have to get under, / Get out and get under, / And fix up his automobile. [Song: *Get Out and Get Under*, 1913, in musical *Pleasure Seekers*, music by Maurice Abrahams]

JOHN COOPER CLARKE 1949–

19 I'd like to be remembered as the Man with that Certain Nothing. [In *Knave* magazine, Mar. 1984]

20 With charm you've got to get up close to see it; style slaps you in the face. [Interview in the *Observer*, 19 May 1985]

PETER CLARKE 1942–

1 The Government [of Clement Attlee] paid for its programme on tick – the tick of a time bomb, as it turned out. [*A Question of Leadership*, 9]

2 Its [the Attlee government's] rhetoric of planning was not matched by a commensurate ability to control the economy. Its response was not *dirigiste* but 'deary me'.

TOM CLARKE

3 Working for the BBC is like working for a cross between the Church and the Post Office; it seldom fails to live down to expectations. [Quoted by Richard Eyre in the *Listener*, 12 Dec. 1987]

PAUL CLAUDEL 1868–1955

4 The poem is not made from these letters that I drive in like nails, but of the white which remains on the paper. [Footnote to *Cinq grandes odes*, I, 'Les muses']

5 *Délivrez-moi de moi-même! délivrez l'être de la condition! / Je suis libre, délivrez-moi de la liberté!* – Deliver me from myself! Deliver my being from its condition! I am free, deliver me from liberty! [II, 'L'esprit et l'eau']

6 *Quelqu'un qui soit en moi, plus moi-même que moi.* – Someone who may be in me, more myself than I. [*Vers d'exil*]

7 *Nous ne naissons pas seuls. Naître, pour tout, c'est connaître. Toute naissance est une connaissance.* – We are not born alone. To be born for each man is a getting to know. Every birth is a getting to know. [*Traité de la connaissance du monde*]

ELDRIDGE CLEAVER 1935–

8 What we're saying today is that you're either part of the solution or you're part of the problem. [Speech in San Francisco, 1968]

JOHN CLEESE 1939– and CONNIE BOOTH 1941–

9 *Que?* [Mañuel's catchphrase in TV series *Fawlty Towers*, 1975 onwards]

10 So Harry says, 'You don't like me any more. Why not?' And he says, 'Because you've got so terribly pretentious.' And Harry says, 'Pretentious? *Moi?*' ['The Psychiatrist']

GEORGES CLEMENCEAU 1841–1929

11 War is much too important a thing to be left to the generals. [Said in 1886. In G. Suarez, *Clemenceau*, but also attr. to Talleyrand, among others]

12 One is always somebody's reactionary. [Quoted by Ernst Gombrich in the *Listener*, 15 Feb. 1979]

13 America is the only nation in history which miraculously has gone directly from barbarism to degeneration without the usual interval of civilization. [Attr. in *Saturday Review*, 1 Dec. 1945]

J. STORER CLOUSTON 1870–1944

14 'Are you afraid of having your pockets picked?' 'Alas!' replied Mr Beveridge, 'it would take two men to do that.' 'Huh!' snorted the Emperor, 'you are so damned strong are you?' 'I mean,' answered his *vis-à-vis* with his polite smile, 'that it would take one man to put something in and another to take it out.' [*The Lunatic at Large*, Pt I, Ch. 2]

15 'Then it was false?' 'As an address it was perfectly genuine, only it didn't happen to be mine.' [III. 5]

HAROLD CLURMAN 1901–1980

16 He [Thornton Wilder] arranges flowers beautifully, but he does not grow them. [*Lies Like Truth*]

IRVIN COBB 1876–1944

17 The mosaic swimming-pool age – just before the era when they had to have a shin-bone of St Sebastian for a clutch-lever. [In F. Scott Fitzgerald, *Pat Hobby Himself*]

18 I've just learnt about his illness; let's hope it's nothing trivial. [In *Treasury of Humorous Quotations*, ed. Evan Esar and Nicolas Bentley. Elsewhere attr. to Winston Churchill on Aneurin Bevan]

19 Why should a worm turn? It's probably just the same on the other side.

CHARLES COBORN 1852–1945

1 'E's all right when you know 'im, / But you've got to know 'im fust. [Song: *'E's all right*]

2 Two lovely black eyes, / Oh, what a surprise! / Only for telling a man he was wrong. / Two lovely black eyes! [*Two Lovely Black Eyes*, 1886]

JAMES COCO 1928–

3 They [American audiences] are so used to getting up and going to the refrigerator that they can't sit still as long as English audiences. [Interview in the *Guardian*, 17 June 1982]

JEAN COCTEAU 1889–1963

4 The essential tact in daring is to know how far one can go too far. [*Le coq et l'arlequin*]

5 But brawling leads to laryngitis. [*Les enfants terribles*, trans. Rosamond Lehmann]

6 The actual tragedies of life bear no relation to one's preconceived ideas. In the event, one is always bewildered by their simplicity, their grandeur of design, and by that element of the bizarre which seems inherent in them.

7 Hugo was a madman who believed he was Hugo. [*Opium*, p. 77]

8 A true poet does not bother to be poetical. Nor does a nursery gardener scent his roses. [*Professional Secrets*]

9 The awful thing about getting old is that you stay young inside. [Quoted by Lawrence Durrell in the *Guardian*, 28 May 1985]

10 The poet is a liar who always speaks the truth. [In Laurence J. Peter, *Peter's Quotations*]

GEORGE M. COHAN 1878–1942

11 We'll be over, we're coming over, / And we won't come back till it's over over there. [US song of 1914–18 War: *Over There*]

LEONARD COHEN 1934–

12 Like a bird on a wire, like a drunk in a midnight choir, / I have tried, in my way, to be free. [Song: *Bird on a Wire*]

13 Suzanne takes you down / To her place by the river / And she feeds you tea and oranges / That come all the way from China. / And you want to travel with her / And you want to travel blind. [Song: *Suzanne*]

MARVIN COHEN 1931–

14 Time is what prevents everything from happening at once. [In the *Guardian*, 21 Apr. 1981]

SIMON COHEN 1931–

15 The probation service have found out that there are two types of person appearing before the courts – those who have problems – and those who are problems. [In the *Magistrate*, June 1983]

TERRY COHEN

16 He who laughs last is generally the last to get the joke. [In P. and J. Holton, *Quote and Unquote*]

DESMOND E. T. COKE 1879–1931

17 His blade struck the water a full second before any other ... until ... as the boats began to near the winning-post, his was dipping into the water twice as often as any other. [Popularly amended to 'All rowed fast but none so fast as stroke.' *Sandford of Merton*, Ch. 12]

FRANK MOORE COLBY 1865–1925

18 Men will confess to treason, murder, arson, false teeth, or a wig. How many of them will own up to a lack of humour? [*Essays*, I]

19 I have found some of the best reasons I ever had for remaining at the bottom simply by looking at the men at the top. [II]

20 Self-esteem is the most voluble of the emotions. [In C. Fadiman, *Reading I Have Liked*]

TERRY COLEMAN 1931–

21 Governor of the Bank of England in the days when the Bank of England was as steady as the Bank of England! [Of Montagu Norman. *The Liners*]

[SIDONIE-GABRIELLE] COLETTE
1873–1954

1 When she raises her eyelids it's as if she were taking off all her clothes. [*Claudine and Annie*]

2 My virtue's still far too small, I don't trot it out and about yet. [*Claudine at School*]

3 Madame Alvarez had taken the name of a Spanish lover now dead, and accordingly had acquired a creamy complexion, an ample bust, and hair lustrous with brilliantine. [*Gigi*]

4 The three great stumbling-blocks in a girl's education, she says, are *homard à l'Américaine*, a boiled egg, and asparagus. Shoddy table manners, she says, have broken up many a happy home.

5 Don't ever wear artistic jewellery; it wrecks a woman's reputation.

6 Don't eat too many almonds; they add weight to the breasts.

7 Jane is rather like one of those refined persons who go out to sew for the rich because they cannot abide contact with the poor. [*The Other One*]

8 If one wished to be perfectly sincere, one would have to admit there are two kinds of love – well-fed and ill-fed. The rest is pure fiction. [In *Lover's Quotation Book*, ed. Helen Handley]

R. G. COLLINGWOOD 1889–1943

9 So, perhaps, I may escape otherwise than by death the last humiliation of an aged scholar, when his juniors conspire to print a volume of essays and offer it to him as a sign that they now consider him senile. [*Autobiography*]

10 History proper is the history of thought. There are no mere events in history. [Epigraph to Sean O'Faolain, *The Irish*]

CHARLES COLLINS *see* FRED W. LEIGH and CHARLES COLLINS

JOHN CHURTON COLLINS 1848–1908

11 Never claim as a right what you can ask as a favour. [In *English Review*, 1914]

MICHAEL COLLINS 1890–1922

12 Early this morning, I signed my death warrant. [On signing the Irish Treaty. He was assassinated a few months afterwards. Letter, 6 Dec. 1921]

NORMAN COLLINS 1907–1982

13 London Belongs to Me. [Title of book]

DAME IVY COMPTON-BURNETT
1884–1969

14 'Well, of course, people are only human,' said Dudley to his brother, 'but it really does not seem much for them to be.' [*A Family and a Fortune*, Ch. 2]

15 People don't resent having nothing nearly as much as too little. I have only just found that out. I am getting the knowledge of the rich as well as their ways.

16 It will be a beautiful family talk, mean and worried and full of sorrow and spite and excitement. I cannot be asked to miss it in my weak state. I should only fret. [10]

17 When I die people will say it is the best thing for me. It is because they know it is the worst. They want to avoid the feeling of pity. As though they were the people most concerned. [*The Mighty and Their Fall*, Ch. 4]

18 There are different kinds of wrong. The people sinned against are not always the best. [7]

19 We must use words as they are used or stand aside from life. [*Mother and Son*, Ch. 9]

20 There is more difference within the sexes than between them. [10]

21 Real life seems to have no plots. [In review in the *Guardian*, Feb. 1973]

RICHARD CONDON 1915–

22 She felt sexual urgings towards Yvonne in the manner that politicians feel an enormous sexual pull toward mirrors. [*Bandicoot*, Ch. 21]

23 He was an unzipped fly caught in forever amber. [*The Ecstasy Business*, Ch. 1]

24 I am you and you are me and what have we done to each other? [*The Manchurian Candidate*, 'The Keener's Manual', epigraph]

25 Cheese. The adult form of milk. [*A Talent for Loving*, Bk I, Ch. 2]

1 In Mexico the gods ruled, the priests interpreted and interposed, and the people obeyed. In Spain, the priests ruled, the king interpreted and interposed, and the gods obeyed. A nuance in an ideological difference is a wide chasm. [6]

2 Television: the key to all minds and hearts because it permits people to be entertained by their government without ever having to participate in it. [In the *Observer*, 'Sayings of the Week', 10 June 1990]

SHANE CONNAUGHTON

3 Jesus must have been an Irishman. After all, He was unmarried, 32 years old, lived at home, and His mother thought He was God. [*Divisions at the Oscar*]

MARC CONNELLY 1890–1980

4 GOD: I'll just r'ar back an' pass a miracle. [*Green Pastures*]

5 Even bein' Gawd ain't a bed of roses.

BILLY CONNOLLY 1942–

6 Your breath's like a badger's bum, an' that. [*The Afternoon After the Morning After the Night Before*]

7 But the great thing about the way Glasgow is now is that if there's a nuclear attack it'll look exactly the same afterwards. [*Gullible's Travels*, 'Scotland']

8 Still you can't worry too much about the future. Life is not a rehearsal.

9 Never trust a man who, when he's alone in a room with a tea-cosy, doesn't try it on. ['Thoughts That Sustain Me']

10 A bird in the hand invariably shits on your wrist.

11 I woke up with an aching head / As usual. / I can't remember going to bed / As usual. / My stomach's feeling very queer, / There's a thunderstorm in my right ear, / It must have been McEwan's beer / As usual. [Written by John Murphy]

12 Marriage is a wonderful invention; but, then again, so is a bicycle repair kit. [In Duncan Campbell, *Billy Connolly, the Authorized Version*, 'Music']

CYRIL CONNOLLY 1903–1974

13 It is closing time in the gardens of the West and from now on an artist will be judged only by the resonance of his solitude or the quality of his despair. [*The Condemned Playground*]

14 A great writer creates a world of his own and his readers are proud to live in it. A lesser writer may entice them in for a moment, but soon he will watch them filing out. [*Enemies of Promise*, Ch. 1]

15 Contemporary books do not keep. The quality in them which makes for their success is the first to go; they turn overnight. [2]

16 I shall christen this style the Mandarin, since it is beloved by literary pundits. It is the style of all those writers whose tendency is to make their language convey more than they mean or more than they feel, it is the style of most artists and all humbugs.

17 The ape-like virtues without which no one can enjoy a public school.

18 Literature is the art of writing something that will be read twice; journalism what will be grasped at once. [3]

19 Puritanism in other people we admire is austerity in ourselves. [9]

20 For most good talkers, when they have run down, are miserable; they know that they have betrayed themselves, that they have taken material which should have a life of its own to dispense it in noises upon the air. [13]

21 Whom the gods wish to destroy they first call promising.

22 If, as Dr Johnson said, a man who is not married is only half a man, so a man who is very much married is only half a writer. [14]

23 There is no more sombre enemy of good art than the pram in the hall.

24 I should like to see the custom introduced of readers who are pleased with a book sending the author some small cash token: anything between half-a-crown and a hundred pounds . . . Not more than a hundred pounds – that would be bad for my character – not

less than half-a-crown – that would do no good to yours.

1 The best that can happen for a writer is to be taken up very late or very early, when either old enough to take its measure, or so young that when dropped by society he has all his life before him. [15]

2 Humorists are not happy men. Like Beachcomber or Saki or Thurber they burn while Rome fiddles. [16]

3 A poet, with the exception of mysterious water-fluent tea-drinking Auden, must be a highly-conscious technical expert.

4 The health of a writer should not be too good, and perfect only in those periods of convalescence when he is not writing.

5 All charming people have something to conceal, usually their total dependence on the appreciation of others.

6 I have always disliked myself at any given moment; the total of such moments is my life. [18]

7 A private school has all the faults of a public school without any of its compensations. [19]

8 Tall, pale, with his flaccid cheeks, large spatulate fingers and supercilious voice, he was one of those boys who seem born old. [Of George Orwell at prep school]

9 The art of getting on at school depends on a mixture of enthusiasm with moral cowardice and social sense. The enthusiasm is for personalities and gossip about them, for a schoolboy is a novelist too busy to write. [21]

10 Boys do not grow up gradually. They move forward in spurts like the hands of clocks in railway stations.

11 In the eighteenth century he would have become Prime Minister before he was thirty; as it was he appeared honourably ineligible for the struggle of life. [Of Sir Alec Douglas-Home as a schoolboy. 23]

12 For the first time I was aware of that layer of blubber which encases an English peer, the sediment of permanent adulation.

13 Were I to deduce any system from my feelings on leaving Eton, it might be called *The Theory of Permanent Adolescence.* [24]

14 I came to America tourist Third with a cheque for ten pounds and I leave plus five hundred, a wife, a mandarin coat, a set of diamond studs, a state room and a bath, and a decent box for the ferret. That's what everybody comes to America to do and I don't think I've managed badly for a beginner. [*A Romantic Friendship, Letters to Noel Blakiston,* Letter, 2 Apr. 1930]

15 I refuse to be famous for a book on Wordsworth, although after all it was all Wordsworth was famous for. [27 Aug. 1962]

16 The more books we read, the clearer it becomes that the true function of a writer is to produce a masterpiece and that no other task is of any consequence. [*The Unquiet Grave,* Ch. 1]

17 'Dry again?' said the Crab to the Rock-Pool. 'So would you be,' replied the Rock-Pool, 'if you had to satisfy, twice a day, the insatiable sea.'

18 It is better to be the lichen on a rock than the President's carnation. Only by avoiding the beginning of things can we escape their ending.

19 There is no fury like an ex-wife searching for a new lover.

20 Life is a maze in which we take the wrong turning before we have learnt to walk.

21 No city should be too large for a man to walk out of in a morning.

22 Everything is a dangerous drug to me except reality, which is unendurable.

23 The civilization of one epoch becomes the manure of the next. Everything over-ripens in the same way. The disasters of the world are due to its inhabitants not being able to grow old simultaneously.

24 Imprisoned in every fat man a thin one is wildly signalling to be let out. [See also 7:14, 286:14, 392:25, 401:20]

25 The true index of a man's character is the health of his wife.

26 We are all serving a life-sentence in the dungeon of self.

27 Others merely live; I vegetate.

28 Our memories are card-indexes consulted

and then returned in disorder by authorities whom we do not control. [3]

1 Better to write for yourself and have no public, than write for the public and have no self. [In *Turnstile One*, ed. V. S. Pritchett]

2 The man who is master of his passions is Reason's slave.

3 Perfect fear casteth out love. [To Philip Toynbee during the Blitz. In obituary in the *Observer*, 1 Dec. 1974]

4 She [Victoria Sackville-West] looked like Lady Chatterley above the waist and the gamekeeper below. [In *Oh, What an Awful Thing to Say!*, comp. W. Cole and L. Phillips]

SIR WILLIAM CONNOR *see* 'CASSANDRA'

JOSEPH CONRAD 1857–1924

5 In plucking the fruit of memory one runs the risk of spoiling its bloom. [*Arrow of Gold*, Author's Note]

6 We live, as we dream – alone. [*Heart of Darkness*, Ch. 1]

7 Exterminate all the brutes! [2]

8 He cried out twice, a cry that was no more than a breath – 'The horror! The horror!' [3]

9 Mistah Kurtz – he dead.

10 A work that aspires, however humbly, to the condition of art should carry its justification in every line. [*The Nigger of the Narcissus*, Preface]

11 It is not the clear-sighted who rule the world. Great achievements are accomplished in a blessed, warm fog. [*Victory*]

12 This could have occurred nowhere but in England, where men and sea interpenetrate, so to speak. [*Youth*]

SHIRLEY CONRAN 1932–

13 Our motto: Life is too short to stuff a mushroom. [*Superwoman*, epigraph]

14 I make no secret of the fact that I would rather lie on a sofa than sweep beneath it. But you have to be efficient if you're going to be lazy. ['The Reason Why']

15 First things first, second things never. ['How to be a Working Wife and Mother']

16 You cannot have everything and certainly cannot dust everything. To cite Conran's Law of Housework – it expands to fill the time available plus half an hour: so obviously it is never finished . . . Keep housework in its place, which, you will remember, is underfoot. [From *Superwoman 2*, in *Telegraph Sunday Magazine*, 30 Oct. 1977]

CONSERVATIVE PARTY PRESS RELEASE

17 This would, at a stroke, reduce the rise in prices, increase productivity and reduce unemployment. [Distributed at press conference, 16 June 1970. Wrongly attr. to Edward Heath at the conference, according to D. Butler and A. Sloman, *British Political Facts 1900–1975*]

A. J. COOK 1885–1931

18 Not a penny off the pay; not a second on the day. [Slogan of coal strike, 1926]

DAN COOK 1926–

19 The opera ain't over till the fat lady sings. [From baseball commentary on US TV, Apr. 1978, in the *Washington Post*, 11 June 1978. Often wrongly ascr. to Dick Motta, coach of Washington Bullets, who adopted it]

PETER COOK 1937–

20 You know, I go to the theatre to be entertained . . . I don't want to see plays about rape, sodomy and drug addiction . . . I can get all that at home. [Caption to cartoon by Roger Law in the *Observer*, 8 July 1962]

21 We exchanged many frank words in our respective languages. [*Beyond the Fringe*]

22 I am very interested in the Universe – I am specializing in the universe and all that surrounds it.

23 I think there's a terrific merit in having no sense of humour, no sense of irony, practically no sense of anything at all. If you're born with these so-called defects you have a very good chance of getting to the top. That's what's enabled her [Mrs Thatcher] to turn Britain into a cross between Singapore and Telford. [In the *Guardian*, 23 July 1988]

ALISTAIR COOKE 1908–

1 Very little is dependable in the politics of a going democracy except the people's conviction that one world-saver at a time is enough. [*America*, Ch. 10]

2 Not since Lincoln had there been such an artful manipulator of the good, the bad, and the bewildered in between. I believe he [Roosevelt] saved the capitalist system by deliberately forgetting to balance the books, by transferring the gorgeous resources of credit from the bankers to the government.

3 The most damning epitaph you can compose about Edward [VIII] – as a prince, as a king, as a man – is one that all comfortable people should cower from deserving: he was at his best only when the going was good. [*Six Men*, Pt II]

4 Trust the French to touch the nerve of the national spirit, or, as they prefer to say about any country but their own, the problem. [*Talk about America*, Ch. 14]

DAME CATHERINE COOKSON 1906–

5 The only sort of four-letter words I use are 'good', 'love', 'warm' and 'kind'. [Interview in John Mortimer, *In Character*]

PRESIDENT CALVIN COOLIDGE 1872–1933

6 There is no right to strike against the public safety by anybody, anywhere, anytime. [Telegram to President of American Federation of Labor, 14 Sept. 1919]

7 One with the law is a majority. [Speech of acceptance as Republican vice-presidential candidate, 27 July 1920]

8 The chief business of the American people is business. [Speech in Washington, 17 Jan. 1925. Commonly misquoted as 'The business of America is business']

9 [When asked what a clergyman had said in a sermon on sin] He said he was against it. [Attr. in J. H. McKee, *Coolidge: Wit and Wisdom*]

10 They hired the money, didn't they? [Of the Allies' war-debt, 1925. Attr., but not authenticated by his biographer, Claude M. Fuess]

CHESTER COOPER 1917–

11 The last crusade. [Of USA's war in Vietnam. In the *Daily Telegraph*, 4 Apr. 1975]

LADY DIANA COOPER 1892–1986

12 Only housemaids mope. [In P. Ziegler, *Lady Diana*]

GILES COOPER 1918–1966

13 Sudanese, called himself a dervish, swallowed a fish-hook, cut himself open, took it out again. If an uneducated savage can do that, you can cut your own hair. [Radio drama *Mathry Beacon*]

14 Plato ... the only five-lettered philosopher ending in o.

15 All schools are hell, nor are we out of them. In a moment you will hear the sound of the second circle: unrestricted boy. [Radio drama *Unman, Wittering and Zigo*]

16 I'm a connoisseur of failure. I can smell it, roll it round my mouth, tell you the vintage and the side of the hill that grew it.

JILLY COOPER 1937–

17 Sex is only the liquid centre of the great Newberry Fruit of friendship. [*Super-Jilly*, jacket]

18 If I were a grouse I'd appeal to the Brace Relations Board. [In the *Guardian*, 28 Dec. 1978]

TOMMY COOPER 1921–1984

19 Just like that! [Catchphrase in comedy act]

20 Last night I dreamt I ate a ten-pound marshmallow. When I woke up the pillow was gone. [Gag in variety act. In John Fisher, *Funny Way to be a Hero*, 'Just a Wolf in Sheep's Clothing']

WILLIAM COOPER 1910–

21 Bolshaw approved of Hitler in so much as he approved of the principle of the Führer's function while feeling that he could fulfil it better himself. [*Scenes from Provincial Life*, Pt I, Ch. 3]

1 If girls aren't ignorant, they're cultured ... You can't avoid suffering. [III. 2]

2 The trouble about finding a husband for one's mistress, is that no other man seems quite good enough. [5]

WENDY COPE 1945–

3 Bloody men are like bloody buses – / You wait for about a year / And as soon as one approaches your stop / Two or three others appear. [*Bloody Men*]

4 I'm sure you'd never exploit one; / I expect you'd rather be dead; / I'm thoroughly convinced of it – / Now can we go to bed? [*From June to December*]

5 It was a dream I had last week / And some kind of record seemed vital. / I knew it wouldn't be much of a poem / But I love the title. [*Making Cocoa for Kingsley Amis*]

6 For we wear each other out with our wakefulness. / For he makes me feel like a light-bulb that cannot switch itself off. [*My Lover*]

7 There are so many kinds of awful men – / One can't avoid them all. She often said / She'd never make the same mistake again: / She always made a new mistake instead. [*Rondeau Redoublé*]

ROBERT COPELAND

8 To get something done a committee should consist of no more than three men, two of whom are absent. [In *Penguin Dictionary of Modern Humorous Quotations*, comp. Fred Metcalf]

AARON COPLAND 1900–1990

9 Recordings are really for people who live in Timbuktu. [On the necessity of live music. In obituary in the *Guardian*, 4 Dec. 1990]

10 If a literary man puts together two words about music, one of them will be wrong. [In Frank Muir, *Frank Muir Book*]

FRANCIS FORD COPPOLA 1939–

11 Your work parallels your life, but in the sense of a glass full of water where people look at it and say, 'Oh, the water's the same shape as the glass!' [Interview in the *Guardian*, 15 Oct. 1988]

RONNIE CORBETT *see* RONNIE BARKER and RONNIE CORBETT

ALAN COREN 1938–

12 An infuriating irritant, like the chap you knew before you were married who is now a bachelor supported by beautiful women and constantly drops in to see you on the way to the airport. [*All Except the Bastard*, 'The Still Centre']

13 I am always on at him to get his claustrophobia looked at but it is not easy to find a doctor who will see him in the middle of a field. [*Bumf*, 'No Bloody Fear']

14 I'm sure the Government knows best. She usually does. ['The Denmark Factor']

15 It turned out that, following the Crucifixion, far and away the most commercially successful area of publishing was religious books! Up until 33 AD it had been gardening and desk diaries, but since the Resurrection it had been religion, definitely. [*The Cricklewood Diet*, 'The Holy Grail']

16 And the Lord God replied unto Adam saying: look, the eternal mystery of how it is *that* there are always pieces of broken blue and white saucers wherever ye dig is the biggest eternal mystery there is. It is so big, *that* even I do not understand it. That is how big it is. ['From the Alternative Version']

17 Some of them words got syllables all over 'em. ['Zuleika Capp']

18 It [his book] also concerns the three most perennially popular subjects currently to be found on the bedside tables of the reading public, viz. golf, cats, and the Third Reich. [*Golfing for Cats*, Foreword]

19 The Act of God designation on all insurance policies; which means, roughly, that you cannot be insured for the accidents that are most likely to happen to you. If your ox kicks a hole in your neighbour's Maserati, however, indemnity is instantaneous. [*The Lady from Stalingrad Mansions*, 'A Short History of Insurance']

20 'Golden hands he's got,' said his father

gloomily. 'A pianist's hands. Or a surgeon's hands.' 'Both,' said his mother. She blew her nose fiercely. 'He could have been both. Operating by day, by night playing Bach.' [*The Sanity Inspector*, 'Wholesale War']

1 Since both its [Switzerland's] national products, snow and chocolate, melt, the cuckoo clock was invented solely in order to give tourists something solid to remember it by. ['And Though They Do Their Best']

2 They [the French] are short, blue-vested people who carry their own onions when cycling abroad, and have a yard which is 3.37 inches longer than other people's. ['All You Need to Know about Europe']

3 The Dutch fall into two quite distinct physical types: the small, corpulent, red-faced Edams, and the thinner, paler, larger Goudas.

4 Apart from cheese and tulips, the main product of the country is advocaat, a drink made from lawyers.

5 'It's your audience for ten a.m., Your Holiness,' murmured the secretary. 'One man?' said the Pope. 'You call that an audience?' ['Believe Me']

6 I sometimes wonder if the manufacturers of foolproof items keep a fool or two on their payroll to test things. [*Seems Like Old Times*, 'August']

7 Frances is as plain as it is possible to be without requiring a licence to enter a public place.

8 Jacob is a German Shepherd. (I have never understood why they aren't called German sheepdogs. What do the Germans call shepherds?) ['January']

9 The self-esteem of the quality writer depends on his belief that those readers who care about good stuff cannot afford to buy it.

10 Between 1984 and 1988 the number of centenarian men in Britain had gone up from 100 to 210. According to my pocket calculator, if this alarming trend continues, in a mere sixty-six years' time the entire male population of this country will be over 100. ['February']

11 As anyone who has ever forked out for a quarter-pound of mixed metaphors will testify, once a bastion falls, the flood-gates open and before you know where you are you're up to the neck in wrung withers. [In *Punch*, 16 Feb. 1972]

12 People who live in large houses shouldn't know Jones. [On BBC radio, 4 Sept. 1977]

13 There is nothing to be pitied in a dumb animal; its dumbness is its salvation, whereas poor man carries the terrible burden of intelligence, and it will surely wipe him out in the not too distant end. The cats and guppies will have the last laugh over the last corpse of the last man: 'If you're so smart, how come you're extinct?' [In *The Times*]

14 Television is more interesting than people. If it were not, we should have people standing in the corners of our rooms.

15 In England you have to know people very intimately indeed before they tell you about the rust in their Volvo. It has never surprised me that there are 50 million Roman Catholics in America, and nearly as many psychiatrists: bean-spilling is the national mania. [Review of Kurt Vonnegut's *Palm Sunday* in the *Sunday Times*, 21 June 1981]

16 Being a personality is not the same as having a personality. [In the *Mail on Sunday*, 12 Mar. 1989]

17 They [VAT booklets] are put together by theologians concerned not merely with the number of angels able to dance on the head of a pin, but with whether the dance may be construed as educational within the meaning of the Act, enabling the pin to be zero-rated, or whether it is an entertainment, rendering the pin liable to an impost of 15 per cent. [In *The Times*, 4 Dec. 1990]

PETER CORNEILLE

18 If anyone wants to know what elephants are like, they are like people only more so. [From *Theatreprint*, 1984, in *Animal Quotations*, ed. G. F. Lamb]

BERNARD CORNFELD 1927–

19 Do you sincerely want to be rich? [Slogan of International Overseas Services]

F. M. CORNFORD 1874–1943

1 Has it ever occurred to you that nothing is ever done until everyone is convinced that it ought to be done, and has been convinced for so long that it is now time to do something else? [*Microcosmographia Academica*]

2 Propaganda is that branch of the art of lying which consists in nearly deceiving your friends without quite deceiving your enemies. [In the *New Statesman*, 15 Sept. 1978]

FRANCES CORNFORD 1886–1960

3 Magnificently unprepared / For the long littleness of life. [*Rupert Brooke*]

4 O why do you walk through the fields in gloves, / Missing so much and so much? / O fat white woman whom nobody loves. [*To a Fat Lady Seen from the Train*]

JOHN CORNFORD 1915–1936

5 Only in constant action was his constant certainty found. / He will throw a longer shadow as time recedes. [In *John Cornford, A Memoir*, ed. Pat Sloan, Pt 2, sect. vii, 'Sergei Mironovich Kirov']

DAME FELICITAS CORRIGAN

6 To me life is just a novitiate eternity. [In the *Observer*, 28 July 1991]

BILLY COTTON 1900–1969

7 Wakey-wakey! [Catchphrase in his *Band Show* on BBC radio and TV, 1950s and 1960s]

PIERRE DE COUBERTIN 1863–1937

8 The most important thing in the Olympic Games is not to win but to take part, just as the most important thing in life is not the triumph but the struggle. [Speech at banquet at close of 1908 games, London]

ÉMILE COUÉ 1857–1926

9 *Tous les jours, à tous points de vue, je vais de mieux en mieux.* – Every day, in every way, I'm getting better and better. [Formula of his faith-cures]

R. COULSON

10 Marriage is not all bed and breakfast. [*Reflections*]

SIR NOËL COWARD 1899–1973

11 Though we all disguise our feelings pretty well, / What we mean by 'Very good' is 'Go to hell'. [*Bitter Sweet*, Act I, sc. ii]

12 I believe that since my life began / The most I've had is just / A talent to amuse. [II. i, 'If Love were All']

13 We have no reliable guarantee that the afterlife will be any less exasperating than this one, have we? [*Blithe Spirit*, I]

14 Never mind, dear, we're all made the same, though some more than others. [*Collected Sketches and Lyrics*, 'The Café de la Paix']

15 We're Regency Rakes / And each of us makes / A personal issue / Of adipose tissue. [*Conversation Piece*, I. iv]

16 There's always something fishy about the French! [vi. See also 282:1]

17 Don't let's be beastly to the Germans. [Lyric: *Don't Let's be Beastly to the Germans*]

18 Don't put your daughter on the stage, Mrs Worthington. [Lyric: *Don't Put Your Daughter on the Stage*]

19 Considering all the time you took forming yourself, Elsie, I'm surprised you're not a nicer little girl than you are. [*Fumed Oak*, Act II, sc. ii]

20 There was a saying, much quoted in the war years, that if an Englishman told you he was a secret agent it was a lie, and that if an American told you the same it was true. [*Future Indefinite*, Pt 4, 2]

21 Poor Little Rich Girl. [Title of song in *On with the Dance*]

22 When it's raspberry time in Runcorn, / In Runcorn, in Runcorn, / The air is like a draught of wine. / The undertaker cleans his sign, / The Hull express goes off the line, / When it's raspberry time in Runcorn. ['Raspberry Time in Runcorn', in *On with the Dance*, 'Fête Galante']

23 The Stately Homes of England, / How beautiful they stand, / To prove the upper

classes / Have still the upper hand. [*Operette*, Act I, sc. vii, 'The Stately Homes of England']

1 And though if the Van Dycks have to go / And we pawn the Bechstein grand. / We'll stand by the Stately Homes of England.

2 Miss Erikson looked more peculiar than ever this morning. Is her spiritualism getting worse? [*Present Laughter*, Act I]

3 Very flat, Norfolk. [*Private Lives*, Act I]

4 Extraordinary how potent cheap music is. [Some versions give 'strange' as the first word]

5 Certain women should be struck regularly, like gongs. [III]

6 But why, oh why, do the wrong people travel, / When the right people stay at home? [*Sail Away*, 'Why Do . . .?']

7 There are bad times just around the corner. / We can all look forward to despair, / It's as clear as crystal / From Bridlington to Bristol / That we can't save democracy / And we don't much care. [Lyric: *There are Bad Times*]

8 I belong to a generation of men, most of which aren't here any more, and we all did the same thing for the same reason, no matter what we thought about politics. [*This Happy Breed*, Act I, sc. iii]

9 A room with a view / And you. [*This Year of Grace*, 'A Room with a View']

10 There's sand in the porridge and sand in the bed, / And if this is pleasure we'd rather be dead. ['Mother's Complaint']

11 Dance, dance, dance little lady, / Leave tomorrow behind. ['Dance Little Lady']

12 Whatever crimes the Proletariat commits / It can't be beastly to the Children of the Ritz. [*Words and Music*, 'The Children of the Rich']

13 Mad dogs and Englishmen go out in the midday sun.

14 The sun never sets on Government House. ['Planters' Wives']

15 Mad about the boy.

16 Television is for appearing on, not watching. [In the *Guardian*, 28 Nov. 1988]

17 Dear 338171 (May I call you 338?) [Opening of Letter to T. E. Lawrence, 25 Aug. 1930, *Letters to T. E. Lawrence*]

18 Never trust men with short legs. Brains too near their bottoms. [In Nancy McPhee, *Book of Insults*]

19 Work is much more fun than fun. [In the *Observer*, 'Sayings of the Week', 21 June 1963]

20 He had just one illusion about them and that was that they were no good. [Of Somerset Maugham's boast that he had no illusions about his fellow men. In Frederic Raphael, *Somerset Maugham and His World*]

21 [When asked by five-year-old Tamsin Olivier what two dogs were doing] The doggie in front has suddenly gone blind, and the other one has very kindly offered to push him all the way to St Dunstan's. [In K. Tynan, *Two Hands Clapping*]

22 Learn the lines and don't bump into the furniture. [Advice to a young actor. Attr.]

HARVEY COX 1929–

23 The Secular City. [Title of book]

TOM CRABTREE ?1924–

24 Some people are born in circumstances which resemble being saddled in the enclosure at Epsom when the race is at Ripon. [In the *Guardian*, 8 Sept. 1977]

EDWARD GORDON CRAIG 1872–1966

25 Farce is the essential theatre. Farce refined becomes high comedy: farce brutalized becomes tragedy. But at the roots of all drama farce is to be found. [*Index to the Story of My Days*]

26 That is what the title of artist means: one who perceives more than his fellows, and who records more than he has seen. [*On the Art of the Theatre*]

HART CRANE 1899–1932

27 Thin squeaks of radio static, / The captured fume of space foams in our ears. [*The Bridge*, 'Cape Hatteras']

28 Stars scribble on our eyes the frosty sagas, / The gleaming cantos of unvanquished space.

29 Our Meistersinger, thou set breath in steel; / And it was thou who on the boldest

heel / Stood up and flung the span on even wing / Of that great Bridge, our Myth, whereof I sing. [Referring to Walt Whitman and Brooklyn Bridge]

1 And hurry along, Van Winkle – it's getting late. ['Van Winkle']

2 The phonographs of hades in the brain / Are tunnels that re-wind themselves, and love / A burnt match skating in a urinal. ['The Tunnel']

3 ... why do I often meet your visage here, / Your eyes like agate lanterns – on and on / Below the toothpaste and the dandruff ads? [Referring to Walt Whitman]

4 The bell-rope that gathers God at dawn / Dispatches me as though I dropped down the knell / Of a spent day. [The Broken Tower]

5 The Cross alone has flown the wave. / But since the Cross sank, much that's warped and cracked / Has followed in its name, has heaped its grave. [The Mermen]

6 And onwards, as bells off San Salvador / Salute the crocus lustres of the stars, / In these poinsettia meadows of her tides. [Voyages, II]

JAMES CREELMAN 1901–1941 and **RUTH ROSE**

7 Oh no, it wasn't the aeroplanes. It was Beauty killed the Beast. [Final words of film King Kong, 1933 version]

FRANCIS CRICK 1916– and **JAMES D. WATSON** 1928–

8 It has not escaped our notice that the specific pairing we have postulated immediately suggests a possible copying mechanism for the genetic material. [Paper announcing discovery of DNA. In Nature, 1953]

QUENTIN CRISP 1908–

9 In the long run, in spite of everything, I have been very lucky. I asked for bread and was given a stone. It turned out to be precious. [How to Become a Virgin, 1]

10 I was given a bed in which four people could have slept without ever being introduced. Everything in America is on wide screen. ['America']

11 Keeping up with the Joneses was a full-time job with my mother and father. It was not until many years later when I lived alone that I realized how much cheaper it was to drag the Joneses down to my level. [The Naked Civil Servant, Ch. 1]

12 As soon as I stepped out of my mother's womb on to dry land, I realized that I had made a mistake – that I shouldn't have come, but the trouble with children is that they are not returnable. [2]

13 Tears were to me what glass beads are to African traders.

14 This woman did not fly to extremes; she lived there. [3]

15 I don't hold with abroad and think that foreigners speak English when our backs are turned. [4]

16 If one is not going to take the necessary precautions to avoid having parents, one must undertake to bring them up. [5]

17 Is not the whole world a vast house of assignation of which the filing system has been lost? [11]

18 There was no need to do any housework at all. After the first four years the dirt doesn't get any worse. [15]

19 ... God, from whose territory I had withdrawn my ambassadors at the age of fifteen. It had become obvious that he was never going to do a thing I said. [16]

20 Life was a funny thing that happened to me on the way to the grave. [18]

21 I became one of the stately homos of England. [24]

22 Sadly I explained that ... the conditions in which anyone could be a famous model had vanished long ago. Those few of us who were still in the racket had dwindled into naked Civil Servants. [29]

23 An autobiography is an obituary in serial form with the last instalment missing.

24 For flavour, Instant Sex will never supersede the stuff you had to peel and cook. [The Sayings of Q.C.]

25 The erroneous but almost universally held idea that culture belongs to France and that for a Frenchman to exhibit talent is a kind of patriotism. [The Wit and Wisdom of Q.C., ed. Guy Kettelhack, Pt 5]

1 It seems that in the United States, Englishmen are regarded as pets, like budgies, that can almost speak American. [7]

2 I have come to represent a sad person's view of a gay person. [From *An Evening with Q.C.*, his one-man show at the Duke of York's Theatre, London, in the *Guardian*, 1 Feb. 1978]

3 [When asked by a US immigration official if he was a practising homosexual] Practising? Certainly not. I'm absolutely perfect. [Quoted by Ray Connolly in the *Sunday Times*, 20 Jan. 1980]

4 In England, the system is benign and the people are hostile. In America, the people are friendly – and the system is brutal! [Interview in the *Guardian*, 23 Oct. 1985]

JULIAN CRITCHLEY, MP 1930–

5 She [Margaret Thatcher] has been beastly to the Bank of England, has demanded that the BBC 'set its house in order' and tends to believe the worst of the Foreign and Commonwealth Office. She cannot see an institution without hitting it with her handbag. [In *The Times*, 21 June 1982]

6 Michael Heseltine cannot see a parapet without ducking below it. [Before Heseltine's resignation from the Cabinet over the Westland affair. In the *Listener*, 2 Jan. 1986]

7 Prima donna inter pares. [Of Margaret Thatcher. Interview in the *Guardian*, 5 Sept. 1987]

8 The Commons was the preserve of the upper class who were just bright enough to get the clever middle class to govern and were kept in power by the deferential working-class vote. [Of the House of Commons in the 1960s. In the *Financial Times*, 28 Nov. 1990]

SIR JOHN CROFTON 1912–

9 The French tipple all the time and kill their livers, and the Scots drink in bouts and kill their neighbours. [At press conference, launching report 'Health Education in the Prevention of Alcohol-related Problems', Edinburgh, 18 Jan. 1985]

RICHMAL CROMPTON 1890–1969

10 Violet Elizabeth [Bott] dried her tears. She saw that they were useless and she did not believe in wasting her effects. 'All right,' she said calmly, 'I'll thcream then. I'll thcream, an' thcream, an' thcream till I'm thick.' [*Just William*]

BING CROSBY 1901–1977

11 Where the blue of the night / Meets the gold of the day, / Someone waits for me. [Song: *Where the Blue of the Night . . .*, words and music by Crosby, Roy Turk and Fred Ahlert, in film *The Big Broadcast of 1936*]

12 There is nothing in the world I wouldn't do for Hope, and there is nothing he wouldn't do for me . . . We spend our lives doing nothing for each other. [In the *Observer*, 'Sayings of the Week', 7 May 1950]

13 Most of them think: 'Well he [Crosby] sings about like I do, you know, when I'm in the bathroom, or in the shower, and feel good and wake up with a gay feeling.' Why they think I'm one of the fellas. [Epigraph to C. Thompson, *Bing*]

14 When Irving Berlin sings you have to hug him to hear him. [BBC TV interview with Michael Parkinson, 1975]

15 Oh – I listen a lot and talk less. You can't learn anything when you're talking.

BING CROSBY and BOB HOPE 1903–

16 Like Webster's Dictionary, we're Morocco bound. [Song: *Road to Morocco*, in film of same title, words by Johnny Burke, music by Jimmy van Heusen]

RICHARD CROSSMAN 1907–1974

17 At last we have a leader who can lie. [On Harold Wilson's becoming Labour Party leader in succession to Gaitskell. *Diaries of a Cabinet Minister*]

18 The Civil Service is profoundly deferential – 'Yes, Minister! No, Minister! If you wish it, Minister!' [22 Oct. 1964]

JOHN CROW 1905–1970

19 Do not think what you want to think until

you know what you ought to know. ['Crow's Law'. In R. V. Jones, *Most Secret War*, Ch. 9]

TOM CRUISE 1962–

1 A lot of the time, what acting is really about is meeting someone's eye. [Interview in the *Guardian*, 28 Feb. 1989]

CONSTANCE CUMMINGS 1910–

2 He [Aneurin Bevan] was like a fire in a room on a cold winter's day. [In Michael Foot, *Aneurin Bevan*, Vol. 1, Ch. 6]

E. E. CUMMINGS 1894–1962

3 who knows if the moon's / a balloon, coming out of a keen city / in the sky – filled with pretty people? [& [AND], 1925, 'Seven Poems, VII']

4 what i want to know is / how do you like your blueeyed boy / Mister Death. [*Collected Poems*, 1938, 31]

5 the flyspecked abdominous female / indubitably tellurian / strolls / emitting minute grins [68]

6 hurries / elsewhere; to blow / incredible wampum.

7 bodies lopped / of every / prettiness, / you hew form truly. [103]

8 Humanity i love you / because you would rather black the boots of / success than enquire whose soul dangles from his / watch-chain which would be embarrassing for both / parties and because you / unflinchingly applaud all / songs containing the words country home and / mother when sung at the old howard [107]

9 a pretty girl who naked is / is worth a million statues [133]

10 (dreaming, / et / cetera, of / Your smile eyes knees and of your Etcetera) / [148]

11 how do you find the sun, ladies? / (graduallyverygradually) 'there is not enough / of it' their hands / minutely / answered [158]

12 when i contemplate her uneyes safely ensconced in thick glass / you try if we are a gentleman not to think of (sh) [201]

13 and the duckbilled platitude lays & lays / and Lays aytash unee [203]

14 responds, without getting annoyed / 'I will not kiss your f.ing flag.' [204]

15 Olaf (upon what were once knees) / does almost ceaselessly repeat / 'there is some shit I will not eat'

16 unless statistics lie he was / more brave than me: more blond than you.

17 lady will you come with me into / the extremely little house of / my mind. [230]

18 squeeze your nuts and open your face [246]

19 he sang his didn't he danced his did [*50 Poems*, 29]

20 Humanity i love you because you / are perpetually putting the secret of / life in your pants and forgetting / it's there and sitting down / on it [*XLI Poems*, 1925, 'La Guerre, II']

21 for whatever we lose (like a you or a me) / it's always ourselves we find in the sea [*Poems 95*, 'maggie and milly and molly and may']

22 (and down went / my Uncle / Sol / and started a worm farm) [*is 5*, 'One, X']

23 While you and i have lips and voices which / are for kissing and to sing with / who cares if some oneeyed son of a bitch / invents an instrument to measure Spring with? [XXXIII]

24 next to of course god america i / love you land of the pilgrims and so forth oh ['*Two*, III']

25 in every language even deafanddumb / thy sons acclaim your glorious name by gorry / by jingo by gee by gosh by gum

26 'then shall the voices of liberty be mute?' / He spoke. And drank rapidly a glass of water

27 a politician is an arse upon which everyone has sat except a man [*1 × 1*, 10]

28 We doctors know / a hopeless case if – listen: there's a hell / of a good universe next door, let's go [14]

29 the Cambridge ladies who live in furnished souls / are unbeautiful and have comfortable minds [*Tulips and Chimneys*, Sonnets-Realities, 1]

30 nobody, not even the rain, has such small hands [*W, LVII*]

VALENTINE CUNNINGHAM 1944–

1 Novel-reading re-enacts the Fall. What keeps the reader going is forbidden fruits, temptation from the tree of knowledge of good and evil. [In the *Observer*, 20 Sept. 1987]

WILL CUPPY 1884–1949

2 Catherine Parr didn't matter. She never committed even low treason. [*The Decline and Fall of Practically Everybody*, V, 'Henry VIII']

3 The Dodo never had a chance. He seems to have been invented for the sole purpose of becoming extinct and that was all he was good for. [*How to Become Extinct*, p. 163]

4 It's easy to see the faults in people I know; it's hardest to see the good. Especially when the good isn't there. [Attr.]

TONY CURTIS 1925–

5 Kissing Marilyn [Monroe] was like kissing Hitler – sure I said that. It wasn't *that* bad. But you can see through that line: there was this woman, beautifully endowed, treating all men like shit. Why did I have to take that? [In *Game*, Sept. 1975]

MICHAEL CURTIZ 1888–1962

6 Nobody should try to play comedy unless they have a circus going on inside. [In David Niven, *The Moon's a Balloon*, Ch. 11]

7 Bring on the empty horses! [Attr. during filming of *The Charge of the Light Brigade*. Niven used for the second volume of his autobiography]

COLIN CURZON

8 I'll tell you in a phrase, my sweet, exactly what I mean: ... Not tonight, Josephine. [*Not Tonight, Josephine*]

EARL CURZON OF KEDLESTON 1859–1925

9 Not even a public figure. A man of no experience. And of the utmost insignificance. [Of Stanley Baldwin's appointment as Prime Minister. In Harold Nicolson, *Curzon: The Last Phase*, Ch. 12]

10 Better send them a Papal Bull. [Marginal comment on misprint in Foreign Office document: '... even the monks of Mount Athos were violating their cows'. In Ronaldshay, *Life of Lord Curzon*, Vol. III, Ch. 15]

11 I never knew that the lower classes had such white skins. [When seeing troops bathing. Attr. in K. Rose, *Superior Person*, Ch. 12]

IVOR CUTLER 1923–

12 If / you are mortar / it is / hard / to feel well-disposed / towards / the / two bricks / you are squashed / between / or / even / a sense of / community. [*A Flat Man*, 'Alone']

D

SIR RALF [later LORD] DAHRENDORF
  1929–

1 It [the Social Democratic Party] promises them [its supporters] a better yesterday. [In the *Observer*, 10 Oct. 1982]

DAILY MIRROR

2 Whose finger on the trigger? [Front-page headline on election day, 25 Oct. 1951. See also 245:12]

3 A good man fallen among politicians. [Of Michael Foot. Editorial, 28 Feb. 1983]

EDOUARD DALADIER 1884–1970

4 *C'est un drôle de guerre.* [Speech in Chamber of Deputies, Paris, 22 Dec. 1939. Became 'It is a phoney war' in trans.]

SALVADOR DALI 1904–1989

5 It is a common error to think of bad taste as sterile; rather, it is good taste, and good taste alone, that possesses the power to sterilize and is always the first handicap to any creative functioning. One has only to consider the good taste of the French: it has encouraged them not to do anything. [In Robert Descharnes and Clovis Prévost, *Gaudi, the Visionary*, Preface]

6 Do you believe that since the earth is round, you will find landscapes everywhere? Does a round face have several noses? There are very few landscapes. They all converge here. Catalonia is the nose of the earth.

7 ... the way an angel cooks a cathedral. [Of Antonio Gaudi. Epigraph to Ch. 1]

8 Picasso is a genius. So am I. Picasso is a Communist. Nor am I. [From Jean Cocteau, *Diaries*, Vol. 2, in the *Sunday Times*, 7 Oct. 1990]

9 I do not paint a portrait to look like the subject, rather does the person grow to look like his portrait. [In *Kiss Me Hardy*, ed. Roger Kilroy, 'The Connoisseur']

SERGEANT DAN DALY [US Marines]

10 Come on, you sons of bitches! Do you want to live for ever? [Attr., Battle of Belleau Wood, 6 June 1918. Echoes Frederick the Great]

PAUL DANIELS 1938–

11 You're going to like this ... not a lot ... but you'll like it! [Catchphrase in conjuring act on TV, from 1980s]

BEI DAO

12 Freedom is nothing but the distance / between the hunter and the hunted. [*The August Sleeper*]

IAN DARK 1950–

13 [When asked whether a boxer was a household name in Belfast] He's not even a household name in his own living-room. [From BBC radio programme *Today*, in the *Listener*, 'Out Takes of the Year', 17/24 Dec. 1987]

MR JUSTICE DARLING 1849–1936

14 The law-courts of England are open to

all men like the doors of the Ritz Hotel. [Also attr. to Lord Justice Sir James Matthew and Judge Sturgess.]

RICHARD DARRÉ 1895–1953

1 *Blut und Boden.* – Blood and soil. [*Law for the Establishment of Hereditary Farms,* 29 Sept. 1933]

CLARENCE DARROW 1857–1938

2 When I was a boy I was told that anybody could become President: I'm beginning to believe it. [In I. Stone, *Clarence Darrow for the Defence,* Ch. 6]

CHARLES GALTON DARWIN 1887–1962

3 The evolution of the human race will not be accomplished in the ten thousand years of tame animals, but in the million years of wild animals, because man is and will always be a wild animal. [*The Next Million Years,* Ch. 7]

HARRY M. DAUGHERTY 1860–1941

4 We sit down about two o'clock in the morning around a table in a smoke-filled room. [Of presidential campaign. Ascr. in *The New York Times,* 21 Feb. 1920, but Daugherty denied he had said 'smoke-filled']

WALTER DAVENPORT 1889–1971

5 An editor: a person who knows precisely what he wants – but isn't quite sure. [Quoted by Bennett Cerf in *Saturday Review Reader,* No. 2]

LIONEL DAVISON 1922–

6 For six days, following an old tradition, this labour continued, and on the seventh ceased. [Of the Six Day War. *Smith's Gazelle,* Ch. 10, sect. i]

ROBERTSON DAVIES 1913–

7 Though academics love bickering they hate rows. [*The Rebel Angels,* 'The New Aubrey II']

8 What he has is wit, not humour, and wit alone never turns inwards. ['Second Paradise VI']

W. H. DAVIES 1871–1940

9 And hear the pleasant cuckoo, loud and long – / The simple bird that thinks two notes a song. [*April's Charms*]

10 A rainbow and a cuckoo's song / May never come together again; / May never come / This side the tomb. [*A Great Time*]

11 It was the Rainbow gave thee birth, / And left thee all her lovely hues. [*The Kingfisher*]

12 Live with proud Peacocks in green parks.

13 What is this life if, full of care, / We have no time to stand and stare? [*Leisure*]

14 Girls scream, / Boys shout; / Dogs bark, / School's out. [*School's Out*]

15 Sweet Stay-at-Home, sweet Well-content. [*Sweet Stay-at-Home*]

BETTE DAVIS 1908–1989

16 I see – she's the original good time that was had by all. [Of a starlet. In Leslie Halliwell, *Filmgoer's Book of Quotes*]

17 Pray to God and say the lines. [Advice to actress Celeste Holm, as quoted by latter]

18 I was never beautiful like Miss Hayworth or Miss Lamarr. I was known as the little brown wren. Who'd want to get me at the end of the picture? [From *Films Illustrated,* Dec. 1979, in *Chambers Film Quotes,* comp. Tony Crawley]

19 I think people need something to look up to, and Hollywood was the only Royalty that America ever had. [Interview in the *Sunday Times,* 20 Sept. 1987]

20 Home is only where you go to when you've nowhere to go. [Quoted by Katharine Whitehorn in the *Observer,* 20 Sept. 1987. See also 368:6]

21 Joan [Crawford] always cries a lot. Her tear ducts must be very close to her bladder. [In Shaun Considine, *Bette and Joan*]

22 Don't let's ask for the moon. We have the stars. [In film *Now, Voyager,* screenplay by Casey Robinson, from novel by Olive Prouty]

MILES DAVIS 1926–1991

1 A legend is an old man with a cane known for what he used to do: I'm still doing it. [In the *Observer*, 'Sayings of the Week', 21 July 1991]

SAMMY DAVIS JR 1925–1990

2 Being a star has made it possible for me to get insulted in places where the average Negro could never hope to get insulted. [*Yes I Can*]

3 I'm a coloured, one-eyed Jew – do I need anything else?

RICHARD DAWKINS 1941–

4 Biology is the study of complicated things that give the appearance of having been designed for a purpose. Physics is the study of simple things that do not tempt us to invoke design. [*The Blind Watchmaker*, Ch. 1]

5 Natural selection ... has no purpose in mind. It has no mind and no mind's eye. It does not plan for the future. It has no vision, no foresight, no sight at all. If it can be said to play the role of watchmaker in nature, it is the blind watchmaker.

6 The Selfish Gene. [Title of book]

7 The welfare state is perhaps the greatest altruistic system the animal kingdom has ever known. [*The Selfish Gene*, Ch. 7]

CLARENCE DAY 1874–1935

8 I meant to be prompt, but it never occurred to me that I had better try to be early. [*Life with Father*, 'Father teaches me to be prompt']

9 Imagine the Lord talking French! Aside from a few odd words in Hebrew, I took it completely for granted that God had never spoken anything but the most dignified English. ['Father interferes'. See also 125:15]

10 'If you don't go to other men's funerals,' he told Father stiffly, 'they won't go to yours.'

11 Father declared he was going to buy a new plot in the cemetery, a plot all for himself. 'And I'll buy one on a corner,' he added triumphantly, 'where I can get out.' [Penultimate para. of book]

12 Books! Bottled chatter! Things that some other simian has formerly said. [*This Simian World*]

MOSHE DAYAN 1915–1981

13 If we lose this war, I'll start another in my wife's name. [Of Six Day War, 1967. Attr.]

14 Whenever you accept our views we shall be in full agreement with you. [Welcoming Cyrus Vance to Israel, in course of Arab–Israeli negotiations. In the *Observer*, 'Sayings of the Week', 14 Aug. 1977]

C. DAY LEWIS 1904–1972

15 Is it birthday weather for you, dear soul? / Is it fine your way, / With tall moon-daisies alight, and the mole / Busy, and elegant hares at play ...? [*Birthday Poem for Thomas Hardy*]

16 I sang as one / Who on a tilting deck sings / To keep men's courage up, though the wave hangs / That shall cut off their sun. [*The Conflict*]

17 All is yet the same as when I roved the heather / Chained to a demon through the shrinking night. [*Emily Brontë*]

18 Now the peak of summer's past, the sky is overcast / And the love we swore would last for an age seems deceit. [*Hornpipe*]

19 Then I'll hit the trail for that promising land; / May catch up with Wystan and Rex my friend, / Go mad in good company, find a good country, / Make a clean sweep or make a clean end. [*The Magnetic Mountain*, 4]

20 Suppose that we, to-morrow or the next day, / Came to an end – in storm the shafting broken, / Or a mistaken signal, the flange lifting – / Would that be premature, a text for sorrow? [*Suppose that we*]

21 It is the logic of our times, / No subject for immortal verse – / That we who lived by honest dreams / Defend the bad against the worse. [*Where are the War Poets?*]

ARCHBISHOP JOOST DE BLANK 1906–1968

22 Christ in this country [South Africa] would quite likely have been arrested under

the Suppression of Communism Act. [In the *Observer*, 'Sayings of the Week', 27 Oct. 1963]

1 I suffer from an incurable disease – colour blindness. [Attr.]

RÉGIS DEBRAY 1941–

2 Revolution in the Revolution? [Title of book]

3 We are never completely contemporaneous with our present. History advances in disguise; it appears on stage wearing the mask of the preceding scene, and we tend to lose the meaning of the play. [*Revolution in the Revolution?*, Ch. 1]

4 Balzac observed all the things that Marx did not see. [*Teachers, Writers, Celebrities*, 'Balzac, or Zoology Today']

MICHEL DEBRÉ 1912–

5 *Europe des patries.* – Europe of the fatherlands. [Speech on taking office as Prime Minister of France, 15 Jan. 1959. Often falsely ascr. to General de Gaulle]

EUGENE V. DEBS 1855–1926

6 While there is a lower class, I am in it; while there is a criminal element, I am of it; while there is a soul in prison, I am not free. [Speech in Cleveland, Ohio, 9 Sept. 1917]

CLAUDE DEBUSSY 1862–1918

7 The odd and pleasant taste of a pink sweet filled with snow. [Of Grieg's music. From *Gil Blas*, 1903, in *Dictionary of Musical Quotations*, ed. I. Crofton and D. Fraser]

8 Music is the arithmetic of sounds as optics is the geometry of light. [In Nat Shapiro, *Encyclopedia of Quotations about Music*]

9 A beautiful sunset that was mistaken for a dawn. [Of Wagner's music. Attr.]

CHARLES DEDERICH

10 Today is the first day of the rest of your life. [Hippie slogan, late 1960s]

SYLVIA DEE

11 They try to tell us we're too young / Too young to really be in love. [Song: *Too Young*, music by Sid Lippman]

WILLIAM [later LORD] DEEDES 1913–

12 Tricky job being Home Secretary – you've got to keep all your feathers in the air. [On receiving life peerage. In the *Observer*, 15 June 1986]

13 You can't make an omelette without frying eggs.

EDGAR DEGAS 1834–1917

14 Monet's pictures are always too draughty for me. [In conversation. In *Memoirs of Julie Manet* (Mme Renoir)]

GENERAL DE GAULLE *see* GAULLE, GENERAL DE

LEN DEIGHTON 1929–

15 Divorce is a system whereby two people make a mistake and one of them goes on paying for it. [In A. Alvarez, *Life after Marriage*]

WALTER DE LA MARE 1873–1956

16 Ann, Ann! / Come! quick as you can! / There's a fish that *talks* / In the frying pan. [*Alas, Alack*]

17 Oh, no man knows / Through what wild centuries / Roves back the rose. [*All That's Past*]

18 Very old are we men: / Our dreams are tales / Told in dim Eden / By Eve's nightingales.

19 Silence and sleep like fields / Of amaranth lie.

20 Far are the shades of Arabia, / Where the Princes ride at noon. [*Arabia*]

21 He is crazed with the spell of far Arabia, / They have stolen his wits away.

22 Has anybody seen my Mopser? – / A comely dog is he, / With hair the colour of a Charles the Fifth, / And teeth like ships at sea. [*The Bandog*]

23 In search of a Fairy, / Whose Rozez he knowzez / Were not honeyed for he. [*The Bees' Song*]

1 Only with beauty wake wild memories – / Sorrow for where you are, for where you would be. [*The Cage*]

2 When I lie where shades of darkness / Shall no more assail mine eyes. [*Fare Well*]

3 Look thy last on all things lovely, / Every hour.

4 Since that all things thou wouldst praise / Beauty took from those who loved them / In other days.

5 God in His pity knows / Why, in her bodice stuck, / Reeks a mock rose. [*The Fat Woman*]

6 Nought but vast sorrow was there – / The sweet cheat gone. [*The Ghost*]

7 He is the Ancient Tapster of this Hostel, / To him at length even we all keys must resign. [*Hospital*]

8 Three jolly gentlemen, / In coats of red, / Rode their horses / Up to bed. [*The Huntsmen*]

9 I can't abear a Butcher, / I can't abide his meat. [*I Can't Abear*]

10 Do diddle di do, / Poor Jim Jay / Got stuck fast / In Yesterday. [*Jim Jay*]

11 'Is there anybody there?' said the Traveller, / Knocking on the moonlit door. [*The Listeners*]

12 'Tell them I came, and no-one answered, / That I kept my word,' he said.

13 And how the silence surged softly backward, / When the plunging hoofs were gone.

14 It's a very odd thing – / As odd as can be – / That whatever Miss T. eats / Turns into Miss T. [*Miss T.*]

15 When music sounds, all that I was I am / Ere to this haunt of brooding dust I came. [*Music*]

16 Softly along the road of evening, / In a twilight dim with rose, / Wrinkled with age, and drenched with dew, / Old Nod, the shepherd, goes. [*Nod*]

17 Three jolly Farmers / Once bet a pound / Each dance the other would / Off the ground. [*Off the Ground*]

18 Slowly, silently, now the moon / Walks the night in her silver shoon. [*Silver*]

19 Who said, 'Peacock Pie'? / The old king to the sparrow: / Who said, 'Crops are ripe'? / Rust to the harrow. [*The Song of the Mad Prince*]

20 Who said, 'Where sleeps she now? / Where rests she now her head, / Bathed in eve's loveliness'? / That's what I said.

21 Who said, 'Ay, mum's the word'? / Sexton to willow.

22 Life's troubled bubble broken.

23 Did not those night-hung houses, / Of quiet, starlit stone, / Breathe not a whisper – 'Stay, / Thou unhappy one; / Whither so secret away?' [*The Suicide*]

24 Too tired to yawn, too tired to sleep: / Poor tired Tim! It's sad for him. [*Tired Tim*]

25 Until we learn the use of living words we shall continue to be waxworks inhabited by gramophones. [In the *Observer*, 'Sayings of the Week', 12 May 1929]

SHELAGH DELANEY 1939–

26 I'm not frightened of the darkness outside. It's the darkness inside houses I don't like. [*A Taste of Honey*, Act I, sc. i]

27 Women never have young minds. They are born three thousand years old.

28 Do you like me more than you don't like me or don't you like me more than you do? [II. ii]

29 The cinema has become more and more like the theatre, it's all mauling and muttering.

FREDERICK DELIUS 1862–1934

30 Admirable, but what language was he singing in? [After a recital of his own songs. In Sir Thomas Beecham, *A Mingled Chime*, Ch. 19]

31 [When asked, 'Why do you write?'] Because I cannot swim. [From *Pourquoi écrivez-vous?*, in the *Sunday Times*, 7 Apr. 1985]

CECIL B. DE MILLE 1881–1959

32 What I have crossed out I didn't like. What I haven't crossed out I'm dissatisfied with. [Of a script. Attr. in Leslie Halliwell, *Filmgoer's Book of Quotes*]

WILLIAM DE MILLE 1878–1955

1 The trouble with Cecil [B. de Mille, William's brother] is that he always bites off more than he can chew – and then chews it. [In Leslie Halliwell, *Halliwell's Filmgoer's Companion*]

JACK DEMPSEY 1895–1983

2 Honey, I forgot to duck. [To his wife after losing his World Heavyweight title to Gene Tunney, 23 Sept. 1926. It was borrowed by President Reagan when he survived an assassination attempt, 1981]

LORD DENNING 1899–

3 To commit suicide was invading the prerogative of the Almighty, by rushing into his presence uncalled for. [Quoting Sir William Blackstone, an 18 cent. lawyer. Speech in House of Lords, 2 Mar. 1961]

NIGEL DENNIS 1912–1989

4 Most acts of assent require far more courage than most acts of protest, since courage is clearly a readiness to risk self–humiliation. [*Boys and Girls Come Out to Play*]

DR ALAN DENT 1905–1978

5 JAMES AGATE: Can ghosts be angry?
DENT: What else is there to do in the shades except take umbrage? [In James Agate, *Ego 2*, 10 Mar. 1934]

SENATOR CHAUNCEY DEPEW
   1834–1928

6 If you will refrain from telling lies about the Republican Party, I'll promise not to tell the truth about the Democrats. [Attr. in J. F. Parker, *If Elected, I Promise* ... See also 359:1]

JACQUES DÉRRIDA 1930–

7 *Il n'y a pas de hors-texte.* – There is nothing outside the text. [In David Lodge, *Nice Work*, 1, 2]

'BUDDY' DE-SYLVA 1895–1950 and
   LEW BROWN 1893–1958

8 The Best Things in Life are Free. [Title of song, 1927, music by Ray Henderson]

DUKE OF DEVONSHIRE 1895–1950

9 Good God, that's done it. He's lost us the tarts' vote. [On hearing Baldwin's attack on the press barons; see 23:6. See also 214:27, 361:12, 401:19. N. Rees, *Quote ... Unquote*, cites Harold Macmillan, the duke's son-in-law, as witness to the two remarks being made in 1931 at a by-election meeting]

PETER DE VRIES 1910–

10 We know the human brain is a device to keep the ears from grating on one another. [*Comfort Me with Apples*, Ch. 1]

11 I think I can say my childhood was as unhappy as the next braggart's.

12 They had lived originally in a dinette apartment in town but had begun to drift apart and needed more room.

13 He believed that the art of conversation was dead. His own small talk, at any rate, was bigger than most people's large.

14 The inscription *Gott Mit Uns*. I must ceaselessly resolve this legend as a declaration that one had gloves. [15]

15 Gluttony is an emotional escape, a sign something is eating us.

16 Probably a fear we have of facing up to the real issues. Could you say we were guilty of Noel Cowardice?

17 I wished now that I had gone to the restaurant across the street where the food had at least the merit of being tasteless. [18]

18 'Where would you place yourself philosophically?' ... 'A self-pitying stoic. I founded the school myself.' [*Consenting Adults*, Ch. 3]

19 'Do you believe in astrology?' 'I don't even believe in astronomy.' [4]

20 Marriage is to courtship as humming is to singing. [6]

21 It is not true that some people need less sleep than others. They simply sleep faster. [7]

22 Or look at it this way. Psychoanalysis is

a permanent fad. [*Forever Panting*, opening words]

1 One woman there had been upstaging us because she had been mugged on Montparnasse. [1]

2 No wonder you've got insomnia. All you ever do is sleep. [2]

3 We must love one another, yes, yes, that's all true enough, but nothing says we have to like each other. [*The Glory of the Hummingbird*, Ch. 1]

4 Anyone informed that the universe is expanding and contracting in pulsations of eighty billion years has a right to ask, 'What's in it for me?'

5 Our church is, I believe, the first split-level church in America. It has five rooms and two baths downstairs ... There is a small worship area at one end. [*The Mackerel Plaza*, Vol. Ch. 1]

6 It is the final proof of God's omnipotence that he need not exist in order to save us. [2]

7 The trouble with treating people as equals is that the first thing you know they may be doing the same thing to you. [*The Prick of Noon*, Ch. 1]

8 You can't be happy with a woman who pronounces both d.s. in Wednesday. [*Sauce for the Goose*]

9 There are times when parenthood seems nothing but feeding the mouth that bites you. [*Tunnel of Love*, Ch. 5]

10 The value of marriage is not that adults produce children but that children produce adults. [8]

11 I was thinking that we all learn by experience, but some of us have to go to summer school. [14]

12 Everybody hates me because I'm so universally liked. [*The Vale of Laughter*, Pt 1, Ch. 1]

13 I am not impressed by the Ivy League establishments. Of course they graduate the best – it's all they'll take, leaving to others the problem of educating the country. They will give you an education the way the banks will give you money – provided you can prove to their satisfaction that you don't need it. [4]

14 I love being a writer. What I can't stand is the paperwork. [In *Writer's Quotation Book*, ed. James Charlton]

LORD DEWAR 1864–1930

15 There are two classes of pedestrians in these days of reckless motor traffic: the quick and the dead. [In George Robey, *Looking Back on Life*, Ch. 28]

SERGE DIAGHILEV 1872–1929

16 *Étonne-moi!* – Astonish me! [To Jean Cocteau, who was dispirited through lack of encouragement, 1912. In *Journals of Jean Cocteau*, Vol. 1]

NEIL DIAMOND 1941–

17 Be as a page that aches for a word / Which speaks on a theme that is timeless. [Song: *Be*]

PHILIP K. DICK 1928–1982

18 Do Androids Dream of Electric Sheep? [Title of book]

19 'Bob, you know something ...' Luckman said at last. 'I used to be the same age as everyone else.' 'I think so was I,' Arctor said. 'I don't know what did it ...' 'Sure, Luckman,' Arctor said, 'you know what did it to all of us.' [*Scanner Darkly*, Ch. 12]

PAUL DICKSON 1939–

20 A businessman needs three umbrellas – one to leave at the office, one to leave at home and one to leave on the train. [In *Playboy*, 1978]

JOAN DIDION 1934–

21 That is one last thing to remember: *writers are always selling somebody out*. [*Slouching towards Bethlehem*, Preface]

MARLENE DIETRICH 1901–1992

22 Once a woman has forgiven her man, she must not reheat his sins for breakfast. [*Marlene Dietrich's ABC*]

23 Detectives are only policemen with

smaller feet. [In Hitchcock film *Stage Fright*, script by Whitfield Cook *et al.* from S. Jepson's *Man Running*]

1 Most women set out to try to change a man, and when they have changed him they do not like him. [In A. Andrews, *Quotations for Speakers and Writers*]

HOWARD DIETZ 1896–1983

2 *Ars gratia artis.* – Art for art's sake. [Motto of MGM film studios]

3 That's Entertainment. [Title of song in musical *The Band Wagon*]

ANNIE DILLARD 1945–

4 It is not you or I that is important. What is important is anyone's coming awake and discovering a place . . . this sparkled mineral sphere, our present world. [From *An American Childhood*, in *New Statesman and Society*, 10 June 1988]

5 I think the dying pray at the last not please but thank you as a guest thanks his host at the door. [*Pilgrim at Tinker Creek*, Ch. 15]

PHYLLIS DILLER 1917–

6 I'll tell you what I don't like about Christmas office parties – looking for a new job afterward. [In *Was It Good for You Too?*, ed. Bob Chieger]

ISAK DINESEN [KAREN BLIXEN] 1885–1962

7 It is a good thing to have a great sorrow. Or should human beings allow Christ to have died on the Cross for the sake of their toothaches? [*Last Tales*, 'Of Hidden Thoughts and Heaven']

8 The tropical night has the companionability of a Roman Catholic cathedral compared to the Protestant churches of the north, which let you in on business only. [*Out of Africa*, 'The Shooting Accident']

9 All my life I have held that you can class people according to how they may be imagined behaving to King Lear. ['Farah and I Sell Out']

10 Pride is faith in the idea that God had, when he made us. A proud man is conscious of the idea, and aspires to realize it. ['On Pride']

11 I wonder if it is really possible to be absolutely truthful when you are alone. Truth, like time, is an idea arising from, and dependent upon, human intercourse. What is the truth about a mountain in Africa that has no name and not even a footpath across it? [*Seven Gothic Tales*, 'The Roads Round Pisa']

12 What is man, when you come to think upon him, but a minutely set, ingenious machine for turning, with infinite artfulness, the red wine of Shiraz into urine? ['The Dreamers'. See also 269:13]

13 I pray thee, good Lord, that I may not be married. But if I am to be married, that I may not be a cuckold. But if I am to be a cuckold, that I may not know. But if I am to know, that I may not mind. ['The Poet'. A saying described as 'the bachelors' prayer']

14 Man and woman are two locked caskets, of which each contains the key to the other. [*Winter's Tales*, 'A Consolatory Tale']

DAVID DIOP 1927–1960

15 This is Africa / Your Africa / That grows again patiently obstinately / And its fruit gradually acquire / The bitter taste of liberty. [In Chinua Achebe, *Anthills of the Savannah*, 10]

LORD DIPLOCK 1907–1985

16 After all, that is the beauty of the common law; it is a maze and not a mortuary. [Morris v. C. W. Martin and Sons Ltd, 1966, in *Dictionary of Legal Quotations*, comp. Simon James and Chantal Stebbings]

WALT DISNEY 1901–1966

17 Supercalifragilisticexpialidocious. [Song in film musical *Mary Poppins*, words by Richard M. and Robert R. Sherman]

18 When You Wish Upon a Star. [Title of song in cartoon film *Pinocchio*, lyric by Ned Washington, music by Leigh Harline]

19 Who's Afraid of the Big Bad Wolf? [Title

of song in cartoon film *Silly Symphony*, lyric and music by Frank E. Churchill and Ann Ronell]

1 Some Day My Prince Will Come. [Title of song in cartoon film *Snow White*, lyric by Larry Morey]

2 Whistle While You Work. [Title of song in *Snow White*, lyric by Larry Morey]

3 Heigh ho, heigh ho! / It's off to work we go. [Song: *Heigh ho*, in *Snow White*]

4 Why should I run for Mayor when I'm already King? [On Ray Bradbury's suggesting that he should run for Mayor of Los Angeles. In the *Listener*, 7 Oct. 1982]

5 There is a natural hootchy-kootchy to a goldfish. [Attr.]

DOM GREGORY DIX 1901–1952

6 It is no accident that the symbol of a bishop is a crook, and the sign of an archbishop is a double-cross. [Quoted by Francis Brown in a letter to *The Times*, 3 Dec. 1977]

MORT DIXON 1892–1956

7 I'm looking over a four-leaf clover / That I overlooked before. [Song: *I'm Looking Over . . .*]

MILOVAN DJILAS 1911–

8 From now on the Party line is that there is no Party line. [Of Yugoslav Communist Party, 1951. In Fitzroy Maclean, *Disputed Barricade*, 15]

9 The New Class. [Title of book]

AUSTIN DOBSON 1840–1921

10 And I wove the thing to a random rhyme, / For the Rose is Beauty, the Gardener, Time. [*A Fancy from Fontenelle*]

11 The ladies of St James's! / They're painted to the eyes, / Their white it stays for ever, / Their red it never dies: / But Phyllida, my Phyllida! / Her colour comes and goes; / It trembles to a lily, – / It wavers to a rose. [*The Ladies of St James's*]

12 I intended an Ode, / And it turned to a Sonnet. [*Rose Leaves*]

13 For I respectfully decline / To dignify the

Serpentine, / And make *hors-d'œuvres* for fishes. [*To 'Lydia Languish'*]

FRANK DOBSON, MP 1940–

14 When Edwina Currie goes to the dentist, it's the dentist who needs the anaesthetic. [In the *Observer*, 14 Sept. 1986]

E. L. DOCTOROW 1931–

15 Like all art and politics, gangsterism is a very important avenue of assimilation into society. [In the *Observer*, 'Sayings of the Week', 7 Oct. 1990]

KEN DODD 1931–

16 The trouble with Freud is that he never played the Glasgow Empire Saturday night. [Interview in ATV programme *The Laughter Makers*. In *The Times*, 7 Aug. 1965]

17 How tickled I am! [Catchphrase in comedy act]

18 What a beautiful day for putting on a kilt, standing upside down in the middle of the road, and saying 'How's that for a table lamp?' [Running gag with many variants. In John Fisher, *Funny Way to be a Hero*, 'How Tickled I Am!']

19 My grandad goes to the Darby and Joan club. I don't know what he does there, but he's got three notches on his walking stick.

20 It's ten years since I went out of my mind. I'd never go back. [In M. Billington, *How Tickled I Am*, Ch. 4]

21 Men's legs have a terribly lonely life – standing in the dark in your trousers all day. [In the *Guardian*, 7 Apr. 1973]

SENATOR ROBERT J. DOLE 1923–

22 History buffs probably noted the reunion at a Washington party a few weeks ago of three ex-presidents: Carter, Ford, and Nixon – See No Evil, Hear No Evil, and Evil. [In *Oh, What an Awful Thing to Say!*, comp. W. Cole and L. Phillips]

'DULCIE DOMUM' [SUE LIMB] 1946–

23 Is love eternal, indestructible: does it, like throw-away plastic packaging, endure

beyond the grave? Own experience suggests that though love can initially degrade, it does, in the end, usefully biodegrade. [In the *Weekend Guardian*, 10–11 Mar. 1990]

1 Annoying to have to lie long after extra-marital relations have been broken off. Like hangover without intoxication. [In the *Weekend Guardian*, 31 Aug.–1 Sept. 1991]

WILLIAM DONALDSON 1935–

2 Dear Major-General Wyldbore Smith, I'm a blunt man, accustomed to plain speaking, so I'll come straight to the point. What's the going price for getting an honour? [*Henry Root Letters*, p. 247]

DR LY VA DONG [Vietnamese doctor resident in Britain]

3 We are Buddhists and we have no expectations. If you travel with the river you have to bend with the river. [In the *Observer*, 12 Mar. 1989]

J. P. DONLEAVY 1926–

4 I got disappointed in human nature as well and gave it up because I found it too much like my own. [*Fairy Tales of New York*, 2]

5 But Jesus, when you don't have any money, the problem is food. When you have money, it's sex. When you have both it's health, you worry about getting ruptured or something. If everything is simply jake then you're frightened to death. [*The Ginger Man*, Ch. 5]

6 When I die I want to decompose in a barrel of porter and have it served in all the pubs in Dublin. I wonder would they know it was me? [31]

ANTAL DORATI 1906–1988

7 What we do should only be recognizable to the orchestra, not the audience. We don't conduct the audience. There are too many conductors who mime. These mime what is being heard, whereas the conductor conducts what is not being heard, but will be in the flash of a second. [Interview at 80 in the *Guardian*, 9 Apr. 1986]

SARAH DOUDNEY 1843–1926

8 But the waiting time, my brothers, / Is the hardest time of all. [*Psalm of Life*, 'The Hardest Time of All']

JAMES DOUGLAS

9 I would rather put a phial of prussic acid in the hands of a healthy boy or girl than the book in question. [Review of Radclyffe Hall's *The Well of Loneliness* in the *Sunday Express*, 1928]

10 If only men could love each other like dogs, the world would be a paradise. [From the *Sunday Express*, in M. Bateman, *This England*, selections from the *New Statesman*, Pt I]

KEITH DOUGLAS 1920–1944

11 Remember me when I am dead / And simplify me when I'm dead. [*Simplify me when I'm dead*]

NATHAN E. DOUGLAS and HAROLD JACOB SMITH

12 It's the duty of a newspaper to comfort the afflicted and to flick the comfortable. [Said by Gene Kelly in film *Inherit the Wind*, based on play by Jerome Lawrence and Robert E. Lee. See also 139:9]

13 I may be rancid butter, but I'm on your side of the bread.

NORMAN DOUGLAS 1868–1952

14 It is the drawback of all sea-side places that half the landscape is unavailable for purposes of human locomotion, being covered by useless water. [*Alone*, 'Mentone']

15 Education is a state-controlled manufactory of echoes. [*How about Europe?*]

16 Bouillabaisse is only good because cooked by the French, who, if they cared to try, could produce an excellent and nutritious substitute out of cigar stumps and empty matchboxes. [*Siren Land*, 'Rain on the Hills']

17 Don Francesco was a fisher of men, and of women. He fished *ad maiorem Dei gloriam*, and for the fun of the thing. It was his way of taking exercise. [*South Wind*, Ch. 2]

1 You can tell the ideals of a nation by its advertisements. [6]

2 Many a man who thinks to found a home discovers that he has merely opened a tavern for his friends. [24]

SIR ALEC DOUGLAS-HOME [EARL OF HOME] 1903–

3 As far as the 14th Earl is concerned, I suppose Mr Wilson, when you come to think of it, is the 14th Mr Wilson. [BBC TV interview, 21 Oct. 1963. See also 406:2]

4 There are two problems in my life. The political ones are insoluble and the economic ones are incomprehensible. [Speech, Jan. 1964]

LADY CAROLINE DOUGLAS-HOME 1937–

5 He is used to dealing with estate workers. I cannot see how anyone can say he is out of touch. [On her father's becoming Prime Minister. In the *Daily Herald*, 21 Oct. 1963]

SIR ARTHUR CONAN DOYLE 1859–1930

6 It is an old maxim of mine that when you have excluded the impossible, whatever remains, however improbable, must be the truth. [*The Adventures of Sherlock Holmes*, 'The Beryl Coronet']

7 Singularity is almost invariably a clue. The more featureless and commonplace a crime is, the more difficult it is to bring it home. ['The Boscombe Valley Mystery']

8 You know my method. It is founded upon the observance of trifles.

9 A little monograph on the ashes of one hundred and forty different varieties of pipe, cigar, and cigarette tobacco.

10 Depend upon it, there is nothing so unnatural as the commonplace. ['A Case of Identity']

11 It has long been an axiom of mine that the little things are infinitely the most important.

12 Crime is common. Logic is rare. Therefore it is upon the logic rather than upon the crime that you should dwell. ['The Copper Beeches']

13 It is my belief, Watson, founded upon my experience, that the lowest and vilest alleys of London do not present a more dreadful record of sin than does the smiling and beautiful countryside.

14 A man should keep his little brain attic stocked with all the furniture that he is likely to use, and the rest he can put away in the lumber-room of his library, where he can get it if he wants it. ['Five Orange Pips']

15 It is quite a three-pipe problem. ['The Red-headed League']

16 I have nothing to do today. My practice is never very absorbing.

17 The giant rat of Sumatra, a story for which the world is not yet prepared. [*The Case Book of Sherlock Holmes*, 'The Sussex Vampire']

18 All other men are specialists, but his specialism is omniscience. [*His Last Bow*, 'The Bruce-Partington Plans']

19 But here, unless I am mistaken, is our client. ['Wisteria Lodge']

20 A cast of your skull, sir, until the original is available, would be an ornament to any anthropological museum. [*The Hound of the Baskervilles*, Ch. 1]

21 A study of family portraits is enough to convert a man to the doctrine of reincarnation. [13]

22 You know my methods, Watson. [*The Memoirs of Sherlock Holmes*, 'The Crooked Man']

23 'Excellent!' I cried. 'Elementary,' said he.

24 He [Professor Moriarty] is the Napoleon of crime. ['The Final Problem']

25 You mentioned your name as if I should recognize it, but beyond the obvious facts that you are a bachelor, a solicitor, a Freemason, and an asthmatic, I know nothing whatever about you. ['The Norwood Builder']

26 A long shot, Watson; a very long shot! ['Silver Blaze']

27 'Is there any point to which you would wish to draw my attention?'
'To the curious incident of the dog in the night-time.'

'The dog did nothing in the night-time.'

'That was the curious incident,' remarked Sherlock Holmes.

1 A bicycle certainly, but not *the* bicycle. I am familiar with forty-two impressions left by tyres. [*The Return of Sherlock Holmes*, 'Priory School']

2 Now, Watson, the fair sex is your department. ['The Second Stain']

3 I have been guilty of several monographs ... one 'Upon the Distinction Between the Ashes of the Various Tobaccos'. In it I enumerate 140 forms ... [*The Sign of Four*, Ch. 1]

4 In an experience of women that extends over many nations and three separate continents, I have never looked upon a face which gave a clearer promise of a refined and sensitive nature. [(Dr Watson), Ch. 2]

5 The most winning woman I ever knew was hanged for poisoning three little children for their insurance money.

6 I never make exceptions. An exception disproves the rule.

7 The Baker Street irregulars. [8]

8 Where there is no imagination there is no horror. [*A Study in Scarlet*, Ch. 5]

9 'I am inclined to think –' said I. 'I should do so,' Sherlock Holmes remarked impatiently. [*The Valley of Fear*, Ch. 1]

10 The vocabulary of 'Bradshaw' is nervous and terse, but limited.

11 Mediocrity knows nothing higher than itself, but talent instantly recognizes genius.

MARGARET DRABBLE 1939–

12 Lord knows what incommunicable small terrors infants go through, unknown to all. We disregard them, we say they forget, because they have not the words to make us remember ... By the time they learn to speak they have forgotten the details of their complaints, and so we never know. They forget so quickly, we say, because we cannot contemplate the fact that they never forget. [*The Millstone*, p. 127]

13 Perhaps the rare and simple pleasure of being seen for what one is compensates for the misery of being it. [*A Summer Bird-cage*, Ch. 7]

14 What fools middle-class girls are to expect other people to respect the same gods as themselves and E. M. Forster. [11]

RUTH DRAPER 1889–1956

15 Sometimes I think I'll not send him to school – but just let his individuality develop. [*The Children's Party*]

16 What is one of the lowest forms of life? ... The earth-worm – exactly! And what does he teach us? ... *To stretch – precisely!* ... He's probably the greatest stretcher in the world! [*A Class in Greek Poise*]

17 As a matter of fact, you know I am rather sorry you should see the garden now, because, alas! it is not looking at its best. Oh, it doesn't *compare* to what it was last year. [*Showing the Garden*]

18 And as for my poor *Glubjullas*, they never came up at all! ... I can't think why, because I generally have great luck with my *Glubjullas*.

JOHN DRINKWATER 1882–1937

19 Moon-washed apples of wonder. [*Moonlit Apples*]

HUGH DRUMMOND

20 Ladies and Gentlemen I give you a toast. It is 'Absinthe makes the tart grow fonder.' [In Seymour Hicks, *Vintage Years*, p. 46]

ALEXANDER DUBČEK 1921–1992

21 Socialism with a Human Face. [Motto of the Prague Spring. In *Rudé Právo*, 19 July 1968. Coined by Radovan Richta, according to *Penguin Dictionary of Political Quotations*, comp. Robert Stewart. See also 177:4]

AL DUBIN 1891–1945

22 Tiptoe through the tulips with me. [Song: *Tiptoe through the Tulips*, in musical *Gold Diggers of Broadway*]

23 You may not be an angel / 'Cause angels are so few, / But until the day that one comes along / I'll string along with you. [*Twenty Million Sweethearts*]

W. E. B. DU BOIS 1868–1963

24 The problem of the twentieth century is

the problem of the colour line. [Address to Pan-African Conference, London, 1900]

KEITH DUCKWORTH 1933–

1 It is better to be un-informed than ill-informed. [In Graham Robson, *Cosworth: The Search for Power*]

MICHAEL DUKAKIS 1933–

2 I find myself in the position of denying non-existent facts. [In the *Independent*, 10 Sept. 1988]

JOHN FOSTER DULLES 1888–1959

3 If EDC [European Defence Community] should fail, the United States might be compelled to make an 'agonizing reappraisal' of its basic policy. [Speech at North Atlantic Council, Paris, 14 Dec. 1953]

4 If you are scared to go to the brink, you are lost. [Interview in *Life* magazine, 16 Jan. 1956]

5 An obsolete conception, and except under very exceptional circumstances it is an immoral and short-sighted conception. [On neutralism. Speech at Iowa State College, 9 June]

6 The world is divided into two groups of people: the Christian anti-Communists, and the others. [Attr.]

DAME DAPHNE DU MAURIER 1907–1989

7 Last night I dreamt I went to Manderley again. [*Rebecca*, opening sentence]

8 It ... was full of dry rot. An unkind visitor said the only reason Menabilly still stood was that the woodworm obligingly held hands. [Interview]

AMERIGO DUMINI

9 My name is Dumini, twelve assassinations. [In George Seldes, *Sawdust Caesar*]

ISADORA DUNCAN 1878–1927

10 Farewell my friends. I am going to glory. [Last words before her scarf became fatally caught in car wheel. In M. Desti, *Isadora Duncan's End*, Ch. 25]

ELAINE DUNDY 1927–

11 I hate champagne more than anything in the world next to Seven-up. [*The Dud Avocado*, Ch. 1]

12 I find I always have to write SOMETHING on a steamed mirror. [See also 113:4]

13 It was one of those nights when the air is blood temperature and it's impossible to tell where you leave off and it begins. [9]

14 I mean, the question actors most often get asked is how they can bear saying the same things over and over again night after night, but God knows the answer to *that* is, don't we all *anyway*; might as well get paid for it.

IAN DUNLOP

15 Shock of the New: Seven Historic Exhibitions of Modern Art. [Title of book, 1972]

DOUGLAS DUNN 1942–

16 It is perfection, to be without hope. [*The Dilemma*]

EITHNE DUNNE [Irish actress] 1917–1988

17 Dear, this is the hardest bloody part I've ever played. [At her death. In obituary in the *Guardian*, 28 Dec. 1988]

FINLEY PETER DUNNE 1867–1936

18 Th' dead ar-re always pop'lar. I knowed a society wanst to vote a monyment to a man an' refuse to help his fam'ly, all in wan night. [*Mr Dooley in Peace and War*, 'On Charity']

19 'Th' American nation in th' Sixth Ward is a fine people,' he says. 'They love th' eagle,' he says, 'on th' back iv a dollar.' ['Oratory on Politics']

20 A fanatic is a man that does what he thinks th' Lord wud do if He knew th' facts iv th' case. [*Mr Dooley's Opinions*, 'Casual Observations']

21 Thrust ivrybody, but cut th' ca-ards.

22 Vice ... is a creature of such heejus mien ... that the more ye see it th' better ye like it. ['The Crusade against Vice']

REV. MGR JAMES DUNNE 1859–1934

1 The English and the Irish are very much alike, except that the Irish are more so. [In conversation, during the Irish Troubles]

2 The quiet Irishman is about as harmless as a powder magazine built over a match factory.

T. E. DUNVILLE

3 A little boy; / a pair of skates; / broken ice; / Heaven's gates! [Music-hall song. In John Fisher, *Funny Way to be a Hero*, 'The Little Dog Laughed . . .']

JACQUELINE DU PRÉ 1945–1987

4 Never mind about present affliction – any moment may be the next. [A favourite quotation of hers. In *With Great Pleasure*, ed. Alec Reid]

5 Don't let the sound of your own wheels drive you crazy.

WILL DURANT 1885–1981

6 The finger that turns the dial rules the air. [*What is Civilization?*]

JIMMY DURANTE 1893–1980

7 Everybody wants to get into da act. [Catchphrase in comedy act]

8 Goodnight Mrs Calabash – wherever you are. [Radio series sign-off, 1942]

9 Imagine waking up in the morning and knowing that's as good as you're going to feel all day. [Of teetotallers. In S. Hoggart, *On the House*, p. 132]

LEO DUROCHER [Manager of Brooklyn Dodgers, baseball team, 1951–4] 1906–

10 Nice guys finish last. [Of New York Giants. According to P. F. Boller Jr and J. George, *They Never Said It*, he really said, 'Nice guys. Finish last', 6 July 1946]

GERALD DURRELL 1925–

11 My Family and Other Animals. [Title of book, 1956]

LAWRENCE DURRELL 1912–1990

12 The Good Lord Nelson had a swollen gland, / Little of the scripture did he understand / Till a woman led him to the promised land / Aboard the Victory, Victory O. [*A Ballad of the Good Lord Nelson*]

13 The novel was invented for the ladies to kill time, / And time was invented to kill the novelist. [From *Endpapers and Inklings*, in *Antaeus: Journals, Notebooks and Diaries*, ed. D. Halpern, p. 93]

14 O men of the Marmion class, sons of the free. [*Mythology*]

15 I love to feel events overlapping each other, crawling over one another like wet crabs in a basket. [*Balthazar*, Pt I]

16 No one can go on being a rebel too long without turning into an autocrat. [II]

17 Somewhere between Calabria and Corfu, the blue really begins. [*Prospero's Cell*, Ch. 1]

18 Poggio's, where people go to watch each other watch each other. [*Tunc*, Ch. 1]

19 I have always tried to arrange my poems for balanced readability – like one does a vase of flowers. How silly it would be to arrange the flowers in the order of their picking. [On the chronology of his poems. *Selected Poems*, Introduction]

20 History is the endless repetition of the wrong way of living, and it'll start again tomorrow, if it's moved from here today. [In the *Listener*, 20 Apr. 1978]

21 Our cathedrals are like abandoned computers now, but they used to be prayer factories once.

22 You can't direct it and it refuses to come. It's as tiring as constipation. It might start tomorrow. [Of writing poetry. Interview in the *Guardian*, 28 May 1985]

23 A poem is what happens when an anxiety meets a technique. [Attr.]

WILL DURST

24 Everything you ever wanted in a Reagan administration, and less. Reagan-lite. [Of President Bush. In the *Guardian*, 27 Apr. 1990]

JEAN CLAUDE DUVALIER ['BABY DOC'] 1951–

1 I am as strong as a monkey's tail. [Boast in Feb. 1986 shortly before fleeing from Haiti]

MRS LILLIAN DYKSTRA

2 He [Thomas E. Dewey] is just about the nastiest little man I've ever known. He struts sitting down. [In J. T. Patterson, *Mr Republican*, Ch. 35]

BOB DYLAN 1941–

3 But to live outside the law, you must be honest. [Song: *Absolutely Sweet Marie*]

4 Beware of bathroom walls that've not been written on. [Song: *Advice for Geraldine on Her Miscellaneous Birthday*. See also 111:12]

5 'There must be some way out of here,' said the joker to the thief, / 'There's too much confusion, I can't get no relief.' [Song: *All along the Watchtower*]

6 All along the watchtower, princes kept the view.

7 How many roads must a man walk down / Before you call him a man? [Song: *Blowin' in the Wind*]

8 Yes, 'n' how many years can some people exist / Before they're allowed to be free? / Yes, 'n' how many times can a man turn his head, / Pretending he just doesn't see? / The answer, my friend, is blowin' in the wind.

9 A Hard Rain's A-Gonna Fall. [Title of song]

10 Oh God said to Abraham, 'Kill me a son.' / Abe says, 'Man, you must be puttin' me on.' [Song: *Highway 61 Revisited*]

11 He not busy being born / Is busy dying. [Song: *It's Alright, Ma (I'm Only Bleeding)*]

12 But even the president of the United States / Sometimes must have / To stand naked.

13 Money doesn't talk, it swears.

14 She takes just like a woman, yes, she does / She makes love just like a woman, yes, she does / And she aches just like a woman / But she breaks just like a little girl. [Song: *Just Like a Woman*]

15 How does it feel / To be without a home / Like a complete unknown / Like a rolling stone? [Song: *Like a Rolling Stone*]

16 She knows there's no success like failure / And that failure's no success at all. [Song: *Love Minus Zero/No Limit*]

17 I ain't gonna work on Maggie's Farm no more. [Song: *Maggie's Farm*]

18 Hey! Mr Tambourine Man, play a song for me. / I'm not sleepy and there is no place I'm going to. [Song: *Mr Tambourine Man*]

19 Ah, but I was so much older then, / I'm younger than that now. [Song: *My Back Pages*]

20 Keep a clean nose / Watch the plain clothes / You don't need a weatherman / To know which way the wind blows. [Song: *Subterranean Homesick Blues*]

21 Twenty years of schoolin' / And they put you on the day shift.

22 I'll let you be in my dreams if I can be in yours. [Song: *Talkin' World War III Blues*]

23 Come mothers and fathers / Throughout the land / And don't criticize / What you can't understand. [Song: *The Times They are A-Changin'*]

24 A song is anything that can walk by itself. [*Bringing It All Back Home*, sleeve notes]

25 [When asked whether he knew what his songs were about] Yeah, some of them are about ten minutes long, others five or six. [Interview, *c.* 1965]

26 Jesus, who's got time to keep up with the times? [Interview in the *Sunday Times*, 1 July 1984]

27 I don't call myself a poet, because I don't like the word. I'm a trapeze artist. [In J. Green, *Book of Rock Quotes*]

E

STEPHEN EARLY 1889–1951

1 Don't worry me – I am an 8 Ulcer Man on 4 Ulcer Pay. [Letter to President Truman, to whom line sometimes attr. because he adopted it; see 378:15. In W. Hillman, *Mr President*, Pt 5, p. 222]

MAX EASTMAN 1883–1969

2 I don't know why it is that we are in such a hurry to get up when we fall down. You might think we would lie there and rest awhile. [*The Enjoyment of Laughter*]

CLINT EASTWOOD 1930–

3 Go ahead, make my day. [In film *Sudden Impact*, screenplay by Joe Stinson]

ABBA EBAN 1915–

4 History teaches us that men and nations behave wisely once they have exhausted all other alternatives. [Speech in London, 16 Dec. 1970]

RICHARD EBERHART 1904–

5 Then the eighty-year-old lady with a sparkle, / A Cambridge lady, hearing of the latest / Suicide, said to her friend, turning off / TV for tea, 'Well, my dear, doesn't it seem / A little like going where you haven't been invited?' [*How It Is*]

JENNY ECLAIR

6 I can eat a man, but I'm not sure of the fibre content. [Interview in *The Times*, 16 Nov. 1985]

UMBERTO ECO 1932–

7 [A novel is] a machine for generating interpretations. [From *Reflections on the Name of the Rose*, in the *Observer*, 7 Apr. 1985]

8 They [the generation of 1968] thought of revolution as instant coffee. [In TV dialogue with Stuart Hall. In the *Listener*, 16 May]

SIR ARTHUR EDDINGTON 1882–1944

9 When Dr Watson watches rats in mazes, what he knows, apart from difficult inferences are certain events in himself. [*Science and the Unseen World*]

10 We used to think that if we knew one, we knew two, because one and one are two. We are finding that we must learn a great deal more about 'and'. [In *Dictionary of Scientific Quotations*, ed. A. L. Mackay]

ANTHONY EDEN, EARL OF AVON 1897–1977

11 REPORTER: If Mr Stalin dies, what will be the effect on international affairs?
EDEN: That is a good question for you to ask, not a wise question for me to answer. [Interview on board *Queen Elizabeth*, 4 Mar. 1953]

12 Everybody is always in favour of general economy and particular expenditure. [In the *Observer*, 'Sayings of the Week', 17 June 1956]

13 We are not at war with Egypt. We are in an armed conflict. [Speech in House of Commons, 4 Nov.]

LADY CLARISSA EDEN 1920–1985

1 During the last few weeks I have felt sometimes that the Suez Canal was flowing through my drawing room. [Of the Suez crisis, when opening Gateshead Conservative Association HQ, 20 Nov. 1956]

DUKE OF EDINBURGH see PRINCE PHILIP, DUKE OF EDINBURGH

THOMAS ALVA EDISON 1847–1931

2 Genius is one per cent inspiration and ninety-nine per cent perspiration. [Newspaper interview, 1903. In *Life*, Ch. 24]

3 They say Wilson has blundered. Perhaps he has but I notice he usually blunders forward. [In John dos Passos, *Mr Wilson's War*, Ch. 2, sect. x]

IRWIN EDMAN 1896–1954

4 Education is the process of casting false pearls before real swine. [In Frank Muir, *Frank Muir Book*]

KING EDWARD VII 1841–1910

5 Let me introduce you to the last king of England. [To Lord Haldane on introducing him to the Prince of Wales, afterwards George V. In D. Sommer, *Haldane of Cloan*, Ch. 15.]

KING EDWARD VIII [DUKE OF WINDSOR] 1894–1972

6 Something must be done. [Speech during tour of unemployment areas in South Wales, 18 Nov. 1936]

7 But you must believe me when I tell you that I have found it impossible to carry the heavy burden of responsibility and to discharge my duties as King as I would wish to do, without the help and support of the woman I love. [Abdication speech, 11 Dec.]

8 The thing that impresses me most about America is the way parents obey their children. [In *Look*, 5 Mar. 1957]

ILYA EHRENBURG 1891–1967

9 The Thaw. [Title of book]

ALBERT EINSTEIN 1879–1955

10 $E = mc^2$
Energy equals mass times the speed of light squared. [Statement of the mass–energy equivalence relationship]

11 The Lord God is subtle but he is not malicious. [Quip first made in May 1921, later carved in German above the fireplace of Fine Hall, the Mathematical Institute of Princeton University]

12 I cannot believe that God plays dice with the cosmos. [In the *Observer*, 'Sayings of the Week' 5 Apr. 1953, but used earlier in letter to Max Born, 4 Dec. 1926. See also 166:1]

13 Science without religion is lame, religion without science is blind. [Paper for conference on science, New York, 9/11 Sept. 1940]

14 If only I had known. I should have become a watchmaker. [Of his making the atom bomb possible, 1945]

15 The release of atom power has changed everything except our way of thinking, and thus we are being driven unarmed towards a catastrophe ... The solution of this problem lies in the heart of humankind. [To US National Commission of Nuclear Scientists, 24 May 1946]

16 Nationalism is an infantile disease. It is the measles of mankind. [*The World as I See It*]

17 If you want to find out anything from the theoretical physicists about the methods they use, I advise you to stick closely to one principle: Don't listen to their words, fix your attention on their deeds.

18 You have got the impression that contemporary physics is based on concepts somewhat analogous to the smile of the absent cat. [Comment on Viscount Samuel, *Essay in Physics*. In John Bowle, *Viscount Samuel*, Ch. 19]

19 As far as the laws of mathematics refer to reality, they are not certain, and as far as they are certain, they do not refer to reality. [In F. Capra, *The Tao of Physics*, Ch. 2]

20 We should take care not to make the intellect our god; it has, of course, powerful muscles, but no personality. [In *Barnes and Noble Book of Quotations*, ed. Robert I. Fitzhenry, 'Intellect']

1 Equations are important to me, because politics is for the present, but an equation is something for eternity. [In Stephen Hawking, *A Brief History of Time*, 'Albert Einstein']

2 Art is the expression of the profoundest thoughts in the simplest way. [In W. Neil, *Concise Dictionary of Religious Quotations*]

3 The process of scientific discovery is, in effect, a continuous flight from wonder. [In Laurence J. Peter, *Peter's Quotations*]

4 Everything should be made as simple as possible, but not simpler. [In *Reader's Digest*, Oct. 1977]

5 Common sense is the collection of prejudices acquired by age eighteen. [In *Scientific American*, Feb. 1976]

6 I know why there are so many people who love chopping wood. In this activity one immediately sees the results. [In Carl Seelig, *Albert Einstein*, Ch. 4.]

7 I don't believe in mathematics. [To Gustave Ferrière. In 5]

8 A theory can be proved by experiment; but no path leads from experiment to the birth of a theory. [In the *Sunday Times*, 18 July 1976]

9 Science can only state what is, not what should be. [From *Out of My Later Years*, in *Practical Wisdom*, ed. Frederick Ungar]

LOREN EISELEY 1907–1977

10 Every man contains within himself a ghost continent – a place circled as warily as Antarctica was circled two hundred years ago by Captain James Cook. [*The Unexpected Universe*, Ch. 1]

PRESIDENT DWIGHT D. EISENHOWER 1890–1969

11 Whatever America hopes to bring to pass in this world must first come to pass in the heart of America. [Inaugural presidential address, 20 Jan. 1953]

12 There is one thing about being President – nobody can tell you when to sit down. [In the *Observer*, 'Sayings of the Week', 9 Aug. 1953]

13 You have a row of dominoes set up. You knock over the first one, and what will happen to the last one is a certainty that it will go over very quickly. [On the strategic importance of Indochina. At press conference, 7 Apr. 1954]

14 The military-industrial complex. [Farewell radio and TV address as President, 17 Jan. 1961]

SIR EDWARD ELGAR 1857–1934

15 I always said God was against art and I still believe it. [After the catastrophic first performance of *The Dream of Gerontius*. Letter, Oct. 1900, in *Faber Book of Letters*]

T. S. ELIOT 1888–1965

16 Pray for us now and at the hour of our birth. [*Animula*]

17 Because I do not hope to turn again / Because I do not hope / Because I do not hope to turn. [*Ash Wednesday*, I]

18 Teach us to care and not to care / Teach us to sit still.

19 Lady, three white leopards sat under a juniper tree / In the cool of the day. [II]

20 At the first turning of the second stair / I turned and saw below / The same shape twisted on the banister. [III]

21 Redeem / The time. Redeem / The unread vision in the higher dream. [IV]

22 Will the veiled sister pray / For children at the gate / Who will not go away and cannot pray. [V]

23 Time present and time past / Are both perhaps present in time future, / And time future contained in time past. [*Four Quartets*, 'Burnt Norton', I]

24 Footfalls echo in the memory / Down the passage which we did not take / Towards the door we never opened / Into the rose-garden.

25 Human kind / Cannot bear very much reality.

26 At the still point of the turning world. [II]

27 In my beginning is my end. ['East Coker', I]

28 The intolerable wrestle / With words and meanings. [II]

29 The houses are all gone under the sea. / The dancers are all gone under the hill.

1 The wounded surgeon plies the steel / That questions the distempered part. [IV]

2 So here I am, in the middle way, having had twenty years – / Twenty years largely wasted, the years of *l'entre deux guerres*. [V]

3 Undisciplined squads of emotion.

4 In my end is my beginning.

5 I do not know much about gods; but I think that the river / Is a strong brown god. ['Dry Salvages', I]

6 The river is within us, the sea is all about us.

7 You are not the same people who left that station / Or who will arrive at any terminus, / While the narrowing rails slide together behind you. [III]

8 Not fare well, / But fare forward, voyagers.

9 Ash on an old man's sleeve / Is all the ash the burnt roses leave, / Dust in the air suspended / Marks the place where a story ended. ['Little Gidding', II]

10 The dove descending breaks the air / With flame of incandescent terror. [IV]

11 Here I am, an old man in a dry month, / Being read to by a boy. [*Gerontion*]

12 In the juvescence of the year / Came Christ the tiger.

13 After such knowledge, what forgiveness? Think now / History has many cunning passages, contrived corridors / And issues.

14 Tenants of the house, / Thoughts of a dry brain in a dry season.

15 The hippopotamus's day / Is passed in sleep; at night he hunts; / God works in a mysterious way – / The Church can feed and sleep at once. [*The Hippopotamus*]

16 We are the hollow men / We are the stuffed men / Leaning together. [*The Hollow Men*, I]

17 Here we go round the prickly pear / At five o'clock in the morning. [V]

18 Between the idea / And the reality / Between the motion / And the act / Falls the Shadow.

19 This is the way the world ends / Not with a bang but a whimper.

20 A cold coming we had of it, / Just the worst time of the year / For a journey. [*Journey of the Magi*]

21 When the evening is spread out against the sky / Like a patient etherised upon a table. [*Love Song of J. Alfred Prufrock*]

22 In the room the women come and go / Talking of Michelangelo.

23 The yellow fog that rubs its back upon the windowpanes.

24 I have measured out my life with coffee spoons.

25 I should have been a pair of ragged claws / Scuttling across the floors of silent seas.

26 And I have seen the eternal Footman hold my coat, and snicker, / And in short, I was afraid.

27 No! I am not Prince Hamlet, nor was meant to be; / Am an attendant lord.

28 I grow old ... I grow old ... / I shall wear the bottoms of my trousers rolled.

29 He always has an alibi, and one or two to spare: / At whatever time the deed took place – Macavity wasn't there! [*Macavity: The Mystery Cat*]

30 I am aware of the damp souls of housemaids / Sprouting despondently at area gates. [*Morning at the Window*]

31 To hear the latest Pole / transmit the Preludes, through his hair and fingertips. [*Portrait of a Lady*]

32 You will see me any morning in the park / Reading the comics and the sporting page. / Particularly I remark / An English countess goes upon the stage.

33 My smile falls heavily among the *bric-à-brac*.

34 The winter evening settles down / With smell of steaks in passage ways. [*Preludes*, I]

35 The worlds revolve like ancient women / Gathering fuel in vacant lots. [IV]

36 Birth, and copulation, and death. / That's all the facts when you come to brass tacks. [*Sweeney Agonistes*, 'Fragment of an Agon']

37 April is the cruellest month, breeding / Lilacs out of the dead land. [*The Waste Land*, 1]

1 I read, much of the night, and go south in the winter. [18]

2 And I will show you something different from either / Your shadow at morning striding behind you / Or your shadow at evening rising to meet you; / I will show you fear in a handful of dust. [27]

3 Madame Sosostris, famous clairvoyante, / Had a bad cold, nevertheless / Is known to be the wisest woman in Europe, / With a wicked pack of cards. [43]

4 Here, said she, / Is your card, the drowned Phoenician Sailor. [46]

5 Unreal City, / Under the brown fog of a winter dawn, / A crowd flowed over London Bridge, so many, / I had not thought death had undone so many. [60]

6 That corpse you planted last year in your garden, / Has it begun to sprout? Will it bloom this year? [71]

7 The Chair she sat in, like a burnished throne, / Glowed on the marble. [77]

8 The change of Philomel, by the barbarous king / So rudely forced. [99]

9 'Jug jug' to dirty ears. [103]

10 My nerves are bad to-night. Yes, bad. [111]

11 When Lil's husband got demobbed, I said – / I didn't mince my words, I said to her myself, / Hurry up please, it's time. [139]

12 Musing upon the king my brother's wreck / And on the king my father's death before him. [191]

13 O the moon shone bright on Mrs Porter / And on her daughter / They wash their feet in soda water. [199]

14 One of the low on whom assurance sits / As a silk hat on a Bradford millionaire. [233]

15 When lovely woman stoops to folly and / Paces about her room again, alone, / She smoothes her hair with automatic hand, / And puts a record on the gramophone. [253]

16 A woman drew her long black hair out tight / And fiddled whisper music on those strings / And bats with baby faces in the violet light / Whistled. [377]

17 Webster was much possessed by death / And saw the skull beneath the skin. [Whispers of Immortality]

18 Uncorseted, her friendly bust / Gives promise of pneumatic bliss.

19 Donne, I suppose, was such another / Who found no substitute for sense. / To seize and clutch and penetrate; / Expert beyond experience.

20 The clock has stopped in the dark. [The Family Reunion, II. iii]

21 Since golden October declined into sombre November / And the apples were gathered and stored, and the land became brown sharp points of death in a waste of water and mud. [Murder in the Cathedral, I]

22 Yet we have gone on living, / Living and partly living.

23 The last temptation is the greatest treason: / To do the right deed for the wrong reason.

24 Clear the air! clean the sky! wash the wind! take stone from stone and wash them. [II]

25 And the wind shall say 'Here were decent godless people; / Their only monument the asphalt road / And a thousand lost golf balls.' [The Rock, Pt 1]

26 He [Hardy] wrote sometimes overpoweringly well, but always very carelessly; at times his style touches sublimity without ever having passed through the stage of being good. [After Strange Gods]

27 We can say of Shakespeare, that never has a man turned so little knowledge to such a great account. [Lecture 'The Classics and the Man of Letters']

28 The only way of expressing emotion in the form of art is by finding an 'objective correlative'; in other words, a set of objects, a situation, a chain of events which shall be the formula of that particular emotion. [Selected Essays, 'Tradition and the Individual Talent']

29 After the erection of the Chinese Wall of Milton, blank verse has suffered not only arrest but retrogression. ['Christopher Marlowe']

30 The majority of poems one outgrows and outlives, as one outgrows and outlives the

majority of human passions. Dante's is one of those that one can only just hope to grow up to at the end of life. ['Dante']

1 Tennyson and Browning are poets, and they think; but they do not feel their thought as immediately as the odour of a rose. A thought to Donne was an experience; it modified his sensibility. ['Metaphysical Poets']

2 In the seventeenth century a dissociation of sensibility set in.

3 [Wit] involves, probably, a recognition, implicit in the expression of every experience, of other kinds of experience that are possible. ['Andrew Marvell']

4 It is our business, as readers of literature, to know what we like. It is our business as Christians, as *well* as readers of literature, to know what we ought to like. It is our business as honest men not to assume that what we like is what we ought to like. ['Charles Whibley']

5 The more perfect the artist, the more completely separate in him will be the man who suffers and the mind which creates. [In 'Palinurus' (Cyril Connolly), *The Unquiet Grave*]

6 Immature poets imitate; mature poets steal. [Quoted by Martin Amis in the *Observer*, 19 Oct. 1980]

7 Poetry is not the expression of, but the escape from, personality. [Quoted by Stephen Spender in the *Observer*, 30 Sept. 1984]

QUEEN ELIZABETH, THE QUEEN MOTHER 1900–

8 I'm glad we've been bombed. It makes me feel I can look the East End in the face. [To policeman, 13 Sept. 1940]

9 My favourite programme is 'Mrs Dale's Diary'. I try never to miss it because it is the only way of knowing what goes on in a middle-class family. [From the *Evening News*, in M. Bateman, *This England*, selections from the *New Statesman*, Pt IV]

10 Oh, do turn it off, it's so embarrassing unless one is there – like hearing the Lord's Prayer when playing canasta. [When the National Anthem was played at a televised Cup Final. In A. Andrews, *Quotations for Speakers and Writers*]

QUEEN ELIZABETH II 1926–

11 I think everybody really will concede that on this, of all days, I should begin my speech with the words 'My husband and I'. [Speech at Silver Wedding Banquet, Guildhall, London, 20 Nov. 1972. The phrase was used as far back as her Christmas Broadcast, 1953]

ALF ELLERTON

12 Belgium Put the Kibosh on the Kaiser. [Title of song of 1914–18 War, sung by Mark Sheridan]

DUKE ELLINGTON 1899–1974

13 Saddest tale told on land or sea / Is the tale they told / When they told the truth on me. [*Saddest Tale*]

MAXINE ELLIOTT 1873–1940

14 I would not marry God. [Cable when her engagement was rumoured. In D. Forbes Robertson, *Maxine*]

ALICE THOMAS ELLIS 1932–

15 To her, religion was mortality and appearance, and she kept it in the same compartment of her mind as her dinner napkins. [*The Clothes in the Wardrobe*, p. 50]

16 Men were made for war. Without it they wandered greyly about, getting under the feet of the women, who were trying to organize the really important things of life. [*The Sin Eater*, p. 70]

17 She detested Protestantism, from the pneumatic sterility of Milton to the ankle socks and hairy calves of the vicar's wife. [77]

18 In the army *they shot cowards*. Homoeopathy, surely, carried to its wildest extreme. [*The 27th Kingdom*, Ch. 15]

19 She is going to go on behaving beautifully and so I shall be forced to behave like a pig to establish the difference between us ... Was it the blameless wonderfulness of God that forced Satan to go and live in the pit, where he could leave his things lying around and put his feet on the table? [*Unexplained Laughter*, p. 24]

1 I'm quite hopeful about life after death. It's life before death I'm not terribly cheerful about. [Interview in the *Observer*, 1 Feb. 1987]

2 Men love women, women love children, children love hamsters, hamsters don't love anybody. [In BBC TV programme *Bookmark*, 16 Dec.]

3 I don't think they [her six children] had a deprived childhood, exactly, but I think I had a deprived motherhood. [In the *Sunday Times Magazine*, 19 June 1988]

HENRY HAVELOCK ELLIS 1859–1939

4 What we call progress is the exchange of one nuisance for another nuisance. [*Impressions and Comments*, 31 July 1912]

5 Every artist writes his own autobiography. [*The New Spirit*, 'Tolstoi', 11]

LUCY ELLMANN 1956–

6 It was Melissa who explained politics to Suzy early on: the Republicans like trees and animals and the countryside, the Democrats like cities and factories and pollution. [*Sweet Desserts*, 'The Heart Operation']

7 The English have adopted Central Heating like some kind of cargo cult ... All the English seem to know is they're supposed to have these sharp-looking metal objects scattered around the walls – they're not interested in heat. But what can one expect in a country where a plug on an electrical device is considered an optional extra? ['Banana Split']

8 Men like war: they do not hold much sway over birth, so they make up for it with death. Unlike women, men menstruate by shedding other people's blood. [In the *Observer Magazine*, 4 Oct. 1992]

BEN ELTON 1959–

9 No one is ever capable of swearing properly in any language other than their own. [*Stark*, 'Love among the Radicals']

BEN ELTON, RIK MAYALL 1958– and LISE MAYER

10 Blimey, that was a bit anarchic! [*The Young Ones Book*]

11 You are a complete and utter bastard!

12 Grown-ups are scared of spots. Spots mean pop music. Spots mean having fun, all things they're too square to understand ... They sneer at acne because they want you to be like them.

13 Even the wars were girly after the Vikings left.

14 Cliff had been worrying about all the things kids worry about – unemployment, the pigs, high rise, spray-on boredom.

15 Of course I'm a feminist. You have to be these days – it's the only way to pull the chicks. [From TV programme *The Young Ones*, in the *Observer*, 24 Apr. 1988]

PAUL ÉLUARD 1895–1952

16 *Adieu tristesse / Bonjour tristesse / Tu es inscrite dans les lignes du plafond.* – Farewell sadness, / Good day sadness. / You are written in the lines on the ceiling. [*La vie immédiate*]

17 *Qui n'a pas vu les ruines du ghetto / Ne connaît pas le destin de son corps.* – Anyone who has not seen the ruins of the ghetto does not know the destiny of his body. [*Varsovie la ville fantastique*]

SIR WILLIAM EMPSON 1906–1984

18 It seemed the best thing to be up and go. [*Aubade*]

19 The heart of standing is you cannot fly.

20 Waiting for the end, boys, waiting for the end. [*Just a Smack at Auden*]

21 Slowly the poison the whole blood stream fills ... / The waste remains, the waste remains and kills. [*Missing Dates*]

22 Seven Types of Ambiguity. [Title of book]

HARRY ENFIELD 1961–

23 Loadsamoney. [TV comic character that became catchphrase]

D. J. ENRIGHT 1920–

24 What odds / Whether the couples walk on the campus and look at / The moon or walk on the moon and look at the earth? /

Just so long as there's somewhere left to walk, to sit, to cycle, / And something left to look at. [*Addictions*]

LEO ENWRIGHT

1 I have a theory about Charles Haughey. Give him enough rope and he'll hang you. [On BBC Radio 4. In the *Guardian*, 31 Jan. 1992]

HANS MAGNUS ENZENSBERGER 1929–

2 What else is Europe but a conglomeration of mistakes? Mistakes that are so diverse that they complement and balance one another. Taken separately, we're each unbearable in our own way. [*Europe, Europe,* 'Polish Incidents']

NORA EPHRON 1941–

3 If you're looking for monogamy, you'd better marry a swan. [In screenplay of film *Heartburn*]

SUSAN ERTZ 1894–1985

4 Millions long for immortality who don't know what to do with themselves on a rainy Sunday afternoon. [*Anger in the Sky*, Ch. 5. See also 186:5]

SENATOR SAM ERVIN 1896–1985

5 That is not executive privilege. It is executive poppycock. [During the Watergate hearings, 1973. In McCrystal *et al.*, *Watergate: The Full Inside Story*]

RENÉ ETIEMBLE 1909–

6 *Parlez-vous Franglais?* [Title of book]

ANTHONY EUWER 1877–1955

7 As a beauty I'm not a great star. / Others are handsomer far; / But my face – I don't mind it / Because I'm behind it; / It's the folk out in front that I jar. [Limerick]

DAME EDITH EVANS 1888–1976

8 When a woman behaves like a man, why doesn't she behave like a nice man? [In the *Observer*, 'Sayings of the Week', 30 Sept. 1956]

9 Death is my neighbour now. [BBC radio interview, a week before her death, 14 Oct. 1976]

EVENING STANDARD

10 My own personal reaction is that most ballets would be quite delightful if it were not for the dancing. [In M. Bateman, *This England*, selections from the *New Statesman*, Pt I]

KENNY EVERETT 1944–

11 It's all done in the best possible taste. [Catchphrase in TV programme *The Kenny Everett Show*, early 1980s]

KURT EWALD

12 Our family is not yet so good as to be degenerating. [*My Little Boy*]

GAVIN EWART 1916–

13 He's very popular among his mates. / I think I'm Auden. He thinks he's Yeats. [*Complete Little Ones*, 'Seamus Heaney']

14 On the Last Day the wrecks will surface over the / sea. ['Resurrection']

15 Miss Twye was soaping her breasts in her bath / When she heard behind her a meaning laugh / And to her amazement she discovered / A wicked man in the bathroom cupboard. [*Miss Twye*]

16 Sex suppressed will go berserk, / But it keeps us all alive. / It's a wonderful change from wives and work / And it ends at half past five. [*Office Friendships*]

W. N. EWER 1885–1976

17 How odd / Of God / To choose / The Jews. [*How Odd*. See also 9:19]

F

CLIFTON FADIMAN 1904–

1 I encountered the mama of dada. [Of Gertrude Stein. *Party of One*, p. 90]

SIR NICHOLAS FAIRBAIRN, MP 1942–

2 The great benefit of the Scots is that they are the only identifiable, civilized European race who do not have the misfortune to have a government. [In the *Independent*, 'Quote Unquote', 16 Nov. 1991]

HANS FALLADA 1893–1947

3 *Kleiner Mann, was nun?* – Little Man, What Now? [Title of book]

FRANTZ FANON 1925–1961

4 However painful it may be for me to accept this conclusion, I am obliged to state it: for the black man there is only one destiny. And it is white. [*Black Skin, White Masks*, Introduction]

5 When people like me, they tell me it is in spite of my colour. When they dislike me, they point out that it is not because of my colour. Either way, I am locked into the infernal circle. [Ch. 1]

6 Violence is man re-creating himself. [*The Wretched of the Earth*, Ch. 1]

7 In guerrilla war the struggle no longer concerns the place where you are, but the place where you are going. Each fighter carries his warring country between his toes. [2]

8 The native intellectual, who takes up arms to defend his nation's legitimacy and who wants to bring proofs to bear out that legitimacy, who is willing to strip himself naked to study the history of his body, is obliged to dissect the heart of his body. [4]

ELEANOR FARJEON 1881–1965

9 Morning has broken / Like the first morning, / Blackbird has spoken / Like the first bird. [Hymn, from poem *Morning Song*]

10 The night will never stay, / The night will still go by, / Though with a million stars / You pin it to the sky; / Though you bind it with the blowing wind / And buckle it with the moon, / The night will slip away / Like sorrow or a tune. [*The Night Will Never Stay*]

HERBERT FARJEON 1887–1945

11 I've danced with a man, who's danced with a girl, who's danced with the Prince of Wales. [*Picnic*]

KING FAROUK OF EGYPT 1920–1965

12 There will soon be only five kings left – the Kings of England, Diamonds, Hearts, Spades and Clubs. [To Lord Boyd-Orr at Cairo Conference, 1948]

J. G. FARRELL 1935–1979

13 The Magistrate . . . had the red hair and ginger whiskers of the born atheist. [*The Siege of Krishnapur*, Pt 1, Ch. 1]

WILLIAM FAULKNER 1897–1962

14 No man can cause more grief than that

one clinging blindly to the vices of his ancestors. [*Intruder in the Dust*, Ch. 3]

1 The Swiss who are not a people so much as a neat clean quite solvent business. [7]

2 Maybe the only thing worse than having to give gratitude constantly all the time, is having to accept it. [*Requiem for a Nun*, Act II, sc. i]

3 Between grief and nothing I will take grief. [*The Wild Palms*]

4 If a writer has to rob his mother, he will not hesitate; the 'Ode to a Grecian Urn' is worth any number of old ladies. [In *Writers at Work*, ed. Malcolm Cowley, First Series]

5 The Long Hot Summer. [Title of film drawn from his stories. He had used the phrase originally in 1928]

6 Democracy is the refuge for your cousin or your uncle that failed in the peanut business. [Speech, 1957. In the *Guardian*, 26 Sept. 1988]

JEAN FAYARD

7 If the French were to play cricket they would all want to be 'batsmen' – the cynosure of all eyes – at the same time, just as nearly all of them want to be Prime Minister. [In *Strangers' Gallery*, ed. A. Synge]

GEORGE FEARON 1901–1972

8 I suppose you're really – an angry young man. [To John Osborne before the first staging of *Look Back in Anger*, 1956. In J. Osborne, *Almost a Gentleman*, Ch. 1. See also 293:16]

VIC [later LORD] FEATHER

9 Industrial relations are like sexual relations. It's better between two consenting parties. [In the *Guardian Weekly*, 8 Aug. 1976]

JULES FEIFFER 1929–

10 No one walks into a party without having a far better party going on inside his head. Every party is going to be that party until we get there. So the key to the boredom and tension at parties is that no one wants to be at the party he's at, he wants to be at the party he's missing. [*Ackroyd*, '1965, February 15']

11 Artists can colour the sky red because they *know* it's blue. Those of us who aren't artists must colour things the way they really are or people might think we're stupid. [*Crawling Arnold*]

12 I know she's alive. I saw her lip curl. [*Sick, Sick, Sick*]

13 There *are* no more policemen. Only police dogs. We've eliminated the middle man. [In the *Observer*, 7 July 1963]

14 At sixteen I was stupid, confused, insecure and indecisive. At twenty-five I was wise, self-confident, prepossessing and assertive. At forty-five I am stupid, confused, insecure and indecisive. Who would have supposed that maturity is only a short break in adolescence? [Caption to drawing in the *Observer*, 3 Feb. 1974]

15 Christ died for our sins. Dare we make his martyrdom meaningless by not committing them? [In Laurence J. Peter, *Peter's Quotations*]

BRUCE FEIRSTEIN 1953–

16 Real Men Don't Eat Quiche. [Title of book]

MARTY FELDMAN 1933–1983

17 Comedy, like sodomy, is an unnatural act. [In *The Times*, 9 June 1969]

18 I won't eat anything that has intelligent life, but I'd gladly eat a network executive or a politician. [In *Cook's Quotation Book*, ed. Maria Polushkin Robbins]

FEDERICO FELLINI 1920–1990

19 She [Greta Garbo] gave cinema the sacredness of mass. [On her death, in the *Independent*, 'Quote Unquote', 21 Apr. 1990]

JAMES FENTON 1949–

20 Oh let us not be condemned for what we are. / It is enough to account for what we do. / Save us from the judge who says: You are your Father's son, / One of your father's crimes – your crime is you. [*Children in Exile*]

1 It is not what they built. It is what they knocked down. / It is not the houses. It is the spaces between the houses. [*A German Requiem*]

EDNA FERBER 1887–1968

2 Being an old maid is like death by drowning, a really delightful sensation after you cease to struggle. [In R. E. Drennan, *Wit's End*, 'Completing the Circle']

LAWRENCE FERLINGHETTI 1919–

3 And he is the mad eye of the fourth person singular / of which nobody speaks. [*He*]

KATHLEEN FERRIER 1912–1953

4 Now I'll have *eine kleine Pause*. [In Gerald Moore, *Am I Too Loud?* Ch. 19. They were the last words he heard her speak, not long before her death]

RICHARD FEYNMAN 1918–1988

5 The most important hypothesis in all of biology, for example, is that everything that animals do, atoms do. In other words, there is nothing that living creatures do that cannot be understood from the point of view that they are made of atoms acting according to the laws of physics. [From *Feynman Lectures on Physics*, Vol. 1, in *Dictionary of Scientific Quotations*, ed. A. L. Mackay]

6 Only one thing is wrong with our noses. They are too far off the ground to be much use. [In the *Independent*, 17 Mar. 1988]

DAME GWEN FFRANGCON-DAVIES 1891–1992

7 My dear, I'm always nervous about doing something for the first time. [On facing death at 101. In the *Observer*, 'Sayings of the Week', 2 Feb. 1992]

ERIC FIELD

8 Towards the end of July 1914 . . . I worked out a draft schedule and wrote an advertisement headed 'Your King and Country need you'. [From *Advertising*, Ch. 2, in *Oxford Dictionary of Modern Quotations*, ed. Tony Augarde]

FRANK FIELD, MP 1942–

9 The House of Lords is a model of how to care for the elderly. [In the *Observer*, 'Sayings of the Week', 24 May 1981]

MICHAEL FIELD [KATHERINE BRADLEY 1846–1914 and EDITH COOPER 1862–1913]

10 His [George Moore's] smile is like sunshine on putty. [*Journals*]

GABRIEL FIELDING 1916–1986

11 It's not what men fight for. They fight in the last resort to impress their mothers. [*The Birthday King*, Ch. 3]

DOROTHY FIELDS 1905–1974

12 Hey! big spender, spend a little time with me. [Song: *Big Spender*]

13 I can't give you anything but love, baby! [Song: *I can't give . . .*]

14 On the Sunny Side of the Street. [Title of song]

DAME GRACIE FIELDS 1898–1979

15 We're going to string old Hitler / From the very highest bough / Of the biggest aspidistra in the world. [Song: *The Biggest Aspidistra*, words and music by J. Harper, W. Haines and T. Connor]

16 I took my harp to a party / But nobody asked me to play. [Song: *I Took my Harp*, words and music by Desmond Carter and Noël Gay]

17 Walter! Walter! Lead me to the altar, / I'll make a better man of you. [Song: *Walter, Walter*, words and music by Will E. Haines, Jimmy Harper and Noël Forrester]

18 Wish Me Luck as You Wave Me Goodbye. [Title of song, words and music by Phil Park and Harry Parr Davies]

19 What Can You Give a Nudist on His Birthday? [Title of song, words and music by Arthur Le Clerq]

W. C. FIELDS 1879–1946

20 A woman is like an elephant – I like to look at 'em, but I wouldn't want to own one. [In film *Mississippi*]

1 Never Give a Sucker an Even Break. [Title of film; the line originated with E. F. Albee]

2 I was in love with a beautiful blonde once, dear. She drove me to drink. That's the one thing I'm indebted to her for. [In *Never Give a Sucker an Even Break*]

3 It's a funny old world – a man's lucky if he gets out of it alive. [In film *You're Telling Me*]

4 [When asked whether he liked children] I do if they're properly cooked! [In *Fields for President*, Ch. 7]

5 A plumber's idea of Cleopatra. [Of Mae West in her films. In Louise Brooks, *Lulu in Hollywood*, 'The Other Face of W. C. Fields']

6 On the whole I would rather be in Philadelphia. [Supposed epitaph. In *Vanity Fair*, June 1925]

7 I must have a drink of breakfast. [In Leslie Halliwell, *Filmgoer's Book of Quotes*]

8 If at first you don't succeed, try again. Then quit. No use being a damn fool about it.

9 [When asked why he never drank water] Fish fuck in it.

10 We lived for days on nothing but food and water. [In Laurence J. Peter, *Peter's Quotations*]

11 Fifteen years ago, I made the line 'It ain't a fit night out for man or beast' a by-word by using it in my sketch in Earl Carroll's *Vanities*. [Letter, 8 Feb. 1944. Also used in his film *The Fatal Glass of Beer*, but he did not claim to have coined it]

EDWARD A. FILENE 1860–1937

12 Why shouldn't the American people take half my money from me? I took all of it from them. [In Arthur M. Schlesinger Jr, *The Coming of the New Deal*, Pt 7, Ch. 2, sect. iv]

ALBERT FINNEY 1936–

13 British people have a Socialist mind and a Conservative heart. [From the *Evening Standard*, 12 Nov. 1970, in *Chambers Film Quotes*, comp. Tony Crawley]

RONALD FIRBANK 1886–1926

14 'O God, help me, Dear,' she prayed, 'this little once, O Lord. For Thou knowest my rights.' [*Caprice*, III]

15 'I hear it's the Hebrew in Heaven, sir – Spanish is seldom spoken,' he exclaimed seraphically. [*The Eccentricities of Cardinal Pirelli*, Ch. 8. See also 101:9]

16 She made a ravishing corpse.

17 'I've never travelled,' Dona Consolation blandly confessed, 'but I dare say, dear, you can't judge Egypt by *Aïda*.' [9]

18 His Weariness the Prince entered the room in all his tinted Orders. [*The Flower beneath the Foot*, Ch. 1]

19 'O, help me heaven,' she prayed, 'to be decorative and to do right.'[2]

20 Beneath the strain of expectation even the little iced sugar cakes upon the tea-table looked green with worry. [3]

21 I feel his books are all written in hotels with the bed unmade at the back of the chair. [4]

22 I remember the average curate at home was something between a eunuch and a snigger.

23 'Basta!' his master replied with all the brilliant glibness of the Berlitz-school. [5]

24 She looks at other women as though she would inhale them.

25 It is said, I believe, that to behold the Englishman at his *best* one should watch him play tip-and-run. [14]

26 As a novelist he was almost successful. His books were watched for . . . but without impatience. [*Vainglory*, 2]

27 The world is disgracefully managed, one hardly knows to whom to complain. [10]

28 All millionaires love a baked apple. [13]

29 She stands, I fear, poor thing, now, for something younger than she looks. [*Valmouth*, Ch. I]

30 'I know of no joy,' she airily began, 'greater than a cool white dress after the sweetness of confession.' [4]

31 And *so* poorly and *so* run down. She says her blood is nothing but rose-water.

32 There was really no joy in pouring out one's sins while he sat assiduously picking his nose. [6]

LOUIS FISCHER 1896–1970

1 But you can burn your fingers on your own chestnuts. [On Stalin's 'burning chestnuts' speech; see 356:6. In the *Nation*, 6 Jan. 1940]

CARRIE FISHER 1956–

2 I'm a product of Hollywood. Fantasy is not unnatural to me: it's my reality. Hollywood people are like everyone else, only more so. They depict reality as opposed to living it. [Interview in the *Weekend Guardian*, 12–13 Jan. 1991]

H. A. L. FISHER 1856–1940

3 Men wiser and more learned than I have discerned in history a plot, a rhythm, a predetermined pattern. These harmonies are concealed from me. I can see only one emergency following on another. [*A History of Europe*, Preface]

4 W.C. [Winston Churchill] is a bigger danger than the Germans by a long way in what is just now imminent in the Dardanelles. [Letter to Bonar Law, May 1915. In Robert Blake, *The Unknown Prime Minister*]

ADMIRAL SIR JOHN [later LORD] FISHER 1841–1920

5 Never contradict
Never explain
Never apologize
(Those are the secrets of a happy life!)
[Letter to *The Times*, 5 Sept. 1919]

M. F. K. FISHER 1908–1992

6 Probably one of the most private things in the world is an egg until it is broken. [From *How to Cook a Wolf*, in Jonathon Green, *Consuming Secrets*]

MELVIN FISHMAN

7 The holes in your Swiss cheese are somebody else's Swiss cheese. [In *The Times Higher Education Supplement*, 15 Jan. 1982]

CLYDE FITCH 1865–1909

8 The Woman in the Case. [Title of play]

ALBERT H. FITZ

9 You are my honey, honeysuckle, I am the bee. [Song: *The Honeysuckle and the Bee*, music by W. H. Penn]

F. SCOTT FITZGERALD 1896–1940

10 In a real dark night of the soul it is always three o'clock in the morning, day after day. [*The Crack-up*]

11 Though the Jazz Age continued, it became less and less of an affair of youth. The sequel was like a children's party taken over by the elders. ['Echoes of the Jazz Age']

12 One of those men who reach such an acute limited excellence at twenty-one that everything afterward savours of anti-climax. [*The Great Gatsby*, Ch. 1]

13 She told me with pride that her husband had photographed her a hundred and twenty-seven times since they had been married. [2]

14 I've been drunk for about a week now, and I thought it might sober me up to sit in a library. [3]

15 Everyone suspects himself of at least one of the cardinal virtues, and this is mine: I am one of the few honest people that I have ever known.

16 There are only the pursued, the pursuing, the busy, and the tired. [4]

17 If you want to kiss me any time during the evening, Nick, just let me know and I'll be glad to arrange it for you. Just mention my name. [6]

18 'What'll we do with ourselves this afternoon?' cried Daisy, 'and the day after that, and the next thirty years?' [7]

19 Her voice is full of money.

20 Gatsby believed in the green light, the orgastic future that year by year recedes before us. It eluded us then, but that's no matter – tomorrow we will run faster, stretch out our arms further . . . And one fine morning – So we beat on, boats against the current, borne back ceaselessly into the past. [9]

21 It's not a slam at *you* when people are rude – it's a slam at the people they've met before. [*The Last Tycoon*, Ch. 1]

1 Writers aren't exactly people. Or, if they're any good, they're a whole *lot* of people trying so hard to be one person.

2 There are no second acts in American lives. ['Notes']

3 His life was a sort of dream, as are most lives with the mainspring left out. [*Notebooks*, C]

4 A man says to another man: 'I'd certainly like to steal your girl.' Second man: 'I'd give her to you, but she's part of a set.' [E]

5 Show me a hero and I will write you a tragedy.

6 Switzerland is a country where very few things begin, but many things end.

7 Hospitality is a wonderful thing. If people really want you, they'll have you even if the cook has just died in the house of small-pox.

8 She was one of those people who would just as soon starve in a garret with a man – if she didn't have to.

9 'What kind of man was he?' 'Well, he was one of those men who come in a door and make any woman with them look guilty.'

10 When he buys his ties he has to ask if gin will make them run.

11 Let me tell you about the very rich. They are different from you and me. [*The Rich Boy*. In *Notebooks*, E, Fitzgerald records Hemingway's rejoinder: 'Yes, they have more money'; but elsewhere Hemingway spoke thus of the rich and Mary Colum gave the put-down]

12 He was not the frock-coated and impressive type of millionaire which has become so frequent since the war. He was rather the 1910 model – a sort of cross between Henry VIII and 'our Mr Jones will be in Minneapolis on Friday'. [H]

13 I entertained on a cruising trip that was so much fun that I had to sink my yacht to make my guests go home. [K]

14 Once tried to get up a ship's party on a ferry boat.

15 When he urinated, it sounded like night prayer. [M]

16 Listen, little Elia, draw your chair up close to the edge of the precipice and I'll tell you a story. [N]

17 An author ought to write for the youth of his own generation, the critics of the next, and the schoolmasters of ever afterwards.

18 Mother always feels the girl is safe if she's with me . . . If I start to hold somebody's hand they laugh at me, and *let* me, just as if it wasn't part of them. As soon as I get hold of a hand they sort of disconnect it from the rest of them. [*This Side of Paradise*, Bk I, Ch. 1]

19 He differed from the healthy type that was essentially middle-class – he never seemed to perspire. [2]

20 Beware of the artist who's an intellectual also. The artist who doesn't fit. [II. 5]

21 One thing I know. If living isn't a seeking for the grail it may be a damned amusing game.

22 A big man has no time really to do anything but just sit and be big. [III. 2]

23 A great social success is a pretty girl who plays her cards as carefully as if she were plain. [Undated letter to Frances Scott Fitzgerald]

24 All good writing is *swimming under water* and holding your breath.

25 Often I think writing is a sheer paring away of oneself leaving always something thinner, barer, more meagre. [Letter to Frances Scott Fitzgerald, 27 Apr. 1940]

26 First you take a drink, then the drink takes a drink, then the drink takes you. [In Jules Feiffer, *Ackroyd*, '1964, May 7'. Elsewhere attr. to Sinclair Lewis]

PENELOPE FITZGERALD 1916–

27 Politics and business can be settled by influence, cooks and doctors can only be promoted on their skill. [*Innocence*, 16]

28 Patience is passive, resignation is active. [32]

29 Duty is what no-one else will do at the moment. [*Offshore*, 1]

BOB FITZSIMMONS 1862–1917

30 The bigger they come, the harder they fall. [Before fight with J. Jeffries, San Francisco, 9 June 1899]

BUD FLANAGAN 1896–1968

1 Underneath the arches / We dream our dreams away. [Song: *Underneath the Arches*]

2 Run, Rabbit. [Title of song, words by Noël Gay and Ralph Butler]

MICHAEL FLANDERS 1922–1975

3 Eating people is wrong. [Song: *The Reluctant Cannibal*, music by Donald Swann]

JAMES ELROY FLECKER 1884–1915

4 For pines are gossip pines the wide world through. [*Brumana*]

5 West of these out to seas colder than the Hebrides I must go, / Where the fleet of stars is anchored and the young star-captains glow. [*The Dying Patriot*]

6 The dragon-green, the luminous, the dark, the serpent-haunted sea. [*The Gates of Damascus*, 'West Gate']

7 We who with songs beguile your pilgrimage / And swear that Beauty lives though lilies die, / We poets of the proud old lineage / Who sing to find your hearts, we know not why, – / What shall we tell you? Tales, marvellous tales / Of ships and stars and isles where good men rest. [*The Golden Journey to Samarkand*, Prologue]

8 When the great markets by the sea shut fast / All that calm Sunday that goes on and on: / When even lovers find their peace at last, / And Earth is but a star, that once had shone.

9 And some to Mecca turn to pray, and I toward thy bed, Yasmin. [*Hassan*, I. ii]

10 For one night or the other night / Will come the Gardener in white, and gathered flowers are dead, Yasmin.

11 Why should the dead be wiser than the living? The dead know only this – that it was better to be alive. [V. i]

12 For lust of knowing what should not be known, / We take the Golden Road to Samarkand. [ii]

13 We are the Pilgrims, master; we shall go / Always a little further; it may be / Beyond that last blue mountain barred with snow / Across that angry or that glimmering sea.

14 What would ye, ladies? It was ever thus. / Men are unwise and curiously planned.

15 I have seen old ships sail like swans asleep / Beyond the village which men still call Tyre. [*The Old Ships*]

16 And with great lies about his wooden horse / Set the crew laughing and forgot his course.

17 It was so old a ship – who knows, who knows? / And yet so beautiful, I watched in vain / To see the mast burst open with a rose / And the whole deck put on its leaves again.

18 A ship, an isle, a sickle moon – / With few but with how splendid stars / The mirrors of the sea are strewn / Between their silver bars. [*A Ship, an Isle, a Sickle Moon*]

19 And old Maeonides the blind / Said it three thousand years ago. [*To a Poet a Thousand Years Hence*]

IAN FLEMING 1908–1964

20 A medium vodka dry martini – with a slice of lemon peel. Shaken and not stirred. [*Dr No*, Ch. 14]

21 Dangerous at both ends and uncomfortable in the middle. [Attr. description of the horse. In *Sunday Times*, 9 Oct. 1966]

CYRIL FLETCHER 1913–

22 Dreaming of thee, dreaming of thee, / Dreaming oh my darling love of thee. [Refrain which became this comedian's catchphrase from a comic recitation of a serious ode by Edgar Wallace. He has written various parodies on it]

23 Pin back your lug-'oles. Odd Ode No. 1 coming up. [Routine in variety and radio comedy act]

24 This is the tale of Margery Spicer / Who leant against a bacon slicer. / And as she jumped back murmured 'Coo, / I think I've lost a slice or two.' . . . / When she got home again she found / The errand boy had called around. / A bag and grocer's bill she saw, / For '5 back rashers one and four'. / She said 'This 'ere ain't half a caution, / They've sent me back my missing portion.' ['Odd Ode': *Margery Spicer*]

25 A fool and his money are soon parted.

What I want to know is how they got together in the first place. [In BBC radio programme, 28 May 1969]

1 There is a compensation for being over forty ... I now do my crossword puzzles in ink. [In BBC radio programme *Does the Team Think?* See also 347:6]

ERROL FLYNN 1909–1959

2 My problem lies in reconciling my gross habits with my net income. [In Jane Mercer, *Great Lovers of the Movies*]

3 If there's anyone listening to whom I owe *money*, I'm prepared to forget it if you are. [In broadcast before leaving Australia. In Leslie Halliwell, *Filmgoer's Book of Quotes*]

MARSHAL FOCH 1851–1929

4 My centre is giving way, my right is in retreat; situation excellent. I am attacking. [Message to Joffre, 8 Sept. 1914, on the eve of First Battle of the Marne]

5 *Victoire, c'est la Volonté!* – The will to conquer is the first condition of victory. [In B. Tuchman, *The Guns of August*, Ch. 3]

JOHN FOLEY

6 Old soldiers never die; / They only fade away! [Song of 1914–18 War, ascr. to Foley in *Oxford Dictionary of Modern Quotations*, ed. Tony Augarde]

HENRY FONDA 1905–1982

7 The best actors do not let the wheels show. [In *Barnes and Noble Book of Quotations*, ed. Robert I. Fitzhenry, 'Acting']

JANE FONDA 1937–

8 A man has every season while a woman only has the right to spring. [In the *Observer*, 'Sayings of the Week', 17 Sept. 1989]

MICHAEL FOOT 1913–

9 A Royal Commission is a broody hen sitting on a china egg. [Speech in House of Commons, 1964]

10 Men of power have no time to read; yet the men who do not read are unfit for power. [*Debts of Honour*]

11 Even a British revolution could not be made with rose-water. [Of Aneurin Bevan. In the *Listener*, 18/25 Dec. 1986]

12 Years later Beaverbrook introduced me to H. G. Wells. He was good, but not as good as his books. [In interview in John Mortimer, *In Character*]

13 It's quite a change to have a Prime Minister who hasn't got any political ideas at all. [Of John Major. In the *Observer*, 'Sayings of the Week', 24 Feb. 1991]

FORD MADOX FORD 1873–1939

14 You cannot be absolutely dumb when you live with a person unless you are an inhabitant of the North of England or the State of Maine. [*The Good Soldier*, Pt III, Ch. 4]

PRESIDENT GERALD FORD 1913–

15 I am a Ford, not a Lincoln ... I am proud – very proud – to be one of 200 million Americans. [On becoming Vice-President, 6 Dec. 1973]

16 I guess it just proves that in America anyone can be President. [On becoming President. In Richard Reeves, *A Ford, Not a Lincoln*, Ch. 4]

HENRY FORD 1863–1947

17 History is more or less bunk. [Interview in the *Chicago Tribune*, 25 May 1916]

18 Any colour, so long as it's black. [Advertisement for Model-T Ford car. Attr. in Allan Nevins, *Ford*, Vol. 2, Ch. 15]

19 What we call evil is simply ignorance bumping its head in the dark. [In the *Observer*, 'Sayings of the Week', 16 Mar. 1930]

20 Exercise is bunk. If you are healthy, you don't need it: if you are sick, you shouldn't take it. [Attr.]

LENA GUILBERT FORD 1870–1916

21 Keep the home-fires burning while your hearts are yearning, / Though your lads are far away, they dream of home. / There's a silver lining through the dark cloud shining: / Turn the dark cloud inside out, till the boys come home. [*Keep the Home Fires Burning*,

music by Ivor Novello, also sometimes credited with first line]

LIEUTENANT-COMMANDER FORGY
[US Naval Chaplain] 1908–1983

1 Praise the Lord and pass the ammunition. [Said at Pearl Harbor, 7 Dec. 1941]

GEORGE FORMBY 1905–1961

2 I'm leaning on a lamp-post at the corner of the street, / In case a certain little lady walks by. [Song: *Leaning on a Lamp-post*, words and music by Noël Gay, in film *Feather Your Nest*]

3 I'll climb this blinking ladder till I get right to the top. / The blushing bride she looks divine, / The bridegroom he is doing fine, / I'd rather have his job than mine, / When I'm cleaning windows. [Song: *When I'm Cleaning Windows*, words and music in collab. F. E. Cliffe and H. Gifford, originally in film *Keep Your Seats Please*]

4 With My Little Stick of Blackpool Rock. [Title of song, words and music by H. Gifford and F. E. Cliffe]

5 If women like them like men like those, / Then why don't women like me? [Song in *Utterly Trivial Knowledge: The Music Game*, ed. John Denny]

E. M. FORSTER 1879–1970

6 It is not that the Englishman can't feel – it is that he is afraid to feel. He has been taught at his public school that feeling is bad form. He must not express great joy or sorrow, or even open his mouth too wide when he talks – his pipe might fall out if he did. [*Abinger Harvest*, 'Notes on the English Character']

7 American women shoot the hippopotamus with eyebrows made of platinum. ['Mickey and Minnie']

8 How rare, how precious is frivolity! How few writers can prostitute all their powers! They are always implying 'I am capable of higher things.' ['Ronald Firbank']

9 Yes – oh dear, yes – the novel tells a story. [*Aspects of the Novel*, 2]

10 *Ulysses* . . . is a dogged attempt to cover the universe with mud. [6]

11 One was left, too, with a gap in Christianity: the canonical gospels do not record that Christ laughed or played. Can a man be perfect if he never laughs or plays? Krishna's jokes may be vapid, but they bridge a gap. [*The Hill of Devi*, 'Gokul Ashtami']

12 Only connect! [*Howards End*, epigraph]

13 They [railway termini] are our gates to the glorious and the unknown. Through them we pass out into adventure and sunshine, and to them, alas! we return. [Ch. 2]

14 Beethoven's Fifth Symphony is the most sublime noise that has ever penetrated into the ear of man. [5]

15 Brahms, for all his grumbling and grizzling, had never guessed what it felt like to be suspected of stealing an umbrella.

16 We are not concerned with the very poor. They are unthinkable, and only to be approached by the statistician or the poet. [6]

17 He believed in sudden conversion, a belief which may be right, but which is peculiarly attractive to the half-baked mind.

18 To speak against London is no longer fashionable. The Earth as an artistic cult has had its day. [13]

19 Give Mr Bast money and don't worry about his ideals. He'll pick up those for himself. [15]

20 There is much to be said for apathy in education. [*Maurice*, Ch. 1]

21 Religion is far more acute than science, and if it only added judgement to insight, would be the greatest thing in the world. [44]

22 Ronny approved of religion as long as it endorsed the National Anthem, but he objected when it attempted to influence his life. [*A Passage to India*, Ch. 5]

23 She felt increasingly . . . that, though people are important, the relations between them are not. [13]

24 'Can you always tell whether a stranger is your friend?' 'Yes.' 'Then you are an Oriental.' [36]

25 Look at them [the Jews] in the railway carriage now. Their faces are anxious and eloquent of past rebuffs. But they are travel-

ling First. [*Pharos and Pharillon*, 'Philo's Little Trip']

1 If I had to choose between betraying my *country* and betraying my *friend*, I hope I should have the guts to betray my *country*. [*Two Cheers for Democracy*, 'What I Believe']

2 So Two cheers for Democracy: one because it admits variety and two because it permits criticism. Two cheers are quite enough; there is no occasion to give three. Only Love the Beloved Republic deserves that. [Final sentence quotes Swinburne]

3 I suggest that the only books that influence us are those for which we are ready, and which have gone a little farther down our particular path than we have yet got ourselves. ['Books That Influenced Me']

4 In no book have I got down more than the people I like, the person I think I am, and the people who irritate me. This puts me among the large body of authors who are not really novelists, and have to get on as best they can with these three categories. [In *Writers at Work*, ed. Malcolm Cowey, First Series]

5 Spoon feeding in the long run teaches us nothing but the shape of the spoon. [In the *Observer*, 'Sayings of the Week', 7 Oct. 1951]

6 One has two duties – to be worried and not to be worried. [4 Jan. 1959]

7 There are writers like Cyril Connolly who give pleasure a bad name. [Attr. by Geoffrey Grigson in the *Guardian*, 30 Sept. 1976]

BRUCE FORSYTH 1928–

8 Didn't he [or she] do well! [Catchphrase in BBC TV programme *The Generation Game*, from early 1970s]

9 Nice to see you – to see you, nice.

FREDERICK FORSYTH 1938–

10 Everyone seems to remember with great clarity what they were doing on November 22nd, 1963, at the precise moment they heard President Kennedy was dead. [*The Odessa File*, opening words. See also 173:1]

SIR GEORGE FOSTER 1847–1931

11 In these somewhat troublesome days

when the great Mother Empire stands splendidly isolated in Europe. [Speech in Canadian House of Commons, 16 Jan. 1896]

MICHEL FOUCAULT 1926–1984

12 One thing in any case is certain: man is neither the oldest nor the most constant problem that has been posed for human knowledge. [*The Order of Things*, Ch. 10, sect. vi]

13 As an archaeology of our thought easily shows, man is an invention of recent date. And one perhaps nearing its end.

JOHN FOWLES 1926–

14 The more abhorrent a news item the more comforting it was to be the recipient since the fact that it had happened elsewhere proved that it had not happened here, was not happening here, and would therefore never happen here. [*The Ebony Tower*, 'Poor Koko']

15 In essence the Renaissance was simply the green end of one of civilization's hardest winters. [*The French Lieutenant's Woman*, Ch. 10]

16 We all write poems; it is simply that poets are the ones who write in words. [19]

17 All perfect republics are perfect nonsense. The craving to risk death is our last great perversion. We come from night, we go into night. Why live in night? [*The Magus*, rev. edn, Ch. 19]

18 It is not only species of animal that die out, but whole species of feeling. And if you are wise you will never pity the past for what it did not know, but pity yourself for what it did. [24]

19 That is the great distinction between the sexes. Men see objects, women see the relationship between objects. Whether the objects need each other, love each other, match each other. It is an extra dimension of feeling we men are without and one that makes war abhorrent to all real women – and absurd. [52]

W. T. R. FOX 1912–

20 The Super Powers. [Title of book, 1944,

coining the phrase; subtitled 'Their Responsibility for Peace']

LEO FRAIN

1 A completely planned economy ensures that when no bacon is delivered, no eggs are delivered at the same time. [In the *Sunday Telegraph*, Jan. 1965]

ANATOLE FRANCE 1844–1924

2 In every well-governed state wealth is a sacred thing; in democracies it is the only sacred thing. [*Penguin Island*]

3 *Le bon critique est celui qui raconte les aventures de son âme au milieu des chefs-d'œuvre.* – A good critic is one who narrates the adventures of his mind among masterpieces. [*La vie littéraire*, I, Preface]

GENERAL FRANCO 1892–1975

4 The destiny of history has united you with myself and the Duce in an indissoluble way. [Letter to Adolf Hitler]

ANNE FRANK 1929–1945

5 I think what is happening to me is so wonderful, and not only what can be seen on my body, but all that is taking place inside. I never discuss myself or any of these things with anybody; that is why I have to talk to myself about them. [*Diary of a Young Girl*, 5 Jan. 1944]

HANS FRANK 1900–1946

6 Our Constitution is the will of the Führer. [In A. Bullock, *Hitler*, Pt VII, 6]

SIR OLIVER [later LORD] FRANKS 1905–92

7 It is a secret in the Oxford sense: you may tell it to only one person at a time. [Quoted by K. Rose in the *Sunday Telegraph*, 30 Jan. 1977]

GEORGE MACDONALD FRASER 1925–

8 I have observed, in the course of a dishonest life, that when a rogue is outlining a treacherous plan, he works harder to con-

vince himself than to move his hearers. [*Flashman*, p. 135]

MICHAEL FRAYN 1933–

9 There is something about a blurb-writer paying his respects to a funny book which puts one in mind of a short-sighted lord mayor raising his hat to a hippopotamus. [*The Best of Beachcomber*, Introduction]

10 If we lived in a featureless desert, we would learn to place the individual grains of sand in a moral and aesthetic hierarchy. [*Constructions*, 10]

11 No woman so naked as one you can see to be naked underneath her clothes. [25]

12 What deeply affects every aspect of a man's experience of the world is his perception that *things could be otherwise*. [42]

13 Ah, *now*! That odd time – the oddest time of all times; the time it always is . . . by the time we've reached the 'w' of 'now' the 'n' is ancient history. [126]

14 I can't help feeling sceptical about the Bible's claim that God made man in his own image. What? Two solemn little Jehovahs to gaze back at him with fathomless wisdom and benevolence? What would have been the fun in that? He could have achieved *that* simply by creating a couple of mirrors, or a closed-circuit television. [157]

15 Each man in his time plays many parts. And not just for long runs as Shakespeare seems to suggest, but in repertory – one part on Monday night, another on Tuesday, and a third at the Wednesday matinée. [160]

16 'Wouldn't it be terrible to be bad?' he says to her right hip. 'You'd never know what a relief it was to stop being good.' [*Sweet Dreams*, p. 75]

17 You can create a good impression on yourself by being right, he realizes, but for creating a good impression on others there's nothing to beat being totally and catastrophically wrong. [76]

18 He recognizes that there is a real divergence of expert opinion between those that believe that men are happy because they are miserable, and those that believe that men are miserable because they are happy; and

wisely arrives at a synthesis of both views. [88]

1 It's not the despair, Laura. I can stand the despair. It's the hope. [Screenplay of film *Clockwise*, sc. 109]

2 There is a painful difference, often obscured by popular prejudice, between reporting something and making it up. [*Clouds*, Act I, sc. i]

3 To be absolutely honest, what I feel really bad about is that I don't feel worse. There's the ineffectual liberal's problem in a nutshell. [In the *Observer*, 8 Aug. 1965]

4 But then people don't usually laugh unless there's something serious at stake. What makes farce funny is seeing someone experience on the stage the terror and panic you feel inside yourself. [Interview in the *Observer*, 17 Sept. 1989]

ARTHUR FREED 1894–1973

5 I'm singing in the rain, just singing in the rain; What a wonderful feeling, I'm happy again. [Song: *Singing in the Rain*, in musical *Hollywood Review of 1929*, music by Nacio Herb Brown]

JOHN FREEMAN 1880–1929

6 Than these November skies / Is no sky lovelier. The clouds are deep; / Into their grey the subtle spies / Of colour creep, / Changing their high austerity to delight, / Till ev'n the leaden interfolds are bright. [*November Skies*]

7 Last night a sword-light in the sky / Flashed a swift terror on the dark. / In that sharp light the fields did lie / Naked and stone-like; each tree stood / Like a tranced woman, bound and stark, / Far off the wood / With darkness ridged the riven dark. [*Stone Trees*]

PAULO FREIRE

8 True generosity consists precisely in fighting to destroy the causes which nourish false charity. [*Pedagogy of the Oppressed*, Ch. 1]

9 The oppressors do not perceive their monopoly of *having more* as a privilege which dehumanizes others and themselves.

10 Liberation, a human phenomenon, cannot be achieved by semi-humans.

MARILYN FRENCH 1929–

11 All men are rapists, and that's all they are. They rape us with their eyes, their laws, and their codes. [*The Women's Room*, Bk 5, Ch. 19]

PERCY FRENCH 1854–1920

12 Where the mountains of Mourne sweep down to the sea. [Song: *The Mountains of Mourne*]

PHILIP FRENCH 1933–

13 I don't know much about philately, but I know what I lick. [In the *Observer Review*, 20 Oct. 1985]

SIR CLEMENT FREUD 1924–

14 If you resolve to give up smoking, drinking and loving, you don't actually live longer; it just seems longer. [Quoting 'a third-rate comedian in Sloane Square'. In the *Observer*, 27 Dec. 1964]

15 [When asked what he thought of New Zealand] I find it hard to say, because when I was there it seemed to be shut. [In BBC radio programme *Quote ... Unquote*, 12 Apr. 1978. Variants ascr. to other people]

16 Attila the Hen. [Nickname for Margaret Thatcher ascr. to him on her resignation, in the *Daily Mail*, 23 Nov. 1990]

SIGMUND FREUD 1856–1939

17 We are so made that we can derive intense enjoyment from a contrast and very little from a state of things. [*Civilization and Its Discontents*, Ch. 2]

18 The myth of King Oedipus, who killed his father and took his mother to wife, reveals, with little modification, the infantile wish, which is later opposed and repudiated by the *barrier against incest*. Shakespeare's *Hamlet* is equally rooted in the soil of the incest-complex, but under a better disguise. [*Five Lectures on Psycho-analysis*, IV]

19 A culture which leaves unsatisfied and drives to rebelliousness so large a number of its members neither has a prospect of continued existence nor deserves it. [*The Future of an Illusion*]

1 The principal task of civilization, its actual *raison d'être*, is to defend us against nature.

2 We believe that civilization has been built up, *under the pressure of the struggle for existence*, by sacrifices in gratification of the primitive impulses. [*Introductory Lectures*]

3 I do not think our successes can compete with those of Lourdes. There are so many more people who believe in the miracles of the Blessed Virgin than in the existence of the unconscious. [*New Introductory Lectures*, Lecture 34]

4 Two women stopped in front of a drugstore, and one said to her companion, 'If you will wait a few moments I'll soon be back,' but she said *movements* instead. She was on her way to buy some castor-oil for her child. [*Psychopathology of Everyday Life*, 5]

5 A woman who is very anxious to get children always reads *storks* instead of *stocks*. [6]

6 Occasionally I have had to admit to myself that the annoying, awkward stepping aside on the street, whereby for some seconds one steps here and there, yet always in the same direction as the other person, until finally both stop facing each other . . . conceals erotic purposes under the mask of awkwardness. [8]

7 When a member of my family complains that he or she has bitten his tongue, bruised her finger, and so on, instead of the expected sympathy I put the question, 'Why did you do that?'

8 Psycho-analysis has revealed to us that the totem animal is really a substitute for the father, and this really explains to us the contradiction that it is usually forbidden to kill the totem animal, that the killing of it results in a holiday, and that the animal is killed and yet mourned. [*Totem and Taboo*, Ch. 4, sect. v]

9 At bottom God is nothing more than an exalted father.

10 The great question . . . which I have not been able to answer, despite my thirty years of research into the feminine soul, is 'What does a woman want?' [Letter to Marie Bonaparte. In Charles Rolo, *Psychiatry in American Life*]

11 I am actually not at all a man of science, not an observer, not an experimenter, not a thinker. I am by temperament nothing but a conquistador – an adventurer. [Letter to Wilhelm Fliess, Feb. 1900]

MAX FRISCH 1911–1991

12 Technology . . . the knack of so arranging the world that we don't have to experience it. [*Homo Faber*, Pt 2]

CHARLES FROHMAN 1860–1915

13 Why fear death? It is the most beautiful adventure in life. [Last words before going down in the *Lusitania*, 7 May 1915]

ERICH FROMM 1900–1980

14 *The affirmation of one's own life, happiness, growth, freedom is rooted in one's captivity to love*, i.e. in care, respect, responsibility, and knowledge. If an individual is able to love productively, he loves himself too; if he can love *only* others, he cannot love at all. [*The Art of Loving*, Ch. 2, sect. 3d]

15 Man has achieved *freedom from* – without yet having *freedom to* – to be himself, to be productive, to be fully awake. [*The Fear of Freedom*, 4]

16 The successful revolutionary is a statesman, the unsuccessful one a criminal. [7]

17 Modern man lives under the illusion that he knows what he wants, while he actually wants what he is supposed to want. [8]

18 The aim of sadism is to transform a man into a thing, something animate into something inanimate, since by complete and absolute control the living loses one essential quality of life – freedom. [*The Heart of Man*]

19 Man always dies before he is fully born. [*Man for Himself*, Ch. 3]

20 Man's main task in life is to give *birth* to himself. [4]

21 In the nineteenth century the problem was that God is dead; in the twentieth century the problem is that man is dead. [*The Sane Society*, Ch. 9]

SIR DAVID FROST 1939–

22 Seriously, though, he's doing a grand

job! [Catchprase in BBC TV series *That Was the Week That Was*, early 1960s]

1 Vote Labour and you build castles in the air. Vote Conservative and you can live in them. [From BBC TV programme *That Was the Week That Was*, 31 Dec. 1962, in *Simpson's Contemporary Quotations*]

2 Hello, good evening, and welcome. [Catchphrase, opening lines of BBC TV series *The Frost Programme*, mid-1960s]

3 Television is an invention that permits you to be entertained in your living room by people you wouldn't have in your home. [From CBC TV programme *David Frost Revue*, 1971, in Jonathon Green, *Says Who?*]

PAUL FROST 1938–

4 A character, no more than a fence, can be strengthened by whitewash. [In *Hodder Book of Christian Quotations*, comp. Tony Castle]

ROBERT FROST 1874–1963

5 Earth's the right place for love; / I don't know where it's likely to go better. [*Birches*]

6 One could do worse than be a swinger of birches.

7 Forgive, O Lord, my little jokes on Thee / And I'll forgive Thy great big one on me. [*Cluster of Faith*]

8 Part of the moon was falling down the west / Dragging the whole sky with it to the hills. [*The Death of the Hired Man*]

9 'Home is the place where, when you have to go there, / They have to take you in.' / 'I should have called it / Something you somehow haven't to deserve.'

10 I would have written of me on my stone: / I had a lover's quarrel with the world. [*Epitaph*]

11 Some say the world will end in fire, / Some say in ice. / From what I've tasted of desire / I hold with those who favour fire, / But if I had to perish twice, / I think I know enough of hate / To say that for destruction ice / Is also great / And would suffice. [*Fire and Ice*]

12 Why make so much of fragmentary blue / In here and there a bird, or butterfly, / Or flower, or wearing-stone, or open eye, / When heaven presents in sheets the solid hue? [*Fragmentary Blue*]

13 The land was ours before we were the land's. / She was our land more than a hundred years / Before we were her people. / Such as we were we gave ourselves outright / (The deed of gift was many deeds of war) / To the land vaguely realizing westward, / But still unstoried, artless, unenhanced, / Such as she was, such as she has become. [*The Gift Outright*]

14 Keep cold, young orchard. Goodbye and keep cold. / Dread fifty above more than fifty below. [*Goodbye and Keep Cold*]

15 This as it will be seen is other far / Than with brooks taken otherwhere in song. / We love the things we love for what they are. [*Hyla Brook*]

16 Something there is that doesn't love a wall. [*Mending Wall*]

17 My apple trees will never get across / And eat the cones under his pines, I tell him. / He only says, 'Good fences make good neighbours'.

18 I met a Californian who would / Talk California – a state so blessed, / He said, in climate, none had ever died there / A natural death. [*New Hampshire*]

19 No wonder poets sometimes have to *seem* / So much more business-like than business men. / Their wares are so much harder to get rid of.

20 I knew a man who failing as a farmer / Burned down his farmhouse for the fire insurance, / And spent the proceeds on a telescope / To satisfy a life-long curiosity / About our place among the infinities. / And how was that for otherworldliness?

21 The bird would cease and be as other birds / But that he knows in singing not to sing. / The question that he frames in all but words / Is what to make of a diminished thing. [*The Oven Bird*]

22 I never dared be radical when young / For fear it would make me conservative when old. [*Precaution*]

23 I shall be telling this with a sigh /

Somewhere ages and ages hence: / Two roads diverged in a wood, and I – / I took the one less travelled by, / And that has made all the difference. [*The Road Not Taken*]

1 Pressed into service means pressed out of shape. [*The Self-seeker*]

2 The best way out is always through. [*A Servant to Servants*]

3 Never tell me that not one star of all / That slip from heaven at night and softly fall / Has been picked up with stones to build a wall. [*A Star in a Stone-boat*]

4 The woods are lovely, dark and deep. / But I have promises to keep, / And miles to go before I sleep. [*Stopping by Woods on a Snowy Evening*]

5 Poetry is a way of taking life by the throat. [*Comment*]

6 A sentence is a sound in itself on which sounds called words may be strung. [Letter to John Bartlett, 22 Feb. 1914]

7 Writing free verse is like playing tennis with the net down. [Address at Milton Academy, Massachusetts, 17 May 1935]

8 WALLACE STEVENS: You write on subjects.
FROST: And you, you write bric-à-brac. [In Robert Francis, *Robert Frost: A Time to Talk*, 'Nov. 1, 1954']

9 People are inexterminable – like flies and bed-bugs. There will always be some that survive in cracks and crevices – that's us. [In the *Observer*, 'Sayings of the Week', 29 Mar. 1959]

10 What do I mean by a phrase? A clutch of words that gives you a clutch at the heart. [Interview in the *Saturday Evening Post*, 16 Nov. 1960]

11 If society fits you comfortably enough, you call it freedom. [In *Esquire* magazine, 1965]

12 That which gets left out of verse and prose in translation. [Definition of poetry. In *The Times Literary Supplement*, 16 Sept. 1989]

13 The brain is a wonderful organ; it starts working the moment you get up in the morning and doesn't stop until you get into the office. [In *Executive's Quotation Book*, ed. James Charlton]

14 A diplomat is a man who always remembers a woman's birthday but never remembers her age. [In *Treasury of Humorous Quotations*, ed. Evan Esar and Nicolas Bentley]

15 The reason why worry kills more people than work is that more people worry than work. [In Barbara Rowes, *Book of Quotes*]

16 A liberal is a man too broad-minded to take his own side in a quarrel. [In *Portable Curmudgeon*, comp. J. Winokur, 'Quotes on "L"']

CHRISTOPHER FRY 1907–

17 Time walks by your side, ma'am, unwilling to pass. [*Curtmantle*, Act II]

18 I know your cause is lost, but in the heart / Of all right causes is a cause that cannot lose. [*The Dark is Light Enough*, III]

19 The Lady's Not for Burning. [Title of play]

20 I travel light; as light, / That is, as a man can travel who will / Still carry his body around because / Of its sentimental value. [*The Lady's Not for Burning*, I]

21 Your innocence is on at such a rakish angle / It gives you quite an air of iniquity.

22 What after all / Is a halo? It's only one more thing to keep clean.

23 Always fornicate / Between clean sheets and spit on a well-scrubbed floor. [II]

24 The moon is nothing / But a circumambulatory aphrodisiac / Divinely subsidized to provoke the world / Into a rising birth-rate. [III]

25 But life and death / Is cat and dog in this double-bed of a world. [*A Phoenix Too Frequent*]

26 He was so punctual, you could regulate / The sun by him.

27 Try thinking of love, or something, / Amor vincit insomnia. [*Sleep of Prisoners*]

ROGER FRY 1866–1934

28 Manet and the Post-Impressionists. [Name of exhibition 'struck out in talk with a journalist'. In Virginia Woolf, *Roger Fry*, Ch. 7]

29 We make buildings for our need, and

then, sacrificing our pockets to art, cover them with a mass of purely nonsensical forms which we hope may turn them into fine architecture. [Letter to *The Times*, 1912. In 8]

1 Art is significant deformity.

2 I've found a perfect description of mysticism – it's the attempt to get rid of mystery. [In 11]

3 Bach almost persuades me to be a Christian.

STEPHEN FRY 1957–

4 Old professors never die, they merely lose their faculties. [*The Liar*, 2. V]

CARLOS FUENTES 1928–

5 You start by writing to live. You end by writing so as not to die. ['The Discovery of Mexico', *Granta*, 22]

6 I always try to tell my critics: Don't classify me, read me. I'm a writer, not a genre. [From *Myself with Others*, in the *Listener*, 16 June 1988]

7 There are people whose external reality is generous because it is transparent, because you can read everything, accept everything, understand everything about them: people who carry their own sun with them. [*The Old Gringo*, 6]

8 To be a gringo in Mexico . . . ah, that is euthanasia. [17]

9 We [Americans] all try to be virtuous. It's our national pastime.

10 The novel is born from the very fact that we do not understand one another any longer, because unitary, orthodox language has broken down. [In the *Guardian*, 24 Feb. 1989]

R. BUCKMINSTER FULLER 1895–1983

11 I am a passenger on the spaceship, Earth. [*Operating Manual for Spaceship Earth*, Ch. 4]

12 One outstandingly important fact regarding Spaceship Earth, and that is that no instruction book came with it.

ROY FULLER 1912–1991

13 As horrible thoughts, / Loud fluttering aircraft slope above his head / At dusk. The ridiculous empires break like biscuits. [*The Middle of a War*]

14 Anyone happy in this age and place / is daft or corrupt. Better to abdicate / From a material and spiritual terrain / Fit only for barbarians. [*Translation*]

15 The poets get a quizzical alien. / They reflect time, I am the very ticking. [*A Wry Smile*]

ALFRED FUNKE 1869–?

16 *Gott strafe England!* – God punish England! [*Schwert und Myrte*]

DOUGLAS FURBER 1885–1961 and
 ARTHUR ROSE ?–1958

17 Any time you're Lambeth way. / Any evening, any day, / You'll find us all doin' the Lambeth walk. [Song: *Doin' the Lambeth Walk*, 1937, music by Noël Gay, revived version sung by Lupino Lane in musical *Me and My Girl*]

WILL FYFFE 1885–1947

18 I'm only a common old working chap, / As anyone here can see, / But when I get a couple of drinks on a Saturday, / Glasgow belongs to me. [Song: *I Belong to Glasgow*]

ROSE FYLEMAN 1877–1957

19 There are fairies at the bottom of our garden. [*Fairies*]

G

CLARK GABLE 1901–1960

1 Frankly, my dear, I don't give a damn. [As Rhett Butler to Scarlett O'Hara [Vivien Leigh] in film *Gone with the Wind*, script by Sidney Howard from Margaret Mitchell's novel]

ZSA ZSA GABOR 1919–

2 I never hated a man enough to give him diamonds back. [In the *Observer*, 'Sayings of the Week,' 28 Aug. 1957]

3 A man in love is incomplete until he has married. Then he's finished. [In *Newsweek*, 28 Mar. 1960]

4 Personally I know nothing about sex because I've always been married. [In the *Observer*, 'Sayings of the Year', 27 Dec. 1987]

5 I haven't known any open marriages, though quite a few have been ajar. [In *Hammer and Tongues*, ed. Michèle Brown and Ann O'Connor, 'Marriage']

6 Macho doesn't prove mucho. [In Barbara Rowes, *Book of Quotes*]

7 I am a marvellous housekeeper. Every time I leave a man, I keep his house. [In *Was It Good for You Too?*, ed. Bob Chieger]

8 [When asked how many husbands she had had] You mean apart from my own? [On US TV, 1985. In *Chambers Film Quotes*, comp. Tony Crawley]

HUGH GAITSKELL 1906–1963

9 Surely the right course is to test the Russians not the bombs. [In the *Observer*, 'Sayings of the Week', 23 June 1957]

10 There are some of us, Mr Chairman, who will fight and fight and fight again to save the party we love. [Speech at Labour Party Conference, Scarborough, 3 Oct. 1960]

11 [European federation would] mean, if this is the idea, the end of Britain as an independent state ... It means the end of a thousand years of history. [Speech at Labour Party Conference, Brighton, 3 Oct. 1962]

12 All terrorists, at the invitation of the Government, end up with drinks at the Dorchester. [Quoted by Dora Gaitskell in letter to the *Guardian*, 23 Aug. 1977]

J. K. GALBRAITH 1908–

13 The Affluent Society. [Title of book]

14 One of the best ways of avoiding necessary and even urgent tasks is to seem to be busily employed on things that are already done. [*The Affluent Society*, Ch. 1, sect. ii]

15 Wealth has never been a sufficient source of honour in itself. It must be advertised and the normal medium is obtrusively expensive goods. [7. v]

16 Inventions that are not made, like babies that are not born, are rarely missed. [9. iii]

17 It is a far, far better thing to have a firm anchor in nonsense than to put out on the troubled seas of thought. [11. iv]

18 In a community where public services

have failed to keep abreast of private consumption things are very different. Here in an atmosphere of private opulence and public squalor, the private goods have full sway. [18. ii]

1 All races have produced notable economists, with the exception of the Irish who doubtless can protest their devotion to higher arts. [*The Age of Uncertainty*, Ch. 1]

2 Much of the world's work, it has been said, is done by men who do not feel quite well. Marx is a case in point. [3]

3 All successful revolutions are the kicking in of a rotten door. The violence of revolutions is the violence of men who charge into a vacuum.

4 This is in the established tradition of social study. Only the man who finds everything wrong and expects it to get worse is thought to have a clear brain. [10]

5 Money is a singular thing. It ranks with love as man's greatest source of joy. And with death as his greatest source of anxiety. Money differs from an automobile, a mistress or cancer in being equally important to those who have it and those who do not. [TV broadcast version, 6th programme]

6 Meetings are indispensable when you don't want to do anything. [*Ambassador's Journal*]

7 Politics is not the art of the possible. It consists in choosing between the disastrous and the unpalatable. [Letter to President Kennedy, 2 Mar. 1962, in above. See also 61:2]

8 Men have been swindled by other men on many occasions. The autumn of 1929 was, perhaps, the first occasion when men succeeded on a large scale in swindling themselves. [*The Great Crash*, Ch. 7]

9 If you can't comfort the afflicted then afflict the comfortable. [Speech to Harvard graduates. See also 108:12]

10 Ken Galbraith described the 'trickle down' theory as meaning that, if you stuffed enough oats into the front end of a donkey, enough would come out of the back end to feed the sparrows. [Denis Healey, *The Time of My Life*, Ch. 25]

PATRICK GALE 1962–

11 What little religion ran in her veins being a condensed Roman Catholicism. [*Facing the Tank*, 18]

LIEUTENANT-GENERAL ADOLF GALLAND 1912–

12 It felt as if angels were pushing. [On his first flight in a jet aircraft, the Messerschmitt 262, May 1943. *The First and the Last*]

PAUL GALLET

13 The man who has made up his mind for all contingencies will often be too quick for one who tries to understand. [*Debates with Historians*, 'Ranke in the Light of the Catastrophe']

14 Freedom to Starve. [Title of book, 1972]

JOHN GALSWORTHY 1867–1933

15 When a Forsyte died – but no Forsyte had as yet died – death being contrary to their principles, they took precautions against it. [*The Forsyte Saga: The Man of Property*, Pt I, Ch. 1]

16 Nobody tells me anything.

17 'Very haughty!' he said, 'the wild Buccaneer.'

18 He would be setting up as a man of property next, with a place in the country.

19 Oh, your precious 'lame ducks'! [II. 12]

20 What is it that gets loose when you begin to fight, and makes you what you think you're not? . . . Begin as you may, it ends in this – skin game. [*The Skin Game*, Act III]

21 When we began this fight, we had clean hands – are they clean now? What's gentility worth if it can't stand fire?

22 The French cook; we open tins. [In *Treasury of Humorous Quotations*, ed. Evan Esar and Nicolas Bentley]

MAHATMA GANDHI 1869–1948

23 [When asked by an interviewer what he thought of Western civilization] I think it would be a good idea. [Attr. in E. F. Schumacher, *Good Work*, Ch. 2]

1 Non-violence is the first article of my faith. It is also the last article of my creed. [Speech in defence against charge of disaffection etc. at Shahi Bag, India, 18 Mar. 1922]

GRETA GARBO 1905–1990

2 [When asked by David Niven, 'Why *did* you give up the movies?'] I had made enough faces. [In David Niven, *Bring on the Empty Horses*, 'Two Queens']

3 I want to be alone. [Attr., but she always insisted she had only said, 'I want to be left alone.' Subsequently used in her film *Grand Hotel*, script by William A. Drake]

FEDERICO GARCÍA LORCA 1899–1936

4 *A las cinco de la tarde. / Eran las cinco en punto de la tarde. / Un niño trajo la blanca sábana / a las cinco de la tarde.* – At five in the afternoon. It was exactly five in the afternoon. A boy brought the white sheet at five in the afternoon. [*Llanto por Ignacio Sánchez Mejías*]

5 *Cuando sale la luna / de cien rostros iguales, / la moneda de plata / solloza en el bolsillo* – When the moon of a hundred identical faces comes out, the silver coins sob in the pocket. [*La luna asoma*]

6 *Ni un solo momento, viejo hermoso Walt Whitman, / he dejado de ver tu barba llena de mariposas* – Not for a moment, beautiful aged Walt Whitman, have I failed to see your beard full of butterflies. [*Oda a Walt Whitman*]

7 *Con el alma de charol / vienen por la carrera.* – With their patent-leather souls, they [the Civil Guards] come along the road. [*Romance de la Guardia civil española*]

8 *El jinete se acercaba / tocando el tambor del llano. / Dentro de la fragua el niño / tiene los ojos cerrados.* – Drumming the plain, the horseman is coming. Inside the smithy the child has closed his eyes. [*Romance de la luna, luna*]

9 *Verde que te quiero verde. / Verde viento. Verde ramas. / El barco sobre el mar / y el caballo en la montaña.* – Green how I love you green. Green wind. Green boughs. The ship on the sea and the horse on the mountain. [*Romance sonambulo*]

GABRIEL GARCÍA MÁRQUEZ 1928–

10 A writer needs a desert island in the morning and the big city at night. As William Faulkner once declared, the perfect home for a writer is a brothel – because in the morning hours it's always calm and in contrast at night there's always a party atmosphere. [In the *Observer*, 24 Oct. 1982]

11 The interpretation of our reality through patterns not our own serves only to make us ever more unknown, ever less free, ever more solitary. [Epigraph to Rana Kabbani, *Europe's Myths of Orient*]

JOSÉ GARCÍA OLIVER [Anarchist Minister of Justice during the Civil War] 1901–

12 Justice, I firmly believe, is so subtle a thing that to interpret it one has only need of a heart. [In Hugh Thomas, *The Spanish Civil War*, Ch. 43]

LEON GARFIELD 1921–

13 Long ago, the Englishman's castle was his home; then that went, and his home became his castle. Now his castle is the nation's and his home is the bank's. [In *Children's Literature in Education*, Ch. 2]

14 Nature herself had created them to be storesmen. They had the very air of having been not so much born as indented for. [*The Drummer Boy*, Ch. 6]

15 The lady of the house was everyone's neighbour, and knew about half as much as God; and whatever had escaped her she made up out of a fund of experience, gleaned from the purchase and sale of buttons. [*The Pleasure Garden*, Ch. 9]

16 Everything had a back door. There was always a way in. The corporal was peculiarly experienced in back doors. All his life had been spent in approaching them. He was confident that, when the time came, he would enter Heaven by a back door. [*The Prisoners of September*, Ch. 14]

17 ... Lady Bullock, who had been at death's door for so long now that one might have been pardoned for mistaking her for its knocker. [29]

JUDY GARLAND 1922–1969

1 I was born at the age of twelve on a Metro-Goldwyn-Mayer lot. [In the *Observer*, 'Sayings of the Week', 18 Feb. 1951]

ALAN GARNER 1934–

2 'There,' he said. 'You'll remember this day, my girl. For the rest of your life.' 'I already have,' said Mary. [*The Stone Book*]

DAVID GARNETT 1892–1981

3 [When asked whether, as a member of the Bloomsbury Group, he did not have homosexual leanings] More leant-upon than leanings, I'd have thought. [Quoted by John Pearson in the *Sunday Times*, 16 Mar. 1980]

MARCUS GARVEY 1887–1940

4 The whole world is run on bluff. No race, no nation, no man has any divine right to take advantage of others. Why allow the other fellow to bluff you? [*Philosophy and Opinions*, p. 7]

GENERAL DE GAULLE 1890–1970

5 *Toute ma vie je me suis fait une certaine idée de la France.* – All my life I have thought of France in a certain way. [*War Memoirs*, Vol. 1: *The Call to Honour*, Ch. 1]

6 *Délibérer est le fait de plusieurs. Agir est le fait d'un seul.* – Deliberation is the work of many men. Action of one alone. [Vol. 2: *Unity*, Ch. 5]

7 France has lost a battle but France has not lost the war. [Broadcast from London after the fall of France, probably composed on 18 June 1940 but not issued until July]

8 I have come to the conclusion that politics are too serious a matter to be left to the politicians. [In Clement Attlee, *Prime Minister Remembers*, Ch. 4]

9 As for me, I have never, in any one of my speeches, spoken of *l'Europe des patries* although it is always claimed that I have. [At press conference, 15 May 1962]

10 You cannot ignore a country with 265 varieties of cheese. [In *Newsweek*, 1 Oct. Often misquoted as 'You cannot govern ...' and dates of first use vary]

11 I myself have become a Gaullist only little by little. [In the *Observer*, 'Sayings of the Year', 29 Dec. 1963]

12 *Les états sont les monstres froids.* – States are frigid monsters. [In the *Listener*, 19 Jan. 1989]

13 [When Jacques Soustelle told him, 'Some of my friends don't approve of your policies.'] Well, change your friends. [Attr.]

14 The graveyards are full of indispensable men. [Attr.]

15 Events have made me the guide of the nation. [Attr.]

PETER GAY 1923–

16 Many historians have heard the music of the past but have transcribed it for penny whistle. [*Freud for Historians*]

SIR ERIC GEDDES 1875–1937

17 We will get everything out of her [Germany] that you can squeeze out of a lemon, and a bit more ... I will squeeze her until you can hear the pips squeak. [Speech at Cambridge, 9 Dec. 1918]

LARRY GELBART 1928–

18 It [the film *Gandhi*] was so boring they shot the leading man at the end of the picture. [In the *Guardian*, 7 Aug. 1986]

19 Generally speaking, the only way of getting any feeling from a TV set is to touch it when you're wet. [In the *Listener*, 17/24 Dec. 1987]

See also BURT SHEVELOVE and LARRY GELBART

SIR BOB GELDOF 1954–

20 I Don't Like Mondays. [Title of song]

JEAN GENET 1910–1986

21 What we need is hatred. From it are our ideas born. [*The Negroes*, epigraph]

PETE GENT 1942–

22 All American males are failed athletes. [In the *Weekend Guardian*, 8–9 July 1989]

KING GEORGE V 1865–1936

1 Wake up, England. [Title given to speech delivered at Guildhall, London, 5 Dec. 1901, when reprinted 10 years later]

2 I can't understand it. I'm really quite an ordinary sort of chap. [Attr. at his jubilee in May 1935]

3 How is the Empire? [Official last words, as quoted in *The Times*, 21 June 1936, but letter from Lord Wigram, 31 Jan. 1936, in *Oxford Dictionary of Modern Quotations*, ed. Tony Augarde, describes the King saying it when reading 'Imperial and Foreign' page of *The Times*]

4 Bugger Bognor! [Attr. dying words when told by his physician he would soon be convalescing in Bognor]

5 That was a rotten way to run a revolution. I could have done it better myself. [Of the General Strike. In *The Times*, 8 May 1986]

KING GEORGE VI 1895–1952

6 Abroad is bloody. [Attr. in W. H. Auden, *A Certain World*]

BOY GEORGE 1961–

7 Sex? – I'd rather have a cup of tea – any day! [With variants. Attr. in 1983]

DANIEL GEORGE 1890–1967 and SAGITTARIUS [OLGA KATZIN] 1896–1987

8 O Freedom, what liberties are taken in thy name! [*The Perpetual Pessimist*]

WILLIAM GERHARDIE 1895–1977

9 She even sighed offensively . . . as if she meant to charge me with the necessity of doing so. [*Futility*, Pt III, Ch. 3]

10 There are as many fools at a university as elsewhere . . . But their folly, I admit, has a certain stamp – the stamp of university training, if you like. It is trained folly. [*The Polyglots*, Ch. 7]

11 We are like icebergs in the ocean: one-eighth part consciousness and the rest submerged beneath the surface of articulate apprehension. [14]

IRA GERSHWIN 1896–1983

12 I got rhythm, / I got music. [Song: *I Got Music*, in musical *Girl Crazy*, music by George Gershwin]

13 Lady, Be Good! [Title of musical, music by George Gershwin]

14 Nice work if you can get it, / And you can get it – if you try. [Song: *Nice Work If You Can Get It*, in musical *A Damsel in Distress*, music by George Gershwin]

15 You'd better dance, little lady! / Dance, little man! / Dance whenever you can! [Song: *Shall We Dance?*, in film of same title, music by George Gershwin]

16 'S wonderful! 'S marvellous – [Song: *'S Wonderful*, in musical *Funny Face*, music by George Gershwin]

17 [When asked, 'Which comes first, the words or the music?'] What usually comes first is the contract. [In the *Guardian*, 18 Aug. 1983, at his death]

18 I've got a whole day's work ahead of me. I'm going to change the ribbon on my typewriter. [On his careful craftsmanship]

IRA GERSHWIN and DU BOSE HEYWARD 1885–1940

19 Oh, I got plenty o' nuthin', / An' nuthin's plenty fo' me. [Song: *I Got Plenty o' Nuthin'*, in musical *Porgy and Bess*, music by George Gershwin]

20 It ain't necessarily so, / It ain't necessarily so – / De t'ings dat yo' li'ble / To read in de Bible – / It ain't necessarily so. [Song: *It Ain't Necessarily So*, in *Porgy and Bess*]

21 Summertime, and the living is easy. [Song: *Summertime*, in *Porgy and Bess*]

PAUL GETTY 1892–1976

22 If you can actually count your money then you are not a really rich man. [In Bernard Levin, *The Pendulum Years*, Ch. 1]

23 The meek shall inherit the earth, but not the mineral rights. [Attr.]

STELLA GIBBONS 1902–1989

24 Something nasty in the woodshed. [*Cold Comfort Farm, passim*]

1 Graceless, Pointless, Feckless and Aimless waited their turn to be milked. [Ch. 3]

WILLA GIBBS

2 The three kinds of services you generally find in the Episcopal churches. I call them either low-and-lazy, broad-and-hazy, or high-and-crazy. [*The Dean*]

WOLCOTT GIBBS 1902–1958

3 Backward ran sentences until reeled the mind. ['Time ... Fortune ... Life ... Luce' (in mockery of style of *Time* magazine), *New Yorker*, 28 Nov. 1936]

KAHLIL GIBRAN 1883–1931

4 If he [a teacher] is indeed wise he does not bid you enter the house of his wisdom, but rather leads you to the threshold of your own mind. [*The Prophet*, 'Of Teaching']

5 Your children are not your children. They are the sons and daughters of Life's longing for itself ... you may strive to be like them, but seek not to make them like you. ['Of Children']

6 You were born together, and together you shall be for evermore ... but let there be spaces in your togetherness. And let the winds of the heavens dance between you. ['Of Marriage']

7 I have never agreed with my other self wholly. The truth of the matter seems to lie between us. [*Sand and Foam*]

8 A bigot is a stone-deaf orator.

9 An exaggeration is a truth that has lost its temper.

10 Disagreement may be the shortest cut between two minds.

11 I discovered the secret of the sea in meditation upon the dewdrop. [*Spiritual Sayings*]

12 It is slavery to live in the mind unless it has become part of the body.

13 The fear of hell is hell itself, and the longing for paradise is paradise itself.

W. W. GIBSON 1878–1962

14 But we, how shall we turn to little things / And listen to the birds and winds and streams / Made holy by their dreams / Nor feel the heart-break in the heart of things? [*A Lament*]

ANDRÉ GIDE 1869–1951

15 *L'acte gratuite* – The unmotivated action. [*Les caves du Vatican, passim*]

16 [When asked to name the greatest French poet] Hugo – alas! [Letter to Paul Valéry. In Claude Martin, *La maturité d'André Gide*, p. 502]

17 The true hypocrite is the one who ceases to perceive his deception, the one who lies with sincerity. [*Journal of 'The Counterfeiters'*, Second Notebook, Aug. 1921]

18 I love small nations. I love small numbers. The world will be saved by the few. [In *The Times Higher Education Supplement*, 15 Jan. 1982]

19 I call journalism everything that will interest less tomorrow than it does today. [Attr.]

SIR JOHN GIELGUD 1904–

20 Style is knowing what sort of play you are in. [On acting. In BBC TV programme *On Acting*, 11 Sept. 1987]

21 Tynan said I had only two gestures, the left hand up, the right hand up – what did he want me to do, bring out my prick? [Interview in John Mortimer, *In Character*]

L. WOLFE GILBERT 1888–1970

22 Waitin' for the *Robert E. Lee*. [Title of Song, 1912, music by Lewis F. Muir]

GILES [CARL RONALD] 1916–

23 Fred's just heard the first cuckoo – and GOT it. [Cartoon caption. In Colin MacInnes, *England, Half English*, 'The Express Families']

ERIC GILL 1882–1940

24 Man cannot live on the human plane, he must be either above or below it. [*Autobiography*, Conclusion]

25 The artist is not a special kind of man but every man a special kind of artist. [In *Art*, 1942]

STRICKLAND GILLILAN 1869–1954

1 Adam / Had 'em. [*On the Antiquity of Microbes*]

ALLEN GINSBERG 1926–

2 America, I'm putting my queer shoulder to the wheel. [*America*]

3 I saw the best minds of my generation destroyed by madness, starving hysterical naked. [*How!*]

4 How we [the Beats] behave in private is actually the ultimate politics. So the original literary inspiration was to behave in public as we do in private. [In Barry Miles, *Ginsberg*, Ch. 17]

5 Poetry is not an expression of the party line. It's that time of night, lying in bed, thinking what you really think, making the private world public, that's what the poet does. [In review in the *Independent*, 20 Jan. 1990]

YEVGENIA GINSBERG 1906–1977

6 All ideologies are relative; the only absolute is the torment that men inflict on each other . . . [In Eric de Mauny, *Russian Prospect*]

NORMAN GINSBURY 1902–

7 If it weren't for his good manners, Leopold could easily pass for an Englishman. [*The First Gentleman*, II. i]

8 I never snub anybody accidentally. [*Viceroy Sarah*, I. ii]

CARLO GINZBURG 1939–

9 Are we the ones who think up myths or is it myths who think us up? [*Clues, Myths and Emblems*, Ch. 5]

GEORGE GIPP 1895–1920

10 One day, when the going is tough and the big game is hanging in the balance, ask the team to win one for the Gipper. I don't know where I'll be, Rock, but I'll know about it and I'll be happy. [Last words, 14 Dec. 1920, to coach Knute Rockne. The legendary football player from Notre Dame University and his pledge became the subject of a film in 1940, with Ronald Reagan as 'The Gipper'. See also 313:13]

JEAN GIRAUDOUX 1882–1944

11 Beauty is always the first to hear about the sins of the world. [*Duel of Angels*, Act I]

12 I said that virtue was the weakness of strong generals, and the strength of weak magistrates.

13 Heroes are men who glorify a life which they can't bear any longer. [III]

14 You know women as well as I do. They are only willing when you compel them, but after that they're as enthusiastic as you are. [*Tiger at the Gates*, Act I]

15 Ask any soldier. To kill a man is to merit a woman.

16 It's odd how people waiting for you stand out far less clearly than people you are waiting for.

17 Often I don't recognize faces, but I always recognize the jewellery.

18 As soon as war is declared it will be impossible to hold the poets back. Rhyme is still the most effective drum.

19 There's no better way of exercising the imagination than the study of law. No poet ever interpreted nature as freely as a lawyer interprets truth.

20 The life of a wife and husband who love each other is never at rest. Whether the marriage is true or false, the marriage portion is the same: elemental discord. [II]

21 I forgot they were talking about me. They sound so wonderfully convincing.

22 Nations, like men, die by imperceptible disorders. We recognize a doomed people by the way they sneeze or pare their nails.

VALÉRY GISCARD D'ESTAING 1926–

23 *Je ne l'aime, ni comme homme, ni comme femme.* – I don't like her [Margaret Thatcher] either as a man or a woman. [From A. Sampson, *The Changing Anatomy of Britain*, in *New Society*, 30 Sept. 1982]

ALEX GLASGOW 1935–

1 Close the coalhouse door, lad. / There's blood inside. [Song: *Close the Coalhouse Door*]

GEORGE GLASS 1910–1984

2 An actor's a guy who, if you ain't talking about him, ain't listening. [In the *Observer*, 'Sayings of the Year', 1 Jan. 1956. Saying sometimes ascr. to Marlon Brando, with whom it was popular, according to Bob Thomas, *Brando*, Ch. 8, and *Oxford Dictionary of Modern Quotations*, ed. Tony Augarde]

MONTAGUE GLASS 1877–1934

3 She was a singer who had to take any note above A with her eyebrows. [In Frank Muir, *Frank Muir Book*]

VICTORIA GLENDINNING 1937–

4 Why are women – most women – more interested in a man after he has made love to them than before? Why are men – most men – more interested in a woman before they have made love to her than after? . . . Men have to *unload*, he thought. The rubbish doesn't care about the feelings of the skip. [*Grown-ups*, Ch. 11]

JOHN GLOAG 1896–1981

5 Architecture cannot lie, and buildings, although inanimate, are to that extent morally superior to men. ['The Significance of Historical Research in Architectural and Industrial Design', paper to the Royal Society of Arts, 20 Mar. 1963]

JOHN A. GLOVER-KIND ?–1918

6 I Do Like to be Beside the Seaside. [Title of song]

MAX GLUCKMAN 1911–

7 A science is any discipline in which the fool of this generation can go beyond the point reached by the genius of the last generation. [*Politics, Law and Ritual*, p. 60]

JEAN-LUC GODARD 1930–

8 Photography is truth. And cinema is truth twenty-four times a second. [In film *Le petit soldat*]

9 To me style is just the outside of content, and content the inside of style, like the outside and inside of the human body – both go together, they can't be separated. [In Richard Roud, *Godard*, Introduction]

10 If I had to define myself I'd say I am 'a painter of letters' as one would say that there are 'men of letters'. [In Jay Leyda, *Voices of Film Experience*]

11 GEORGE FRANJU: Movies should have a beginning, a middle and an end.
GODARD: Certainly, but not necessarily in that order. [In *Time* magazine, 14 Sept. 1981]

CHARLES GODFREY ?–1935

12 When we go to meet the foe, / It's the English-speaking race against the world. [Song: *We're Brothers of the Selfsame Race*]

FRED GODFREY

13 Who were you with last night? / Out in the pale moonlight. [Song: *Who were You with Last Night?*, 1912, in collab. Mark Sheridan]

A. D. GODLEY 1856–1925

14 What is this that roareth thus? / Can it be a Motor Bus? / Yes, the smell and hideous hum / Indicat Motorem Bum. [*The Motor Bus*]

JOSEF GOEBBELS 1897–1945

15 Our Government of gentlemen . . . [In the *Observer*, 'Sayings of the Week', 22 Oct. 1933]

16 We can be prepared, without butter, but not without guns, for example. [Speech in Berlin, 17 Jan. 1936. Echoed later that year by Goering; see 146:2]

17 An iron curtain would at once descend on this territory. [*Das Reich*, 25 Feb. 1945. See also 80:6, 352:4]

18 This was the Angel of History! We felt its wings flutter through the room. Was that not the future we awaited so anxiously? [On hearing of Roosevelt's death. *Diary*, 12 Apr. 1945]

1 Whoever says the first word to the world is right. [In *The Media in British Politics*, ed. Ben Pimlott and Jean Seaton]

HERMANN GOERING 1893–1946

2 Guns will make us powerful; butter will only make us fat. [Broadcast, Summer 1936. The juxtaposition was also used that year by Josef Goebbels; see 145:17]

3 I herewith commission you to carry out all preparations with regard to . . . a *total solution* of the Jewish question in those territories of Europe which are under German influence. [Instructions to Heydrich, 31 July 1941. In W. L. Shirer, *The Rise and Fall of the Third Reich*, Bk v, Ch. 27]

4 They [the British] entered the war to prevent us from going into the East, not to have the East come to the Atlantic. [On the possibilities of splitting the Grand Alliance. In G. M. Gilbert, *Nuremberg Diary*]

See also under JOHST, HANNS

IVAN GOFF 1910– and BEN ROBERTS 1916–1984

5 Made it, Ma . . . Top of the World! [Said by James Cagney in film *White Heat*]

RUBE GOLDBERG 1883–1970

6 No matter how thin you slice it, it's still baloney. [In B. Gill, *Here at the New Yorker*, Ch. 13. But Eric Partridge, *Dictionary of Catch-phrases*, judges it to be a US catch-phrase of the late 1930s]

SIR WILLIAM GOLDING 1911–1993

7 Life should serve up its feast of experience in a series of courses. [*Close Quarters*, 17]

8 Philip is a living example of natural selection. He was as fitted to survive in this modern world as a tapeworm in an intestine. [*Free Fall*, Ch. 2]

9 Ralph wept for the end of innocence, the darkness of man's heart, and the fall through the air of the true, wise friend called Piggy. [*Lord of the Flies*, Ch. 12]

10 The theme defeats structuralism, for it is an emotion. The theme of *Lord of the Flies* is grief, sheer grief, grief, grief, grief. [*A Moving Target*, title essay]

11 Sleep is when all the unsorted stuff comes flying out as from a dustbin upset in a high wind. [*Pincher Martin*, Ch. 6]

12 Eighteen is a good time for suffering. One has all the necessary strength, and no defences. [*The Pyramid*, p. 12]

13 With lack of sleep and too much understanding I grow a little crazy, I think, like all men at sea who live too close to each other and too close thereby to all that is monstrous under the sun and moon. [*Rites of Passage*, final words]

EMMA GOLDMAN 1869–1940

14 If there's no dancing count me out. [Of the Russian Revolution. In the *New Statesman*, 1 Mar. 1985]

WILLIAM GOLDMAN 1931–

15 As far as the film-making process is concerned, stars are essentially worthless and absolutely essential. [*Adventures in the Screen Trade*, Pt 1, Ch. 1]

16 Today, a million dollars is what you pay a star you don't want.

17 You can't make a 'Hamlet' without breaking a few egos. [Of the screenwriter's problems over the star system. In the *Observer*, 8 Apr. 1984]

EDWARD GOLDSMITH 1928–

18 Consider that human beings are made up of a small and very unimpressive array of raw materials. They are 80 per cent water and the market value of the chemicals in their production is not much in excess of one pound. [*The Great U-turn*, Ch. 7]

SIR JAMES GOLDSMITH 1933–

19 The private sector is that part of the economy the Government controls and the public sector is the part that nobody controls. [In the *Observer*, 'Sayings of the Week', 25 Mar. 1979]

20 When you marry your mistress you create a job vacancy. [In the *Independent Magazine*, 22 Apr. 1989]

1 If you see a bandwagon, it's too late. [In Jeffrey Robinson, *The Risk Takers*]

SENATOR BARRY GOLDWATER 1909–

2 I would remind you that extremism in the defence of liberty is no vice. And let me remind you also that moderation in the pursuit of justice is no virtue. [Speech on accepting Republican nomination, San Francisco, 16 July 1964, but he attr. it to Cicero]

3 A government that is big enough to give you all you want is big enough to take it all away. [Speech at West Chester, Pennsylvania, 21 Oct. 1964]

4 You've got to forget about this civilian. Whenever you drop bombs, you're going to hit civilians. [Speech in New York, 23 Jan. 1967]

SAMUEL GOLDWYN 1882–1974

5 For years I have been known for saying 'include me out': but today I am giving it up for ever. [Address at Balliol College, Oxford, 1 Mar. 1945. He always denied it was actually first said at Association of Motion Picture Producers, 1933]

6 Let's have some new clichés. [In the *Observer*, 'Sayings of the Week', 24 Oct. 1948]

7 Why should people go out and pay money to see bad films when they can stay at home and see bad television for nothing? [9 Sept. 1956]

8 A wide screen just makes a bad film twice as bad. [Said on 9 Sept. 1956]

9 His [Joseph M. Schenk's] verbal contract is worth more than the paper it's written on. [Became Goldwynized to: A verbal contract isn't worth the paper it's written on. In Carol Easton, *Search for Goldwyn*]

10 Chaplin is no business man – all he knows is that he can't take anything less. [In Charles Chaplin, *My Autobiography*, Ch. 19]

11 I read part of it all the way through. [In Philip French, *The Movie Moguls*, Ch. 4]

12 We have all passed a lot of water since then. [In discussion with Ezra Goodman. 9]

13 What we want is a story that starts with an earthquake and works its way up to a climax. [In Leslie Halliwell, *Filmgoer's Book of Quotes*]

14 My *Toujours* Lautrec! [In Lillian Ross, *Picture*, 'Throw the Little Old Lady Down the Stairs!']

15 How'm I gonna do decent pictures when all my good writers are in jail? ... Don't misunderstand me, they all ought to be hung. [Quoted by Dorothy Parker in *Writers at Work*, ed. Malcolm Cowley, First Series]

16 That H-bomb. It's dynamite. [In A. Scott Berg, *Goldwyn*]

17 Anybody who goes to see a psychiatrist ought to have his head examined. [Attr., but probably invented by one of his staff]

18 Deep below the glitter, it's all solid tinsel. [Attr. in the *Guardian*, 11 Apr. 1984]

19 Every director bites the hand that lays the golden egg. [Attr. in Alva Johnston, *The Great Goldwyn*, Ch. 1]

20 I'll give you a definite maybe. [Attr.]

21 In two words: im-possible. [Attr. (by Charles Chaplin?) but apocryphal. In Johnston, *The Great Goldwyn*]

22 It's more than magnificent – it's mediocre. [Attr.]

23 Tell me, how did you love my picture? [Attr. in J. R. Colombo, *Colombo's Hollywood*]

24 Too caustic? To hell with cost; we'll make the picture anyway. [Attr. in A. K. Adams, *Cassell's Book of Humorous Quotations*]

25 We're overpaying him but he's worth it.

26 You ought to take the bull between the teeth. [Attr.]

DR I. J. GOOD 1916–

27 When I hear the word 'gun' I reach for my culture. [*The Scientist Speculates*. See also 196:12]

SIR CRISPIN GOODALL

28 The atmosphere knows no boundaries, and the winds carry no passports. [On the greenhouse effect. In the *Independent*, 'Quote Unquote', 13 May 1989]

JOE GOODWIN 1889–1943 and LARRY SHAY 1897–1988

29 When you're smiling the whole world

smiles with you. [Song: *When You're Smiling*, music by Mark Fisher]

MIKHAIL GORBACHEV 1931–

1 It is sometimes said that face-to-face you don't see the other person's face. [After his second summit meeting with President Reagan, Oct. 1986]

2 We need the free competition of minds. [Speech to the Central Committee, Feb. 1988]

3 So shall we break up the union because of sausage? [Responding to Lithuanian complaints about shortages in the shops. In the *Independent*, 'Quote Unquote', 13 Jan. 1990]

RICHARD GORDON 1921–

4 I began to suffer an attack of *terror celibans*, or bachelor's panic. [*Doctor at Sea*, Ch. 1]

5 The established English custom of dropping the national mantle of self-consciousness at Christmastime and revealing the horrible likeness of the charade underneath. [*Doctor in the House*, Ch. 10]

BISHOP CHARLES GORE 1853–1932

6 If there *is* to be a resurrection we must hold on to our toasting forks. [Said while in delirium. In C. A. Alington, *Things Ancient and Modern*, Ch. 5]

7 But for the miracles, I should consider Nero the ideal man. [Attr.]

MAXIM GORKY 1868–1936

8 Everyone knows that it is much harder to turn word into deed than deed into word. [From 'On Plays', In *USSR in Construction*, Apr. 1937]

9 You must write for children in the same way as you do for adults, only better. [Attr.]

EDMUND GOSSE 1849–1928

10 We were as nearly bored as enthusiasm would permit. [On a Swinburne play. In Christopher Hassall, *Edward Marsh*, Ch. 6]

11 There always seemed to me a worm slumbering at the root of his talent. [On Flecker's death. Letter to Edward Marsh, Jan. 1915]

RICHARD GOTT 1938–

12 Development in the Third World usually means the over-development of objects and the underdevelopment of people. [In the *Guardian*, 30 Nov. 1976]

GERALD GOULD 1885–1936

13 The telephone directory is, because of its rigorous selection and repression, a work of art compared to the wastepaper basket. And [James Joyce's] *Ulysses* is a wastepaper basket. [*The English Novel*]

STEPHEN J. GOULD 1941–

14 Life is a copiously branching bush, continually pruned by the grim reaper of extinction, not a ladder of predictable progress. [On evolution. *Wonderful Life*, Ch. 1]

15 Science is all those things which are confirmed to such a degree that it would be unreasonable to withhold one's provisional consent. [Lecture on evolution, Cambridge, 1984. In *Dictionary of Scientific Quotations*, ed. A. L. Mackay]

ANA ANGARIKA GOVINDA 1898–

16 A Guru is far more than a teacher in the ordinary sense of the word. A teacher gives knowledge, but a Guru gives himself. [*The Way of the White Clouds*, 6]

LEW [later LORD] GRADE 1906–

17 When a little girl asked me what two and two make, I'm supposed to have answered, 'It depends if you're buying or selling' . . . Not true! [*Still Dancing*, Ch. 12]

18 All my shows are great. Some of them are bad. But they are all great. [In the *Observer*, 'Sayings of the Week', 14 Sept. 1975]

19 [On being told that the actor playing Christ in TV series was not married to the girl he was living with] What about it? Do you want to crucify the boy? [Attr.]

GRAFFITI

20 Amnesia rules er – ? – ? [In a pub in London W1]

21 Blow your mind – smoke gunpowder. [In Robert Reisner, *Graffiti*]

1 Death is the greatest kick of all, that's why they save it for last.

2 Don't take your wife into a brothel, they'll charge you corkage! [In *Wine Graffiti Book*, comp. 'The Four Muscateers']

3 Dregs? That's what he sediment.

4 Dyslexia Rules – K.O.? [In a Birmingham lavatory]

5 An eye for an eye – soon the whole world will be blind. [On a wall by the Grand Union Canal, Paddington, London]

6 Fighting for peace is like fucking for chastity. [In *Knave* magazine, Mar. 1977]

7 God is not Dead but Alive and Well and working on a Much Less Ambitious Project. [In a Greenwich pub. In the *Guardian*, 'London Letter', 27 Nov. 1975]

8 Happiness is Slough in your rear view mirror. [Car sticker sighted in London, 12 Mar. 1981]

9 Help the police, beat yourself up, OK? [In *London Graffiti*, photographed by Jac Charoux]

10 Hey, hey, L.B.J., how many kids did you kill today? [At period of Vietnam War. In Robert Reisner, *Graffiti*]

11 How come there's only one Monopolies Commission? [In *Book of Business Quotations*, comp. Eugene Weber]

12 I'd give my right hand to be ambidextrous. [In a pub in Camden, London. US version in Robert Reisner, *Graffiti*]

13 If God had meant us to fly, he'd have given us tickets.

14 If Margaret Thatcher is the answer, then it must have been a bloody silly question. [In gentlemen's lavatory on Irish Sealink ferry]

15 Incest – a game the whole family can play. [In Robert Reisner, *Graffiti*]

16 Is there intelligent life on earth? Yes, but I'm only visiting. [In Cambridge. Quoted by Norman Shrapnel in the *Guardian*, 17 Oct. 1970]

17 Is there life before death? [On estate in Lower Falls Road, Belfast. In Sheila Hancock, *Ramblings of an Actress*, Ch. 6]

18 *Je suis Marxiste, tendance Groucho.* [In Paris 1968]

19 Jesus saves but he couldn't on my wages. [In *London Graffiti*, photographed by Jac Charoux]

20 Jesus was a typical man – they always say they'll come back but you never see them again. [In *Woman Talk 2*, ed. Michèle Brown and Ann O'Connor]

21 Just one nuclear bomb can ruin your whole day. [In the *Spectator*, 24/31 Dec. 1988]

22 Keep your city clean – *Eat a pigeon.* [In *Spoken in Jest*, ed. Gillian Bennett]

23 Life is like a rainbow: you get all the colours of the rectum.

24 Man is preceded by forest, followed by desert. [In France during the student revolt, 1968]

25 My mother made me a Lesbian.
Get her to knit one for me too. [On campus at Sussex University, England]

26 No Pope here.
Lucky Pope. [In Londonderry, Northern Ireland, 1977]

27 Nostalgia isn't what it used to be.

28 Nuclear Waste fades your genes. [In *London Graffiti*, photographed by Jac Charoux]

29 One hundred thousand lemmings can't be wrong. [At Balliol College, Oxford. In the *Guardian*, 6 Dec. 1975]

30 One orgasm in the bush is worth two in the hand. [In Robert Reisner, *Graffiti*]

31 Red brothers, go back to your reservations. [In Prague during 1968 uprising. In *Studies in Comparative Communism*, July 1968]

32 Russian circus in town. Do not feed the animals. [In Czechoslovakia, 1968. In Robert Reisner, *Graffiti*]

33 Save water – *Dilute it!* [In *Spoken in Jest*, ed. Gillian Bennett]

34 Take a cannibal to lunch. [In Robert Reisner, *Graffiti*, as pseudo-graffito]

35 *Three* wise men – are you serious? [From *c.* 1984; used as epigraph to Julian Barnes, *Staring at the Sun*, Pt 2]

36 To do is to be – Rousseau.
To be is to do – Sartre.
Doobedoobedoobedoo – Sinatra. [Quoted by

Ronald Fletcher in BBC radio programme *Quote . . . Unquote*, 5 Apr. 1978]

1 Two persons in every one in Woolwich are schizophrenic. [In lavatory in theatre at Woolwich. In *The Times*, 3 May 1978]

2 We aim to please. You aim too please. [In gentlemen's lavatory of New York restaurant]

3 We are the writing on your wall. [At 144 Piccadilly, London, when taken over by squatters]

4 When God created man, she was only experimenting. I always thought men were a phallusy. [In ladies' lavatory]

5 When you've Adam, doesn't it make you Eve? [In *Picking on Men Again*, comp. Judy Allen and Dyan Sheldon]

HARRY GRAHAM 1874–1936

6 'There's been an accident!' they said, / 'Your servant's cut in half: he's dead!' / 'Indeed!' said Mr Jones, 'and please / Send me the half that's got my keys.' [*Ruthless Rhymes*, 'Mr Jones']

7 Billy, in one of his nice new sashes, / Fell in the fire and was burnt to ashes; / Now, although the room grows chilly, / I haven't the heart to poke poor Billy. ['Tender Heartedness']

8 Late last night I slew my wife, / Stretched her on the parquet flooring; / I was loth to take her life, / But I *had* to stop her snoring! [*When Grandma Fell off the Boat*, 'Necessity']

W. S. GRAHAM 1918–1986

9 So here we are, you and I, / Thought up out of silence for an instant here / Under the ancient hardware of the sky. [*In Memoriam: Burns Singer*]

GLORIA GRAHAME 1925–1981

10 I've been rich and I've been poor; believe me rich is better. [In film *The Big Heat*, screenplay by S. Boehm from novel by W. P. McGivern. See also 233:6]

KENNETH GRAHAME 1859–1932

11 'O Mr Hodgitts!' I heard her cry, 'you are brave! for my sake do not be rash!' He was not rash. [*The Golden Age*, 'The Burglars']

12 Monkeys, who very sensibly refrain from speech, lest they should be set to earn their livings. ['The Magic Ring']

13 There is nothing – absolutely nothing – half so much worth doing as simply messing about in boats. [*The Wind in the Willows*, Ch. 11. See also 153:8]

14 The clever men at Oxford / Know all that there is to be knowed. / But they none of them know one half as much / As intelligent Mr Toad. [10, Song]

15 'But we don't want to teach 'em,' replied the Badger. 'We want to learn 'em . . .' [11]

PERCY GRAINGER 1882–1961

16 Salvation Army Booth objected to the devil having all the good tunes. I object to jazz and vaudeville having all the best instruments! [Preface to *Spoon River*. In John Bird, *Percy Grainger*, Appendix C]

ANTONIO GRAMSCI 1891–1937

17 [Hegemony] is the 'spontaneous' consent given by the great masses of the population to the general direction imposed on social life by the dominant . . . group. [*Prison Notebooks*, 'The Intellectuals']

18 To wait until one has grown to half the voters plus one is the programme of cowardly souls who wait for socialism by a royal decree countersigned by two ministers. [In A. Pozzolini, *Antonio Gramsci: An Introduction to His Thought*, Ch. 2]

19 Pessimism of the spirit; optimism of the will. [Attr. description of intelligence]

CARY GRANT 1904–1986

20 [In reply to telegram to his agent asking, 'How old Cary Grant?'] Old Cary Grant fine. How you? [In Leslie Halliwell, *Filmgoer's Book of Quotes*]

GÜNTER GRASS 1927–

21 In a devious way I am uncomplicated. [*From the Diary of a Snail*]

1 What novel – or what else in the world – can have the epic scope of a photograph album? May our Father in Heaven, the untiring amateur who each Sunday snaps us from above, at an unfortunate angle that makes for hideous foreshortening, and pastes our pictures, properly exposed or not, in his album, guide me safely through this album of mine. [*The Tin Drum*, 'The Photograph Album']

2 Even bad books are books and therefore sacred. ['Rasputin and the Alphabet']

3 One of the mistakes the Germans made, in this century and also in the time before, was that they were not brave enough to be afraid. [In Channel 4 TV programme *Voices*, 27 June 1985]

4 The job of a citizen is to keep his mouth open. [In *Contradictory Quotations*, ed. M. Rogers]

A. P. GRAVES 1846–1931

5 Och! Father O'Flynn, you've the wonderful way wid you. [*Father O'Flynn*]

6 Checkin' the crazy ones, coaxin' onaisy ones, / Liftin' the lazy ones on wid the stick.

ROBERT GRAVES 1895–1985

7 No escape, / No such thing: to dream of new dimensions, / Cheating checkmate by painting the king's robe / So that he slides like a queen. [*The Castle*]

8 Children are dumb to say how hot the day is, / How hot the scent is of the summer rose. [*The Cool Web*]

9 Counting the beats, / Counting the slow heart beats, / The bleeding to death of time in slow heart beats, / Wakeful they lie. [*Counting the Beats*]

10 A gaping silken dragon, / Puffed by the wind, suffices us for God. [*The Cuirassiers of the Frontier*]

11 Yet love survives, the word carved on the sill / Under antique dread of the headsman's axe. [*End of Play*]

12 I dung on my grandfather's doorstep, / Which is a reasonable and loving due / To hold no taint of spite or vassalage / And understood only by him and me. [*Front Door Soliloquy*]

13 This house is jealous of its nastiness.

14 To be mad is not easy, / Will earn him no money, / But a niche in the news. [*The Halls of Bedlam*]

15 Christ of his gentleness, / Thirsting and hungering / Walked in the wilderness; / Soft words of grace he spoke / Unto lost desert-folk / That listened wondering. [*In the Wilderness*]

16 These dusty-featured Lollocks / Have their nativity in all disordered / Backs of cupboard drawers. [*Lollocks*]

17 Across two counties he can hear / And catch your words before you speak. / The woodlouse or the maggot's weak / Clamour rings in his sad ear, / And noise so slight it would surpass / Credence. [*Lost Love*]

18 Is it not the height of silent humour / To cause an unknown change in the earth's climate? [*The Meeting*]

19 Stirring suddenly from long hibernation, / I knew myself once more a poet / Guarded by timeless principalities / Against the worm of death. [*Mid-winter Waking*]

20 Those famous men of old, the Ogres – / They had long beards and stinking armpits, / They were wide-mouthed, long-yarded and great-bellied / Yet of no taller stature, Sirs, than you. [*Ogres and Pygmies*]

21 The thundering text, the snivelling commentary.

22 Any honest housewife would sort them out, / Having a nose for fish, an eye for apples. [*The Poets*]

23 You reading over my shoulder, peering beneath / My writing arm. [*The Reader over My Shoulder* (also title of a book of criticism)]

24 What, then, was war? No mere discord of flags / But an infection of the common sky / That sagged ominously upon the earth / Even when the season was the airiest May? [*Recalling War*]

25 Take your delight in momentariness, / Walk between dark and dark – a shining space / With the grave's narrowness, though not its peace. [*Sick Love*]

26 Why have such scores of lovely, gifted

girls / Married impossible men? [*A Slice of Wedding Cake*]

1 'How is your trade, Aquarius, / This frosty night?' / 'Complaints is many and various / And my feet are cold,' says Aquarius. [*Star-talk*]

2 Love is a universal migraine / A bright stain on the vision / Blotting out reason. [*Symptoms of Love*]

3 They carry / Time looped so river-wise about their house / There's no way in by history's road / To name or number them. [*Through Nightmare*]

4 To bring the dead to life / Is no great magic. / Few are wholly dead: / Blow on a dead man's embers / And a live flame will start. [*To Bring the Dead to Life*]

5 To evoke posterity / Is to weep on your own grave, / Ventriloquizing for the unborn. [*To Evoke Posterity*]

6 'What did the mayor do?' / 'I was coming to that.' [*Welsh Incident*]

7 It's an old story – f's for s's – / But good enough for them, the suckers. [*Wm. Brazier*]

8 Goodbye to All That. [Title of book]

9 Nowadays, to curse effectively one cannot rely merely on breaches of religious or semi-religious taboos; a reality or at least a plausibility must be invoked. [*Occupation: Writer*, 'Lars Porsena']

10 For a woman to have a *liaison* is almost always pardonable, and occasionally, when the lover chosen is sufficiently distinguished, even admirable; but in love as in sport, the amateur status must be strictly maintained.

11 I should define a good poem as one that makes complete sense; and says all it has to say memorably and economically, and has been written for no other than poetic reasons. [*Steps*, 'Talk on the Legitimate Criticism of Poetry']

12 If there's no money in poetry, neither is there poetry in money. [Speech at London School of Economics, 6 Dec. 1963]

13 Nine-tenths of English poetic literature is the result either of vulgar careerism, or of a poet trying to keep his hand in. Most poets are dead by their late twenties. [In the *Observer*, 11 Nov. 1962]

14 To be a poet is a condition rather than a profession. [In *Horizon* questionnaire, 1946]

15 Only in a world where there are cranes and horses . . . can poetry survive. [In Derek Walcott, *Map of the New World*, 'Sea Cranes']

16 Prose books are the show dogs I breed and sell to support my cat. [Of his loyalty to poetry. In *Book of Days*, ed. Neal T. Jones, 26 July]

ROBERT GRAVES and ALAN HODGE 1915–1979

17 At the superior nudist camps, a nice class distinction was made: the butlers and maids who brought along the refreshments were forced to admit their lower social standing by wearing loincloths and aprons respectively. [*The Long Week End*, Ch. 16]

ALASDAIR GRAY 1934–

18 Art is the only work open to people who can't get along with others and still want to be special. [*Lanark*, Bk 3, Ch. 1]

19 Glasgow, the sort of industrial city where most people live nowadays but nobody imagines living. [Ch. 11]

20 Of course in nature the only end is death, but death hardly ever happens when people are at their best. That is why we like tragedies. They show men ending energetically with their wits about them and deserving to do it. [Bk 1, Interlude]

HAROLD GRAY 1894–1968

21 Little Orphan Annie. [Title of American comic strip serial, 1925. Derived from song by J. W. Riley]

SIMON GRAY 1936–

22 Sixth-form teachers are something like firemen called in to quench flames that are already out. [*Butley*, Act II]

23 REG: Just one of those historical romances where the hero shoves his sword into assorted villains and his cock into assorted ladies. It won't get the reviews but it'll make us money.
BEN: If he did it the other way round you might get both.

1 STEPHEN: What have you got against having children?
SIMON: Well Steve, in the first place there isn't enough room. In the second place they seem to start by mucking up their parents' lives, and then go on in the third place to muck up their own. In the fourth place it doesn't seem right to bring them into a world like this in the fifth place and in the sixth place I don't like them very much in the first place. OK? [*Otherwise Engaged*, Act II]

SPALDING GRAY 1941–

2 Some say that the Thais are the nicest people that money can buy, because they like to have fun. [*Swimming to Cambodia*, Pt 1]

ROCKY GRAZIANO 1922–1990

3 Somebody Up There Likes Me. [Catch-phrase and title of autobiography]

CELIA GREEN 1935–

4 The way to do research is to attack the facts at the point of greatest astonishment. [*The Decline and Fall of Science*, 'Aphorisms']

5 The remarkable thing about the human mind is its range of limitations.

6 In an autocracy, one person has his way; in an aristocracy, a few people have their way; in a democracy, no one has his way.

HANNAH GREEN [JOANNE GREENBERG] 1932–

7 I Never Promised You a Rose Garden. [Title of book]

MICHAEL GREEN 1927–

8 Coarse sailing is not mucking around in boats, but boating around in muck. [*The Art of Coarse Sailing*, blurb. See also 150:13]

GRAHAM GREENE 1904–1991

9 At one with the One, it didn't mean a thing beside a glass of Guinness on a sunny day. [*Brighton Rock*, Pt 1, Ch. 1]

10 He trailed the clouds of his own glory after him; hell lay about him in his infancy. He was ready for more deaths. [II. 2]

11 Those who marry God ... can become domesticated too – it's just as humdrum a marriage as all the others. [*A Burnt-out Case*, Ch. 1]

12 What's the good of a lie if it's seen through? When I tell a lie no-one can tell it from the gospel truth. Sometimes I can't even tell it myself. [*The Captain and the Enemy*, Pt 1, Ch. 1]

13 His slang ... was always a little out of date as though he had studied in a dictionary of popular usage, but not in the latest edition. [*The Comedians*, Pt 1, Ch. 1, sect. i]

14 However great a man's fear of life ... suicide remains the courageous act, the clear headed act of a mathematician. The suicide has judged by the laws of chance – so many odds against one, that to live will be more miserable than to die. His sense of mathematics is greater than his sense of survival. [4. i]

15 I have often noticed that a bribe ... has that effect – it changes a relation. The man who offers a bribe gives away a little of his own importance; the bribe once accepted, he becomes the inferior, like a man who has paid for a woman. [iii]

16 We mustn't complain too much of being comedians – it's an honourable profession. If only we could be good ones the world might gain at least a sense of style. We have failed – that's all. We are bad comedians, we aren't bad men. [II. 5. ii]

17 Catholics and Communists have committed great crimes, but at least they have not stood aside, like an established society, and been indifferent. I would rather have blood on my hands than water like Pilate. [III. 4. iv]

18 He would certainly have despised Christ for being the son of a carpenter, if the New Testament had not proved in time to be such a howling commercial success. [*Dr Fischer of Geneva*, Ch. 7]

19 To me comfort is like the wrong memory at the wrong place or time: if one is lonely one prefers discomfort. [*The End of the Affair*, Pt I, Ch. 1]

20 He spoke with the faintest foreign accent and it was difficult to determine whether he was Jewish or of an ancient English family.

He gave the impression that very many cities had rubbed him smooth. [*A Gun for Sale*, Ch. 4, sect. iii]

1 So many of his prayers had remained unanswered that he had hopes that this one prayer of his had lodged all the time like wax in the Eternal ear. [*Monsignor Quixote*, Pt 1, Ch. 1]

2 Perhaps we are all fictions, father, in the mind of God.

3 The believer will fight another believer over a shade of difference: the doubter fights only with himself. [4]

4 A solitary laugh is often a laugh of superiority. [9]

5 Hail Mary, quite contrary! [*Our Man in Havana*, Pt 1, Ch. 2]

6 There is always one moment in childhood when the door opens and lets the future in. [*The Power and the Glory*, Pt I, Ch. i]

7 That whisky priest, I wish we had never had him in the house. [ii and *passim*]

8 Of course, before we *know* he is a saint, there will have to be miracles. [IV]

9 Insanity is a kind of innocence. [*The Quiet American*, Pt III, Ch. 2, ii]

10 Fame is a powerful aphrodisiac. [In *Radio Times*, 10 Sept. 1964]

11 I have to watch my characters crossing the room, lighting a cigarette. I have to see everything they do, even if I don't write it down. So my eyes get tired. [On his method of writing. Interview with John Mortimer in the *Sunday Times*, 16 Mar. 1980]

12 The world is not black and white. More like black and grey. [In the *Observer*, 'Sayings of the Year', Dec. 1982]

13 I'm not very conscious of His presence, but I hope that He is still dogging my footsteps. [In the *Observer*, 'Sayings of the Week', 9 Sept. 1984]

14 We're all unbelievers within our own faiths.

15 Sentimentality – that's what we call the sentiment we don't share. [In A. Andrews, *Quotations for Speakers and Writers*. See also 257:6]

ANDY GREENHALGH ?1945–

16 I'm a great lover. I can make sex last . . . ooh . . . twenty minutes. That includes going out to dinner first, of course. [In the *Guardian*, 14 July 1987]

BILL GREENWELL

17 Trendy is emulating your children while they emulate your parents. [In the *New Statesman*, 18 June 1982]

DICK GREENWOOD [Rugby Union coach for England] 1941–

18 It didn't demoralize us, but it moralized them. [On mistake that led to defeat by Wales. In the *Guardian*, 'Sporting Life 1985', 24 Dec. 1985]

GERMAINE GREER 1939–

19 Man is jealous because of his *amour propre*; woman is jealous because of her lack of it. [*The Female Eunuch*, 'Egotism']

20 Women have very little idea of how much men hate them. ['Loathing and Disgust']

21 Women are reputed never to be disgusted. The sad fact is that they often are, but not with men, they are most often disgusted with themselves.

22 The tragedy of machismo is that a man is never quite man enough. [From 'My Mailer Problem', in *Picking on Men*, comp. Judy Allen]

23 Britain's two female figureheads are a woman who can't tell a joke and a woman who can't understand one. [In the *Sunday Times Magazine*, 19 Jan. 1986]

HUBERT GREGG 1914–

24 Maybe it's because I'm a Londoner / That I love London so. [Song: *Maybe It's because I'm a Londoner*, 1949]

PHILIPPA GREGORY [also KATE WEDD] 1954–

25 Any cyclist will confirm that in hilly country the slope is always steeper the side you are going up. This is one of the great

mysteries of Nature. [In the *Guardian*, 12 Oct. 1985]

1 Kate Wedd is not my real name. It is a nom de plume. It is actually my aunt's name; so it is, if you wish, le nom de plume de ma tante. [23 May 1987]

JOYCE GRENFELL 1910–1979

2 George – don't do that. ['Nursery Sketches', *passim*, and in her book of same title]

3 Nikolas, you can manage a big crown, can't you? You've just the ears for it. I think if you pull your ears down a bit that will hold it up. [*George – Don't Do That*, 'Nativity Play']

4 All right, you shall be a cauliflower – only be it *gently*. ['Flowers']

JULIAN GRENFELL 1888–1915

5 And he is dead who will not fight, / And who dies fighting has increase. [*Into Battle*]

CLIFFORD GREY 1887–1941

6 Another little drink wouldn't do us any harm. [Song in musical *The Bing Boys*, 1916, music by Nat Ayer]

7 If you were the only girl in the world, / And I were the only boy. [Song: *If you were the Only Girl*]

SIR EDWARD GREY [later LORD GREY OF FALLODEN] 1862–1933

8 The lamps are going out all over Europe; we shall not see them lit again in our lifetime. [On the eve of war, 3 Aug. 1914]

9 The United States is like a gigantic boiler. Once the fire is lighted under it there is no limit to the power it can generate. [In Winston S. Churchill, *Their Finest Hour*, Ch. 32]

D. W. GRIFFITH 1874–1948

10 Viewed as drama, the [Great] War is somewhat disappointing. [In Leslie Halliwell, *Filmgoer's Book of Quotes*]

MERVYN GRIFFITH-JONES 1909–1978

11 Would you allow your wife or your ser-vant to read this book? [Presenting the case for the prosecution of *Lady Chatterley's Lover*, 20 Oct. 1960, at Old Bailey, London]

LEON GRIFFITHS 1928–1992

12 'Er indoors. [Catchphrase in TV series *Minder*]

13 A nice little earner.

14 My son, the world is your lobster. [From above, in obituary in the *Guardian*, 16 June 1992]

TREVOR GRIFFITHS 1935–

15 It's the sort of suit you walk into a tailor's in and ask for the cheapest suit in the shop and he says you're wearing it. [*The Comedians*, Act I]

16 Cough and the world coughs with you. Fart and you stand alone.

17 Had a look at the alligators. Just floating handbags, really. [II]

18 The intellectual's problem is not vision, it's commitment. You enjoy biting the hand that feeds you, but you'll never bite it off. [*The Party*, Act I]

19 There's nowt'll replace the formative intellectual matrices of a really well-run Sunday School. By Christ. [II]

JO [later LORD] GRIMOND 1913–

20 He had a mind like a beautiful Clapham Junction, through which lines slid off at every sort of tangent. [Of an Oxford friend killed in the war. Contribution to book *My Oxford*]

GEORG GRODDECK

21 Whatever you blame, that you have done yourself. [In 'Palinurus' (Cyril Connolly), *The Unquiet Grave*, Pt III]

JOHN GUARE 1938–

22 Having a rich friend is like drowning and your friend makes lifeboats. But the friend gets touchy if you say one word: lifeboat. [*Six Degrees of Separation*, opening scene]

1 I think avoiding humiliation is the core of tragedy and comedy. [In the *Observer*, 'Sayings of the Week', 23 Oct. 1988]

GIOVANNI GUARESCHI 1908–1968

2 I had to do everything to stay alive and succeeded almost completely by dedicating myself to a precise programme which is summarized in my slogan 'I will not die even if they kill me.' [*The Little World of Don Camillo*, 'How I Got Like This']

PHILIP GUEDALLA 1889–1944

3 Any stigma, as the old saying is, will serve to beat a dogma. [*Ministers and Men*, 'Ministers of State']

4 It was Quintilian or Max Beerbohm who said, 'History repeats itself: historians repeat each other.' [*Supers and Supermen*, 'Some Historians']

5 The cheerful clatter of Sir James Barrie's cans as he went round with the milk of human kindness. ['Some Critics']

6 The work of Henry James has always seemed divisible by a simple dynastic arrangement into three reigns: James I, James II, and the Old Pretender.

7 An Englishman is a man who lives on an island in the North Sea governed by Scotsmen. ['Some More Frenchmen']

8 Biography is a very definite region bounded on the north by history, on the south by fiction, on the east by obituary, and on the west by tedium. [In the *Observer*, 'Sayings of the Week', 3 Mar. 1929]

9 The twentieth century is only the nineteenth speaking with a slight American accent. [Attr.]

TEXAS GUINAN 1884–1933

10 Hello, sucker! [Welcome to nightclub customers]

11 Fifty million Frenchmen can be wrong. [Attr. in *New York World-Telegram*, 21 Mar. 1931, when denied entry into France]

12 A politician is a fellow who will lay down your life for his country. [In *Hammer and Tongues*, ed. Michèle Brown and Ann O'Connor, 'Politics']

ARTHUR GUITERMAN 1871–1943

13 The Prophet's Cam-u-el, that primal Desert Ship. [*The Legend of the First Cam-u-el*]

14 Don't tell your friends about your indigestion: / 'How are you!' is a greeting, not a question. [*A Poet's Proverbs*, 'Of Tact'. See also 366:13]

SACHA GUITRY 1885–1957

15 God, how pretty you are on the phone, tonight! [*Elles et toi*]

16 Vanity is other people's pride. [*Jusqu'à nouvel ordre*]

NUBAR GULBENKIAN 1896–1972

17 The best number for a dinner party is two – myself and a dam' good head waiter. [In the *Daily Telegraph*, 14 Jan. 1965]

THOM GUNN 1929–

18 The group's name on the left, The Knights, / And on the right the slogan Born to Lose. [*Black Jackets*]

19 I saw that lack of love contaminates. / You know I know you know I know you know. [*Carnal Knowledge*]

20 We stand on a white terrace and confer; / This is the last camp of experience. [*From the Highest Camp*]

21 One is always nearer by not keeping still. [*On the Move*]

JOHN GUNTHER 1901–1970

22 Ours is the only country deliberately founded on a good idea. [*Inside America*]

GEORGE GURDJIEFF 1868–1949

23 He can be called a remarkable man who stands out from those around him by the resourcefulness of his mind, and who knows how to be restrained in the manifestations which proceed from his nature, at the same time conducting himself justly and tolerantly towards the weakness of others. [*Meetings with Remarkable Men*, Introduction]

DOROTHY GURNEY 1858–1932

24 The kiss of the sun for pardon. / The

song of the birds for mirth. / One is nearer God's Heart in a garden / Than anywhere else on earth. [*God's Garden*]

IVOR GURNEY 1890–1937

1 The songs I had are withered / Or vanished clean, / Yet there are bright tracks / Where I have been. [*The songs I had*]

ARLO GUTHRIE 1947–

2 I don't know, but I've been told / That the streets of heaven have all been sold. [Song. In J. Green, *Book of Rock Quotes*]

3 The world has shown me what it has to offer ... it's a nice place to visit, but I wouldn't want to live there. [In *Wit and Wisdom of Rock and Roll*, ed. Maxim Jakubowski]

WOODY GUTHRIE 1912–1967

4 Some will rob you with a six gun, / And some with a fountain pen. [Song: *Pretty Boy Floyd*]

5 So Long, It's Been Good to Know Yuh. [Title of song]

6 This Land is Your Land, this Land is My Land. [Song: *This Land is Your Land*]

H

JOHN HABBERTON 1842–1921

1 Want to shee the wheels go wound. [*Helen's Babies*, 1]

ARCHBISHOP JOHN HABGOOD 1927–

2 Has it occurred to you that the lust for certainty may be a sin? [In BBC TV Programme *On the Record*, 8 Dec. 1988]

OTTO HAHN 1879–1968

3 But God can't want that. [Of the possibility of releasing atomic energy. Said in 1939, recalled in the *Guardian*, 17 Apr. 1987]

EARL HAIG 1861–1928

4 FOCH: Are the men in good heart?
HAIG: They never were in better heart, and are longing for a fight. [*Diaries*, 12 Sept. 1915]

5 Like the feather pillow he bears the mark of the last person who sat on him. [Of the Earl of Derby. Letter to Lady Haig, 14 Jan. 1918]

6 Every position must be held to the last man: there must be no retirement. With our backs to the wall, and believing in the justice of our cause, each one of us must fight on to the end. [Order to the British troops, 12 Apr.]

EMPEROR HAILE SELASSIE OF ABYSSINIA 1892–1975

7 We have finished the job, what shall we do with the tools? [Telegram in 1941 to Winston Churchill, echoing his 'Give us the tools, and we will finish the job'; see 79:20. In Edward Marsh, *Ambrosia and Small Beer*, Ch. 4]

LORD HAILSHAM [QUINTIN HOGG] 1907–

8 Conservatives do not believe that political struggle is the most important thing in life . . . The simplest among them prefer fox-hunting – the wisest religion. [*The Case for Conservatism*, p. 10]

9 The Conservatives do not believe it necessary, and, even if it were, we should oppose it. [From the *Oxford Mail*, in M. Bateman, *This England*, selections from the *New Statesman*, Pt III]

10 A great party is not to be brought down because of a scandal by a woman of easy virtue and a proved liar. [On the Profumo affair. In BBC TV interview, 13 June 1963]

11 If the British public falls for this [Labour policies], I say it will be stark, staring bonkers. [At press conference at Conservative Central Office before general election, 12 Oct. 1964]

12 God doesn't count on his hands, you know. [On reaching 80. In BBC radio programme *Law in Action*, 9 Oct. 1987]

J. B. S. HALDANE 1892–1964

13 Shelley and Keats were the last English poets who were at all up to date in their chemical knowledge. [*Daedalus or Science and the Future*]

1 There is no great invention, from fire to flying, which has not been hailed as an insult to some god.

2 The conservative has but little to fear from the man whose reason is the servant of his passions, but let him beware of him in whom reason has become the greatest and most terrible of passions.

3 It took man 250,000 years to transcend the hunting pack. It will not take him so long to transcend the nation.

4 If human beings could be propagated by cutting, like apple trees, aristocracy would be biologically sound. [*The Inequality of Man*, title essay]

5 The higher animals are not larger than the lower because they are more complicated. They are more complicated because they are larger. [*Possible Worlds*, 'On Being the Right Size']

6 An angel whose muscles developed no more power weight for weight than those of an eagle or a pigeon would require a breast projecting for about four feet to house the muscles engaged in working its wings, while to economize in weight, its legs would have to be reduced to mere stilts.

7 Christian Science is so often therapeutically successful because it lays stress on the patient's believing in his or her own health rather than in Noah's Ark or the Ascension. ['Duty of Doubt']

8 My own suspicion is that the universe is not only queerer than we suppose, but queerer than we *can* suppose. [Title essay]

VISCOUNT HALDANE 1856–1928

9 I was a little exhausted when I arrived [at the War Office] ... and asked the tall ex-Guards soldier in attendance for a glass of water. 'Certainly, sir: Irish or Scotch?' [Letter. In Dudley Sommer, *Haldane of Cloan*, Ch. 8]

10 Yes, I consider Lötze's classroom was my spiritual home. [Remark at Mrs Humphry Ward's, later distorted by Professor Oncken, so that it referred to Germany. In 22]

H. R. HALDEMAN 1926–

11 Once the toothpaste is out of the tube, it is awfully hard to get it back in. [Comment to John Dean on Watergate affair, 8 Apr. 1973]

GENERAL FRANZ HALDER

12 It is hardly too much to say that the campaign against Russia has been won in fourteen days. [Diary note, 3 July 1941. In W. L. Shirer, *The Rise and Fall of the Third Reich*, Ch. 23]

ÉLIE HALÉVY 1870–1937

13 The Socialists believe in two things which are absolutely different and perhaps even contradictory: freedom and organization. [In W. R. Inge, *The End of an Age*]

BILL HALEY 1925–1985

14 See You Later, Alligator! [Title of song, 1956, written by R. Guidry]

JERRY HALL

15 My mother said it was simple to keep a man, you must be a maid in the living room, a cook in the kitchen and a whore in the bedroom. I said I'd hire the other two and take care of the bedroom bit. [In the *Observer*, 'Sayings of the Year', 29 Dec. 1985]

HENRY HALL 1898–1989

16 This is Henry Hall speaking, and tonight is my guest night. [Catchphrase in BBC radio programme, from 1934]

SIR PETER HALL 1930–

17 I don't regard Brecht as a man of iron-grey purpose and intellect, I think he is a theatrical whore of the first quality. [In Frank Muir, *Frank Muir Book*]

18 Bottoms on seats. [His policy for the National Theatre, London. In the *Spectator*, 10 May 1980. Often becomes 'bums on seats']

STUART HALL 1932–

19 Politics does not reflect majorities, it constructs them. [In *Marxism Today*, July 1987]

MARGARET HALSEY 1910–

1 Englishwomen's shoes look as if they had been made by someone who had often heard shoes described, but had never seen any. [*With Malice Toward Some*, Pt 2]

GENERAL SIR IAN HAMILTON 1853–1947

2 Dig, dig, dig! [Instructions at Gallipoli campaign, 1916]

WILLIE HAMILTON, MP 1917–

3 The tourists who come to our island take in the Monarchy along with feeding the pigeons in Trafalgar Square. [*My Queen and I*, Ch. 9]

DAG HAMMARSKJÖLD 1905–1961

4 Pray that your loneliness may spur you into finding something to live for, great enough to die for. [*Diaries*, 1951]

5 In the last analysis, it is our conception of death which decides our answers to all the questions that life puts to us. [1958]

6 I don't know Who – or what – put the question, I don't know when it was put. I don't even remember answering. But at some moment I did answer *Yes* to Someone – or Something – and from that hour I was certain that existence is meaningful and that, therefore, my life, in self-surrender, had a goal. [*Markings*, 'Whitsunday 1961']

OSCAR HAMMERSTEIN II 1895–1960

7 June is Bustin' Out All Over. [Title of song in musical *Carousel*, music by Richard Rodgers]

8 I Whistle a Happy Tune. [Title of song in musical *The King and I*, I, music by Richard Rodgers]

9 Hello, Young Lovers, Wherever You Are. [Title of song in *The King and I*]

10 The last time I saw Paris, her heart was warm and gay, / I heard the laughter of her heart in every street café. [Song: *The Last Time I Saw Paris*, in musical *Lady be Good*]

11 Oh, what a beautiful mornin'! / Oh, what a beautiful day! [Song: *Oh, What a Beautiful Mornin'*, in musical *Oklahoma!*, music by Richard Rodgers]

12 The corn is as high as an elephant's eye.

13 Ol' man river, dat ol' man river, / He must know sumpin', but don't say nothin', / He just keeps rollin', he keeps on rollin' along. [Song: *Ol' Man River*, in musical *Show Boat*, I, music by Jerome Kern]

14 Tired of living, / And scared of dying.

15 The hills are alive with the sound of music / With songs they have sung / For a thousand years. [Title song in musical *The Sound of Music*, music by Richard Rodgers]

16 Some enchanted evening, / you may see a stranger / Across a crowded room. [Song: *Some Enchanted Evening*, in musical *South Pacific*, I, music by Richard Rodgers]

17 I'm Gonna Wash That Man Right Out of My Hair. [Title of song in *South Pacific*]

KATHARINE HAMNETT

18 I have always said that the best clothes are invisible . . . they make you notice the person. [In the *Independent*, 'Quote Unquote', 11 Mar. 1989]

CHRISTOPHER HAMPTON 1946–

19 You know very well that unless you're a scientist, it's much more important for a theory to be shapely, than for it to be true. [*The Philanthropist*, sc. 1]

20 You see, always divide people into two groups. Those who live by what they know to be a lie, and those who live by what they believe, falsely, to be the truth. [6]

21 If I had to give a definition of capitalism I would say: the process whereby American girls turn into American women. [*Savages*, sc. 16]

22 You have wants the way other people have toothache. Kind of dull and general. [*Treats*, sc. 6]

23 Asking a working writer what he thinks about critics is like asking a lamp-post how it feels about dogs. [In the *Sunday Times Magazine*, 16 Oct. 1977]

SHEILA HANCOCK 1942–

24 He [Kenneth Williams] suffers fools by

gladly making them suffer. [*Ramblings of an Actress*, Ch. 1]

TONY HANCOCK 1924–1968

1 Flippin' kids! [Catchphrase in BBC radio comedy series *Educating Archie*, 1950s]

2 It's red hot, mate. I hate to think of this sort of book getting into the wrong hands. As soon as I've finished this, I shall recommend they ban it. [BBC TV comedy series *Hancock's Half Hour*, 'The Missing Page', scripts by Ray Galton and Alan Simpson]

3 I'm having a little reunion of my old army pals. The Third East Cheam Light Horse. Three of the heaviest drinkers who ever set foot inside a pair of army boots. ['The Reunion Party']

4 He was the only man I knew who came back from Dunkirk with two women ... Well it's too far for one to row, isn't it?

5 And when I'm finally called, by the Great Architect, and he says 'What did you do?' I shall just bring me book out and say, 'Here you are, add that lot up.' ['The Blood Donor']

6 I came in here in all good faith to help my country. I don't mind giving a reasonable amount [of blood], but a pint ... why that's very nearly an armful. I'm sorry. I'm not walking around with an empty arm for anybody.

7 Why kill time when you can kill yourself? [In film *The Rebel*, script by Ray Galton and Alan Simpson]

TERRY HANDS 1941–

8 English actresses are mistresses and French ones clever daughters. [Attr. in the *Sunday Times Magazine*, 26 Nov. 1978]

MINNY MAUD HANFF 1880–1942

9 Since then they called him Sunny Jim. [Advertisement for Force, a breakfast food, *c.* 1903]

CLIFFORD HANLEY 1922–

10 A born leader of men is somebody who is afraid to go anywhere by himself. [In conversation. In *Scottish Quotations*, comp. Alan Bold]

JAMES HANLEY 1901–1985

11 That is the art of living that your price shall suit everybody. [*Drift*, Ch. 2]

12 You talk about walking in the wilderness, but what else *is* the world but that, and besides, aren't we all walking in one kind of wilderness or another, since only we can make them. [*A Walk in the Wilderness*, title story]

BRIAN HANRAHAN 1949–

13 I'm not allowed to say how many planes joined the raid but I counted them all out and I counted them all back. [On British attack in Falklands War. BBC broadcast, 1 May 1982]

OTTO HARBACH 1873–1963

14 Smoke Gets In Your Eyes. [Title of song in musical *Roberta*, music by Jerome Kern]

MAJOR-GENERAL HARBORD 1866–1947

15 I met the great little man [Colonel House], the man who can be silent in several languages. [In John Dos Passos, *Mr Wilson's War*, Ch. 3, sect. xv]

E. Y. 'YIP' HARBURG 1898–1981

16 Brother, Can You Spare a Dime? [Title of song in musical *New Americana*, music by Jay Gorney]

17 Say, it's only a paper moon, / Sailing over a cardboard sea. [Song: *Paper Moon*, in musical *Take a Chance*]

18 Someday I'll wish upon star. [Song: *Over the Rainbow*, in film *The Wizard of Oz*, music by Harold Arlen]

19 Somewhere over the rainbow, / Way up high: / There's a land that I heard of / Once in a lullaby.

GILBERT HARDING 1907–1960

20 I would like to quote what a judge said not long ago – that all his experience both as Counsel and Judge had been spent in sorting out the difficulties of people who, upon the recommendation of people they did not know, signed documents which they did

not read, to buy goods they did not need, with money they had not got. [TV answer to question on subject of hire purchase. In *Gilbert Harding and His Friends*]

1 [When asked by Mae West's manager, 'Can't you sound a bit more sexy when you interview her?'] If, sir, I possessed the power of conveying unlimited sexual attraction through the potency of my voice, I would not be reduced to accepting a miserable pittance from the BBC for interviewing a faded female in a damp basement.

MIKE HARDING 1944–

2 It was the Puritans who put an end to the practice of dancing, as well as discontinuing the tradition of kings wearing heads on their shoulders. [In *Apt and Amusing Quotations*, ed. G. F. Lamb, 'History']

REV. E. J. HARDY

3 How to be Happy though Married. [Title of book, 1910]

OLIVER HARDY 1892–1957

4 Another nice mess you've gotten me into. [To Stan Laurel. Catchphrase in film comedies]

THOMAS HARDY 1840–1928

5 When the Present has latched its postern behind my tremulous stay, / And the May month flaps its glad green leaves like wings, / Delicate-filmed as new-spun silk, will the neighbours say, / 'He was a man who used to notice such things'? [*Afterwards*]

6 Where once we danced, where once we sang, Gentlemen, / The floors are shrunken, cobwebs hang. [*An Ancient to Ancients*]

7 The bower we shrined to Tennyson, / Gentlemen, / Is roof-wrecked; damps there drip upon / Sagged seats, the creeper-nails are rust, / The spider is sole denizen.

8 Any little old song / Will do for me. [*Any little old song*]

9 So zestfully canst thou sing? / And all this indignity, / With God's consent, on thee! / Blinded ere yet a-wing. [*The Blinded Bird*]

10 The Immanent Will that stirs and urges everything. [*The Convergence of the Twain*]

11 Yet hear – no doubt to your surprise – / I am grieving, for his sake, / That I have escaped the sacrifice / I was distressed to make! [*Cross-currents*]

12 So little cause for carolings / Of such ecstatic sound / Was written on terrestrial things / Afar or nigh around, / That I could think there trembled through / His happy good-night air / Some blessed Hope, whereof he knew / And I was unaware. [*The Darkling Thrush*]

13 His landmark is a kopje-crest / That breaks the veldt around; / And foreign constellations west / Each night above his mound. [*Drummer Hodge*]

14 Smile out; but still suffer: / The paths of love are rougher / Than thoroughfares of stones. [*The End of the Episode*]

15 We two kept house, the Past and I. [*The Ghost of the Past*]

16 O man-projected Figure, of late / Imaged as we, thy knell who shall survive? / Whence came it we were tempted to create / One whom we can no longer keep alive? [*God's Funeral*]

17 Crass Casualty obstructs the sun and rain, / And dicing Time for gladness casts a moan . . . / These purblind Doomsters had as readily strown / Blisses about my pilgrimage as pain. [*Hap*]

18 Well, World, you have kept faith with me, / Kept faith with me; / Upon the whole you have proved to be / Much as you said you were. [*He never expected much*]

19 I am the family face; / Flesh perishes, I live on, / Projecting trait and trace / Through time to times anon, / And leaping from place to place / Over oblivion. [*Heredity*]

20 I need not go / Through sleet and snow / To where I know / She waits for me: / She will tarry there / Till I find it fair, / And have time to spare / From company. [*I need not go*]

21 Who holds that if way to the Better there be, it exacts a full look at the Worst. [*In Tenebris*, II]

22 Only a man harrowing clods / In a slow

silent walk / With an old horse that stumbles and nods / Half asleep as they stalk. [*In the Time of 'The Breaking of Nations'*]

1 Yonder a maid and her wight / Come whispering by: / War's annals will cloud into night / Ere their story die.

2 She chose her bearers before she died / From her fancy-men. [*Julie-Jane*]

3 Let me enjoy the earth no less / Because the all-enacting Might / That fashioned forth its loveliness / Had other aims than my delight. [*Let me enjoy*]

4 There's not a modest maiden elf / But dreads the final Trumpet, / Lest half of her should rise herself, / And half some sturdy strumpet! [*The Levelled Churchyard*]

5 'Well, though it seems / Beyond our dreams,' / Said Liddell to Scott, / 'We've really got / To the very end.' [*Liddell and Scott*]

6 What of the faith and fire within us / Men who march away / Ere the barncocks say / Night is growing gray, / Leaving all that here can win us? [*Men who march away*]

7 In the third-class seat sat the journeying boy, / And the roof-lamp's oily flame / Played down on his listless form and face, / Bewrapt past knowing to what he was going, / Or whence he came. [*Midnight on the Great Western*]

8 And both of us, scorning parochial ways, / Had lived like the wives in the patriarchs' days. [*Over the Coffin*]

9 Christmas Eve, and twelve of the clock. / 'Now they are all on their knees.' [*Oxen*]

10 If someone said on Christmas Eve, / 'Come see the oxen kneel . . .' / I should go with him in the gloom, / Hoping it might be so.

11 Queer are the ways of a man I know. [*The Phantom Horsewoman*]

12 The Roman Road runs straight and bare / As the pale parting-line in hair. [*The Roman Road*]

13 There was Life – pale and hoar; / And slow it said to me, / 'Twice-over cannot be!' [*A Second Attempt*]

14 A pinch of unseen, unguarded dust. [*Shelley's Skylark*]

15 'What do you think of it, Moon, / As you go? / Is life much or no?' / 'O, I think of it, often think of it / As a show / God ought surely to shut up soon, / As I go.' [*To the Moon*]

16 A star looks down at me, / And says: 'Here I and you / Stand, each in our degree: / What do you mean to do?' [*Waiting Both*]

17 This is the weather the cuckoo likes / And so do I. [*Weathers*]

18 When I set out for Lyonnesse, / A hundred miles away, / The rime was on the spray. [*When I set out for Lyonnesse*]

19 Who's in the next room? – who? / I seemed to see / Somebody in the dawning passing through, / Unknown to me. [*Who's in the next room?*]

20 You were the sort that men forget; / Though I – not yet! – / Perhaps not ever. [*You were the Sort That Men Forget*]

21 A local cult, called Christianity. [*The Dynasts*, 1. vi]

22 To persons standing alone on a hill during a clear midnight such as this, the roll of the world eastward is almost a palpable movement. [*Far from the Madding Crowd*, Ch. 2]

23 A nice unparticular man. [8]

24 Ethelberta breathed a sort of exclamation, not right out, but stealthily, like a parson's damn. [*The Hand of Ethelberta*]

25 Done because we are too menny. [*Jude the Obscure*, Pt VI, Ch. 2]

26 Life's Little Ironies. [Title of volume of stories]

27 All her shining keys will be took from her, and her cupboards opened, and things a' didn't wish seen, anybody will see; and her little wishes and ways will all be as nothing. [*The Mayor of Casterbridge*, Ch. 18]

28 The long, laborious road, dry, empty, and white. It was quite open to the heath on each side, and bisected that vast dark surface like the parting-line on a head of black hair, diminishing and bending away on the furthest horizon. [*The Return of the Native*, Ch. 2]

29 A little one-eyed, blinking sort o' place. [*Tess of the D'Urbervilles*, Ch. 1]

1 'Justice' was done, and the President of the Immortals, in Aeschylean phrase, had ended his sport with Tess. [59]

2 Good, but not religious-good. [*Under the Greenwood Tree*, I, Ch. 2]

3 I like a story with a bad moral ... all good stories have a coarse touch or a bad moral, depend on't. If the story-tellers could ha' got decency and good morals from true stories, who'd have troubled to invent parables? [8]

4 Silent? ah, he is silent! He can keep silence well. That man's silence is wonderful to listen to. [II. 5]

5 You was a good man, and did good things. [*The Woodlanders*, Ch. 48]

6 Oh, but I admire it [the *Iliad*] greatly. Why, it's in the *Marmion* class! [To T. E. Lawrence, who disparaged the work. In Robert Graves, *Goodbye to All That*, Ch. 28]

DAVID HARE 1947–

7 I sometimes think that if the Lord Jesus returned today, the Church of England would ask him to set out his ideas on a single sheet of A4. [*Racing Demon*, Act I, sc. 4]

8 When you get angry, they tell you, count to five before you reply. Why should I count to five? It's what happens *before* you count to five which makes life interesting. [*Secret Rapture*, Sc. 7]

9 The theatre is the best way of showing the gap between what is said and what is seen to be done, and that is why, ragged and gap-toothed as it is, it has still a far healthier potential than some poorer, abandoned arts. [In the *Sunday Times Magazine*, 26 Nov. 1978, 'The Playwright as Historian']

10 She's got everything she wants and yet she seems furious all day. [Of Margaret Thatcher. In the *Independent*, 6 Oct. 1988]

11 The English are very good at hiding emotions, but without suggesting there is anything passionate to hide. [In the *Observer Magazine*, 26 May 1989]

12 A gift for dialogue qualifies you to be a playwright no more than a gift for mixing sand and water qualifies you to build cathedrals. [In the *Independent on Sunday*, 26 May 1991]

See also **HOWARD BRENTON** and **DAVID HARE**

MAURICE E. HARE 1886–1967

13 There once was a man who said, 'Damn! / It is borne in upon me I am / An engine that moves / In predestinate grooves; / I'm not even a bus, I'm a tram.' [Limerick]

W. F. HARGREAVES 1846–1919

14 I'm Burlington Bertie: I rise at ten thirty. [Song: *Burlington Bertie from Bow*, 1915, sung by Ella Shields]

15 I walk down the Strand / With my gloves on my hand, / And I walk down again / With them off.

16 P. C. 49. [Title of song]

MERRILY HARPUR 1948–

17 You can't make a silk purse out of a sow's ear, but you can make the most lovely homemade wine. [*The Nightmares of Dream Topping*]

18 A man is about thirty-eight before he stockpiles enough socks to be able to get one truly matching pair. [In *Femail on Sunday*, 7 July 1985]

J. P. HARRINGTON 1865–?

19 Be Good. If You Can't be Good, be Careful! [Title of song, music by James W. Tate]

20 Now your country calls you far across the sea, / To do a soldier's duty / For England, home and beauty. [Song: *The Girls You Leave Behind You*]

J. P. HARRINGTON and GEORGE LE BRUNN ?–1905

21 Everything in the Garden's Lovely! [Title of music-hall song, sung by Marie Lloyd]

CHARLES K. HARRIS 1865–1930

22 Many a heart is aching, if you could read them all, / Many the hopes that have vanished, after the ball. [Song: *After the Ball*, 1892, in show *A Trip to Chinatown*]

CLIFFORD HARRIS

1 You called me Baby Doll a year ago. [Song: *A Broken Doll*, 1916, music by James W. Tate]

FENELLA HARRISON 1944–

2 The world is an increasingly treeless jungle. [' "Words of Wisdom" for an Unborn child', in *The Times*, 21 Apr. 1988]

TONY HARRISON 1937–

3 Class v. class, bitter as before, / The unending violence of US and THEM, / personified in 1984 / by Coal Board MacGregor and the NUM. [*V*]

4 I have always disliked the idea of an arts ghetto in which poetry is kept on a life-support system. [In the *Observer*, 23 July 1989]

LORENZ HART 1895–1943

5 Bewitched, Bothered and Bewildered. [Title of song in musical *Pal Joey*, music by Richard Rodgers]

6 That's Why the Lady is a Tramp. [Title of song in musical *Babes in Arms*]

7 With a Song in My Heart. [Title of song in musical *Spring is Here*, 1929]

RUPERT HART-DAVIS 1907–

8 President Kennedy is a great one for the girls, and during the election his opponents said that if he got to the White House they only hoped he would do for fornication what Eisenhower did for golf. [Letter, 25 Feb. 1961, *Lyttelton–Hart-Davis Letters*, ed. Rupert Hart-Davis, Vol. 3]

L. P. HARTLEY 1895–1972

9 The past is a foreign country: they do things differently there. [*The Go-between*, opening words]

WILLIAM HARTSON 1947–

10 A game to subdue the turbulent spirit, or to worry a tranquil mind. [*The Kings of Chess*, Ch. I]

SIR JOHN HARVEY-JONES 1924–

11 It is, of course, a particularly British characteristic to think that every man is the same under the skin, and that Eskimos are really only would-be old Etonians wearing fur coats. [*Making It Happen*, 6]

MINNIE HASKINS 1875–1957

12 And I said to the man who stood at the gate of the year: 'Give me a light that I may tread safely into the unknown.' And he replied: 'Go out into the darkness and put your hand into the hand of God. That shall be to you better than light and safer than a known way.' [*The Desert*, Introduction. Quoted by King George VI in his Christmas Broadcast, 1939]

CHRISTOPHER HASSALL 1912–1963

13 Some Day My Heart Will Awake. [Title of song in operetta *King's Rhapsody*, Act I, music by Ivor Novello]

14 She's genuinely bogus. [Of Dame Edith Sitwell. Attr.]

H. DE CRONIN HASTINGS 1902–1986

15 Worm's eye view. [Caption to photograph in *Architectural Review*, c. 1932, and *passim*]

CAPTAIN GEORGE HASWELL

16 Gentlemen, before the barrage lifts! [Toast before Battle of the Somme, 1916. In E. Bush, *Salute the Soldier*]

ROY HATTERSLEY, MP 1932–

17 The Fabians are 100 years old. In many ways they always have been. [On centenary of the Fabian Society. In the *Guardian*, 17 Mar. 1984]

18 The Treasury operates like one of those First World War howitzers that landed their shells on targets that gunners never saw. Home Office policy is hand to hand fighting. [In the *Guardian*, 18 July 1987]

DEREK HATTON [Deputy leader of Liverpool Council] 1948–

19 They were looking for a peg to hang a

Hatton. [Of the Militant Inquiry into Labour politics in Liverpool. In the *Observer*, 'Sayings of the Week', 23 Feb. 1986]

STEPHEN HAWKING 1942–

1 God not only plays dice. He also sometimes throws the dice where they cannot be seen. [From *Nature*, 1975, 257.362, in *Dictionary of Scientific Quotations*, ed. A. L. Mackay. See also 115:12]

IAN HAY [JOHN HAY BEITH] 1876–1952

2 Funny peculiar, or funny ha-ha? [*The Housemaster*, III. Catchphrase appears but does not originate here]

WILL HAY 1888–1949

3 MASTER: They split the atom by firing particles at it, at 5,500 miles a second.
BOY: Good heavens. And they only split it? [In music-hall and radio comedy sketches *The Fourth Form at St Michael's, passim*]

4 MASTER: Well, who *was* Noah's wife?
BOY: Joan of Arc.

S. I. HAYAKAWA 1908–1992

5 It is not true that we have only one life to live; if we can read, we can live as many more lives and as many kinds of lives as we wish. [In *Writer's Quotation Book*, ed. James Charlton]

J. MILTON HAYES 1884–1940

6 There's a one-eyed yellow idol to the north of Khatmandu; / There's a little marble cross below the town; / And a broken-hearted woman tends the grave of 'Mad Carew', / While the yellow god forever gazes down. [*The Green Eye of the Little Yellow God*, written, 1911, with Cuthbert Clarke]

7 The Whitest Man I Know. [Title of song, music by R. Fenton Gower. See also 198:23, 221:14]

ARTHUR GARFIELD HAYS 1881–1954

8 When there's a rift in the lute, the business of the lawyer is to widen the rift and gather the loot. [In A. Andrews, *Quotations for Speakers and Writers*]

DENIS [later LORD] HEALEY 1917–

9 Their [The Conservatives'] Europeanism is nothing but imperialism with an inferiority complex. [In the *Observer*, 'Sayings of the Week', 7 Oct. 1962]

10 That part of his speech was rather like being savaged by a dead sheep. [On being attacked in a parliamentary debate by Geoffrey Howe over his Budget proposals, House of Commons, 14 June 1978]

11 Mrs Thatcher is doing for monetarism what the Boston Strangler did for door-to-door salesmen. [Speech in House of Commons, 15 Dec. 1979]

12 His [Harold Wilson's] short-term opportunism, allied with a capacity for self-delusion which made Walter Mitty appear unimaginative, often plunged the Government into chaos. [*The Time of My Life*, Ch. 16]

13 The party of the state owners has become the party of the estate agents. [Of the Conservatives. In the *Financial Times*, 28 Nov. 1990]

14 Not just a female Franco, but a Pétain in petticoats. [Of Mrs Thatcher. In Hugh Rawson, *Dictionary of Invective*]

15 Keith Joseph? . . . A wonderful mixture of Rasputin and Tommy Cooper. [Interview in John Mortimer, *In Character*]

16 He hasn't got the Tebbit touch. I'm afraid you can't turn a spaniel into a Rottweiler. [On John Major's demonstrating aggression during election campaign. To journalists in North Kensington, London, 21 Mar. 1992]

SEAMUS HEANEY 1939–

17 That's the borderline that poetry / Operates on too, always in between / What you would like to happen and what will – / Whether you like it or not. [*The Cure at Troy*, p. 2]

18 Once in a lifetime / The longed-for tidal wave / Of justice can rise up, / And hope and history rhyme. [77]

19 Between my finger and my thumb / The squat pen rests; snug as a gun. [*Digging*]

1 We are voluptuaries of the morning after. [*Holding Course*]

2 Keep your eye clear / as the bleb of the icicle, / trust the feel of what nubbed treasure / your hands have known. [*North*]

3 You lose more of yourself than you redeem / Doing the decent thing. [*Station Island*, XII]

4 When they spoke of the mammon of iniquity / The coins in my pockets reddened like stove-lids. [*Terminus*]

5 Auden of the last years, when he had begun to resemble in his own person an ample, flopping, ambulatory volume of the OED in carpet-slippers. [In *London Review of Books*, 4 June 1987]

6 I never wrote with an audience in mind. If you're writing poems, you truly forget about an audience – it's the poet himself who *listens in*. [Interview in the *Sunday Times*, 7 Oct. 1990]

W. R. HEARST 1863–1951

7 [When newspaper artist Frederic Remington cabled to be allowed home since there was no war in Cuba for him to cover] Please remain. You furnish the pictures and I'll furnish the war. [Cable, 1898]

8 Stop running those dogs on your page. I wouldn't have them peeing on my cheapest rug. [To editor who was publishing Thurber's drawings. In James Thurber, *The Years with Ross*, Ch. 7]

SIR EDWARD HEATH 1916–

9 It is the unpleasant and unacceptable face of capitalism. [Of the Lonrho affair In House of Commons, 15 May 1973]

10 I was, however, approached by Chinese journalists, one of whom observed how interesting it was that I combined politics – which is practical, and music – which is fantasy. I replied they had it the wrong way round! [In the *Sunday Times*, 8 Jan. 1989]

See also under CONSERVATIVE PARTY PRESS RELEASE

FRED HEATHERTON [DESMOND COX 1903–1966 HAROLD BOX 1903–1981 and IRWIN DASH 1892–1984]

11 I've got a loverly bunch of cocoanuts, / There they are a-standing in a row, / Big ones, small ones, some as big as your head. [Song: *I've Got a Lovely Bunch of Cocoanuts*, 1948]

12 Singing roll or bowl a ball, a penny a pitch.

BEN HECHT 1893–1964

13 I'll tell you briefly what I think of newspapermen: the hand of God reaching down into the mire couldn't elevate one of them to the depths of degradation – not by a million miles. [Screenplay of film *Nothing Sacred*]

14 A city where wise guys peddle gold bricks to each other and Truth, crushed down to earth, rises again as phoney as a glass eye. [Of New York]

15 Starlet is a name for any woman under thirty not actively employed in a brothel. [In *Hollywood Anecdotes*, ed. Paul F. Boller Jr and Kristin Thompson]

ERIC HEFFER, MP 1922–1991

16 They are nothing else but a load of kippers, two-faced with no guts. [Of the Conservative Party. Said in House of Commons, n.d.]

MARTIN HEIDEGGER 1889–1976

17 Only when we turn thoughtfully toward what has already been thought, will we be turned to use for what must still be thought. [*Identity and Difference*]

18 We are too late for the gods, too early for Being. [In review in *The Times Literary Supplement*, 1 July 1965]

19 Poetry proper is never merely a higher mode (melos) of everyday language. It is rather the reverse: everyday language is a forgotten and therefore used up poem, from which there hardly resounds a call any longer. [From *Language*, in Bruce Chatwin, *Songlines*, p. 35]

JASCHA HEIFETZ 1901–1987

20 I would rather starve where food is good.

[To his friends on going to Paris in the 1920s. In David Dubal, *Evenings with Horowitz*, Ch. 28]

CYNTHIA HEIMEL

1 If You Can't Live without Me, Why aren't You Dead?! [Title of book, ascr. by Heimel to John Crowley]

ROBERT HEINLEIN 1907–1979

2 Stranger in a Strange Land. [Title of book]

WERNER HEISENBERG 1901–1976

3 An expert is someone who knows some of the worst mistakes that can be made in his subject, and how to avoid them. [*Physics and Beyond*]

4 Natural science does not simply describe and explain nature, it is part of the interplay between nature and ourselves. [*Physics and Philosophy*]

JOSEPH HELLER 1923–

5 'You're crazy,' Clevinger shouted vehemently, his eyes filling with tears. 'You've got a Jehovah complex.' [*Catch-22*, Ch. 2]

6 He was a self-made man who owed his lack of success to nobody. [3]

7 He had decided to live for ever or die in the attempt.

8 He disapproved of Adolf Hitler, who had done such a great job of combating un-American activities in Germany. [4]

9 Even when he cheated he couldn't win, because the people he cheated against were always better at cheating too.

10 There was only one catch and that was Catch-22, which specified that a concern for one's own safety in the face of dangers that were real and immediate was the process of a rational mind. [5]

11 There was little she hadn't tried and less she wouldn't. [8]

12 Some men are born mediocre, some men achieve mediocrity, and some men have mediocrity thrust upon them. With Major Major it had been all three. [9]

13 Hungry Joe collected lists of fatal diseases and arranged them in alphabetical order so that he could put his finger without delay on any one he wanted to worry about. [17]

14 Good God, how much reverence can you have for a Supreme Being who finds it necessary to include such phenomena as phlegm and tooth-decay in His divine system of Creation? [18]

15 Frankly, I'd like to see the government get out of war altogether and leave the whole field to private industry. [24]

16 I want those letters to be sincere letters. I want them filled up with lots of personal details so there'll be no doubt I mean every word you say. [25]

17 Prostitution gives her an opportunity to meet people. It provides fresh air and wholesome exercise, and it keeps her out of trouble. [33]

18 I'll let you in on a secret about my son Solomon: he was dead serious when he proposed cutting the baby in half, that *putz*. I swear to God. The dumb son of a bitch was trying to be fair, not shrewd. [*God Knows*, 1]

19 And a man who lay with a beast, said the Lord, would surely die. And if he doesn't lie with a beast, I would have countered, he won't die? [2]

20 Abraham . . . circumcised himself. Now this is not an easy thing to do – try it sometime and see.

21 But in Bethlehem things like that are always happening. Some people say it has something to do with the drinking water. [6]

22 Almost one out of every four people in the world is Chinese, you know, even though many of them might not look it. [*Good as Gold*, 5]

23 If Richard Nixon was second-rate, what in the world *is* third-rate? [6]

24 Kissinger brought peace to Vietnam the same way Napoleon brought peace to Europe: by losing. [7]

25 He gave fifty thousand dollars secretly to Henry Kissinger. Imagine – for fifty thousand dollars then you might have bought a small Klee or Bonnard or a large Jackson Pollock, and all he got for his money was a medium-sized Kissinger. [8]

LILLIAN HELLMAN 1905–1984

1 It is a mark of many famous people that they cannot part with their brightest hour. [*Pentimento*, 'Theatre']

2 For anybody of my generation, so eager for the neurosis, yours if you could manage it, if desperate somebody else's . . .

3 The English don't raise their voices, Arthur, although they may have other vulgarities. ['Arthur W. A. Cowan']

4 I am suspicious of guilt in myself and in other people: it is usually a way of not thinking, or of announcing one's own fine sensibilities the better to be rid of them fast. [*Scoundrel Time*]

5 I cannot and will not cut my conscience to fit this year's fashions. [Letter to House Committee of un-American Activities, 19 May 1952]

6 People change and forget to tell each other. [From *Toys in the Attic*, in *Simpson's Contemporary Quotations*]

ERNEST HEMINGWAY 1899–1961

7 But did thee feel the earth move? [*For Whom the Bell Tolls*, Ch. 13]

8 All modern American literature comes from one book by Mark Twain called *Huckleberry Finn*. [*The Green Hills of Africa*, Ch. 1]

9 If you are lucky enough to have lived in Paris as a young man, then wherever you go for the rest of your life, it stays with you, for Paris is a moveable feast. [To a friend, 1950; used as epigraph to *A Moveable Feast*]

10 A man can be destroyed but not defeated. [*The Old Man and the Sea*]

11 DOROTHY PARKER: Exactly what do you mean by 'guts'?
HEMINGWAY: I mean grace under pressure. [Interview with Parker in the *New Yorker*, 30 Sept. 1929. In J. F. Kennedy, *Profiles in Courage*, Ch. 1]

12 All good books are alike in that they are truer than if they had really happened. [In *Esquire* magazine, Dec. 1934]

13 I started out very quiet and I beat Mr Turgenev. Then I trained hard and I beat Mr de Maupassant. I've fought two draws with Mr Stendhal, and I think I had an edge in the last one. But nobody's going to get me in any ring with Mr Tolstoy unless I'm crazy or I keep getting better. [From the *New Yorker*, 13 May 1950, in Lillian Ross, *Portrait of Hemingway*]

14 Old Corndrinking Mellifluous. [Of William Faulkner. In Carlos Baker, *Ernest Hemingway, A Life Story*]

15 A serious writer is not to be confounded with a solemn writer. A serious writer may be a hawk or a buzzard or even a popinjay, but a solemn writer is always a bloody owl. [In Cyril Connolly, *Enemies of Promise*, Ch. 8]

16 If people bring so much courage to this world, the world has to kill them . . . It kills the very good and very gentle and the very brave impartially. [In Arthur M. Schlesinger Jr, *A Thousand Days*]

17 Never think that war, no matter how necessary nor how justified, is not a crime. [In *The Norton Book of Modern War*, ed. Paul Fussell, Introduction]

SIR NEVILE HENDERSON 1882–1942

18 He [Goering] may be a blackguard, but not a dirty blackguard. [Speech at Sleaford, reported in *News Chronicle*. In M. Bateman, *This England*, selections from the *New Statesman*, Pt II]

ARTHUR W. D. HENLEY

19 Nobody Loves a Fairy When She's Forty. [Title of song, 1934]

ADRIAN HENRI 1932–

20 Love is a fanclub with only two fans. [*Love is . . .*]

21 I wanted your soft verges / But you gave me the hard shoulder. [*Song of a Beautiful Girl Petrol-pump Attendant*]

LENNY HENRY 1958–

22 Know what I mean, Harry? [Catchphrase, borrowed from boxer Frank Bruno]

23 Sometimes they ask you to crack a joke for them when you meet them on the street. But if I was walking along with a couple of pipes and met a passing welder I wouldn't ask him to weld the pipes. [Interview in the *Guardian*, 31 Aug. 1988]

O. HENRY [W. S. PORTER] 1862–1910

1 Esau, that swapped his copyright for a partridge. [*Cupid à la Carte*]

2 The road lay curling around wood and dale like a ribbon lost from the robe of a careless summer. [*The Defeat of the City*]

3 Busy as a one-armed man with the nettle-rash pasting on wall-paper. [*The Ethics of Pig*]

4 About the only job left that a woman can beat a man in is female impersonator in vaudeville. [*The Hand That Rules the World*]

5 Men to whom life had appeared as a reversible coat – seamy on both sides. [*The Hiding of Black Bill*]

6 It couldn't have happened anywhere but in little old New York. [*A Little Local Colour*]

7 Baghdad-on-the-Subway. [Of New York. *A Madison Square Arabian Night*, also in other stories]

8 A burglar who respects his art always takes his time before taking anything else. [*Makes the Whole World Kin*]

9 If men knew how women pass the time when they are alone, they'd never marry. [*Memoirs of a Yellow Dog*]

10 He had the artistic metempsychosis which is half drunk when sober and looks down on airships when stimulated. [*A Midsummer Masquerade*]

11 Satan . . . is a hard boss to work for . . . When other people are having their vacation is when he keeps you the busiest. As old Dr Watts or St Paul or some other diagnostician says: 'He always finds somebody for idle hands to do.'

12 It was beautiful and simple as all truly great swindles are. [*The Octopus Marooned*]

13 Whenever he saw a dollar in another man's hands he took it as a personal grudge, if he couldn't take it any other way.

14 There are two times when you never can tell what is going to happen. One is when a man takes his first drink; and the other is when a woman takes her latest.

15 He was outwardly decent and managed to preserve his aquarium, but inside he was impromptu and full of unexpectedness.

16 There is always hope for a man who, when sober, will not concede or acknowledge that he was ever drunk. [*The Rubaiyat of a Scotch Highball*]

17 A straw vote only shows which way the hot air blows. [*A Ruler of Men*]

18 The best grafts in the world are built up on copybook maxims and psalms and proverbs and Esau's fables. They seem to kind of hit off human nature. [*A Tempered Wind*]

19 Take it from me – he's got the goods. [*The Unprofitable Servant*]

20 Turn up the lights, I don't want to go home in the dark. [Last words, 5 June 1910, quoting popular song; see 403:20]

KATHARINE HEPBURN 1907–

21 Nature, Mr Allnut, is what we are put into this world to rise above. [To Humphrey Bogart in film *The African Queen*, screenplay by James Agee and John Huston]

22 He gave her class and she gave him sex. [Of Fred Astaire and Ginger Rogers. On former's death, in the *Guardian*, 23 June 1987]

SIR A. P. HERBERT 1890–1971

23 Don't let's go to the dogs tonight, / For mother will be there. [*Don't let's go*]

24 Not huffy or stuffy, not tiny or tall, / But fluffy, just fluffy, with no brains at all. [*I Like Them Fluffy*]

25 It may be life, but ain't it slow? [*It May be Life*]

26 For Kings and governments may err / But never Mr Baedeker. [*Mr Baedeker, or Britons Abroad*]

27 Other people's babies – / That's my life! / Mother to dozens, / And nobody's wife. [*Other People's Babies*]

28 Nothing is wasted, nothing is in vain: / The seas roll over but the rocks remain. [*Tough at the Top*]

29 Holy Deadlock. [Title of book]

30 People must not do things for fun. We are not here for fun. There is no reference to fun in any Act of Parliament. [*Uncommon Law*, 'Is It a Free Country?']

1 The critical period in matrimony is breakfast time. ['Is Marriage Lawful?']

2 The Treasury are never happy; even in Paradise they will be worried about excessive imports. [In the *Observer*, 'Sayings of the Week', 19 Apr. 1964]

F. HUGH HERBERT 1897–1958

3 Don't you think it's better for a girl to be preoccupied with sex than occupied? [Said by Maggie McNamara in film *The Moon is Blue*]

OLIVER HERFORD 1863–1935

4 King Barumph has a whim of iron. [*Excuse It Please*, 'Impossible Pudding']

5 Only the young die good. [In A. Andrews, *Quotations for Speakers and Writers*]

6 Diplomacy – lying in state. [In Laurence J. Peter, *Peter's Quotations*]

OLIVER HERFORD and ADDISON MIZNER

7 The wages of gin is breath. [*The Cynic's Calendar*]

ÉDOUARD HERRIOT 1872–1957

8 When it's a question of peace one must talk to the Devil himself. [In the *Observer*, 'Sayings of the Week', 21 Sept. 1953]

JAMES HERRIOT [J. A. WIGHT] 1916–

9 I have long held the notion that if a vet can't catch his patient there's nothing much to worry about. [*Vet in Harness*]

JUNE HERSHEY

10 Deep in the Heart of Texas. [Title of song, 1941, music by Don Swander]

WERNER HERZOG 1942–

11 Film is not the art of scholars but of illiterates. Film culture is not analysis but agitation of the mind. [In the *Guardian*, 8 Sept. 1977]

HERMANN HESSE 1877–1962

12 If you hate a person, you hate something in him that is part of yourself. What isn't part of ourselves doesn't disturb us. [*Demian*, Ch. 6]

13 When dealing with the insane, the best method is to pretend to be sane. [*Prose und Feuilletons*]

14 The man of power is ruined by power, the man of money by money, the submissive man by subservience, the pleasure seeker by pleasure. [*Steppenwolf*, 'Treatise on the Steppenwolf']

15 The bourgeois is consequently by nature a creature of weak impulses, anxious, fearful of giving himself away and easy to rule. Therefore, he has substituted majority for power, law for force, and the polling booth for responsibility.

16 As a body everyone is single, as a soul never.

17 I believe that the struggle against death, the unconditional and self-willed determination to live, is the motive power behind the lives and activities of all outstanding men.

LORD JUSTICE HEWART 1870–1943

18 A long line of cases shows that it is not merely of some importance, but it is of fundamental importance, that justice should not only be done, but should manifestly and undoubtedly be seen to be done. [Rex v. Sussex Justices, 9 Nov. 1923]

SEYMOUR HICKS 1871–1949

19 You will recognize, my boy, the first sign of age: it is when you go out into the streets of London and realize for the first time how young the policemen look. [*Between Ourselves*]

GEORGE V. HIGGINS 1939–

20 A contemporary comforted me with the observation that it's nice, as one approaches fifty, to discover what one wants to be when one grows up. [In the *Guardian*, 17 June 1988]

JACK HIGGINS [HARRY PATTERSON] 1929–

21 The Eagle Has Landed. [Title of book. See also 10:5]

CHRISTOPHER HILL 1912–

22 Only very slowly and late have men

come to realize that unless freedom is universal it is only extended privilege. [*The Century of Revolution*, Ch. 20]

GEOFFREY HILL 1932–

1 He considers the lilies, the rewards. / There is no substitute for a rich man. [*To the (Supposed) Patron*]

JOE HILL 1879–1915

2 Work and pray, live on hay. / You'll get pie in the sky when you die. [Song: *The Preacher and the Slave*]

3 Don't waste any time mourning – organize! [Letter to W. D. Haywood, the day before being shot by firing squad, Utah State Penitentiary, 19 Nov. 1915]

PATTI SMITH HILL 1868–1946 and MILDRED J. HILL ?–1935

4 Happy birthday to you, happy birthday to you. [Song: *Happy Birthday*]

SIR EDMUND HILLARY 1919–

5 Well, we knocked the bastard off! [To George Lowe after the conquest of Everest. *Nothing Venture*, Ch. 10. See also 367:13]

FRANK HILLEBRAND 1893–1963

6 Home, James and Don't Spare the Horses. [Title of song, ascr. by Denis Norden in the *Guardian*, 'Notes and Queries', 18 June 1990]

ALICE, LADY HILLINGDON 1857–1940

7 I am happy now that Charles calls on my bedchamber less frequently than of old. As it is, I now endure but two calls a week and when I hear his steps outside my door I lie down on my bed, close my eyes, open my legs and think of England. [*Journal*, 1912]

JAMES HILTON 1900–1954

8 Anno domini – that's the most fatal complaint of all in the end. [*Good-bye, Mr Chips*, Ch. 1]

HEINRICH HIMMLER 1900–1945

9 We shall never be rough and heartless when it is not necessary, that is clear. We Germans, who are the only people in the world who have a decent attitude towards animals, will also assume a decent attitude towards these human animals. [Speech, 4 Oct. 1943]

PAUL HINDEMITH 1895–1963

10 Today unexplored regions of the stringed instruments' fingerboard are non-existent; even the arctic zones of the eternal rosin (near the bridge) have become a habitable abode for fearless climbers. [*A Composer's World*, Ch. 7, sect. ii]

EMPEROR HIROHITO OF JAPAN 1901–1989

11 We have resolved to endure the unendurable and suffer what is insufferable. [After dropping of atomic bomb on Hiroshima, Aug. 1945. Quoted by A. J. P. Taylor in the *Listener*, 9 Sept. 1976]

12 You can't imagine the extra work I had when I was a god. [On visit to London, as band played 'God Save the Queen']

SIR ALFRED HITCHCOCK 1899–1980

13 Actors are cattle. [Attr. In Leslie Halliwell, *Filmgoer's Book of Quotes*. He claimed he had said that actors should be *treated* like cattle]

14 Drama is life with the dull bits left out.

15 There is no terror in a bang, only in the anticipation of it.

16 The length of the film should be directly related to the endurance of the human bladder. [In Leslie Halliwell, *Halliwell's Filmgoer's Companion*, 8th edn]

17 For me the cinema is not a slice of life, but a piece of cake. [In the *Sunday Times Magazine*, 6 Mar. 1977]

RAYMOND HITCHCOCK 1865–1929

18 When You're All Dressed Up and No Place to Go. [Title of song, 1912, written by G. Whiting; British version became 'Nowhere']

CHRISTOPHER HITCHENS 1949–

1 Like everyone else of my generation, I can remember exactly where I was standing and what I was doing on the day that President John Fitzgerald Kennedy nearly killed me. [Of the Cuban missile crisis. *Prepared for the Worst*. See also 130:10]

2 To listen even briefly to Ronald Reagan is to realize that he is a man upon whose synapses the termites have dined long and well.

ADOLF HITLER 1889–1945

3 With a suitcase full of clothes and underwear in my hand and an indomitable will in my heart, I set out for Vienna . . . I too hoped to become 'something'. [*Mein Kampf*, Ch. 1]

4 All those who are not racially pure are mere chaff. [2]

5 The art of leadership . . . consists in consolidating the attention of the people against a single adversary and taking care that nothing will split up that attention. [3]

6 Only constant repetition will finally succeed in imprinting an idea on the memory of the crowd. [6]

7 The broad masses of the people . . . will more easily fall victims to a big lie than to a small one. [10]

8 I have never delivered a firebrand speech. [Said in 1933. In the *Observer*, 'Sayings of Our Times', 31 May 1953]

9 The victor will not be asked afterwards whether he told the truth or not. In starting and waging a war it is not right that matters, but victory. [In W. L. Shirer, *The Rise and Fall of the Third Reich*, Ch. 16]

10 According to the English there are two countries in the world today which are led by adventurers: Germany and Italy. But England, too, was led by adventurers when she built her Empire. Today she is ruled merely by incompetents. [To Ciano. In A. Bullock, *Hitler*, Pt VI, 6]

11 I go the way that Providence dictates with the assurance of a sleepwalker. [Speech at Munich, 15 Mar. 1936, after successful reoccupation of the Rhineland]

12 If artists do see fields blue they are deranged, and should go to an asylum. If they only pretend to see them blue, they are criminals and should go to prison. [Speech in Munich on occasion of 'Degenerate Art' exhibition, July 1937]

13 It [the Sudetenland] is the last territorial claim that I have to make in Europe. [Speech, 26 Sept. 1938]

14 Well, he [Chamberlain] seemed such a nice old gentleman, I thought I would give him my autograph as a souvenir. [After Munich. Attr.]

15 We cannot tolerate any more the tutelage of governesses. [Referring to Great Britain after Munich. In Winston S. Churchill, *The Gathering Storm*, Ch. 18]

16 Rather than go through it [his meeting with Franco] again, . . . I would prefer to have three or four of my teeth out. [To Mussolini. From Ciano's *Diplomatic Papers*, in Winston S. Churchill, *Their Finest Hour*, Ch. 26]

17 We have mastered a destiny which broke another man [Napoleon] a hundred and thirty years ago. [Speech to the Reichstag, 26 Apr. 1942. In A. Bullock, *Hitler*, Pt XII, 3]

18 I am not annoyed with Hungary, but she has missed the bus. [In conversation with Darányi. In A. J. P. Taylor, *The Origins of the Second World War*, Ch. 9]

19 Is Paris burning? [On the liberation of Paris, 25 Aug. 1944. In L. Collins and D. Lapierre, *Is Paris Burning?*, Ch. 6]

20 I don't see much future for the Americans . . . Everything about the behaviour of American society reveals that it's half judaized, and the other half negrified. How can one expect a state like that to hold together? [*Hitler's Secret Conversations*]

21 On land I am a hero, but on water I am a coward. [To von Runstedt. In Milton Shulman, *Defeat in the West*]

EDWARD HOAGLAND 1932–

22 The forties are the old age of youth and the fifties the youth of old age. [From *Learning to Eat Soup*, in *Antaeus: Journals, Notebooks and Diaries*, ed. D. Halpern, p. 232]

RUSSELL HOBAN 1925–

1 If the past cannot teach the present and the father cannot teach the son, then history need not have bothered to go on, and the world has wasted a great deal of time. [*The Lion of Boaz-Jachin and Jachin-Boaz*, Ch. 1]

2 Everything that is found is always lost again, and nothing that is found is ever lost again. [2]

3 When you suffer an attack of nerves you're being attacked by the nervous system. What chance has a man got against a system? [13]

4 There were times when it seemed to him that the different parts of him were not all under the same management. [15]

5 After all, when you come right down to it, how many people speak the same language even when they speak the same language? [27]

6 Sometimes there's nothing but Sundays for weeks on end. Why can't they move Sunday to the middle of the week so you could put it in the OUT tray on your desk? [32]

7 'Who can know anybody?' said the bookshop owner. 'Every person is like thousands of books. New, reprinting, in stock and out of stock, fiction, non-fiction, poetry, rubbish. The lot. Different every day. One's lucky to be able to put his hand on the one that's wanted, let alone know it.'

8 'NIGHT BATTLE ON MEADOW BORDER RESULTS IN . . .' He paused and flew lower, in some confusion as to who had won and who had lost. 'VICTORY!' he concluded. [*The Mouse and His Child*, Ch. 3]

9 Don't think too much youwl grow hair on the in side of your head. [*Riddley Walker*, 10]

10 His eyes look as if he's pawned his real ones and is wearing paste. [*Turtle Diary*, Ch. 2]

11 The sign said: 'The Green Turtle, *Chelonia mydas*, is the source of turtle soup . . .' I am the source of William G. soup if it comes to that. Everyone is the source of his or her kind of soup. In a town as big as London that's a lot of soup walking about. [3]

12 But when I don't smoke I scarcely feel as if I'm living. I don't feel as if I'm living unless I'm killing myself. [7]

13 Me, what's that after all? An arbitrary limitation of being bounded by the people before and after and on either side. Where they leave off I begin, and vice versa. [11]

14 Only a certain number of things can happen and whatever can happen *will* happen. The differences in scale and costume do not alter the event. Oedipus went to Thebes, Peter Rabbit into Mr McGregor's garden, but the story is essentially the same: life points only towards the terror. [12]

15 And now it seems she's on my wavelength. That's all I need. My mind isn't much of a comfort to me but at least I thought it was private. [21]

16 Nothing to be done really about animals. Anything you do looks foolish. The answer isn't in us. It's almost as if we're put here on earth to show how silly they aren't. [42]

17 I'd always assumed I was the central character in my own story but now it occurred to me I might in fact be only a minor character in someone else's. [51]

18 Explorers have to be ready to die lost. [Interview in *The Times*, 1975]

E. J. HOBSBAWM 1917–

19 The only certain thing about the future is that it will surprise even those who have seen furthest into it. [*The Age of Empire, 1875–1914*, final sentence]

20 Like the radish, red outside, white inside, and always on the side the bread is buttered. [Of the leaders of the French Third Republic. *The Invention of Tradition*, ed. E. J. Hobsbawm and Terence Ranger]

21 This was the kind of war which existed in order to produce victory parades. [Of Falklands War, 1982. In *Marxism Today*, Jan. 1983]

SIR HAROLD HOBSON 1904–1992

22 The United States, I believe, are under the impression that they are twenty years in advance of this country; whilst, as a matter of actual verifiable fact, of course, they are

just about six hours behind it. [*The Devil in Woodford Wells*, Ch. 8]

EDWARD WALLIS HOCH 1849–1925

1 There is so much good in the worst of us, / And so much bad in the best of us, / That it hardly becomes any of us / To talk about the rest of us. [*Good and Bad*. Authorship not absolutely certain]

ROLF HOCHHUTH 1931–

2 Cursed are the peacemakers. [*The Representative*, Act I, sc. i]

DAVID HOCKNEY 1937–

3 All you can do with most ordinary photographs is stare at them – they stare back, blankly – and presently your concentration begins to fade. They stare you down. I mean, photography is all right if you don't mind looking at the world from the point of view of a paralysed cyclops – *for a split second*. [In *Cameraworks*, as told to Lawrence Weschler]

4 Art has to move you and design does not, unless it's a good design for a bus. [At press conference for his retrospective at Tate Gallery, London, 25 Oct. 1988]

5 My interest in the photocopier was philosophical really. Beyond a shadow of doubt, it's that technology that brought down communism. [In the *Guardian*, 13 Sept. 1990]

6 Of course all painting, no matter what you're painting, is abstract in that it's got to be organized. [From *David Hockney*, in *Dictionary of Art Quotations*, comp. Ian Crofton]

RALPH HODGSON 1871–1962

7 'Twould ring the bells of Heaven / The wildest peal for years, / If Parson lost his senses / And people came to theirs. [*The Bells of Heaven*]

8 See an old unhappy bull, / Sick in soul and body both. [*The Bull*]

9 Reason has moons, but moons not hers / Lie mirror'd on her sea, / Confounding her astronomers, / But, O! delighting me. [*Reason Has Moons*]

10 I climbed a hill as light fell short, / And rooks came home in scramble sort, / And filled the trees and flapped and fought / And sang themselves to sleep. [*The Song of Honour*]

11 When stately ships are twirled and spun / Like whipping tops and help there's none / And mighty ships ten thousand ton / Go down like lumps of lead.

12 Without a wish, without a will, / I stood upon that silent hill / And stared into the sky until / My eyes were blind with stars and still / I stared into the sky.

13 Time, you old gipsy man, / Will you not stay, / Put up your caravan / Just for one day? [*Time, You Old Gipsy Man*]

RUDOLF HOESS [Commandant of Auschwitz] 1900–1947

14 Another improvement that we made ... was that we built our gas-chambers to accommodate two thousand people at one time. [Affidavit. In A. Bullock, *Hitler*, Pt XII]

SAMUEL HOFFENSTEIN 1890–1947

15 The stars, like measles, fade at last. [*The Mimic Muse*, V]

16 Though women tempt you more than plenty, / Your rate is half a girl in twenty. / In short, from grace you never fell yet – / And what do you get? On all sides hell yet! [*Poems in Praise of Practically Nothing*, First Series]

17 You buy some flowers for your table; / You tend them tenderly as you're able; / You fetch them water from hither and thither – / What thanks do you get for it all? They wither. [Second Series]

18 I think of all the corpses / Worm-eaten in the shade; / I cannot chew my peanuts / Or drink my lemonade: / Good God, I am afraid! [*The Shropshire Lad's Cousin*]

19 Babies haven't any hair; / Old men's heads are just as bare; – / Between the cradle and the grave / Lies a haircut and a shave. [*Songs of Faith in the Year after Next*, 8]

20 We [Hollywood people] are the croupiers in a crooked gambling house. [In Lillian Ross, *Picture*, 'Throw the Little Old Lady Down the Stairs!' See also 315:9]

ERIC HOFFER 1902–1983

1 When people are free to do as they please, they usually imitate each other. [*The Passionate State of Mind*, Ch. 1]

2 It's easier to love humanity as a whole than to love one's neighbour. [In *The New York Times Magazine*, 15 Feb. 1959]

AL HOFFMAN 1902–1960 and **DICK MANNING** 1912–

3 It Takes Two to Tango. [Title of song, 1952]

GENERAL MAX HOFFMANN 1869–1927

4 LUDENDORFF: The English soldiers fight like lions.
HOFFMANN: True. But don't we know that they are lions led by donkeys. [Of 1915 battles. In A. Clark, *The Donkeys*]

DOUGLAS R. HOFSTADTER 1945–

5 Is the soul greater than the hum of its parts? [*The Mind's I*, composed with Daniel C. Dennett, 11, 'Reflections']

LANCELOT HOGBEN 1895–1975

6 This is not the age of pamphleteers. It is the age of engineers. The spark-gap is mightier than the pen. Democracy will not be salvaged by men who talk fluently, debate forcefully and quote aptly. [*Science for the Citizen*, 'Epilogue']

QUINTIN HOGG *see* **HAILSHAM, LORD**

SIR RICHARD HOGGART 1918–

7 The Uses of Literacy. [Title of book]

8 If we felt in our heart that we were *always* doctoring our experiences, our attempts to reach others would all be at bottom forms of salesmanship, not attempts to tell things as we think they really are. [From BBC Reith Lectures, in the *Listener*, Dec. 1971]

SIMON HOGGART 1946–

9 The President's answers totter forward, as if supported by a walking frame, never quite reaching the question and sometimes not even starting out. [Of President Reagan. In the *Observer*, 1987]

10 At the moment, he [President Bush] would love to save the planet, though not if it means offending General Motors. [10 Dec. 1989]

SIR WILLIAM [later LORD] HOLFORD 1907–1975

11 Large buildings in London and elsewhere today are too often designed in the lift going to lunch. [In the *Observer*, 'Sayings of the Week', 5 June 1960]

BILLIE HOLIDAY 1915–1959

12 I've been making a comeback but nobody ever tells me where I've been. [In *New Woman*, July 1989]

REV. HENRY SCOTT HOLLAND 1847–1914

13 Death is nothing at all. I have only slipped away into the next room. I am I and you are you. [Attr. in *Dictionary of Twentieth Century Quotations*, ed. Nigel Rees]

STANLEY HOLLOWAY 1890–1982

14 Sam, Sam, pick oop tha' musket. [Monologue *Old Sam*, 1929, written with Wolseley Charles]

REV. J. H. HOLMES 1879–1964

15 The universe is not hostile, nor yet is it friendly. It is simply indifferent. [*The Sensible Man's View of Religion*]

LARRY HOLMES

16 It's hard being black. You ever been black? I was black once – when I was poor. [Quoted by J. Bernard in the *Spectator*, 11 July 1987]

GUSTAV HOLST 1874–1934

17 Never compose anything unless the not composing of it becomes a positive nuisance to you. [Letter to W. G. Whittaker. In Nat

Shapiro, *Encyclopedia of Quotations about Music*]

WINIFRED HOLTBY 1898–1935

1 God give me work while I may live and life till my work is done. [Inscription on her grave]

MIROSLAV HOLUB 1923–

2 I believe / that only what cannot be trimmed / is a head. / There is much promise / in the circumstance / that so many people have heads. [*A Boy's Head*]

3 But above all / we have / the ability / to sort peas, / to cup water in our hands, / to seek / the right screw / under the sofa / for hours. / This / gives us / wings. [*Wings*, trans. Ian Milner and George Theiner]

4 What we need now is socialism with a human *head*. [Quoted by W. L. Webb in the *Guardian*, 13 July 1987. See also 110:21]

PRESIDENT HERBERT HOOVER 1874–1964

5 The American system of rugged individualism. [Campaign speech in New York, 22 Oct. 1928]

6 The grass will grow in the streets of a hundred cities, a thousand towns; the weeds will overrun the fields of millions of farms if that protection is taken away. [On the removal of the protective tariff. Speech, 31 Oct. 1932]

7 Older men declare war. But it is youth that must fight and die. And it is youth that must inherit the tribulation, the sorrow, and the triumphs that are the aftermath of war. [Speech at Republican National Convention, Chicago, 27 June 1944]

ANTHONY HOPE [SIR ANTHONY HOPE HAWKINS] 1863–1933

8 Economy is going without something you do want in case you should, some day, want something you probably won't want. [*The Dolly Dialogues*, 12]

9 Unless one is a genius, it is best to aim at being intelligible. [15]

10 'Boys will be boys –'
'And even that wouldn't matter if we could only prevent girls from being girls.' [16]

11 '*Bourgeois*,' I observed, 'is an epithet which the riff-raff apply to what is respectable, and the aristocracy to what is decent.' [17]

12 He is very fond of making things which he does not want, and then giving them to people who have no use for them.

13 Good families are generally worse than any others. [*The Prisoner of Zenda*, Ch. 1]

14 His foe was folly and his weapon wit. [Inscription on tablet to Sir W. S. Gilbert]

BOB HOPE 1903–

15 They are doing things on the screen these days that the French don't even put on postcards. [In Leslie Halliwell, *Filmgoer's Book of Quotes*]

16 The box they buried entertainment in. [Of TV. In *New Society*, 10 Jan. 1985]

17 You know you're getting old when the candles cost more than the cake. [In *Hodder Book of Christian Quotations*, comp. Tony Castle]

18 A bank is a place that will lend you money if you can prove you don't need it. [In Alan Harrington, *Life in the Crystal Palace*, 'The Tyranny of Forms']

See also BING CROSBY and BOB HOPE

CHRISTOPHER HOPE 1944–

19 One foot in the nineteenth century and the other in Woolworths. [Of Pretoria. *White Boy Running*, Ch. 2]

LAURENCE HOPE [ADELA FLORENCE NICOLSON] 1865–1904

20 Less than the dust beneath thy chariot wheel, / Less than the weed that grows beside thy door. [*Indian Love Lyrics*, 'Less than the Dust']

21 Pale hands I loved beside the Shalimar, / Where are you now? Who lies beneath your spell? ['Pale Hands I Loved']

EDWARD HOPPER 1882–1967

1 What I wanted to do was to paint sunlight on the side of a house. [In catalogue to Hayward Gallery exhibition, London, 1981]

ALISTAIR HORNE 1925–

2 To sum up on Joffre, it might be said that the war was very nearly lost with him, but that it would almost certainly have been lost without him. [*The Price of Glory*, Ch. 2]

KENNETH HORNE 1900–1969 and RICHARD MURDOCH 1907–1990

3 Oh, jolly D.! [Dudley Davenport. Catchphrase in BBC radio comedy series *Much Binding-in-the-Marsh*, during 1939–45 War and after]

4 Read any good books lately?

5 Good morning sir – was there something? [Sam Costa]

6 Not a word to Bessie about this! [Spoken by Horne]

7 When I was in Sidi Barrani . . .

DONALD HORNIG 1920–

8 Aside from being tremendous it was one of the most aesthetically beautiful things I have ever seen. [Of first atomic test. *The Decision to Drop the Bomb*]

VLADIMIR HOROWITZ 1904–

9 The piano is the easiest instrument to play in the beginning, and the hardest to master in the end. [In David Dubal, *Evenings with Horowitz*, Ch. 7]

LIEUTENANT-GENERAL SIR BRIAN HORROCKS 1895–1985

10 I have always regarded the forward edge of the battlefield as the most exclusive club in the world. [*A Full Life*]

ZILPHIA HORTON 1907–1957

11 We Shall Overcome. [Title of song, original version. Later additions by Pete Seeger, Frank Hamilton, Guy Carawan]

COLONEL EDWARD HOUSE 1858–1938

12 My ambition has been so great it has never seemed to me worth while to try to satisfy it. [In John Dos Passos, *Mr Wilson's War*, Ch. 1, sect. ii]

GEOFFREY HOUSEHOLD 1900–1988

13 I have noticed that what cats most appreciate in a human being is not the ability to produce food which they take for granted – but his or her entertainment value. [*Rogue Male*]

14 It's easy to make a man confess the lies he tells to himself; it's far harder to make him confess the truth.

A. E. HOUSMAN 1859–1936

15 The Grizzly Bear is huge and wild; / He has devoured the infant child. / The infant child is not aware / He has been eaten by the bear. [*Infant Innocence*]

16 The Queen of air and darkness / Begins to shrill and cry, / 'O young man, O my slayer, / To-morrow you shall die.' [*Last Poems*, 3]

17 Pass me the can, lad; there's an end of May. [9]

18 May will be fine next year as like as not: / Oh ay, but then we shall be twenty-four.

19 We for a certainty are not the first / Have sat in taverns while the tempest hurled / Their hopeful plans to emptiness, and cursed / Whatever brute and blackguard made the world.

20 The troubles of our proud and angry dust / Are from eternity, and shall not fail. / Bear them we can, and if we can we must. / Shoulder the sky, my lad, and drink your ale.

21 But men at whiles are sober / And think by fits and starts, / And if they think, they fasten / Their hands upon their hearts. [10]

22 I, a stranger and afraid / In a world I never made. [12]

23 For so the game is ended / That should not have begun. / My father and my mother

/ They had a likely son, / And I have none. [14]

1 And then the clock collected in the tower / Its strength and struck. [15, 'Eight O'Clock']

2 Made of earth and sea / His overcoat for ever, / And wears the turning globe. [20]

3 The fairies break their dances / and leave the printed lawn. [21]

4 The young man feels his pockets / And wonders what's to pay.

5 These, in the day when heaven was falling. / The hour when earth's foundations fled, / Followed their mercenary calling / And took their wages and are dead.

6 Their shoulders held the skies suspended; / They stood, and earth's foundations stay; / What God abandoned, these defended, / And saved the sum of things for pay. [37, 'Epitaph on an Army of Mercenaries']

7 Until from grass and clover / The upshot beam would fade, / And England over / Advanced the lofty shade. [41, 'Fancy's Knell']

8 Tomorrow, more's the pity, / Away we both must hie, / To air the ditty / And to earth I.

9 The rainy Pleiads wester, / Orion plunges prone, / The stroke of midnight ceases, / And I lie down alone. [More Poems, 11]

10 Loveliest of trees, the cherry now / Is hung with bloom along the bough. [A Shropshire Lad, 2]

11 Now, of my threescore years and ten, / Twenty will not come again.

12 About the woodlands I will go / To see the cherry hung with snow.

13 Clay lies still, but blood's a rover; / Breath's a ware that will not keep. / Up, lad; when the journey's over / There'll be time enough for sleep. [4, 'Reveille']

14 Lie down, lie down, young yeoman; / The sun moves always west; / The road one treads to labour / Will lead one home to rest, / And that will be the best. [7]

15 A neck God made for other use / Than strangling in a string. [9]

16 Lovers lying two by two / Ask not whom they sleep beside, / And the bridegroom all

night through / Never turns him to the bride. [12]

17 When I was one-and-twenty / I heard a wise man say, / 'Give crowns and pounds and guineas / But not your heart away.' [13]

18 Oh, when I was in love with you, / Then I was clean and brave. [18]

19 And silence sounds no worse than cheers / After death has stopped the ears. [19, 'To an Athlete Dying Young']

20 In summertime on Bredon / The bells they sound so clear; / Round both the shires they ring them / In steeples far and near, / A happy noise to hear.

21 Here of a Sunday morning / My love and I would lie, / And see the coloured counties, / And hear the larks so high / About us in the sky. [21, 'Bredon Hill']

22 'Come all to church, good people,' – / Oh, noisy bells, be dumb; / I hear you, I will come.

23 They carry back bright to the coiner the mintage of man, / The lads that will die in their glory and never be old. [23]

24 Is my team ploughing, / That I was used to drive? [27]

25 No change, though you lie under / The land you used to plough.

26 The goal stands up, the keeper / Stands up to keep the goal.

27 The flag of morn in conqueror's state / Enters at the English gate: / The vanquished eve, as night prevails, / Bleeds upon the road to Wales. [28, 'The Welsh Marches']

28 Today the Roman and his trouble / Are ashes under Uricon. [31]

29 From far, from eve and morning / And yon twelve-winded sky, / The stuff of life to knit me / Blew hither: here am I. [32]

30 White in the moon the long road lies. [36]

31 Into my heart an air that kills / From yon far country blows: / What are those blue remembered hills, / What spires, what farms are those? [40]

32 That is the land of lost content, / I see it shining plain, / The happy highways where I went / And cannot come again.

33 And the feather pate of folly / Bears the falling of the sky. [49]

1 Think no more; 'tis only thinking / Lays lads underground.

2 With rue my heart is laden / For golden friends I had, / For many a rose-lipt maiden / And many a lightfoot lad. [54]

3 Malt does more than Milton can / To justify God's ways to man. [62]

4 Ale, man, ale's the stuff to drink / For fellows whom it hurts to think.

5 Mithridates, he died old.

6 Good religious poetry ... is likely to be most justly appreciated and most discriminately relished by the undevout. [*The Name and Nature of Poetry*]

7 Even when poetry has a meaning, as it usually has, it may be inadvisable to draw it out ... Perfect understanding will sometimes almost extinguish pleasure.

8 If a line of poetry strays into my memory, my skin bristles so that the razor ceases to act.

9 Cambridge has seen many strange sights. It has seen Wordsworth drunk, it has seen Porson sober. I am a greater scholar than Wordsworth and I am a greater poet than Porson. So I fall betwixt and between. [Speech, on leaving University College, London, to take up the Chair of Latin at Cambridge, 1911. In R. P. Graves, *A. E. Housman, the Scholar-poet*, Ch. 5]

10 I find Cambridge an asylum, in every sense of the word. [On coming from Oxford. Attr.]

11 I'll tell that story on the golden floor. [On being told a joke when he was dying. Attr. by the Rev. J. Plowden-Wardlaw, Vicar of St Edward the Great, Cambridge]

SIR GEOFFREY HOWE 1927–

12 It's rather like sending your opening batsmen to the crease only for them to find the moment the first balls are bowled that their bats have been broken before the game by the team captain. [Explaining his resignation from Mrs Thatcher's Cabinet. Speech in House of Commons, 13 Nov. 1990]

WILLIAM DEAN HOWELLS 1837–1920

13 Some people can stay longer in an hour than others can in a week. [Attr. in *Treasury of Humorous Quotations*, ed. Evan Esar and Nicolas Bentley]

SIR FRANKIE HOWERD 1922–1992

14 Nowadays you can't be filthy unless you've got a degree. [In BBC TV programme *That Was the Week That Was*, 6 Apr. 1963]

15 I was *amazed!* [Catchphrase in comedy act]

16 Mock ye not!

17 I think most broken-hearted clowns would be much more broken-hearted if they weren't clowns; and the only really broken-hearted clowns that I know are those that are not working or [are] unemployed. [Interview on BBC Radio 4. In the *Listener*, 21 May 1987]

18 It's television, you see. If you are not on the thing every week, the public think you are either dead or deported. [In the *Independent*, 'Quote Unquote', 16 Mar. 1991]

ANGELA DE HOYOS ?1940–

19 No one told me / So how was I to know / that in the paradise / of crisp white cities / snakes still walk upright? [Quoted by Reyner Banham in *New Society*, 22 Jan. 1988]

ELBERT HUBBARD 1856–1915

20 Life is just one damned thing after another. [*One Thousand and One Epigrams*. Elsewhere attr. to F. W. O'Malley. See also 261:11]

21 Never explain – your friends do not need it and your enemies will not believe you anyway. [*Motto Book*]

22 One machine can do the work of fifty ordinary men. No machine can do the work of one extraordinary man. [*Roycroft Dictionary and Book of Epigrams*]

23 Little minds are interested in the extraordinary; great minds in the commonplace.

24 You had better be a round peg in a square hole than a square peg in a square hole. The latter is in for life, while the first is only an indeterminate sentence. [In W. H. Auden and L. Kronenberger, *Faber Book of Aphorisms*]

FRANK McKINNEY 'KIN' HUBBARD
1868–1930

1 Nobody ever forgets where he buried a hatchet. [*Abe Martin's Broadcast*, 1930]

DAVID HUGHES 1930–

2 Childhood's a risk we all take. [*The Pork Butcher*, p. 114]

HOWARD HUGHES 1905–1976

3 You're like a pay toilet, aren't you? You don't give a shit for nothing. [To Robert Mitchum. Quoted by Mitchum in interview in the *Observer*, 5 Feb. 1989]

4 That man's ears make him look like a taxi-cab with both doors open. [Of Clark Gable. In Charles Higham and Joel Greenberg, *Celluloid Muse*]

LANGSTON HUGHES 1902–1967

5 Because just *one* drop of black blood makes a coloured man. *One* drop – you are a Negro! . . . Black is powerful. [*Simple Takes a Wife*, p. 85]

RICHARD HUGHES 1900–1976

6 Nature is as wasteful of promising young men as she is of fish-spawn. It's not just getting them killed in wars: mere middle age snuffs out ten times more talent than ever wars and sudden death do. [*The Fox in the Attic*, Bk I, Ch. 18]

7 For a politician rises on the backs of his friends (that's probably all they're good for), but it's through his enemies he'll have to govern afterwards. [II. 20]

8 History has to use second-hand timber when she builds a new edifice – like those awkward post-war chickenhouses people build out of bits of army huts and old ammo-boxes, with 'W.D.' stamped all over them and costly enigmatical fittings too much trouble to unscrew. [III. 31]

ROBERT HUGHES ?1938–

9 Histories do not break off clean, like a glass rod; they fray, stretch, and come undone, like a rope. [*The Shock of the New*, Ch. 8]

10 It is no wonder that Hockney, the Cole Porter of figurative painting, should so often and so exaggeratedly have been taken for Mozart.

TED HUGHES 1930–

11 But Oedipus he had the luck / For when he hit the ground / He bounced up like a jackinabox / And knocked his Daddy down. [*Crow*, 'Song for a Phallus']

12 It took the whole of Creation / To produce my foot, my each feather: / Now I hold creation in my foot. [*Hawk Roosting*]

13 The world rolls under the long thrust of his heel. / Over the cage floor the horizons come. [*The Jaguar*]

JOSEPHINE HULL 1886–1957

14 Playing Shakespeare is very tiring. You never get to sit down unless you're a King. [In *Time* magazine, 16 Nov. 1953]

T. E. HULME 1883–1917

15 I walked abroad, / And saw the ruddy moon lean over a hedge / Like a red-faced farmer. / I did not stop to speak, but nodded, / And round about were the wistful stars / With white faces like town children. [*Autumn*]

CARDINAL BASIL HUME 1923–

16 Oh, I just keep plugging away. At its best it's like being in a dark room with someone you love. You can't see them; but you know they're there. [Of prayer. Interview in John Mortimer, *In Character*]

VICE-PRESIDENT HUBERT HUMPHREY
1911–1978

17 Here we are the way politics ought to be in America, the politics of happiness, the politics of purpose and the politics of joy. [Speech in Washington, 27 Apr. 1968]

BARRY HUMPHRIES 1934–

18 At Sunday School I was always in demand, especially for our annual Passion Play and Pageant, and I was always given the *meatier* rolls. [*Dame Edna's Coffee Table Book*, 'My Wonderful Career']

JAMES HUNEKER 1860–1921

1 Lawyers earn their bread in the sweat of their browbeating. [From *Painted Veils*, in *Quotable Lawyer*, ed. D. Shrager and E. Frost]

STAN HUNT

2 Why do you have to be a nonconformist like everybody else? [Cartoon caption in the *New Yorker*. Often wrongly attr. to James Thurber]

HERMAN HUPFELD 1894–1951

3 You must remember this; / A kiss is just a kiss, / A sigh is just a sigh – / The fundamental things apply / As time goes by. [Song: *As Time Goes By*, used in film *Casablanca*]

SADDAM HUSSEIN 1937–

4 The revolution chooses its enemies. [In the *Guardian*, 10 Dec. 1990]

5 The great, the jewel and the mother of battles has begun. [At the outset of the Gulf War, 17 Jan. 1991]

ALDOUS HUXLEY 1894–1963

6 There are few who would not rather be taken in adultery than in provincialism. [*Antic Hay*, 10]

7 Mr Mercaptan went on to preach a brilliant sermon on that melancholy sexual perversion known as continence. [18]

8 Lady Capricorn, he understood, was still keeping open bed. [21]

9 'Going to the Feelies this evening, Henry?' enquired the Assistant Predestinator. 'I hear the new one at the Alhambra is first-rate. There's a love scene on a bearskin rug; they say it's marvellous. Every hair of the bear reproduced.' [*Brave New World*, Ch. 3]

10 Our Ford . . . had been the first to reveal the appalling dangers of family life.

11 Oh, she's a splendid girl. Wonderfully pneumatic.

12 The sexophones wailed like melodious cats under the moon. [5]

13 Judd remained for him the Oldest Friend whom one definitely dislikes. [*Brief Candles*, 'After the Fireworks']

14 We participate in a tragedy; at a comedy we only look. [*The Devils of Loudun*, Ch. 11]

15 I was seeing what Adam had seen on the morning of his creation – the miracle, moment by moment, of naked existence. [*The Doors of Perception*]

16 Consistency is contrary to nature, contrary to life. The only completely consistent people are the dead. [*Do What You Will*, 'Wordsworth in the Tropics']

17 Good is that which makes for unity; Evil is that which makes for separateness. [*Ends and Means*]

18 The fact that the Matthew Passion, for example, the Hammerklavier Sonata, had had human authors was a source of hope. It was just conceivable that humanity might some day and somehow be made a little more John-Sebastian-like. [*Eyeless in Gaza*, Ch. 22]

19 People will insist . . . on treating the *mons Veneris* as though it were Mount Everest. [30]

20 Death . . . It's the only thing we haven't succeeded in completely vulgarizing. [31]

21 The quality of moral behaviour varies in inverse ratio to the number of human beings involved. [*Grey Eminence*, Ch. 10]

22 'Bed,' as the Italian proverb succinctly puts it, 'is the poor man's opera.' [*Heaven and Hell*]

23 I can sympathize with people's pains, but not with their pleasures. There is something curiously boring about somebody else's happiness. [*Limbo*, 'Cynthia']

24 'But I should like to come,' Miss Spence protested, throwing a rapid Gioconda at him. [*Mortal Coils*, 'The Gioconda Smile', i]

25 She was a machine-gun riddling her hostess with sympathy. [ii]

26 She was one of those indispensables of whom one makes the discovery, when they are gone, that one can get on quite as well without them. ['Nuns at Luncheon']

27 For Lawrence, existence was one continuous convalescence; it was as though he were newly reborn from a mortal illness every day

of his life. What these convalescent eyes saw, his most casual speech would reveal. [*The Olive Tree*, 'D. H. Lawrence']

1 The picture-papers are more than half-filled with photographs of bathing nymphs – photographs that make one understand the ease with which St Anthony rebuffed his temptations. [*On the Margin*, 'Beauty in 1920']

2 Forgetting that several excuses are always less convincing than one. [*Point Counter Point*, Ch. 1]

3 He had cured her, he remembered, of a passion for Burne-Jones, but never, alas, of her prejudice in favour of virtue. [4]

4 A correspondence course of passion was, for her, the perfect and ideal relationship with a man. [5]

5 Brought up in an epoch when ladies apparently rolled along on wheels, Mr Quarles was peculiarly susceptible to calves. [20]

6 Parodies and caricatures are the most penetrating of criticisms. [28]

7 Happiness is like coke – something you get as a by-product in the process of making something else. [30]

8 Burlap walked home. He was feeling pleased with himself and the world at large. 'I accept the Universe', was how, only an hour before, he had concluded his next week's leader. [37]

9 You never see animals going through the absurd and often horrible fooleries of magic and religion ... Only man behaves with such gratuitous folly. It is the price he has to pay for being intelligent but not, as yet, quite intelligent enough. [*Texts and Pretexts*, 'Amor Fati']

10 I'm afraid of losing my obscurity. Genuineness only thrives in the dark. Like celery. [*Those Barren Leaves*, Pt 1, Ch. 1]

11 At thirty-three ... Lilian Aldwinkle appealed to all the instinctive bigamist in one. She was eighteen in the attics and widow Dido on the floors below. [2]

12 'It's like the question of the authorship of the *Iliad*,' said Mr Cardan. 'The author of that poem is either Homer or, if not Homer, somebody else of the same name.' [V. 4]

13 How appallingly thorough these Germans always managed to be, how emphatic! In sex no less than in war – in scholarship, in science. Diving deeper than anyone else and coming up muddier. [*Time Must Have a Stop*, 6]

14 There's only one corner of the universe you can be certain of improving, and that's your own self. [7]

15 There isn't any formula or method. You learn to love by loving – by paying attention and doing what one thereby discovers has to be done. [30]

16 A million million spermatozoa, / All of them alive: / Out of their cataclysm but one poor Noah / Dare hope to survive. / And among that billion minus one / Might have chanced to be / Shakespeare, another Newton, a new Donne – / But the One was Me. [*The Fifth Philosopher's Song*]

17 But when the wearied Band / Swoons to a waltz, I take her hand, / And there we sit in peaceful calm, / Quietly sweating palm to palm. [*Frascati's*]

18 Beauty for some provides escape, / Who gain a happiness in eyeing / The gorgeous buttocks of the ape / Or Autumn sunsets exquisitely dying. [*The Ninth Philosopher's Song*]

19 He [T. S. Eliot] likes to look on the bile when it's black. [In Edward Marsh, *Ambrosia and Small Beer*, Ch. 5, sect. i]

20 He [T. E. Lawrence] is one of those great men for whom one feels intensely sorry, because he was nothing but a great man. [Letter to V. Ocampo, 1946. In J. Wintle and R. Kenin, *Dictionary of Biographical Quotation*]

SIR JULIAN HUXLEY 1887–1975

21 We all know how the size of sums of money appears to vary in a remarkable way according as they are being paid in or paid out. [*Essays of a Biologist*, Ch. 5]

22 Sooner or later, false thinking brings wrong conduct. [7]

23 Operationally, God is beginning to resemble not a ruler but the last fading smile of a cosmic Cheshire cat. [*Religion without Revelation*, Ch. 3]

Edward Hyams

EDWARD HYAMS 1910–1975

1 Assassination ... should be used as the vote should ideally be used, that is, bearing in mind only the public good and regardless of personal interest. [*Killing No Murder*, Ch. 10]

DOLORES IBÁRRURI ['LA PASIONARIA'] 1895–1989

1 It is better to die on your feet than to live on your knees! [Republican slogan broadcast in the Spanish Civil War, but coined by Emiliano Zapata in Mexico in 1910. In Hugh Thomas, *The Spanish Civil War*, Ch. 16]

2 *¡no pasarán!* – They shall not pass. [Rallying cry to Spanish Republicans in Civil War, 1936. The call echoes the French *Ils ne passeront pas* of 1916 at Verdun. See also 11:28, 295:14]

HAROLD L. ICKES 1874–1952

3 I am against government by crony. [On resigning as US Secretary of the Interior, Feb. 1946]

4 The trouble with Senator Long is that he is suffering from halitosis of the intellect. That's presuming Emperor Long has an intellect. [In Arthur M. Schlesinger Jr, *The Politics of Upheaval*, Pt II, Ch. 14, sect. v]

ERIC IDLE *see* MONTY PYTHON'S FLYING CIRCUS

MICHAEL IGNATIEFF 1947–

5 Political utopias are a form of nostalgia for an imagined past projected on to the future as a wish. [*The Needs of Strangers*, Ch. 4]

6 We need words to keep us human. Being human is an accomplishment like playing an instrument. It takes practice. [Conclusion]

IVAN D. ILLICH 1926–

7 Our hope of salvation lies in our being surprised by the Other. Let us learn always to receive further surprises. [*Celebration of Awareness*, Ch. 9]

8 In both rich and poor nations consumption is polarized while expectation is equalized. [12]

9 Man must choose whether to be rich in things or in the freedom to use them. [*Deschooling Society*, Ch. 4]

10 We must rediscover the distinction between hope and expectation. [7]

REV. CHARLES INGE 1868–1957

11 This very remarkable man / Commends a most practical plan: / You can do what you want / If you don't think you can't, / So don't think you can't if you can. [*On M. Coué*]

W. R. INGE, DEAN OF ST PAUL'S 1860–1954

12 What we know of the past is mostly not worth knowing. What is worth knowing is mostly uncertain. Events in the past may roughly be divided into those which probably never happened and those which do not matter. [*Assessments and Anticipations*, 'Prognostications']

13 When our first parents were driven out of Paradise, Adam is believed to have remarked to Eve: 'My dear, we live in an age of transition.' ['Work']

1 I called democracy a superstition and a fetish: and I repeat that it is plainly both. [*The Church and the Age*, Preface]

2 The aim of education is the knowledge not of fact but of values. [*The Church in the World*, Oct. 1932]

3 Universal suffrage almost inevitably leads to government by mass bribery, an auction of the worldly goods of the unrepresented minority. [*The End of an Age*, Ch. 1]

4 The enemies of Freedom do not argue; they shout and they shoot. [4]

5 Most of us, though we are bidden to look forward to an eternity of calm fruition, cannot spend an evening without trying to escape from a gentleman whom we know slightly and find, it seems, an intolerable bore – ourselves. [6. See also 121:4]

6 The effect of boredom on a large scale in history is underestimated. It is a main cause of revolutions, and would soon bring to an end all the static Utopias and the farmyard civilization of the Fabians.

7 The command 'Be fruitful and multiply' [was] promulgated according to our authorities, when the population of the world consisted of two persons. [*More Lay Thoughts of a Dean*, Pt I, 6]

8 Personalize your sympathies, depersonalize your antipathies. [IV. 1]

9 The vulgar mind always mistakes the exceptional for the important.

10 Many people believe that they are attracted by God or by nature, when they are only repelled by man.

11 To become a popular religion, it is only necessary for a superstition to enslave a philosophy. [*Outspoken Essays*, Second Series, 'The Idea of Progress']

12 Christianity promises to make men free; it never promises to make them independent. [*The Philosophy of Plotinus*]

13 A man may build himself a throne of bayonets, but he cannot sit on it.

14 Literature flourishes best when it is half a trade and half an art. [*The Victorian Age*, p. 49]

15 Our day of political pride is over. A great race we are and shall remain; a great power we have been and are no longer. [*Diary*, Sept. 1914]

16 The proper time to influence the character of a child is about a hundred years before he is born. [In the *Observer*, 21 July 1929]

17 I think middle age is the best time, if we can escape the fatty degeneration of the conscience which often sets in at about fifty. [In the *Observer*, 'Sayings of the Week', 8 June 1930]

18 Worry is the interest paid on trouble before it falls due. [14 Feb. 1932]

19 When Arthur Balfour launched his scheme for peopling Palestine with Jewish immigrants, I am credibly informed that he did not know there were Arabs in the country. [From the *Evening Standard*, in M. Bateman, *This England*, selections from the *New Statesman*, Pt I]

20 A nation is a society united by a delusion about its ancestry and by a common hatred of its neighbours. [In Sagittarius and D. George, *The Perpetual Pessimist*]

21 Christianity is good news: not good advice. [In *Geoffrey Madan's Notebooks*, ed. J. A. Gere and John Sparrow, 'Livres sans nom']

22 Christ says, 'Judge not,' *but we must judge*. [Attr.]

23 Religion is a way of walking, not a way of talking. [Attr.]

24 We tolerate shapes in human beings that would horrify us if we saw them in a horse. [Attr.]

RICHARD INGRAMS 1937–

25 I have come to regard the law courts [in the Strand] not as a cathedral but rather as a casino. [In the *Guardian*, 30 July 1977]

26 My own motto is publish and be sued. [As editor of *Private Eye*. In BBC radio programme, 4 May 1977]

RICHARD INGRAMS and JOHN WELLS 1936–

27 So we set off, on a lovely May morning, with Mr Haines at the wheel of his Mini, and myself, Harold and Lady Forkbender in the back. [*Mrs Wilson's Diary*, 30 May 1975]

SIR THOMAS INSKIP

1 The years that the locust hath eaten. [Applying Joel 2:25 to wasted years, 1931–5; said in 1939. In Winston S. Churchill, *The Gathering Storm*, Ch. 5]

EUGENE IONESCO 1912–

2 He made the best-looking corpse in Great Britain! And he never looked his age. Poor old Bobby! He'd been dead for four years and he was still warm. A living corpse if ever there was one. [*The Bald Prima Donna*, Act I]

3 Describe a circle, stroke its back and it turns vicious.

4 We haven't the time to take our time. [*Exit the King*]

5 It's our own mediocrity that makes us let go of love, makes us renounce it. True Love doesn't know the meaning of renunciation, is not even aware of that problem, never resigns itself; resignation is for beaten people, as beaten paths are for beaten men. [*The Hermit*, trans. Richard Seaver]

6 Look at yourself with one eye, listen to yourself with the other. [*Improvisation*]

7 I'm going into the next room to pack my bags and you'll never see me again, except at mealtimes and at odd moments during the day and night for a cup of tea and a bun. [*Jacques or Obedience*]

8 You'll probably say that progress can be good or bad, like Jews or Germans or films! [*Maid to Marry*]

9 A nose that can see is worth two that sniff. [*The Motor Show*]

10 Life is an abnormal business. [*Rhinoceros*, Act I]

11 There are more dead people than living. And their numbers are increasing. The living are getting rarer. [II]

12 You can only predict things after they've happened. [III]

13 If God exists, what's the good of literature? If God does not exist, what's the point of writing? [Interview in the *Guardian*, 14 Sept. 1990]

WILLIAM WALLACE IRWIN

14 Statistics show that of those who contract the habit of eating, very few ever survive. [In *Cook's Quotation Book*, ed. Maria Polushkin Robbins]

CHRISTOPHER ISHERWOOD
1904–1986

15 I am a camera with its shutter open, quite passive, recording, not thinking. [*Goodbye to Berlin*, 'A Berlin Diary']

16 The common cormorant or shag / Lays eggs inside a paper bag / The reason you will see no doubt / It is to keep the lightning out / But what these unobservant birds / Have never noticed is that herds / Of wandering bears may come with buns / And steal the bags to hold the crumbs. [In *The Poet's Tongue*, ed. W. H. Auden and John Garrett]

J

ALAN JACKSON 1938–

1 O Knox he was a bad man / he split the Scottish mind. / The one half he made cruel / and the other half unkind. [In *Scottish Quotations*, comp. Alan Bold]

GLENDA JACKSON, MP 1936–

2 The important thing in acting is to be able to laugh and cry. If I have to cry, I think of my sex life. If I have to laugh, I think of my sex life. [Quoted by Kim Basinger in *Playboy*, May 1986]

KEVIN JACKSON 1955–

3 They were not long, the days of whine and neuroses. [In review of TV programme (subtitled 'A History of the Teenager, 1950–1990') in the *Independent*, 21 Feb. 1990]

'JOE' JACOBS [US boxing manager] 1896–1940

4 I should of stood [have stayed] in bed. [At World Baseball Series, Oct. 1935. In J. Lardner, *Strong Cigars and Lovely Women*]

5 We was robbed! [After Max Schmeling (whose manager he was) was declared loser in heavyweight-boxing title fight with Jack Sharkey, 21 June 1932]

W. W. JACOBS 1863–1943

6 'Dealing with a man,' said the night-watchman thoughtfully, 'is as easy as a tee-totaller walking along a nice wide pave-ment; dealing with a woman is like the same teetotaller, arter four or five whiskies, trying to get up a step that ain't there.' [*Deep Water*, 'Husbandry']

7 'Sailor men 'ave their faults,' said the night-watchman, frankly. 'I'm not denying it. I used to 'ave myself when I was at sea.' [*The Lady of the Barge*, 'Bill's Paper Chase']

8 A nice, quiet gal she was, and there wasn't much went on that she didn't hear. I've known 'er to cry for hours with the ear-ache, pore gal. [*Odd Craft*, 'Dixon's Return']

9 Mr Joseph Gibbs finished his half-pint . . . with the slowness of a man unable to see where the next was coming from. [*Ship's Company*, 'Friends in Need']

10 When I told my missis once I should never dream of being jealous of *her*, instead of up and thanking me for it, she spoilt the best frying-pan we ever had. ['Good Intentions']

HOWARD JACOBSON 1942–

11 Arthur Twinbarrow, who specialized in all the twentieth-century poets whose first or second names were Tom or Thomas. [*Coming from Behind*, Ch. 2]

12 On street corners prostitutes who must have fallen below any standards of dress or appearance set by the EEC stood in their oldest clothes. [4]

13 He had been brought up to spot a gentile as someone who ordered pints in pubs. [7]

14 Symbols drove Sefton to distraction. To him they were like fleas in the double bed of

literature. He was aware that they might be in there somewhere but he could never find them himself. [8]

1 Sefton wasn't excessively or unreasonably Oedipal – he didn't want his father entirely out of the way; but it wouldn't do any harm if he just moved to one side a bit. [10]

2 I journeyed to the centre of dialogue; wherever it was I thought I'd been I'd never in fact set foot outside a conversation. [Of Tasmania. From *In the Land of Oz*, in *The Times Literary Supplement*, 25 Sept. 1987]

3 She was no different from all other mothers, (how could she be?) in that while she wanted me, in a general way, to be married, she didn't want me, in a specific way, to have a wife. [*Peeping Tom*, Pt 1, 7. 5]

4 I am unable to pass a theatre without wanting to walk in, and am unable to listen to a single word from an actor without wanting to walk out again. [In the *Listener*, 23 Jan. 1986]

MICK JAGGER 1943–

5 It's all right letting yourself go, as long as you can let yourself back. [In J. Green, *Book of Rock Quotes*]

MICK JAGGER and KEITH RICHARD
     1943–

6 We all need someone we can bleed on. [Song: *Let It Bleed*]

7 I can't get no satisfaction. [Song: *Satisfaction*]

CARWYN JAMES [Rugby coach]
     1929–1983

8 Get your retaliation in first. [To British Lions team, 1971. In the *Guardian*, 7 Nov. 1989]

CLIVE JAMES 1939–

9 One parent is enough to spoil you but discipline takes two. [*Unreliable Memoirs*, Ch. 1]

10 Having a character that consists mainly of defects, I try to correct them one by one,

but there are limits to the altitude that can be attained by hauling on one's own bootstraps. [3]

11 I could never achieve the grim face essential to success in paramilitary organizations. [Of himself as a Cub. 6]

12 Generally it is our failures that civilize us. Triumph confirms us in our habits.

13 I had also mastered the art of laughing at myself a fraction of a second before anybody else did. [10]

14 The essence of a class system is not that the privileged are conscious of their privileges, but that the deprived are conscious of their deprivation. [12]

15 Even a luxury liner is really just a bad play surrounded by water. [17]

16 Aden was a revelation. Until then my belief in God's indifference had been theoretical.

17 She [Marilyn Monroe] was good at playing abstract confusion in the same way that a midget is good at being short. [*Visions before Midnight*]

18 I don't suggest that her face has been lifted, but there is a possibility that her body has been lowered. [Of character in BBC TV series *Dallas*. In the *Observer*, 19 Apr. 1981]

C. L. R. JAMES 1901–1989

19 Time would pass, old empires would fall and new ones take their place, the relations of countries and the relations of classes had to change, before I discovered that it is not quality of goods and utility which matter, but movement; not where you are or what you have, but where you have come from, where you are going and the rate at which you are getting there. [*Beyond a Boundary*, Ch. 8]

20 Cricket is first and foremost a dramatic spectacle. It belongs with the theatre, ballet, opera and the dance. [16]

21 The rich are only defeated when running for their lives. [*Black Jacobins*, Ch. 3]

HENRY JAMES 1843–1916

22 Strether had at this very moment to recognize the truth that wherever one paused in Paris the imagination reacted before one could stop it. [*The Ambassadors*, Bk II, Ch. 2]

1 'Decent men don't go to Cannes with the – well with the kind of ladies you mean.' 'Don't they?' Strether asked with an interest in decent men that amused her. 'No: elsewhere, but not to Cannes. Cannes is different.' [III. 2]

2 She seemed, with little cries and protests and quick recognitions, movements like the darts of some fine high-feathered free-pecking bird, to stand before life as before some full shop window. You could fairly hear, as she selected and pointed, the tap of her tortoise-shell against the glass. [V. 1]

3 One of those types who don't keep you explaining – minds with doors as numerous as the many-tongued cluster of confessionals at St Peter's. You might confess to her with confidence in Roumelian, and even Roumelian sins. [3]

4 The deep well of unconscious cerebration. [The American, Preface]

5 We must grant the artist his subject, his idea, his donné: our criticism is applied only to what he makes of it. [The Art of Fiction, 'Partial Portraits']

6 The historian, essentially, wants more documents than he can really use; the dramatist only wants more liberties than he can really take. [The Aspern Papers]

7 London doesn't love the latent or the lurking, has neither time, nor taste, nor sense for anything less discernible than the red flag in front of the steam-roller. It wants cash over the counter and letters ten feet high. [The Awkward Age, I. 2]

8 He had not supposed at the moment – in the fifties and the sixties – that he passed for old-fashioned, but life couldn't have left him so far in the rear had the start between them originally been fair. [V. 17]

9 Little Aggie differed from any young person he had ever met in that she had been deliberately prepared for consumption and in that furthermore the gentleness of her spirit had immensely helped the preparation. [18]

10 The men, the young and the clever ones, find it a house ... with intellectual elbow-room, with freedom of talk. Most English talk is a quadrille in a sentry-box. [19]

11 People talk about the conscience, but it seems to me one must just bring it up to a certain point and leave it there. You can let your conscience alone if you're nice to the second housemaid. [VI. 23]

12 What could the thing that was to happen to him be, after all, but just this thing that had begun to happen? Her dying, her death, his consequent solitude – that was what he had figured as the beast in the jungle. [The Beast in the Jungle]

13 She had indeed no sense of humour and, with her pretty way of holding her head on one side, was one of those persons whom you want, as the phrase is, to shake, but who have learnt Hungarian by themselves. [The Figure in the Carpet, V]

14 Vereker's secret, my dear man – the general intention of his books: the string the pearls were strung on, the buried treasure, the figure in the carpet. [XI]

15 He lacked ... the light hand with which Corvick had gilded the gingerbread – he laid on the tinsel in splotches.

16 She would have liked for instance ... to marry; and nothing in general is more ridiculous, even when it has been pathetic, than a woman who has tried and has not been able. [The Golden Bowl, Bk I, Pt ii, Ch. 10]

17 It takes a great deal of history to produce a little literature. [Hawthorne, Ch. 1]

18 In her position – that of a young person spending, in framed and wired confinement, the life of a guinea-pig or a magpie. [In the Cage, Ch. 1]

19 Cats and monkeys, monkeys and cats – all human life is there. [The Madonna of the Future]

20 We work in the dark – we do what we can – we give what we have. Our doubt is our passion, and our passion is our task. The rest is the madness of art. [The Middle Years, 1893]

21 The Real Thing. [Title of story]

22 The flowers at Waterbath would probably go wrong in colour and the nightingales sing out of tune; but she remembered to have heard the place described as possessing those advantages that are usually spoken of as natural. [The Spoils of Poynton, Ch. 1]

1 He might have been a fine young man with a bad toothache, with the first even of his life. What ailed him, above all, she felt, was that trouble was new to him. [8]

2 He was so particularly the English gentleman and the fortunate settled normal person . . . He had kind safe eyes and a voice which, for all its clean fullness, told the quiet tale of its having never had once to raise itself. [*The Wings of the Dove*, Bk I, Ch. 1]

3 It was an oddity of Mrs Lowder's that her face in speech was like a lighted window at night, but that silence immediately drew the curtain. [II. 2]

4 She was all for scenery – yes; but she wanted it human and personal, and all she could say was that there would be in London – wouldn't there? – more of that kind than anywhere else. [III. 2]

5 He was for ever carrying one well-kept Italian hand to his heart and plunging the other straight into her pocket, which, as she had instantly observed him to recognize, fitted it like a glove. [VII. 3]

6 The time-honoured bread-sauce of the happy ending. [*Theatricals*, Second Series]

7 Dearest Alice, I could come back to America (could be carried back on a stretcher) to die – but never, never to live. [Letter to his sister-in-law, Alice James, *The Letters of Henry James*, sel. and ed. Percy Lubbock, Vol. 2]

8 But then I'm a battered old novelist and it's my business to comprehend. [Letter to Edward Marsh, 1915]

9 It is art that *makes* life, makes interest, makes importance, for our consideration and application of these things, and I know of no substitute whatever for the force and beauty of its process. [Letter to H. G. Wells, 10 July 1915]

10 Summer afternoon – summer afternoon; to me those have always been the two most beautiful words in the English language. [In Edith Wharton, *A Backward Glance*, Ch. 10]

11 So here it is at last, the distinguished thing! [Said by a 'voice' heard as he suffered his first stroke, often wrongly described as his last words. In 14]

12 Kidd, turn off the light to spare my blushes. [Said to the maid after Edmund Gosse had told him he had been awarded the Order of Merit. In James S. Bain, *A Bookseller Looks Back*]

13 Tell the boys to follow, to be faithful, to take me seriously. [Last recorded words, said to Alice James. In H. Montgomery Hyde, *Henry James at Home*, Ch. 7, iv]

14 It was like morning prayers in a workhouse. [Of a would-be Elizabethan production of *Hamlet*. Attr.]

WILLIAM JAMES 1842–1910

15 I think you will practically recognize the two types of mental make-up that I mean if I head the columns by the titles 'tender-minded' and 'tough-minded' respectively. [*Pragmatism*]

16 There is no more miserable human being than one in whom nothing is habitual but indecision. [*Principles of Psychology*, Ch. 4]

17 The art of being wise is the art of knowing what to overlook. [22]

18 The whole drift of my education goes to persuade me that the world of our present consciousness is only one of many worlds of consciousness that exist. [*The Varieties of Religious Experience*, Lecture 20]

19 Waking consciousness, as we call it, is but one special type of consciousness, whilst all about it, parted from it by the flimsiest of screens, there lie potential forms of consciousness entirely different.

20 The moral flabbiness born of the bitch-goddess Success. [Letter to H. G. Wells, 11 Sept. 1906]

21 [James] was being teased by a theological colleague who said to him: 'A philosopher is like a blind man in a dark cellar, looking for a black cat that isn't there.' 'Yes,' said William James, 'and the difference between philosophy and theology is that theology finds the cat.' [In A. J. Ayer, *On Making Philosophy Intelligible*]

22 Whenever two people meet there are really six people present. There is each man as he sees himself, each man as the other person sees him, and each man as he really is. [In Laurence J. Peter, *Peter's Quotations*]

23 [Environment is] a big, booming, buzzing

confusion. [In Peter F. Smith, *The Dynamics of Urbanism*, Ch. 2]

1 A great many people think they are thinking when they are merely rearranging their prejudices. [Attr. in Clifton Fadiman, *American Treasury*]

2 The perfection of rottenness. [Of a book by Santayana. Attr.]

STORM JAMESON 1897–1986

3 She did not so much cook as assassinate food. [Attr.]

RANDALL JARRELL 1914–1965

4 President Robbins was so well adjusted to his environment that sometimes you could not tell which was the environment and which was President Robbins. [*Pictures from an Institution*, Pt I, Ch. 4]

5 To Americans English manners are far more frightening than none at all. [5]

6 For her there were two species: writers and people; and the writers were really people, and the people weren't. [9]

7 She looked at me the way you'd look at a chessman if it made its own move. [II. 1]

8 She was so thin you could have recognized her skeleton. [3]

9 The people I'm used to just have more marriages and more Matisses than the people you're used to. [III. 6]

10 It is better to entertain an idea than to take it home to live with you for the rest of your life. [IV. 9]

11 I decided that Europeans and Americans are like men and women: they understand each other worse, and it matters less, than either of them suppose. [10]

12 You Americans do not rear children, you *incite* them; you give them food and shelter and applause.

13 In the United States, there one feels free ... Except from the Americans – but every pearl has its oyster.

14 Is an institution always a man's shadow shortened in the sun, the lowest common denominator of everybody in it? [V. 9]

15 It was the speech a vain average would make to an audience of means. [VI. 4]

16 The people who live in a Golden Age usually go around complaining how yellow everything looks. [From *A Sad Heart at the Supermarket*, in *Oxford Book of Aphorisms*, chosen by J. Gross]

17 It is a piece of prose that has something wrong with it. [Defining the novel. Quoted by Frank Tuohy in *The Times Literary Supplement*, 14 Jan. 1983. See also 335:17]

18 Oscar Williams's new book is pleasanter and a little quieter than his old, which gave the impression of having been written on a typewriter by a typewriter. [In *The Times Literary Supplement*, 11 July 1986]

19 I felt quite funny when Freud died. It was like having a continent disappear. [Letter to Allen Tate, Sept. 1939, *Letters*, ed. Mary Jarrell]

ALFRED JARRY 1873–1907

20 By my green candle, shit, madam, certainly I'm satisfied with the way things are. After all, aren't I Captain of the Dragoons, confidential adviser to King Wenceslas, decorated with the order of the Red Eagle of Poland, and ex-King of Aragon – what more do you want? [*King Ubu*, Act 1, sc. i, trans. M. Benedikt and G. E. Wellwarth]

SIR ANTHONY JAY 1936–

21 The class in which one half wouldn't be seen dead with the other. [Of the middle class. Quoted by Robert Robinson in the *Sunday Times Magazine*, 11 May 1980]

See also **JONATHAN LYNN** and **SIR ANTHONY JAY**

DOUGLAS [later LORD] JAY 1907–

22 Fair Shares for All is Labour's Call. [Slogan at North Battersea by-election, London, June 1946]

PETER JAY 1937–

23 As the Prime Minister [his father-in-law, James Callaghan] put it to me ... he saw his role as being that of Moses. [Speech in Washington, Aug. 1977]

SIR JAMES JEANS 1887–1946

1 Life exists in the universe only because the carbon atom possesses certain exceptional properties. [*The Mysterious Universe*, Ch. 1]

2 The universe begins to look more like a great thought than a great machine.

3 The universe shows evidence of a designing or controlling power that has ... the tendency to think in the way which, for want of a better word, we describe as mathematical.

4 Science should leave off making pronouncements: the river of knowledge has too often turned back on itself.

SIR GLADWYN JEBB [later LORD GLADWYN] 1900–

5 He [Anthony Eden] has antennae in all directions, but no brain. He doesn't read papers, he only sniffs them. [In *The Second World War Diary of Hugh Dalton 1940–45*, ed. Ben Pimlott, 2 Sept. 1943]

REV. EDWARD JEFFREY 1932–

6 People expect the clergy to have the grace of a swan, the friendliness of a sparrow, the strength of an eagle and the night hours of an owl – and some people expect such a bird to live on the food of a canary. [In the *Observer*, 'Sayings of the Week', 14 June 1964]

LAMBERT JEFFRIES

7 I prefer a bike to a horse. The brakes are more easily checked. [In *Apt and Amusing Quotations*, ed. G. F. Lamb, 'Horse']

LENA [later LADY] JEGER 1915–

8 It is a sad woman who buys her own perfume. [In the *Observer*, 'Sayings of the Week', 20 Nov. 1955]

ANN JELLICOE 1927–

9 That white horse you see in the park could be a zebra synchronized with the railings. [*The Knack*, Act III]

ALAN JENKINS 1926–

10 There's absolutely no side here, but plenty of edge. [Of the poet Paul Muldoon. In the *Sunday Times*, 14 Dec. 1986]

RT REV. DAVID JENKINS, BISHOP OF DURHAM 1925–

11 I wouldn't put it past God to arrange a virgin birth if he wanted to, but I very much doubt if he would – because it seems to be contrary to the way in which he deals with persons and brings his wonders out of natural personal relationships. [In *Church Times*, 4 May 1984]

12 As I get older I seem to believe less and less and yet to believe what I do believe more and more. [In the *Observer*, 'Sayings of the Week', 6 Nov. 1988]

ROY [later LORD] JENKINS 1920–

13 There are always great dangers in letting the best be the enemy of the good. [Maiden speech as Home Secretary in the House of Commons. In the *Sunday Times*, 8 June 1975]

14 The politics of the left and centre of this country are frozen in an out-of-date mould which is bad for the economic and political health of Britain and increasingly inhibiting for those who live within the mould. Can it be broken? [Speech to Parliamentary Press Gallery, 9 June 1980. Also used by others at foundation of the Social Democratic Party, prompting the phrase: 'Breaking the mould of British politics']

15 He [Anthony Eden] liked private life punctuated by bursts of public adulation. [From *A Gallery of Twentieth Century Portraits*, in the *Observer*, 6 Nov. 1988]

ELIZABETH JENNINGS 1926–

16 Now deep in my bed / I turn and the world turns on the other side. [*In the Night*]

PAUL JENNINGS 1918–1989

17 Resistentialism is concerned with what Things think about men. [*Even Oddlier*, 'Developments in Resistentialism']

18 When numbered pieces of toast and marmalade were dropped on various samples of carpet arranged in quality, from coir matting to the finest Kirman rugs, the marmalade-

downwards-incidence (μδι) varied indirectly with the quality of the carpet (Qc) – the Principle of the Graduated Hostility of Things.

1 Ventre's stark dictum that *les choses sont contre nous*.

2 In this concept of Activated Sludge two perfectly opposite forces are held in perfect equilibrium, like all those electrons, mesons, neutrons, protons and morons in the atom. [*The Jenguin Pennings*, 'Activated Sludge']

3 Ventre offers us a grand vision of the Universe as One Thing – the Ultimate Thing (Dernière Chose). And it is against us. ['Report on Resistentialism']

4 Of all musicians, flautists are most obviously the ones who know something we don't know. ['Flautists Flaunt Afflatus']

5 They have collective farms, why not the collective unconscious? ['Intourist on Capital']

6 Wembley, adj. Suffering from a vague *malaise*. 'I feel a bit w. this morning.' ['Ware, Wye, Watford']

7 It is difficult to decide whether translators are heroes or fools. They must surely know that the Afrikaans for 'Hamlet, I am thy father's ghost' sounds something like 'Omlet, ek is de papa spook.' [From 'On Beatrix Potter Translated', in the *Observer*. In Stephen Potter, *The Sense of Humour*, Ch. 3]

8 To hear some people talk, you would think humour was an aspect of satire, instead of the other way round. Satire is simply humour in uniform. [In obituary in the *Guardian*, 1 Jan. 1990]

JEROME K. JEROME 1859–1927

9 It is impossible to enjoy idling thoroughly unless one has plenty of work to do. [*Idle Thoughts of an Idle Fellow*, 'On Being Idle']

10 Love is like the measles; we all have to go through it. ['On Being in Love']

11 The Passing of the Third Floor Back. [Title of play]

12 I want a house that has got over all its troubles; I don't want to spend the rest of my life bringing up a young and inexperienced house. [*They and I*]

13 I never read a patent medicine advertise-ment without being impelled to the conclusion that I am suffering from the particular disease therein dealt with in its most virulent form. [*Three Men in a Boat*, Ch. 1]

14 The only malady I could conclude I had not got was housemaid's knee.

15 It is a curious fact, but nobody ever is sea-sick – on land.

16 I like work: it fascinates me. I can sit and look at it for hours. I love to keep it by me: the idea of getting rid of it nearly breaks my heart. [15]

C. E. M. JOAD 1891–1953

17 It all depends what you mean by . . . [In BBC radio series *The Brains Trust*, 1940s, *passim*]

18 Conscience was the barmaid of the Victorian soul. Recognizing that human beings were fallible and that their failings, though regrettable, must be humoured, conscience would permit, rather ungraciously perhaps, the indulgence of a number of carefully selected desires. Once the appointed limit was reached, conscience would rap on the bar of the soul. 'Time's up, gentlemen,' she would say, 'we close at ten-thirty.' [*Under the Fifth Rib*, Ch. 9]

19 Whenever I look inside myself I am afraid. [In the *Observer*, 'Sayings of the Week', 8 Nov. 1942]

20 My life is spent in a perpetual alternation between two rhythms, the rhythm of attracting people for fear I may be lonely and the rhythm of trying to get rid of them because I know that I am bored. [12 Dec. 1948]

21 There was never an age in which useless knowledge was more important than in our own. [30 Sept. 1951]

22 It will be said of this generation that it found England a land of beauty and left it a land of beauty spots. [In the *Observer*, 'Sayings of Our Times', 31 May 1953]

POPE JOHN XXIII 1881–1963

23 Men are like wine. Some turn to vinegar, but the best improve with age. [In Gerald Brenan, *Thoughts in a Dry Season*, 'Life']

1 It often happens that I wake at night and begin to think about a serious problem and decide I must tell the Pope about it. Then I wake up completely and remember I am the Pope. [In H. Fesquet, *Wit and Wisdom of Good Pope John*]

2 Anybody can be Pope; the proof of this is that I have become one.

3 Who is ruling the Church, John, you or the Holy Ghost? [To himself when waking up unwell. Attr. in *The Times*, Sept. 1977]

4 I am able to follow my own death step by step. Now I move softly towards the end. [Said two days before his death. In the *Guardian*, 3 June 1963]

POPE JOHN PAUL I 1912–1978

5 Bishops vary just as much as books. Some are like eagles, soaring high above us, bearing important messages; others are nightingales, who sing God's praises in a marvellous way; and others are poor wrens, who simply squawk away on the lowest branch of the ecclesiastical tree, trying to express the odd thought on some great subject. [*Illustrissimi*, 'Letter to Mark Twain']

POPE JOHN PAUL II 1920–

6 Adultery in your heart is committed not only when you look with excessive sexual desire at a woman who is not your wife, but also if you look in the same manner at your wife. [At Vatican Synod. In the *Observer*, 'Sayings of the Week', 12 Oct. 1980]

AUGUSTUS JOHN 1878–1961

7 W. R. RODGERS: What do you think of life? JOHN: There's nothing more terrifying. [In the *Sunday Times*, 1 Dec. 1963]

GLYNIS JOHNS 1923–

8 I think the Swiss have sublimated their sense of time into clock-making. [Attr.]

ARTE JOHNSON 1934–

9 Very interesting ... but stupid! [Catchphrase as German soldier in US TV comedy series *Rowan and Martin's Laugh-in*,

1967–73. In *Very Interesting ... but Stupid!*, comp. Nigel Rees]

SENATOR HIRAM JOHNSON 1866–1945

10 The first casualty when war comes is truth. [Speech in US Senate, 1918, can be traced back to Aeschylus]

PRESIDENT LYNDON B. JOHNSON 1908–1973

11 Boys, I may not know much, but I know chicken shit from chicken salad. [Of Richard Nixon's 'Checkers' Speech, 24 Sept. 1952. In *Morrow Book of Quotations in American History*, ed. Joseph R. Conlin]

12 Every man has a right to a Saturday night bath. [In the *Observer*, 'Sayings of the Week', 13 Mar. 1960]

13 This administration today, here and now, declares unconditional war on poverty in America. [Annual Message to the Congress on the State of the Union, 8 Jan. 1964]

14 In short ... we must be constantly prepared for the worst, and constantly acting for the best ... strong enough to win a war and ... wise enough to prevent one.

15 For the first time in our history it is possible to conquer poverty. [In the *Observer*, 'Sayings of the Week', 22 Mar.]

16 For in your time we have the opportunity to move not only toward the rich society and the powerful society, but upward to the Great Society. [Speech at University of Michigan, Ann Arbor, 22 May]

17 We are not about to send American boys 9 or 10,000 miles away from home to do what Asian boys ought to be doing for themselves. [Speech at Akron University, Ohio, 21 Oct.]

18 Nail those coonskins to the wall, boys! [To soldiers going to Vietnam War. In Arthur Miller, *Timebends*, 8]

19 I am going to build the kind of nation that President Roosevelt hoped for, President Truman worked for and President Kennedy died for. [Speech in Dec. 1964]

20 [When asked why he kept J. Edgar Hoover at the FBI] I'd much rather have that fellow inside my tent pissing out, than

outside my tent pissing in. [Said in 1964. Quoted by J. K. Galbraith in the *Guardian Weekly*, 18 Dec. 1971]

1 [When asked why he had not involved the public more in the question of Vietnam] If you have a mother-in-law with only one eye and she has it in the centre of her forehead, you don't keep her in the living room. [In D. Halberstam, *The Best and the Brightest*, Ch. 19]

2 I don't want loyalty. I want *loyalty*. I want him to kiss my ass in Macy's window at high noon and tell me it smells like roses. I want his pecker in my pocket. [20]

3 Jerry Ford is so dumb that he can't fart and chew gum at the same time. [In R. Reeves, *A Ford, Not a Lincoln*, Ch. 1]

4 When you're up to your ass in alligators, just stop a moment and ask yourself why you decided to drain the swamp in the first place. [Attr.]

5 If you're in politics and you can't tell when you walk into a room who's for you and who's against you, then you're in the wrong line of work. [In B. Mooney, *The Lyndon Johnson Story*]

PAUL JOHNSON 1928–

6 For me this is a vital litmus test: no intellectual society can flourish where a Jew feels even slightly uneasy. [In the *Sunday Times Magazine*, 6 Feb. 1977]

7 It does not always pay to have a golden tongue unless one has the ability to hold it. [Of Lord Curzon. In the *Listener*, 5 June 1986]

PHILANDER JOHNSON 1866–1939

8 Cheer up, the worst is yet to come. [*Shooting Stars*]

R. W. JOHNSON 1943–

9 Monarchy is, in a secular age, Britain's own curious form of religion – it is publicly far easier to say one doesn't believe in God than to say one doesn't believe in monarchy. [In review of Tom Nairn's *The Enchanted Glass* in *London Review of Books*, 7 July 1988]

ALVA JOHNSTON 1880–1950

10 Anyone who extends to him [Mayor La Guardia] the right hand of fellowship is in danger of losing a couple of fingers. [Arthur M. Schlesinger Jr, *The Politics of Upheaval*, Pt I, Ch. 8, sect. iii]

JILL JOHNSTON 1929–

11 All women are Lesbians, except those who don't know it yet. [From *Dialogue on Women's Liberation*, in *Contradictory Quotations*, ed. M. Rogers]

HANNS JOHST 1890–1978

12 When I hear anyone talk of culture, I reach for my revolver. [*Schlageter*. The German actually reads 'I reach for the safety catch on my Browning'. Usually attr. wrongly to Hermann Goering. See also 147:27]

AL JOLSON 1886–1950

13 You ain't heard nothin' yet. [In first talking film, *The Jazz Singer*, July 1927]

AL JOLSON, 'BUDDY' DE-SYLVA
　　1895–1950 and **JOSEPH MAYER**

14 California Here I Come. [Title of song in musical *Bombo*, 1924]

RICHARD JONES

15 The sun's gonna shine in my back do' some day. [Song: *Troubled in Mind*. Alan Lomax, *Folk Songs of North America*, No. 313]

R. V. JONES 1911–

16 I sometimes think that strategy is nothing but tactics talked through a brass hat! [*Most Secret War*, Ch. 51]

TERRY JONES 1942– and **MICHAEL PALIN** 1943–

17 This book features many of the less savoury aspects of human behaviour. But you have been warned. We believe that it is far better we should face reality, however horrible, than stick our heads, sand-like, into an ostrich. [*Dr Fegg's Encyclopaedia of All World Knowledge*, Publisher's Foreword]

See also MONTY PYTHON'S FLYING CIRCUS

ERICA JONG 1942–

1 The zipless fuck is the purest thing there is. And it is rarer than the unicorn. And I have never had one. [*Fear of Flying*, Ch. 1]

JANIS JOPLIN 1943–1970

2 She [Bessie Smith] showed me the air and taught me how to fill it. [In C. Albertson, *Bessie*]

3 On stage I make love to twenty-five thousand people; then I go home alone. [In *Barnes and Noble Book of Quotations*, ed. Robert I. Fitzhenry, 'Acting']

SIR KEITH [later LORD] JOSEPH 1918–

4 Problems reproduce themselves from generation to generation. If I refer to this as a 'cycle of deprivation' I do not want to be misunderstood. [Speech to Pre-school Playgroups Association, London, 29 June 1972]

5 We need inequality in order to eliminate poverty. [In Audrey Hilton, *This England, 74–78*, 'Political Persuasion']

MICHAEL JOSEPH 1897–1958

6 Authors are easy enough to get on with – if you are fond of children. [In the *Observer*, 'Sayings of the Week', 29 May 1949]

JAMES JOYCE 1882–1941

7 The devil mostly speaks a language called Bellsybabble which he makes up himself as he goes along but when he is very angry he can speak quite bad French very well though some who have heard him say that he has a strong Dublin accent. [*The Cat and the Devil*]

8 riverrun, past Eve and Adam's, from swerve of shore to bend of bay, brings us by a commodius vicus of recirculation back to Howth Castle and Environs. [*Finnegans Wake*, 1939, Pt I, p. 1]

9 the redaction known as the Sayings Attributive to H. C. Earwicker, prize on schillings, postlots free. [36]

10 Have you heard of one Humpty Dumpty / How he fell with a roll and a rumble / And curled up like Lord Olafa Crumble / By the butt of the Magazine Wall, / (Chorus) Of the Magazine Wall, / Hump, helmet and all? ['The Ballad of Persse O'Reilly', 45]

11 He was fafafather of all schemes for to bother us / Slow coaches and immaculate contraceptives for the populace.

12 Like the bumping bull of the Cassidys / All your butter is in your horns.

13 Mind my duvetyne dress above all! It's golded silvy, the newest sextones with princess effect. For Rutland blue's got out of passion. [148]

14 The Mookse and the Gripes.
Gentes and laitymen, fullstoppers and semicolonials, hybreds and lubberds!
Eins within a space and a wearywide space it wast ere wohned a Mookse. [152]

15 Nuvoletta in her lightdress, spunn of sisteen shimmers, was looking down on them, leaning over the bannistars and listening all she childishly could. [157]

16 Shem is as short for Shemus as Jem is joky for Jacob. [169]

17 Shem was a sham and a low sham and his lowness creeped out first via foodstuffs. [170]

18 O / tell me all about / Anna Livia! I want to hear all / about Anna Livia. Well, you know Anna Livia? Yes, of course, we all know Anna Livia. Tell me all. Tell me now. [196]

19 Can't hear with the waters of. The chittering waters of. Flittering bats, fieldmice bawk talk. Ho! Are you not gone ahome? [215]

20 Dark hawks near us. Night! Night! My ho head halls. I feel as heavy as yonder stone.

21 Beside the rivering waters of, hitherandthithering waters of Night! [216]

22 Voyaging after maidens, belly jonah hunting the polly joans. [II. 323]

23 Reefer was a wenchman. One can smell off his wetsments how he is coming from a beach of promisck.

1 *Three quarks for Muster Mark!* [383]

2 The Gracehoper was always jigging ajog, hoppy on akkant of his joyicity. [III. 414]

3 *The thing pleased him andt, and andt, / He larved ond he larved on he merd such a nauses / The Gracehoper feared he would mixplace his fauces.* [418]

4 Write it, damn you, write it! What else are you good for? [*Giacomo Joyce*]

5 Envoy: Love me, love my umbrella.

6 A Portrait of the Artist as a Young Man. [Title of book]

7 Ireland is the old sow that eats her farrow. [*A Portrait of the Artist as a Young Man*, Ch. 5]

8 I go to encounter for the millionth time the reality of experience, and to forge in the smithy of my soul the uncreated conscience of my race. Old father, old artificer, stand me now and ever in good stead. [Final words of Stephen Daedalus]

9 The snotgreen sea. The scrotumtightening sea. [*Ulysses*, Penguin edn, 1992, p. 3]

10 When I makes tea I makes tea, as old mother Grogan said. And when I makes water I makes water. [13]

11 History, Stephen said, is a nightmare from which I am trying to awake. [42]

12 The Roman, like the Englishman who follows in his footsteps, brought to every new shore on which he set his foot (on our shore he never set it) only his cloacal obsession. He gazed about him in his toga and he said: It is meet to be here. Let us construct a water-closet. [166]

13 As we read in the first chapter of Guinness'es. [167]

14 I caught a cold in the park. The gate was open. [171]

15 St Thomas ... writing of incest from a standpoint different from that of the new Viennese school. [264]

16 We call it DBC because they have damn bad cakes. [320]

17 Gold by bronze heard iron steel. [348]

18 A face on him as long as a late breakfast. [420]

19 They believe in rod, the scourger almighty, creator of hell upon earth and in Jacky Tar, the son of a gun, who was conceived of unholy boast, born of the fighting navy, suffered under rump and dozen, was sacrificed flayed and curried, yelled like bloody hell, the third day he arose again from bed, steered into haven, sitteth on his beamend till further orders whence he shall come to drudge for a living and be paid. [427]

20 There's a bloody sight more pox than pax about that boyo. [Of Edward VII. 429]

21 A dream of wellfilled hose. [480]

22 There have been cases of shipwreck and somnambulism in my client's family. [589]

23 I regard him as the whitest man I know. He is down on his luck at present owing to the mortgaging of his extensive property at Agendath Netaim in faraway Asia Minor, slides of which will now be shown. [590. See also 166:7, 221:14]

24 I belong to the *faubourg Saint-Patrice* called Ireland for short. [748]

25 Your battles inspired me – not the obvious material battles but those that were fought and won behind your forehead. [Letter to Henrik Ibsen, March 1901]

C. G. JUNG 1875–1961

26 A more or less superficial layer of the unconscious is undoubtedly personal. I call it the personal unconscious. But this personal unconscious rests upon a deeper layer, which does not derive from personal experience and is not a personal acquisition but is inborn. The deeper layer I call the collective unconscious ... It has contents and modes of behaviour that are more or less the same everywhere and in all individuals. [*Archetypes and the Collective Unconscious*]

27 Encounters with people of so many different kinds and on so many different psychological levels have been for me incomparably more important than fragmentary conversations with celebrities. The finest and most significant conversations of my life were anonymous. [*Memories, Dreams, Reflections*, Ch. 4]

1 The pendulum of the mind oscillates between sense and nonsense, not between right and wrong. [5]

2 All the eagles and other predatory creatures that adorn our coats of arms seem to me to be apt psychological representations of our true nature. [9. ii]

3 A man who has not passed through the inferno of his passions has never overcome them. [iv]

4 As far as we can discern, the sole purpose of human existence is to kindle a light in the darkness of mere being. [11]

5 Every form of addiction is bad, no matter whether the narcotic be alcohol or morphine or idealism. [12]

6 Among all my patients in the second half of life – that is to say over thirty-five – there has not been one whose problem in the last resort was not that of finding a religious outlook on life. [*Modern Man in Search of His Soul*]

7 Nothing has a stronger influence psychologically on their environment, and especially on their children, than the unlived life of the parents. [*Paracelsus*]

8 Religion, it might be said, is the term that designates the attitude peculiar to a consciousness which has been altered by the experience of the *numinosum*. [*Psychology and Religion*, Ch. 1]

9 Solitude is for me a fount of healing which makes my life worth living. Talking is often a torment for me and I need many days of silence to recover from the futility of words. [*Letters*, Vol. 2, 1951–61]

10 Show me a sane man and I will cure him for you. [Quoted by Vincent Brome in the *Observer*, 19 July 1975]

11 The true leader is always led. [In the *Guardian Weekly*, 30 Oct. 1976]

12 [When asked if he believed in God] I do not believe ... I know. [In Laurens van der Post, *Jung and the Story of Our Time*]

13 We need more understanding of human nature, because the only real danger that exists is man himself ... We know nothing of man, far too little. His psyche should be studied because we are the origin of all coming evil. [In BBC TV 'Face to Face' interview with John Freeman, 22 Oct. 1959]

14 Everything better is purchased at the price of something worse. [Quoted by W. L. Webb in the *Guardian*, 27 Dec. 1984]

15 A human being would certainly not grow to be seventy or eighty years old if this longevity had no meaning to the species. The afternoon of human life must also have a significance of its own and cannot be merely a pitiful appendage to life's morning. [In *Practical Wisdom*, ed. Frederick Ungar, 'Youth and Old Age']

16 But what if I should discover that the enemy himself is within me, that I myself am the enemy that must be loved – what then? [Attr.]

ERNST JÜNGER 1895–

17 Evolution is far more important than living. [In Albert Camus, *The Rebel*, Ch. 3]

NORTON JUSTER 1929–

18 'Isn't that lovely?' she sighed. 'It's my favourite programme – fifteen minutes of silence – and after that there's a half hour of quiet and then an interlude of lull.' [*The Phantom Tollbooth*, Ch. 12]

19 Did you know that if a beaver two feet long with a tail a foot and a half long can build a dam twelve feet high and six feet wide in two days, all you would need to build the Kariba Dam is a beaver sixty-eight feet long with a fifty-one-foot tail? [14]

20 As long as the answer is right, who cares if the question is wrong?

21 Infinity is a dreadfully poor place. They can never manage to make ends meet. [16]

K

PAULINE KAEL 1919–

1 When I see those ads with the quote 'You'll have to see this picture twice', I know it's the kind of picture I don't want to see once. [*Deeper into Movies*, 'Waiting for Orgy']

2 She's playing herself – and it's awfully soon for that. [Of Barbra Streisand in *What's Up, Doc?* 'Collaboration and Resistance']

3 It's the tragedy of TV that instead of drawing upon new experience and fresh sources of comedy it cannibalizes old pop culture. When movies do the same now, they aren't even imitating movies, they're imitating TV. The result is too infantile to be called decadent; it's pop culture for those with bad memories for pop culture, or so young they have no memories.

4 The words 'Kiss Kiss Bang Bang', which I saw on an Italian movie poster, are perhaps the briefest statement imaginable of the basic appeal of movies. This appeal is what attracts us and ultimately what makes us despair when we begin to understand how seldom movies are more than this. [*Kiss Kiss Bang Bang*, 'A Note on the Title']

5 [Cecil B.] De Mille made small-minded pictures on a big scale – they're about as Promethean as a cash register. ['Epics']

FRANZ KAFKA 1883–1924

6 You've been taken on as Land Surveyor, as you say, but, unfortunately, we have no need of a Land Surveyor. There wouldn't be the least use for one here. The frontiers of our little state are marked out and all officially recorded. [*The Castle*, Ch. 5]

7 It's a working principle of the Head Bureau that the very possibility of error must be ruled out of account. The ground principle is justified by the consummate organization of the whole authority.

8 There's no fixed connection with the Castle, no central exchange which transmits our calls further. When anybody calls up the Castle from here the instruments in all the subordinate departments ring, or rather they would ring if practically all the departments . . . didn't leave their receivers off.

9 Officials are highly educated, but one-sided; in his own department an official can grasp whole trains of thought from a single word, but let him have something from another department explained to him by the hour, he may nod politely, but he won't understand a word of it. [15, 'Petitions']

10 As Gregor Samsa awoke one morning from uneasy dreams he found himself transformed in his bed into a gigantic insect. [*Metamorphosis*, opening words]

11 You may object that it is not a trial at all; you are quite right, for it is only a trial if I recognize it as such. [*The Trial*, 2, 'First Interrogation']

12 It's often safer to be in chains than to be free. [8]

13 Let me remind you of the old maxim: people under suspicion are better moving than at rest, since at rest they may be sitting in the balance without knowing it, being weighed together with their sins.

1 'But I am not guilty,' said K.; 'it's a misunderstanding. And if it comes to that, how can any man be called guilty?' [9]

2 If the French were German in their essence, then how the Germans would admire them! [*The Diaries of Franz Kafka*, 17 Dec. 1910]

3 Don't despair, not even over the fact that you don't despair. [21 July 1913]

4 If there is a transmigration of souls, then I am not yet on the bottom rung. My life is a hesitation before birth. [24 Jan. 1922]

5 Every revolution evaporates, leaving behind only the slime of a new bureaucracy. [*The Great Wall of China: Aphorisms, 1917–1919*]

6 We need the books that affect us like a disaster, that grieve us deeply, like the death of someone we loved more than ourselves, like being banished into forests far from everyone, like suicide. A book must be the axe for the frozen sea inside us. [Letter to Oskar Pollack, 27 Jan. 1904]

E. J. KAHN JR 1884–1972

7 'I get out of bed,' he [Kahn] said, 'and throw up and take a shower and shave and have breakfast ...' 'You throw up every morning?' 'Of course,' Kahn said. 'Doesn't everyone?' [Brendan Gill, *Here at the 'New Yorker'*, Ch. 12]

GUS KAHN 1886–1941

8 Yes sir, That's my Baby; / No sir, Don't mean maybe; / Yes sir, That's my Baby now. [Song: *Yes Sir, That's My Baby*, 1925, music by Walter Donaldson]

9 All God's Chillun Got Rhythm. [Title of song, 1937, in film *A Day at the Races*, in collab. Walter Jurmann and Bronislaw Kaper]

GUS KAHN, RAYMOND B. EGAN 1890–1952 and RICHARD A. WHITING

10 There's nothing surer, / The rich get rich and the poor get poorer, / In the meantime, in between time, / Ain't we got fun. [Song: *Ain't We Got Fun*, 1921, in film *By the Light of the Silvery Moon*]

JAN KALINA

11 We all piss in the swimming pool. Because I piss from the diving board, I am guilty? [Said to the Czech secret police, who answered yes. Reported in BBC TV programme *Tiny Revolutions*, 22 Sept. 1981]

WALTER KANE

12 Hughes was the only man I ever knew who had to die to prove he had been alive. [In J. Phelan, *Howard Hughes, The Hidden Years*]

STEFAN KANFER 1933–

13 Philosophy is concerned with two matters: soluble questions that are trivial and critical questions that are insoluble. [In *Time* magazine, 19 Apr. 1982]

DR TED KAPTCHUK 1947–

14 Health is an episode between two illnesses. [Interview in the *Guardian*, 2 July 1986]

RYSZARD KAPUŚCIŃSKI 1932–

15 In a rich country, money is a piece of paper with which you buy goods on the market. You are only a customer. Even a millionaire is only a customer, nothing more. And in a poor country? In a poor country, money is a wonderful thick hedge, dazzling and always blooming, which separates you from everything else. [*The Emperor*, 'Throne']

16 Words that open our eyes to the world are always the easiest to remember. [*Shah of Shahs*, 'Daguerreotypes']

17 Authority cannot put up with a nation that gets on its nerves; the nation cannot tolerate an authority it has come to hate. ['Dead Flame']

ERICH KÄSTNER 1899–1974

18 *Kennst Du das Land, wo die Kanonen blühn? Du kennst es nicht? Du wirst es kennen lernen.* – Do you know the land where the cannon flower grew? You don't? But you will. [*Bei Durchsicht meiner Bücher*, 'Kennst Du das Land, wo die Kanonen blühn?']

19 *Da hat mir kürzlich und mitten im Bett*

*eine Studentin der Jurisprudenz erklärt: Jungfern-
schaft sei, möglicherweise, ganz nett, besäss aber
kaum noch Sammlerwert.* – Recently and in
the middle of bed, a girl student of law
informed me that virginity might possibly be
quite nice, but had now hardly any collector's value. ['*Moralische Anatomie*']

1 *Wo sonst die Linie 56 hält / war eine Art
von Urwald aufgestellt. / Und Orang Utans
hingen in den Zweigen.* – Where once the
number 2 bus used to stop / They'd set a
kind of pristine jungle up / And apes –
orang-outangs – hung on the trees. [*Doktor
Erich Kästners Lyrische Hausapotheke*, '*Gefähr-
liches Lokal*' ('Dangerous Establishment'),
trans. Michael Hamburger]

2 *Weil man mich dann zum Telephone rief /
(ein Kunde wollte mich geschäftlich sprechen),
war ich genötigt, plötzlich aufzubrechen. / Als
ich zurückkam, sah ich, dass ich schlief . . .* –
Because they called me to the phone (old
Deeping, / My senior clerk, to tell me he was
sick). / I was obliged to make my exit quick.
/ When I came back I saw that I was sleeping.

3 *Wenn Frauen Fehler machen wollen, / dann
soll man ihnen nicht in Wege stehen.* – When
women want to make mistakes, one should
not prevent them. ['*Hotelsolo für eine Männer-
stimme*']

4 *Nun bin ich beinah 40 Jahre / und habe
eine kleine Versfabrik.* – Now I am almost 40
and have a little verse-factory. ['*Kurzgefasster
Lebenslauf*']

GEORGE S. KAUFMAN 1889–1961

5 Satire is something that closes on Saturday night. [In R. E. Drennan, *Wit's End*]

6 One man's Mede is another man's Per-
sian.

7 [On Raoul Fleischmann's saying he was
fourteen before he knew he was a Jew] That's
nothing. I was sixteen before I knew I was a
boy.

8 [When asked by a poor bridge partner,
'How should I have played that hand?'] Under
an assumed name. [In Scott Meredith, *George
S. Kaufman and the Algonquin Round Table*]

9 The trouble with incest is that it gets
you involved with relatives. [In *Was it Good
for You Too?*, ed. Bob Chieger]

10 I like terra firma – the more firma, the
less terra. [In *Barnes and Noble Book of Quotations*, ed. Robert I. Fitzhenry]

11 God finally caught his eye. [Mock epitaph
on a waiter. In *Portable Curmudgeon*, comp. J.
Winokur, but also used in poem by D.
McCord, 1935]

MILLARD KAUFMAN 1917–

12 I am consumed with apathy. [In film
Bad Day at Black Rock, scripted with Don
McGuire]

PATRICK KAVANAGH 1905–1967

13 Unlearnedly and unreasonably poetry is
shaped / Awkwardly but alive in the unmeas-
ured womb. [*Art McCooey*]

14 Cassiopeia was over / Cassidy's hanging
hill, / I looked and three whin bushes rode
across / The horizon – the Three Wise Kings.
[*Christmas Childhood*]

15 Come Dance with Kitty Stobling. [Title of
poem]

P. J. KAVANAGH 1931–

16 Mary lived by wondering what lay round
the corner, I lived by knowing there was no
corner. [*A Happy Man*, Ch. 12]

17 I sometimes think that whenever men
want to cool down their lives women instinc-
tively want to hot them up, and vice versa.
[13]

18 Now you can reach forty and get no
nearer a real grief than the television news.
[*People and Weather*, 4]

19 He [Charlie Parker] always filled me with
a kind of despair, because he played the way I
would have liked to write, and this wasn't
possible for me or anyone else. He made poetry
seem word-bound. [*The Perfect Stranger*, Ch. 5]

20 You had to follow the clues inside yourself, even if they led to incoherence, to crazi-
ness, and people happened to you on the
way. You didn't collect them like stamps.

21 Try not to despise yourself too much –
it's only conceit. [*A Song and Dance*, Ch. 6]

1 But long ago he had decided never to be afraid of the deafeningly obvious, it is always news to somebody.

TED KAVANAGH 1892–1958

2 'After you, Claude.' / 'No, after you, Cecil.' [Catchphrase in BBC radio comedy series *Itma*, 1940s]

3 Can I do you now, sir? [Mrs Mop]

4 Don't forget the diver.

5 Foonf speaking.

6 I don't mind if I do. [Colonel Chinstrap]

7 I go – I come back.

8 It's being so cheerful as keeps me going. [Mona Lott]

9 TTFN. [Ta-ta for now]

10 Wot, me? In my state of health! [Charles Atlas]

DANNY KAYE 1913–1987

11 All my relations are muscle-bound from jumping to conclusions. [In film *The Secret Life of Walter Mitty*, script by Ken Englund and Everett Freeman]

NIKOS KAZANTZAKIS 1883–1957

12 The doors of heaven and hell are adjacent and identical: both green, both beautiful. [*The Last Temptation*, Ch. 18]

FRED KEATING

13 I've just spent an hour talking to Tallulah [Bankhead] for a few minutes. [In *Woman Talk 2*, comp. Michèle Brown and Ann O'Connor]

TOM KEATING 1917–1984

14 The feeling came upon me, and I . . . did sixteen [Samuel] Palmers in a weekend. [*The Fake's Progress: Tom Keating's Story*, as told to Frank and Geraldine Norman]

VICTOR KEEGAN 1940–

15 Thinking is an area where the Government has made one of its most spectacular economies. It is now done by a very small number of people. Often by one person (who has to double up by running the country as well). [In the *Guardian*, 13 Feb. 1989]

CHRISTINE KEELER

16 A few days on your feet and we'll soon have you back in bed. [Quoting her doctor. In Montgomery Hyde, *A Tangled Web*, p. 269]

BRIAN KEENAN 1950–

17 [After four and a half years' captivity in Beirut, when asked what he would do] I'm going to visit all the countries in the world, eat all the food in the world, drink all the drink and make love, I hope, to all the women in the world, and maybe then get a good night's sleep. [On arrival at Dublin, 25 Aug. 1990]

18 They took away my liberty, not my freedom. [Describing his captivity in Lebanon. At Dublin news conference after his release, 30 Aug. 1990]

GARRISON KEILLOR 1942–

19 Some people wear a watch – on the one hand. On the other hand they don't look at it very often. [*Lake Wobegon Days*, 'Summer']

20 If God had not meant everyone to be in bed by ten-thirty, He would never have provided the ten o'clock newscast. ['News']

21 For years I worried because my penis hangs slightly to the left, and finally read in a book that this is within the realm of the normal, but then wondered, what sort of person would read books like that?

22 Some luck lies in not getting what you thought you wanted but getting what you have, which once you have it you may be smart enough to see is what you would have wanted had you known. ['Revival']

23 They say such nice things about people at their funerals that it makes me sad to realize I'm going to miss mine by just a few days. ['Lecture in San Francisco', 13 Dec. 1984]

PENELOPE KEITH 1940–

24 Shyness is just egoism out of its depth. [In the *Observer*, 'Sayings of the Week', 3 July 1988]

HANS KELLER 1919–1985

1 In order to prove its phoniness beyond reasonable doubt, a profession has to create grave problems which it then fails to solve. [*Criticism*, Pt 1, Ch. 1]

2 The Law and Morality are, naturally enough, brothers-in-law rather than natural brothers. [3]

3 For it is of the nature of art that the artist cannot suffer alone.

4 Laziness is the extreme virtue of the ungifted. [In the *Sunday Times Review*, 23 Feb. 1986]

WALTER KELLY 1913–1973

5 We have met the enemy, and he is us. [In strip cartoon 'Pogo', parodying Captain Oliver Hazard Perry (1785–1819), 'We have met the enemy and he is ours', at Battle of Lake Erie, 10 Sept. 1813]

SALLY KEMPTON ?1943–

6 It's hard to fight an enemy with outposts in your head. [Of feminism. In *Esquire* magazine, 1970]

JAAN KENBROVIN [JAMES BROCKMAN ?–1967, JAMES KENDIS ?–1946 and NATHANIEL VINCENT ?–1979]

7 I'm Forever Blowing Bubbles. [Title of song, 1919, music by John William Kellette]

HOWARD KENDALL [Manager of Everton Football Club] 1946–

8 We were firing on all blanks. [In the *Guardian*, 'Quotes of the Season', 30 May 1987]

FLORYNCE KENNEDY 1916–

9 If men could get pregnant abortion would be a sacrament. [In *Ms*, Mar. 1973]

JIMMY KENNEDY 1902–1984

10 Bless 'em all! Bless 'em all! / The long and the short and the tall. [Song: *Bless 'Em All*, 1940, music by Jimmy Hughes and Frank Lake]

11 Red Sails in the Sunset. [Title of song in show *Provincetown Follies*, 1935, music by Hugh Williams (Wilhelm Grosz)]

12 If you go down to the woods today / You're sure of a big surprise . . . / For every bear that ever there was / Will gather there for certain because / Today's the day the teddy bears have their picnic. [Song: *The Teddy Bears' Picnic*, music by John W. Bratton]

JIMMY KENNEDY and MICHAEL CARR 1904–1968

13 South of the Border – down Mexico way. [Song: *South of the Border*, 1939]

14 We're Gonna Hang Out the Washing on the Siegfried Line. [Title of song]

PRESIDENT JOHN F. KENNEDY 1917–1963

15 We stand today on the edge of a new frontier. [Speech on his adoption as Democratic presidential candidate, 15 July 1960]

16 Let the word go forth from this time and place, to friend and foe alike, that the torch has been passed to a new generation of Americans – born in this century, tempered by war, disciplined by a hard and bitter peace. [Inaugural address as President, 20 Jan. 1961]

17 In the past, those who foolishly sought power by riding on the back of the tiger ended up inside.

18 Let us never negotiate out of fear. But let us never fear to negotiate.

19 All this will not be finished in the first 100 days. Nor will it be finished in the first 1,000 days, nor in the life of this Administration, not even perhaps in our lifetime on this planet. But let us begin.

20 And so, my fellow Americans: ask not what your country can do for you – ask what you can do for your country. My fellow citizens of the world: ask not what America will do for you, but what together we can do for the freedom of man.

21 I think it's the most extraordinary collection of talent, of human knowledge, that has ever been gathered together at the White

House – with the possible exception of when Thomas Jefferson dined alone. [At a dinner for Nobel prizewinners, 29 Apr. 1962]

1 The war against hunger is truly mankind's war of liberation. [Speech at opening of World Food Congress, 4 June 1963]

2 If we cannot now end our differences, at least we can help make the world safe for diversity. [Address at American University, Washington, 10 June]

3 All free men, wherever they may live, are citizens of Berlin. And therefore, as a free man, I take pride in the words: 'Ich bin ein Berliner'. [Speech at West Berlin City Hall, 26 June]

4 When power narrows the areas of man's concern, poetry reminds him of the richness and diversity of his existence. When power corrupts, poetry cleanses. [Address at Dedication of the Robert Frost Library, Amherst College, Massachusetts, 26 Oct.]

5 In free society art is not a weapon ... Artists are not engineers of the soul. [See also 356:9]

6 I believe in an America that is on the march. [In Saturday Review, 'Ideas, Attitudes, Purposes from His Speeches and Writings', 7 Dec.]

7 The people of the world respect a nation that can see beyond its own image.

8 The basic problems facing the world today are not susceptible to a military solution.

9 Do you realize the responsibility I carry? I'm the only person standing between Nixon and the White House. [Said on 13 Oct. 1960 to Arthur M. Schlesinger Jr. In the latter's A Thousand Days, Ch. 3]

10 [When asked how he became a war hero] It was involuntary. They sank my boat. [In 4]

11 We must use time as a tool not as a couch. [In the Observer, 'Sayings of the Week', 10 Dec. 1961]

JOSEPH P. KENNEDY 1888–1969

12 Dear Jack. Don't buy a single vote more than necessary. I'll be damned if I'm going to pay for a landslide. [Wire to his son John

F. Kennedy. In speech of the latter in Washington, 1958]

13 When the going gets tough, the tough get going. [In J. H. Cutler, Honey Fitz, p. 291]

SENATOR ROBERT KENNEDY 1925–1968

14 About one fifth of the people are against everything all the time. [Speech at University of Pennsylvania, 6 May 1964]

15 Always forgive your enemies but never forget their names. [In game Quotations]

HUGH E. KEOUGH ?–1912?

16 The race is not always to the swift, but that is where to look. [Quoted by F. P. Adams in the Atlantic Monthly, Aug. 1942]

JEROME KERN 1885–1945

17 [When asked about Irving Berlin's place in American music] Irving Berlin is American music. [In Berlin's obituary in the Guardian, 25 Sept. 1989]

JACK KEROUAC 1922–1969

18 We tiptoed around each other like heartbreaking new friends. [On the Road, Pt I, Ch. 1]

19 We're really all of us bottomly broke. I haven't had time to work in weeks. [7]

20 I had nothing to offer anybody except my own confusion. [II. 3]

21 You know this really is a beat generation. [To John Clellon Holmes. In Playboy, June 1959. Kerouac ascr. the coinage to Herbert Huncke]

JEAN KERR 1923–

22 If you can keep your head when all about you are losing theirs, it's just possible you haven't grasped the situation. [Please Don't Eat the Daisies, Introduction]

23 I make mistakes; I'll be the second to admit it. [The Snake Has All the Lines, 'I Was a Sand Crab']

24 I'm tired of all this nonsense about beauty being only skin-deep. That's deep

enough. What do you want – an adorable pancreas? ['Mirror, Mirror']

SENATOR ROBERT S. KERR [of OKLAHOMA] 1896–1963

1 Eisenhower is the only living unknown soldier. [Letter to Goodman Ace, 19 July 1960. In Groucho Marx, *The Groucho Letters*]

LORNA KERR-WALKER

2 Sure, Reagan promised to take senility tests. But what if he forgets? [In the *Pacific Sun*, 21 Mar. 1981]

GERALD KERSH 1911–1968

3 The habitual liar always imagines that his lie rings true. No miracle of belief can equal his childlike faith in the credulity of the people who listen to him; and so it comes to pass that he fools nobody as completely as he fools himself. [*Night and the City*]

4 They Died with Their Boots Clean. [Title of book]

KEN KESEY 1935–

5 But it's the truth even if it didn't happen. [*One Flew over the Cuckoo's Nest*, Pt I]

JOSEPH KESSELRING 1902–1967

6 Arsenic and Old Lace. [Title of play]

THOMAS KETTLE 1880–1916

7 It is with ideas as with umbrellas, if left lying about they are peculiarly liable to change of ownership. [From his wife's memoir, in *Book of Irish Quotations*, ed. Sean McMahon, but other claimants]

8 Life is a cheap *table d'hôte* in a rather dirty restaurant, with time changing the plates before you've had enough of anything.

SIDNEY KEYES 1922–1943

9 He never loved the frenzy of the sun / Nor the clear seas. / He came with hero's arms and bullock's eyes / Afraid of nothing but his nagging gods. [*Dido's Lament for Aeneas*]

10 There is no virtue now in blind reliance / On place or person or the forms of love. / The storm bears down the pivotal tree, the cloud / Turns to the net of an inhuman fowler / And drags us from the air. [*The Kestrels*]

JOHN MAYNARD [later LORD] KEYNES 1883–1946

11 He [Clemenceau] had one illusion – France; and one disillusion – mankind. [*Economic Consequences of the Peace*, Ch. 3]

12 Like Odysseus, the President [Woodrow Wilson] looked wiser when seated.

13 A study of the history of opinion is a necessary preliminary to the emancipation of the mind. I do not know which makes a man more conservative – to know nothing but the present, or nothing but the past. [*End of Laissez-faire*, Pt 1]

14 There is no harm in being sometimes wrong – especially if one is promptly found out. [*Essays in Biography*]

15 The Economic Problem, as one may call it for short, the problem of want and poverty and the economic struggle between classes and nations, is nothing but a frightful muddle, a transitory and *unnecessary* muddle. [*Essays in Persuasion*, Preface]

16 Whenever you save 5s. you put a man out of work for a day. [II, 'Inflation and Deflation']

17 Regarded as a means the business man is tolerable; regarded as an end he is not so satisfactory. [IV, 'A Short View of Russia']

18 If the Treasury were to fill old bottles with banknotes, bury them at suitable depths in disused coalmines which are then filled up to the surface with town rubbish, and leave it to private enterprise on well-tried principles of *laissez-faire* to dig the notes up again . . . there need be no more unemployment and, with the help of the repercussions, the real income of the community . . . would probably become a good deal larger than it actually is. [*The General Theory of Employment*, Bk iii, Ch. 10]

19 The importance of money essentially flows from its being a link between the present and the future. [v. 21]

1 It is better that a man should tyrannize over his bank balance than over his fellow citizens. [vi. 24]

2 The ideas of economists and political philosophers, both when they are right and when they are wrong, are more powerful than is commonly understood. Indeed the world is ruled by little else. Practical men, who believe themselves to be quite exempt from any intellectual influences, are usually the slaves of some defunct economist.

3 But this *long run* is a misleading guide to current affairs. *In the long run* we are all dead. [*A Tract on Monetary Reform*, Ch. 3]

4 It is Enterprise which builds and improves the world's possessions . . . If Enterprise is afoot, wealth accumulates whatever may be happening to Thrift; and if Enterprise is asleep, Wealth decays, whatever Thrift may be doing. [*Treatise on Money*]

5 I work for a Government I despise for ends I think criminal. [When working at the Treasury. In letter to Duncan Grant, Dec. 1917]

6 'Sound' finance may be right psychologically; but economically it is a depressing influence. [In the *Observer*, 'Sayings of Our Times', 1932]

7 The recent gyrations of the dollar have looked to me more like a gold standard on the booze than the ideal managed currency which I hope for. [1933]

8 BONHAM CARTER: What do you think happens to Mr Lloyd George when he is alone in the room?
KEYNES: When he is alone in the room there is nobody there. [Recalled by Lady Violet Bonham Carter in Romanes Lecture, Oxford, 1963]

9 A man with his ears so close to the ground that he cannot hear the words of an upright man. [Definition of an American politician. In BBC TV programme *Horizon*, 6 Jan. 1981]

10 No, I don't know his telephone number. But it was up in the high numbers. [Attr.]

VIKTOR KHAVKIN

11 It has become the fashion here [Moscow] to stick your hand in someone else's pocket and when they catch you, you say, 'Ah, you don't understand market relations.' [In the *Guardian*, 22 May 1992]

NIKITA S. KHRUSHCHEV 1894–1971

12 If anyone believes our smiles involve the abandonment of the teaching of Marx, Engels, and Lenin he deceives himself poorly. Those who wait for that must wait until a shrimp learns to whistle. [Impromptu speech at Moscow dinner for East German visitors, 17 Sept. 1955]

13 Comrades! We must abolish the cult of the individual decisively, once and for all. [Speech to secret session of 20th Congress of Communist Party, 25 Feb. 1956. Often becomes 'the cult of personality']

14 Every year humanity takes a step towards Communism. Maybe not you, but at all events your grandson will surely be a Communist. [In conversation with Sir William Hayter, June 1956]

15 Whether you like it or not, history is on our side. We will bury you. [At Moscow reception, 18 Nov.]

16 If you cannot catch a bird of paradise, better take a wet hen. [In *Time* magazine, 6 Jan. 1958]

17 Politicians are the same all over. They promise to build a bridge even where there is no river. [Impromptu remark on visit to the USA at Glen Cove, NY, Oct. 1960. Repeated in Yugoslavia, 21 Aug. 1963]

18 When you are skinning your customers, you should leave some skin on to grow so that you can skin them again. [Addressing British businessmen. In the *Observer*, 'Sayings of the Week', 28 May 1961]

19 They talk about who won and who lost. Human reason won. Mankind won. [On the Cuban crisis. In the *Observer*, 11 Nov. 1962]

20 If you start throwing hedgehogs under me, I shall throw two porcupines under you. [In the *Observer*, 'Sayings of the Week', 10 Nov. 1963]

21 If you feed people just with revolutionary slogans they will listen today, they will listen tomorrow, they will listen the day after tomorrow, but on the fourth day they will say 'To hell with you.' [In *The New York Times*, 4 Oct. 1964]

1 We had no use for the policy of the Gospels: if someone slaps you, just turn the other cheek. We had shown that anyone who slapped us on our cheek would get his head kicked off. [*Khrushchev Remembers*, Vol. 2]

2 I don't like the life here in New York. There is no greenery. It would make a stone sick. [In *Barnes and Noble Book of Quotations*, ed. Robert I. Fitzhenry, 'America']

BENEDICT KIELY 1919–

3 In Ireland there's a precedent for everything. Except commonsense. [*Nothing Happens in Carmincross*, 'The Landing']

KEN KIFF 1935–

4 With what I do the imagery is part of a continuous body. It hasn't rushed in for a quick shout. [Of his painting. In the *New Statesman*, 17 Jan. 1986]

KEVIN KILLANE

5 Thatcherism is best explained as that philosophy which seeks to create a New Jerusalem based on the high principles of the Ideal Home Exhibition, its hymns couched in the rhetoric of the tupperware party. [In *Lower Than Vermin*, ed. M. Rowson, 'Further Reflections on Dumb Chums']

JOYCE KILMER 1888–1918

6 I think that I shall never see / A poem lovely as a tree. [*Trees*. See also 278:6]

7 Poems are made by fools like me, / But only God can make a tree.

THOMAS KILROY 1934–

8 To be effective propaganda has to be confirmation, at some level, of people's desires. [*Double Cross*, Pt 2]

MARTIN LUTHER KING JR 1929–1968

9 I want to be the white man's brother, not his brother-in-law. [In *New York Journal-American*, 10 Sept. 1962]

10 I am coming to feel that the people of ill will have used time much more effectively than the people of goodwill. We will have to repent in this generation not merely for the vitriolic words and actions of the bad people, but for the appalling silence of the good people. [Letter from Birmingham City Jail, Alabama, 16 Apr. 1963]

11 I have a dream that my four little children will one day live in a nation where they will not be judged by the colour of their skin but by the content of their character. [Speech in Washington on completion of civil rights march, 28 Aug.]

12 I just want to do God's will. And He's allowed me to go up to the mountain. And I've looked over, and I've seen the promised land. I may not get there with you, but I want you to know tonight that we as a people will get to the promised land. [Speech at Memphis, Tennessee, 3 Apr. 1968, on the eve of his assassination]

13 A riot is at bottom the language of the unheard. [*Chaos or Community*, Ch. 4]

14 Our scientific power has outrun our spiritual power. We have guided missiles and misguided men. [*Strength to Love*, Ch. 7]

15 We have flown the air like birds and swum the sea like fishes, but have yet to learn the simple act of walking the earth like brothers. [In the *Guardian*, 4 Apr. 1983]

STODDARD KING 1889–1933

16 There's a long, long trail a-winding / Into the land of my dreams. [Song: *There's a Long, Long Trail*, music by Zo Elliott]

HUGH KINGSMILL 1889–1949

17 What still alive at twenty-two. / A clean, upstanding chap like you! / Sure, if your throat is hard to slit, / Slit your girl's and swing for it. [Parody of Housman. In H. Pearson and M. Muggeridge, *About Kingsmill*]

18 But bacon's not the only thing / That's cured by hanging from a string. [Parody of Housman]

19 Friends are God's apology for relations. [*The Best of Hugh Kingsmill*, ed. Michael Holroyd, Introduction]

20 Society is based on the assumption that everyone is alike and no one is alive.

MILES KINGTON 1941–

1 The ideal civil servant should have complete loyalty to the truth, and protect it from being known at all times. [Imaginary quotation from Sir Robert Armstrong. In *The Times*, 1 Jan. 1987. See also 14:6, 379:22]

2 Americans get nervous abroad. As a result they tend either to travel in groups or bomb Libya. [In the *Independent*, 29 Mar. 1989]

3 Cinemas and theatres are always bigger inside than they are outside.

4 It is better to have loved a short man, than never to have loved a tall. ['Cod' Albanian proverb. In the *Independent*, 27 Dec. 1991]

NEIL KINNOCK, MP 1942–

5 [To heckler who said, 'At least Mrs Thatcher has got guts' in reference to Falklands War] And it's a pity people had to leave theirs on the ground at Goose Green in order to prove it. [In TV election programme, 5 June 1983]

6 [US Secretary of State] Mr Schultz went off his pram. [On visit to Washington, 14 Feb. 1984]

7 I would die for my country but I would never let my country die for me. [Speech at Labour Party Conference, 30 Sept. 1986]

8 You have the right to speak and the right to be wrong, and you use both rights extensively. [To Ken Livingstone, MP, of his opinions on the IRA, at Labour National Executive, 25 Nov. 1987]

9 When I hear the Prime Minister feeling sorry for the rest of the world I understand at last why she's taken to calling herself 'we'. It makes her feel less lonely. [Speech in House of Commons, 21 Nov. 1989]

10 If these people ever travelled the road to Damascus, they would only do so on a return ticket. [Of the Conservative Party. In the *Independent*, 'Quote Unquote', 20 Apr. 1991]

11 Thatcherism was Toryism without regrets; Majorism is Toryism with regrets. [In the *Observer*, 'Sayings of the Week', 13 July 1992]

RUDYARD KIPLING 1865–1936

12 When you've shouted 'Rule Britannia', when you've sung 'God save the Queen', / When you've finished killing Kruger with your mouth. [*The Absent-minded Beggar*]

13 He's an absent-minded beggar, and his weaknesses are great – / But we and Paul must take him as we find him. / He's out on active service, wiping something off a slate – / And he's left a lot of little things behind him!

14 Duke's son – cook's son – son of a hundred kings – / (Fifty thousand horse and foot going to Table Bay!).

15 Pass the hat for your credit's sake, and pay – pay – pay!

16 Back to the army again, sergeant, / Back to the army again. / Out o' the cold an' the rain. [*Back to the Army Again*]

17 Seven men from all the world back to town again, / *Rollin' down the Ratcliffe Road drunk and raising Cain.* [*The Ballad of the 'Bolivar'*]

18 Oh, East is East, and West is West, and never the twain shall meet, / Till Earth and Sky stand presently at God's great Judgment Seat; / But there is neither East nor West, Border, nor Breed, nor Birth, / When two strong men stand face to face, though they come from the ends of the earth! [*The Ballad of East and West*]

19 Four things greater than all things are, – / Women and Horses and Power and War. [*The Ballad of the King's Jest*]

20 It was not preached to the crowd, / It was not taught by the State. / No man spoke it aloud, / When the English began to hate. [*The Beginnings*]

21 And a woman is only a woman, but a good cigar is a smoke. [*The Betrothed*]

22 Oh, where are you going to, all you Big Steamers, / With England's own coal, up and down the salt seas? [*Big Steamers*]

23 There's a little red-faced man, / Which is Bobs. / Rides the tallest 'orse 'e can – / Our Bobs. [*Bobs* – Lord Roberts]

24 (Boots – boots – boots – boots – movin' up and down again!) / There's no discharge in the war! [*Boots*]

1 I've a head like a concertina, I've a tongue like a button-stick, / I've a mouth like an old potato, and I'm more than a little sick. [*Cells*]

2 Teach us delight in simple things, / And mirth that has no bitter springs. [*The Children's Song*]

3 The coastwise lights of England watch the ships of England go! [*The Coastwise Lights*]

4 We have fed our sea for a thousand years / And she calls us, still unfed, / Though there's never a wave of all her waves / But marks our English dead.

5 They know the worthy General as 'that most immoral man'. [*A Code of Morals*]

6 Until thy feet have trod the Road / Advise not wayside folk. [*The Comforters*]

7 We know that the tail must wag the dog, for the horse is drawn by the cart; / But the Devil whoops, as he whooped of old: 'It's clever, but is it Art?' [*The Conundrum of the Workshops*]

8 Till the Devil whispered behind the leaves, / 'It's pretty, but is it Art?'

9 If once you have paid him the Danegeld / You never get rid of the Dane. [*Danegeld*]

10 O they're hangin' Danny Deever in the mornin'! [*Danny Deever*]

11 The 'eathen in 'is blindness bows down to wood and stone; / 'E don't obey no orders unless they is 'is own. [*The 'Eathen*]

12 The 'eathen in 'is blindness must end where 'e began, / But the backbone of the Army is the Non-commissioned Man!

13 Who are neither children nor gods, but men in a world of men! [*England's Answer*]

14 Winds of the World, give answer! They are whimpering to and fro – / And what should they know of England who only England know? [*The English Flag*]

15 Because to force my ramparts your nutshell navies came.

16 Cock the gun that is not loaded, cook the frozen dynamite – / But oh, beware my Country, when my Country grows polite! [*Et Dona Ferentes*]

17 Something lost behind the Ranges. Lost and waiting for you. Go! [*The Explorer*]

18 For the female of the species is more deadly than the male. [*The Female of the Species*]

19 The Hun is at the gate! [*For All We Have and Are*]

20 What stands if Freedom fall? / Who dies if England live?

21 So 'ere's to you, Fuzzy-Wuzzy, at your 'ome in the Soudan; / You're a pore benighted 'eathen but a first-class fightin' man. [*'Fuzzy-Wuzzy'*]

22 'E's all 'ot sand an' ginger when alive, / An' 'e's generally shammin' when 'e's dead.

23 To the legion of the lost ones, to the cohort of the damned. [*Gentlemen-Rankers*]

24 Gentlemen-Rankers out on the spree, / Damned from here to Eternity.

25 Oh, Adam was a gardener, and God who made him sees / That half a proper gardener's work is done upon his knees. [*The Glory of the Garden*, 8]

26 But when it comes to slaughter / You will do your work on water, / An' you'll lick the bloomin' boots of 'im that's got it. [*Gunga Din*]

27 The uniform 'e wore / Was nothin' much before, / An' rather less than 'arf o' that be'ind.

28 An' for all 'is dirty 'ide / 'E was white, clear white inside / When 'e went to tend the wounded under fire.

29 You're a better man than I am, Gunga Din!

30 Ere yet we loose the legions – / Ere yet we draw the blade, / Jehovah of the Thunders, / Lord God of Battles aid! [*Hymn before Action*]

31 If you can keep your head when all about you / Are losing theirs and blaming it on you. [*If –*]

32 If you can meet with Triumph and Disaster / And treat those two impostors just the same.

33 If you can talk with crowds and keep your virtue, / Or walk with kings – nor lose the common touch.

1 If you can fill the unforgiving minute / With sixty seconds' worth of distance run, / Yours is the Earth and everything that's in it, / And – which is more – you'll be a Man, my son!

2 There are nine and sixty ways of constructing tribal lays, / And – every – single – one – of – them – is – right! [*In the Neolithic Age*]

3 *No doubt but ye are the People – your throne is above the King's. / Whoso speaks in your presence must say acceptable things.* [*The Islanders*]

4 Then ye returned to your trinkets; then ye contented your souls / With the flannelled fools at the wicket or the muddied oafs at the goals.

5 And I'd like to roll to Rio / Some day before I'm old! [*Just So Stories*, 'The Beginning of the Armadilloes']

6 I keep six honest serving-men / (They taught me all I knew); / Their names are What and Why and When / And How and Where and Who. [Follows 'The Elephant's Child']

7 We get the Hump – / Cameelious Hump – / The Hump that is black and blue! ['How the Camel Got His Hump']

8 'Confound Romance!' . . . And all unseen / Romance brought up the nine-fifteen. [*The King*]

9 For Allah created the English mad – the maddest of all mankind! [*Kitchener's School*]

10 There's times when you'll think that you mightn't, / There's times when you know that you might; / *But the things you will learn from the Yellow and Brown, / They'll 'elp you a lot with the White!* [*The Ladies*]

11 An' I learned about women from 'er!

12 I've taken my fun where I've found it / An' now I must pay for my fun.

13 For the Colonel's Lady an' Judy O'Grady / Are sisters under their skins!

14 Have it *jest* as you've a mind to, but I've proved it time on time, / If you want to change her nature you have *got* to give her lime. [*The Land*]

15 Thus said the Lord in the Vault above the Cherubim / Calling to the Angels and the Souls in their degree. [*The Last Chantey*]

16 And Ye take mine honour from me if Ye take away the sea!

17 Then stooped the Lord, and he called the good sea up to Him, / And 'stablishèd its borders unto all eternity.

18 *And the ships shall go abroad / To the Glory of the Lord / Who heard the silly sailor-folk and gave them back their sea!*

19 Now this is the Law of the Jungle – as old and as true as the sky. [*The Law of the Jungle*]

20 We have had an Imperial lesson, it may make us an Empire yet! [*The Lesson*]

21 There's a whisper down the field where the year has shot her yield, / And the ricks stand grey to the sun, / Singing: – 'Over then, come over, for the bee has quit the clover, / And your English summer's done'. [*The Long Trail*]

22 You have heard the beat of the off-shore wind. / And the thresh of the deep-sea rain; / You have heard the song – how long? how long? / Pull out on the trail again!

23 Pull out, pull out on the Long Trail – the trail that is always new!

24 There be triple ways to take, of the eagle or the snake, / Or the way of a man with a maid.

25 Predestination in the stride o' yon connectin'-rod. [*McAndrew's Hymn*]

26 Though Thy Power brings / All skill to naught, Ye'll understand a man must think o' things.

27 Ye thought? Ye are not paid to think.

28 Lord, send a man like Robbie Burns to sing the Song o' Steam!

29 On the road to Mandalay, / Where the flyin'-fishes play, / An' the dawn comes up like thunder outer China 'crost the Bay! [*Mandalay*]

30 A-wastin' Christian kisses on an 'eathen idol's foot.

31 An' there ain' no buses runnin' from the Bank to Mandalay.

32 Tho' I walks with fifty 'ousemaids outer Chelsea to the Strand, / An' they talks a lot o' lovin', but wot do they understand?

33 Ship me somewhere east of Suez, where

the best is like the worst, / Where there aren't no Ten Commandments, an' a man can raise a thirst: / For the temple-bells are callin', an' it's there that I would be – / By the old Moulmein Pagoda, looking lazy at the sea.

1 And your rooms at college was beastly – more like a whore's than a man's. [*The 'Mary Gloster'*]

2 Stiff-necked Glasgow beggar! I've heard he's prayed for my soul, / But he couldn't lie if you paid him, and he'd starve before he stole.

3 'Not least of our merchant princes.' Dickie, that's me, your dad!

4 King Solomon drew merchantmen, / Because of his desire / For peacocks, apes and ivory, / From Tarshish unto Tyre. [*The Merchantmen*]

5 My new-cut ashlar takes the light / Where crimson-blank the windows flare. [*'My New-cut Ashlar'*]

6 I will out and batter the family priest, / Because my Gods have afflicted me! [*Natural Theology*]

7 And the end of the fight is a tombstone white with the name of the late deceased, / And the epitaph drear: 'A fool lies here who tried to hustle the East'. [*Naulahka*, Ch. 5, epigraph]

8 Daughter am I in my mother's house, / But mistress in my own. [*Our Lady of the Snows*]

9 The toad beneath the harrow knows / Exactly where each tooth-point goes; / The butterfly upon the road / Preaches contentment to that toad. [*Pagett MP*]

10 To my own Gods I go. / It may be they shall give me greater ease / Than your cold Christ and tangled Trinities. [*Plain Tales from the Hills*, 'Lisbeth', epigraph]

11 Brothers and Sisters, I bid you beware / Of giving your heart to a dog to tear. [*The Power of the Dog*]

12 King over all the children of pride / Is the Press – the Press – the Press! [*The Press*]

13 Little Tin Gods on Wheels. [*Public Waste*]

14 God of our fathers, known of old, / Lord of our far-flung battle-line. [*Recessional*]

15 The tumult and the shouting dies; / The Captains and the Kings depart: / Still stands thine ancient sacrifice, / An humble and a contrite heart. / Lord God of Hosts, be with us yet, / Lest we forget – lest we forget!

16 Such boastings as the Gentiles use, / Or lesser breeds without the Law.

17 Gawd, 'oo knows all I cannot say, / Look after me in Thamesfontein [London]. [*The Return*]

18 There's never a law of God or man runs north of Fifty-three. [*The Rhyme of the Three Sealers*]

19 *Brother, thy tail hangs down behind!* [*Road-song of the 'Bandar-Log'*]

20 Shillin' a day, / Bloomin' good pay – / Lucky to touch it, a shillin' a day. [*Shillin' a Day*]

21 Brandy for the Parson, / 'Baccy for the Clerk; / Laces for a lady, letters for a spy, / Watch the wall, my darling, while the Gentlemen go by! [*A Smuggler's Song*]

22 'E's a kind of a giddy harumfrodite – soldier an' sailor too! [*Soldier an' Sailor too!*]

23 The God of Fair Beginnings / Hath prospered here my hand – [*The Song of Diego Valdez*]

24 If blood be the price of admiralty, / Lord God, we ha' paid in full! [*The Song o' the Dead*]

25 Keep ye the Law – be swift in all obedience – / Clear the land of evil, drive the road and bridge the ford. [*A Song of the English*]

26 Through the Jungle very softly flits a shadow and a sigh – / He is Fear, O Little Hunter, he is Fear! [*The Song of the Little Hunter*]

27 'Let us now praise famous men' – / Men of little showing – / For their work continueth, / And their work continueth, / Broad and deep continueth, / Greater than their knowing! [*Stalky and Co.*, 'School Song']

28 You may carve it on his tombstone, you may cut it on his card, / That a young man married is a young man marred. [*The Story of the Gadsbys*]

29 Our blunt, bow-headed, whale-backed Downs. [*Sussex*]

30 Here through the strong and shadeless

days / The tinkling silence thrills; / Or little, lost, Down churches praise / The Lord who made the hills.

1 And the Long Man of Wilmington / Looks naked towards the shires.

2 God gives all men all earth to love, / But, since man's heart is small, / Ordains for each one spot shall prove / Belovèd over all. / Each to his choice, and I rejoice / The lot has fallen to me / In a fair ground – in a fair ground – / Yea, Sussex by the Sea!

3 For the sin ye do by two and two ye must pay for one by one! [*Tomlinson*]

4 The Devil he blew upon his nails, and the little devils ran, / And he said: 'Go husk this whimpering thief that comes in the guise of a man.'

5 'Ye have scarce the soul of a louse,' he said, / 'But the roots of sin are there.'

6 Oh, it's Tommy this, an' Tommy that, an' 'Tommy, go away'; / But it's 'Thank you, Mr Atkins', when the band begins to play. [*Tommy*]

7 We aren't no thin red 'eroes, nor we aren't no blackguards too. / But single men in barracks, most remarkable like you; / And if sometimes our conduck isn't all your fancy paints, / Why, single men in barracks don't grow into plaster saints.

8 Of all the trees that grow so fair, / Old England to adorn, / Greater are none beneath the Sun, / Than Oak and Ash and Thorn. [*A Tree Song*]

9 How very little, since things were made, / Things have altered in the building trade. [*A Truthful Song*]

10 But a fool must follow his natural bent / (Even as you and I!). [*The Vampire*]

11 Each in his place, by right, not grace, / Shall rule his heritage – / The men who simply do the work / For which they draw the wage. [*The Wage-Slaves*]

12 They shut the road through the woods / Seventy years ago. [*The Way through the Woods*]

13 All the people like us are We, / And every one else is They. [*We and They*]

14 When the Earth's last picture is painted and the tubes are twisted and dried. [*When Earth's Last Picture*]

15 And, each in his separate star, / Shall draw the Thing as he sees it for the God of things as they are!

16 When 'Omer smote 'is bloomin' lyre, / He'd 'eard men sing by land an' sea; / An' what he thought 'e might require, / 'E went an' took – the same as me! [*When 'Omer Smote*]

17 Your new-caught, sullen peoples / Half devil and half child. [*The White Man's Burden*]

18 Take up the White Man's burden – / And reap his old reward: / The blame of those ye better, / The hate of those ye guard.

19 'Ave you 'eard o' the Widow at Windsor / With a hairy gold crown on 'er 'ead? [*The Widow at Windsor*]

20 Hands off o' the sons o' the Widow, / Hands off o' the goods in 'er shop.

21 And you can't refuse when you get the card, / And the Widow gives the party. [*The Widow's Party*]

22 They rest awhile in Zion, / Sit down and smile in Zion; / Ay, even jest in Zion; / In Zion, at their ease. [*Zion, 1914–18*]

23 He travels the fastest who travels alone. [*The Winners*]

24 'How are you, sir?' 'Loungin' round and sufferin', my son.' [*Debits and Credits*, 'The United Idolaters']

25 He was confined to heavings and shruggin's and copious *Mong Jews*! The French are very badly fitted with relief-valves. [*A Diversity of Creatures*, 'The Horse Marines']

26 He was in a highly malleable condition and full o' *juice de spree*.

27 He spoke and wrote trade-English – a toothsome amalgam of Americanisms and epigrams. ['The Village That Voted the Earth was Flat']

28 Politics are not my concern ... They impressed me as a dog's life without a dog's decencies.

29 Good hunting! [*The Jungle Book*, 'Kaa's Hunting']

30 A man-cub is a man-cub, and he must learn *all* the Law of the Jungle.

1 What the *Bandar-log* think now the jungle will think later.

2 Nothing but foolish words, and little picking thievish hands.

3 'We be of one blood, thou and I,' Mowgli answered, '. . . my kill shall be thy kill if ever thou art hungry.'

4 The Cat. He walked by himself, and all places were alike to him. [*Just So Stories*, 'The Cat That Walked by Himself']

5 An Elephant's Child – who was full of 'satiable curtiosity. ['The Elephant's Child']

6 The great grey-green, greasy Limpopo River, all set about with fever trees.

7 There lived a Parsee from whose hat the rays of the sun were reflected in more-than-oriental splendour. ['How the Rhinoceros Got His Skin']

8 Men are as chancy as children in their choice of playthings. [*Kim*, Ch. 10]

9 One does not own to the possession of money in India. [11]

10 You haf too much Ego in your Cosmos. [*Life's Handicap*, 'Bertran and Bimi']

11 What's the good of argifying? ['On Greenhow Hill']

12 The Light That Failed. [Title of book]

13 Never praise a sister to a sister, in the hope of your compliments reaching the proper ears. [*Plain Tales from the Hills*, 'False Dawn']

14 The silliest woman can manage a clever man; but it needs a very clever woman to manage a fool. ['Three and – an Extra']

15 But that is another story.

16 She was as immutable as the hills. But not quite so green. ['Venus Annodomini']

17 The two men seemed to agree about everything, but when grown-ups agree they interrupt each other almost as much as if they were quarrelling. [*Rewards and Fairies*, 'The Wrong Thing']

18 Being kissed by a man who didn't wax his moustache was – like eating an egg without salt. [*Soldiers Three*, 'The Gadsbys, Poor Dear Mamma']

19 Steady the Buffs.

20 A member of the most ancient profession in the world. ['On the City Wall']

21 I gloat! Hear me gloat! [*Stalky and Co.*, 'In Ambush']

22 'Twiggez-vous?' 'Nous twiggons.' ['Slaves of the Lamp', Pt 1]

23 'This man', said M'Turk, with conviction, 'is the Gadarene Swine.' [The Flag of Their Country']

24 The God who Looks after Small Things had caused the visitor that day to receive two weeks' delayed mails in one. [*Traffics and Discoveries*, 'The Captive']

25 'Tisn't beauty, so to speak, nor good talk necessarily. It's just IT. ['Mrs Bathurst']

26 Words are, of course, the most powerful drug used by mankind. [Speech, 14 Feb. 1923]

27 Power without responsibility – the prerogative of the harlot throughout the ages. [See 23:6, 104:9, 361:12, 401:19]

JAMES KIRKWOOD 1924–1989

28 I want out of the freak show and into the main tent. [*P.S. Your Cat is Dead*]

29 With all this horse shit – there must be a pony! [*There Must be a Pony*, cover]

HENRY KISSINGER 1923–

30 The conventional army loses if it does not win. The guerrilla wins if he does not lose. [*Foreign Affairs*, XIII, 'The Vietnam Negotiations', Jan. 1969]

31 There cannot be a crisis next week. My schedule is already full. [In *The New York Times Magazine*, 1 June 1969]

32 We are all the President's men. [Said in 1970 of the invasion of Cambodia. In M. and B. Kalb, *Kissinger*, Ch. 7]

33 Power is the ultimate aphrodisiac. [In *The New York Times*, 19 Jan. 1971]

34 Within a decade no child will go to bed hungry . . . no family will fear for its next day's bread. [At World Food Conference, June 1974]

35 Castro is without any question a remarkable man. I think it is important for Americans to understand that individuals who go into the mountains to lead a revolution are not motivated by economic considerations. If

they were, they would be bank presidents and not revolutionaries. [TV interview, May 1975]

1 Even a paranoid can have enemies. [In *Time* magazine, 24 Jan. 1977. Also ascr. to Delmore Schwartz]

2 The superpowers often behave like two heavily-armed blind men feeling their way around a room, each believing himself in mortal peril from the other, whom he assumes to have perfect vision. [In the *Observer*, 'Sayings of the Week', 30 Sept. 1979]

3 Clearly, security without values is like a ship without a rudder. But values without security are like a rudder without a ship. [In the *Observer*, 9 Mar. 1986]

A. I. KITAIGORODSKII 1914–

4 A first-rate theory predicts; a second-rate theory forbids; and a third-rate theory explains after the event. [Lecture in Amsterdam, Aug. 1975. In *Dictionary of Scientific Quotations*, ed. A. L. Mackay]

FRED KITCHEN 1872–1950

5 We're in, Meredith, we're in! [Catchphrase from Fred Karno sketch *The Bailiff*, 1907]

LORD KITCHENER 1850–1916

6 I don't mind your being killed, but I object to your being taken prisoner. [To the Prince of Wales, on his asking to go to the Front. In Viscount Esher, *Journal*, 18 Dec. 1914]

EARTHA KITT 1928–

7 I want an old-fashioned house / With an old-fashioned fence / And an old-fashioned millionaire. [Song: *Old-fashioned Girl*, by Marve Fisher]

PAUL KLEE 1879–1940

8 Art does not reproduce what we see. Rather, it makes us see. [*Creative Credo*]

9 An *active* line on a walk, moving freely, without goal. A walk for a walk's sake. [*Pedagogical Sketchbook*, I. 1]

10 The father of the arrow is the thought: how do I expand my reach? [IV. 37]

11 I cannot be grasped in this world, for I am as much at home with the dead as with the yet unborn – a little closer to the heart of creation than is usual, if still not close enough. [Extract from *Diary*, inscribed on his grave as an epitaph]

B. KLIBAN 1935–1990

12 Cat: one Hell of a nice animal, frequently mistaken for a meatloaf. [*Cat*]

JOHN KNAPPSWOOD 1903–1989

13 Commit no thesis. [Inscription for a poet's tomb]

FLETCHER KNEBEL 1911–

14 It is now proved beyond doubt that smoking is one of the leading causes of statistics. [In *Reader's Digest*, Dec. 1961]

CHARLES KNIGHT and KENNETH LYLE

15 Here we are! here we are!! here we are again!!! / There's Pat and Mac and Tommy and Jack and Joe. / When there's trouble brewing, / When there's something doing, / Are we downhearted? / No! Let 'em all come! [Song: *Here we are! Here we are again!!*, 1914, sung by Mark Sheridan]

MGR RONALD KNOX 1888–1957

16 There once was a man who said, 'God / Must find it exceedingly odd / If he finds that this tree / Continues to be / When there's no one about in the quad'. [Limerick. See also 9:21]

17 We love the windows bright / With red and yellow paints / Presenting to our sight / The better class of Saints. [Hymn parody. In Evelyn Waugh, *Ronald Knox*, Pt I, Ch. 5]

18 It is so stupid of modern civilization to have given up believing in the devil when he is the only explanation of it. [*Let Dons Delight*, Ch. 8]

19 Greet him like Etonians without a single word, / Absolutely silent and infinitely bored. [*On the Right Method of Greeting a New Headmaster*]

1 A loud noise at one end and no sense of responsibility at the other. [Definition of a baby. Quoted by C. Blakemore in the BBC Reith Lecture, in the *Listener*, 9 Dec. 1976]

2 A bad sailor keeps clear of the engine room. [On his avoidance of Rome. Quoted by Archbishop Roberts in review in the *Guardian*, 8 Mar. 1973]

3 It's not the taste of water I object to. It's the after-effects. [In *Geoffrey Madan's Notebooks*, ed. J. A. Gere and John Sparrow, 'Extracts and Summaries']

4 Everyone's afraid of dying but no one is afraid of being dead. [Quoted by Cardinal Basil Hume in interview in John Mortimer, *In Character*]

ARTHUR KOESTLER 1905–1983

5 Only in a decaying and doomed civilization did people imagine that they could eat their cake and have it; and that was precisely why they were doomed. [*The Age of Longing*, Pt ii, Ch. 2]

6 One may not regard the world as a sort of metaphysical brothel for emotions. [*Darkness at Noon*, 'The Second Hearing', 7]

7 The definition of the individual was: a multitude of one million divided by one million. ['The Grammatical Fiction', 2]

8 Two half-truths do not make a truth, and two half-cultures do not make a culture. [On the 'Two Cultures'. *The Ghost in the Machine*, Preface]

9 Behaviourism is indeed a kind of flat-earth view of the mind. Or, to change the metaphor: it has replaced the anthropomorphic fallacy – ascribing to animals human faculties and sentiments – with the opposite fallacy: denying man faculties not found in lower animals; it has substituted for the erstwhile anthropomorphic view of the rat, a ratomorphic view of man. [Ch. 1]

10 God seems to have left the receiver off the hook, and time is running out. [18]

11 Just as one could not feel the pull of a magnet with one's skin, so one could not hope to grasp in cognate terms the nature of ultimate reality. It was a text written in invisible ink; and though one could not read it, the knowledge that it existed was sufficient to alter the texture of one's existence. [*The Invisible Writing*, Ch. 33]

12 The most persistent sound which reverberates through men's history is the beating of war drums. [*Janus: A Summing Up*, Prologue]

13 A writer's ambition should be to trade a hundred contemporary readers for ten readers in ten years' time and for one reader in a hundred years' time. [Interview in *The New York Times Book Review*, 1 Apr. 1951]

14 If the creator had a purpose in equipping us with a neck, he surely meant us to stick it out. [In *Encounter*, May 1970]

15 A publisher who writes is like a cow in a milk bar. [To Anthony Blond. In *The Wit of Publishing*, ed. R. Huggett]

16 Liking a writer and then meeting the writer is like liking goose liver and then meeting the goose. [In the *International Herald Tribune*, 24–5 Apr. 1982]

17 Thou shalt not carry moderation unto excess. [Last entry in his final notebook. In George Mikes, *Arthur Koestler: The Story of a Friendship*]

PROFESSOR LEOPOLD KOHR and KIRKPATRICK SALE 1937–

18 The Beanstalk Principle – For every animal, object, institution or system there is an optimal limit beyond which it should not grow. [Manifesto of *The Fourth World*. In the *Guardian*, 25 Nov. 1987]

OSKAR KOKOSHKA 1886–1980

19 If you last you'll see your reputation die three times. [At age of 80. In Ian Hamilton, *Robert Lowell*]

ALEXANDRA KOLLONTAI 1872–1952

20 KOLLONTAI: I regard sex like a glass of water, from which I drink when I am thirsty. LENIN: But who wants to drink a glass of dirty water? [In Georgie Anne Geyer, *The Young Russians*, Ch. 15]

ALFRED KORZYBSKI 1879–1950

21 The map is not the territory. [Slogan. In Fritjof Capra, *The Tao of Physics*, Ch. 2]

JERZY KOSINSKI 1933–1991

1 I rent everything, other than the gift of life itself, which was given to me without any predictable lease, a gift that can be withdrawn at any time. [In interview three days before committing suicide, in the *Weekend Guardian*, 25–6 May 1991]

ERNIE KOVACS 1919–1962

2 A medium, so called because it is neither rare nor well done. [Of television. In Leslie Halliwell, *Filmgoer's Book of Quotes*]

LARRY KRAMER 1935–

3 The rest of the world goes on out there, all around us [gays under the threat of AIDS], as if nothing is happening, going on with their own lives and not knowing what it's like, what we're going through. We're living through war, but where they're living it's peacetime, and we're all in the same country. [*The Normal Heart*, Act II, sc. 11]

KARL KRAUS 1874–1936

4 How is the world ruled and how do wars start? Diplomats tell lies to journalists and then believe what they read. [*Aphorisms and More Aphorisms*]

5 Art is spectral analysis. Art is light synthesis. [*Half-truths and One-and-a-half Truths*, 'Riddles', trans. Harry Zohn]

6 Only he is an artist who can make a riddle out of a solution.

7 Artists have a right to be modest and a duty to be vain.

8 One must read all writers twice – the good as well as the bad. The one will be recognized; the other, unmasked.

9 Where shall I find the time to do all this non-reading?

10 Heinrich Heine so loosened the corsets of the German language that today even little salesmen can fondle her breasts.

11 One cannot dictate an aphorism to a typist. It would take far too long.

12 An aphorism never coincides with the truth: it is either a half-truth or one-and-a-half truths.

13 Newspapers have roughly the same relationship to life as fortune-tellers to metaphysics. ['In hollow heads']

14 Journalists write because they have nothing to say, and have something to say because they write.

15 Psychoanalysis is that mental illness for which it regards itself as therapy.

16 A woman who cannot be ugly is not beautiful. ['Not for women']

17 Solitude would be an ideal state if one were able to pick the people one avoids. ['Lord, forgive the . . .']

18 There are people who can never forgive a beggar for their not having given him anything.

V. K. KRISHNA MENON 1898–1982

19 That expression 'positive neutrality' is a contradiction in terms. There can be no more positive neutrality than there can be a vegetarian tiger. [In *The New York Times*, 18 Oct. 1960]

J. KRISHNAMURTI 1895–1986

20 Happiness comes uninvited; and the moment you are conscious that you are happy, you are no longer happy. [*The Penguin Krishnamurti Reader*, 'Questions and Answers']

21 Constantly to seek the purpose of life is one of the odd escapes of man. If he finds what he seeks it will not be worth that pebble on the path. [*The Second Penguin Krishnamurti Reader*, Ch. 14]

22 The constant assertion of belief is an indication of fear.

23 Meditation is not a means to an end. It is both the means and the end.

24 Religion is the frozen thought of men out of which they build temples. [In the *Observer*, 'Sayings of the Week', 22 Apr. 1928]

25 I maintain that Truth is a pathless land, and you cannot approach it by any path whatsoever, by any religion, by any sect. [Speech in Holland, 3 Aug. 1929. In the *Guardian* at his death, 19 Feb. 1986]

KRIS KRISTOFFERSON 1936– and FRED FOSTER

1 Freedom's just another word for nothin' left to lose, / And nothin' ain't worth nothin' but it's free. [Song: *Me and Bobby McGee*]

LOUIS KRONENBERGER 1904–1980

2 The trouble with us in America isn't that the poetry of life has turned to prose, but that it has turned to advertising copy. [*Company Manners*, 'The Spirit of the Age']

PRESIDENT PAULUS KRUGER 1825–1904

3 They [the British] have asked for my trousers, and I have given them; for my coat, I have given that also; now they want my life, and that I cannot give. [Speech in Raad, 7 Sept. 1899]

JOSEPH WOOD KRUTCH 1893–1970

4 The most serious charge which can be brought against New England is not Puritanism but February. [*Twelve Seasons*, 'February']

STANLEY KUBRICK 1928–

5 The great nations have always acted like gangsters, and the small nations like prostitutes. [In the *Guardian*, 5 June 1963]

STANLEY KUBRICK, TERRY SOUTHERN 1926– and PETER GEORGE 1924–1966

6 I do not avoid women – but I do deny them my bodily essence. [Said by Sterling Hayden in film *Dr Strangelove: Or How I Stopped Worrying and Learned to Love the Bomb*]

7 Gentlemen, you can't fight in here. This is the War Room. [From *Dr Strangelove*, in Alexander Walker, *Stanley Kubrick Directs*]

8 If you want to know what I think, I think you're some kind of a deviated prevert.

THOMAS KUHN 1922–

9 There is no appropriate scale available with which to weigh the merits of alternative paradigms: they are incommensurable. [*The Structure of Scientific Revolution*, p. 65]

MILAN KUNDERA 1929–

10 The territory where no one possesses the truth, but where everyone has the right to be understood. [Of the novel. From *The Art of the Novel*, in the *Observer*, 5 June 1988]

11 Women don't look for handsome men, they look for men with beautiful women. [*The Book of Laughter and Forgetting*, Pt 1, 8]

12 The only reason people want to be masters of the future is to change the past. [17]

13 According to my calculations there are two or three new fictional characters baptized on earth every second. [4. 1]

14 All man's life among men is nothing more than a battle for the ears of others.

15 People fascinated by the idea of progress never suspect that every step forward is also a step on the way to the end. [6. 17]

16 The novelist teaches the reader to comprehend the world as a question. [Afterword]

17 Alas, solitude is not very likely, there is so little of it in life, so what can we expect after death! After all, the dead far outnumber the living! [*Immortality*, Pt 1, 3]

18 No one can give anyone else the gift of the idyll; only an animal can do so, because only animals were not expelled from Paradise. [*The Unbearable Lightness of Being*, Pt 7, 4]

19 A man able to think isn't defeated – even when he is defeated. [Interview with Philip Roth in the *Sunday Times Magazine*, 20 May 1984]

20 Only a great cynic would be an optimist these days.

L

HENRY LABOUCHERE 1831–1912

1 He [Labouchere] did not object, he once said, to Gladstone's always having the ace of trumps up his sleeve, but only to his pretence that God put it there. [A. L. Thorold, *Life of H.L.*, Ch. 15]

LABOUR PARTY

2 Yesterday's Men. [Of the Conservatives. 1970 election slogan, ascr. to David Kingsley, Dennis Lyons and Peter Lovell-Davis in *Oxford Dictionary of Modern Quotations*, ed. Tony Augarde]

JANET LACEY 1903–1988

3 Need not Greed. [Slogan of Christian Aid]

ALAN LADD 1913–1964

4 A man's gotta do what a man's gotta do. [In film *Shane*, screenplay by A. B. Guthrie Jr, from novel by Jack Schaefer]

JOHN LAHR 1941–

5 In front of the small screen, life becomes fiction, and fiction life. [In the *Independent on Sunday*, 29 Sept. 1991]

R. D. LAING 1927–1989

6 Schizophrenia cannot be understood without understanding despair. [*The Divided Self*, Ch. 2]

7 Few books today are forgivable. [*The Politics of Experience*, Introduction]

8 We are born into a world where alienation awaits us.

9 Before we can ask such an optimistic question as 'What is a personal relationship?', we have to ask if a personal relationship is possible, or, *are persons possible* in our present situation? [Ch. 1]

10 Children do not give up their innate imagination, curiosity, dreaminess easily. You have to love them to get them to do that. [3]

11 We are effectively destroying ourselves by violence masquerading as love. [4]

12 It seems to us that *without exception* the experience and behaviour that gets labelled schizophrenic is *a special strategy that a person invents in order to live in an unlivable situation.* [5]

13 Madness need not be all breakdown. It may also be break-through. It is potential liberation and renewal as well as enslavement and existential death. [6]

14 True guilt is guilt at the obligation one owes to oneself to be oneself. False guilt is guilt felt at not being what other people feel one ought to be or assume that one is. [*Self and Others*, Ch. 10]

A. J. LAMB 1870–1928

15 She's a Bird in Gilded Cage. [Title of song, 1900, music by H. von Tilzer]

GEORGE LAMMING 1927–

16 The English language no longer belongs

to the English. It's an export reject. [In BBC radio programme *Third World*, on Caribbean writing, 1958]

GIUSEPPE DI LAMPEDUSA 1896–1957

1 If we want things to stay as they are, things will have to change. [*The Leopard*, Ch. 1]

WILLIAM JAMES LAMPTON 1859–1917

2 Same old slippers, / Same old rice, / Same old glimpse of / Paradise. [*June Weddings*]

SIR OSBERT LANCASTER 1908–1986

3 The resulting style, known as Bankers Georgian, always preserves something of the air of a Metro-Goldwyn-Mayer production of *The School for Scandal*. [*Pillar to Post*, 'Bankers Georgian']

4 'Fan vaulting' ... an architectural device which arouses enormous enthusiasm on account of the difficulties it has all too obviously involved but which from an aesthetic standpoint frequently belongs to the 'Last-supper-carved-on-a-peach-stone' class of masterpiece. ['Perpendicular']

5 A hundred and fifty accurate reproductions of Anne Hathaway's cottage, each complete with central heating and garage. ['Stockbrokers Tudor']

6 Searching the scriptures for hints of things to come, preferably unpleasant, has always been a favourite pastime of extreme Protestantism. [*With an Eye to the Future*, Ch. 1]

7 For sheer pleasure few methods of progression can compare with the perambulator. The motion is agreeable, the range of vision extensive, and one has always before one's eyes the rewarding spectacle of a grown-up maintaining prolonged physical exertion. [In *The Times Literary Supplement*, 12 June 1981]

ELSA LANCHESTER 1902–1986

8 She looked as though butter wouldn't melt in her mouth – or anywhere else. [Of Maureen O'Hara. In Leslie Halliwell, *Filmgoer's Book of Quotes*]

ANN LANDERS 1918–

9 One out of four people in this country is mentally unbalanced. Think of your three closest friends – and if they seem okay then you're the one! [In *Kiss Me Hardy*, ed. Roger Kilroy]

ANDREW LANG 1844–1912

10 *I* am the batsman and the bat, / *I* am the bowler and the ball, / The umpire, the pavilion cat, / The roller, pitch, and stumps, and all. [*Brahma*, imitating Emerson]

11 He uses statistics as a drunken man uses lamp-posts – for support rather than illumination. [In *Dictionary of Scientific Quotations*, ed. A. L. Mackay]

JULIA LANG 1921–

12 Are you sitting comfortably? Then I'll begin. [Catchphrase in BBC radio programme *Listen with Mother*, 1950s to 1980s]

FREDERICK LANGBRIDGE 1849–1923

13 Two men look out through the same bars: / One sees the mud, and one the stars. [*Cluster of Quiet Thoughts*, 1896]

HALVARD LANGE 1902–1970

14 We do not regard Englishmen as foreigners. We look on them only as rather mad Norwegians. [In the *Observer*, 'Sayings of the Week', 9 Mar. 1957]

DAVID LARDNER

15 The plot was designed in a light vein that somehow became varicose. [In Bennett Cerf, *Try and Stop Me*]

RING LARDNER 1885–1933

16 I have known what it was like to be hungry, but I always went right to a restaurant. [*The Lardners: My Family Remembered*]

17 He [Present Taft] looked at me as if I was a side dish he hadn't ordered. [In A. K. Adams, *Home Book of Humorous Quotations*]

1 You know you've had a few too many when you come home and find cold scrambled eggs on top of last night's lamb chops. [In R. E. Drennan, *Wit's End*]

2 Frenchmen drink wine just like we used to drink water before Prohibition.

PHILIP LARKIN 1922–1985

3 Sexual intercourse began / in nineteen sixty-three / – (Which was rather late for me) – / Between the end of the *Chatterley* ban / And the Beatles' first LP. [*Annus Mirabilis*]

4 To prove / Our almost-instinct almost true: / What will survive of us is love. [*An Arundel Tomb*]

5 Religion used to try, / That vast moth-eaten musical brocade / Created to pretend we never die. [*Aubade*]

6 Hatless, I take off / My cycle-clips in awkward reverence. [*Church-going*]

7 A serious house on serious earth it is.

8 On me your voice falls as they say love should, / Like an enormous yes. [*For Sidney Bechet*]

9 Marrying left your maiden name disused. [*Maiden Name*]

10 Clearly money has something to do with life / – In fact, they've a lot in common, if you enquire: / You can't put off being young until you retire. [*Money*]

11 Perhaps being old is having lighted rooms / Inside your head, and people in them, acting. / People you know, yet can't quite name. [*The Old Fools*]

12 In this way I spent youth, / Tracing the trite untransferable / Truss-advertisement, truth. [*Send No Money*]

13 Get stewed: / Books are a load of crap. [*A Study of Reading Habits*]

14 Here's to the whitest man I know, / Though white is not my favourite colour. [*Sympathy in White Major*. See also 166:7, 198:23]

15 They fuck you up, your mum and dad. / They may not mean to, but they do. / They fill you with the faults they had / And add some extra, just for you. [*This be the Verse*]

16 Man hands on misery to man, / It deepens like a coastal shelf. / Get out as early as you can, / And don't have any kids yourself.

17 Why should I let the toad *work* / Squat on my life? [*Toads*]

18 I thought of London spread out in the sun, / Its postal districts packed like squares of wheat. [*The Whitsun Weddings*]

19 Deprivation is for me what daffodils were for Wordsworth. [*Required Writing*, 'An Interview with the *Observer*']

20 It was that verse about becoming again as a little child that caused the first sharp waning of my Christian sympathies. If the Kingdom of Heaven could be entered only by those fulfilling such a condition I knew I should be unhappy there. ['The Savage Seventh']

21 Far too many relied on the classic formula of a beginning, a muddle, and an end. [Of modern novels. Speech on judging the Booker Prize, 1977. In *New Fiction*, Jan. 1978]

22 I can't understand these chaps who go round American universities explaining how they write poems: It's like going round explaining how you sleep with your wife. [Quoted by John Updike in *The New York Times*, 17 Aug. 1986]

23 [When asked whether, despite his known dislike of travel, he would not like to visit China] Yes, so long as I can get there and back in a day. [In the *Guardian*, 27 Sept. 1988]

CHRISTOPHER LASCH 1932–

24 Nothing succeeds like the appearance of success. [From *The Culture of Narcissism*, in Jonathon Green, *Cynic's Lexicon*]

HAROLD LASKI 1893–1950

25 Every phrase and gesture was studied. Now and again when she said something a little out of the ordinary she wrote it down herself in a notebook. *It was like watching someone organizing her own immortality.* [On sitting next to Virginia Woolf at lunch. In letter of George Lyttelton, 27 Oct. 1955, *Lyttelton–Hart-Davis Letters*, ed. Rupert Hart-Davis, Vol. 1]

1 Both of us carry on the teaching of Karl Marx; you in your way, I in his. [Quoted by Brian Jackson in *New Society*, 17 Mar. 1983]

2 De mortuis nil nisi bunkum. [Attr.]

HAROLD LASSWELL 1902–1978

3 Politics: Who Gets What, When, How. [Title of book]

SIR HARRY LAUDER 1870–1950

4 I love a lassie. [Song]

5 Just a wee deoch-an-duoris / Before we gang awa' . . . / If y' can say / It's a braw brecht moonlecht necht, / Yer a' recht, that's a'. [Song]

6 Keep right on to the end of the road. [Song]

7 O! it's nice to get up in the mornin', / But it's nicer to stay in bed. [Song]

8 Roamin' in the gloamin', / By the bonny banks of Clyde. [Song]

CHARLES LAUGHTON 1899–1962

9 I had to throw too many of his kind out of our hotel when I was sixteen. [On refusing to play Falstaff. In James Agate, *Ego 1*, 1933]

WILLIAM L. LAURENCE 1888–1977

10 At first it [the first atomic explosion] was a giant column that soon took the shape of a supramundane mushroom. [In *The New York Times*, 26 Sept. 1945]

PIERRE LAVAL 1883–1945

11 If peace is a chimaera, I am happy to have caressed her. [Said in 1935. In the *Observer*, 'Sayings of Our Times', 31 May 1953]

D. H. LAWRENCE 1885–1930

12 Creatures that hang themselves up like an old rag, to sleep; / And disgustingly upside down. / Hanging upside down like rows of disgusting old rags / And grinning in their sleep. / Bats! [*Bats*]

13 Me or the Mexican who comes to chop wood / All the same, / All humanity is jam to you. [*Bibbles*]

14 You must always be a-waggle with LOVE.

15 Is it the secret of the long-nosed Etruscans? / The long-nosed, sensitive footed, subtly-smiling Etruscans, / Who made so little noise outside the cypress groves? [*Cypresses*]

16 Evil, what is evil? / There is only one evil, to deny life / As Rome denied Etruria / And mechanical America Montezuma still.

17 Don't be sucked in by the su-superior, / don't swallow the culture-bait. [*Don'ts*]

18 Along the avenue of cypresses, / All in their scarlet cloaks and surplices / Of linen, go the chanting choristers, / The priests in gold and black, the villagers. [*Giorno dei Morti*]

19 O pity the dead that are dead, but cannot make / the journey, still they moan and beat / against the silvery adamant walls of life's exclusive city. [*The Houseless Dead*]

20 How beastly the bourgeois is especially the male of the species. [*How Beastly the Bourgeois Is*]

21 Too much of the humble Willy wet-leg / And the holy can't-help-it touch. [*Now It's Happened*]

22 A snake came to my water-trough / On a hot, hot day, and I in pyjamas for the heat, / To drink there. [*Snake*]

23 And so, I missed my chance with one of the lords / Of life. / And I have something to expiate; / A pettiness.

24 Not I, not I, but the wind that blows through me! / A fine wind is blowing the new direction of Time. [*Song of a Man Who Has Come Through*]

25 Thought is not a trick, or an exercise, or a set of dodges. / Thought is a man in his wholeness wholly attending. [*Thought*]

26 The English people on the whole are surely the *nicest* people in the world, and everyone makes everything so easy for everybody else, that there is almost nothing to resist at all. [*Dull London*]

27 To the Puritan all things are impure. [*Etruscan Places*, 'Cerveteri']

1 Cuckoos, like noise falling in drops off the leaves. [*Fantasia of the Unconscious*, Ch. 4]

2 Morality which is based on ideas, or on an ideal, is an unmitigated evil. [7]

3 When Eve ate this particular apple, she became aware of her own womanhood, mentally. And mentally she began to experiment with it. She has been experimenting ever since. So has man. To the rage and horror of both of them.

4 Every race which has become selfconscious and idea-bound in the past has perished.

5 To make the mind an absolute ruler is as good as making a Cook's tourist-interpreter a king and a god, because he can speak several languages and make an Arab understand that an Englishman wants fish for supper. [11]

6 Death is the only pure, beautiful conclusion of a great passion. [15]

7 Better passion and death than any more of these 'isms'. No more of the old purpose done up in aspic. Better passion and death.

8 You may be the most liberal Liberal Englishman, and yet you cannot fail to see the categorical difference between the responsible and the irresponsible classes. [*Kangaroo*, Ch. 1]

9 'We don't like to have anybody overhead here,' said Kangaroo. 'We don't even care to go upstairs, because then we're one storey higher than our true, groundfloor selves.' [6]

10 What do the facts we know *about* a man amount to? Only two things we can know of him, and this by pure soul-intuition: we can know if he is true to the flame of life and love which is inside his heart, or if he is false to it. [7]

11 The indifference – the fern-dark indifference of this remote golden Australia. Not to care – from the bottom of one's soul, not to care. [10]

12 Life makes no absolute statement. It is all Call and Answer.

13 The highest function of *mind* is its function of messenger. [16]

14 Man's ultimate love for man? Yes, yes, but only in the separate darkness of man's love for the present, unknowable God. [17]

15 We have all lost the war. All Europe. [*The Ladybird*, title story]

16 It's all this cold-hearted fucking that is death and idiocy. [*Lady Chatterley's Lover*, Ch. 14]

17 This is John Thomas marryin' Lady Jane. [15]

18 A man's most dangerous moment . . . is when he's getting into his shirt. Then he puts his head in a bag.

19 But tha mun dress thysen, an' go back to thy stately homes of England, how beautiful they stand. Time's up! Time's up for Sir John, an' for little Lady Jane! Put thy shimmy on, Lady Chatterley!

20 No absolute is going to make the lion lie down with the lamb unless the lamb is inside. [*The Later D. H. Lawrence*]

21 It is as if the life had retreated eastwards. As if the Germanic life were slowly ebbing away from contact with western Europe, ebbing to the deserts of the east. [*A Letter from Germany*, 1924]

22 The identifying ourselves with the visual image of ourselves has become an instinct; the habit is already old. The picture of me, the me that is *seen*, is me. [*Phoenix*, 'Art and Morality']

23 Neither can you expect a revolution, because there is no new baby in the womb of our society. Russia is a collapse, not a revolution.

24 Sentimentalism is the working off on yourself of feelings you haven't really got. ['John Galsworthy']

25 Pornography is the attempt to insult sex, to do dirt on it. ['Pornography and Obscenity']

26 Russia will certainly inherit the future. What we already call the greatness of Russia is only her pre-natal struggling. [Preface to Leo Shestov, *All Things are Possible*]

27 No matter how much of a shabby animal you may be, you can learn from Dostoyevsky and Chekhov, etc., how to have the most tender, unique, coruscating soul on earth. ['Preface to Mastro-don Gesualdo']

1 It is no good casting out devils. They belong to us, we must accept them and be at peace with them. ['The Reality of Peace']

2 We know these new English Catholics. They are the last words in Protest. They are Protestants protesting against Protestantism. [Review of Eric Gill's *Art Nonsense*]

3 I am a man, and alive . . . For this reason I am a novelist. And being a novelist, I consider myself superior to the saint, the scientist, the philosopher, and the poet, who are all great masters of different bits of man alive, but never get the whole hog. ['Why the Novel Matters']

4 Only in the novel are *all* things given full play.

5 My destiny has been cast among cocksure women. Perhaps when man begins to doubt himself, woman, who should be nice and peacefully hen-sure, becomes instead insistently cocksure. She develops convictions, or she catches them. And then woe betide everybody. ['Women are so Cocksure']

6 To every man who struggles with his own soul in mystery, a book that is a book flowers once, and seeds, and is gone. ['A Bibliography of D.H.L.']

7 'It [Mexico] is a country where men despise sex, and live for it,' said Ramón. 'Which is suicide.' [*The Plumed Serpent*, Ch. 25]

8 He daren't quite bite. Not that he was really afraid of the others. He was afraid of himself, once he let himself go. [*St Mawr*]

9 The modern pantheist not only sees the god in everything, he takes photographs of it.

10 Judas is the last god, and, by heaven, the most potent.

11 And suddenly she craved again for the more absolute silence of America. English stillness was so soft, like an inaudible murmur of voices, of presences.

12 There's nothing so artificial as sinning nowadays. I suppose it once was real.

13 Be a good animal, true to your animal instincts. [*The White Peacock*, Pt II, Ch. 2]

14 I think more of a bird with broad wings flying and lapsing through the air, than anything, when I think of metre. [Letter to Edward Marsh, Nov. 1913]

15 I like to write when I feel spiteful: it's like having a good sneeze. [Letter to Lady Cynthia Asquith, Nov. 1913]

16 The ordinary novel would trace the history of the diamond – but I say, 'Diamond, what! This is carbon.' And my diamond may be coal or soot and my theme is carbon. [Letter to Edward Garnett, 5 June 1914]

17 I cannot get any sense of an enemy – only of a disaster. [Letter to Edward Marsh, Autumn 1914]

18 Individuals do not *vitally* concern me any more. Only a *purpose* vitally concerns me. [Letter to Lady Ottoline Morrell, 29 July 1915]

19 They are great parables, the novels [Dostoyevsky's], but false art. They are only parables. All the people are *fallen angels* – even the dirtiest scrubs. This I cannot stomach. People are not fallen angels, they are merely people. [Letter to J. Middleton Murry and Katherine Mansfield, 17 Feb. 1916]

20 I am only half there when I am ill, and so there is only half a man to suffer. To suffer in one's whole self is so great a violation, that it is not to be endured. [Letter to Catherine Carswell, 16 Apr. 1916]

21 The autumn always gets me badly, as it breaks into colours. I want to go south, where there is no autumn, where the cold doesn't crouch over one like a snow-leopard waiting to pounce. The heart of the North is dead, and the fingers are corpse fingers. [Letter to J. Middleton Murry, 3 Oct. 1924]

22 I'm not sure if a mental relation with a woman doesn't make it impossible to love her. To know the *mind* of a woman is to end in hating her. Love means the pre-cognitive flow . . . it is the honest state before the apple. [Letter to Dr Trigant Burrow, 3 Aug. 1927]

23 I am tired of being told there is no such animal by animals who are merely different. [Letter to J. Middleton Murry, 20 May 1929]

24 Whatever the sun may be, it is certainly not a ball of flaming gas. [In C. K. Ogden and I. A. Richards, *Meaning of Meaning*]

JEROME LAWRENCE 1916–

25 A neurotic is the man who builds a

castle in the air. A psychotic is the man who lives in it. A psychiatrist is the man who collects the rent. [In Laurence J. Peter, *Peter's Quotations*]

T. E. LAWRENCE 1888–1935

1 Many men would take the death-sentence without a whimper to escape the life-sentence which fate carries in her other hand. [*The Mint*, Pt I, Ch. 4]

2 The trumpets came out brazenly with the last post ... Our eyes smarted against our wills. A man hates to be moved to folly by a noise. [III. 9]

3 I loved you, so I drew these tides of men into my hands and wrote my will across the sky in stars. [*Seven Pillars of Wisdom*, Dedication]

4 All men dream: but not equally. Those who dream by night in the dusty recesses of their minds wake in the day to find that it was vanity: but the dreamers of the day are dangerous men, for they may act their dream with open eyes, to make it possible. [Ch. 1]

5 We were a self-centred army without parade or gesture, devoted to freedom, the second of man's creeds, a purpose so ravenous that it devoured all our strength, a hope so transcendent that our earlier ambitions faded in its glare.

6 I meant once to write a book on the background of Christ ... Galilee and Syria, social, intellectual and artistic of 40 BC. It would make an interesting book. As good as Renan's *Life of Jesus* should have been, if only he had had the wit to leave out the central figure. [Letter to Sir Herbert Baker, 20 Jan. 1928]

7 I fancy, for myself, that they are rather out of touch with reality; by reality I mean shops like Selfridges, and motor buses, and the *Daily Express*. [Of James Joyce and fellow expatriate authors in Paris. Letter to W. Hurley, 1 Apr. 1929]

8 I'm re-reading it [*Lady Chatterley's Lover*] with a slow deliberate carelessness. [Letter to Edward Marsh, 18 Apr. 1929]

9 In some ways it's a horrible little book. Like over-brewed tea. [Of *The Mint*]

IRVING LAYTON 1912–

10 In Pierre Elliott Trudeau, Canada has at last produced a political leader worthy of assassination. [*The Whole Bloody Bird*, 'Obo II']

SIR EDMUND LEACH 1910–1989

11 Crimes are created by Parliament; it needs a policeman to make a criminal. You don't become a criminal by breaking the law, but by getting found out. [*Runaway World*, Ch. 3]

12 Far from being the basis of the good society, the family, with its narrow privacy and tawdry secrets, is the source of all our discontents.

13 Gods are no more likely to achieve their private ambitions than are mere men who suffer the slings and arrows of outrageous fortune, but gods have much more fun. [6]

STEPHEN LEACOCK 1869–1944

14 Advertising may be described as the science of arresting the human intelligence long enough to get money from it. [*Garden of Folly*, 'The Perfect Salesman']

15 A single room is that which has no parts and no magnitude. [*Literary Lapses*, 'Boarding-House Geometry']

16 The landlady of a boarding-house is a parallelogram – that is, an oblong angular figure, which cannot be described, but which is equal to anything.

17 Any two meals at a boarding-house are together less than two square meals.

18 On the same bill and on the same side of it there should not be two charges for the same thing.

19 Get your room full of good air, then shut up the windows and keep it. It will keep for years. Anyway, don't keep using your lungs all the time. Let them rest. ['How to Live to be 200']

20 I detest life-insurance agents; they always argue that I shall some day die, which is not so. ['Insurance Up to Date']

21 The great man ... walks across his century and leaves the marks of his feet all over

it, ripping out the dates on his goloshes as he passes. ['The Life of John Smith']

1 Astronomy teaches the correct use of the sun and the planets. ['A Manual of Education']

2 Electricity is of two kinds, positive and negative. The difference is, I presume, that one comes a little more expensive, but is more durable; the other is a cheaper thing, but the moths get into it.

3 There are no handles to a horse, but the 1910 model has a string to each side of its face for turning its head when there is anything you want it to see. ['Reflections on Riding']

4 It takes a good deal of physical courage to ride a horse. This, however, I have. I get it at about forty cents a flask, and take it as required.

5 He flung himself from the room, flung himself upon his horse and rode madly off in all directions. [*Nonsense Novels*, 'Gertrude the Governess']

6 The general idea, of course, in any first-class laundry is to see that no shirt or collar ever comes back twice. [*Winnowed Wisdom*, Ch. 6]

TIMOTHY LEARY 1920–

7 If you take the game of life seriously, if you take your nervous system seriously, if you take your sense organs seriously, if you take the energy process seriously, you must turn on, tune in, and drop out. [*The Politics of Ecstasy*, Ch. 21]

MARY LEASE 1853–1933

8 Kansas had better stop raising corn and begin raising hell. [Attr.]

F. R. LEAVIS 1895–1978

9 The only way to escape misrepresentation is never to commit oneself to any critical judgement that makes an impact – that is, never *say* anything. [*The Great Tradition*, Ch. 1]

10 He [Rupert Brooke] energized the Garden-Suburb ethos with a certain original talent and the vigour of a prolonged adolescence. His verse exhibits . . . something that is rather like Keats's vulgarity with a Public School accent. [*New Bearings in English Poetry*, Ch. 2]

11 The Sitwells belong to the history of publicity rather than of poetry.

12 The question 'This is so, isn't it?' expecting the answer 'Yes, but –' [Lectures, *passim*]

FRAN LEBOWITZ ?1948–

13 Never judge a cover by its book. [*Metropolitan Life*]

14 Food is an important part of a balanced diet. ['Food for Thought and Vice Versa']

15 Being a woman is of special interest only to aspiring male transsexuals. To actual women, it is simply a good excuse not to play football. ['Letters']

16 I am not personally a parent. But I do have two godchildren and am expecting a third. I am naturally concerned for their future. If I ruled the world you could bet your boots that none of them would ever set their eyes on any such contraptions as digital clocks and pocket calculators. But alas, I do not rule the world and that, I am afraid, is the story of my life – always a godmother, never a God. ['Digital Clocks and Pocket Calculators']

17 Original thought is like original sin: both happened before you were born to people you could not possibly have met. [*Social Studies*, 'People']

18 Great people talk about ideas, average people talk about things, and small people talk about wine.

19 Never allow your child to call you by your first name. He hasn't known you long enough. ['Parental Guidance']

20 Do not elicit your child's political opinions. He doesn't know any more than you do.

21 Remember that as a teenager you are at the last stage in your life when you will be happy to hear that the phone is for you. ['Tips for Teens']

22 I am not the type who wants to go back to the land; I am the type who wants to go back to the hotel. ['Things']

23 A dog who thinks he is man's best friend

is a dog who obviously has never met a tax lawyer.

1 There are two modes of transport in Los Angeles: car and ambulance. Visitors who wish to remain inconspicuous are advised to choose the latter. ['Lesson One']

2 If you're going to America, bring your own food. ['Fran Lebowitz's Travel Hints']

STANISLAW LEC 1909–1966

3 Is it progress if a cannibal uses knife and fork? [*Unkempt Thoughts*]

4 When smashing monuments, save the pedestals – they always come in handy.

5 In a war of ideas it is people who get killed.

JOHN LE CARRÉ 1931–

6 The only decent diplomat is a deaf Trappist. [*A Perfect Spy*, 3]

7 Publishers can get their minds halfway round anything. [*The Russia House*, Ch. 5]

8 The Spy Who Came in from the Cold. [Title of book]

9 A committee is an animal with four back legs. [*Tinker, Tailor, Soldier, Spy*, Pt III, Ch. 34]

LE CORBUSIER 1887–1965

10 *Une maison est une machine-à-habiter.* – A house is a machine for living in. [*Vers une architecture*]

11 The snail lives in its shell ... Industrialization must lead the snail back to his shell. A sensible dream.

BERT LEE 1880–1946, HARRIS WESTON and IRVING TAYLOR

12 Knees up, Mother Brown! [Title of song, 1938]

GYPSY ROSE LEE 1914–1970

13 God is love but get it in writing. [Catchphrase]

14 Royalties are nice and all but shaking the beads brings in money quicker. [In L. L. Levinson, *Bartlett's Unfamiliar Quotations*, 'Authorship']

15 Men aren't attracted to me by my mind. They're attracted by what I don't mind. [In *Woman Talk*, comp. Michèle Brown and Ann O'Connor]

HARPER LEE 1926–

16 Shoot all the bluejays you want, if you can hit 'em, but remember it's a sin to kill a mockingbird. [*To Kill a Mockingbird*, II. 10]

JENNIE [later LADY] LEE 1904–1988

17 Nye was born old and died young. [Of her husband, Aneurin Bevan. In Michael Foot, *Aneurin Bevan*, Ch. 6]

LAURIE LEE 1914–

18 Effie M. was a monster. Six foot high and as strong as a farm horse. No sooner had she decided that she wanted Uncle Tom than she knocked him off his bicycle and told him. [*Cider with Rosie*, 'The Uncles']

THÉO LEFÈVRE [Belgian Prime Minister] 1914–1973

19 In Western Europe there are now only small countries – those that know it and those that don't know it yet. [In the *Observer*, 'Sayings of the Year', 1963]

RICHARD LE GALLIENNE 1866–1947

20 The cry of the Little Peoples goes up to God in vain, / For the world is given over to the cruel sons of Cain. [*The Cry of the Little Peoples*]

21 She's somewhere in the sunlight strong, / Her tears are in the falling rain, / She calls me in the wind's soft song, / And with the flowers she comes again. [*Song*]

22 What of the Darkness? Is it very fair? [*What of the Darkness?*]

ERNEST LEHMAN 1920–

23 The Sweet Smell of Success. [Title of film, scriped with Clifford Odets]

ROSAMOND LEHMANN 1901–1990

24 The trouble with Ian [Fleming] is that he

227

gets off with women because he can't get on with them. [In J. Pearson, *The Life of Ian Fleming*]

TOM LEHRER 1928–

1 He gives the kids free samples, / Because he knows full well / That today's young innocent faces / Are tomorrow's clientele. [Song: *The Old Dope Pedlar*]

2 Once all the Germans were warlike and mean / But that couldn't happen again. / We taught them a lesson in 1918, / And they've hardly bothered us since then. [Song: *Sleep, Baby, Sleep*]

3 Life is like a sewer. What you get out of it depends on what you put into it. [Preamble to song *We Will All Go Together When We Go*]

4 It is a sobering thought that when Mozart was my age he had been dead for two years. [In Nat Shapiro, *Encyclopedia of Quotations about Music*]

FRED W. LEIGH ?–1924

5 There was I, waiting at the church, / Waiting at the church, waiting at the church, / When I found he'd left me in the lurch, / Lor', how it did upset me . . . / Can't get away to marry you today – / My wife won't let me! [Song: *Waiting at the Church*, 1906, music by Henry E. Pether, sung by Vesta Victoria]

FRED W. LEIGH and GEORGE ARTHURS

6 A Little of What You Fancy Does You Good. [Title of song, 1915, sung by Marie Lloyd]

FRED W. LEIGH and CHARLES COLLINS ?–1923

7 My old man said, 'Follow the van, / Don't dilly dally on the way!' [Song: *My Old Man Said, 'Follow the Van'*, 1919, sung by Marie Lloyd]

8 Why am I always a bridesmaid never a blushing bride? [Music-hall song: *Why am I Always a Bridesmaid?*, 1917, written with Lily Morris, who also sang it]

C. A. LEJEUNE 1897–1973

9 Me no leica. [Review of film *I am a Camera*]

GENERAL CURTIS LEMAY 1906–1990

10 My solution to the problem [of North Vietnam] would be to tell them frankly that they've got to draw in their horns and stop their aggression, or we're going to bomb them back into the Stone Age. [*Mission with LeMay*, p. 565]

'JUSTE LE MOT'

11 [When Marc Chagall said his picture had not only magic but also truth in it] Magic realism, then! [Quoted by G. Cabrera Infante in *The Times Literary Supplement*, 18 Oct. 1985]

VLADIMIR ILYICH [ULYANOV] LENIN 1870–1924

12 If it were necessary to give the briefest possible definition of imperialism, we should have to say that imperialism is the monopoly stage of capitalism. [*Imperialism, the Highest Stage of Capitalism*, Ch. 7]

13 History generally, and the history of revolutions in particular, is always richer in content, more varied, more many-sided, more lively and more 'subtle' than even the best parties and the most class-conscious vanguards of the most advanced classes imagine. [*'Left-wing' Communism*, Ch. 10]

14 One step forward, two steps back . . . It happens in the lives of individuals, and it happens in the history of nations and in the development of parties. [*One Step Forward, Two Steps Back*]

15 Democracy is a *state* which recognizes the subordination of the minority to the majority, i.e. an organization for the systematic use of force by one class against another, by one section of the population against another. [*The State and Revolution*, Ch. 4, sect. vi]

16 So long as the state exists there is no freedom. When there is freedom there will be no state. [5. iv]

17 Under socialism *all* will govern in turn and will soon become accustomed to no one governing. [6. iii]

1 'A decisive victory of the revolution over tsarism' is the *revolutionary-democratic dictatorship of the proletariat and the peasantry.* [*Two Tactics of Social-democracy*, Ch. 6]

2 Every cook has to learn how to govern the state. [*Will the Bolsheviks Retain Government Power?*]

3 To proclaim in advance the dying away of the state will be a violation of historical perspective. [At 7th Party Congress, Mar. 1918]

4 Communism is Soviet power plus the electrification of the whole country. [Slogan promoting the electrification programme. At Congress of Soviets, 22 Dec. 1920]

5 I can't listen to music too often. It affects your nerves; you want to say nice, stupid things and stroke the heads of people who could create such beauty while living in this vile hell. And now you must not stroke anyone's head – you might get your hand bitten off. You have to hit them on the head, without any mercy. [To Maxim Gorky of Beethoven's 'Appassionata' Sonata. In M. Lasky, *Utopia and Revolution*, Pt 1, Ch. 2. See also 304:16]

6 Who, whom? We or they? [Epigraph to Fitzroy Maclean, *Disputed Barricade*, Pt 3]

7 He [G. Bernard Shaw] is a good man fallen among Fabians. [In Arthur Ransome, *Six Weeks in Russia in 1919*, 'Notes of Conversations with Lenin']

8 It is true that liberty is precious – so precious that it must be rationed. [In Sidney and Beatrice Webb, *Soviet Communism*, Ch. 12]

JOHN LENNON 1940–1980

9 We're more popular than Jesus Christ now. I don't know which will go first. Rock and roll or Christianity. [*The Beatles' Illustrated Lyrics*]

10 His wife a former beauty queer, regarded him with a strange but burly look. [In *His Own Write*, 'No Flies on Frank']

11 For the past 17 years the fabled fibe had been forming into adventures on varicose islands and secrete vallets with their famous ill bred dog. ['The Famous Five']

12 Jumble Jim, whom shall remain nameless, was slowly but slowly asking his way through the underpants. ['On Safairy']

13 Will people in the cheaper seats clap your hands? All the rest of you just rattle your jewellery. [At Royal Variety Performance, 15 Nov. 1963]

14 Some people like ping-pong, other people like digging over graves. They're all escapes from now. People will do anything rather than be here now. [In *Playboy Interviews*, ed. G. Barry Golson, 12]

15 Nothing happened in the sixties except that we all dressed up. [In *Wit and Wisdom of Rock and Roll*, ed. Maxim Jakubowski]

16 Life is what happens to us while we're making other plans. [Song: *Beautiful Boy*]

JOHN LENNON and PAUL McCARTNEY 1942–

17 All You Need is Love. [Title of song]

18 How does it feel to be one of the beautiful people, now that you know who you are? [Song: *Baby You're a Rich Man*]

19 For I don't care too much for money, / For money can't buy me love. [Song: *Can't Buy Me Love*]

20 All the lonely people, where do they all come from? / All the lonely people, where do they all belong? [Song: *Eleanor Rigby*]

21 I'm fixing a hole where the rain gets in and stops my mind from wandering where it will go. [Song: *Fixing a Hole*]

22 If there's anything that you want, / If there's anything I can do, / Just call on me, / And I'll send it along with love from me to you. [Song: *From Me to You*]

23 I've got to admit it's getting better. / It's a little better all the time. [Song: *Getting Better*]

24 Give Peace a Chance. [Title of song]

25 It's been a hard day's night. [Song: *A Hard Day's Night*, and also film title]

26 When I caught a glimpse of Rita, / Filling in a ticket in her little white book. / In a cap she looked much older, / And the bag across her shoulder, made her look a little like a milit'ry man. / Lovely Rita, Meter Maid. [Song: *Lovely Rita*]

1 Picture yourself in a boat on a river with tangerine trees and marmalade skies. / Somebody calls you, you answer quite slowly a girl with kaleidoscope eyes. [Song: *Lucy in the Sky with Diamonds*]

2 Bang! Bang! Maxwell's Silver Hammer came down upon her head. / Clang! Clang! Maxwell's Silver Hammer made sure that she was dead. [Song: *Maxwell's Silver Hammer*]

3 He's a real Nowhere Man. / Sitting in his Nowhere Land, / Making all his nowhere plans for nobody. / Doesn't have a point of view, / Knows not where he's going to, / Isn't he a bit like you and me? [Song: *Nowhere Man*]

4 Sergeant Pepper's Lonely Hearts Club Band. [Title of song]

5 She loves you, yeh, yeh, yeh, / And with a love like that you know you should be glad. [Song: *She Loves You*]

6 She's leaving home after living alone for so many years. [Song: *She's Leaving Home*]

7 She's got a ticket to ride, but she don't care. [Song: *Ticket to Ride*]

8 Will you still need me, will you still feed me, / When I'm sixty-four? [Song: *When I'm Sixty-four*]

9 I get by with a little help from my friends. [Song: *With a Little Help from My Friends*]

10 We all live in a yellow submarine, yellow submarine, yellow submarine. [Song: *Yellow Submarine*, and also film title]

DAN LENO 1860–1904

11 Ah what is man? Wherefore does he why? Whence did he whence? Whither is he withering? [*Dan Leno Hys Booke*, Ch. 1]

12 I see the world as a football, kicked about by the higher powers, with me clinging on by my teeth and toenails to the laces. [In Desmond MacCarthy, *Theatre*]

ELMORE LEONARD 1925–

13 If it sounds like writing, I rewrite it. [From *Newsweek*, 22 Apr. 1985, in *Simpson's Contemporary Quotations*]

HUGH LEONARD 1926–

14 In seventy years the one surviving fragment of my knowledge, the only indisputable poor particle of certainty in my entire life is that in a public house lavatory incoming traffic has the right of way. [*Da*]

15 My grandmother made dying her life's work. [*Home before Night*, opening sentence]

16 The problem with Ireland is that it's a country full of genius, but with absolutely no talent. [Interview in *The Times*, Aug. 1977]

ALAN JAY LERNER 1918–1986

17 An Englishman's way of speaking absolutely classifies him. / The moment he talks he makes some other Englishman despise him. [*My Fair Lady*, Act I, sc. i, music by Frank Loewe]

18 All I want is a room somewhere, / Far away from the cold night air; / With one enormous chair ... / Oh, wouldn't it be loverly?

19 They're always throwin' goodness at you / But with a little bit of luck / A man can duck! [ii]

20 Don't talk of June! / Don't talk of fall! / Don't talk at all / Show me! [II. ii]

21 I'm getting married in the morning, / Ding dong! the bells are gonna chime. / Pull out the stopper! / Let's have a whopper! / But get me to the church on time! [iii]

22 Why can't a woman be more like a man? / Men are so honest, so horribly square; / Eternally noble, historically fair. [iv]

23 I've grown accustomed to the trace / Of something in the air, / Accustomed to her face. [vi]

24 [When asked by Andrew Lloyd Webber, 'Hey, why do people take an instant dislike to me?'] Because it saves time. [In the *Observer*, 30 Apr. 1989]

EMMANUEL LE ROY-LADURIE 1929–

25 Some [historians] should be labelled parachutists: the others might more fittingly be called truffle hunters. [Quoted by David Cannadine in the *Guardian*, 6 Nov. 1987]

DORIS LESSING 1919–

1 When old settlers say 'One has to understand the country,' what they mean is, 'You have to get used to our ideas about the native.' They are saying, in effect, 'Learn our ideas, or otherwise get out; we don't want you.' [*The Grass is Singing*, Ch. 1]

2 When a white man in Africa by accident looks into the eyes of a native and sees the human being (which it is his chief preoccupation to avoid), his sense of guilt, which he denies, fumes up in resentment and he brings down the whip. [8]

ALFRED LESTER 1874–1925

3 Call out the Boys of the Old Brigade, / Who made Old England free – / Send out my Mother, my Sister and my Brother, / But for God's sake don't send me! [Song of 1914–18 War: *Conscientious Objector's Lament*]

W. R. LETHABY 1857–1931

4 Art is not a special sauce applied to ordinary cooking; it is the cooking itself if it is good. [*Form in Civilization*, 'Art and Workmanship']

5 Art is thoughtful workmanship.

OSCAR LEVANT 1906–1972

6 Strip the phoney tinsel off Hollywood and you'll find the real tinsel underneath. [*Memoirs of an Amnesiac*]

7 She [Zsa-Zsa Gabor] not only worships the Golden Calf, she barbecues it. [Attr.]

VICTOR DE LEVELAYE [Belgian lawyer]

8 V for Victory! [Anti-Nazi graffito initiated by him, 14 Jan. 1941. In *Ultimate Trivia Quiz Game Book*, ed. M. and A. Hiron]

HAROLD [later **LORD**] **LEVER** 1914–

9 [When asked, 'Would you still have married your wife if she hadn't had two million pounds?'] I would have married her if she had only had one million pounds! [In S. Hoggart, *Back in the House*, p. 6]

LORD LEVERHULME 1851–1925

10 Half the money I spend on advertising is wasted, and the trouble is I don't know which half. [In David Ogilvy, *Confessions of an Advertising Man*, Ch. 3. Quoted by John Wanamaker and sometimes wrongly attr. to him]

ADA LEVERSON 1865–1936

11 People were not charmed with Eglantine because she herself was charming, but because she was charmed. [*Love at Second Sight*]

12 You don't know a woman until you've had a letter from her. [*Tenterhooks*, Ch. 7]

13 Thou canst not serve both cod and salmon. [On being offered a choice of fish at a dinner party. In *The Times*, 7 Nov. 1970]

14 [When told by Wilde that a devoted apache used to follow him about Paris with a knife in his hand] I'm sure he had a fork in the other. [Attr.]

PRIMO LEVI 1919–1987

15 We had finished our coffee, which was loathsome, as in all countries . . . where the accent of the word for coffee falls on the first syllable. [*The Wrench*]

BERNARD LEVIN 1928–

16 Jehovah's Witnesses, awaiting the Last Day with the quiet kind of satisfaction that a man gets in the dry season when he knows his neighbour's house is not insured against fire. [*The Pendulum Years*, Ch. 1]

17 Paul Getty, who had always been vastly, immeasurably wealthy, and yet went about looking like a man who cannot quite remember whether he remembered to turn the gas off before leaving home.

18 [Tony] Benn flung himself into the Sixties technology with the enthusiasm (not to say language) of a newly enrolled Boy Scout demonstrating knot-tying to his indulgent parents. [11]

19 One [of the Harolds, Macmillan and Wilson] played the part of the last aristocrat . . . advancing through life with a paralysed shuffle, an assortment of facial tics, a voice which was the distilled essence of all the confidence-tricksters who ever went home and entertained the children after the

day's work was done. The role assumed by the other was that of the purposive, technologically-equipped, full twentieth-century citizen, leaning forward when he walked, like a man trying not to fall over if the bus starts with a jerk, his voice the ingratiating wheedle of the toucher who wants yet another fiver to tide him over to pay-day, and will do anything to get it. [12]

1 Only one man took the full measure of this astonishing truth, and that man the one who knew what Macmillan was made of for the best of all reasons; Harold Wilson was made of the same stuff. Between them, then, Walrus and Carpenter, they divided up the Sixties.

2 The silence went straight from rapt to fraught without pausing at pregnant. [In *The Times*, 17 Oct. 1974]

3 Once, when a British Prime Minister sneezed, men half a world away would blow their noses. Now when a British Prime Minister sneezes nobody else will even say 'Bless You'. [8 June 1976]

4 It [a production of Brecht's *The Days of the Commune*] has the depth of a cracker-motto, the drama of a dial-a-recipe service and the eloquence of a conversation between a speak-your-weight machine and a whoopee-cushion. [In the *Sunday Times*, 6 Nov. 1977]

5 Whom the mad would destroy they first make Gods. [Of Mao Zedong, 1967. In *Dictionary of Contemporary Quotations*, ed. J. Green]

EUGEN LEVINÉ

6 We Communists are dead men on leave. [At his trial. In R. Leviné-Meyer, *Leviné: The Life of a Revolutionary*, Ch. 3]

CLAUDE LÉVI-STRAUSS 1908–

7 The anthropologist respects history, but he does not accord it a special value. He conceives it as a study complementary to his own: one of them unfurls the range of human societies in time, the other in space. [*The Savage Mind*]

8 Our own society is the only one which we can transform and yet not destroy, since the changes which we should introduce would come from within. [*World on the Wane*]

ANDRE LE VOT 1921–

9 He [Fitzgerald] knew we pay for everything: this was what he was paid to know. [From *F. Scott Fitzgerald: A Biography*, in *New Society*, 19 Apr. 1984]

CECIL DAY LEWIS *see* DAY LEWIS, C.

C. S. LEWIS 1898–1963

10 Humanity does not pass through phases as a train passes through stations: being alive, it has the privilege of always moving yet never leaving anything behind. [*The Allegory of Love*, Ch. 1]

11 There is wishful thinking in Hell as well as on earth. [*The Screwtape Letters*, Preface]

12 Gratitude looks to the past and love to the present; fear, avarice, lust and ambition look ahead. [15]

13 There must be several young women who would render the Christian life intensely difficult to him if only you could persuade him to marry one of them. [19]

14 He's vulgar, Wormwood. He has a vulgar mind. [Of God. 22]

15 She's the sort of woman who lives for others – you can always tell the others by their hunted expression. [26]

16 Fatigue makes women talk more and men less. [30]

17 This extraordinary pride in being exempt from temptation that you have not yet risen to the level of. Eunuchs boasting of their chastity. [In Brian Aldiss and Kingsley Amis, *Spectrum IV*]

18 Leavis demands moral earnestness; I prefer morality ... I mean I'd sooner live among people who don't cheat at cards than among people who are earnest about not cheating at cards.

19 Courage is not simply *one* of the virtues but the form of every virtue at the testing point, which means at the point of highest reality. [In 'Palinurus', (Cyril Connolly), *The Unquiet Grave*, Ch. 3]

1 All except the best men would rather be called wicked than vulgar. [In the *Guardian*, 21 Aug. 1980]

2 No book is really worth reading at the age of ten which is not equally (and often far more) worth reading at the age of fifty and beyond. [In *Writer's Quotation Book*, ed. James Charlton]

D. B. WYNDHAM LEWIS 1891–1961

3 I am one of those unfortunates to whom death is less hideous than explanations. [*Welcome to All This*]

See also under SEARLE, RONALD

'FURRY' LEWIS 1893–1981

4 [When asked why he had never married] Why the hell should I get a wife when the man next door's got one? [At age of 87 in 1980. In *Was It Good for You Too?*, ed. Bob Chieger]

SIR GEORGE CORNEWALL LEWIS

5 Life would be tolerable, were it not for its amusements. [In Sagittarius and D. George, *The Perpetual Pessimist*]

JOE E. LEWIS 1901–1971

6 I've been rich, and I've been poor and believe me, rich is better. [In Barbara Rowes, *Book of Quotes*. See also 150:10]

JOHN LEWIS [PARTNERSHIP]

7 We are never knowingly undersold. [Shop slogan. Ascr. to John S. Lewis, *c.* 1920, in *Oxford Dictionary of Modern Quotations*, ed. Tony Augarde]

PERCY WYNDHAM LEWIS 1882–1957

8 It is to what I have called the Apes of God that I am drawing your attention – *those prosperous mountebanks who alternately imitate and mock at and traduce those figures they at once admire and hate.* [*The Apes of God*, Pt III]

9 The soul started at the knee-cap and ended at the navel. [XII]

10 'Dying for an idea,' again, sounds well enough, but why not let the idea die instead of you? [*The Art of Being Ruled*, Pt I, Ch. 1]

11 The goitrous torpid and squinting husks provided by Matisse in his sculpture are worthless except as tactful decorations for a mental home. [XII. 7]

12 If you must go nowhere, step out. [*The Human Age*, Bk I: *The Childermass*, closing words]

13 The revolutionary simpleton is everywhere. [*Time and Western Man*, Bk I, Ch. 6]

14 The root of the comic is to be sought in the sensations resulting from the observations of a thing behaving like a person. But from that point of view all men are necessarily comic; for they are all things, or physical bodies, behaving as persons. [*The Wild Body*]

ROSA LEWIS

15 I knew him before he was born. [In D. Fielding, *The Duchess of Jermyn Street*, Ch. 9]

SINCLAIR LEWIS 1885–1951

16 He was nimble in the calling of selling houses for more than people could afford to pay. [*Babbitt*, Ch. 1]

17 To George F. Babbitt ... his motor-car was poetry and tragedy, love and heroism. The office was his pirate ship, but the car his perilous excursion ashore. [3]

18 In other countries, art and literature are left to a lot of shabby bums living in attics and feeding on booze and spaghetti, but in America the successful writer or picture-painter is indistinguishable from any other decent business man. [14]

19 Our American professors like their literature clear and cold and pure and very dead. [Address on receiving the Nobel Prize, Stockholm, 12 Dec. 1930]

ROBERT LEY 1890–1945

20 *Kraft durch Freude.* – Strength through joy. [German Labour Front slogan, first used 2 Dec. 1933]

[WLADZIU VALENTINO] LIBERACE 1919–1987

21 I cried all the way to the bank. [Reaction

to hostile criticism in 1954. In Bob Thomas, *Liberace: The True Story*]

1 I've done my bit for motion pictures. I've stopped making them.

MAX LIEBERMANN 1847–1935

2 I can piss the old boy in the snow. [To a portrait-painter who complained that he could not draw von Hindenburg's features. In Igor Stravinsky and Robert Craft, *Conversations with Stravinsky*]

A. J. LIEBLING 1904–1963

3 The chief industry in my part of the country is getting by. [*Back Where I Came From*, 'Getting By']

4 Freedom of the press is guaranteed only to those who own one. [In R. Kluger, *The Paper: The Life and Death of the New York Herald Tribune*]

KARL LIEBNECHT

5 We are fighting for the gates of heaven. [In the abortive German revolution, 1918–19. In Albert Camus, *The Rebel*, Ch. 3]

BEATRICE LILLIE 1894–1989

6 I'll simply say here that I was born Beatrice Gladys Lillie at an extremely tender age because my mother needed a fourth at meals. [*Every Other Inch a Lady*, Ch. 1]

VACHEL LINDSAY 1879–1931

7 It is portentous, and a thing of state / That here at midnight, in our little town / A mourning figure walks, and will not rest, / Near the old courthouse pacing up and down. [*Abraham Lincoln Walks at Midnight*]

8 And who will bring white peace / That he may sleep upon his hill again?

9 Then I saw the Congo, creeping through the black, / Cutting through the jungle with a golden track. [*The Congo*, 1]

10 Mumbo-Jumbo is dead in the jungle. [3]

11 Booth died blind and still by faith he trod, / Eyes still dazzled by the ways of God. [*General William Booth Enters Heaven*]

ERIC LINKLATER 1889–1974

12 With a heavy step Sir Matthew left the room and spent the morning designing mausoleums for his enemies. [*Juan in America*, Prologue]

13 It is notorious that we speak no more than half-truths in our ordinary conversation, and even a soliloquy is likely to be affected by the apprehension that walls have ears. [II. 4]

14 I've been married six months. She looks like a million dollars, but she only knows a hundred and twenty words and she's only got two ideas in her head. The other one's hats. [5]

15 'There won't be any revolution in America,' said Isadore. Nikitin agreed. 'The people are too clean. They spend all their time changing their shirts and washing themselves. You can't feel fierce and revolutionary in a bathroom.' [V. 3]

16 'I dislike burdens,' said Juan, 'and at my back I often hear Time's winged chariot changing gear.' [*Juan in China*]

17 All I've got against it [golf] is that it takes you so far from the club house. [*Poet's Pub*, Ch. 3]

18 Authors and uncaptured criminals ... are the only people free from routine. [23]

MAGNUS LINKLATER 1942–

19 Teenage sex-change priest in mercy dash to Palace. [The newspaper editor's dream headline. In BBC radio programme, 18 Sept. 1976]

LIN YUTANG 1895–1976

20 The German philosophers are the most frivolous of all – they count truths like lovers but seldom propose to marry them. [Attr.]

MAUREEN LIPMAN 1946–

21 It's the place where the sky is always blue and so are the screenwriters. Where the story line is accepted on Monday by the twenty-four-year-old head of a studio, and rejected on the Thursday by his sixteen-year-old replacement. [Of Los Angeles. *How was it for You?*, 'Travels with Me aren't']

1 You know the worst thing about oral sex? The view. [In *Dictionary of Outrageous Quotations*, comp. C. R. S. Marsden]

WALTER LIPPMAN 1889–1974

2 In a free society the state does not administer the affairs of men. It administers justice among men who conduct their own affairs. [*An Enquiry into the Principles of a Good Society*]

LISTENER

3 A patriot is a man who loves his country: a nationalist is one who hates everyone else's. ['Begrudgery: Tall Poppy Syndrome', 1 Dec. 1988]

RICHARD LITTLE 1944–

4 He's the kind of guy you'd like to have around when you want to be alone. With a little effort he could become an anonymity. [Of George Bush. In TV programme on night of US presidential election, 9 Nov. 1988]

MAXIM LITVINOV 1876–1951

5 Peace is indivisible. [Speech on 22 Feb. 1920, repeated with variants on several occasions]

PENELOPE LIVELY 1933–

6 Wars are fought by children – conceived by their mad demonic elders and fought by boys. [*Moon Tiger*, Ch. 8]

7 Giving presents is one of the most possessive of things we do ... It's the way we keep a hold on other people. Plant ourselves in their lives.

8 One never, of course, knows what people in portraits are thinking about. [*Next to Nature, Art*, Ch. 10]

KEN LIVINGSTONE, MP 1945–

9 We are the dirty armpit of Europe. [In the *Independent*, 'Quote Unquote', 18 Mar. 1989]

10 Historians will write of Britain in the eighties that this was the decade the locusts ate. [13 Jan. 1990]

HAROLD LLOYD 1893–1971

11 [When asked his age at over seventy] I am just turning forty and taking my time about it. [In *The Times*, 23 Sept. 1970]

MARIE LLOYD 1870–1922

12 I'm one of the ruins that Cromwell knocked about a bit. [Song, 1912, words and music by Harry Bedford and Terry Sullivan]

13 Oh, mister porter, what shall I do? / I wanted to go to Birmingham, but they've carried me on to Crewe. [Song: *Oh, Mister Porter*, words by George Le Brunn]

DAVID, EARL LLOYD GEORGE 1863–1945

14 You cannot feed the hungry on statistics. [Speech on Tariff Reform, 1904. In Malcolm Thomson, *David Lloyd George*, Ch. 8]

15 Mr Balfour's Poodle. [Description of House of Lords, in reply to a claim that the Lords were 'the watchdog of the nation'. Speech in House of Commons, 26 June 1907]

16 A fully equipped Duke costs as much to keep up as two Dreadnoughts, and Dukes are just as great a terror, and they last longer. [Speech on the Budget, 9 Oct. 1909]

17 What is our task? To make Britain a fit country for heroes to live in. [Speech, 24 Nov. 1918]

18 May I ask of Protestants and Catholics alike that in these days of rejoicing [Christmas] we shall not forget the pitiful Madonna of the Slums with her pallid children. [Speech in London, 18 Dec. 1925]

19 Every man has a House of Lords in his own head. Fears, prejudices, misconceptions – those are the peers, and they are hereditary. [Speech at Cambridge, 1927]

20 The world is becoming like a lunatic asylum run by lunatics. [In the *Observer*, 8 Jan. 1933]

21 Winston [Churchill] would go up to his Creator and say that he would very much like to meet His Son, about Whom he had

heard a great deal and, if possible, would like to call on the Holy Ghost. Winston *loved* meeting people. [In A. J. Sylvester, *Diary*, 2 Jan. 1937]

1 He [Ramsay MacDonald] had sufficient conscience to bother him, but not sufficient to keep him straight. [29 Aug. 1938]

2 If we are going in without the help of Russia we are walking into a trap. [Speech in House of Commons, 3 Apr. 1939]

3 Doctrinaires are the vultures of principle. They feed upon principle after it is dead. [Quoted by Dingle Foot in the *Guardian*, 17 Jan. 1963]

4 I am opposed to Titanic seamanship in politics and as an old mariner I would not drive the ship on to the ice floes that have drifted into our seas from the frozen wastes of the Tory past.

5 When they circumcised Herbert Samuel they threw away the wrong bit. [Quoted by John Grigg in the *Listener*, 7 Sept. 1978]

6 He [Neville Chamberlain] saw foreign policy through the wrong end of a municipal drainpipe. [In Leon A. Harris, *The Fine Art of Political Wit*, Ch. 6]

7 He [Field-Marshal, Lord Haig] was brilliant to the top of his army boots. [Attr. in J. Wintle, *Dictionary of War Quotations*]

8 The Right Hon. gentleman [Sir John Simon] has sat so long on the fence that the iron has entered his soul. [Attr., speech in House of Commons]

DAVID LODGE 1935–

9 Literature is mostly about having sex and not much about having children; life is the other way round. [*The British Museum is Falling Down*, Ch. 4]

10 The British, he thought, must be gluttons for satire: even the weather forecast seemed to be some kind of spoof, predicting every possible combination of weather for the next twenty-four hours without actually committing itself to anything specific. [*Changing Places*, Ch. 2]

11 Walt Whitman who laid end to end words never seen in each other's company before outside of a dictionary. [5]

12 I can understand why the pure of heart are generally religious people. If you believed that there was a fanlight in your mind, through which an old man with a beard was perpetually peering, taking down notes, you would think twice about throwing orgies in there. [*Ginger, You're Barmy*, 4]

13 There's a proposal to install contraceptive machines in the students' cloakrooms at college ... It's a very special machine, designed for Catholics ... You put contraceptives in and get money out. [*How Far Can You Go?*, Ch. 3]

14 As to our universities, I've come to the conclusion that they are élitist where they should be egalitarian and egalitarian where they should be élitist. [*Nice Work*, 5. 4]

15 Conversation is like playing tennis with a ball made of Krazy Putty that keeps coming back over the net in a different shape. [*Small World*, Pt 1, 1]

16 The world is a global campus, Hilary, you'd better believe it. The American Express card has replaced the library pass. [2]

17 Yeah, you remember kissing. It used to come between saying 'Hi' and fucking. I'm an oldfashioned guy. [2. 2]

SIR OLIVER LODGE 1851–1940

18 This Universe must not fail. [Attr.]

FRANK LOESSER 1910–1969

19 I'd like to get you / On a slow boat to China. [Song: *Slow Boat to China*, 1948]

20 See what the boys in the back room will have, / And tell them I'm having the same. [Song in film *Destry Rides Again*, 1939, music by Frederick Hollander, sung by Marlene Dietrich]

CHRISTOPHER LOGUE 1926–

21 For example, he [Brecht] composed / Plays that staged by us promote / All the values he opposed. [*Christopher Logue's ABC*, B]

22 Said Marx: 'Don't be snobbish, we seek to abolish / The 3rd Class, not the 1st.' [M]

JACK LONDON 1876–1916

1 In an English ship, they say, it is poor grub, poor pay, and easy work; in an American ship, good grub, good pay, and hard work. And this is applicable to the working populations of both countries. [*The People of the Abyss*, Ch. 20]

HUEY LONG 1893–1935

2 I looked around at the little fishes present, and said 'I'm the Kingfish.' [In Arthur M. Schlesinger Jr, *The Politics of Upheaval*, Bk I, Ch. 4, sect. v]

LORD LONGFORD 1905–

3 The male sex still constitute in many ways the most obstinate vested interest one can find. [Speech in House of Lords, 23 June 1963]

ALICE ROOSEVELT LONGWORTH 1884–1980

4 If you can't say anything good about someone, sit right here by me. [Embroidered on a cushion in her sitting room]

5 He [Calvin Coolidge] looked as if he had been weaned on a pickle. [In conversation, 1924. In *Morrow Book of Quotations in American History*, ed. Joseph R. Conlin]

ANITA LOOS 1893–1981

6 So this gentleman said a girl with brains ought to do something else with them besides think. [*Gentlemen Prefer Blondes*, Ch. 1]

7 Gentlemen always seem to remember blondes.

8 Any girl who was a lady would not even think of having such a good time that she did not remember to hang on to her jewelry. [4]

9 The Eyefull Tower is devine.

10 Kissing your hand may make you feel very good but a diamond and safire bracelet lasts forever.

11 So then Dr Froyd said all I needed was to cultivate a few inhibitions and get some sleep. [5]

12 Back to the mink-lined rut. [On being forced back to Hollywood after the Wall Street crash. In obituary in the *Guardian*, 20 Aug. 1981]

13 I'm furious about the Women's Liberationists. They keep getting up on soap-boxes and proclaiming that women are brighter than men. That's true, but it should be kept very quiet or it ruins the whole racket. [In the *Observer*, 'Sayings of the Year', 30 Dec. 1973]

LYDIA LOPOKOVA [LADY KEYNES] 1891–1981

14 I dislike being in the country in August, because my legs get so bitten by barristers. [Attr. in Robert L. Heilbroner, *The Worldly Philosophers*, Ch. 9]

FEDERICO GARCÍA LORCA *see* GARCÍA LORCA, FEDERICO

KONRAD LORENZ 1903–1989

15 It is a good morning exercise for a research scientist to discard a pet hypothesis every day before breakfast. It keeps him young. [*On Aggression*, Ch. 2]

16 The long-sought missing link between animals and the really humane being is ourselves. [Epigraph to Christa Wolf, *Accident*]

LORD LOTHIAN 1882–1940

17 A limitation of armaments by political appeasement. [Letter to *The Times*, May 1934]

18 After all they are only going into their own back garden. [Of Hitler's military reoccupation of the Rhineland, 1936. In Winston S. Churchill, *The Second World War*, Vol. 1, Ch. 11]

LOTHIAN PARENTS ACTION GROUP, SCOTLAND

19 It will be a great day when our schools have all the resources they need and the air force has to hold a cake-sale to buy a bomber. [Slogan. In the *Observer*, 25 May 1986]

EMILY LOTNEY

20 A converted cannibal is one who, on

Friday, eats only fishermen. [In Laurence J. Peter, *Peter's Quotations*, 'Religion']

JAMES LOVELOCK 1919–

1 If we think only of ourselves and degrade the earth, then it will respond by replacing humans with a more amenable species. It will live but we may die. I think we should see ourselves as members of a very democratic planetary community and remember that, in a democracy, we can be voted out. [Interview in the *Sunday Times*, 1 Oct. 1989]

ROBERT LOVEMAN 1864–1923

2 It is not raining rain to me, / It's raining violets. [*April Rain*]

SIR DAVID LOW 1891–1963

3 I do not know whether he [Walt Disney] draws a line himself. I hear that at his studio he employs hundreds of artists to do the work. But I assume that his is the direction, the constant aiming after improvement in the new expression . . . it is the direction of a real artist. It makes Disney, not as a draughtsman but as an artist who uses his brains, the most significant figure in graphic art since Leonardo. [In R. Schickel, *Walt Disney*, Ch. 20]

4 Gad, sir, Lord Coot is right. War brings out the best in a man – and it stays out. [Colonel Blimp in cartoon in the *Evening Standard*]

ROBERT LOWELL 1917–1977

5 Yours the lawlessness / of something simple that has lost its law. [*Caligula*]

6 If we see light at the end of the tunnel, / It's the light of the oncoming train. [*Day by Day*. See also 310:7]

7 The man is killing time – there's nothing else. [*The Drinker*]

8 The monument sticks like a fishbone / in the city's throat. [*For the Union Dead*]

9 This is death / To die and know it. This is the Black Widow, death. [*Mr Edwards and the Spider*]

10 They died / When time was open-eyed, / Wooden and childish; only bones abide / There, in the nowhere, where their boats were tossed / Sky-high, where mariners had fabled news / of IS, the whited monster. [*The Quaker Graveyard in Nantucket*]

11 The Lord survives the rainbow of His will.

12 But I suppose even God was born / too late to trust the old religion – / all those setting out / that never left the ground, / beginning in wisdom, dying in doubt. [*Tenth Muse*]

13 Gored by the climacteric of his want, / he stalls above me like an elephant. [*To Speak of the Woe That is in Marriage*]

MALCOLM LOWRY 1909–1957

14 Where are the children I might have had? You may suppose I might have wanted them. Drowned to the accompaniment of the rattling of a thousand douche bags. [*Under the Volcano*, Ch. 10]

15 How alike are the groans of love to those of the dying. [12]

SUZANNE LOWRY

16 Keeping body and soul together is never as difficult as trying to keep them separate. [On prostitution. In the *Guardian*, 24 May 1974]

E. V. LUCAS 1868–1938

17 I have noticed that the people who are late are so often much jollier than the people who have to wait for them. [*365 Days and One More*]

F. L. LUCAS 1894–1967

18 Human temperaments are too diverse; we can never agree how drunk we like our art to be. [*Literature and Psychology*, Ch. 10]

GEORGE LUCAS 1944–

19 The Empire Strikes Back. [Title of film]

20 May the Force be with you. [Catchphrase in film *Star Wars*]

CLARE BOOTH LUCE 1903–1987

1 A man's home may seem to be his castle on the outside; inside, it is more often his nursery. [In Fidelis Morgan, *Misogynist's Source Book*]

DOCTOR KARL LUEGER [Mayor of Vienna from 1897]

2 Science is what one Jew copies from another. [In the *Sunday Times*, 12 June 1966]

3 I decide who is a Jew. [In A. Bullock, *Hitler*, Pt I, 1. Sometimes wrongly attr. to Goering]

ALISON LURIE 1926–

4 That is the worst thing about being a middle-class woman ... you have more knowledge of yourself and the world; you are equipped to make choices, but there are none left to make. [*The War between the Tates*, 3]

SIR EDWIN LUTYENS 1869–1944

5 [When asked at a committee what should be done with the Crystal Palace] Put it under a glass case. [In Elisabeth Lutyens, *A Goldfish Bowl*, Ch. 2]

6 This piece of cod passes all understanding. [In R. Lutyens, *Sir Edwin Lutyens*, p. 74]

7 The answer is in the plural and they bounce. [Before a Royal Commission. Attr.]

ELISABETH LUTYENS 1906–1983

8 All living artists compete with the towering dead with their nightingales and psalms. [*A Goldfish Bowl*, Ch. 2]

ROSA LUXEMBURG 1871–1919

9 Freedom is always and exclusively freedom for the one who thinks differently. [*The Russian Revolution*, sect. 4]

ROBERT LYND 1879–1949

10 No human being believes that any other human being has a right to be in bed when he himself is up. [In *Apt and Amusing Quotations*, ed. G. F. Lamb, 'Bed']

JONATHAN LYNN 1943– and SIR ANTHONY JAY 1936–

11 The Official Secrets Act is not to protect secrets but to protect officials. [*Yes Minister*, Ch. 7]

12 We're all equals ... A team. Like the Cabinet, except that we're all on the same side. [*Yes Prime Minister*, Vol. 1, 'Party Games']

13 The first rule of politics is Never Believe Anything Until It's Been Officially Denied.

14 If he was the sole entrant in an intelligence contest, he'd come third.

15 I'm afraid he's at an even greater disadvantage in understanding economics, Prime Minister. He's an economist. ['A Real Partnership']

16 But the point about government is that no one has control. Lots of people have the power to stop something happening – but almost nobody has the power to *make* anything happen. We have a system of government with the engine of a lawn-mower and the brakes of a Rolls-Royce.

17 The opposite of peaceful coexistence is warlike non-existence. ['A Victory for Democracy']

18 After all, one never trusts anyone that one has deceived. ['The Smokescreen']

19 You mean, your statistics are facts, but my facts are just statistics.

20 Is something a blow against freedom just because it can seriously damage your wealth?

21 Annie couldn't see why religion has nothing to do with bishops so I explained to her that they are basically managers in fancy dress. ['The Bishop's Gambit']

22 It's one of those irregular verbs, isn't it? 'I have an independent mind, you are eccentric, he is round the twist'?

23 So that means you need to know things even when you don't need to know them. You need to know them not because you need to know them but because you need to know whether or not you need to know. And if you don't need to know you still need to know so that you know that there was no need to know. [2, 'Man Overboard']

1 The definition of a non-aligned country is that it is non-aligned with the United States. ['A Diplomatic Incident']

2 The basic rule of the City was that if you are incompetent you have to be honest, and if you're crooked you have to be clever. The reasoning is that, if you are honest, the chaps will rally round if you make a pig's breakfast out of your business dealings. Conversely, if you are crooked, no one will ask questions so long as you are making substantial profits. ['A Conflict of Interest']

3 'Irregularity' means there's been a crime but you can't prove it. 'Malpractice' means there's been a crime and you can prove it.

4 A completely honest answer always gives you the advantage of surprise in the House of Commons. ['The Tangled Web']

5 I thought that when I became Prime Minister I'd have power. And what have I got? *Influence!* ['The National Education'. See also 252:8, 366:1]

GEORGE LYTTELTON 1883–1962

6 It is not what old men forget that shadows their senescence, but what they remember. [Letter, 27 Oct. 1955, *Lyttelton–Hart-Davis Letters*, ed. Rupert Hart-Davis, Vol. 2]

LADY CONSTANCE LYTTON
1869–1923

7 The first time you meet Winston [Churchill] you see all his faults and the rest of your life you spend in discovering his virtues. [In Christopher Hassall, *Edward Marsh*, Ch. 7]

M

GENERAL DOUGLAS MacARTHUR
1880–1964

1 I shall return. [Speech in Adelaide, Australia, after leaving the Philippines, 20 Mar. 1942]

DAME ROSE MACAULAY 1889–1958

2 Here is one of the points about this planet which should be remembered; into every penetrable corner of it, and into most of the impenetrable corners, the English will penetrate. [*Crewe Train*, Pt 1, Ch. 1]

3 Gentlemen know that fresh air should be kept in its proper place – out of doors – and that, God having given us indoors and out-of-doors, we should not attempt to do away with this distinction. [5]

4 'Take my camel, dear', said my aunt Dot, as she climbed down from this animal on her return from High Mass. [*The Towers of Trebizond*, Ch. 1]

5 It was a book to kill time for those who like it better dead. [In *Treasury of Humorous Quotations*, ed. Evan Esar and Nicolas Bentley]

6 The great and recurrent question about abroad is, is it worth getting there? [Attr.]

GENERAL A. C. McAULIFFE
1898–1975

7 Nuts! [Reply to German demand to surrender Bastogne, 22 Dec. 1944]

GEORGE MacBETH 1932–1992

8 To leave great themes unfinished is / Perhaps the most satisfying exercise / Of power. [*The Spider's Nest*]

SIR DESMOND MacCARTHY
1877–1952

9 The whole of art is an appeal to a reality which is not without us but in our minds. [*Theatre*, 'Modern Drama']

10 It [Post-Impressionist painting] may ... appear ridiculous to those who do not recall the fact that a good rocking-horse has often more of the true horse about it than an instantaneous photograph of a Derby winner. [Introduction to exhibition 'Manet and His Contemporaries,' 1910]

11 [Journalists are] more attentive to the minute hand of history than to the hour hand. [In Kenneth Tynan, *Curtains*, Pt 2]

JOSEPH McCARTHY 1885–1943

12 In my sweet little Alice blue gown, / When I first wandered out in the town. [Song: *Alice Blue Gown*, in musical *Irene*, 1919, Act 1, music by Harry Tierney]

13 You made me love you, / I didn't want to do it. [Song, music by James V. Monaco]

SENATOR JOSEPH R. McCARTHY
1908–1957

14 McCarthyism is Americanism with its sleeves rolled. [Speech in Wisconsin, 1952. In R. Rovere, *Senator Joe McCarthy*, Ch. 1]

MARY McCARTHY 1912–1989

1 Stepping into his new Buick convertible he [the American] knows that he would gladly do without it, but imagines that to his neighbour, who is just backing *his* out of the driveway, this car is the motor of life. [*On the Contrary*, 'America the Beautiful']

2 When an American heiress wants to buy a man, she at once crosses the Atlantic. The only really materialistic people I have ever met have been Europeans.

3 American life, in large cities at any rate, is a perpetual assault on the senses and the nerves; it is out of asceticism, out of unworldliness, precisely, that we bear it.

4 The American character looks always as if it had just had a rather bad haircut, which gives it, in our eyes at any rate, a greater humanity than the European, which even among its beggars has an all too professional air.

5 The immense popularity of American movies abroad demonstrates that Europe is the unfinished negative of which America is the proof.

6 An interviewer asked me what book I thought best represented the modern American Woman. All I could think of to answer was: *Madame Bovary*. ['Characters in Fiction']

7 There are no new truths, but only truths that have not been recognized by those who have perceived them without noticing. A truth is something that everyone can be shown to know and to have known, as people say, all along. ['The *Vita activa*']

8 And I don't feel the attraction of the Kennedys at all ... I don't think they are Christians; they may be Catholics but they are not Christians, in my belief anyway. [In the *Observer*, 14 Oct. 1979]

9 Every word she [Lillian Hellman] writes is a lie, including 'and' and 'the'. [Discussing the 1930s in TV interview on *Dick Cavett Show*, 25/26 Jan. 1980]

PAUL McCARTNEY 1942–

10 [When asked if the Beatles were to be reunited] You cannot reheat a soufflé. [In J. Green, *Book of Rock Quotes*]

See also **JOHN LENNON** and **PAUL McCARTNEY**

JOHN McCRAE 1872–1918

11 In Flanders fields the poppies blow / Between the crosses, row on row. [*In Flanders Fields*]

DEREK McCULLOCH [UNCLE MAC] 1897–1967

12 Goodnight children...everywhere. [Closing catchphrase to BBC radio programme *Children's Hour*, 1940s]

REV. JOSEPH McCULLOCH 1908–1990

13 We have just buried the Church of England. [To David Edwards at the funeral of Archbishop William Temple. In obituary in the *Guardian*, 7 Mar. 1990]

W. D. H. McCULLOUGH 1901–1978 and 'FOUGASSE' 1887–1965

14 A professor of anatomy once declared that there are only fourteen types of woman – young women, women who are really wonderful all things considered, and the twelve most famous women in history – and the same applies to Bridge partners. Over and above this, they are usually either so good that you lose all your self-confidence, or so bad that you lose all your money. [*Aces Made Easy*]

HUGH MacDIARMID 1892–1978

15 I'll ha'e nae hauf-way hoose, but aye be whaur / Extremes meet – it's the only way I ken / To dodge the curst conceit o' bein' richt / That damns the vast majority o' men. [*A Drunk Man looks at the Thistle*, 141–4]

16 'Let there be Licht,' said God, and there was / A little. [2100–2101]

17 Hauf his soul a Scot maun use / Indulgin' in illusions, / And hauf in gettin' rid o' them / And comin' to conclusions. [2388–9]

18 Killing / Is the ultimate simplification of life. [*England's Double Knavery*]

19 (Though England prefers victims who begin by being restive, / They taste better

afterwards – like birds / Cooked while their blood is still warm.)

1 There are plenty of ruined buildings in the world but no ruined stones. [*On a Raised Beach*]

2 To an Englishman something is what it is called: to a Scotsman something is what it is. [Epigraph to Lewis Grassic Gibbon and Hugh MacDiarmid, *Scottish Scene*]

BETTY MacDONALD 1908–1958

3 In high school and college my sister Mary was very popular with the boys, but I had braces on my teeth and got high marks. [*The Egg and I*, Ch. 2]

4 The days slipped down like junket, leaving no taste on the tongue. [4]

RAMSAY MacDONALD 1866–1917

5 Tomorrow every Duchess in London will be wanting to kiss me! [On forming the national government, 25 Aug. 1931. In Viscount Snowden, *Autobiography*]

6 Let them [France and Germany] especially put their demands in such a way that Great Britain could say that she supported both sides. [In A. J. P. Taylor, *The Origins of the Second World War*, Ch. 3]

WILLIAM C. MacDONALD

7 It took God longer to write the Bible than it has taken Him to build the British Empire. [*Modern Evangelism*]

IAN McEWAN 1948–

8 Looking after children is one way of looking after yourself. [*Black Dogs*, Preface]

9 Her eyes, nose, mouth, skin, all might have been designed in committee to meet the barest requirements of feasibility. [*The Comfort of Strangers*, Ch. 6]

10 Shall there be womanly times, or shall we die? [*Or Shall We Die?*]

ARTHUR McEWEN ?–1907

11 News is anything that makes a reader say 'Gee whiz!' . . . News is whatever a good editor chooses to print. [In *Colliers*, 18 Feb. 1911]

PHYLLIS McGINLEY 1905–1978

12 I'm happy the great ones are thriving, / But what puzzles my head / Is the thought that they need reviving. / I had never been told they were dead. [*On the Prevalence of Literary Revivals*]

FELIX McGLENNON ?–1943

13 They may build their ships, my lads, and think they know the game, / But they can't build boys of the bulldog breed / Who made old England's name. [*Sons of the Sea*]

ROGER McGOUGH 1937–

14 You will put on a dress of guilt / and shoes with broken high ideals. [*Comeclose and Sleepnow*]

15 Let me die a youngman's death / not a clean & inbetween / the sheets holy-water death / not a famous-last-words / peaceful out of breath death. [*Let Me Die A Youngman's Death*]

16 When I'm 73 / & in constant good tumour / may I be mown down at dawn / by a bright red sports car / on my way home / from an allnight party.

17 Or when I'm 91 / with silver hair / & sitting in a barber's chair / may I rival gangsters / with hamfisted tommyguns bust in / & give me a short back & insides.

18 Winter has been sacked / for negligence / It appears he left / the sun on all day. [*Sky in the Pie*, 'March ingorders']

WILLIAM McILVANNEY 1936–

19 There is a kind of laughter people laugh at public events, as if a joke were a charity auction and they want to be seen to be bidding. [*The Big Man*, Ch. 1]

COLIN MacINNES 1914–1976

20 In England, pop art and fine art stand resolutely back to back. [*England, Half English*, 'Pop Songs and Teenagers']

21 The decorations are like those of the embassy of a nation about to go into voluntary liquidation. ['See You at Mabel's']

1 A coloured man can tell, in five seconds dead, whether a white man likes him or not. If the white man *says* he does, he is instantly – and usually quite rightly – mistrusted. ['A Short Guide for Jumbles']

DENIS MACKAIL 1892–1971

2 A first night was notoriously distracting owing to the large number of people who stand about looking famous. [*How Amusing*]

SIR COMPTON MACKENZIE 1883–1972

3 Women do not find it difficult nowadays to behave like men; but they often find it extremely difficult to behave like gentlemen. [*On Moral Courage*]

4 The present school is not fit for children at all ... 'How many water-closets have you?' one of these wise men from the East ... was asking me at the last meeting ... 'How many water-closets, General? The whole island is a water-closet,' I said. [*Whisky Galore*, Ch. 3]

THOMAS McKEOWN 1912–1988

5 Wine experts are of two kinds, gastronomic and intellectual, distinguishable according to whether on sight of the bottle they reach for their glass or their glasses. [In *Perspectives in Biology and Medicine*, Summer 1981, 'It Has Been Said']

6 The dramatist changes the props but keeps the players. The Almighty does the reverse. [Spring 1983]

H. S. MACKINTOSH

7 Give me that song of Picardy: / 'He has been duped – the station-master!' [*Ballades and Other Verse*, 'Il est cocu – le chef de gare!']

SHIRLEY MACLAINE 1934–

8 I've made so many movies playing a hooker that they don't pay me in the regular way any more. They leave it on the dresser. [In *New Woman*, July 1989]

SIR FITZROY MACLEAN 1911–

9 They [the Soviets] are Communists just as the Victorians were Christians. They attend CP meetings and lectures on Marxism-Leninism at regular intervals in exactly the same way as the Victorians attended church on Sunday. They believe in world revolution just as implicitly as the Victorians believed in the Second Coming. And they apply the principles of Marxism in their private lives to just about the same extent as the Victorians applied the principles of the Sermon on the Mount. Neither more nor less. [*Back to Bokhara*]

ARCHIBALD MACLEISH 1892–1982

10 A poem should be palpable and mute / As a globed fruit, / Dumb / As old medallions to the thumb ... / A poem should be equal to / Not true ... / A poem should not mean / But be. [*Ars Poetica*]

11 For history's a twisted root / With art its small, translucent fruit / And never the other way round.

12 We have learned the answers, all the answers: / It is the question that we do not know. [*The Hamlet of A. Macleish*]

13 History, like a badly constructed concert hall, has occasional dead spots where the music can't be heard. [In the *Observer*, 'Sayings of the Week', 12 Feb. 1967]

IAIN MACLEOD 1913–1970

14 History is too serious to be left to historians. [In the *Observer*, 'Sayings of the Week', 16 July 1961]

MARSHALL McLUHAN 1911–1980

15 The new electronic interdependence re-creates the world in the image of a global village. [*The Gutenberg Galaxy*]

16 For tribal man space was the uncontrollable mystery. For technological man it is time that occupies the same role. [*The Mechanical Bride*, 'Magic That Changes Mood']

17 If the nineteenth century was the age of the editorial chair, ours is the century of the psychiatrist's couch. [*Understanding Media*, Introduction]

18 The medium is the message. This is merely to say that the personal and social consequences of any medium ... result from

the new scale that is introduced into our affairs by each extension of ourselves or by any new technology. [Ch. 1]

1 A hot medium is one that extends one single sense in 'high definition'. High definition is the state of being well filled with data. A photograph is, visually, 'high definition' ... Telephone is a cool medium or one of low definition, because the ear is given a meagre amount of information. [2]

2 The car has become the carapace, the protective and aggressive shell, of urban and suburban man. [22]

3 Television brought the brutality of war into the comfort of the living room. Vietnam was lost in the living rooms of America – not on the battlefields of Vietnam. [In the *Montreal Gazette*, 16 May 1975]

4 Gutenberg made everybody a reader. Xerox makes everybody a publisher. [From interview in the *Washington Post*, in the *Guardian Weekly*, 12 June 1977]

5 North Americans have a peculiar bias. They go outside to be alone and they go home to be social. [In the *Sunday Times Magazine*, 26 Mar. 1978]

HAROLD MACMILLAN, [later LORD STOCKTON] 1894–1986

6 You've never had it so good. [Speech on financial situation at Bedford, 20 July 1957; originally US presidential election slogan, 1952; reuse attr. to Oliver Poole]

7 There ain't gonna be no war. [At press conference in London after Geneva Summit, 24 July 1955]

8 I thought the best thing to do was to settle up these little local difficulties, and then turn to the wider vision of the Commonwealth. [Said at London Airport, 7 Jan. 1958, referring to resignation of Treasury Ministers]

9 Jaw-jaw is better than war-war. [Said at Canberra, 30 Jan. See also 80:14]

10 When you're abroad you're a statesman: when you're at home you're just a politician. [Speech, 1958. In the *Observer*, 28 July 1963]

11 The wind of change is blowing through this Continent, and whether we like it or not, this growth of national consciousness is a political fact. [Speech in Cape Town, 3 Feb. 1960]

12 Fifteen fingers on the safety catch. [Speech in House of Commons, 30 May, on breakdown of summit conference on nuclear disarmament. See also 99:2]

13 It is the duty of Her Majesty's government ... neither to flap nor to falter. [In the *Observer*, 'Sayings of the Week', 19 Nov. 1961]

14 What happened at Brussels yesterday was bad, bad for us, bad for Europe and bad for the whole free world. [On General de Gaulle's vetoing Britain's entry to the European Community, TV broadcast, 15 Jan. 1963]

15 After a long experience of politics I have never found that there is any inhibition caused by ignorance as regards criticism. [Speech in House of Commons, 11 July]

16 'How do you treat a cold?' One nanny said, 'Feed a cold' – she was a neo-Keynesian. Another nanny said, 'Starve a cold' – she was a monetarist. [Maiden speech in House of Lords at age of 90, 13 Nov. 1984]

17 First of all the Georgian silver goes, and then all that nice furniture that used to be in the saloon. Then the Canalettos go. [On privatization. Speech to Tory Reform Group, 8 Nov. 1985]

18 We, my dear Mr [Richard] Crossman are Greeks in the Roman Empire. You will find the Americans much as the Greeks found the Romans – a great big, vulgar, bustling people, more vigorous than we are, but also more idle, with more unspoilt virtues but also more corrupt. [In obituary in *The Times*, 30 Dec. 1986]

19 [Rab Butler] was a sweet man, and very loyal to me. [Pause] Yet I can always see him dressed in a soutane, conspiring in the corridors of the Vatican. [Quoted by Alistair Horne at Macmillan's death in the *Sunday Times*, 4 Jan. 1987]

20 Spending half his time thinking about adultery, the other half about second-hand ideas passed on by his advisers. [Of President Kennedy]

LOUIS MacNEICE 1907–1963

1 And we who have been brought up to think of 'Gallant Belgium' / As so much blague / Are now prepared again to essay good through evil / For the sake of Prague. [*Autumn Journal*, VII]

2 A howling radio for our paraclete.

3 It's no go the merrygoround, it's no go the rickshaw, / All we want is a limousine and a ticket for the peepshow. / Their knickers are made of crêpe-de-chine, their shoes are made of python, / Their halls are lined with tiger rugs and their walls with heads of bison. [*Bagpipe Music*]

4 It's no go the picture palace, it's no go the stadium, / It's no go the country cot with a pot of pink geraniums, / It's no go the Government grants, it's no go the elections, / Sit on your arse for fifty years and hang your hat on a pension.

5 It's no go, my honey love, it's no go, my poppet; / Work your hands from day to day, the winds will blow the profit. / The glass is falling hour by hour, the glass will fall for ever, / But if you break the bloody glass you won't hold up the weather.

6 Between the enormous fluted Ionic columns / There seeps from heavily jowled or hawk-like foreign faces / The guttural sorrow of the refugees. [*The British Museum Reading Room*]

7 When our brother Fire was having his dog's day / Jumping the London streets with millions of tin cans / Clanking at his tail, we heard some shadow say / 'Give the dog a bone'. [*Brother Fire*]

8 Ordinary men ... / Put up a barrage of common sense to baulk / Intimacy but by mistake interpolate / Swear-words like roses in their talk. [*Conversation*]

9 Crumbling between the fingers, under the feet, / Crumbling behind the eyes, / Their world gives way and dies / And something twangs and breaks at the end of the street. [*Débâcle*]

10 Time was away and somewhere else, / There were two glasses and two chairs / And two people with one pulse. [*Meeting Point*]

11 In the beginning and in the end the only decent / Definition is tautology: man is man, / Woman woman, and tree tree. [*Plain Speaking*]

12 He can discover / A selfish motive for anything – and collect / His royalties as recording angel. [*The Satirist*]

HECTOR McNEIL 1907–1955

13 It's easy to be brilliant if you are not bothered about being right. [Of Richard Crossman. In Denis Healey, *The Time of My Life*, Ch. 5]

'SUGGS' McPHERSON [Of pop group Madness] 1961–

14 In London town a man gets mugged every twenty minutes. He's getting very sick of it. [In *New Musical Express*, 20/27 Dec. 1986]

SALVADOR DE MADARIAGA 1886–1978

15 Considering how bad men are, it is wonderful how well they behave. [*Morning without Noon*, Pt 1, Ch. 14]

16 It is not armaments that cause war, but wars that cause armaments. [Pt 1, Ch. 9]

17 A professor said, 'People are not interested in freedom but in ham and eggs.' To which I retorted, 'Ten years in prison with only ham and eggs for breakfast would cure that.' [In BBC TV programme *Viewpoint*, 14 Oct. 1969]

18 First the sweetheart of the nation, then the aunt, woman governs America because America is a land of boys who refuse to grow up. [In Sagittarius and D. George, *The Perpetual Pessimist*]

19 In politics, as in grammar, one should be able to tell the substantives from adjectives. Hitler was a substantive; Mussolini only an adjective. Hitler was a nuisance; Mussolini was bloody. Together a bloody nuisance. [Attr.]

BEN MADDOW 1909–1992 and JOHN HUSTON 1906–1987

20 Crime is only a left-handed form of

human endeavour. [In film *The Asphalt Jungle*, from novel of W. R. Burnett]

BRENDA MADDOX 1932–

1 I wish I wrote books like other people do, from beginning to end . . . For me, writing a book is like doing a jigsaw puzzle under house arrest. [In the *Listener*, 16 Oct. 1986]

MAURICE DE MAETERLINCK
1862–1949

2 *Il n'y a de morts.* – There are no dead. [*L'oiseau bleu* (*The Blue Bird*), Act IV, sc. ii]

HERB MAGIDSON 1906–1986

3 Music, Maestro, Please. [Title of Song]

MAGNUS MAGNUSSON 1929–

4 My wife says I'm Scotch by absorption. [In the *Listener*, 21 May 1987]

GUSTAV MAHLER 1860–1911

5 At last, fortissimo! [On visiting Niagara. In K. Blaukopf, *Mahler*, Ch. 8]

6 A symphony must be like the world. It must contain everything. [To Jean Sibelius in Helsingfors, Finland, 1907]

7 Both my marriages were failures! Number one departed and number two stayed. [On Swiss radio, Dec. 1987]

DEREK MAHON 1941–

8 What do you know / Of the revolutionary theories advanced / By turnips, or the sex life of cutlery? / Everything is susceptible, Pythagoras said so. [*Mute Phenomena*]

MOLLY MAHOOD 1919–

9 Naming the parts does not show us what makes the gun go off. [From *Shakespeare's Wordplay*, p. 19, in Walter Redfern, *Puns*, Introduction]

NORMAN MAILER 1923–

10 Sentimentality is the emotional promiscuity of those who have no sentiment. [*Cannibals and Christians*, p. 51]

11 And she gave me a sisterly kiss. Older sister. [*The Deer Park*]

12 The horror of the Twentieth Century was the size of each event, and the paucity of the reverberation. [*Fire on the Moon*, Pt 1, Ch. 2]

13 Ultimately a hero is a man who would argue with the Gods, and awakens devils to contest his vision. [*Presidential Papers*, Special Preface]

14 But then the country is our religion. The true religion of America has always been America. [Interview in *Time Out*, 27 Sept.–3 Oct. 1984]

15 He [Marlon Brando] is our greatest actor, our noblest actor, and he is also our national lout. [In the *Observer*, 1 Jan. 1989]

16 Novels don't always come your way . . . It's like falling in love. You can't say: 'Oh, gee, I think I'm ready to fall in love,' and then meet some woman who'd be perfect. When a novel comes, it's a grace. Something in the cosmos has forgiven you long enough so that you can start. [Interview in the *Weekend Guardian*, 5–6 Oct. 1991]

17 The greatest mind ever to stay in prep school. [Of J. D. Salinger. In *Oh, What an Awful Thing to Say!*, comp. W. Cole and L. Phillips]

JOHN MAJOR, MP 1943–

18 I am my own man. [On becoming Prime Minister. In the *Independent*, 'Quote Unquote', 1 Dec. 1990]

BERNARD MALAMUD 1914–1986

19 There is no life that can be recaptured wholly; as it was. Which is to say that all biography is ultimately fiction. [*Dubin's Lives*, p. 20]

20 'Mourning is a hard business,' Cesare said. 'If people knew there'd be less death.' [*Idiots First*, 'Life is Better Than Death']

21 Levin wanted friendship and got friendliness; he wanted steak and they offered spam. [*A New Life*, sect. vi]

22 There comes a time in a man's life when to get where he has to go – if there are no doors or windows he walks through a wall. [*Rembrandt's Hat*, 'Man in the Drawer']

MALCOLM X 1925–1965

1 It's just like when you've got some coffee that's too black, which means it's too strong. What do you do? You integrate it with cream, you make it weak . . . It used to wake you up, now it puts you to sleep. [On Black Power and the Civil Rights movement. *Malcolm X Speaks*, Ch. 14]

GEORGE MALLABY 1902–1978

2 Never descend to the ways of those above you. [*From My Level*]

G. H. L. MALLORY 1886–1924

3 [When asked why he wanted to climb Everest] Because it's there. [In John Hunt, *The Ascent of Everest*, Ch. 1]

MAE MALOO

4 There's one thing to be said for inviting trouble: it generally accepts. [In *Reader's Digest*, Sept. 1976]

ANDRÉ MALRAUX 1901–1976

5 A revolution only remains victorious through methods which are alien to those that made it. And sometimes even through sentiments which are similarly alien. [From *L'espoir*, in Fitzroy Maclean, *Back to Bokhara*]

6 England is never as great as when she is alone. And France is never France when she fights for herself . . . When the French fight for mankind they are wonderful. When they fight for themselves, they are nothing. [In Bruce Chatwin, *What am I Doing Here*, 'André Malraux']

7 Here is a man who questioned life, but did not know in what name he questioned life. [Of T. E. Lawrence]

8 In France intellectuals are usually incapable of opening an umbrella.

DAVID MAMET 1947–

9 Film is the least realistic of art forms. [Interview in the *Guardian*, 16 Feb. 1989]

MANCHESTER GUARDIAN

10 If Mr Eliot had been pleased to write in demotic English *The Waste Land* might not have been, as it just is to all but anthropologists and literati, so much wastepaper. [In Virginia Woolf, *The Common Reader*, First Series, 'How It Strikes a Contemporary']

LORD MANCROFT 1914–1987

11 Happy is the man with a wife to tell him what to do and a secretary to do it. [In the *Observer*, 'Sayings of the Week', 18 Dec. 1966]

12 If [your wife] happens to be travelling anywhere without you and you want her back in a hurry, send her a copy of your local newspaper with a little paragraph cut out. [In *Punch*, 27 Jan. 1971]

13 Money is the sixth sense that helps you to enjoy the other five. It would therefore be nice if Providence could think less about money itself, and more about the sort of people to whom it is given. [From *Punch*, in obituary in the *Independent*, 18 Sept. 1987. See also 256:18]

NELSON MANDELA 1918–

14 There is no easy walk to freedom. [Quoted by Donald Woods in the *Observer*, 8 Jan. 1978]

NADEZHDA MANDELSTAM 1899–1980

15 Silence is the real crime against humanity. [In *In a Dark Time*, ed. N. Humphrey and R. J. Lifton]

OSIP MANDELSTAM 1891–1938

16 No, I am no one's contemporary – ever. / That would have been above my station . . . / How I loathe that other with my name. / He certainly never was me. [*Poems*, No. 141, trans. Clarence Brown and W. S. Merwin]

17 Star-salt is melting in the barrel, / icy water is turning blacker, / death's growing purer, misfortune saltier, / the earth's moving nearer to truth and to dread. [216]

18 But whenever there's a snatch of talk / it turns to the Kremlin mountaineer, / the ten thick worms his fingers, / his words like measures of weight, / the huge laughing cockroaches on his top lip, / The glitter of his boot-rims. [286, *Stalin Epigram*]

1 The people need poetry that will be their own secret / To keep them awake forever, / And bathe them in the bright-haired wave / Of its breathing. [287]

2 Now I'm dead in the grave with my lips moving / And every schoolboy repeating my words by heart. [306]

3 You took away the oceans and all the room. / You gave me my shoe-size in earth and bars around it. [307]

4 Do preserve what I've said for its taste of misfortune and smoke. [Quoted by Michael Schmidt in the *New Statesman*, 17 Oct. 1980]

5 It's in the margins we'll find the poems. [Attr.]

RUBY MANIKAN [Indian church leader]

6 If you educate a man you educate a person, but if you educate a woman you educate a family. [In the *Observer*, 'Sayings of the Week', 30 Mar. 1947]

HERMAN J. MANKIEWICZ 1897–1953

7 You know it's hard to hear what a bearded man is saying. He can't speak above a whisker. [In R. E. Drennan, *Wit's End*]

8 There, but for the Grace of God goes God. [Of Orson Welles, during the making of the film *Citizen Kane*. In *The Citizen Kane Book*. Also ascr. to Winston Churchill on Stafford Cripps]

9 People never sat at his [Charlie Chaplin's] feet. He went to where people were sitting and stood in front of them. [In Kenneth Tynan, *Show People*, 'Louise Brooks']

10 That man [a fellow scriptwriter] is so bad he shouldn't be left alone in a room with a typewriter. [Attr.]

HERMAN J. MANKIEWICZ and ORSON WELLES 1915–1985

11 It [death] is the only disease you don't look forward to being cured of. [In film *Citizen Kane*]

12 I guess Rosebud is just a piece in a jigsaw puzzle – a missing piece.

JOSEPH L. MANKIEWICZ 1909–1993

13 Fasten your safety belts; it's going to be a bumpy night. [Said by Bette Davis in film *All about Eve*]

14 It is about time the piano realized it has not written the concerto.

15 I admit I may have seen better days, but I am still not to be had for the price of a cocktail – like a salted peanut.

16 All playwrights should be dead for three hundred years.

17 Eve would ask Abbott to give her Costello.

18 The best friend of a boy is his mother, of a man his horse; only it's not clear when the transition takes place. [In A. Andrews, *Quotations for Speakers and Writers*]

THOMAS MANN 1875–1955

19 Our capacity for disgust, let me observe, is in proportion to our desires; that is in proportion to the intensity of our attachment to the things of this world. [*The Confessions of Felix Krull*, Pt I, Ch. 5]

20 A great truth is a truth whose opposite is also a great truth. [*Essay on Freud*. See also 45:2]

21 What we call mourning for our dead is perhaps not so much grief at not being able to call them back as it is grief at not being able to want to do so. [From *The Magic Mountain*, in *Oxford Book of Aphorisms*, chosen by J. Gross]

22 Instead of leading the world, America appears to have resolved to buy it. [Letter, 1947. In *Morrow Book of Quotations in American History*, ed. Joseph R. Conlin]

23 In the long run a harmful truth is better than a useful lie. [Quoted by Arthur Koestler on leaving the Communist Party. In Koestler's obituary in the *Guardian*, 4 Mar. 1983]

24 We should know how to inherit, because inheriting is culture. [Quoted by Hans Werner Henze in *Music and Politics*]

25 Every intellectual attitude is latently political. [In the *Observer*, 11 Aug. 1974]

FREDERIC MANNING 1887–1935

26 They were singularly brave men, these

Prussian machine-gunners, but the extreme of heroism, alike in foe or friend, is indistinguishable from despair. [*Her Privates We*, 1]

JAYNE MANSFIELD 1933–1967

1 [When asked by Robin Day, 'Is it true you led a tiger down Sunset Boulevard by a pink ribbon?'] Yes, I like pink. [TV interview. In the *Guardian*, 23 Dec. 1989]

KATHERINE MANSFIELD 1888–1923

2 If there was one thing he hated more than another it was the way she had of waking him in the morning ... It was her way of establishing her grievance for the day. [*Bliss*, 'Mr Reginald Peacock's Day']

3 He stands, smiling encouragement, like a clumsy dentist. [*The Garden Party*, 'Bank Holiday']

4 She couldn't possibly go back to the gentleman's flat; she had no right to cry in strangers' houses. ['Life of Ma Parker']

5 E. M. Forster never gets any further than warming the teapot. He's a rare fine hand at that. Feel this teapot. Is it not beautifully warm? Yes, but there ain't going to be no tea. [*Journal*, May 1917]

6 Whenever I prepare for a journey I prepare as though for death. Should I never return, all is in order. This is what life has taught me. [1922]

MAO ZEDONG 1893–1976

7 The enemy advances, we retreat; the enemy camps, we harass; the enemy tires, we attack; the enemy retreats, we pursue. [Letter, 5 Jan. 1930, but in fact quoting a letter from the Front Committee to the Central Committee of the Chinese Communist Party]

8 If you want knowledge, you must take part in the practice of changing reality. If you want to know the taste of a pear, you must change the pear by eating it yourself. [*On Practice*, July 1937]

9 Politics is war without bloodshed while war is politics with bloodshed. [*On Protracted War*, May 1938]

10 Every Communist must grasp the truth, 'Political power grows out of the barrel of a gun.' [Speech to Central Committee, Communist Party, 6 Nov.]

11 We are advocates of the abolition of war, we do not want war; but war can only be abolished through war, and in order to get rid of the gun it is necessary to take up the gun.

12 We should support whatever the enemy opposes and oppose whatever the enemy supports. [Newspaper interview, 16 Sept. 1939]

13 All reactionaries are paper tigers. [Talk with the American correspondent Anna Louise Strong, Aug. 1946]

14 The atom bomb is a paper tiger which the United States reactionaries use to scare people.

15 Letting a hundred flowers blossom and a hundred schools of thought contend is the policy for promoting the progress of the arts and the sciences. [*On the Correct Handling of Contradictions*, 27 Feb. 1957]

16 For the sake of the achievement of a specific political goal, it is possible to sacrifice half mankind. [Speech at meeting in Moscow, Nov. 1957. In *Pravda*, 26 Aug. 1973]

17 To read too many books is harmful. [In the *New Yorker*, 7 Mar. 1977]

18 The peaceful population is the sea in which the guerrilla swims like a fish. [In R. Taber, *The War of the Flea*]

19 A fat man should not play the concertina. [In *Quote ... Unquote Book of Love, Death and the Universe*, ed. Nigel Rees]

20 The government burns down whole cities while the people are forbidden to light lamps. [Attr.]

HERBERT MARCUSE 1898–1979

21 The revolt of a population injected with needs they are unable to satisfy. [Definition of revolution. 'Warsaw Diary', *Granta*, 16]

JOHNNY MARKS 1909–1985

22 Rudolph, the Red-nosed Reindeer / Had a very shiny nose. [Song: *Rudolph, the Red-nosed Reindeer*]

LAURENCE MARKS 1948– and
MAURICE GRAN 1949–

1 In the good old days, you got ill, you were poor, you died. Today, everyone seems to think they have the right to be cured. Result of this sloppy socialist thinking? More poor people. [YTV series *The New Statesman*, 'Sex is Wrong']

GEORGE MARKSTEIN 1929–1987 and
DAVID TOMBLIN

2 I am not a number – I am a free man! [Catchphrase in TV series *The Prisoner*, 1967, said by political prisoner Number Six]

GABRIEL GARCÍA MÁRQUEZ *see*
GARCÍA MÁRQUEZ, GABRIEL

DON MARQUIS 1878–1937

3 but wotthehell wotthehell / oh i should worry and fret / death and I will coquette / there's a dance in the old dame yet / toujours gai toujours gai [*archy and mehitabel*, III, 'the song of mehitabel']

4 a / whole scuttleful of chef douvres what / you mean is hors douvres mehitabel i / told her what i mean is grub [XI, 'why mehitabel jumped']

5 live so that you / can stick out your tongue / at the insurance / doctor [XII, 'certain maxims of archy']

6 procrastination is the / art of keeping / up with yesterday

7 i do not care / what a dogs / pedigree may be . . . / millionaires and / bums taste / about alike to me

8 an optimist is a guy / that has never had / much experience

9 it's cheerio / my deario that / pulls a lady through [XXIV, 'cheerio my deario']

10 always being / misunderstood by some / strait laced / prune faced bunch / of prissy mouthed / sisters of uncharity

11 archy she told me / it is merely a plutonic / attachment / and the thing can be / believed for the tom / looks like one of pluto's demons [XXX, 'the old trouper']

12 he had a voice / that used to shake / the ferryboats / on the north river

13 you want to know / whether i believe in ghosts / of course i do not believe in them / if you had known / as many of them as i have / you would not / believe in them either [XXXIII, 'ghosts']

14 jamais triste archy jamais triste / that is my motto [XLVI, 'mehitabel sees paris']

15 there is always / a comforting thought / in time of trouble when / it is not our trouble [*archy does his part*, 'comforting thoughts']

16 did you ever / notice that when / a politician / does get an idea / he usually / gets it all wrong [*archys life of mehitabel*, XL, 'archygrams']

17 now and then / there is a person born / who is so unlucky / that he runs into accidents / which started out to happen / to somebody else [XLI, 'archy says']

18 The art of newspaper paragraphing is / to stroke a platitude until it purrs like an epigram. [*New York Sun*: 'The Sun Dial']

19 An idea isn't responsible for the people who believe in it.

20 Poetry is what Milton saw when he went blind.

21 If you want to get rich from writing, write the sort of thing that's read by persons who move their lips when reading to themselves. [In *Writer's Quotation Book*, ed. James Charlton]

SIR NEVILLE MARRINER 1924–

22 Only really very tall conductors can deal adequately with slow music. [In the *Listener*, 14 Mar. 1985]

MOORE MARRIOTT 1885–1949

23 Next train's gone! [In film *Oh, Mr Porter!*, screenplay by J. O. C. Orton, Val Guest and Marriott Edgar, 1938]

SIR EDWARD MARSH 1874–1953

24 Why is it that the sudden mention of an aunt is so deflating to a poem? [*Ambrosia and Small Beer*, Ch. 5]

25 If you call Le Gallienne a minor poet you

might just as well call a street lamp a minor planet. [Letter. In Christopher Hassall, *Edward Marsh*, Ch. 6]

1 He told me his object in life is to influence people for good, but he can't make up his mind whether to spread out his influence thin over 'millions' or give it in strong doses to a small circle of intimates. [In 7]

2 Dear Roger Fry whom I love as a man but detest as a movement. [In 11]

3 Praise of one's friends is always more unmixed pleasure than of oneself, because there isn't the slightest discomfort of doubting inwardly whether it is deserved. [Letter to Henry James, Spring 1915]

ARTHUR MARSHALL 1910–1989

4 It's all part of life's rich pageant. [Monologue *The Games Mistress*, on gramophone record, 1937]

SYBIL MARSHALL 1913–

5 Education must have an end in view, for it is not an end in itself. [*An Experiment in Education*, Ch. 4]

VICE-PRESIDENT T. R. MARSHALL 1854–1925

6 What this country needs is a really good five-cent cigar. [Supposedly said to Henry M. Rose. In the *New York Tribune*, 4 Jan. 1920]

DEAN MARTIN 1917–

7 You're not drunk if you can lie on the floor without holding on. [In Paul Dickson, *Official Rules*]

KINGSLEY MARTIN 1897–1969

8 I should always prefer influence to power. [*Father Figures*. See also 240:4, 366:1]

9 Wherever you go, the weather is, without exception, exceptional. [Quoted by Katharine Whitehorn in the *Observer*, 26 June 1988]

STEVE MARTIN

10 Talking about music is like dancing about architecture. [In the *Independent*]

HOLT MARVELL *see under* MASCHWITZ, ERIC

CHICO MARX 1891–1961

11 Mustard's no good without roast beef. [In film *Monkey Business*, script by S. J. Perelman, Will B. Johnstone and Arthur Sheekman]

12 You can't fool me, there ain't no Sanity Clause. [In film *A Night at the Opera*, script by George S. Kaufman, M. Ryskind and A. Boasberg]

13 [When caught by his wife, kissing a chorus girl] I wasn't kissing her, I was whispering in her mouth. [In Groucho Marx and R. J. Anobile, *Marx Brothers Scrapbook*, Ch. 24]

GROUCHO MARX 1895–1977

14 Didn't I tell you not to go over Australia? / Didn't I tell you Australia was up? [In film *Animal Crackers*, script by Bert Kalmar]

15 What's a thousand dollars? Mere chicken feed. A poultry matter. [In film *The Cocoanuts*, script by George S. Kaufman and M. Ryskind]

16 JUDY: May I have one of your pictures? GROUCHO: Why . . . I haven't got one. I could give you my foot prints, but they're upstairs in my socks. [In film *A Day at the Races*, screenplay by Robert Pirosh, George Seaton and George Oppenheimer]

17 [Feeling patient's pulse] Either he's dead, or my watch has stopped.

18 [On throwing his watch into the handbasin before carrying out an operation] Better rusty than missin'.

19 Send two dozen roses to Room 424 and put 'Emily. I love you' on the back of the bill.

20 [Putting his arms around Emily] If I hold you any closer, I'll be in back of you.

21 Emily, I've a little confession to make. I really am a horse doctor. But marry me, and I'll never look at any other horse.

22 If you can't leave in a taxi you can leave in a huff. If that's too soon, you can leave in a minute and a huff. [In film *Duck Soup*, script by Bert Kalmar, Harry Ruby, Arthur Sheekman and Nat Perrin]

1 You know you haven't stopped talking since I came here? You must have been vaccinated with a phonograph needle.

2 Dig trenches? With our men being killed off like flies? There isn't time to dig trenches. We'll have to buy them ready made.

3 Remember, men, we're fighting for this woman's honour; which is probably more than she ever did.

4 In my day a college widow stood for something. She stood for plenty. [In film *Horse Feathers*, script by Bert Kalmar, Harry Ruby, S. J. Perelman and Will B. Johnstone]

5 I'll bet your father spent the first year of your life throwing rocks at the stork. [In film *The Marx Brothers at the Circus*, script by Irving Brecher]

6 Do you suppose I could buy back my introduction to you? [In film *Monkey Business*, script by S. J. Perelman, Will B. Johnstone and Arthur Sheekman]

7 LUCILLE: ... But from the time he got the marriage licence I've led a dog's life.
GROUCHO: Are you sure he didn't get a dog's licence?

8 I've worked myself up from nothing to a state of extreme poverty.

9 Be back next Thursday and bring a specimen of your money.

10 He's an uncle on my father's side. And if he's on my father's side, I'll fight on my mother's. [In radio show *Flywheel, Shyster and Flywheel*, 1933, scripts ed. Michael Barson]

11 Please accept my resignation. I don't want to belong to any club that will accept me as a member. [*Groucho and Me*, Ch. 26]

12 I only cite these annoyances to show you that it isn't necessary to have relatives in Kansas City to be unhappy. [Letter to Goodman Ace, 18 Jan. 1951, *The Groucho Letters*]

13 They say a man is as old as the woman he feels. In that case I'm eighty-five. [*The Secret Word is Groucho*]

14 I've been around so long I can remember Doris Day before she was a virgin. [In Leslie Halliwell *Filmgoer's Book of Quotes*. Also ascr. to Oscar Levant]

15 Any man who says he can see through a woman is missing a lot. [In P. and J. Holton, *Quote and Unquote*]

16 I didn't like the play, but then I saw it under adverse conditions – the curtain was up. [In Laurence J. Peter, *Peter's Quotations*]

17 I was so long writing my review that I never got around to reading the book.

18 Military intelligence is a contradiction in terms. [In A. Spiegelman and B. Schneider, *Whole Grains*. See also 315:10]

19 I never forget a face, but I'll make an exception in your case. [In the *Guardian*, 18 June 1965. See also 363:10]

20 She got her good looks from her father – he's a plastic surgeon. [In *New Woman*, Apr. 1989]

21 Since my daughter is only half-Jewish, could she go in the water up to her knees? [When excluded from a smart Californian beach club on racial grounds. In obituary by Philip French in the *Observer*, 21 Aug. 1977]

22 Time wounds all heels. [In the *Sunday Telegraph*, 21 Aug. 1977]

23 No, Groucho is not my real name. I'm breaking it in for a friend. [Attr.]

JAN MASARYK 1886–1948

24 The trouble with bridges is that in peace-time the horses crap all over them – and when war comes they're the first things to be blown up. [On Czechoslovakia being described as a bridge. In the *New Statesman*, 10 Feb. 1981]

ERIC MASCHWITZ 1901–1969

25 A Nightingale Sang in Berkeley Square. [Title of song]

26 These Foolish Things Remind Me of You. [Title of song, 1936, under pseudonym Holt Marvell, music by Jack Strachey]

JOHN MASEFIELD 1878–1967

27 Coming in solemn beauty like slow old tunes of Spain. [*Beauty*]

28 Best trust the happy moments. What they gave / Makes man less fearful of the certain grave, / And gives his work

compassion and new eyes. / The days that make us happy make us wise. [*Biography*]

1 Oh some are fond of Spanish wine, and some are fond of French. [*Captain Stratton's Fancy*]

2 Quinquireme of Nineveh from distant Ophir / Rowing home to haven in sunny Palestine, / With a cargo of ivory, / And apes and peacocks, / Sandalwood, cedarwood and sweet white wine. [*Cargoes*]

3 Dirty British coaster with a salt-caked smoke stack, / Butting through the Channel in the mad March days, / With a cargo of Tyne coal, / Road-rail, pig-lead, / Firewood, iron-ware, and cheap tin-trays.

4 Out into street I ran uproarious, / The devil dancing in me glorious. [*The Everlasting Mercy*]

5 I did not shrink, I did not strive, / The deep peace burnt my me alive.

6 Laugh and be merry, remember, better the world with a song. / Better the world with a blow in the teeth of a wrong. [*Laugh and be Merry*]

7 What am I, Life? A thing of watery salt / Held in cohesion by unresting cells, / Which work they know not why, which never halt, / Myself unwitting where their master dwells? [*Lollingdon Downs*, Sonnet 37]

8 From the Gallows Hill to the Tineton Copse / There were ten ploughed fields, like ten full-stops. [*Reynard the Fox*]

9 One road leads to London, / One road runs to Wales, / My road leads me seawards / To the white dipping sails. [*Roadways*]

10 I must down to the seas again, to the lonely sea and the sky, / And all I ask is a tall ship and a star to steer her by, / And the wheel's kick and the wind's song and the white sail's shaking. / And a grey mist on the sea's face and a grey dawn breaking. [*Sea Fever*]

11 I must down to the sea again, for the call of the running tide / is a wild call and a clear call that may not be denied.

12 I must down to the seas again, to the vagrant gypsy life, / To the gull's way and the whale's way where the wind's like a whetted knife; / And all I ask is a merry yarn from a laughing fellow-rover, / And quiet sleep and a sweet dream when the long trick's over.

13 Life's battle is a conquest for the strong; / The meaning shows in the defeated thing. [*The 'Wanderer'*]

14 It's a warm wind, the west wind, full of birds' cries. [*The West Wind*]

15 In those days, as a little child, I was living in Paradise, and had no need of the arts, that at best are only a shadow of Paradise. [*So Long to Learn*]

JACKIE MASON 1931–

16 I have enough money to last me the rest of my life unless I buy something. [*Jackie Mason's America*]

17 England is the only country where food is more dangerous than sex. [*The World According to Me*]

18 If an Englishman gets run down by a truck he apologizes to the truck. [In the *Observer*, 'Sayings of the Week', 23 Sept. 1990]

19 I did spend the night with my manager, who is also my wife and has all my money. I am the first guy who ever got married for his own money. [In the *Weekend Guardian*, 23–4 Nov. 1991]

LORD [formerly ROY] MASON 1924–

20 I went underground as a miner at 14 and worked 14 years in a seam which was 1 foot 10 inches high. Even the mice were bow-legged. [Maiden speech in House of Lords, Nov. 1987]

WALT MASON 1862–1939

21 He's the Man Who Delivers the Goods. [*The Man Who Delivers the Goods*]

JOHN MASTERS 1914–1983

22 Join a Highland regiment, me boy. The kilt is an unrivalled garment for fornication and diarrhoea. [Quoting a major of Highlanders. In *Bugles and a Tiger*]

GEORGE MATHEW

1 We cannot help the birds of sadness flying over our heads, / But we need not let them build their nests in our hair. [Alleged Chinese saying. In James Agate, *Ego 1*, 1933]

AIDAN MATHEWS 1956–

2 Cheerfulness is a quiet condition; glee, on the other hand, is only desperation on a good day. [*Lipstick on the Host*, title story]

3 Men who call women ladies generally treat them as maids.

TOM MATHEWS 1925–

4 Why did you keep me on tiptoe so long if you weren't going to kiss me? [When Henry Luce eventually decided against a British edition of *Time*. In the *Observer*, 19 May 1963]

MELISSA MATHISON 1950–

5 ET phone home. [In film *ET: The Extra-terrestrial*]

HENRI MATISSE 1869–1954

6 I don't know whether I believe in God or not. I think, really, I'm some kind of Buddhist. But the essential thing is to put oneself in a frame of mind which is close to that of prayer. [In Françoise Gilot and Carlton Lake, *Life with Picasso*, Pt 6]

7 Exactitude is not truth. [Essay title. In *Matisse on Art*, ed. J. D. Flam]

8 [When questioned about the afterlife at the age of 80] I wouldn't mind turning into a vermilion goldfish. [In *Simpson's Contemporary Quotations*]

9 One can't live in a house kept by country aunts. One has to go off into the jungle to find simpler ways which don't stifle the spirit. [In the *Observer*, 7 Oct. 1984]

10 Whoever devotes himself to painting should begin by cutting out his own tongue. [In the *Independent*, 2 Oct. 1991]

MTUTUZELI MATSHOBA

11 Police stations were like toilets, as they are to all blacks here [in South Africa, more particularly Soweto]. [*Call Me Not a Man*, Autobiographical Note]

WALTER MATTHAU 1920–

12 Poker exemplifies the worst aspects of capitalism that have made our country so great. [In *Business Quotations*, comp. Rolf White]

BRANDER MATTHEWS 1852–1929

13 A gentleman need not know Latin, but he should at least have forgotten it. [Advice to Dr Joseph Shipley]

VICTOR MATURE 1915–

14 I don't want to be gummed to death. [Of the toothless animal in film *Androcles and the Lion*. Quoted by Angela Carter in the *Guardian*, 19 Aug. 1988]

REGINALD MAUDLING 1917–1977

15 There comes a time in every man's life when he must make way for an older man. [In Smoking Room of House of Commons on being dropped from Mrs Thatcher's Shadow Cabinet. In the *Guardian*, 20 Nov. 1976]

16 Britain has lost its pride but retained its conceit. [In Peter Madgwick *et al.*, *Britain since 1945*, Ch. 1]

W. SOMERSET MAUGHAM 1874–1965

17 You know, of course, that the Tasmanians, who never committed adultery, are now extinct. [*The Bread-winner*, III]

18 I don't think you want too much sincerity in society. It would be like an iron girder in a house of cards. [*The Circle*, Act I]

19 A woman will always sacrifice herself if you give her the opportunity. It is her favourite form of self-indulgence. [III]

20 When married people don't get on they can separate, but if they're not married it's impossible. It's a tie that only death can sever.

21 It's not the seven deadly virtues that make a man a good husband, but the three

hundred pleasing amiabilities. [*The Constant Wife*, Act I]

1 It's only if a man's a gentleman that he won't hesitate to do an ungentlemanly thing. Mortimer is on the boundary line and it makes him careful. [II]

2 The only places John likes on the Continent are those in which it's only by an effort of the imagination that you can tell you're not in England. [III]

3 We have long passed the Victorian Era when asterisks were followed after a certain interval by a baby. [See also 411:19]

4 JOHN: Do you think I can't be a lover as well as a husband?
CONSTANCE: My dear, no one can make yesterday's cold mutton into tomorrow's lamb cutlets.

5 The degree of a nation's civilization is marked by its disregard for the necessities of existence. [*Our Betters*, I]

6 It was such a lovely day I thought it was a pity to get up. [II]

7 My dear, she's been my greatest friend for fifteen years, I know her through and through, and I tell you that she hasn't got a single redeeming quality. [III]

8 Hypocrisy is the most difficult and nerve-racking vice that any man can pursue; it needs an unceasing vigilance and a rare detachment of spirit. It cannot, like adultery or gluttony, be practised at spare moments; it is a whole time job. [*Cakes and Ale*, Ch. 1]

9 Poor Henry [James], he's spending eternity wandering round and round a stately park and the fence is just too high for him to peep over and they're having tea just too far away for him to hear what the Countess is saying. [9]

10 'But I can do nothing unless I am in complete possession of the facts.' 'Obviously you can't cook them unless you have them.'

11 From the earliest times the old have rubbed it into the young that they are wiser than they, and before the young had discovered what nonsense this was they were old too, and it profited them to carry on the imposture.

12 I forget who it was that recommended men for their soul's good to do each day two things they disliked ... it is a precept that I have followed scrupulously; for every day I have got up and I have gone to bed. [*The Moon and Sixpence*, Ch. 1]

13 Impropriety is the soul of wit. [4]

14 It is not true that suffering ennobles the character; happiness does that sometimes, but suffering, for the most part, makes men petty and vindictive. [17]

15 A woman can forgive a man for the harm he does her ... but she can never forgive him for the sacrifices he makes on her account. [41]

16 Like all weak men he laid an exaggerated stress on not changing one's mind. [*Of Human Bondage*, Ch. 37]

17 People ask you for criticism, but they only want praise. [50]

18 Money is like a sixth sense, without which you cannot make a complete use of the other five. [51. See also 248:13]

19 For to write good prose is an affair of good manners. It is, unlike verse, a civil art ... Poetry is baroque. [*The Summing Up*, Ch. 12]

20 Most people have a furious itch to talk about themselves and are restrained only by the disinclination of others to listen. Reserve is an artificial quality that is developed in most of us as the result of innumerable rebuffs. [19]

21 I would sooner read a time-table or a catalogue than nothing at all ... They are much more entertaining than half the novels that are written. [25]

22 I'll give you my opinion of the human race in a nutshell ... Their heart's in the right place, but their head is a thoroughly inefficient organ. [55]

23 The artist's egoism is outrageous; it must be; he is by nature a solipsist and the world exists only for him to exercise upon it his powers of creation. [61]

24 Casting my mind's eye over the whole of fiction, the only absolutely original creation I can think of is Don Quixote. [*10 Novels and their Authors*, Ch. 1, sect. i]

25 Music-hall songs provide the dull with

wit, just as proverbs provide them with wisdom. [*A Writer's Notebook*, 1892]

1 Men have an extraordinarily erroneous opinion of their position in nature; and the error is ineradicable. [1896]

2 There are times when I look over the various parts of my character with perplexity. I recognize that I am made up of several persons and that the person that at the moment has the upper hand will inevitably give place to another. But which is the real one? All of them or none?

3 American women expect to find in their husbands a perfection that English women only hope to find in their butlers.

4 The highest activities of consciousness have their origins in physical occurrences of the brain just as the loveliest melodies are not too sublime to be expressed by notes. [1902]

5 I can't think of a single Russian novel in which one of the characters goes to a picture gallery. [1917]

6 Sentimentality is only sentiment that rubs you up the wrong way. [1941. See also 154:15]

7 I've always been interested in people, but I've never liked them. [In the *Observer*, 'Sayings of the Week', 28 Aug. 1949]

8 I am sick of this way of life. The weariness and sadness of old age make it intolerable. I have walked with death in hand, and death's own hand is warmer than my own. I don't wish to live any longer. [Remarks to the press on his 90th birthday. In M. B. Strauss, *Family Medical Quotations*]

BILL MAULDIN 1921–

9 'He's right, Joe, when we ain't fightin' we should act like sojers.' [*Up Front*, cartoon caption]

ANDRÉ MAUROIS 1885–1967

10 In England there is only silence or scandal. [Attr.]

JAMES MAXTON 1885–1946

11 If my friend cannot ride two horses –

what's he doing in the bloody circus? [On the political difficulties of straddling the Independent Labour Party and Labour Party, at Scottish ILP Conference, Jan. 1931. In G. McAllister, *James Maxton*]

12 Sit down, man. You're a bloody tragedy. [To Ramsay MacDonald on the occasion of the last speech he made in House of Commons. Attr.]

ELAINE MAY 1947–

13 I like a moral issue so much more than a real issue. [Quoted by Gore Vidal in the *New Statesman*, 4 May 1973]

VLADIMIR MAYAKOVSKY 1893–1930

14 Oh for just / one / more conference / regarding the eradication of all conferences! [*In re Conferences*, trans. Herbert Marshall]

15 Always to shine, / and everywhere to shine, / and, to the very last, / to shine, – / thus runs / my motto / and the sun's. [*A Most Extraordinary Adventure*]

16 Our planet / is poorly equipped / for delight / One must snatch / gladness / from the days that are. / In this life / it's not difficult to die. / To make life / is more difficult by far. [*Sergei Yessenin*]

17 Art is not a mirror to reflect the world, but a hammer with which to shape it. [In the *Guardian*, 11 Dec. 1974]

LOUIS B. MAYER 1885–1957

18 The number one book of the ages was written by a committee, and it was called The Bible. [To writers who complained of changes made to their work. In Leslie Halliwell, *Filmgoer's Book of Quotes*]

19 Throw the little old lady down the stairs! Throw the mother's good, home-made chicken soup in the mother's face! *Step* on the mother! *Kick* her! That is *art*, they say. Art! [In Lillian Ross, *Picture*, 'Throw the Little Old Lady Down the Stairs!']

CHARLES H. MAYO 1865–1939

20 Specialist – a man who knows more and more about less and less. [In *Modern Hospital*, Sept. 1938, but he did not claim as his own. Elsewhere ascr. to Nicholas Butler]

HUGHES MEARNS 1875–1965

1 As I was going up the stair / I met a man who wasn't there. / He wasn't there again today. / I wish, I wish he'd go away. [*The Psycho-ed*]

SIR PETER MEDAWAR 1915–1987

2 No scientist is admired for failing in the attempt to solve problems that lie beyond his competence. The most he can hope for is the kindly contempt earned by the Utopian politician. If politics is the art of the possible, research is surely the art of the soluble. Both are immensely practical-minded affairs. [Review of Arthur Koestler's *Art of Creation* in the *New Statesman*, 19 June 1964; used in *The Art of the Soluble*, Introduction]

3 Scientific discovery is a private event, and the delight that accompanies it, or the despair of finding it illusory does not travel. [*Hypothesis and Imagination*]

4 There is no spiritual copyright in scientific discoveries, unless they should happen to be quite mistaken. Only in making a blunder does a scientist do something which, conceivably, no one might ever do again. [*Pluto's Republic*]

GITA MEHTA 1943–

5 We have all been buggered by the shuttle. Shuttle diplomacy. Shuttle religion. Shuttle fantasy. [*Karma Cola*, II. 7]

6 The art of dialling has replaced the art of dialogue. [VIII. 2]

GOLDA MEIR 1898–1978

7 Pessimism is a luxury that a Jew never can allow himself. [In the *Observer*, 'Sayings of the Year', 29 Dec. 1974]

8 I don't know whether Sadat and Begin deserve the Nobel Prize, but they both deserve Oscars. [Of the Camp David Agreement. Said in 1977, recalled in the *Guardian*, 19 Nov. 1987, on the 10th anniversary of the initiative]

ANDREW MELLON 1855–1937

9 A nation is not in danger of financial disaster merely because it owes itself money. [Said in 1933. In the *Observer*, 'Sayings of Our Times', 31 May 1953]

THOMAS MELLOR 1880–1926

10 I Wouldn't Leave My Little Wooden Hut for You. [Title of song]

H. L. MENCKEN 1880–1956

11 I can't remember a single masculine figure created by a woman who is not, at bottom, a booby. [*In Defence of Women*, Ch. 1, sect. i]

12 We must respect the other fellow's religion, but only in the sense and to the extent that we respect his theory that his wife is beautiful and his children smart. [Notebooks, *Minority Report*, 1]

13 Men always try to make virtues of their weaknesses. Fear of death and fear of life become piety. [54]

14 It is now quite lawful for a Catholic woman to avoid pregnancy by a resort to mathematics, though she is still forbidden to resort to physics and chemistry. [62]

15 The capacity of human beings to bore one another seems to be vastly greater than that of any other animals. Some of their most esteemed inventions have no other apparent purpose, for example, the dinner party of more than two, the epic poem, and the science of metaphysics. [67]

16 Men are the only animals who devote themselves assiduously to making one another unhappy. It is, I suppose, one of their godlike qualities. Jahweh, as the Old Testament shows, spends a large part of His time trying to ruin the business and comfort of all other gods. [93]

17 War will never cease until babies begin to come into the world with larger cerebrums and smaller adrenal glands. [164]

18 A nun, at best, is only half a woman, just as a priest is only half a man. [221]

19 Whenever one comes to close grips with so-called idealism, as in war time, one is shocked by its rascality. [223]

20 Why assume so glibly that the God who presumably created the universe is still run-

ning it? It is certainly perfectly conceivable that He may have finished it and then turned it over to lesser gods to operate. [298]

1 The chief contribution of Protestantism to human thought is its massive proof that God is a bore. [309]

2 Science, at bottom, is really anti-intellectual. It always distrusts pure reason, and demands the production of objective fact. [412]

3 The great artists of the world are never Puritans, and seldom even ordinarily respectable. [*Prejudices*, First Series, 16]

4 To sum up: 1. The cosmos is a gigantic fly-wheel making 10,000 revolutions a minute. 2. Man is a sick fly taking a dizzy ride on it. 3. Religion is the theory that the wheel was designed and set spinning to give him the ride. [*Prejudices*, Third Series, 'Ad Imaginem dei creavit illum', Coda]

5 Poetry is a comforting piece of fiction set to more or less lascivious music. ['The Poet and his Art']

6 Faith may be defined briefly as an illogical belief in the occurrence of the improbable. ['Types of Men']

7 He [the businessman] is the only man who is for ever apologizing for his occupation.

8 The man who boasts that he habitually tells the truth is simply a man with no respect for it. It is not a thing to be thrown about loosely, like small change; it is something to be cherished and hoarded, and disbursed only when absolutely necessary.

9 Every man sees in his relatives, and especially in his cousins, a series of grotesque caricatures of himself.

10 No healthy male ever really thinks or talks of anything save himself. [*Prejudices*, Fourth Series, 'Reflections on Monogamy', 8]

11 No man is genuinely happy, married, who has to drink worse gin than he used to drink when he was single. [14]

12 I've made it a rule never to drink by daylight and never to refuse a drink after dark. [In the *New York Post*, 18 Sept. 1945]

13 Opera in English, is, in the main, just

about as sensible as baseball in Italian. [In Frank Muir, *Frank Muir Book*]

14 The chief value of money lies in the fact that one lives in a world in which it is over-estimated. [Attr.]

PIERRE MENDÈS-FRANCE 1907–1982

15 To govern is to choose. [Attr.]

KARL MENNINGER 1893–1990

16 Illness is in part what the world has done to a victim, but in a larger part it is what the victim has done with his world, and with himself. [Quoted in Susan Sontag, *Illness as Metaphor*, Ch. 6]

SIR YEHUDI [later LORD] MENUHIN 1916–

17 Music creates order out of chaos; for rhythm imposes unanimity upon the divergent, melody imposes continuity upon the disjointed, and harmony imposes compatibility upon the incongruous. [Quoted by Anthony Storr in the *Sunday Times*, 10 Oct. 1976]

18 Holding a violin is like holding a young bird. It is vibrating under your touch and you must hold it without squeezing it ... It is a good thing to cultivate the feeling of those sympathetic vibrations in dealing with people. [In the *Daily Mail*, 15 Mar. 1977]

DAVID MERCER 1928–1980

19 What is an audience to an actor, after all, but a vast tit? [TV play *On the Eve of Publication*]

JOHNNY MERCER 1909–1976

20 Ma Moma done tol' me, / When I was in knee pants. [Song: *Blues in the Night*]

21 Days of wine and roses laugh and run away, / Like a child at play. [Song: *Days of Wine and Roses*]

22 I'm an old cow-hand / From the Rio Grande. [Song: *I'm an Old Cow-hand*]

22 Jeepers Creepers – where you get them peepers? [Song: *Jeepers Creepers*]

24 Strange as a will-o'-the-wisp, / Crazy as

a loon, / Sad as a gypsy, / Serenading the moon. [Song: *Skylark*]

1 That old black magic has me in its spell. [Song: *That Old Black Magic*]

2 You must have been a beautiful baby, / 'Cos baby just look at you now. [Song: *You Must Have Been a Beautiful Baby*]

VIVIAN MERCIER 1919–1989

3 Godot is a play in which nothing happens – twice. [Review of text of *Waiting for Godot*, in the *Irish Times*, 18 Feb. 1956]

ETHEL MERMAN 1908–1984

4 She's OK if you like talent. [Of fellow-actress Mary Martin. In *Hammer and Tongues*, ed. Michèle Brown and Ann O'Connor, 'Acting']

BOB MERRILL 1890–1977

5 How Much is That Doggie in the Window? [Title of song]

6 People who need people are the luckiest people in the world. [Song: *People Who Need People*, in musical *Funny Girl*]

DIXON MERRITT 1879–1972

7 A wonderful bird is the pelican, / His bill will hold more than his belican. / He can take in his beak / Enough food for a week, / But I'm darned if I know how the helican. [*The Pelican*]

E. H. W. MEYERSTEIN 1889–1952

8 It [the last movement of Beethoven's Ninth Symphony] is the song of the angels sung by earth spirits. [Letter to his mother, 21 Oct. 1908]

9 It is pre-Whitman, and therefore pre-Pound and pre-Eliot, but not prepossessing. [Describing poem by Clough, to R. N. Green-Armitage, 2 Sept. 1940]

SIR FRANCIS MEYNELL 1891–1975

10 So conscious he how short time was / For all he planned to do within it / He nothing did at all, alas, / Save note the hour – and file the minute. [*For a Functionary*]

11 What woman has this old cat's graces? / What boy can sing as the thrush sings? [*Man and Beast*]

JAMES MICHIE 1889–1952

12 Up in the heavenly saloon / Sheriff sun and rustler moon / Gamble, stuck in the sheriff's mouth / The fag end of an afternoon. [*Arizona Nature Myth*]

BETTE MIDLER 1945–

13 When it's three o'clock in New York, it's still 1938 in London. [From *The Times*, 1978, in *Penguin Dictionary of Modern Humorous Quotations*, comp. Fred Metcalf]

14 People say that I have it all, and I have to say: 'Well, could I give just a little bit of it back?' Because I've really had enough. [In *New Woman*, July 1989]

15 The worst part of having success is to try finding someone who is happy for you. [Attr. in *Penguin Dictionary of Modern Humorous Quotations*, comp. Fred Metcalf]

LUDWIG MIES VAN DER ROHE 1886–1969

16 Less is more. [In the *New York Herald Tribune*, 28 June 1959]

GEORGE MIKES 1912–1987

17 The Swiss managed to build a lovely country around their hotels. [*Down with Everybody*]

18 Continental people have sex life; the English have hot-water bottles. [*How to be an Alien*]

19 The trouble with tea is that originally it was quite a good drink.

20 In England it is bad manners to be clever, to assert something confidently. It may be your personal view that two and two make four, but you must not state it in a self-assured way, because this is a democratic country and others may be of a different opinion.

21 To employ an English charwoman is a compromise between having a dirty house and cleaning it yourself.

22 It was twenty-one years ago that Eng-

land and I first set foot on each other. I came for a fortnight; I have stayed ever since. [*How to be Inimitable*]

1 The one class you do *not* belong to and are not proud of at all is the lower-middle class. No one ever describes himself as belonging to the lower-middle class.

2 When you go to New York you notice that you need two hands to open a letter box while you fly a plane with one hand. [In the *International Herald Tribune*, 24–5 Apr. 1982]

GENERAL MILLÁN ASTRAY Y TERREROS 1879–1954

3 Long live death! Down with intelligence! [Slogan in Spanish Civil War. In Hugh Thomas, *The Spanish Civil War*, 42]

EDNA ST VINCENT MILLAY 1892–1950

4 Euclid alone / Has looked on Beauty bare, Fortunate they / Who, though once only and then but far away, / Have heard her massive sandal set on stone. [*Euclid alone has looked on Beauty bare*]

5 I came upon no wine / So wonderful as thirst. [*Feast*]

6 My candle burns at both ends; / It will not last the night; / But, ah, my foes, and oh, my friends – / It gives a lovely light. [*A Few Figs from Thistles*, 'First Fig']

7 Safe upon solid rock the ugly houses stand: / Come and see my shining palace built upon the sand. ['Second Fig']

8 Blessed be death that cuts in marble / What would have sunk in dust. [*Keen*]

9 Who builds her a house with love for timber, / Builds her a house of foam; And I'd rather be bride to a lad gone down / Than widow to one safe home.

10 And if I loved you Wednesday, / Well what is that to you? / I do not love you Thursday – / So much is true. [*Thursday*]

11 It is not true that life is one damn thing after another – it is one damn thing over and over. [Capping Elbert Hubbard; see 180:20. Letter to A. D. Fiske, 24 Oct. 1930, *Letters of Edna St Vincent Millay*]

ALICE DUER MILLER 1874–1942

12 In a world where England is finished and dead; / I do not wish to live. [*The White Cliffs*]

ARTHUR MILLER 1915–

13 The word 'now' is like a bomb through the window, and it ticks. [*After the Fall*, Act 1]

14 A suicide kills two people, Maggie, that's what it's for! [II]

15 All organization is and must be grounded on the idea of exclusion and prohibition just as two objects cannot occupy the same space. [*The Crucible*, Act I]

16 There are many who stay away from church these days because you hardly ever mention God any more.

17 I have not moved from there to there without I think to please you, and still an everlasting funeral marches round your heart. [II]

18 Oh, Elizabeth, your justice would freeze beer!

19 He's liked, but he's not well liked. [*Death of a Salesman*, Act I]

20 The world is an oyster, but you don't crack it open on a mattress.

21 Never fight fair with a stranger, boy. You'll never get out of the jungle that way.

22 I still feel – kind of temporary about myself.

23 Willy Loman never made a lot of money. His name was never in the paper. He's not the finest character that ever lived. But he's a human being, and a terrible thing is happening to him. So attention must be paid.

24 A small man can be just as exhausted as a great man.

25 Everybody likes a kidder, but nobody lends him money.

26 He's a man way out there in the blue, riding on a smile and a shoeshine. And when they start not smiling back – that's an earthquake . . . A salesman is got to dream, boy. It comes with the territory. [II, 'Death Requiem']

27 Years ago a person, he was unhappy, didn't know what to do with himself – he'd go to church, start a revolution – *something.* Today you're unhappy? Can't figure it out? What is the salvation? Go shopping. [*The Price*, Act I]

1 The time comes when you realize that you haven't merely been specializing in something – something has been specializing in you. [2]

2 A man comes into a great hotel and says, I am a messenger. Who is this man? He disappears walking, there is no noise, nothing. Maybe he will never come back, maybe he will never deliver the message. But a man who rides up on a great machine, this man exists. He will be given messages. [*A View from the Bridge*, Act I]

3 A good newspaper, I suppose, is a nation talking to itself. [In the *Observer*, 'Sayings of the Week', 26 Nov. 1961]

4 Why should I go [to Marilyn Monroe's funeral]? She won't be there. [Attr.]

HENRY MILLER 1891–1980

5 The world does seem to become one, however much its component elements may resist. Indeed, the stronger the resistance the more certain is the outcome. *We resist only what is inevitable.* [*Big Sur and the Oranges of Hieronymus Bosch*]

6 Sex is one of the nine reasons for reincarnation . . . The other eight are unimportant.

7 All my good reading, you might say, was done in the toilet . . . There are passages of *Ulysses* which can be read only in the toilet – if one wants to extract the full flavour of their content. [*Black Spring*, 'Paris and Its Suburbs']

8 Though I've never read a line of Homer I believe the Greek of today is essentially unchanged. If anything he is more Greek than he ever was. [*The Colossus of Maroussi*, Ch. 1]

9 Every man with a belly full of the classics is an enemy of the human race. [*Tropic of Cancer*, 'Dijon']

JONATHAN MILLER 1934–

10 I'm not really a Jew; just Jew-ish, not the whole hog. [*Beyond the Fringe*]

11 They do those little personal things people sometimes do when they think they are alone in railway carriages; things like smelling their own armpits.

12 The human body is private property. We have to have a search warrant to look inside, and even then an investigator is confined to a few experimental tappings here and there, some gropings on the party wall, a torch flashed rather hesitantly into some of the dark corners. [From BBC TV programme *The Body in Question*, 'Perishable Goods', in the *Listener*, 15 Feb. 1979]

13 There is such relish in England for anything that doesn't succeed. [Interview in the *Sunday Times*, 4 Dec. 1988]

MAX MILLER 1895–1963

14 That's what I like about you, you're quick, aren't you? [Running gag in variety act]

15 I like the girls who do, / I like the girls who don't; / I hate the girl who says she will / And then she says she won't. / But the girl that I like best of all / And I think you'll say I'm right – / Is the one who says she never has / But looks as though she . . . / 'Ere listen . . . [From song: *The Girls Who Do*, in *The Max Miller Blue Book*]

SPIKE MILLIGAN 1918–

16 It was Battery Sergeant-Major 'Jumbo' Day. His hair was so shorn his neck seemed to go straight up the back of his hat. [*Adolf Hitler: My Part in His Downfall*, 'I Join the Regiment']

17 Some people are always late, like the late King George V. [*The Bald Twit Lion*]

18 A baby Sardine / Saw her first submarine: / She was scared and watched through a peephole. / 'Oh, come, come, come,' / Said the Sardine's mum, / 'It's only a tin full of people.' [*A Book of Milliganimals*, 'Sardines']

19 I said to the First Officer, 'Gad, that sun's hot,' to which he replied, 'Well, you shouldn't touch it.' [*A Dustbin of Milligan*, 'Letters to Harry Secombe', I]

20 I shook hands with a friendly Arab . . . I still have my right hand to prove it.

1 He told me he had the sea in his blood, and believe me you can see where it gets in. [II]

2 What a beautiful morning it's been out on deck ... Only on the third class tourist class passengers' deck was it a sultry overcast dull morning, but then if you do things on the cheap you must expect these things.

3 By Midday in Colombo, the heat is so unbearable that the streets are empty save for thousands of Englishmen taking mad dogs for walks. [III]

4 Nowadays, the old prison has been turned into a first-class hotel with a service that any Michelin guide would be only too pleased to condemn. [V]

5 He walked with a pronounced limp. L-I-M-P, pronounced 'limp'. ['The Great Man']

6 I thought I saw Jesus on a tram. / I said 'Are you Jesus?' / He said 'Yes I am.' [*Open Heart University*]

7 Painful though it was, / I cut my last winter rose for her. / She turned it inside out / To see who the manufacturer was. ['Trust']

8 His thoughts, few that they were, lay silent in the privacy of his head. [*Puckoon*, Ch. 1]

9 Tank heaven the ground broke me fall. [2]

10 I'm a hero wid coward's legs, I'm a hero from the waist up.

11 When she saw the sign 'Members only' she thought of him. [3]

12 Money can't buy friends, but you can get a better class of enemy. [6]

13 A thousand hairy savages / Sitting down for lunch / Gobble gobble glup glup / Munch munch munch. [*Silly Verse for Kids*]

14 'Do you come here often?'
'Only in the mating season.' [Running gag in BBC radio comedy series *The Goon Show*, 1950s]

15 You silly twisted boy!

16 I'm walking backwards for Christmas.

17 The dreaded lergy.

18 It's all in the mind, you know.

19 He's fallen in the water.

20 PETER SELLERS: In South America.
HARRY SECOMBE: That's abroad, isn't it?
SELLERS: It all depends on where you're standing. [*The Goon Show*, 'The Affair of the Lone Banana']

21 Not so loud, you fool – remember – even people have ears. ['The Marie Celeste']

22 SECOMBE: Gad, Bloodnok, I admire your guts.
BLOODNOK: What, are they showing? [Variations in other instalments]

23 MORIARTY: How are you at Mathematics?
SECOMBE: I speak it like a native. ['Dishonoured']

24 BLUEBOTTLE: Enter Bluebottle – where's the sausiges? [Also other instalments]

25 BLUEBOTTLE: What do you want, my Capitain – as if I didn't know! ['The Great Bank of England Robbery', and repeated elsewhere]

26 Are you going to come quietly, or do I have to use earplugs? ['The Great Mustard and Cress Shortage']

27 Contraceptives should be used on every conceivable occasion. [*The Last Goon Show of All*]

28 And then the monsoons came, and they couldn't have come at a worse time, bang in the middle of the rainy season. [In the *Telegraph Sunday Magazine*, 26 June 1977]

29 We [the Goons] were a crowd of idiots existing as idiots together and doing things like climbing Mount Everest from the inside. [Interview in the *Observer Magazine*, 17 Apr. 1988]

30 One day the don't-knows will get in, and then where will we be? [On results of a pre-election poll. Attr.]

31 Don't you think it's going to be rather wet for the horses? [On having the Boat Race course described to him. Attr.]

SPIKE MILLIGAN and ERIC SYKES
1923–

32 A floor so cunningly laid that no matter where you stood it was always under your feet. [BBC radio comedy series *The Goon Show*, 'The China Story']

1 To conserve energy we marched lying down and only stood up to sleep. ['The Siege of Fort Night']

2 It's only 80 miles as the crow flies – and our crow is a sick man.

A. J. MILLS 1872–? and BENNETT SCOTT

3 All the Nice Girls Love a Sailor. [Title of song, 1909]

A. J. MILLS and HARRY CASTLING

4 Just Like the Ivy I'll Cling to You. [Title of song, 1903]

A. J. MILLS, FRED GODFREY and BENNETT SCOTT

5 Take me back to dear old Blighty, / Put me on the train to London Town. [Song: *Take me back to Dear Old Blighty*, 1917]

A. A. MILNE 1882–1956

6 They're changing guard at Buckingham Palace – / Christopher Robin went down with Alice. / Alice is marrying one of the guard. / 'A soldier's life is terrible hard,' / Says Alice. [*When We Were Very Young*, 'Buckingham Palace']

7 James James / Morrison Morrison / Weatherby George Dupree / Took great / Care of his Mother / Though he was only three. ['Disobedience']

8 You must never go down to the end of the town if you don't go down with me.

9 John had / Great Big / Waterproof / Boots on; / John had a / Great Big / Waterproof / Hat; / John had a / Great Big / Waterproof / Mackintosh – / And that / (Said John) / Is / That. ['Happiness']

10 The King asked / The Queen, and / The Queen asked / The Dairymaid: / 'Could we have some butter for / The Royal slice of bread?' ['The King's Breakfast']

11 Nobody, my darling, could call me / A fussy man – / BUT / I do like a little bit of butter to my bread!

12 And some of the bigger bears try to pretend / That they came round the corner to look for a friend; / And they'll try to pretend that nobody cares / Whether you walk on the lines or the squares. ['Lines and Squares']

13 Hush! Hush! Whisper who dares! / Christopher Robin is saying his prayers! ['Vespers']

14 If the English language had been properly organized ... then there would be a word which meant both 'he' and 'she', and I could write, 'If John or May comes, heesh will want to play tennis,' which would save a lot of trouble. [*The Christopher Robin Birthday Book*]

15 And nobody knows / (Tiddely pom), / How cold my toes / (Tiddely pom), / How cold my toes / (Tiddely pom), / Are growing. [*House at Pooh Corner*, Ch. 1]

16 Tiggers don't like honey. [2]

17 'Well, I sort of made it up,' said Pooh ... 'it comes to me sometimes.' 'Ah!' said Rabbit, who never let things come to him, but always went and fetched them. [5]

18 He respects Owl, because you can't help respecting anybody who can spell TUESDAY, even if he doesn't spell it right.

19 When you are a Bear of Very Little Brain, and you Think of Things, you find sometimes that a Thing which seemed very Thingish inside you is quite different when it gets out into the open and has other people looking at it. [6]

20 For one person who dreams of making fifty thousand pounds, a hundred people dream of being left fifty thousand pounds. [*If I May*, 'The Future']

21 I wrote somewhere once that the third rate mind was only happy when it was thinking with the majority, the second rate mind was only happy when it was thinking with the minority, and the first rate mind was only happy when it was thinking. [*War with Honour*]

22 Isn't it funny / How a bear likes honey? / Buzz! Buzz! Buzz! / I wonder why he does? [*Winnie-the-Pooh*, Ch. 1]

23 How sweet to be a Cloud / Floating in the Blue!

24 When Rabbit said, 'Honey or condensed

milk with your bread?' he was so excited that he said, 'Both,' and then, so as not to seem greedy, he added, 'But don't bother about the bread, please.' [2]

1 I am a Bear of Very Little Brain and long words Bother Me. [4]

2 I have decided to catch a Heffalump. [5]

3 I'm giving him a Useful Pot to Keep Things In. [6]

4 'Pathetic,' he said. 'That's what it is. Pathetic.'

5 Time for a little something.

6 Kanga and Baby Roo. [7]

7 On Monday, when the sun is hot, / I wonder to myself a lot: / 'Now is it true, or is it not, / That what is which and which is what?'

8 An Expotition to the North Pole. [8, heading]

EWART MILNE ?–1987

9 I ween it is between those twain / That once is seen: that twice is not seen! [*Once More to Tourney*, 'Grandmer's Busy Day']

LORD MILNER 1854–1925

10 If we believe a thing to be bad, and if we have a right to prevent it, it is our duty to try to prevent it and to damn the consequences. [Speech in Glasgow, 26 Nov. 1909]

CZESLAW MILOSZ 1911–

11 Those who harm simple / people and who laugh at their / injuries will not be safe. / For the poet remembers. [Inscription at the martyrs' monument, Gdansk shipyard, Poland]

12 In the West people make free with words like 'freedom' and 'the spirit' but few ever think to ask a man whether he has enough money for lunch. [*Visions from San Francisco Bay*]

CARDINAL JÓZSEF MINDSZENTY 1892–1975

13 The singing bird forgets its cage. [In the *Observer*, 5 May 1991]

DR S. MINTZ 1922–

14 What do you experience with your first mouthful of hot fudge sundae? It's not surprising that we carry it over to describe the intensity of love and sex. [In the *Weekend Guardian*, 29–30 Dec. 1990]

ADRIAN MITCHELL 1932–

15 The man who believes in giraffes would swallow anything. [*Loose Leaf Poem*]

16 A sinking pool for learning to drown.

17 He gets the odd villain. / A couple of revolutionaries / Whose graves keep catching fire / But mostly they're a decent mob, the dead. [*Please Keep off the Dead*]

18 It's hard to see Christ for priests. That happens when / A poet engenders generations of advertising men. [*Quite Apart from the Holy Ghost*]

19 Most people ignore most poetry because most poetry ignores most people. [*Poems*, 'Introduction']

20 Poetry is an extra hand. It can caress or tickle. It can clench and fight. The hand is hot. Take it or leave it. ['Poetry Lives', *Sunday Times*, 13 Feb. 1972]

ARTHUR MITCHELL ?1926–

21 We must avoid duplication of effort, because that is being done by others. [On retiring as President of the Machine Tool Technology Association. In the *Independent*, 3 Mar. 1990]

AUSTIN MITCHELL, MP 1934–

22 In modern Britain forward-looking politicians spend much of their time looking back. [In the *Guardian*, 15 Apr. 1983]

23 Barristers may be gentlemen trying to be lawyers, and solicitors are lawyers trying to be gentlemen. But . . . neither is very good at either. [6 June 1990]

JONI MITCHELL 1945–

24 They paved paradise / And put up a parking lot. [Song: *Big Yellow Taxi*]

25 I've looked at life from both sides now / From win and lose and still somehow / It's

life's illusions I recall / I really don't know life at all. [Song: *Both Sides Now*]

1 My old man / He's a singer in the park / He's a walker in the rain / He's a dancer in the dark. [Song: *My Old Man*]

2 But when he's gone / Me and them lonesome blues collide. / The bed's too big. / The frying pan's too wide.

JULIAN MITCHELL 1935–

3 At Oxford he had been deliberately Byronic, and the Don Juan attitude was still there in emergencies. An enemy had once told him to his face that he needed more buckle and less swash. [*As Far as You Can Go*, Pt 1, Ch. 2]

4 It has been said that a careful reading of *Anna Karenina*, if it teaches you nothing else, will teach you how to make strawberry jam. [In *Radio Times*, 30 Oct. 1976]

SUSAN LANGSTAFF MITCHELL 1866–1926

5 Some men kiss and do not tell, some kiss and tell; but George Moore told and did not kiss. [In O. St John Gogarty, *As I Was Going Down Sackville Street*, Ch. 5]

ROBERT MITCHUM 1917–

6 The only thing wrong with performing was that you couldn't phone it in. [Quoted by Robert Robinson in the *Sunday Times Magazine*, 11 May 1980]

7 Marry me, and you'll be farting through silk. [When proposing to his future wife. Ascr. in interview in the *Guardian*, 23 June 1984]

JESSICA MITFORD 1917–

8 I have nothing against undertakers personally. It's just that I wouldn't want one to bury my sister. [Attr. in *Saturday Review*, 1 Feb. 1964]

NANCY MITFORD 1904–1973

9 All the heat there was seemed to concentrate in the Hons' cupboard, which was always stifling. Here we would sit, huddled up on the slatted shelves, and talk for hours about life and death. [*The Pursuit of Love*, Ch. 2]

10 Aunt Sadie ... so much disliked hearing about health that people often took her for a Christian Scientist, which, indeed, she might have become had she not disliked hearing about religion even more. [4]

11 I have only read one book in my life, and that is *White Fang*. It's so frightfully good I've never bothered to read another.

12 English women are elegant until they are ten years old, and perfect on grand occasions. [In L. and M. Cowan, *The Wit of Women*]

13 I love children – especially when they cry and somebody takes them away. [In *Dictionary of Outrageous Quotations*, comp. C. R. S. Marsden]

DIMITRI MITROPOULOS 1896–1960

14 I never used a score when conducting my orchestra ... Does a lion tamer enter a cage with a book on how to tame a lion? [Said in 22 Jan. 1951. In Nat Shapiro, *Encyclopedia of Quotations about Music*]

PRESIDENT FRANÇOIS MITTERRAND 1916–

15 Nonetheless, I am wary of globe-trotters: true knowledge is sedentary. [*The Wheat and the Chaff*]

16 Mere ability is not sufficient to explain great destinies: the last yards are run alone. [Of Henry Kissinger]

17 One day Mrs Thatcher comes to me and says Britain is under-developed, and 48 hours later she is reminding me that Britain is a world power. [In the *Observer*, 'Sayings of the Week', 29 Nov. 1987]

18 She [Margaret Thatcher] has the mouth of Marilyn Monroe and the eyes of Caligula. [In Denis Healey, *The Time of My Life*, Ch. 23]

19 We are part of the continent of Europe, not just a balcony overlooking the Atlantic. [In *Libération*, Nov. 1988]

WILSON MIZNER 1876–1933

20 Be nice to people on your way up be-

cause you'll meet 'em on your way down. [In A. Johnston, *The Legendary Mizners*, Ch. 4. Also attr. to Jimmy Durante]

1 If you steal from one author it's plagiarism. If you steal from many it's research.

2 A trip through a sewer in a glass-bottomed boat. [Of Hollywood. See also 390:8]

3 Working for Warner Bros is like fucking a porcupine: it's a hundred pricks against one. [In David Niven, *Bring on the Empty Horses*, 'Degrees of Friendliness']

4 A fellow who is always declaring he's no fool usually has his suspicions. [In A. Andrews, *Quotations for Speakers and Writers*]

GENERAL EMILIO MOLA 1887–1937

5 We have four columns advancing on Madrid. The fifth column will arise at the proper time. [Radio speech, Oct. 1936]

CLAUS MOLLER [Danish management guru]

6 I have 25 years' experience equals I have one year's experience, and it is 24 years old. [In BBC TV programme *Business Matters*, 11 Apr. 1988. See also 68:5]

V. M. MOLOTOV 1890–1986

7 The British Outer Mongolia. [Of the House of Lords. In the *Listener*, 17/24 Dec. 1987. See also 35:17]

GENERAL SIR JOHN MONASH 1865–1931

8 I don't care a damn for your loyal service when you think I am right; when I really want it most is when you think I am *wrong*. [Attr. in Colin MacInnes, *England, Half English*, 'Joshua Reborn']

COSMO MONKHOUSE 1840–1901

9 There was an old party of Lyme, / Who married three wives at one time, / When asked, 'Why the third?' / He replied, 'One's absurd, / And bigamy, sir, is a crime!' [Limerick]

JEAN MONNET 1888–1979

10 He [Jean Monnet] liked to divide politicians into those who want to *be someone* and those who want to *do something*. [Lord (Roy) Jenkins, in the *Observer*, 25 Nov. 1990, in reference to Margaret Thatcher, who 'outstandingly' belonged to the second category]

HAROLD MONRO 1879–1932

11 When the tea is brought at five o'clock, / And all the neat curtains are drawn with care, / The little black cat with bright green eyes / Is suddenly purring there. [*Milk for the Cat*]

12 The white saucer like some full moon descends / At last from the clouds of the table above.

13 That star-enchanted song falls through the air / From lawn to lawn down terraces of sound, / Darts in white arrows on the shadowed ground; / While all the night you sing. [*The Nightingale near the House*]

MARILYN MONROE 1926–1962

14 JOURNALIST: Didn't you have anything on?
MONROE: I had the radio on. [Of photograph in calendar. In *Time* magazine, 11 Aug. 1952]

15 Isn't there any other part of a matzo you can eat? [On having matzo balls for dinner for the third time at Arthur Miller's parents. Quoted by Sir Laurence Olivier in BBC TV programme]

THOMAS L. MONSON

16 Our very business in life is not to get ahead of others, but to get ahead of ourselves. [Attr.]

C. E. MONTAGUE 1867–1928

17 War hath no fury like a non-combatant. [*Disenchantment*, Ch. 16]

18 A gifted small girl has explained that pins are a great means of saving life, 'by . . . not swallowing them'. [*Dramatic Values*]

19 I was born below par to th' extent of two whiskies. [*Fiery Particles*]

EUGENIO MONTALE 1896–1981

20 Parody is just originality in a second-hand suit. [In the *Listener*, 7 June 1990]

FIELD-MARSHAL [later VISCOUNT] MONTGOMERY 1887–1976

21 This sort of thing may be tolerated by

the French, but we are British – thank God. [On Homosexuality Bill, in House of Lords, 24 May 1965]

L. M. MONTGOMERY 1874–1942

1 People who haven't red hair don't know what trouble is. [*Anne of Green Gables*, Ch. 7]

MONTY PYTHON'S FLYING CIRCUS 1969–1974

2 [Ferndean School Report on God] Progress and conduct: I am afraid that I am severely disappointed in God's works. All three of Him have shown no tendency to improve and He merely sits at the back of the class talking to himself. He has shown no interest in Rugger, asked to be excused Prayers, and moves in a mysterious way. [*The Brand New Monty Python Book*]

3 I'm a lumberjack / And I'm OK / I sleep all night / And I work all day. [*Monty Python's Big Red Book*]

4 It's not pining, it's passed on. This parrot is no more. It's ceased to be. It's expired. It's gone to meet its maker. This is a late parrot. It's a stiff. Bereft of life it rests in peace. It would be pushing up the daisies if you hadn't nailed it to the perch. It's rung down the curtain and joined the choir invisible. It's an ex-parrot. [BBC TV comedy series, programme of 14 Dec. 1969]

5 Nudge, nudge, wink, wink. Know what I mean? [Running gag in series, with variants]

6 And now for something completely different.

7 In your report here, it says that you are an appallingly dull person. Our experts describe you as an appallingly dull fellow, unimaginative, timid, spineless, easily dominated, no sense of humour, tedious company and irresistibly drab and awful. And whereas in most professions these would be considered drawbacks, in accountancy they are a positive boon. [In film *And Now for Something Completely Different*]

DORIS LANGLEY MOORE 1902–1989

8 The Churches grow old but do not grow up. [*The Vulgar Heart*, Ch. 2]

GEORGE MOORE 1852–1933

9 All reformers are bachelors. [*The Bending of the Bough*, I]

10 A man travels the world over in search of what he needs and returns home to find it. [*The Brook Kerith*, Ch. 11]

11 Acting is therefore the lowest of the arts, if it is an art at all. [*Mummer-worship*]

12 I had to keep you waiting till the strain of composition had worn off my face. [In O. St John Gogarty, *As I Was Going Down Sackville Street*, Ch. 17]

13 To be aristocratic in Art one must avoid polite society. [In Cyril Connolly, *Enemies of Promise*, Ch. 15]

GERALD MOORE 1899–1987

14 Am I Too Loud? [Title of autobiography]

MARIANNE MOORE 1887–1972

15 Openly, yes, / with the naturalness / of the hippopotamus or the alligator / when it climbs out on the bank to / experience the / sun, I do these / things which I do, which please / no one but myself. [*Black Earth*]

16 My father used to say, / 'Superior people never make long visits.' [*Silence*]

17 Nor was he insincere in saying, 'Make my house / your inn.' / Inns are not residences.

18 If 'compression is the first grace of style,' / you have it. [*To a Snail*]

19 Any writer overwhelmingly honest about pleasing himself is almost sure to please others. [In *Writer's Quotation Book*, ed. James Charlton]

T. STURGE MOORE 1870–1944

20 Two buttocks of one bum. [Of Belloc and Chesterton. In Stephen Potter, *The Sense of Humour*, Ch. 1]

POP MORAND

21 Keeping Up With the Joneses. [Title of cartoon strip which first appeared in 1914 and ran till 1958]

ALBERTO MORAVIA 1907–1990

1 The ratio of literacy to illiteracy is constant, but nowadays the illiterates can read and write. [Quoted by Mary McCarthy in the *Observer*, 14 Oct. 1979]

ERIC MORECAMBE 1926–1984 and
ERNIE WISE 1925–

2 Q: What do you think of the show so far? A: Rubbish. [Running gag in TV show *The Morecambe and Wise Show*, scripts by Eddie Braben]

3 Short, fat, hairy legs.

4 Well, there's no answer to that.

CHRISTIAN MORGENSTERN 1871–1914

5 *Ein Knie geht einsam durch die Welt. Es ist ein Knie, sonst nichts.* – There wanders through the world a knee, / A knee and nothing more. [*Galgenlieder, 'Das Knie'*, trans. R. F. C. Hull]

6 *Im Winkel König Fahrenheit / hat still sein Mus gegessen / – 'Ach Gott, sie war doch schön, die Zeit, / da man nach mir gemessen!'* – In the corner King Fahrenheit / quietly ate his pap. / 'Oh God, those were fine times / when they measured by me.' [*Kronprätendenten'*]

7 *Es war einmal ein Lattenzaun, / mit Zwischenraum, hindurchzuschaun. / Ein Architekt, der dieses sah, / stand eines Abends plötzlich da – / und nahm den Zwischenraum heraus / und baute draus ein grosses Haus.* – There was a fence with spaces you / Could look through if you wanted to. / An architect who saw this thing / Stood there one summer evening, / Took out the spaces with great care / And built a castle in the air. [*'Der Lattenzaun'*]

8 *Es gibt ein Gespenst / das frisst Taschentücher; / es begleitet dich / auf deiner Reise.* – There is a ghost / That eats handkerchiefs; / It keeps you company / On all your travels. [*'Gespenst'*]

9 *Palmström baut sich eine Geruchs-Orgel / und spielt darauf v. Korfs Nieswurz-Sonate.* – Palmström builds himself a Smell-organ / and plays von Korf's sneeze-wort [hellebore] sonata on it. [*'Die Geruchs-Orgel'*]

10 *Zwar ein Werk, wie allerwärts, / doch zugleich ein Werk – mit Herz.* – Though clockwork in its outward part / It hides within – a tender heart.

11 *Und er kommt zu dem Ergebnis: / 'Nur ein Traum war das Erlebnis. / Weil,' so schliesst er messerscharf, / 'nicht sein kann, was nicht sein darf.'* – And so he comes to the conclusion / The whole affair was an illusion. / 'For look,' he cries triumphantly, / 'What's not permitted CANNOT be!' [*'Die unmögliche Tatsache'*]

CHRISTOPHER MORLEY 1890–1957

12 Why do they put the Gideon Bibles only in the bedrooms [of hotels], where it's usually too late? And not in the bar-room downstairs? [*Contribution to a Contribution*]

13 A human being: an ingenious assembly of portable plumbing. [*Human Being*, Ch. 11. See also 106:12]

14 There are three ingredients in the good life: learning, earning and yearning. [*Parnassus on Wheels*, Ch. 10]

15 Life is a foreign language: all men mispronounce it. [*Thunder on the Left*, Ch. 14]

16 Prophets were twice stoned – first in anger; then, after their death, with a handsome slab in the graveyard. [*Where the Blue Begins*, Ch. 11]

17 My theology, briefly, is that the universe was dictated but not signed. [In A. Andrews, *Quotations for Speakers and Writers*]

ROBERT MORLEY 1908–1992

18 The British tourist is always happy abroad so long as the natives are waiters. [In the *Observer*, 'Sayings of the Week', 20 Apr. 1958]

19 Beware of the conversationalist who adds 'in other words'. He is merely starting afresh. [6 Dec. 1964]

20 What have I done to achieve longevity? Woken up each morning and tried to remember not to wear my hearing aid in the bath. [In *London Review of Books*, 20 Mar. 1986]

21 France has for centuries blocked our way to Europe. Before the invention of the aeroplane we had to step over it to get anywhere.

[In *Apt and Amusing Quotations*, ed. G. F. Lamb, 'France']

1 No man is lonely while eating spaghetti. [In Jonathon Green, *Consuming Passions*]

J. E. MORPURGO 1918–

2 Austria is Switzerland, speaking pure German and with history added. [*The Road to Athens*]

DESMOND MORRIS 1918–

3 There are one hundred and ninety-three living species of monkeys and apes. One hundred and ninety-two of them are covered with hair. The exception is a naked ape self-named *Homo sapiens*. [*The Naked Ape*, Introduction]

4 He [*Homo sapiens*] is proud that he has the biggest brain of all the primates, but attempts to conceal the fact that he also has the biggest penis.

5 Clearly, then, the city is not a concrete jungle, it is a human zoo. [*The Human Zoo*, Introduction]

JAMES [later JAN] MORRIS 1926–

6 The master illusion of Spain is the conviction that the Spaniards are a people different, when they are only a people separate. [*The Presence of Spain*]

JIM MORRISON 1943–1971

7 The old get old, the young get stronger, / They've got the guns but we got the numbers. [Song: *Five to One*]

TONI MORRISON 1931–

8 In this country American means white. Everybody else has to hyphenate. [In the *Observer*, 'Sayings of the Week', 2 Feb. 1992. See also 323:9, 406:22]

[STEVEN] MORRISSEY 1959–

9 The kind people have a wonderful dream / Margaret on the guillotine / because people like you make me feel so tired / when will you die? [Song: *Margaret on the Guillotine*]

JOHN MORTIMER 1923–

10 Farce is a form of drama which seems to me often more true to the facts of life as we know them than many great tragedies. [*Clinging to the Wreckage*]

11 He [James Anderton] had the look of deep and complacent satisfaction which men assume when they speak of having been beaten in childhood. [*In Character*]

12 Matrimony and murder both carry a mandatory life sentence. [*Rumpole for the Defence*, 'Rumpole and the Boat People']

13 Most of what's most interesting in life goes on below the belt. [*Summer's Lease*, Ch. 9]

14 Eddy was a tremendously tolerant person, but he wouldn't put up with the Welsh. He always said, surely there's enough English to go round. [*Two Stars for Comfort*, Act I, sc. ii]

15 When I was a boy at school I never minded the lessons. I just resented having to work terribly hard at playing. [*A Voyage round My Father*, Act I]

16 No brilliance is needed in the law. Nothing but common sense, and relatively clean finger nails.

17 The immortality of the soul! What a boring conception! Can't think of anything worse than living for infinity in a great transcendental hotel, with nothing to do in the evenings. [II]

18 That deep mistrust of the English upper classes which can best be learned at Harrow. [In the *Sunday Times Magazine*, 31 Aug. 1986]

19 The shelf life of the modern hard-back author is somewhere between the milk and the yoghurt. [When opening the Antiquarian Book Fair, London, 23 June 1987]

20 Hell must be a place where you are only allowed to read what you agree with. [On the furore over Salman Rushdie's *Satanic Verses*. In the *Sunday Times Books*, 5 Mar. 1989]

21 American is the language in which people say what they mean as Italian is the language in which they say what they feel. English is the language in which what a character means or feels has to be deduced from what he or she says, which may be quite the opposite. [In the *Mail on Sunday*, 26 Mar.]

22 Green and true blue are colours which

don't, unfortunately, mix. [In the *Guardian*, 8 Mar. 1990]

J. B. MORTON ['BEACHCOMBER']
1893–1979

1 A Mrs Tasker is accused of continually ringing the doorbell of a Mrs Renton, and then, when the door is opened, pushing a dozen red-bearded dwarfs into the hall and leaving them there. [*The Best of Beachcomber*, ed. Michael Frayn, 1, 'The Case of the Twelve Red-bearded Dwarfs']

2 The Doctor is said to have invented an extraordinary weapon which will make war less brutal. It is described as a very powerful liquid which rots braces at a distance of a mile. [5, 'Bracerot']

3 He [Dr Smart-Allick of Narkover] said it was not always the timid fellow, with four conventional aces in his hand, who won the highest honours. 'It is often,' he said, 'the fifth ace that makes all the difference between success and failure.' [8, 'The Drama at Badger's Earth']

4 She has a Rolls body and a Balham mind. [9, 'A Foul Innuendo']

5 KEEPING THEIR END UP
Not many of our old families can boast that a Savile Row tailor calls four times a year at their country estate to measure the scarecrows in the fields for new suits.

6 Behind every beetle you will find a good mother-beetle. [10, 'Open Letter to Sir James Barrie']

7 I shall never forget my mother's horror and my father's cry of joy when, for the first time in my life, I said angrily to my father, 'That's not the hand I dealt you, Dad.' [11, 'The Life and Times of Captain de Courcy Foulenough']

8 To fairy flutes, / As the light advances, / In square black boots / The cabman dances. [12, 'The Saga of the Saucy Mrs Flobster: The Dancing Cabman']

9 SIXTY HORSES WEDGED IN A CHIMNEY
The story to fit this sensational headline has not turned up yet. [13, 'Mr Justice Cocklecarrot: Home Life']

10 'Does it occur to you,' asked a voice, 'that the absence of a dead body from a room does not necessarily prove that someone is dead? Your dead body is not in the kitchen, but you are not dead.' [15, 'Dead Man's Alibi']

11 Last night Cocklecarrot exclaimed, with his customary lucidity, that if a cow with handlebars is a bicycle, within the meaning of the Act, then a bicycle with four legs instead of two wheels is a cow. [17, 'If so be That']

12 Dr Strabismus (Whom God Preserve) of Utrecht is carrying out research work with a view to crossing salmon with mosquitoes. He says it will mean a bite every time for fishermen. [*By the Way*, Jan., Tail-piece]

13 I used to be able to shoot the rind off an apple stored in a loft at the top of a cast-iron lighthouse. [13 Aug., 'On the Moors: Social Jottings']

14 One disadvantage of being a hog is that at any moment some blundering fool may try to make a silk purse out of your wife's ear. [Sept., Tail-piece]

15 Hush, hush, / Nobody cares! / Christopher Robin / Has / Fallen / Down- / Stairs. [18 Dec., 'Now We are Sick']

16 Iron Nostril Balzarotti, the man who tried to stuff the Severn Tunnel with sage and onions. [*Beachcomber: The Works of J. B. Morton*, ed. Richard Ingrams]

17 ROLAND MILK, the limp-wristed poet: Before I die I want to do something big and clean in the world.
LADY CABSTANLEIGH: Go and wash an elephant.

18 Gone to that country from whose Bourne no Hollingsworth returns. [*Gallimaufry*, 'Another True Story']

19 The English are very fond of humour, but they are afraid of wit. For wit is like a sword, but humour is like a jester's bladder. [From the *Spectator*, in the *Sunday Times*, 27 Sept. 1987]

20 Wagner is the Puccini of music. [Attr.]

ROGERS MORTON 1914–1979

21 I'm not going to rearrange the furniture on the deck of the Titanic. [Of President

Ford's campaign for re-election. In the *Washington Post*, 16 May 1976]

SIR CLAUS MOSER 1922–

1 Education costs money, but then so does ignorance. [Speech at British Association, Swansea, 20 Aug. 1990]

LEONARD MOSLEY 1913–

2 In parliamentary life, he [Curzon] was to be one who stayed to get his feet wet before deciding that a ship was sinking. [*The Glorious Fault*]

SIR OSWALD MOSLEY 1896–1980

3 'Can't' will be the epitaph of the British Empire – unless we wake up in time. [Speech at Manchester, 9 Dec. 1937]

4 The opponents of our people are the money lords and the press lords who control the old parties. Britain is now ruled by King Bunk and King Bank. [Speech, 5 Mar. 1956]

5 I am not, and never have been, a man of the right. My position was on the left and is now in the centre of politics. [Letter to *The Times*, 26 Apr. 1968]

HOWARD MOSS 1922–1987

6 There are no rocks / At Rockaway, / There are no sheep / At Sheepshead Bay, / There's nothing new / In Newfoundland, / And silent is / Long Island Sound. [*Geography: A Song*]

ROBERT MOTHERWELL 1915–1991

7 Perhaps – I say perhaps because I do not know how to reflect except by opening my mind like a glass-bottomed boat so that I can watch what is swimming below – painting becomes sublime when the artist transcends his personal anguish, when he projects in the midst of a shrieking world an expression of living and its end that is silent and ordered. [*A Tour of the Sublime (The Ides of Art)*, 'Tiger's Eye', 1 Dec. 1948]

8 Having a retrospective is making a will. [In F. O'Hara, *Robert Motherwell*]

ANDREW MOTION 1952–

9 I've never lost sight / of losing you now. [*A Dying Race*]

10 He [Seamus Heaney] does address one of the major themes, childhood, in a fabulous way. He puts the shine back on things that I did know once. [In the *Guardian*, 25 June 1987]

FERDINAND MOUNT 1939–

11 And while no doubt talent will find its own level, it remains true that the son-in-law also rises. [Of promotion in business. From the *Spectator*, in the *New Statesman*, 12 Oct. 1984]

LORD LOUIS MOUNTBATTEN 1900–1979

12 I say in all sincerity that the nuclear arms race has no military purpose. Wars cannot be fought with nuclear weapons. Their existence only adds to our perils because of the illusions which they have generated. [Speech at Strasbourg, 11 May 1979]

13 You've no idea what it costs to keep the old man [Mahatma Gandhi] in poverty. [In *Utterly Trivial Knowledge: The Pure Trivia Game*, ed. Margaret Hickey]

KITTY MUGGERIDGE ?1905–

14 He rose without trace. [Of David Frost. To Malcolm Muggeridge, mid-1960s]

MALCOLM MUGGERIDGE 1903–1990

15 An orgy looks particularly alluring seen through the mists of righteous indignation. [*The Most of Malcolm Muggeridge*, 'Dolce Vita in a Cold Climate']

16 The orgasm has replaced the Cross as the focus of longing and the image of fulfilment. ['Down with Sex']

17 Macmillan seemed, in his very person, to embody the national decay he supposed himself to be confuting. He exuded a flavour of moth-balls. [*Tread Softly for You Tread on My Jokes*, 'England, Whose England']

18 He [Anthony Eden] is not only a bore but he bores for England. ['Boring for England', reprinted in Edward Hyams, *Newstatesmanship*]

19 Never forget that only dead fish swim with the stream. [Reported as said to him in Manchester, *Radio Times*, 9 July 1964]

1 Writing about travels is nearly always tedious, travelling being, like war and fornication, exciting but not interesting. [Review of *Diaries of Evelyn Waugh* in the *Observer*, 5 Sept. 1976]

2 The fallacy of the liberal mind is to see good in everything. That has been of great assistance to the devil. [Interview in John Mortimer, *In Character*]

3 God seems to me to be an artist ... rather than a judge. He has created the drama, and the parts of the play that are wicked and dreadful may be necessary to the whole creation in a way we can't understand. Life is a drama and not a progress.

MUHAMMAD ALI *see* ALI, MUHAMMAD

EDWIN MUIR 1887–1959

4 It was not meant for human eyes, / That combat on the shabby patch / Of clods and trampled earth that lies / Somewhere beneath the sodden skies / For eye of toad or adder to catch. [*The Combat*]

5 We have seen / Good men made evil wrangling with the evil, / Straight minds grown crooked fighting crooked minds. / Our peace betrayed us; we betrayed our peace. / Look at it well. This was the good town once. [*The Good Town*]

6 Oh these deceits are strong almost as life, / Last night I dreamt I was in the labyrinth, / And woke far on. I did not know the place. [*The Labyrinth*]

7 There is a road that turning always / Cuts off the country of Again. / Archers stand there on every side / And as it runs Time's deer is slain, / And lies where it has lain. [*The Road*]

8 See him, the gentle Bible beast, / With lacquered hoofs and curling mane, / His wondering journey from the East / Half-done, between the rock and plain. [*The Toy Horse*]

9 The life of every man is an endlessly repeated performance of the life of man. [*An Autobiography*, Ch. 1]

FRANK MUIR 1920–

10 Dogs, like horses, are quadrupeds. That

is to say, they have four rupeds, one at each corner, on which they walk. [In Frank Muir and Denis Norden, *You Can't Have Your Kayak and Heat It*, 'Ta-ra-ra-boom-de-ay!']

11 It has been said that a bride's attitude towards her betrothed can be summed up in three words: Aisle. Altar. Hymn. [In Frank Muir and Denis Norden, *Upon My Word!*, 'A Jug of Wine', but perhaps of earlier origin]

12 I'd gone to the South of France for six months, to finish my latest book. I'm a very slow reader. [In foreword to Ronnie Barker, *It's Goodnight from Him*]

FRANK MUIR and DENIS NORDEN 1922–

13 Q: What are you – a sorcerer? A: Only at home. In company I drink out of the cup. [BBC radio comedy series *Take It from Here*, 1957, No. 216]

PAUL MULDOON 1951–

14 The mind's a razor / on the body's strop. [*Meeting the British*, 'The Soap-pig']

KEN MULLEN 1943–

15 Even if it's grim, we'll bare it. [Advertisement for *The Times*, from Leo Burnett Advertising Agency]

16 Our sages know their onions.

17 Prose without the con.

18 I'm very modest. I tend to hide my light under a peck. [In conversation]

HERBERT J. MULLER 1905–1980

19 Few have heard of Fra Luca Parioli, the inventor of double-entry book-keeping; but he has probably had much more influence on human life than has Dante or Michelangelo. [*The Uses of the Past*, Ch. 8]

BRIAN MULRONEY 1939–

20 I am not denying anything I didn't say. [In *Oxford Book of Canadian Political Anecdotes*]

LEWIS MUMFORD 1895–1990

21 If you fall in love with a machine there

is something wrong with your love life. If you worship a machine there is something wrong with your religion. [*Art and Technics*]

1 Every generation revolts against its fathers and makes friends with its grandfathers. [*The Brown Decades*, Ch. 1]

2 New York is the perfect model of a city, not the model of a perfect city. [*My Work and Days*]

3 Today, the notion of progress in a single line without goal or limit seems perhaps the most parochial notion of a very parochial century. [*Technics and Civilization*, Ch. 8, sect. xii]

4 In the city time becomes visible. [In L. L. Levinson, *Bartlett's Unusual Quotations*]

H. H. MUNRO *see* SAKI

DAME IRIS MURDOCH 1918–

5 In philosophy, if you aren't moving at a snail's pace you aren't moving at all. [(Socrates) *Acastos: Two Platonic Dialogues*]

6 All art deals with the absurd and aims at the simple. Good art speaks truth, indeed *is* truth, perhaps the only truth. [*The Black Prince*, 'Bradley Pearson's Foreword']

7 Writing is like getting married. One should never commit oneself until one is amazed at one's luck.

8 I think being a woman is like being Irish . . . Everyone says you're important and nice but you take second place all the same. [*The Red and the Green*]

9 'We aren't getting anywhere. You know that as well as I do.' 'One doesn't have to get anywhere in a marriage. It's not a public conveyance.' [*A Severed Head*, Ch. 3]

10 People will endlessly conceal from themselves that good is only good if one is good for nothing. The whole history of philosophy, the whole theology, is the act of concealment. [*The Time of the Angels*, Ch. 17]

11 Everything I write probably is *Hamlet* in disguise. [Interview in the *Guardian*, 15 Sept. 1980]

12 All art is full of magic and trickery, but in a novel the whole thing can subside into an ocean of reflection and continuous thought – at least in a traditional novel – whereas in theatre you are really jumping from place to place like a mountain goat. [Interview in the *Weekend Guardian*, 22–23 Apr. 1989]

RICHARD MURDOCH *see* KENNETH HORNE and RICHARD MURDOCH

RUPERT MURDOCH 1931–

13 The Third World never sold a newspaper. [In the *Observer*, 1 Jan. 1978]

C. W. MURPHY, WILL LETTERS, JOHN CHARLES MOORE and WILLIAM C. McKENNA

14 Has anybody here seen Kelly? / Kelly from the Isle of Man? [Song: *Has Anybody Here Seen Kelly?*, 1909, sung by Florrie Forde]

CAPTAIN ED MURPHY 1918–

15 If anything can go wrong it will. [Murphy's Law, various versions. Also ascr. to George Nichols. In P. Dickson, *The Official Rules*]

DAVID MURRAY 1888–1962

16 A reporter is a man who has renounced everything in life but the world, the flesh, and the devil. [In the *Observer*, 'Sayings of the Week', 5 July 1931]

FRED MURRAY ?–1922

17 Ginger, You're Barmy! [Title of song, 1912, sung by Harry Champion]

18 When she play'd for Mister Gee, / She could always find the key, / Tho' she'd never had a lesson in her life. [Song: *She'd Never Had a Lesson . . .*]

FRED MURRAY and GEORGE EVERARD

19 And it's all right in the summer time, / In the summer time it's lovely! / While my old man's painting hard, / I'm posing in the old back yard. / But oh, oh! In the wintertime / It's another thing you know, / With a

little red nose, / And very little clothes, / And the stormy winds do blow. [Song: *It's All Right in the Summer Time*]

FRED MURRAY and R. P. WESTON
?–1936

1 I'm Henery the Eighth, I am ... I got married to the widder next door. / She's been married seven times before, / Hevery one was a Henery, / She wouldn't have a Willy or a Sam. [Song: *I'm Henery the Eighth*, 1911, sung by Harry Champion]

SIR GILBERT MURRAY 1866–1957

2 Experience dulls the edges of all our dogmas. [Attr.]

LES A. MURRAY 1938–

3 Where two or three / are gathered together, that / is about enough. [*Company*]

EDWARD R. MURROW 1908–1965

4 This – is London. [First words in broadcasts to USA from London, 1938–45]

5 He [Winston Churchill] mobilized the English language and sent it into battle to steady his fellow countrymen and hearten those Europeans upon whom the long dark night of tyranny had descended. [Broadcast, 30 Nov. 1954]

ROBERT MUSIL 1880–1942

6 Progress would be wonderful – if only it would stop. [Attr.]

BENITO MUSSOLINI 1883–1945

7 CURZON: What is your foreign programme?
MUSSOLINI: My foreign policy is 'Nothing for Nothing'. [In George Seldes, *Sawdust Caesar*, Ch. 12]

8 Fascism is not an article for export. [German press report, 1932. In Ch. 24]

9 I should be pleased, I suppose, that Hitler has carried out a revolution on our lines. But they are Germans. So they will end by ruining our idea. [In Christopher Hibbert, *Benito Mussolini*, Pt II, Ch. 1]

10 Believe! Obey! Fight! [Fascist slogan]

11 The Italians will laugh at me; every time Hitler occupies a country he sends me a message. [Remark to Ciano. In Alan Bullock, *Hitler*, Pt VIII, 12]

12 We cannot change our policy now. After all, we are not political whores.

13 Live every day as if it was your last, but think as if you will live for ever. [In address by Gianfranco Fini, the Italian neo-Fascist leader, at the funeral of two Fascist veterans, Rome, 24 May 1988]

N

VLADIMIR NABOKOV 1899–1977

1 All hygienes have their hyenas. [*The Enchanter*, p. 22]

2 There are aphorisms that, like airplanes, stay up only while they are in motion. [*The Gift*, Ch. 1]

3 Lolita, light of my life, fire of my loins. My sin, my soul, Lo-lee-ta: the tip of the tongue taking a trip of three steps down the palate to tap, at three, on the teeth. Lo. Lee. Ta. [*Lolita*, opening sentences]

4 I am sufficiently proud of my knowing something to be modest about my not knowing all.

5 As to the rest, I am no more guilty of imitating 'real life' than 'real life' is responsible for plagiarizing me. [*Nabokov's Dozen*, Bibliographical Note]

6 Like so many ageing college people, Pnin had long ceased to notice the existence of students on the campus. [*Pnin*, Ch. 3, sect. vi]

7 Discussion in class, which means letting twenty young blockheads and two cocky neurotics discuss something that neither their teacher nor they know. [6. x]

8 Poor Knight! he really had two periods, the first – a dull man writing broken English, the second – a broken man writing dull English. [*The Real Life of Sebastian Knight*, Ch. 1]

9 I think like a genius, I write like a distinguished author, and I speak like a child. [*Strong Opinions*, Foreword]

10 [When asked if he believed in God] I know more than I can express in words, and the little I can express would not have been expressed, had I not known more. [Ch. 3]

11 Satire is a lesson, parody is a game. [6]

12 One of those 'Two Cultures' is really nothing but utilitarian technology; the other is B-grade novels, ideological fiction, popular art. Who cares if there exists a gap between such 'physics' and such 'humanities'? Those Eggheads are terrible Philistines. A real good head is not oval but round.

13 A good laugh is the best pesticide. [9]

14 A novelist is, like all mortals, more fully at home on the surface of the present than in the ooze of the past. [20]

15 Actually I always loathed the Viennese quack. I used to stalk him down dark alleys of thought, and now we shall never forget the sight of old, flustered Freud seeking to unlock his door with the point of his umbrella. [TV Interview. In the *Listener*, 24 Mar. 1977]

SHIVA NAIPAUL 1945–1985

16 Too much thinking, in my opinion, is not becoming to Toryism. It ought not to be encouraged. Thought is a Socialist temptation, not a Tory one. [In the *Spectator*, 28 May 1983]

V. S. [later SIR VIDIA] NAIPAUL 1932–

17 He said that he had learnt to trample on the past. In the beginning it had been like trampling on a garden; later it had been like walking on ground. [*Bend in the River*, Ch. 8]

1 I'm a lucky man. I carry the world within me. You see, Salim, in this world beggars are the only people who can be choosers. Everyone else has his side chosen for him. [9]

2 'But the man is a BA!' 'And LLB. I know, I wouldn't trust an Aryan with my great-grandmother.' [*A House for Mr Biswas*, Ch. 3]

3 They say there's good and bad everywhere. There's no good and bad here. They're just Africans. [*In a Free State*, Ch. 6]

IAN NAIRN 1930–1983

4 Subtopia. [Title of article in *Architectural Review*, June 1955]

SIR LEWIS NAMIER 1888–1960

5 One would expect people to remember the past and to imagine the future. But in fact ... they imagine ... [history] in terms of their own experience, and when trying to gauge the future they cite supposed analogies from the past: till, by a double process of repetition, they imagine the past and remember the future. [From *Conflicts*, pp. 69–70, in John Kenyon, *The History Men*]

FRIDTJOF NANSEN 1861–1930

6 The difficult is what takes a little time; the impossible is what takes a little longer. [Also attr. to others. Variant form was motto placarded at South-East Asia HQ in 1939–45 War. See also 394:17]

R. K. NARAYAN 1906–

7 The saying is that Madras is hot for ten months of the year and hotter for two. [*The Bachelor of Arts*, Ch. 7]

OGDEN NASH 1902–1971

8 A bit of talcum / Is always walcum. [*The Baby*]

9 Oh, what a tangled web do parents weave / When they think that their children are naïve. [*Baby, What Makes the Sky Blue?*]

10 The camel has a single hump; / The dromedary two; / Or else the other way around. / I'm never sure. Are you? [*The Camel*]

11 The song of canaries / Never varies, / And when they're moulting / They're pretty revolting. [*The Canary*]

12 The cow is of the bovine ilk; / One end is moo, the other, milk. [*The Cow*]

13 One would be in less danger / From the wiles of the stranger / If one's own kin and kith / Were more fun to be with. [*Family Court*]

14 God in His wisdom made the fly / And then forgot to tell us why. [*The Fly*]

15 Women would rather be right than reasonable. [*Frailty, Thy Name is a Misnomer*]

16 Another difference between me and Samuel Taylor Coleridge is more massive in design: / People used to interrupt him while he was dreaming his dreams, but they interrupt me while I am recounting mine. [*I Can Hardly Wait for the Sandman*]

17 Who wants my jellyfish? / I'm not sellyfish. [*The Jellyfish*]

18 The trouble with a kitten is / THAT / Eventually it becomes a / CAT. [*The Kitten*]

19 Beneath this slab / John Brown is stowed. / He watched the ads, / And not the road. [*Lather as You Go*]

20 Do you think my mind is maturing late, / Or simply rotted early? [*Lines on Facing Forty*]

21 Do you know my friend Mr Betts? / I wish I could remember as accurately as he forgets. [*Mr Betts's Mind a Kingdom Is*]

22 Tell me, O Octopus, I begs, / Is those things arms, or is they legs? / I marvel at thee, Octopus; / If I were thou, I'd call me Us. [*The Octopus*]

23 Children aren't happy with nothing to ignore, / And that's what parents were created for. [*The Parent*]

24 Middle-aged life is merry, and I love to lead it. [*Peekaboo, I Almost See You*]

25 I prefer to forget both pairs of glasses and pass my declining years saluting strange women and grandfather clocks.

26 He tells you when you've got on / too

much lipstick, / And helps you with your girdle / when your hips stick. [*The Perfect Husband*]

1 Candy is dandy, / But liquor is quicker. [*Reflection on Ice-breaking*]

2 When Ah itchez, Ah scratchez. [*Requiem*]

3 What chills the finger not a bit / Is so frigid upon the fundament. [*Samson Agonistes*]

4 In spite of her sniffle, / Isabel's chiffle. [*The Sniffle*]

5 Some girls with a snuffle, / Their tempers are uffle, / But when Isabel's snivelly / She's snivelly civilly, / And when she is snuffly / She's perfectly luffly.

6 I think that I shall never see / A billboard lovely as a tree. / Perhaps unless the billboards fall, / I'll never see a tree at all. [*Song of the Open Road*. See also 208:6]

7 The turtle lives 'twixt plated decks / Which practically conceal its sex. / I think it clever of the turtle / In such a fix to be so fertile. [*The Turtle*]

8 Gently my eyelids close; / I'd rather be good than clever; / And I'd rather have my facts all wrong / Than have no facts whatever. [*Who Did Which?*]

9 Life is not having been told that the man has just waxed the floor. [*You and Me and P. B. Shelley*]

10 Plus ça change, plus c'est la memsahib. [Attr.]

TERRY NATION

11 We will exterminate . . . [Daleks' chorus in BBC TV series *Dr Who*, from 1960s]

JOHN NAUGHTON 1933–

12 Proust is to life as an empty orchestra pit is to music. [In the *Observer Review*, 24 Feb. 1991]

13 So [actionable] too is the imputation that the man [Lord Dacre] would mow his own grass. The former Regius Professor of History is so grand that he probably sends his lawn out to be cut. [In the *Observer*, 7 July]

MARTINA NAVRATILOVA 1956–

14 I'm not just involved in tennis but committed. Do you know the difference between involvement and commitment? Think of ham and eggs. The chicken is involved. The pig is committed. [From *Newsweek Magazine*, in the *International Herald Tribune*, 3 Sept. 1982]

JAMES NAYLOR 1860–1945

15 King David and King Solomon / Led merry, merry lives. [*Ancient Authors*]

GRANNI NAZZANO

16 My only hobby is laziness, which naturally rules out all the others. [Attr.]

JOSEPH NEEDHAM 1900–

17 *Laboratorium est oratorium*. The place where we do our scientific work is a place of prayer. [In *Dictionary of Scientific Quotations*, ed. A. L. Mackay]

JAWAHARLAL NEHRU 1889–1964

18 Long years ago we made a tryst with destiny, and now the time comes when we shall redeem our pledge, not wholly, or in full measure. [In the *Guardian*, 8 Dec. 1984]

PABLO NERUDA 1904–1973

19 *Lo que tengo en mí está en medio de las olas. / Un rayo de agua, un día para mí, un fondo férreo.* – What I have in myself is in the midst of the waves. / A flash of water, a day to myself, a depth of iron. [*Vals*]

20 Poetry is an act of peace. Peace goes into the making of a poet as flour goes into the making of bread. [*Memoirs*, Ch. 6]

E. NESBIT 1858–1924

21 Oh! little brown brother, / Are you awake in the dark? [*Baby Seed Song*]

W. D. NESBIT

22 Let's Keep the Glow in Old Glory and the Free in Freedom Too. [Title of song]

RICHARD NEVILLE 1931–

23 Is marijuana addictive? Yes, in the sense

that most of the really pleasant things in life are worth endlessly repeating. [*Playpower*]

ALLAN NEVINS 1890–1971

1 Offering Germany too little, and offering even that too late. [*Current History*, May 1935]

H. W. NEVINSON 1856–1941

2 He [H. Scott Holland] used to run as if the Holy Grail were just round the corner, and he might catch it if only he could run fast enough. [*In the Dark Backward*]

ANTHONY NEWLEY 1931– and **LESLIE BRICUSSE** 1931–

3 Stop the World, I Want to Get Off. [Title of musical]

ERNEST NEWMAN 1868–1959

4 His [Stravinsky's] music used to be original. Now it is aboriginal. [From *Musical Times*, 1921, in *Dictionary of Musical Quotations*, comp. I. Crofton and D. Fraser]

5 I sometimes wonder which would be nicer – an opera without an interval, or an interval without an opera. [In *Berlioz, Romantic and Classic*, essays ed. Peter Heyworth]

6 My dear boy, you may help a lame dog over a stile but he is still a lame dog on the other side. [To Heyworth in answer to the suggestion that Newman should do something to encourage young composers]

7 The higher the voice the smaller the intellect. [Attr. by Heyworth]

PAUL NEWMAN 1925–

8 There are two Newman's Laws. First, it's useless to put on your brakes when you're upside down. Second, just when things look darkest, they go black. [In *Playboy*, Apr. 1983]

9 Why have hamburger out when you've got steak at home? That doesn't always mean it's tender. [Of marriage. In the *Observer*, 'Sayings of the Week', 11 Mar. 1984, but earlier variants on this line]

NEWS OF THE WORLD

10 All human life is there. [Newspaper's slogan]

SIR JOHN NEWSOM 1910–1971

11 *All* education is, in a sense, vocational, vocational for living. ['The Education Women Need', *Observer*, 6 Sept. 1964]

NEW STATESMAN

12 A radical – one who not only knows all the answers but keeps on thinking up new questions. [Undated]

THE NEW YORK TIMES

13 All the news that's fit to print. [Newspaper's slogan, devised by Adolph S. Ochs, 1896]

BEVERLEY NICHOLS 1899–1983

14 It is only to the gardener that time is a friend, giving each year more than he steals. [*Merry Hall*, Feb. 1957]

ROBERT NICHOLS 1893–1944

15 [When asked what music he liked best] The sound of my own voice. [In Edward Marsh, *Ambrosia and Small Beer*, Ch. 5, sect. i]

BASIL NICHOLSON

16 There's enough acid in your stomach to burn a hole in the carpet. [Advertisement headline for digestive tablet]

17 Horlicks guards against Night Starvation. [Advertising slogan, attr. May be by another member of the firm of J. Walter Thompson]

VIVIAN NICHOLSON 1936–

18 [When asked what she was going to do with record football pools win] Spend, spend, spend. [In Sept. 1961. Also used as title of her autobiography]

SIR HAROLD NICOLSON 1886–1968

19 He [T. S. Eliot] is without pose and full of poise. He makes one feel that all cleverness

is an excuse for thinking hard. [*Diaries and Letters, 1930–1939*, 2 Mar. 1932]

1 I do not consider that efficiency need be mated to extreme delicacy or precision of touch ... It should possess a sweeping gesture – even if that gesture may at moments sweep the ornaments from the mantelpiece. [*Small Talk*, 'On Being Efficient']

REINHOLD NIEBUHR 1892–1971

2 God grant me the serenity to accept things I cannot change, courage to change things I can, and wisdom to know the difference. [Attr., but never claimed by him, probably 18 cent. German, if not earlier]

3 Man's capacity for evil makes democracy necessary and man's capacity for good makes democracy possible. [*The Children of Light and the Children of Darkness*, Foreword]

4 Man is always worse than most people suspect, but also generally better than most people dream. [In the *Guardian*, 15 July 1988]

MARTIN NIEMÖLLER 1892–1984

5 In Germany, the Nazis came for the Communists and I didn't speak up because I was not a Communist. Then they came for the Jews and I didn't speak up because I was not a Jew. Then they came for the trade unionists and I didn't speak up because I was not a trade unionist. Then they came for the Catholics and I was a Protestant so I didn't speak up. Then they came for me ... By that time there was no one to speak up for anyone. [Attr. in *Congressional Record*, 14 Oct. 1968]

FLORENCE NIGHTINGALE 1820–1910

6 Too kind – too kind. [When handed the insignia of the Order of Merit on her deathbed. In Lytton Strachey, *Eminent Victorians*]

ANAÏS NIN 1903–1977

7 Perhaps a child, like a cat, is so much inside of himself that he does not see himself in the mirror. [*Diary of A.N.*, Vol. 2, Mar. 1937]

8 The sculptor must himself feel that he is not so much inventing or shaping the curve of a breast or shoulder as delivering the image from its prison. [Vol. 5, Spring 1948]

DAVID NIVEN 1910–1983

9 George [Sanders], a giant grizzly of a man, had a face, even in his twenties, which looked as though he had rented it on a long lease and had lived in it so long he didn't want to move out. [*Bring on the Empty Horses*, Ch. 2]

LARRY NIVEN 1938–

10 [When asked at a science-fiction convention, 'What is the best advice you have ever been given?'] On my twenty-first birthday my father said, 'Son, here's a million dollars. Don't lose it.' [Attr.]

PRESIDENT RICHARD NIXON 1913–

11 You won't have Nixon to kick around any more, gentlemen. This is my last Press Conference. [After losing election for governorship of California, 7 Nov. 1962]

12 Let us begin by committing ourselves to the truth, to see it like it is and to tell it like it is, to find the truth, to speak the truth and live with the truth. That's what we'll do. [Speech accepting Republican nomination in presidential election, Miami, 8 Aug. 1968]

13 You can say that this Administration will have the first complete, far-reaching attack on the problem of hunger in history. Use all the rhetoric, so long as it doesn't cost money. [From official minutes of White House meeting, 17 Mar. 1969]

14 This is the greatest week in the history of the world since the creation. [Of man's first moon-landing. Said on board the *Hornet*, 24 July]

15 The great silent majority of my fellow Americans – I ask for your support. [TV address on Vietnam War, 3 Nov.]

16 There can be no whitewash at the White House. [TV address on the Watergate crisis, 30 Apr. 1973. In C. Bernstein and B. Woodward, *All the President's Men*]

17 I welcome this kind of examination because people have got to know whether or not their President is a crook. Well, I'm not a crook. [At press conference, 11 Nov.]

1 If some of my judgements were wrong, and some were wrong, they were made in what I believed at the time to be the best interest of the nation. [Resignation speech, 8 Aug. 1974]

2 I let down my friends, I let down my country. I let down our system of government. [In the *Observer*, 'Sayings of the Week', 8 May 1977]

3 When the President does it, that means it is not illegal. [TV interview with David Frost, 20 May]

LOUIS NIZER 1902–

4 When a man points a finger at someone else, he should remember that four of his fingers are pointing at himself. [*My Life in Court*]

DAVID NOBBS 1935–

5 'This one's going to be a real winner', said C.J. 'I didn't get where I am today without knowing a real winner when I see one.' [BBC TV series, 1976–1980, *The Fall and Rise of Reginald Perrin*, 'Thursday', and running catchphrase]

6 They [Sunday evening trains] are full of people going from where they chose to be to where they have to be. [From *Pratt of the Argus*, in *The Times Literary Supplement*, 20 May 1988]

MILTON NOBLES 1847–1924

7 The villain still pursued her. [*Phoenix*, Act 1, sc. iii]

A. J. NOCK 1873–1945

8 It is an economic axiom as old as the hills that goods and services can be paid for only with goods and services. [*Memoirs of a Superfluous Man*, III, Ch. 3]

DENIS NORDEN 1922–

9 It's a funny kind of month, October. For the really keen cricket fan it's when you discover that your wife left you in May. [In *She* magazine, Oct. 1977]

10 The snows of yesterday can't be re-freezed. [In BBC radio programme *My Word*, 5 Oct.]

11 If all the world's a stage, and all the men and women merely players, where do all the audiences come from. [30 Nov.]

12 You know how God dictated the Ten Commandments to Moses? Well if, instead of Moses, he had dictated them to a temp – we would now all be working on only Four Commandments. [In Frank Muir and Denis Norden, *Upon My Word!*, 'Old Father Thames']

See also FRANK MUIR and DENIS NORDEN

FRANK NORMAN 1931–1981

13 Fings Ain't Wot They Used T'Be. [Title of musical, music by Lionel Bart, derived from song, 1939, by Mercer Ellington and Ted Persons]

LORD NORTHCLIFFE 1865–1922

14 It is hard news that catches readers. Features hold them. [In T. Clarke, *My Northcliffe Diary*]

15 When I want a peerage, I will pay for it like an honest man. [In Reginald Pound and Geoffrey Harmsworth, *Northcliffe*, Ch. 11]

16 Never put on the table of Demos what you would not have on your own table. [Quoted by Claud Cockburn in BBC TV programme *Read All About It*, 28 July 1975]

17 They are only ten. [Said to have been written up in his offices to remind the staff of their readership's mental age]

MARY NORTON 1903–1992

18 We don't talk fancy grammar and eat anchovy toast. But to live under the kitchen doesn't say we aren't educated. [*The Borrowers*, Ch. 5]

19 If you're born in India, you're bilingual. And if you're bilingual, you can't read. Not so well. [9]

20 But we *are* Borrowers . . . like you're a – a Human Bean or whatever it's called. [10]

JACK NORWORTH 1879–1959

21 Oh! shine on, shine on, harvest moon /

Up in the sky. / I ain't had no lovin' / Since April, January, June or July. [Song: *Shine On, Harvest Moon*, 1908, music by Nora Bayes]

IVOR NOVELLO 1893–1951

1 There's something Vichy about the French. [In Edward Marsh, *Ambrosia and Small Beer*, Ch. 4. See also 93:16]

2 And Her Mother Came Too. [Title of song, in collab. Dion Titheradge, in show *A to Z*, 1921]

See also under FORD, LENA GUILBERT, and WEISSMULLER, JOHNNY

ALFRED NOYES 1880–1958

3 Go down to Kew in lilac-time, in lilac-time, in lilac-time. [*The Barrel Organ*]

PATRICK NUTTGENS 1930–

4 The challenge for the modern architect is the same as the challenge for all of us in our lives: to make out of the ordinary something out-of-the-ordinary. [From BBC TV programme *Architecture for Everyman*, in the *Listener*, 1 Mar. 1979]

5 Banister Fletcher's *History of Architecture* which no one has ever read completely except in hospital. [In *The Times Higher Education Supplement*, 10 Jan. 1986]

PRESIDENT JULIUS NYERERE 1921–

6 Our desire is to be friendly to every country in the world, but we have no desire to have a friendly country choosing our enemies for us. [In Robert Andrews, *Routledge Dictionary of Quotations*, 'Alliances']

PHILIP OAKES 1928–

1 I could see that childhood was an invention of grown-ups, a fiction we were required to take on trust in case we demanded something better. [In the *Listener*, 9 Mar. 1989]

MICHAEL OAKESHOTT 1901–1990

2 Our predicament is not the difficulty of attaining happiness, but the difficulty of avoiding the misery to which the pursuit of happiness exposes us. [In obituary in the *Guardian*, 22 Dec. 1990]

CAPTAIN LAWRENCE 'TITUS' OATES 1880–1912

3 I am just going outside, and may be some time. [Last words, 16 Mar. 1912. In R. F. Scott's diary, *Scott's Last Expedition*, Ch. 20]

CONOR CRUISE O'BRIEN 1917–

4 It [Dublin] is a city where you can see a sparrow fall to the ground, and God watching it. [Attr.]

EDNA O'BRIEN 1932–

5 To Crystal, hair was the most important thing on earth. She would never get married because you couldn't wear curlers in bed. [*Winter's Tales*, 8, 'Come into the Drawing Room, Doris']

6 The vote, I thought, means nothing to women. We should be armed. [Epigraph to Erica Jong, *Fear of Flying*, Ch. 16]

FLANN O'BRIEN [MYLES NA GOPALEEN] 1911–1966

7 The conclusion of your sylloglsm, I said lightly, is fallacious, being based upon licensed premises. [*At Swim-Two-Birds*, Ch. 1]

8 The pocket was the first instinct of humanity and was used long years before the human race had a trousers between them – the quiver for arrows is one example and the pouch of a kangaroo is another.

9 A second thought is never an odd thought.

10 Evil is even, truth is an odd number and death is a full stop.

11 I dedicate these pages to my Guardian Angel, impressing upon him that I'm only fooling and warning him to see to it that there is no misunderstanding when I go home. [*The Dalkey Archive*, dedication]

12 A thing of duty is a boy for ever. [On the perennial youthfulness of policemen. In the *Listener*, 24 Feb. 1977]

OBSERVER

13 Can the world of God be found in a pool of limelight? [Profile of Rabbi Julia Neuberger, 22 June 1986]

14 Unlike a classical dictatorship, in which the lines of conflict run between government and the governed, in modern Communist societies this line runs through each person, for everyone in his or her own way is both a victim and a supporter of the system. [Profile of Vaclav Havel, 29 Jan. 1989]

SEAN O'CASEY 1880–1964

1 I killin' meself workin', an' he sthruttin' about from mornin' till night like a paycock! [*Juno and the Paycock*, Act I]

2 He's an oul' butty o' mine – oh, he's a darlin' man, a daarlin' man.

3 The whole worl's in a state o' chassis.

4 I often looked up at the sky an' assed meself the question – what is the stars, what is the stars?

5 The Polis as Polis, in this city, is Null an' Void! [3]

6 It's only a little cold I have; there's nothing derogatory wrong with me. [*The Plough and the Stars*, I]

7 There's no reason to bring religion into it. I think we ought to have as great a regard for religion as we can, so as to keep it out of as many things as possible.

8 A man should always be drunk, Minnie, when he talks politics – it's the only way in which to make them important. [*The Shadow of a Gunman*, Act I]

9 English literature's performing flea. [Of P. G. Wodehouse. In Wodehouse's *Performing Flea*, 'Postscript']

ADOLPH S. OCHS *see under* THE NEW YORK TIMES

FLANNERY O'CONNOR 1925–1964

10 I don't deserve any credit for turning the other cheek as my tongue is always in it. [From *The Habit of Being*, in *Simpson's Contemporary Quotations*]

CLIFFORD ODETS 1906–1963

11 Go out and fight so life shouldn't be printed on dollar bills. [*Awake and Sing*, Act I]

DAVID OGG 1887–1965

12 In the nineteenth century the average length of life for clergymen was eighty-one years, for politicians seventy-seven years and for atheists and sceptics sixty-four years. [From *Europe of the Ancien Régime*, in Gerald Brenan, *Thoughts in a Dry Season*, 'Religion',

who comments, 'So it paid then to believe in God']

DAVID OGILVY 1911–

13 At 60 miles an hour the loudest noise in this new Rolls-Royce comes from the electric clock. [Advertisement, derived from technical report on car]

14 Every soldier carries a marshal's baton in his pack [Napoleon]. Yes, but don't let it stick out. [*Confessions of an Advertising Man*, Ch. 10]

GEOFFREY O'HARA 1882–1967

15 K-K-K-Katy, beautiful Katy, / You're the only g-g-g-girl that I adore, / When the m-m-m-moon shines over the cow-shed, / I'll be waiting at the k-k-k-kitchen door. [Song: *K-K-K-Katy*]

PATRICK O'KEEFE 1872–1934

16 Say it with flowers. [Slogan for Society of American Florists, 1917]

TIM O'LEARY ?–1991

17 You are as old as the last time you changed your mind. [In the *Observer*, 'Sayings of the Week', 25 Sept. 1983]

SIR LAURENCE [later LORD] OLIVIER 1907–1989

18 Realism doesn't mean copying art back into life. It means making life into art: not just accepting the facts of life but elevating them. [Kenneth Harris, *Kenneth Harris Talking to*: 'Sir Laurence Olivier']

19 Shakespeare – the nearest thing in incarnation to the eye of God.

20 I often think that could we creep behind the actor's eyes, we would find an attic of forgotten toys and a copy of the Domesday Book. ['Olivier on Acting', *The New York Times*, 26 Oct. 1986]

21 There are no great parts. Some are a bit longer than others, that's all. [In Gary O'Connor, *Ralph Richardson: An Actor's Life*, Pt II, Ch. 25]

22 [When asked the greatest secret of an actor's success] Sincerity, sincerity. Once you

can fake that you can achieve anything. [In Michael Shea, *Influence*, Ch. 15]

AUSTIN O'MALLEY 1858–1932

1 An Englishman thinks seated; a Frenchman, standing; an American, pacing; an Irishman afterward. [In A. Andrews, *Quotations for Speakers and Writers*]

F. W. O'MALLEY *see under* HUBBARD, ELBERT

EUGENE O'NEILL 1888–1953

2 For de little stealin' dey gits you in jail soon or late. For de big stealin' dey makes you emperor and puts you in de Hall o' Fame when you croaks. [*The Emperor Jones*]

3 A Long Day's Journey into Night. [Title of play]

4 Our lives are merely strange dark interludes in the electric display of God the Father. [*Strange Interlude*, sc. ix]

GEORGE OPPENHEIMER 1904–1967

5 It rolls off my back like a duck. [Parodying Samuel Goldwyn. In Philip French, *The Movie Moguls*, Ch. 4]

J. ROBERT OPPENHEIMER 1904–1967

6 We knew the world would not be the same. [After first atomic test. *The Decision to Drop the Bomb*]

7 The physicists have known sin; and this is a knowledge which they cannot lose. [Lecture at Massachusetts Institute of Technology, 25 Nov. 1947]

SUSIE ORBACH 1946–

8 Fat is a Feminist Issue. [Title of book]

ROBERT ORBEN 1927–

9 Old people shouldn't eat health foods. They need all the preservatives they can get. [In *Cook's Quotation Book*, ed. Maria Polushkin Robbins]

BARONESS ORCZY 1865–1947

10 We seek him here, we seek him there, / Those Frenchies seek him everywhere. / Is he in heaven? – Is he in hell? / That demmed elusive Pimpernel? [*The Scarlet Pimpernel*, Ch. 12]

P. J. O'ROURKE 1947–

11 Australia is not very exclusive ... On the visa application they still ask if you've been convicted of a felony – although they are willing to give you a visa even if you haven't been. [*Holidays in Hell*]

12 So everyone's a fool outside their own country. America, having emerged from World War II as the only country with any money left, got a 20-year head start on being fools overseas. [Interview in the *Observer*, 15 Jan. 1989]

JOSÉ ORTEGA Y GASSET 1883–1955

13 I am I plus my surroundings, and if I do not preserve the latter, I do not preserve myself. [*Meditations of Quixote*]

14 Minorities are individuals or groups of individuals especially qualified. The masses are the collection of people not especially qualified. [*The Revolt of the Masses*, Ch. 1]

15 The epoch of the masses is the epoch of the colossal. We are living ... under the brutal empire of the masses. [2]

16 The world is the sum-total of our vital possibilities. [4]

17 Revolution is not the uprising against pre-existing order, but the setting-up of a new order contradictory to the traditional one. [6]

18 Civilization consists in the attempt to reduce violence to the *ultima ratio*, the final argument. [8]

JOE ORTON 1933–1967

19 I'd the upbringing a nun would envy and that's the truth. Until I was fifteen I was more familiar with Africa than my own body. [*Entertaining Mr Sloane*, Act I]

20 Persuade her. Cut her throat but persuade her! [III]

21 It's all any reasonable child can expect if the dad is present at the conception.

22 FAY: Have you known him long?

HAL: We shared the same cradle.

FAY: Was that economy or malpractice?
[*Loot*, Act I]

1 Every luxury was lavished on you – atheism, breast-feeding, circumcision. I had to make my own way.

2 Policemen, like red squirrels, must be protected.

3 Reading isn't an occupation we encourage among police officers. We try to keep the paper work down to a minimum. [II]

4 PRENTICE: You did have a father?

GERALDINE: Oh, I'm sure I did. My mother was frugal in her habits, but she'd never economize unwisely. [*What the Butler Saw*, Act I]

5 You were born with your legs apart. They'll send you to the grave in a Y-shaped coffin.

6 This is a boy, sir. Not a girl. If you're baffled by the difference it might be as well to approach both with caution. [II]

7 The whole trouble with Western society today is the lack of anything worth concealing. [Diary. In J. Lahr, *Prick Up Your Ears*]

GEORGE ORWELL [ERIC BLAIR]
1903–1950

8 Man is the only creature that consumes without producing. [*Animal Farm*, Ch. 1]

9 Four legs good, two legs bad. [3]

10 Napoleon had commanded that once a week there should be held something called a Spontaneous Demonstration. [9]

11 He intended, he said, to devote the rest of his life to learning the remaining twenty-two letters of the alphabet.

12 All animals are equal, but some animals are more equal than others. [10]

13 The creatures outside looked from pig to man, and from man to pig, and from pig to man again; but already it was impossible to say which was which.

14 I'm fat, but I'm thin inside. Has it ever struck you that there's a thin man inside every fat man, just as they say there's a statue inside every block of stone? [*Coming up for Air*, I. 3. See also 7:14, 88:24, 392:25, 401:20]

15 Before the war, and especially before the Boer War, it was summer all the year round. [II. 1]

16 If the war didn't happen to kill you it was bound to start you thinking. After that unspeakable idiotic mess you couldn't go on regarding society as something eternal and unquestionable, like a pyramid. You knew it was just a balls-up. [8]

17 He was an embittered atheist (the sort of atheist who does not so much disbelieve in God as personally dislike Him). [*Down and Out in Paris and London*, Ch. 30]

18 The novel is practically a Protestant form of art; it is a product of the free mind, of the autonomous individual. [*Inside the Whale*, II]

19 Probably the Battle of Waterloo *was* won on the playing-fields of Eton, but the opening battles of all subsequent wars have been lost there. [*The Lion and the Unicorn*, 'England, Your England']

20 A family with the wrong members in control – that, perhaps, is as near as one can come to describing England in a phrase. ['The Ruling Class']

21 Big Brother is watching you. [*1984*, Pt I, Ch. 1]

22 Only the Thought Police mattered.

23 War is Peace / Freedom is Slavery / Ignorance is Strength.

24 Newspeak was the official language of Oceania. [Footnote]

25 His mind . . . fetched up with a bump against the Newspeak word *doublethink*.

26 Who controls the past controls the future . . . Who controls the present controls the past. [3]

27 The Two Minutes Hate.

28 The proles are not human beings. [5]

29 Hate Week.

30 It is brought home to you . . . that it is only because miners sweat their guts out that superior persons can remain superior. [*The Road to Wigan Pier*, Ch. 2]

31 This business of petty inconvenience and indignity, of being kept waiting about, of having to do everything at other people's convenience is inherent in working-class life. A thousand influences constantly press a working man into a *passive* role. He does not act, he is acted upon. [3]

1 I sometimes think that the price of liberty is not so much eternal vigilance as eternal dirt. [4]

2 There can hardly be a town in the South of England where you could throw a brick without hitting the niece of a bishop. [7]

3 Comrade X, it so happens, is an old Etonian. He would be ready to die on the barricades, in theory anyway, but you notice that he still leaves his bottom waistcoat button undone. [8]

4 As with the Christian religion, the worst advertisement for Socialism is its adherents. [II]

5 The typical socialist . . . a prim little man with a white-collar job, usually a secret teetotaller and often with vegetarian leanings.

6 The underlying motive of many Socialists, I believe, is simply a hypertrophied sense of order. The present state of affairs offends them not because it causes misery, still less because it makes freedom impossible, but because it is untidy; what they desire, basically, is to reduce the world to something resembling a chessboard.

7 The higher-water mark, so to speak, of Socialist literature is W. H. Auden, a sort of gutless Kipling.

8 Man is not, as the vulgarer hedonists seem to suppose, a kind of walking stomach; he has also got a hand, an eye, and a brain. Cease to use your hands, and you have lopped off a huge chunk of your consciousness. [12]

9 It is usual to speak of the Fascist objective as the 'beehive state', which does a grave injustice to bees. A world of rabbits ruled by stoats would be nearer the mark.

10 We of the sinking middle class . . . may sink without further struggles into the working class where we belong, and probably when we get there it will not be so dreadful as we feared, for, after all, we have nothing to lose but our aitches. [13]

11 The aim of a joke is not to degrade the human being but to remind him that he is already degraded. [Collected Essays, 'Funny but Not Vulgar']

12 Objective consideration of contemporary phenomena compels the conclusion that success or failure in competitive activities exhibits no tendency to be commensurate with innate capacity, but that a considerable element of the upredictable must invariably be taken into account. Paraphrase of Ecclesiates, Ch. 9, 11. ['Politics and the English Language']

13 The inflated style is itself a kind of euphemism. A mass of Latin words falls upon the facts like soft snow, blurring the outlines and covering up all the details. The great enemy of clear language is insincerity.

14 In prose, the worst thing one can do with words is surrender to them.

15 The Catholic and the Communist are alike in assuming that an opponent cannot be both honest and intelligent. ['The Prevention of Literature']

16 The quickest way of ending a war is to lose it. [Shooting an Elephant, 'Second Thoughts on James Burnham']

17 Serious sport has nothing to do with fair play. It is bound up with hatred, jealousy, boastfulness, disregard of all rules and sadistic pleasure in witnessing violence. In other words, it is war minus the shooting. ['The Sporting Spirit']

18 For casual reading – in your bath, for instance, or late at night when you are too tired to go to bed, or in the odd quarter of an hour before lunch – there is nothing to touch a back number of the Girl's Own Paper. [In Fortnightly Review, Nov. 1936]

19 If liberty means anything at all, it means the right to tell people what they do not want to hear. ['The Freedom of the Press', proposed preface to Animal Farm]

20 One cannot really be a Catholic and grown-up. [Of Evelyn Waugh. Notebook, undated, before Mar. 1949]

21 At 50, everyone has the face he deserves. [Notebook, 17 Apr. 1949]

JOHN OSBORNE 1929–

22 Don't clap too hard – it's a very old building. [The Entertainer, vii]

23 But I have a go, lady, don't I? I have a go. I do.

24 Never believe in mirrors or newspapers. [The Hotel in Amsterdam, Act I]

1 He really deserves some sort of decoration ... a medal inscribed 'For Vaguery in the Field'. [*Look Back in Anger*, I]

2 I'm not mentioned at all because my name is a dirty word.

3 I don't think one 'comes down' from Jimmy's university. According to him, it's not even red brick, but white tile. [II. i]

4 They spend their time mostly looking forward to the past.

5 Poor old Daddy – just one of those sturdy old plants left over from the Edwardian Wilderness, that can't understand why the sun isn't shining any more. [ii]

6 There aren't any good, brave causes left. [III. i]

7 JENNY: What was known as art silk –
TIM: Like art cinema –
JENNY: It wasn't really silk at all. [*Under Plain Cover*]

8 This is a letter of hate. It is for you my countrymen. I mean those men of my country who have defiled it ... I only hope it (my hate) will keep me going. I think it will. I think it will sustain me in the last few months. Till then, damn you England. [Letter to the *Tribune*, 18 Aug. 1961]

FRANK OTTER

9 I am of the opinion that had your father spent more of your mother's immoral earnings on your education you would not even then have been a gentleman. [In Seymour Hicks, *Vintage Years*]

P. D. OUSPENSKY 1878–1947

10 Truths that become old become decrepit and unreliable; sometimes they may be kept going artificially for a certain time, but there is no life in them ... Ideas can be too old. [*A New Model of the Universe*, Preface to 2nd edn]

11 Man, as he is, is not a genuine article. He is an imitation of something, and a very bad imitation. [*The Psychology of Man's Possible Evolution*, Ch. 2]

DAVID [later LORD] OWEN 1938–

12 We are fed up with fudging and mudging, with mush and slush. [Speech at Labour Party Conference, Blackpool, 2 Oct. 1980]

WILFRED OWEN 1893–1918

13 My subject is war, and the pity of War. The Poetry is in the pity. [*Poems*, Preface]

14 What passing-bells for those who die as cattle? / Only the monstrous anger of the guns. / Only the stuttering rifles' rapid rattle / Can patter out their hasty orisons. [*Anthem for doomed Youth*]

15 And bugles calling for them from sad shires.

16 And each slow dusk a drawing-down of blinds.

17 And in the happy no-time of his sleeping / Death took him by the heart. [*Asleep*]

18 The old Lie: *Dulce et decorum est / Pro patria mori.* [*Dulce et decorum est*]

19 Move him into the sun – / Gently its touch awoke him once / At home. [*Futility*]

20 Red lips are not so red / As the stained stones kissed by the English dead. / Kindness of wooed and wooer / Seems shame to their love pure. [*Greater Love*]

21 Whatever mourns when many leave these shores: / Whatever shares / The eternal reciprocity of tears. [*Insensibility*]

22 So secretly, like wrongs hushed-up, they went. / They were not ours: / We never heard to which front these were sent. [*The Send-off*]

23 My soul looked down from a vague height with Death. / As unremembering how I rose or why, / And saw a sad land, weak with sweats of dearth. [*The Show*]

24 It seemed that out of battle I escaped / Down some profound dull tunnel, long since scooped / Through granites which titanic wars had groined. [*Strange Meeting*]

25 One sprang up, and stared / With piteous recognition in fixed eyes, / Lifting distressful hands, as if to bless.

26 'Strange friend,' I said, 'here is no cause to mourn.' / 'None,' said the other, 'save the undone years, / The hopelessness. Whatever hope is yours / Was my life also; I went

hunting wild / After the wildest beauty in the world.'

1 Courage was mine, and I had mystery, / Wisdom was mine, and I had mastery: / To miss the march of the retreating world / Into vain citadels that are not walled.

AMOS OZ 1939–

2 I will tell you that this nation [Israel] of four million citizens is really an uneasy coalition of four million prime ministers, if not four million self-appointed prophets and messiahs. ['Israel', *Granta*, 17]

P

VANCE PACKARD 1914–

1 The Hidden Persuaders. [Title of book]

WALTER PAGE 1855–1918

2 The English have three vegetables and two of them are cabbage. [In Jonathon Green, *Consuming Passions*]

SATCHEL PAIGE [Baseball player and sage] *c.* 1906–1982

3 Go very light on vices such as carrying on in society. The social ramble ain't restful. [*Six Rules for a Long Life*]

MICHAEL PALIN *see* TERRY JONES and MICHAEL PALIN, and MONTY PYTHON'S FLYING CIRCUS

K. M. PANIKKAR 1895–1963

4 If an ambassador says yes, it means perhaps; if he says perhaps, it means no; if he ever said no, he would cease to be an ambassador. [In *New Light's Dictionary of Quotations*, comp. Ved Bhushan]

EMMELINE PANKHURST 1858–1928

5 We have to free half of the human race, the women, so that they can help to free the other half. [In Naim Attallah, *Women*]

BORIS PANKIN [Russian Ambassador to Britain] 1931–

6 Recession is when you have to tighten the belt. Depression is when there is no belt to tighten. We are probably in the next degree of collapse when there are no trousers as such. [In the *Independent*, 'Quote Unquote', 25 July 1992]

EDWARD PARAMORE 1895–1956

7 Hard-boiled as a picnic egg. [*The Ballad of Yukon Jake*]

BHIKU PAREKH 1935–

8 Those who make history can afford to forget or retain nostalgic memories of it, those made by it daily live in this shadow. [In *New Statesman and Society*, 9 Sept. 1988]

CHARLIE PARKER 1920–1955

9 Music is your own experience, your thoughts, your wisdom. If you don't live it, it won't come out of your horn. [In Nat Shapiro and Nat Hentoff, *Hear Me Talkin' to Ya*]

DOROTHY PARKER 1893–1967

10 Here's my strength and my weakness, gents, / I loved them until they loved me. [*Ballade at Thirty-Five*]

11 You will be frail and musty / With peering, furtive head, / While I am young and lusty / Among the roaring dead. [*Braggart*]

12 He lies below, correct in cypress wood, / And entertains the most exclusive worms. [*Epitaph for a Very Rich Man*]

13 Some men break your heart in two, / Some men fawn and flatter, / Some men never look at you; / And that cleans up the matter. [*Experience*]

1 Four be the things I'd been better without: / Love, curiosity, freckles, and doubt. [*Inventory*]

2 There was nothing more fun than a man. [*The Little Old Lady in Lavender Silk*]

3 But I, despite expert advice, / Keep doing things I think are nice, / And though to good I never come – / Inseparable my nose and thumb! [*Neither Bloody nor Bowed*]

4 Men seldom make passes / At girls who wear glasses. [*News Item*. See also 64:4]

5 Why is it no one ever sent me yet / One perfect limousine, do you suppose? / Ah no, it's always just my luck to get / One perfect rose. [*One Perfect Rose*]

6 If, with the literate, I am / Impelled to try an epigram, / I never seek to take the credit; / We all assume that Oscar said it. [*Oscar Wilde*]

7 Whose love is given over-well / Shall look on Helen's face in hell, / Whilst they whose love is thin and wise / May view John Knox in paradise. [*Partial Comfort*]

8 Guns aren't lawful; / Nooses give; / Gas smells awful; / You might as well live. [*Résumé*]

9 Accursed from their birth they be / Who seek to find monogamy, / Pursuing it from bed to bed – / I think they would be better dead. [*Reuben's Children*]

10 Where's the man could ease a heart, / Like a satin gown? [*The Satin Dress*]

11 Lady, Lady, should you meet / One whose ways are all discreet, / One who murmurs that his wife / Is the lodestar of his life, / One who keeps assuring you / That he never was untrue, / Never loved another one . . . / Lady, lady, better run! [*Social Note*]

12 'And if he never came,' said she, / 'Now what on earth is that to me? / I wouldn't have him back!' / I hope / Her mother washed her mouth with soap. [*Story*]

13 The man she had was kind and clean / And well enough for every day, / But oh, dear friends, you should have seen / The one that got away! [*Tombstones in the Starlight*, 'The Fisherwoman']

14 By the time you swear you're his, / Shivering and sighing, / And he vows his passion is / Infinite, undying – / Lady, make a note of this: / One of you is lying. [*Unfortunate Coincidence*]

15 He's really awfully fond of coloured people. Well, he says himself, he wouldn't have white servants. [*Arrangement in Black and White*]

16 All I say is, nobody has any business to go around looking like a horse and behaving as if it were all right. You don't catch horses going around looking like people, do you? [*Horsie*]

17 I bet you could get into the subway without using anybody's name. [*Just a Little One*]

18 Three highballs, and I think I'm St Francis of Assisi.

19 And I'll stay off Verlaine too; he was always chasing Rimbauds. [*The Little Hours*]

20 How do people go to sleep? I'm afraid I've lost the knack. I might try busting myself smartly over the temple with the nightlight. I might repeat to myself, slowly and soothingly, a list of quotations beautiful from minds profound; if I can remember any of the damn things.

21 I'm never going to be famous. My name will never be writ large on the roster of Those Who Do Things. I don't do anything. Not one single thing. I used to bite my nails, but I don't even do that any more.

22 I know there was something, something pretty terrible, too. Not just plain terrible. This was fancy terrible; this was terrible with raisins in it. Ah, yes, I have it. This is my birthday. [*The Middle or Blue Period*]

23 Sorrow is tranquillity remembered in emotion. [*Sentiment*]

24 How do you do, Mr Jukes? And how is that dear little brother of yours, with the two heads? [*The Waltz*]

25 There was I, trapped. Trapped like a trap in a trap.

26 Wit's End. [Nickname for Alexander Woollcott's New York apartment. In James Thurber, *The Years with Ross*, Ch. 15]

27 [When asked whether she had enjoyed a cocktail party] Enjoyed it! One more drink and I'd have been under the host. [In R. E. Drennan, *Wit's End*]

1 You can't teach an old dogma new tricks.

2 Salary is no object. I only want to keep body and soul apart. [On discussing a job with a prospective employer]

3 This is not a novel to be tossed aside lightly. It should be thrown with great force. [Book review]

4 How could they tell? [On being told that ex-President Coolidge had died. Similar joke ascr. to Wilson Mizner in A. Johnston, *Legend of a Sport; the New Yorker*]

5 The affair between Margot Asquith and Margot Asquith will live as one of the prettiest love stories in all literature. [From review of Margot Asquith's *Autobiography* in the *New Yorker*, 22 Oct. 1927, in *The Penguin Dorothy Parker*]

6 And it is that word 'hummy', my darlings, that marks the first place in *The House at Pooh Corner* at which Tonstant Weader Fwowed up. [Review of A. A. Milne's book, 20 Oct. 1928]

7 I was fired from there [her convent school], finally, for a lot of things, among them my insistence that the Immaculate Conception was spontaneous combustion. [In *Writers at Work*, ed. Malcolm Cowley, First Series]

8 As artists they're rot, but as providers they're oil wells; they gush ... And there was that poor sucker Flaubert rolling around on his floor for three days looking for the right word.

9 Hollywood money isn't money. It's congealed snow, melts in your hand, and there you are.

10 You can lead a whore to culture but you can't make her think. [Speech to American Horticultural Society. In J. Keats, *You Might as Well Live*, Pt 1, Ch. 2]

11 This is on me. [Suggested epitaph for her own tombstone. In 5]

12 It serves me right for putting all my eggs in one bastard. [On going into hospital to get an abortion. In II. 3]

13 Oh, don't worry about Alan ... Alan will always land on somebody's feet. [Of her husband on the day their divorce became final. In IV. 1]

14 Brevity is the Soul of Lingerie. [Caption for a fashion magazine. In Alexander Woollcott, *While Rome Burns*, 'Our Mrs Parker']

15 The House Beautiful ... is the play lousy. [Play review in *Vanity Fair*]

16 That woman speaks eighteen languages, and can't say No in any of them.

17 If all the girls attending it [a Yale prom] were laid end to end, I wouldn't be at all surprised.

18 Excuse my dust. [Alternative epitaph]

19 She ran the whole gamut of her emotions from A to B. [Of Katharine Hepburn in play *The Lake*, 1933]

20 Seventy-two suburbs in search of a city. [Of Los Angeles, but others are attr. with the description. In Leslie Halliwell, *Filmgoer's Book of Quotes*]

21 [When told someone was very nice to her inferiors] Where does she find them? [In letter of Rupert Hart-Davis, 22 Jan. 1956, *Lyttelton–Hart-Davis Letters*, ed. Rupert Hart-Davis, Vol. 1]

22 Just before they made S. J. Perelman, they broke the mould. [Quoted by Alan Coren in the *Observer*, 29 Nov. 1987]

23 Why, after all, should readers never be harrowed? Surely there is enough happiness in life without having to go to books for it. [Attr.]

ROSS PARKER 1914–1974 and
HUGHIE CHARLES 1907–

24 There'll always be an England / While there's a country lane, / Wherever there's a cottage small / Beside a field of grain. [Song: *There'll Always be an England*]

STEWART PARKER 1941–1988

25 A car is just a hard shell of aggression, for the soft urban mollusc to secrete itself in. It's a form of disguise. All its parts are hidden. [*Spokesong*, Act II]

TONY PARKER 1923–

26 I don't believe in heaven or hell, they're here; you choose which one you're going to be a lodger in. [Quoting lighthouse keeper describing his life in *Lighthouse*, Ch. 20]

CECIL [later LORD] PARKINSON 1931–

1 I have my own Parkinson's Law: in politics people give you what they think you deserve and deny you what they think you want. [In the *Observer*, 'Sayings of the Week', 25 Nov. 1990]

C. NORTHCOTE PARKINSON 1909–1993

2 Work expands so as to fill the time available for its completion. General recognition of this fact is shown in the proverbial phrase. 'It is the busiest man who has time to spare.' [*Parkinson's Law*, Ch. 1]

3 The rise in the total of those employed is governed by Parkinson's Law and would be much the same whether the volume of work were to increase, diminish or even disappear.

4 Seven officials are now doing what one did before. This is where Factor 2 comes into operation. For these seven make so much work for each other that all are fully occupied and A is actually working harder than ever.

5 It might be termed the Law of Triviality. Briefly stated, it means that the time spent on any item of the agenda will be in inverse proportion to the sum involved. [3]

6 The age of Frustration will not always be the same ... but its symptoms are easy to recognize. The man who is denied the opportunity of taking decisions of importance begins to regard as important the decisions he is allowed to take. He becomes fussy about filing, keen on seeing that pencils are sharpened, eager to ensure that the windows are open (or shut) and apt to use two or three different-coloured inks. [10]

7 It is now known ... that men enter local politics solely as a result of being unhappily married.

DOLLY PARTON 1946–

8 [When asked how long it took to do her hair] I don't know. I'm never there. [In the *Independent*, 'Quote Unquote', 17 Feb. 1990]

BORIS PASTERNAK 1890–1960

9 Gardens, ponds, palings, the creation, / foamed with the purity of tears, / are only categories of passion, / hoarded by the human heart. [*Definition of the Creative Power*, trans. J. M. Cohen]

10 And yet the order of the acts is planned, / The way's end destinate and unconcealed. / Alone. Now is the time of Pharisees. / *To live is not like walking through a field.* [*Hamlet*, trans. Henry Kamen]

11 When the heart dictates the line / it sends a slave on to the stage / and there's an end of art and there's / a breath of earth and destiny. [*Oh, had I known*, trans. J. M. Cohen]

12 No bad man can be a good poet. [In Ilya Ehrenburg, *Truce*]

KENNETH PATCHEN 1911–1972

13 God must have loved the People in Power, for he made them so very like their own image of him. [Quoted by Adrian Mitchell in the *Guardian*, 1 Feb. 1972]

ANDREW PATERSON 1864–1941

14 Once a jolly swagman camped by a billabong, / Under the shade of a coolibah tree, / And he sang as he sat and waited till his billy boiled, / 'You'll come a-waltzing, Matilda, with me.' [*Waltzing Matilda*]

BRIAN PATTEN 1946–

15 And the rightful owner of the music, / tiny and no longer timid, sang, / for the rightful owners of the song. [*Interruption at the Opera House*]

LESLIE PAUL 1905–

16 Angry Young Man. [Title of book, 1951. See also 123:8]

WOLFGANG PAULI 1900–1958

17 So young, and already so unknown? [Of another scientist. In E. Regis, *Who Got Einstein's Office?*]

TOM PAULIN 1949–

18 It's one thing being British / but you need a white skin to be English / then you can shout things in public places / at kids with a different complexion. [*Chucking It Away* (after Heinrich Heine)]

1 See this word *tradition* / it'll squeak if you touch it / then break up like a baked turd / into tiny wee bits. [*The Good Lord must persecute me*]

2 What the wrong gods established / no army can ever save. [*A Partial State*]

3 The deadlands of the mullahs / Where young men dream of laws / As simple as the gallows. [*Song for February*]

CESARE PAVESE 1908–1950

4 The richness of life lies in the memories we have forgotten. [*This Business of Living: A Diary 1935–1950*]

5 One nail drives out another. But four nails make a cross. [16 Aug. 1950]

ANNA PAVLOVA 1885–1931

6 An artist should know all about love and learn to live without it. [In the *Guardian*, 5 Oct. 1987]

OCTAVIO PAZ 1914–

7 Great art is always an invention that begins as an imitation. [*Convergences*]

8 Memory is not what we remember, but that which remembers us. Memory is a present that never stops passing. [*The Curse*: used as epigraph to David Suzuki and Peter Knudtson, *Genethics*, Ch. 1]

9 Mexicans are descended from the Aztecs, Peruvians from the Incas and Argentinians from the ships. [Ascr. in the *Observer*, 16 June 1990]

NORMAN VINCENT PEALE 1898–

10 The Power of Positive Thinking. [Title of book]

EDWARD PEARCE 1939–

11 Television has devalued politicians of all parties. It has thrown them back on their own merits. [From *Hummingbirds and Hyenas*, in the *Guardian*, 3 Oct. 1985]

12 On the side of the angels but he isn't doing them any good. [Of Norman Willis, General Secretary of the TUC. From *Looking down on Mrs Thatcher*, in *New Society*, 21 Sept. 1987]

13 We [the British] have . . . elevated servility into one of the fine arts. Yet we make no impact at all on the world we have lost. Britain is a tin can tied to a dog's tail, but a tin can fitted with a silencer. [Of Britain's subservience to the USA on the eve of Gulf War. In the *Guardian*, 9 Jan. 1991]

PHILIPPA PEARCE 1920–

14 Then, suddenly, when Ben could hardly see, he saw clearly. He saw clearly that you couldn't have impossible things, however much you wanted them. He saw that if you didn't have the possible things, then you had nothing. [*A Dog So Small*, Ch. 19]

LESTER PEARSON 1897–1972

15 Not only did he [Dean Acheson] not suffer fools gladly, he did not suffer them at all. [In *Time* magazine, 25 Oct. 1971]

16 Diplomacy is letting someone else have your way. [From the *Observer*, 18 Mar. 1965, in Jonathon Green, *Says Who?*]

COMMANDER R. PEARY 1856–1920

17 The Eskimo had his own explanation. Said he: 'The devil is asleep or having trouble with his wife, or we should never have come back so easily.' [*The North Pole*]

WESTBROOK PEGLER 1894–1969

18 He [Edward VIII] will go from resort to resort getting more tanned and more tired. [On the king's abdication. In Alistair Cooke, *Six Men*, Pt II]

CHARLES PÉGUY 1873–1914

19 The Social Revolution will be moral, or it will not be. [*Basic Verities*]

20 What will God say to us if some of us go to him without the others? [In W. Neil, *Concise Dictionary of Religious Quotations*]

C. S. PEIRCE 1839–1914

21 Young fogey. [Coinage ascr. to him in 1909 by Alan Watkins in the *Observer*, 26 May 1985]

SEAN PENN 1960–

1 The difference between being a director and being an actor is the difference between being the carpenter banging the nails into the wood, and being the piece of wood the nails are being banged into. [Interview in the *Guardian*, 28 Nov. 1991]

S. J. PERELMAN 1904–1979

2 Crazy Like a Fox [Title of book]

3 I guess I'm just an old mad scientist at bottom. Give me an underground laboratory, half a dozen atomsmashers, and a beautiful girl in a diaphanous veil waiting to be turned into a chimpanzee, and I care not who writes the nation's laws. [*Crazy Like a Fox*, 'Captain Future, Block that Kick']

4 A feeling of emulsion swept over me. ['The Love Decoy']

5 He bit his lip in a manner which immediately awakened my maternal sympathy, and I helped him bite it.

6 There had been a heavy fall of talcum several hours before and as far as the ground could see the eye was white.

7 Philomène was a dainty thing, built somewhat on the order of Lois de Fee, the lady bouncer. She had the rippling muscles of a panther, the solidity of a water buffalo, and the lazy insolence of a shoe salesman. ['Kitchen Bouquet']

8 For years I have let dentists ride roughshod over my teeth; I have been sawed, hacked, chopped, whittled, bewitched, bewildered, tattooed, and signed on again; but this is cuspid's last stand. ['Nothing but the Tooth']

9 You've a sharp tongue in your head, Mr Essick. Look out it doesn't cut your throat. [*The Rising Gorge*, 'All Out . . .']

10 Love is not the dying moan of a distant violin – it's the triumphant twang of a bedspring. [In A. Andrews, *Quotations for Speakers and Writers*]

SHIMON PERES 1923–

11 Most of them [Israeli observers who study overseas systems] are like the lawyer who appeared before the jury and said: 'The following are the conclusions on which I base my facts.' [Attr.]

GABRIEL PÉRI [French communist] 1902–1941

12 In a few minutes I am going out to shape all the singing tomorrows. [Before his execution by the Germans in 1941. In A. Andrews, *Quotations for Speakers and Writers*]

JUAN PERÓN 1895–1974

13 If I had not been born Perón, I would have liked to be Perón. [In the *Observer*, 'Sayings of the Week', 21 Feb. 1960]

MARSHAL PÉTAIN 1856–1951

14 They shall not pass. [Attr. at Battle of Verdun, 26 Feb. 1916. Also used in General Nivelle's Order of the Day, 23 June 1916, as 'You will not let them pass!' and adopted in the Spanish Civil War. See 11:28, 185:2]

15 One does not fight with men against material; it is with material served by men that one makes war. [In Alistair Horne, *The Price of Glory*, Ch. 27]

16 To make a union with Great Britain would be fusion with a corpse. [On Churchill's proposal for Anglo-French union, 1940. In Winston S. Churchill, *Their Finest Hour*, Ch. 10]

ZARKO PETAN

17 Cowards' hearts beat faster than heroes' but last longer. [In *The Times*, 15 June 1977]

18 In the theatre, the director is God – but unfortunately, the actors are atheists.

JOHN PETER 1938–

19 His [Samuel Beckett's] statement of desolation has its own impersonal dignity and you can derive from it whatever comfort you can: otherwise there is always God, economics, or Ibsen. [On Beckett's death, in the *Sunday Times*, 31 Dec. 1989]

20 You can hold a mirror up to nature or a mirror up to art; I don't think you should

hold a mirror up to another mirror. [Review of Michael Frayn's play *Look Look* in the *Sunday Times*, 22 Apr. 1990]

LAURENCE J. PETER 1919–1990

1 The modern child will answer you back before you've said anything. [*Peter's Quotations*, 'Childhood']

2 A pessimist is a man who looks both ways before crossing a one-way street. ['Optimism – Pessimism']

LAURENCE J. PETER and RAYMOND HULL 1918–1985

3 *The Peter Principle*: In a Hierarchy Every Employee Tends to Rise to his Level of Incompetence. [*The Peter Principle*, Ch. 1]

4 Work is accomplished by those employees who have not yet reached their level of incompetence.

5 Competence, like truth, beauty and contact lenses, is in the eye of the beholder. [3]

6 The watchword for Side-Issue Specialists is *Look after the molehills and the mountains will look after themselves.* [13]

7 If you don't know where you are going, you will probably end up somewhere else. [15]

8 *Lateral Arabesque* – a pseudo-promotion consisting of a new title and a new work place. [Glossary]

JAN PETRZAK

9 Once we [the Poles] had socialism without social justice, now we have capitalism without capital. [In the *Observer*, 'Sayings of the Week', 15 Apr. 1990]

SIR NIKOLAUS PEVSNER 1902–1983

10 Hearty, robust and revolting. [Of a church. *Buildings of England: London, except the Cities of London and Westminster*]

DR WILLIAM LYON PHELPS 1865–1913

11 Instead of selecting a subject, modern biographers pick a victim. It's getting so that good men are afraid to die. [Quoted by Magnus Magnusson in the *Guardian*, 8 Apr. 1982]

PRINCE PHILIP, DUKE OF EDINBURGH 1921–

12 I include 'pidgin-English' ... even though I am referred to in that splendid language as 'Fella belong Mrs Queen'. [Speech at English-speaking Union Conference, Ottawa, 29 Oct. 1958]

13 Just at this moment we are suffering a national defeat comparable to any lost military campaign, and what is more it is self-inflicted ... I think it is about time we pulled our finger out. [Speech to businessmen in London 17 Oct. 1961]

14 The rest of the world most certainly does not owe us a living.

15 I never see any home cooking. All I get is fancy stuff. [In the *Observer*, 'Sayings of the Week', 28 Oct. 1962]

16 The biggest waste of water in the country by far. You spend half a pint and flush two gallons. [Attr., speech, 1965]

17 If you stay here much longer you'll go back with slitty eyes. [Remark to British student during state visit to China, 16 Oct. 1986]

18 I don't think doing it for money makes it any more moral. I don't think a prostitute is more moral than a wife, but they are doing the same thing. [Of killing animals. Speech in London, 6 Dec. 1988]

19 This [Buckingham Palace] isn't ours. it's a tied cottage. [In *Royal Quotes*, sel. Noel St George]

EMO PHILIPS

20 I'm not a fatalist; even if I were, what could I do about it? [In TV programme *Saturday Live*, 8 Mar. 1986]

MELANIE PHILLIPS 1951–

21 Pity our poor dear queen. She finds herself increasingly the head of not so much the royal family as the royal one-parent family. [On the break-up of the marriage of the Duke and Duchess of York. In the *Guardian*, 21 Mar. 1992]

NORAH [later LADY] PHILLIPS
1910–1992

1 On the subject of confused people, I liked the store detective who said he'd seen a lot of people so confused that they'd stolen things, but never one so confused that they'd paid twice. [In the *Sunday Telegraph*, 14 Aug. 1977]

2 I have found that people are usually much more moved by economics than by morals. [In the *Independent*, 'Quote Unquote', 30 Mar. 1991]

STEPHEN PHILLIPS 1864–1915

3 A man not old, but mellow, like good wine. [*Ulysses*, Act III, sc. ii]

TOM PHILLIPS 1937–

4 The test of a good portrait is that if you take it down, you have the feeling that somebody has left the room. [Interview in the *Observer*, 1 Oct. 1989]

EDEN PHILLPOTTS 1862–1961

5 His father's sister had bats in the belfry and was put away. [*Peacock House*, 'My First Murder']

EDITH PIAF 1915–1963

6 *Non, je ne regrette rien.* [Title of song, words by Michael Vaucaire]

PABLO PICASSO 1881–1973

7 Every human being is a whole colony. [In Françoise Gilot and Carlton Lake, *Life with Picasso*, Pt 1]

8 God is really only another artist. He invented the giraffe, the elephant, and the cat. He has no real style. He just goes on trying other things.

9 You must always work not just within but below your means. If you can handle three elements, handle only two. If you can handle ten, then handle only five. In that way the ones you do handle, you handle with more ease, more mastery, and you create a feeling of strength in reserve. [2]

10 For me a painting is a dramatic action in the course of which reality finds itself split apart.

11 Beginning with Van Gogh, however great we may be, we are all, in a measure, auto-didacts – you might almost say primitive painters. Painters no longer live within a tradition and so each one of us must re-create an entire language.

12 There are two professions . . . whose practitioners are never satisfied with what they do: dentists and photographers. Every dentist would like to be a doctor and every photographer would like to be a painter.

13 Every positive value has its price in negative terms, and you never see anything very great which is not, at the same time, horrible in some respect. The genius of Einstein leads to Hiroshima.

14 That's why painters live so long. While I work I leave my body outside the door, the way Moslems take off their shoes before entering the mosque. [3]

15 If I telegraph one of my canvases to New York . . . any house-painter should be able to do it properly. A painting is a sign – just like the sign that indicates a one-way street. [5]

16 I hate that aesthetic game of the eye and the mind . . . played by these connoisseurs, these mandarins who 'appreciate' beauty. What *is* beauty, anyway? There's no such thing. I never 'appreciate', any more than I 'like'. I love or I hate. [6]

17 Don't talk to me about Bonnard . . . That's not painting, what he does. He never goes beyond his own sensibility. He doesn't know how to choose.

18 Aragon is a saint, but perhaps not a hero.

19 My sculptures are plastic metaphors. It's the same principle as in painting. I've said that a painting shouldn't be a *trompe l'oeil* but a *trompe l'esprit*. I'm out to fool the mind rather than the eye. And that goes for sculpture too.

20 Lingerie is on the next floor. [To Peggy Guggenheim when she arrived at his studio in 1939 with a list of pictures she wanted to buy. In J. B. Weld, *Peggy: The Wayward Guggenheim*]

1 Painting is a blind man's profession. He paints not what he sees, but what he feels, what he tells himself about what he has seen. [In Jean Cocteau, *Journals*, 'Childhood']

2 You do something, and then somebody else comes along and does it pretty. [To Gertrude Stein. Quoted by F. Scott Fitzgerald in letter to Frances Scott Fitzgerald, 7 May 1940]

3 Art is a lie which makes us realize the truth. [In D. Ashton, *Picasso on Art*]

4 A green parrot is also a green salad and a green parrot. He who makes it only a green parrot diminishes its reality. [In *Education and Imagination*, ed. Kieran Egan and Dan Nadaner, 'What Happened to Imagination?']

5 I never made a painting as a work of art. It's all research. [Quoted by David Hockney in interview in the *Observer*, 16 Nov. 1988]

6 Picasso insisted everything was miraculous. It was miraculous, he said, 'that one did not melt in one's bath'. [Attr. by Jean Cocteau]

DR H. R. PICKARD

7 If you give a girl an inch nowadays she will make a dress of it. [In the *Observer*, 'Sayings of the Week', 7 Oct. 1928]

MARY PICKFORD 1893–1979

8 Douglas [Fairbanks] had always faced a situation the only way he knew how, by running away from it. [*Sunshine and Shadow*]

WILFRED PICKLES 1904–1978

9 Have a Go! [Title of BBC radio quiz show, 1946–1967]

10 Are you courting? [Catchphrase in *Have a Go!*]

11 Give him the money, Barney. [Addressed to Barney Colehan]

12 In Cornwall it's Saturday before you realize it's Thursday.

CHARLES PIERCE [Female impersonator]

13 I'd rather be black than gay because when you're black you don't have to tell your mother. [In *Penguin Dictionary of Modern Humorous Quotations*, comp. Fred Metcalf]

LESTER PIGGOTT 1935–

14 Eating's going to be a whole new ball game, and I may have to buy a new pair of trousers. [On his retirement from racing. In the *Observer*, 'Sayings of the Week', 3 Nov. 1985]

HAROLD PINTER 1930–

15 I got this mate in Shepherd's Bush. In the convenience. Well, he was in the convenience. Run about the best convenience they had. [*The Caretaker*, Act I]

16 I said to this monk, here, I said, ... you haven't got a pair of shoes, have you, a pair of shoes, I said, enough to keep me on my way ... Piss off, he said to me.

17 If only I could get down to Sidcup! I've been waiting for the weather to break. He's got my papers, this man I left them with, it's got it all down there, I could prove everything.

18 Shirts like these don't go far in the winter-time. I mean that's one thing I know for a fact. No, what I need is a kind of a shirt with stripes, a good solid shirt, with stripes going down. [II]

19 I mean, don't forget the earth's about five thousand million years old, at least. Who can afford to live in the past? [*The Homecoming*, Act II]

20 In other words, apart from the known and the unknown, what else is there?

21 I've been the whole hog plenty of times. Sometimes ... you can be happy ... and not go the whole hog. Now and again ... you can be happy ... without going any hog.

22 In my day nobody changed. A man was. Only religion could alter him, and that at least was a glorious misery. [*No Man's Land*, Act II]

23 'But what would you say your plays were *about*, Mr Pinter?' 'The weasel under the cocktail cabinet.' [Exchange at a new writers' brains trust. In J. Russell Taylor, *Anger and After*, Ch. 7]

1 The more acute the experience the less articulate its expression. [Programme note to *The Room*, and *The Dumb Waiter*]

2 The great thing about writing plays is you don't think. [In the *Observer*, 'Sayings of the Week', 25 Oct. 1988]

3 One way of looking at speech is to say it is a constant stratagem to cover nakedness. [In *Barnes and Noble Book of Quotations*, ed. Robert I. Fitzhenry, ' Words']

SIR DAVID PIPER 1918–1990

4 A magnanimous tribute by Imperial England to a gallant if muddle-headed girl. [On statue of Joan of Arc at Stanhope Gate, Hyde Park. *The Companion Guide to London*]

LUIGI PIRANDELLO 1867–1936

5 Six Characters in Search of an Author. [Title of play]

ROBERT M. PIRSIG 1928–

6 When people are fanatically dedicated to political or religious faiths or any other kind of dogmas or goals, it's always because these dogmas or goals are in doubt. [*Zen and the Art of Motorcycle Maintenance*, Pt II, Ch. 13]

7 Mental reflection is so much more interesting than TV it's a shame more people don't switch over to it. They probably think what they hear is unimportant but it never is. [III. 17]

8 One thing about pioneers that you don't hear mentioned is that they are invariably, by their nature, mess-makers. [21]

9 One geometry cannot be more true than another; it can only be more *convenient*. Geometry is not true, it is advantageous. [22. Echoes Henri Poincaré]

10 Traditional scientific method has always been at the very *best*, 20–20 hindsight. It's good for seeing where you've been. [24]

11 We keep passing unseen through little moments of other people's lives.

12 That's the classical mind at work, runs fine inside but looks dingy on the surface. [25]

WILLIAM B. PITKIN 1878–1953

13 Life Begins at Forty. [Title of book, 1932]

RUTH PITTER 1897–1992

14 The seldom female in a world of males! [*The Kitten's Eclogue*, IV]

FIONA PITT-KETHLEY 1954–

15 I believe in equality. Bald men should marry bald women. [Interview in the *Guardian*, 21 Nov. 1990]

16 Sanity is not being caught by a psychiatrist. [In the *Guardian*, 8 May 1991]

WILLIAM PITTS 1900–1980

17 It is the overtakers who keep the undertakers busy. [In the *Observer*, 'Sayings of the Week', 22 Dec. 1963]

MAX PLANCK 1858–1947

18 I regard consciousness as fundamental. I regard matter as derivative from consciousness. We cannot get behind consciousness. [Interview with J. W. N. Sullivan. In Kenneth Walker, *The Circle of Life*, Pt II, Ch. 3]

ALAN PLATER 1935–

19 Writers tend to hang around the edges of society, designated court jesters who know they've landed the best job in the court. They also know that they win in the end. [In the *Listener*, 2 Mar. 1989]

SYLVIA PLATH 1932–1963

20 A man in black with a Meinkampf look. [*Daddy*]

21 So daddy, I'm finally through. / The black telephone's off at the root, / The voices just can't worm through.

22 Dying / Is an art, like everything else. / I do it exceptionally well. [*Lady Lazarus*]

23 Love set you going like a fat gold watch. [*Morning Song*]

24 Winter is for women – / The woman still at her knitting, / At the cradle of Spanish walnut, / Her body a bulb in the cold and too dumb to think. [*Wintering*]

KEN PLATT 1922–

1 Daft as a brush. [Catchphrase in comedy act, from 1940s. In Nigel Rees, *Dictionary of Twentieth Century Quotations*]

2 I won't take my coat off – I'm not stopping. [Catchphrase, 1950s]

FRANCIS PLAYER [Gary Player's father]

3 Never invest in anything that eats while you sleep. [Advice to Gary Player and his brother. In the *Observer*, 24 Feb. 1991]

WILLIAM PLOMER 1903–1973

4 Out of that bungled, unwise war / An alp of unforgiveness grew. [*The Boer War*]

5 A pleasant old buffer, nephew to a lord, / Who believed that the bank was mightier than the sword, / And that an umbrella might pacify barbarians abroad: / Just like an old liberal / Between the wars. [*Father and Son: 1939*]

6 With first-rate sherry flowing into second-rate whores, / And third-rate conversation without one single pause: / Just like a couple / Between the wars.

7 Who strolls so late, for mugs a bait, / In the mists of Maida Vale, / Sauntering past a stucco gate / Fallen, but hardly frail? [*French Lisette*]

8 On a sofa upholstered in panther skin / Mona did researches in original sin. [*Mews Flat Mona*]

9 So never say to D'Arcy, 'Be your age!' – / He'd shrivel up at once or turn to stone. [*The Playboy of the Demi-world: 1938*]

10 It's so utterly out of the world! / So fearfully wide of the mark! / A Robinson Crusoe existence will pall / On that unexplored side of the Park – / Not a soul will be likely to call! [*A Shot in the Park*]

11 She had only taken one bite out of the tiny piece of bread and butter on her plate, and her little finger was like a hook on which to hang a whole system of genteel behaviour. [*I Speak of Africa*, 'Saturday, Sunday, Monday']

CHRISTOPHER PLUMMER 1927–

12 Working with her [Julie Andrews] is like being hit over the head with a Valentine card. [In *Utterly Trivial Knowledge: The Music Game*, ed. John Denny]

JOSEPH PLUNKETT 1887–1916

13 I see His blood upon the rose / And in the stars the glory of His eyes. [*I See His Blood*]

HENRI POINCARÉ 1854–1912

14 Science is built of facts, as a house is built of stones; but an accumulation of facts is no more a science than a heap of stones is a house. [*Science and Hypothesis*, Ch. 9]

15 Thought is only a flash between two long nights, but this flash is everything. [In H. L. Mencken, *New Dictionary of Quotations*]

A. W. POLLARD 1859–1944

16 He is a bad man who does not pay to the future at least as much as he has received from the past. [In the *Observer*, 'Sayings of the Week', 31 July 1927]

QUINTON POLLARD

17 If you can see the French coast, it means that it is going to rain; if you can't see it, then it's already raining. [Attr.]

CHANNING POLLOCK 1880–1946

18 No man in the world has more courage than the man who can stop after eating one peanut. [In Jonathon Green, *Consuming Secrets*]

JACKSON POLLOCK 1912–1956

19 Painting is self-discovery. Every good artist paints what he is. [In F. V. O'Connor, *Jackson Pollock*]

PRESIDENT GEORGES POMPIDOU 1911–1974

20 A statesman is a politician who places himself at the service of the nation. A politician is a statesman who places the nation at his service. [In the *Observer*, 'Sayings of the Year', 30 Dec. 1973]

MICHAEL POPE ?–?1940

21 A fire has destroyed the Chameleon at

Strood, / Which makes me exceedingly glad; / For the waitresses there were disgustingly rude / And the food was incredibly bad. [*Capital Levities*, 'Epitaph on a Country Inn Destroyed by Fire']

DR SAXTON POPE

1 And so, stoic and unafraid, departed the last wild Indian of America [named Ishi]. He closed a chapter in history. He looked upon us as sophisticated children – smart but not wise. We knew many things and much that is false. He knew nature, which is always true. [In Theodora Kroeber, *Ishi in Two Worlds*, Epilogue]

SIR KARL POPPER 1902–

2 Our knowledge can only be finite, while our ignorance must necessarily be infinite. [*Conjectures and Refutations*]

3 But I shall certainly admit a system as empirical or scientific only if it is capable of being *tested* by experience. These considerations suggest that not the *verifiability* but the *falsifiability* of a system is to be taken as a criterion of demarcation ... *It must be possible for an empirical scientific system to be refuted by experience.* [*The Logic of Scientific Discovery*, Ch. 1, sect. vi]

4 This civilization has not yet fully recovered from the shock of its birth – the transition from the tribal or 'closed society', with its submission to magical forces, to the 'open society' which sets free the critical powers of man. [*The Open Society and Its Enemies*, Introduction]

5 We may become the makers of our fate when we have ceased to pose as its prophets.

6 We must plan for freedom, and not only for security, if for no other reason than that only freedom can make security secure. [21]

7 There is no history of mankind, there is only an indefinite number of histories of all kinds of aspects of human life. And one of these is the history of political power. This is elevated into the history of the world. [25]

8 Science must begin with myths, and with the criticism of myths. ['Philosophy of Science: A Personal Report', in *British Philosophy in the Mid-century*, ed. C. A. Mace]

9 Don't ask *what are* questions, ask *what do* questions, don't ask *why* questions, ask *how* questions. [Quoted by Bernard Levin in the *Sunday Times Books*, 16 Apr. 1989]

JACK POPPLEWELL 1911–

10 Horses for courses, yes – but not at table if you please. [*Dear Children*]

11 Wife (borrowing mink coat from her husband's mistress), 'We shared the skunk – why not the mink?' [*Every Other Evening*]

COLE PORTER 1891–1964

12 But I'm always true to you, darlin', in my fashion, / Yes, I'm always true to you, darlin', in my way. [Song: *Always True to You in My Fashion*, in musical *Kiss Me, Kate*]

13 But now, God knows, / Anything goes. [Song: *Anything Goes*, and also title of musical]

14 And we suddenly know, what heaven we're in, / When they begin the beguine. [Song: *Begin the Beguine*, in musical *Jubilee*]

15 Don't Fence Me In. [Title of song in film *Hollywood Canteen*]

16 I Get a Kick out of You. [Title of song in *Anything Goes*]

17 I love Paris in the springtime. [Song: *I Love Paris*, in musical *Can-Can*]

18 It's delightful, / It's delicious, / It's delectable, / It's delirious. [Song: *It's De-Lovely*, in musical *Red Hot and Blue*]

19 I've Got You Under My Skin. [Title of song in musical *Born to Dance*]

20 It's not 'cause I wouldn't / It's not 'cause I shouldn't / And, Lord knows, it's not 'cause I couldn't, / It's simply because I'm the laziest gal in town. [Song: *The Laziest Gal in Town*, in musical *Stage Fright*, sung by Marlene Dietrich]

21 Birds do it, bees do it, / Even educated fleas do it. / Let's do it, let's fall in love. [Song: *Let's Do It*, in musical *Paris*; these words added later]

22 If you want to buy my wares, / Follow me and climb the stairs. / Love for sale. [Song: *Love for Sale*, in musical *The New Yorkers*]

1 Miss Otis regrets she's unable to lunch today. [Song: *Miss Otis Regrets*, in musical *Hi Diddle Diddle*]

2 My heart belongs to Daddy / 'Cause my Daddy, he treats me so well. [Song: *My Heart Belongs to Daddy*, in musical *Leave It to Me*]

3 Night and day you are the one, / Only you beneath the moon and under the sun. [Song: *Night and Day*, in musical *Gay Divorce*]

4 And his cheques, I fear, / Mean that sex is here / To stay. [Song: *Sex is Here to Stay*]

5 HE: Have you heard it's in the stars / Next July we collide with Mars? / SHE: Well, did you evah! What a swell party this is. [Song: *Well, Did You Evah!*, in film *High Society*]

6 Who wants to be a millionaire? I don't. [Song: *Who Wants to be a Millionaire?*, in *High Society*]

7 You're the top! You're the Eiffel Tower! [Song: *You're the Top*, in *Anything Goes*]

PETER PORTER 1929–

8 London is full of chickens on electric spits, / Cooking in windows where the public pass. / This, say the chickens, is their Auschwitz, / And all poultry eaters are psychopaths. [*Annotations of Auschwitz*]

9 Who would be loved / If he could be feared and hated, yet still / Enjoy his lust, eat well and play the flute? [*Soliloquy at Potsdam*]

10 Some of us may die. / Remember, statistically / It is not likely to be you. / All flags are flying fully dressed / On Government buildings – the sun is shining / Death is the least we have to fear. [*Your Attention Please*]

ROY PORTER 1946–

11 Civilization gets the historians it deserves. [In the *Observer*, 30 Oct. 1988]

BEATRIX POTTER 1866–1943

12 I am worn to a ravelling. [*The Tailor of Gloucester*]

13 I am undone and worn to a thread-paper for I have NO MORE TWIST.

14 I shall tell you a tale of four little rabbits whose names were Flopsy, Mopsy, Cottontail and Peter. [*The Tale of Peter Rabbit*]

15 You may go into the field or down the lane, but don't go into Mr McGregor's garden.

16 It is said that the effect of eating too much lettuce is 'soporific'. [*The Tale of the Flopsy Bunnies*]

DENNIS POTTER 1935–

17 People think bleakness is despair, but it's not. There is always that last place. [Profile in the *Listener*, 20 Nov. 1986]

GILLIE POTTER 1887–1975

18 Good evening, England. This is Gillie Potter speaking to you in basic English. [Catchphrase in BBC radio broadcasts as the 'Squire of Hogsnorton'. In John Fisher, *Funny Way to be a Hero*, '. . . To See Such Fun']

STEPHEN POTTER 1900–1969

19 Gamesmanship or, The Art of Winning Games without Actually Cheating. [Title of book]

20 *How to be one up* – how to make the other man feel that something has gone wrong, however slightly. [*Lifemanship*, 1]

21 There was one ploy of Gattling's which I found particularly effective, and I believe it must have been about this time that I first murmured to myself the word 'Lifemanship'.

22 If you have nothing to say, or, rather, something extremely stupid and obvious, say it, but in a 'plonking' tone of voice – i.e. roundly, but hollowly and dogmatically. [3]

23 Just as there are OK-words in conversationship so there are OK-*people to mention* in Newstatesmanship. [5]

24 Donsmanship he defines as 'the art of criticizing without actually listening'. [6]

25 A good general rule is to state that the bouquet is better than the taste, and vice versa. [*One-upmanship*, Ch. 14]

EZRA POUND 1885–1972

26 Winter is icumen in, / Lhude sing Goddamm. / Raineth drop and staineth slop, /

And how the wind doth ramm! / Sing: God-damm. [*Ancient Music*]

1 Hang it all, Robert Browning, / There can be but one 'Sordello'. [*Cantos*, II]

2 And the life goes on, mooning upon bare hills; / Flame leaps from the hand, the rain is listless, / Yet drinks the thirst from our lips, / solid as echo. [VII]

3 Go to hell Apovitch. Chicago aint the whole punkin. [XII]

4 'I am not your fader but your moder,' quod he. / 'Your father was a rich merchant in Stambouli.'

5 And even I can remember / A day when the historians left blanks in their writings, / I mean for things they didn't know. [XIII]

6 The blossoms of the apricot / blow from the east to the west, / And I have tried to keep them from / falling.

7 To the beat of the measure / From star-up to the half-dark / From half-dark to half-dark / Unceasing the measure. [XXXIX]

8 *With Usura* / With usura hath no man a house of good stone / each block cut smooth and well fitting. [XLV]

9 Said Paterson: / Hath benefit of interest in all / the moneys which it, the bank, creates out of / nothing. [XLVI]

10 Pull down thy vanity / Thou art a beaten dog beneath the hail, / A swollen magpie in a fitful sun, / Half black half white / Nor knowst'ou wing from tail / Pull down thy vanity. [LXXXI]

11 Bah! I have sung women in three cities, / But it is all the same; / And I will sing of the sun. [*Cino*]

12 Of all those young women / not one has enquired the cause of the world / Nor the modus of lunar eclipses / Nor whether there be any patch left of us / After we cross the infernal ripples [*Homage to Sextus Propertius*]

13 For three years, out of key with his time, / He strove to resuscitate the dead art / Of poetry; to maintain 'the sublime' / In the old sense. Wrong from the start. [*Hugh Selwyn Mauberley*, 'E. P. Ode pour l'élection de son sépulcre', I]

14 Observed the elegance of Circe's hair / Rather than the mottoes on sundials.

15 Caliban casts out Ariel. [III]

16 Walked eye-deep in hell / believing in old men's lies, then unbelieving / came home, home to a lie. [IV]

17 There died a myriad, / And of the best, among them, / For an old bitch gone in the teeth, / For a botched civilization. [V]

18 Dowson found harlots cheaper than hotels. ['Siena mi fe; disfecemi Maremma']

19 And give up verse, my boy, / there's nothing in it. ['Mr Nixon']

20 The apparition of these faces in the crowd; / Petals on a wet black bough. [*In a Station of the Metro*]

21 She is dying piece-meal / of a sort of emotional anaemia. / And round about there is a rabble / of the filthy, sturdy, unkillable infants / of the very poor. [*Lustra*, 'The Garden']

22 The author's conviction . . . is that music begins to atrophy when it departs too far from the dance; that poetry begins to atrophy when it gets too far from music. [*ABC of Reading*, 'Warning']

23 Any general statement is like a cheque drawn on a bank. Its value depends on what is there to meet it. [Ch. 1]

24 Literature is news that *stays* news. [2]

25 Rhythm is a form cut into TIME, as a design is determined SPACE. ['Treatise on Reading', I]

26 Real education must ultimately be limited to men who insist on knowing: the rest is mere sheep-hearding. [8]

27 Great Literature is simply language charged with meaning to the utmost possible degree. [*How to Read*, Pt II]

28 The difference between a gun and a tree is a difference of tempo. The tree explodes every spring. [In *Criterion*, July 1937]

29 I once told Fordie [Ford Madox Ford] that if he were placed naked and alone in a room without furniture, I would come back in an hour and find total confusion. [In V. S. Pritchett, *The Working Novelist*]

ANTHONY POWELL 1905–

30 He fell in love with himself at first sight and it is a passion to which he has

always remained faithful. Self-love seems so often unrequited. [*The Acceptance World*, Ch. 1]

1 Dinner at the Huntercombes' possessed 'only two dramatic features – the wine was a farce and the food a tragedy'. [4]

2 All men are brothers, but thank God, they aren't all brothers-in-law. [*At Lady Molly's*, Ch. 4]

3 All the same, you know parents – especially step-parents – are sometimes a bit of a disappointment to their children. They don't fulfil the promise of their early years. [*A Buyer's Market*, Ch. 2]

4 There is a strong disposition in youth, from which some individuals never escape, to suppose that everyone else is having a more enjoyable time than we are ourselves. [4]

5 People think that because a novel's invented, it isn't true. Exactly the reverse is the case. Biography and memoirs can never be wholly true, since they cannot include every conceivable circumstance of what happened. The novel can do that. [*Hearing Secret Harmonies*, Ch. 3]

6 You knew that château-bottled shit Widmerpool. [7]

7 One of the worst things about life is not how nasty the nasty people are. You know that already. It is how nasty the nice people can be.

8 Growing old is like being increasingly penalized for a crime you haven't committed. [*Temporary Kings*, Ch. 1]

9 Borrit ... once spoke of the Masai tribe holding, as a tenet of faith, that all cows in the world belong to them. Ada, in similar manner, arrogated to herself all the world's gossip, sources other than her own a presumption. [3]

10 If you don't spend every morning of your life writing, it's awfully difficult to know what to do otherwise. [Interview in the *Observer*, 3 Apr. 1984]

ENOCH POWELL 1912–

11 The life of nations no less than that of men is lived largely in the imagination. [Said in 1946. Epigraph to Martin J. Wiener, *English Culture and the Decline of the Industrial Spirit, 1850–1980*]

12 As I look ahead, I am filled with foreboding. Like the Roman, I seem to see 'the River Tiber foaming with much blood'. [Speech in Birmingham, 20 Apr. 1968]

13 I always refer to my opponents as Miss Hughes. [On election campaign for South Down, Northern Ireland, June 1983]

14 Above any other position of eminence that of Prime Minister is filled by fluke. [In the *Observer*, 'Sayings of the Week', 8 Mar. 1987]

15 Always looking at himself in mirrors to make sure that he was sufficiently outrageous. [Of Byron. In the *Sunday Times Books*, 8 May 1988]

16 [When asked why he rarely listened to music now] I don't like things ... which interfere with one's heart strings. It doesn't do to awaken longings that can't be fulfilled. [Interview in John Mortimer, *In Character*. See also 229:5]

ROBERT POWELL 1909–

17 People are either escapists or Buddhists in this world. [*Zen and Reality*, 'Thoughts on Life']

SANDY POWELL 1900–1982

18 Can you hear me, mother? [Catchphrase coined in early days of radio comedy. In *Can You Hear Me, Mother?*, Ch. 3]

DAVID POWNALL 1938–

19 Doctor Livingstone thought that football was God in the same way as his fellow Glaswegians. All the rules are the same as those of God. Would God allow us to be offside? Of course not. To molest the unprotected goalkeeper? Never. [*The Raining Tree War*, Ch. 5]

JOHN COWPER POWYS 1872–1963

20 We have at any rate one advantage over Time and Space. We think *them* whereas it is extremely doubtful whether *they* think *us*! [*Art of Happiness*, 1929, p. 39]

1 He combined scepticism of everything with credulity about everything ... and I am convinced this is the true Shakespearean way wherewith to take life. [*Autobiography*]

JOSEPH PRESCOTT

2 The trouble with many travellers is that they take themselves along. [*Aphorisms and Other Observations*, 'Travel']

3 There are no foreign books; there are only foreign readers. ['Literature']

4 Alexander Graham Bell invented an extension of the umbilical cord. ['Miscellany']

5 All flesh is grass under a power mower. ['Variations']

JACQUES PRÉVERT 1900–1977

6 *La mère fait du tricot / Le fils fait la guerre / Elle trouve ça tout naturel la mère / Et le père qu'est-ce qu'il fait le père?* – The mother is knitting, the son is fighting in the war. The mother finds this quite natural, and what's the father up to? [*Familiale*]

7 *Notre Père qui êtes aux cieux / Restez-y / Et nous resterons sur la terre / Qui est quelquefois si jolie.* – Our Father that art in heaven, stay there and we will stay on earth which is sometimes so pretty. [*Pater Noster*]

ANDRÉ PREVIN 1929–

8 The basic difference between classical music and jazz is that in the former the music is always greater than its performance – whereas the way jazz is performed is always more important than what is being played. [In Nat Shapiro, *Encyclopedia of Quotations about Music*]

DORY PREVIN 1937–

9 I have flown to star-stained heights / on bent and battered wings / in search of mythical kings, mythical kings. / Sure that everything of worth was in the sky / and not the earth. [Song: *Mythical Kings and Iguanas*]

FRANK PREWETT

10 Alas, no maid shall get him / For all her love, / Where he sleeps a million strong. [*Voices of Women*]

J. B. PRIESTLEY 1894–1984

11 Comedy, we may say, is society protecting itself – with a smile. [*George Meredith*]

12 The earth is nobler than the world we have put upon it. [*Johnson over Jordon*, Act 3]

13 A number of anxious dwarfs trying to grill a whale. [Of politicians. *Outcries and Asides*]

14 I can't help feeling wary when I hear anything said about the masses. First you take their faces from 'em by calling 'em the masses and then you accuse 'em of not having any faces. [*Saturn over the Water*, Ch. 2]

15 Our great-grandchildren, when they learn how we began this war by snatching glory out of defeat ... may also learn how the little holiday steamers made an excursion to hell and came back glorious. [On Dunkirk. BBC radio broadcast, 5 June 1940]

16 Our trouble is that we drink too much tea. I see in this the slow revenge of the Orient, which has diverted the Yellow River down our throats. [In the *Observer*, 'Sayings of the Week', 15 May 1949]

17 It is hard to tell where MCC ends and the Church of England begins. [In the *New Statesman*, 20 July 1962]

18 A good holiday is one spent among people whose notions of time are vaguer than yours. [In *Penguin Dictionary of Modern Humorous Quotations*, comp. Fred Metcalf]

19 I am not yet a very mean old man, but I am moving in that direction. I view with increasing distaste those guests who can leave an inch or so of good wine in their glasses. [In obituary in *The Times*, 16 Aug. 1984]

20 If I were compelled to choose between living in West Bromwich and Florence, I should make straight for West Bromwich. [Quoted at his memorial service, Westminster Abbey, 2 Oct. 1984]

V. S. [later SIR VICTOR] PRITCHETT 1900–

21 Dickens was not the first or the last

novelist to find virtue more difficult to portray than the wish for it. [*Books in General*, 'Oliver Twist']

1 The detective novel is the art-for-art's-sake of yawning Philistinism. ['The Roots of Detection']

2 Smollett's temper was, in some respects, a new, frost-bitten bud of civilization, of which sick, divided and impossible men are frequently the growing point. ['The Unhappy Traveller']

3 Chekhov has the art of showing us farce as inverted poetry. [*Chekhov: A Spirit Set Free*]

4 The principle of procrastinated rape is said to be the ruling one in all the great bestsellers. [*The Living Novel*, 'Clarissa']

5 He watched his restless hands, surprised they had remembered to come with him. [*Mr Beluncle*, 15]

6 If evil does not exist, what is going to happen to literature? [23]

7 It is the role of the poet to look at what is happening in the world and to know that quite other things are happening. [*The Myth Makers*]

8 Human beings are simply archaic, ivy-covered ruins, preserved by the connoisseur, and they stand out oddly in the new world of the masses. [*New Writing and Daylight*, 'The Future of Fiction']

P. J. PROBY [JAMES MARCUS SMITH]
1938–

9 I think God is groovy. He had a great publicity agent. [In J. Green, *Book of Rock Quotes*]

MARJORIE PROOPS ?1911–

10 The Iron Maiden. [Of Margaret Thatcher. Headline in the *Daily Mirror*, 5 Feb. 1975. See also 367:15]

MARCEL PROUST 1871–1922

11 Perhaps the immobility of the things that surround us is forced upon them by our conviction that they are themselves and not anything else, by the immobility of our conception of them. [*Remembrance of Things Past: Swann's Way*, 'Overture', trans. C. K. Scott Moncrieff and Terence Kilmartin]

12 The taste was that of the little piece of madeleine which on Sunday mornings at Combray . . . when I went to say good morning to her in her bedroom, my aunt Léonie used to give me, dipping it first in her own cup of tea or tisane.

13 The life which, of all the various lives we lead concurrently, is the most episodic, the most full of vicissitudes; I mean the life of the mind. ['Combray']

14 Swann, who behaved simply and casually with a duchess, would tremble for fear of being despised, and would instantly begin to pose, when in the presence of a housemaid. ['Swann in Love']

15 In his younger days a man dreams of possessing the heart of the woman whom he loves; later, the feeling that he possesses a woman's heart may be enough to make him fall in love with her.

16 There are only two classes of people, the magnanimous, and the rest.

17 With the wisdom invariably shown by people who, not being in love themselves, feel that a clever man should only be unhappy about a person who is worth his while, which is rather like being astonished that anyone should condescend to die of cholera at the bidding of so insignificant a creature as the comma bacillus.

18 People often say that, by pointing out to a man the faults of his mistress, you succeed only in strengthening his attachment to her, because he does not believe you; yet how much more if he does!

19 For what we suppose to be our love or our jealousy is never a single, continuous and indivisible passion. It is composed of an infinity of successive loves, of different jealousies, each of which is ephemeral, although by their uninterrupted multiplicity they give us the impression of continuity, the illusion of unity.

20 To think that I've wasted years of my life, that I've longed to die, that I've experienced my greatest love, for a woman who didn't appeal to me, who wasn't even my type.

1 The countries which we long for occupy, at any given moment, a far larger place in our actual life than the country in which we happen to be.

2 In theory one is aware that the earth revolves, but in practice one does not perceive it, the ground upon which one treads seems not to move, and one can live undisturbed. So it is with Time in one's life. [*Within a Budding Grove*, 'Madame Swann at Home']

3 No doubt very few people understand the purely subjective nature of the phenomenon that we call love, or how it creates, so to speak, a supplementary person, distinct from the person the world knows by the same name, a person most of whose constituent elements are derived from ourselves.

4 A powerful idea communicates some of its power to the man who contradicts it.

5 Just as priests, having the widest experience of the human heart, are best able to pardon the sins which they do not themselves commit, so genius, having the widest experience of the human intelligence, can best understand the ideas most directly in opposition to those which form the foundations of its own works.

6 There can be no peace of mind in love, since the advantage one has secured is never anything but a fresh starting-point for further desires.

7 One becomes moral as soon as one is unhappy.

8 It is our noticing them that puts things in a room, our growing used to them that takes them away again and clears a space for us. ['Place-names']

9 As to the pretty girls who went past, from the day on which I had first known that their cheeks could be kissed, I had become curious about their souls.

10 He strode rapidly across the whole width of the hotel, seeming to be in pursuit of his monocle, which kept darting away in front of him like a butterfly.

11 In later life we look at things in a more practical way, in full conformity with the rest of society, but adolescence is the only period in which we learn anything.

12 To strip our pleasures of imagination is to reduce them to their own dimensions, that is to say to nothing.

13 The most exclusive love for a person is always a love for something else.

14 The human face is indeed, like the face of the God of some oriental theogony, a whole cluster of faces, juxtaposed on different planes so that one does not see them all at once. ['Elstir']

15 Every person is destroyed when we cease to see him; after which his next appearance is a new creation, different from that which immediately preceded it, if not from them all.

16 And so when studying faces, we do indeed measure them, but as painters, not as surveyors.

17 She's the sort of woman who does a tremendous lot for her old governesses. [*The Guermantes Way*, Ch. 1]

18 We strive all the time to give our life its form, but we do so by copying willy-nilly, like a drawing, the features of the person we are and not of the person we should like to be.

19 As soon as he ceased to be mad he became merely stupid. There are maladies which we must not seek to cure because they alone protect us from others that are more serious.

20 Everything we think of as great has come to us from neurotics. It is they and they alone who found religions and create great works of art. The world will never realize how much it owes to them, and what they have suffered in order to bestow their gifts on it. ['Decline and Death of My Grandmother']

21 Neurosis has an absolute genius for malingering. There is no illness which it cannot counterfeit perfectly ... If it is capable of deceiving the doctor, how should it fail to deceive the patient?

22 In the pathology of nervous diseases, a doctor who doesn't talk too much nonsense is a half-cured patient, just as a critic is a poet who has stopped writing verse and a policeman a burglar who has retired from practice.

1 A dead writer can at least be illustrious without any strain on himself. [2]

2 It has even been said that the highest praise of God consists in the denial of him by the atheist who finds creation so perfect that he can dispense with a creator.

3 His hatred of snobs derived from his snobbishness, but made the simple-minded (in other words, everyone) believe that he was immune from snobbishness.

4 It's far more difficult to disfigure a great work of art than to create one. [*Cities of the Plain*, Pt II, Ch. 1]

5 I was beginning to learn the exact value of the language, spoken or mute, of aristocratic affability, an affability that is happy to shed balm upon the sense of inferiority of those to whom it is directed, though not to the point of dispelling that inferiority, for in that case it would no longer have any *raison d'être*.

6 I hope, for his own sake, that he has younger people than me at his disposal if he wishes to ask for bad advice, especially if he means to follow it.

7 Good-bye, I've barely said a word to you, but it's always like that at parties – we never really see each other, we never say the things we should like to; in fact it's the same everywhere in this life. Let's hope that when we are dead things will be better arranged.

8 I've sometimes regretted living so close to Marie . . . because although I'm very fond of her, I'm not quite so fond of her company.

9 Illness is the most heeded of doctors: to kindness and wisdom we make promises only; pain we obey.

10 If habit is a second nature it prevents us from knowing whose cruelties it lacks as well as its enchantments.

11 I have a horror of sunsets, they're so romantic, so operatic. [2]

12 If the eyes are sometimes the organ through which our intelligence is revealed, the nose is generally the organ in which stupidity is most readily displayed.

13 Distances are only the relation of space to time and vary with it. [3]

14 Albertine never related facts that were damaging to her, but always other facts which could be explained only by the former, the truth being rather a current which flows from what people say to us, and which we pick up, invisible though it is, than the actual thing they have said.

15 Happiness is beneficial for the body, but it is grief that develops the powers of the mind. [*Time Regained*, Ch. 2, trans. C. K. Scott Moncrieff, Terence Kilmartin and Andreas Mayor]

16 War . . . does not escape the laws of our old Hegel. It is a state of perpetual becoming.

17 Life deceives us so much that we come to believing that literature has no relation with it and we are astonished to observe that the wonderful ideas books have presented to us are gratuitously exhibited in everyday life, without risk of being spoilt by the writer.

18 For all the fruitful altruisms of Nature develop in an egotistical mode; human altruism which is not egoism is sterile, it is that of a writer who interrupts his work to receive a friend who is unhappy, to accept some public function or to write propaganda articles.

DAVID PROWSE

19 It [the new one pound coin] should . . . be called the 'Thatcher' because it was 'thick, brassy and wanted to be a sovereign'. [From *Western Morning News*, in *This England, 1979–1988*]

JOHN PUDNEY 1909–1977

20 Do not despair / For Johnny Head-in-Air. / He sleeps as sound / As Johnny Underground. [Lines scribbled on an envelope during an air raid in 1941. Later used for film *The Way to the Stars*]

PUNCH

21 I'm afraid you've got a bad egg, Mr Jones!
  Oh no, my Lord, I assure you! Parts of it are excellent! [Vol. cix, p. 222, 1895]

22 Look here, Steward, if this is coffee, I want tea; but if this is tea, then I wish for coffee. [cxxiii. 44, 1902]

1 Darling only one more instalment and Baby will be *ours*. [In Robert Graves and Alan Hodge, *The Long Weekend*, Ch. 11]

COMMANDER HARRY PURSEY, MP
1891–1980

2 There we were, one foot on a bar of soap and the other in the gutter. [Attr.]

MARIO PUZO 1920–

3 I'll make him an offer he can't refuse. [In novel, Ch. 1, and film *The Godfather*, screenplay with Francis Ford Coppola]

4 GEORGE MANDEL: 'He's [Joseph Heller's] got something called Guillain-Barré.'

'My God,' Mario blurted out. 'That's terrible.' A surprised George murmured, 'Hey, Mario, you know about Guillain-Barré?'

'No, I never heard nothing about it,' Mario replied. 'But when they name any disease after two guys, it's got to be terrible.' [Joseph Heller and Speed Vogel, *No Laughing Matter*, p. 44]

Q

Q MAGAZINE

1 Perfectly balanced – chips on both shoulders. [Of musician Billy Joel. In the *New Statesman*, 12 Sept. 1986. See also 11:1]

VICE-PRESIDENT DANIEL QUAYLE 1947–

2 What a waste it is to lose one's mind – or not to have a mind. [Speech to United Negro College Fund (whose motto is 'A mind is a terrible thing to waste'). In the *Observer*, 8 Oct. 1989]

SIR ARTHUR QUILLER COUCH 1863–1944

3 Know you her secret none can utter? / – Hers of the Book, the tripled Crown? [*Alma Mater*]

WILLARD QUINE 1908–

4 Statements are sentences, but not all sentences are statements. [*Elementary Logic*, opening sentence]

5 This is the old Platonic riddle of nonbeing. Nonbeing must in some sense be, otherwise what is it that there is not? This tangled doctrine might be nicknamed Plato's beard; historically it has proved tough, frequently dulling the edge of Occam's razor. [*From a Logical Point of View*, 'On What There is']

ANTHONY [later LORD] QUINTON 1925–

6 Architecture is the most inescapable of the higher arts. [From *The Times*, 1982, in *Dictionary of Art Quotations*, comp. Ian Crofton]

SIR JOHN QUINTON 1929–

7 Bankers sometimes look on politicians as people who, when they see light at the end of the tunnel, order more tunnel. [In the *Independent*, 15 Apr. 1989. See also 238:6]

R

JONATHAN RABAN 1942–

1 In this miniature inverted cluster, the British had hit by chance on a perfect symbol of themselves. The Falklands held a mirror up to our own islands, and it reflected, in brilliantly sharp focus, all our injured belittlement, our sense of being beleaguered, neglected and misunderstood. [*Coasting*, Ch. 3]

2 If poems can teach one anything, Larkin's teach that there is no desolation so bleak that it cannot be made habitable by style. If we live inside a bad joke, it is up to us to learn, at best and worst, to tell it well. [6]

JOHN RAE 1931–

3 A mother has an innate ability for aggravating the wounds of her offspring's pride. This is inevitable since the relationship between mother and child is a most unnatural one; other species have the good sense to banish their young at an early age. [*The Custard Boys*, Ch. 13]

4 War is, after all, the universal perversion. We are all tainted: if we cannot experience our perversion at first hand we spend our time reading war stories, the pornography of war; or seeing war films, the blue films of war; or titillating our senses with the imagination of great deeds, the masturbation of war.

GEORGE RAFT 1895–1980

5 She stole everything but the cameras. [As Mae West's co-star on her film début.

In Leslie Halliwell, *Filmgoer's Book of Quotes*]

CRAIG RAINE 1944–

6 Tell me, is he bright enough to find / that memo pad you call your mind? [*Rich*, 'Attempt at Jealousy']

7 The mind is a museum / to be looted at night. ['The Grey Boy']

8 It's a bit like talking to the *Encyclopaedia Britannica* – but an unauthorized version, an alternative route to knowledge, well off the main trunk roads. [Of Ted Hughes. In the *Sunday Times*, 23 Dec. 1984]

SIR WALTER A. RALEIGH 1861–1922

9 I wish I loved the Human Race; / I wish I loved its silly face; / I wish I liked the way it walks; / I wish I liked the way it talks; / And when I'm introduced to one / I wish I thought *What Jolly Fun!* [*Laughter from a Cloud*, 'Wishes of an Elderly Man']

10 We could not lead a pleasant life, / And 'twould be finished soon, / If peas were eaten with the knife, / And gravy with the spoon. / Eat slowly; only men in rags / And gluttons old in sin / Mistake themselves for carpet bags / And tumble victuals in. ['Stans puer ad mensam']

11 An anthology is like all the plums and orange peel picked out of a cake. [Letter to Mrs Robert Bridges, 15 Jan. 1915, *Letters*, Vol. II]

12 There is no one thing to be found in books which it is a disgrace not to know. [Attr.]

AYN RAND 1905–1982

1 So you think that money is the root of all evil. Have you ever asked what is the root of money? [In *Executive's Quotation Book*, ed. James Charlton]

JAMES RANDI 1928–

2 The New Age? It's just the old age stuck in a microwave oven for 15 seconds. [In the *Observer*, 'Sayings of the Week', 14 Apr. 1991]

DAVID RANDOLPH 1934–

3 The kind of opera that starts at six o'clock and after it has been going three hours, you look at your watch and it says 6.20. [Of *Parsifal*. In Frank Muir, *Frank Muir Book*]

JOHN CROWE RANSOM 1888–1974

4 Here lies a lady of beauty and high degree. / Of chills and fevers she died, of fever and chills. [*Here Lies a Lady*]

5 And if no Lethe flows beneath your casement, / and when ten years have not brought full effacement, / Philosophy was wrong, and you may meet. [*Parting at Dawn*]

6 Two evils, monstrous either one apart, / Possessed me, and were long and loath at going: / A cry of Absence, Absence, in the heart, / And in the wood the furious winter blowing. [*Winter Remembered*]

ARTHUR RANSOME 1884–1967

7 BETTER DROWNED THAN DUFFERS IF NOT DUFFERS WONT DROWN [*Swallows and Amazons*, Ch. 1]

P. V. NARASIMHA RAO 1921–

8 Decisions are easier, you know, when there are no choices left. [First interview as Indian Prime Minister with foreign journalist, in the *Observer*, 7 July 1991]

FREDERIC RAPHAEL 1931–

9 This [Cambridge] is the city of perspiring dreams. [*The Glittering Prizes*, 'An Early Life']

10 I come from suburbia, Dan, personally, I don't ever want to go back. It's the one place in the world that's further away than anywhere else. ['A Sex Life']

11 I find it quite remarkable, don't you, how people always take offence when a conversation ceases to be personal? ['An Academic Life']

12 We thought philosophy ought to be patient and unravel people's mental blocks. Trouble with doing that is, once you've unravelled them, their heads fall off. ['A Double Life']

13 He was cautious, but he was careful not to show it. [*Oxbridge Blues*, 'The Muse']

14 If you were to give a little more tongue to your cheek.

15 Homosexuals, like Jews, often find themselves numbered among their enemies' best friends. [In *3: Radio Three Magazine*, Oct. 1982]

16 From the accountants' point of view, war was simply a speeded up kind of peace, with conspicuously increased consumption. [In *New Society*, 10 May 1984]

17 What adultery was to the nineteenth century novel espionage is to today's. The sincerity of defection is common to both. [In *The Times Literary Supplement*, 3 Apr. 1987]

18 Duplicity lies at the heart of language: only Trappists avoid the trap. [In the *Sunday Times*, 31 May]

19 Today's superstars may be more famous than God (and have more reliable agents). [In the *Sunday Times Books*, 22 May 1988]

20 The old jibe is that Jews are like everyone else, only more so; British Jews, they like to think, are like other Jews, only less so. [In the *Listener*, 20 Apr. 1989]

SIR TERENCE RATTIGAN 1911–1977

21 The headmaster said you ruled with a rod of iron. He called you the Himmler of the lower fifth. [*The Browning Version*]

22 She has ideas above her station ... How would you say that in French? ... you can't say au-dessus de sa gare. It isn't that sort of station. [*French without Tears*, Act I]

1 You can be in the Horse Guards and still be common, dear. [*Separate Tables*, 'Table Number Seven']

2 In future I trust that a son of mine will at least show enough sense to come in out of the rain. [*The Winslow Boy*, Act I]

3 A nice, respectable, middle-class, middle-aged maiden lady, with time on her hands and the money to help her pass it . . . Let us call her Aunt Edna . . . Aunt Edna is universal, and to those who may feel that all the problems of the modern theatre might be solved by her liquidation, let me add that . . . she is also immortal. [*Collected Plays*, Vol. II, Preface]

IRINA RATUSHINSKAYA 1954–

4 In order to understand birds / You have to be a convict. / And if you share your bread – It means your time is done. [*No, I am Not Afraid*, 'The Sparrows of Butyrki']

5 We have learned, indeed, to throw time into tins / And have stirred in the condensed night at all times. / This century grows even darker, and the next will not come soon, / To wipe clean the names off yesterday's prison wall. ['Pencil Letter']

GWEN RAVERAT 1885–1957

6 But she never, never missed the train. I think she felt that it would not have been sporting to start in time; it would not have given the train a fair chance of getting away without her. [*Period Piece*, Ch. 5]

7 I have defined Ladies as people who did not do things themselves. [7]

TED RAY 1906–1977

8 Ee, it was agony, Ivy. [Catchphrase in BBC radio comedy series *Ray's a Laugh*, 1950s]

CLAIRE RAYNER 1931–

9 It [motherhood] is a dead-end job. You've no sooner learned the skills than you are redundant. [In the *Weekend Guardian*, 15–16 Dec. 1960]

SIR HERBERT READ 1893–1968

10 I saw him stab / And stab again / A well-killed Boche. / This is the happy warrior. / This is he . . . [*The Happy Warrior*]

11 It [Europe] will be a gay world. There will be lights everywhere except in the minds of men, and the fall of the last civilization will not be heard above the din. [In Richard Hoggart and Douglas Johnson, *An Idea of Europe*]

NANCY REAGAN 1921–

12 A woman is like a teabag. It's only when she's in hot water that you realize how strong she is. [Address to US Women's Congress. In the *Observer*, 'Sayings of the Week', 29 Mar. 1981]

PRESIDENT RONALD REAGAN 1911–

13 Tell them to go out there with all they got and win just one for the Gipper. [In film *Knute Rockne, All American*, 1940, screenplay by Robert Buckner. See also 144:10]

14 Keeping up with Governor Brown [in governorship of California race in 1966] is like reading *Playboy* while your wife turns the pages. [In the *Observer Review*, 5 Jan. 1986]

15 You can tell a lot about a fellow's character from the way he eats jelly beans. [In the *Daily Mail*, 22 Jan. 1981]

16 Honey, I forgot to duck. [To Nancy Reagan on entering hospital after assassination attempt, 30 Mar., quoting Jack Dempsey; see 104:2]

17 She [Margaret Thatcher] is the best man in England. [To reporters, 7 Jan. 1983]

18 My fellow Americans, I am pleased to tell you I have just signed legislation that will outlaw Russia for ever. We begin bombing in five minutes. [Rehearsal for TV programme, transmitted in error, 13 Aug. 1984]

19 I've been burning the midday oil. [Of US bombing of Libya. Speech to Annual Dinner of White House Correspondents Association, Washington, 16 Apr. 1986]

20 They say hard work never hurt anybody, but I figure why take the chance!

21 All in all, not bad. Not too bad at all.

[Verdict on his own presidency. Speech on US TV. In the *Independent*, 'Quote Unquote', 14 Jan. 1989]

1 You can't massacre an idea, you cannot run tanks over hope. [Of Chinese repression of student demonstrations. Churchill Lecture at Guildhall, London, 13 June]

2 Where's the Rest of Me? [Title of autobiography, taken from line in his most famous film, *King's Row*]

3 There is nothing wrong with America that together we can't fix. [In Robert Andrews, *Routledge Dictionary of Quotations*, 'America']

ROBERT REDFORD 1937–

4 He [Paul Newman] has the attention span of a bolt of lightning. [In *The New York Times*, 28 Sept. 1986]

LYNN REDGRAVE 1943–

5 A smart girl is one who knows how to play tennis, piano and dumb. [In the *Guardian*, 22 May 1992]

PETER REDGROVE 1932–

6 He sighs, and the waves are a city of doors slamming; / God's arm engloves this tree and brandishes it. [*The Affianced*]

7 For sixpence he can get drunk / And be a torero, the government, or a saint. [*Malagueño*]

HENRY REED 1914–1986

8 It is, we believe, / Idle to hope that the simple stirrup-pump / Can extinguish hell. [*Chard Whitlow (Mr Eliot's Sunday Evening Postscript)*]

9 To-day we have naming of parts. Yesterday / We had daily cleaning. And tomorrow morning, / We shall have what to do after firing. But to-day, / To-day we have naming of parts. [*Lessons of the War*, I, 'Naming of Parts']

10 They call it easing the Spring: it is perfectly easy / If you have any strength in your thumb: like the bolt, / And the breech, and the cocking-piece, and the point

of balance, / Which in our case we have not got.

11 You must never be over-sure. You must say, when reporting: / At five o'clock in the central sector is a dozen / Of what appear to be animals; whatever you do, / Don't call the bleeders *sheep*.

12 And the various holds and rolls and throws and breakfalls / Somehow or other I always seemed to put / In the wrong place. And as for war, my wars / Were global from the start. [III, 'Unarmed Combat']

13 In a civil war, a general must know – and I'm afraid it's a thing rather of instinct than of practice – he must know exactly when to move over to the other side. [BBC radio drama *Not a Drum was Heard: The War Memoirs of General Gland*]

14 I dream quite a bit, myself. Only when I'm asleep, of course. Curious thing is it's always the same dream . . . Not that I mind, of course, I'm not one to hanker after change the whole time. [BBC radio drama *The Primal Scene, as It Were*]

15 If one doesn't get birthday presents it can remobilize very painfully the persecutory anxiety which usually follows birth.

16 The sooner the tea's out of the way, the sooner we can get out the gin, eh? [BBC radio drama *The Private Life of Hilda Tablet*]

17 Of course, we've all dreamed of reviving the castrati; but it's needed Hilda to take the first practical steps towards making them a reality . . . She's drawn up a list of well-known singers who she thinks would benefit from . . . treatment . . . It's only a question of getting them to agree.

JOHN REED 1887–1920

18 Ten Days That Shook the World. [Title of book on Russian Revolution]

LOU REED 1942–

19 Give me your tired your poor I'll piss on 'em / That's what the Statue of Bigotry says / Your poor huddled masses, let's club 'em to death / and get it over with and just dump 'em on the boulevard. [Song: *Dirty Blvd*]

REX REED 1938–

1 In Hollywood, if you don't have happiness you send out for it. [In J. R. Colombo, *Colombo's Hollywood*, 'Hollywood the Bad']

GEORGE REEDY 1917–

2 You know that nobody is strongminded around a President; . . . it is always: 'yes sir,' 'no sir' (the 'no sir' comes when he asks whether you're dissatisfied). [In *The White House*, ed. R. Gordon Hoxie]

C. B. REES

3 Beethoven's Fifth Symphony may be Fate – or Kate – knocking at the door. That is up to you. [In *Penguin Music Magazine*, 1946]

LEONARD REES

4 Damn it, man, I could cut the Lord's Prayer! [In James Agate, *Ego 1*]

MAX REGER 1873–1916

5 I am sitting in the smallest room of my house. I have your review before me. In a moment it will be behind me. [Letter to critic Rudolph Louis, 7 Feb. 1906]

CHARLES A. REICH 1928–

6 The Greening of America. [Title of book]

WILHELM REICH 1897–1957

7 Every kind of destructive action by itself is the reaction of the organism to the denial of the gratification of a vital need, especially the sexual. [*The Function of the Orgasm*]

8 The few bad poems which occasionally are created during abstinence are of no great interest. [*The Sexual Revolution*]

GOTTFRIED REINHARDT 1913–

9 Hollywood people are afraid to leave Hollywood. Out in the world, they are frightened . . . Sam Hoffenstein used to say we are the croupiers in a crooked gambling house. And it's true. Everyone of us thinks, You know, I really don't deserve a swimming pool. [In Lillian Ross, *Picture*, 'Throw the Little Old Lady Down the Stairs!' See also 175:20]

10 You know, there are three kinds of intelligence – the intelligence of man, the intelligence of the animal, and the intelligence of the military. In that order. [In 'Piccolos under Your Name, Strings under Mine'. See also 253:18]

11 Money is good for bribing yourself through the inconveniences of life. [In 'Looks Like We're Still in Business']

LORD REITH 1889–1971

12 Despotism tempered by assassination. [On the best form of government. In the *Observer*, 12 Nov. 1972]

ERICH MARIA REMARQUE 1898–1970

13 *Im Westen nichts Neues.* – All Quiet on the Western Front. [Title of book]

M. J. RENDALL 1862–1950

14 Nation shall speak peace unto nation. [Motto of BBC, 1927]

DR DAVID REUBEN 1933–

15 Everything You've Always Wanted to Know about Sex, but were Afraid to Ask. [Title of book]

CHARLES REVSON 1906–1975

16 In the factory we make cosmetics. In the store we sell hope. [In A. Tobias, *Fire and Ice*, Ch. 8]

EBEN REXFORD 1848–1916

17 Darling, I am growing old, / Silver threads among the gold. [*Silver Threads among the Gold*]

BURT REYNOLDS 1936–

18 When an actor marries an actress they both fight for the mirror. [Interview in the *Guardian*, 12 Mar. 1988]

MALVINA REYNOLDS 1900–1978

19 They're all made out of ticky-tacky, and they all look just the same. [Song: *Little Boxes* about the tract houses in the hills south of San Francisco, sung by Pete Seeger]

OLIVER REYNOLDS 1957–

1 Bad luck was always / As welcome as / A sandy foreskin. [*Acholba*]

CECIL RHODES 1853–1902

2 Remember that you are an Englishman, and have consequently won first prize in the lottery of life. [In Peter Ustinov, *Dear Me*, Ch. 4]

3 So little done, so much to do. [Last words. In Lewis Michell, *Life of Rhodes*, Vol. 2, Ch. 39]

JEAN RHYS 1894–1979

4 The feeling of Sunday is the same everywhere, heavy, melancholy, standing still. Like when they say, 'As it was in the beginning, is now, and ever shall be, world without end.' [*Voyage in the Dark*, Ch. 4]

MIRELLA RICCIARDI

5 My husband Lorenzo says he can't live more than a few weeks with me because I take up all the oxygen. [In the *Guardian*, 31 Mar. 1982]

GRANTLAND RICE 1880–1954

6 For when the One Great Scorer comes / To write against your name. / He marks – not that you won or lost – / But how you played the game. [*Alumnus Football*]

TIM RICE 1944–

7 Don't Cry for Me, Argentina. [Title of song in musical *Evita*, music by Andrew Lloyd Webber]

MANDY RICE-DAVIES 1944–

8 He would, wouldn't he? [When told Lord Astor had denied any involvement with her, at trial of Stephen Ward, 28 June 1963]

9 Call me Lady Hamilton. [When asked for autograph during Profumo scandal, 1963. In H. Montgomery Hyde, *A Tangled Web*, p. 256]

KEITH RICHARD [formerly RICHARDS] 1943–

10 I've never had problems with drugs, only policemen. [In *Wit and Wisdom of Rock and Roll*, ed. Maxim Jakubowski]

11 If you're gonna get wasted, get wasted elegantly.

See also MICK JAGGER and KEITH RICHARD

FRANK RICHARDS 1876–1971

12 'My esteemed chums,' murmured Hurree Jamset Ram Singh. 'This is not an occasion for looking the gift horse in the mouthfulness.' [*Bunter's Last Fling*, Ch. 5]

13 The fat owl of the Remove. [Nickname for Bunter, with variants, throughout series]

I. A. RICHARDS 1893–1979

14 Anything is valuable that will satisfy an appetency without involving the frustration of some equal or *more important* appetency. [*Principles of Literary Criticism*]

15 To be forced by desire into any unwarrantable belief is a calamity.

16 It [poetry] is a perfectly possible means of overcoming chaos. [*Science and Poetry*, Ch. 7]

SIR JAMES RICHARDS 1907–1992

17 There are three kinds of man you must never trust: a man who hunts south of the Thames, a man who has soup for lunch, and a man who waxes his moustache. [Quoting his father. *Memoirs of an Unjust Fella*]

SIR RALPH RICHARDSON 1902–1983

18 God is very economical, don't you think? Wastes nothing. Yet also the opposite. [In Kenneth Tynan, *Show People*]

19 It's like Edith Evans – she used to open a window to her heart and then slam it shut, so that you'd come back the next night to see more. [Of styles of acting]

20 In music, the punctuation is absolutely strict, the bars and the rests are absolutely defined. But our punctuation cannot be quite strict, because we have to relate it to the audience. In other words, we are continually changing the score.

1 There are lots of reasons why people become actors. Some to hide themselves, and some to show themselves. [Interview with Russell Harty on LWT, Sept. 1975. In above]

2 Alexander Korda continuously makes people do things against their will but seldom against their interest. [In Gary O'Connor, *Ralph Richardson: An Actor's Life*, Pt I, Ch. 18]

3 Travelling broadens the mind ... [No] it narrows it. Jesus never travelled; not more than a hundred miles; Michelangelo, Rembrandt, Milton: they are people who made a journey of scarcely any consequence at all and subsequently never travelled further. Travel is for people without imagination: dullards, clods; those who need to animate the landscape, otherwise they see nothing there at all. [In II. 20]

4 You might say he [Shakespeare's Henry V] was a cold bath king, that he was a scoutmaster, yes. But you must remember he is the *exaltation* of scoutmasters. [To Laurence Olivier. In 22]

5 Acting is merely the art of keeping a large group of people from coughing. [In 26]

6 Acting is to some extent a controlled dream. In one part of your consciousness it really and truly is happening. But, of course, to make it true to the audience all the time, the actor must, at any rate some of the time, believe himself that it is really true. [In III. 39]

7 You've got to perform in a role hundreds of times. In keeping it fresh one can become a large, madly humming, demented refrigerator. [In *Time* magazine, 21 Aug. 1978]

8 The audience didn't realize how odd he [Charlie Chaplin] was because he was so near to reality in his madness. [In BBC TV programme *The Michael Parkinson Show*, 13 Dec. 1980]

9 The most precious things in speech are pauses. [Attr. See also 338:16]

MORDECAI RICHLER 1931–

10 And furthermore did you know that behind the discovery of America there was a Jewish financier? [*Cocksure*, Ch. 24]

11 'I'm world-famous,' Dr Parks said, 'all over Canada.' [*The Incomparable Atuk*, Ch. 4]

HANS RICHTER 1843–1916

12 Your damned nonsense can I stand twice or once, but sometimes always, by God, never! [To orchestra at rehearsal. In *Utterly Trivial Knowledge: The Music Game*, ed. John Denny]

CHRISTOPHER RICKS 1933–

13 *Qui s'accuse s'excuse.* [From *Dickens and the Twentieth Century*, 'Great Expectations', in *Oxford Book of Aphorisms*, chosen by John Gross]

EDGELL RICKWORD 1898–1982

14 My soul's a trampled duelling ground where Sade, / the gallant marquis, fences for his life / against the invulnerable retrograde / Masoch, his shade, more constant than a wife. [*Chronique Scandaleuse*]

15 The oldest griefs of summer seem less sad / than drone of mowers on suburban lawns / and girls' thin laughter, to the ears that hear / the soft rain falling of the failing stars. [*Regrets*, II]

W. PETT RIDGE 1857–1930

16 He took her up in his arms in the way of a bachelor who in his time has had amateur experience of the carrying of nieces. [*Lost Property*, Pt I, Ch. 8]

17 Gertie recommended her to adopt the habit of not magnifying grievances; if you wanted to view trouble, you could take opera-glasses, but you should be careful to hold them the wrong way round. [*Love at Paddington Green*, Ch. 4]

18 'How did you think I managed at dinner, Clarence?' 'Capitally!' 'I had a knife and two forks left at the end,' she said regretfully. [6]

19 Ballard admitted he was no hand at giving descriptions; the man was apparently a gentleman and the woman – well, not exactly a lady, although she had a very fine flow of language. [*Mrs Galer's Business*, Ch. 6]

SIR WILLIAM RIDGEWAY ?–1926

1 I'm not so deaf as the man who said family prayers kneeling on the cat. [Attr. in *Letters of A. E. Housman*, ed. H. Maas, p. 427]

NICHOLAS [later LORD] RIDLEY 1929–1993

2 This is all a German racket designed to take over the whole of Europe. It has to be thwarted. This rushed take over by the Germans on the worst possible basis, with the French behaving like poodles to the Germans, is absolutely intolerable. [Interview in the *Spectator*, 14 July 1990]

DAVID RIESMAN 1909–

3 The Lonely Crowd. [Title of book]

RAINER MARIA RILKE 1875–1926

4 *O Bäume Lebens, o wann winterlich? / Wir sind nicht einig. Sind nicht wie die Zug- / vögel verständigt. Überholt und spät, / so drängen wir uns plötzlich Winden auf / und fallen ein auf teilnahmslosen Teich.* – O trees of life, when will it be winter for you? We are not at one. We are not of one mind like the migratory birds. Overtaken and late, we suddenly hurry up-wind and fall on the indifferent pond. [*Duineser Elegien*, 4]

5 *Uns aber, wo wir Eines meinen ganz, / ist schon des andern Aufwand fühlbar. Feindschaft / ist uns das Nächste.* – But we, when we are entirely intent on one thing, can feel the pull of another. Hostility comes easiest to us.

6 *Wer zeigt ein Kind, so wie es steht? Wer stellt / es ins Gestirn und gibt das Mass des Abstands / ihm in die Hand?* – Who will show a child, as it really is? Who will place it in its constellation and put the measure of distance in its hand?

7 *den ganzen Tod, noch vor dem Leben so / sanft zu enthalten und nicht bös zu sein, / ist unbeschreiblich.* – To contain the whole of death so gently even before life has begun, and not be angry – this is beyond description.

8 *Plätze, o Platz in Paris, unendlicher Schauplatz, / wo die Modistin, Madame Lamort, / die*

ruhlosen Wege der Erde, endlose Bänder, / schlingt und windet. – Squares, O square in Paris, endless showplace where the modiste, Madame Lamort, loops and winds endless ribbons, the restless roads of the world. [5]

9 *ihre Türme aus Lust, ihre / längst, wo Boden nie war, nur aneinander / lehnenden Leitern, bebend.* – Their towers of pleasure, their ladders that have for so long now leaned against each other, where there was no ground, trembling.

10 *Feigenbaum, seit wie lange schon ists mir bedeutend, / wie du die Blüte beinah ganz überschlägst / und hinein in die zeitig entschlossene Frucht, / ungerühmt, drängst dein reines Geheimnis.* – Fig-tree, for a long time now I have found meaning in the way you almost entirely overleap the stage of blossom and thrust your pure mystery, unsung, into the early set fruit. [6]

11 *Wunderlich nah ist der Held doch den jugendlich Toten.* – The hero is strangely akin to those who die young.

12 *War er nicht Held schon in dir, O Mutter, begann nicht / dort schon, in dir, seine herrische Auswahl?* – Was he not already a hero inside you, O mother? Did not his imperious choice already begin there, in you?

13 *abgewendet schon, stand er am Ende der Lächeln, anders.* – But already withdrawn, he stood at the end of smiles, different.

14 *Unser / Leben geht hin mit Verwandlung.* – Our life passes in transformation. [7]

15 *Wo einmal ein dauerndes Haus war, / schlägt sich erdachtes Gebild vor, quer, zu Erdenklichem / völlig gehörig.* – Where once a lasting house was, obliquely an invented picture starts up, which belongs entirely to the imaginary.

16 *o Glück der Mücke, die noch innen hüpft, / selbst wenn sie Hochzeit hat: denn Schooss ist alles.* – O joy of the gnat, that still leaps inwards even in the act of wedding; for womb is all! [8]

17 *so leben wir und nehmen immer Abschied.* – Thus we live, for ever taking leave.

18 *Hier ist des Säglichen Zeit, hier seine Heimat. / Sprich und bekenn.* – Here is the time of the tellable, here is its home. Speak and proclaim. [9]

1 *Preise dem Engel die Welt, nicht die unsäg-liche, ihm / kannst du nicht grosstun mit herrlich Erfühltem; im Weltall, / wo er fühlender fühlt, bist du ein Neuling. Drum zeig / ihm das Ein-fache.* – Praise the world to the angel, not the untellable. You cannot impress him with the splendour you have felt; in the cosmos where he feels with greater feeling you are a novice. So show him the simple thing.

2 *beklebt mit Plakaten des 'Todlos', / jenes bitteren Biers, das den Trinkenden süss scheint.* – Stuck with placards for 'Deathless', that bitter beer that tastes sweet to its drinkers. [10]

3 *Das war der Seelen wunderliches Bergwerk.* – That was the wonderful mine of souls. [*Orpheus, Eurydike, Hermes*]

4 *Sie war schon aufgelöst wie langes Haar / und hingegeben wie gefallner Regen / und aus-geteilt wie hundertfacher Vorrat.* – She was already loosened like long hair, given up like fallen rain, and divided like a hundredfold store.

5 *Ist er ein Hiesiger? Nein, aus beiden / Reichen erwuchs seine weite Natur.* – Is he a man of this side? No, his broad nature grew from both realms. [*Die Sonette an Orpheus*, I. 6]

6 *Nicht sind die Leiden erkannt, / nicht ist die Liebe gelernt, / und was im Tod uns entfernt, / ist nicht entschleiert.* – Sorrows are not known, love is not learnt, and what removes us in death is not revealed. [19]

7 *Frühling ist wiedergekommen. Die Erde – ist wie ein Kind, das Gedichte / weiss.* – Spring has returned. The earth is like a child that knows poems. [21]

8 *Alles das Eilende / wird schon vorüber sein; / denn das Verweilende / erst weiht uns ein.* – All that is hurrying will soon be past; for that which stays gives us our first initiation. [23]

9 *O du verlorener Gott! Due unendliche Spur! / Nur weil dich reissend zuletzt die Feindschaft verteilte, / sind wir die Hörenden jetzt und ein Mund der Natur.* – O thou lost God! O endless trace! Only because hostility finally tore you to pieces are we now the listeners and a mouthpiece of Nature. [26]

10 *O dieses ist das Tier, das es nicht gibt.* – O this is the animal that does not exist. [II. 4]

11 *Alles Erworbene bedroht die Maschine.* – The machine threatens all achievement. [10]

12 *Sei allem Abschied voran, als wäre er hinter / dir, wie der Winter der eben geht.* – Be ahead of all farewells, as if they were behind you, like the winter that is just departing. [12]

13 *Alle die dich suchen, versuchen dich. / Und die, so dich finden, binden dich / an Bild und Gebärde.* – All who seek you tempt you, and as soon as they find you, bind you to an image and a posture. [*Das Stundenbuch, 'Alle welche dich suchen'*]

14 *Die Könige der Welt sind alt / und werden keine Erben haben.* – The kings of the earth are old and will have no heirs. [*'Die Könige der Welt sind alt'*]

15 *Was wirst du tun, Gott, wenn ich sterbe? / Ich bin dein Krug (wenn ich zerscherbe?)* – What will you do, God, if I die? I am your pitcher (if I break?). [*'Was wirst du tun, Gott'*]

16 It was the sinister, princely death which the chamberlain had carried with him and had himself nourished during his whole life. [*Notebooks of Malte Laurids Brigge*, Pt I]

17 A good marriage is that in which each appoints the other guardian of his solitude. [Letter. In *Barnes and Noble Book of Quota-tions*, ed. Robert I. Fitzhenry, 'Marriage']

NIKOLAI RIMSKY-KORSAKOV
1844–1908

18 I have already heard it [Debussy's music]. I had better not go: I will start to get accustomed to it and finally like it. [In Igor Stravinsky and Robert Craft, *Conversations with Stravinsky*]

R. L. RIPLEY 1893–1949

19 Believe It or Not. [Title of newspaper feature]

JOAN RIVERS 1933–

20 I saw my first porno film recently – a Jewish porno film – one minute of sex and nine minutes of guilt. [In *Hammer and Tongues*, ed. Michèle Brown and Ann O'Connor, 'Guilt']

TOM ROBBINS 1936–

21 Amnesia is not knowing who one is and

wanting desperately to find out. Euphoria is not knowing who one is and not caring. Ecstasy is knowing exactly who one is – and still not caring. [*Another Roadside Attraction*]

1 Among the Haida Indians of the Pacific Northwest, the verb for 'making poetry' is the same as the verb 'to breathe'.

2 Human beings were invented by water as a device for transporting itself from one place to another.

MICHAEL ROBERTS 1902–1948

3 More often than prose or mathematics, poetry is received in a hostile spirit, as if its publication were an affront to the reader. [*Faber Book of Modern Verse*, Introduction]

R. C. ROBERTSON-GLASCOW 1901–1965

4 [When asked by Ben Travers what bowling to Hobbs and Sandham had been like] It's like trying to bowl to God on concrete. [In Ben Travers, *94 Declared*]

SIR GEORGE ROBEY 1869–1954

5 The Prime Minister of Mirth. [Sobriquet of unknown origin]

6 Desist! [Said with raised eyebrows and lifted hand to quell applause. In A. E. Wilson, *The Prime Minister of Mirth*, Ch. 3]

7 The inmate of a lunatic asylum was writing a letter. A man looked over his shoulder and asked: 'To whom are you writing?' The inmate replied: 'I am writing to myself.' 'What are you saying?' asked the other man. 'Oh, I shan't know till I get it tomorrow,' said the inmate. [In 12]

8 I stopped, I looked and I listened. [Song in musical *The Bing Boys*, words by Clifford Grey. See also 383:4]

9 They knew her by the pimple, / The pimple on her nose. [Song: *The Simple Pimple*]

LEO ROBIN 1900–1984

10 Diamonds are a Girl's Best Friend. [Title of song in musical *Gentlemen Prefer Blondes*, music by Jule Styne]

11 Thanks for the Memory. [Title of song in musical *Big Broadcast*, music by Ralph Rainger]

EDWIN ARLINGTON ROBINSON 1869–1935

12 Friends / To borrow my books and set wet glasses on them. [*Captain Craig*, II]

13 I shall have more to say when I am dead. [*John Brown*]

14 Miniver loved the Medici, / Albeit he had never seen one; / He would have sinned incessantly / Could he have been one. [*Miniver Cheevy*]

JOAN ROBINSON 1903–1983

15 Being innocent of mathematics, I had to think. [Of her economics. In obituary in the *New Statesman*, 19 Aug. 1983]

MARY ROBINSON, PRESIDENT OF IRELAND 1944–

16 The fifth province is not anywhere here or there, north or south, east or west. It is a place within each of us – that place that is open to the other, that swinging door which allows us to venture out and others to venture in. [In the *Independent*, 19 May 1991]

ROBERT ROBINSON 1927–

17 I don't like going for walks in the country because it's so easy to turn round and go home again that you can't help wondering whether it's worthwhile setting out in the first place. [*Dog Chairman*, 'Aiming, Shooting and Missing']

18 Leisure is work you volunteer for. ['Try a Grasshopper']

19 And he [J. B. Priestley] gives us what only the rare ones give us: a sense that we are collaborating, rather than simply paying to go in. He admits us to the country of ourselves. ['Priestley']

20 The longest-lived editor is the one least distinguishable from his average reader. ['Our Betters']

21 I've always felt it was the car which went down to the showroom to choose the man, not the other way round, and Volvos like to pick a dentist who is going to send his son to a not quite first-rate public school. ['The Place of the Volvo']

1 Nobody ever makes up nicknames, a nickname is your real identity, jumping out from behind you like an afreet. ['Nicknames']

2 Certain people are born with natural false teeth. [In BBC radio programme *Stop the Week*, 1977]

3 The national dish of America is menus. [In BBC TV programme *Robinson's Travels*, Aug. 1977]

J. M. ROBSON ?1900–1982

4 Theory is often just practice with the hard bits left out. [In *The Library*, 1985, VI. 7]

JAMES W. RODGERS ?–1960

5 [When asked if he had any last request before he was shot] Why yes – a bullet proof vest! [In Jonathon Green, *Famous Last Words*]

JOHN RODKER

6 It [*The Good Soldier*] is the finest French novel in the English language. [Quoted by Ford Madox Ford in a dedicatory letter to the novel]

THEODORE ROETHKE 1908–1963

7 Over this damp grave I speak the words of my love; / I, with no rights in this matter, / Neither father nor lover. [*Elegy for Jane*]

8 In a dark time the eye begins to see. [*In a Dark Time*]

9 I wake to sleep, and take my waking slow. / I learn by going where I have to go. [*The Waking*]

E. W. ROGERS 1864–1913

10 Ev'ry member of the force / Has a watch and chain, of course; / If you want to know the time, / Ask a P'liceman! [*Ask a P'liceman*]

11 Hi-tiddley-hi-ti. [Title of song]

R. C. ROGERS 1862–1912

12 The hours I spent with thee, dear heart, / Are as a string of pearls to me; / I count them over, every one apart, / My rosary. [*My Rosary*]

SIR RICHARD ROGERS 1933–

13 You should be able to read a building. It should be what it does. [In Walter Neurath Memorial Lecture, London University, Mar. 1990]

WILL ROGERS 1879–1935

14 I was born because it was a habit in those days, people dident know anything else. [*Autobiography*, Ch. 1]

15 Communism is like prohibition, it's a good idea but it won't work. [Nov. 1927]

16 I never was much on this Book reading, for it takes em too long to describe the colour of the eyes of all the Characters. [14]

17 England elects a Labour Government. When a man goes in for politics over here, he has no time to labour, and any man that labours has no time to fool with politics. Over there politics is an obligation; over here it's a business.

18 You can't say civilization don't advance, however, for in every war they kill you a new way.

19 It's great to be great but it's greater to be human. [15]

20 Half our life is spent trying to find something to do with the time we have rushed through life trying to save.

21 Everybody is ignorant, only on different subjects. [*The Illiterate Digest*]

22 Everything is funny as long as it's happening to somebody else.

23 It [Income Tax] has made more liars out of the American people than Golf.

24 A comedian can only last till he either takes himself serious or his audience takes him serious. [Newspaper article, 1931]

25 Being a hero is about the shortest-lived profession on earth. [In *Saturday Review*, 25 Aug. 1962, 'A Rogers Thesaurus']

26 I don't make jokes – I just watch the government and report the facts.

27 The more you read about politics, you got to admit that each party is worse than the other.

28 They got him [Pancho Villa] in the

morning editions, but the afternoon ones let him get away.

1 See what'll happen to you if you don't stop biting your finger-nails. [On the Venus de Milo. In Bennett Cerf, *Shake Well before Using*. Elsewhere ascr. to Noël Coward]

2 My folks didn't come over on the *Mayflower*, but they were there to meet the boat. [In *Treasury of Humorous Quotations*, ed. Evan Esar and Nicolas Bentley]

3 So live that you wouldn't be ashamed to sell the family parrot to the town gossip.

ROMAIN ROLLAND 1866–1944

4 It's the artist's job to create sunshine when there isn't any. [*Jean Christophe: La foire sur la place*]

SIR HUMPHREY DAVY ROLLESTON 1862–1944

5 First they [physicians] get *on*, then they get *honour*, then they get *honest*. [In David Ogilvy, *Confessions of an Advertising Man*]

SIGMUND ROMBERG 1887–1951

6 A love song is just a caress set to music. [In Nat Shapiro, *Encyclopedia of Quotations about Music*]

ELEANOR ROOSEVELT 1884–1962

7 Remember, no one can make you feel inferior without your consent. [In *Catholic Digest*, Aug. 1960]

PRESIDENT FRANKLIN D. ROOSEVELT 1882–1945

8 The forgotten man at the bottom of the economic pyramid. [Broadcast speech, 7 Apr. 1932]

9 I pledge you – I pledge myself – to a new deal for the American people. [Speech at convention, Chicago, 2 July]

10 Let me assert my firm belief that the only thing we have to fear is fear itself. [First inaugural address, 4 Mar. 1933]

11 In the field of world policy I would dedicate this nation to the policy of the good neighbour.

12 This generation of Americans has a rendezvous with destiny. [Speech accepting renomination, 27 June 1936]

13 We have always known that heedless self-interest was bad morals; we know now that it is bad economics. [Second inaugural address, 20 Jan. 1937]

14 I see one-third of a nation ill-housed, ill-clad, ill-nourished.

15 The change in the moral climate of America.

16 Quarantine the aggressors. [Speech at Chicago, 5 Oct.]

17 He may be a son of a bitch, but he's our son of a bitch. [Of Nicaraguan dictator 'Tacho' Somoza, 1938. In Jonathon Green, *Says Who?*]

18 The trouble is that when you sit around a table with a Britisher he usually gets 80 per cent of the deal and you get what's left. [In John Morton Blum, *From the Morgenthau Diaries*, Vol. I: *Years of Crisis, 1928–1938*]

19 A radical is a man with both feet planted firmly in the air. A reactionary is a somnambulist walking backwards. A conservative is a man with two perfectly good legs who, however, has never learned how to walk forward. A liberal is a man who uses his legs and his hands at the behest of his head. [Radio address, 26 Oct. 1939]

20 I have told you once and I will tell you again – your boys will not be sent into any foreign wars. [Election speech, 30 Oct. 1940]

21 The best immediate defence of the United States is the success of Great Britain defending itself. [At press conference, 17 Dec. In Winston S. Churchill, *Their Finest Hour*, Ch. 28]

22 We must be the great arsenal of democracy. [*Fireside Chat*, radio address, 29 Dec.]

23 A world founded upon four essential freedoms. The first is freedom of speech and expression – everywhere in the world. The second is freedom of every person to worship God in his own way – everywhere in the world. The third is freedom from want ... everywhere in the world. The fourth is freedom from fear ... anywhere in the world. [Speech, 6 Jan. 1941]

24 Never before have we had so little time

in which to do so much. [*Fireside Chat*, radio address, 23 Feb. 1942]

1 It is fun to be in the same decade with you. [To Churchill, in answer to congratulations on his 60th birthday. In Winston S. Churchill, *The Hinge of Fate*, Ch. 4]

2 Stalin hates the guts of all your top people. He thinks he likes me better, and I hope he will continue to do so. [In 11]

3 Defeat of Germany means the defeat of Japan, probably without firing a shot or losing a life. [In 25]

4 The only limit to our realization of tomorrow will be our doubts of today. [Address written for Jefferson Day dinner to have been given 13 Apr. 1945. He died on the 12th]

PRESIDENT THEODORE ROOSEVELT
1858–1919

5 I wish to preach, not the doctrine of ignoble ease, but the doctrine of the strenuous life. [Speech at Chicago, 10 Apr. 1899]

6 Speak softly and carry a big stick: you will go far. [Speech at Chicago, 2 Apr. 1903]

7 A man who is good enough to shed his blood for his country is good enough to be given a square deal afterwards. More than that no man is entitled to, and less than that no man shall have. [Speech at Springfield, Illinois, 4 July]

8 The men with the muck-rakes are often indispensable to the well-being of society but only if they know when to stop raking the muck. [At laying of corner-stone, House of Representatives, 14 Apr. 1906]

9 Hyphenated Americanism. [Speech in New York, 12 Oct. 1915. See also 270:8, 406:22]

10 One of our defects as a nation is a tendency to use what have been called 'weasel words'. When a weasel sucks eggs the meat is sucked out of the egg. If you use a 'weasel word' after another there is nothing left of the other. [Speech in St Louis, Missouri, 31 May 1916]

11 There can be no fifty-fifty Americanism in this country. There is room here for only one hundred per cent Americanism. [Speech at Saratoga, New York, 19 July 1918]

12 The lunatic fringe in all reform movements. [*Autobiography*, Ch. 7]

13 No man is justified in doing evil on the ground of expediency. [*The Strenuous Life*, 'Latitude and Longitude among Reformers']

14 The most successful politician is he who says what everybody is thinking most often and in the loudest voice. [In *Treasury of Humorous Quotations*, ed. Evan Esar and Nicolas Bentley]

NED ROREM 1923–

15 To see itself through, music must have an idea or magic. The best has both. Music with neither dies young, though sometimes rich. [*Pure Contraption*]

16 It isn't evil that's running the earth, but mediocrity. The crime is not that Nero played while Rome burned, but that he played badly. [From *Final Diary*, in *Simpson's Contemporary Quotations*]

AMANDA ROS [MRS ANNA ROSS]
1860–1939

17 I don't believe in publishers who wish to butter their bannocks on both sides while they'll hardly allow an author to smell treacle. I consider they are too grabby together and like Methodists they love to keep the Sabbath and everything else they can lay their hands on. [Letter to Lord Ponsonby, 1910]

ARTHUR ROSE see DOUGLAS FURBER
and ARTHUR ROSE

BILLY ROSE [WILLIAM ROSENBERG]
1899–1966

18 Does the Spearmint Lose Its Flavour on the Bedpost Overnight. [Title of song, 1924, in musical *Be Yourself*, written with Marty Bloom, music by Ernest Breuer]

19 Me and My Shadow [Title of song, 1927, in show *Delmar's Revels*, music by Al Jolson]

20 Never invest your money in anything that eats or needs repainting. [In the *New York Post*, 1957]

EARL OF ROSEBERY 1847–1929

1 The Empire is a Commonwealth of Nations. [Speech at Adelaide, S. Australia, 18 Jan. 1884]

2 It is beginning to be hinted that we are a nation of amateurs. [Rectorial address, Glasgow University, 16 Nov. 1900]

3 I must plough my own furrow alone. [Speech at City of London Liberal Club, 19 July 1901]

4 You have to clean your plate. [Advice to the Liberal Party. Speech at Chesterfield, 16 Dec.]

BERNARD ROSENBERG

5 Radical: A person whose left hand does not know what his other left hand is doing. [In Laurence J. Peter, *Peter's Quotations*]

ETHEL 1916–1953 and JULIUS ROSENBERG 1918–1953

6 We are innocent, as we have proclaimed and maintained from the time of our arrest. This is the whole truth. To forsake this truth is to pay too high a price even for the priceless gift of life – for life thus purchased we could not live out in dignity and self-respect. [Petition for clemency filed 19 Jan. 1953 before execution for espionage]

HAROLD ROSENBERG 1906–1978

7 The modern painter begins with nothingness. That is the only thing he copies. The rest he invents. [Of Jackson Pollock. In the *Guardian*, 23 Nov. 1989]

ISAAC ROSENBERG 1890–1918

8 The darkness crumbles away – / It is the same old druid Time as ever. [*Break of Day in the Trenches*]

9 Droll rat, they would shoot you if they knew / Your cosmopolitan sympathies / (And God knows what antipathies).

10 Earth has waited for them, / All the time of their growth / Fretting for their decay: / Now she has them at last. [*Dead Man's Dump*]

11 Death could drop from the dark / As easily as song. [*Returning, We Hear the Larks*]

LEO ROSENBERG

12 First you forget names, then you forget faces, then you forget to pull your zipper up, then you forget to pull your zipper down. [In Laurence J. Peter, *Peter's Quotations*, 'Old Age']

EUGEN ROSENSTOCK-HUESSY 1888–1959

13 He who believes in nothing still needs a girl to believe in him. [In W. H. Auden, *A Certain World*]

ALAN S. C. ROSS 1907–1978

14 U and Non-U, An Essay in Sociological Linguistics. [Title of essay, included in *Noblesse Oblige*]

HAROLD W. ROSS 1892–1951

15 You can exclude noise by soundproofing your mind. [Quoting anonymous authority. In James Thurber, *The Years with Ross*, Ch. 3]

16 Is Moby Dick the whale or the man? [In 4]

17 The *New Yorker* will be the magazine which is not edited for the old lady from Dubuque. [On founding the *New Yorker*, 1925. Later she became 'the little old lady']

18 I don't want you to think I'm not incoherent. [In 5]

19 Thurber is the greatest unlistener I know.

20 WOMAN AT ZOO: Is that a male or a female hippopotamus?
KEEPER: Madam, I don't see how that could interest anybody except another hippopotamus. [Tale of unknown origin, told by Ross]

21 I understand the hero keeps getting in bed with women, and the war wasn't fought that way. [On Hemingway's *A Farewell to Arms*. In 7]

22 On one of Mr Benchley's manuscripts he [Ross] wrote in the margin opposite 'Andromache', 'Who he?' Mr Benchley wrote back, 'You keep out of this.' [Quoted by Dorothy Parker in *Writers at Work*, ed. Malcolm Cowley, First Series]

JEAN ROSTAND 1894–1977

1 To be adult is to be alone. [*Thoughts of a Biologist*]

LEO C. ROSTEN 1908–

2 Anybody who hates dogs and babies can't be all bad. [Of W. C. Fields at Masquers' Club Dinner, Hollywood, 16 Feb. 1939. Often misquoted as 'children and dogs' and wrongly attr. to Fields]

PHILIP ROTH 1933–

3 In Israel it's enough to live – you don't have to do anything else and you go to bed exhausted. Have you ever noticed that Jews shout? Even one ear is more than you need. [*The Counterlife*, 2]

4 What makes you a normal Jew, Nathan, is how you are riveted by Jewish abnormality. [3]

5 Since I was a little girl I always wanted to be Very Decent to People. Other little girls wanted to be nurses and pianists. They were less dissembling. [*Letting Go*, Pt I, Ch. 1]

6 My first impression of her had been clear and sharp: profession – student; inclinations – neurotic.

7 It's the little questions from women about tappets that finally push men over the edge.

8 It's a family joke that when I was a tiny child I turned from the window out of which I was watching a snowstorm, and hopefully asked, 'Momma, do we believe in winter?' [*Portnoy's Complaint*]

9 Doctor, my doctor, what do you say – let's put the id back in yid!

10 A Jewish man with parents alive is a fifteen-year-old boy, and will remain a fifteen-year-old boy till they die.

11 In America everything goes and nothing matters, while in Europe nothing goes and everything matters. [Interview in *Time* magazine, Nov. 1983]

FIRST LORD ROTHERMERE 1868–1940

12 Hats off to France. [Title of article in the *Daily Mail*, 1923, supporting French occupation of the Ruhr]

GEORGES ROUAULT 1871–1958

13 For me, painting is a way to forget life. It is a cry in the night, a strangled laugh. [In Laurence J. Peter, *Peter's Quotations*]

M. E. ROURKE 1867–1933

14 And when I told them how beautiful you are / They didn't believe me! They didn't believe me! [Song: *They Didn't Believe Me*, music by Jerome Kern]

DAN ROWAN 1922–1987 and DICK MARTIN 1922–

15 Very interesting . . . but stupid! [Catchphrase in US TV comedy series *Rowan and Martin's Laugh-in*, 1967–73]

16 This is beautiful downtown Burbank.

17 Sock it to me!

SHEILA ROWBOTHAM 1943–

18 Men will often admit other women are oppressed but not you. [*Woman's Consciousness, Man's World*]

EDWARD C. ROWLAND

19 Mademoiselle from Armenteers, / Hasn't been kissed for forty years, / Hinky pinky, parley-voo. [Song of 1914–18 War: *Mademoiselle from Armentières*. Authorship uncertain; also ascr. to Alfred J. Walden (under pseudonym of Harry Wincott)]

HELEN ROWLAND 1875–1950

20 A man never knows how to say goodbye; a woman never knows when to say it. [*Reflections of a Bachelor Girl*]

21 It is easier to keep half a dozen lovers guessing than to keep one lover after he has stopped guessing.

22 A husband is what is left of the lover after the nerve has been extracted. [*The Rubaiyat of a Bachelor*]

RICHARD ROWLAND ?1881–1947

23 The lunatics have taken over the asylum. [When United Artists was taken over by

Chaplin, Pickford, Fairbanks and Griffith. In Leslie Halliwell, *Filmgoer's Book of Quotes*]

MAUDE ROYDEN 1876–1956

1 The Church should go forward along the path of progress and be no longer satisfied only to represent the Conservative Party at prayer. [Speech at Queen's Hall, London, 16 July 1917. In *Oxford Dictionary of Modern Quotations*, ed. Tony Augarde]

NAOMI ROYDE-SMITH ?1875–1964

2 I know two things about the horse / And one of them is rather coarse. [In Frances and Vera Meynell, *Weekend Book*]

BERNICE RUBENS 1928–

3 The acid test of a good piece of writing, even if it is of violence and cruelty, is that it must make one's ears water. [In the *Sunday Times*, 3 Apr. 1988]

PAUL RUBENS 1875–1917

4 We Don't Want to Lose You but We Think You Ought to Go. [Song of 1914–18 War: *Your King and Country Want You*, sung by Alice Delysia]

ARTUR RUBINSTEIN 1887–1982

5 [When told by Stephen Spender he looked like a cross between Bertrand Russell and Chopin] Bertrand Russell – good. But anyone can look like Chopin. [In Stephen Spender, *Journals, 1939–1983*, ed. J. Goldsmith, 16 Mar. 1975]

6 Don't tell me how talented you are. Tell me how hard you work. [In David Dubal, *Evenings with Horowitz*, Ch. 43]

MICHAEL RUBINSTEIN 1920–

7 To be and not to be, that is the answer. [In conversation]

RITA RUDNER 1956–

8 Men who have a pierced ear are better prepared for marriage – they've experienced pain and bought jewellery. [On Channel 4 TV, 5 Dec. 1989]

ARCHBISHOP ROBERT [later LORD] RUNCIE 1921–

9 In the middle ages people were tourists because of their religion, whereas now they are tourists because tourism is their religion. [In the *Observer*, 'Sayings of the Week', 11 Dec. 1988]

SIR STEVEN RUNCIMAN 1903–

10 Unlike Christianity, which preached a peace that is never achieved, Islam unashamedly came with a sword. [*A History of the Crusades*, 'The First Crusade']

DAMON RUNYON 1884–1946

11 Now of course this is strictly the old ackamarackus, as the Lemon Drop Kid cannot even spell arthritis, let alone have it. [*Furthermore*, 'The Lemon Drop Kid']

12 Any time you see him he is generally by himself because being by himself is not apt to cost him anything. ['Little Miss Marker']

13 If this little doll is sitting in your joint all afternoon . . . the best thing to do right now is to throw a feed into her as the chances are her stomach thinks her throat is cut.

14 Personally, I consider a taxicab much more convenient and less expensive than an old-fashioned victoria if you wish to get to some place, but of course guys and dolls engaged in a little offhand guzzling never wish to get any place in particular, or at least not soon. ['Princess O'Hara']

15 My boy . . . always try to rub up against money, for if you rub up against money long enough, some of it may rub off on you. ['A Very Honourable Guy']

16 Even Mr Justin Veezee is not so oldfashioned as to believe any doll will go to his apartment just to look at etchings nowadays. ['What, No Butler?']

17 'In fact,' Sam the Gonoph says, 'I long ago came to the conclusion that all life is six to five against.' [*More Than Somewhat*, 'A Nice Price']

18 Angie the Ox is an importer himself, besides enjoying a splendid trade in other lines, including artichokes and extortion. ['The Old Doll's House']

1 She is a smart old broad. It is a pity she is so nefarious. [*Runyon à la carte*, 'Broadway Incident']

2 At such an hour the sinners are still in bed resting up from their sinning of the night before, so they will be in good shape for more sinning a little later on. ['The Idyll of Miss Sarah Brown']

3 I quietly give Girondel a boff over his pimple with a blackjack and flatten him like a welcome mat. ['A Light in France']

4 I step over to his table and give him a medium hello, and he looks up and gives me a medium hello right back, for, to tell the truth, Maury and I are never bosom friends.

5 I remarked that his eyes were open so he must be awake. 'The one on your side is,' said a backer, 'but the one on the other side is closed. He is sleeping one-eyed.' [*Short Takes*, 'Bed-Warmers']

6 I once knew a chap who had a system of just hanging the baby on the clothes line to dry and he was greatly admired by his fellow citizens for having discovered a wonderful innovation on changing a diaper. ['Diaper Dexterity']

7 A free-loader is a confirmed guest. He is the man who is always willing to come to dinner. ['Free-loading Ethics']

8 I do not approve of guys using false pretences on dolls, except, of course, when nothing else will do. [*Take It Easy*, 'It Comes up Mud']

9 These citizens are always willing to bet that what Nicely-Nicely dies of will be overfeeding and never anything small like pneumonia, for Nicely-Nicely is known far and wide as a character who dearly loves to commit eating. ['Lonely Heart']

10 He is without strict doubt a Hoorah Henry, and he is generally figured as nothing but a lob as far as doing anything useful in this world is concerned. ['Tight Shoes']

11 Much as he is opposed to lawbreaking, he is not bigoted about it. [Attr.]

SALMAN RUSHDIE 1947–

12 Making our way in this West stuffed with money, power and things, this North that taught us how to see from its privileged point of view. But maybe we were the lucky ones; we knew that other perspectives existed. We had seen the view from elsewhere. [On his visit to Nicaragua. *The Jaguar Smile*, final words]

13 Most of what matters in your life takes place in your absence. [*Midnight's Children*, Bk II, 'Alpha and Omega']

14 The modern world lacks not only hiding places, but certainties. ['Outside the Whale', *Granta*, 11]

15 Any community worthy of the name needs what I call the family virtues – acceptance, tolerance, compassion and forgiveness. [In the *Observer*, 'Sayings of the Week', 26 Feb. 1989]

16 To burn a book is not to destroy it. One minute of darkness will not make us blind. [Review of Gabriel García Márquez's *Clandestine in Chile* in the *Weekend Guardian*, 14–15 Oct.]

17 Literature is the one place in any society where, within the secrecy of our own heads, we can hear *voices talking about everything in every possible way*. [Lecture 'Is Nothing Sacred?', at Institute of Contemporary Arts, London, 6 Feb. 1990]

18 The world has always felt a long way away to Americans. Its important battles have always been internal, its most feared enemies within. [In the *Independent on Sunday*, 10 Feb. 1991]

DEAN RUSK 1909–

19 I wouldn't make the slightest concession for moral leadership. It's much overrated. [Said in 1962. In D. Halberstam, *The Best and the Brightest*, Ch. 16]

20 We're eyeball to eyeball, and the other fellow just blinked. [On the Cuban missile crisis, 24 Oct. 1962. In Eric de Mauny, *Russian Prospect*]

JOANNA RUSS 1937–

21 First you have to liberate the children (because they're the future) and then you have to liberate the men (because they've been so deformed by the system) and then if

there's any liberation left you can take it into the kitchen and eat it. [*On Strike against God*, p. 84]

BERTRAND, LORD RUSSELL
1872–1970

1 Three passions, simple but overwhelmingly strong, have governed my life: the longing for love, the search for knowledge, and unbearable pity for the suffering of mankind. [*Autobiography*, Vol. I, Prologue]

2 I was told that the Chinese said they would bury me by the Western Lake and build a shrine to my memory. I have some slight regret that this did not happen, as I might have become a god, which would have been very *chic* for an atheist. [II, Ch. 3]

3 One of the great drawbacks to self-centred passions is that they afford so little variety in life. The man who loves only himself cannot, it is true, be accused of promiscuity in his affections, but he is bound in the end to suffer intolerable boredom from the inevitable sameness of the object of his devotion. [17]

4 ... the nuns who never take a bath without wearing a bathrobe all the time. When asked why, since no man can see them, they reply 'Oh, but you forget the good God.' [*The Basic Writings*, Pt II, Ch. 7]

5 The megalomaniac differs from the narcissist by the fact that he wishes to be powerful rather than charming, and seeks to be feared rather than loved. To this type belong many lunatics and most of the great men of history. [*The Conquest of Happiness*, Ch. 1]

6 Suspicion of one's own motives is especially necessary for the philanthropist and the executive. [8]

7 To be without some of the things you want is an indispensable part of happiness.

8 Of all forms of caution, caution in love is perhaps the most fatal to true happiness. [12]

9 Man is not a solitary animal, and so long as social life survives, self-realization cannot

be the supreme principle of ethics. [*History of Western Philosophy*, 'Romanticism']

10 Broadly speaking, we are in the middle of a race between human skill as to means and human folly as to ends. [*Impact of Science on Society*, 1952, Ch. 7]

11 Really high-minded people are indifferent to happiness, especially other people's.

12 Brief and powerless is Man's life; on him and all his race the slow, sure doom falls pitiless and dark. [*Mysticism and Logic*, 'A Free Man's Worship']

13 Mathematics possesses not only truth, but supreme beauty – a beauty cold and austere, like that of sculpture. [Ch. 4]

14 Mathematics may be defined as the subject in which we never know what we are talking about, nor whether what we are saying is true.

15 Pure mathematics consists entirely of assertions to the effect that, if such and such a proposition is true of *anything*, then such and such another proposition is true of that thing. It is essential not to discuss whether the first proposition is really true, and not to mention what the anything is, of which it is supposed to be true. [5]

16 Organic life, we are told, has developed gradually from the protozoon to the philosopher and this development, we are assured, is indubitably an advance. Unfortunately it is the philosopher, not the protozoon, who gives us this assurance. [6]

17 Better the world should perish than that I or any other human being should believe a lie ... that is the religion of thought, in whose scorching flames the dross of the world is being burnt away. [10]

18 Matter ... a convenient formula for describing what happens where it isn't. [*An Outline of Philosophy*]

19 Only on the firm foundation of unyielding despair can the soul's edifice henceforth be built. [*Philosophical Essays*, 2]

20 I think that bad philosophers may have a certain influence, good philosophers, never. [In the *Observer*, 'Sayings of the Week', 24 Apr. 1955]

21 The collection of prejudices which is

called political philosophy is useful provided that it is not called philosophy. [In the *Observer*, 'Sayings of the Year', 1962]

1 All intellectuals should suffer a certain amount of persecution as early in life as possible. Not too much. That is bad for them. But a certain amount. [In Kenneth Harris, *Kenneth Harris Talking to:* 'Bertrand Russell']

2 There's a Bible on that shelf there. But I keep it next to Voltaire – poison and antidote.

3 Hume seems to me to have been the only one of the great philosophers who wanted to get at the truth. The rest all wanted to get at something else, something that would flatter humanity, or suit their prejudices, or refute their enemies.

4 What men really want is not knowledge but certainty. [Quoted by G. M. Carstairs in the *Listener*, 30 July 1964]

5 Many people would sooner die than think. In fact they do. [Epigraph to A. Flew, *Thinking about Thinking*]

6 You may reasonably expect a man to walk a tightrope safely for ten minutes; it would be unreasonable to do so without accident for two hundred years. [Of the nuclear confrontation of the superpowers. In D. Bagley, *The Tightrope Men*]

7 The stars are in one's brain. [In R. D. Laing, *Politics of Experience*, Ch. 1]

8 The average man's opinions are much less foolish than they would be if he thought for himself. [Attr.]

9 Few people can be happy unless they hate some person, nation or creed. [Attr.]

10 Patriots always talk of dying for their country, and never of killing for their country. [Attr.]

11 To die for one's beliefs is to put too high a price on conjecture. [Attr.]

CLAUDE RUSSELL 1919–

12 Curious how much more room dirty clothes take up than clean ones, when you're packing – quite out of proportion to the amount of dirt they contain. [In Edward Marsh, *A Number of People*]

GEORGE WILLIAM RUSSELL [Æ]
1867–1935

13 A literary movement: five or six people who live in the same town and hate each other. [Attr. in *Book of Irish Quotations*, ed. Sean McMahon]

WILLY RUSSELL 1947–

14 The main purpose of marriage is rearing children and when that's done you should be free to renew your option – about twenty years seems like a reasonable term to me. [Interview in the *Guardian*, 20 Oct. 1987]

ERNEST [later LORD] RUTHERFORD
1871–1937

15 Well, I made the wave, didn't I? [In answer to the jibe 'Lucky fellow, Rutherford, always on the crest of the wave.' In C. P. Snow, *The Two Cultures and the Scientific Revolution*]

16 Science is divided into two categories, physics and stamp-collecting. [In J. D. Bernal, *The Social Function of Science*]

17 The energy produced by the breaking down of the atom is a very poor kind of thing. Anyone who expects a source of energy from the transformation of these atoms is talking moonshine. [From *Physics Today*, 1970, in *Dictionary of Scientific Quotations*, ed. A. L. Mackay. Often misquoted as 'nuclear power is moonshine']

GILBERT RYLE 1900–1976

18 Philosophy is the replacement of category-habits by category-disciplines. [*The Concept of Mind*, Introduction]

19 Many people can talk sense with concepts but cannot talk sense about them; they know by practice how to operate with concepts, anyhow inside their chosen fields, but they cannot state the logical regulations governing their use. They are like people who know their way about their own parish, but cannot construct or read a map of it, much less of the region, or continent in which their parish lies.

20 A myth is, of course, not a fairy story. It is the presentation of facts belonging

to one category in the idioms appropriate to another. To explode a myth is accordingly not to deny the facts but to re-allocate them.

1 The dogma of the Ghost in the Machine. [Ch. 1]

2 So too Plato was, in my view, a very unreliable Platonist. He was too much of a philosopher to think that anything he had said was the last word. It was left to his disciples to identify his footmarks with his destination. [*Dilemmas*, Ch. 1]

S

OLIVER SACKS 1933–

1 Health is infinite and expansive in mode, and reaches out to be filled with the fullness of the world; whereas disease is finite and reductive in mode, and endeavours to reduce the world to itself. [*Awakenings*, 'Perspectives']

2 This seems to be the nature of thought that it leads to its own starting point, the timeless home of the mind. [*A Leg to Stand On*, final words]

3 The Man Who Mistook His Wife for a Hat. [Title of Book]

WINIFRED SACKVILLE STONER JR

4 In fourteen hundred and ninety-two / Columbus sailed the ocean blue. [In the *Observer*, 10 Feb. 1991]

VICTORIA SACKVILLE-WEST 1892–1962

5 The greater cats with golden eyes / Stare out between the bars. [*King's Daughter*, II. 1]

6 The country habit has me by the heart,/ For he's bewitched for ever who has seen, / Not with his eyes but with his vision, Spring / Flow down the woods and stipple leaves with sun. [*The Land*, 'Winter']

7 Forget not bees in winter, though they sleep, / For winter's big with summer in her womb. ['Spring']

8 All craftsmen share a knowledge. They have held / Reality down fluttering to a bench. ['Summer']

MICHAEL SADLEIR 1888–1957

9 Fanny by Gaslight. [Title of book]

FRANÇOISE SAGAN 1935–

10 I like men to behave like men – strong and childish. [In *Dictionary of Contemporary Quotations*, ed. Jonathon Green]

11 Marriage? It's like asparagus eaten with vinaigrette or hollandaise, a matter of taste but of no importance. [In the *Guardian*, 21 June 1988]

MORT SAHL 1926–

12 People tell me there are a lot of guys like me, which doesn't explain why I'm lonely. [In E. Lax, *Woody Allen and His Comedy*, Ch. 12]

13 Beverly Hills is very exclusive. For instance, their fire department won't make house calls. [Attr. in *Penguin Dictionary of Modern Humorous Quotations*, comp. Fred Metcalf]

14 Washington could not tell a lie; Nixon could not tell the truth; Reagan cannot tell the difference. [In the *Observer*, 'Sayings of the Week', 18 Oct. 1987]

15 Reagan won because he ran against Jimmy Carter. Had he run unopposed he would have lost. [In *The Other 637 Best Things Anybody Ever Said*, comp. Robert Byrne]

16 Would you buy a second-hand car from this man? [Of President Nixon. Attr.]

ANTOINE DE SAINT-EXUPÉRY
1900–1944

1 Grown-ups never understand anything for themselves, and it is tiresome for children to be always and forever explaining things to them. [*The Little Prince*, Ch. 1]

2 It is much more difficult to judge oneself than to judge others. [10]

3 It is only with the heart that one can see rightly; what is essential is invisible to the eye. [21]

4 You become responsible, forever, for what you have tamed. You are responsible for your rose.

5 Philosophy is a battle against the bewitchment of our intelligence by means of language. [Attr.]

LEE [JOHN L.] ST JOHN

6 Archibald – certainly not! [Title of song made popular *c.* 1910–20 by George Robey]

SAKI [H. H. MUNRO] 1870–1916

7 You can't expect a boy to be depraved until he has been to a good school. [*A Baker's Dozen*]

8 I believe I once considerably scandalized her by declaring that clear soup was a more important factor in life than a clear conscience. [*The Blind Spot*]

9 Addresses are given to us to conceal our whereabouts. [*Cross Currents*]

10 'I believe I take precedence,' he said coldly; 'you are merely the club Bore: I am the club Liar.' [*A Defensive Diamond*]

11 One of those strapping florid girls that go so well with autumn scenery or Christmas decorations in church. [*Esmé*]

12 Waldo is one of those people who would be enormously improved by death. [*The Feast of Nemesis*]

13 Children with Hyacinth's temperament don't know better as they grow older; they merely know more. [*Hyacinth*]

14 In baiting a mouse-trap with cheese, always leave room for the mouse. [*The Infernal Parliament*]

15 I might have been a gold-fish in a glass bowl for all the privacy I got. [*The Innocence of Reginald*]

16 The people of Crete unfortunately make more history than they can consume locally. [*The Jesting of Arlington Stringham*]

17 He's simply got the instinct for being unhappy highly developed. [*The Matchmaker*]

18 There's nothing in Christianity or Buddhism that quite matches the sympathetic unselfishness of an oyster.

19 All decent people live beyond their incomes nowadays, and those who aren't respectable live beyond other people's. A few gifted individuals manage to do both.

20 His socks compelled one's attention without losing one's respect. [*Ministers of Grace*]

21 The young have aspirations that never come to pass, the old have reminiscences of what never happened. [*Reginald at the Carlton*]

22 There may have been disillusionments in the lives of the medieval saints, but they would scarcely have been better pleased if they could have foreseen that their names would be associated nowadays chiefly with racehorses and the cheaper clarets.

23 The cook was a good cook, as cooks go; and as cooks go she went. [*Reginald on Besetting Sins*]

24 She took to telling the truth; she said she was forty-two and five months. It may have been pleasing to the angels, but her elder sister was not gratified.

25 People may say what they like about the decay of Christianity; the religious system that produced green Chartreuse can never really die. [*Reginald on Christmas Presents*]

26 Even the Hooligan was probably invented in China centuries before we thought of him. [*Reginald on House-parties*]

27 Every reformation must have its victims. You can't expect the fatted calf to share the enthusiasm of the angels over the prodigal's return. [*Reginald on the Academy*]

28 I think she must have been very strictly brought up, she's so desperately anxious to do the wrong thing correctly. [*Reginald on Worries*]

1 Her frocks are built in Paris, but she wears them with a strong English accent.

2 I always say beauty is only sin deep. [*Reginald's Choir Treat*]

3 Temptation came to him, in middle age, tentatively and without insistence, like a neglected butcher-boy who asks for a Christmas box in February for no more hopeful reason than that he didn't get one in December. [*The Reticence of Lady Anne*]

4 His 'Noontide Peace', a study of two dun cows under a walnut tree, was followed by 'A Mid-day Sanctuary', a study of a walnut tree with two dun cows under it. [*The Stalled Ox*]

5 This story has no moral. If it points out an evil, at any rate it suggests no remedy. [*The Unbearable Bassington*, Author's Note]

6 The woman who can sacrifice a clean unspoiled penny stamp is probably unborn. [Ch. 1]

7 A woman whose dresses are made in Paris and whose marriage has been made in Heaven might be equally biased for and against free imports. [9]

8 Sherard Blaw, the dramatist who had discovered himself, and who had given so ungrudgingly of his discovery to the world. [13]

9 The English have a proverb: 'Conscience makes cowboys of us all.' [*Wratislav*]

J. D. SALINGER 1919–

10 Sex is something I really don't understand too hot. You never know *where* the hell you are. I keep making up these sex rules for myself, and then I break them right away. [*The Catcher in the Rye*, Ch. 9]

11 I was about half in love with her by the time we sat down. That's the thing about girls. Every time they do something pretty, even if they're not much to look at, or even if they're sort of stupid, you fall half in love with them, and then you never know *where* you are. [10]

12 He looked like the kind of a guy that wouldn't talk to you much unless he wanted something off you. He had a lousy personality. [11]

13 The thing is, it's really hard to be roommates with people if your suitcases are much better than theirs – if yours are really good ones and theirs aren't. You think if they're intelligent and all, the other person, and have a good sense of humour, that they don't give a damn whose suitcases are better, but they do. [15]

14 They didn't act like people and they didn't act like actors. It's hard to explain. They acted more like they knew they were celebrities and all. I mean they were good, but they were *too* good. [17]

15 Take most people, they're crazy about cars ... and if they get a brand-new car already they start thinking about trading it in for one that's even newer. I don't even like *old* cars. I mean they don't even interest me. I'd rather have a goddam horse. A horse is at least *human*, for God's sake.

16 The trouble with girls is, if they like a boy, no matter how big a bastard he is, they'll say he has an inferiority complex, and if they *don't* like him, no matter how nice a guy he is, or how big an inferiority complex he has, they'll say he's conceited. Even smart girls do it. [18]

17 Sally said I was a sacrilegious atheist. I probably am. The thing Jesus *really* would've liked would be the guy that plays the kettle drums in the orchestra.

18 For Esmé, with Love and Squalor. [Title of story]

19 Poetry, surely, is a crisis, perhaps the only actionable one we can call our own. [*Seymour: An Introduction*]

20 Probably passed on, these many years, of an overdose of garlic, the way all New York barbers eventually go.

21 A confessional passage has probably never been written that didn't stink a little bit of the writer's pride in having given up his pride.

22 One of the thousand reasons I quit going to the theatre when I was about twenty was that I resented like hell filing out of the theatre just because some playwright was forever slamming down his silly curtain.

LORD SALISBURY 1893–1972

23 He [Iain Macleod, Colonial Secretary] has

adopted, especially in his relationship to the white communities of Africa, a most unhappy and an entirely wrong approach. He has been too clever by half. [Speech in House of Lords, 7 Mar. 1961]

ANDREW SALKEY 1928–

1 Culture come when you buck up / on you'self. / It start when you' body make shadow / on the lan', / an' you know say / that you standin' up into mirror / underneat' you. [*Jamaica: A Long Poem*]

2 [When asked to give an oxymoron] Sincerely, Nixon. [In PBS programme *All Things Considered*, Washington, 1980]

HARRY SALTZMAN 1915–

3 [When Ken Russell told him he would like to make a film on Tchaikovsky] You can't do Tchaikovsky . . . Dimitri Tiomkin's gonna do that, *and he's already writing the music.* [In J. Baxter, *An Appalling Talent*]

ANTHONY SAMPSON 1926–

4 Members rise from CMG (known sometimes in Whitehall as 'Call me God') to the KCMG ('Kindly Call me God') to . . . the GCMG ('God Calls me God'). [*Anatomy of Britain*, Ch. 18]

5 In America, journalism is apt to be regarded as an extension of history: in Britain, as an extension of conversation.

GEOFFREY SAMPSON 1944–

6 To my mind by far the greatest danger in scholarship . . . is not that the individual may fail to master the thought of a school but that a school may succeed in mastering the thought of the individual. [*Schools of Linguistics*, Preface]

GEORGE SAMPSON 1873–1950

7 The well-meaning people who talk about education as if it were a substance distributable by coupon in large or small quantities never exhibit any understanding of the truth that you cannot teach anybody anything that he does not want to learn. [*Seven Essays*, i. XIX]

HERBERT [later LORD] SAMUEL 1870–1963

8 Without doubt the greatest injury . . . was done by basing morals on myth, for sooner or later myth is recognized for what it is, and disappears. Then morality loses the foundation on which it has been built. [Romanes Lecture, 1947]

9 Democracy is like a hobby-horse: it will carry you nowhere unless you use your own legs. [In the *Observer*, 'Sayings of the Week', 27 Mar. 1927]

10 Hansard is history's ear, already listening. [18 Dec. 1949]

11 A library is thought in cold storage. [In his *Book of Quotations*, 'Books']

12 A friend in need is a friend to be avoided. [In the *Sunday Telegraph Magazine*, 27 Nov. 1977]

13 A difficulty for every solution. [Of the Civil Service. Attr.]

RAPHAEL SAMUEL 1934–

14 Ideologically, in its craving for authority figures, it [the Conservative Party] has replaced the Altar and the Throne by the police. [In the *Guardian*, 2 Dec. 1985]

CARL SANDBURG 1878–1967

15 Hog Butcher for the World. [Of Chicago in *Chicago*]

16 When Abraham Lincoln was shovelled into the tombs, / he forgot the copperheads and the assassin . . . / in the dust, in the cool tombs. [*Cool Tombs*]

17 The fog comes / on little cat feet. [*Fog*]

18 Pile the bodies high at Austerlitz and Waterloo, / Shovel them under and let me work – / I am the grass; I cover all. [*Grass*]

19 The people will live on. / The learning and blundering people will live on. / They will be tricked and sold and again sold / And go back to the nourishing earth for rootholds. [*The People, Yes*]

20 Sometimes they'll give a war and nobody will come.

21 I am an idealist. I don't know where I'm going but I'm on my way. ['Incidentals']

1 Poetry is the achievement of the synthesis of hyacinths and biscuits. ['Poetry Considered', *Atlantic Monthly*, Mar. 1923]

2 Slang is a language that rolls up its sleeves, spits on its hands and goes to work. [In *The New York Times*, 13 Feb. 1959]

GEORGE SANTAYANA 1863–1952

3 The young man who has not wept is a savage, and the old man who will not laugh is a fool. [*Dialogues in Limbo*, Ch. 3]

4 The barbarian is the man who regards his passions as their own excuse for being; who does not domesticate them either by understanding their cause or by conceiving their ideal goal. [*Egotism in German Philosophy*]

5 As the Latin languages are not composed of two diverse elements, as English is of Latin and German, so the Latin mind does not have two spheres of sentiment, one vulgar and the other sublime. All changes are variations on a single key, which is the key of intelligence. [*Interpretations of Poetry and Religion*]

6 The Bible is literature, not dogma. [*Introduction to the Ethics of Spinoza*]

7 Fanaticism consists of redoubling your effort when you have forgotten your aim. [*The Life of Reason*, Vol. 1, Introduction]

8 Happiness is the only sanction of life; where happiness fails, existence remains a mad lamentable experiment. [Ch. 10]

9 Progress, far from consisting in change, depends on retentiveness ... Those who do not remember the past are condemned to repeat it. [12]

10 England is the paradise of individuality, eccentricity, heresy, anomalies, hobbies, and humours. [*Soliloquies in England*, 'The British Character']

11 Trust the man who hesitates in his speech and is quick and steady in action, but beware of long arguments and long beards.

12 Friendship is almost always the union of a part of one mind with a part of another; people are friends in spots. ['Friendships']

13 The truth, which is a standard for the naturalist, for the poet is only a stimulus. ['Ideas']

14 There is no cure for birth and death save to enjoy the interval. ['War Shrines']

15 It is a great advantage for a system of philosophy to be substantially true. [*The Unknowable*]

16 Life is not a spectacle or a feast; it is a predicament. [In Sagittarius and D. George, *The Perpetual Pessimist*]

JOHN SINGER SARGENT 1856–1925

17 A portrait is a picture in which there is just a tiny little something not quite right about the mouth. [In *Anecdotes of Modern Art*, ed. Donald Hall and Pat Corrington-Wykes, but ascr. to Eugene Speicher, 1883–1962, in Frank Muir, *Frank Muir Book*. See also 192:17]

18 Every time I paint a portrait I lose a friend. [In *Treasury of Humorous Quotations*, ed. Evan Esar and Nicolas Bentley]

ROBERT W. SARNOFF 1918–

19 Finance is the art of passing currency from hand to hand until it finally disappears. [In *Executive's Quotation Book*, ed. James Charlton]

LESLIE SARONY 1897–1985

20 Ain't It Grand to be Blooming Well Dead? [Title of song, 1932]

WILLIAM SAROYAN 1908–1981

21 Now what? [Last words. In the *Guardian*, 14 Feb. 1985]

JEAN-PAUL SARTRE 1905–1980

22 I hate victims who respect their executioners. [*Altona*, Act I]

23 When one does nothing, one believes oneself responsible for everything.

24 An American is either a Jew, or an anti-Semite, unless he is both at the same time.

25 Man is a useless passion. [*Being and Nothingness*, Pt IV, Ch. 2]

26 In reality, people read because they want to write. Anyway, reading is a sort of rewriting. [*Between Existentialism and Marxism*, 'The Purposes of Writing']

1 Man is condemned to be free. [*Existentialism is a Humanism*]

2 Life is nothing until it is lived; but it is yours to make sense of, and the value of it is nothing other than the sense you choose.

3 Human life begins on the other side of despair. [*The Flies*, Act III, sc. ii]

4 Hell is other people. [*Huis clos* (*In Camera*), sc. v]

5 Three o'clock is always too late or too early for anything you want to do. [*Nausea*, Friday, trans. Robert Baldick]

6 A man is always a teller of tales, he lives surrounded by his stories and the stories of others, he sees everything that happens to him through them; and he tries to live his life as if he were recounting it. [Saturday, noon]

7 Doctors, priests, magistrates, and officers know men as thoroughly as if they had made them. [Shrove Tuesday]

8 Things are entirely what they appear to be and *behind* them ... there is nothing. [Monday]

9 My thought is *me*: that is why I can't stop. I exist by what I think ... and I can't prevent myself from thinking.

10 They think about Tomorrow, in other words simply about another today; towns have only one day at their disposal which comes back exactly the same every morning. [Tuesday at Bouville]

11 I know perfectly well that I don't want to do anything; to do something is to create existence – and there's quite enough existence as it is. [One hour later]

12 The world could get along very well without literature; it could get along even better without man. [*What is Literature?*]

13 I distrust the incommunicable; it is the source of all violence.

14 These modest yet proud middle-class people considered beauty above their means or below their condition; they allowed it to titled women and prostitutes. [*Words*, Pt 1, trans. Irene Clephane]

15 Families naturally prefer widows to unmarried mothers, but only just.

16 Dying is not everything: you have to die in time.

17 I realized afterwards that it is possible to know everything about our affections except their strength; that is to say, their sincerity.

18 I was ready to admit – if only I had been old enough to understand them – all the right-wing truths which an old left-wing man taught me through his actions: that Truth and Myth are one and the same thing, that you have to simulate passion to feel it and that man is a creature of ceremony.

19 At the time, a refined family had to include at least one delicate child. I was a perfect subject because I had some thought of dying at birth.

20 Polite Society believed in God so that it need not talk of Him.

21 She believed in nothing; only her scepticism kept her from being an atheist.

22 Like all dreamers, I mistook disenchantment for truth. [2]

23 I confused things with their names: that is belief.

24 In whatever circle of hell we live, I think that we are free to break it. And if people do not break it, then they stay there of their own free will. So they put themselves in hell freely. [In *L'Express*, 11–17 Oct. 1965]

25 I am not fond of the word psychological. There is no such thing as psychological. Let us say that one can improve the biography of the person. [In R. D. Laing, *The Divided Self*, Ch. 8]

26 In the first days of the revolt you must kill: to shoot down a European is to kill two birds with one stone, to destroy an oppressor and the man he oppresses at the same time: there remain a dead man, and a free man. [In Preface to F. Fanon, *The Wretched of the Earth*]

27 Evil is the product of the ability of humans to make abstract that which is concrete. [In *New Society*, 31 Dec. 1970]

28 We make little revolutions, but there is not a human end, nothing concerning man, only disorders. [Last interview before his death, in *Le nouvel observateur*, 24 Mar. 1980]

SIEGFRIED SASSOON 1886–1967

29 If I were fierce and bald and short of breath, / I'd live with scarlet Majors at the

Base, / And speed glum heroes up the line to death. [*Base Details*]

1 I'd like to see a Tank come down the stalls, / Lurching to rag-time tunes, or 'Home, sweet Home', / And there'd be no more jokes in Music-halls / To mock the riddled corpses round Bapaume. ['*Blighters*']

2 Soldiers are citizens of death's grey land, / Drawing no dividend from time's tomorrows. [*Dreamers*]

3 Everyone suddenly burst out singing. [*Everyone Sang*]

4 The song was wordless; / The singing will never be done.

5 'He's a cheery old card,' grunted Harry to Jack / As they slogged up to Arras with rifle and pack ... / But he did for them both by his plan of attack. [*The General*]

6 Safe with his wound, a citizen of life, / He hobbled blithely through the garden gate, / And thought: 'Thank God they had to amputate!' [*The One-legged Man*]

7 Here was the world's worst wound. And here with pride / 'Their name liveth for ever,' the Gateway claims. / Was ever an immolation so belied / As these intolerably nameless names? [*On Passing the New Menin Gate*]

8 There must be crowds of ghosts among the trees, – / Not people killed in battle – they're in France / But horrible shapes – old men who died / Slow natural deaths – old men with ugly souls, / Who wore their bodies out with nasty sins. [*Repression of War Experience*]

9 My stretcher was popped into an ambulance which took me to a big hospital at Denmark Hill. At Charing Cross a woman handed me a bunch of flowers and a leaflet by the Bishop of London who earnestly advised me to lead a clean life and attend Holy Communion. [*Memoirs of an Infantry Officer*, Pt VIII, 4]

10 I am making this statement as a wilful defiance of military authority because I believe that the War is being deliberately prolonged by those who have the power to end it. [Letter in X. 3]

VIDAL SASSOON 1928–

11 The only place where success comes

before work is in a dictionary. [On BBC radio, quoting one of his teachers]

ERIK SATIE 1866–1925

12 My doctor has always told me to smoke. He even explains himself: 'Smoke, my friend. Otherwise someone else will smoke in your place.' [*Memoirs of an Amnesiac*]

13 M. Ravel has refused the Légion d'Honneur but all his music accepts it. [In James Harding, *Erik Satie*, Ch. 21]

14 I came to this world very young at a very old time. [In Pierre-Daniel Templier, *Erik Satie*, Ch. 1, trans. E. L. and D. S. French]

15 I had the pleasure of meeting myself last Monday at Darius Milhaud's, where I was lunching with Auric.

16 The musician is perhaps the most modest of animals, but he is also the proudest. It is he who invented the sublime art of ruining poetry. [In 2]

17 I want to compose a piece for dogs, and I already have my décor. The curtain rises on a bone. [In 3]

VICTOR SAVILLE 1897–1979

18 She had a heart. It photographed. [Of Jessie Matthews, who appeared in the film *Evergreen*, directed by Saville. In her obituary in the *Guardian*, 21 Aug. 1981]

DOROTHY L. SAYERS 1893–1957

19 I can't see that she could have found anything nastier to say if she'd thought it out with both hands for a fortnight. [*Busman's Holiday*, 'Prothalamion']

HENRY J. SAYERS 1855–1932

20 Ta-ra-ra-boom-de-ay! [Title of song, 1891, sung by Lottie Collins]

ALEXEI SAYLE 1952–

21 In fact when somebody from Hampstead is drowning, all their previous furniture passes in front of them. [From BBC TV programme *Comic Roots*, in the *Listener*, 1 Sept. 1983]

AL SCALPONE 1913–

1 The family that prays together stays together. [Slogan of Roman Catholic Rosary Crusade, first broadcast 6 Mar. 1947. In Father Patrick Peyton, *All for Her*]

HUGH [later LORD] SCANLON 1913–

2 Here we are again with both feet firmly planted in the air. [On his union's attitude to the Common Market. In the *Observer*, 'Sayings of the Year', 30 Dec. 1973]

3 Liberty is conforming to the majority. [In the *Observer*, 'Sayings of the Week', 14 Aug. 1977]

GERALD SCARFE 1936–

4 I'm looking for a Get Well card with a hint of insincerity. [*Seven Deadly Sins*, cartoon caption]

JONATHAN SCHELL 1943–

5 A nuclear holocaust, widely regarded as 'unthinkable' but never as undoable, appears to confront us with an action that we can perform but cannot quite conceive. [*The Fate of the Earth*, I]

EGON SCHIELE 1890–1918

6 Man is a rope stretched between the beast and the superhuman: a rope stretched across the abyss. [In TV film by J.-L. Fournier, 12 July 1977]

FIELD-MARSHAL VON SCHLIEFFEN 1833–1913

7 When you march into France, let the last man on the right brush the Channel with his sleeve. [Of the Schlieffen plan. In B. Tuchman, *The Guns of August*, Ch. 2]

8 Only make the right wing strong.

MICHAEL SCHMIDT 1947–

9 A church can be so broadened that the roof falls in. [In *PN Review*, No. 61, 1988, Editorial]

ARTUR SCHNABEL 1882–1951

10 I am attracted only to music which I consider to be better than it can be performed. [*My Life and Music*, Pt II, Ch. 1]

11 It is easier to gain fame than to retain it. [4]

12 I don't think there was ever a piece of music that changed a man's decision on how to vote. [8]

13 Interpretation is a free walk on firm ground. [10]

14 I know two kinds of audience only – one coughing and one not coughing. [See also 4:5]

15 Applause is a receipt, not a bill. [In explanation of his refusal to give encores. In I. Kolodin, *Musical Life*]

16 The notes I handle no better than many pianists. But the pauses between the notes – ah, that is where the art resides. [In the *Chicago Daily News*, 11 June 1958. See also 317:9]

17 The sonatas of Mozart are unique; they are too easy for children, and too difficult for artists. [In Nat Shapiro, *Encyclopedia of Quotations about Music*]

ARTHUR SCHNITZLER 1862–1931

18 Women always want to be our last love, and we their first. [In *Practical Wisdom*, ed. Frederick Ungar]

19 World history is a conspiracy of diplomats against common sense.

ARNOLD SCHOENBERG 1874–1951

20 Once, in the army, I was asked if I was really the composer Arnold Schoenberg. 'Somebody had to be,' I said. [*Letters*]

21 For whom, then, do they [aesthetic laws] exist? For the critic? He who can distinguish a good fruit from a bad with his palate does not have to be able to express the distinction through a chemical formula and does not need the formula to recognize the distinction. [*The Theory of Harmony*, Ch. 22, trans. Roy Carter]

22 Art should be cold. [In Artur Schnabel, *My Life and Music*, Pt II, Ch. 9, but elsewhere ascr. to Stravinsky]

23 Very well, I can wait. [Attr., when told his violin concerto needed a soloist with six

fingers. In Nat Shapiro, *Encyclopedia of Quotations about Music*. Another version is: 'I want the little finger to become longer. I can wait']

1 There is still much good music to be written in C. major. [In J. Machlis, *Introduction to Contemporary Music*]

CONGRESSWOMAN PATRICIA SCHROEDER 1940–

2 He [Ronald Reagan] has achieved a political breakthrough – the Teflon-coated presidency. He sees to it that nothing sticks to him. [In *Oh, What an Awful Thing to Say!*, comp. W. Cole and L. Phillips]

3 We've got the kind of President [Ronald Reagan] who thinks arms control means some kind of deodorant. [In the *Observer*, 'Sayings of the Week', 9 Aug. 1987]

B. P. SCHULBERG 1892–1957

4 Czar of all the rushes. [Of Louis B. Mayer, head of MGM. In Leslie Halliwell, *Filmgoer's Book of Quotes*]

BUDD SCHULBERG *see under* BRANDO, MARLON

CHARLES M. SCHULZ 1922–

5 Happiness is a Warm Puppy. [Title of book]

6 Good Grief, Charlie Brown. [Catchphrase in 'Peanuts' strip cartoon]

7 LINUS: You got sort of nervous when she walked by, didn't you, Charlie Brown?
CHARLIE BROWN: What makes you think I got nervous?
LINUS: You tied your peanut butter sandwich in a knot.

8 That's the only dog I know who can smell someone just *thinking* about food.

9 Never try to lick ice-cream off a hot sidewalk.

10 Jogging is very beneficial. It's good for your legs and your feet. It's also very good for the ground. It makes it feel needed. [(Snoopy) In *Kiss Me Hardy*, ed. Roger Kilroy, 'Golf World']

11 I've developed a new philosophy – I only dread one day at a time. [In *Barnes and Noble Book of Quotations*, ed. Robert I. Fitzhenry, 'Philosophy']

E. F. SCHUMACHER 1911–1977

12 Small is Beautiful. [Title of book subtitled 'A Study of Economics as if People Mattered']

13 The heart of the matter, as I see it, is the stark fact that world poverty is primarily a problem of two million villages, and thus a problem of two thousand million villagers. [*Small is Beautiful*, 13]

14 After all, for mankind as a whole there are no exports. We did not start developing by obtaining foreign exchange from Mars or the moon. Mankind is a closed society. [14]

15 Any intelligent fool can make things bigger, more complex, and more violent. It takes a touch of genius – and a lot of courage – to move in the opposite direction. [In obituary in the *Guardian*, 6 Sept. 1977]

WALTER SCHWARZ 1930–

16 Your average Frenchman, seeing another Frenchman, assumes he's an enemy unless he proves a friend. In Britain, it's the other way round. [In the *Guardian Weekly*, 9 Sept. 1984]

17 But Normans don't joke until they've known you for twenty years, and then never about food.

ALBERT SCHWEITZER 1875–1965

18 'Hullo! friend,' I call out. 'Won't you lend us a hand?' 'I am an intellectual and don't drag wood about,' came the answer. 'You're lucky,' I reply. 'I too wanted to become an intellectual, but I didn't succeed.' [*More from the Primeval Forest*, Ch. 5]

LEONARDO SCIASCIA 1921–1989

19 Really premeditated crimes are those that are not committed. [From *1912 + 1*, in *The Times Literary Supplement*, 20 Mar. 1987]

C. P. SCOTT 1846–1932

20 Comment is free but facts are sacred. [In the *Manchester Guardian*, 5 May 1921]

1 Television? No good will come of this device. The word is half Greek and half Latin. [Attr.]

CAPTAIN R. F. SCOTT 1868–1912

2 Had we lived, I should have had a tale to tell of the hardihood, endurance and courage of my companions which would have stirred the heart of every Englishman. These rough notes and our dead bodies must tell the tale. ['Message to the Public', *Journal*, Mar. 1912]

3 For God's sake look after our people. [29 Mar. 1912]

4 I have done this to show what an Englishman can do. [Note found on his frozen corpse in the Antarctic. In Bruce Chatwin, *What am I Doing Here*, 'André Malraux']

RONNIE SCOTT 1927–

5 Even the mice eat next door. [Of his jazz club. In *Ultimate Trivia Quiz Game Book*, ed. M. and A. Hiron]

RONALD SEARLE 1920–

6 The Terror of St Trinian's. [Title of book by Timothy Shy (D. B. Wyndham Lewis), illustrated by Searle]

7 Though loaded firearms were strictly forbidden at St Trinian's to all but Sixth-Formers ... one or two of them carried automatic acquired in the holidays, generally the gift of some indulgent relative. [*The Terror of St Trinian's*, Ch. 3]

8 It was at this precise moment that a brilliant idea recurred to Angela Menace. That very night she would set fire to the School. [6]

9 In the spring ... your lovely Chloë lightly turns to one mass of spots. [7]

SIR HARRY SECOMBE 1921–

10 My advice if you insist on slimming: Eat as much as you like – just don't swallow it. [In the *Daily Herald*, 5 Oct. 1962]

ALAN SEEGER 1888–1916

11 I have a rendezvous with Death / At some disputed barricade. [*I Have a Rendezvous with Death*]

PETE SEEGER 1919–

12 Where have all the flowers gone? / Young girls picked them them every one. [Song: *Where Have All the Flowers Gone?*, words by Derek Collyer, 1936–85, and David Cummings, 1934–]

ERICH SEGAL 1937–

13 Love means never having to say you're sorry. [Last line of film *Love Story*, and novel, Ch. 13]

GERALD SEGAL

14 There are four sides to every issue: your side, my side, the right side and the United Nations' side. [In the *Sunday Times*, 19 June 1988]

JACQUES SÉGUÉLA

15 Don't Tell My Mother I Work in Advertising – She Thinks I'm a Piano-player in a Brothel. [Title of book]

GEORGE SELDES 1890–1970

16 Sawdust Caesar. [Title of biography of Benito Mussolini]

H. GORDON SELFRIDGE 1857–1947

17 The Great Principles on which we will build this Business are as everlasting as the Pyramids. [Preliminary announcement on Selfridge's store]

18 The customer is always right. [Shop slogan]

W. C. SELLAR 1898–1951 and R. J. YEATMAN 1897–1968

19 For every person wishing to teach there are thirty not wanting to be taught. [*And Now All This*, Introduction]

20 To confess that you are totally Ignorant about the Horse, is social suicide: you will be despised by everybody, especially the horse. [*Horse Nonsense*]

21 1066 and All That. [Title of book]

22 The Roman Conquest was, however, a Good Thing. [*1066 and All That*, Ch. 1]

1 The Venomous Bead (author of *The Rosary*). [3]

2 The Memorable Round Table made to have the Conferences at, so that it was impossible to say who was top knight. [6]

3 Whenever he returned to England he always set out again immediately for the Mediterranean and was therefore known as Richard Gare de Lyon. [17]

4 '*Honi soie qui mal y pense*' ('Honey, your silk stocking's hanging down'). [24]

5 Finding, however, that he was not memorable, he very patriotically abdicated in favour of Henry IV, part II. [26]

6 Lumbago and the Laxative Islands. [11]

7 Napoleon's armies always used to march on their stomachs, shouting: 'Vive l'Intérieur!' [48]

8 He [Gladstone] spent his declining years trying to guess the answer to the Irish Question; unfortunately whenever he was getting warm, the Irish secretly changed the question. [57]

9 America became top nation and history came to a full stop. [62]

10 Do not on any account attempt to write on both sides of the paper at once. [Test paper 5]

RICHARD SELZER 1928–

11 Not that it is a disservice to a man to be made mindful of his death, but, at three o'clock in the morning, it is less than philosophy. [*Confessions of a Knife*, 'The Surgeon as Priest']

12 The liver, doted upon by the French, assaulted by the Irish, disdained by the Americans, and chopped up with egg, onion, and chicken fat by the Jews. ['Liver']

13 As for the brain, it is all mystery and memory and electricity.

14 What is man, the son of man, asks the biochemist, but a container of salt solution in a state of more or less saturation? ['Stone']

15 Pissing in his shoe keeps no man warm for long. ['In Praise of Senescence']

MAURICE SENDAK 1928–

16 There must be more to life than having everything! [*Higglety Pigglety Pop!*, Ch. 1]

MACK SENNETT 1880–1960

17 Anyone who tells you he has discovered something new is a fool, or a liar or both. [In James Agee, *Agee on Film*, Vol. 1]

ROBERT W. SERVICE 1874–1958

18 Ah! the clock is always slow; / It is later than you think. [*It is Later Than You Think*]

19 This is the Law of the Yukon, that only the Strong shall thrive; / That surely the Weak shall perish, and only the Fit survive. [*The Law of the Yukon*]

20 Back of the bar, in a solo game, sat Dangerous Dan McGrew, / And watching his luck was his light o' love, the lady that's known as Lou. [*The Shooting of Dan McGrew*]

VIKRAM SETH 1952–

21 Ten hostages is terrorism; / A million, and it's strategy. / To ban books is fanaticism; / To threaten in totality / All culture and all civilization, / All humankind and all creation, / This is a task of decorous skill / And needs high statesmanship and will. [*The Golden Gate*, 7. 31]

22 How ugly babies are! How heedless / Of all else than their bulging selves – / Like sumo wrestlers, plush with needless / Kneadable flesh – like mutant elves / ... (A pity that the blubbering blobs / Come unequipped with volume knobs). [13. 47]

DR SEUSS [THEODOR SEUSS GEISEL] 1904–1991

23 Adults are obsolete children. [In L. L. Levinson, *Bartlett's Unfamiliar Quotations*]

ATHENE SEYLER 1889–1990

24 A woman ought to dance as she moves in a seventeenth century play, to sail in an eighteenth century one, to swim in a nineteenth century dress (with tiny, even steps under crinoline or bustle), and to stride in the twentieth century. [Of acting. In obituary in the *Guardian*, 14 Sept. 1990]

JOHN SEYMOUR 1914–

25 We don't have television. It stops you

from doing anything useful – you watch other people live instead of living yourself. [In the *Sunday Times Magazine*, 12 Feb. 1989]

DELPHINE SEYRIG 1932–1990

1 I think the real reason one loves acting lies in this conception of the gesture bound by personality. Even actors who don't admit it actually play much more than the text. They act because they are inventing a character. [In obituary in the *Guardian*, 17 Oct. 1990]

PETER SHAFFER 1926–

2 Rehearsing a play is making the word flesh. Publishing a play is reversing the process. [*Equus*, A Note on the Text]

3 All my wife has ever taken from the Mediterranean – from that whole vast intuitive culture – are four bottles of Chianti to make into lamps, and two china condiment donkeys labelled Sally and Peppy. [Act I, sc. xviii]

4 The Normal is the good smile in a child's eyes – all right. It is also the dead stare in a million adults. It both sustains and kills – like a God. It is the Ordinary made beautiful; it is also the Average made lethal. [xix]

5 Passion, you see, can be destroyed by a doctor. It cannot be created. [II. xxxv]

THE SHAH OF IRAN 1919–1980

6 My real opposition is myself. [Interview in *Le monde*, 1 Oct. 1976]

IDRIES SHAH 1924–

7 Quite a common observation is: 'It takes all sorts to make a world.' This may well be true: but if it is – where are they all? [*Reflections*, 'The Difference between Saying and Doing']

8 A certain person may have, as you say, a wonderful presence: I do not know. What I do know is that he has a perfectly delightful absence. ['Presence and Absence']

BILL SHANKLY 1914–1981

9 Some people think football is a matter of

life and death. I don't like that attitude. I can assure them it is much more serious than that. [In the *Sunday Times*, 4 Oct. 1981]

TOM SHARPE 1928–

10 The South African Police would leave no stone unturned to see that nothing disturbed the even terror of their lives. [*Indecent Exposure*, Ch. 1]

11 Skullion had little use for contraceptives at the best of times. Unnatural, he called them, and placed them in the lower social category of things along with elastic-sided boots and made-up bow ties. Not the sort of attire for a gentleman. [*Porterhouse Blue*, Ch. 9]

G. BERNARD SHAW 1856–1950

12 Whether you think Jesus was God or not, you must admit that he was a first-rate political economist. [*Androcles and the Lion*, Preface, 'Jesus as Economist']

13 All great truths begin as blasphemies. [*Annajanska*]

14 Breakages, Limited, the biggest industrial corporation in the country. [*The Apple Cart*, I]

15 I never resist temptation, because I have found that things that are bad for me do not tempt me. [II]

16 What use are cartridges in battle? I always carry chocolate instead. [*Arms and the Man*, I]

17 You are a very poor soldier: a chocolate cream soldier!

18 My father is a very hospitable man: he keeps six hotels.

19 I never apologize! [III]

20 You're not a man, you're a machine.

21 Every genuine scientist must be ... a metaphysician. [*Back to Methuselah*, Preface]

22 Make me a beautiful word for doing things tomorrow, for that surely is a great and blessed invention. [Pt I, Act I]

23 The He-Ancient. [Character in Pt V]

24 He is a barbarian, and thinks that the customs of his tribe and island Britain are the laws of nature. [*Caesar and Cleopatra*, II]

25 When a stupid man is doing something

he is ashamed of, he always declares that it is his duty. [III]

1 We have no more right to consume happiness without producing it than to consume wealth without producing it. [*Candida*, I]

2 It is easy – terribly easy – to shake a man's faith in himself. To take advantage of that to break a man's spirit is devil's work.

3 I'm only a beer teetotaller, not a champagne teetotaller. [III]

4 The worst sin towards our fellow creatures is not to hate them, but to be indifferent to them: that's the essence of inhumanity. [*The Devil's Disciple*, II]

5 I never expect a soldier to think. [III]

6 The British soldier can stand up to anything except the British War Office.

7 Stimulate the phagocytes. Drugs are a delusion. [*The Doctor's Dilemma*, I]

8 All professions are conspiracies against the laity.

9 It's easier to replace a dead man than a good picture. [II]

10 All Shaw's characters are himself: mere puppets stuck up to spout Shaw. [*Fanny's First Play*, Epilogue]

11 The one point on which all women are in furious secret rebellion against the existing law is the saddling of the right to a child with the obligation to become the servant of a man. [*Getting Married*, Preface]

12 Physically there is nothing to distinguish human society from the farm-yard except that children are more troublesome and costly than chickens and women are not so completely enslaved as farm stock.

13 What God hath joined together no man shall ever put asunder: God will take care of that. [Play itself]

14 Has he attained the seventh degree of concentration? [*Heartbreak House*, I]

15 When our relatives are at home, we have to think of all their good points or it would be impossible to endure them. But when they are away, we console ourselves for their absence by dwelling on their vices.

16 She married a numskull.

17 Go anywhere in England where there are natural, wholesome, contented, and really nice English people: and what do you always find? That the stables are the real centre of the household. [III]

18 The captain is in his bunk, drinking bottled ditchwater; and the crew is gambling in the forecastle ... Do you think the laws of God will be suspended in favour of England because you were born in it?

19 My way of joking is to tell the truth. It's the funniest joke in the world. [*John Bull's Other Island*, Act II]

20 We must be thoroughly democratic, and patronize everybody without distinction of class.

21 What really flatters a man is that you think him worth flattering. [IV]

22 There are only two qualities in the world: efficiency and inefficiency; and only two sorts of people: the efficient and the inefficient.

23 Nobody can say a word against Greek: it stamps a man at once as an educated gentleman. [*Major Barbara*, Act I]

24 He is always breaking the law. He broke the law when he was born: his parents were not married.

25 I am a sort of collector of religions; and the curious thing is that I find I can believe in them all. [II]

26 I am a Millionaire. That is my religion.

27 I cant talk religion to a man with bodily hunger in his eyes.

28 Wot prawce Selvytion nah?

29 Alcohol is a very necessary article ... It enables Parliament to do things at eleven at night that no sane person would do at eleven in the morning.

30 He never does a proper thing without giving an improper reason for it. [III]

31 He knows nothing; and he thinks he knows everything. That points clearly to a political career.

32 Nothing is ever done in this world until men are prepared to kill one another if it is not done.

33 CUSINS: Do you call poverty a crime?

UNDERSHAFT: The worst of all crimes. All the other crimes are virtues beside it.

1 Like all young men, you greatly exaggerate the difference between one young woman and another.

2 Give women the vote, and in five years there will be a crushing tax on bachelors. [*Man and Superman*, Preface]

3 Effectiveness of assertion is the alpha and omega of style.

4 A lifetime of happiness! No man alive could bear it: it would be hell on earth. [I]

5 The more things a man is ashamed of, the more respectable he is.

6 Vitality in a woman is a blind fury of creation. She sacrifices herself to it.

7 The true artist will let his wife starve, his children go barefoot, his mother drudge for his living at seventy, sooner than work at anything but his art.

8 Your pious English habit of regarding the world as a moral gymnasium built expressly to strengthen your character in.

9 Very nice sort of place, Oxford, I should think, for people that like that sort of place. [II]

10 It is a woman's business to get married as soon as possible, and a man's to keep unmarried as long as he can.

11 Marry Ann; and at the end of a week you'll find no more inspiration in her than in a plate of muffins.

12 As a rule there is only one person an English girl hates more than she hates her eldest sister; and thats her mother.

13 Lying hardly describes it. I overdo it. I get carried away in an ecstasy of mendacity.

14 MENDOZA: I am a brigand. I live by robbing the rich.
TANNER: I am a gentleman. I live by robbing the poor. [III]

15 There is plenty of humbug in hell.

16 Hell is full of musical amateurs: music is the brandy of the damned.

17 An Englishman thinks he is moral when he is only uncomfortable.

18 If you go to Heaven without being naturally qualified for it, you will not enjoy yourself there.

19 In the arts of peace Man is a bungler.

20 As an old soldier I admit the cowardice: it's as universal as sea sickness, and matters just as little.

21 What is virtue but the Trade Unionism of the married?

22 Those who talk most about the blessings of marriage and the constancy of its vows are the very people who declare that if the chain were broken and the prisoners left free to choose, the whole social fabric would fly asunder. You cannot have the argument both ways. If the prisoner is happy, why lock him in? If he is not, why pretend that he is?

23 There are two tragedies in life. One is to lose your heart's desire. The other is to gain it. [IV. Echoes Oscar Wilde]

24 Do not do unto others as you would they should do unto you. Their tastes may not be the same. ['Maxims for Revolutionists', 'The Golden Rule']

25 Do not love your neighbour as yourself. If you are on good terms with yourself it is an impertinence; if on bad, an injury.

26 The golden rule is that there are no golden rules.

27 He who slays a king and he who dies for him are alike idolaters. ['Idolatry']

28 Democracy substitutes election by the incompetent many for appointment by the corrupt few. ['Democracy']

29 He who can, does. He who cannot, teaches. ['Education']

30 Marriage is popular because it combines the maximum of temptation with the maximum of opportunity. ['Marriage']

31 Titles distinguish the mediocre, embarrass the superior, and are disgraced by the inferior. ['Titles']

32 If you strike a child, take care that you strike it in anger, even at the risk of maiming it for life. A blow in cold blood neither can nor should be forgiven. ['How to Beat Children']

33 Beware of the man whose god is in the skies. ['Religion']

34 Self-denial is not a virtue; it is only the effect of prudence on rascality. ['Virtues and Vices']

1 In heaven an angel is nobody in particular. ['Greatness']

2 The most intolerable pain is produced by prolonging the keenest pleasure. ['Beauty and Happiness']

3 The reasonable man adapts himself to the world; the unreasonable one persists in trying to adapt the world to himself. Therefore all progress depends on the unreasonable man. ['Reason']

4 Hell is paved with good intentions, not with bad ones. ['Good Intentions']

5 Home is the girl's prison and the woman's workhouse. ['Women in the Home']

6 Every man over forty is a scoundrel. ['Stray Sayings']

7 It is dangerous to be sincere unless you are also stupid.

8 There is nothing so bad or so good that you will not find an Englishman doing it; but you will never find an Englishman in the wrong. He does everything on principle. He fights you on patriotic principles; he robs you on business principles; he enslaves you on imperial principles. [*Man of Destiny*]

9 The injury to the child would be far less if the voluptuary said frankly: 'I beat you because I like beating you; and I shall do it whenever I can contrive an excuse for it.' [*Misalliance*, Preface]

10 Heaven, as conventionally conceived, is a place so inane, so dull, so useless, so miserable, that nobody has ever ventured to describe a whole day in heaven, though plenty of people have described a day at the seaside.

11 The secret of being miserable is to have leisure to bother about whether you are happy or not.

12 A great devotee of the Gospel of Getting On. [*Mrs Warren's Profession*, IV]

13 The fickleness of the women I love is only equalled by the infernal constancy of the women who love me. [*The Philanderer*, II]

14 There is only one religion though there are a hundred versions of it. [*Plays Pleasant*, Preface]

15 He's a gentleman: look at his boots. [*Pygmalion*, I]

16 I dont want to talk grammar. I want to talk like a lady. [II]

17 PICKERING: Have you no morals, man?
DOOLITTLE: Can't afford them, Governor. Neither could you if you was as poor as me. [II]

18 Undeserving poverty is my line. Taking one station in society with another, it's – it's – well, it's the only one that has any ginger in it, to my taste.

19 My aunt died of influenza: so they said ... But it's my belief they done the old woman in. [III]

20 Gin was mother's milk to her.

21 Not bloody likely.

22 Tied me up and delivered me into the hands of middle class morality. [V]

23 West wind, wanton wind, wilful wind, womanish wind, false wind from over the water, will you never blow again? [*St Joan*, III]

24 How can what an Englishman believes be heresy? It is a contradiction in terms. [IV]

25 Assassination is the extreme form of censorship. [*The Shewing-up of Blanco Posnet*, 'The Limits of Toleration']

26 I have a technical objection to making sexual infatuation a tragic theme. Experience proves that it is only effective in the comic spirit. [*Three Plays for Puritans*, Preface]

27 So much for Bardolatry!

28 It does not follow ... that the right to criticize Shakespear involves the power of writing better plays. And in fact ... I do not profess to write better plays.

29 BETTER THAN SHAKESPEAR? [Of his own work. Crossheading]

30 No woman can shake off her mother. There should be no mothers, only women. [*Too True to be Good*, Act III]

31 We're from Madeira, but perfectly respectable, so far. [*You Never Can Tell*, Act I]

32 Well, sir, you never can tell. That's a principle in life with me, sir, if you'll excuse my having such a thing, sir. [II]

33 He's the very incarnation of intellect. You can hear his mind working. [IV]

34 My speciality is being right when other people are wrong.

1 All matches are unwise. It's unwise to be born; it's unwise to be married; it's unwise to live; and it's unwise to die.

2 With the single exception of Homer, there is no eminent writer, not even Sir Walter Scott, whom I can despise so entirely as I despise Shakespear when I measure my mind against his . . . It would positively be a relief to me to dig him up and throw stones at him. [*Dramatic Opinions and Essays*, Vol. ii, p. 52]

3 I could not write the words Mr Joyce used: my prudish hand would refuse to form the letters. [*Table-talk of G.B.S.*]

4 Martyrdom is the only way in which a man can become famous without ability. [In Preface to 1908 reprint of *Fabian Essays*]

5 Like fingerprints, all marriages are different. [In C. Pulling, *They were Singing*, Ch. 5]

6 We are a nation of governesses. [In the *New Statesman*, 12 Apr. 1913]

7 A perpendicular expression of a horizontal desire. [Of dancing. In the *New Statesman*, 23 Mar. 1962]

8 If he [T. E. Lawrence] hides in a quarry he puts red flags all round. [In the *Guardian*, 22 Jan. 1963]

9 The trouble, Mr Goldwyn, is that you are only interested in art and I am only interested in money. [When declining to sell Goldwyn the screen rights of his plays. In Philip French, *The Movie Moguls*, Ch. 4]

10 England and America are two countries separated by the same language. [Attr. in *Reader's Digest*, Nov. 1942]

11 LORD NORTHCLIFFE: The trouble with you, Shaw, is that you look as if there were famine in the land.
SHAW: The trouble with you, Northcliffe, is that you look as if you were the cause of it. [Attr.]

12 If all economists were laid end to end, they would not reach a conclusion. [Attr.]

SIR HARTLEY [later LORD]
  SHAWCROSS 1902–1989

13 We are the masters at the moment – and not only for the moment, but for a very long time to come. [Said in House of Commons in a debate on the trade unions, 2 Apr. 1946]

14 The so-called new morality is too often the old immorality condoned. [In the *Observer*, 'Sayings of the Week', 17 Nov. 1963]

PATRICK SHAW-STEWART
  1888–1917

15 I saw a man this morning / Who did not wish to die: / I ask, and cannot answer, / If otherwise would I. [In Evelyn Waugh, *Ronald Knox*, Pt 1, Ch. 4]

MICHAEL SHEA 1938–

16 Dr Robert Runcie, the Archbishop of Canterbury, has in the past been accused of nailing his colours firmly to the fence. [*Influence*, Ch. 12]

LLOYD SHEARER

17 [David] Selznick gave the impression that he stormed through life demanding to see the manager – and that, when the manager appeared, Selznick would hand him a twenty-page memo announcing his instant banishment to Elba. [In R. Behlmer, *Memo from David O. Selznick*, Foreword]

A. F. SHELDON 1868–1935

18 He profits most who serves best. [*Motto for International Rotary*]

DYAN SHELDON 1946–

19 If life were a candy bar, she'd eat the wrapper. [*Dreams of an Average Man*, 7]

20 It is no wonder, he thinks, that God sent his only son to earth and not his only daughter. She would have really fucked up everything: arbitrarily deciding not to go about her father's business because it seemed too nebulous; refusing to walk on water because she didn't want to take her shoes off, getting her feet wet, look like a fool; leaving town before the crucifixion because she suddenly remembered a date she had elsewhere. [*Victim of Love*, 3]

GILBERT SHELTON 1939–

21 Grass will carry you through times of no money better than money through times of

no dope. [Motto in strip cartoon 'Fabulous Furry Freak Brothers']

ROBERT SHELTON 1926–

1 He [Bob Dylan] is like all of us, only more so. [In the *Sunday Times*, 11 Oct. 1987]

ROBERT E. SHERWOOD 1896–1955

2 It is disappointing to report that George Bernard Shaw appearing as George Bernard Shaw is sadly miscast in the part. Satirists should be heard and not seen. [Review of Shaw play]

BURT SHEVELOVE 1915–1982 and LARRY GELBART 1928–

3 A Funny Thing Happened on the Way to the Forum. [Title of musical, music and lyrics by Stephen Sondheim]

EMMANUEL [later LORD] SHINWELL 1884–1986

4 We know that the organized workers of the country are our friends. As for the rest, they don't matter a tinker's cuss. [Speech at Electrical Trades Union Conference, Margate, Kent, 7 May 1947]

5 There was nowhere else to go. [Attr., on accepting a peerage]

CLEMENT K. SHORTER 1858–1926

6 The latest definition of an optimist is one who fills up his crossword puzzle in ink. [In the *Observer*, 'Sayings of the Week', 22 Feb. 1925. See also 129:1]

DIMITRI SHOSTAKOVICH 1906–1975

7 Creative reply of a Soviet artist to just criticism. [Epigraph to his Fifth Symphony]

8 He [Puccini] wrote marvellous operas, but dreadful music. [In conversation with Benjamin Britten. In Lord Harewood, *The Tongs and the Bones*]

JEAN SIBELIUS 1865–1957

9 Pay no attention to what the critics say; no statue has ever been put up to a critic. [In B. de Törne, *Sibelius: A Close-up*, Ch. 2]

WALTER SICKERT 1860–1942

10 Nothing links man to man like the frequent passage from hand to hand of cash. [In *New Age*, 28 July 1910]

MAURICE SIGLER 1901–1961

11 Little Man, You've Had a Busy Day. [Title of song, written with Al Hoffman]

FRANK SILVER 1892–1960 and IRVING CONN 1898–1961

12 Yes, we have no bananas, / We have no bananas today. [Song: *Yes, We Have No Bananas*]

SIME SILVERMAN 1873–1933

13 Sticks Nix Hick Pix. [On Midwestern reaction to films about poor hillbillies. Headline in *Variety*]

GEORGES SIMENON 1903–1989

14 I read the Penal Code and the Bible. The Bible is a cruel book. Perhaps the cruellest book ever written. [Interview in John Mortimer, *In Character*]

NEIL SIMON 1927–

15 It's like paradise, with a lobotomy. [Of Los Angeles. Said by Jane Fonda in film *California Suite*]

16 I got brown sandwiches and green sandwiches ... It's either very new cheese or very old meat. [*The Odd Couple*, Act I, and said by Walter Matthau in film of same title]

17 You've got to be missing for forty-eight hours before you're missing. The worst he could be is lost.

18 Twelve years doesn't mean you're a *happy* couple. It just means you're a *long* couple.

PAUL SIMON 1942–

19 Like a bridge over troubled water, / I will ease your mind. [Song: *Bridge over Troubled Water*]

20 Here's to you, Mrs Robinson, / Jesus loves you more than you will know. [Song: *Mrs Robinson*]

1 People talking without speaking, / People listening without hearing, / People writing songs that voices never shared. / No one dared. [Song: *Sound of Silence*]

2 The words of the prophets are written / On the subway walls and tenement halls.

REV. F. A. SIMPSON

3 How can one believe in the divinity of Our Lord ... when he was so unconscionably rude to His mother? [Quoted by Rev. Eric James in the *Listener*, 30 Oct. 1980]

HAROLD SIMPSON ?–1955

4 Down in the Forest Something Stirred. [Title of song, 1915, music by Landon Ronald]

N. F. SIMPSON 1919–

5 I eat merely to put food out of my mind. [*The Hole*]

6 MRS EDO: Sid just had another bad night worrying about being so different from the people he sees round him.
MRS MESO: Has he tried resembling anybody?

7 He went to Dr Bunch – he's been going to him for years – and complained about his ribs, and told him they seemed to be giving him claustrophobia.

8 Knocked down a doctor? With an ambulance? How could she? It's a contradiction in terms. [*One-way Pendulum*, Act I]

9 It'll do him good to lie there unconscious for a bit. Give his brain a rest.

10 In sentencing a man for one crime, we may well be putting him beyond the reach of the law in respect of those crimes which he has not yet had an opportunity to commit. The law, however, is not to be cheated in this way. I shall therefore discharge you.

11 There's somebody at the door wanting you to form a government. [*A Resounding Tinkle*, Act I, sc. i]

12 If he's a criminal, he's in plain clothes – that's all I can say.

13 The small of my back is too big, doctor.

ROBERT SIMPSON 1921–

14 Let us reserve the term 'advanced' for those [composers] who deserve it – dead these five centuries or alive now. [Talk on BBC radio, 1976]

GEORGE R. SIMS 1847–1922

15 It is Christmas Day in the workhouse. [*Dragonet Ballads*, 'In the Workhouse: Christmas Day']

ISAAC BASHEVIS SINGER 1904–1991

16 Art ... can also in its small way attempt to mend the mistakes of the eternal builder in whose image man was created. [*Death of Methuselah*, Author's Note]

17 Children don't read to find their identity, to free themselves from guilt, to quench the thirst for rebellion or to get rid of alienation. They have no use for psychology. They detest sociology. They still believe in God, the family, angels, devils, witches, goblins, logic, clarity, punctuation, and other such obsolete stuff ... When a book is boring, they yawn openly. They don't expect their writer to redeem humanity, but leave to adults such childish illusions. [Speech on receiving the Nobel Prize for Literature. In the *Observer*, 17 Dec. 1978]

DAME EDITH SITWELL 1887–1964

18 Jane, Jane, / Tall as a crane, / The morning light creaks down again. [*Aubade*]

19 The fire was furry as a bear. [*Dark Song*]

20 Don Pasquito / Hid where the leaves drip with sweet ... / But a word stung him like a mosquito ... / For what they hear, they repeat! [*Façade*, 'I do like to be beside the Seaside']

21 'See me dance the polka' / Said Mr Wagg like a bear. ['Polka']

22 Lily O'Grady, / Silly and shady, / Longing to be / A lazy lady. ['Popular Song']

23 Do not take a bath in Jordan, / Gordon, / On the holy Sabbath, on the peaceful day! ['Scotch Rhapsody']

24 Under great yellow flags and banners of the ancient Cold / Began the huge migrations

/ From some primeval disaster in the heart of Man. [*The Shadow of Cain*]

1 Who dreamed that Christ has died in vain? / He walks again on the Seas of Blood, He comes in the terrible Rain.

2 Still falls the Rain – / Dark as the world of man, black as our loss – / Blind as the nineteen hundred and forty nails / Upon the Cross. [*Still Falls the Rain*]

3 Virginia Woolf, I enjoyed talking to her, but thought *nothing* of her writing. I considered her 'a beautiful little knitter'. [Letter to G. Singleton, 11 July 1955]

4 I have often wished I had time to cultivate modesty ... But I am too busy thinking about myself. [In the *Observer*, 'Sayings of the Week', 30 Apr. 1950]

SIR OSBERT SITWELL 1892–1969

5 Do you remember Mr Goodbeare, the carpenter, / Godfearing and bearded Mr Goodbeare, / Who worked all day / At his carpenter's tray? [*Elegy for Mr Goodbeare*]

6 In reality, *killing time* / Is only the name for another of the multifarious ways / By which Time kills us. [*Milordo Inglese*]

7 Now the nimble fingers are no more nimble, / And the silver thimble lies cold and tarnished black. [*Miss Mew's Window-box*]

8 She did not recognize her enemy, / She thought him Dust: / But what is Dust, / Save Time's most lethal weapon, / Her faithful ally and our sneaking foe? [*Mrs Southern's Enemy*]

9 But He was never, well, / What I call / A Sportsman; / For forty days / He went out into the desert / – And never shot anything. [*Old Fashioned Sportsmen*]

10 Our poverty, then, signified chiefly that we were no longer allowed to throw down pennies, done up in screws of paper, to the conductors of German bands. [*The Scarlet Tree*, Bk III, Ch. 1]

11 When younger he [Sir George Sitwell] had invented many other things; at Eton, for example, a musical toothbrush which played 'Annie Laurie' as you brushed your teeth and a small revolver for killing wasps. [IV. 1]

12 The artist, like the idiot or clown, sits on the edge of the world, and a push may send him over it. [2]

13 We attended stables, as we attended church, in our best clothes, thereby no doubt showing the degree of respect due to horses, no less than to the deity.

14 Education: In the holidays from Eton. [Entry in *Who's Who*, 1929]

ROBIN SKELTON 1925–

15 A man does not write poems about what he knows, but about what he does not know. [*Teach Yourself Poetry*]

ROBERT [later LORD] SKIDELSKY 1939–

16 The only way biography as an undertaking can recover its main function of good storytelling is to go back to its roots. These roots lie in ancestor worship. [In *The Times Literary Supplement*, 13 Nov. 1987]

PROFESSOR B. F. SKINNER 1904–1990

17 Indeed one of the ultimate advantages of an education is simply coming to the end of it. [*The Technology of Teaching*]

18 Education is what survives when what has been learnt has been forgotten. [In *New Scientist*, 21 May 1964]

CORNELIA OTIS SKINNER 1901–1979

19 Woman's virtue is man's greatest invention. [Attr.]

DR FREDERIK VAN ZYL SLABBERT 1940–

20 The relationship between this present parliament [that of President Botha in South Africa] and democracy is akin to that between prostitution and marriage. Both have to do with the same issue, but with entirely different preoccupations and practices. [Interview in the *Guardian*, 22 May 1987]

ELIZABETH SMART 1913–1986

21 By Grand Central Station I Sat Down and Wept. [Title of book]

OLEG SMIRNOFF [Russian representative of Pepsi-Cola]

1 A cooperative is private enterprise in a state economy. That's like a newspaper inside a prison. It cannot operate freely. [In Hedrick Smith, *The New Russians*, Pt 3, p. 285]

ALFRED E. SMITH 1873–1944

2 William Randolph Hearst gave him [Ogden Mills] the kiss of death. [Of Hearst's support for Smith's opponent for governorship of New York State. In *The New York Times*, 25 Oct. 1926. Cited as origin of term in John Bartlett, *Familiar Quotations*, and *Oxford Dictionary of Modern Quotations*, ed. Tony Augarde]

SIR CYRIL SMITH, MP 1928–

3 Parliament is the longest running farce in the West End. [Said in July 1973. In *Big Cyril*, Ch. 8]

EDGAR SMITH 1857–1938

4 You may tempt the upper classes / With your villainous demi-tasses, / But Heaven will protect the Working Girl. [Song: *Heaven Will Protect the Working Girl*]

F. E. SMITH *see* **BIRKENHEAD, EARL OF**

GEORGE JOSEPH SMITH [Murderer of the Brides in the Bath]

5 Sir – In answer to your application regarding my parentage, my mother was a bus-horse, my father a cab-driver, my sister a rough-rider over the Arctic regions. My brothers were all gallant sailors on a steamroller. [Letter to father-in-law produced at trial. In Edward Marjoribanks, *Life of Sir Edward Marshall Hall*, Ch. 10]

GODFREY SMITH 1926–

6 Degrees are like false teeth. You'd rather not be without them, but you don't flaunt the fact you've got them to the world. [In *Directory of Opportunities for Graduates*, 1957, 'Academic Anonymous']

7 Opera is the theatre of the absurd set to music. [In the *Sunday Times*, 15 Nov. 1987]

IAN SMITH 1919–

8 I don't believe in black majority rule ever in Rhodesia . . . not in a thousand years. I believe in blacks and whites working together. [Broadcast speech, 20 Mar. 1976]

JOHN SMITH, MP 1935–

9 We were promised a New Statesman, and what have we got instead? The Spectator. [Of John Major's handling of the sterling crisis. Speech at Labour Party Conference, Blackpool, 29 Sept. 1992]

LOGAN PEARSALL SMITH 1865–1946

10 There are two things to aim at in life: first, to get what you want; and, after that, to enjoy it. Only the wisest of mankind achieve the second. [*Afterthoughts*, 1]

11 How awful to reflect that what people say of us is true!

12 Solvency is entirely a matter of temperament and not of income.

13 There are few sorrows, however poignant, in which a good income is of no avail.

14 What music is more enchanting than the voices of young people, when you can't hear what they say? [2]

15 I cannot forgive my friends for dying: I do not find these vanishing acts of theirs at all amusing.

16 Most people sell their souls, and live with a good conscience on the proceeds. [3]

17 A friend who loved perfection would be the perfect friend, did not that love shut his door on me.

18 It is the wretchedness of being rich that you have to live with rich people. [4]

19 We need two kinds of acquaintances, one to complain to, while we boast to the others.

20 A best-seller is the gilded tomb of a mediocre talent. [5]

21 What I like in a good author is not what he says, but what he whispers.

22 I might give my life for my friend, but he had better not ask me to do up a parcel. [6]

23 People say that life is the thing, but I prefer reading.

1 There is more felicity on the far side of baldness than young men can possibly imagine. [*Last Words*]

2 Thank heavens, the sun has gone in, and I don't have to go out and enjoy it.

3 Is it seemly that I, at my age, should be hurled with my books of reference, and bed-clothes, and hot-water bottle, across the sky at the unthinkable rate of nineteen miles a second? As I say, I don't like it at all. [*Trivia*, I, 'Vertigo']

4 The thought that my mind is really nothing but an empty sieve – often this, too, disconcerts me. ['Dissatisfaction']

5 Is there then no friend? No one who hates Ibsen and problem plays, and the Supernatural, and Switzerland and Adultery as much as I do? Must I live all my life as mute as a mackerel, companionless and uninvited, and never tell anyone what I think of my famous contemporaries? [II, 'Loneliness']

6 What a bore it is, waking up in the morning always the same person. ['Green Ivory']

7 [When asked shortly before his death if he had discovered any meaning in life] There is a meaning, at least for me, there is one thing that matters – to set a chime of words tinkling in the mind of a few fastidious people. [In obituary appreciation by Cyril Connolly in the *New Statesman*, 9 Mar. 1946]

DAME MAGGIE SMITH 1933–

8 One went to school, one wanted to act, one started to act, and one's still acting. [Of her career. In profile in the *Sunday Times*, 1 Jan. 1989]

PATTI SMITH 1946–

9 Jesus died for somebody's sins but not mine. [Record album *Horses*, opening line]

REGINALD DORMAN SMITH 1899–1971

10 Let 'Dig for Victory' be the motto for everyone with a garden. [Radio broadcast to encourage vegetable growing, 4 Oct. 1939]

STEVIE SMITH 1902–1971

11 A Good Time was Had by All. [Title of book, 1937, ascr. as source of phrase in Eric Partridge, *Dictionary of Catch-phrases*]

12 'O Charley, Charley, do not go upon the water' / Cries a friendly swan, 'with the Duke's daughter.' [*The Magic Morning*]

13 Shall I tell you the signs of a New Age coming? / It is a sound of drubbing and sobbing / Of people crying, We are old, we are old / And the sun is going down and becoming cold. [*The New Age*]

14 I was much too far out all my life. / And not waving but drowning. [*Not Waving but Drowning*]

15 Oh to become sensible about social advance at seventeen is to be lost. [*Parents*]

16 Private Means is dead, / God rest his soul, / Officers and fellow-rankers said. [*Private Means is Dead*]

17 The crux and Colonel of the whole matter, / (As you can read in the Journal, if it's not tattered) / Lies in the Generals, Collapse, Debility, Panic and Uproar, / Who are too old in any case / To go to War.

18 It [my poetry] does as well for telling atom secrets as for knowing whatever Mabel's been up to lately. [In the *Observer*, 9 Nov. 1969]

THORNE SMITH 1892–1934

19 Stevens' mind was so tolerant that he could have attended a lynching every day without becoming critical. [*The Jovial Ghosts*, Ch. 11]

20 'I find it rather sad. Mrs Hart had a hard life.' 'You mean she led a hard life,' declared Marion. 'She was a trull before she could toddle.' [*Topper Takes a Trip*, Ch. 14]

C. P. [later LORD] SNOW 1905–1980

21 'I grant you that he's not two-faced,' I said. 'But what's the use of that when the one face he has got is so peculiarly unpleasant?' [*The Affair*, Ch. 4]

22 The official world, the corridors of power. [*Homecomings*, Ch. 22. Later used as title of novel]

1 I like humour dry. Charles's splashes. [*The Search*, Pt III, Ch.2]

2 The Two Cultures. [Title of article in the *New Statesman*, 6 Oct. 1956, on the gulf between the arts and the sciences]

3 When scientists are faced with an expression of the traditional culture it tends . . . to make their feet ache. [*The Two Cultures*, 4]

ETHEL [later VISCOUNTESS SNOWDEN 1881–1951

4 We were behind the 'iron curtain' at last! [*Through Bolshevik Russia*, 1920. The phrase was later used by Goebbels (see 145:18) and taken up by Winston Churchill in his Fulton speech in 1946 (see 80:6). Derived from the safety curtain in a theatre]

PHILIP [later VISCOUNT] SNOWDEN 1864–1937

5 It would be desirable if every Government, when it comes into power, should have its old speeches burned. [In C. E. Bechofer Roberts ('Ephesian'), *Philip Snowden*, Ch. 12.]

GARY SNYDER 1930–

6 Taste all, and hand the knowledge down. [*Turtle Island*, 'Ethnobotany']

STEVEN SODERBERGH 1963–

7 Some of the worst films of all time have been made by people who think too much. [Interview in the *Guardian*, 7 Sept. 1989]

ALEXANDER SOLZHENITSYN 1918–

8 The whole of his life had prepared Podduyev for living, not for dying. [*Cancer Ward*, Pt I, Ch. 8, trans. N. Bethell and D. Burg]

9 The Rusanovs loved the People, their great People. They served the People and were ready to give their lives for the People. But as the years went by they found themselves less and less able to tolerate actual human beings, those obstinate creatures who were always resistant, refusing to do what they were told and, besides, demanding something for themselves. [14]

10 Nowadays we don't think much of a man's love for an animal; we laugh at people who are attached to cats. But if we stop loving animals, aren't we bound to stop loving humans too?

11 The camps had taught him that people who say nothing carry something within themselves. [II. 10]

12 Capitalism was doomed ethically before it was doomed economically, a long time ago.

13 One of the [zoo] cages had a notice on it: 'White owls do not do well in captivity.' So they know that! And they still lock them up! What sort of degenerate owls, he wondered, did so well in captivity? [14]

14 You took my freedom away a long time ago and you can't give it back because you haven't got it yourself. [*The First Circle*, Ch. 17, trans. M. Guybon]

15 You only have power over people so long as you don't take *everything* away from them. But when you've robbed a man of everything he's no longer in your power – he's free again.

16 They don't sell tickets to the past. [37]

17 Their teacher had advised them not to read Tolstoy's novels, because they were very long and would easily confuse the clear ideas which they had learned from reading critical studies of him. [40]

18 For a country to have a great writer is like having a second government. That is why no regime has ever loved great writers, only minor ones. [57]

19 None of us who lived close to her perceived that she was that one righteous person without whom, as the saying goes, no city can stand.
   Nor the world. [*Matryona's House*, final words, trans. M. Glenny]

20 Prayers are like those appeals of ours. Either they don't get through or they're returned with 'rejected' scrawled across 'em. [*One Day in the Life of Ivan Denisovich*, trans. R. Parker]

21 When truth is discovered by someone else, it loses something of its attractiveness. [*Candle in the Wind*, sc. iii]

22 Forget the outside world. Life has differ-

ent laws in here. This is Campland, an invisible country. It's not in the geography books, or the psychology books or the history books. This is the famous country where ninety-nine men weep while one laughs. [*The Lovegirl and the Innocent*, Act I, sc. iii, trans. N. Bethell and D. Burg]

1 In our country the lie has become not just a moral category but a pillar of the State. [In the *Observer*, 'Sayings of the Year', 29 Dec. 1974]

ANASTASIO SOMOZA [Dictator of Nicaragua] 1925–1980

2 Indeed, you won the elections, but I won the count. [To an opponent who accused him of rigging the elections. In the *Guardian*, 17 June 1977. See also 360:8]

STEPHEN SONDHEIM 1930–

3 The shiny stuff is tomatoes. / The salad lies in a group. / The curly stuff is potatoes. / The stuff that moves is soup. / Anything that is white is sweet. / Anything that is brown is meat. / Anything that is grey, don't eat. [On airways food. Song: *Do I Hear a Waltz?*]

4 Everything's Coming Up Roses. [Title of song in musical *Gypsy*]

5 It's not talk of God / And the decade ahead / That allows you to get through the worst. / It's 'you do' and 'I don't' and 'nobody said that' / And 'who brought the subject up first?' [Song: *It's the Little Things*, in musical *Company*]

6 Send in the Clowns. [Title of song in musical *A Little Night Music*]

7 One's impossible, two is dreary, / Three is company, safe and cheery. [Song: *Side by Side by Side*]

SUSAN SONTAG 1933–

8 Illness is the night-side of life, a more onerous citizenship. Everyone who is born holds dual citizenship, in the kingdom of the well and in the kingdom of the sick. Although we all prefer to use only the good passport, sooner or later each of us is obliged, at least for a spell, to identify ourselves as citizens of that other place. [*Illness as Metaphor*, opening words]

9 A large part of the popularity and persuasiveness of psychology comes from its being a sublimated spiritualism: a secular, ostensibly scientific way of affirming the primacy of 'spirit' over matter. [Ch. 7]

10 A photograph is not only an image (as a painting is an image), an interpretation of the real; it is also a trace, something directly stencilled off the real, like a footprint or a death mask. [*On Photography*]

11 When we're afraid we shoot. But when we're nostalgic we take pictures.

CHARLES SORLEY 1895–1915

12 Give them not praise. For, deaf, how should they know / It is not curses heaped on each gashed head? [*When You See Millions of the Mouthless Dead*]

DUNCAN SPAETH

13 I know why the sun never sets on the British Empire; God wouldn't trust an Englishman in the dark. [In Gyles Brandreth, *The Last Word*]

NANCY SPAIN 1917–1964

14 Only a fool would make the bed every day. [In Quentin Crisp, *The Naked Civil Servant*, Ch. 15]

DAME MURIEL SPARK 1918–

15 She doesn't have anything to do with youth clubs. There are classes within classes in Peckham. [*The Ballad of Peckham Rye*, Ch. 3]

16 A short neck denotes a good mind ... You see, the messages go quicker to the brain because they've shorter to go. [7]

17 The one certain way for a woman to hold a man is to leave him for religion. [*The Comforters*, Ch. 1]

18 Parents learn a lot from their children about coping with life. [6]

19 'And you say it's [Proust] about something in particular?' ... 'Well, it's about everything in particular, isn't it?' [*A Far Cry from Kensington*, Ch. 6]

20 All the nice people were poor; at least, that was a general axiom, the best of the rich being poor in spirit. [*The Girls of Slender Means*, Ch. 1]

1 Selwyn Macgregor, the nicest boy who ever committed the sin of whisky. [*The Go-away bird*, 'A Sad Tale's Best for Winter']

2 I enjoyed the mealtimes more than the meals. [*The Only Problem*, 8]

3 Give me a girl at an impressionable age, and she is mine for life. [*The Prime of Miss Jean Brodie*, Ch. 1]

4 If you had been mine when you were seven you would have been the crème de la crème.

5 But I did not remove my glasses, for I had not asked for her company in the first place, and there is a limit to what one can listen to with the naked eye. [*Voices at Play*, 'The Dark Glasses']

6 Do you think it pleases a man when he looks into a woman's eyes and sees a reflection of the British Museum Reading Room? [In L. and M. Cowan, *The Wit of Women*]

7 I wouldn't take the Pope too seriously. He's a Pole first, a Pope second, and maybe a Christian third. [In the *Observer*, 'Sayings of the Week', 4 June 1989]

JOHNNY SPEIGHT 1920–

8 You silly moo. [Catchphrase in BBC TV comedy series *Till Death Do Us Part*]

9 They start bloody wars they can't afford ... That old fool Chamberlain that was ... 'Peace in our time' ... Didn't give a thought to the cost of it – didn't enter his head to go into a few figures – get an estimate – soppy old sod. ['The Bird Fancier']

10 Well, your natives have that. They have *sounds* for things, but it's not language. I mean, a dog barks but it's not language. I mean, yer Jocks an' yer Irish they've got that, they've got sounds. Yer Gaelic ... but it's no good to 'em 'cept for talking among themselves. They wanna talk to other people, they've got to learn English.

11 If Her Majesty stood for Parliament – if the Tory Party had any sense and made Her its leader instead of that grammar school twit Heath – us Tories, mate, would win every election we went in for. ['I Can Give It Up']

12 ALF: That's the one [religion] you got to belong to. No good belonging to any of the others. But who knows which one is His? I mean, that's your problem, annit? 'Cos God ain't said nothing for years, He aint ...
MIKE: You ought to join all the religions – don't take any chances ... ['Sex before Marriage']

13 Don't be daft. You don't get any pornography on there, not on the telly. Get filth, that's all. The only place you get pornography is in yer Sunday papers. ['Royal Variety Performance 1972']

14 'Cos as the Lord Jesus said, it will be easier for a needle to pass through the eye of a camel than for a rich man to enter the Kingdom of Heaven. ['If We Want a Proper Democracy ...']

CARDINAL SPELLMAN 1889–1967

15 Pray as if everything depended on God, and work as if everything depended upon man. [In Lewis C. Henry, *Best Quotations for All Occasions*]

SIR STANLEY SPENCER 1891–1959

16 Painting is saying 'Ta' to God. [Quoted by his daughter, Shirin, in the *Observer*, 7 Feb. 1988]

17 I no more like people personally than I like dogs. When I meet people I am only apprehensive whether they will bite me, which is reasonable and sensible. [In Maurice Collis, *Stanley Spencer, a Biography*, Ch. 17]

SIR STEPHEN SPENDER 1909–

18 Different living is not living in different places / But creating in the mind a map. [*Different Living*]

19 After the first powerful manifesto / The black statement of pistons, without more fuss / But gliding like a queen, she leaves the station. [*The Express*]

20 But let the wrong cry out as raw as wounds / This Time forgets and never heals, far less transcends. [*In Railway Halls*]

21 I think continually of those who were truly great. / Who, from the womb, remembered the soul's history / Through corridors of light. [*I think continually of those*]

1 Born of the sun, they travelled a short while towards the sun / And left the vivid air signed with their honour.

2 My parents kept me from children who were rough / And who threw words like stones and who wore torn clothes. [*My parents kept me from children who were rough*]

3 Pylons, those pillars / Bare like nude giant girls that have no secret. [*The Pylons*]

4 Only the lucid friend to aerial raiders / The brilliant pilot moon, stares down / Upon this plain she makes a shining bone. [*Two Armies*]

5 Who live under the shadow of a war, / What can I do that matters? [*Who Live under the Shadow*]

6 People sometimes divide others into those you laugh at and those you laugh with. The young Auden was someone you could laugh-at-with. [Address at W. H. Auden's memorial service, Oxford, 27 Oct. 1973]

7 He [W. H. Auden] had an open mind about sex but a closed one about clocks. [*Journals, 1939–83*, ed. John Goldsmith, 22 Jan. 1975]

HILDE SPIEL 1911–

8 Malice is like a game of poker or tennis; you don't play it with anyone who is manifestly inferior to you. [*The Darkened Room*]

STEVEN SPIELBERG 1947–

9 Close Encounters of the Third Kind. [Title of film, written and directed by him]

MICKEY SPILLANE 1918–

10 Don't stand too near the window, honey, someone might blow you a kiss. [In film *Kiss Me Deadly*, script by A. I. Bezzerides]

11 Those big-shot writers ... could never dig the fact that there are more salted peanuts consumed than caviar. [In *Writer's Quotation Book*, ed. James Charlton]

DR BENJAMIN SPOCK 1903–

12 You know more than you think you do. [*Baby and Child Care*, opening words]

13 To win in Vietnam, we will have to exterminate a nation. [*Dr Spock on Vietnam*, Ch. 7]

REV. W. A. SPOONER 1844–1930

14 Kinquering Congs their titles take. [Announcing the hymn in New College Chapel, 1879]

15 I remembered your name perfectly, but I just can't think of your face. [Attr., but apocryphal]

16 Let us drink to the queer old Dean. [Attr.]

17 Sir, you have tasted two whole worms: you have hissed all my mystery lectures and been caught fighting a liar in the quad; you will leave Oxford by the next town drain. [Attr., but apocryphal]

SIR CECIL SPRING-RICE 1859–1918

18 I vow to thee, my country – all earthly things above – / Entire and whole and perfect, the service of my love. [*I vow to thee, my Country*]

19 And there's another country, I've heard of long ago.

20 And her ways are ways of gentleness, and all her paths are peace.

21 I am the Dean of Christ Church, Sir: / There's my wife; look well at her. / She's the Broad and I'm the High; / We are the University. [*The Masque of Balliol*]

BRUCE SPRINGSTEEN 1949–

22 Nobody wins unless everybody wins. [Catchphrase. In Dave Marsh, *Glory Days*, Ch. 12]

SIR JOHN SQUIRE 1884–1958

23 It did not last: the Devil howling, 'Ho! / Let Einstein be!' restored the status quo. [*Answer to Pope's Epitaph on Sir Isaac Newton*]

24 But I'm not so think as you drunk I am. [*Ballade of Soporific Absorption*]

25 But Shelley had a hyper-thyroid face. [*Ballade of the Glandular Hypothesis*]

26 Full many a vice is born to blush unseen, / Full many a crime the world does not discuss, / Full many a pervert lives to reach

a green / Replete old age, and so it was with us. [*If Gray had had to write his Elegy in the Cemetery of Spoon River*]

1 At last incapable of further harm, / The lewd forefathers of the village sleep.

SRI AUROBINDO

2 Nothing to the supernatural sense is really finite; it is founded on a feeling of all in each and each in all. [*The Synthesis of Yoga*]

MR JUSTICE STABLE 1923–

3 It would be much better if young women should stop being raped much earlier in the proceedings than some of them do. [In the *Observer*, 'Sayings of the Week', 8 Jan. 1961]

HENRY DE VERE STACPOOLE
1863–1931

4 In home-sickness you must keep moving – it is the only disease that does not require rest. [*The Bourgeois*]

JOSEPH STALIN 1879–1953

5 The state is an instrument in the hands of the ruling class for suppressing the resistance of its class enemies. [On 'Proletarian democracy'. *Foundations of Leninism*, sect. 4/6]

6 The tasks of the party are ... to be cautious and not allow our country to be drawn into conflicts by warmongers who are accustomed to have others pull the chestnuts out of the fire for them. [Speech to the 8th Congress of the Communist Party, 6 Jan. 1941. See also 126:1]

7 To govern is not to write resolutions and distribute directives; to govern is to control the implementation of the directives. [In N. McInnes, *The Communist Parties of Western Europe*, Ch. 3]

8 The Pope! How many divisions has he got? [To French Prime Minister Laval, who asked him to encourage Catholicism to please the Pope, 13 May 1935. In W. S. Churchill, *The Second World War*, Vol. 1, Ch. 8, but also quoted by President Truman as said to Churchill at Potsdam Conference]

9 Writers are the engineers of human souls. [In *Barnes and Noble Book of Quotations*, ed. Robert I. Fitzhenry, 'Writers and Writing'. See also 205:5]

10 The party is the rallying-point for the best elements of the working class. [Attr.]

JOHN STALKER 1939–

11 Crime and its components have always been an unself-conscious adjunct of show-business. [In the *Sunday Times*, 22 Apr. 1990]

COL. CHARLES E. STANTON
1859–1933

12 Lafayette, we are here! [At Lafayette's grave, Paris, 4 July 1917]

FRANK L. STANTON 1857–1927

13 Sweetes' li'l' feller, / Everybody knows; / Dunno what to call 'im, / But he's mighty lak' a rose! [*Sweetes' Li'l' Feller*]

OLAF STAPLEDON 1886–1950

14 That strange blend of the commercial traveller, the missionary, and the barbarian conqueror, which was the American abroad. [*Last and First Men*, Ch. 3, sect. i]

CHRISTINA STEAD 1902–1983

15 A self-made man is one who believes in luck and sends his son to Oxford. [*House of All Nations*, 'Credo']

16 If all the rich men in the world divided up their money amongst themselves, there wouldn't be enough to go round.

WICKHAM STEED 1876–1956

17 The famous 'AEIOU' policy – *Austriae est imperare orbi universo* (to Austria belongs universal rule). [*The Hapsburg Monarchy*]

SIR DAVID STEEL 1938–

18 Experience has shown that the only sure way to run a small business in Tory Britain is to start with a large one. [Speech at Liberal Party Assembly, Llandudno, Wales, 18 Sept. 1981]

1 To listen to some people in politics, you'd think 'nice' was a four letter word. [Party Political Broadcast on ITV for the Social Democrats, in the *Listener*, 5 Feb. 1987]

LINCOLN STEFFENS 1866–1936

2 I have seen the future and it works. [To Bernard Baruch after a visit to the Soviet Union in 1919. In *Autobiography*, Ch. 18. See also 64:3, 376:6]

3 City government is of the people, by the rascals, for the rich. [In *The Times*, 18 July 1977]

GERTRUDE STEIN 1874–1946

4 Hemingway, remarks are not literature. [*Autobiography of Alice B. Toklas*, Ch. 7]

5 Native always means people who belong somewhere else, because they had once belonged somewhere. That shows that the white race does not really think they belong anywhere because they think of everybody else as native. [*Everybody's Autobiography*, Ch. 1]

6 Anything scares me, anything scares anyone but really after all considering how dangerous everything is nothing is really very frightening. [2]

7 Two things are always the same the dance and war. One might say anything is the same but the dance and war are particularly the same because one can see them. That is what they are for. [5]

8 Pigeons on the grass alas. [*Four Saints in Three Acts*, III. iii]

9 In the United States there is more space where nobody is than where anybody is. That is what makes America what it is. [*The Geographical History of America*]

10 Ida never sighed, she just rested. When she rested she turned a little and she said, yes dear. She said that very pleasantly. That was all of Ida's life just then. [*Ida*, Pt II]

11 It is difficult never to have been younger but Ida almost was she almost never had been younger.

12 Disillusionment in living is the finding out nobody agrees with you not those that are fighting for you. Complete disillusion-ment is when you realize that no one can for they can't change. [*The Making of Americans*]

13 Rose is a rose is a rose is a rose. [*Sacred Emily*]

14 The first of the last generation. [Of F. Scott Fitzgerald. In J. M. Brinnin, *The Third Rose*]

15 A village explainer, excellent if you were a village, but if you were not, not. [Of Ezra Pound. In Malcolm Cowley, *Exile's Return*]

16 You should only read what is truly good or what is frankly bad. [In Ernest Hemingway, *A Moveable Feast*, 3]

17 That's what you all are ... All of you young people who served in the war. You are a lost generation. [See also 373:7]

18 Anything one is remembering is a repetition, but existing as a human being, that is being, listening and hearing is never repetition. [In David Lodge, *Changing Places*, Ch. 5]

19 Just before she [Stein] died she asked, 'What *is* the answer?' No answer came. She laughed and said, 'In that case what is the question?' Then she died. [D. Sutherland, *Gertrude Stein: A Biography of Her Work*, Ch. 6]

JOHN STEINBECK 1902–1968

20 Man, unlike any other thing organic or inorganic in the universe, grows beyond his work, walks up the stairs of his concepts, emerges ahead of his accomplishments. [*The Grapes of Wrath*, Ch. 14]

21 Okie use' to mean you was from Oklahoma. Now it means you're scum. Don't mean nothing itself, it's the way they say it. [18]

GLORIA STEINEM 1934–

22 A woman without a man is like a fish without a bicycle. [Attr. in *Quotable Women*, comp. Elaine Partnow]

23 I can't mate in captivity. [On why she has never married. In *The Other 637 Best Things Anybody Ever Said*, comp. Robert Byrne]

GEORGE STEINER 1929–

24 I think we must all learn to be guests of

each other. [Interview in the *Guardian*, 19 May 1981]

WILHELM STEKEL 1868–1940

1 The mark of the immature man is that he wants to die nobly for a cause, while the mark of the mature man is that he wants to live humbly for one. [In J. D. Salinger, *The Catcher in the Rye*, Ch. 24]

JAMES STEPHENS 1882–1950

2 I heard a bird at dawn / Singing sweetly on a tree, / That the dew was on the lawn, / And the wind was on the lea; / But I didn't listen to him, / For he didn't sing to me. [*The Rivals*]

3 I heard a sudden cry of pain! / There is a rabbit in a snare. [*The Snare*]

4 Finality is death. Perfection is finality. Nothing is perfect. There are lumps in it. [*The Crock of Gold*, Bk 1, Ch. 4]

5 Men come of age at sixty, women at fifteen. [In the *Observer*, 'Sayings of the Week', 1 Oct. 1944]

PAMELA STEPHENSON

6 I scramble into my clothes – whatever's lying in a heap on the floor. I do, however, put on a clean pair of underpants each morning – by Friday I've got seven pairs on. [In the *Sunday Times Magazine*, 'Life in the Day of', 13 June 1982]

ANDREW B. STERLING 1874–1955

7 Meet Me in St Louis, Louis. [Title of song, music by Kerry Mills]

ISAAC STERN 1920–

8 It was in Russia that I had all my primary training: I didn't come to the United States till I was ten months old. [Interview in the *Guardian*, 16 Feb. 1987]

RICHARD G. STERN 1928–

9 When love gets to be important to someone, it means that he hasn't been able to manage something else. Falling in love seems to me an almost sure sign of failure. Except for the very few who have a talent for it. [*Golk*, Ch. 2, iii]

WALLACE STEVENS 1879–1955

10 What counted was mythology of self, / Blotched out beyond unblotching. [*The Comedian as the Letter C*, I]

11 The only emperor is the emperor of ice-cream. [*The Emperor of Ice-cream*]

12 Poetry is the supreme fiction, madame. / Take the moral law and make a nave of it / And from the nave build haunted heaven. [*A High-toned Old Christian Woman*]

13 They said, 'You have a blue guitar, / You do not play things as they are.' / The man replied, 'Things as they are / Are changed upon the blue guitar.' [*The Man with the Blue Guitar*]

14 In the high west there burns a furious star. / It is for fiery boys that star was set / And for sweet-smelling virgins close to them. [*Le Monocle de Mon Oncle*]

15 If sex were all, then every trembling hand / Could make us squeak, like dolls, the wished-for words. [*Le Monocle de Mon Oncle*]

16 She bathed in her still garden, while / The red-eyed elders watching, felt / The basses of their beings throb / In witching chords, and their thin blood / Pulse pizzicati of Hosanna. [*Peter Quince at the Clavier*]

17 Beauty is momentary in the mind – / The fitful tracing of a portal; / But in the flesh it is immortal.

18 I do not know which to prefer, / The beauty of inflections / Or the beauty of innuendoes, / The blackbird whistling / Or just after. [*Thirteen Ways of Looking at the Blackbird*]

19 I had as lief be embraced by the porter at the hotel / As to get no more from the moonlight / Than your moist hand. [*Two Figures in Dense Violet Night*]

ADLAI STEVENSON 1900–1965

20 A lie is an abomination unto the Lord, and a very present help in trouble. [Speech, Springfield, Illinois, Jan. 1951]

21 Let's talk sense to the American people. Let's tell them the truth, that there are no

gains without pains. [Speech accepting Democratic presidential nomination, Chicago, 26 July 1952]

1 I would make a proposition to my Republican friends ... That if they will stop telling lies about the Democrats, we will stop telling the truth about them. [Campaign remark, Fresno, California, 10 Sept. In *Respectfully Quoted*, ed. Suzy Platt. Described as a favourite line of Stevenson, it in fact reverses original of Senator Chauncey Depew; see 104:6]

2 There is no evil in the atom; only in men's souls. [Speech in Hartford, Connecticut, 18 Sept.]

3 My definition of a free society is a society where it is safe to be unpopular. [Speech in Detroit, 7 Oct.]

4 A funny thing happened to me on the way to the White House. [On his defeat in presidential election. Speech in Washington, 13 Dec.]

5 God bless mother and daddy, my brother and sister, and save the King. And, oh God, do take care of yourself, because if anything happens to you we're all sunk. [Speech at Harvard Business School, 6 June 1959]

6 Flattery is all right – if you don't inhale. [Speech, 1 Feb. 1961]

7 She [Eleanor Roosevelt] would rather light candles than curse the darkness, and her glow has warmed the world. [Address to the United Nations General Assembly, 7 Nov. 1962, on her death]

8 Power corrupts, but lack of power corrupts absolutely. [In the *Observer*, Jan. 1963. Parody of Lord Acton; see *New Penguin Dictionary of Quotations*]

9 They remind me of a very tired rich man who said to his chauffeur 'Drive off that cliff, James, I want to commit suicide.' [In A. Andrews, *Quotations for Speakers and Writers*]

10 A politician is a statesman who approaches every question with an open mouth. [In Leon A. Harris, *The Fine Art of Political Wit*. Also ascr. to Arthur Goldberg describing diplomats]

REV. JOHN STEWART 1909–

11 It has been well said that the quarrel

between capitalism and communism is whether to sit upstairs or downstairs in a bus going the wrong way. [Letter to the *Listener*, 18 Dec. 1986]

MARK STEYN

12 It's hard enough to write a good drama, it's much harder to write a good comedy, and it's hardest of all to write drama with comedy. [In the *Independent*, 21 Feb. 1990]

JOHN STILL

13 The memories of men are too frail a thread to hang history from. [*The Jungle Tide*, Ch. 5]

MARY [later LADY] STOCKS
1891–1975

14 It is clearly absurd that it should be possible for a woman to qualify as a saint with direct access to the Almighty while she may not qualify as a curate. [*Still More Commonplace*]

MERVYN STOCKWOOD, BISHOP OF SOUTHWARK 1913–

15 A psychiatrist is a man who goes to the Folies-Bergère and looks at the audience. [In the *Observer*, 'Sayings of the Week', 15 Oct. 1961, but probably of earlier origin]

I. F. STONE 1907–1989

16 If you live long enough, the venerability factor creeps in; you get accused of things you never did and praised for virtues you never had. [In Laurence J. Peter, *Peter's Quotations*]

ROBERT STONE 1937–

17 People are getting to be a disgrace to the planet. [*A Flag for Sunrise*, Ch. 6]

G. M. STONIER [FANFARLO]
1903–1985

18 I explain my theory of optimo-pessimism. [*Shaving through the Blitz*, Ch. 5]

TOM STOPPARD 1937–

19 Why are you bothering to lie to me? You

are like a man on a desert island refusing to admit to his companion that he ate the last coconut. [*Artist Descending a Staircase*]

1 Skill without imagination is craftsmanship and gives us many useful objects such as wickerwork picnic baskets. Imagination without skill gives us modern art.

2 That's why he comes over as a sanctimonious busybody with an Energen roll where his balls ought to be. [*Dirty Linen*]

3 *The Times* has published no rumours; it's only reported the facts, namely that other, less responsible papers are publishing certain rumours.

4 If you took away everything in the world that had to be invented, there'd be nothing left except a lot of people getting rained on. [*Enter a Free Man*, Act I]

5 A circle is the longest distance to the same point. [*Every Good Boy Deserves Favour*]

6 What is known as common sense, whose virtue, uniquely among virtues, is that everybody has it. [*Jumpers*, Act I]

7 To attempt to sustain the attention of rival schools of academics by argument alone is tantamount to constructing a Gothic arch out of junket.

8 It's not the voting that's democracy, it's the counting. [See also 353:2]

9 If rationality were the criterion of things being allowed to exist, the world would be a gigantic field of soya beans!

10 I can't think of anyone more susceptible to the Rad-Lib philosophy: 'No problem is insoluble given a big enough plastic bag.'

11 Do you think every *sole meunière* comes to you untouched by suffering? [II]

12 Do not despair – many are happy much of the time; more eat than starve, more are healthy than sick, more curable than dying; not so many dying as dead; and one of the thieves was saved. Hell's bells and all's well – half the world is at peace with itself, and so is the other half; vast areas are unpolluted; millions of children grow up without suffering deprivation, and millions, while deprived, grow up without suffering cruelties, and millions, while deprived and cruelly treated, none the less grow up. No laughter is sad and many tears are joyful. [Coda]

13 A foreign correspondent is someone who lives in foreign parts and corresponds, usually in the form of essays containing no new facts. Otherwise he's someone who flies around from hotel to hotel and thinks the most interesting thing about any story is the fact that he has arrived to cover it. [*Night and Day*, Act I]

14 The media. It sounds like a convention of spiritualists.

15 A lady, if surprised by melancholy, might go to bed with a chap, once; or a thousand times if consumed by passion. But twice, Wagner, *twice* . . . a lady might think she'd be taken for a tart.

16 MILNE: No matter how imperfect things are, if you've got a free press everything is correctable, and without it everything is conceivable.

RUTH: I'm with you on the free press. It's the newspapers I can't stand.

17 I don't like to give offence by giving notice – in a servant it looks presumptuous. [*On the Razzle* (adapted from Johann Nestroy, *Einen Jux will er sich machen*), Act I]

18 ANDERSON: Tomorrow is another day, McKendrick.

MCKENDRICK: Tomorrow, in my experience, is usually the same day. [*Professional Foul*]

19 I was taken once to Convent Garden to hear a woman called Callas in a sort of foreign musical with no dancing which people were donating kidneys to get tickets for. [*The Real Thing*, Act I, sc. 2]

20 Gallons of ink and miles of typewriter ribbon expended on the misery of the unrequited lover; not a word about the utter tedium of the unrequiting. [4]

21 We do on the stage the things that are supposed to happen off. Which is a kind of integrity, if you look on every exit being an entrance somewhere else. [*Rosencrantz and Guildenstern are Dead*, Act I]

22 You're familiar with the tragedies of antiquity, are you? The great homicidal classics?

23 We're *actors* – we're the opposite of people! [II]

24 We have been left so much to our own

devices – after a while one welcomes the uncertainty of being left to other people's.

1 Eternity is a terrible thought. I mean, where's it going to end?

2 The bad end unhappily, the good unluckily. That is what tragedy means.

3 Life is a gamble, at terrible odds – if it was a bet, you wouldn't take it. [III]

4 An essentially private man who wished his total indifference to public notice to be universally recognized. [*Travesties*, Act I]

5 What a bloody country [Switzerland], even the cheese has got holes in it!

6 War is capitalism with the gloves off and many who go to war know it but they go to war because they don't want to be a hero.

7 It is a librarian's duty to distinguish between poetry and a sort of belle-litter.

8 What is an artist? For every thousand people there's nine hundred doing the work, ninety doing well, nine doing good, and one lucky bastard who's the artist. [Also used with slightly different wording in *Artist Descending a Staircase*]

9 I learned three things in Zürich during the war. I wrote them down. Firstly, you're either a revolutionary or you're not, and if you're not you might as well be an artist as anything else. Secondly, if you can't be an artist, you might as well be a revolutionary . . . I forget the third thing. [II]

10 My problem is that I am not frightfully interested in anything, except myself. And of all forms of fiction autobiography is the most gratuitous. [*Lord Malquist and Mr Moon*, Pt II, 3]

11 I agree with everything you say but I would attack to the death your right to say it – Voltaire (the younger). [Parody of Voltaire, attr.; see *New Penguin Dictionary of Quotations*]

12 The House of Lords, an illusion to which I have never been able to subscribe – responsibility without power, the prerogative of the eunuch throughout the ages. [VI. 1. See also 23:6, 104:9, 214:27, 401:19]

13 I do not pretend to understand the universe. It is a great deal bigger than I am [2]

14 I write fiction because it's a way of making statements I can disown, and I write plays because dialogue is the most respectable way of contradicting myself. [TV interview. In the *Guardian*, 21 Mar. 1973]

15 A truth is always a compound of two half-truths, and you never reach it, because there is always something more to say.

16 I doubt that art needed Ruskin any more than a moving train needs one of its passengers to shove it. [In *The Times Literary Supplement*, 3 June 1977]

17 I write to get out of jail. [In the *Observer Review*, on his 50th birthday, 28 June 1987]

18 Plays work through metaphor. In the end the best play about Vietnam will probably turn out to have been written by Sophocles. [Interview in the *Guardian*, 18 Mar. 1988]

19 Interviews are funny things because I keep having to improvise what I think I think I think. In fact I never give it a thought. [Interview in the *Observer*, 29 July 1990]

JACK TREVOR STORY 1917–1991

20 Live Now, Pay Later. [Title of book]

REX STOUT 1886–1975

21 There are two kinds of statistics, the kind you look up and the kind you make up. [*Death of a Doxy*, Ch. 9]

22 'I'll discuss it with you,' she said, in a voice that could have been used to defrost her refrigerator. [*Three Witnesses*, 'Die Like a Dog', III]

JOHN STRACHEY 1901–1963

23 Becoming an Anglo-Catholic must surely be a sad business – rather like becoming an amateur conjurer. [*The Coming Struggle for Power*, Pt III, Ch. 11]

24 Mr MacDonald has become . . . an actor – and that type of actor which the cruel French call a '*m'as-tu vu?*' 'Have you seen me as the Prime Minister? – My greatest role, I assure you,' Mr MacDonald is anxiously asking the nation. Yes, we have seen him. [V. 17]

25 Fascism means war. [Slogan, 1930s]

LYTTON STRACHEY 1880–1932

1 'Before she came,' said a soldier, 'there was cussin' and swearin', but after that it was as 'oly as a church.' The most cherished privilege of the fighting man was abandoned for the sake of Miss Nightingale. [*Eminent Victorians*, 'Florence Nightingale']

2 Yet her conception of God was certainly not orthodox. She felt towards Him as she might have felt towards a glorified sanitary engineer; and in some of her speculations she seems hardly to distinguish between the Deity and the Drains.

3 It should not merely be useful and ornamental; it should preach a high moral lesson. [On the Prince Consort's plans for the Great Exhibition. *Queen Victoria*, Ch. 4, vii]

4 Mr Gladstone was in his shirt-sleeves at Hawarden, cutting down a tree, when the royal message was brought to him. 'Very significant,' he remarked, when he had read the letter, and went on cutting down his tree. [8. i]

5 The Faery [Queen Victoria], he determined, should henceforth wave her wand for him [Disraeli] alone. [iii]

6 First I write one sentence: then I write another. That's how I write. And so I go on. But I have a feeling writing ought to be like running through a field. [In conversation with Max Beerbohm. In Virginia Woolf, *A Writer's Diary*, 1 Nov. 1938]

7 [When asked at a military tribunal before which he had registered as a conscientious objector, 'What would you do if you saw a German soldier trying to violate your sister?'] I would try to get between them. [In Robert Graves, *Good-bye to All That*, Ch. 23]

8 If this is dying, I don't think much of it. [Dying words. In Michael Holroyd. *Lytton Strachey*, Pt V, Ch. 17, sect. viii]

EUGENE STRATTON 1861–1918

9 I know she likes me, / 'Cause she says so. [Song: *The Lily of Laguna*, 1912, written by Leslie Stuart]

10 Little Dolly Daydream, pride of Idaho. [Song: *Little Dolly Daydream*, written by Leslie Stuart]

HENRY G. STRAUSS [later LORD CONESFORD] 1892–1974

11 I have every sympathy with the American who was so horrified by what he had read of the effects of smoking that he gave up reading. [In A. Andrews, *Quotations for Speakers and Writers*]

IGOR STRAVINSKY 1882–1971

12 It is not art that rains down upon us in the song of a bird; but the simplest modulation, correctly executed, is already art. [*Poetics of Music*, Ch. 2]

13 A renewal is fruitful only when it goes hand in hand with tradition. [5]

14 Rachmaninov's immortalizing totality was his scowl. He was a six-and-a-half-foot-tall scowl. [Igor Stravinsky and Robert Craft, *Conversations with Stravinsky*]

15 Nothing is likely about masterpieces, least of all whether there will be any. ['The Future of Music']

16 The very people who have done the breaking through are themselves often the first to try to put a scab on their achievement. ['Advice to Young Composers']

17 Academism results when the reasons for the rule change, but not the rule. ['Some Musical Questions']

18 A good composer does not imitate; he steals. [In Peter Yates, *Twentieth Century Music*, Pt 1, Ch. 8]

19 Film music should have the same relationship to the film drama that somebody's piano-playing in my living-room has on the book I'm reading. [In *Music Digest*, Sept. 1946]

20 My music is best understood by children and animals. [In the *Observer*, 'Sayings of the Week', 8 Oct. 1961]

21 I had another dream the other day about music critics. They were small and rodent-like with padlocked ears, as if they had stepped out of a painting by Goya. [In the *Evening Standard*, 29 Oct. 1969]

22 What does von K[arajan]'s conducting really do to Mozart? He opens his bier, unclasps his hands from his bosom, and folds them behind his head. [In the *Guardian*, 18 July 1989]

AUGUST STRINDBERG 1849–1912

1 I loathe people who keep dogs. They are cowards who haven't got the guts to bite people themselves. [*A Madman's Diary*]

ERICH VON STROHEIM 1885–1957

2 The man who cut my picture [*Greed*] had nothing on his mind but a hat. [In Kevin Brownlow, *Hollywood: The Pioneers*, Ch. 22]

REV. G. A. STUDDERT KENNEDY 1883–1929

3 When Jesus came to Birmingham, they simply passed him by, / They never hurt a hair of him, they only let him die. [*The Unutterable Beauty* – 'Indifference']

TERRY SULLIVAN ?–1950

4 She sells sea-shells on the sea-shore. / The shells she sells are sea-shells, I'm sure. [Song: *She Sells Sea-shells*, 1908, in show *The Beauty Shop*, music by Harry Gifford]

SUSAN SUSSMAN 1942–

5 Moving up the steep hill of a relationship had to be easier on tandem than unicycle, especially if the other person wasn't pedalling in the opposite direction. [*The Dieter*, Ch. 23]

GRAHAM SUTHERLAND 1903–1980

6 To 'portray' (used in the best sense) has become synonymous with 'betray'. [Of portraiture. In the *Guardian*, 9 June 1978]

SHIN'ICHI SUZUKI 1898–

7 Teaching music is not my main purpose. I want to make good citizens. If a child hears fine music from the day of his birth, and learns to play it himself, he develops sensitivity, discipline and endurance. He gets a beautiful heart. [In *Reader's Digest*, Nov. 1973]

ITALO SVEVO 1861–1928

8 Whenever I look at a mountain I always expect it to turn into a volcano. [*Confessions of Zeno*]

9 There are three things I always forget. Names, faces, and – the third I can't remember. [Attr. See also 253:19]

GRAHAM SWIFT 1949–

10 What is a photograph? It's something defined, with an edge ... A long time after the event it is still there, and when you look at it you shut out everything else. It becomes an icon, a totem, a curio. A photo is a piece of reality? A fragment of the truth? [*Out of This World*, 'Harry']

11 A photo is a reprieve, an act of suspension, a charm. If you see something terrible or wonderful, that you can't take in or focus your feelings on ... take a picture of it, hold the camera to it. Look again when it's safe.

12 Life is one tenth Here and Now, nine-tenths a history lesson. For most of the time the Here and Now is neither now nor here. [*Waterland*, 8]

13 People die when curiosity goes. People have to find out, people have to know. How can there be any true revolution till we know what we're made of? [27]

ERIC SYKES *see* SPIKE MILLIGAN and ERIC SYKES

ARTHUR SYMONS 1865–1945

14 As a perfume doth remain / In the folds where it hath lain, / So the thought of you, remaining / Deeply folded in my brain, / Will not leave me: all things leave me: / You remain. [*Memory*]

J. M. SYNGE 1871–1909

15 When I was writing 'The Shadow of the Glen' I got more aid than any learning would have given me from a chink in the floor of the old Wicklow house where I was staying, that let me hear what was being said by the servant girls in the kitchen. [*The Playboy of the Western World*, Preface]

16 I'd know his way of spitting, and he astride the moon. [III]

17 Oh, my grief, I've lost him surely. I've lost the only Playboy of the Western World. [Closing words]

THOMAS SZASZ 1920–

1 A child becomes an adult when he realizes that he has a right not only to be right but also to be wrong. [*The Second Sin*, 'Childhood']

2 Masturbation: the primary sexual activity of mankind. In the nineteenth century it was a disease; in the twentieth, it's a cure. ['Sex']

3 A teacher should have maximal authority and minimal power. ['Education']

4 Happiness is an imaginary condition, formerly often attributed by the living to the dead, now usually attributed by adults to children, and by children to adults. ['Emotions']

5 The proverb warns that, 'You should not bite the hand that feeds you.' But maybe you should, if it prevents you from feeding yourself. ['Control and Self-control']

6 The stupid neither forgive nor forget; the naïve forgive and forget; the wise forgive but do not forget. ['Personal Conduct']

7 Two wrongs don't make a right, but they make a good excuse. ['Social Relations']

8 Psychiatrists classify a person as neurotic if he suffers from his problems in living, and as psychotic if he makes others suffer. ['Psychiatry']

9 If you talk to God, you are praying; if God talks to you, you have schizophrenia. If the dead talk to you, you are a spiritualist; if God talks to you, you are a schizophrenic. ['Schizophrenia']

ALBERT SZENT-GYÖRGYI 1893–1986

10 Discovery consists of seeing what everybody has seen and thinking what nobody has thought. [In I. J. Good, *The Scientist Speculates*, p. 15]

T

ROBERT TABER 1921–

1 The guerrilla fights the war of the flea, and his military enemy suffers the dog's disadvantages: too much to defend; too small, ubiquitous, and agile an enemy to come to grips with. [*The War of the Flea*, Ch. 2]

JOSEPH TABRAR 1857–1931

2 Daddy wouldn't buy me a bow-wow, bow-wow, / I've got a little cat / And I'm very fond of that. [Song: *Daddy Wouldn't Buy Me a Bow-wow*]

3 In over a year and a half / I've only sung it once, / And I don't suppose I shall sing it again / For months and months and months. [Song: *For Months and Months and Months*]

SIR RABINDRANATH TAGORE 1861–1941

4 He who wants to do good knocks at the gate; he who loves finds the door open. [*Stray Birds*, 83]

S. G. TALLENTYRE 1868–?

5 The crowning blessing of life – to be born with a bias to some pursuit. [*The Friends of Voltaire*]

BOOTH TARKINGTON 1869–1946

6 There are two things that will be believed of any man whatsoever, and one of them is that he has taken to drink. [*Penrod*, Ch. 10]

ALLEN TATE 1899–1979

7 Row upon row with strict impunity / The headstones yield their names to the element. [*Ode to the Confederate Dead*]

8 Autumn is desolation in the plot / Of a thousand acres, where these memories grow / From the inexhaustible bodies that are not / Dead, but feed the grass, row after rich row.

9 The brute curiosity of an angel's stare / Turns you like them to stone.

10 Now that the salt of their blood / Stiffens the saltier oblivion of the sea.

BERNIE TAUPIN 1950–

11 Goodbye Norma Jean / Though I never knew you at all / You had the grace to hold yourself / While those around you crawled. / They crawled out of the woodwork / And they whispered into your brain / Set you on the treadmill / And made you change your name. [Song: *Candle in the Wind*]

TOM TAUSSIK

12 The difference between Los Angeles and yogurt is that yogurt has real culture. [From *Legless in Gaza*, in *Contradictory Quotations*, ed. M. Rogers]

R. H. TAWNEY 1880–1962

13 As long as men are men, a poor society cannot be too poor to find a right order of life, nor a rich society too rich to have need to seek it. [*The Acquisitive Society*]

A. J. P. TAYLOR 1906–1990

1 He [Lord Northcliffe] aspired to power instead of influence, and as a result forfeited both. [*English History, 1914–1945*, Ch. 1. See also 240:4, 252:8]

2 History gets thicker as it approaches recent times. [Biblography]

3 Communism continued to haunt Europe as a spectre – a name men gave to their own fears and blunders. But the crusade against Communism was even more imaginary than the spectre of Communism. [*The Origins of the Second World War*, Ch. 2]

4 Lenin was the first to discover that capitalism 'inevitably' caused war; and he discovered this only when the First World War was already being fought. Of course he was right. Since every great state was capitalist in 1914, capitalism obviously 'caused' the First World War; but just as obviously it had 'caused' the previous generation of Peace. [6]

5 A racing tipster who only reached Hitler's level of accuracy would not do well for his clients. [7]

6 All change in history, all advance, comes from non-conformity. If there had been no troublemakers, no dissenters, we should still be living in caves. [From *The Troublemakers*, in the *Guardian* on his 80th birthday, 22 Mar. 1986]

7 He [Napoleon III] was what I often think is a dangerous thing for a statesman to be – a student of history; and like most of those who study history, he learned from the mistakes of the past how to make new ones. [In the *Listener*, 6 June 1963]

8 A promoted clown. [Of Mussolini. In the *Spectator*, 28 May 1983]

9 [When asked as a young man if he had strongly held left-wing views] No. I have extreme views, weakly held. [Quoted by R. W. Johnson in *London Review of Books*, 8 May 1986]

10 Most Prime Ministers would not be interesting unless they had been Prime Ministers (and some are not interesting even then). [In *New Society*, 17 Oct. 1986]

11 Leo Amery would have been prime minister had he not been two inches too short and his speeches two pages too long. [In *The Times Literary Supplement*, 26 Aug. 1988]

12 Great events do not necessarily have great causes. [In obituary in the *Independent*, 8 Sept. 1990]

BERT LESTON TAYLOR 1866–1921

13 A bore is a man who, when you ask him how he is, tells you. [*The So-called Human Race*, p. 163. See also 156:14]

ELIZABETH TAYLOR 1912–1975

14 Life persists in the vulnerable, the sensitive . . . They carry it on. The invulnerable, the too heavily armoured perish. [*A Wreath of Roses*, Ch. 5]

15 He loved himself only as much as self-respect required, and the reason why he saw himself so clearly was that he looked not often, but suddenly, so catching himself unawares. [9]

16 It is very strange . . . that the years teach us patience; that the shorter our time, the greater our capacity for waiting. [10]

NORMAN [later LORD] TEBBIT 1931–

17 [When asked if he was backing the Republican slate in the 1980 US presidential election] Well, I'm a George Bush man myself. I support the double ticket: Reagan and a heart-attack. [In S. Hoggart, *Back in the House*]

18 He [Tebbit's father] didn't riot. He got on his bike and he looked for work. And he kept on looking until he found it. [Speech at Conservative Party Conference, Blackpool, 15 Oct. 1981. Commonly misquoted as 'On your bike']

19 I suppose the Prince of Wales feels extra sympathy towards those who've got no job because, in a way, he's got no job. [In BBC TV programme *Panorama*, Nov. 1987]

20 I have not got a single enemy I would not want. [In the *Independent*, 'Quote Unquote', 16 Feb. 1991]

PIERRE TEILHARD DE CHARDIN
1881–1955

1 Faith has need of the whole truth. [*The Appearance of Man*]

2 Individual human beings are so subtly developed through the centuries that it is strictly impermissible to compare any two men who are not contemporaries – that is to say are taken from two quite different times. [Ch. 17, sect. ii]

3 From an evolutionary point of view, man has stopped moving, if he ever did move. [*The Phenomenon of Man*, Postscript]

WILLIAM TEMPLE, ARCHBISHOP OF CANTERBURY 1881–1944

4 If a man is going to be a villain, in heaven's name let him remain a fool. [*Mens Creatrix*]

5 Unless all existence is a medium of Revelation, no particular revelation is possible. [*Nature, Man and God*]

6 Personally, I have always looked on cricket as organized loafing. [Remark to parents when Headmaster of Repton School]

7 It is a mistake to suppose that God is only, or even chiefly, concerned with religion. [In R. V. C. Bodley, *In Search of Serenity*, Ch. 12]

8 The Christian Church is the one organization in the world that exists purely for the benefit of non-members. [In *Hodder Book of Christian Quotations*, comp. Tony Castle]

9 It is not the ape, nor the tiger in man that I fear, it is the donkey. [Attr.]

10 I believe in the Church. One Holy, Catholic and Apostolic, and I regret that it nowhere exists. [Attr.]

EDITH TEMPLETON 1916–

11 Women are like teeth. Some tremble and never fall and some fall and never tremble. [*The Surprise of Cremona*, 'Urbino']

12 Raphael is the life itself, he is at once in the battle and above it.

SHERPA TENZING NORGAY
1914–1986

13 We've done the bugger! [Attr., on conquering Mount Everest, 29 May 1953. See also 172:5]

DAME ELLEN TERRY 1848–1928

14 How Henry would have loved it! [At Sir Henry Irving's funeral, 1905. In Robert Hitchens, *Yesterdays*]

MARGARET [later LADY] THATCHER
1925–

15 I stand before you tonight in my green chiffon evening gown . . . the Iron Lady of the Western World. Me? [Taking up term used of her by Soviet newspaper *Red Star*. Speech in Dorking, Surrey, 31 Jan. 1976. See also 306:10]

16 I don't mind how much my ministers talk, as long as they do what I say. [In the *Observer*, 'Sayings of the Week', 27 Jan. 1980]

17 You turn if you want to – the lady's not for turning. [In denying the possibility of her making a U-turn over economic policy. Closing speech at Conservative Party Conference, Brighton, 11 Oct. Phrase ascr. to Ronald Millar as her speech-writer]

18 Rejoice, rejoice. [On hearing British troops had retaken South Georgia during Falklands War, 25 Apr. 1982. Echoes St Francis]

19 I always say that if you want a speech made you should ask a man, but if you want something done you should ask a woman. [At AGM of Townswomen's Guild, 26 July]

20 We can do business together. [Of Mr Gorbachev. In *The Times*, 18 Dec. 1984]

21 We must try to find ways to starve the terrorist and the hijacker of the oxygen on which they depend. [Speech to London branch of American Bar Association, 15 July 1985]

22 No one would remember the Good Samaritan if he'd only had good intentions. He had money as well. [TV interview, 6 Jan. 1986]

23 There is no such thing as society. There

are individual men and women and there are families. [In *Woman's Own*, 31 Oct. 1987]

1 The cocks may crow, but it's the hen that lays the egg. [At a private dinner party, 1987. Quoted by Robert Skidelsky in the *Sunday Times Books*, 9 Apr. 1989]

2 It is not the creation of wealth that is wrong, but love of money for its own sake. [Speech to the General Assembly of the Church of Scotland, Edinburgh, 21 May 1988]

3 We have become a grandmother. [On TV, 3 Mar. 1989]

4 Every prime minister should have a Willie. [Of her deputy, Lord Whitelaw. Quoted by Godfrey Smith in the *Sunday Times*, 12 Mar.]

5 I fight on; I fight to win. [Outside 10 Downing Street, 21 Nov. 1990, on the eve of her resignation as Prime Minister]

6 Home is where you come to when you have nothing better to do. [In the *Independent*, 'Quote Unquote', 11 May 1991. Misquoted as her attitude to domesticity, rather than a reference to children's attitudes. See also 100:20]

[NORMAN] THELWELL 1923–

7 The Effluent Society. [Title of book of cartoons, 1971]

STEFAN THEMERSON 1910–1988

8 Contrary to what clergymen and policemen believe, gentleness is biological and aggression is cultural. [In obituary in the *Guardian*, 8 Sept. 1988]

PAUL THEROUX 1941–

9 They say that if the Swiss had designed these mountains [the Alps], they'd be rather flatter. [*The Great Railway Bazaar*, Ch. 2]

10 Extensive travelling induces a feeling of encapsulation, and travel, so broadening at first, contracts the mind. [21]

11 The Japanese have perfected good manners and made them indistinguishable from rudeness. [28]

12 In Turkey it was always 1952, in Malaysia 1937; Afghanistan was 1910 and Bolivia

1949. It is twenty years ago in the Soviet Union, ten in Norway, five in France. It is always last year in Australia and next week in Japan. [*The Kingdom by the Sea*, Ch. 1]

13 No one looks more like a displaced person than an Indian in an overcoat. [*My Secret History*, IV. 1]

14 In the best comedy, there is clearly something wrong, but it is secret and unstated – not even implied. Comedy is the public version of a private darkness. [V. 7]

15 All writing, even the clumsy kind, exposes in its loops and slants a yearning deeper than an intention, the soul of the writer flopping on the clothes-peg of his exclamation mark. [*Saint Jack*, Ch. 1]

16 A foreign swear-word is practically inoffensive except to the person who has learnt it early in life and knows its social limits. [12]

17 He [S. J. Perelman] was too much of an Anglophile to like England greatly. [Introduction to S. J. Perelman, *The Last Laugh*]

DYLAN THOMAS 1914–1953

18 Her fist of a face died clenched on a round pain; / And sculptured Ann is seventy years of stone. [*After the Funeral*]

19 Where blew a flower may a flower no more / Lift its head to the blows of the rain; / Though they be mad and dead as nails, / Heads of the characters hammer through daisies; / Break in the sun till the sun breaks down, / And death shall have no dominion. [*And death shall have no dominion*]

20 Before I knocked and flesh let enter, / With liquid hands tapped on the womb, / I who was shapeless as the water / That shaped the Jordan near my home / Was brother to Mnetha's daughter / And sister to the fathering worm. [*Before I Knocked*]

21 The conversation of prayers about to be said / Turns on the quick and the dead, and the man on the stairs / Tonight shall find no dying but alive and warm. [*The Conversation of Prayer*]

22 Do not go gentle into that good night. / Rage, rage against the dying of the light. [*Do not go gentle into that good night*]

23 Ears in the turrets hear / Hands grumble

on the door, / Eyes in the gables see / The fingers at the locks. [*Ears in the turrets hear*]

1 Oh as I was young and easy in the mercy of his means, / Time held me green and dying / Though I sang in my chains like the sea. [*Fern Hill*]

2 The force that through the green fuse drives the flower / Drives my green age. [*The force that through the green fuse*]

3 The hand that signed the treaty bred a fever, / And famine grew, and locusts came; / Great is the hand that holds dominion over / Man by a scribbled name. [*The hand that signed the paper*]

4 The hunchback in the park / A solitary mister. / Propped between trees and water. [*The Hunchback in the Park*]

5 And the wild boys innocent as strawberries

6 The world is half the devil's and my own, / Daft with the drug that's smoking in a girl / And curling round the bud that forks her eye. [*If I were Tickled by the Rub of Love*]

7 Man be my metaphor.

8 Light breaks where no sun shines; / Where no sea runs, the waters of the heart / Push in their tides. [*Light breaks where no sun shines*]

9 My birthday began with the water- / Birds and the birds of the winged trees flying my name. [*Poem in October*]

10 And I rose / In rainy autumn / And walked abroad in a shower of all my days.

11 A child's / Forgotten mornings when he walked with his mother / Through the parables / Of sun light / And the legends of the green chapels.

12 It was my thirtieth / Year to heaven stood there then in the summer noon.

13 A process in the weather of the heart / Turns damp to dry; the golden shot / Storms in the freezing tomb. [*A Process in the Weather of the Heart*]

14 And I must enter again the round / Zion of the water bead / And the synagogue of the ear of corn. [*A refusal to mourn the death, by fire, of a child in London*]

15 Deep with the first dead lies London's daughter, / Robed in the long friends, / The grains beyond age, the dark veins of her mother, / Secret by the unmourning water /

Of the riding Thames. / After the first death, there is no other.

16 Shall gods be said to thump the clouds / When clouds are cursed by thunder? [*Shall gods be said to thump the clouds?*]

17 The ball I threw while playing in the park / Has not yet reached the ground. [*Should lanterns shine*]

18 This bread I break was once the oat, / This wine upon a foreign tree / Plunged in its fruit; / Man in the day or wind at night / Laid the crops low, broke the grape's joy. [*This bread I break*]

19 It is a winter's tale / That the snow blind twilight ferries over the lakes / And floating fields from the farm in the cup of the vales. [*A Winter's Tale*]

20 It is spring, moonless night in the small town, starless and bible-black. [*Under Milk Wood*]

21 The boys are dreaming wicked or of the bucking ranches of the night and the jolly-rodgered sea.

22 I'm Jonah Jarvis, come to a bad end, very enjoyable.

23 Every night of her married life she has been late for school.

24 . . . kissed her once by the pigsty when she wasn't looking and never kissed her again although she was looking all the time.

25 Straightfaced in his cunning sleep he pulls the legs of his dreams.

26 Nothing grows in our garden, only washing. And babies.

27 Oh, isn't life a terrible thing, thank God?

28 The ship's clock in the bar says half past eleven. Half past eleven is opening time. The hands of the clock have stayed still at half past eleven for fifty years. It is always opening time in the Sailors Arms.

29 Oh I'm a martyr to music. [Mrs Organ Morgan]

30 I love you until Death do us part and then we shall be together for ever and ever.

31 I see you got a mermaid in your lap he said and he lifted his hat. He is a proper Christian.

32 Portraits of famous bards and preachers, all fur and wool from the squint to the knee-caps.

1 Johann Sebastian mighty Bach. Oh Bach fach.

2 I missed the chance of a lifetime, too. Fifty lovelies in the rude and I'd left my Bunsen burner home. [*Portrait of the Artist as a Young Dog*, 'One Warm Saturday']

3 Too many of the artists of Wales spend too much time talking about the position of the artists of Wales. There is only one position for an artist anywhere: and that is upright. [*Quite Early One Morning*, Pt 2, 'Wales and the Artist']

4 I read somewhere of a shepherd who, when asked why he made, from within fairy rings, ritual observances to the moon to preserve his flocks, replied: 'I'd be a damn' fool if I didn't!' [*Collected Poems*, Author's Note]

5 The land of my fathers. My fathers can have it. [In John Ackerman, *Dylan Thomas*]

6 Dylan himself once defined an alcoholic as a man you don't like who drinks as much as you do. [Constantine Fitzgibbon, *Life of Dylan Thomas*, Ch. 6]

EDWARD THOMAS 1878–1917

7 Yes. I remember Adlestrop – / The name, because one afternoon / Of heat the express-train drew up there / Unwontedly. It was late June. [*Adlestrop*]

8 All are behind, the kind / And the unkind too, no more / To-night than a dream. The stream / Runs softly and drowns the Past, / The dark-lit stream has drowned the Future and the Past. [*The Bridge*]

9 I have come to the borders of sleep, / The unfathomable deep / Forest where all must lose / Their way. [*Lights Out*]

10 All was foretold me; naught / Could I foresee; / But I learned how the wind would sound / After these things should be. / [*The New House*]

11 The green elm with the one great bough of gold / Lets leaves into the grass slip, one by one. [*October*]

12 Out in the dark over the snow / The fallow fawns invisible go / With the fallow doe; / And the winds blow / Fast as the stars are slow. [*Out in the Dark*]

13 The new moon hangs like an ivory bugle / In the naked frosty blue. [*The Penny Whistle*]

14 Merrily / Answered staid drinkers, good bedmen and all bores: / 'At Mrs Greenland's Hawthorn Bush,' said he / 'I slept.' [*A Private*]

15 I love roads: / The goddesses that dwell / Far along them invisible / Are my favourite gods. [*Roads*]

16 Now all the roads lead to France / And heavy is the tread / Of the living; but the dead / Returning lightly dance.

17 I like the dust on the nettles, never lost / Except to prove the sweetness of a shower. [*Tall Nettles*]

18 Open your eyes to the air / That has washed the eyes of the stars / Through all the dewy night: / Up with the light, / To the old wars; / Arise, arise. [*The Trumpet*]

19 When these old woods were young / The thrushes' ancestors / As sweetly sung / In the old years. [*Under the Woods*]

20 Out of us all / That make rhymes, / Will you choose / Sometimes – / As the winds use / A crack in a wall / Or a drain, / Their joy or their pain / To whistle through – / Choose me, / You English words? [*Words*]

GWYN THOMAS 1913–1981

21 I wanted a play that would paint the full face of sensuality, rebellion and revivalism. In South Wales these three phenomena have played second fiddle only to Rugby Union which is a distillation of all three. [*Jackie the Jumper*, Introduction]

22 A bit like God in his last years, the Alderman. [*The Keep*, Act I]

23 A good voice but too autocratic for oratorio. [II]

24 There are still parts of Wales where the only concession to gaiety is a striped shroud. [In *Punch*, 18 June 1958]

IRENE THOMAS 1920–

25 Protestant women may take the Pill. Roman Catholic women must keep taking the *Tablet*. [Attr. in conversation]

LEWIS THOMAS 1913–

1 It has been one of the great errors of our time to think that by thinking about thinking, and then talking about it, we could possibly straighten out and tidy up our minds ... It is all very well to be aware of your awareness, even proud of it, but never try to operate it. You are not up to the job. [*Late Night Thoughts*, 'The Attic of the Brain']

R. S. THOMAS 1913–

2 We will listen instead to the wind's text / Blown through the roof, or the thrush's song / In the thick bush that proved him wrong, / Wrong from the start, for nature's truth / Is primary and her changing seasons / Correct out of a vaster reason / The vague errors of the flesh. [*The Minister*, final lines]

3 We were a people taut for war; the hills / Were no harder, the thin grass / Clothed them more warmly than the coarse / Shirts our small bones. [*Welsh History*]

4 An impotent people, / Sick with inbreeding, / Worrying the carcase of an old song. [*Welsh Landscape*]

E. P. THOMPSON 1924–

5 Humankind must at last grow up. We must recognize that the Other is ourselves. [*Beyond the Cold War*]

6 For two decades the State, whether Conservative or Labour administrations, has been taking liberties, and these liberties were once ours. [*Writing by Candlelight*, Introduction]

7 This 'going into Europe' will not turn out to be the thrilling mutual exchange supposed. It is more like nine middle-aged couples with failing marriages meeting in a darkened bedroom in a Brussels hotel for a Group Grope. [On the Europe debate. In the *Sunday Times*, 27 Apr. 1975]

PAUL THOMPSON 1935–

8 Personal moral reliability was crucial to business success [in the early nineteenth century]. The warm hassock in the numbered pew and the scrubbed doorstep to the weeded garden were the credit cards of yesterday. [In *New Society*, 15 May 1987]

DAVID THOMSON 1914–1988

9 The vice of meanness, condemned in every other country, is in Scotland translated into a virtue called 'thrift'. [*Nairn in Darkness and Light*, p. 70]

10 Even stroking a cat may be regarded by strict Presbyterians as a carnal sin. [185]

ROY THOMSON [later LORD THOMSON OF FLEET] 1894–1976

11 A stake in commercial television is the equivalent of having a licence to print money. [On the profit in commercial TV in Britain, Aug. 1957. In R. Braddon, *Roy Thomson*, Ch. 32]

JEREMY THORPE 1929–

12 Greater love hath no man than this, that he lay down his friends for his life. [Of Macmillan's swingeing Cabinet reshuffle on 13 July 1962. In Bernard Levin, *The Pendulum Years*, Ch. 12]

ROSE H. THORPE 1850–1939

13 As she climbed the dusty ladder on which fell no ray of light, – / Up and up, her white lips saying, 'Curfew shall not ring to-night.' [*Curfew Must Not Ring Tonight*]

JAMES THURBER 1894–1961

14 'I think this calls for a drink' has long been one of our national slogans. [*Alarms and Diversions*, 'Merry Christmas']

15 'Poe,' I said, 'was perhaps the first great nonstop literary drinker of the American nineteenth century. He made the indulgences of Coleridge and De Quincey seem like a bit of mischief in the kitchen with the cooking sherry.' ['The Moribundant Life . . .']

16 I was seized by the stern hand of Compulsion, that dark, unseasonable Urge that impels women to clean house in the middle of the night. ['There's a Time for Flags']

17 She developed a persistent troubled frown which gave her the expression of

someone who is trying to repair a watch with his gloves on. [*The Beast in Me and Other Animals*, 'Look Homeward, Jeannie']

1 All right, have it your way – you heard a seal bark. [Cartoon caption]

2 That's my first wife up there, and this is the present Mrs Harris.

3 Grandog. [*The Dogs*, Preface]

4 Early to rise and early to bed makes a male healthy and wealthy and dead. [*Fables for Our Time*, 'The Shrike and the Chipmunks']

5 You might as well fall flat on your face as lean over too far backward. ['The Bear Who Let It Alone']

6 You can fool too many of the people too much of the time. ['The Owl Who Was God']

7 It is better to have loafed and lost than never to have loafed at all. ['The Courtship of Arthur and Al']

8 Though statisticians in our time have never kept the score, Man wants a great deal here below and Woman even more. [*Further Fables for Our Time*, 'The Godfather and His Godchild']

9 Ashes to ashes, and clay to clay, if the enemy doesn't get you your own folks may. ['The Peacelike Mongoose']

10 No man ... who has wrestled with a self-adjusting card table can ever quite be the man he once was. [*Let Your Mind Alone*, 'Sex *ex* Machina']

11 He was chewing on a splinter of wood and watching the moon come up lazily out of the old cemetery in which nine of his daughters were lying, and only two of them were dead. ['Bateman Comes Home']

12 It's a naïve domestic Burgundy without any breeding, but I think you'll be amused by its presumption. [*Men, Women and Dogs*, cartoon caption]

13 You wait here and I'll bring the etchings down.

14 I said the hounds of Spring are on Winter's traces – but let it pass, let it pass!

15 Well, if I called the wrong number, why did you answer the phone?

16 Laissez faire and let laissez faire is what I believe in.

17 I say she used to be no better than she ought to be, but she is now.

18 The War between Men and Women. [Cartoon sequence]

19 I myself have accomplished nothing of excellence except a remarkable and, to some of my friends, unaccountable expertness in hitting empty ginger ale bottles with small rocks at a distance of thirty paces. [*My Life and Hard Times*, Preface]

20 They [humorists] lead, as a matter of fact, an existence of jumpiness and apprehension. They sit on the edge of the chair of Literature. In the house of Life they have the feeling that they have never taken off their overcoats.

21 I suppose that the high-water mark of my youth in Columbus, Ohio, was the night the bed fell on my father. [Ch. 1]

22 Her own mother lived the latter years of her life in the horrible suspicion that electricity was dripping invisibly all over the house. [2]

23 When the dam broke, or, to be more exact, when everybody in town *thought* that the dam broke. [3]

24 The ghost that got into our house on the night of November 17, 1915, raised such a hullabaloo of misunderstandings that I am sorry I didn't just let it keep on walking, and go to bed. [4]

25 Q: We have cats the way most people have mice. [Signed] Mrs C. L. FOOTLOOSE
A: I see you have. I can't tell from your communication whether you wish advice or are just boasting. [*The Owl in the Attic*]

26 Why don't you get dressed, then, and go to pieces like a man? [*The Seal in the Bedroom*, cartoon caption]

27 'We all have flaws,' he said, 'and mine is being wicked.' [*The 13 Clocks*, Ch. 8]

28 If he knew where he was going, it is not apparent from this distance. He fell down a great deal during this period, because of a trick he had of walking into himself. [On himself as a child. *The Thurber Carnival*, Preface]

29 There is, of course, a certain amount of drudgery in newspaper work, just as there is

'n teaching classes, tunnelling into a bank, or being President of the United States. I suppose that even the most pleasurable of imaginable occupations, that of batting baseballs through the windows of the RCA Building, would pall a little as the days ran on. ['Memoirs of a Drudge']

1 Humour ... is emotional chaos remembered in tranquillity. [In the New York Post, 29 Feb. 1960]

2 We are an ideal couple and have not had a harsh word in the seven weeks of our married life. [Letter to Herman and Dorothy Miller, Aug. 1935, Selected Letters from J.T., ed. Helen Thurber and Edward Weeks]

3 He [Henry James] would have been most unhappy now, I'm sure, in an age when the male sometimes doesn't even take off his hat, or the woman her overcoat. (In bed, of course, I mean.) [Letter to Herman and Dorothy Miller, Oct. 1936]

4 Humour is counterbalance. Laughter need not be cut out of anything, since it improves anything. The power that created the poodle, the platypus and people has an integrated sense of both comedy and tragedy. [Letter to Frances Glennon, June 1959]

5 The old cliché 'the dignity of man' is proved only in the breach. It is only when he falls down that we appreciate how straight he can stand.

6 I loathe the expression 'What makes him tick'. It is the American mind, looking for simple and singular solution, that uses the foolish expression. A person not only ticks, he also chimes and strikes the hour, falls and breaks and has to be put together again, and sometimes stops like an electric clock in a thunderstorm. [PS]

7 'You are all a lost generation,' Gertrude Stein said to Hemingway. We weren't lost. Knew where we were, all right, but we wouldn't go home. Ours was the generation that stayed up all night. Indeed we spent so little time in bed most of us had only one child. [PPS. See also 357:17]

8 You are constantly distracted by the sight of the flowers and the buds bursting. I can sit here and I don't get distracted by flying birds or the sight of a pretty girl going by. Of course ... I can still hear a pretty girl go by. [On the advantages of blindness to a writer. In Alistair Cooke, Talk about America, Ch. 15]

9 [When asked his opinion of a play] It had only one fault. It was kind of lousy. [In P. G. Wodehouse, Performing Flea, 1947–52]

10 She said he proposed something on their wedding night her own brother wouldn't have suggested. [In Kiss Me Hardy, ed. Roger Kilroy, 'Family Circle']

11 God bless ... God damn! [Last words, quoted by Paul Theroux in the Sunday Times, 31 Jan. 1982, who comments, 'As a judgement on the world it is very nearly perfect.']

See also under HUNT, STAN

THWACKHURST

12 'You have ruined all the graffiti. You can't find anything in a piss-house now but political remarks ... And just when the spread of popular education was bringing the graffiti lower on the walls.' 'Lower on the walls?' 'Sure. Don't you see the little children were beginning to add their quota, when all this damn politics comes along.' [In O. St John Gogarty, As I Was Going Down Sackville Street, Ch. 4]

BARON THYSSEN 1927–

13 Collecting is an activity that is not quite normal. There are no logical reasons you do it. They can come later. [In the Independent, 'Quote Unquote', 15 Oct. 1988]

TIANANMEN DECLARATION

14 What we need is not a perfect saviour but a perfect democratic system ... Rather ten devils to check each other than one mandarin with absolute power. [Issued in Tiananmen Square, Beijing, 2 June 1989, by Liu Xiaobo, Zhou Duo, Hou Dejian and Gao Xin]

COL. PAUL W. TIBBETTS [Pilot of Enola Gay] 1915–

15 A mushroom of boiling dust up to 20,000 feet. [Description of Hiroshima explosion, 6 Aug. 1945]

PAUL TILLICH 1886–1965

1 Neurosis is the way of avoiding non-being by avoiding being. [*The Courage to Be*, Pt 2, Ch. 7]

2 Faith is the state of being ultimately concerned. [*Dynamics of Faith*, Ch. 1]

3 Life could not continue without throwing the past into the past, liberating the present from its burden. [*The Eternal Now*, Pt II, Ch. 1]

4 You must forget everything traditional that you have learned about God, perhaps even the word itself. [*The Shaking of the Foundations*, 'The Depth of Existence']

5 Boredom is rage spread thin. [In *Barnes and Noble Book of Quotations*, ed. Robert I. Fitzhenry, 'Bores']

HARRY TILZER [ALBERT VON TILZER] 1878–1956

6 Come, Come, Come and have a drink with me / Down at the old 'Bull and Bush'. [Song: *Down at the Old Bull and Bush*, sung by Florrie Forde]

THE TIMES

7 In my childhood it was said by all: 'A child of ten can go on the road of a town playing with a golden ball in perfect safety under British rule.' [In *The Times*]

8 Good prose is the selection of the best words; poetry is the best words in the best order; and journalese is any old words in any old order. [Quoted by Adam Brewer in letter to paper, 21 Aug. 1987]

PETER TINNISWOOD 1936–

9 It is a fact not generally known that in her youth Queen Victoria had the makings of a cricketer of considerable stature. [*Tales from a Long Room*, p. 19]

10 Nine children! No wonder she had such trouble with her run-up. [25]

CHARLES TOBIAS *see* LEW BROWN, CHARLES TOBIAS and SAM H. STEPT

JUDITH TODD

11 My father [Sir Garfield Todd] taught me a long time ago that you just keep throwing your bread upon the water, and if you're lucky it will come back as ham sandwiches. [Interview in the *Sunday Times Magazine*, 21 Jan. 1990]

ALIVIN TOFFLER 1928–

12 Future Shock. [Title of book, derived from term 'Culture Shock']

PALMIRO TOGLIATTI 1893–1964

13 The experience accomplished in the building of a socialist society in the Soviet Union cannot contain instructions for resolving all the questions which may present themselves to us and to Communists in other countries ... There is established ... a polycentric system. [Speech to the Central Committee of Italian Communist Party, 24 June 1956]

J. R. R. TOLKIEN 1892–1973

14 In a hole in the ground there lived a hobbit. [*The Hobbit*, Ch. 1]

15 One Ring to rule them all, One Ring to find them, / One Ring to bring them all and in the darkness bind them. [*The Lord of the Rings*, Pt I: *The Fellowship of the Ring*, Ch. 2]

16 The night was tailing against the morning of which it was bereaved, and the cold was cursing the warmth for which it hungered. [8]

17 The stories [*The Lord of the Rings*] were made rather to provide a world for the languages than the reverse. To me a name comes first and the story follows. [Letter. In the *Observer*, 23 Aug. 1981]

18 My political opinions lean more and more to anarchy. The most improper job of any man, even saints, is bossing other men. There is only one bright spot and that is the growing habit of disgruntled men of dynamiting factories and power stations. I hope that, encouraged now as patriotism, may remain a habit. [Letter to his son Christopher (in the RAF), *Letters of J.R.R.T.*, ed. Humphrey Carpenter. In the *Guardian*, 20 Aug. 1982]

TATAYANA TOLSTAYA 1951–

1 Russia is an enormous lunatic asylum. There is a heavy padlock on the door, but there are no walls. [In the *Guardian*, 19 Mar. 1992]

LEO TOLSTOY 1828–1910

2 Historians are like deaf people who go on answering questions that no one has asked them. [In Manning Clark, *A Discovery of Australia*, 'Being an Historian']

3 How do peasants die? [Deathbed words, attr. in Kenneth Clark, *Civilization*, Ch. 13]

NICHOLAS TOMALIN 1931–1973

4 *Tout comprendre, c'est tout pardonner*, and *tout pardonner* makes very dull copy. [Quoted by James Cameron on BBC radio, Nov. 1976]

RUDOLPHE TOMASCHEK 1895–?

5 Modern Physics is an instrument of [world] Jewry for the destruction of Nordic science ... True physics is the creation of the German spirit. [In W. L. Shirer, *The Rise and Fall of the Third Reich*, Ch. 8]

CALVIN TOMKINS 1925–

6 Living Well is the Best Revenge. [Title of book, 1971, quoting old Spanish proverb]

LILY TOMLIN 1939–

7 If truth is beauty, how come no one has their hair done in the library? [In *Was It Good for You Too?* ed. Bob Chieger]

8 If sex is so personal, why are we expected to share it with someone else?

9 We're all in this together by ourselves. [In *Hammer and Tongues*, ed. Michèle Brown and Ann O'Connor, 'Life']

10 If love is the answer, could you rephrase the question? [In Barbara Rowes, *Book of Quotes*]

CHARLES TOMLINSON 1927–

11 Everything we see / Teaches the time that we are living in. [*Poem for My Father*]

H. M. TOMLINSON 1873–1958

12 I will never believe again that the sea was ever loved by anyone whose life was married to it. [*The Sea and the Jungle*, Ch. 1]

JOHN KENNEDY TOOLE 1937–1969

13 Mother doesn't cook ... she burns. [*A Confederacy of Dunces*, I. 3]

14 Her logic was a combination of half-truths and clichés, her worldview a compound of misconceptions deriving from a history of our nation as written from the perspective of a subway tunnel. [V. 3]

15 The human desire for food and sex is relatively equal. If there are armed rapes why should there not be armed hot dog thefts? [VII. 1]

16 You can always tell employees of the government by the total vacancy which occupies the space where most other people have faces. [IX. 1]

GENERAL OMAR TORRIJOS HERRERA

17 When you find grass uncut in a village cemetery you know it is a bad village. If they don't look after the dead, they won't look after the living. [In Graham Greene, *Getting to Know the General*]

PAUL TORTELIER 1914–1990

18 If I died tomorrow, I wouldn't be afraid to meet the composer. [Of his special affection for playing Tchaikovsky's Rococo Variations. In obituary in the *Guardian*, 19 Dec. 1990]

ARTURO TOSCANINI 1867–1957

19 After I die, I shall return to earth as the doorkeeper of a bordello and I won't let a one of you in. [To his orchestra at rehearsal. In N. Lebrecht, *Discord*]

20 For Strauss the composer I take off my hat. For Strauss the man I put it on again. [In Antony Storr, *The School of Genius*]

MICHEL TOURNIER 1924–

21 Nakedness is a luxury in which a man may only indulge without peril to himself when he is warmly surrounded by the multitude of his fellows. [*Friday or the Other Island*, Ch. 2]

F. H. TOWNSEND

1 O Cuckoo, shall I call thee bird, / Or but a wandering voice? / State the alternative preferred / And reasons for your choice. [Parody of Wordsworth's *To the Cuckoo*]

PETE TOWNSHEND 1945–

2 I hope I die before I get old. [Song: *My Generation*]

3 I was born with a plastic spoon in my mouth. [Song: *Substitute*]

ARNOLD TOYNBEE 1889–1975

4 America is a large, friendly dog in a very small room. Every time it wags its tail it knocks over a chair. [Broadcast news summary, 14 July 1954]

5 The human race's prospects of survival were considerably better when we were defenceless against tigers than they are today when we have become defenceless against ourselves. [In the *Observer*, 'Sayings of the Year,' 1963]

PHILIP TOYNBEE 1916–1981

6 I have seen the future and it does not work. [Of the USA. In the *Observer*, 27 Jan. 1974. See also 64:3, 357:2]

7 He [John Middleton Murry] was the type of man who is always trying to live beyond his moral means. [In the *Observer*, 12 Jan. 1975]

SPENCER TRACY 1900–1967

8 There were times my pants were so thin I could sit on a dime and tell if it was heads or tails. [Of his early struggles. In L. Swindell, *Spencer Tracy*]

BARBARA TRAPIDO 1941–

9 Yeats, William Butler . . . Brother of the more famous Jack, of course. [*Brother of the More Famous Jack*, 4]

10 It was one of those weddings where the bride's and groom's families stand out like opposing football teams, wearing their colours. All the decent hats were, thank God, on our side. [50]

11 Ali . . . could often not purchase a toothbrush without making the act appear eccentric. [*Noah's Ark*, 8]

12 'Poetry is for women, I suppose?' she said. 'Created by men with women in mind? Like Crimplene.' [25]

BEN TRAVERS 1886–1980

13 I think about death a great deal – almost all the time, but then anyone of my age [93] would. Each morning you open your eyes and you think, what again? [In the *Sunday Times Magazine*, 10 Aug. 1980]

14 This is where the real fun starts. [Suggested epitaph. In the *Listener*, 31 Dec. 1981]

MERLE TRAVIS 1917–1983

15 Some people say a man is made out of mud, A poor man's made out of muscle and blood. / Muscle and blood and skin and bone / A mind that's weak and a back that's strong. . . . I owe my soul to the company store. [Song: *Sixteen Tons*, 1947, sung by Tennessee Ernie]

SIR HERBERT BEERBOHM TREE 1853–1917

16 FELLOW-MEMBER [after a scene at the Garrick Club]: When I joined all the members were gentlemen.
TREE: I wonder why they left. [In Hesketh Pearson, *Beerbohm Tree*, Ch. 5]

17 The only man who wasn't spoilt by being lionized was Daniel. [In 12]

18 A whipper-snapper of criticism who quoted dead languages to hide his ignorance of life. [Of A. B. Walkley]

19 She has kissed her way into society. I don't like her. But don't misunderstand me: my dislike is purely platonic. [Of an actress who was better as a lover than on the stage]

20 My poor fellow, why not carry a watch? [To a man who was staggering in the street under the weight of a grandfather clock]

21 Sirs, I have tested your machine. It adds a new terror to life and makes death a long-felt want. [To a gramophone company who asked for a testimonial. [In 19]

1 God is a sort of burglar. As a young man you knock him down; as an old man you try to conciliate him, because he may knock you down. [In 21]

2 His face shining like Moses, his teeth like the Ten Commandments, all broken. [Of Israel Zangwill]

3 He is an old bore; even the grave yawns for him.

4 Ladies, just a little more virginity, if you don't mind. [To a 'collection of damsels that had been dragged into the theatre as ladies in waiting to the queen' in his production of *Henry VIII*. In Alexander Woollcott, *Shouts and Murmurs*, 'Capsule Criticism']

HERBERT TRENCH 1865–1923

5 O dreamy, gloomy, friendly trees. [*O Dreamy, Gloomy, Friendly Trees*]

6 Come, let us make love deathless, thou and I. [*To Arolilia*, 2]

G. M. TREVELYAN 1876–1962

7 Education . . . has produced a vast population able to read but unable to distinguish what is worth reading. [*English Social History*, Ch. 18]

8 Walpole . . . even when Prime Minister was said to open his gamekeeper's letters first of the batch. [*History of England*, Bk V, Ch. 2]

9 Nelson, born in a fortunate hour for himself and for his country, was always in his element and always on his element. [5]

10 The poetry of history lies in the quasi-miraculous fact that once, on this earth, on this familiar spot of earth, walked other men and women as actual as we are today, thinking their own thoughts, swayed by their own passions but now all gone, vanishing one after another, gone as utterly as we ourselves shall be gone like ghosts at cock-crow. [In the *Guardian*, 26 Sept. 1991]

HUGH TREVOR-ROPER [LORD DACRE] 1914–

11 [James I] remained an omniscient umpire whom no one consulted. [*Archbishop Laud*]

LIONEL TRILLING 1905–1975

12 We are all ill: but even a universal sickness implies an idea of health. [*The Liberal Imagination*, 'Art and Neurosis']

13 It would seem that Americans have a kind of resistance to looking closely at society. ['Manners, Morals and the Novel']

14 We who are liberal and progressive know that the poor are our equals in every sense except that of being equal to us. ['Princess Casamassima']

TOMMY TRINDER 1909–1989

15 You lucky people! [Catchphrase used in variety and radio comedy act]

16 They're overpaid, overfed, oversexed and over here. [Of the GIs. Attr. by Alan Brien in the *Sunday Times*, 4 Jan. 1976]

LEON TROTSKY 1874–1940

17 Revolution by its very nature is sometimes compelled to take in more territory than it is capable of holding. Retreats are possible – when there is territory to retreat from. [*Diary in Exile*, 15 Feb. 1935]

18 Old age is the most unexpected of all the things that happen to a man.

19 The vengeance of history is more terrible than the vengeance of the most powerful Secretary General. [*Final Testament* (written 10 days before his murder)]

20 The 23rd of February was International Woman's Day . . . It had not occurred to anyone that it might become the first day of the revolution. [*History of the Russian Revolution*, Pt 1, Ch. 7]

21 The revolution does not choose its paths: it made its first steps towards victory under the belly of a Cossack's horse.

22 The English and French bourgeoisie created a new society after their own image. The Germans came later, and they were compelled to live for a long time on the pale gruel of philosophy. [10]

23 Revolutions are always verbose. [II. 12]

24 Civilization has made the peasantry its pack animal. [III. 1]

25 In practice a reformist party considers

unshakable the foundations of that which it intends to reform. [5]

1 Insurrection is an art, and like all arts it has its laws. [6]

2 There is a limit to the application of democratic methods. You can inquire of all the passengers as to what type of car they like to ride in, but it is impossible to question them as to whether to apply the brakes when the train is at full speed and accident threatens.

3 From being a patriotic myth, the Russian people have become an awful reality. [7]

4 Armed insurrection stands in the same relation to revolution that revolution as a whole does to evolution. It is the critical point when accumulating quantity turns with an explosion into quality. [9]

5 For us, the tasks of education in socialism were closely integrated with those of fighting. Ideas that enter the mind under fire remain there securely and for ever. [*My Life*, Ch. 35]

6 It was the supreme expression of the mediocrity of the apparatus that Stalin himself rose to his position. [40]

7 We only die when we fail to take root in others. [In Trevor Griffiths, *The Party*, Act II]

8 Patriotism to the Soviet State is a revolutionary duty, whereas patriotism to a bourgeois state is treachery. [Epigraph to Fitzroy Maclean, *Disputed Barricade*, Pt 1]

9 The end may justify the means as long as there is something that justifies the end. [In A. Pozzolini, *Antonio Gramsci: An Introduction to His Thought*, Preface]

10 I myself took this job [Commissar for Foreign Relations] so I would have more time for Party work. All there is to do is to publish the secret treaties. Then I will close the shop. [In A. Ulam, *Expansion and Coexistence*]

11 An ally has to be watched just like an enemy.

FRANÇOIS TRUFFAUT 1932–1984

12 I've always had the impression that real militants are like cleaning women, doing a thankless, daily but necessary job. But you,

you're the Ursula Andress of militancy, you make a brief appearance, just enough time for the cameras to flash, you make two or three startling remarks and then you disappear again, trailing clouds of self-serving mystery. [Letter to Jean-Luc Godard, May–June 1973]

PRESIDENT HARRY TRUMAN
1884–1972

13 The buck stops here. [Notice on his presidential desk]

14 If we see that Germany is winning the war we ought to help Russia, and if Russia is winning we ought to help Germany, and in that way let them kill as many as possible. [In *The New York Times*, 24 July 1941, the day the Nazis invaded Russia]

15 An eight-ulcer man on a four-ulcer job, and all four ulcers working. [Letter to the *Washington Post* on unflattering reviewer of his daughter's song recital, 5 Dec. 1950. The remark was originally made by Stephen Early in a letter to Truman; see 114:1]

16 I have found the best way to give advice to your children is to find out what they want and then advise them to do it. [Interview with Margaret Truman in TV programme *Person to Person*, 27 May 1955]

17 It's a recession when your neighbour loses his job; it's a depression when you lose your own. [In the *Observer*, 'Sayings of the Week', 6 Apr. 1958]

18 A politician is a man who understands government, and it takes a politician to run a government. A statesman is a politician who's been dead ten or fifteen years. [Impromptu speech to Reciprocity Club, Washington, 11 Apr.]

19 You don't set a fox to watching the chickens just because he has a lot of experience in the hen house. [On Vice-President Nixon's candidacy for the presidency. Speech, 30 Oct. 1960]

20 I didn't fire him [General MacArthur] because he was a dumb son of a bitch, although he was, but that's not against the law for generals. If it was, half to three-

quarters of them would be in gaol. [Interview. In Merle Miller, *Plain Speaking*, 24]

1 I sit here all day trying to persuade people to do the things they ought to have sense enough to do without my persuading them ... That's all the powers of the President amount to. [In R. E. Neustadt, *Presidential Power*]

2 What's a statesman anyway? I'll tell you what he is – he's just a politician no one is afraid of any more. [In the *Observer*, 11 May 1986]

3 I was in search of a one-armed economist so that the guy could never make a statement and then say 'on the other hand ...' [In *Time* magazine, 30 Jan. 1989]

4 'Sartor Resartus' is simply unreadable, and for me that always sort of spoils a book. [In *Barnes and Noble Book of Quotations*, ed. Robert I. Fitzhenry, 'Books']

MARINA TSVETAYEVA 1892–1941

5 I have two enemies in all the world, / two twins inseparably fused: / the hunger of the hungry and the fullness of the full. [*If the soul were born with pinions*, trans. Elaine Feinstein]

6 I ask around all Paris, for it's / only in stories or pictures / that people rise to the skies: / where is your soul gone, where? [*Epigraph*]

7 The poet from afar has taken speech, / Speech takes the poet far. A poet's speech begins a great way off. / A poet is carried away by speech. [*The Poet*]

BARBARA W. TUCHMAN 1912–1989

8 Dead battles, like dead generals, hold the military mind in their dead grip. [*The Guns of August*, Ch. 2]

9 No more distressing moment can ever face a British government than that which requires it to come to a hard and fast and specific decision. [Of Aug. 1914. 9]

SOPHIE TUCKER ?1884–1966

10 I'm the last of the red-hot mommas. [Title of song, written by Jack Yellen, which became her sobriquet]

11 Life begins at forty. [Title of song, written by Jack Yellen]

ROY TURK 1892–1934, FRED AHLERT 1892–1952, and HARRY RICHMAN 1895–1972

12 Walking My Baby Back Home. [Title of song, 1930, in show *Navy Blues*]

W. J. TURNER 1889–1946

13 When I was but thirteen or so / I went into a golden land, / Chimborazo, Cotopaxi / Took me by the hand. [*Romance*]

BISHOP DESMOND TUTU 1931–

14 When the missionaries first came to Africa they had the Bible and we had the land. They said 'let us pray'. We closed our eyes. When we opened them, we had the Bible and they had the land. [In the *Observer*, 'Sayings of the Week', 16 Dec. 1984]

JULIAN TUWIM 1894–1954

15 There are two kinds of blood, the blood that flows in the veins and the blood that flows out of them. [*We, the Polish Jews*]

MARK TWAIN [S. L. CLEMENS] 1835–1910

16 There was things which he stretched, but mainly he told the truth. [*The Adventures of Huckleberry Finn*, Ch. 1]

17 *Pilgrim's Progress*, about a man who left his family, it didn't say why. The statements was interesting, but tough. [17]

18 All kings is mostly rapscallions. [23]

19 There are three kinds of lies – lies damned lies and statistics. [Quoting Benjamin Disraeli, in *Autobiography*, Pt V, Ch. 1. Often wrongly attr. to Twain]

20 If there was two birds sitting on a fence, he would bet you which one would fly first. [*The Celebrated Jumping Frog*]

21 Soap and education are not as sudden as a massacre, but they are more deadly in the long run. [*The Facts Concerning the Recent Resignation*]

22 Truth is the most valuable thing we have. Let us economize it. [*Following the Equator*, Ch. 7. See also 14:6, 209:1]

23 I admire him [Cecil Rhodes], I frankly

confess it; and when his time comes I shall buy a piece of the rope for a keepsake.

1 It is by the goodness of God that in our country we have those three unspeakably precious things: freedom of speech, freedom of conscience, and the prudence never to practise either of them. [20]

2 They spell it Vinci and pronounce it Vinchy; foreigners always spell better than they pronounce. [*Innocents Abroad*, Ch. 19]

3 Guides cannot master the subtleties of the American joke.

4 Lump the whole thing! Say that the Creator made Italy from designs by Michael Angelo! [27]

5 Are you going to hang him *anyhow* – and try him afterward? [*Innocents at Home*, Ch. 5]

6 When I'm playful I use the meridians and parallels of latitude for a seine, and drag the Atlantic Ocean for whales! I scratch my head with the lightning and purr myself to sleep with the thunder! [*Life on the Mississippi*, Ch. 3]

7 All the modern inconveniences. [43]

8 At bottom he [Carlyle] was probably fond of them [the Americans], but he was always able to conceal it. [*My First Lie*]

9 What a good thing Adam had. When he said a good thing he knew nobody had said it before. [*Notebooks*, p. 67]

10 Familiarity breeds contempt – and children. [237]

11 An experienced, industrious, ambitious, and often quite picturesque liar. [*Private History of a Campaign That Failed*]

12 Cauliflower is nothing but cabbage with a college education. [*Pudd'nhead Wilson*, Ch. 5, epigraph]

13 All say, 'How hard it is to die' – a strange complaint to come from the mouths of people who have had to live. [10]

14 It is difference of opinion that makes horse races. [19]

15 They make a mouth at you and say thank you 'most to death, but there ain't-a-going to *be* no core. [*Tom Sawyer Abroad*, Ch. 1]

16 The cross of the Legion of Honour has been conferred upon me. However, few escape that distinction. [*A Tramp Abroad*, Ch. 8]

17 Some of his words were not Sunday-school words. [20]

18 This poor little one-horse town. [*The Undertaker's Chat*]

19 There was worlds of reputation in it, but no money. [*A Yankee at the Court of King Arthur*, Ch. 9]

20 A classic is something that everybody wants to have read and nobody wants to read. [Speech 'The Disappearance of Literature']

21 The report of my death is exaggerated. [Cable from London to the Associated Press, 1897. Slightly varying versions exist]

'TWEETY-PIE'

22 I t'ought I saw a puddy-tat ... [Catchphrase in the 'Sylvester and Tweety-Pie' cartoon series]

KENNETH TYNAN 1927–1980

23 William Congreve is the only sophisticated playwright England has produced; and like Shaw, Sheridan and Wilde, his nearest rivals, he was brought up in Ireland. [*Curtains*, 1, 'The Way of the World']

24 Forty years ago he [Noël Coward] was Slightly in *Peter Pan*, and you might say he has been wholly in *Peter Pan* ever since. ['A Tribute to Mr Coward']

25 A special virtue attaches to plays which remind the drama of how much it can do without and still exist. By all the known criteria, Samuel Beckett's 'Waiting for Godot' is a dramatic vacuum. Pity the critic who seeks a chink in its armour, for it is all chink. ['Waiting for Godot']

26 A novel is a static thing that one moves through; a play is a dynamic thing that moves past one. ['Cards of Identity']

27 What, when drunk, one sees in other women, one sees in Garbo sober. [2, 'Garbo']

28 If his [Noël Coward's] face suggested an old boot, it was unquestionably hand-made. [*The Sound of Two Hands Clapping*, 'In Memory of Mr Coward']

1 A good drama critic is one who perceives what is happening in the theatre of his time. A great drama critic also perceives what is not happening. [*Tynan Right and Left*, Foreword]

2 A critic is a man who knows the way but can't drive the car. [In *The New York Times Magazine*, 9 Jan. 1966]

3 Something between bland and grandiose: blandiose perhaps. [Of Ralph Richardson's voice. In the *Observer Magazine*, 'Tynan on Richardson', 18 Dec. 1977]

4 Of whom it might be said her soul is showing. [Of Peggy Ashcroft. In the *Observer* on her 80th birthday, 20 Dec. 1987]

GEORGE TYRRELL 1861–1909

5 That's this country [Ireland] all over! Not content with a contradiction in terms, it must go on to an antithesis in ideas. 'Temperance Hotel'! You might as well speak of a celibate kip [brothel]! [In O. St John Gogarty, *As I Was Going Down Sackville Street*, Ch. 25]

U

SAJI UMALATOVA 1953–

1 You [President Gorbachev] have listened to the applause of the West and forgotten whose president you are. [Speech at Congress of People's Deputies, Moscow. In the *Guardian*, 18 Dec. 1990]

MIGUEL DE UNAMUNO 1864–1937

2 *La vida es duda, / y la fe sin la duda es sólo muerte.* – Life is doubt, and faith without doubt is nothing but death. [*Poesías*, 1907]

3 Selfish old age is nothing more than childhood in which there is awareness of death. [*Abel Sanchez*, Ch. 38]

4 And killing time is perhaps the essence of comedy, just as the essence of tragedy is killing eternity. [*San Manuel Bueno*, Prologue]

5 It is not usually our ideas that make us optimists or pessimists, but it is our optimism or pessimism, of physiological or pathological origin . . . that makes our ideas. [*The Tragic Sense of Life*, Ch. 1]

6 My work . . . is to shatter the faith of men here, there and everywhere, faith in affirmation, faith in negation, and faith in abstention from faith, and this for the sake of faith in faith itself. [Conclusion]

7 May God deny you peace but give you glory! [Closing words]

8 They [the Franco rebels] will conquer, but they will not convince. [Said at the end of his life]

UNESCO

9 Since wars begin in the minds of men, it is in the minds of men that the defence of peace must be constructed. [Constitution, adopted 16 Nov. 1945, Preamble. Both Clement Attlee and Archibald Macleish, chairman of US delegation to 1945 conference, credited with authorship; see *Respectfully Quoted*, ed. Suzy Platt]

JOHN UPDIKE 1932–

10 A healthy male adult bore consumes each year one and a half times his own weight in other people's patience. [*Assorted Prose*, 'Confessions of a Wild Bore']

11 The founding fathers in their wisdom decided that children were an unnatural strain on parents. So they provided jails called schools, equipped with tortures called education. School is where you go between when your parents can't take you and industry can't take you. [*The Centaur*, Ch. 4]

12 In general the churches, visited by me too often on weekdays . . . bore for me the same relation to God that billboards did to Coca-Cola: they promoted thirst without quenching it. [*A Month of Sundays*, Ch. 2]

13 Americans have been conditioned to respect newness, whatever it costs them. [18]

14 Donald is considerably to the right of our Lord and Saviour Jesus Christ!

15 It is hard, of course, to console or advise professional consolers and advisers; rote phrases, professional sympathy, even an emphatic patience are brusquely shunted aside.

At a convention of masseurs no one turns his back. [25]

1 Everybody who tells you how to act has whisky on their breath. [*Rabbit, Run*]

2 The difficulty with humorists is that they will mix what they believe with what they don't; whichever seems likelier to win an effect.

3 Celebrity is a mask that eats into the face. [In the *Independent*, 'Quote Unquote', 11 Mar. 1989]

RALPH R. UPTON

4 Stop; look; listen. [Notice devised in 1912 for American railway crossings. See also 320:8]

RICHARD USBORNE 1910–

5 A monstrous aunt can be funny. A monstrous mother would be tragic. [*Wodehouse at Work to the End*, Ch. 2]

6 Lovely Pamela, who found / One sure way to get around / Goes to bed beneath this stone / Early, sober, and alone. [*Epitaph on a Party Girl*]

7 Definition of a slogan: a form of words for which memorability has been *bought*. [In letter to editors, 1964]

SIR PETER USTINOV 1921–

8 I was irrevocably betrothed to laughter, the sound of which has always seemed to me the most civilized music in the world. [*Dear Me*, Ch. 3]

9 I do not believe that friends are necessarily the people you like best, they are merely the people who got there first. [5]

10 I sometimes wished he [his father] would realize that he was poor instead of being that most nerve-racking of phenomena, a rich man without money. [6]

11 Thanks to the movies, gunfire has always sounded unreal to me, even when being fired at. [7]

12 I am an optimist, unrepentant and militant. After all, in order not to be a fool an optimist must know how sad a place the world can be. It is only the pessimist who finds this out anew every day. [9]

13 Revolutions have never succeeded unless the establishment does three-quarters of the work. [15]

14 I can take no allegiance to a flag if I don't know who's holding it. [16]

15 I believe that the Jews have made a contribution to the human condition out of all proportion to their numbers: I believe them to be an immense people. Not only have they supplied the world with two leaders of the stature of Jesus Christ and Karl Marx, but they have even indulged in the luxury of following neither one nor the other.

16 In my day, there were things that were done, and things that were not done, and there was even a way of doing things that were not done. [Quoting *Photo Finish*, in 17]

17 Once we are destined to live out our lives in the prison of our mind, our one duty is to furnish it well. [In 20]

18 I prefer our military past. The harm's done and there it is. As for being a General, well at the age of four with paper hats and wooden swords we're all Generals. Only some of us never grow out of it. [*Romanoff and Juliet*, Act I]

19 A diplomat these days is nothing but a head-waiter who's allowed to sit down occasionally.

20 This is a free country, madam. We have a right to share your privacy in a public place.

21 Sometimes I wish I could fall in love. Then at least you know who your opponent is! [II]

22 Laughter would be bereaved if snobbery died. [In the *Observer*, 'Sayings of the Week', 13 Mar. 1955]

23 If Botticelli were alive today he'd be working for *Vogue*. [21 Oct. 1962]

24 The difference between an ordinary democracy and a people's democracy is that in a people's democracy opinion cannot be freely expressed and therefore goes unheeded, whereas in an ordinary democracy like those in the West, opinion can be freely expressed and therefore goes unheeded. [Rectorial address, University of Dundee, 17 Oct. 1968]

1 I kept wishing he [Laurence Olivier] would put on a false nose and be himself again. [In the *Sunday Times Books*, 16 July 1989]

V

HORACE ANNESLEY-VACHELL
1861-1955

1 In nature there are no rewards or punishments; there are consequences. [*The Face of Clay*, Ch. 10]

LUDVÍK VACULÍK 1926–

2 Truth is not victorious; truth is simply what is left when everything else has gone to pot. [*A Cup of Coffee with my Interrogator*. Quoted by W. L. Webb in the *Guardian*, 6 Nov. 1987]

ROGER VADIM 1928–

3 She [Brigitte Bardot] was the type of flower that one waters but does not cut. [From *Bardot, Deneuve and Fonda*, in the *Sunday Times*, 6 Apr. 1986]

AMANDA VAIL 1921-1966

4 Sometimes I think if there was a third sex men wouldn't get so much as a glance from me. [*Love Me Little*, Ch. 6]

5 We talked a lot about life. There was nothing else to talk about. [8]

6 'Parents are strange,' Amy said, 'for their age.' [10]

7 'American girls do have regrets,' Amy said 'That is what distinguishes them from French girls.'

PAUL VALÉRY 1871-1945

8 Talent without genius comes to little. Genius without talent is *nothing*. [*At Moments*, 'The Beautiful is Negative']

9 The poet is the most defenceless of all beings – for the good reason that he is always walking on his hands. [*Bad Thoughts and Not So Bad*, B]

10 Cognition reigns but does not rule. [D]

11 A serious man has few ideas. A man of many ideas cannot be serious. [I]

12 Truth is naked; but under the skin lies the anatomy. [M]

13 A man who wishes to impose his opinions on others is unsure of their value. He has to uphold them by all possible means. He adopts a special tone of voice, thumps the table, smiles on some and browbeats others. In short, he borrows from his body the wherewithal to bolster up his mind. [N]

14 The able man is the one who makes mistakes according to the rules. [Q]

15 The painter should not paint what he sees, but what will be seen. [S]

16 God made everything out of nothing. But the nothingness shows through. [T]

17 A poem is never finished, only abandoned. [*Literature*]

18 Of two possible words always choose the lesser. [*Odds and Ends*, 'Advice to the Writer']

19 The great man dies twice; once as a man and once as a great man. ['Notebook B (1910)']

20 A man is more complex, infinitely more so, than his thoughts. [*Odds and Ends*, VII]

21 *Variation on Descartes*: Sometimes I think; and sometimes I *am*. [VIII]

22 Politics is the art of preventing people from minding their own business. [*Rhumbs*]

1 It is wisest to write in 'B-natural'. But many write in 'B-sharp'.

2 In every enthusiast there lurks a false enthusiast; in every lover a feigned lover; in every man of genius a pseudo-genius. [*Suite*, 'Duties']

3 'Thinkers' are people who re-think; who think that what was thought before was never thought *enough*. ['Thinkers']

4 Man is only man at the surface. Remove his skin, dissect, and immediately you come to machinery. [In W. H. Auden, *A Certain World*]

VIVIEN VAN DAMM ?1889–1960

5 We Never Closed. [Slogan of London's Windmill Theatre during 1939–45 War, when he was its manager. *Tonight and Every Night*, Ch. 18]

SIR LAURENS VAN DER POST 1906–

6 Neither Heaven nor Hell are hereafter. Hell is time arrested within and refusing to join in the movement of wind and stars. Heaven is the boulder rock unrolled to let new life out: it is man restored to all four of his seasons rounding for eternity. [*The Seed and the Sower*]

7 'The story is like the wind,' the Bushman prisoner said. 'It comes from a far off place, and we feel it.' [*A Story Like the Wind*]

BARTOLOMEO VANZETTI 1888–1927

8 If it had not been for these things, I might have lived out my life talking at street corners to scorning men. I might have died, unmarked, unknown, a failure. Now we [Sacco and himself] are not a failure. This is our career and our triumph. Never in our full life could we hope to do such work for tolerance, for justice, for man's understanding of man as now we do by accident. Our words – our lives – our pains – nothing! The taking of our lives – lives of a good shoemaker and a poor fish-pedlar – all! That last moment belongs to us – that agony is our triumph. [On receiving the death sentence. Letter to his son, 9 Apr. 1927]

VARIETY [US show-business magazine]

9 Egghead marries hourglass. [On announce-ment of Arthur Miller's marriage to Marilyn Monroe. Quoted by Godfrey Smith in the *Sunday Times*, 11 Nov. 1984]

MICHAEL VAUCAIRE *see under* PIAF, EDITH

MAJOR-GENERAL HARRY VAUGHAN 1893–1981

10 If you don't like the heat, get out of the kitchen. [In *Time* magazine, 28 Apr. 1952. Often quoted by President Truman and wrongly ascr. to him; elsewhere phrase de-scribed as proverbial]

RALPH VAUGHAN WILLIAMS 1872–1958

11 I realize now it [his London Symphony] is not as boring as I thought it was. [Quoted by Sir Adrian Boult in broadcast, 1 Aug. 1965]

12 I don't know whether I like it [his Fourth Symphony], but it is what I meant.

THORSTEIN VEBLEN 1857–1929

13 Safe and sane business management . . . reduces itself in the main to a sagacious use of sabotage. [*The Nature of Peace*, Ch. 7]

14 The outcome of any serious research can only be to make two questions grow where only one grew before. [*The Place of Science in Modern Civilization*]

15 Conspicuous consumption of valuable goods is means of reputability to the gentleman of leisure. [*Theory of the Leisure Class*, Ch. 4]

CARL VAN VECHTEN 1880–1964

16 There are, I have discovered, two kinds of people in this world, those who long to be understood and those who long to be misun-derstood. It is the irony of life that neither is gratified. [*The Blind Bow-boy*]

TOM VERNON 1939–

17 You can stay stupid in a village, but if you take your stupidity to the town, the traffic runs you over. [*Fat Man in the Kitchen*]

DR HENDRIK VERWOERD [Prime Minister of South Africa] 1901–1966

18 We did what God wanted us to do. [In

the *Observer*, 'Sayings of the Week', 26 Mar. 1961]

BORIS VIAN 1920–1959

1 What interests me isn't the happiness of every man, but that of each man. [*Moon Indigo*]

VICKY [VICTOR WEISZ] 1913–1966

2 Introducing Super-Mac. [Caption to cartoon of Macmillan as Superman, *Evening Standard*, 6 Nov. 1958]

GORE VIDAL 1925–

3 When Ronald Reagan's career in show business came to an end, he was hired to impersonate, first a California Governor and then an American President. [*Armageddon*, title essay]

4 Ronnie [Reagan] never stopped talking, even though he never had anything to say except what he had just read in *Reader's Digest*, which he studied the way Jefferson did Montesquieu. ['Ronnie and Nancy']

5 A candidate should not mean but be. [*The Best Man*]

6 A radical theory I had always held but dared not openly formulate: that boredom in the arts can be, under the right circumstances, dull. [*Myra Breckinridge*, Ch. 21]

7 Like all analysts Randolph is interested only in himself. In fact, I have often thought that the analyst should pay the patient for allowing himself to be used as a captive looking-glass. [37]

8 Don't you realize, Dwight, you have nothing to say, only to add? [To Dwight Macdonald. *Two Sisters*]

9 He will lie even when it is inconvenient, the sign of a true artist.

10 American writers want to be not good but great; and so are neither.

11 The astronauts! . . . Rotarians in outer space.

12 Never have children, only grandchildren.

13 John Barth, a perfect U-novelist [university] whose books are written to be taught,

not to be read. [In *Writers at Work*, ed. George Plimpton, Fifth Series]

14 He [Norman Mailer] is now what he wanted to be: the patron saint of bad journalism.

15 INTERVIEWER: Why do you prefer movies to the theatre?

VIDAL: I'm embarrassed by live actors. They're always having a much better time than I am.

16 Whenever a friend succeeds, a little something inside me dies. [In the *Sunday Times Magazine*, 16 Sept. 1973]

17 I'm all for bringing back the birch, but only between consenting adults. [On a David Frost TV programme about corporal punishment. In above]

18 [Commercialism is] doing well that which should not be done at all. [From BBC TV programme *Success Story*, in the *Listener*, 7 Aug. 1975]

19 It is not enough to succeed. Others must fail. [In G. Irvine, *Antipanegyric for Tom Driberg*, 8 Dec. 1976]

20 A triumph of the embalmer's art. [Of Ronald Reagan. In the *Observer*, 26 Apr. 1981]

21 It's a country evenly divided between conservatives and reactionaries. [Of the USA. Interview in the *Observer*, 16 Sept. 1984]

22 I don't think literature is ever finished in any country which has more prizes than it has writers. [In the *Observer*, 'Sayings of the Week', 27 Sept. 1987]

23 I suspect one of the reasons we create fiction is to make sex exciting. [In *The Times Literary Supplement*, 2 Oct.]

24 Different cultures. You [the British] are too modest – in a very vain way. We [the Americans] are too busy – in a very humble way, of course. [Interview in the *Observer Magazine*, 15 Nov.]

25 A genius with the IQ of a moron. [Of Andy Warhol. In the *Observer*, 18 June 1989]

26 Every twenty years the middle-aged celebrate the decade of their youth. [In the *Observer Review*, 27 Aug.]

1 Prometheus stole fire from Heaven so that we could not only cook dinner but one another.

2 We fight wars which we lose, then we make films showing how we won them and the films make more money than the war lost. [In the *Weekend Guardian*, 4–5 Nov.]

VINCENT DE VIGNAUD 1901–1978

3 Nothing holds up the progress of science so much as the right idea at the wrong time. [In R. V. Jones, *Most Secret War*, Ch. 9]

STEPHEN VIZINCZEY 1933–

4 The great nineteenth-century English novelists are Gogol, Dostoevsky, Tolstoy, Stendhal and Balzac in English. [*Truth and Lies in Literature*, p. 14]

5 Great writers are not those who tell us we shouldn't play with fire but those who make our fingers burn. [161]

6 I was told I am a true cosmopolitan: I am unhappy everywhere. [In the *Guardian*, 7 Mar. 1968]

VLADIMIR VOINOVICH 1932–

7 A meeting is an occasion when people gather together, some to say what they do not think, and others not to say what they really do. [Of the USSR. In the *Listener*, 10 Nov. 1988]

KURT VONNEGUT 1922–

8 One of the main effects of war, after all, is that people are discouraged from being characters. [*Slaughterhouse 5*, Ch. 7]

9 And so it goes ... [Catchphrase in above]

10 Hatred is like vitamins, you do feel better. [In conversation with Heinrich Böll on TV programme *Voices*. In the *Listener*, 4 July 1985]

11 Unanticipated invitations to travel are dancing lessons from God. [Quoted by David Mamet in interview in the *Guardian*, 16 Feb. 1989]

ANDREI VOZNESENSKY 1933–

12 it is time / For you to run out of me and I / Out of you. [*Autumn in Sigulda*, trans. W. H. Auden]

13 The art of creation / is older than the art of killing. [*Poem with a Footnote*]

14 Genius is in the planet's blood. / You're either a poet or a Lilliputian. [*Who Are We?*, trans. S. Moss]

DIANA VREELAND 1903–1989

15 Pink is the navy blue of India. [Attr. in *Rolling Stone*, 11 Aug. 1977]

JANE WAGNER

1 I refuse to be intimidated by reality any more. After all, what is reality anyway? Nothin' but a collective hunch ... I made some studies, and reality is the leading cause of stress among those in touch with it. [Spoken by Lily Tomlin as the Bag-lady in *Search for Signs of Intelligent Life in the Universe*]

2 I've always wanted to *be* somebody, but now I see I should have been more specific.

JOHN WAIN 1925–

3 The lesson is that dying men must groan; / And poets groan in rhymes that please the ear. / But still it comes expensive, you must own. [*Don't let's spoil it all, I thought we were going to be such good friends*]

4 Poetry is to prose as dancing is to walking. [Talk on BBC radio, 13 Jan. 1976]

DEREK WALCOTT 1930–

5 A man living with English in one room. [Of Joseph Brodsky. *Forest of Europe*]

6 Hawks have no music. [*Hawk*]

7 Maturity is the assimilation of the features of every ancestor. [*Is Massa Dead?*, 'The Muse of History']

8 Epic / follows the plough, metre the ring of the anvil; / prophecy divines the figurations of storks, and awe / the arc of the stallion's neck. [*Map of the New World*, III, 'Sea Cranes']

9 He had no idea how time could be re-worded / Which is the historian's task. [*Omeros*, Ch. XVIII, 1]

10 The worst crime is to leave a man's hands empty. / Men are born makers, with that primal simplicity / In every maker since Adam. [XXVIII. 2]

11 Was he the only fisherman left in the world / using the old ways, who believed his work was prayer, / who caught only enough, since the sea had to live. [LX]

12 A lot of contemporary verse sounds like, you know, 'Someone hit me.' Whereas in a narrative you know exactly who hit you. [Interview in the *Independent*, 10 Nov. 1990]

GEORGE WALD 1906–

13 It would be a poor thing to be an atom in a universe without physicists. And physicists are made of atoms. A physicist is an atom's way of knowing about atoms. [From Foreword to L. J. Henderson, *The Fitness of the Environment*, in *Dictionary of Scientific Quotations*, ed. A. L. Mackay]

PRESIDENT LECH WALESA 1947–

14 Wherever there are three Poles there are four political parties. [Interview in the *Independent*, 4 Dec. 1989]

ARTHUR WALEY 1889–1965

15 It is not difficult to censor foreign news, / What is hard today is to censor one's own thoughts, – / To sit by and see the blind man / On the sightless horse, riding into the bottomless abyss. [*Censorship*]

1 In the early dusk, down an alley of green moss, / The garden-boy is leading the cranes home. [*The Cranes*, trans. from the Chinese of Po-Chü-I]

ALICE WALKER 1944–

2 'Tea' to the English is really a picnic indoors. [*The Color Purple*, p. 116]

3 Any God I ever felt in church I brought in with me. And I think all the other folks did too. They come to church to *share* God not find God. [165]

4 When I found out I thought God was white, and a man, I lost interest. [166]

5 I think it pisses God off if you walk by the color purple in a field somewhere and don't notice it. What it do when it pissed off? I ast. Oh, it make something else. People think pleasing God is all God care about. But any fool living in the world can see it always trying to please us back. [167]

6 Womanist is to feminist as purple is to lavender. [In the *Guardian*, 17 May 1986]

JAMES J. WALKER 1881–1946

7 Will you love me in December / As you did in May? [Song: *Will You Love Me in December?*, music by Ernest R. Ball]

8 A reformer is a guy who rides through a sewer in a glass-bottomed boat. [Speech as Mayor of New York, 1928. See also 267:2]

GENERAL SIR WALTER WALKER 1912–

9 Britain has invented a new missile. It's called the civil servant – it doesn't work and it can't be fired. [In the *Observer*, 'Sayings of the Year', 3 Jan. 1982]

MAX WALL 1908–1990

10 Wall is the name – Max Wall. My father was the Great Wall of China. He was a brick. [Opening patter to variety act]

11 To me Adler will always be Jung. [Telegram to his friend Larry Adler on his 60th birthday in 1974]

12 I was born there because I wanted to be near my parents. [In obituary in the *Guardian*, 23 May 1990]

VICE-PRESIDENT HENRY WALLACE 1888–1965

13 The century on which we are entering – the century which will come out of this war – can be and must be the century of the common man. [Speech, 8 May 1942]

GRAHAM WALLAS 1858–1932

14 The little girl had the makings of a poet in her who, being told to be sure of her meaning before she spoke, said: 'How can I know what I think till I see what I say?' [*The Art of Thought*, Ch. 4]

WALL STREET JOURNAL

15 A true gentleman is a man who knows how to play the bagpipes – but doesn't. [In *Reader's Digest*, Mar. 1976]

SIR ALAN WALTERS 1926–

16 Money is used to pay bills and credit is used to delay paying them. [In the *Observer*, 'Sayings of the Week', 26 Mar. 1989]

SIR WILLIAM WALTON 1902–1983

17 It's just as difficult to overcome success as it is to overcome failure. [On receiving the Order of Merit, 1967. In Susanna Walton, *William Walton: Behind the Façade*, p. 179]

18 [When asked by Gillian Widdicombe what he remembered of a week under intensive care, just after his 80th birthday] It was very quiet. Didn't see a soul, not even Ben Britten's. Then there was a fanfare, but it wasn't one of mine. Bliss, I suppose. [In obituary in the *Observer*, 13 Mar. 1983]

WENDY WARD

19 The worst moment for an atheist is when he feels grateful and has no one to thank. [In P. and J. Holton, *Quote and Unquote*]

ANDY WARHOL 1927–1987

20 I always thought I'd like my tombstone to be blank. No epitaph, and no name. Well, actually I'd like it to say 'figment'. [*America*]

21 It's the place where my prediction from the sixties finally came true: 'In the future

everyone will be famous for fifteen minutes.'
[*Andy Warhol's Exposures*, 'Studio 54']

1 Try the Andy Warhol New York City
Diet: when I order in a restaurant, I order
everything I don't want, so I have a lot to
play around with while everyone else eats.
[*From A to B and Back Again*, 'Beauty']

2 An artist is someone who produces
things that people don't need to have but
that he – for *some reason* – thinks it would be
a good idea to give them. ['Atmosphere']

3 That's what show business is for – to
prove that it's not what you are that counts,
it's what they *think* you are. [*POPism*, '1967']

4 I guess it was just being in the wrong
place at the right time. That's what assassination is all about. ['1968–9']

5 Heaven and Hell are Just One Breath
Away. [Title of last picture]

6 The most exciting attractions are between two opposites that never meet. [In
Barbara Rowes, *Book of Quotes*]

JACK WARNER 1895–1981

7 Mind my bike! [Catchphrase in BBC radio
series *Garrison Theatre*, of 1939–45 War]

8 Evening, all. [Catchphrase in BBC TV
series *Dixon of Dock Green*, from 1950s, original scripts by Ted Willis]

JACK L. WARNER [of Warner Bros] 1892–1981

9 [When told Ronald Reagan was running
for the governorship of California in 1966]
No, No! Jimmy Stewart for governor, Reagan
for best friend. [In *Morrow Book of Quotations
in American History*, ed. Joseph R. Conlin]

CHIEF JUSTICE EARL WARREN 1891–1974

10 Many people consider the things which
government does for them to be social
progress, but they consider the things government does for others as socialism. [In Laurence J. Peter, *Peter's Quotations*]

KEITH WATERHOUSE 1929–

11 The 50s face was angry, the 60s face

was well-fed, the 70s face was foxy. Perhaps
it was the right expression: there was a lot
to be wary about. [In the *Observer Magazine*,
30 Dec. 1979]

12 MISTRESS: Do you mind if we have separate bills? You see, I don't sleep with him any
more. [*Jeffrey Bernard is Unwell*, Act I. The
play is based on the life and writings of Ber-
nard]

13 I wonder what it's like to be a tortoise.
Not a barrel of laughs, I shouldn't imagine.
You can't be frivolous or facetious if you're a
tortoise, can you? And think of the danger of
being turned into a pair of hair-brushes . . .
But you do have a home to go to.

DOUGLAS WATKINSON

14 It [golf] is the unthinkable in pursuit of
the unsinkable. [*Dragon's Tail*]

JAMES D. WATSON 1928–

15 The thought could not be avoided that
the best home for a feminist was in another
person's lab. [*The Double Helix*, Ch. 2]

16 Already for thirty-five years he [Francis
Crick] had not stopped talking and almost
nothing of fundamental value had emerged.
[8]

17 I was twenty-five and too old to be unusual. [29]

18 It is necessary to be somewhat underem-
ployed if you want to do something significant.
[In H. Judson, *The Eighth Day of Creation*]

See also **FRANCIS CRICK** and **JAMES D. WATSON**

SIR WILLIAM WATSON 1858–1935

19 April, April, / Laugh thy girlish laughter;
/ Then, the moment after, / Weep thy girlish
tears! [*April*]

20 The staid, conservative, / Came-over-
with-the-Conqueror type of mind. [*A Study
in Contrasts*, I. i. 42]

DAVID WATT 1932–1987

21 It was like reading a hostile analysis of
goldfish written by a cat. [Of Richard Crossman's descriptions in his *Diaries of a Cabinet*

Minister of Harold Wilson's government. *Inquiring Eye*, ed. Ferdinand Mount]

ARTHUR WAUGH 1866–1943

1 He [the dog] is unhappy and wants to tell us about it, which, after all, is all that most literature is. [In *Waugh on Women*, ed. Jacqueline McDonnell]

EVELYN WAUGH 1903–1966

2 I expect you'll be becoming a schoolmaster, sir. That's what most of the gentlemen does, sir, that gets sent down for indecent behaviour. [*Decline and Fall*, Prelude]

3 We class schools, you see, into four grades: Leading School, First-rate School, Good School, and School. [I. 1]

4 That's the public-school system all over. They may kick you out, but they never let you down. [3]

5 Meanwhile you will write an essay on 'self-indulgence'. There will be a prize of half a crown for the longest essay, irrespective of any possible merit. [5]

6 For generations the British bourgeoisie have spoken of themselves as gentlemen, and by that they have meant, among other things, a self-respecting scorn of irregular perquisites. It is the quality that distinguishes the gentleman from both the artist and the aristocrat. [6]

7 There aren't many left like him nowadays, what with education and whisky the price it is. [7]

8 We can trace almost all the disasters of English history to the influence of Wales. [8]

9 'The Welsh,' said the Doctor, 'are the only nation in the world that has produced no graphic or plastic art, no architecture, no drama. They just sing,' he said with disgust, 'sing and blow down wind instruments of plated silver.'

10 I have noticed again and again since I have been in the Church that lay interest in ecclesiastical matters is often a prelude to insanity.

11 I have often observed in women of her type a tendency to regard all athletics as inferior forms of fox-hunting. [10]

12 I'm one of the blind alleys off the main road of procreation. [12]

13 I haven't been to sleep for over a year. That's why I go to bed early. One needs more rest if one doesn't sleep. [II. 3]

14 There is a species of person called a 'Modern Churchman' who draws the full salary of a beneficed clergyman and need not commit himself to any religious belief. [4]

15 'But you married?' 'Yes, mum, but it was in the war, and he was very drunk.' [5]

16 Services are voluntary – that is to say, you must either attend all or none. [III. 1]

17 He stood twice for Parliament, but so diffidently that his candidature passed almost unnoticed.

18 I came to the conclusion many years ago that almost all crime is due to the repressed desire for aesthetic expression.

19 Anyone who has been to an English public school will always feel comparatively at home in prison. [4]

20 Instead of this absurd division into sexes they ought to class people as static and dynamic. [7]

21 Only when one has lost all curiosity has one reached the age to write an autobiography. [*A Little Learning*, opening words]

22 That impersonal insensitive friendliness that takes the place of ceremony in that land [the USA] of waifs and strays. [*The Loved One*]

23 What did your Loved One pass on from?

24 You never find an Englishman among the underdogs – except in England of course.

25 Enclosing every thin man, there's a fat man demanding elbow-room. [*Officers and Gentlemen*, Interlude. See also 7:14, 88:24, 286:14, 401:20]

26 '*The Beast* stands for strong mutually antagonistic governments everywhere,' he said. 'Self-sufficiency at home, self-assertion abroad,' [*Scoop*, Bk I, Ch. 1, 3]

27 Up to a point, Lord Copper.

28 Yes, cider and tinned salmon are the staple diet of the agricultural classes. [1. 4]

29 Feather-footed through the plashy fen passes the questing vole. [2. 1]

1 Personally I can't see that foreign stories are ever news – not *real* news. [5. 1]

2 News is what a chap who doesn't care much about anything wants to read. And it's only news until he's read it. After that it's dead.

3 The better sort of Ishmaelites have been Christian for many centuries and will not publicly eat human flesh uncooked in Lent, without special and costly dispensation from their bishop. [II. 1. 1]

4 As there was no form of government common to the peoples thus segregated, nor tie of language, history, habit, or belief, they were called a Republic.

5 'I will not stand for being called a woman in my own house,' she said. [1. 9]

6 Other nations use 'force'; we Britons alone use 'Might'. [5. 1]

7 Creative Endeavour lost her wings, Mrs Ape. [*Vile Bodies*, Ch. 1]

8 Particularly against books the Home Secretary is. If we can't stamp out literature in the country, we can at least stop it being brought in from outside. [2]

9 When the war broke out she took down the signed photograph of the Kaiser and, with some solemnity, hung it in the men-servants' lavatory; it was her one combative action. [3]

10 She had heard someone say something about an Independent Labour Party, and was furious that she had not been asked. [4]

11 I feel my full income when that young man is mentioned. [6]

12 All this fuss about sleeping together. For physical pleasure I'd sooner go to my dentist any day.

13 We are all American at puberty; we die French. [*Diaries*, ed. M. Davie, 'Irregular Notes', 18 July 1961]

14 Punctuality is the virtue of the bored. [26 Mar. 1962]

15 One can write, think and pray exclusively of others; dreams are all egocentric. [5 Oct. 1962]

16 One forgets words as one forgets names. One's vocabulary needs constant fertilizing or it will die. [25 Dec. 1962]

17 It was announced that the trouble was not 'malignant' . . . I remarked that it was a typical triumph of modern science to find the only part of Randolph that was not malignant and remove it. [On Randolph Churchill's having a lung removed. Mar. 1964]

18 Really, to spend millions of pounds of public money in letting off invisible fireworks. [Of space travel. From *Letters*, ed. Mark Amory, in *The Times Literary Supplement*, 7 Nov. 1980]

19 No admittance on business. [Notice on his house gate]

20 I do not aspire to advise my sovereign in her choice of servants. [On why he didn't vote at elections. In *A Little Order*, ed. D. Gallagher]

21 Manners are especially the need of the plain. The pretty can get away with anything. [In the *Observer*, 'Sayings of the Year', 1962]

22 All fictional characters are flat. A writer can give an illusion of depth by giving an apparently stereoscopic view of a character – seeing him from two vantage points; all a writer can do is give more or less information about a character, not information of a different order. [Interview in *Paris Review*, 1963]

23 No writer before the middle of the 19th century wrote about the working classes other than as grotesques or as pastoral decorations. Then when they were given the vote certain writers started to suck up to them.

24 [In reply to Graham Greene, who had said that he intended to write a political novel] I wouldn't give up writing about God at this stage, if I was you. It would be like P. G. Wodehouse dropping Jeeves half-way through the Wooster series. [In Christopher Sykes, *Evelyn Waugh*]

25 Simply a radio personality who outlived his prime. [Of Winston Churchill]

26 I put the words down and push them a bit. [In obituary in *The New York Times*, 11 Apr. 1966]

LORD WAVELL 1883–1950

27 'The best confidential report I ever heard

of,' said Lord Wavell, 'was also the shortest. It was by one Horse Gunner of another, and ran, "Personally I would not breed from this officer." ' [In Gilbert Harding, *Treasury of Insult*]

F. E. WEATHERLY 1848–1929

1 Where are the boys of the Old Brigade? [*The Old Brigade*]

2 Roses are flowering in Picardy, / But there's never a rose like you. [*Roses of Picardy*]

BEATRICE WEBB 1858–1943

3 If I ever felt inclined to be timid as I was going into a room full of people, I would say to myself, 'You're the cleverest member of one of the cleverest families in the cleverest class of the cleverest nation in the world, why should you be frightened?' [In Bertrand Russell, *Portraits from Memory*, VIII]

GEFFREY WEBB and EDWARD J. MASON 1913–1971

4 An everyday story of country folk. [Subtitle to BBC radio serial *The Archers*, from 1951]

SIDNEY WEBB, LORD PASSFIELD 1859–1947

5 First let me insist on what our opponents habitually ignore, and indeed, they seem intellectually incapable of understanding, namely the inevitable gradualness of our scheme of change. [Presidential speech at Labour Party Conference, London, 26 June 1923]

MAX WEBER 1864–1920

6 The Protestant Ethic and the Spirit of Capitalism. [Title of book]

ANTON VON WEBERN 1883–1945

7 Music is natural law as related to the sense of hearing. [*The Path to the New Music*, two lectures trans. Leo Black]

KATE WEDD *see* GREGORY, PHILIPPA

DAME VERONICA WEDGWOOD 1910–

8 History is lived forward but it is written in retrospect. [In Salman Rushdie, *The Jaguar Smile*, Epilogue]

SIMONE WEIL 1909–1943

9 All sins are attempts to fill voids. [*Gravity and Grace*, p. 27]

10 Culture is an instrument wielded by professors to manufacture professors, who when their turn comes will manufacture professors. [*The Need for Roots*]

11 What a country calls its vital economic interests are not the things which enable its citizens to live, but the things which enable it to make war. Petrol is more likely than wheat to be a cause of international conflict.

12 Every time we really pay attention we destroy some of the evil within. [*Waiting on God*]

MAX WEINREICH

13 A language is a dialect that has an army and a navy. [In Leo Rosten, *The Joys of Yiddish*, Preface]

PETER WEISS 1916–1982

14 We invented the Revolution / but we don't know how to run it. [*The Marat / Sade*, sc. xv, trans. G. Skelton and A. Mitchell]

15 When I wrote / I always wrote with action in mind / kept sight of the fact / that writing was just a preparation. [xxviii]

JOHNNY WEISSMULLER 1904–1984

16 Me Tarzan, you Jane. [Misquotation from film *Tarzan the Ape-man*, 1932, screenplay by Ivor Novello, from novel by Edgar Rice Burroughs. Actual words were 'Tarzan, Jane']

PRESIDENT CHAIM WEIZMANN OF ISRAEL 1874–1952

17 Difficult things take a long time, the impossible takes a little longer. [In V. Weizmann, *The Impossible Takes Longer*. See also 277:6]

C. F. VON WEIZSÄCKER 1912–

1 Body and soul are not two substances but one. They are man becoming aware of himself in two different ways. [In *Hodder Book of Christian Quotations*, comp. Tony Castle]

PRESIDENT RICHARD VON WEIZSÄCKER OF GERMANY 1920–

2 In England life is not governed by ideas, ideas are born from life. [In the *Observer*, 'Sayings of the Week', 6 July 1986]

RAQUEL WELCH 1940–

3 The mind can also be an erogenous zone. [In J. R. Colombo, *Colombo's Hollywood*]

FAY WELDON 1931–

4 Christianity really is a man's religion: there's not much in it for women except docility, obedience, who-sweeps-a-room-as-for-thy-cause, downcast eyes and death in childbirth. For the men it's better: all power and money and fine robes, the burning of heretics – fun, fun, fun! – and the Inquisition fulminating from the pulpit. [*The Heart of the Country*, 'Love Your Enemy']

5 To journey is better than to arrive – or so say those who have already arrived. ['Doing It All Wrong']

6 It's full time work being on social security. They really make you earn your living. ['Driven Mad']

7 Men are so romantic, don't you think? They look for a perfect partner when what they should be looking for is perfect love. [Interview in the *Sunday Times*, 6 Sept. 1987]

8 I didn't set out to be a feminist writer. I just look at the sheep out of the window and watch their behaviour. [Interview in the *Observer*, 30 Apr. 1989]

9 I think if you had ever written a book you were absolutely pleased with, you'd never write another. The same probably goes for having children. [Interview in the *Guardian*, 28 Nov. 1991]

10 Nature's only interest is in having you procreate, then it throws you away. [In the *Guardian*, 15 Jan. 1992]

ORSON WELLES 1915–1985

11 It's the biggest trainset a boy ever had. [Of the Hollywood studio where he was to make his first film. In *Book of Hollywood Quotes*, ed. Gary Herman]

12 In Italy for thirty years under the Borgias they had warfare, terror, murder, bloodshed – they produced Michelangelo, Leonardo da Vinci and the Renaissance. In Switzerland they had brotherly love, five hundred years of democracy and peace, and what did they produce . . . ? The cuckoo clock. [Harry Lime's parting speech in film *The Third Man*, script by Graham Greene, but Welles contributed this himself]

13 I started at the top and worked my way down. [In Leslie Halliwell, *Filmgoer's Book of Quotes*]

14 I'm just in love with making movies. Not very fond of movies – I don't go to them much. I think it's very harmful for movie-makers to see movies, because you either imitate them or worry about not imitating them. [From TV programme *Arena*, in the *Listener*, 17 Oct. 1985]

15 I've always dreamed of being a popular entertainer, and the only way has been to use magic, which I love. I have to do magic on television because I've never had a friend who has asked me to do a trick. [Interview, quoted at his death in the *Guardian*, 19 Oct. 1985]

16 It is not 'politics' which is the arch-enemy of art, it is neutrality which robs us of the sense of tragedy. [Letter on the subject of Eugene Ionesco. In the *Guardian*, 14 Sept. 1990]

See also HERMAN J. MANKIEWICZ and ORSON WELLES

MME WELLINGTON KOO

17 The air is thick with the wings of birds coming home to roost. [After Munich crisis. Attr.]

H. G. WELLS 1866–1946

18 It was a room to eat muffins in. [*The Autocracy of Mr Parham*, Bk 2, Ch. III]

19 The cat is the offspring of a cat and the

dog of a dog, but butlers and lady's maids do not reproduce their kind. They have other duties. [*Bealby*, Pt I, Ch. 1]

1 He was quite sure that he had been wronged. Not to be wronged is to forgo the first privilege of goodness. [IV. 1]

2 Miss Madeleine Philips was making it very manifest to Captain Douglas that she herself was a career; that a lover with any other career in view need not – as the advertisements say – apply. [V. 5]

3 He had one peculiar weakness; he had faced death in many forms but he had never faced a dentist. The thought of dentists gave him just the same sick horror as the thought of Socialism. [VIII. 1]

4 Cossar was a large-bodied man with gaunt inelegant limbs casually placed at convenient corners of his body, and a face like a carving abandoned as altogether too unpromising for completion. [*The Food of the Gods*]

5 Roöötten Beëëastly Silly Hole! [*The History of Mr Polly*, Ch. I, 2]

6 Mr Polly went into the National School at six, and he left the private school at fourteen, and by that time his mind was in much the same state that you would be in, dear reader, if you were operated on for appendicitis by a well-meaning boldly enterprising, but rather overworked and underpaid butcher boy, who was superseded towards the climax of the operation by a left-handed clerk of high principles but intemperate habits – that is to say, it was in a thorough mess.

7 And then came the glorious revelation of that great Frenchman whom Mr Polly called Raboo-loose.

8 '*Language*, man!' roared Parsons; 'why, it's LITERATURE!' [3]

9 'Sesquippledan,' he would say. 'Sesquippledan verboojuice.' [5]

10 'The High Egrugious is fairly on,' he said, and dived down to return by devious subterranean routes to the outfitting department. [II. 2]

11 'Smart Juniors,' said Polly to himself, 'full of Smart Juniosity. The Shoveacious Cult.' [III. 1]

12 'You're a Christian?' 'Church of England,' said Mr Polly. 'Mm,' said the employer, a little checked. 'For good all round business work, I should have preferred a Baptist.'

13 I'll make a gory mess of you. I'll cut bits orf you. [IX. 6]

14 Arson, after all, is an artificial crime . . . A large number of houses deserve to be burnt. [X. 1]

15 Of course he had no desire to place himself on an equality in any way with Ibsen; still the fact remained that his own experience in England and America and the colonies was altogether more extensive than Ibsen could have had. Ibsen had probably never seen 'one decent bar scrap' in his life. [*Kipps*, Bk I, Ch. 4, sect. iv]

16 'I'm a Norfan, both sides,' he would explain, with the air of one who had seen trouble. [6. i]

17 'It's giving girls names like that [Euphemia],' said Buggins, 'that nine times out of ten makes 'em go wrong, It unsettles 'em. If ever I was to have a girl, if ever I was to have a dozen girls, I'd call 'em all Jane.' [ii]

18 Of course we can Learn even from Novels, Nace Novels that is, but it isn't the same thing as serious reading. [II. 2. i]

19 He felt like some lonely and righteous man dynamited into Bliss. [ii]

20 You can't have money like that and not swell out. [4. ii]

21 He found that a fork in his inexperienced hand was an instrument of chase rather than capture. [7. vi]

22 Everybody hates house-agents because they have everybody at a disadvantage. All other callings have a certain amount of give and take; the house-agent simply takes. [III. 1. iii]

23 One book's very like another – after all what is it? Something to read and done with. It's not a thing that matters like print dresses or serviettes – where you either like 'em or don't, and people judge you by. [3. iii]

24 I was thinking jest what a Rum Go everything is. [viii]

25 The Social Contract is nothing more nor

less than a vast conspiracy of human beings to lie to and humbug themselves and one another for the general Good. Lies are the mortar that binds the savage individual man into the social masonry. [*Love and Mr Lewisham*, Ch. 23]

1 Notice the smug suppressions of his face. In his mouth are Lies in the shape of false teeth.

2 Human history becomes more and more a race between education and catastrophe. [*The Outline of History*, Ch. 15]

3 I sometimes think that if Adam and Eve had been merely engaged, she would not have talked with the serpent; and the world had been saved an infinity of misery. [*Select Conversations with an Uncle*]

4 The Shape of Things to Come. [Title of book, 1933]

5 Now it is on the whole more convenient to keep history and theology apart. [*A Short History of the World*, Ch. 37]

6 'I'll call my article', meditated the war correspondent, '"Mankind *versus* Ironmongery".' [*Short Stories*, 'The Land Ironclads']

7 He had the face of a saint, but he had rendered this generally acceptable by growing side-whiskers. ['The Last Trump']

8 Cynicism is humour in ill-health.

9 He was a practical electrician but fond of whisky, a heavy red-haired brute with irregular teeth. He doubted the existence of the Deity but accepted Carnot's cycle, and he had read Shakespeare and found him weak in chemistry. ['The Lord of the Dynamos']

10 Bricklayers kick their wives to death, and dukes betray theirs; but it is among the small clerks and shopkeepers nowadays that it comes most often to the cutting of throats. ['The Purple Pileus']

11 The third peculiarity of aerial warfare was that it was at once enormously destructive and entirely indecisive. [*The War in the Air*, 1908, Ch. 8]

12 ... my epitaph. That, when the time comes, will manifestly have to be: 'I told you so. You *damned* fools.' (The italics are mine.) [1941. *The War of the Worlds*, Preface originally written 1907]

13 The War to End War. [Title of book, 1914]

14 It seems to me that I am more to the left than you, Mr Stalin. [Interview with Stalin in the *New Statesman*, 27 Oct. 1934]

15 There is no reason whatever to believe that the order of nature has any greater bias in favour of man that it had in favour of the ichthyosaur or the pterodactyl. [In Sagittarius and D. George, *The Perpetual Pessimist*]

16 If Max [Beaverbrook] gets to Heaven he won't last long. He will be chucked out for trying to pull off a merger between Heaven and Hell ... after having secured a controlling interest in key subsidiary companies in both places, of course. [In A. J. P. Taylor, *Beaverbrook*, Ch. 8]

ARNOLD WESKER 1932–

17 You breed babies and you eat chips with everything. [*Chips with Everything*, I. ii]

18 Every place I look at I work out the cubic feet, and I say it will make a good warehouse or it won't. Can't help myself. One of the best warehouses I ever see was the Vatican in Rome. [vi]

19 BERNARD LEVIN: Wesker is not as wonderful as he thinks he is.

WESKER: You are *exactly* as wonderful as you think you are. [Quoted by Steven Berkoff in the *Sunday Times Books*, 9 July 1989]

MAE WEST 1892–1980

20 Keep cool and collect. [In film *Belle of the Nineties*, screenplay by West]

21 A man in the house is worth two in the street.

22 I'm glad you like my Catherine. I liked her too. She ruled thirty million people and had three hundred lovers. I did the best I could in a couple of hours. [Curtain speech after performance of play *Catherine the Great*. In Peter S. Hay, *Broadway Anecdotes*]

23 It ain't no sin to crack a few laws now and then, just so long as you don't break any. [In film *Every Day's a Holiday*, screenplay by West]

24 I have a lot of respect for that dame

[Delilah]. There's one lady barber that made good. [In film *Going to Town*, screenplay by West]

1 She's the kind of girl who climbed the ladder of success, wrong by wrong. [In film *I'm no Angel*, screenplay by West]

2 Beulah, peel me a grape.

3 When I'm good I'm very good, but when I'm bad I'm better.

4 It's not the men in my life but the life in my men.

5 Give a man a free hand and he'll run it all over you. [In film *Klondike Annie*, screenplay by West]

6 Between two evils, I always pick the one I never tried before.

7 Goodness, what beautiful diamonds! WEST: Goodness had nothing to do with it, dearie! [In film *Night after Night*, script by Vincent Lawrence]

8 Is that a gun in your pocket or are you just glad to see me? [In film *She Done Him Wrong*, screenplay by Harvey Thaw and J. Bright from West's play *Diamond Lil*]

9 Why don't you come up some time, see me? [Usually misquoted as 'Come up and see me sometime']

10 I was once so poor I didn't know where my next husband was coming from.

11 I'm tired, send one of them home. [On being told that ten men were waiting to meet her at home. In J. Weintraub, *Peel Me a Grape*]

12 I used to be Snow White ... but I drifted.

13 You can say what you like about long dresses, but they cover a multitude of shins.

14 [When asked what she wanted to be remembered for] Everything. [In the *Observer Weekend Review*, 30 Nov. 1969]

15 RED SKELTON: Oh, Miss West, I've heard so much about you.
WEST: Yeah, honey, but you can't prove a thing. [In TV programme *The Red Skelton Show*]

16 The guy's no good – he never was any good ... his mother should have thrown *him* away and kept the stork. [In *Hammer and Tongues*, ed. Michèle Brown and Ann O'Connor, 'Men']

17 She's one of the finest women who ever walked the streets. [In Leslie Halliwell, *Filmgoer's Book of Quotes*]

NATHANAEL WEST 1903–1940

18 Are-you-in-trouble? – Do-you-need-advice? – Write-to-Miss-Lonelyhearts-and-she-will-help-you. [*Miss Lonelyhearts*]

19 When they ask for bread don't give them crackers as does the Church, and don't, like the State, tell them to eat cake. Explain that man cannot live by bread alone, and give them stones. ['Miss Lonelyhearts and the dead pan']

20 Goldsmith ... smiled, bunching his fat cheeks like twin rolls of smooth pink toilet paper. ['In the dismal swamp']

DAME REBECCA WEST 1892–1983

21 Margaret Thatcher's great strength seems to be the better people know her, the better they like her. But, of course, she has one great disadvantage – she is a daughter of the people and looks trim, as the daughters of the people desire to be. Shirley Williams has such an advantage over her because she's a member of the upper-middle class and can achieve that kitchen-sink-revolutionary look that one cannot get unless one has been to a really good school. [Interview with Jilly Cooper in the *Sunday Times*, 25 July 1976]

22 There are two kinds of imperialists – imperialists and bloody imperialists. [Review in first issue of the *Freewoman*, 23 Nov. 1911. In Victoria Glendinning, *Rebecca West*, Pt 1, Ch. 10]

23 The Old Maid among novelists. [Review of H. G. Wells's *Marriage*, 19 Sept. 1912]

24 I only know that people call me a feminist whenever I express sentiments that differentiate me from a doormat or a prostitute. [Said in 1913. In the *Observer*, 25 July 1982]

25 Our four uncles. [Wells, Bennett, Shaw and Galsworthy. In Stephen Potter, *The Sense of Humour*, Ch. 1]

1 He [Michael Arlen] is every other inch a gentleman. [In Glendinning, *Rebecca West*, Pt 3, Ch. 5, but also ascr. to Alexander Woollcott]

2 There is, of course, no reason for the existence of the male sex except that one sometimes needs help with moving the piano. [In Pt 6, Ch. 5]

3 It is sometimes very hard to tell the difference between history and the smell of a skunk. [Epigraph to *Voices from the Great War*, ed. Peter Vansittart]

4 A telephone exchange without enough subscribers. [Of Edward VII. In *The Times Educational Supplement*, 8 May 1987]

R. P. WESTON ?–1936

5 Some soldiers send epistles, say they'd sooner sleep in thistles / Than the saucy, soft, short shirts for soldiers, sister Susie sews. [Song: *Sister Susie's Sewing Shirts for Soldiers*, 1914, music by Herman E. Darewski, sung by Jack Norworth]

R. P. WESTON, F. J. BARNES ?–1917 and MAURICE SCOTT

6 Hush! Here comes a Whizz-Bang! [Title of song]

R. P. WESTON and BERT LEE 1880–1946

7 Good-bye-ee! good-bye-ee! / Wipe the tear, baby dear, from your eye-ee. / Tho' it's hard to part, I know, / I'll be tickled to death to go. / Don't cry-ee! – don't sigh-ee! – / There's a silver lining in the sky-ee! – / Bonsoir, old thing! cheerio! chin-chin! / Nahpoo! Toodle-oo! Good-bye-ee! [Song: *Good-bye-ee*, 1918]

8 With her head tucked underneath her arm / She walks the Bloody Tower! [Song: *With Her Head Tucked underneath Her Arm*, 1934, sung by Stanley Holloway]

9 Brahn Boots, I asks yer, brahn boots! [Monologue *Brahn Boots*, 1940, performed by Stanley Holloway]

GENERAL WEYGAND 1867–1965

10 In three weeks England will have her neck wrung like a chicken. [At the fall of France, Apr. 1940. In Winston S. Churchill, *Their Finest Hour*, Ch. 10. Churchill answered, 'Some chicken; some neck!'; see 79:24]

EDITH WHARTON 1862–1937

11 An unalterable and unquestioned law of the musical world required that the German text of French operas sung by Swedish artists should be translated into Italian for the clearer understanding of English speaking audiences. [*The Age of Innocence*, Bk I, Ch. I]

12 What can you expect of a girl who was allowed to wear black satin at her coming-out ball? [V]

13 New York tolerated hypocrisy in private relations; but in business matters it exacted a limpid and impeccable honesty. [II. XXVI]

14 She was like a disembodied spirit who took up a great deal of room. [*The House of Mirth*, Bk I, Ch. 2]

15 Mrs Peniston was one of the episodic persons who form the padding of life. [3]

16 No *divorcées* were included, except those who had shown signs of penitence by being remarried to the very wealthy. [5]

17 Of course, being fatally poor and dingy, it was wise of Gerty to have taken up philanthropy and symphony concerts. [8]

18 Miss Farish, who was accustomed, in the way of happiness, to such scant light as shone through the cracks of other people's lives. [14]

19 She keeps on being queenly in her own room, with the door shut. [II. 1]

20 Paying for what she doesn't get rankles so dreadfully with Louisa; I can't make her see that it's one of the preliminary steps to getting what you haven't paid for. [2]

21 Blessed are the pure in heart for they have so much more to talk about. [In *John O'London's Weekly*, 10 Apr. 1932]

22 What a horror it is for a whole nation to be developing without the sense of beauty, and eating bananas for breakfast. [Letter to Sara Norton, 19 Aug. 1904, *Letters of E.W.*, ed. R. W. B. and Nancy Lewis]

HUGH WHEELER 1912–

23 To lose a lover or even a husband or two

during the course of one's life can be vexing. But to lose one's teeth is a catastrophe. [Musical *A Little Night Music*, music by Stephen Sondheim]

1 Solitaire is the only thing in life that demands absolute honesty.

E. B. WHITE 1899–1985

2 Commuter – one who spends his life / In riding to and from his wife; / A man who shaves and takes a train, / And then rides back to shave again. [*The Commuter*]

3 All poets who, when reading from their own works, experience a choked feeling, are major. For that matter, all poets who read from their own works are major, whether they choke or not. [*How to Tell a Major Poet from a Minor Poet*]

4 It is easier for a man to be loyal to his club than to his planet; the by-laws are shorter, and he is personally acquainted with the other members. [*One Man's Meat*]

5 As in the sexual experience, there are never more than two persons present in the act of reading – the writer who is the impregnator, and the reader who is the respondent. [*The Second Tree from the Corner*]

6 The dream of the American male is for a female who has an essential languor which is not laziness, who is unaccompanied except by himself, and who does not let him down. He desires a beautiful, but comprehensible creature who does not destroy a perfect situation by forming a complete sentence. ['Notes on our Time']

7 To perceive Christmas through its wrapping becomes more difficult with every year. ['Time Present']

8 Democracy is the recurrent suspicion that more than half the people are right more than half of the time. [*The Wild Flag*]

9 MOTHER: It's broccoli dear.
CHILD: I say it's spinach, and I say the hell with it. [Caption to cartoon by Carl Rose in the *New Yorker*, 28 Dec. 1928]

10 Thurber wrote the way a child skips rope, the way a mouse waltzes. [From the *New Yorker*, on Thurber's death in 1961, in the *Guardian*, 29 Jan. 1982]

PATRICK WHITE 1912–1990

11 As I see it, the little that is subtle in the Australian character comes from the masculine principle in its women, the feminine in its men. [*Flaws in the Glass*, title essay, p. 155]

12 It was perhaps doubtful if anyone would ever notice Mrs Poulter or Mrs Dun unless life took its cleaver to them. [*The Solid Mandala*, Ch. 1]

13 'I dunno,' Arthur said. 'I forget what I was taught. I only remember what I've learnt.' [2]

14 He would have liked to sit down and talk with someone about the flat things, as blameless as paper, about which it is necessary to talk. It is not possible with parents, any more than with corkscrews. His mother would bore right in, hoping to draw something out. [*The Tree of Man*, Ch. 16]

15 Conversation is imperative if gaps are to be filled, and old age, it is the last gap but one. [22]

T. H. WHITE 1906–1964

16 Seventeen years ago, come Michaelmas, and been after the Questing Beast ever since. Boring, very. [*The Sword in the Stone*, Ch. 2]

17 But I unfortunately was born at the wrong end of time, and I have to live *backwards* from in front. [3]

WILLIAM ALLEN WHITE 1868–1944

18 All dressed up, with nowhere to go. [On the Progressive Party in 1916, after Theodore Roosevelt retired from the presidential campaign]

W. L. WHITE 1900–1973

19 They were Expendable. [Title of book, 1942]

A. N. WHITEHEAD 1861–1947

20 Unfortunately, life is an offensive, directed against the repetitious mechanism of the Universe. [*Adventures of Ideas*, Ch. 5]

21 Language is incomplete and fragmentary, and merely registers a stage in the

average advance beyond ape-mentality. But all men enjoy flashes of insight beyond meanings already stabilized in etymology and grammar. [15]

1 It is more important that a proposition be interesting than that it be true. [16]

2 The deliberate aim at Peace very easily passes into its bastard substitute, Anaesthesia. [20]

3 Knowledge does not keep any better than fish. [*Aims of Education*, Pt III, Ch. 4]

4 There are no whole truths; all truths are half-truths. It is trying to treat them as whole truths that plays the devil. [*Dialogues*, Prologue]

5 Civilization advances by extending the number of important operations which we can perform without thinking about them. [*An Introduction to Mathematics*, Ch. 5]

6 Philosophy is the product of wonder. [*Nature and Life*, Ch. 1]

7 A dead Nature aims at nothing. It is the essence of life that it exists for its own sake, as the intrinsic reaping of value.

8 Science can find no individual enjoyment in Nature: science can find no aim in Nature; science can find no creativity in Nature; it finds mere rules of succession. [2]

9 The European philosophical tradition . . . consists of a series of footnotes to Plato. [*Process and Reality*, Pt 2, Ch. 1]

10 An instant of time, without duration, is an imaginative logical construction. Also each duration of time mirrors in itself all temporal durations. [*Science and the Modern World*, Ch. 4]

11 The fact of the instability of evil is the moral order of the world. [In Victor Gollancz, *A Year of Grace*]

12 A science which hesitates to forget its founders is lost. [Attr.]

KATHARINE WHITEHORN 1926–

13 Hats divide generally into three classes: offensive hats, defensive hats, and shrapnel. [In *Shouts and Murmurs*, a selection from the *Observer* 1962–3, 'Hats']

14 Filing is concerned with the past; anything you actually need to see again has to do with the future. [*Sunday Best*, 'Sorting Out']

15 I wouldn't say when you've seen one Western you've seen the lot; but when you've seen the lot you get the feeling you've seen one. ['Decoding the West']

16 They are not quite my friends, but I know them better than many who are; they aren't related to me, but they might as well be. They are the close friends of *my* close friends – my friends-in-law. ['Best Friend Once Removed']

17 My brother cuts the time it takes to read a newspaper by skipping everything in the future tense; and it's amazing what he doesn't miss. ['Never-Never Land']

18 Have you ever taken anything out of the clothes basket because it had become, relatively, the cleaner thing? [In the *Observer*, 1964, 'On Shirts']

19 The power to get other people to do things has been the prerogative of the harlot throughout the ages – and of the manager. [In the *Observer*, 26 May 1985. See also 23:6, 104:9, 214:27, 361:12]

20 In answer to: Inside every thin woman there's a fat woman trying to get out, I always think it's: Outside every thin woman there's a fat man trying to get in. [In BBC radio programme *Quote, Unquote*, 27 July. See also 7:14, 88:24, 286:14, 392:25]

21 I have known couples stay up till three in the morning, each hoping the other would finally give in and make the bed. Perhaps after all our mothers were right, when they warned us that as you lie in your bed, so you must make it. [In the *Observer*, 28 Aug.]

22 As ridiculous to approve of property and let a few men have a grossly unfair share of it, as say you are all for marriage, and then let one man have all the wives. [In the *Observer*, 29 June 1986]

23 'She's the sort of women who lives for others' – and you can tell the others by their hunted look. [30 Apr. 1989]

24 A good listener is not someone who has nothing to say. A good listener is a good talker with a sore throat. [In Herbert V. Prochnow, *The Public Speaker's Treasure Chest*]

WILLIAM [later LORD] WHITELAW 1918–

1 I have always said it is a great mistake to prejudge the past. [At his first press conference after being appointed Ulster Secretary, 1972]

2 They [Labour Ministers] are going about the country stirring up complacency. [During 1974 election. In Simon Hoggart, On the House, p. 38. Frequently misquoted as 'stirring up apathy']

3 Those who say that I am not in agreement with the [Conservative immigration] policy are, rightly or wrongly, quite wrong. [39]

WILLIAM H. WHYTE 1917–

4 This book is about the organization man ... I can think of no other way to describe the people I am talking about. They are not workers, nor are they the white-collar people in the usual, clerk sense of the word. These people only work for the Organization. The ones I am talking about belong to it as well. [The Organization Man, Ch. 1]

NORBERT WIENER 1894–1964

5 We have decided to call the entire field of control and communication theory, whether in the machine or in the animal, by the name of Cybernetics, which we form from the Greek [for] steersman. [Cybernetics]

RICHARD WILBUR 1921–

6 Most women know that sex is good for headaches. [In the Observer, 'Sayings of the Week', 1 Nov. 1987]

BILLY WILDER 1906–

7 I've met a lot of hardboiled eggs in my time, but you're twenty minutes. [In film Ace in the Hole, scripted with Lesser Samuels and Walter Newman]

8 HOLDEN: You used to be in pictures, you used to be big.

SWANSON: I am big. It's the pictures that got small. [In film Sunset Boulevard, scripted with Charles Brackett and D. M. Marshman]

9 Why don't you slip out of those wet clothes and into a dry Martini. [In film The Major and the Minor, scripted with Charles Brackett. Line spoken by Robert Benchley, who sometimes is given credit; ascr. also to Alexander Woollcott]

10 MARILYN MONROE: Water polo? Isn't that terribly dangerous?

TONY CURTIS: I'll say! I had two ponies drown under me. [In film Some Like It Hot, scripted with I. A. L. Diamond]

11 Well nobody's perfect. [In Some Like It Hot, last lines, as Joe E. Brown is told by his bride-to-be, Jack Lemmon, that he is not a woman]

12 Hindsight is always twenty-twenty. [In J. R. Colombo, Colombo's Hollywood]

13 France is a country where the money falls apart in your hands and you can't tear the toilet paper. [In Leslie Halliwell, Filmgoer's Book of Quotes]

14 You have Van Gogh's ear for music. [To Cliff Osmond. Attr.]

See also CHARLES BRACKETT and BILLY WILDER

THORNTON WILDER 1897–1975

15 For what human ill does not dawn seem to be an alleviation? [The Bridge of San Luis Rey, Ch. 3]

16 Most everybody in the world climbs into their graves married. [Our Town, Act II]

17 My advice to you is not to inquire why or whither, but just enjoy your ice-cream while it's on your plate, – that's my philosophy. [The Skin of Our Teeth, Act I]

18 We'll trot down to the movies and see how girls with wax faces live. [III]

19 When you're at war you think about a better life; when you're at peace you think about a more comfortable one.

20 Success is paralysing only to those who have never wished for anything else. [Journals, 1939–61, ed. Donald Gallup]

21 A living is made, Mr Kemper, by selling something that everybody needs at least once a year. Yes, sir! And a million is made by producing something that everybody needs every day. You artists produce something that nobody needs at any time. [The Matchmaker, Act I]

1 Ninety-nine per cent of the people in the world are fools and the rest of us are in great danger of contagion.

2 Marriage is a bribe to make a housekeeper think she's a householder.

3 The best part of married life is the fights. The rest is merely so-so. [II]

4 AMBROSE: That old man with one foot in the grave!
MRS LEVI: And the other three in the cash box. [III]

5 There's nothing like eavesdropping to show you that the world outside your head is different from the world inside your head.

6 That's not a friend, that's an employer I'm trying out for a few days.

7 Never support two weaknesses at the same time. It's your combination sinners – your lecherous liars and your miserly drunkards – who dishonour the vices and bring them into bad repute.

8 But there comes a moment in everybody's life when he must decide whether he'll live among human beings or not – a fool among fools or a fool alone. [IV]

EMPEROR WILHELM II 1859–1941

9 We have fought for our place in the sun and won it. Our future is on the water. [Speech at Elbe regatta, Hamburg, 18 June 1901, but phrase of earlier origin]

10 You will be home before the leaves have fallen from the trees. [To troops leaving for the Front, Aug. 1914. In B. Tuchman, *The Guns of August*, Ch. 9]

11 A contemptible little army. [Of British Expeditionary Force. Order at Aix-la-Chapelle HQ, 19 Aug. 1914]

12 I would have liked to go to Ireland, but my grandmother [Queen Victoria] would not let me. Perhaps she thought I wanted to take the little place. [In H. Montgomery Hyde, *Carson*, Ch. 9, sect. vi]

GEORGE WILL 1941–

13 The unpleasant sound emitting from [Vice-President] Bush as he traipses from one conservative gathering to another is a thin, tinny 'arf' – the sound of a lap-dog. [In the *Washington Post*, 30 Jan. 1986]

14 Football combines the two worst things about America: it is violence punctuated by committee meetings. [In the *Observer*, 'Sayings of a Year', 30 Dec. 1990]

GEOFFREY WILLANS 1911–1958 and RONALD SEARLE 1920–

15 Lately things are a bit different. The oiks have become v. well dressed certainly beter than pauncefootes pater and their skools are quite remarkable with all those windows to let the sunshine in. [*How to be Topp*, Ch. 2]

16 Cads have always a grandmother who is the DUCHESS of BLANK hem hem. They are inclined to cheat at conkers having baked them for 300 years in the ancestral ovens. [4]

17 Still xmas is a good time with all those presents and good food and i hope it will never die out or at any rate not until i am grown up and have to pay for it all. [11]

EMLYN WILLIAMS 1905–1987

18 They say I died in 1974, but I have racked my brain and cannot recall anything untoward happening that year. [On the premature announcement of his death. In obituary in the *Guardian*, 26 Sept. 1987]

19 You just got into the new wave as the tube doors were closing. [To dramatist John Mortimer. In obituary in the *Sunday Times*, 27 Sept. 1987]

HARRY WILLIAMS 1874–1924

20 I'm Afraid to Go Home in the Dark. [Title of song, music by Jack Judge]

21 In the Shade of the Old Apple Tree. [Title of song, music by E. von Alstyne]

22 Good-bye Piccadilly, Farewell Leicester Square; / It's a long, long way to Tipperary, but my heart's right there! [*It's a Long Way to Tipperary*, music by Jack Judge]

HEATHCOTE WILLIAMS 1941–

23 From space, the planet is blue. / From space, the planet is the territory / Not of humans, but of the whale. / Blue seas cover

seven-tenths of the earth's surface, / And are the domain of the largest brain ever created, / With a fifty-million-year-old smile. [*Whale Nation*, opening lines]

MARY LOU WILLIAMS 1910–1981

1 My back is breakin', I'm fallin' down, I'm on a level with the ground – / Lord, when I've done the best I can I want my crown. [Song: *I Want My Crown*]

RAYMOND WILLIAMS 1921–1988

2 A very large part of English middle-class education is devoted to the training of servants ... In so far as it is, by definition, the training of upper servants, it includes, of course, the instilling of that kind of confidence which will enable the upper servants to supervise and direct the lower servants. [*Culture and Society*, Ch. 3, Conclusion]

3 The human crisis is always a crisis of understanding: what we genuinely understand we can do.

4 When art communicates, a human experience is actively offered and actively received. Below this activity threshold there can be no art. [*The Long Revolution*, Pt I, Ch. 1, sect. vi]

5 Nationalism is in this sense like class. To have it, and to feel it, is the only way to end it. If you fail to claim it, or give it up too soon, you will be merely cheated, by other classes and other nations. [*Second Generation*]

ROBIN WILLIAMS 1952–

6 I did drugs to keep going. But performing in itself is a drug. And taking cocaine is like being a haemophiliac in a razor factory. [In the *Sunday Times Magazine*, 25 Sept. 1988]

TENNESSEE WILLIAMS 1911–1983

7 It is a terrible thing for an old woman to outlive her dogs. [*Camino Real*, Prologue]

8 The most dangerous word in any human tongue is the word for brother. It's inflammatory. [Block 2]

9 Caged birds accept each other but flight is what they long for. [7]

10 *Make voyages! – Attempt them!* there's nothing else. [8]

11 We're all of us guinea pigs in the laboratory of God. Humanity is just a work in progress. [12]

12 Cat on a Hot Tin Roof. [Title of play]

13 I'm not living with you. We occupy the same cage. [*Cat on a Hot Tin Roof*, I]

14 You can be young without money but you can't be old without it.

15 BRICK: Well, they say nature hates a vacuum, Big Daddy.

BIG DADDY: That's what they say, but sometimes I think that a vacuum is a hell of a lot better than some of the stuff that nature replaces it with. [II]

16 That Europe's nothin' on earth but a great big auction, that's all it is.

17 For time is the longest distance between two places. [*The Glass Menagerie*, sc. vii]

18 We're all of us sentenced to solitary confinement inside our own skins, for life! [*Orpheus Descending*, Act 2, sc. 1]

19 A Streetcar Named Desire. [Title of play]

20 I can't stand a naked light bulb, any more than I can a rude remark or a vulgar action. [*A Streetcar Named Desire*, Act II, sc. iii]

21 Poker shouldn't be played in a house with women.

22 I have always depended on the kindness of strangers. [Blanche's final words in xi]

23 If people behaved in the way nations do they would all be put in straitjackets. [BBC interview]

WILLIAM CARLOS WILLIAMS 1883–1963

24 Obviously, in a plutocracy / the natural hero / is the man who robs a bank. [*Childe Harold to the Round Tower Came*]

25 Minds like beds always made up, / (more stony than a shore) / unwilling or unable. [*Patterson*, I, Preface]

26 Divorce is / the sign of knowledge in our time.

27 so much depends / upon / a red wheel / barrow / glazed with rain / water / beside the white / chickens. [*Spring and Fall*, 21, 'The Red Wheelbarrow']

28 This is just to say / I have eaten / the plums / that were in / the icebox / and

which / you were probably / saving / for breakfast. / Forgive me / they were delicious / so sweet / and so cold. [*This is just to say*]

1 Liquor and love / rescue the cloudy sense / banish its despair / give it a home. [*The World Narrowed to a Point*]

WENDELL WILLKIE 1892–1944

2 The constitution does not provide for first and second class citizens. [*An American Programme*, Ch. 2]

3 There exists in the world today a gigantic reservoir of good will toward us, the American people. [*One World*, Ch. 10]

4 Freedom is an indivisible word. If we want to enjoy it, and fight for it, we must be prepared to extend it to everyone, whether they are rich or poor, whether they agree with us or not, no matter what their race or the colour of their skin. [13]

GARY WILLS 1934–

5 Like much of America [Reagan] contained contradictions, but never experienced them. [*Reagan's America: Innocents at Home*]

SIR ANGUS WILSON 1913–1991

6 She was more than ever proud of the position of the bungalow, so almost in the country. [*A Bit off the Map*, 'A Flat Country Christmas']

7 I have no concern for the common man except that he should not be so common. [*No Laughing Matter*]

8 'God knows how you Protestants can be expected to have any sense of direction,' she said. 'It's different with us. I haven't been to mass for years, I've got every mortal sin on my conscience, but I know when I'm doing wrong. I'm still a Catholic.' [*The Wrong Set*, 'Significant Experience']

CHARLES E. WILSON 1890–1961

9 For years I thought what was good for the country was good for General Motors, and vice versa. [To a Congressional Committee, 15 Jan. 1953. Often misquoted as 'What's good for General Motors is good for the country']

10 A bigger bang for a buck. [Of the H-Bomb tested at Bikini in 1954. In W. Safire, *Political Dictionary*]

EARL WILSON 1907–

11 Gossip is hearing something you like about someone you don't. [In *New Woman*, Apr. 1989]

EDMUND WILSON 1895–1972

12 A point of view (I invented this). 'I always give the whores as little as possible: I don't think that prostitution ought to be encouraged.' [*The Twenties*, 'After the War']

13 Of all the great Victorian writers, he [Dickens] was probably the most antagonistic to the Victorian age itself. [*The Wound and the Bow*, 'The Two Scrooges']

14 No two people read the same book. [Quoted by John Russell in the *Sunday Times*, 25 July 1971]

HAROLD [later LORD] WILSON 1916–

15 The school I went to in the north was a school where more than half the children in my class never had any boots and shoes to their feet. They wore clogs, because they lasted longer than shoes of comparable price. [Speech in Birmingham, 28 July 1948. Misquoted to suggest his schoolmates went barefoot; see 58:6]

16 All these financiers, all the little gnomes of Zürich and the other financial centres, about whom we keep on hearing. [Speech in House of Commons, 12 Nov. 1956]

17 This party is a moral crusade, or it is nothing. [At Labour Party Conference, 1 Oct. 1962]

18 If I had the choice between smoked salmon and tinned salmon. I'd have it tinned. With vinegar. [In the *Observer*, 11 Nov.]

19 There is something utterly nauseating about a system of society which pays a harlot 25 times as much as it pays its Prime Minister, 250 times as much as it pays its Members of Parliament, and 500 times as much as it pays some of its ministers of religion. [On the case of Christine Keeler. Speech in House of Commons, June 1963]

1 The Britain that is going to be forged in the white heat of this revolution will be no place for restrictive practices or out-dated methods on either side of industry. [Speech at Labour Party Conference, 1 Oct.]

2 After half a century of democratic advance the whole process has ground to a halt with a 14th Earl. [On Sir Alec Douglas-Home's becoming Prime Minister. Speech in Manchester, 19 Oct. For retort, see 109:3]

3 Everybody should have an equal chance – but they shouldn't have a flying start. [In the *Observer*, 'Sayings of the Year', 1963]

4 A week is a long time in politics. [Probably said in 1964 at parliamentary lobby after sterling crisis, but variant recorded as early as 1960. In N. Rees, *Quote . . . Unquote*]

5 It does not mean, of course, that the pound here in Britain in your pocket or purse or in your bank has been devalued. [In prime ministerial broadcast on TV announcing devaluation, 19 Nov. 1967]

6 Get your tanks off my lawn, Hughie! [To Hugh Scanlon of the TUC during confrontation over union reform, at Chequers, 1 June 1969]

7 I believe the greatest asset a head of state can have is the ability to get a good night's sleep. [BBC radio interview in *The World Tonight*, 16 Apr. 1975]

8 The monarch is a labour-intensive industry. [In the *Observer*, 'Sayings of the Week', 13 Feb. 1977]

9 I have always said about Tony [Benn] that he immatures with age. [From BBC TV programme *Pebble Mill*, in Jad Williams, *Tony Benn*, Ch. 37]

10 Hence the practised performances of latter-day politicians in the game of musical daggers; never be left holding the dagger when the music stops. [*The Governance of Britain*, Ch. 2]

11 I'm an optimist, but an optimist who carries a raincoat. [In *New Woman*, Sept. 1989]

SANDY WILSON 1924–

12 She says it's nicer, much nicer in Nice. [*The Boy Friend*, Act II]

13 DULCIE: The modern buildings that you see / Are often most alarming.
LORD B: But I am sure that you'll agree.
DULCIE: A ruin
LORD B: Can be charming. [III]

14 Its never too late to have a fling / For autumn is just as nice as spring, / And it's never too late to fall in love.

PRESIDENT T. WOODROW WILSON
1856–1924

15 I would never read a book if it were possible to talk half an hour with the man who wrote it. [Advice to his students at Princeton, 1900]

16 Business underlies everything in our national life, including our spiritual life. Witness the fact that in the Lord's Prayer the first petition is for daily bread. No one can worship God or love his neighbour on an empty stomach. [Speech in New York, 1912]

17 There is such a thing as a man being too proud to fight. [Address at Philadelphia, 10 May 1915]

18 Armed neutrality. [Message to Congress, 26 Feb. 1917]

19 The world must be made safe for democracy. [Address to Congress, 2 Apr.]

20 The right is more precious than peace.

21 America . . . is the prize amateur nation of the world. Germany is the prize professional nation. [Speech to officers of the fleet, Aug.]

22 There are a great many hyphens left in America. For my part, I think the most unAmerican thing in the world is a hyphen. [Of double-barrelled names. Speech at St Paul, Minnesota, 9 Sept. 1919. See also 270:8, 323:9]

23 Never murder a man who is committing suicide. [Of Governor Hughes's election campaign. In John Dos Passos, *Mr Wilson's War*, Pt II, Ch. 10, sect. x]

24 Once lead this people into war and they'll forget there ever was such a thing as tolerance. [III. 2. xii]

25 People will endure their tyrants for years, but they tear their deliverers to pieces if a

millennium is not created immediately. [Said to George Creel. Heading to V. 22]

1 Tell me what's right and I'll fight for it. [To his experts at Versailles Peace Conference, 1919]

2 The war we have just been through, though it was shot through with terror, is not to be compared with the war we would have to face next time.

3 It [D. W. Griffith's film *Birth of a Nation*] is like writing history with lightning and my only regret is that it is all so terribly true. [In D. J. Boorstin, *The Image*, Ch. 4]

ROBB WILTON 1881–1957

4 The day war broke out. [Catchphrase in comedy act, from 1940s]

ARTHUR WIMPERIS 1874–1953

5 I've gotter motter – / Always merry and bright! ['My Motter', from *The Arcadians*, III]

6 My dear fellow a unique evening! I wouldn't have left a turn unstoned. [On a vaudeville show. In E. Short, *Fifty Years of Vaudeville*]

ARTHUR WIMPERIS and HERMAN FINCK

7 I'm Gilbert, the Filbert, / The Colonel of the Knuts. [Song: *Gilbert the Filbert*, 1914, in *The Passing Show*]

8 On Sunday I walk out with a soldier, / On Monday I'm taken by a tar, / On Tuesday I'm out with a baby Boy Scout, / On Wednesday an Hussar. [Song: *On Sunday I Walk out with a Soldier*, 1914]

9 And on Saturday I'm willing, / If you'll only take the shilling, / To make a man of every one of you.

MARTY WINCH

10 It's better to be wanted for murder than not to be wanted at all. [*Psychology in the Wry*]

DUCHESS OF WINDSOR 1896–1986

11 One can never be too thin or too rich. [Attr.]

MICHAEL WINNER 1935–

12 A team effort is a lot of people doing what I say. [In the *Observer Magazine*, 8 May 1983]

D. A. WINSTANLEY

13 Gow has an inferiority complex about other people. [In *Geoffrey Madan's Notebooks*, ed. J. A. Gere and John Sparrow, 'Anecdotes']

JEANETTE WINTERSON 1959–

14 I asked why he was a priest, and he said if you have to work for anybody an absentee boss is best. [*The Passion*, 1]

15 I was happy but happy is an adult word. You don't have to ask a child about happy, you see it. They are or they are not. Adults talk about being happy because largely they are not.

16 I have met a great many people on their way towards God and I wonder why they have chosen to look for him rather than themselves. [*Sexing the Cherry*, p. 102]

17 I don't hate men, I just wish they'd try harder. They all want to be heroes and all we want is for them to stay at home and help with the housework and the kids. That's not the kind of heroism they enjoy. [127]

18 It is a fact that, up north, cemeteries are a way of life. [In the *Guardian*, 7 Aug. 1991]

JOHN WISDOM 1904–

19 ... Another sort of doubt which I venture to call 'philosophical', though I cannot here present all the excuses for stretching the word to cover all doubts of this sort. Examples of this sort are, 'Can a man keep a promise by mistake?', 'Is a zebra without stripes a zebra?' [*Other Minds*]

20 [Asking whether Ludwig Wittgenstein has made a key contribution to modern philosophy] is like asking whether one can play chess without the queen. [Quoted by Frederic Raphael in *New Society*, 30 May 1985]

ERNIE WISE 1925–

21 My video recorder records programmes I

don't want to see, and then plays them back when I'm out. [In *Apt and Amusing Quotations*, ed. G. F. Lamb, 'Television']

See also **ERIC MORECAMBE** and **ERNIE WISE**

LUDWIG WITTGENSTEIN 1889–1951

1 Philosophy, as we use the word, is a fight against the fascination which forms of expression exert upon us. [*The Blue Book*, p. 27]

2 If there were a verb meaning 'to believe falsely', it would not have any significant first person, present indicative. [*Philosophical Investigations*, Pt 2, sect. 10]

3 In order to draw a limit to thinking, we should have to be able to think both sides of this limit. [*Tractatus Logico-philosophicus*, Preface]

4 The world is everything that is the case. [1. 1]

5 All philosophy is 'Critique of language' . . . [4.0031]

6 Philosophy is not a theory but an activity. [4.112]

7 Everything that can be said can be said clearly. [4.116]

8 In logic process and result are equivalent. (Therefore no surprises.) [6.1261]

9 Whereof one cannot speak, thereof one must be silent. [7]

10 Ethics does not treat of the world. Ethics must be a condition of the world, like logic. [In W. H. Auden, *A Certain World*]

P. G. [later **SIR PELHAM**] WODEHOUSE 1881–1975

11 Chumps always make the best husbands. When you marry, Sally, grab a chump. Tap his forehead first, and if it rings solid, don't hesitate. All the unhappy marriages come from the husbands having brains. What good are brains to a man? They only unsettle him. [*The Adventures of Sally*, Ch. 10]

12 Unlike the male codfish which, suddenly finding itself the parent of three million five hundred thousand little codfish, cheerfully resolves to love them all, the British aristocracy is apt to look with a somewhat jaundiced eye on its younger sons. [*Blandings Castle*, 'The Custody of the Pumpkin']

13 It is never difficult to distinguish between a Scotsman with a grievance and a ray of sunshine.

14 He was either a man of about a hundred and fifty who was rather young for his years or a man of about a hundred and ten who had been aged by trouble. ['Lord Emsworth Acts for the Best']

15 'What ho!' I said, 'What ho!' said Motty. 'What ho! What ho!' 'What ho! What ho! What ho!' After that it seemed rather difficult to go on with the conversation. [*Carry On, Jeeves*, 'Jeeves and the Unbidden Guest']

16 Honoria . . . is one of those robust, dynamic girls with the muscles of a welter-weight and a laugh like a squadron of cavalry charging over a tin bridge. ['The Rummy Affair of Old Biffy']

17 He looked haggard and careworn, like a Borgia who has suddenly remembered that he has forgotten to shove cyanide in the consommé, and the dinner-gong due any moment. ['Clustering around Young Bingo']

18 I can't do with any more education. I was full up years ago. [*The Code of the Woosters*, Ch. 1]

19 He spoke with a certain what-is-it in his voice, and I could see that, if not actually disgruntled, he was far from being gruntled.

20 His whole attitude recalled irresistibly to the mind that of some assiduous hound who will persist in laying a dead rat on the drawing-room carpet, though repeatedly apprised by word and gesture that the market for same is sluggish or even non-existent.

21 It is no use telling me that there are bad aunts and good aunts. At the core they are all alike. Sooner or later, out pops the cloven hoof. [2]

22 Big chap with a small moustache and the sort of eye that can open an oyster at sixty paces.

23 'Oh Bertie,' she said in a low voice like beer trickling out of a jug, 'you ought not to be here!' [3]

1 He paused, and swallowed convulsively, like a Pekingese taking a pill.

2 'Have you ever seen Spode eat asparagus?' 'No.' 'Revolting. It alters one's whole conception of Man as Nature's last word.' [4]

3 He felt like a man who, chasing rainbows, has had one of them suddenly turn and bite him in the leg. [*Eggs, Beans and Crumpets*, 'Anselm Gets His Chance']

4 The only thing that prevented a father's love from faltering was the fact that there was in his possession a photograph of himself at the same early age, in which he, too, looked like a homicidal fried egg. ['Sonny Boy']

5 'But you said they were like a couple of love-birds.' 'Quite. But even with love-birds circumstances can arise which will cause the female love-bird to get above herself and start throwing her weight about.' ['All's Well with Bingo']

6 The fishy glitter in his eye became intensified. He looked like a halibut which had been asked by another halibut to lend it a couple of quid till next Wednesday. [*A Few Quick Ones*, 'The Word in Season']

7 Her voice trailed away in a sigh that was like the wind blowing through the cracks in a broken heart. [*Full Moon*, Ch. 10]

8 As is so often the case with butlers, there was a good deal of Beach. Julius Caesar, who liked to have men about him who were fat, would have taken to him at once. He was a man who had made two chins grow where only one had been before, and his waistcoat swelled like the sail of a racing yacht. [*Galahad at Blandings*, Ch. 2]

9 To My Daughter, LEONORA, without whose never-failing sympathy and encouragement this book would have been finished in half the time. [*The Heart of a Goof*, dedication]

10 I turned to Aunt Agatha, whose demeanour was now rather like that of one who, picking daisies on the railway, has just caught the down express in the small of the back. [*The Inimitable Jeeves*, Ch. 4]

11 He had a pair of shaggy eyebrows which gave his eyes a piercing look which was not at all the sort of thing a fellow wanted to encounter on an empty stomach. [8]

12 It was one of those cold, clammy, accusing sort of eyes – the kind that makes you reach up to see if your tie is straight: and he looked at me as I were some sort of unnecessary product which Cuthbert the Cat had brought in after a ramble among the local ash-cans. [10]

13 Jeeves coughed one soft, low, gentle cough like a sheep with a blade of grass stuck in its throat. [13]

14 I'm not lugged into Family Rows. On the occasions when Aunt is calling to Aunt like mastodons bellowing across primeval swamps and Uncle James's letter about Cousin Mabel's peculiar behaviour is being shot round the family circle ('Please read this carefully and send it on to Jane'), the clan has a tendency to ignore me. [16]

15 There's no doubt that Jeeves's pick-me-up will produce immediate results in anything short of an Egyptian mummy.

16 It was my Uncle George who discovered that alcohol was a food well in advance of modern medical thought.

17 Into the face of the young man who sat on the terrace of the Hotel Magnifique at Cannes there had crept a look of furtive shame, the shifty, hangdog look which announces that an Englishman is about to talk French. [*The Luck of the Bodkins*, Ch. 1]

18 It is a good rule in life never to apologize. The right sort of people do not want apologies, and the wrong sort take a mean advantage of them. [*The Man Upstairs*, title story]

19 It was the look which caused her to be known in native bearer and halfcaste circles as 'Mgobi-'Mgumbi, which may be loosely translated as She On Whom It Is Unsafe To Try Any Oompus-Boompus. [*Money in the Bank*, Ch. 8]

20 New York's a small place when it comes to the part of it that wakes up just as the rest is going to bed. [*My Man Jeeves*, 'The Aunt and the Sluggard']

21 I don't owe a penny to a single soul – not counting tradesmen, of course. ['Jeeves and the Hard-boiled Egg']

1 In this matter of shimmering into rooms the chappie [Jeeves] is rummy to a degree.

2 He moves from point to point with as little uproar as a jellyfish.

3 She fitted into my biggest armchair as if it had been built round her by someone who knew they were wearing armchairs tight about the hips that season. ['Jeeves and the Unbidden Guest']

4 I gave Motty the swift east-to-west.

5 What with excellent browsing and sluicing and cheery conversation and what-not, the afternoon passed quite happily.

6 Another slightly *frappé* silence.

7 As a rule, from what I've observed, the American captain of industry doesn't do anything out of business hours. When he has put the cat out and locked up the office for the night, he just relapses into a state of coma from which he emerges only to start being a captain of industry again. ['Leave It to Jeeves']

8 I was so darned sorry for poor old Corky that I hadn't the heart to touch my breakfast. I told Jeeves to drink it himself.

9 I spent the afternoon musing on Life. If you come to think of it, what a queer thing Life is! So unlike anything else, don't you know, if you see what I mean. ['Rallying round Old George']

10 Looking soiled and crumpled, like a Roman Emperor who has sat up too late over the Falernian wine. [*The Old Reliable*, Ch. 7]

11 '... you can't stick lighted matches between the toes of an English butler. He would raise his eyebrows and freeze you with a glance. You'd feel as if he had caught you using the wrong fork.' [17]

12 He had described Adela as looking like a Welsh rarebit about to come to the height of its fever, and it was such a Welsh rarebit at the critical stage of its preparation that she now resembled. [20]

13 One of the foulest cross-country runs that ever occurred outside Dante's *Inferno*. [*Psmith Journalist*, Ch. 30]

14 'I may as well inform you that it is not twenty-four hours since she turned me down.' 'Turned you down?' 'Like a bedspread. In this very garden.' [*Right Ho, Jeeves*, Ch. 15]

15 'How much gin did you put in the jug?' 'A liberal tumblerful, sir.' 'Would that be a normal dose for an adult defeatist, do you think?' [16]

16 It just shows, what any member of Parliament will tell you, that if you want real oratory, the preliminary noggin is essential. Unless pie-eyed you cannot hope to grip. [17]

17 It was a confusion of ideas between him and one of the lions he was hunting in Kenya that had caused A. B. Spottsworth to make the obituary column. He thought the lion was dead, and the lion thought it wasn't. [*Ring for Jeeves*, Ch. 1]

18 We may say what we will against the aristocracy of England ... but we cannot deny that in certain crises blood will tell. An English peer of the right sort can be bored nearer to the point where mortification sets in, without showing it, than anyone else in the world. [*Something Fresh*, Ch. 3]

19 To attract attention in the dining-room of the Senior Conservative Club between the hours of one and two-thirty, you have to be a mutton chop, not an earl.

20 Like so many substantial Americans, he had married young and kept on marrying, springing from blonde to blonde like the chamois of the Alps leaping from crag to crag. [*Summer Moonshine*, Ch. 2]

21 I can honestly say that I always look on Pauline as one of the nicest girls I was ever engaged to. [*Thank You, Jeeves*, Ch. 6]

22 'Alf Todd,' said Ukridge, soaring to an impressive burst of imagery, 'has about as much chance as a one-armed blind man in a dark room trying to shove a pound of melted butter into a wild cat's left ear with a red-hot needle.' [*Ukridge*, Ch. 5]

23 'That,' I replied cordially, 'is what it doesn't do nothing else but.' [6]

24 The stationmaster's whiskers are of a Victorian bushiness and give the impression of having been grown under glass. [*Uncle Dynamite*, Ch. 1]

1 He was prepared to coo to him like a turtledove; or as nearly like a turtledove as was within the scope of one whose vocal delivery was always reminiscent of a bad-tempered toastmaster. [3]

2 He blinked, like some knight of King Arthur's court, who, galloping to perform a deed of derring-do, has had the misfortune to collide with a tree. [5]

3 Say what you will, there is something fine about our old aristocracy. I'll bet Trotsky couldn't hit a moving secretary with an egg on a dark night. [*Uncle Fred in the Springtime*, Ch. 11]

4 Bingo uttered a stricken woofle like a bull-dog that has been refused cake. [*Very Good, Jeeves!*, 'Jeeves and the Impending Doom']

5 The Right Hon. was a tubby little chap who looked as if he had been poured into his clothes and had forgotten to say 'When!'

6 I once got engaged to his daughter, Honoria, a ghastly dynamic exhibit who read Nietzsche and had a laugh like waves breaking on a stern and rock-bound coast. ['Jeeves and the Yule-tide Spirit']

7 If I had had to choose between him and a cockroach as a companion for a walking-tour, the cockroach would have had it by a short head. ['The Spot of Art']

8 And closing the door with the delicate caution of one brushing flies off a sleeping Venus, he passed out of my life. ['Jeeves and the Old School Chum']

9 He groaned slightly and winced, like Prometheus watching his vulture dropping in for lunch. [In Richard Usborne, *Wodehouse at Work to the End*, Ch. 10]

CHARLOTTE WOLF 1904–1986

10 Women have always been the guardians of wisdom and humanity which makes them natural, but usually secret, rulers. The time has come for them to rule openly, but together with and not against men. [*Bisexuality: A Study*, Ch. 2]

HUMBERT WOLFE 1886–1940

11 You cannot hope / To bribe or twist, / Thank God! / the British journalist. / But seeing what / the man will do / Unbribed, there's / no occasion to. [*The Uncelestial City*, Bk 1, 'Over the Fire']

THOMAS WOLFE 1900–1938

12 Most of the time we think we're sick, it's all in the mind. [*Look Homeward, Angel*, Pt I, Ch. 1]

13 Making the world safe for hypocrisy. [III. 36]

TOM WOLFE 1931–

14 Yes, the labour movement was truly religious, like Judaism itself. It was one of those things you believed in for all mankind and didn't care about for a second in your own life. [*The Bonfire of the Vanities*, Ch. 8]

15 Yale [Law School] is terrific for anything you wanna do, so long as it don't involve people with sneakers, guns, dope, or sloth. [16]

16 The Kandy-kolored Tangerine-flake Streamline Baby. [Title of book]

17 Radical Chic. [Title of book]

18 The Right Stuff. [Title of book and film on US space programme]

19 Pornography was the great vice of the Seventies; plutography – the graphic depiction of the acts of the rich – is the great vice of the Eighties. [Interview in the *Sunday Times Magazine*, 10 Jan. 1988]

VICTORIA WOOD 1953–

20 I mean, in my day, in a magazine, you didn't have sex, you had a row of dots. [*Barmy*, 'No Gossip'. See also 256:3]

21 I'm all for killing animals and turning them into handbags, I just don't want to have to eat them. [On being vegetarian. Interview in the *Independent*, 7 Oct. 1987]

22 Our bed's only MFI; it won't take multiple orgasm. [Stage performance at Strand Theatre, London, Oct. 1990]

23 The only possible way there'd be an uprising in this country would be if they banned car boot sales and caravanning.

LIEUTENANT-COMMANDER TOMMY WOODROOFFE 1899–1978

1 The Fleet's lit up. It is like fairyland; the ships are covered with fairy lights. [BBC radio commentary at the Coronation Review of the Royal Navy at Spithead, 20 May 1937]

VIRGINIA WOOLF 1882–1941

2 Somewhere, everywhere, now hidden, now apparent in whatever is written down, is the form of a human being. If we seek to know him, are we idly occupied? [*The Captain's Death Bed*, 'Reading']

3 The poet gives us his essence, but prose takes the mould of the body and mind entire.

4 The interest in life does not lie in what people do, nor even in their relations to each other, but largely in the power to communicate with a third party, antagonistic, enigmatic, yet perhaps persuadable, which one may call life in general. [*The Common Reader*, First Series, 'On Not Knowing Greek']

5 Life is not a series of gig lamps symmetrically arranged: life is a luminous halo, a semi-transparent envelope surrounding us from the beginning of consciousness to the end. ['Modern Fiction']

6 She [Charlotte Brontë] does not attempt to solve the problems of human life; she is even unaware that such problems exist; all her force, and it is the more tremendous for being constricted, goes into the assertion, 'I love', 'I hate', 'I suffer'. ['Jane Eyre']

7 *Middlemarch*, the magnificent book which with all its imperfections is one of the few English novels for grown up people. ['George Eliot']

8 Those comfortably padded lunatic asylums which are known euphemistically as the stately homes of England. ['Lady Dorothy Nevill']

9 A good essay must have this permanent quality about it; it must draw its curtain round us, but it must be a curtain that shuts us in not out. ['The Modern Essay']

10 Trivial personalities decomposing in the eternity of print.

11 In or about December, 1910, human *character* changed. ['Mr Bennett and Mrs Brown']

12 Each had his past shut in him like the leaves of a book known to him by heart; and his friends could only read the title. [*Jacob's Room*, Ch. 5]

13 It's not catastrophes, murders, deaths, diseases, that age and kill us; it's the way people look and laugh, and run up the steps of omnibuses. [6]

14 There is in the British Museum an enormous mind. Consider that Plato is there cheek by jowl with Aristotle; and Shakespeare with Marlowe. This great mind is hoarded beyond the power of any single mind to possess it. [9]

15 'The guns?' said Betty Flanders, half asleep ... Again, far away, she heard the dull sound, as if nocturnal women were beating great carpets. [13]

16 Life itself, every moment of it, every drop of it, here, this instant, now, in the sun, in Regent's Park, was enough. Too much, indeed. [*Mrs Dalloway*]

17 Rigid, the skeleton of habit alone upholds the human frame.

18 A woman must have money and a room of her own if she is to write fiction. [*A Room of One's Own*, Ch. 1]

19 Women have served all these centuries as looking-glasses possessing the magic and delicious power of reflecting the figure of man at twice its natural size. [2]

20 So that is marriage, Lily thought, a man and a woman looking at a girl throwing a ball. [*To the Lighthouse*, Ch. 13]

21 I have lost friends, some by death ... others through sheer inability to cross the street. [*The Waves*]

22 Let a man get up and say, 'Behold, this is the truth', and instantly I perceive a sandy cat filching a piece of fish in the background. Look, you have forgotten the cat, I say.

23 On the outskirts of every agony sits some observant fellow who points.

24 Never have I read such tosh. As for the first two chapters we will let them pass,

but the 3rd, 4th, 5th, 6th – merely the scratching of pimples on the body of the boot-boy at Claridges. [Of James Joyce's *Ulysses*. Letter to Lytton Strachey, 24 Aug. 1922]

1 All raw, uncooked, protesting. A descendant, oddly enough, of Mrs [Humphry] Ward: interest in ideas; makes people into ideas. [Of Aldous Huxley's *Point Counter Point*. *A Writer's Diary*, 23 Jan. 1935]

2 A man or woman of thoroughbred intelligence galloping across open country in pursuit of an idea. [Definition of a highbrow. In Kenneth Tynan, *Curtains*, Pt 1]

3 In the play we recognize the general . . . in the novel, the particular. [In 2]

4 Nothing is stronger than the position of the dead among the living. [Quoted by Penelope Lively in the *Sunday Times*, 2 Apr. 1989]

ALEXANDER WOOLLCOTT 1887–1943

5 All the things I really like to do are either illegal, immoral, or fattening. [*The Knock at the Stage Door*]

6 I am in no need of your God-damned sympathy. I ask only to be entertained by some of your grosser reminiscences. [*Letter to a Rex O'Malley*, 1942]

7 A broker is a man who runs your fortune into a shoestring. [In R. E. Drennan, *Wit's End*]

8 Harold Ross, a man who knew nothing . . . and had a contempt for anything he didn't understand, which was practically everything. [In James Thurber, *The Years with Ross*, Ch. 15]

9 Woollcott himself used to brag that he was the best writer in America, but had nothing to say.

DAVID WRIGHT 1920–

10 It is not the hearing that one misses but the over-hearing. [*Deafness: A Personal Account*]

FRANK LLOYD WRIGHT 1869–1959

11 Give me the luxuries of life and I will willingly do without the necessities. [*Autobiography*, Bk 2, p. 108]

12 The physician can bury his mistakes, but the architect can only advise his client to plant vines. [In *The New York Times Magazine*, 4 Oct. 1953]

13 The land is the simplest form of architecture. Building upon the land is as natural to man as to other animals, birds or insects. In so far as he was more than an animal, his building became what we call architecture. While he was true to earth his architecture was creative. [In *New Light's Dictionary of Quotations*, comp. Ved Bhushan]

KIT WRIGHT 1944–

14 I like my face in the mirror, / I like my voice when I sing. / My girl says it's just infatuation – / I know it's the real thing. [*Every Day in Every Way*]

MRS WRIGHT

15 Eh! but it would make a grand Co-op! [Of All Souls College, Oxford. In E. M. Wright's biography of Professor J. Wright]

PETER WRIGHT 1916–

16 No one should have been allowed to become Prime Minister who has made twelve trips to Moscow. [Of Harold Wilson. In David Leigh, *The Wilson Plot*]

WUER KAIXI

17 A black sun has appeared in the sky of my motherland. [Of the violent suppression of demonstration in Tiananmen Square, Beijing. In the *Observer*, 'Sayings of the Week', 2 July 1989]

WOODROW [later LORD] WYATT 1919–

18 A man falls in love through his eyes, a woman through her ears. [*To the Point*, p. 107]

JANE WYMAN 1914–

19 Ask him [her former husband, Ronald Reagan] the time, and he'll tell you how the

watch was made. [In *Utterly Trivial Knowledge: The Pure Trivia Game*, ed. Margaret Hickery]

TAMMY WYNETTE 1942– and BILLY SHERRILL 1936–

1 Stand by Your Man. [Title of song]

JON WYNNE-TYSON 1924–

2 The wrong sort of people are always in power because they would not be in power if they were not the wrong sort of people. [Book review in *The Times Literary Supplement*]

ADMIRAL ISOROKU YAMAMOTO
1884–1943

1 I fear we have only awakened a sleeping giant, and his reaction will be terrible. [After Japanese attack on Pearl Harbor, 1941. Quoted by A. J. P. Taylor in the *Listener*, 9 Sept. 1976]

JUDGE LÉON R. YANKWICH
1888–1975

2 There are no illegitimate children – only illegitimate parents. [Decision in State District Court for the Southern District of California, June 1928, quoting columnist O. O. McIntyre]

GENE YASENAK

3 Kissing is a means of getting two people so close together that they can't see anything wrong with each other. [In *Was It Good for You Too?*, ed. Bob Chieger]

W. B. YEATS 1865–1939

4 That William Blake / Who beat upon the wall / Till Truth obeyed his call. [*An Acre of Grass*]

5 I said, 'A line will take us hours maybe; / Yet if it does not seem a moment's thought, / Our stitching and unstitching has been naught.' [*Adam's Curse*]

6 Better go down upon your marrow-bones / And scrub a kitchen pavement, or break stones / Like an old pauper, in all kinds of weather; / For to articulate sweet sounds together / Is to work harder than all these.

7 His element is so fine / Being sharpened by his death. / To drink from the wine-breath / While our gross palates drink from the whole wine. [*All Souls' Night*]

8 Nothing can stay my glance / Until that glance run in the world's despite / To where the damned have howled away their hearts, / And where the blessed dance.

9 When I was young, / I had not given a penny for a song / Did not the poet sing it with such airs / That one believed he had a sword upstairs. [*All Things Can Tempt Me*]

10 O body swayed to music, O brightening glance, / How can we know the dancer from the dance? [*Among School Children*, 8]

11 Bring the balloon of the mind / That bellies and drags in the wind / Into its narrow shed. [*The Balloon of the Mind*]

12 That dolphin-torn, that gong-tormented sea. [*Byzantium*]

13 Now that my ladder's gone, / I must lie down where all the ladders start, / In the foul rag-and-bone shop of the heart. [*The Circus Animals' Desertion*]

14 There's more enterprise / In walking naked. [*A Coat*]

15 Suddenly I saw the cold and rook-delighting heaven / That seemed as though ice burned and was but the more ice. [*The Cold Heaven*]

16 The years like great black oxen tread the world, / And God the herdsman goads them on behind, / And I am broken by their passing feet. [*The Countess Cathleen*, IV]

1 I would be ignorant as the dawn / That has looked down / On that old queen measuring a town / With the pin of a brooch. [*The Dawn*]

2 Yet always when I look death in the face, / When I clamber to the heights of sleep, / Or when I grow excited with wine, / Suddenly I meet your face. [*A Deep-Sworn Vow*]

3 Down by the salley gardens my love and I did meet: / She passed the salley gardens with little snow-white feet. / She bid me take love easy, as the leaves grow on the tree; / But I, being young and foolish, with her would not agree. [*Down by the Salley Gardens*]

4 I have met them at close of day / Coming with vivid faces / From counter or desk among grey / Eighteenth-century houses. / I have passed with a nod of the head / Or polite meaningless words. [*Easter 1916*]

5 All changed, changed utterly: / A terrible beauty is born.

6 The fascination of what's difficult. / Has dried the sap out of my veins, and rent / Spontaneous joy and natural content / Out of my heart. [*The Fascination of What's Difficult*]

7 I swear before the dawn comes round again / I'll find the stable and pull out the bolt.

8 One that is ever kind said yesterday: / 'Your well-belovèd's hair has threads of grey, / And little shadows come about her eyes.' [*The Folly of Being Comforted*]

9 Time can but make her beauty over again.

10 O heart! O heart! if she'd but turn her head, / You'd know the folly of being comforted.

11 The little fox he murmured, / 'O what of the world's bane?' / The sun was laughing sweetly, / The moon plucked at my rein; / But the little red fox murmured, / 'O do not pluck at his rein, / He is riding to the townland, / That is the world's bane.' [*The Happy Townland*]

12 What tumbling cloud did you cleave, / Yellow-eyed hawk of the mind, / Last evening? that I, who had sat / Dumbfounded before a knave, / Should give to my friend / A pretence of wit. [*The Hawk*]

13 I have drunk ale from the Country of the Young / And weep because I know all things now. [*He Thinks of his Past Greatness*]

14 I have spread my dreams under your feet; / Tread softly because you tread on my dreams. [*He wishes for the Cloths of Heaven*]

15 Processions that lack high stilts have nothing that catches the eye. [*High Talk*]

16 Out-worn heart, in a time out-worn, / Come clear of the nets of wrong and right. [*Into the Twilight*]

17 Nor law, nor duty bade me fight, / Nor public men, nor cheering crowds, / A lonely impulse of delight / Drove to this tumult in the clouds. [*An Irish Airman Foresees his Death*]

18 I will arise and go now, and go to Innisfree, / And a small cabin build there, of clay and wattles made: / Nine beanrows will I have there, a hive for the honey-bee, / And live alone in the bee-loud glade. [*The Lake Isle of Innisfree*]

19 And I shall have some peace there, for peace comes dropping slow, / Dropping from the veils of the morning to where the cricket sings.

20 And evening full of the linnet's wings.

21 The wind blows out of the gates of the day, / The wind blows over the lonely of heart, / And the lonely of heart is withered away. [*The Land of Heart's Desire*]

22 The land of faery, / Where nobody gets old and godly and grave, / Where nobody gets old and crafty and wise, / Where nobody gets old and bitter of tongue.

23 All things uncomely and broken, all things worn out and old, / The cry of a child by the roadway, the creak of a lumbering cart, / The heavy steps of the ploughman, splashing the wintry mould, / Are wronging your image that blossoms a rose in the deeps of my heart. [*The Lover tells of the Rose in his Heart*]

24 I shudder and I sigh to think / That even Cicero / And many-minded Homer were / *Mad as the mist and snow*. [*Mad as the Mist and Snow*]

1 We had fed the hearts on fantasies, / The heart's grown brutal from the fare. [*Meditations in Time of Civil War*, VI]

2 Time drops in decay, / Like a candle burnt out. [*The Moods*]

3 Why, what could she have done, being what she is? / Was there another Troy for her to burn? [*No Second Troy*]

4 A pity beyond all telling / Is hid in the heart of love. [*The Pity of Love*]

5 An intellectual hatred is the worst. [*A Prayer for My Daughter*]

6 Rose of all Roses, Rose of all the World! [*The Rose of Battle*]

7 Who dreamed that beauty passes like a dream? [*The Rose of the World!*]

8 Under the passing stars, foam of the sky, / Lives on this lonely face.

9 That is no country for old men. The young / In one another's arms, birds in the trees / – Those dying generations – at their song, / The salmon-falls, the mackerel-crowded seas. [*Sailing to Byzantium*]

10 An aged man is but a paltry thing, / A tattered coat upon a stick, unless / Soul clap its hands and sing, and louder sing / For every tatter in its mortal dress.

11 A Roman Caesar is held down / Under this hump. [*The Saint and the Hunchback*]

12 Turning and turning in the widening gyre / The falcon cannot hear the falconer; / Things fall apart; the centre cannot hold; / Mere anarchy is loosed upon the world, / The blood-dimmed tide is loosed, and everywhere / The ceremony of innocence is drowned; / The best lack all conviction, while the worst / Are full of passionate intensity. [*The Second Coming*]

13 And what rough beast its hour come round at last, / Slouches towards Bethlehem to be born?

14 Far-off, most secret and inviolate Rose, / Enfold me in my hour of hours. [*The Secret Rose*]

15 A woman of so shining loveliness / That men threshed corn at midnight by a tress, / A little stolen tress.

16 When shall the stars be blown about the sky, / Like the sparks blown out of a smithy, and die?

17 Romantic Ireland's dead and gone, / It's with O'Leary in the grave. [*September 1913*]

18 He that crowed out eternity / Thought to have crowed it in again. [*Solomon and the Witch*]

19 We have gone round and round / In the narrow theme of love / Like an old horse in a pound. [*Solomon to Sheba*]

20 And pluck till time and times are done / The silver apples of the moon, / The golden apples of the sun. [*The Song of Wandering Aengus*]

21 The brawling of a sparrow in the eaves, / The brilliant moon and all the milky sky, / And all that famous harmony of leaves, / Had blotted out man's image and his cry. [*The Sorrow of Love*]

22 Civilization is hooped together, brought / under a rule, under the semblance of peace / By manifold illusion. [*Supernatural Songs*, 'Meru']

23 What shall I do with this absurdity – / O heart, O troubled heart – this caricature, / Decrepit age that has been tied to me / As to a dog's tail? [*The Tower*, 1]

24 It seems that I must bid the Muse go pack, / Choose Plato and Plotinus for a friend / Until imagination, ear and eye, / Can be content with argument and deal / In abstract things; or be derided by / A sort of battered kettle at the heel.

25 Death and life were not / Till man made up the whole, / Made lock, stock and barrel / Out of his bitter soul. [3]

26 When you are old and grey and full of sleep, / And nodding by the fire, take down this book. [*When you are old*]

27 But one man loved the pilgrim soul in you, / And loved the sorrows of your changing face.

28 Love fled / And paced upon the mountains overhead / And hid his face amid a crowd of stars.

29 Unwearied still, lover by lover, / They paddle in the cold / Companionable streams or climb the air. [*The Wild Swans at Coole*]

1 Much did I rage when young, / Being by the world oppressed, / But now with flattering tongue / It speeds the parting guest. [*Youth and Age*]

2 We make out of the quarrel with others, rhetoric, but of the quarrel with ourselves, poetry. [*Anima Hominis*, 5]

3 It is so many years before one can believe enough in what one feels even to know what the feeling is. [*Autobiographies*, 'Reveries XXX']

4 He [Wilfred Owen] is all blood, dirt and sucked sugar stick. [Letter, 21 Dec. 1936, *Letters on Poetry to Dorothy Wellesley*]

5 Too true, too sincere. The Muse prefers the liars, the gay and warty lads. [Of James Reeves's *The Natural Need*. In Robert Graves and Alan Hodge, *The Long Weekend*, Ch. 25]

6 People are responsible for their *opinions*, but Providence is responsible for their morals. [In Christopher Hassall, *Edward Marsh*, Ch. 6]

7 The young men are mad jealous of their leaders for being shot. [Said by old Irish cabinet-maker after Easter Week rising. Reported in letter to Lord Haldane; see D. Sommer, *Haldane of Cloan*, Ch. 23]

8 When I try to put all into a phrase I say 'Man can embody truth, but he cannot know it.' [Letter just before his death. In Jonathon Green, *Famous Last Words*]

9 O'CONNOR: How are you?
YEATS: Not very well, I can only write prose today. [Attr.]

JACK YELLEN 1892–1991

10 Happy Days are Here Again. [Title of song]

See also under TUCKER, SOPHIE

PRESIDENT BORIS YELTSIN 1931–

11 You can make a throne from bayonets, but you can't sit on it for long. [From the top of a tank during the coup against Gorbachev. In the *Independent* 'Quote Unquote', 24 Aug. 1991]

12 You don't understand the Russian spirit.

People here do not understand the concept of buying and selling land. The land is like a mother. You don't sell your mother. [In the *Guardian*, 7 Dec.]

YEVGENY YEVTUSHENKO 1933–

13 No Jewish blood runs among my blood, / but I am as bitterly and hardly hated / by every anti-semite / as if I were a Jew. By this / I am a Russian. [*Babiy Yar*, trans. R. Milner-Gulland and P. Levi]

14 The hell with it. Who never knew / the price of happiness will not be happy. [*Lies*]

15 A poet in Russia is more than a poet. [In the *Guardian*, 20 Apr. 1987]

ANDREW YOUNG 1885–1971

16 For still I looked on that same star, / That fitful, fiery Lucifer, / Watching with mind as quiet as moss / Its light nailed to a burning cross. [*The Evening Star*]

17 It was the time of year / Pale lambs leap with thick leggings on / Over small hills that are not there, / That I climbed Eggardon. [*A Prehistoric Camp*]

18 Stars lay like yellow pollen / That from a flower has fallen; / And single stars I saw / Crossing themselves in awe; / Some stars in sudden fear / Fell like a falling tear. [*The Stars*]

19 The Swallows twisting here and there / Round unseen corners of the air / Upstream and down so quickly passed / I wondered that their shadows flew as fast. [*The Swallows*]

EDWARD YOUNG 1879–1960

20 Born Originals, how comes / it to pass that we die / Copies? [Epigraph to Jacob Golomb, *Inauthenticity and Authenticity*]

G. M. YOUNG 1882–1959

21 Great prose may occur by accident: but not great poetry. [In *Geoffrey Madan's Notebooks*, ed. J. A. Gere and John Sparrow, 'Extracts and Summaries']

MICHAEL [later LORD] YOUNG
   1915–

1 The Rise of the Meritocracy. [Title of book]

2 The Chipped White Cups of Dover. [Title of pamphlet]

WALDEMAR YOUNG, JOHN F.
   BALDERSTON, ACHMED
   ABDULLAH, GROVER JONES and
   WILLIAM SLAVENS McNUT

3 We have ways of making men talk. [In film *The Lives of a Bengal Lancer*, 1935]

Z

ISRAEL ZANGWILL 1864–1926

1 No Jew was ever fool enough to turn Christian unless he was a clever man. [*Children of the Ghetto*, I. 7]

2 Scratch the Christian and you find the pagan – spoiled. [II. 6]

3 America is God's Crucible, the great Melting Pot where all the races of Europe are melting and re-forming. [*The Melting Pot*, I]

4 The law of dislike for the unlike will always prevail. And whereas the unlike is normally situated at a safe distance, the Jews bring the unlike into the heart of *every milieu*, and must there defend a frontier line as large as the world. [*Speeches, Articles and Letters*, 'The Jewish Race']

DARRYL F. ZANUCK 1902–1979

5 For God's sake don't say yes until I've finished talking. [In Philip French, *The Movie Moguls*, Ch. 5]

6 If two men on the same job agree all the time, then one is useless. If they disagree all the time, then both are useless. [In the *Observer*, 'Sayings of the Week', 23 Oct. 1949]

FRANK ZAPPA 1940–

7 Rock journalism is people who can't write interviewing people who can't talk for people who can't read. [In *Rolling Stone*, 1970]

ROBERT ZEMECKIS 1952–

8 Where we're going we don't need roads. [In film *Back to the Future*, 1985, written and directed by Zemeckis. The line much loved and used by President Reagan]

ZHOU ENLAI 1898–1976

9 [When asked what he thought of the French Revolution] It is too early to say. [At the bicentenary of the Revolution. In the *Guardian*, 2 May 1989]

RONALD L. ZIEGLER [Press Secretary to President Nixon] 1939–

10 This is an operative statement. The others are inoperative. [Statement to White House press corps, 1973, admitting the untruth of earlier denials of government involvement in Watergate affair]

LUIS DE ZULUETA

11 The Church complains of persecution when it is not allowed to persecute. [Speech in the Cortes, 1936]

Index

a. is sin without God 65:18
all art deals with the a. 274:6
one's a.. And bigamy, sir, is a crime 267:9
something a. about the past 30:4
theatre of the a. set to music 350:7
Absurdity: a. . . . this caricature 417:23
Abuse: go on, a. me 31:9
to a. a man is a lover-like thing 69:15
Abyss: riding into the bottomless a. 389:15
rope stretched across the a. 338:6
Academic: a.s love bickering 100:7
rival schools of a.s 360:7
Academism: a. results when the reasons 362:17
Accent: a. of . . . coffee 231:15
English without an a. 34:24
wears them with a strong English a. 333:1
with a slight American a. 156:9
Acceptable: must say a. things 211:3
Access: that discovered a. 49:10
Accident: a. threatens 378:2
a.s . . . happen to somebody else 251:17
no a. that the symbol of a bishop 107:6
problem of habitual a.s 34:19
prose may occur by a. 418:21
without a. for two hundred years 329:6
Accidentally: never snub anybody a. 144:8
Accompaniment: a. of . . . douche bags 238:14
Accomplishment: ahead of his a.s 357:20
Accountancy: in a. they are a positive boon 268:7
someone who finds a. too exciting 8:20
Accountant: an a.. If they come any greyer 24:17
Accursed: a. power which stands 32:32
Accuse: qui s'a. s'excuse 317:13
Accused: a. of every death 67:4
a. of things you never did 359:16
Accusing: clammy, a. sort of eyes 409:12
Accustomed: get a. to it and finally like it 319:18
I've grown a. to her face 230:23
Ace: fifth a. makes all the difference 271:3
Ache: a.s just like a woman 113:14
be as a page that a.s for a word 105:17
Acheson, Dean 294:15
Achievement: great a. . . . in a blessed, warm fog 89:11
machine threatens all a. 319:11
scab on their a. 362:16
Acid: enough a. . . . to burn a hole 279:16
Ackamarackus: strictly the old a. 326:11
Acne: it goes with acne 46:1
sneer at a. 120:12
Acquaintance: we need two kinds of a.s 350:19
Acre: peaceful a.s 13:10
plot of a thousand a.s 365:8
Act: a. because they are inventing 342:1
A. of God designation 91:19
between the motion and the a. 117:18
easier to a. than to think 13:13
everybody who tells you how to a. 383:1
wants to get into da a. 112:7
yet the order of the a.s is planned 293:10
Act of Parliament: no . . . fun in any A. 170:30

Acte: l'a. gratuite 143:15
Acted: a. more like . . . celebrities 333:14
he does not act, he is a. upon 286:31
Acting: a. is . . . a controlled dream 317:6
a. is about . . . meeting someone's eye 97:1
a. is the lowest form of the arts 268:11
a. . . . keeping . . . from coughing 317:5
important thing in a. 188:2
not so much a. as reacting 63:9
one's still a. 351:8
real reason one loves a. 342:1
Action: a. [is the work] of one alone 141:6
unmotivated a. 143:15
world can only be grasped by a. 54:2
wrote with a. in mind 394:15
Activated: concept of A. Sludge 194:2
Active: resignation is a. 127:28
Activity: not a theory but an a. 408:6
two hours a day of a. 58:13
Actor: a. . . . ain't talking 145:2
a. . . . French call 'm'as-tu vu?' 361:24
a.s are atheists 295:18
a.s are cattle 172:13
best a.s do not let the wheels show 129:7
didn't act like a.s 333:14
director and . . . an a. 295:1
embarrassed by live a.s 387:15
good a. does not make his entry 47:7
good a.s and send them cheap 28:1
reasons why people become a.s 317:1
remember I'm an a. 69:18
single word from an a. 189:4
we're a.s – . . . opposite of people 360:23
when an a. marries an actress 315:18
Actress: fame of the a. is transitory 25:10
next worst to an a. 69:18
when an actor marries an a. 315:18
Actresses: English a. are mistresses 161:8
Actual: as a. as we are today 377:10
Actuary: a. . . . accountancy too exciting 8:20
Acute: a. limited excellence 126:12
more a. the experience 299:1
Ad: watched the a.s, and not the road 277:19
Adam: A. had 'em 144:1
A. was a gardener 210:25
every maker since A. 389:10
if A. and Eve had been merely engaged 397:3
what A. had seen on . . . his creation 182:15
what a good thing A. had 380:9
when A. and Eve were dispossessed 47:19
when you've A. 150:5
Adamant: a. for drift 79:10
Adapt: reasonable man a.s himself 345:3
Add: a. that lot up 161:5
nothing to say, only to a. 387:8
Adder: eye of toad or a. to catch 273:4
Addiction: a. to silk underwear 65:7
every form of a. is bad 199:5
terminal point of a. 19:3
Address: as an a. it was . . . genuine 84:14
Addresses: a. . . . to conceal whereabouts 332:9

Against: a. whom? 2:13
  fifth of the people are a. everything 205:14
  he said he was against it [sin] 90:9
Agate: eyes like a. lanterns 95:3
Age: after a certain a. 65:11
  a. shall not weary them 43:2
  astonishing any of us choose old a. 22:4
  best improve with a. 194:23
  decrepit a. . . . tied to me 417:23
  drives my green a. 369:2
  first sign of a. 171:19
  immatures with a. 406:9
  never remembers her a. 136:14
  never say to D'Arcy, 'Be your a.' 300:9
  old a. stuck in a microwave 312:2
  old age is always fifteen years older 27:6
  same a. as everyone else 105:19
  somewhere a.s and a.s hence 135:23
  unhoped serene that men call a. 54:10
  wrinkled with a. 103:16
Aged: a. by trouble 408:14
  a. man is but a paltry thing 417:10
  beauty of an a. face 64:16
Agendath Netaim 198:23
Agent: more reliable a.s [than God] 312:19
Aggression: a. is cultural 368:8
Aggressor: quarantine the a.s 322:16
Agir: *a. est le fait d'un seul* 141:6
Agitation: a. of the mind 171:11
Agonizing: a. reappraisal 111:3
Agony: it was a., Ivy 313:8
  outskirts of every a. 412:23
  that a. is our triumph 386:8
Agree: I a. with everything you say 361:11
  if two men on the same job a. 420:6
  nobody a.s with you 357:12
  question of getting them to a. 314:17
  when grown-ups a. 214:17
  with her would not a. 416:3
Agreed: meaning only in so far as it is not a.
  65:17
  never a. with my other self 143:7
Agricultural: diet of the a. classes 392:28
  fault of the A. Extension Service 11:17
Agriculture: problems with Soviet A. 11:5
Agua: *un rayo de a.* 278:19
Ahead: always wise to look a. 82:4
  be a. of all farewells 319:12
  get a. of ourselves 267:16
  lust and ambition look a. 232:12
Ahem: poets get a quizzical a. 137:15
Ahome: Ho! are you not going a.? 197:19
Aid: a. that is . . . without strings 53:25
  unhearing a. 43:8
Aida: you can't judge Egypt by *A* 125:17
AIDS 217:3
Aim: deliberate a. at Peace 401:2
  forgotten your a. 335:7
  no a. in Nature 401:8
  two things to a. at in life 350:10
  we a. to please. You a. too please 150:2

what is our a.? 79:14
Aime: *je ne l'aime, ni comme homme* 144:23
Air: a. force has to hold a cake-sale 237:19
  a. is blood temperature 111:13
  a. is like a draught of wine 93:22
  a. is thick with the wings 395:17
  both feet . . . in the a. 338:2
  clear the a. 118:24
  climb the a. 417:29
  dispense it in noise upon the a. 87:20
  dove descending breaks the a. 117:10
  drags us down from the a. 206:10
  fall through the air of . . . Piggy 146:9
  fresh a. and royalties 15:6
  fresh a. . . . in its proper place 241:3
  keep all your feathers in the a. 102:12
  open your eyes to the a. 370:18
  room full of good a. 225:19
  showed me the a. 197:2
  to a. the ditty 179:8
  unseen corners of the a. 418:19
  vivid a. signed with their honour 355:1
  which way the hot a. blows 170:17
Aircraft: a. slope above his head 137:13
Airiest: season was the a. May 151:24
Airplane: aphorisms . . . like a.s 276:2
Airport: a. is a free-range womb 56:1
  as pretty as an a. 1:14
Airship: looks down on a.s 170:10
Aisle: A. Altar. Hymn 273:11
Aitches: nothing to lose but our a. 287:10
Ajar: few [marriages] have been a. 138:5
Akkant: hoppy on a. of his joyicity 198:2
Alamein: before A. we never had a v. 81:17
Album: guide me safely through this a. 151:1
Alcohol: a. is a very necessary article 343:29
  discovered a. was a food 409:16
Alcoholic: a. . . . a man you don't like 370:6
Alderman: God in his last years, the A. 370:22
Aldershot: burnished by A.'s sun 40:19
Ale: a. from the Country of the Young 416:13
  a. out of an English flagon 74:18
  a.'s the stuff to drink 180:4
  shoulder the sky . . . drink your a. 178:20
  twopenny a. and cheese 74:19
Alexander: A.'s Ragtime Band 39:2
Algebra: relation . . . that a. bears 19:22
  what is a.? 26:14
Alibi: he always has an a. 117:29
  mortar or the a. 65:29
Alice: Christopher Robin went down with A.
  264:6
  in my sweet little A. blue gown 241:12
Alien: sentiments . . . similarly a. 248:5
Alienation: a. awaits us 219:8
Alike: everyone is a. 208:20
Alimony: a. is like buying oats 21:11
Alive: a. with him [Winston Churchill] 70:7
  better to be a. 128:11
  Dickens' world is . . . a. 71:5
  everyone is alike and no one is a. 208:20

had to die to prove he had been a. 201:12
lucky if he gets out of it [world] a. 125:3
never knew Lord Jones was a. 77:20
no dying but a. and warm 368:21
not while I'm a. 42:3
she's a.. I saw her lip curl 123:12
still alive at twenty-two 208:17
to be the one who comes out a. 51:3
wish they were the only one a. 19:5
All: a. in each and each in a. 356:2
a. that I was I am 103:15
good time was had by a. 351:11
you know what did it to a. of us 105:19
All-enacting: a. might that fashioned 163:3
All-powerful: a. for impotence 79:10
All Souls College, Oxford 413:15
Allah: A. created the English mad 211:9
Allegiance: no a. to a flag 383:14
Alleviation: dawn seem to be an a. 402:15
Alley: down an a. of green moss 390:1
lowest and vilest a.s of London 109:13
Alligator: a.s, just floating handbags 155:17
see you later, a. 159:14
up to your ass in a.s 196:4
Allnight: way home from an a. party 243:16
Ally: a. has to be watched 378:11
faithful a. and our sneaking foe 349:8
Almighty: A. in His infinite wisdom 80:2
direct access to the A. 359:14
prerogative of the A. 104:3
Almonds: a. . . . add weight 86:6
Almost-instinct: our a. almost true 221:4
Alone: absolutely truthful when you are a. 106:11
a., a. about the dreadful wood 17:13
a. . . . there is nobody there 207:8
early, sober, and a. 383:6
I want to be a. 140:3
last yards are run a. 266:16
leave a thing a. 77:7
leaving home after living a. 230:6
left a. with our day 18:26
live a. in the bee-loud glade 416:18
make love . . . then I go home a. 197:3
never so great as when she is a. 248:6
no one exists a. 18:19
to be adult is to be a. 325:1
we live as we dream – a. 89:6
Alp: a. of unforgiveness grew 300:4
Alpha: a. and omega of style 344:3
Alps 368:9
Altar: Aisle. A.. Hymn 273:11
replaced the A. and the Throne 334:14
Walter! Lead me to the a. 124:17
Altered: a. in the building trade 213:9
Alternative: a.s . . . not chosen themselves 46:8
considering the a. . . . it's not too bad 78:9
exhausted all . . . a.s 114:4
state the a. preferred 376:1
sun shone, having no a. 28:23
weigh the merits of a. paradigms 218:9
Altitude: a. . . . attained by hauling 189:10

Altruism: fruitful a.s of nature 308:18
Altruistic: greatest a. system 101:7
Alvarez: Madame A. had taken the name 86:3
Always: mine was a. that 28:17
Amaranth: sleep like fields of a. 102:19
Amateur: a. status must be . . . maintained 152:10
becoming an a. conjurer 361:23
disease that affects a.s 76:19
Father in Heaven, the untiring a. 151:1
hell is full of musical a.s 344:16
nation of a.s 324:2
prize a. nation 406:21
sure sign of an a. 59:7
Amazed: I was a. 180:15
Ambassador: British A. in Berlin 72:1
if an a. says yes 290:4
withdrawn my a.s at the age of fifteen 95:19
Amber: unzipped fly caught in forever a. 86:23
Ambidextrous: my right hand to be a. 149:12
Ambiguity: seven types of a. 120:22
Ambition: my a. has been so great 178:12
Ambitious: much less a. project 149:7
Ambivalence: a. . . . . chief characteristic 53:6
Ambulance: knocked down . . . with an a.? 348:8
Ambulatory: a. volume of the OED 167:5
America 85:3
  see also USA; United States
A. became top nation 341:9
A. contained contradictions 405:5
A. . . . engaged in high moral principle 60:13
A. . . . from barbarism to degeneration 84:13
A. has a new delicacy 76:1
A. is a land of boys 246:18
A. is a large, friendly dog 376:4
A. is God's crucible 420:3
A. is so big and everyone is working 33:26
A. . . . is the prize amateur nation 406:21
A. means white 270:8
A. seems to have resolved to buy it 249:22
A. that is on the march 205:6
behind the discovery of A. 317:10
best writer in A. 413:9
came to A. tourist Third 88:14
cultural centre of A. 34:11
England and A. . . . are separated 346:10
everything in A. is on wide screen 95:10
50 million Roman Catholics in A. 92:15
first come to pass in the heart of A. 116:11
God bless A. 39:9
going to A., bring your own food 227:2
greening of A. 315:6
impresses me most about A. 115:8
in A. anyone can be President 129:16
in A. everything goes 325:11
in A. the . . . system is brutal 96:4
in A. . . . two classes of travel 34:26
last wild Indian of A. 301:1
many hyphens left in A. 406:22
mechanical A. 222:16
moral climate of A. 322:15
more absolute silence of A. 224:11

national dish of A. 321:3
negative of which A. is the proof 242:5
next to . . . god a. i love you 97:24
nothing wrong with A. 314:3
only royalty A. ever had 100:19
religion of A. has always been A. 247:14
to A. to die 191:7
two worst things about A. 403:14
what makes A. what it is 357:9
woman governs A. 246:18
American: A. girls do have regrets 385:7
all A. at puberty 393:13
all A. males are failed athletes 141:22
A. abroad 356:13
A. as apple pie 56:9
A. captain of industry 410:7
A. character . . . greater humanity 242:4
A. Express has replaced 236:16
A. girls turn into A. women 160:21
A. heiress wants to buy a man 242:2
A. history . . . men hating 49:11
A. is either a Jew or an anti-Semite 335:24
A. life . . . is a perpetual assault 242:3
A. literature comes from one book 169:8
A. nation in th' Sixth Ward 111:19
A. . . . people say what they mean 270:21
A. people take half my money 125:12
A. professors like their literature 233:19
A. ship, good grub 237:1
A. society is half judaized 173:20
A. system of rugged individualism 177:5
A. [thinks] pacing 285:1
A. women like quiet men 10:1
A. women shoot the hippopotamus 130:7
A.s a . . . vulgar bustling people 245:18
A.s are like men and women 192:11
A.s are polite by telling the truth 49:12
A.s . . . conditioned to repect newness 382:13
A.s do not rear children 192:12
A.s get nervous abroad 209:2
A.s have a kind of resistance 377:13
[A.s] are too busy 387:24
budgies that can almost speak A. 96:1
business of the A. people is business 90:8
contradictions of A. life 53:26
dream of the A. Male 400:6
for the good of A. prose 8:7
free . . . except from the A.s 192:13
go round A. universities 221:22
goodwill toward us, the A. people 405:3
greatest A. friend 81:23
I don't see much future for the A.s 173:20
Irving Berlin *is* A. music 205:17
like so many substantial A.s 410:20
liver, . . . disdained by the A.s 341:12
19th [century] . . . with an A. accent 156:9
no second acts in A. lives 127:2
probably fond of them [A.s] 380:8
proud to be one of 200 million A.s 129:15
represented the modern A. woman 242:6
subtleties of the A. joke 380:3

success happens to an A. writer 8:7
talk sense to the A. people 358:21
therapy . . . the tenth A. muse 54:7
world. . . . a long way away to A.s 327:18
Americanism: A. with its sleeves rolled up 241:14
hyphenated A. 323:9
no fifty-fifty A. 323:11
toothsome amalgam of A.s and epigrams
    213:27
Amery, Leo: A. . . . prime minister 366:11
Amiabilities: three hundred . . . a.s 255:21
Amiably: do a. here, O God 64:13
Ammunition: pass the a. 130:1
Amnesia: a. is not knowing 319:21
    a. rules er – ? – ? 148:20
    apart from my a. 12:24
Amor: a. vincit insomnia 136:27
Amputate: thank God they had to a. 337:6
Amuse: talent to a. 93:12
Amused: a. by its presumption 372:12
Amusement: were it not for its a.s 233:5
Amusing: damned a. game 127:21
Anaemia: emotional a. 303:21
Anaesthesia: bastard substitute, A. 401:2
Anaesthetic: dentist who needs the a. 107:14
Analogy: a. . . . is the least misleading 61:15
Analyser: I'm an a. trying to leave out 29:9
Analysis: hostile a. of goldfish 391:21
    in a. with a strict Freudian 5:20
Analyst: a. should pay the patient 387:7
Anarchic: that was a bit a. 120:10
Anarchist: a.s who love God 69:19
    to a real a. a poke in the eye 69:19
Anarchy: a. is loosed upon the world 417:12
    my opinions lean . . . to a. 374:18
    when we apply it, you call it a. 77:10
    you do not even get a. 77:22
Anatomy: under the skin lies the a. 385:12
Ancestor: features of every a. 389:7
    roots lie in a. worship 349:16
    thrushes' a.s as sweetly sung 370:19
    vices of his a.s 122:14
Ancestry: delusion about its a. 186:20
Anchored: fleet of stars is a. 128:5
Anchovy: we don't . . . eat a. toast 281:18
Ancient: a. tapster of this hostel 103:7
    most a. profession in the world 214:20
    worlds revolve like a. women 117:35
And: including 'and' and 'the' 242:9
    learn a great deal more about 'and' 114:10
Anderton, James 270:11
Andress, Ursula: A. of militancy 378:12
Andrews, Julie 300:12
Android: a.s dream of electric sheep? 105:18
Andromache: A., Who he? 324:22
Angel: a. . . . breast projecting 159:6
    a. of history 145:18
    a. out of heaven brings you 75:9
    a.s are so few 110:23
    a.s can fly 77:8
    a.s play only Bach in praising God 26:29

born of risen apes, not fallen a.s 13:10
calling to the A. and the Souls 211:15
collect his royalties as recording a. 246:12
curiosity of an a.'s stare 365:9
felt as if a.s were pushing 139:12
in heaven an a. is nobody 345:1
not fallen a.s 224:19
number of a.s able to dance 92:17
on the side of the a.s 294:12
pleasing to the a.s 332:24
praise the world to the a. 319:1
share the enthusiasm of the a.s 332:27
song of the a.s 260:8
the difference from a person and an a. 8:18
Anger: a. of men who have no opinions 76:21
  monstrous a. of the guns 288:14
Anglo-Catholic: becoming an A. 361:23
Anglo-Irishman 31:3
Anglophile: too much of an A. 368:17
Angry: a. young man 123:8, 293:16
  that a. or that glimmering sea 128:13
Anguish: transcends his . . . anguish 272:7
Animal: a. that does not exist 319:10
  a.s going through . . . fooleries 183:9
  a.s were not expelled from Paradise 218:18
  a.s who are merely different 224:23
  a.s will not look 18:26
  attitude towards these human a.s 172:9
  if we stop loving a.s 352:10
  I'm all for killing a.s 411:21
  man is a wild a. 100:3
  multitude of a.s which scamper 54:1
  my family and other a.s 112:11
  nothing to be done really about a.s 174:16
  some a.s are more equal 286:12
  true to your a. instincts 224:13
  understood by children and a.s 362:20
  what appear to be a.s 314:11
Ankle: a. socks . . . of the vicar's wife 119:17
  women who wear a. socks 36:16
Ann: A., A.! Come quick as you can 102:16
Anna Karenina 266:4
Anna Livia: O tell me all about A. 197:18
Anno Domini: A. – . . . fatal complaint 172:8
Annoyed: responds without getting a. 97:14
Annoying: a. to have to lie 108:1
Anonymity: he could become an a. 235:4
Anonymous: conversations . . . were a. 199:27
Another: that is a. story 214:15
Answer: a., . . . blowin' in the wind 113:8
  a. is in the p. and they bounce 239:7
  a. isn't in us 174:16
  a. yes without having asked 65:10
  a. you back before you've said 296:1
  believe that men were the a. 25:18
  I ask and cannot a. 346:15
  if love is the a. 375:10
  if Margaret Thatcher is the a. 149:14
  learned the a.s, all the a.s 244:12
  that is the a. 326:7
  there's no answer to that 269:4

why did you a, the phone? 372:15
Answered: tell them I came, and no one a. 103:12
  their hands minutely a. 97:11
Ant: a. sandwich 11:2
Antagonistic: a, enigmatic 412:4
  a. to the Victorian age 405:13
Antarctica: warily as A. was circled 116:10
Antennae: a. in all directions 193:5
Anthology: a. is like all the plums 311:11
Anthony, St 183:1
Anthropologist: a. respects history 232:7
Anthropology: drama is a form of a. 42:26
Anthropomorphic: a. fallacy 216:9
Anti-clerical: understand a. things 33:18
Anti-climax: savours of a. 126:12
Anti-Communist: Christian a.s 111:6
Anti-intellectual: science is really a. 259:2
Anti-Semite: Jew or an a. 335:24
Anti-social: a. and dangerous character 35:2
Antidote: poison and a. 329:2
Antipathies: cosmopolitan sympathies . . . and a.
  324:9
  depersonalize your a. 186:8
Antique: a., dread of the headsman's axe 151:11
Antiquity: tragedies of a. 360:22
Antithesis: a. in ideas 381:5
Anvil: ring of the a. 389:8
Anxiety: a. meets a technique 112:23
  a. which . . . follows birth 314:15
  his greatest source of a. 139:5
Anxious: a. to be someone 48:6
Anybody: a., anywhere, anytime 90:6
  'a. there?' said the traveller 103:11
Anything: a. goes 301:13
  a. you can do 39:6
  do a. rather than be here now 229:14
  he laughs like a. 75:3
  I don't want to do a. 336:11
  if there's a. that you want 229:22
  nobody tells me a. 139:16
  not to mention what the a. is 328:15
  wot's the good of a. [hanyfink] 78:6
Apart: you mean a. from my own? 138:8
Apathy: consumed with a. 202:12
  much to be said for a. 130:20
Ape: advance beyond a. – mentality 400:21
  a.s – orang utangs hang in the trees 202:1
  a.s of God 233:8
  born of risen a.s 13:10
  cargo of ivory, and a.s and peacocks 254:2
  gorgeous buttocks of the a. 183:18
  it is not the a., nor the tiger 367:9
  naked a. 270:3
  peacocks, a.s and ivory 212:4
Ape-like: a. virtues 87:17
Aphorism: a. never coincides 217:12
  a.s that, like airplanes stay up 276:2
  one cannot dictate an a. 217:11
Aphrodisiac: fame is a powerful a. 154:10
  moon . . . circumambulatory a. 136:24
  power is the ultimate a. 214:33

427

Apologies: people do not want a.s 409:18
Apologize: Englishman a.s to the truck 254:18
  I never a. 342:19
  never a. 126:5
  never to a. 409:18
Apologizing: for ever a. 259:7
Apology: a. for the Devil 61:22
  friends are God's a. for relations 208:19
Apparatus: mediocrity of the a. 378:6
Apparition: a. of these faces 303:20
Appeal: prayers are like those a.s of ours 352:20
  they just lose their a. 12:6
Appear: entirely what they a. 336:8
Appearance: a. of having been designed 101:4
  next a. is a new creation 307:15
  religion was mortality and a. 119:15
Appearing: for a. on, not watching 94:16
Appeasement: political a. 237:17
Appeaser: a. . . . feeds a crocodile 82:19
Appendicitis: operated on for a. 396:6
Appendix: a. put back in 64:11
Appetency: equal or more important a. 316:14
Applaud: a. all songs 97:8
Applause: a. is a receipt, not a bill 338:15
  a. of the West 382:1
  a. the echo of a multitude 42:7
  food and shelter and a. 192:12
Apple: a. trees will never get across 135:17
  a. wood of Hereford 74:13
  all millionaires have baked a. 125:28
  American as a. pie 56:9
  a.s fell and the swallows 68:14
  a.s were gathered and stored 118:21
  don't sit under the a. tree 56:15
  having . . . an eye for a.s 151:22
  honest state before the a. 224:22
  moon-washed a.s of wonder 110:19
  propagated by cutting, like a. trees 159:4
  shade of the old a. tree 403:21
  shoot the rind off an apple 271:13
  silver a.s of the moon 417:20
Apply: lover . . . need not a. 396:2
Appointment: a. by the corrupt few 344:28
Appreciate: a., any more than I like 297:16
Appreciation: a. of others 88:5
Apprehension: articulate a. 142:11
  jumpiness and a. 372:20
  passionate a. of form 31:15
  respect and a. 52:13
Apprehensive: a. whether they . . . bite 354:17
Apprentice: time for me to become an a. 28:11
Apricot: blossoms of the a. 303:6
April: A. is the cruellest month 117:37
  A., laugh thy girlish laughter 391:19
Aptitude: our . . . a.s, however slight 38:8
Aquarium: managed to preserve his a. 170:15
Arab: know there were A.s in the country 186:19
  shook hands with a friendly A. 262:20
Arabesque: lateral a. 296:8
Arabia: crazed with the spell of far A. 102:21
  far are the shades of A. 102:20

Aragon: A. is . . . not a hero 297:17
Arbeit: *A. macht frei* 19:24
Arc: a. of a stallion's neck 389:8
Arch-enemy: a. of art 395:16
Archaeologist: a. is the best husband 78:15
Archaeology: a. of our thought 131:13
Archbishop: a. had come to see me 58:20
  sign of an a. 107:6
Archer: a.s stand there on every side 273:7
Arches: underneath the a. 128:1
Archibald: A., certainly not 332:6
Architect: a. can only . . . plant vines 413:12
  finally called, by the Great A. 161:5
  I was meant to be a sculptor or a. 70:1
Architecture: a. cannot lie 145:5
  a. is the most inescapable of . . . arts 310:6
  a. was the work of . . . civil servants 83:8
  it's modern a. 24:13
  land is the simplest . . . a. 413:13
  like dancing about a. 252:10
  may turn them into fine a. 136:29
  opera, next to Gothic a. 83:7
  rise and fall of English a. 41:5
  shining at new styles of a. 18:23
Arctic: a. zones of the eternal rosin 172:10
  rough-rider over the A. regions 350:5
Area: sprouting despondently at a. gates 117:30
Argentina: don't cry for me, A. 316:7
Argentinian: A.s from the ships 294:9
Argifying: what's the good of a.? 214:11
Argue: enemies of freedom do not a. 186:4
Argument: a. . . . in religion 41:20
  beware of long a.s 335:11
  detected only once in . . . an a. 37:6
  final a. 285:18
Ariel: Caliban casts out A. 303:15
Arise: I will a. and go now 416:18
  to the old wars; A., a. 370:18
Aristocracy: a. . . . badly educated 77:25
  a. to what is decent 177:11
  a. would be biologically sound 159:4
  British a. . . . looks 408:12
  say what we will against the a. 410:18
  something fine about our old a. 411:3
Aristocrat: honour is a luxury for a.s 76:15
Aristocratic: language of a. affability 308:5
Aristotle: Plato is there . . . with A. 412:14
Arithmetic: a. of sounds 102:8
  one [language] in which you do a. 66:8
  take sides against a. 79:5
Arlen, Michael: 399:2
Arm: hero's a.s and bullock's eyes 206:9
  I'm not walking around with an empty a. 161:6
  let me stay in your a.s 63:7
  stretch out our a.s further 126:20
Arm-chair: a. for my steed 65:2
Armada: Mosquito A. 81:9
Armaments: [it is] wars that cause a. 246:16
Armchair: wearing a.s tight 410:3
Armed: a. hot dog thefts 375:15
  a. neutrality 406:18

in a state of a. conflict 114:13
we [women] should be a. 283:6
Armenteers: mademoiselle from A. 325:19
Armful: that's very nearly an a. 161:6
Armies: crush the spring leaf with your a. 5:3
    interested in a. and fleets 17:11
Armoured: too heavily a. perish 366:14
Armpit: dirty a. of Europe 235:9
    like smelling their own a.s 262:11
    long beards and stinking a.s 151:20
Arms: a. control means . . . deodorant 339:3
Army: a. is a peasant's idea of order 53:10
    back to the a. again 209:16
    contemptible little a. 403:11
    dialect that has an a. and a navy 394:13
    hitched him up to the A. 17:14
    in the a. they *shot* cowards 119:18
    join the A., see the world 12:27
    Newman's . . . gone into the a. 69:17
    no a. can ever save 294:2
    self-centred a. without parade 225:5
    this is the a., Mr Jones 39:11
    we are Fred Karno's a. 12:19
Around: one sure way to get a. 383:6
Arrange: French a. 70:14
    glad to a. it [a kiss] for you 126:17
Arras: slogged up to A. 337:5
Arrested: Christ would have been a. 101:22
Arrive: a. at any terminus 117:7
Arrived: I've a. and to prove it, I'm here 62:12
    so say those who have already a. 395:5
Arrow: father of the a. is the thought 215:10
    research is like shooting an a. 2:12
    white a.s on the shadowed ground 267:13
Ars: *A. gratia artis* 106:2
Arse: politician is an a. 97:27
    sit on your a. for fifty years 246:4
Arsenal: a. of democracy 322:22
Arsenic: a. and old lace 206:6
Arson: a. . . . is an artificial crime 396:14
Arsonist: phoenix who runs with a.s 34:6
Art: acting . . . lowest form of the a.s 268:11
    all a. deals with the absurd 274:6
    all a. is full of magic 274:12
    all a. is the same 29:11
    always said God was against a. 116:15
    arch-enemy of a. 395:16
    a. and religion are [an] escape 31:16
    a. . . . can go on mattering 48:5
    a. . . . can . . . mend the mistakes 348:16
    a. . . . chief means of breaking bread 19:13
    a. does not imitate life 53:11
    a. does not reproduce what we see 215:8
    a. for a.s sake 106:2
    a. ghetto in which poetry is kept 165:4
    a. greater than life 67:15
    a. has to move you 175:4
    a. is a lie 298:3
    a. is an appeal to a reality 241:9
    a. is . . . involved with the female 83:5
    a. is light synthesis 217:5

a. is meant to disturb 50:16
a. is not a mirror 257:17
a. is not a special sauce 231:4
a. is not a weapon 205:5
a. is significant deformity 137:1
a. is spectral analysis 217:5
a. is the history of revivals 61:18
a. is thoughtful workmanship 231:5
a. its small, translucent fruit 244:11
a. . . . left to . . . shabby bums 233:18
a. . . . life is all right 43:7
a. of living that your price 161:11
a. . . . profoundest thoughts 116:2
a. . . . rather than the article 82:3
a. should be cold 338:22
a. . . . to people who can't get along 152:18
a.s . . . only a shadow of Paradise 254:15
aspires . . . to the condition of a. 89:10
B-grade novels . . . popular a. 276:12
directory is . . . a work of a. 148:13
disfigure a great work of a. 308:4
dying is an a. 299:22
every work of art . . . is simple 76:24
great a. is always an invention 294:7
half a trade and half an a. 186:14
how drunk we like our a. to be 238:18
I doubt that a. needed Ruskin 361:16
if there's a clash . . . it is bad a. 71:9
it's a. that makes life 191:9
it's clever, but is it A.? 210:7
least realistic of a. forms 248:9
like all art it has its laws 378:1
making life into a. 284:18
most inescapable of the higher a.s 310:6
no one will take to a. 31:18
object of a. is to give life shape 12:23
painting as a work of a. 298:5
pop a. and fine a. 243:20
rest is the madness of a. 190:20
sacrificing our pockets to a. 136:29
significant figure in graphic a. 238:3
simplest modulation . . . is . . . a. 362:12
sombre enemy of good art 87:23
that is a., they say. A.! 257:19
their [Irish] devotion to higher a.s 139:1
to be aristocratic in a. 268:13
what was known as a. silk 288:7
when a. communicates 404:4
you are only interested in a. 346:9
Artefact: remembered by their a.s 27:16
Arthritis: a., and I don't deserve that 37:13
    cannot even spell a. 326:11
Artichoke: a.s and extortion 326:18
Article: art . . . rather than the a. 82:3
Articulate: a. apprehension 142:11
    a. sweet sounds together 415:6
    more a. its expression 299:1
Artificer: old a. stand me 198:8
Artificial: arson . . . is an a. crime 396:14
    nothing so a. as sinning 224:12
Artisan: employment to the a. 33:5

Artist: a. . . . can make a riddle 217:6
  a. cannot suffer alone 204:3
  a. disappears into it [landscape] 47:18
  a. . . . is by nature a solipsist 256:23
  a. like the idiot or clown 349:12
  a. should know all about love 294:6
  a. who doesn't fit 127:20
  a. who uses his brains 238:3
  a. who's an intellectual also 127:20
  a. will betray . . . by . . . sincerity 76:22
  a. . . . with the worst possible ordeal 40:6
  a. writes his own autobiography 120:15
  a.s are not engineers of the soul 205:5
  a.s can colour the sky red 123:11
  a.'s egoism is outrageous 256:23
  a.s have a right to be modest 217:7
  a.'s job to create sunshine 322:4
  a.s . . . people don't need 391:2
  a.s produce [what] nobody needs 402:21
  as a.s they're rot 292:8
  creative reply of a Soviet a. 347:7
  from now on an a. will be judged 87:13
  gentleman from . . . the a. 392:6
  God . . . an a. . . . rather than a judge 273:3
  God is really only another a. 297:8
  great a.s . . . are never Puritans 259:3
  if a.s do see fields blue 173:12
  let the a. have just enough to eat 31:18
  man is a special kind of a. 143:25
  more perfect the a. 119:5
  one lucky bastard who's the a. 361:8
  only a mediocre a. 48:10
  only one position for an a. 370:3
  portrait of the a. as a young man 198:6
  sensitiveness . . . of the true a. 30:24
  style of most a.s and all humbugs 87:16
  too difficult for a.s 338:17
  true a. will let his wife starve 344:7
  we must grant the a. his subject 190:5
  what the title of a. means 94:26
  you might as well be an a. 361:9
Artistic: a. and spiritual life 75:23
  a. metempsychosis 170:10
  a. temperament is a disease 76:19
  don't ever wear a. jewellery 86:5
  earth as an a. cult 130:18
Aryan: I wouldn't trust an A. 277:2
Ascension: rather than in . . . the A. 159:7
Ascent: a. of man 54:1
Asceticism: out of a. . . . that we bear it 242:3
Ascot: A. . . . where the horses own 57:17
Ash: a. on an old man's sleeve 117:9
  oak and a. and thorn 213:8
Ashamed: doing something he is a. of 342:25
  more things a man is a. of 344:5
Ashes: a. of . . . tobacco 109:9
  a. under Uricon 179:28
  sour grapes and a. 15:8
Ashlar: my new-cut a. 212:5
Asian: what A. boys ought to be doing 195:17
Ask: a. not what your country 204:20

but were afraid to a. 315:15
  I a. and cannot answer 346:15
Asleep: not to fall a. is distinguished 34:3
  old ships sail like swans a. 128:15
Asparagus: a. . . . with vinaigrette 331:11
  Spode eat a. 409:2
Asphalt: a. jungle 59:19
  only monument the a. road 118:25
Aspidistra: biggest a. in the world 124:15
Aspiration: a.s that never come to pass 332:21
  Gothic . . . is all . . . a. 52:1
Aspire: a.s . . . to the condition of art 89:10
  do not a. to advise my sovereign 393:20
Asquith, A.A., Earl of Oxford 46:3
  A. is good and immoral 82:5
Asquith, Margot 292:5
Ass: kiss my a. in Macy's window 196:2
  up to your a. in alligators 196:4
Assail: darkness shall no more a. 103:2
Assassin: a. . . . in the dust 334:16
Assassinate: a. food 192:3
Assassination: a. is . . . censorship 345:25
  a. should be used as the vote 184:1
  despotism tempered by a. 315:12
  Dumini, twelve a.s 111:9
  political leader worthy of a. 225:10
  what a. is all about 391:4
Assent: a. require far more courage 104:4
Assertion: effectiveness of a. 344:3
Assiduously: a. picking his nose 125:32
Assignation: vast house of a. 95:17
Assimilation: a. of the features 389:7
  avenue of a. into society 107:15
Associate: Ali Baba and the Forty A.s 33:22
Assumed: [bridge] under an a. name 202:8
Assurance: a. sits as a silk hat 118:14
Astaire, Fred 16:5, 39:19, 170:21
Asterisk: a.s . . . followed . . . by a baby 256:3
Asthma: Count A. 18:24
Astonish: a. me 105:16
Astonishment: a. at our own existence 75:23
  point of greatest a. 153:4
  your a.'s odd 9:21
Astor, Nancy, Viscountess 16:7
Astor, William Waldorf, Viscount 316:8
Astride: he a. the moon 363:16
Astronaut: a.s! . . . Rotarians in outer space
  387:11
Astronomer: confounding her a.s 175:9
Astronomy: a. teaches the . . . sun 226:1
  I don't even believe in a. 104:19
Asunder: no man will ever put a. 343:13
Asylum: Cambridge an a., in every sense 180:10
  comfortably padded . . . a.s 412:8
  deranged and should go to an a. 173:12
  lunatics have taken over the a. 325:23
  Russia is an enormous . . . a. 375:1
Athanasian: A. creed in public 19:1
Atheism: every luxury . . . a. 286:1
Atheist: a. . . . no invisible means of support 57:14
  a. who finds creations so perfect 308:2

actors are a.s 295:18
embittered a. 286:17
ginger whiskers of the born a. 122:13
I am an a. still, thank God 58:14
sacrilegious a. 333:17
scepticism kept her from being an a. 336:21
very *chic* for an a. 328:2
worst moment for an a. 390:19
Athens: burn with A. and with Rome 65:4
Athlete: American males are failed a.s 141:22
Athletic: a.s as inferior . . . fox-hunting 392:11
high a. qualifications 81:15
Atkins: thank you Mr A. 213:6
Atlantic: balcony overlooking the A. 266:19
Battle of the A. 81:14
drag the A. for whales 380:6
not to have the East come to the A. 146:4
Atlas: immense improbable a. 17:9
Atmosphere: a. knows no boundaries 147:28
Atom: a. . . . has changed everything 115:15
a.s acting according to . . . physics 124:5
a.'s way of knowing about a.s 389:13
bomb: a. is a paper tiger 250:14
breaking down of the a. 329:17
carbon a. possesses . . . qualities 193:1
does as well for telling a. secrets 351:18
no evil in the a. 359:2
protons and morons in the a. 194:2
they only split it? [the a.] 166:3
Atomic: energy 158:3
explosion 222:10
way to win an a. war 50:2
Atomic bomb 82:3, 172:11, 178:8, 285:6
Atrophy: music begins to a. 303:22
Attachment: a. to the things of this world 249:19
strengthening his a. 306:18
Attack: a. . . . your right to say it 361:11
Attend: a. all or none 392:15
Attention: a. . . . against a single adversary 173:5
a. must be paid 261:22
a. span of a bolt of lightning 314:4
every time we really pay a. 394:12
thank him for his kind a.s 75:9
wish to draw my a. 109:27
Attic: a. of forgotten toys 284:20
beauty crieth in an a. 62:7
brain a. . . . with all the furniture 109:14
eighteen in the a.s 183:12
Attila: A. the Hen 133:16
Attire: a. for a gentleman 342:11
Attitude: every intellectual a. 249:25
Attlee, Clement [later Earl] 10:4, 82:5, 82:6, 84:1, 84:2
Mr A. combines a limited outlook 80:13
Attracted: a. by God or by nature 186:10
Attracting: rhythm of a. people 194:20
Attraction: a.s for their coming week 18:8
most exciting a.s 391:16
Attractive: faithful . . . in the least a. 65:6
Attractiveness: loses some of its a. 352:21
Attributed: a. by the living to the dead 364:4

Auction: a. of the worldly goods 186:3
if a joke were a charity 243:19
nothin' . . . but a . . . a. 404:16
Auden, W.H.: A., a sort of gutless Kipling 287:7
A. . . . an ample . . . OED 167:5
A. had an open mind about sex 355:7
A. . . . you could laugh-at-with 355:6
[A.] didn't love God 10:8
I think I'm A. 121:13
mysterious, . . . tea-drinking A. 88:3
Audience: [American a.s] can't sit still 85:3
a. of means 192:15
a. . . . one not coughing 338:14
drama is when the a. cries 67:10
Folies-Bergère and looks at the a. 359:15
I never wrote with an a. in mind 167:6
one man? . . . You call that an a? 92:5
play chooses its a. 37:1
sure . . . the a. is still there 50:5
take its a.s seriously 25:11
we don't conduct the a. 108:7
what is an a. . . . but a vast tit? 259:19
where do all the a. come from? 281:11
Aufgestellt: war eine Art von Urwald a. 202:1
Aufwand: des andern A. fühlbar 318:5
Aufzubrechen: plötzlich a. 202:2
August: A. for the people 17:6
Aunt: a. is so deflating to a poem 251:24
adopted a. of lone abnormal me 40:23
bad a.s and good a.s 408:21
his a.s who are not married 75:11
house kept by country a.s 255:9
monstrous a. can be funny 383:5
when A. is calling to A. 409:14
Auschwitz: this . . . is their A. 302:8
Austen, Jane: as A. wrote about manners 45:15
Austerity: high a. to delight 133:7
we admire a. in ourselves 87:19
Austerlitz: pile the bodies high at A. 334:18
Australia: A. is not very exclusive 285:11
being lost in A. 73:13
didn't I tell you A. was up? 252:14
indifference of this . . . A. 223:12
last year in A. 368:12
Australian: subtle in the A. character 400:11
Austria: A. is Switzerland 270:2
Austriae: A. est imperare orbi universo 356:17
Auswahl: begann nicht . . . seine herrische A. 318:12
Author: allow an a. to smell treacle 323:17
a.s and uncaptured criminals 234:18
a.s are easy . . . to get on with 197:6
a.s who are not really novelists 131:4
I write like a distinguished a. 276:9
sending the a. some small cash token 87:24
shelf-life of the modern hard-back a. 270:19
six characters in search of an a. 299:5
Authorities: a. whom we do not control 88:28
Authority: a. cannot put up with a nation 201:17
craving for a. figures 334:14
maximal a. and minimal power 364:3
no morality can be founded on a. 20:5

Auto-didact: we are all . . . a.s 297:11
Autobiographies: a. tell more lies 62:10
Autobiography: a. is an obituary in serial form 95:23
  a. is the most gratuitous 361:10
  age to write an a. 392:21
  every artist writes his own a. 120:5
Autocrat: rebel . . . without being an a. 112:16
Autocratic: too a. for oratorio 370:23
Autograph: I would give him my a. 173:14
Automatic: a. acquired in the holidays 340:7
  smoothes her hair with a. hand 118:15
Automobile: fix up his a. 83:18
  money differs from an a. 139:5
Autonomous: a. individual 286:18
Autumn: a. is desolation 365:8
  a. is just as nice as spring 406:14
  A. sunsets exquisitely dying 183:18
  go well with the autumn scenery 332:11
  I rose in rainy a. 369:10
  south, where there is no a. 224:21
Aventures: a. de son âme 132:3
Average: a. made lethal 342:4
  a. man's opinions 329:8
  speech a vain a. would make 192:15
Aviator: poor a. lay dying 12:15
Avoid: one can't a. them all 91:7
  to pick the people one a.s 217:17
Avoided: few errors they have ever a. 80:6
  friend to be a. 334:12
Avoiding: a. non-being by a. being 374:1
A-waggle: a. with love 222:14
Awake: coming a. and discovering a place 106:4
  freedom to be fully a. 134:15
  some day my heart will a. 165:13
Aware: man becoming a. of himself 395:1
Awareness: aware of your a. 371:1
  a. of death 382:3
Away: seen the one that got a. 291:13
Awe: a. the . . . stallion's neck 389:8
  treated dreams with the proper a. 66:22
Awful: how a. . . . what people say 350:11
  so many kinds of a. men 91:7
Awkward: a. squad 64:13
Awkwardness: under the mask of a. 134:6
Axe: a. for the frozen sea inside us 201:6
  antique dread of the headsman's a. 151:11
  no a.s are being ground 56:4
  swinging his a. to fell kings 58:12

B

B-natural: wisest to write in B. 386:1
BBC: B. . . . a cross between the Church 84:3
BO: man who has cured himself of B. 56:7
Babbit, George F. 233:18
Babies: anybody who hates dogs and b. 325:2
  b. haven't any hair 175:19
  b. outside greengrocers' shops 49:10

b. that are not born 138:17
b. . . . with larger cerebrums 258:17
how ugly b. are! 341:22
only washing. And b. 369:26
other people's b. 170:27
putting milk into b. 80:3
you breed b. and you eat chips 397:17
Baby: asterisks were followed . . . by a b. 256:3
  b. in an ox's stall 40:9
  bats with b. faces 118:16
  first b. laughed for the first time 26:10
  hanging the b. on the clothes line 327:6
  never put a hot b. on a cold slab 10:20
  proposed cutting the b. in half 168:18
  that's a beautiful b. 10:18
  walking my b. back home 379:12
  yes sir. That's my b. 201:17
  you called me B. Doll a year ago 165:1
  you must have been a beautiful b. 260:2
Baccy: 'b. for the clerk 212:21
Bach, J.S.: B. . . . persuades me to be a Christian 137:3
  if B. wriggles 61:17
  Johann Sebastian mighty B. 370:1
  little John-Sebastian-like 182:18
  operating by day, by night playing B. 91:20
  play only B. in praising God 26:29
Bachelor: all reformers are b.s 268:9
  b. supported by beautiful women 91:12
  b. who . . . has had amateur experience 317:16
  b.'s baby suffocating 17:14
  b.'s panic 148:4
  crushing tax on b.s 344:2
Back: b. that's strong 376:15
  b. us or sack us 63:14
  boys in the b. room 236:20
  everything had a b. door 140:16
  it rolls off my b. like a duck 285:5
  my b. is breakin' 404:1
  no one turns his b. 382:15
  small of my b. is too big 348:13
  with our b.s to the wall 158:6
Backbone: b. of the army 210:12
Backing: I'm b. Britain 12:1
Backward: b. ran sentences 143:3
  lean over too far b. 372:5
  silence surged softly b. 103:13
Backwardness: big advantage of b. 23
Backwards: I'm walking b. for Christmas 263:16
  live b. from in front 400:17
  walk out b. 11:11
Bacon: b.'s not the only thing 208:18
  leant against a b. slicer 128:24
Bad: all in all, not b. 313:21
  b. for us, b. for Europe 245:14
  b. times just around the corner 94:7
  cleanest . . . way of having a b. time 73:19
  considering how b. men are 246:15
  defend the b. against the worse 101:21
  I won't make you feel b. 36:15
  like to be told how b. things are 79:22

no b. man can be a good poet 293:11
nothing so b. or so good 345:8
only read what is . . . frankly bad 357:16
so much b. in the best of us 175:1
television for nothing 147:7
things that are b. for me 342:15
when I'm b. I'm better 398:3
Badger: breath's like a b.'s bum 87:6
Badly: worth doing b. 77:15
Badness: b. of her b. 26:15
Baedeker: never Mr B. 170:26
Baffled: if you're b. by the difference 286:6
Baghdad: B.-on-the-Subway 170:7
Bagpipes: play the b. – but doesn't 390:15
Bailey, Bill: won't you come home, B? 67:1
Bait: for mugs a b. 300:7
Baker Street: B. irregulars 110:7
Balance: in the b. without knowing it 200:13
    point of b. . . . we have not got 314:10
Balanced: b. – chips on both shoulders 310:1
Balcony: b. overlooking the Atlantic 266:19
    sat on his b. eating his dog 24:3
Bald: b. men should marry b. women 299:15
    fierce and b. and short of breath 336:29
    fight between two b. men 47:3
    God a bad time for making him b. 50:12
Baldness: felicity on the far side of b. 351:1
Baldwin, Stanley, Earl 82:9. 98:9, 104:9
Balfour, Arthur, Lord 82:5, 186:19
    Mr B.'s poodle 235:15
Balham: Rolls body and a B. mind 271:4
Balkans: place her low down in the B. 64:19
Ball, Lucille 14:9
Ball: after the b. 164:22
    b. I threw when playing 369:17
    black satin at her coming-out b. 399:12
    Energen roll where his b.s ought to be 360:2
    playing with a golden b. 374:7
    ten b.s in the air 10:12
Ball-floor: dance on this b. 44:8
Ballet: b. of bloodless categories 49:23
    b.s . . . not for the dancing 121:10
Balloon: bring the b. of the mind 415:11
    who knows if the moon's a b. 97:3
Balls-up: you knew it was just a b. 286:16
Balm: shed b. upon the . . . inferiority 308:5
Baloney: it's still b. 146:6
Balzac, Honoré de 102:4
Ban: I shall recommend they b. it 161:2
Banality: b. of evil 13:12
Banana: b.s for breakfast 399:22
    path . . . bestrewn by b. skins 62:8
    yes, we have no b.s 347:12
Band: when the b. begins to play 213:6
Bandar-log: what the B. think now 214:1
Bänder: endlose B., schlingt und windet 318:8
Bandwagon: if you see a b. 147:1
Bane: what of the world's b.? 416:11
Bang: bigger b. for a buck 405:10
    no terror in a b. 172:15
    not with a b. but a whimper 117:19

Banish: b. their young at an early age 311:3
Banister: same shape twisted on the b. 116:20
Bank: b. . . . if you . . . don't need it 177:18
    B. of Miracles 56:20
    b. was mightier than the sword 300:5
    beastly to the B. of England 96:5
    from the B. to Mandalay 211:31
    hero is the man who robs a b. 404:24
    his home is the b.'s 140:13
    I cried all the way to the b. 233:21
    King Bunk and King B. 272:4
    moneys which it, the b., creates 303:9
    robbing a b. compared to founding 51:19
    steady as the B. of England 85:21
    tunnelling into a b. 372:29
    tyrannize over his b. balance 207:1
    way the b.s will give you money 105:13
Bank-rate: artefacts, not their b.s 27:16
Banker: B.'s Georgian 220:3
    from the b.s to the government 90:2
Bankhead, Tallulah: hour talking to B. 203:13
Banknote: fill old bottles with b.s 206:18
Bannock: butter their b.s on both sides 323:17
Bapaume: riddled corpses round B. 337:1
Baptist: I should have preferred a B. 396:12
Baptized: new fictional characters b. 218:13
Bar: one decent b. scrap 396:15
    shoe-size in earth and b.s around it 249:3
    two men look out through the same b.s 220:13
Barba: b. llena de mariposas 140:6
Barbarian: b. conqueror, . . . American abroad
    356:13
    b. . . . regards his passions 335:4
    terrain fit only for b.s 137:14
    umbrella might pacify b.s abroad 300:5
    what will become of us without b.s 71:1
Barbarism: gone from b. to degeneration 84:13
    political b. 78:13
Barbarous: b. king so rudely forced 118:8
Barbecue: Golden Calf, she b.s it 231:7
Barber: only lady b. that made good 397:24
    way all New York barbers . . . go 333:20
Barber-shop: light burns low in the b. 43:10
Bard: famous b.s and preachers 369:32
Bardolatry: so much for B. 345:27
Bardot, Brigitte 385:3
Bare: b. like nude giant girls 355:3
    even if it's grim, we'll b. it 273:15
Barefoot: let his . . . children go b. 344:7
Bargain: b. on the part of the wolves 45:11
Bark: you heard a seal b. 372:1
Barking: without b. his shins 72:15
Barmaid: b. of the Victorian soul 194:18
Barmy: Ginger, you're b.! 274:17
Barncock: ere the b.s say 163:6
Baronet: half mad b. 61:1
Baroque: poetry is b. 256:19
Barracks: single men in b. 213:7
Barrage: b. of common-sense to baulk intimacy
    246:8
    before the b. lifts 165:16

b. word for doing things tomorrow 342:22
bachelor supported by b. women 91:12
black is b. 9:2
both green, both b. 203:12
half mad baronet, half b. woman 61:1
House B. . . . is the play lousy 292:15
how b. they stand 93:23
O you b. doll 56:19
Oh, what a b. mornin' 160:11
one of the b. people 229:18
Ordinary made b. 342:4
small is b. 339:12
so old a ship . . . and yet so b. 128:17
when I told them how b. you are 325:14
woman who cannot be ugly is not b. 217:16
[women] look for men with b. women 218:11
you must have been a b. baby 260:2
Beautifully: go on behaving b. 119:19
Beauty: as a b. I'm no great star 121:7
   b. and the lust for learning 30:21
   b. at low temperatures *is* b. 53:15
   b. being only skin-deep 205:24
   b. cold and austere 328:13
   b. crieth in an attic 62:7
   b. for some provides escape 183:18
   b. is always the first to hear 144:11
   b. is momentary in the mind 358:17
   b. is only sin deep 333:2
   b. killed the beast 95:7
   b. lives though lilies die 128:7
   b. of an aged face 64:16
   b. of inflections 358:18
   b. passes like a dream 417:7
   b. took from those who loved them 103:4
   considered b. above their means 336:14
   Euclid alone has looked on b. bare 261:4
   for England, home and b. 164:20
   here lies a lady of b. 312:4
   left it [England] a land of b. spots 194:22
   make her b. over again 416:9
   mandarins who 'appreciate' b. 297:17
   only with b. wake wild memories 103:1
   permanence more than . . . b. 70:9
   rose is b. 107:10
   terrible b. is born 416:5
   what is b., anyway? 297:16
   wife a former b. queer 229:10
   wildest b. in the world 288:26
Beaver: b. sixty-eight feet long 199:19
Beaverbrook, Lord: B. is like the town tart 27:14
   if Max [B.] gets to heaven 397:16
Because: b. I do not hope to turn 116:17
Bechstein: pawn the B. grand 94:1
Beckett, Samuel: 295:19, 380:25
Becoming: state of perpetual b. 308:16
Bed: all I want is a warm b. 53:3
   b. beneath this stone 383:6
   b. fell on my father 372:21
   b. . . . . four people could have slept 95:10
   b. . . . . is the poor man's opera 182:22
   b. unmade at the back of the chair 125:21

b. would be . . . supreme experience 77:13
b.'s too big 266:2
deep, deep peace of the double b. 65:1
desert sighs in the b. 18:5
every day I have . . . gone to b. 256:12
everyone to be in b. by ten-thirty 203:20
fool would make the b. every day 353:14
I should of stood in b. 188:4
I towards thy b., Yasmin 128:9
in b., of course, I mean 373:3
keeps getting in b. with women 324:21
lie in b., so must you make it 401:21
marriage is not all b. and breakfast 93:10
might go to b. with a chap once 360:15
minds like b.s always made up 404:25
musical b.s 4:17
no child will go to b. hungry 214:34
now can we go to bed? 91:4
our b.'s only MFI 411:22
pursuing it from b. to b. 291:9
right to be in b. when he . . . is up 239:10
rode their horses up to b. 103:8
soon have you back in b. 203:16
spent so little time in b. 373:7
stay in b. all day 34:19
still keeping open b. 182:8
that's why I go to b. early 392:13
Bedmen: good b. and all bores 370:14
Bedpost: on the b. overnight 323:18
Bedroom: comment in the b. 21:12
   doesn't matter what you do in the b. 64:20
   take care of the b. bit 159:15
Bedspread: turned down like a b. 410:14
Bedspring: triumphant twang of a b. 295:10
Bee: b. has quit the clover 211:21
   does a grave injustice to b.s 287:9
   I am the b. 126:9
   sting like a b. 5:11
Bee-loud: live alone in the b. glade 416:18
Beef: eat b. on our knees 11:13
   mustard's no good without roast b. 252:11
Beefy: b. ATS without . . . hats 40:11
Beehive: b. state 287:9
Beer: b. and wine remain 5:15
   b. b. glorious b. 8:10
   bitter b. that tastes sweet 319:2
   I'm only here for the b. 3:15
   only a b. teetotaller 343:3
   voice like b. trickling 408:23
   your justice would freeze b. 261:18
Beerbohm, Max: Quintilian or B. 156:4
Beethoven, Ludwig van: B.'s Fifth . . . Fate – or
      Kate 315:3
   B.'s Fifth . . . most sublime noise 130:14
   roll over, B. 39:13
Beetle: behind every b. 271:6
Beetroot: Lord's Prayer in b. 15:25
Beggar: b.s are the only . . . choosers 277:1
   people who can never forgive a b. 217:18
Begin, Menachem 258:8
Begin: b. the beguine 301:14

but let us b. 204:19
where very few things b. 127:6
you leave off and it b.s 111:13
Beginner: managed badly for a b. 88:14
Beginning: avoiding the b. of things 88:18
    God of my fair b.s 212:23
    in my b. is my end 116:27
    in the end is my b. 117:4
    is there no b. to your talents 8:9
    no b., no end 47:14
    not even the b. of the end 79:26
Beguile: with songs b. your pilgrimage 128:7
Beguine: begin the b. 301:14
Begun: everything has already b. before 64:6
Behave: wonderful how well they b. 246:15
Behaving: b. to King Lear 106:9
Behaviour: best b. one isn't . . . at one's best 36:20
    whole system of genteel b. 300:11
Behaviourism: b. . . . flat-earth view 216:9
    of course, B. works 18:31
Behind: all are b. 370:8
    b. them . . . there is nothing 336:8
    in a moment it will be b. me 315:5
    left a lot of little things b. him 209:13
    ride two horses with one b. 5:22
Being: light in the darkness of mere b. 199:4
    too early for b. 167:18
Beleaguered: b., . . . and misunderstood 311:1
Belfry: bats in the b. 297:5
Belgium: B. put the Kibosh on the Kaiser 119:12
    'Gallant B.' as so much blague 246:1
Belgrade: never shoot a film in B. 55:19
Belief: any unwarrantable b. 316:15
    arrive at new b.s 39:15
    b. without evidence 42:15
    commit himself to any religious b. 392:14
    constant assertion of b. 217:22
    illogical b. in the . . . improbable 259:6
    satire is dependant on strong b.s 55:13
    things with their names: that is b. 336:23
    to die for one's b.s 329:11
Believe: b. enough in what one feels 418:3
    b. in the divinity of Our Lord 348:3
    b. it or not 319:19
    B.! Obey! Fight! 275:10
    he who b.s in nothing 324:13
    I b. in relationships 50:18
    I can believe in them all [religions] 343:25
    I do not believe [in God] . . . I know 199:12
    I don't b. in mathematics 116:7
    men who really believe in themselves 76:28
    never b. anything until . . . denied 239:13
    they didn't b. me 325:14
    to b. what I do b. more and more 193:12
    verb . . . 'to b. falsely' 408:2
    what we b. is not necessarily true 31:20
    you would not believe in them either 251:13
Believed: two things that will be b. 365:6
Believer: b. will fight another b. 154:3
Belittlement: all our injured b. 311:1
Bell, Alexander Graham 305:4

Bell: b.s of hell go ting-a-ling-a-ling 12:10
    b.s off San Salvador 95:6
    b.s they sound so clear 179:20
    t'would ring the b.s of heaven 175:7
Bell-rope: b. that gathers God at dawn 95:4
Belle-litter: poetry and b. 361:7
Bellies: b. and drags in the wind 415:11
Belloc, Hilaire 268:20
Bellow, Saul, B. 34:13
Bellsybabble: devil mostly speaks . . . B. 197:7
Belly: b. full of the classics 262:9
    b. jonah hunting the polly joans 197:22
    b. of a Cossack horse 377:21
    embrace me, b. 18:15
Belong: b. somewhere else 357:5
    b.. to it [the organization] 402:4
    one [religion] you got to b. to 354:12
Beloved: Love the B. Republic 131:2
    prove b. over all 213:2
Below: belt without hitting b. it 15:20
    life goes on b. the belt 270:13
Belt: b. without hitting below it 15:20
    life goes on below the b. 270:13
Ben-Gurion, David 39:16
Bench: grass is growing on the Front B. 16:8
Benchley, Robert 324:22
Bend: b. over backwards and forwards 10:21
    b. with the river 108:3
    if it b.s it's funny 5:23
Benign: b. indifference of the universe 65:25
    in England the system is b. 96:4
Benn, Tony: B. . . . enthusiasm of a Boy Scout
        231:18
    T. immatures with age 406:9
Bennett, Arnold 398:25
Bent: fool must follow his natural b. 213:10
Bereaved: laughter would be b. 383:22
Beresford, Lord Charles 78:20
Bergère: b. ô tour Eiffel 13:3
Bergwerk: der Seelen wunderliches B. 319:3
Berkeley Square: a nightingale sang in B. 253:25
Berlin, Irving: B. is American music 205:17
    when B. sings you have to hug him 96:14
Berlin: British Ambassador in B. 72:1
Berliner: ich bin ein B. 205:3
Berlitz-school: glibness of the B. 125:23
Bermuda: trip to B. is over in two weeks 6:16
Bernard, Jeffrey 391:13
Bernstein, Leonard 47:14
Berserk: sex suppressed will go b. 121:16
Bespangled: Jack Frost dancing b. 80:17
Bessie: not a word to B. about this 178:7
Best: at his b. only when the going was good 90:3
    b. be the enemy of the good 193:13
    b. behaviour one isn't . . . at one's b. 36:20
    b. improve with age 194:23
    b. lack all conviction 417:12
    b. of nothing 72:8
    b. thing to get up and go 120:18
    b. things in life are free 104:8
    constantly acting for the b. 195:14

do your worst, and we will do our b. 79:23
good is better than the b. 36:17
so much bad in the b. of us 175:1
where the b. is like the worst 211:33
Best-seller: b. because it is great or vice versa 46:17
b. . . . because it was selling 46:18
b. . . . tomb of a mediocre talent 350:20
Bet: b. you which one would fly 379:20
if it was a b., you wouldn't take it 361:3
three jolly farmers once b. a pound 103:17
Bethlehem: in B. things like that 168:21
slouches towards B. 417:13
Betray: synonymous with 'b'. 363:6
Betrayed: b. our soldiers 81:20
Betrothed: b. to laughter 383:8
Better: be b. off than you are 59:16
blame of those ye b. 213:18
everything b. is purchased 199:14
getting b. and b. 93:9
I can do b. 39:6
if way to the b. there be 162:21
it's a little b. all the time 229:23
more ye see it th' b. ye like it 111:22
used to be no b. 372:17
when I'm bad I'm b. 398:3
when you have nothing b. to do 368:6
where it's likely to go b. 135:5
you're a b. man than I am 210:29
Between: give a damn what goes on in b. 29:17
I would try to get between them 362:7
truth . . . seems to lie b. us 143:7
Bevan, Aneurin 41:19, 97:2
Nye [B.] was born old and died young 227:17
Beverly Hills: B. is very exclusive 331:13
Bevin, Ernest 10:14
Beware: b. of bathroom walls 113:4
Bewildered: bewitched, bothered and b. 165:5
good, the bad and the b. in between 90:2
Bewitched: b., bothered and bewildered 165:5
b. for ever who has seen 331:6
Bewitchment: b. of our intelligence 332:5
Bewrapt: b. past knowing 163:7
Beyond: b. that last blue mountain 128:13
Bias: b. in favour of man 397:15
born with a b. to some pursuit 365:5
history must not be written with b. 41:4
Bible: B. by way of the Cross 22:15
B. is a cruel book 347:14
B. is literature, not dogma 335:6
B. . . . is a lesson in how not to write 72:14
B. . . . next to Voltaire 329:2
b.-ridden, white South 8:13
B. . . . was written by a c. 257:18
longer to write the B. 243:7
see him, the gentle B. beast 273:8
t'ings dat yo' . . . to read in de B. 142:20
we had the B. and they had the land 379:14
world's best-seller 46:17
Bible-black: starless and b. 369:20
Bickering: academics love b. 100:7

Bicycle: b. certainly, but not *the* b. 110:1
delirious b.s 13:7
fish without a b. 357:22
if a cow with handlebars is a b. 271:11
knocked him off his b. and told him 227:18
so is a b. repair kit 87:12
Bier: he opens his b. 362:22
Big: I always liked b. women 70:1
I *am* b. 402:8
just sit and be b. 127:22
more easily fall victim to a b. lie 173:7
that is how big it is 91:16
Bigamist: instinctive b. 183:11
Bigamy: b. is having one husband too many 9:1
one's absurd. And b., sir, is a crime 267:9
Bigger: b. bang for a buck 405:10
b. they come the harder they fall 127:30
theatres are always b. inside 209:3
Bigot: b. is a stone-deaf orator 143:8
followed by the priests and b.s 65:29
Bigoted: he is not b. about it 327:11
Bigotry: b. [is] the anger of men 76:21
Statue of B. 314:19
Bike: I prefer a b. to a horse 193:7
mind my b.! 391:7
on his b. and he looked for work 366:18
Bild: so dich finden, binden dich an B. 319:13
Bile: look on the b. when it's black 183:19
Bilingual: if you're b., you can't read 281:19
Bill: 'I love you' on the back of the b. 252:19
money is used to pay b.s 390:16
Billboard: b. lovely as a tree 278:6
b.s did to Coca-Cola 382:12
Billy: haven't the heart to poke poor B. 150:7
Bind: b. it with the blowing wind 122:10
in the darkness b. them 374:15
Biochemist: man, . . . asks the b. 341:14
Biodegrade: in the end, usefully b. 107:23
Biographer: modern b.s pick a victim 296:11
Biography: all b. is ultimately fiction 247:19
b. . . . can never be wholly true 304:5
b. . . . can recover its main function 349:16
b. is a very definite region 156:8
b. is about chaps 37:16
b. is . . . life after death 66:29
improve the b. of the person 336:25
Biological: gentleness is b. 368:8
Biology: b. is . . . complicated things 101:4
Birch: b., . . . between consenting adults 387:17
Birches: swinger of the b. 135:6
Bird: b. in a gilded cage 219:15
b.s coming home to roost 395:17
b.s cooked while their blood 242:19
b.s do it, bees do it 301:21
b.s in their little nests 33:8
b.s of sadness flying over 255:1
caged b.s accept each other 404:9
cease and be as other b.s 135:21
I heard a b. at dawn 358:2
like a b. on a wire 85:12
no b. can contradict 18:27

b. man on the sightless horse 389:15
does the B. Man own his escort? 1:6
like two heavily-armed b. men 215:2
minute of darkness will not make us b. 327:6
my eyes were b. with stars 175:12
old Maeonides the b. said it 128:19
painting is a b. man's profession 298:1
religion without science is b. 115:13
soon the whole world will be b. 149:5
what Milton saw when he went b. 251:20
you want to travel b. 85:13
Blinded: b. ere yet a-wing 162:9
see, no longer b. 55:8
Blindfold: his reader may enter b. 72:15
Blindness 373:8
Blinked: other fellow just b. 327:20
Blinking: one-eyed, b. sort o' place 163:29
Bliss: dynamited into b. 396:19
promise of pneumatic b. 118:18
Bliss Sir Arthur: B. I suppose 390:18
Blisses: b. about my pilgrimage 162:17
Blister: they gave her b.s 21:17
Blitz: b. of a boy 70:20
Block: each b. cut smooth 303:8
Blockhead: twenty young b.s 276:7
Blond: more b. than you 97:16
Blonde: b. to make a bishop kick 72:6
Gentlemen . . . remember b.s 237:7
in love with a beautiful b. 125:2
save you a b. for a shilling 12:13
springing from b. to b. 410:20
Blood: air is b. temperature 111:13
b. and soil 100:1
b., dirt and sucked sugar stick 418:4
b., toil, tears and sweat 79:13
b.'s a rover 179:13
can't be all of the B. royal 15:4
cooked while their b. is still warm 242:19
drop of black b. makes a coloured man 181:5
giving a reasonable amount [of b.] 161:6
good enough to shed his b. 323:7
he had the sea in his b. 263:1
her b. is nothing but rose-water 125:31
I see His b. upon the rose 300:13
if b. be the price of admiralty 212:24
made out of muscle and b. 376:15
rather have b. on my hands than water 153:17
River Tiber foaming with much b. 304:12
salt of their b. stiffens 365:10
show business with b. 57:8
there's b. inside 145:1
thin b. pulse pizzicati 358:16
two kinds of b. 379:15
walks again on the Seas of B. 349:1
we be of one b. 214:3
Bloodless: ballet of b. categories 49:23
Bloodshed: war is politics with b. 250:9
Bloody: abroad is b. 142:6
b. men are like b. buses 91:3
not b. likely 345:21
she walks the B. Tower 399:8

something wrong with our b. ships 28:3
what b. good are we? 12:19
where's the b. horse? 65:3
Bloom: cherry now is hung with b. 179:10
lose our hair, our teeth! Our b.! 28:16
risk of spoiling its b. 89:5
sort of b. on a woman 26:20
will it b. this year? 118:6
Blooming: grand to be b. well dead 335:20
Bloomingdale's 10:3
Blossom: blossomed Sarah, and I b. 40:1
b.s of the apricot 303:6
letting a hundred flowers b. 250:15
overleap the stage of b. 318:10
Blotched: b. out beyond unblotching 358:10
Blotting: b. out reason 152:2
Blow: b. in cold blood 344:32
b. incredible wampum 97:6
b. on a dead man's embers 152:4
b. out, you bugles 54:10
b. your mind – smoke gunpowder 148:21
thou hast a good job. Don't b. it 6:11
will you never b. again 345:23
Blowing: answer . . . is b. in the wind 113:8
Blubber: b. which encases an English peer 88:12
Blubbering: b. blobs come unequipped 341:22
Blue: beyond that last b. mountain 128:13
b. birds over the white cliffs of Dover 60:5
b. really begins 112:17
b. remembered hills 179:32
cloud floating in the b. 264:23
green and true b. 270:22
heard it most of all in the b.s 83:3
if artists do see fields b. 173:12
in the naked frosty b. 370:13
lonesome b. collide 266:2
so much of fragmentary b. 135:12
where the b. of the night 96:11
you have a b. guitar 358:13
Blueeyed: how do you like your b. boy 97:4
Blue-vested: short b. people 92:2
Bluff: whole world run on b. 141:4
Blunder: b. . . . . no one might ever do again 258:4
he usually b.s forward 115:13
so grotesque a b. 37:18
Blundering: b. people will live on 334:19
Blunt: b., bow-headed, whale-backed Downs
212:29
b. man accustomed to plain speaking 108:2
Blurb-writer: something about a b. 132:9
Blurring: draw a line without b. it 80:10
Blush: full many a vice is born to b. 355:26
Blushes: spare my b. 191:12
Blushing: b. bride she looks divine 130:3
Blut: B. und Boden 100:1
Blüte: wie du die B. beinah 318:10
Boarding house: landlady of a b. is a parallelogram
225:16
meals at a b. . . . . less than . . . square 225:17
Boast: while we b. to the others 350:19
Boasting: advice or are just b. 372:25

such b.s as the Gentiles use 212:16

Boat: B. Race 263:31
b.s against the current 126:20
come in and sink my b.s 6:30
messing about in b.s 150:13
their b.s were tossed sky-high 238:10
they sank my b. 205:10

Boating: b. around in muck 153:8

Boche: well-killed B. 313:10

Bodice: why, in her b. stuck 103:5

Bodies: b. lopped of every prettiness 97:7
pile the b. high at Austerlitz 334:18

Body: b. and mind entire 412:3
b. and soul are not two substances 395:1
b. odour 3:2
carry his body around 136:20
dissect the heart of his b. 122:18
her b. a bulb in the cold 299:24
her b. has been lowered 189:18
I leave my b. outside the door 297:14
keep b. and soul apart 292:2
keeping b. and soul together 238:16
more familiar with Africa than my own b.
285:19
no contact with my own b. 36:4
O b. swayed to music 415:10
Rolls b. and a Balham mind 271:4
when you' b. make shadow 334:1
you too can have a b. like mine 16:12

Boer: especially before the B. War 286:15

Boff: b. over his pimple 327:3

Bog: Russian people . . . floundering in the b. 82:1

Bogart, Humphrey 21:3
B.'s a helluva nice guy till 11.30 p.m. 73:12

Bogey: b.s are . . . libidinous 52:18

Bognor: bugger B. 142:4

Bogus: genuinely b. 165:14

Bois: fuyez les b. 13:8

Bolivia: B. [it was always] 1949 368:12

Bolshevism: afraid of bits of B. 75:16

Bolt: pull out the b. 416:7

Bomb: b. them back into the Stone Age 228:10
come, friendly b.s 40:18
drop b.s, . . . hit civilians 147:4
ears like b.s 70:20
lead us to the Buddha or to the b. 67:11
test the Russians not the b.s 138:9
the word 'now' is like a b. 261:13
what time is it by your b.? 11:10

Bombed: I'm glad we've been b. 119:8

Bomber: cake-sale to buy a b. 237:19

Bombing: learn to get used to it [b.] 79:18
we begin b. in five minutes 313:18

Bone: circumstance break men's b.s 75:25
curtain rises on a b. 337:17
only b.s abide 238:10
our small b.s 371:3
this plain she makes a shining b. 355:4

Bone-fed: field and wood, all b. loam 44:11

Boneless: B. Wonder 79:7

Bonjour: b. tristesse 120:16

Bonkers: stark, staring b. 158:11

Bonnard: don't talk to me about B. 297:17

Bony: some b. structure under the muck 72:10

Booby: woman who is not . . . a b. 258:11

Book: accessories . . . are my reference b.s 22:7
against b.s the Home Secretary is 393:8
all good b.s are alike 169:12
bad b.s, but . . . well written 49:15
bishops vary just as much as b.s 195:5
b. chooses its readers 37:1
b. getting into the wrong hands 161:2
b. in question 108:9
b. known to him by heart 412:12
b. . . . . represented . . . American woman 242:6
b. . . . . sold . . . because it was selling 46:18
b. that is a b. flowers once 224:6
b. would have been finished 409:9
b. you were absolutely pleased with 395:9
b.s are a load of crap 221:13
b.s are all written in hotels 125:21
b.s! Bottled chatter 101:12
b.s one ought to read 36:10
b.s one remembers best 36:11
b.s that affect us like a disaster 201:6
b.s were watched for 125:26
contemporary b.s do not keep 87:15
do not throw this b. about 32:26
even bad b.s are b.s and . . . sacred 151:2
every person is like thousands of b.s 174:7
few b.s are forgivable 219:7
forgetting to balance the b.s 90:2
friends to borrow my b.s 320:12
go away and write a b. about it 48:15
God has written all the b.s 61:22
happiness . . . without . . . b.s 292:23
hers of the b. 310:3
his b.s were read 32:33
horrible little b. 225:9
I have only read one b. in my life 266:11
I never was much on this B. reading 321:16
I would never read a b. 406:15
in no b. have I ever got down 131:4
long had a taste for bad b.s 49:15
lusting after b.s 52:18
Middlemarch, the magnificent b. 412:7
more b.s than they have tickets for 52:18
never got round to reading the b. 253:17
never judge a cover by its b. 226:13
no b. is worth reading at . . . ten 233:2
no foreign b.s; . . . only foreign readers 305:3
no one thing to be found in b.s 311:12
no two people read the same b. 405:14
not as good as his b.s 129:12
one b.'s very like another 396:23
only b.s that influence us 131:3
read any good b.s lately? 15:14, 178:4
read b.s like that 203:21
reader brings as much to the b. 36:11
some b.s are undeservedly forgotten 19:4
take down this b. 417:26
to ban b.s is fanaticism 341:21

to burn a b. is not to destroy it 327:16
to read too many b.s is harmful 250:17
when a b. is boring, they yawn openly 348:17
whose b.s are written to be taught 387:12
wonderful ideas b. have presented 308:17
writing a b. is . . . a jigsaw puzzle 247:1
Bookmark: pound notes as b.s 54:8
Boot: before the truth has got its b.s on 63:12
　black the b.s of success 97:8
　b., . . . unquestionably hand-made 380:28
　b.s – b.s – b.s – movin' up and down 209:24
　brahn b.s, I asks yer 399:9
　children . . . never had any b.s 405:15
　criticism .. made him jump out of his b.s 76:4
　died with their b.s clean 206:4
　drinkers . . . inside a pair of army b.s 161:3
　he's a gentleman: look at his b.s 345:15
　if he went to school without b.s 58:5
　you'll lick the bloomin' b.s 210:26
Boot-boy: body of the b. at Claridges 412:24
Boot-rims: glitter of his b. 248:18
Bootstrapper: physicist . . . is a b. 78:11
Boot-straps: hauling on one's own b. 189:10
Booth, General 150:16
Booze: gold standard on the b. 207:7
　you can tell a man who b.s 60:3
Bordello: doorkeeper of a b. 375:20
Border: south of the b. 204:13
　'stablished its b.s unto all eternity 211:17
Borderline: b. that poetry operates on 166:17
Bore: all their b.s abroad 45:17
　B. a person who talks 42:8
　b., . . . ask him how he is 366:13
　b. . . . waking up . . . as the same person 351:6
　b. who's here today 25:14
　b.s for England 272:18
　capacity of human beings to b. 258:15
　club b. 332:10
　everyone is a b. to someone 51:24
　God is a b. 259:1
　good bedmen and all b.s 370:14
　healthy male adult b. 382:10
　his mother would b. right in 400:14
　if your husband is a b. 34:10
　intolerable b. – ourselves 186:5
Bored: b. as enthusiasm would permit 148:10
　b. . . . mortification sets in 410:18
　I feel a little b. 74:5
　I know I am b. 194:20
　realize you're b. 48:9
　silent and infinitely b. 215:19
　virtue of the b. 393:14
Boredom: b. in the arts can be . . . dull 387:6
　b. is rage spread thin 374:5
　effect of b. . . . in history 186:6
　spray-on b. 120:14
Borgia: B. who has forgotten 408:17
　I dined last night with the B.s 30:9
　in Italy . . . under the B.s 395:12
Boring: b. about . . . happiness 182:23
　b., very 400:16

not as b. as I thought it was 386:11
so b. they shot the leading man 141:18
when a book is b. 348:17
Born: b. at an extremely tender age 234:6
　b. at the age of twelve 141:1
　b. at the wrong end of time 400:17
　b. because it was a habit 321:14
　b. in this century, tempered by war 204:16
　b. into uncongenial surroundings 76:16
　b. of the sun 355:1
　b. old 88:8
　b. old and died young 227:17
　b. originals 418:20
　b. three thousand years old 103:27
　b. . . . to be near my parents 390:12
　B. to Lose 156:18
　b. with a bias to some pursuit 365:5
　b. with a plastic spoon 376:3
　b. with your legs apart 286:5
　dies before he is fully b. 134:19
　I knew him before he was b. 233:15
　it's unwise to be b. 346:1
　not busy being b. is busy dying 113:11
　not so much b. as indented for 140:14
　one is not b. a woman 28:7
　towards Bethlehem to be b. 417:13
　we are all b. mad 29:7
　we are not b. alone 84:7
Borne: b. back . . . into the past 126:20
Borrow: b. more books than . . . tickets 52:18
Borrower: but we are B.s 281:20
Bös: und nicht b. zu sein 318:7
Boss: absentee b. is best 407:14
　hand of the b.'s daughter 23:1
Bossing: b. other men 374:18
Boston: B. Strangler did for . . . salesmen 166:11
　B., the home of the bean 47:8
　God made B. on a wet Sunday 72:19
Botched: for a b. civilization 303:17
Both: b. . . . but don't bother about the bread 264:24
　unless he is b. at the same time 335:24
Botha, P.W. 349:20
Bothered: bewitched, b. and bewildered 165:5
Bott, Violet Elizabeth 96:10
Botticelli, Sandro: if B. were alive today 383:23
　man's opinion on B. 76:9
Bottle: hitting empty ginger ale b.s 372:19
Bottled: b. chatter 101:12
　introduced b. water into India 69:13
Bottom: b. of the economic pyramid 322:8
　b.s on seats 159:18
　brains too near their b.s 94:18
　knocked the b. out of B.'s dream 74:4
　reasons . . . for remaining at the b. 85:19
　wear the b.s of my trousers rolled 117:28
Bottomley, Horatio: Ah, B., sewing? 47:12
Bottomly: really all of us b. broke 205:19
Bough: petals on a wet black b. 303:20
Bought: memorability has been b. 383:7
Bouillabaisse: b. is only good 108:16

Boulevard: dump 'em on the b. 314:19
Bounce: in the plural and they b. 239:7
Boundaries: atmosphere knows no b. 147:28
Boundary: Mortimer is on the b. line 256:1
Bouquet: b. is better than the taste 302:25
Bourgeois: b. . . . an epithet which the riff-raff
    apply 177:11
  b. is . . . a creature of weak impulses 171:15
  how beastly the b. is 222:20
  patriotism to a b. state 378:8
Bourgeoisie: b. created a new society 377:22
Bourne: B. no Hollingsworth returns 271:18
Bournemouth: B. . . . call 'her' 41:3
Bovril: she will be made into B. 15:23
Bow-headed: b., whale-backed Downs 212:29
Bow-legged: even the mice were b. 254:20
Bow-wow: B. public park manner 26:24
Bower: b. we shrined to Tennyson 162:7
Bowl: trying to b. to God on concrete 320:4
Box: b. they buried entertainment in 177:16
Boxing: b.'s . . . show business with blood 57:8
Boy: and I were the only b. 155:7
  being read to by a b. 117:11
  b. . . . his hand in his pocket 26:17
  b.s are dreaming wicked 369:21
  b.s do not grow up gradually 88:10
  b.s in the back room 236:20
  b.s . . . into any foreign war 322:20
  b.s of the Old Brigade 231:3, 394:1
  b.s will be b.s 177:10
  land of b.s who refuse to grow up 246:18
  little b.; a pair of skates 112:3
  mad about the b. 94:15
  men that were b.s when I was a b. 33:11
  one of those b.s . . . born old 88:8
  see if the b.s are still there 27:7
  tell the b.s to follow 191:13
  thing of duty is a b. forever 283:12
  this is a b., sir 286:6
  till the b.s come home 129:21
  Tuesday . . . with a baby B. Scout 407:8
  unrestricted b. 90:15
  what b. can sing as the thrush 260:11
Brace: b. ourselves to our duties 79:17
  B. Relations Board 90:18
  b.s on my teeth and got high marks 243:3
  liquid which rots b.s 271:2
Bracket: I put a b. round it thus 80:18
Bradford: silk hat on a B. millionaire 118:14
Bradshaw: vocabulary of B. 110:10
Braggart: as unhappy as the next b.'s 104:11
Brahms, Johannes: B., for all his grumbling
    130:15
  thought life was going to be like B. 36:9
Brain: antennae . . . but no b. 193:5
  bear of very little b. 264:19, 265:1
  b. attic stocked with . . . furniture 109:14
  b. got no better; but it buzzed more 80:11
  b. is a wonderful organ 136:13
  b., it is all mystery and memory 341:13
  b., it's my second favourite organ 6:7

b. . . . to keep the ears from grating 104:10
b. . . . with which we think we think 42:9
b.s too near their bottoms 94:18
cells and fibres in one human b. 43:15
deeply folded in my b. 363:14
disorders in the strongest b. 40:5
domain of the largest b. 403:23
fluffy, with no b.s at all 170:24
girl with b.s 237:6
give his b. a rest 348:9
his b.s go to his head 15:21
messages go quicker to the b. 353:16
origins in . . . the b. 257:4
phonographs of Hades in the b. 95:2
stars are in one's b. 329:7
thought to have a clear b. 139:4
thoughts of a dry b. 117:14
what good are b.s to a man? 408:11
whispered into your b. 365:11
Brake: b.s are more easily checked 193:7
  b.s on when you're upside down 279:8
  trapping b.s and briars 44:5
  whether to apply the b.s 378:2
Brandishes: engloves this tree and b. it 314:6
Brando, Marlon: [B.] is also our national lout 247:15
Brandt, Willy 14:12
Brandy: b. for the parson 212:21
  music is the b. of the damned 344:16
Brass: tactics talked through a b. hat 196:16
  when you come to b. tacks 117:36
Brave: aren't any good, b. causes left 288:6
  b. man may become a coward 76:2
  more b. than me 97:16
  not b. enough to be afraid 151:3
Braver: b. in another language 55:12
Braw: b. brecht moonlecht necht 222:5
Brawling: b. leads to laryngitis 85:5
  b. of a sparrow 417:21
Bread: breaking b. with the dead 19:13
  but don't bother about the b. 264:24
  butter for the royal slice of b. 264:10
  first petition for daily b. 406:16
  I asked for b. and was given stone 95:9
  if you share your b. 313:4
  I'm on your side of the b. 108:13
  on the side the b. is buttered 174:20
  this is b. I break 369:18
  throwing your b. on the water 374:11
  when they ask for b. 398:19
Bread-sauce: b. of the happy ending 191:6
Breadline: I'd be . . . on the b. 57:1
Break: as long as you don't b. any 397:23
  b. a man's spirit is devil's work 343:2
  b.s just like a little girl 113:14
  never give a sucker an even b. 125:1
Breakage: B.s, Limited 342:14
Breakdown: madness need not be all b. 219:13
Breakfast: bananas for b. 399:22
  b. food of love 4:7
  critical period in matrimony is b. time 171:1
  drink of b. 125:7

eats cheese for b. 25:2
face . . . as long as a late b. 198:18
heart to touch my b. 410:8
marriage is not all bed and b. 93:10
must not reheat his sins for b. 105:22
Breaking: b. it [name] in for a friend 253:23
Breakneck: riding at b. speed 43: 17
Breakthrough: madness . . . may be b. 219:13
Breakwater: within these b.s 17:9
Breast: almonds . . . add weight to the b.s 86:6
b. projecting for about four feet 159:6
salesmen can fondle her b.s 217:10
secondary characteristic, like b.s 16:18
soaping her b.s in the bath 121:15
Breast-feeding: every luxury . . . b. 286:1
Breastbone: hand of stone on your white b. 70:19
Breath: b. you take is someone else's last 66:19
b.'s a ware that will not keep 179:13
b.'s like a badger's bum 87:6
cry that was no more than a b. 89:8
fierce and bald and short of b. 336:29
Heaven and Hell . . . one b. away 391:5
peaceful out of b. death 243:15
wages of gin is b. 171:7
whisky on their b. 383:1
writing is . . . holding your b. 127:24
Breathe: b. not a whisper 103:23
making poetry is . . . to b. 320:1
we b., we change 28:16
Breathing: hear heavy b. again 45:8
Breathless: b., we flung us 54:14
Brecht, Bertolt 232:4, 236:21
B. . . . theatrical whore 159:17
Breed: lesser b.s without the law 212:16
would not breed from this officer 393:27
Brevity: b. is the soul of lingerie 292:14
Bribe: b. once accepted 153:15
cannot hope to b. or twist 411:11
marriage is a b. 403:2
Bribed: b. not to be b. 77:17
Bribery: government by mass b. 186:3
Bribing: b. yourself through the inconveniences 315:11
Bric-à-brac: my smile . . . among the *b.* 117:33
you write b. 136:8
Brick: b.s with ephemeral straw 64:12
cannot see through a b. wall 19:6
not even red b. 288:3
throw a b. without hitting the niece 287:2
well-disposed towards the two b.s 98:12
Bricklayer: b.s kick their wives 397:10
Bride: blushing b. she looks divine 130:3
b. to a lad gone down 261:9
jealousy to the b. 26:13
Bridegroom: b. . . . never turns him 179:16
Bridesmaid: always a b. 228:8
Bridge: and the same applies to b. partners 242:14
b. even where there is no river 207:17
like a b. over troubled water 347:19
that great b., our Myth 94:29
trouble with b.s 253:24

Women, and Champagne, and B. 32:32
Bridlington: from B. to Bristol 94:7
Brief: b. and powerless is man's life 328:12
Brigade: between the fire b. and the fire 79:4
boys of the Old B. 231:3, 394:1
Brigand: b.s demand your money 61:28
Bright: b., nimble, . . . comprehending 80:17
b. tracks where I have been 157:1
Brightest: part with their b. hour 169:1
Brighton: B. is Dublin without priests 31:12
high time B. was relieved 47:11
Brilliance: no b. is needed in the law 270:16
Brilliant: b. to the top of his army boots 236:17
dullard envy of b. men 30:18
easy to be b. 246:13
far less b. pen than mine 30:5
Brilliantine: hair lustrous with b. 86:3
Bring: b. [bwing] another 48:14
Brink: scared to go to the b. 111:4
Bristle: skin b.s . . . razor ceases to act 180:8
Bristol: from Bridlington to B. 94:7
Britain: Battle of B. 79:16, 81:14
B. a fit country for heroes 235:17
B. has lost its pride 255:16
B. is a tin can tied to a dog's tail 294:13
class, you can only get in B. 49:3
customs of his tribe and island B. 342:24
end of B. as an independent state 138:11
I'm backing B. 12:1
no longer speak for B. 14:17
British: bribe . . . the B. journalist 411:11
B. . . . have a Socialist mind 125:13
B. have . . . a taste for bad books 49:15
[B.] have elevated servility 13
B. Jews . . . are like other Jews 312:20
B. love permanence 70:9
B. must be gluttons for satire 236:10
B. Outer Mongolia 267:7
B. revolution could not be made 129:11
B. soldier can stand up to anything 343:6
B. tourist is always happy abroad 269:18
[B.] are too modest – in a vain way 387:24
can ever face a B. government 379:9
conversation is never easy for the B. 49:6
dirty B. coaster 254:3
Hitler never understood . . . the B. 58:4
it's one thing being B. 293:18
perfect safety under B. rule 374:7
structure of the . . . B. sentence 80:19
we are B. – thank God 267:21
British Empire: B. . . . last for a thousand years 79:17
'can't' . . . epitaph of the B. 272:3
liquidation of the B. 80:1
longer . . . than to build the B. 243:7
why the sun never sets on the B. 353:13
British Museum: B. an enormous mind 412:14
except perhaps in the B. 83:6
reflection of the B. Reading Room 354:6
British Rail: county . . . cut off by B. 49:16
Britisher: sit round a table with a B. 322:18
Briton: every B. is at heart a Tory 37:5

we B.s use 'Might' 393:6
Britten, Benjamin 390:18
Broad: b. of Church and . . . mind 41:2
  she's the B. and I'm the High 355:21
Broadened: church can be so b. 338:9
Brocade: vast moth-eaten musical b. 221:5
Broccoli: President is never going to eat b. 60:10
Broke: all of us bottomly b. 205:19
Broken: bats . . . b. . . . by the team captain 180:12
  b. by their passing feet 415:16
  b. pictorial space 38:16
  like the Ten Commandments, all b. 377:2
  morning has b. 122:9
  uncomely and b. 416:23
Broken-down: I write in a b. patois 72:13
Broken-hearted: b. clowns 180:17
Broker: b. . . . runs your fortune 413:7
Bronchitis: unless he or she has b. 4:5
Brontë, Charlotte 412:6
Brood: her b. had gone from her 64:17
Brooding: haunt of b. dust 103:15
Broody: b. hen sitting on a china egg 129:9
Brook: b. taken otherwise than in song 135:15
Brooke, Rupert: B. energized the Garden-Suburb
   ethos 226:10
Brooklyn: B. . . . the heart of the Old World 6:19
Brothel: don't take your wife into a b. 149:2
  metaphysical b. for emotions 216:6
  not actively employed in a b. 167:15
  perfect home for a writer is a b. 140:10
  piano-player in a b. 340:15
  played the piano . . . in a b. 10:4
  upstairs a b. 50:3
Brother: b., can you spare a dime? 161:16
  Big B. is watching you 286:21
  her own b. wouldn't have suggested 373:10
  little brown b., are you awake 278:21
  O my b.s 58:18
  that dear little b. of yours 291:24
  walking the earth like b.s 208:15
  white man's b. not his b.-in-law 208:9
  word for b. It's inflammatory 404:8
Brother-in-law: law and morality are . . . b.s 204:2
  thank God, they aren't all b.s 304:2
  white man's brother, not his b. 208:9
Browbeating: sweat of their b. 182:1
Brown: b. [brahn] boots, I asks yer 399:9
Browning, Robert: hang it all, Robert B. 303:1
  Tennyson and B. are poets 119:1
Browsing: excellent b. and sluicing 410:5
Brush: daft as a b. 300:1
Brussels: B. hotel for a Group Grope 371:7
Brutal: system is brutal 96:4
Brutality: b. of war 245:3
Brute: b. curiosity of an angel's stare 365:9
  exterminate all the b.s 89:7
  whatever b. and blackguard 178:20
Bu: j'ai b. l'été 13:9
Bubble: I'm forever blowing b.s 204:7
  life's troubled b. broken 103:22
Buccaneer: haughty . . . the wild b. 139:17

Buck: bigger bang for a b. 405:10
  b. stops here 378:13
Bucking: b. ranches of the night 369:21
Buckingham Palace: [B.] . . . it's a tied cottage
  296:19
  changing guard at B. 264:6
Buckle: b. it with the moon 122:10
  more b. and less swash 266:3
Bud: b. that forks her eye 369:6
Buddha: to the B. or to the bomb 67:11
Buddhism: nothing in . . . B. . . . matches 332:18
Buddhist: B.s and we have no expectations 108:3
  I'm some kind of B. 255:6
  people are either escapists or B.s 304:17
Budgies: b. . . . almost speak American 96:1
Buffer: pleasant old b. 300:5
Buffs: Steady the B. 214:19
Bugger: b. Bognor 142:4
  b. Sunday 44:18
  we've done the b. 367:13
Buggered: b. by the shuttle 258:5
Bugle: b.s calling for them 288:15
  new moon hangs like an ivory b. 370:13
Builder: eternal b. in whose image 348:16
Building: b.s are . . . morally superior 145:5
  destroy a b. 47:15
  read a b. 321:13
  things have altered in the b. trade 213:9
  we make b.s for our need 136:29
Built: it is not what they b. 124:1
Bulb: can't stand a naked light b. 404:20
Bulging: all else than their b. selves 341:22
Bull: bumping b. of the Cassidys 197:12
  b. who carried his own china shop 82:11
  down at the old 'B. and Bush' 374:6
  see an old unhappy b. 175:8
  take the b. between the teeth 147:26
  taking the b. by both horns 15:9
Bulldog: boys of the b. breed 243:13
  b. . . . refused cake 411:4
Buller, General Sir Redvers: what he [B.] said was
  obscure 81:1
Bullet: b. with my name on it 10:13
  where the b.s all go in 70:19
  yes – a b. proof vest 321:5
Bullock: hero's arms and b.'s eyes 206:9
Bum: breath's like a badger's b. 87:6
  instead of a b., . . . what I am 50:14
  left to . . . shabby b.s 233:18
  millionaires and b.s 251:7
  two buttocks of one b. 268:20
Bumpy: it's going to be a b. night 249:13
Bungalow: b., so almost in the country 405:6
Bungled: b., unwise war 300:4
Bungler: in . . . peace Man is a b. 344:19
Bunk: exercise is b. 129:20
  history is more or less b. 129:17
  King B. and King Bank 272:4
Bunkum: de mortuis nil nisi b. 222:2
Bunsen burner: left my B. at home 370:2
Burbank: beautiful downtown B. 325:16

Burden: b. of intelligence 92:13
I dislike b.s 234:16
white man's b. 213:18
Bureaucracy: slime of a new b. 201:5
Burgandies: b. . . . resembling . . . soap 7:9
Burglar: b. who has retired 307:22
b. who respects his art 170:8
Burgundy: naïve domestic B. 372:12
Buried: b. the Church of England 242:13
forgets where he b. a hatchet 181:1
Burke, Edmund 14:6
Burlington Bertie: I'm B. 164:14
Burly: strange but b. look 229:10
Burn: b. while Rome fiddles 88:3
b. with Athens and with Rome 65:4
b. your fingers on your own chestnuts 126:1
doesn't cook . . . she b.s 375:13
to b. a book is not to destroy it 327:16
trying to b. down everything 49:11
Burne-Jones, Sir Edward: passion for B. 183:3
Burning: b. of the leaves 42:29
is Paris b.? 173:19
keep the home-fires b. 129:21
Burnished: b. by Aldershot's sun 40:19
chair . . . like a b. throne 118:7
Burns, Robert: man like B. to sing 211:28
Burnt: old speeches b. 352:5
Burst: everyone suddenly b. out singing 337:3
Bury: b. my heart at Wounded Knee 35:12
we will b. you 207:15
Bus: b. going the wrong way 359:11
good design for a b. 175:4
missed the b. 72:2, 173:18
not even a b., I'm a tram 164:13
once the number 2 bus used to stop 202:1
Buses: bloody men are like bloody b. 91:3
b. running from the Bank to Mandalay 211:31
Bush, President George 60:10, 176:10, 235:4
I'm a B. man myself 366:17
sound emitting from B. 403:13
Bush: life is a copiously branching b. 148:14
one orgasm in the b. 149:30
Busiest: b. man has time to spare 293:2
Business: as a means the b. man is tolerable 206:17
b. as usual 78:21
b. can be settled by influence 127:27
b. of the wealthy man 33:5
b. underlies everything 406:16
chief b. of the American people is b. 90:8
churches . . . let you in on b. only 106:8
have ye any *other* b.? 68:16
it's my b. to comprehend 191:8
moral liability was crucial to b. 371:8
neat clean quite solvent b. 123:1
no admittance on b. 393:19
no b. like show b. 39:4
not to go about her father's b. 346:20
only sure way to run a small b. 356:18
over here it [politics] is a b. 321:17
preventing people from minding their own b.
385:22

safe and sane b. management 386:13
we can do b. together 367:20
Business-like: more b. than business men 135:19
Businessman: b. . . . for ever apologizing 259:7
b. needs three umbrellas 105:20
Bust: acquired . . . an ample b. 86:3
uncorseted, her friendly b. 118:18
undivided b. 24:12
Bustin': June is b. out all over 160:7
Busy: little man you've had a b. day 347:11
not b. being born is b. dying 113:11
pursuing, the b. and the tired 126:16
Butcher: hog b. for the world 334:15
I can't abear a b. 103:9
like a neglected b. boy 333:3
overworked and underpaid b. boy 396:6
when you go to a b. 50:22
Butler, R.A. [later Lord] 245:19
Butler: b.s . . . do not reproduce 395:19
b.s ought to know their place 32:18
hope to find in their b.s 257:3
toes of an English b. 410:11
Butter: all your b. is in your horns 197:12
b. for the royal slice of bread 264:10
b. their bannocks on both sides 323:17
b. will only make us fat 146:2
b. wouldn't melt in her mouth 220:8
I may be rancid b. 108:13
melted b. into a . . . left ear 410:22
without b., but not without guns 145:16
Buttered: on the side the bread is b. 174:20
Butterflies: beard full of b. 140:6
Butterfly: b. . . . preaches contentment 212:9
float like a b. 5:11
here and there a bird, or b. 135:12
Buttock: gorgeous b.s of the ape 183:18
two b.s of one bum 268:20
Button: bottom waistcoat b. undone 287:3
purchase and sale of b.s 140:15
Button-stick: tongue like a b. 210:1
Butty: he's an oul' b. o' mine 284:2
Buy: b. back my introduction to you 253:6
don't b. a single vote 205:12
stop me and b. one 3:22
Buying: depends if you're b. or selling 148:17
Buzzard: writer may be a hawk or a b. 169:15
Buzzed: brain . . . b. more 80:11
Buzzing: big, booming, b. confusion 191:23
Bwing: another 48:14
By-law: b.s are shorter 400:4
Byron, George Gordon, Lord 304:15
B. – would be forgotten today 30:29
Byronic: deliberately B. 266:3
Byzantium: Soldan of B. is smiling 74:20

C

C. major: much good music to be written in C. 339:1
Cabbage: c. with a college education 380:12

two of the are c. 290:2

Cabin: small c. build there 416:18

Cabinet: all equals . . . like the C. 239:12
dark as the inside of a C. Minister 69:22

Cabman: c. dances 271:8

Cabots: C. talk only to God 47:8

Cad: c. have always a grandmother 403:16
cocoa is a c. and coward 75:10

Caesar: Roman C. is held down 417:11
sawdust C. 340:16

Café: in every street c. 160:10

Cage: bird in a gilded c. 219:15
over the c. floor the horizons come 181:13
singing bird forgets its c. 265:13
we occupy the same c. 404:13

Cain: cruel sons of C. 227:20

Cake: c. is . . . a piece of cake 172:17
candles cost more than the c. 177:17
don't tell them . . . to eat c. 398:19
enough white lies to ice a c. 15:24
orange peel picked out of a c. 311:11
your c. and eat it; . . . get fat 25:15

Cake-sale: air force has to hold a c. 237:19

Calabash: goodnight Mrs C. 112:8

Calabria: between C. and Corfu 112:17

Calamities: c. are of two kinds 42:10

Calamity: unwarrantable belief is a c. 316:15

Calculate: c. coldly about the unknown 43:16

Calculating: desiccated c. machine 41:11

Calf: c. won't get much sleep 6:12
fatted c. to share the enthusiasm 332:27

Caliban: C. casts out Ariel 303:15

California: C. – a state so blessed 135:18
C. here I come 196:14
C., the department-store state 72:8

Caligula: eyes of C. 266:18

Call: c. on me , and I'll send it along 229:22
clear c. may not be denied 254:11
life . . . is all c. and answer 223:12
may I call you 338? 94:17
not a soul will be likely to c. 300:10
till truth obeyed his call 415:4

Callaghan, James [later Lord] 22:13, 192:23

Callas, Maria: woman called C. 360:19

Called: something is what it is c. 243:2

Calves: hairy c. of the vicar's wife 119:17
particularly susceptible to c. 183:5

Cambridge: C. has seen many strange sights 180:9
[C.] is the city of perspiring dreams 312:9
C. ladies . . . in furnished souls 97:29
C. lady, hearing of the latest suicide 114:5
C. people rarely smile 54:19
I find C. an asylum, in every sense 180:10
put gently back at . . . C. 30:7

Cambridgeshire: C. . . . Men who Understand 54:18

Camel: c. has a single hump 277:10
c. is a horse designed by a committee 9:4
pass through the eye of a camel 354:14
take my c., dear 241:4

Cameo: hardly more affable than a c. 30:17

Camera: c. relieves us of the burden 38:12
hold the c. to it 363:11
I am a c. with its shutter open 187:15
stole everything but the c.s 311:5
time for the c.s to flash 378:12

Camp: last c. of experience 156:20

Camper: bogus c.s 13:7

Campeurs: faux c. 13:7

Campland: C., an invisible country 352:22

Campus: walk on the c. and look at the moon 120:24
world is a global campus 236:16

Can: pass me the c., lad 178:17

Canaan: white streams of C. 13:1

Canada: C. is . . . square 35:22
national mental illness . . . of C. 17:4
world-famous . . . all over C. 317:11

Canal: Suez C. . . . through my drawing room 115:1

Canaletto: then the C.s go 245:17

Canaries: song of c. never varies 277:11

Canasta: Lord's Prayer when playing c. 119:10

Cancer: money differs from . . . c. 139:5

Candidate: c. should not mean but be 387:5

Candidature: c. passed almost unnoticed 392:17

Candle: by my green c., shit, madam 192:20
c.s cost more than the cake 177:17
like a c. burnt out 417:2
my c. burns at both ends 261:6
rather light c.s 359:7
white c. in a holy place 64:16

Candy: c. is dandy 278:1
if life were a c. bar 346:19

Cane: white c. knocking into knowledge 68:2

Cannes: elsewhere, but not to C. 190:1

Cannibal: c. . . . orders the waiter 37:12
converted c. . . . eats only fishermen 237:20
progress if a c. uses knife and fork 227:3
take a c. to lunch 149:34

Cannon: where the c. flower grew 201:18

Cannot: he who c., teaches 344:29

Canonical: c. gospels do not record 130:11

Canons: c. ironiques 13:7

Can't: c. . . . epitaph of the British Empire 272:3
don't think you c. if you can 185:11

Canto: c. of unvanquished space 94:28

Cap-à-pie: armed c. to defend himself 52:6

Capable: c. of higher things 130:8

Capitain: what do you want, my C. 263:25

Capitalism: c. 'caused' the . . . War 366:4
c. is the exploitation of man by man 11:16
c. was doomed ethically 352:12
c. whereby American girls turn into . . . women 160:21
c. with the gloves off 361:6
c. without capital 296:9
imperialism is the monopoly stage of c. 228:12
making c. out of socialism 22:10
quarrel between c. and communism 359:11
spirit of c. 394:6
unacceptable face of c. 167:9

theology finds the c. 191:21
what woman has this old c.'s graces? 260:11
you have forgotten the c. 412:22
Cat-call: if there are c.s 50:5
Cataclysm: out of their c. 183:16
Catalogue: everything in the c. 72:10
Catalonia: C. is the nose of the earth 99:6
Catamite: in bed with my c. 58:20
Catastrophe: lose one's teeth is a c. 399:23
not c.s . . . that age and kill us 412:13
race between education and c. 397:2
unarmed towards a c. 115:15
Catch: c.-22 168:10
Catching: they thought it was c. 43:12
Categories: ballet of bloodless c.s 49:23
Category-habit: replacement of c.s 329:18
Cathedral: c.s . . . abandoned computers 112:21
not a c. but . . . a casino 186:25
qualifies you to build c.s 164:12
Catherine the Great: you liked my C. 397:22
Catholic: came for the C.s 280:5
C. and grown-up 287:20
C. and the Communist are alike 287:15
C. woman to avoid pregnancy 258:14
C.s . . . are the last word in protest 224:2
C.s . . . have committed great crimes 153:17
church he . . . did not attend was C. 7:15
I'm still a C. 405:8
Kennedys . . . may be C. 242:8
machine, designed for C.s 236:13
mate for life, like pigeons or C.s 6:3
Catholicism: C. – . . . die now and pay later 6:1
Cattle: actors are c. 172:13
those who die as c. 288:14
Caught: c. only enough 389:11
Cauliflower: c. . . . cabbage with . . . education
380:12
you shall be a c. 155:4
Cause: aren't any good, brave c.s left 288:6
as if you were the c. of it 346:11
c. that cannot lose 136:18
great c. of cheering us all up 37:3
great events do not . . . have great c.s 366:12
wants to die nobly for a c. 358:1
Causeway: found . . . the c. 82:1
Caustic: too c.? To hell with cost 147:24
Caution: approach both with c. 286:6
c. in love is . . . fatal 328:8
c. of one brushing flies 411:8
Cautious: c., . . . careful not to show it 312:13
Cavalry: c. charging over a tin bridge 408:16
Cave: stand at the jaws of the c. 8:4
we should still be living in c.s 366:6
Caviar: more salted peanuts . . . than c. 355:11
Ceauşescu, President Nicolae 71:4
Cecil: after you, C. 203:2
Cedar: Unicorn among the c.s 18:4
Ceiling: long enough to draw on the c. 77:13
writing in the lines of the c. 120:16
Celebrities: acted more like . . . c. 333:14
conversations with c.s 198:27

Celebrity: c. is a mask 383:3
c. . . . known for his well-knownness 46:16
c. . . . works hard 5:12
they liked c. in those days 43:12
Celery: thrives in the dark. Like c. 183:10
Celibacy: world c. championships 32:3
Celibans: terror c. 148:4
Celibate: c. kip 381:5
Cell: cohesion by unresting c.s 254:7
Cemeteries: c. are a way of life 407:18
Corde avoided c. 33:25
Cemetery: c. in which nine . . . daughters 372:11
complete unanimity in a c. 4:1
grass uncut in a . . . c. 375:17
living half in a c. 52:11
Censer: clank of c.s 4:10
Censor: c. one's own thoughts 389:15
Censorship: extreme form of c. 345:25
Centenarian: number of c. men in Britain 92:10
Central: assumed I was the c. character 174:17
Central heating: English have adopted c. 120:7
Centre: c. cannot hold 417:12
c. is giving way 129:4
sex is only the liquid c. 90:17
Centuries: what wild c. 102:17
Century: c. of the common man 390:13
great man . . . walks across his c. 225:21
this c. grows even darker 313:5
Cerebration: well of unconscious c. 190:4
Cerebrum: babies . . . with larger c.s 258:17
Ceremony: c. in that land of waifs 392:22
c. of innocence is drowned 417:12
man is a creature of c. 336:18
Cerrados: el nino tiene los ojos c. 140:8
Certain: as far as they are c. 115:19
c. little lady 130:2
only c. thing about the future 174:19
Certainties: modern world lacks . . . c. 327:14
Certainty: his constant c. found 93:5
lust for c. may be a sin 158:2
not knowledge but c. 329:4
Chaff: not racially pure are mere c. 173:4
Chagall, Marc 228:11
Chain: safer . . . in c.s than . . . free 200:12
sang in my c.s like the sea 369:1
Chained: c. to a demon 101:17
Chair: c. . . . like a burnished throne 118:7
c. up close to the . . . precipice 127:16
c.s are being brought in 17:20
edge of the c. of literature 372:20
Chairman: C. of Ego, Inc. 18:25
Chaise-longue: hurly-burly of the c. 65:1
Challenging: c. Israel to peace 13:5
Chamberlain, Neville: [C.] . . . a nice old gentleman
173:14
[C.] saw foreign policy through . . . a drainpipe
236:5
that old fool C. 354:9
Chamberlain: death . . . . c. had carried 319:16
Chameleon: destroyed the C. at Strood 300:21
Chamois: like the c. of the Alps 410:20

wars are fought by c. 235:6
way parents obey their c. 115:8
weapon to keep c. good 54:9
what have you got against having c.? 153:1
what is he doing with the c. 70:18
when they started life as c. 7:16
when they think their c. are naïve 277:9
where are the c. I might have had? 238:14
white faces like town c. 181:15
write for c. . . . as for adults 148:9
your c. are not your c. 143:5
Chill: of c.s and fevers she died 312:4
Chimborazo: golden land, C. 379:13
Chime: c. of words tinkling in the mind 351:7
    he also c.s 373:6
Chimney: sixty horses wedged in a c. 271:9
Chin: two c. . . . where only one 409:8
China 221:23
    bull who carried his own c. shop 82.11
    father was the Great Wall of C. 390:10
    slow boat to C. 236:19
    there [C.] and back in a day 221:23
Chinamen: agree with C. but not with me 33:8
Chinese: C., . . . might not look it 168:22
    C. Wall of Milton 118:29
Chink: it is all c. 380:25
Chip: c. on each shoulder 11:1
    c.s on both shoulders 310:1
    c.s with everything 397:17
Chittering: c. waters of 197:19
Chocolate: c. cream soldier 342:17
    eating an entire box of c. liqueurs 67:8
    I always carry c. instead 342:16
Choice: of playthings 214:8
    courage is when you have c.s 8:14
    easier. . . . when there are no c.s 312:8
    equipped to make c.s 239:4
    imperious c. already begin there 318:12
    reasons for your c. 376:1
Choir: drunk in a midnight c. 85:12
Choke: major, whether they c. or not 400:3
Cholera: condescend to die of c. 306:17
Choose: doesn't know how to c. 297:17
    to c. the Jews 121:17
    to govern is to c. 259:15
    will you c. sometimes 370:20
Chooser: only people who can be c.s 277:1
Chop: people who c. off heads 47:17
Chopin, Frédéric: anyone can look like C. 326:5
    gap between Dorothy and C. 2:11
Chopping: people who love c. wood 116:6
Chord: play the c. of C major 29:14
    throb in witching c.s 358:16
Chorister: go the chanting c.s 222:18
Chortling: c. by officials 81:11
Chorus-girl: meeting with a pretty c. 65:12
Chose: c. to be to where they have to be 281:6
Chose: les c.s sont contre nous 194:1
Christ, see Jesus Christ
Christ Church: I am the Dean of C. 355:21
Christendom: half of C. worships a Jew 9:6

Christian: Bach . . . persuades me to be a C. 137:3
    C. anti-Communists, and the others 111:6
    C. Church . . . exists for . . . non-members 367:8
    C. ideal has been found difficult 77:16
    C. kisses on an 'eathen idol's foot 211:30
    fool enough to turn C. 420:1
    he is a proper C. 369:31
    just as the Victorians were C.s 244:9
    maybe a C. third 354:7
    render the C. life intensely difficult 232:13
    scratch the C. 420:2
    souls of C. people 74:3
    teachers were called by their c. names 22:1
    they [Kennedys] are not C.s 242:8
    waning of my C. sympathies 221:20
Christian Science: C. is . . . therapeutically
    successful 159:7
Christian Scientist: took her for a C. 266:10
Christianity: C. is . . . a man's religion 395:4
    C. is good news: not good advice 186:21
    C. naturally, but why journalism? 24:1
    C. preached a peace . . . never achieved 326:10
    C. promises to make men free 186:12
    gap in C. 130:11
    local cult, called C. 163:21
    nothing in C. . . . that quite matches 332:18
    rock and roll or C. 229:9
    say what they like about C. 332:25
Christmas: C. box in February 333:3
    C. Day in the workhouse 348:15
    C. Eve, and twelve of the clock 163:9
    C. through its wrapping 400:7
    don't like about C. office parties 106:6
    dreaming of a white C. 39:10
    go well with . . . the C. decorations 332:11
    I'm walking backwards for C. 263:16
    Socialist Revolution as if it were C. 68:8
Christmastime: self-consciousness at C. 148:5
Christopher Robin: C. has fallen downstairs
    271:15
    C. is saying his prayers 264:13
    C. went down with Alice 264:6
Chronicle: young men read c.s 76:20
Chuck: c. it, Smith 74:3
Chump: c.s . . . make the best husbands 408:11
Church: attended stables as we attended c. 349:13
    between the C. and the Post Office 84:3
    came to c. to share God 390:3
    c. as he goes to the bathroom 44:16
    c. can be so broadened 338:9
    C. can feed and sleep at once 117:15
    c. complains of persecution 420:11
    c. he currently did not attend 7:15
    c.'s restoration in 1883 40:13
    come all to c. good people 179:22
    first split-level c. in America 105:5
    get me to the c. on time 230:21
    I believe in the C. 367:10
    many who stay away from c. 261:16
    'oly as a c. 362:1
    people . . . who go to c. when abroad 19:19

Protestant c.s of the north 106:8
stands the C. clock 55:1
straying away from the c. 57:2
who is ruling the C. 195:3
Church of England: C. would ask him to set out his ideas 164:7
we have just buried the C. 242:13
where MCC ends and C. begins 305:17
Churches: c. . . . bore for me 382:12
c. grow old but do not grow up 268:8
martyrs do not build c. 65:29
Churchill, Randolph: part of R. . . . not malignant 393:17
Churchill, Winston 15:19, 16:7, 41:14, 70:7, 158:7, 295:16, 323:1, 352:4, 393:24
C. is a bigger danger than the Germans 126:4
C. liked thinking aloud 46:3
first time you meet C. 240:6
he [C.] mobilized the English language 275:5
W. is back 81:7
W. loved meeting people 235:21
W. with his hundred horse-power mind 23:11
Churchman: Modern C. . . . draws the full salary 392:14
Cicero: C. and many-minded Homer 416:24
Cider: c. and tinned salmon 392:28
Cigar: fifty-cent c. 2:1
good c. is a smoke 209:21
really good five-cent c. 252:6
substitute out of c. stumps 108:16
Cinco: eran las c. en punto de la tarde 140:4
Cinema: c. . . . are always bigger inside 209:3
c. has become . . . like the theatre 103:29
c. is not a slice of life 172:17
c. is truth twenty-four times a second 145:8
Circle: c. is the longest distance 360:5
describe a c. 187:3
locked into the infernal c. 122:5
sound of the second c. 90:15
Circulation: wages of sin are increased c. 13:11
Circumambulatory: c. aphrodisiac 136:24
Circumcised: c. Herbert Samuel 236:4
Circumcision: every luxury . . . c. 286:1
Circumstance: c.s break men's bones 75:25
died . . . under very good c.s 52:12
from c.s to ecstasy 31:16
Circumvent: to c. death 66:7
Circus: c. going on inside 98:6
class . . . like the c. people 52:5
what's he doing in the bloody c.? 257:11
Citadel: vain c.s that are not walled 288:27
Cities: government burns down whole c. 250:20
I have sung women in three c. 303:11
many c. had rubbed him smooth 153:20
paradise of crisp white c. 180:19
real c. have something else 72:10
Citizen: c. means something in the City 75:13
c. of life 337:6
c.s of death's grey land 337:2
first and second class c.s 405:2
free men . . . are c.s of Berlin 205:3

I want to make good c.s 363:7
job of a c. 151:4
Citizenship: dual c. in the kingdom 353:8
City: basic rule of the C. 240:1
big c. at night 140:10
c. government is of the people 357:3
c. is a . . . human jungle 270:5
citizen means something in the C. 75:13
every c. has sex and age 38:15
in the c. time becomes visible 274:4
keen c. in the sky 97:3
no c. should be too large 88:21
perfect model of a c. 274:2
sacred city of the mind 65:4
Secular C. 94:23
seventy-two suburbs in search of a c. 292:20
unreal c. 118:5
without whom . . . no c. can stand 352:19
Civil guard: c. . . . hard-hatted race 68:11
Civil servant: c. should have complete loyalty to the truth 209:1
naked C.s 95:22
new missile . . . called the c. 390:9
wonderfully gifted c.s 83:8
Civil Service: C. is . . . deferential 96:18
Civilian: forget about this c. 147:4
Civilization: can't say c. don't advance 321:18
c. advances by extending 401:5
c. gets the historians it deserves 302:11
c. has made the peasantry 377:24
c. has not recovered 301:4
c. is hooped together 417:22
c. of one epoch 88:23
c. . . . the attempt to reduce violence 285:18
c.s are remembered by their artefacts 27:16
degree of a nation's c. 256:5
fall of the last c. 313:11
farmyard c. of the Fabians 186:6
for a botched c. 303:17
it [c.] would be a good idea 139:23
nasty, vulgar sort of c. 59:4
new, frost-bitten bud of c. 306:2
principal task of c. 134:1
strong c. . . . can replace things 47:15
threaten in totality all . . . c. 341:21
usual interval of c. 84:13
Civilize: our failures that c. us 189:12
Civilized: most c. music in the world 383:8
Claim: never c. as of right 86:11
Clairvoyante: Madam Sosostris, famous c. 118:3
Clamber: c. to the heights of sleep 416:edit
Clamour: c. of the day 71:6
maggot's weak c. rings 151:17
Clan: c. has a tendency to ignore me 409:14
Clap: don't c. too hard 287:22
Clapham: like a beautiful C. Junction 155:20
Claret: cheaper c.s 332:22
Claridges: after a week at C. 52:12
body of the boot-boy at C. 412:24
Class: abolish the 3rd C. not the 1st 236:22
c. . . . half wouldn't be seen dead 192:21

c., I mean, real c. 49:3
c. v. c., bitter as before 165:3
cleverest c. 394:3
essence of a c. system 189:14
first and second c. citizens 405:2
force by one c. against another 228:15
he gave her c. and she gave him sex 170:22
I coulda had c. 50:14
nationalism is . . . like c. 404:5
new c. 107:9
poets . . . are outside the c. system 52:5
resistance of its c. enemies 356:5
upper c. who were just bright enough 96:8
while there is a lower c., I am in it 102:6
without distinction of c. 343:20
Classes: c. within c. in Peckham 353:15
comfort came in with the middle c. 31:19
lower c. had such white skins 98:117
mistrust of the English upper c. 270:18
only two c. of people 306:16
responsible and irresponsible c. 223:8
struggle between c. and nations 206:15
upper c. have still the upper hand 93:23
vanguards of the most advanced c. 228:13
Classic: belly full of the c.s 262:9
c. . . . wants to have read 380:20
c.s . . . one ought to read 36:10
great homicidal c.s 360:22
Classical: c. mind at work 299:12
Classifies: way of speaking . . . c. him 230:17
Classify: Germans c. 70:14
Claude: after you, C. 203:2
Claustrophobia: get his c. looked at 91:13
his ribs . . . giving him c. 348:7
Claw: c.s loosen 40:3
pair of ragged c.s 117:25
Clay: c. lies still 179:13
of c. and wattles made 416:18
Clean: be c., be tidy, oil the clock 18:30
c. house in the middle of the night 371:16
c. life and attend Holy Communion 337:9
c. the sky 118:24
keep your city c. – eat a pigeon 149:22
make a c. sweep or make a c. end 101:19
that c.s up the matter 290:13
then I was c. and brave 179:18
when a soldier sees a c. face 51:8
you have to c. your plate 324:4
Clean-limbed: c. American boys 9:20
Cleaner: relatively the c. thing 401:18
Cleanest: c. . . . way of having a bad time 73:19
Cleaning: militants are like c. women 378:12
Clear: c. the air 118:24
Clear-sighted: not the c. who rule 89:11
Clearing-house: c. of the world 71: 13
Clearly: can be said c. 408:7
Cleaver: unless life took its c. 400:12
Clemenceau, Georges: [C.] had one illusion –
France 206:11
Clenched: c. on a round pain 368:18
Cleopatra: I dreamed I was C. 3:14

plumber's idea of 125:5
Clerc: trahison des c.s 35:10
Clergy: c. . . . on the food of a canary 193:6
Clergyman: salary of a beneficed c. 392:14
Clergymen: contrary to what c. . . . believe 368:8
length of life for c. 284:12
Clerical: lissom, c., printless toe 54:17
Clerk: left-handed c. of high principles 396:6
small c.s and shopkeepers 397:10
Clever: bad manners to be c. 260:20
c. enough to get all that money 77:19
if you're crooked you have to be c. 240:1
it's c., but is it Art? 210:7
too c. by half 333:23
unless he was a c. man 420:1
Cleverest: c. class of the c. nation 394:3
Cleverness: c. is an excuse for thinking 279:19
Cliché 42:4
combination of half-truths and c.s 375:14
C. is but pauperized Ecstasy 1:5
c. is dead poetry 52:2
c. is not a c. 1:5
c.s old and new 82:12
English abounds in c.s 52:2
for fear of c.s 53:11
let's have some new c.s 147:6
old c. 'the dignity of man' 373:5
see also Clitch
Client: here . . . is our c. 109:19
Clientele: tomorrow's c. 228:1
Climacteric: c. of his want 238:13
Climate: heaven for c. . . . hell for company 26:7
moral c. of America 322:15
unknown change in the earth's c. 151:18
whole c. of opinion 17:15
wife provides the c. 51:26
Climax: works its way up to a c. 147:13
Climb: c. upon my knee, Sonny Boy 56:13
c.s into their graves married 402:16
Climber: abode for fearless c.s 172:10
Clinging: c. to their crosses 74:2
Clitch: c. c. c. 42:4
Cloacal: c. obsession 198:12
Clock: be clean, be tidy, all the c. 18:30
c. collected . . . its strength 179:1
c. has stopped in the dark 118:20
c. is always slow 341:18
closed one [mind] about c.s 355:7
electric c. in a thunderstorm 373:6
hands of c.s in railway stations 88:10
hands of the c. have stayed still 369:28
loudest noise . . . from the electric c. 284:13
stands the Church c. 55:1
Clock-making: sublimated . . . in c. 195:8
Clockwork: c. in its outward part 269:10
who ever heard of a c. orange 58:19
Clod: c.s in a slow silent walk 162:22
turned her into the c. she was 7:5
Clogs: c. because they lasted longer 405:15
Close: c. encounters of the third kind 355:9
c. the coalhouse door 145:1

so c. together 415:3

Close-up: tragedy when seen in c. 73:2

Closed: we never c. 386:5

Closer: c. to the ground as children 36:5
  if I hold you any c. 252:20

Closing: c. time in the gardens of the West 87:13
  if you stay till c. time 70:17

Cloth: wearing a c. coat 24:4

Clothes: anything out of the c. basket 401:18
  best c. are invisible 160:18
  hanging the baby on the c. line 327:6
  more room dirty c. take 329:12
  poured into his c. 411:5
  take off your c. for the doctor 70:19
  taking off all her c. 86:1
  who wore torn c. 355:2

Clothes-peg: c. of his exclamation mark 368:15

Cloud: c. turns to the net 206:10
  gods be said to thump the c.s 369:16
  how sweet to be a c. 264:23
  trailed the c. of his own glory 153:10
  tumult in the c.s 416:17
  turn the dark c. inisde out 129:21
  what tumbling c. did you cleave 416:12

Cloven: out pops the c. hoof 408:21

Clover: bee has quit the c. 211:21
  I'm looking over a four-leaf c. 107:7

Clown: artist, like the idiot or c. 349:12
  broken-hearted c.s 180:17
  I remain . . . a c. 73:1
  promoted c. 366:8
  send in the c.s 353:6

Club: c. . . . in favour of the poor member 77:9
  c. that will accept me as a member 253:11
  dance at the Golf C., my victor and I 40:20
  easier . . . to be loyal to his c. 400:4
  most exclusive club in the world 178:10
  rode politely in the c. 74:5
  you are merely the c. bore 332:10

Clue: follow the c.s inside yourself 202:20
  singularity is . . . a c. 109:7

Clunk: c. click, every trip 3:4

Clutch: c. at the heart 136:10
  seize and c. and penetrate 118:19

Clutch-lever: St Sebastian for a c. 84:17

Co-op: it would make a grand C. 413:15

Coaches: slow c. and . . . contraceptives 197:11

Coal: England's own c. 209:22
  hot c.s in his mouth 45:14
  island . . . made of c. 41:9
  piece of c. up his ass 53:4

Coal Board: C. MacGregor and the NUM 165:3

Coalhouse: close the c. door 145:1

Coalition: c. of four million 289:1

Coarse: all good stories have a c. touch 164:3
  c. sailing . . . boating around in muck 153:8
  one of them is rather c. 326:2

Coastal: it deepens like a c. shelf 221:16

Coaster: dirty British c. 254:3

Coastwise: c. lights of England 210:3

Coat: hold my c. and snicker 117:26

I won't take my c. off 300:2
  tattered c. upon a stick 417:10

Coates, Eric: C.. And very nice too 36:9

Coaxin': c. onaisy ones 151:6

Cobweb: floors are shrunken , c.s hang 162:6

Cobweb-covered: dusty, c., maimed 62:7

Coca-Cola: billboards did to C. 382:12

Cocaine: c. isn't habit-forming 24:6

Cock: c. into assorted ladies 152:23
  c. may crow 368:1
  c. the gun that is not loaded 210:16
  two people, himself and his c. 22:5

Cockcrow: like ghosts at c. 377:10

Cockroach: c. would have had it 411:7
  composed by an intelligent c. 67:16

Cockroaches: c. on his top lip 248:18

Cocksure: cast among c. women 224:5

Cocktail: had for the price of a c. 249:15
  weasel under the c. cabinet 298:23

Cocoa: c. is a cad and coward 75:10

Coconut: admit he ate the last c. 359:19
  lovely bunch of c.s 167:11

Cocoon: live wrapped tight in a c. 68:6

Cod: piece of c. passes all understanding 239:6
  serve both c. and salmon 231:13

Code: they rape us with their c.s 133:11

Coded: read more c. signs 38:13

Codfish: unlike the male c. 408:12

Coerce: not force people . . . we c. them 47:10

Coffee: accent of . . . c. 231:15
  c. that's too black 248:1
  if this is c., I want tea 308:22
  measured out my life with c. spoons 117:24
  revolution as instant c. 114:8

Coffin: kid or a c. 26:16
  to the grave in a Y-shaped c. 286:5

Cognition: c. reigns but does not rule 385:10

Cohesion: held in c. by unresting cells 254:7

Cohn, Harry 11:20

Cohort: c. of the damned 210:23

Coin: c.s in my pocket reddened 167:4

Coiner: carry back bright to the c. 179:13

Coir: c. matting to . . . Kirman rugs 193:18

Coke: happiness is like c. 183:7

Cold: able to feel hot and think c. 69:14
  art should be c. 338:22
  blow c. blood 344:32
  called a c. a c. 37:2
  caught a cold in the park 198:14
  c. and rook-delighting heaven 415:15
  c. bath king 317:4
  c. coming we had of it 117:20
  c. companionable streams 417:29
  c. war 27:5
  c. was cursing the warmth 374:16
  'Feed a c.' – . . . a neo-Keynesian 245:16
  flags and banners of the ancient C. 348:24
  her body a bulb in the c. 299:24
  imperatives of c. and . . . daylight 53:15
  keep c., young orchard 135:14
  leapt straight past the common c. 20:11

Madam Sosostris . . . had a bad c. 118:3
spy who came in from the c. 227:8
Cold-bloodedly: c. handed over 51:16
Colder: c. than the Hebrides 128:5
Coleridge, Samuel Taylor: 277:16
 indulgences of C. 371:15
Collaborating: sense that we are c. 320:19
Collapse: c. debility, panic and uproar 351:17
Colleague: c. had far more weight here 33:22
Collect: keep cool and c. 397:20
Collecting: c. is . . . not quite normal 373:13
Collection: c. of prejudices 116:4
Collective: c. security 35:11
 c. unconscious 194:5, 198:26
 nothin' but a c. hunch 389:1
Collector: c. of religions 343:25
 hardly any c.'s value 201:19
College: cabbage with a c. education 380:12
 your rooms at c. was beastly 212:1
Collide: misfortune to c. with a tree 411:2
Colonel: C. of the Knuts 407:7
 crux and C. of the whole matter 351:17
 C's lady and Judy O'Grady 211:13
Colonized: c. the Isle of Wight 32:5
Colony: every human being is a whole c. 297:7
 we were an empire, now . . . a c. 35:19
Colossal: epoch of the c. 285:15
Colour: all c.s and none 75:16
 all the c.s of the rectum 149:23
 any c., so long as it's black 129:18
 c. things the way they really are 123:11
 describe the c. of the eyes 321:16
 hair the c. of a Charles the Fifth 102:22
 her c. comes and goes 107:11
 incurable disease – c. blindness 102:1
 judged by the c. of their skin 208:11
 nailing his c.s . . . to the fence 346:16
 not because of my c. 122:5
 problem of the c. line 110:24
 winter is . . . low on c.s 53:15
Colourable: give c. reasons 72:15
Coloured: awfully fond of c. people 291:15
 c. counties 179:21
 c. man can tell 244:1
 c., one-eyed Jew 101:3
 c. pencil long enough to draw 77:13
 drop of black blood makes a c. man 181:5
 everybody's c. 29:23
Colourless: c. green ideas 78:12
Columbus, Christopher: C. sailed the ocean blue
 331:4
Comb: fight . . . over a c. 47:3
Combat: c. on the shabby patch of clods 273:4
Combating: c. un-American activities 168:8
Combative: her one c. action 393:9
Combination: c. sinners 403:7
Combustion: Immaculate Conception was
 spontaneous c. 292:7
Come: c. on and hear 39:2
 c. up some time, see me? 398:9
 it c.s to me sometimes 264:17

let 'em all c. 215:15
shape of things to c. 397:4
Comeback: c. but nobody ever tells me 176:12
Comedian: bad c.s: not bad men 153:16
 c. can only last 321:24
Comedy: all I need to make c. 72:20
 at a c. we only look 182:14
 c. . . . into an open sewer and die 55:21
 c. . . . is society protecting itself 305:11
 c. is the public version 368:14
 c. is tragedy interrupted 20:4
 c., like sodomy 123:17
 core of tragedy and c. 156:1
 essence of c. 382:4
 farce refined becomes high c. 94:25
 hardest . . . to write drama with c. 359:12
 life is . . . a comedy in long-shot 73:2
 nobody should try to play c. 98:6
 sense of both c. and tragedy 373:4
Comely: c. dog is he 102:22
Comfort: c. is like the wrong memory 153:19
 c. . . . with the middle classes 31:19
 easy speeches that c. cruel men 74:24
 I tell you naught for your c. 74:9
 my mind isn't much of a c. to me 174:15
 newspaper to c. the afflicted 108:12
Comfortable: afflict the c. 139:9
 baith grand and c. 26:8
 c. minds 97:29
 c. people should cower from deserving 90:3
 feeling c. in the universe 64:9
 flick the c. 108:12
Comforted: folly of being c. 416:10
Comforting: c. . . . in time of trouble 251:15
Comic: all men are necessarily c. 233:14
 c.s and the sporting page 117:32
 only effective in the c. spirit 345:26
Coming: cold c. we had of it 117:20
Comma bacillus: insignificant . . . as the c. 306:17
Commandment: science knows only one c. 51:5
 Ten C.s, all broken 377:2
 there aren't no Ten C.s 211:33
 working on only Four C.s 281:12
 wouldn't have been ten c. 49:20
Comment: c. is free but facts are sacred 339:20
 thick walls and running c. 34:16
Commentary: snivelling c. 151:21
Commercial: blend of the c. traveller 356:13
Commercialism: c. is doing well 387:18
Commission: Royal C. is a broody hen 129:9
Commit: c. no thesis 215:13
Commitment: between involvement and c. 278:14
Committee: camel is a horse designed by a c. 9:4
 c. is an animal 227:9
 c. should consist of three men 91:8
 designed in c. 243:9
 number one book was written by a c. 257:18
 violence punctuauted by c. meetings 403:14
Commodius: c. vicus of recirculation 197:8
Common: beauty of the c. law 106:16
 century of the c. man 390:13

Conclusion: art of drawing sufficient c.s 61:12
  c. of your syllogism 283:7
  c.s on which I base my facts 295:11
  muscle-bound from jumping to c.s 203:11
  they would not reach a c. 346:12
Concrete: absence of c. 66:5
  city is not a c. jungle 270:5
  make abstract that which is c. 336:27
  trying to bowl to God on c. 320:4
Condemned: c. for what we are 123:20
Condensed: c. Roman Catholicism 139:11
Condescend: c. to die of cholera 306:17
Condition: c. rather than a profession 152:14
Conducive: c. to our own welfare 61:7
Conduct: false thinking brings wrong c. 183:22
  our c. isn't all your fancy paints 213:7
Conducting: c. himself justly and tolerantly
  156:23
  never used a score when c. 266:14
Conductor: tall c.s can deal . . . with slow music
  251:22
  third-rate foreign c.s 29:20
  too many c.s who mime 108:7
Confer: on the white terrace and c. 156:20
Conference: c. is a gathering of important people
  5:13
  c. regarding the eradication of all c.s 257:14
  made to have the C.s at 341:2
  naked into the c. chamber 41:13
Confess: c. to her with confidence 190:3
  easy to . . . c. the lies he tells 178:14
  men will confess to . . . a wig 85:18
Confession: sweetness of c. 125:30
Confessional: c. . . . that didn't stink 333:21
  many-tongued cluster of c.s 190:3
Confidence: going wrong with c. 9:12
Confinement: framed and wired c. 190:18
Confirmed: all those things which are c. 148:15
Conflict: cause of international c. 394:11
  in a state of armed c. 114:13
  never in the field of human c. 79:19
Conformity: reward for c. 56:18
Confronted: c. with what they do 14:1
Confuse: c. the clear ideas 352:17
Confused: c. things with their names 336:23
  so c. that they'd paid twice 297:1
Confusion: big, booming, buzzing c. 191:23
  find total c. 303:29
  good at playing abstract c. 189:17
  nothing to offer . . . except my own c. 205:20
  too much c., I can't get no relief 113:5
Congo: C., creeping through the black 234:9
Congreve, William: C. is the only sophisticated
  playwright 380:23
Conjecture: too high a price on c. 329:11
Conjurer: becoming an amateur c. 361:23
Conkers: inclined to cheat at c. 403:16
Connaissance: toute naissance est une c. 84:7
Connect: only c.! 130:12
Connoisseur: c. of failure 90:16
  ruins preserved by the c. 306:8

Connolly, Cyril: C. . . . give pleasure a bad name
  131:17
Conquer: c. but . . . not convince 382:8
  possible to c. poverty 195:15
Conquered: c. people tend to be witty 34:8
Conqueror: came-over-with-the-C. 391:20
Conquest: c. for the strong 254:13
Conquistador: c. – an adventurer 134:11
Conscience: c. . . . barmaid of the Victorian soul
  194:18
  c. makes cowboys of us all 333:9
  c. to fit this year's fashions 169:5
  fatty degeneration of the c. 186:17
  freedom of c. 380:1
  let your c. alone 190:11
  live with a good c. on the proceeds 350:16
  more important . . . than a clear c. 332:8
  sufficient c. to bother him 236:1
  uncreated c. of my race 198:8
Conscious: so c. he how short time was 260:10
  wood of c. evil 17:13
Consciousness: activities of c. 257:4
  c. altered by . . . numinosum 199:8
  lopped off a huge chunk of your c. 287:8
  one-eighth part c. 142:11
  waking c. is . . . special type of c. 191:18
  we cannot get behind c. 299:18
  world of our c. is only one of many 191:18
Consent: feel inferior without your c. 322:7
  withhold one's provisional c. 148:15
Consenting: better between two c. parties 123:9
Consequence: damn the c.s 265:10
  in nature . . . there are c.s 385:1
Conservatism: c. . . . leave things alone 77:7
Conservative: c. is a man with two . . . good legs
  322:19
  c. who has been arrested 9:9
  C.'s Europeanism is . . . imperialism 166:9
  divided between c.s and reactionaries 387:21
  healthy stomach is nothing if not c. 61:14
  make me c. when old 135:22
  Socialist mind and a C. heart 125:13
  vote C. and . . . live in them 135:1
  which makes a man more c. 206:13
Conservative Party 166:9, 167:16
  C. at prayer 326:1
  it [C.] has replaced the Altar 334:14
Consistency: c. is contrary to nature 182:16
Console: c. . . . professional consolers 382:15
Consommé: cyanide in the c. 408:17
Conspiring: c. in the . . . Vatican 245:19
Constancy: infernal c. of the women 345:13
Constant: in c. action was his c. certainty found
  93:5
Constellation: foreign c.s west 162:13
  place it in its c. 318:6
Constipation: as tiring as c. 112:22
Constitution: c. is the will of the Fürher 132:6
Consulted: umpire no one c. 377:11
Consume: c. wealth without producing it 343:1
  c.s without producing 286:8

Consumed: c. with apathy 202:12
Consumption: c. is polarized 185:8
  conspicuous c. of valuable goods 386:15
  conspicuously increased c. 312:16
  deliberately prepared for c. 190:9
Contact lenses: c., . . . eye of the beholder 296:5
Contagion: great danger of c. 403:1
Contemplation: left for c. 40:13
Contemporaneous: never completely c. 102:3
Contemporaries: c. pass exams 40:25
  two men who are not c. 367:2
  what I think of my famous c. 351:5
Contemporary: c. books do not keep 87:15
  c. physics is based on concepts 115:18
  c. verse sounds like 389:12
  I am no one's c. – ever 248:16
  the more c. history becomes 66:27
Contempt: c. earned by the Utopian 258:2
  c. for anything he didn't understand 413:8
Contemptible: c. little army 403:11
Contender: I coulda been a c. 50:14
Content: natural c. out of my heart 416:6
  this is the land of lost c. 179:32
Continence: perversion known as c. 182:7
Continent: ghost c. 116:10
  iron curtain has descended across the C. 80:7
  like having a c. disappear 192:19
  only places John likes on the C. 256:2
Continental: C. people have sex life 260:18
Contingencies: all c. . . . too quick 139:13
Continual: c. flight from wonder 116:3
Continuity: c. upon the disjointed 259:17
  impression of c. 306:19
Contraception: story about oral c. 6:21
Contraceptive: best c. is . . . water 10:2
  c.s . . . on every conceivable occasion 263:27
  little use for c.s 342:11
  put c.s in and get money out 236:13
  slow coaches and immaculate c.s 197:11
Contract: travel . . . c.s the mind 368:10
  verbal c. is worth more 147:9
  what usually comes first is the c. 142:17
Contradict: man who c.s it [idea] 307:4
  never c. 126:5
Contradicting: way of c. myself 361:14
Contradiction: America contained c.s 405:5
  c. in terms 253:19, 345:24, 348:8, 381:15
  c. of my time 27:1
Contradictory: c. to the traditional 285:17
Contraire: au c. 48:13
Contrary: c. to their principles 139:15
  Hail Mary, quite c. 154:5
Contrast: enjoyment from a c. 133:17
Contribute: c. to science 51:5
Contrived: c. corridors and issues 117:13
Control: c. and communication theory 402:5
Controlling: c. interest in the key 397:16
Convalescence: c. when he is not writing 88:4
  for Lawrence, existence was . . . c. 182:27
Convenience: about the best c. they had 298:15
  do everything at other people's c. 286:31

Convenient: it can only be more c. 299:9
Conventional: c. army loses 214:30
Conversation: c. is imperative 400:15
  c. is like playing tennis 236:15
  c. is never easy 49:6
  c. of prayers about to be said 368:21
  finest . . . c.s of my life 198:27
  journalism . . . as an extension of c. 334:5
  never . . . set foot inside a c. 189:2
  third-rate c. 300:6
  when a c. ceases to be personal 312:11
Conversationalist: c. who adds 269:19
Converse: spend in pure c. 55:8
Conversion: believed in sudden c. 130:17
Conveyance: not a public c. 274:9
Convict: you have to be a c. 313:4
Conviction: best lack all c. 417:12
  every c. begins as a whim 56:5
Convince: conquer but . . . not c. 382:8
  works harder to c. himself 132:8
Convinced: I'm thoroughly c. of it 91:4
Convincing: sound so wonderfully c. 144:21
Cook, Captain James 116:10
Cook: as c. go she went 332:23
  c. the frozen dynamite 210:16
  c.s . . . promoted on their skill 127:27
  C.'s tourist-interpreter a king 223:5
  doesn't c. . . . she burns 375:13
  even if the c. has just died 127:7
  every c. has to learn to govern 229:2
  not only c. dinner but one another 387:25
  not so much c. as assassinate food 192:3
  stuff you had to peel and c. 95:24
  where the c.s are French 9:23
  you can't c. [the facts] 256:10
Cooked: if they're properly cooked 125:4
Cooking: art . . . is the c. itself 231:4
  c. in windows where the public pass 302:8
  I never see any home c. 296:15
Cool: c. white dress after . . . confession 125:30
  keep c. and collect 397:20
  whenever men want to c. down 202:17
Coolidge, President Calvin 292:4
  [C.] . . . weaned on a pickle 237:5
Coonskin: nail those c.s to the wall 195:18
Cooper, Lady Diana 67:16
Cooper, Gary: in a world of C.s 23:4
Cooper, Tommy: Rasputin and C. 166:15
Cooperative: c. is private enterprise 350:1
Copies: nothingness . . . the only thing he c. 324:7
  we die c. 418:20
Coping: learn . . . about c. with life 353:18
Copperhead: he forgot the c.s 334:16
Copulation: birth, and c., and death 117:36
Copy: makes very dull c. 375:4
Copybook: c. maxims and psalms 170:18
Copying: c. . . . genetic material 95:8
  c. willy-nilly, like a drawing 307:18
Copyright: spiritual c. in scientific discoveries 258:4
  swapped his c. for a partridge 170:1

c. is . . . to risk self-humiliation 104:4
c. is when you have choices 8:14
c. to change things I can 280:2
c. was mine 288:27
no man in the world has more c. 300:18
to keep men's c. up 101:16
Course: experience in a series of c.s 146:7
forgot his c. 128:16
horses for c.s 301:10
Court: c. him, elude him 44:8
c.s not a cathedral but . . . a casino 186:25
landed the best job in the c. 299:19
Courthouse: near the old c. 234:7
Courting: are you c.? 298:10
Courtship: marriage is to c. 104:20
Cousin: c. . . . in the peanut business 123:6
c.s, a series of grotesque caricatures 259:9
Covent Garden: C. to hear . . . Callas 360:19
Cover: he has arrived to c. it 360:13
never judge a c. by its book 226:13
Cow: all c. in the world belong 304:9
cheaper . . . than to keep a c. 61:26
c. is of the bovine ilk 277:12
c. with handlebars is a bicycle 271:11
How Now, Brown C. 2:9
two dun c.s under a walnut tree 333:4
violating their c.s 98:10
we had ten c.s 11:17
why buy the c. 48:21
Cow-hand: I'm an old c. 259:22
Coward, Noël 104:16, 380:24, 380:28
Coward: cocoa is a cad and c. 75:10
c.s' hearts beat faster 295:17
drunkard through being a c. 76:2
hero wid c.'s legs 263:10
in they army they *shot* c.s 119:18
on water I am a c. 173:21
Cowardice: c. . . . as universal as sea sickness 344:20
great faith in his c. 52:10
guilty of Noel C. 104:16
Cowardly: programme, of c. souls 150:18
Cowboy: conscience makes c.s of us all 333:9
Crab: wet c.s in a basket 112:15
Crack: c. a few laws 397:23
c. in the tea-cup opens a lane 18:5
c.s in a broken heart 409:7
c.s of other people's lives 399:18
don't c. it open on a mattress 261:20
Cracked: blessed are the c. 9:3
Cracker: don't give them c.s 398:19
Cracker-motto: depth of a c. 232:4
Cradle: between the c. and the grave 175:19
c. of Spanish walnut 299:24
shared the same c. 285:22
Craftsmen: all c. share a knowledge 331:8
Cram: c.s with cans of poisoned meat 75:3
Crane: Jane, Jane, tall as a c. 348:18
leading the c.s home 390:1
world where there are c.s and horses 152:15
Crank: apprenticeship as a c. 56:5
Crap: books are a load of c. 221:13

Crass: c. casualty obstructs the sun 162:17
Craving: c. to escape death 131:17
Crawford, Joan 100:21
Crawled: c. out of the woodwork 365:11
Crazed: c. with the spell of far Arabia 102:21
Crazy: checkin' the c. ones 151:6
c. about cars 333:15
c. like a fox 295:2
low-and-hazy, . . . or high-and-c. 143:2
own wheels drive you c. 112:5
Cream: you integrate it with c. 248:1
Create: c. one whom we can no longer keep alive
162:16
mind which c.s 119:5
Created: it [passion] cannot be c. 342:5
Creation: art of c. is older 388:13
blind fury of c. 344:6
greatest week . . . since the c. 280:14
hate into his dearest c. 59:1
little closer to the heart of c. 215:11
next appearance is a new c. 307:15
now I hold c. in my foot 181:12
what Adam had seen on . . . his c. 182:15
Creative: C. Endeavour lost her wings 393:7
c. reply of a Soviet artist 347:7
Creativity: no c. in Nature 401:8
Creator: C. made Italy 380:4
he can dispense with a c. 308:2
Creature: nothing that living c.s do 124:5
Credence: so slight it would pass c. 151:17
Credit: c. cards of yesterday 371:8
c. is used to delay paying 390:16
faces as thin as c. cards 8:2
gorgeous resources of c. 90:2
nothing I can take c. for 44:4
Credulity: c. about everything 305:1
Creed: freedom, the second of man's c.s 225:5
last article of my c. 140:1
Creeper-nail: c.s are rust 162:7
Crème: c. de la c. 354:4
Crêpe-de-chine: knickers are made of c. 246:3
Crete: C. . . . make more history 332:16
Crew: set the c. laughing 128:16
Crick, Francis 391:16
Cricket: c. as organized loafing 367:6
c. fan . . . your wife left you in May 281:9
c. is . . . a dramatic spectacle 189:20
if the French were to play c. 123:7
not in support of c. 31:2
to where the c. sings 416:19
Cricketer: makings of a c. 374:9
Cricklewood: Midland, bound for C. 40:15
Cried: c. all the way to the bank 233:21
c. at all his own weddings 21:3
you suddenly c. and turned away 54:15
Cries: drama is when the audience c. 67:10
Crime: arson . . . is an artificial c. 396:14
c. and its components 356:11
c. and you can't prove it 240:2
c. is a left-handed form 246:20
c. is common 109:12

if d. is present at the conception 285:21
Dada: I encountered the mama of d. 122:1
Daddy: d., I'm finally through 299:21
  D. wouldn't buy me a bow-wow 365:2
  my heart belongs to D. 302:2
  what did you do in the Great War, d.? 3:26
Daemon: divine d. is absolute 31:18
Daffodil: what d.s were for Wordsworth 221:19
Daft: anyone happy . . . is d. or corrupt 137:14
  d. as a brush 300:1
  d. with the drug that's smoking 369:6
Dagger: left holding the d. 406:10
Daily Express: D. is read 3:31
Daintily: I must have things d. served 40:12
Daisies: hammer through d. 368:19
  picking d. on the railway 409:10
Dam: thought that the d. broke 372:23
Damascus: D. . . . on a return ticket 209:10
Damn: d. the consequences 265:10
  d. you England 288:8
  frankly, my dear, I don't give a d. 138:1
  one d. thing over and over 261:11
  stealthily, like a parson's d. 163:24
Damnation: addiction is . . . d. 19:3
Damned: d. from here to eternity 210:24
  I told you so. You d. fools 397:12
  lies, d. lies and statistics 379:19
  music is the brandy of the d. 344:16
  one d. thing after another 180:20
  where the d. have howled 415:8
Damp: d. souls of housemaids 117:30
  d.s there drip upon sagged seats 162:7
  turns d. to dry 369:13
Dance: can d. a little 16:5
  come d. with me Kitty Stobling 202:15
  d. and war are . . . the same 357:7
  d. . . . educational within the . . . Act 92:17
  d., little lady 94:11, 142:15
  d. on this ball-floor 44:8
  dead returning lightly d. 370:16
  departs too far from the d. 303:22
  each d. the other would 103:17
  fairies break their d.s 179:3
  I am the Lord of the D. 69:11
  see me d. the polka 348:21
  there's a d. in the old dame yet 251:3
  where the blessed d. 415:8
  winds of the heavens d. 143:6
  woman ought to dance as she moves 341:24
Danced: d. with the Prince of Wales 122:11
  he d. his did 97:19
  where once we d. 162:6
Dancer: d. in the dark 266:1
  d.s are all gone under the hill 116:29
  know the d. from the dance 415:10
Dancing: as d. is to walking 389:4
  d. lessons from God 388:11
  [d.] a perpendicular expression 346:7
  delightful if it were not for the d. 121:10
  if there's no d. count me out 146:14
  like d. about architecture 252:10

Puritans who put an end to . . . d. 162:2
Dandruff: below the . . . d. ads 95:3
Dandy: candy is d. 278:1
Danegeld: once you have paid him the D. 210:9
Danger: d. from the . . . stranger 277:13
Dangerous: d. at both ends 128:21
  D. Dan McGrew 341:20
  it is d. to be sincere 345:7
  when they are no longer d. 47:16
Daniel: only man . . . was D. 376:17
Danny Deever: hangin' D. in the mornin' 210:10
Dante Alighieri 273:19
Dante's *Inferno*: outside D. 410:13
Darby: D. and Joan club 107:19
Dardanelles: imminent in the D. 126:4
Daring: essential tact in d. 85:4
Dark: afraid to go home in the d. 403:20
  clock has stopped in the d. 118:20
  d. as the inside of a Cabinet Minister 69:22
  d. as the world of man 349:2
  d., the serpent-haunted sea 128:6
  death could drop from the d. 324:11
  genuineness only thrives in the d. 183:10
  I don't want to go home in the d. 170:20
  ignorance bumping its head in the d. 129:19
  in a d. room with someone you love 181:16
  in a d. time the eye begins to see 321:8
  never to refuse a drink after d. 259:12
  nightmare of the d. 17:16
  out in the d. over the snow 370:12
  real d. night of the soul 126:10
  trust an Englishman in the d. 353:13
  walk between d. and d. 151:25
  we work in the d. 190:20
  with darkness ridged the riven d. 133:7
Darkest: when things look d. 279:8
Darkness: curse the d. 359:7
  d. crumbles away 324:8
  d. inside houses I don't like 103:26
  go out into the d. 165:12
  in the d. bind them 374:15
  lie where shades of d. 103:2
  one minute of d. 327:16
  public version of a private d. 368:14
  what of the d.? Is it very far? 227:22
Darling: d. of the music-halls 43:5
  oh, he's a d. [darlin'] man 284:2
  poor d.s [the Jews] 33:19
Date: consult the Book of D.s 50:8
  remembered she had a d. elsewhere 346:20
  ripping out the d.s on his goloshes 225:21
Daughter: d. am I in my mother's house 212:8
  don't put your d. on the stage 93:18
  fame is rot: d.s are the thing 26:5
  French [actresses are] clever d.s 161:8
  his only son . . . and not his only d. 346:20
  Mrs Porter and her d. 118:13
  trim as the d.s of the people 398:21
  where you wash your dirty d. 12:18
David, King: D. and King Solomon 278:15
Dawn: brown fog of a winter d. 118:5

d. comes up like thunder 211:29
d. seem to be an alleviation 402:15
God at d. 95:4
grey d. breaking 254:10
I heard a bird at d. 358:2
I swear before the d. 416:7
ignorant as the d. 416:1
noises at d. 18:27
spectral dance, before the d. 54:17
sunset that was mistaken for a d. 102:9
without the hope of d. 4:11
Dawning: in the d. passing through 163:19
Dawson of Penn, Bertrand, Lord: D. was not a
   good doctor 16:2
Day, Doris: D. before she was a virgin 253:14
Day: and the d. after that 126:18
d. to myself 278:19
d. war broke out 407:4
d.s of wine and roses laugh 259:21
d.s slipped down like junket 243:4
every d. in every way 93:9
go ahead, make my d. 114:3
gold of the d. 96:11
happily ever after on a d. to d. basis 45:9
I only dread one d. at a time 339:11
it's been a hard d.'s night 229:25
long d.'s journey into night 285:3
met them at close of d. 416:4
night and d. you are the one 302:3
not a second on the d. 89:18
some d. my heart will awake 165:13
some d. my prince will come 107:1
swallows crossed off the d.s 68:14
ten d.s that shook the world 314:18
there and back in a d. 221:23
they put you on the d. shift 113:21
twenty-four hour d. has come to stay 30:1
what a day! Two salmon this morning 71:16
Daydream: little Dolly D. 362:10
Daylight: imperatives of cold and . . . d. 53:15
never to drink by d. 259:12
de Gaulle, General Charles: [G.] is like a female
   llama 82:13
De Mille, Cecil B.: D. made small movies 200:5
De Quincey, Thomas: indulgences of . . . D. 371:15
Dead: absence of a d. body from a room 271:10
after that it's d. 393:2
among the roaring d. 290:11
as much at home with the d. 215:11
cliché is d. poetry 52:2
consistent people are the d. 182:16
d. . . . and he was still warm 187:2
d. are the imagination 38:6
d. ar-re always pop'lar 111:18
d. battles, like d. generals 379:8
d. far outnumber the living 218:7
d. men on leave 232:6
d. or deported 180:18
d. returning lightly dance 370:16
d. to life is no great magic 152:4
d. writer can at least be illustrious 308:1

deal to be said for being d. 37:17
deep with the first d. 369:15
democracy of the d. 77:27
easier to replace a d. man 343:9
easy for your d. to visit you 33:25
England mourns for her d. 43:1
few are wholly d. 152:4
gathered flowers are d. 128:10
grand to be blooming well d. 335:20
Harrow is the house of the d. 18:23
he is d. who will not fight 155:5
healthy and wealthy and d. 372:4
he's d., or my watch has stopped 252:17
I expect you'd rather be dead 91:4
I had never been told they were d. 243:12
I think they would be better d. 291:9
if the d. talk to you 364:9
if they don't look after the d. 375:17
if this is pleasure we'd rather be d. 94:10
in the long run we are all d. 207:3
inexhaustible bodies that are not d. 365:8
lane to the land of the d. 18:5
literature . . . very d. 233:19
mad and d. as nails 368:19
many more d. people than living 187:11
more to say when I am d. 320:13
no one is afraid of being d. 216:4
only d. fish swim with the stream 272:19
only two of them were dead 372:11
our d. bodies must tell the tale 340:2
pity the d. that are d. 222:19
playwrights should be d. 249:16
position of the d. among the living 413:4
quoted d. languages 376:18
savaged by a d. sheep 166:10
simplify me when I am d. 108:11
still as the d. 44:9
there are no d. 247:2
there remain a d. man and a free man 336:26
they're a decent mob, the d. 265:17
to make sure he was d. 10:22
took their wages and are d. 179:5
towering d. with their nightingales 239:8
turns on the quick and the d. 368:21
when I am d., . . . it may be said 32:33
when we are d. things will be better 308:7
why aren't you d.? 168:1
why should the d. be wiser 128:11
Deadeye: d. of earth 71:6
Deadland: d.s of the mullahs 294:3
Deadlock: holy d. 170:29
Deadly: more d. in the long run 379:21
Deaf: d. as the man who said . . . prayers 318:1
d., how should they know 353:12
historians are like d. people 375:2
Deafanddumb: every language even d. 97:25
Deafeningly: afraid of the d. obvious 203:1
Deal: new d. for the American people 322:9
Dean: I am the D. of Christ Church 355:21
queer old d. 355:16
sly shade of a Rural D. 54:17

Deary me: not *dirigiste* but d. 84:2
Death: after d. has stopped the ears 179:19
  armed against all d.'s endeavour 55:4
  at d.'s door for so long 140:17
  awareness of d. 382:3
  being cured of [d.] 249:11
  birth, and copulation, and d. 117:36
  Black Widow, d. 238:19
  blessed be d. that cuts in marble 261:8
  citizens of d.'s grey land 337:2
  contain the whole of d. 318:7
  craving to escape d. 131:17
  d. and I will coquette 251:3
  d. and life were not . . . made 417:25
  d. as his greatest . . . anxiety 139:5
  d. being contrary to their principles 139:15
  d. comes to everyone 38:11
  d. . . . conclusion of a great passion 223:6
  d. could drop from the dark 324:11
  d. had undone so many 118:5
  d. hardly ever happens . . . at their best 152:20
  d. is a full stop 283:10
  d. is an acquired trait 6:27
  d. is less hideous than explanations 233:3
  d. is my neighbour now 121:9
  d. is nothing at all 176:13
  d. is the greatest kick 149:1
  d. is the least we have to fear 302:10
  d. must take me for someone else 28:22
  d. of someone we loved 201:6
  d. shall have no dominion 368:19
  d. . . . succeeded in vulgarizing 182:20
  d. . . . the most beautiful adventure 134:13
  d. took him by the heart 288:17
  d. which decides our answers 160:5
  d. will find me 55:9
  d.'s growing purer 248:17
  d.'s own hand is warmer than my own 257:8
  enormously improved by d. 332:12
  finality is d. 358:4
  flirting with d. 38:14
  follow my own d. step by step 195:4
  from a vague height with d. 288:23
  glum heroes up the line to d. 336:29
  he was ready for more d.s 153:10
  I love you until d. do us part 369:30
  I think about d. a great deal 376:13
  if people knew there'd be less d. 247:20
  inbetween the sheets holy-water d. 243:15
  is there life before d.? 149:17
  kiss of d. 350:2
  let me die a youngman's d. 243:15
  life before d. I'm not cheerful about 120:1
  like a footprint or a d. mask 353:10
  long live d.! 261:3
  makes d. a long-felt want 376:21
  much possessed by d. 118:17
  no cure for birth and d. 335:14
  nothing but d. 382:2
  only certain form of life after d. 66:29
  our own d.s we mourn for 51:27

  peaceful out of breath d. 243:15
  prepare as though for d. 250:6
  rendezvous with d. 340:11
  report of my d. is exaggerated 380:21
  sharp points of d. 118:21
  sharpened by his d. 415:7
  sinister, princely d. 319:16
  struggle against d. 171:17
  they make up for it with d. 120:8
  tie that only d. can sever 255:20
  to circumvent d. 66:7
  until the arrival of d. 39:21
  what removes us in d. 319:6
  when I look d. in the face 416:2
Death-sentence: d. without a whimper 225:1
Deathless: 'D'. that bitter beer 319:2
  let us make love d. 377:6
Debauchee: *D.* pursued pleasure 42:11
Debussy, Claude 319:18
Decade: d. the locusts ate 235:10
  fun to be in the same d. 323:1
  talk of God and the d. ahead 353:5
Decadent: too infantile to be called d. 200:3
Decay: fretting for their d. 324:10
  seemed to embody the national d. 272:17
  time drops in d. 417:2
Deceased: with the name of the late d. 212:7
Deceit: d.s are strong almost as life 273:6
  love . . . seems d. 101:18
Deceive: fail to d. the patient 307:21
Deceived: anyone that one has d. 239:28
Deceiving: nearly d. your friends 93:2
December: will you love me in D. 390:6
Decencies: dog's life without a dog's d. 213:28
Decent: d. godless people 118:25
  d. . . . live beyond their incomes 332:19
  d. men don't go to Cannes 190:1
  doing the d. thing 167:3
  wanted to be Very D. to People 325:5
Decided: d.s only to be undecided 79:10
Decision: d.s are easier 312:8
  hard and fast and specific d. 379:9
  important the d.s he has to take 293:6
Decisive: d. blows are . . . left-handed 35:13
Deck: one who on a tilting d. sings 101:16
  whole d. put on its leaves again 128:17
Declension: hidden under a lot of d.s 59:4
Decline: d. to dignify the Serpentine 107:13
  went into a bit of a d. 1:16
Decompose: d. in a barrel of porter 108:6
Decomposing: d. in . . . print 412:10
Decoration: d.s . . . of a nation 243:21
Decorative: to be d. and to do right 125:19
Decorous: task of d. skill 341:21
Decry: their works remain to d. them 25:10
Dedicated: when people are fanatically d. 299:6
Deduced: d. the rest logically 36:4
Deed: at whatever time the d. took place 117:29
  fix your attention on their d.s 115:17
  harder to turn word into d. 148:8
Deep: d., d. peace of the double bed 65:1

d. in the heart of Texas 171:10
Defeat: after Alamein we never had a d. 81:17
  d. is an orphan 82:22
  d. without a war 79:11
  in d.: defiance 81:4
  in d. he [Kaiser] fled 82:14
  in d. unbearable 82:16
Defeated: man able to think isn't d. 218:19
  man can be destroyed but not d. 169:10
  meaning shows in the d. thing 254:13
Defeatist: normal dose for an adult d. 410:15
Defect: character . . . of d.s 189:10
  chief d. of Henry King 32:12
  with these so-called d.s 89:23
Defection: sincerity of d. 312:17
Defence: d. of peace 382:9
  d. of philosophic doubt 23:16
  necessary strength and no d.s 146:12
  only d. is offence 23:7
  think about the d. of England 23:8
Defenceless: d. against ourselves 376:5
Defend: d. our island, whatever the cost 79:15
  d. the bad against the worse 101:21
Defended: what God abandoned: these d. 179:6
Defensive: d. hats, and shrapnel 401:13
Deferential: d. working-class vote 96:8
Defiance: in defeat: d. 81:4
Defined: something d., with an edge 363:10
Definite: d. maybe 147:20
Definition: one single sense in high d. 245:1
  only decent d. is tautology 246:11
Deflating: mention of an aunt is so d. 251:24
Deformed: d. by the system 327:21
Deformity: art is significant d. 137:1
Defrost: d. her refrigerator 361:22
Degenerating: family is not yet . . . d. 121:12
Degeneration: fatty d. of the conscience 186:17
  gone from barbarism to d. 84:13
Degradation: depths of d. 167:13
Degrade: if we . . . d. the earth 238:1
  though love can initially d. 107:23
Degraded: he is already d. 287:11
Degree: d.s are like false teeth 350:6
  filthy unless you've got a d. 180:14
  I and you stand, each in our d. 163:16
  my d. was a kind of inoculation 36:8
Deity: between the D. and the Drains 362:2
  doubted the existence of the D. 397:9
Deliberation: d. is the work of many 141:6
Délibérer: d. est le fait de plusieurs 141:6
Delicacy: America has a new d. 76:1
Delicate: family had to include . . . d. child 336:19
Delicate-filmed: d. as new-spun silk 162:5
Delight: had other aims than my d. 163:3
  leaping light for your d. 17:23
  lonely impulse of d. 416:17
  planet is poorly equipped for d. 257:16
  take your d. in momentariness 151:25
  teach us to d. in simple things 210:2
Delightful: it's d., it's delicious 301:18
Delighting: but, O! d. me 175:9

Delilah 397:24
Deliver: man who d.s the goods 254:21
Deliverance: not to assign to this d. 81:10
Deliverer: tear their d.s to pieces 406:25
Délivrez: d. moi de moi-même 84:5
Delusion: d. about its ancestry 186:20
  drugs are a d. 343:7
Demi-tasses: your villainous d. 350:4
Demobbed: when Lil's Husband got d. 118:11
Democracies: in d. it is . . . sacred 132:2
Democracy: arsenal of d. 322:22
  between . . . parliament and d. 349:20
  can't save d. and we don't much care 94:7
  d. a superstition and a fetish 186:1
  d. . . . election by the incompetent 344:28
  d. is . . . force by one class 228:15
  d. is half spoilt at a stroke 77:18
  d. is like a hobby-horse 334:9
  d. is the recurrent suspicion 400:8
  d. is the refuge for your cousin 123:16
  d. is the worst form of government 80:9
  d. means government by discussion 16:13
  d. means government by the uneducated 77:25
  d. of the dead 77:27
  d. resumed her reign 32:32
  d. will not be salvaged 176:6
  evil makes d. necessary 280:3
  in a d., no one has his way 153:6
  not the voting that's d. 360:8
  ordinary d. and a people's d. 383:24
  politics of a going d. 90:1
  two cheers for D. 131:2
  understand d. but can't do it 14:13
  world . . . safe for d. 406:19
Democrat: D. like cities and factories 120:6
  telling lies about the D.s 359:1
  truth about the D.s 104:6
Democratic: application of d. methods 378:2
  d., and patronize everybody 343:20
  d. planetary community 238:1
  perfect d. system 373:14
  this is a d. country 260:20
Demon: chained to a d. 101:17
Demonic: their mad d. elders 235:6
Demonstration: Spontaneous D. 286:10
Demoralize: d. us but it moralized them 154:18
  perfectly d. the nation 40:5
Demos: table of D. 281:16
Demotic: pleased to write in d. English 248:10
Denial: d. of the gratification 315:7
Denied: until it's been officially d. 239:13
Denizen: spider is sole d. 162:7
Dentist: d. would like to be a doctor 297:12
  encouragement like a clumsy d. 250:3
  I have let d.s ride rough-shod 295:18
  I'd sooner go to my dentist 393:12
  never faced a d. 396:3
  when Edwina Currie goes to the d. 107:14
Deny: d. you what they think you want 293:1
  only one evil, to d. life 222:16
Denying: d. non-existent facts 111:2

innocent children and d.s 83:11
no good casting out d.s 224:1
question of peace . . . talk to the D. 171:8
rather ten d.s to check 373:14
to break a man's spirit is d.'s work 343:2
world is half the d.'s 369:6
Devious: in a d. way I am uncomplicated 150:21
Devon: D., glorious D. 47:19
Devotee: d. of the Gospel of Getting On 345:12
Devotion: sameness of the object of his d. 328:3
Dew: d. was on the lawn 358:2
  drenched with d. 103:16
Dewdrop: meditation upon the d. 143:11
Dewey, Thomas 113:2
Día: un d. para mi 278:19
Diagnosis: wait for the doctor's d. 73:6
Diagnostician: St Paul or some other d. 170:11
Dial: finger that turns the d. 112:6
Dial-a-recipe: drama of a d. service 232:4
Dialect: d. that has an army and a navy 394:13
Dialectics: d., a kind of false teeth 66:26
Dialling: d. has replaced . . . dialogue 258:6
Dialogue: d. . . . contradicting myself 361:14
  dialling has replaced . . . d. 258:6
  gift for d. qualifies you 164:12
  journeyed to the centre of d. 189:2
Diamond: d. and safire bracelet lasts forever
    237:10
  d.s are a girl's best friend 320:;10
  in two weeks you'd have a d. 53:4
  my d. may become soot 224:16
  to give him d.s back 138:2
Diaper: innovation on changing a d. 327:6
Diaries: gardening and desk d. 91:15
Diarrhoea: fornication and d. 254:22
Dice: God not only plays d. 166:1
Dicing: d. time for gladness 162:17
Dick: at Dirty D.'s and Sloppy Joe's 18:16
Dickens, Charles: a bit like D. 59:1
  D. was not the first . . . novelist 305:21
  D.'s world is not life-like 71:5
  he [D.] was . . . most antagonistic 405:13
  London . . . hasn't changed since . . . D. 38:15
  put to D. as children 36:18
Dictated: d. but not signed 269:17
Dictatorship: unlike a classical d. 283:14
Dictionary: d. of popular usage 153:13
  sucess comes before work . . . in a d. 337:11
Did: he d. for them both 337:5
Dido: widow D. . . . below 183:12
Die: better to d. on your feet 185:1
  come back to America to d. 191:7
  created to pretend we never d. 221:5
  d. to prove he had been alive 201:12
  d. when we fail to take root 378:7
  d.s before he is fully born 134:19
  good men are afraid to d. 296:11
  great man d.s twice 385:19
  hope I d. before I get old 376:2
  how hard it is to d. 380:13
  if I should d. think only this of me 55:5

it's not difficult to d. 257:16
it's not that I'm afraid to d. 6:13
it's unwise to d. 346:1
I've longed to d. 306:20
man . . . who did not wish to d. 346:15
never let my country d. for me 209:7
only the young d. good 171:5
people d. when curiosity goes 363:13
pie in the sky when you d. 172:2
some of us may d. 302:10
sooner d. than think 329:5
they only let him d. 363:3
those who d. as cattle 288:14
to d. . . . awfully big adventure 26:12
to d. for one's beliefs 329:11
wants to d. nobly for a cause 358:1
we d. copies 418:20
we d. French 393:13
we want to d. together 71:4
what will you do, God, if I d.? 319:15
when I d. . . . best thing for me 86:17
when they d. by thousands 75:3
when will you d.? 270:9
will not d. even if they kill me 156:2
womanly times or shall we d.? 243:10
Died: born old and d. young 227:17
  d. to save their country 32:28
  d. with their boots clean 206:4
  dreamed that Christ had d. in vain? 349:1
  if I d. tomorrow 375:18
  if snobbery d. 383:22
  little children d. in the streets 17:11
  they say I d. in 1974 403:18
  you got ill, you were poor, you d. 251:1
Dies: man d. when he wants 12:25
  no hero is mortal till he d. 18:21
Diet: Andy Warhol New York City D. 391:1
  d. of the agricultural classes 392:28
  important part of a balanced d. 226:14
Difference: d. between one young woman 344:1
  more d. between the sexes 86:20
  that has made all the d. 135:23
  wisdom to know the d. 280:2
Different: d. from the people he sees round him
    348:6
  d. living 354:18
  now for something completely d. 268:6
  something d. from either 118:2
Differently: freedom for the one who thinks d.
    239:9
  they do things d. there 165:9
Difficult: d. is what takes a little time 277:6
  d. things take a long time 394:17
  fascination of what's d. 416:6
Difficulties: little local d. 245:8
  sorting out the d. of people 161:20
Difficulty: d. for every solution 334:13
Dig: d. d. d. 160:2
  d. for victory 351:10
Digesting: d. time 19:14
Digestion: few radicals have good d.s 61:14

Dignify: d. the Serpentine 107:13
Dignity: in d. and self-respect 324:6
Dilly: don't d. dally on the way 228:7
Dilute: save water – d. it 149:33
Dilution: d. in the universal 71:7
Dime: brother, can you spare a d.? 161:16
  I could sit on a d. 376:8
Dimension: dream of new d.s 151:7
  reduce them to their own d.s 307:12
Diminished: what to make of a d. thing 135:21
Dined: d. at the table of history 70:7
  d. last night with the Borgias 30:9
  more d. against than dining 48:12
  when asked if he had d. 48:13
Dinette: d. apartment in town 104:12
Dingy: d. on the surface 299:12
  fatally poor and d. 399:17
Dinner: always willing to come to d. 327:7
  best number for a d. party is two 156:17
  d. party of more than two 258:15
  how did you think I managed at d. 317:18
  same compartment . . . as her d. napkins
    119:15
  that includes going out to d. first 154:16
Dinner-gong: d. due any moment 408:17
Diplomacy: d. . . . someone else have your way
    294:16
  d. is the art of saying 'Nice Doggie' 70:16
  d. – lying in state 171:6
  d. means the art of nearly deceiving 60:17
Diplomat: conspiracy of d.s against common sense
    338:19
  d. . . . nothing but a head-waiter 383:19
  d. . . . remembers a woman's birthday 136:14
  d.s tell lies . . . then believe 217:4
  only decent d. is a dead Trappist 227:6
Direct: you can't d. it [poetry] 112:22
Directing: d. and being directed 28:5
Direction: rode madly off in all d.s 226:5
Directive: implementation of d.s 356:7
Director: d. and . . . an actor 295:1
  d. of a film is treated 52:13
  in the theatre, the d. is God 295:18
Dirigiste: not d. but 'deary me' 84:2
Dirt: d. doesn't get any worse 95:18
  he picked her up out of the d. 7:5
  price of liberty is . . . eternal d. 287:1
Dirty: d. house and cleaning it yourself 260:21
  more room d. clothes take 329:12
  my name is a d. word 288:2
Disagreement: d. . . . shortest cut 143:10
Disappear: he d.s walking 262:2
Disappointed: d. in human nature 108:4
Disappointing: War is . . . d. 155:10
Disaster: books that affect us like a d. 201:6
  d. of the world 88:23
  meet with triumph and d. 210:32
  nation not in danger of financial d. 258:9
  primeval d. in the heart of Man 348:24
Disastrous: d. and the unpalatable 139:7
Discernible: less d. than the red flag 190:7

Discharge: d. my duties as king 115:7
  I shall therefore d. you 348:10
  no d. in the war 209:24
Disciples: left to his d.s to identify 330:2
Discipline: d. needs two [parents] 189:9
Disciplined: d. by a hard . . . peace 204:16
Discobolus: D. . . . turneth his face 62:7
Disconnect: d. it from the rest of them 127:18
Discontent: source of all our d.s 225:12
Discord: elemental d. 144:20
  no mere d. of flags 151:24
Discovery: d. consists of seeing 364:10
  d. is . . . a continual flight 116:3
  d. is a private event 258:3
  d., it moves in mighty leaps 20:11
Discretion: d. without having tumbled 37:10
Discuss: crime the world does not d. 355:26
Discussion: d. in class 276:7
Disease: collected lists of fatal d.s 168:13
  d. is finite 331:1
  name any d. after two guys 309:4
  nationalism is an infantile d. 115:16
  nineteenth century it was a d. 364:2
  suffering from the particular d. 194:13
  there is no cure for this d. 32:13
Disenchantment: mistook d. for truth 336:22
Disfavour: viewed with great d. by me 81:11
Disfigure: d. a great work of art 308:3
Disgrace: d. not to know 311:12
  d. to the planet 359:17
  intellectual d. 17:17
  O the d. of it 30:13
Disgraced: d. by the inferior 344:31
Disgruntled: growing habit of d. men 374:18
Disguise: d. our feelings pretty well 93:11
  history advances in d. 102:3
Disgust: capacity for d. 249:19
Disgusted: women are . . . d. 154:21
Disillusion: one d. – mankind 206:11
Disillusionment: d. in living 357:12
Dislike: d. before first sight 82:15
  d. is purely platonic 376:19
  friend whom one definitely d.s 182:13
  law of d. for the unlike 420:4
  personally d. Him 286:17
Disliked: do each day two things they d. 256:12
  I have always d. myself 116
Disliking: be someone without d. things 48:6
Disney, Walt: D. . . . the most significant figure
    238:3
Disorder: d.s in the strongest brain 40:5
  nothing concerning man, only d.s 336:28
Disown: making statements I can d. 361:14
Dispensation: special and costly d. 393:3
Displaced: looks more like a d. person 368:12
Disprove: exception d.s the rule 110:6
Disraeli, Benjamin 362:5, 379:19
Disregard: d. for the necessities 256:5
Dissatisfied: what I haven't crossed out I'm d. with
    103:32
  when he asks whether you're d. 315:2

Dissect: d. the heart of his body 122:8
Dissembling: they were less d. 325:15
Dissenter: if there had been . . . no d.s 366:6
Disservice: mindful of his d. 341:11
Dissipated: still keep looking so d. 34:20
Dissolution: lingering d. 28:13
Dissolve: government to d. the people 51:22
Distance: d. between the hunter 99:12
  d.s are only the relation of space 308:13
  measure of d. in its hand 318:6
  sixty seconds' worth of d. 211:1
Distempered: questions the d. part 117:1
Distillation: d. of all three 370:21
Distinction: few escape that d. 380:16
Distinguishable: d. from his average reader 320:20
Distinguished: at last, the d. thing 191:11
  lover chosen is sufficiently d. 152:10
Distressful: lifting d. hands 288:25
Distrust: d. of our senses 64:9
  d. one another 49:1
Disturb: art is meant to d. 50:16
  part of ourselves doesn't d. us 171:12
Ditchwater: drinking bottled d. 343:18
Dithering: d., drunken and dumb 43:11
Diver: don't forget the d. 203:4
Diversity: make the world safe for d. 205:2
Divide: people sometimes d. others 355:6
Dividend: no d. from time's tomorrows 337:2
Divinely: d. given best of him 67:13
Divinity: believe in the d. of Our Lord 348:3
Division: how many d.s has he got? 356:8
Divorce: d. is something you always have 6:16
  d. is the sign of knowledge 404:26
  d. . . . two people make a mistake 102:15
Divorced: demand to be d. 75:11
Divorcée: no *d.s* were included 399:16
Do: can I d. you now, sir? 203:3
  get other people to d. things 401:19
Doc: what's up D.? 58:8
Doctor: capable of deceiving the d. 307:21
  d. . . . in the middle of a field 91:13
  d. who doesn't talk . . . nonsense 307:22
  d. whose office plants have died 45:7
  d.s . . . know men 336:7
  d.s . . . promoted on their skill 127:27
  every dentist would like to be a d. 297:12
  illness is the most heeded of d.s 308:9
  knocked down a d.? With an ambulance? 348:8
  never have died, had he had another d. 16:2
  passion can be destroyed by a d. 342:5
  take off your clothes for the d. 70:19
  tongue at the insurance d. 251:5
  we d.s know a hopeless case 97:28
Doctoring: d. our experiences 176:8
Doctrinaire: d.s are the vultures 236:3
Doctrine: d. is something you kill for 35:20
  d. of the strenuous life 323:5
Document: d.s which they did not read 161:20
Dodo: d. never had a chance 98:3
Dog: all the d.s of Europe bark 17:16
  America is a large, friendly d. 376:4

beaten d. beneath the hail 303:10
comely d. is he 102:22
d. did nothing in the night-time 109:27
d. who has never met a tax lawyer 226:23
d.'s disadvantages 365:1
d.'s life without a d.'s decencies 213:29
d.s bark, school's out 100:14
d.s go on with their doggy life 18:3
don't let's go to the d.s tonight 170:23
Englishmen taking mad d.s for walks 263:3
giving your heart to a d. 212:11
he didn't get a d.'s licence 253:7
lamp-post how it feels about d.s 160: 23
like people . . . than I like d.s 354:17
love each other like d.s 108:10
mad d.s and Englishmen 94:13
only police d.s 123:13
other d.'s phone calls 5:24
outlive her d.s 404:7
people who keep d.s . . . are cowards 363:1
sat on his balcony eating his d. 24:3
show d.s . . . to support my cat 152:16
showbusiness is worse than d. eat d. 5:24
some shadow say 'Give the d. a bone' 246:7
still a lame d. on the other side 279:6
stop running those d.s 167:8
to compose a piece for d.s 337:17
woman who is really kind to d.s 30:20
Dog: anybody who hates d.s and babies 325:2
Doggie: d. in front has suddenly gone blind 94:21
  how much is the d. in the window? 260:5
  the art of saying 'Nice D.' 70:16
Dogging: still d. my footsteps 154:13
Dogma: Bible is literature, not d. 335:6
  dulls the edges of all our d.s 275:2
  stigma . . . will serve to beat a d. 156:3
  teach an old d. new tricks 292:1
  these d.s or goals are in doubt 299:6
Dogmatically: hollowly and d. 302:21
Doing: d. what comes naturally 39:3
Doll: O you beautiful d. 56:19
  you called me Baby D. a year ago 165:1
Dollar: love th' eagle on th' back iv a d. 111:19
  printed on d. bills 284:11
  recent gyrations of the d. 207:7
  saw a d. in another man's hands 170:13
Dolphin-torn: d. . . . . sea 415:12
Domain: d. of the largest brain 403:23
Domesday Book: toys and . . . the D. 284:20
Domestic: respectable d. establishment 36:3
Domesticate: does not d. them [passions] 335:4
Dominant: direction . . . by the d. 150:17
Dominion: death shall have no d. 368:19
  hand that holds d. 369:3
Dominoes: row of d.s set up 116:13
Don: d.s admirable! D.s of might 33:4
  remote and ineffectual d. 33:3
Don John: D. . . . . is going to the war 74:21
Don Juan: D. attitude was still there 266:3
Done: d. because we are too menny 163:25
  ever d. until . . . it ought to be d. 93:1

my belief they d. the old woman in 345:19
so little d., so much to do 316:3
something d. . . . ask a woman 367:19
something must be d. 115:6
things that were not d. 383:16
Donkey: I fear . . . the d. 367:9
  lions led by d.s 176:4
  oats into the front end of a d. 139:10
  two china condiment d.s 342:3
Donne, John: D., I suppose, was such another 118:19
  new D. 183:16
  thought to D. was an experience 119:1
Donné: his subject, his idea, his *d.* 190:5
Donsmanship: d. . . . the art of criticizing 302:24
Don't-know: one day the d. will get in 263:30
Doobedoobedoobedoo: d. – Sinatra 149:36
Doom: slow, sure d. falls pitiless 328:12
Doomed: capitalism was d. ethically 352:12
  precisely why they were d. 216:5
  we recognize a d. people 144:22
Doomster: purblind d.s 162:17
Door: at death's d. for so long 140:17
  city of d.s slamming 314:6
  did not that love shut his d. 350:17
  d. opens and lets the future in 154:6
  d.s of heaven and hell 203:12
  everything had a back d. 140:16
  hands grumble on the d. 368:23
  in little girls is slamming d.s 32:25
  kicking of a rotten d. 139:3
  leave my body outside the d. 297:14
  O for d.s to be open 18:24
  somebody at the d. 348:11
  towards the d. we never opened 116:24
  who loves finds the d. open 365:4
  world beats a path past his d. 32:6
Door-to-door: did for d. salesmen 166:11
Doorkeeper: d. of a bordello 375:19
Doormat: d. or a prostitute 398:24
Doorstep: I dung on my grandfather's d. 151:12
  scrubbed d. to the weeded garden 371:8
Dope: money through times of no d. 346:21
  proper share . . . of d. and drink 18:25
Dorchester: terrorists . . . at the D. 138:12
Dostoyevsky, F.M. 223:27, 224:19
Dots: you had a row of d.s 411:20
Double: deep, deep peace of the d. bed 65:1
  joke with a d. meaning 25:12
Double-bed: d. of literature 188:14
  this d. of a world 136:24
Double-cross: sign . . . is a d. 107:6
Doublethink: Newspeak word d. 286:25
Doubt: defence of philosophic d. 23:16
  d. . . . I . . . call 'philosophical' 407:19
  d.s about him [Jesus Christ] 36:13
  d.s of today 323:4
  in d. about this or that 61:16
  in wisdom, dying in d. 238:12
  let us never, never d. 33:6
  life is d. 382:2

our d. is our passion 190:20
  these dogmas or goals are in d. 299:6
Doubter: d. fights only with himself 154:3
Douche: rattling of . . . douche bags 238:14
Doughnut: d. and only see the hole 9:7
Douglas-Home, Sir Alec 88:11, 109:5
Douleurs: roi de mes d. 13:8
Dove: d. descending breaks the air 117:10
Dover: chipped white cups of D. 419:2
  think about the chalk cliffs of D. 23:8
  white cliffs of D. 60:5
Down: let go, Sir! D., Sir! Put it d. 32:15
  worked my way d. 395:13
Downhearted: are we d.? 215:15
Downs: bow-headed, whale-backed D. 212:29
Downstairs: d. a billiard saloon 50:3
Drag: d. the Joneses down to my level 95:11
Dragon: before he killed the d. 74:18
  d. of years 40:3
  silken d. puffed by the wind 151:10
Dragon-green: d. the luminous, the dark 128:6
Dragoon: aren't I Captain of the D.s 192:20
Drain: decided to d. the swamp 196:4
  Deity and the D.s 362:2
  next town d. 355:17
  pale owing to the d.s 15:3
Drainage: that does not require main d. 52:15
Drainpipe: wrong end of a municipal d. 236:6
Drama: as d., the [Great] War 155:10
  at the roots of all d. farce 94:25
  d. is a form of anthropology 42:26
  d. is life with the dull bits left out 172:14
  d. is when the audience cries 67:10
  good d. critic 381:1
  life is a d. and not a progress 273:3
  to write d. with comedy 359:12
Dramatic: cricket is . . . a d. spectacle 189:20
  God . . . the best of the d. poets 59:1
  painting is a d. action 297:10
Dramatist: d. changes the props 244:6
  d. only wants more liberties 190:6
  d. who had discovered himself 333:8
Drank: d. rapidly a glass of water 97:26
Draughty: d., like an abandoned temple 67:9
  Monet's pictures are always too d. 102:14
Draw: d. the thing as he sees it 213:15
Drawback: being royal has many . . . d.s 15:7
Drawing: back to the old d. board 14:8
  d. . . . of an untaught child 44:15
Drawing-down: d. of blinds 288:16
Drawing room: Suez . . . through my d. 115:1
Dread: d. of games 40:22
  d.s the final trumpet 163:4
  I only d. one day at a time 339:11
  nearer to truth and to d. 248:17
Dreaded: d. lergy 263:17
Dream: act their d. with open eyes 225:4
  acting is . . . a controlled d. 317:6
  all men d.: but not equally 225:4
  androids d. of electric sheep 105:18
  beauty passes like a d. 417:7

better than most people d. 280:4
bottom out of Bottom's d. 74:4
city of perspiring d.s 312:9
d. of the American Male 400:6
d. our d.s away 128:1
d.s are all egocentric 393:15
d.s, . . . rarely . . . accomplished 13:10
facts are better than d. 81:8
Germans painted their d. 2:16
guided d. 46:21
his life was a sort of d. 127:3
I being poor, have only my d.s 418:1
I d. quite a bit . . . asleep 314:14
I have a d. 208:11
I'll let you be in my d.s 113:22
I'll take the other 22 in d.s 58:13
it was a d. I had last week 91:5
kind people have a wonderful d. 270:9
Klee treated d.s with the proper awe 66:22
land of my d.s 208:16
made holy by their d.s 143:14
no more tonight than a d. 370:8
our d.s are tales told in dim Eden 102:18
pulls the legs of his d.s 369:25
salesman is got to d. 261:26
they d. of home 129:21
though it seems – beyond our d.s 163:5
we live as we d. – alone 89:6
we who lived by honest d.s 101:21
while I am recounting mine [d.s] 277:16
you tread on my d.s 416:14
Dreamed: d. that Christ had died in vain 349:1
Dreamer: d.s of the day are dangerous 225:4
Dreaming: boys are d. wicked 369:21
    d. of a white Christmas 39:10
    d. of thee 128:22
    d. of your etcetera 97:10
Dreamt: d. I went to Manderley 111:7
Dreamy: O d., gloomy, friendly trees 377:5
Dreary: one's impossible, two is d. 353:7
Dregs: d.? That's what he sediment 149:2
Drenched: wrinkled . . . and d. with dew 103:16
Dress: adjust your d. before leaving 82:12
    put on a d. of guilt 243:14
    tha mun d. thysen 223:19
Dressed: all d. up and no place to go 60:4, 172:18
    d. up, with nowhere to go 400:18
    flags are flying fully d. 302:10
Dresser: they leave it on the d. 244:8
Dresses: long d. . . . cover a multitude 398:13
    matters like print d. 396:23
Drift: adamant for d. 79:10
    d. of a club . . . in favour of the rich 77:9
Drifted: Snow White . . . but I d. 398:12
Drink: another little d. 155:6
    bad as drunkenness – or so good as d. 75:21
    come and have a d. with me 374:6
    d. a pinta milka day 3:5
    d. from the wine-breath 415:7
    d. of breakfast 125:7
    d.s as much as you do 370:6

everybody . . . is three d.s behind 45:1
I think this calls for a d. 371:14
man takes his first d. 170: 14
never to refuse a d. after dark 259:12
rarely d. alone where I am known 7:1
she drove me to d. 125:2
that he has taken to d. 365:6
then the d. takes you 127:26
told Jeeves to d. it himself 410:8
we d. too much tea 305:16
willing to taste any d. once 63:1
yet d.s the thirst from our lips 303:2
Drinker: d.s . . . inside a pair of army boots 161:3
    first great nonstop literary d. 371:15
    merrily answered staid d.s 370:14
Drinking: to do with the d. water 168:21
Dripping: electricity was d. 372:22
Drive: d. my green age 369:2
Driver: as long as he was in the d.'s seat 28:10
    carts to good d.s 51:1
Drôle: d. de guerre 99:4
Droll: d. rat, they would shoot you 324:9
Drone: d. of mowers on suburban lawns 317:15
Drop: turn on, tune in, and d. out 226:7
Dross: d. of the world is being burnt 328:17
Drown: sinking pool for learning to d. 265:16
Drowned: BETTER D. THAN DUFFERS 312:7
    d. Phoenician sailor 118:4
    d. to the accompaniment 238:14
Drowning: d., a . . . delightful sensation 124:2
    it's put me against drowning 46:20
    not waving but d. 351:14
    throwing a d. man both ends 21:9
Drubbing: sound of d. and sobbing 351:13
Drudge: d. for a living 198:19
Drudgery: d. in newspaper work 372:29
Drug: daft with the d. that's smoking 369:6
    d.s are a delusion 343:7
    everything is a dangerous d. 88:22
    most powerful d. used by mankind 214:26
    never had problems with d.s 316:10
    performing . . . is a d. 404:6
Drug-taking 57:5
Druid: same old d. time as ever 324:8
Drum: faint sound of d.s 68:15
    rhyme is still the most effective d. 144:18
Drunk: a man should always be d. 284:8
    concede . . . that he was ever d. 170:16
    d. for about a week now 126:14
    half d. when sober 170:10
    how d. we like our art to be 238:18
    in the war and he was very d. 392:15
    like a d. in a midnight choir 85:12
    my mother, d. or sober 76:6
    not d. if you can lie on the floor 252:7
    not so think as you d. I am 355:24
    what, when d., one sees 380:27
Drunkard: d. through being a coward 76:2
    miserly d.s 403:7
    rolling English D. 74:27
Drunkenness: anything so bad as d. 75:21

Dry: d. . . . like an abandoned temple 67:9
  I like humour d. 352:1
  turns damp to d. 369:13
Dublin 283:4
  D. without priests 31:12
  served in all the pubs in D. 108:6
  [the devil] has a strong D. accent 197:7
Duchess: behaved simply . . . with a d. 306:14
  every D. . . . wanting to kiss me 243:5
Duck: Honey, I forgot to d. 104:2, 313:16
  it rolls off my back like a d. 285:5
  one more bite and it would be a d. 24:18
  your precious lame d.s 139:19
Duckbilled: d. platitude 97:13
Duda: la vida es d. 382:2
Due: reasonable and loving d. 151:12
Duelling: trampled d. ground 317:14
Duffer: BETTER DROWNED THAN D.S 312:7
Duke: drawing room full of d.s 19:7
  d.'s son – cook's son 209:14
  d.s betray theirs [wives] 397:10
  fully equipped D. 235:16
  water . . . with the D.'s daughter 351:12
Dulce et decorum est: old lie: D. 288:18
Dull: life with the d. bits left out 172:14
  songs provide the d. with wit 256:25
Dullard: d.'s envy of brilliant men 30:18
Dulles, John Foster 82:11
Dullness: d. . . . is like halitosis 43:13
Dumb: cannot be absolutely d. 129:14
  d. as old medallions to the thumb 244:10
  d. son of a bitch 378:20
  Oh, noisy bells be d. 179:22
  play tennis, piano and d. 314:5
  too d. to think 299:24
Dumbness: d. is its salvation 92:13
Dumini: D., twelve assassinations 111:9
Dung: d. on my grandfather's doorstep 151:12
Dunkirk: came back from D. with two women 161:4
  tale of the D. beaches will shine 81:9
Dunn, Miss Joan Hunter 40:19
Dunstan's, St: push him . . . to D. 94:21
Duped: d. – the station-master 244:7
Duplication: avoid d. of effort 265:21
Duplicity: d. lies at the heart 312:18
  d. with honour 34:2
Duration: mirrors . . . all temporal d.s 401:10
Dusk: each slow d. 288:16
Dust: cannot d. everything 89:16
  d. in the air suspended 117:9
  excuse my d. 292:18
  fear in a handful of d. 118:2
  I like the d. on the nettles 370:17
  less than the dust 177:20
  mushroom of boiling d. 373:15
  richer d. concealed 55:5
  this haunt of brooding d. 103:15
  troubles of our proud and angry d. 178:20
  unexpected d. mop 72:15
  unseen, unguarded d. 163:14

what is d. 349:8
what of vile d.? 74:26
what would have sunk in d. 261:8
Dustbin: d. upset in a high wind 146:11
Dusty: d., cobweb-covered, maimed 62:7
Dusty-featured: d. Lollocks 151:16
Dutch: as I'd swop for my dear old D. 78:7
  D. . . . two distinct . . . types 92:3
Duties: discharge my d. as king 115:7
Duty: declares that it is his d. 342:25
  d. is what no-one else will do 127:29
  only one d., and that is to love 65:23
  pleasure is a safer guide than d. 62:3
  thing of d. is a boy forever 283:12
Duvetyne: mind my d. dress above all 197:13
Dwarf: dozen red-bearded d.s into the hall 271:1
  d.s trying to grill a whale 305:13
Dwelling: d. on their good vices 343:15
Dyb dyb dyb 21:8
Dying: Autumn sunsets exquisitely d. 183:18
  d. generations 417:9
  d. is an art 299:22
  d. is not everything 336:16
  d. men must groan 389:3
  d. now and done for 41:1
  d. pray at the last 106:5
  d. religion always interferes 77:23
  grandmother made d. her life's work 230:15
  her d., . . . his consequent solitude 190:12
  I cannot forgive my friends for d. 350:15
  if this is d. 362:8
  [immortality] through not d. 6:28
  no d. but alive and warm 368:21
  not busy being born is busy d. 113:11
  not so many d. as dead 360:12
  prepared . . . for living, not for d. 352:8
  scared of d. 160:14
  she is d. piece-meal 303:21
  some thought of d. at birth 336:19
  there are so many ways of us d. 22:4
  time held me green and d. 369:1
Dylan, Bob: he [D.] is like all of us 347:1
Dynamic: class people as static and d. 392:20
  ghastly d. exhibit 411:6
Dynamite: cook the frozen d. 210:16
  that H-bomb. It's d. 147:16
Dynamited: d. into bliss 396:19
Dynamiting: d. factories 374:18
Dynastic: simple d. arrangements 156:6
Dyslexia: d. rules – K.O.? 149:4

E

E = mc² 115:10
EEC: standards . . . set by the E. 188:12
ET: E. phone home 255:5
Each: all in e. and e. in all 356:2
  e. in his place, by right 213:11
Eagle: E. has landed 10:5, 171:21

e. on th' back iv a dollar 111:19
e.s . . . adorn our coats of arms 199:2
Ear: battle for the e.s of others 218:14
  death has stopped the e.s 179:19
  e. make him look like a taxi-cab 181:4
  e.s in the turrets hear 368:23
  e.s like bombs 70:20
  e.s like errant wings 74:14
  e.s so close to the ground 207:9
  even people have e.s 263:21
  finest e. of any English poet 19:16
  Hansard is history's e. 334:10
  jug jug to dirty e.s 118:9
  keep both e.s to the ground 9:18
  keep the e.s from grating 104:10
  like wax in the Eternal e. 154:1
  make one's e.s water 326:3
  men who have a pierced e. 326:8
  one e. is more than you need 325:3
  rhymes that please the e. 389:3
  shout about my e.s 74:15
  Van Gogh's e. for music 402:14
  wag my great, long, furry e.s 37:15
  woman [falls in love] through her e.s 413:18
  you've got just the e.s for it 155:3
Earache: cry for hours with the e. 188:8
Earl: ground to a halt with a 14th E. 406:2
  mutton chop not an E. 410:19
Early: decide whether too e. or too late 66:18
  e., sober, and alone 383:6
  never occured to me . . . to be e. 101:8
  too e. for being 167:18
  too e. to say 420:9
Earned: old age . . . what we have e. 51:25
Earner: nice little e. 155:13
Earnest: e. about not cheating at cards 232:18
Earning: learning, e. and yearning 269:14
Earplug: or do I have to use e.s? 263:26
Earth: air the ditty and to e. 179:8
  back to the nourishing e. 334:19
  did thee feel the e. move? 169:7
  don't forget the e.'s . . . old 298:19
  e. as an artistic cult 130:18
  e. has waited for them 324:10
  e. is but a star 128:8
  e. is like a child 319:7
  e. is nobler than the world 305:12
  e. is one, but the world is not 57:6
  e. tideless and inert 23:17
  e. which is sometimes so pretty 305:7
  e. will grow worse 75:4
  e.'s moving nearer to truth 248:17
  e.'s the right place for love 135:5
  hour when e.'s foundations fled 179:5
  immersion of the hands in the e. 16:17
  inherit the e., but not the mineral 142:23
  is there intelligent life on e.? 149:16
  it isn't evil that's running the e. 323:16
  kings of the e. are old 319:14
  let me enjoy the e. no less 163:3
  of e. and sea his overcoat 179:2

one is aware that the e. revolves 307:2
passenger on the spaceship, E. 137:11
song of the angels sung by e. spirits 260:8
walk on the moon and look at the e. 120:24
you gave me shoe-size in e. 249:3
your's is the e. 211:1
Earth-woman: lowest form of life . . . e. 110:16
Earthquake: e. . . . up to a climax 147:13
  not smiling back – that's an e. 261:26
Earwicker, H.C.: Sayings Attributive to E. 197:9
Ease: doctrine of ignoble e. 323:5
Easing: they call it e. the spring 314:10
East: E. is E. and West is West 209:18
  have the E. come to the Atlantic 146:4
  one of these wise men from the E. 244:4
  tried to hustle the E. 212:7
East End: look the E. in the face 119:8
East-to-west: swift e. 410:4
Eastern: full of e. promise 3:10
Eastwards: life had retreated e. 223:21
Easy: e. to shake a man's belief 343:2
  no e. walk to freedom 248:14
  none of which is e. 8:19
  not an e. thing to do – try it 168:20
  Oh as I was young and e. 369:1
  she bid me take love e. 416:3
  summertime, and the living is e. 142:21
Eat: anything that e.s while you sleep 300:3
  don't want to have to e. them 411:21
  e. as much as you like 340:10
  e. . . . to put food out of my mind 348:5
  e. well and play the flute 302:9
  even the mice e. next door 340:5
  gladly e. a network executive 123:18
  I can e. a man 114:6
  invest . . . in anything that e.s 323:20
  just enough to e. 31:18
  more e. than starve 360:12
  while everyone else e.s 391:1
Eating: dearly loves to commit e. 327:9
  e. people is wrong 128:3
  e. without chewing 58:17
  e.'s . . . a whole new ball game 298:14
  habit of e., very few ever survive 187:14
  sign that something is e. us 104:15
Eavesdropping: nothing like e. 403:5
Eccentric: making the act appear e. 376:11
  you are e., he is round the twist 239:22
Ecclesiastes: 287:12
Ecclesiastical: branch of the e. tree 195:5
Ecclesiologist: keen e. 41:2
Echo: solid as e. 303:2
Echo-chamber: tyranny sets up its own e. 73:14
Echoes: manufactory of e. 108:15
Economic: bottom of the e. pyramid 322:8
  calls its vital e. interests 394:11
  E. Problem . . . a frightful muddle 206:15
  e. [problems] are incomprehensible 109:4
Economical: e. with the truth 14:6
  God is very e. 316:18
Economics: God, e., or Ibsen 295:19

moved by e. than by morals 297:2
we know now it is bad e. 322:13
Economies: most spectacular e. 203:15
Economist: disadvantage . . . he's an e. 239:15
  e.s with the exception of the Irish 139:1
  ideas of e.s . . . are more powerful 207:2
  if all e.s were laid end to end 346:12
  Jesus . . . a first rate political e. 342:12
  one-armed e. 379:3
  slaves of some defunct e. 207:2
Economize: let us e. it 379:22
  she'd never e. unwisely 286:4
Economy: completely planned e. 132:1
  e. and particular expenditure 114:12
  e. is going without something 177:8
  e. or malpractice? 285:22
  trouble about a free market e. 14:11
Ecstasy: e. is knowing 319:21
  e. of mendacity 344:13
  escape from circumstances to e. 31:16
Ecstatic: carolings of such e. sound 162:12
Eczema: silk, too often hides e. 65:7
Edam: small corpulent, red-faced E.s 92:3
Eden, Sir Anthony: 42:4, 60:19, 82:11, 193:5,
  193:15
  E. . . . bores for England 272:18
  E., half mad baronet 61:1
Eden: tales told in dim E. 102:18
Edge: no side here, but plenty of e. 193:10
Edifice: can the soul's e. . . . be built 328:19
Edited: his wife . . . e. him 55:22
Edition: got him in the morning e.s 321:28
Editor: e. . . . knows . . . what he wants 100:5
  good e. chooses to print 243:243
  longest-lived e. 320:20
  trust your e. . . . sleep on straw 73:17
Editorial: age of the e. chair 244:17
Educate: e. a whole family 249:6
Educated: e. beyond . . . common sense 9:8
  fingers must be e. 71:11
  stamps a man as an e. gentleman 343:23
Education: advantages of an e. 349:17
  all e. is . . . vocational 279:11
  apathy in e. 130:20
  cabbage with a college e. 380:12
  can't do with any more e. 408:18
  e. and whisky being the price it is 392:7
  e. but it never went to my head 36:8
  e. costs money, . . . so does ignorance 272:1
  e. . . . distributable by coupon 334:7
  e. . . . has produced a vast population 377:7
  e. in socialism 378:5
  E.: in the holidays from Eton 349:14
  e. indispensable to . . . society 80:22
  e. is a sieve as well as a lift 73:3
  e. is . . . casting false pearls 115:4
  e. is not an end in itself 252:5
  e. is the soul of society 78:1
  e. is what survives 349:18
  e. . . . knowledge . . . of values 186:2
  e. . . . manufactory of echoes 108:15

e. the way the banks 105:13
English middle-class e. 404:2
enough e. to make me immune 36:8
race between e. and catastrophe 397:2
real e. must ultimately be limited 303:26
soap and e. 379:21
struggle . . . between e. and propaganda 57:12
stumbling-blocks in a girl's e. 86:4
tortures called e. 382:11
Edward VII 399:4
  E. . . . best type of sporting publican 4:3
Edward VIII [formerly Prince of Wales] 215:6,
  294:18
  most damning epithet . . . about E. 90:3
Edwardian: E. Wilderness 288:5
Eel: e.s get used to skinning 79:18
Effacement: brought full e. 312:5
Effect: likelier to win an e. 383:2
Effectiveness: e. of assertion 344:3
Efficiency: e. . . . a sweeping gesture 280:1
Efficient: e. and the inefficient 343:22
  e. if you're going to be lazy 89:14
Effluent: e. society 368:7
Effort: avoid duplication of e. 265:21
  e. nearly killed her 32:21
  only e. worth making 48:11
  redoubling you e. 335:7
Egalitarian: where they should be e. 236:14
Egg: all my e.s in one bastard 292:12
  e. until it is broken 126:6
  e. without salt 71:3, 214:18
  e.'s way of making another e. 61:10
  go to work on an e. 3:11
  hand that lays the golden e. 147:19
  hard-boiled as a picnic e. 290:7
  hen that lays the e.s 368:1
  homicidal fried e. 409:4
  lay one more bloody e. 20:9
  lays e.s inside a paper bag 187:16
  making e.s out of an omelette 22:9
  met a lot of hard-boiled e.s 402:7
  no e.s delivered 132:1
  omelette without frying e.s 102:13
  sitting on a china e. 129:9
Eggardon: I climbed E. 418:17
Egghead: e. marries hourglass 386:9
  E.s are terrible Philistines 276:12
Ego: Hamlet without breaking a few e.s 146:17
  too much e. in your cosmos 214:10
Egocentric: dreams are all e. 393:15
Egoism: altruism which is not e. 308:18
  artist's e. is outrageous 256:23
  shyness is just e. out of its depth 203:24
Egotist: E. more interested in himself 42:13
Egregious: High E. is fairly on 396:10
Egypt: we are not at war with E. 114:13
  you can't judge E. by Aida 125:17
Eiffel: bergère ô tour E. 13:3
  you're the E. Tower 302:7
Eight-ulcer: e. man on a four-ulcer job 378:15
Eighteen: e. in the attics 183:12

wake up, E. 142:1
watch the ships of E. go 210:3
who made old E.'s name 243:13
you can tell you're not in E. 256:2
English: Allah created the E. mad 211:9
anyone . . . raped and speaks E. 31:13
blubber which encases an E. peer 88:12
broken man writing dull E. 276:8
choose me, you E. words 370:20
disasters of E. history 392:8
E. abounds in clichés 52:2
E. actresses are mistresses 161:8
E. ale out of an E. flagon 74:18
E. and the . . . Irish more so 112:1
E. are polite by telling lies 49:12
E. are very good at hiding emotions 164:11
E. countess goes upon the stage 117:32
E. don't raise their voices 169:3
E. five minutes 31:23
E. God is not so dominant 68:4
E. have adopted central heating 120:7
E. have hot-water bottles 260:18
E. have three vegetables 290:2
E. is the language . . . to be deduced 270:21
E. language no longer belongs to the E. 219:16
E. . . . language of an imaginative race 52:2
E. language . . . properly organized 264:14
E. literature's performing flea 284:9
E. manners are far more frightening 192:5
E. may not like music 29:19
E. never draw a line 80:10
E. peer of the right sort 410:18
E. people . . . are . . . the nicest 222:26
E. ship, . . . poor grub 237:1
E.-speaking race against the world 145:12
E. stillness was so soft 224:11
E., unofficial rose 54:16
E. will penetrate 241:2
E. women are elegant until . . . ten 266:12
E. women only hope to find 257:3
enters at the E. gate 179:27
especially if he went among the E. 26:21
finest French novel in the E. language 321:6
living with E. in one room 389:5
mistrust of the E. upper classes 270:18
mobilized the E. language 275:5
most dignified E. 101:9
most embarrassed people . . . E. 36:15
need a white skin to be E. 293:18
particularly the E. gentleman 191:2
pious E. habit 344:8
really nice E. people 343:17
rise and fall of E. architecture 41:5
rolling E. drunkard 74:27
so deeply rooted in E. character 61:7
speak E. when our backs are turned 95:15
speak E. without an accent 34:24
stones kissed by the E. dead 288:20
tea to the E. 390:2
there's enough E. to go round 270:14
they've got to learn E. 354:10

to employ an E. charwoman 260:21
under an E. heaven 55:7
understanding of E. . . . audiences 399:11
wears them with a strong E. accent 333:1
what the E. call character 36:19
when success happens to an E. writer 8:6
when the E. began to hate 209:20
within these breakwaters E. is spoken 17:9
your E. summer's done 211:21
Englishman: can what an E. believes be heresy?
    345:24
could easily pass for an E. 144:7
E. and remained one for years 31:3
E. apologizes to the truck 254:18
E. is about to talk French 409:17
E. likes to imagine himself at sea 66:6
E. . . . lives on an island 156:7
E. thinks he is moral 344:17
E. thinks seated 285:1
E. told you he was a secret agent 93:20
E. wants fish for supper 223:5
E.'s way of speaking 230:17
God wouldn't trust an E. in the dark 353:13
never find an E. among the underdogs 392:24
never find an E. in the wrong 345:8
not that the E. can't feel 130:6
remember that you are an E. 316:2
show what an E. can do 340:4
stirred the heart of every E. 340:2
to an E. something is what it is called 243:2
to outwit an E., touch him 25:20
Englishmen: behold the E. at his best 125:25
create Frenchmen in the image of E. 80:2
E. taking mad dogs for walks 263:3
if all E. were like him 32:5
in the United States E. are . . . pets 96:2
mad dogs and E. 94:13
we do not see E. as foreigners 220:14
Englishwomen: E.'s shoes 160:1
Englove: God's arm e.s this tree 314:6
Enigma: mystery inside an e. 79:12
Enjoy: get what you want . . . e. it 350:10
I don't have to go out and e. it 351:2
Enjoyable: come to a bad end, very e. 369:22
everyone else is having a more e. time 304:4
Enjoyment: no individual e. in Nature 401:8
Enlightenment: triumph of E. 34:9
Enormous: conceived in an e. room 83:6
Enough: I've really had e. 260:14
patriotism is not e. 71:2
wouldn't be e. to go round 356:16
Ensconced: safely e. in thick glasses 97:12
Enslave: e.s you on imperial principles 345:8
Enslavement: madness . . . is e. 219:13
Enterprise: if e. is afoot 207:4
more e. in walking naked 415:14
only forms of free e. 53:7
Entertain: better to e. an idea 192:10
e.s the most exclusive worms 290:12
Entertained: e. by . . . reminiscences 413:6
Entertainer: dreamed of being a . . . e. 395:15

Entertainment: box they buried e. in 177:16
  cats . . . appreciate . . . e. 178:13
  no connection with . . . e. 64:18
Enthusiasm: bored as e. would permit 148:10
  e. moves the world 23:18
Enthusiast: in every e. there lurks 386:2
Entire: e. and whole and perfect 355:18
Entitled: more than that no man is e. to 323:7
Entrant: e. in an intelligence contest 239:14
Entry: happens to be a Second E. 2:10
Envelope: we see the e. they are 14:14
Environment: e. is full of uncertainties 73:6
  [e.] is a big, booming, . . . confusion 191:23
  heredity is just e. stored 58:16
  tell which was the e. 192:4
Environs: back to Howth Castle and E. 197:8
Envy: made e. legitimate 39:19
  upbringing a nun would e. 285:19
Ephemeral: bricks with e. straw 64:12
Epic: e. follows the plough 389:8
Epigram: amalgam of Americanisms and e.
    213:27
  impelled to try an e. 291:6
  until it purrs like an e. 251:18
Episcopal: services in the E. churches 143:2
Episodic: one of the e. persons 399:15
Epistle: some soldiers send e.s 399:5
Epitaph: no e., and no name 390:20
Epoch: civilization of one e. 88:23
  e. of the masses 285:15
Epsom: saddled in the enclosure at E. 94:24
Epstein, Jacob 9:24, 67:15
Equal: everybody . . . an e. chance 406:3
  poor are our e.s 377:14
  some animals are more e. 286:12
  trouble with treating people as e.s 105:7
  we're all e.s . . . like the Cabinet 239:12
Equality: e. in the servants' hall 26:3
  Liberty, E., Adultery! 34:9
Equalized: expectation is e. 185:8
Equation: e. is something for eternity 116:1
Equator: no more a . . . nation than the e. 79:8
Equivalent: process and result are e. 408:8
'Er: 'e. indoors 155:12
Erben: die Könige . . . werden keine E. haben 319:14
Erde: die E. † ist wie ein Kind 319:7
Erfühltem: nicht grosstun mit herrlich E. 319:1
Erikson: Miss, E. looked more peculiar 94:2
Erogenous: mind can also be an e. zone 395:3
Erotic: e. practices . . . diversified 34:5
  e. purposes under the mask 134:6
Error: few e.s they have ever avoided 80:6
  possibility of e. must be ruled out 200:7
  time for the destruction of e. 17:20
  vague e.s of the flesh 371:2
Erworbene: alles E. bedroht die Maschine 319:11
Esau: E., . . . copyright for a partridge 170:1
  proverbs and E.'s fables 170:18
Escape: beauty for some provides e. 183:18
  no e.. No such thing 151:7
Escapist: either e.s or Buddhists 304:17

Eskimo: E.s . . . would-be Etonians 165:11
Espionage: e. is to today's [century] 312:17
Essay: e. good through evil 246:1
  e.s containing no new facts 360:13
  good e. must have this 412:9
  longest e., irrespective of merit 392:5
  volume of e.s and offer it to him 86:9
Essence: deny them my bodily e. 218:6
  e. of comedy 382:4
  poet gives us his e. 412:3
Essential: what is e. is invisible 332:3
Establishment: e. does . . . the work 383:13
Estate: party of e. agents 166:13
  used to dealing with e. workers 109:5
Estimate: get an e. – soppy old sod 354:9
Etat: é.s sont les monstres froids 141:12
Etcetera: dreaming . . . of your e. 97:10
Etching: I'll bring the e.s down 372:13
  just to look at his e.s 326:16
Eternal: e. footman 117:26
  e. triangle 10:6
  love e., indestructible 107:23
  pulse in the e. mind 55:6
Eternity: crowed out e. 417:18
  e. is a terrible thought 361:1
  e. of calm fruition 186:5
  from here to e. 210:24
  killing e. 382:4
  life is just a novitiate e. 93:6
Ethelberta: E. breathed 163:24
Ethic: e.s does not treat of the world 408:10
  grub first, then e.s 51:18
  supreme principle of e.s 328:9
Ethic: Protestant e. 394:6
Ethically: capitalism was doomed e. 352:12
Eton: feelings on leaving E. 88:13
  in the holidays from E. 349:14
  spiritually I was at E. 40:24
  won on the playing-fields of E. 286:19
Etonian: Eskimos . . . would-be E.s 165:11
  greet him like E.s 215:19
Étonne: É.-moi 105:16
Etruria: as Rome denied E. 222:16
Etruscan: subtly-smiling E.s 222:15
Euclid: E. . . . looked on beauty bare 261:4
Eunuch: between a e. and a snigger 125:22
  e.s boasting of their chastity 232:17
  prerogative of the e. 361:12
Euphemism: style is . . . a kind of e. 287:13
Euphoria: e. is not knowing 319:21
Europe: all the dogs of E. bark 17:16
  bad for us, bad for E. 245:14
  dirty armpit of E. 235:9
  E. . . . a conglomeration of mistakes 121:2
  E. des patries 102:5, 141:9
  E. is the unfinished negative 242:5
  E. of the father-lands 102:5
  [E.] will be a gay world 313:11
  E's nothin' but a . . . auction 404:16
  German racket . . . to take over . . . E. 318:2
  'going into E.' will not turn out 371:7

in E. nothing goes 325:11
lamps are going out all over E. 155:8
Napoleon brought peace to E. 168:24
races of E. are melting 420:3
United States of E. 80:8
we have all lost the war. All E. 223:15
wisest woman in E. 118:3
European: E. Community 245:14
   E. philosophical tradition 401:9
   E.s and Americans . . . men and women 192:11
   greater h. than the E. 242:4
   materialistic people . . . E.s 242:2
   to shoot down a E. 336:26
Europeanism: E. is imperialism 166:9
Euthanasia: ah, that's e. 137:8
Evacuation: wars are not won by e.s 81:10
Evanescent: e. bricks 64:12
Evans, Edith 316:19
Evaporate: every revolution e.s 201:5
Eve: Adam and E. had been merely engaged 397:3
   bathed in E.'s loveliness 103:20
   doesn't it make you E. 150:5
   E. saw her reflection 42:6
   E. would ask Abbott 249:17
   fallen sons of E. 75:7
   tales told . . . by E.'s nightingales 102:18
   when E. ate this particular apple 223:3
Evening: e., all 391:8
   e. full of the linnet's wings 416:20
   e. is spread out against the sky 117:21
   good e. England 302:18
   some enchanted e. 160:16
Event: certain e.s in himself 114:9
   e.s overlapping each other 112:15
   great e.s do not . . . have great causes 366:12
Ever: do you want to live for e.? 99:10
Ever-flowing: e. stream of time 69:3
Everest: 172:5, 248:3, 367:13
   climbing Mount E. from the inside 263:29
   mons Veneris as . . . Mount E. 182:19
Everidge, Dame Edna 66:28
Everybody: e. needs every day 402:21
Everyday: e. language is a . . . poem 167:19
   e. story of country folk 394:4
Everyone: e. suddenly burst out singing 337:3
Everything 398:14
   because you can . . . understand e. 137:7
   e. that is the case 408:4
   e. you've always wanted to know 315:15
   e.'s coming up roses 353:4
   laid hands on e. 66:14
   more to life than having e. 341:16
   most of e. and the best of nothing 72:8
   responsible for e. 335:23
   when you've robbed a man of e. 352:15
   you can't have e. 6:5
Evidence: all e. supports that myth 46:12
   belief without e. 42:15
Evil: all e. shed away 55:6
   banality of e. 13:12
   between two e.s 398:6

clear the land of e. 212:25
destroy some of the e. within 394:12
E. cannot imagine Good 19:2
e. is even 283:10
e. is not . . . wholly e. 5:8
e. is simply ignorance 129:19
e. is the product of the ability 336:27
e. makes for separateness 182:17
e. on the ground of expediency 323:13
e. wrangling with the e. 273:5
if e. does not exist 306:6
instability of e. 401:11
it isn't e. that's running the earth 323:16
man's capacity for e. 280:3
no e. in the atom 359:2
only one e., to deny life 222:16
origin of all coming e. 199:13
see no e., hear no e., and e. 107:22
speechless e. 17:8
two e.s, monstrous either one 312:6
wood of conscious e. 17:13
Evoke: e. posterity is to weep 152:5
Evolution: cultural e. 54:1
   e. is far more important than living 199:17
   relation to . . . e. 378:4
Ex-parrot: it's an e. 268:4
Ex-wife: e. searching for a new lover 88:19
Exactitude: e. is not truth 255:7
Exaggerated: report of my death is e. 380:21
Exaggeration: e. is a truth 143:9
   nothing is true except the e.s 2:17
Exaltation: e. of scoutmasters 317:4
Exam: contemporaries pass e.s 40:25
Exasperating: afterlife any less e. 93:13
Excellence: acute limited e. 126:12
   e. of the strong man 46:8
Excellent: situation e. 129:4
Exception: e. disproves the rule 110:6
   I'll make an e. in your case 253:19
Exceptional: mistakes the e. for the important 117
   weather is, without exception, e. 252:9
Excess: carry moderation unto e. 216:17
Exchequer: salmon this morning and . . . the E.
   this afternoon 71:16
Exciting: travelling . . . e. but not interesting 273:1
Exclamation: clothes-peg of his e. mark 368:15
   Ethelberta breathed a sort of e. 163:24
Exclusion: idea of e. and prohibition 261:15
Exclusive: adamant walls of life's e. city 222:19
   entertains the most e. worms 290:12
Excursion: e. to hell 305:15
Excuse: cleverness is an e. for thinking 279:19
   if you'll e. me having such a thing 345:32
   qui s'accuse s'e. 317:13
   several e.s are . . . less convincing 183:2
   two wrongs . . . make a good e. 364:7
Executioner: respect their e.s 335:22
Executive: e. poppycock 121:5
   philanthropist and the e. 328:6
Exercise: e. is bunk 129:20
   his way of taking e. 108:17

Exertion: prolonged physical e. 220:7
Exhausted: small man can be just as e. 261:24
Exile: in e. he [Kaiser] remarried 82:14
  not abrupt e. 17:21
Exist: animal that does not e. 319:10
  [God] need not e. . . . to save us 105:6
  I e. by what I think 336:9
  I regret that it nowhere e.s 367:10
  no one e.s alone 18:19
  satisfy myself that it still e.s 29:14
Existed: knowledge that it e. 216:11
Existence: alter the texture of one's e. 216:11
  astonishment at our own e. 75:23
  disregard for the necessities of e. 256:5
  e. is meaningful 160:6
  e. remains a mad . . . experiment 335:8
  know more about it than its bare e. 61:6
  miracle . . . of naked e. 182:15
  prospect of continued e. 133:19
  quite enough e. as it is 336:11
  richness and diversity of his e. 205:4
  sole purpose of human e. 199:4
  struggle for e. 134:2
  unless all e. is a medium 367:5
Existential: madness is . . . e. death 219:13
Existing: e. as a human being 357:18
Exit: every e. being an entrance 360:21
  obliged to make my e. quick 202:2
Exotic: e. marriages 34:10
Expectation: beneath the strain of e. 125:20
  distinction between hope and e. 185:10
  e. is equalized 185:8
  our talents and our e.s 46:13
  present of immediate e. 38:12
  seldom fails to live down to e.s 84:3
  we are Buddhists and we have no e.s 108:3
Expediency: evil on the ground of e. 323:13
Expendable: they were e. 400:19
Expenditure: particular e. 114:12
Expensive: how . . . e. it is to be poor 23:2
  obtrusively e. goods 138:15
  still it comes e. 389:3
Experience: doctoring our e.s 176:8
  e. dulls the edges of . . . dogmas 275:2
  e. in the hen house 378:19
  e. isn't interesting 48:2
  e. of the carrying of nieces 317:16
  e. of women . . . over many nations 110:4
  expert beyond e. 118:19
  feast of e. in a series of courses 146:7
  last camp of e. 156:20
  learn by e., but . . . summer school 105:11
  man of no e. 98:9
  more acute the e. 299:1
  music is your own e. 290:9
  one year's e., and it's 24 years old 267:6
  one year's e. thirty times 68:5
  optimist . . . has never had much e. 251:8
  reality of e. 198:8
  tested by e. 301:3
  trying every e. once 27:12

widest e. of the human intelligence 307:5
wit involves . . . e. 119:3
Experienced: e., industrious . . . liar 380:11
Experiment: existence remains a mad . . . e. 335:8
  from e. to . . . a theory 116:8
Experimenting: e. ever since 223:3
Expert: e. beyond experience 118:19
  e. . . . has made all the mistakes 45:3
  e. . . . knows more and more 60:18
  e. . . . knows the worst mistakes 168:3
  highly-conscious technical e. 88:3
Expertise: not e. but uncertainties 53:8
Expiate: something to e.; a pettiness 222:23
Explain: e.s after the event 215:4
  never e. 126:5
  never e. – your friends do not need it 180:21
Explainer: village e. 357:15
Explanation: I do loathe e.s 26:9
  less hideous than e.s 233:3
Exploit: you would never e. one 91:4
Exploitation: you apply it, I call it e. 77:10
Explorer: e.s have to be ready to die 174:18
Explosion: how to reverse e.s 66:16
Export: [English language] is an e. reject 219:16
  Fascism is not an article for e. 275:8
  for mankind . . . there are no e.s 339:14
Expotition: e. to the North Pole 265:8
Express: e. in the small of her back 409:10
  e.-train drew up there unwontedly 370:7
  little I can e. 276:10
  never keen to e. themselves 49:6
Expression: e. of the mediocrity 378:6
  forms of e. 408:1
  more articulate its e. 299:1
Exteemed: my e. chums 316:12
Exterminate: e. a nation 355:13
  e. all the brutes 89:7
  we will e. 278:11
Extinct: how come you're e.? 92:13
  invented for . . . becoming e. 98:3
  Tasmanians . . . are now e. 255:17
Extinction: grim reaper of e. 148:14
Extol: how shall we e. thee 37:14
Extortion: artichokes and e. 326:18
Extramarital: believe in e. relationships 6:3
Extraordinary: interested in the e. 180:23
  work of one e. man 180:22
Extreme: aye be whaur e.s meet 242:15
  did not fly to e.s; she lived there 95:14
  e. views weakly held 366:9
Extremism: e. in the defence of liberty 147:2
Eye: acting is . . . meeting someone's e. 97:1
  chewing gum for the e.s 56:12
  clammy, accusing sort of e.s 409:12
  compassion and new e.s 253:28
  darkness shall no more assail mine e.s 103:2
  e. clear as the bleb of the icicle 167:2
  e. for an e. soon . . . blind 149:5
  e. that can open an oyster 408:22
  e.s have it 24:19
  e.s . . . if he's pawned his real ones 174:10

e.s in the gable see 368:23
e.s like agate lanterns 95:3
e.s of Caligula 266:18
e.s still dazzled by the ways of God 234:11
e.s . . . through which our intelligence 308:12
fool the mind rather than the e. 297:19
God finally caught his e. 202:11
greater cats with golden e.s 331:5
hand is more important than the e. 54:2
in a dark time the e. begins to see 321:8
in the stars the glory of His e.s 300:13
kind safe e.s 191:2
less of this than meets the e. 24:7
like a fish hook into an open e. 17:3
listen to with the naked e. 354:5
little shadows come about her e.s 416:8
locked and frozen in each e. 17:17
look at yourself with one e. 187:6
mad e. of the fourth person singular 124:1
man falls in love through his e.s 413:18
mother-in-law with only one e. 196:1
nearest thing to the e. of God 284:19
not meant for human e.s 273:4
only their e.s move 68:6
open your e.s to the air 370:18
painted to the e.s 107:11
piteous recognition in fixed e.s 288:25
scribble on our e.s the frosty sagas 94:28
seeing with a child's e. 46:15
smoke gets in your e.s 161:14
stretch one's e.s 32:21
that man's [Mussolini's] e.s 45:12
two lovely black e.s 85:2
you'll go back with slitty e.s 296:17
Eyeball: e. to e. and . . . just blinked 327:20
Eyebrow: e. made of platinum 130:7
take any not above A with her e.s 145:3
Eye-deep: walked e. in hell 303:16
Eyefull: E. Tower is devine 237:9
Eyelid: when she raises her e.s 86:1

F

Fabian: farmyard civilization of the F.s 186:6
F.s are 100 years old 165:17
good man fallen among F.s 229:7
Face: accuse 'em of not having any f.s 305:14
beauty of an aged f. 64:16
can't think of your f. 355:15
cluster of f.s, juxtaposed 307:14
coming with vivid f.s 416:4
does a round f. have several noses? 99:6
don't recognize f.s 144:17
every man is responsible for his f. 65:11
everyone has the f. he deserves 287:21
f. anything except the future 53:2
f. . . . as long as a late breakfast 198:18
f. . . . as though he had rented it 280:9
f. like a carving abandoned 396:4

f. like . . . Cardinal Newman's 69:17
f. . . . of a . . . sensitive nature 110:4
f. shining like Moses 377:2
f. suggested an old boot 380:28
f.-to-f. you don't see the . . . f. 148:1
f.s as thin as credit cards 8:2
f.s . . . to express rage or loathing 7:13
50s f. was angry 391:11
hawk-like foreign f.s 246:6
her f. in speech 191:3
her fist of a f. 368:18
hid his face amid . . . stars 417:28
I like my f. in the mirror 413:14
I've grown accustomed to her f. 230:23
keeping your f. or your figure 69:12
lives on this lonely f. 417:8
made enough f.s 140:2
make kinder the f. of the nation 60:13
mask that eats into the f. 383:3
might as well fall flat on your f. 372:5
my f. – I don't mind it 121:7
never forget a f. 253:19
no f., only two profiles 16:3
one f. he has got is so . . . unpleasant 351:21
open your f. 97:18
private f.s in public places 17:24
Shelley had a hyper-thyroid f. 355:25
slept-in f. 24:21
Socialism with a human f. 110:21
sorrows of your changing f. 417:27
style slaps you in the f. 83:20
voice without a f. 18:20
when I look death in the f. 416:2
when studying f.s, we . . . measure 307:16
where most people have f.s 375:16
Fact: accumulation of f.s 300:14
comment is free but f.s are sacred 339:20
conclusions on which I base my f.s 295:11
denying non-existent f.s 111:2
f.s are better than dreams 81:8
f.s that were damaging 308:14
knowledege not of f. but of values 186:2
legend becomes f. 31:22
life will give you all the f.s 18:28
Lord wud do if He knew th' f.s 111:20
my f.s are just statistics 239:19
not just accepting the f.s of life 284:18
not neglect the known f.s 38:3
not to deny the f.s 329:20
rather have my f.s all wrong 278:8
take sides against the obvious f.s 79:5
that's all the f.s 117:36
you can't cook them [f.s] 256:10
Factor: where F. 2 comes into operation 293:4
Factory: in the f. we make cosmetics 315:16
Faculties: they merely lose their f.s 137:4
Faculty: f. sport 4:17
Fad: psychoanalysis is a permanent f. 104:22
Fade: nuclear waste f.s your genes 149:28
they only f. away 129:6
Faded: f. female in a damp basement 162:1

Fader: I am not your f. but your moder 303:4

Fading: not so much that he was f. away 22:2

Faery: F. should . . . wave her wand 362:5
   land of f. 416:22

Fafafather: f. of all schemes for to bother us
   197:11

Fag: pop out for a packet of f.s 22:6

Fahrenheit: King F. quietly ate his pap 269:6
   König F. hat still sein Mus gegessen 269:6

Fail: I was sure I would not f. 81:8
   others must f. 387:19
   try again. f. again. f. better 29:1

Failed: light that f. 214:12

Failure: connoisseur of f. 90:16
   falling in love . . . sign of f. 358:9
   it is our f.s that civilize us 189:12
   no success like f. 113:16
   now we are not a f. 386:8

Fair: f. sex is your department 110:2
   f. shares for all 192:22
   never fight f. with a stranger 261:21
   sport has nothing to do with f. play 287:17
   trying to be f., not shrewd 168:18

Fairbanks, Douglas: F. faced a situation . . . by
   running away 298:8

Fairies: f. at the bottom of our garden 137:19
   f. break their dances 179:3
   I don't believe in f. 26:11
   that was the beginning of f. 26:10

Fairy: from within f. rings 370:4
   in search of a f. 102:23
   myth is not a f. story 329:20
   nobody loves a f. when she's forty 169:19
   to f. flutes as the light advances 271:8
   vale and the pastoral f.-tale 44:12

Fairyland: it's like f. 412:1

Faith: all unbelievers within our own f.s 154:14
   f. . . . being ultimately concerned 374:2
   f. . . . belief in the . . . improbable 259:6
   F. belief without evidence 42:15
   f. has need of the whole truth 367:1
   f. in f. itself 382:6
   f. is something you die for 35:20
   f. without doubt 382:2
   it's an article of f. 32:7
   reason is itself an act of f. 77:2
   still by f. he trod 234:11
   sudden explosions of f. 51:28
   what of the f. and fire within us 163:6
   world, you have kept f. with me 162:18

Fake: sincerity. Once you can f. that 284:22

Falcon: f. cannot hear the falconer 417:12

Falklands War 174:21
   F. held a mirror up 311:1
   F. thing . . . fight between two bald men 47:3

Fall: chance that you will f. out 34:19
   harder they f. 127:30
   how do you f., sir? 17:12
   hurry to get up when we f. down 114:2
   novel-reading re-enacts the F. 98:1
   only when he f.s down 373:5

some tremble and never f. 367:11

tank heaven the ground broke me f. 263:9

things f. apart 417:12

Fallacy: f. of the liberal mind 273:2
   Pathetic F. 4:4
   see also Phallusy

Fallen: f. but hardly frail 300:7
   f. sons of Eve 75:7
   home before the leaves have f. 403:10

Falling: tried to keep them from f. 303:6

Fallow: f. fawns invisible go 370:12

False: all modesty is f. 36:12
   degrees are like f. teeth 350:6
   f. pearls before real swine 115:4
   f. teeth when he was twenty-seven 36:1
   f. thinking brings wrong conduct 183:22
   using f. pretences on dolls 327:8

Falsely: verb . . . 'to believe f.' 408:2

Falsifiability: verifiability but the f. 301.3

Falstaff: too many of his [F's] kind 222:9

Falter: neither to flap nor to f. 245:13

Fame: easier to gain f. than to retain 338:11
   f. is a powerful aphrodisiac 154:10
   f. is rot 26:5
   trying to avoid f. 34:13

Familiarity: f. breeds . . . children 380:10

Families: f. . . . prefer widows 336:15
   good f. are . . . worse off 177:13

Family: appalling dangers of f. life 182:10
   beautiful f. talk 86:16
   educate a whole f. 249:6
   f. had to include . . . delicate child 336:19
   f. is not yet . . . degenerating 121:12
   f. that prays together 338:1
   f. virtues 327:15
   f., with its narrow privacy 225:12
   f. with the wrong members in control 286:20
   I am the f. face 162:19
   incest – a game the whole f. can play 149:15
   lugged into F. Rows 409:14
   man in a f. is appointed to buy meat 10:15
   man who left his f. 379:17
   my f. and other animals 112:11
   no f. will fear for . . . bread 214:34
   royal one-parent f. 296:21
   study of f. portraits 109:21

Famine: as if there were f. in the land 346:11
   bred a fever, and f. grew 369:3

Famished: I hear a f. [famisht] howl 40:1

Famous: become f. without ability 346:4
   everyone . . . f. for fifteen minutes 390:21
   f. fibe 229:11
   f. for a book on Wordsworth 88:15
   f. for being f. 14:15
   f.-last-words . . . death 243:15
   I'm never going to be f. 291:21
   let us now praise f. men 212:27
   mark of many f. people 169:1
   stand about looking f. 244:2
   those f. men of old, the Ogres 151:20

Fan: f. vaulting . . . enthusiasm 220:4

Fanatic: f. does what he thinks 111:20
    f. is a great leader 56:5
Fanaticism: f. . . . redoubling your effort 335:7
    to ban books is f. 341:21
Fancied: he [W.H.Auden] just fancied him 10:8
Fanclub: f. with only two fans 169:20
Fancy: all I get is f. stuff 296:15
    little of what you f. does you good 228:6
    managers in f. dress 239:21
Fancy-men: bearers . . . from her f. 163:2
Fanfare: f., but it wasn't one of mine 390:18
Fanlight: f. in your mind 236:12
Fanny: F. by gaslight 331:9
Fantasies: fed the hearts on f. 417:1
Far: f. are the shades of Arabia 102:20
    how f. one can go too f. 85:4
Far-off: f., . . . and inviolate rose 417:14
Faraway: quarrel in a f. country 71:18
Farce: f. as inverted poetry 306:3
    f. is . . . more true to . . . life 270:10
    f. is the essential theatre 94:25
    f. . . . theatre of the surrealist 37:20
    Parliament is the longest running f. 350:3
    what makes f. funny 133:4
    wine was a f. 304:1
Fare: not f. well, but f. forward 117:8
Farewell: be ahead of all f.s 319:12
    f. my friends, I am going to glory 111:10
Farm: work on Maggie's F. 113:17
Farmer: like a red-faced f. 181:5
    three jolly f.s once bet a pound 103:17
    to the f.'s children you beckon 17:7
Farmhouse: burnt down his f. 135:20
    f.s with their white faces 44:5
Farmyard: distinguish human society from the f. 343:12
    f. civilization of the Fabians 186:6
    I might have been a f. hen 20:8
Farnsworth, Philo T.: if it weren't for F. 69:1
Fart: f. and chew gum at the same time 196:3
    f. and you stand alone 155:16
Farther: look f. than you can see 82:4
Farting: f. through silk 266:7
Fascination: f. of what's difficult 416:6
    f. which . . . expression 408:1
Fascism: bold experiment of F. 57:13
    F. is not an article for export 275:8
    F. . . . is the future 41:18
    F. means war 361:25
Fascist: F. objective 287:9
Fashion: conscience to fit this year's f.s 169:5
    true to you, darlin', in my f. 301:12
Fast: f. as the stars are slow 370:12
    none so f. as stroke 85:17
Faster: they simply sleep f. 104:21
Fastidious: mind of a few f. people 351:7
Fat: all f. women look the same 17:1
    f. is a feminist issue 285:8
    f. man demanding elbow-room 392:25
    f. man should not play the concertina 250:19
    f. man trying to get in 401:20

imprisoned in every f. man 88:24
O f. white woman whom nobody loves 93:4
outside every f. man 7:14
thin man inside every f. man 286:14
till the f. lady sings 89:19
your cake and eat it; . . . you get f. 25:15
Fatal: collected lists of f. diseases 168:13
    most f. complaint 172:8
Fatalist: I am not a f.; even if I were 296:20
Fatally: f. poor and dingy 399:17
Fate: become the makers of our f. 301:5
    f. wrote her a . . . tragedy 30:10
    their f. must always be the same 18:22
    we know the f. of none 40:2
Father: after all, I'm your f. 28:18
    bed fell on my f. 372:21
    dreading to find its F. 17:13
    f. entirely out of the way 189:1
    f. of the arrow is the thought 215:10
    f.'s love from faltering 409:4
    from her f. – he's a plastic surgeon 253:20
    generation revolts against its f.s 274:1
    God is . . . an exalted f. 134:9
    if he's on my f.'s side 253:10
    if . . . the f. cannot teach the son 174:1
    men liking their f.s 49:11
    mothers and f.s throughout the land 113:23
    my f. . . . had a likely son 178:23
    my f.s can have it 370:5
    neither f. nor lover 321:7
    not to go about her f.'s business 346:20
    one of your f.'s crimes 123:20
    Our F. that art in heaven, stay there 305:7
    problem in finding a lost f. 26:30
    substitute for the f. 134:8
    told the truth about his f. 36:13
    victory finds a hundred f.s 82:23
    what's the f. up to? 305:6
    you did have a f.? 286:4
Father-lands: Europe of the f. 102:5
Fatherhood: mirrors and f. are abominable 47:1
Fathering: sister to the f. worm 368:20
Fatigue: f. makes women talk more 232:16
Fattening:: illegal, immoral, or f. 413:5
Fatty: f. degeneration of the conscience 186:17
Faubourg: f. Saint-Patrice 198:14
Fauce: mixplace his f.s 198:3
Faulkner, William 169:14
Fault: f.s in people I know 98:4
    f.s of his mistress 306:18
    fix you up with the f.s they had 221:15
    it has only one fault 373:9
    meet Winston you see all his f. 240:6
Favour: what you can ask as a f. 86:11
Fawn: fallow f.s invisible go 370:12
Fe: la f. sin la duda 382:2
Fear: belief is an indication of f. 217:22
    can she who shines so calm be f.? 44:6
    f., . . . and ambition look ahead 232:12
    F. and the Muse stand watch 4:11
    f. in a handful of dust 118:2

f. of death and f. of life 258:13
f. of hell is hell 143:13
freedom from f. 322:23
he is F., O little hunter 212:26
heroism . . . indistinguishable from f. 249:26
never f. to negotiate 204:18
perfect f. casteth out love 89:3
stars in sudden f. 418:18
thing we have to f. is f. itself 322:10
why f. death? 134:13
Feared: f. rather than loved 328:5
its most f. enemies within 327:18
who would be loved if he could be f. 302:9
Fearful: less f. of the certain grave 253:28
Fearfully: so f. wide of the mark 300:10
Feasibility: barest requirements of f. 243:9
Feast: Paris is a moveable f. 169:9
Feather: f. pate of folly 179:33
keep all your f.s in the air 102:12
like the f. pillow, he bears the mark 158:5
Feather-bed: f. of correctitude 37:10
Feather-footed: f. through the plashy fen 392:29
Feature: f.s hold them [readers] 281:14
f.s of every ancestor 389:7
February: most serious charge is . . . F. 218:4
Fed: f. the hearts on fantasies 417:1
Fee: answered as they took their f.s 32:13
Feeding: f. the mouth that bites you 105:9
prevents you from f. yourself 364:5
Feel: good as you're going to f. all day 112:9
man is as old as the woman he f.s 253:13
Feelies: going to the F. this evening 182:9
Feeling: can't put things out of his f.s 70:4
disguise our f. pretty well 93:11
f. from a TV set 141:19
f. is bad form 130:6
know what the f. is 418:3
Feet: always land on somebody's f. 292:13
always under your f. 263:32
better to die on your f. 185:1
both f. . . . in the air 322:19, 338:2
few days on your f. 203:16
fog comes on little cat f. 334:17
it tends to make their f. ache 352:3
palms before my f. 74:15
policemen with smaller f. 105:23
put his f. on the table 119:19
stayed to get his f. wet 272:2
suddenly found my f. 36:4
very nice f. and plenty of money 15:10
Fehler: wenn frauen f. machen wollen 202:3
Feigenbaum: F. seit wie lange schon 318:10
Feindschaft: F. ist uns das Nächste 318:5
Felicity: f. on the far side of baldness 351:1
Fell: he f. down a great deal 372:28
Fella: f. belong Mrs Queen 296:12
they think I'm one of the f.s 96:13
Fellow: f.s whom it hurts to think 180:4
Fellow-man: way to love my f. 75:15
Felony: if you've been convicted of a f. 285:11
Female: Britain's two f. figureheads 154:23

faded f. in a damp basement 162:1
f. impersonator in vaudeville 170:4
f. of the species is more deadly 210:18
f. who has an essential languor 400:6
involved with the f. principle 83:5
seldom f. in a world of males 299:14
Feminine: f. in its men 400:11
Feminism: f. is an insurrection 29:12
Feminist: best home for a f. 391:15
didn't set out to be a f. writer 395:8
fat is a f. issue 285:8
f. . . . to pull the chicks 120:15
f. whenever I express sentiments 398:24
triumph of the f. movement 66:28
womanist is to f. 390:6
Femme fatale: f. limb 68:10
Fen: through the plashy f. 392:29
Fence: animal who can sit on the f. 9:18
don't f. me in 301:15
good f.s make good neighbours 135:17
milk through the f. 48:21
nailing his colours . . . to the f. 346:16
sat so long on the f. 236:8
Férreo: un fondo f. 278:19
Ferret: decent box for the f. 88:14
Ferries: twilight f. over the lakes 369:19
Ferryboat: ship's party on a f. 127:14
voice that used to shake the f.s 251:12
Fertile: turtle . . . to be so f. 278:7
Fertilizing: vocabulary needs . . . f. 393:16
Fetched: always went and f. them 264:17
Fetid: f. compartment of the . . . bookshop 26:1
Fetish: superstition and a f. 186:1
Fever: bred a f., and famine grew 369:3
Few: so much owed by so many to so f. 79:19
world will be saved by the f. 143:18
Fibe: famous f. 229:11
Fibre: not quite sure of the f. content 114:6
Fickleness: f. of the woman I love 345:13
Fiction: biography . . . bounded . . . by f. 156:8
biography is ultimately f. 247:19
continuous fiction 41:17
f. a way of making statements 361:14
f. is piss 55:24
f. is to make sex exciting 387:23
f. set to . . . lascivious music 259:5
f. we were required to take on trust 283:1
house of f. has many windows 49:2
life becomes f. and f. life 219:5
more lies than . . . f. 62:10
perhaps we are all f.s 154:2
poetry is the supreme f. 358:12
rest is pure f. 86:8
room . . . if she is to write f. 412:18
Fictional: all f. characters are flat 393:22
new f. characters baptized 218:14
Fiddle: burn while Rome f.s 88:3
communicates to us through his f. 67:13
many a good tune played on an old f. 62:5
Fiddled: f. whisper music 118:16
Field: doctor . . . in the middle of a f. 91:13

floating f.s from the farm 369:19
never in the f. of human conflict 79:19
sleep like f.s of amaranth 102:19
walk through the f.s in gloves 93:4
we shall fight in the f.s 79:15
Fieldmice: f. bawk talk 197:19
Fierce: f. and bald and short of breath 336:29
Fiery: for f. boys that star was set 358:14
Fifteen: acquired before the age of f. 70:15
famous for f. minutes 390:21
f. fingers on the safety catch 245:12
f.-year-old boy till they die 325:10
women [come of age] at f. 358:5
Fifth: f. ace makes all the difference 271:3
f. column will arise 267:5
f. province is not anywhere 320:16
Himmler of the lower f. 312:21
one f. of the people are against 205:14
Fifties: f. the youth of old age 173:22
Fifty: as one approaches f. 171:20
at f. you have the choice 69:12
Fifty-fifty: no f. Americanism 323:11
Fifty-three: law . . . runs north of f. 212:18
Fig-leaf: f. . . . into a price tag 34:15
Fig-tree: f. . . . I have found meaning 318:10
Fight: Believe! Obey! F.! 275:10
best part . . . is the f.s 403:3
end of the f. is a tombstone white 212:7
f. against the fascination 408:1
f. and f. and f. again 138:10
f. in here. This is the War Room 218:7
f. two days in three 32:1
f.s you on patriotic principles 345:8
gets loose when you begin to f. 139:20
go out and f. 284:11
he is dead who will not f. 155:5
I f. on; I f. to win 368:5
longing for a f. 158:4
men . . . f. to impress their mothers 124:11
never f. fair with a stranger 261:21
nor law, nor duty bade me f. 416:17
right and I'll f. for it 407:1
too proud to f. 406:17
we shall f. on the beaches 79:15
Fighting: between two periods of f. 42:21
cherished privilege of the f. man 362:1
first-class f. man 210:21
when we ain't f. 257:9
who dies f. has increase 155:5
Figment: I'd like it to say 'f'. 390:20
Figuration: f. of storks 389:8
Figure: f. in the carpet 190:14
keeping your face or your f. 69:12
wit to leave out the central f. 225:6
Filbert: Gilbert the F. 407:7
File: note the hour – and f. the minute 260:10
Filing: f. is concerned with the past 401:14
f. system has been lost 95:17
watch them f. out 87:14
Fillet: rise in the price of f. steak 83:12
Film: bad f. twice as bad 147:8

f. culture . . . is agitation 171:11
f. is operating with a laser 63:10
f. is the least realistic of art forms 248:9
f. music . . . the same relationship 362:19
great art of f.s 55:15
length of the f. . . . human bladder 172:16
like Jews or Germans or f.s 187:8
worst f.s of all time 352:7
Film-acting: f. is . . . reacting 63:9
Film-making 46:14, 146:15
Filthy: f. unless you've got a degree 180:14
Final: dreads the f. trumpet 163:4
f. argument 285:18
Finality: f. is death 358:4
Finance: f. is . . . passing currency 335:19
'sound' f. . . . depressing influence 207:6
Financial: if only for f. reasons 6:14
nation not in danger of f. disaster 258:9
Finchley: Lord F. tried to mend 33:5
Find: people have to f. out 363:13
Fine: is it f. your way 101:15
Fineness: f. or accuracy of suppression 33:20
Finest: this was their f. hour 79:17
Finger: between my f. and my thumb 166:19
fifteen f.s on the safety catch 245:12
f.-lickin' good 3:9
f. that turns the dial 112:6
f.s are corpse f.s 224:21
f.s at the locks 368:23
f.s he outstretches from [his nose] 29:25
f.s must be educated 71:11
f.s on your own chestnuts 126:1
four of his f.s are pointing 281:4
in danger of losing a couple of f.s 196:10
little f. was like a hook 300:11
nimble f.s are no more nimble 349:7
time we pulled our f. out 296:13
what chills the f. not a bit 278:3
whose f. on the trigger 99:2
Finger nail: relatively clean f.s 270:16
Fingerboard: unexplored regions of the . . . f.
172:10
Fingerprint: f. . . . from being under someone's
thumb 25:1
like f.s, all marriages are different 346:5
Fingertip: through his hair and f.s 117:31
Fings: f. ain't wot they used t'be 281:13
Finish: we will f. the job 79:21
Finished: married. Then he's f. 138:3
Finite: disease is f. 331:1
knowledge can only be f. 301:2
nothing . . . is really f. 356:2
Fire: between the f. brigade and the f. 79:4
brother F. was having his dog's day 117
enter the mind under f. 378:5
every time she shouted 'F.!' 32:24
f. department won't make house calls 331:13
F. Next Time 22:16
f. was furry as a bear 348:19
gentility worth if it can't stand f. 139:21
I didn't f. him 378:20

suffers f.s by . . . making them suffer 160:24
what f.s middle-class girls are 110:14
Fooleries: f. of magic and religion 183:9
Fooling: I'm only f. 283:11
Foolish: anything you do looks f. 174:16
   I, being young and f. 416:3
   less f. than . . . if he thought 329:8
   nothing but f. words 214:2
   these f. things remind me of you 253:26
   to be silly is not to be f. 36:22
Foolproof: manufacturers of f. items 92:6
Foonf: F. speaking 203:5
Foot, Michael 22:13, 99:3
Foot: England and I first set f. 260:22
   f. and nose disease 41:7
   now I hold creation in my f. 181:12
   one f. in the nineteenth century 177:19
Football: f. combines . . . worst things 403:14
   f. is a matter of life and death 342:9
   good excuse not to watch f. 226:15
   I see the world as a f. 230:12
   like opposing f. teams 376:10
   thought that f. was God 304:19
Footfall: f.s echo in the memory 116:24
Footman: eternal f. hold my coat 117:26
Footmark: identify his f.s 330:2
Footnote: f.s to Plato 401:9
Footpath: not even a f. across it 106:11
Footprint: looking for a man's f. 30:16
   my f. . . . are upstairs 252:16
Footstep: He is still dogging my f.s 154:13
Forbid: second-rate theory f.s 215:4
Forbidden: f. fruits, temptation 98:1
   hinting at the f. 17:7
Force: ev'ry member of the f. 321:10
   f. that through the green fuse 369:2
   law for f. 171:15
   may the F. be with you 238:20
   other nations use 'f'. 393:6
Ford, Ford Madox 303:29
Ford, President Gerald: F. is so dumb 196:3
   I am a F. not a Lincoln 129:15
Ford: bridge the f. 212:25
Forebears: thankful to their f. 66:10
Forecastle: crew is gambling in the f. 343:18
Forefathers: lewd f. of the village 356:1
Forehead: tap his f. first 408:11
Foreign: f. stories . . . not *real* news 393:1
   f. swear-word is . . . inoffensive 368:16
   lives in f. parts and corresponds 360:13
   no f. books . . . are only f. readers 305:3
   not be sent into any f. war 322:20
   past is a f. country 165:9
   so f. . . . low down in the Balkans 64:19
   some corner of a f. field 55:5
Foreigner: f.s always spell better 380:2
   f.s speak English 95:15
Foreshortening: angle that makes for f. 151:1
Foreskin: welcome as a sandy f. 316:1
Forest: down in the f. something stirred 348:4
   preceded by f., followed by desert 149:24

unfathomable deep f. 370:9
Foretold: all was f. me 370:10
Forever: day it rained f. 49:21
   I'm f. blowing bubbles 204:7
Forfeited: f. the confidence 51:22
Forge: f. in the smithy of my soul 198:8
Forged: Britain that is going to be f. 406:1
Forget: change and f. to tell each other 169:6
   do not quite f. 75:1
   don't f. the diver 203:4
   f. both pairs of glasses 277:25
   f. everything traditional 374:4
   f. not bees in winter 331:7
   f. . . . such a thing as tolerance 406:24
   f. the outside world 352:22
   f. to pull your zipper down 324:12
   f. what I was taught 400:13
   f.s where he buried a hatchet 181:1
   hesitates to forget its founders 401:12
   lest we f. 212:15
   never f. their names 205:15
   not what old men f. 240:5
   one f.s words as one f.s names 393:16
   painting is a way to f. life 325:13
   prepared to f. it 129:3
   remember as accurately as he f.s 277:21
   singing bird f.s its cage 265:13
   sort that men f. 163:20
   they [infants] never f. 110:12
   thing I will never entirely f. 75:12
   three things I always f. 363:9
   wise forgive but do not f. 364:6
   you f. the good God 328:4
Forgetting: f. to balance the books 90:2
Forgivable: few books are f. 219:7
Forgive: f. me they were delicious 404:28
   f. your enemies but never forget 205:15
   I cannot f. my friends for dying 350:15
   people who can never f. a beggar 217:18
   stupid neither f. nor forget 364:6
   woman . . . never forgive sacrifices 256:15
Forgiveness: knowledge, what f.? 117:13
Forgotten: child's f. mornings 369:11
   f. man at the bottom 322:8
   should at least have f. it [Latin] 255:13
   what has been learnt has been f. 349:18
Fork: bud that f.s her eye 369:6
   caught you using the wrong f. 410:11
   f. in his inexperienced hand 396:21
   f. in the other [hand] 231:14
Forkbender: Harold and Lady F. 186:27
Form: passionate apprehension of f. 31:15
   significant f. 31:14
   strive . . . to give our life its f. 307:18
Formative: f. intellectual matrices 155:19
Formerly: not what we were f. told 44:10
Forming: time you took f. yourself 93:19
Formula: f. for describing what happens 328:18
Fornicate: f. between clean sheets 136:23
Fornicated: f. and read the papers 65:8
Fornication: for f. what Eisenhower did 165:8

garment for f. and diarrhoea 254:22
war and f., . . . not interesting 273:1
Forster, E.M.: F. never gets any further 250:5
same gods as themselves and F. 110:14
trouble began with F. 59:11
Forsyte: no F. has as yet died 139:15
Fortescue, Charles Augustus 32:10
Forties: f. are the old age of youth 173:22
Fortissimo: at last, f.! 247:5
Fortnight: came for a f.; I have stayed 260:22
Fortune: f. into a shoestring 413:7
good f. to others 42:10
if you want to make a f. 64:10
makes a wheel – or a f. 44:19
Fortune-teller: f.s to metaphysics 217:13
Forty: every man over f. is a scoundrel 345:6
f. and get no nearer a real grief 202:18
just turning f. and taking my time 235:11
life begins at f. 299:13, 379:11
nobody loves a fairy when she's f. 169:19
Forty-two: Universe and Everything is F. 1:13
Forum: on the way to the F. 347:3
Forward: he usually blunders f. 115:3
history is lived f. 394:8
looking f. to the past 288:4
not fare well, but fare f. 117:8
step f. . . . step . . . to the end 218:15
Forward-looking: f. politicians 265:22
Found: criminal . . . by getting f. out 225:11
f. is always lost again 174:2
Foundation: firm f. of unyielding despair 328:19
unshakable the f.s 377:25
Founder: forget its f.s 401:12
Founding: robbing a bank compared to f. 51:19
Fount, white f.s falling in the courts 74:20
Fountain: some rob you with a . . . f. pen 157:4
Four: f. be the thing 291:1
f. sides to every issue 340:14
one in every f. people is Chinese 168:22
Four-footed: parody on all f. things 74:14
Four-leaf: I'm looking over a f. clover 107:7
Four-letter: only sort of f. words I use 90:5
Fourteenth: f. Mr Wilson 109:3
Fourth: mother needed a f. at meals 234:6
Fowler: net of an inhuman f. 206:10
Fox: crazy like a f. 295:2
hare better than that of the f. 44:14
little f., he murmured 416:11
set a f. to watching chickens 378:19
Fox-hunting: f. – the wisest religion 158:8
good sense of f. society 83:9
inferior . . . f. 392:11
Fraction: short words and vulgar f.s 80:14
Fragile: we are essentially f. 22:4
Fragment: to carry his f.s away 12:15
Frail: fallen but hardly f. 300:7
too f. a thread to hang history 359:13
you will be f. and musty 290:11
France: all the r.s lead to F. 370:16
[Clemenceau] had one illusion – F. 206:11
culture belongs to F. 95:25

five [years ago] in F. 368:12
F. . . . a lot of French horns 24:5
F. . . . can't tear the toilet paper 402:13
F. has lost a battle . . . not the war 141:7
hats off to F. 325:12
never F. when she fights for herself 248:6
step over it [F.] to get anywhere 269:21
thought of F. in a certain way 141:5
une certaine idée de la F. 141:5
Francis of Assisi, St: I think I'm F. 291:18
Franco, General: 173:16, 382:8
not just a female F. 166:14
Franglais: parlez-vous F.? 121:6
Frank: f. words in our respective languages 89:21
Frappé: slightly *f.* silence 410:6
Fraud: great men of history are f.s 45:10
Freak: I want out of the f. show 214:28
Freckle: love, curiosity, f.s, and doubt 291:1
Free: best things in life are f. 104:8
Christianity promises to make men f. 186:12
everybody favours f. speech 56:4
f. verse . . . playing tennis 136:7
I am not a number – I am a f. man 251:2
man is condemned to be f. 336:1
mother of the f. 37:14
safer to be in chains than to be f. 200:12
so that they can f. the other half 290:5
sons of the f. 112:14
soul in prison, I am not f. 102:6
there remain a dead man and a f. man 336:26
tried, in my way to be f. 85:12
trouble about a f. market economy 14:11
truth that makes men f. 4:2
why does f. love cost so much? 12:9
Free-loader: f. is a confirmed guest 327:7
Free-range: f. womb 56:1
Freedom: elbow-room, with f. of talk 190:10
enemies of f. do not argue 186:4
essential quality of life – f. 134:18
four essential f.s 322:23
f. and organization 159:13
f. for some 18:27
f. for the one who thinks differently 239:9
f. is an indivisible word 405:4
f. is slavery 286:23
f. is . . . the distance 99:12
f. of conscience 380:1
f. of speech 380:1
f. of the press . . . who own one 234:4
f., the second of man's creeds 225:5
f. there will be no state 228:16
f. to be fully awake 134:15
f. to starve 139:14
f.'s just another word for nothin' 218:1
glow in Old Glory and the free in f. 278:22
if society fits . . . you call it f. 136:11
is something a blow against f. 239:20
no easy walk to f. 248:14
O f., what liberties are taken 142:8
only f. can make security secure 301:6
they took away my liberty, not my f. 203:18

together we can do for the f. of man 204:20
took my f. away a long time ago 352:14
unless f. is universal 171:22
what stands if f. fall? 210:20
Freelance 35:7
Freemasonry: women . . . have a . . . f. 30:29
Freeze: your justice would f. beer 261:18
Frei: Arbeit macht f. 19:24
French 92:2
distinguishes them from F. girls 385:7
Englishman is about to talk F. 409:17
finest F. novel in . . . English 321:6
F. [actresses are] clever daughters 161:8
F. are very badly fitted 213:25
F. arrange 70:14
F. cook: we open tins 139:22
F. don't even put on their postcards 177:15
F. five minutes 31:23
F. needed only to paint a vegetable 2:16
F. operas sung be Swedish artists 399:11
F. order and clarity 52:1
F. . . . poodles to the Germans 318:2
F. tipple all the time 96:9
good because cooked by the F. 108:16
good taste of the F. 99:5
Heaven is where the cooks are F. 9:23
how would you say that in F.? 312:22
if the F. were German 201:2
if the F. were to play cricket 123:7
if you can see the F. coast 300:17
imagine the Lord talking F.! 101:9
liver, doted upon by the F. 341:12
may be tolerated by the F. 267:21
some are fond of F. 254:1
something fishy about the F. 93:16
something Vichy about the F. 282:1
speak quite bad F. very well 197:7
trust the F. to touch the nerve 90:4
we die F. 393:13
French Revolution 47:17, 420:9
Frenchies: those F. seek him everywhere 285:10
Frenchman: F., seeing another F. 339:16
F. [thinks] standing 285:1
Frenchmen: fifty million F. can be wrong 156:11
F. drink wine like we . . . drink water 221:2
F. in the image of Englishmen 80:2
F. to exhibit talent 95:25
Frenzy: never loved the f. of the sun 206:9
Fresh: f. air . . . in its proper place 241:3
Fret: I should only f. 86:16
Fretting: f. for their decay 324:10
Freud, Sigmund: F. felt that it should be limited to
    women 6:8
I felt quite funny when F. died 192:19
if F. had worn a kilt 59:10
old, flustered F. 276:15
trouble with F. 107:16
Freude: Kraft durch F. 233:20
Freudian: in analysis with a strict F. 5:20
Friday: by F. I've got seven pairs on 358:6
on F., eats only fishermen 237:20

Friend: among their enemies' best f.s 312:15
answer, my f. is blowin' in the wind 113:8
betraying my f. 131:1
breaking it [name] in for a f. 253:23
change your f.s 141:13
closest f.s – and if they seem okay 220:9
come round the corner to look for a f. 264:12
diamonds are a girl's best f. 320:10
enemy unless he proves a f. 339:16
even your best f. won't tell you 3:7
farewell my f.s, I am going to glory 111:10
f. . . . comes to hear your lectures 49:5
f. in need is a f. to be avoided 334:12
f. who loved perfection 350:17
f. whom one definitely dislikes 182:13
f.s are God's apology for relations 208:19
f.s . . . got there first 383:9
f.s-in-law 401:16
f.s to borrow my books 320:12
funerals of our f.s 51:27
his f.s were very good to him 32:14
how to win f.s and influence people 68:3
I cannot forgive my f.s for dying 350:15
I don't trust him. We're f.s 51:7
I have lost f.s 412:21
I let down my f.s 281:2
I might give my life for my f. 350:22
is there then no f. 351:5
laughter and the love of f.s 32:27
lay down his f.s for his life 371:12
like heart-breaking new f.s 205:18
man's f. likes him but leaves him 77:6
much-loved and elegant f. 73:5
nearly deceiving all your f.s 60:17
nearly deceiving your f.s 93:2
never explain – your f.s do not need it 180:21
not a f. . . . an employer 403:6
not quite my f.s 401:16
of the two, the f. is the nicer 22:5
only seeing the King and a few f.s 16:1
paint a portrait I lose a f. 335:18
people are f.s in spots 335:12
Plato and Plotinus for a f. 417:24
praise of one's f.s is 252:3
rises on the backs of his f.s 181:7
robed in the long f.s 369:15
tavern for his f.s 109:2
tell whether a stranger is your f. 130:24
to the gardener that time is a f. 279:14
whenever a f. succeeds 387:16
with a little help from my f.s 230:9
worst f. and enemy is but death 55:3
yourself and a f., if you have one 82:22
Friendliness: impersonal insensitive f. 392:22
wanted friendship and got f. 247:21
Friendly: f. country choosing our enemies 282:6
O dreamy, gloomy, f. trees 377:5
so f. and so large 18:6
uncorseted, her f. bust 118:18
Friendship: great Newberry Fruit of f. 90:17
Fright: bad one in a hell of a f. 69:21

491

Frighten: in the street and f. the horses 64:20
Frightened: why should you be f.? 394:3
Frightening: nothing is . . . f. 357:6
Frightfulness: f. is not a remedy 79:3
Frigid: f. upon the fundament 278:3
  states are f. monsters 141:12
Fringe: lunatic f. 323:12
Frivolity: how precious is f. 130:8
Frivolous: German . . . are the most f. 234:20
Frock: her f.s are built in Paris 333:1
Froid: états sont les monstres f.s 141:12
Front: never heard to which f. 288:22
Frontier: f. . . . as large as the world 420:4
  f.s of our little state 200:6
  on the edge of a new f. 204:15
Frost, Robert 4:12
Frosty: scribble . . . the f. sagas 94:28
Frown: persistent troubled f. 371:17
Frozen: locked and f. in each eye 17:17
  religion is the f. thought of men 217:24
Frucht: hinein in die zeitig entschlossene F. 318:10
Frugal: mother was f. in her habits 286:4
Frugality: f. only . . . a virtue 48:1
Frühling: F. ist wiedergekommen 319:7
Fruit: f. . . . acquire the bitter taste 106:15
  f. of memory 89:5
Fruitful: be f. and multiply 6:23, 186:7
  renewal is f. 362:13
Frustration: age of f. 293:6
Fry, Roger: dear F. whom I . . . detest 252:2
Frying: anyone who can pick up a f. pan 60:1
  fish that talks in the f. pan 102:16
  f. pan's too wide 266:2
  omelette without f. eggs 102:13
  spoilt the best f. pan we ever had 188:10
Fuchsia: f. drenched with rain 4:6
Fuck: fish f. in it 125:9
  they f. you up, your mum and dad 221:15
  zipless f. is the purest thing 197:1
Fucked: really f. up everything 346:20
Fucking: all this cold-hearted f. 223:16
  come between 'Hi' and f. 236:17
  f. a porcupine 267:3
  f. for chastity 149:6
Fudge: first mouthful of hot f. sundae 265:14
Fudging: fed up with f. and mudging 288:12
Fuel: gathering f. in vacant lots 117:35
Führer: principle of the F.'s function 90:21
  purer F. 9:19
  will of the F. 132:6
Fulfil: f. it better himself 90:21
Fulfilment: every f. is slavery 65:21
  however much the f. may be complicated 76:24
Full: f. up years ago 408:18
Fullness: f. of the full 379:5
Full-stop: death is a f. 283:10
  f. put just at the right place 21:1
  ten ploughed fields, like ten f.s 254:8
Fullstoppers: f. and semi-colonials 197:14
Fulminating: f. from the pulpit 395:4
Fume: captured f. of space 94:27

Fun: ain't we got f. 201:10
  and for the f. of the thing 108:17
  burning of heretics – f., f., f. 395:4
  f. to be in the same decade 323:1
  I wish I thought *What jolly f.* 311:9
  if one's own kin and kith were more f. 277:13
  most f. I've ever had without laughing 5:18
  no reference to f. in any Act 170:30
  nothing more f. than a man 291:2
  now I must pay for my f. 211:12
  sitting inside making f. of you 66:9
  where the real f. starts 376:14
  work is much more f. than f. 94:18
Fundament: frigid upon the f. 278:3
Fundamental: f. desire to take . . . courses 48:18
  f. things apply 182:3
  I regard consciousness as f. 299:18
Funeral: as if you were off to a f. supper 50:22
  attended his f. . . . to make sure 10:22
  everlasting f. marches round 261:17
  f. of our friends we grieve for 51:27
  if you don't go to other men's f.s 101:10
  nice things . . . at their f.s 203:23
Funny: being sane . . . knowing what's funny 7:17
  f. because I had said it 76:27
  f. . . . happening to somebody else 321:22
  f. old world 125:3
  f. peculiar, or f. ha-ha? 166:2
  f. thing . . . on the way to the Forum 347:3
  f. thing . . . on the way to the grave 95:20
  f. thing . . . on the way to the White House 359:4
  if it bends it's f. 5:23
  isn't it f. how a bear likes honey? 264:22
  monstrous aunt can be f. 383:5
Fur: all f. and wool 369:32
Furious: f. that she had not been asked 393:10
  she seems f. all day 164:10
Furnace: being thrown into the f. 33:24
Furnish: duty is to f. it well 383:17
Furnished: live in f. souls 97:29
Furniture: alone . . . without furniture 303:29
  don't bump into the f. 94:22
  previous f. passes in front of them 337:21
Furrow: plough my own f. alone 324:3
Furry: fire was f. as a bear 348:19
Further: always a little f. 128:13
  f. away than anywhere else 312:10
Fury: no f. like an ex-wife 88:19
  no fury like a non-combatant 267:17
Fuse: force that through the green f. 369:2
Fusion: f. with a corpse 295:16
Fuss: minimum of f. and no explanation 44:16
Fussy: nobody . . . could call me a f. man 264:11
Future: does not pay to the f. 300:16
  door opens and lets the f. in 154:6
  empires of the f. 80:4
  face anything except the f. 53:2
  f. is not what it was 9:5
  f. is propaganda 53:5
  F. . . . our affairs prosper 42:16

f. refusing to be born 41:18
f. shock 374:12
f. we awaited so anxiously 145:18
link between the present and the f. 206:19
man with a great f. behind him 69:7
much f. for the Americans 173:20
never place one's trust in the f. 72:4
only certain thing about the f. 174:19
orgastic f. that . . . recedes 126:20
our f. is on the water 403:9
past projected on to the f. 185:5
prose in our f. 53:17
remember the f. 277:5
Russia will . . . inherit the f. 223:26
seen the f. – it was being repaired 64:3
seen the f. and it does not work 376:6
seen the f. and it works 357:2
skipping . . . the f. tense 401:17
time f. contained in time past 116:23
to see again has to do with the f. 401:14
want to be masters of the f. 218:12
we have no f. 45:15
who controls the past controls the f. 286:26
Fuzzy-Wuzzy: 'ere's to you, F. 210:21

G

Gable, Clark 181:4
Gable: eyes in the g. see 368:23
Gabor, Zsa-Zsa: [G.] not only worships the Golden
    Calf 231:7
Gadarene: this man . . . is the G. Swine 214:23
Gael: great G.s of Ireland 74:10
Gaelic: Yer G. . . . it's no good to 'em 354:10
Gai: toujours g. toujours g. 251:3
Gaiety: only concession to g. 370:24
Gain: there are no g.s without pains 358:21
Gaitskell, Hugh 41:11
Gal: laziest g. in town 301:20
Gallant: g. if muddle-headed girl 299:4
    very g. gentleman 16:11
Gallienne: if you call Le G. a minor poet 251:25
Gallon: you can get a couple of g. in it 70:17
Galloping: g. across open country 413:2
    g. obsolescence 35:18
Gallows: g. in my garden 74:6
    laws as simple as the g. 294:3
Gallows Hill: from G. to Tineton Copse 254:8
Galsworthy, John 398:25
Gamble: life is a g., at terrible odds 361:3
    sheriff sun and rustlers moon g. 260:12
Gambling: croupiers in a crooked g. house 175:20
Game: big g. is hanging in the balance 144:10
    but how you played the g. 316:6
    dread of g.s 40:22
    g. at which two can play 30:26
    g. of the eye and the mind 297:16
    parody is a g. 276:11
    return g. between a man and his stars 28:24

skin g. 139:20
so the g. is ended 178:23
Gamekeeper: g. below [the waist] 89:4
    g.'s letters first 377:8
Gamesmanship: g. or the art of winning 302:19
Gamut: g. of her emotions from A to B 292:19
Gandhi, Mahatma: costs to keep the old man [G.]
    in poverty 272:13
Gangster: nations have always acted like g.s 218:5
    rival g.s with . . . tommyguns 243:17
Gangsterism: g. is . . . assimilation 107:15
Gaol: half . . . would be in g. 378:20
    woman's place was in the g. 50:4
Gap: g. between what is said 164:9
    g. in the market 3:31
    old age, . . . last g. but one 400:15
Gaping: g. silken dragon 151:10
Garbage: all the g. is on television 6:18
    living in a g. dump 73:9
Garbo, Greta 67:9
    G. gave cinema the sacredness of mass 123:19
    one sees in G. sober 380:27
Garden: doorstep to the weeded g. 371:8
    everything in the g.'s lovely 164:21
    fairies at the bottom of our g. 137:19
    g. . . . is not looking at its best 110:17
    g. of the West 87:13
    gallows in my g. 74:6
    g.s, ponds, palings, the creation 293:9
    men going into their own back g. 237:18
    nearer to God's heart in a g. 156:24
    nothing grows in our g. 369:26
    she bathed in her still g. 358:16
    weed the g., wind the clock 18:30
Garden-Suburb: G. ethos 226:10
Gardener: g., Time 107:10
    half a proper g.'s work 210:25
    nor does a nursery g. scent his roses 85:8
    only to the g. that time is a friend 279:14
    will come the G. in white 128:10
Gardening: g. and desk diaries 91:15
    g. is not a rational act 16:17
Gare: you can't say au-dessus de sa g. 312:22
Garlic: no such thing as a little g. 21:10
    passed on . . . of an overdose of g. 333:20
Garret: starve in a g. with a man 127:18
Garter: G. . . . to keep a woman 42:17
    he ended . . . a knight of the g. 16:15
Gas: g. smells awful 291:8
    g. was on in the Institute 40:17
Gas-chamber: g.s to accommodate two thousand
    175:14
Gas-mask: digging trenches and trying on g.s
    71:18
Gaslight: Fanny by g. 331:9
Gate: fighting for the g.s of heaven 234:5
    g.s to the glorious 130:13
    knocks at the g. 365:4
    man who stood at the g. of the year 165:12
    pray for children at the g. 116:22
    sprouting despondently at area g. 117:30

Gathered: g. flowers are dead 128:10
two or three are g. together 275:3
Gaullist: G. only little by little 141:11
Gave: I never g. away anything 55:16
Gay: g. and warty lads 418:5
I'd rather be black than g. 298:13
sad person's view of a g. person 96:2
we're g. and we're proud 12:7
Gear: time's winged chariot changing g. 234:16
Gebild: schlägt sich erdachtes G. vor 318:15
Gedichte: wie ein Kind, das G. weiss 319:7
Gee-string: g. of very respectable dimensions 69:6
Geheimnis: drängst dein reines G. 318:10
Gemessent: Zeit da man nach mir g. 269:6
Gene: nuclear waste fades your g.s 149:28
selfish g. 101:6
General: at . . . four . . . we're all g.s 383:18
dead battles, like dead g.s 379:8
g. economy 114:12
G.s . . . too old . . . to go to war 351:17
not against the law for g.s 378:20
not the job of a g. to be winning 24:20
recognize the g. 413:3
too important to be left the g.s 84:11
weakness of strong g.s 144:12
worthy G. as 'that most immoral man' 210:5
General Motors: good for G. and vice versa 405:9
not if it means offending G. 176:10
Generating: g. interpretations 114:7
Generation: dying g.s 417:9
first of the last g. 357:14
g. gives the next g. advice 44:3
g. revolts against its fathers 274:1
g. that stayed up all night 373:7
lost g. 357:17, 373:7
problems reproduce themselves from g. to g.
197:4
this really is a beat g. 205:21
torch has been passed to a new g. 204:16
Generosity: do without g. 65:14
true g. consists in fighting 133:8
Genetic: mechanism for the g. material 95:8
Genitals: different attitude to g. 59:10
Genius: g. . . . best understand the ideas 307:5
g. . . . has two great ideas 54:4
g. is in the planet's blood 388:14
g. is one per cent inspiration 115:2
g. of the last generation 145:7
G. . . . reaction against one.s training 38:2
g. . . . to move in the opposite direction 339:15
g. what man possesses 11:3
g. which does what it must 25:6
g. with the IQ of a moron 387:25
g. without talent is nothing 385:8
I think like a g. 276:9
in every . . . g. a pseudo-g. 386:2
Ireland is . . . full of g. 230:16
organizing g. 41:9
talent instantly recognizes g. 110:11
took to be a mark of g. 38:8
unless one is a g. 177:9

what a g., that Picasso 71:8
what a g. the Labour Party has 70:6
Geniuses: g. are the luckiest of mortals 19:12
Genre: writer not a g. 116
Genteel: whole system of g. behaviour 300:11
Gentes: g. and laitymen 197:14
Gentile: g. . . . who orders pints in pubs 188:13
such boastings as the G.s use 212:16
Gentility: what's g. worth 139:21
Gentleman: every other inch a g. 399:2
g. farmer who raises goose-flesh 39:1
g. from . . . the artist 392:6
g.. I live by robbing the poor 344:14
g. . . . knows how to play the bagpipes 390:15
g. need not know Latin 255:13
g. whom we know slightly 186:5
g. . . . won't hesitate 256:1
g. . . . wouldn't hit a woman 5:14
he's a g.: look at his boots 345:15
if we are a g. not to think of (sh) 97:12
not quite a g. 15:2
not the sort of attire for a g. 342:11
so particularly the English g. 191:2
such a nice old g. 173:14
tea . . . is a g. at least 75:10
very gallant g. 16:11
what a g. is to a gent 23:12
would not even then have been a g. 288:9
Gentleman-Rankers: g. out on the spree 210:24
Gentlemen: all the members were g. 376:16
g. always seem to remember blondes 237:7
g. trying to be lawyers 265:23
government of g. 145:15
three jolly g., in coats of red 103:8
while the g. go by 212:21
women . . . difficult to behave like g. 244:3
Gentleness: g. is biological 368:8
g. of her spirit 190:9
her ways are ways of g. 355:20
Gents: g., I loved them 290:10
Genuinely: g. bogus 165:14
Genuineness: g. only thrives in the dark 183:10
Geographical: g. change . . . does not work 39:18
Geography: g. is about maps 37:16
g. of one's own nature 48:11
g. spares them the immediate experience 78:13
Geometry: g. is not true, it is advantageous 299:9
g. of light 102:8
George St: G. he was for England 74:18
George the Third: G. ought never to have occured
37:18
George V 40:10
G. . . . would never have died 16:2
George: G. – don't do that 155:2
somebody had called him G. 17:14
Georgian: Bankers Georgian 220:3
German: all the G.s were warlike and mean 228:2
conductors of G. bands 349:10
creation of the G. spirit 375:5
don't let's be beastly to the G.s 93:17
G. in a forest 66:6

G. is someone who cannot tell a lie 2:19
G. philosophers are the most frivolous 234:20
G. racket . . . to take over . . . Europe 318:2
G.s. . . . will end by ruining ou idea 275:9
G.s classify 70:14
G.s . . . compelled to live 377:22
G.s . . . not brave enough to be afraid 151:3
G.s painted their dream 2:16
good or bad, like Jews or G.s or films 187:8
how . . . thorough these G.s 183:13
if the French were G. 201:2
Switzerland, speaking pure G. 270:2
Winston Churchill is a bigger danger than the
   G.s 126:4
we G.s . . . decent attitude 172:9
what do the G.s call shepherds? 92:8
where the engineers are G. 9:23
Germanic: G. life . . . ebbing away 223:21
Germany 80:5, 141:17, 243:6
   combating un-American activities in G. 168:8
   defeat of G. means the defeat of Japan 323:3
   G. . . . prize professional nation 406:21
   G., the Nazis came for the Communists 280:5
   G. was rearming and we must rearm 23:10
   if . . . G. is winning 378:14
   offering G. too little . . . too late 279:1
   this country is at war with G. 72:1
Geruchs-Orgel: Plamström baut sich eine G. 269:9
Gespenst: es gibt ein G. das frisst Taschentücher
   269:8
Gestirn: wer stellt es ins G. 318:6
Gesture: g. bound by personality 342:1
   only two g.s 143:21
Getting: Gospel of G. On 345:12
Getty, Paul: G. . . . to turn the gas off 231:17
Ghastly: g. good taste 41:5
Ghetto: arts g. in which poetry is kept 165:4
Ghetto: ruines du g. 120:17
Ghost: can g.s be angry? 104:5
   crowds of g.s among the trees 337:8
   g. continent 116:10
   g. stories written for g.s 5:5
   g. that eats handkerchiefs 269:8
   g. that got into our house 372:24
   g.s have taken their places 44:5
   g.s with rifles 68:11
   know whether I believe in g.s 251:3
   like g.s at cockcrow 377:10
Giaconda: throwing a rapid G. at him 182:24
Giant: awakened a sleeping g. 415:1
   bare like nude g. girls 355:3
   [Victorians] were lame g.s 77:26
   when the war of the g.s is over 81:22
Gideon Bible: G.s only in the bedrooms 269:12
Gielgud, John: Mr G. had the most meaningless
   legs 56:10
Gift: deed of g. was many deeds of war 135:13
   g. horse in the mouthfulness 316:12
   g. of oneself 12:21
   g. that can be withdrawn 217:1
Gig lamp: life is not a series of g.s 412:5

Gilbert: G., the Filbert 407:7
Gilded: g. tomb of a mediocre talent 350:20
   invite with g. edges 18:24
Gin: ask if g. will make the [ties] run 127:10
   drinking g. in the lowest kind of inn 74:22
   g. was mother's milk to her 345:20
   hair as white as g. 70:18
   little drops of g. 9:27
   no need for g. and tonic 20:7
   sooner we can get out the g. 314:16
   wages of g. is breath 171:7
   worse g. than . . . when he was single 259:11
Ginger: G., you're barmy! 274:17
   hitting empty g. ale bottles 372:19
   only one that has any g. in it 345:18
Gipper: win just one for the G. 144:10, 313:13
Gipsies: class of their own, like . . . g. 52:5
Gipsy: time, you old g. man 175:13
Giraffe: he [God] invented the g. 297:8
   man who believes in g.s 265:15
Girdle: helps you with your g. 277:26
Girl: diamonds are a g.'s best friend 320:10
   even smart g.s do it 333:16
   giant g.s that have no secret 355:3
   gifted g.s married impossible men 151:26
   g. throwing a ball 412:20
   g. to believe in him 324:14
   g.'s thin laughter 317:15
   g.s who do 262:15
   give me a g. at an impressionable age 354:3
   if g.s aren't ignorant, they're cultured 91:1
   if you were the only g. in the world 155:7
   nicest g.s I was ever engaged to 410:21
   poor little rich g. 93:21
   prevent g.s from being g.s 177:10
   see how g. with wax faces live 402:18
   still hear a pretty g. 373:8
   who needs a whole g. 53:18
   young g.s picked them every one 340:12
   your rate is half a g. in twenty 175:16
Girlish: April, laugh thy g. laughter 391:19
Girl's Own Paper: nothing to touch the G. 287:18
Give: g. us [gizza] a job 43:18
   I can't g. you anything but love 124:13
Giving: g. each year more than he steals 279:14
Gizza: g. job, go on gizzit! 43:18
Glacier: g. knocks in the cupboard 18:5
Glad: May month flaps its g. green leaves 162:5
   or are you just g. to see me? 398:8
   you know you should be g. 230:5
Gladness: dicing time for g. casts a moan 162:17
   g. of her g. 26:15
   snatch g. from the days 257:16
Gladstone, William Ewart 362:4
   G. always having the ace of trumps 219:1
   G. read Homer for fun 80:20
   G. . . . spent his declining years 341:8
Glamour: to take the sex out of g. 67:18
Glance: nothing can stay my g. 415:8
   O brightening g. 415:10
Gland: Lord Nelson had a swollen g. 112:12

Glasgow: G. belongs to me 137:18
  G. . . . nobody imagines living 152:19
  great thing about the way G. is now 87:7
  he never played the G. Empire 107:16
  stiff-necked G. beggar 212:2
Glass: as phoney as a glass eye 167:14
  hate you through the g. 44:8
  if you break the bloody g. 246:5
  put it under a g. case 239:5
  reach for their g. or their glasses 244:5
  water's the same shape as the g. 91:11
  what g. beads are to African traders 95:13
  whiskers . . . grown under g. 410:24
Glass-bottomed: mind like a g. boat 272:7
  through a sewer in a g. boat 267:2, 390:8
Glasses: but I did not remove my g. 354:5
  girls who wear g. 64:4, 291:4
  prefer to forget both pairs of g. 277:25
  reach for their glass or their g. 244:5
  there were two g. and two chairs 246:10
Gleaming: g. cantos of unvanquished space 94:28
Glee: g. . . . desperation on a good day 255:2
Glibness: g. of the Berlitz-school 125:23
Gliding: g. like a queen she leaves 354:19
Glimmering: that angry or that g. sea 128:13
Glitter: below the g., its solid tinsel 147:18
Gloamin': roamin' in the g. 222:8
Gloat: I g.! Hear me g.! 214:21
Global: g. village 244:15
  my wars were g. from the start 314:12
Globally: think g. 12:8
Globe: wears the turning g. 179:2
Globe-trotter: I am wary of g.s 266:15
Glorify: g. a lfe which they can't bear 144:13
Glorious: devil dancing in me g. 254:4
  g. misery 298:22
Glory: deny you peace but give you g. 382:7
  farewell my friends, I am going to g. 111:10
  in the stars the g. of His eyes 300:13
  Land of Hope and G. 37:14
  trailed the clouds of his own g. 153:10
  what price g.? 8:11
Glove: *Gott Mit Uns*. . . . one had g.s 104:14
  repair a watch with his g.s on 371:17
  walk through the fields in g. 93:4
Glow: g. in Old Glory 278:22
  her g. has warmed the world 359:7
  young star-captains g. 128:5
Glubjullas: great luck with my G. 110:18
Glum: g. heroes up the line to death 336:29
Glutton: g. old in sin 311:10
Gluttony: g. is an emotional escape 104:15
Gnat: O joy of the g. 318:6
Gnome: little g.s of Zürich 405:16
Go: best thing to get up and g. 120:18
  g. ahead, make my day 114:3
  g. on. I can't g. on. I'll g. on 29:2
  have a g.! 298:9
  I g. – I come back 203:7
  I have a g., lady 287:23
  in the name of God, g. 7:8

we think you ought to g. 326:4
  why should I go? She won't be there 262:4
Goad: g.s them on behind 415:16
Goal: keeper stands up to keep the g. 179:26
  these dogmas or g.s are in doubt 299:6
Goalkeeper: molest the unprotected g. 304:19
Goat: g.s . . . sheep from broken homes 49:17
God: absurd is sin without G. 65:18
  Act of G. designation 91:19
  afraid of nothing but his nagging g.s 206:9
  always a godmother, never a G. 226:16
  always said G. was against art 116:15
  America is G.'s crucible 420:3
  any G. I ever felt in church 390:3
  argue with the G.s 247:13
  bearded lips of G. 58:19
  before the g.s that made the g.s 74:8
  being G. [Gawd] ain't a bed of roses 87:5
  believed in G. so that it need not talk 336:20
  bell-rope that gathers G. at dawn 95:4
  blameless wonderfulness of G. 119:19
  Cabots talk only to G. 47:8
  can the world of G. be found 283:13
  concept of G. has any validity 22:17
  conception of G. was . . . not orthodox 362:2
  didn't love G., he just fancied him 10:8
  easier to say one doesn't believe in G. 196:9
  electric display of G. the Father 285:4
  English G. is not so dominant 68:4
  even G. was born too late 238:12
  everything traditional . . . about G. 374:4
  extra work I had when I was a g. 172:12
  eyes still dazzled by the ways of G. 234:11
  final proof of G.'s omnipotence 105:6
  give up writing about G. 393:24
  gives G. a bad time 50:12
  G. . . . an artist . . . rather than a judge 273:3
  G. and carpeting 6:19
  G. as a working hypothesis 46:6
  G. believed in him 39:16
  G. Bless America 39:9
  G. bless . . . G. damn! 373:11
  G. bless the USA so large 18:6
  G. calls me G. 334:4
  G. can't want that 158:3
  G. created man, she was only experimenting 150:4
  G. doesn't count on his hands 158:12
  G. don't come when you want him 10:7
  G. finally caught his eye 202:11
  G., from whose territories 95:19
  G. has written all the books 61:22
  G. . . . he's an underachiever 6:2
  G. in drag 24:12
  G. in his last years 370:22
  G. is a bore 259:1
  G. is a sort of burglar 377:1
  G. is . . . an exalted father 134:9
  G. is groovy 306:9
  G. is Love – I dare say 61:23
  G. is love but get it in writing 227:13

G. is . . . not a ruler 183:23
G. is not dead but alive and well 149:7
G. is really only another artist 297:8
G. . . . is still running it 258:20
G. is subtle but . . . not malicious 115:11
G. is very economical 316:18
G. . . . left the receiver off the hook 216:10
G. made the wicked grocer 75:2
G. . . . moves in a mysterious way 268:2
G. must have loved the people in power 293:13
G. not only plays dice 166:1
G. of my fair beginnings 212:23
G. of our fathers, known of old 212:14
G. of things as they are 213:15
G. plays dice with the cosmos 115:12
G. reaching down into the mire 167:13
G. said to Abraham 113:10
G. . . . the best of the dramatic poets 59:1
G. the herdsman goads 415:16
G. was a mistake 66:18
G. who let us prove his existence 46:9
G. who looks after small things 214:24
G. works in a mysterious way 117:15
[G.] well adjusted for an only child 6:24
G.'s arm engloves this tree 314:6
g.s be said to thump the clouds 369:16
G.s have much more fun 225:13
going back to G. 57:2
hailed as an insult to some g. 159:1
hardly ever mention G. any more 261:16
highest praise of G. 308:2
His mother thought he was G. 87:3
honest G.'s the noblest work of man 61:27
how odd of G. 121:17
I am an atheist still, thank G. 58:14
I do not know much about g.s 117:5
I just want to do G's will 208:12
I might have become a g. 328:2
I thought G. was white, and a man 390:4
I would not marry G. 119:14
idea that G. had, when he made us 106:10
if G. exists 187:13
if G. had been a Liberal 49:20
if G. had meant us to fly 149:13
if G. had meant us to have group sex 49:14
if G. talks to you 364:9
imagine G. taking French! 101:9
imagine G. without man's immortality 65:20
in Mexico the g.s ruled 87:1
in the theatre, the director is G. 295:18
it paid then to believe in G. 284:12
it took G. longer to write the Bible 243:7
it's like kissing G. 57:5
knew about half as much as G. 140:15
laws of G. will be suspended 343:18
man whose g. is the skies 344:33
man's ignorance of the g.s 61:9
may G. deny you peace 382:7
men that G. made mad 74:10
mistake to suppose that G. 367:7
more famous than G. 312:19

my belief in G.'s indifference 189:16
my favourite g.s 370:15
my G.s have afflicted me 212:6
nearer to G.'s heart in a garden 156:24
nearest thing to the eye of G. 284:19
never decreed that a g. mustn't pay 51:2
next to . . . g. america i love you 97:24
no G., but try getting a plumber 6:10
no man will ever put asunder: G. will 343:13
no wonder . . . G. sent his only son 346:20
not so much disbelieve in G. 286:17
O thou lost G. 319:9
oh G., take care of yourself 359:5
painting is saying 'Ta' to G. 354:16
pleasing G. is all G. care about 390:5
praise G. when you can 44:18
pray as if everything depended on G. 354:15
present, unknowable G. 223:14
problem was that G. is dead 131:21
put your hand into the hand of G. 165:12
respect the same g.s as themselves 110:14
river is a strong brown g. 117:5
severely disappointed in G.'s works 268:2
Short Story Conference with G. 1:4
suffices us for G. 151:10
sustains and kills – like a G. 342:4
take care not to make the intellect our G.
    115:20
talk of G. and the decade ahead 353:5
there, but for the grace of G. goes G. 82:10,
    249:8
there is always G., economics, or Ibsen 295:19
they [children] still believe in G. 348:17
they first make G.s 232:5
they ought to have left G. alone 33:19
those who marry G. 153:11
to my own G.s I go 212:10
too late for the g.s 167:18
trying to bowl to G. on concrete 320:4
way towards G. 407:16
we did not ask what G. wanted us to do 386:18
we're in G.'s hands now 51:9
what . . . G. thinks of money 25:7
what God abandoned 179:6
what is the prose for G.? 25:9
what the wrong g.s established 294:2
what will G. say 294:20
what will you do, G., if I die? 319:15
when we write. . . . G. 8:1
whether I believe in G. or not 255:6
whom the g.s wish to destroy 87:21
why G. singles people out 59:8
world . . . is nearer to G. 46:7
worship G. in his own way 322:23
worship G. . . . on an empty stomach 406:16
would G. allow us to be offside? 304:19
yellow g. forever gazes down 166:6
you forget the good G. 328:4
yours faithfully, G. 9:21
God-made: some G. object 71:9
God-men: g. say when die go sky 9:22

Goddamm: lhude sing G. 302:26
Goddesses: g. that dwell far along them 370:15
Godfearing: g. and bearded Mr Goodbeare 349:5
Godiva, Lady: if she were cast as G. 9:25
Godless: decent g. people 118:25
Godly: where nobody gets . . . g. 416:22
Godmother: always a g., never a God 226:16
Godot: G. . . . nothing happens – twice 260:3
    waiting for G. 29:4
Goering, Hermann: [G.] . . . a blackguard 169:18
Goes: and so it g. 388:9
Going: best only when the g. was good 90:3
    I don't know where I'm g. 334:21
    long and loath at g. 312:6
    when the g. gets tough. 205:13
    where we're g. 420:8
Gold: g. by bronze heard iron steel 198:17
    g. of the day 96:11
    g. standard on the booze 207:7
    guys peddle g. bricks 167:14
    rarer gifts than g. 54:10
    silver threads among the g. 315:17
    something more dependable. Solid g. 69:20
Golded: g. silvy 197:13
Golden: g. hands he's got 91:20
    g. October 118:21
    g. road to Samarkand 128:12
    I went into a g. land 379:13
    my heart is laden for g. friends 180:2
    pay to have a g. tongue 196:7
    people who live in a G. Age 192:16
    playing with a g. ball 374:7
    story of the g. floor 180:11
    there are no g. rules 344:26
Golden Calf: not only worships the G. 231:7
Goldfish: g. in a glass bowl 332-15
    hostile analysis of g. 391:21
    natural hootchy-kootchy to a g. 107:5
    turning into a vermilion g. 255:8
Goldwyn, Sam: 346:9
Golf: 391:14
    earnest protest against g. 31:2
    g., cats, and the Third Reich 91:18
    [g.] takes you . . . from the club house 234:17
    more liars . . . than g. 321:23
    thousand lost g. balls 118:25
    we dance at the G. Club 40:20
    what Eisenhower did for g. 165:8
Goloshes: dates on his g. 225:21
Gone: g. as . . . we ourselves shall be g. 377:10
Gong: strong g.s groaning 74:21
    struck regularly, like g.s 94:5
Gong-tormented: that . . . g. sea 415:12
Good: appalling silence of the g. people 208:10
    at his best only when the going was g. 90:3
    can't say anything g. about someone 237:4
    feeling rather a g. chap 7:19
    four legs g. 286:9
    g. but not religious-good 164:2
    g., but they were *too* g. 333:14
    G. can imagine Evil 19:2

g. [end] unluckily 361:2
g. for the country 405:9
g. is better than the best 36:17
g. is only g. if one is g. for nothing 274:10
g. . . . makes for unity 182:17
g. man fallen among politicians 99:3
g. men are afraid to die 296:11
g. old days . . . wished we were dead 28:15
g. or bad, like Jews or Germans or films 187:8
G. Samaritan . . . had money as well 367:22
g. time that was had by all 100:16
g. time was had by all 351:11
g. use of bad rubbish 38:4
g. war 51:6
Guinness is g. for you 3:12
hardest to see the g. 98:4
he who wants to do g. 365:4
if you can't be g., be careful 164:19
if you're very g. in this life 20:2
language of g. 17:8
letting the best be the enemy of the g. 193:13
man's capacity for g. 280:3
men have never been g. 26:28
misplaced g. 5:8
no other man seems quite g. enough 91:2
nothing so bad or so g. 345:8
only read what is truly g. 357:16
only the young die g. 171:5
policy of the g. neighbour 322:11
rather be g. than clever 278:8
relief . . . to stop being g. 132:16
Roman Conquest was . . . a G. *Thing* 340:22
see g. in everything 273:2
so much g. in the worst of us 175:1
there's no g. and bad here 277:3
they love the G. 54:20
this was the g. town once 273:5
to g. I never come 291:3
what we like is not necessarily g. 31:20
what we mean by 'Very g.' 93:11
when he said a g. thing 380:9
when I'm g. I'm very very g. 398:3
you was a g. man and did g. things 164:5
you've never had it so g. 245:6
Good-bye-ee: Nahpoo! Toodle-oo! G.! 399:7
Good-night: trembled through his happy g. air
    162:12
Goodbeare: godfearing and bearded Mr G. 349:5
Goodbye: g. and keep cold 135:14
    g. Norma Jean 365:11
    g. to all that 152:8
    man never knows how to say g. 325:20
    wish me luck as you wave me g. 124:18
Goodbye: g. Piccadilly 403:22
Goodness: first privilege of g. 396:1
    g. has nothing to do with it 398:7
    g. only knowses 75:8
    My G.. My Guinness 3:19
    they're always throwin' g. at you 230:19
Goodnight: g. children . . . everywhere 242:12
    g. from me . . . g. from him 25:13

g. Mrs Calabash – wherever you are 112:8
Goods: buy g. they did not need 161:20
g. and sevices can be paid for 281:8
man who delivers the g. 254:21
take it from me – he's got the g. 170:19
Goodwill: g. toward . . . American people 405:3
in peace: g. 81:4
Goons: [the G.] were a crowd of idiots 263:29
Goose: then meeting the g. 216:16
Goose-flesh: farmer who raises g. 39:1
Goose Green: on the ground at G. 209:5
Gorbachev, Mikhail 367:20, 382:1, 418:11
Gored: g. by the climacteric 238:13
Gorgeous: g. resources of credit 90:2
Gorry: by g. by jingo, by gee 97:25
Gory: I'll make a g. mess of you 396:13
Gospel: G. of Getting On 345:12
no use for the policy of the G.s 208:1
Gossip: all the world's g. 304:9
g. is hearing something you like 405:11
pines are g. pines 128:4
sell the family parrot to the town g. 322:3
Gothic: cars . . . great G. cathedrals 27:2
G. arch out of junket 360:7
G. . . . is all revolt 52:1
G. opera next to G. architecture 83:7
Gott: G. . . . one had gloves 104:14
G. strafe England 137:16
o du verlorener G.! 319:9
was wirst du tun, G., wenn ich sterbe? 319:15
Gotta: a man's g. do what a man's g. do 219:4
Gouda: thinner, paler, larger G.s 92:3
Govern: clever middle class to g. 96:8
every cook has to learn to g. 229:2
go out and g. New South Wales 32:20
Labour is not fit to g. 79:2
to g. is not to write resolutions 356:7
to g. is to choose 259:15
Governesses: tremendous lot for her old g. 307:17
tutelage of g. 173:15
we are a nation of g. 346:6
Governing: become accustomed to no one g.
228:17
Government: at the door wanting you to form a g.
348:11
be a torero, the g. or a saint 314:7
between the g. and the governed 283:14
can ever face a British g. 379:9
city g. is of the people 357:3
crawl in to a g. 41:19
democracy is the worst form of g. 80:9
democracy means g. by the uneducated 77:25
duty of H.M.G. 245:13
entertained by their g. 87:2
every g. carries a health warning 11:26
forfeited the confidence of the g. 51:22
from the bankers to the g. 90:2
good g. . . . is a bad one in . . . fright 69:21
g. by crony 185:3
g. by discussion 16:13
g. by mass bribery 186:3

g. knows best. She usually does 91:14
g. of gentlemen 145:15
g. that is big enough to give you all 147:3
g. to dissolve the people 51:22
g. with the engine of a lawn-mower 239:16
it's no go the G. grants 246:4
Kings and g.s may err 170:16
let down our system of g. 281:2
misfortune to have a g. 122:2
mutually antagonistic g.s 392:26
no . . . g. common to the peoples 393:4
politician to run a g. 378:18
see the g. get out of war 168:15
sun never sets on G. House 94:14
tell employees of the g. 375:16
things g. does for them 391:10
watch the g. and report the facts 321:26
work for a G. I despise 207:5
Gown: in my sweet little Alice blue g. 241:12
Goya: stepped out of a painting by G. 362:21
Grace, W.G. 31:2
Grace: clergy to have the g. of a swan 193:6
each in his place, by right, not g. 213:11
from g. you never fell yet 175:16
g. to hold yourself 365:11
g. under pressure 169:11
what woman has this old cat's g.? 260:11
Gracchopper: g. was always jigging a jog 198:2
Graceless: G. . . . waited . . . to be milked 143:1
Gradient: altered g. at another rate 17:21
Gradually: g. very g. 97:11
Gradualness: inevitable g. 394:5
Graffiti: g. lower on the walls 373:12
Graft: best g.s in the world 170:18
Grail: living isn't a seeking of the g. 127:21
what . . . to do with the G. 30:30
Grain: g.s beyond age 369:15
place individual g.s of sand 132:10
Grammar: I don't want to talk g. 345:16
meanings stabilized in . . . g. 400:21
we don't talk fancy g. 281:18
Gramophone: puts a record on the g. 118:15
waxworks inhabited by g.s 103:25
Grand: to be baith g. and comfortable 26:8
Grand Central Station: by G. I sat down and wept
349:21
Grandchildren: never have children, only g.
387:12
Grandfather: g. turned into a grandmother 4:12
I dung on my g.'s doorstep 151:12
makes friends with its g.s 274:1
saluting strange women and g. clocks 277:25
Grandiose: between bland and g. 381:3
Grandmother: cads have always a g. 403:16
my g. would not let me 403:12
slaughter of the G.s 17:14
we have become a g. 368:3
Grandson: your g. . . . a Communist 207:14
Granite: g.s which titanic wars 288:24
Grant, Cary: old G. fine. How you 150:20
Grape: broke the g.'s joy 369:18

peel me a g. 398:2
sour g.s and ashes 15:8
Grass: all flesh is g. 305:5
from g. and clover the upshot beam 179:7
future is propoganda. So is g. 53:5
g. grows green on the battlefield 79:1
g. is growing on the Front Bench 16:8
g., row after rich row 365:8
g. uncut in a . . . cemetery 375:17
g. will carry you through 346:21
g. will grow in the streets 177:5
I am the g.; I cover all 334:18
is the g. emptier now? 36:5
kissed the lovely g. 54:14
pigeons on the g. alas 357:8
rather eat g. standing up 11:13
sheep with . . . g. in its throat 409:13
thin g. clothed them more warmly 371:3
White Horse . . . was cut out of the g. 74:8
Grateful: when he feels g. 390:19
Gratification: g. of a vital need 315:7
Gratitude: g. looks to the past 232:12
worse than having to give g. 123:2
Gratuite: l'acte g. 115
Gratuitous: autobiography is the most g. 361:10
Grave: by my g. you'd pray to have me back 69:2
climbs into their g.s married 402:16
endure beyond the g. 107:23
even the g. yawns for him 377:3
funny thing . . . on the way to the g. 95:20
give birth astride of a g. 29:8
g.'s narrowness, though not its peace 151:15
have their g.s at home 74:16
heaped to its g. 95:5
in the g. with my lips moving 249:1
less fearful of the certain g. 253:28
over this damp g. I speak 321:7
with O'Leary in the g. 417:17
Graveyard: bone to pick with g.s 28:19
g.s are full of indispensable men 141:14
Greasy: great grey-green, g. Limpopo 214:6
Great: definition of a g. work 47:18
everything we think of as g. 307:20
g. enough to die for 160:4
g. history and . . . small lives 80:5
g. man dies twice 385:20
g. man . . . walks across his century 225:21
g. men of history are frauds 45:10
G. Society 195:16
happy the g. ones are thriving 243:12
it's g. to be g. 321:19
nothing but a g. man 183:20
real g. man . . . makes every man feel g. 75:24
some . . . are bad. But they are all g. 148:18
those who were truly g. 354:21
what did you do in the G. War 3:26
Great Britain: G. has lost an Empire 1:8
G. . . . supported both sides 243:6
success of G. defending itself 322:21
Great-grandmother: Aryan with my g. 277:2
Greatest: I am the g. 5:10

Greatness: in our past there is g. 53:17
Greed: need not g. 219:3
not for everyone's g. 57:15
Greek: G. . . . more G. than he ever was 262:8
G.s had a word for it 4:13
G.s in the Roman Empire 245:18
half G. and half Latin 340:1
nobody can say a word against G. 343:23
unknown to the G.s 46:22
Green: both g., both beautiful 203:12
cakes . . . looked g. with worry 125:20
drives my g. age 369:2
force that through the g. fuse 369:2
Gatsby believed in the g. light 126:20
g. and true blue . . . don't . . . mix 270:22
g. end of . . . hardest winters 131:15
g. how I love you 140:9
g. parrot is also a g. salad 298:4
g. replete old age 355:26
legends of the g. chapels 369:11
time held me g. and dying 369:1
Greene, Graham 393:24
Greenfly: make sure there weren't any g. 20:3
Greengrocer: babies outside g.s' shops 49:10
Greening: g. of America 315:6
Greet: g. him like Etonians 215:19
Greeting: g. a corpse 23:14
'How are you' is a g. not a question 156:14
Grey: anything that is g., don't eat 353:3
old and g. and full of sleep 417:26
Grey-green: great g., greasy Limpopo 214:6
Greyly: wandered g. about 119:16
Grief: between g. and nothing I will take g. 123:3
g. at not being able to call then back 249:21
g. . . . develops . . . the mind 308:15
Lord of the Flies is g. sheer g. 146:10
oldest g.s of summer 317:14
Grieg, Edvard: 102:7
Grievance: establishing her g. for the day 250:2
not magnifying g.s 317:17
Scotsman with a g. 408:13
Grieving: g., . . . escaped the sacrifice 162:11
Grim: g. face essential to success 189:11
Gringo: g. in Mexico . . . euthanasia 137:8
Grizzling: grumbling and g. 130:15
Grizzly: g. bear is huge and wild 178:15
Groan: how alike are the g.s of love 238:15
poets g. in rhymes 389:3
Groaning: strong gongs g. 74:21
Grocer: God made the wicked g. 75:2
Groovy: God is g. 306:9
Grope: Brussels hotel for a Group G. 371:7
Groping: laid our g. hands away 55:8
Gross: g. habits with my net income 129:2
Ground: as far as the g. could see 295:6
good for the g. 339:10
tank heaven the g. broke me fall 263:9
Groundfloor: our true g. selves 223:9
Group: Brussels hotel for a G. Grope 371:7
g.'s name on the left 156:18
if God had meant us to have g. sex 49:14

Grouse: if I were a g. I'd appeal 90:18

Grow: churches g. old but do not g. up 268:8
g. again patiently 106:15
humankind must at last g. up 371:5
limit beyond which it should not g. 216:18
millions . . . none the less grow up 360:12
some of us never g. out of it 383:18
what one wants to be when one g.s up 171:20

Growling: low g. noises 1:15

Grown-up: cannot really be a Catholic and g. 287:20
g. maintaining . . . physical exertion 220:7
g.s are scared of spots 120:12
g.s never understand anything 332:1
not until I'm g. and have to pay 403:17
when g.s agree 214:17

Grub: g. first, then ethics 51:18

Grudge: he took it as a personal g. 170:13

Gruel: pale g. of philosophy 377:22

Grumbling: Brahms, for all his g. 130:15

Gruntled: far from g. 408:19

Guarantee: no one can g. success in war 81:13

Guard: changing g. at Buckingham Palace 264:6
hate of those ye g. 213:18

Guardian: dedicate these pages to my G. Angel 283:11
G. is read 3:31
g. of his solitude 319:17

Guerre: le fils fait la g. 305:6
que la g. est jolie 12:26
years of l'entre deux g.s 117:2

Guerrilla: g. fights the war of the flea 365:1
g. war . . . place where you are going 122:7
g. wins if he does not lose 214:30
sea in which the g. swims 250:18

Guesses: who . . . g. where we go? 58:12

Guessing: one lover after he has stopped g. 325:21

Guest: free-loader is a confirmed g. 327:7
g. thanks his host at the door 106:5
g.s of each other 357:24
speeds the parting g. 418:1
tonight is my g. night 159:16

Guggenheim, Peggy 297:20

Guide: g. of the nation 141:15
g.s cannot master . . . American joke 380:3

Guided: g. missiles and misguided men 208:14

Guile: urban, squat, and packed with g. 54:19

Guilt: dress of g. 243:14
false g. . . . not what. . . one ought to be 219:14
natural classification of g. 21:16
nine minutes of g. 319:20
sense of g. . . . fumes up in resentment 231:2

Guilty: g. of Noel Cowardice 104:16
how can any man be called g.? 201:1
I piss from the diving board I am g.? 201:11
make any woman with them look g. 127:19

Guinea: worth a g. a box 3:28

Guinea pig: g.s in the laboratory of God 404:11
spending . . . the life of a g. 190:18

Guinness: glass of G. on a sunny day 153:9
G. is good for you 3:12

My Goodness. My G. 3:19
read in the first chapter of G.'es 198:13

Guitar: one man and his g. against the world 83:3
you have a blue g. 358:13

Gum: chewing g. for the eyes 56:12
fart and chew g. at the same time 196:3

Gummed: I don't want to be g. to death 255:14

Gummidge, Worzel: Labour . . . led by G. 22:13

Gun: as snug as a g. 166:19
as the g.s boom far 74:21
difference between a g. and a tree 303:28
g. will make us powerful 146:2
got the g.s but we got the numbers 270:7
g.s aren't lawful 291:8
ironic g.s 13:7
is that a g. in your pocket 398:8
its g.s will not be wanted 52:6
monstrous anger of the g.s 288:14
necessary to take up the g. 250.11
power grows out of the barrel of a g. 250:10
show us what makes the g. go off 247:9
some rob you with a six g. 157:4
when the g.s begin to rattle 25:8
without butter, but not without g.s 145:16
word 'g.' I reach for my culture 147:27

Gunfire: g. . . . . unreal to me 383:11

Gunga Din: better man than I am, G. 210:29

Gunpowder: blow your mind – smoke g. 148:21

Guppies: cats and g. will have the last laugh 92:13

Guru: g. gives himself 148:16

Gutenberg, Johann: G. made everybody a reader 245:4

Guts: [g.] on the ground at Goose Green 209:5
g.s. What, are they showing? 263:22
g.s to betray my country 131:1
what do you mean by 'g.'? 169:11

Gutter: and the other in the g. 309:2

Guzzling: little off-hand g. 326:14

Gym: flare was up in the g. 40:17

Gymnasium: g. . . . . strengthen character 344:8

Gypsy: sad as a g. serenading the moon 259:23
to the vagrant g. life 254:12

Gyration: recent g.s of the dollar 207:7

Gyre: turning in the widening g. 417:12

H

H-Bomb 405:10
that H.. It's dynamite 147:16

Haar: schon augelöst wie langes H. 319:4

Habit: gross h.s with my net income 129:2
if h. is second nature 308:10
it was a h. in those days 321:14
pulling h.s out of rats 60:9
triumph confirms us in our h.s 189:12

Habit-forming: cocaine isn't h. 24:6

Habitual: nothing is h. but indecision 191:16

Had: good time that was h. by all 100:16

Hades: phonographs of H. in the brain 95:2

Haemophiliac: h. in a razor factory 404:6
Haida: among the H. Indians 320:1
Haig, Douglas, Earl 28:9
   [H.] was brilliant to the top 236:8
Hail: H. Mary quite contrary 154:5
Haines, Joe: H. at the wheel of his Mini 186:27
Hair: babies haven't any h. 175:19
   compassionate h. 7:22
   drew her long black h. out tight 118:16
   driving taxi cabs and cutting h. 59:20
   every h. of the bear reproduced 182:9
   grow h. on the inside of your head 174:9
   h. as white as gin 70:18
   h. done in the library 375:7
   h. has threads of grey 416:8
   h. the colour of a Charles the Fifth 102:22
   h. was the most important thing 283:5
   loosened like the long h. 319:4
   Preludes through his h. 117:31
   they never hurt a h. of him 363:3
   wash that man right out of my h. 160:17
   you can cut your own h. 90:13
Hair-brushes: turned into a pair of h. 391:13
Haircut: lies a h. and a shave 175:19
Half: 'arf the sound of a lap-dog 403:13
   'arf the world full of savages 70:2
   h. the people are right 400:8
   hated each other at h. sight 64:15
   I am only h. there when I am ill 224:20
   I don't know which h. 231:10
   send me the h. that's got my keys 150:6
   too clever by h. 333:23
   you fall h. in love with them 333:11
Half-a-crown: h. – that would be bad 87:24
Half-baked: attractive to the h. mind 130:17
Half-caste: known in . . . h. circles 409:19
Half-dark: from h. to h. 303:7
Half-truth: all truths are h.s 401:4
   combination of h.s and clichés 375:14
   truth is a compound of two h.s 361:15
   we speak no more than h.s 234:13
Halibut: h. asked by another h. 409:6
Halitosis: cured himself of . . . h. 56:7
   dullness is like h. 43:13
   h. of the intellect 185:4
Hall, Henry: this is H. speaking 159:16
Hall-porter: necessity for h.s 76:15
Halo: h. is . . . to keep clean 136:22
   special h. round what is written 64:8
Haloes: reason saints wear h. 24:14
Ham: come back as h. sandwiches 374:11
   in prison with only h. and eggs 246:17
Hamburger: why have h. out 279:9
Hamilton, Lady: call me Lady H. 316:9
Hamlet: Afrikaans for 'H. . .' 194:7
   everything I write . . . is *H.* in disguise 274:11
   H. . . . rooted in . . . incest-complex 133:18
   H. without breaking a few egos 146:17
   I am not Prince H. 117:27
Hammer: characters h. through daisies 368:19
   h. to shape [the world] 257:17

Maxwell's silver h. 230:2
Hammerklavier Sonata: H. . . . had human authors
   182:18
Hampstead: when somebody from H. is drowning
   337:21
Hamster: h.s don't love anybody 120:2
   h.s mate one day in three 32:1
Hand: affectionately by both your h.s 42:14
   as soon as I get hold of a h. 127:18
   cease to use your h.s 287:8
   give a man a free h. 398:5
   H. a singular instrument 42:18
   h. is hot. Take it or leave it 265:20
   h. is the cutting edge of the mind 54:2
   h. that holds dominion over Man 369:3
   h. that signed the treaty 369:3
   hath prospered here my h. 212:23
   h.s grumble on the door 368:23
   h.s minutely answered 97:11
   h.s off the sons of the Widow 213:20
   I can't see anything but h.s 27:17
   I still have my h. to prove it 262:20
   no more . . . than your moist h. 358:19
   nobody . . . has such small h.s 97:30
   pianist's h.s. Or a surgeon's h.s 91:20
   put your h. into the h. of God 165:12
   that's not the h. I dealt you Dad 271:7
   then say 'on the other h.' 379:3
   to leave a man's h.s empty 389:10
   wear a watch – on the one h. 203:19
   woodworm obligingly held h.s 111:8
   worth two [orgasms] in the h. 149:30
Hand-made: unquestionably h. 380:28
Hand-to-hand: policy is h. fighting 165:18
Handbag: alligators, just floating h.s 155:17
   hitting it with her h. 96:5
   turning them into h.s 411:21
Handkerchief: ghost that eats h.s 269:8
Handle: if you can h. three elements 297:9
   no h.s to a horse 226:4
Handlebar: cow with h.s is a bicycle 271:11
Handsome: women don't look for h. men 218:11
Hang: enough rope and he'll h. you 121:1
   h. him anyhow 380:5
   h. it all, Robert Browning 303:1
   h. out the washing 204:14
   I will not h. myself today 74:7
Hang-gliding: mice have taken up h. 32:2
Hanged: h. for poisoning . . . children 110:5
Hangover: like h. without intoxication 108:1
Hanker: not one to h. after change 314:14
Hansard: H. is history's ear 334:10
Hanyfink: wot's the good of h.? 78:6
Happen: power to make anything h. 239:16
   tell what is going to h. 170:14
   this thing that had begun to h. 190:12
   what h.s where it isn't 328:18
   what you would like to h. 166:17
   whatever can h. *will* h. 174:14
Happening: perceives what is not h. 381:1
   quite other things are h. 306:7

when the English began to h. 209:20
Hated: h. each other at half sight 64:15
Hathaway, Anne: H.'s cottage, . . . with central
  heating 220:5
Hatless: h., I take off my cycle-clips 221:6
Hatred: common h. of its neighbours 186:20
  deep burning h. for the Tory Party 40:10
  h. is like vitamins 388:10
  intellectual h. is the worst 417:5
  no h. or bitterness towards anyone 71:2
  what we need is h. 141:21
Hatton, Derek: peg to hang a H. 165:19
Hauf-way: I'll ha'e nae h. hoose 242:15
Haughey, Charles: H. . . . give him enough rope
  121:1
Haughty: h. barbers cutting . . . hair 43:10
  very h. . . . the wild buccaneer 139:17
Haunt: h. of brooding dust 103:15
Haunted: from the nave build h. heaven 358:12
Haus: und baute draus ein grosses H. 269:7
  wo einmal ein dauerndes H. war 318:15
Haute Lorraine: wine they . . . make in H. 74:12
Hawk: dark h.s near us 197:20
  h.s have no music 389:6
  writer may be a h. or a buzzard 169:15
  yellow-eyed h. of the mind 416:12
Hayworth, Rita 100:18
Hazy: low-and-h., . . . or high and crazy 143:2
He-Ancient 342:23
Head: brother of yours, with the two h.s 291:24
  curses heaped on each gashed h. 353:12
  enemy with outposts in your h. 204:6
  good h. is not oval but round 276:12
  h. is a thoroughly inefficient organ 256:22
  h. of the characters hammer 368:19
  hands and legs at the behest of his h. 322:19
  her h. tucked underneath her arm 399:8
  hit them on the h. without any mercy 229:5
  if you can keep your head 205:22, 210:31
  lift its h. to the blows 368:19
  monstrous h. and sickening cry 74:14
  my ho h. halls 197:20
  only what cannot be trimmed is a h. 177:2
  peering, furtive h. 290:11
  people who chop off h.s 47:17
  Socialism with a human h. 177:4
  some as big as your h. 167:11
  tell if it was h.s or tails 376:8
  their h.s fall off 312:12
  tradition of kings wearing h.s 162:2
  within the secrecy of our own h.s 327:17
  world outside your h. 403:5
Head-ache: writers . . . give h.s 1:7
Head-waiter: h. allowed to sit 383:19
Headache: sex is good for h.s 402:6
Headmaster: h.s have powers 80:21
  most formidable h. . . . a headmistress 24:12
Headsman: antique dread of the h.'s axe 151:11
Headstone: h.s yield their names 365:7
Heal: time forgets and never h.s 354:20
Health: government carries a h. warning 11:26

h., his honour and his quality 44:10
h. is an episode between illnesses 201:14
h. is infinite 331:1
h. of a writer should not be too good 88:4
h. of his wife 88:24
idea of h. 377:12
old people shouldn't eat h. foods 285:9
patient believing in . . . own h. 159:7
seriously damage your h. 239:20
Wot, me? In my state of h.! 203:10
Healthy: h. and wealthy and dead 372:4
  h. type . . . essentially middle-class 127:19
  if you are h., you don't need it 129:20
  more are h. than sick 360:12
  no h. male . . . talks of anything 259:10
Heaney, Seamus: [S.] puts the shine back 272:10
Heaped: h. to its grave 95:5
Hear: come on and h. 39:2
  h., know, and say 55:8
  still h. a pretty girl 373:8
  what they do not want to h. 287:19
  what they h., they repeat 348:20
  you can h. his mind working 345:33
Heard: conducts what is not being h. 108:7
  I have already h. it 319:18
  satirists should be h. and not seen 347:2
  you ain't h. nothin' yet 196:13
Hearing: listening without h. 348:1
  natural law as related to . . . h. 394:7
  not the h. one misses but the over-h. 413:10
Hearing aid: wear my h. in the bath 269:20
Hearsay: contemporary h. 66:27
Hearst, William Randolph: H. gave him the kiss of
  death 350:2
Heart: apart from an occasional h. attack 35:6
  beware of giving your h. to a dog 212:11
  bury my h. at Wounded Knee 35:12
  clutch at the h. 136:10
  come to pass in the h. of America 116:11
  committed adultery in my h. 69:9
  counting the slow h. beats 151:9
  country habit has me by the h. 331:6
  cracks in a broken h. 409:7
  death took him by the h. 288:17
  deep in the h. of Texas 171:10
  fasten their hands upon their h.s 178:21
  feeling that he posseses a woman's h. 306:15
  give crowns . . . but not your h. away 179:17
  h. has its reasons 41:8
  h. may think it knows better 48:3
  h. of standing 120:19
  half as many h.s lost to her 30:14
  he gets a beautiful h. 363:7
  heart-break in the h. of things 143:14
  hid in the h. of love 417:4
  hoarded by the human h. 293:9
  howled away their h.s 415:8
  h.s at peace under an English heaven 55:7
  h.'s grown brutal on the fare 417:1
  h.s that we broke long ago 18:17
  interfere with one's h. strings 304:16

into my h. an air that kills 179:31
it hides within a tender h. 269:10
King of H.s . . . hasn't a moustache 63:3
lonely of h. is withered away 416:21
man could ease a h. 291:10
many a h. is aching 164:22
my h. belongs to Daddy 302:2
my h.'s right there 403:22
never were in better h. 158:4
O, h., O troubled h. 417:23
O h.! O h.! if she'd but turn 416:10
one is to lose your h.'s desire 344:23
only with the h. that one can see 332:3
open a window to her h. 316:19
out-worn h., in a time out-worn 416:16
primeval disaster in the h. of Man 348:24
process in the weather of the h. 369:13
rag-and-bone shop of the h. 415:13
Sergeant Pepper's lonely h.s club 230:4
she had a h. 337:18
sing to find your h.s 128:7
Socialist mind and a Conservative h. 125:13
some day my h. will awake 165:13
some men break your h. in two 290:13
stirred the h. of every Englishman 340:2
their h. is in their boots 74:23
while your h.s are yearning 129:21
with a song in my h. 165:7
Heart-attack: Reagan and a h. 366:17
Heart-breaking: like h. new friends 205:18
Hearty: h., robust and revolting 296:10
Heat: if you don't like the h. 386:10
  white h. of this revolution 406:1
Heath, Sir Edward: grammar school twit H.
  354:11
Heathen: h. ['eathen] in his blindness 210:11
  Higgins is a h. 75:11
  poor benighted h. ['eathen] 210:21
Heather: over the h. the west wind blows 18:14
  same as when I roved the h. 101:17
Heaven: broken ice; H.'s gates 112:3
  cold and rook-delighting h. 415:15
  doors of h. and hell are adjacent 203:12
  enter H. by a back door 140:16
  fighting for the gates of h. 234:5
  from the nave build haunted h. 358:12
  go to H. without being . . . qualified 344:18
  H. and Hell . . . one breath away 391:5
  h. goes in for something more dependable 69:20
  h. . . . is so inane, so dull 345:107
  H. is the boulder rock 386:6
  h. is where the police are British 9:23
  h. of all their wish 54:13
  H. will protect the working girl 350:4
  Hebrew in H. 125:15
  I don't believe in h. or hell 292:26
  if it's h. for climate 26:7
  in h. an angel is nobody 345:1
  is he in h.? 285:10
  merger between H. and Hell 397:16
  my thirtieth year to h. 369:12

Our Father that art in h., stay there 305:7
road from h. to Hereford 74:12
streets of h. have all been sold 157:2
these in the day when h. was falling 179:4
under an English h. 55:7
ventured to describe a day in h. 345:10
winds of the h.s dance between you 143:6
Heavenly: up in the h. saloon 260:12
Heaving: confined to h.s and shruggin's 213:25
Heavy: I feel as h. as yonder stone 197:20
Hebrew: few odd words in H. 101:9
  H. in Heaven 125:15
Hebrides: colder than the H. 128:5
Hedge: thick h., dazzling 201:15
Hedgehog: if you start throwing h.s 207:20
Heejus: creature of h. mien 111:22
Heel: long thrust of his h. 181:13
  on the boldest h. 94:29
  time wounds all h.s 253:22
Heesh: h. will want to play tennis 264:14
Heffalump: I have decided to catch a h. 265:2
Hegel, G.F.W.: laws of our old H. 308:16
Hegemony: [h.] . . . 'spontaneous' consent 150:17
Heigh ho: h. h.! 107:3
Height: h. of silent humour 151:18
  struggle towards the h.s 65:19
Heimat: hier seine H. 318:18
Heine, Heinrich: H. loosened the corsets 217:10
Heineken: H.. Refreshes the parts 3:13
Heinz: Beanz Meanz H. 3:1
Heir: old and will have no h.s 319:14
Heiress: American h. wants to buy a man 242:2
Held: war er nicht H. schon in dir 318:12
  wunderlich nah ist der H. 318:11
Helen: look on H.'s face in hell 291:7
Hell: all schools are h. 90:15
  believe in existence of h. 29:24
  bells of h. go ting-a-ling-a-ling 12:10
  doors of heaven and h. are adjacent 203:12
  fear of h. is h. itself 143:13
  fourth day . . . 'To h. with you' 207:21
  go to h. Apovitch 303:3
  go to h. like lambs 74:23
  h. for company 26:7
  h. is full of musical amateurs 344:16
  h. is other people 336:4
  h. is paved with good intentions 69:20, 345:4
  H. is time arrested 386:6
  h. is where the police are German 9:23
  h. lay about him in his infancy 153:10
  H. . . . where you 270:20
  h. without the hygiene 24:22
  half so wicked as Lord George H. 30:8
  H.'s bells and all's well 360:12
  if Hitler invaded H. 81:16
  in whatever circle of h. we live 336:24
  merger between Heaven and H. 397:16
  on all sides h. yet 175:16
  plenty of humbug in h. 344:15
  put themselves in h. freely 336:24
  stirrup-pump can extinguish h. 314:8

that's what h. must be like 28:15
'Very good' is 'Go to h.' 93:11
wishful thinking in H. 232:11
Hellman, Lillian: every word [H.] writes 242:9
Hello: give him a medium h. 327:4
h., sucker 156:10
h., young lovers 160:9
Help: all here on earth to h. others 19:15
h. and support of the woman I love 115:7
h. me, Dear, . . . this little once 125:14
having to call 'H.' 46:20
very present h. 358:20
with a little h. from my friends 230:9
Hemingway, Ernest 357:4
Hen: Attila the H. 133:16
better take a wet h. 207:16
h. is only an egg's way 61:10
h. that lays the eggs 368:1
Hen-sure: woman who should be . . . h. 224:5
Henry V: H. was a cold bath king 317:4
Henry VIII: cross between H. and 'our Mr Jones'
127:12
I'm H. [Henery] the Eighth 275:1
Hepburn, Katharine 292:19
Herdsman: God the h. goads 415:16
Here: H. and Now is neither now nor h. 363:12
h. today and h. tomorrow 25:14
h. we are again! 215:15
we're h. because we're h. 12:20
we're h. because we're queer 31:10
would therefore never happen h. 131:14
Hereafter: I shall believe in . . . the h. 63:13
Heredity: h. is just environment stored 58:16
Hereford: road from heaven to H. 74:13
Heresies: h. . . . explosions of faith 51:28
religions are kept alive by h. 51:28
Heresy: an Englishman believes be h. 345:24
Heretic: burning of h.s – fun, fun, fun 395:4
Heritage: we have come into our h. 54:11
Hermit: spoiled h. 29:10
Hero: already a h. inside you 318:12
because they don't want to be a h. 361:6
h. and I will write you a tragedy 127:5
h. from the waist up 263:10
h. is . . . akin to those who die young 318:11
h. is the man who robs a bank 404:24
h. keeps getting in bed with women 324:21
h. . . . the shortest-lived profession 321:25
h. . . . would argue with the Gods 247:13
h.'s arms and bullock's eyes 206:9
no h. is mortal till he dies 18:21
on land I am a h. 173:21
saint, but perhaps not a h. 297:18
Heroes: fit country for h. to live in 235:17
h. glorify a life which they can't bear 144:13
land that is in need of h. 51:4
Heroism: h. . . . indistinguishable from fear 249:26
not the . . . h. they enjoy 407:17
Herself: she's playing h. 200:2
Herz: doch zugleich ein Werk † mit H. 269:10
Heseltine, Michael: H. cannot see a parapet 96:6

Hesitate: h.s to forget its founders 401:12
trust the man who h.s 335:11
Hesitation: my life is a h. before birth 201:4
Hesper: slippered H. 54:16
Hew: you h. form truly 97:8
Hi-tiddley-hi-ti 321:11
Hibernation: stirring . . . from long h. 151:19
Hick: sticks nix h. pix 347:13
Hidden: h. persuaders 290:1
now h., now apparent 412:2
Hide: prefer having nothing to h. 65:15
some to h. themselves 317:1
taxidermist leaves the h. 67:2
Hiding: world lacks not only h. places 327:14
writing always means h. something 64:7
Hierarchical: language of h. authority 53:24
Hierarchy: moral and aesthetic h. 132:10
Hiesiger: ist er ein H.? 319:5
High: she's the Broad and I'm the H. 355:21
High-feathered: h. free-pecking bird 190:2
High-minded: h. people are indifferent 328:11
Highball: three h.s . . . I'm St Francis 291:18
Higher: h. animals are not larger 159:5
h. the voice the smaller the intellect 279:7
Highmindedness: honourable h. 50:10
Highway: happy h.s where I went 179:32
Hijacker: starve the . . . h. 367:21
Hill: dancers are all gone under the h. 116:29
h.s are alive with the sound of music 160:15
h.s that are not there 418:17
h.s were no harder 371:3
I climbed a h. as light fell short 175:10
praise the Lord who made the h.s 212:30
side of the h. that grew it 90:16
steep h. of a relationship 363:5
we shall fight in the h.s 79:15
Hills: immutable as the h.s 214:16
Himmler: H. of the lower fifth 312:21
Hindenberg, P. von 234:2
Hindsight: h.. . . . good for seeing 299:10
h. is always twenty-twenty 402:12
raise h. to the status of a profession 49:18
Hinting: h. at the wicked 17:7
Hippopotamus: h. as an enormous mistake 76:3
h.'s day is passed in sleep 117:15
interest anybody except another h. 324:20
raising his hat to a h. 132:9
shoot the h. with eyebrows 130:7
shoot the h. with . . . platinum 32:9
Hire: h. the other two 159:15
now he would have to h. a hall 33:25
Hired: they h. the money 90:10
Hiroshima 373:15
genius of Einstein leads to H. 297:13
Historia: h. me absolvera 70:13
Historian: h. . . . wants more documents 190:6
h.s are like deaf people 375:2
h.s it deserves 302:11
h.s left blanks in their writings 303:5
h.s repeat each other 156:4
[h.s] should be labelled parachutists 230:25

that is the h.'s task 389:9
typical 49:18
Historical: violation of h. perspective 229:3
Historically: people think too h. 52:11
Histories: h. do not break off clean 181:9
History: all change in h. 366:6
  angel of h. 145:18
  bounded on the north by h. 156:8
  can't get at the truth by writing h. 52:7
  destiny of h. 132:4
  dined at the table of h. 70:7
  disasters of English h. 392:8
  discerned in h. a plot 126:3
  effect of boredom . . . in h. 186:6
  end of a thousand years of h. 138:11
  great h. and . . . small lives 80:5
  great men of h. are frauds 45:10
  h. advances in disguise 102:3
  h. and the smell of skunk 399:3
  h. . . . badly constructed concert hall 244:13
  h. becomes more and more a race 397:2
  h. gets thicker 366:2
  h. has created something new in the USA 34:2
  h. has many cunning passages 117:13
  h. has to use second-hand timber 181:8
  h. . . . is a nightmare 198:11
  h. is about men liking their fathers 49:11
  h. is in the shit sense 55:24
  h. is lived forward 394:8
  h. is more or less bunk 129:17
  h. . . .is more subtle 228:13
  h. is on our side 207:15
  h. is too serious to be left 244:14
  h. must not be written with bias 41:4
  h. . . . must not neglect the known facts 38:3
  h. need not have bothered to go on 174:1
  h. of art is the h. of revivals 61:18
  h. proper is the h. of thought 86:10
  h. . . . repetition of the wrong way 112:20
  h. teaches us that men . . . behave wisely 114:4
  h. to produce a little literature 190:17
  h. to the defeated 18:26
  h. will absolve me 70:13
  [h.] in terms of their own experience 277:5
  Hansard is h.'s ear 334:10
  he closed a chapter in h. 301:1
  hope and h. rhyme 166:18
  h.'s a twisted root 244:11
  in h. lie like bones 19:23
  in h. . . . only a negative learning 66:25
  keep h. and theology apart 397:5
  lunatics and . . . great men of h. 328:5
  man is a h.-making creature 19:8
  minute hand of h. 241:11
  more h. than they can consume 332:16
  most of those who study h. 366:7
  music . . . is an imitation of h. 19:10
  nine tenths a h. lesson 363:12
  no mere events in h. 86:10
  no way in by h.'s road 152:3
  persistent sound . . . through men's h. 216:12

poetry of h. 377:10
pure German with h. added 270:2
remember the soul's h. 354:21
sinister phenomena in intellectual h. 66:5
Thames is liquid h. ['istory] 59:21
the more contemporary h. becomes 66:27
there is no h. of mankind 301:7
those who make h. 290:8
too frail a thread to hang h. from 359:13
unloading h. 81:18
vengeance of h. 377:19
world h. is a conspiracy of diplomats 338:19
writing h. with lightning 407:3
Hit: h. list was longer 53:21
  h. the trail for that . . . land 101:19
Hitch-hiker: H.'s Guide to the Galaxy 1:11
Hitchcock, Alfred 39:1
Hitler, Adolf 11:4, 79:22, 132:4, 132:6, 237:18
  Bolshaw approved of H. 90:21
  every time H. occupies a country 275:11
  H. . . . defence against . . . Communism 57:16
  H. . . . get away with what he had got 72:2
  H. has carried out a revolution 275:9
  H. showed . . . loyalty to Mussolini 58:5
  H. was a nuisance 246:19
  H., who had done such a great job 168:8
  if H. invaded Hell 81:16
  like kissing H. 98:5
  only one purpose, the destruction of H. 81:16
  people H. never understood 58:4
  so was H. [literate] 53:21
  string old H. from the . . . bough 124:15
  tipster who only reached H.'s level 366:5
Hitlerism: H. is . . . of Jewish origin 78:2
Hive: h. for the honey-bee 416:18
Hoarded: h. by the human heart 293:9
Hoare, Sir Samuel 46:19
Hobbies: h. and humours 335:10
Hobbit: there lived a h. 374:14
Hobbled: h. . . . through the garden gate 337:6
Hobbs, Jack 320:4
Hobby: particular h. was getting ordained 25:4
Hobby-horse: democracy is like a h. 334:9
Hockney, David: H. . . . taken for Mozart 181:10
Hoe: hard row to h. 75 20
Hog: disadvantage of being a h. 271:14
  h. butcher for the world 334:15
  happy . . . without going any h. 298:21
Hold: in order to h. it against them 66:25
Holding: if I don't know who's h. it 383:14
Hole: h. when the cheese is gone 51:10
  h. where the rain gets in 229:21
  h.s in your Swiss cheese 126:7
  if you know of a better h. ['ole] 22:9
  smallest h. a man can hide his head in 77:1
Holland, H. Scott 279:2
Holland 92:4
Hollow: we are the h. men 117:16
Hollywood 175:20, 237:12
  H. money isn't money 292:9
  H. people are afraid to leave H. 315:9

H. people are like everyone else 126:2
H. was the only royalty 100:19
in H., if you don't have happiness 315:1
Los Angeles has H. – and hates it 72:10
strip the phoney tinsel off H. 231:6
Holy: h. deadlock 170:29
made h. by their dreams 143:14
not the fault of the h. 54:9
one H., Catholic and Apostolic Church 367:10
too much of the . . . h. can't-help-it 222:21
Holy Ghost: would like to call on the H. 235:21
you or the H.? 195:3
Holy Grail: H. were just round the corner 279:2
Holy-water: h. death 243:15
Home: at h. you're just a politician 245:10
based on the . . . Ideal H. Exhibition 208:5
build a h. for the truth 72:16
country h. and mother 97:8
for England, h. and beauty 164:20
go home to be social 245:5
h. . . . a tavern for his friends 109:2
h. before the leaves have fallen 403:10
h. is the girl's prison 345:5
h. is where you come home to 368:6
h. is where you go to 100:20
h., James and don't spare the horses 172:6
h. . . . they have to take you in 135:9
here is its h. 318:18
his h. is the bank's 140:13
house is not a h. 2:15
how does it feel to be without a h. 113:15
I can get all that at h. 89:20
I'm tired, send one of them h. 398:11
keep the h.-fires burning 129:21
lead one h. to rest 179:14
more difficult it is to bring it h. 109:7
no misunderstanding when I go h. 283:11
people you wouldn't have in your h. 135:3
returns h. to find [what he needs] 268:10
right people stay at h. 94:6
sheep from broken h.s 49:17
stately h.s of England 93:23
walking my baby back h. 379:12
what is it to be at h. 28:13
won't you come home, Bill Bailey 67:1
you do have a h. to go to 391:13
Home Office: H. . . . hand-to-hand fighting 165:18
Home Secretary: against books the H. is 393:8
tricky job being H. 102:12
Home-sickness: in h. . . . keep moving 356:4
Homer: H. ['Omer] smote 'is bloomin' lyre 213:16
if not H., somebody else 183:12
many-minded H. 416:24
Mr Gladstone read H. for fun 80:20
though I have never read a line of H. 262:8
with the single exception of H. 346:2
Homicidal: great h. classics 360:22
h. fried egg 409:4
Homme: ni comme h., ni comme femme 144:23
Homo: one of the stately h.s of England 95:21
Homo sapiens: H. has . . . the biggest penis 270:4

Homoeopathy: h. . . . carried to . . . extreme 119:18
Homosexual: h.s . . . numbered 312:15
Homosexuality 141:3, 268:21
Hon: H.'s cupboard 266:9
Honest: fine thing to be h. 82:9
h. answer gives you . . . surprise 240:3
h. in one way or another 12:22
h. state before the apple 224:22
I am one of the few h. people 126:15
incompetent you have to be h. 240:1
outside the law, you must be h. 113:3
pay for it like an h. man 281:15
she was poor but she was h. 12:17
then they get h. 322:5
Honesty: limpid and impeccable h. 399:13
solitaire demands absolute h. 400:1
Honey: H., I forgot to duck 313:16
H., your silk stocking's hanging 341:4
is there h. still for tea? 55:1
isn't it funny how a bear likes h.? 264:22
it's no go my h. love 246:5
Tiggers don't like h. 264:16
Honeyed: not h. for he 102:23
Honeysuckle: you are my honey, h. 126:9
Honour: fighting for this woman's h. 253:3
going price for getting an h. 108:2
h. and the sword 74:24
h. has come back, as a king 54:11
h. if we can the vertical man 17:10
h. is a luxury for aristocrats 76:15
his h. and his quality taken 44:10
take mine h. from me 211:16
vivid air signed with their h. 355:1
Honourably: h. ineligible 88:11
Hoof: when the plunging h.s were gone 103:13
Hook: h. on which to hang a whole system 300:11
like a h. into an eye 17:3
Hooker: so many movies playing a h. 244:8
Hooligan: H. . . . invented in China 332:26
Hooped: civilization is h. together 417:22
Hoorah Henry: without strict doubt a H. 327:10
Hootchy-kootchy: natural h. to a goldfish 107:5
Hooter: because the h. hoots 74:23
Hoover, J. Edgar 195:20
right back of H. 57:1
Hope, Bob: nothing I wouldn't do for H. 96:12
Hope: because I do not h. to turn again 116:17
cannot run tanks over h. 314:1
distinction between h. and expectation 185:10
h. and history rhyme 166:18
h. is the power of being cheerful 76:14
h. so transcendent 225:6
in the store we sell h. 315:16
Land of H. and Glory 37:14
many the h.s that have vanished 164:22
perfection, to be without h. 111:16
some blessed h. 162:12
stand the despair. It's the h. 133:1
Hopeful: h. disposition 79:6
quite h. about life after death 120:1

Humour: cynicism is h. in ill-health 397:8
  h. is counterbalance 373:4
  h. . . . is emotional chaos 373:1
  h. is like a jester's bladder 271:19
  hobbies and h.s 335:10
  I like h. dry 352:1
  merit in having no sense of h. 89:23
  own up to a lack of h. 85:18
  ridiculous but no sense of h. 4:18
  satire is simply h. in uniform 194:8
  unconscious h. 61:19
Hump: cameelious h. 211:7
Humpty Dumpty: have you heard of one H.
    197:10
Hun: H. is at the gate 210:19
Hunch: nothin' but a collective h. 389:1
Hunchback: h. in the park 369:4
Hundred: first h. days 204:19
  h. eyes were fixed on her 30:14
  how it will tell a h. years hence 61:16
Hundredfold: divided like a h. store 319:4
Hung: they all ought to be h. 147:15
Hungarian: learnt H. by themselves 190:13
Hungary: I am not annoyed with H. 173:18
Hunger: bodily h. in his eyes 343:27
  h. allows no choice 18:19
  h. of the hungry 379:5
  war against h. 205:1
Hungering: thirsting and h. 151:15
Hungry: feed the h. on statistics 235:14
  no child will go to bed h. 214:34
  what it was like to be h. 220:16
  where human beings went h. 14:12
Hunt: at night he h.s 117:15
  h.s south of the Thames 316:17
Hunted: tell . . . by their h. expression 232:15
  tell . . . by their h. look 401:23
Hunter: h. and hunted 53:22, 99:12
Hunting: Good H.! 213:29
  I went h. wild 288:26
  transcend the h. pack 159:3
Hunting-horns: memories are h. 13:2
Hurly-burly: h. of the chaise-longue 65:1
Hurries: h. elsewhere 97:6
Hurry: h. to get up when we fall down 114:2
  h. up please, it's time 118:11
  so who's in a h.? 35:4
Hurrying: all that is h. 319:8
Hurt: wish to hurt 54:5
Hurting: once it has stopped h. 48:5
Husband: archaeologist is the best h. 78:15
  being a h. is a whole-time job 37:8
  bigamy is having one h. too many 9:1
  chumps . . . make the best h.s 408:11
  finding a h. for one's mistress 91:2
  h. is what is left of the lover 325:22
  h. [provides] the landscape 51:26
  if your h. is a bore 34:10
  in their h.s a perfection 257:3
  my h. and I 119:11
  to lose . . . a h. or two 399:23

where my next h. was coming from 398:10
Hush: h., h.. Nobody cares 271:15
  h.! h.! whisper who dares 264:13
Hushed: wrongs h. up 288:22
Husk: goitrous torpid and squinting h.s 233:11
Hussar: on Wednesday an H. 407:8
Hut: wouldn't leave my little wooden h. 258:10
Hyacinth: synthesis of h.s and biscuits 335:1
Hybreds: h. and lubberds 197:14
Hyena: all hygienes have their h.s 276:1
Hygiene: all h.s have their hyenas 276:1
  hell without the h. 24:22
Hymn: Aisle. Altar. H.. 273:11
Hyper-thyroid: Shelley had a h. face 355:25
Hypertrophied: h. sense of order 287:6
Hyphen: many h.s left in America 406:22
Hyphenate: everybody else has to h. 270:8
Hyphenated: h. Americanism 323:9
Hypocrisy: h. is . . . a whole time job 256:8
  homage to virtue . . . we call it h. 62:2
  New York tolerated h. 399:13
  world safe for h. 411:13
Hypocrite: h. . . . lies with sincerity 143:17
  see far enough into a h. 76:12
Hypothesis: discard a pet h. every day 237:15
  God as a working h. 46:6
Hypothetics: highest degree in h. 61:4

I

I: greatest concentration is in . . . I 66:11
  I am I and you are you 176:13
  I and Thou 57:11
IMF: I. running our financial affairs 35:19
Ibsen, Henrik: God, economics, or I. 295:19
  no one who hates I. 351:5
  on an equality . . . with I. 396:15
Ice: as though I. burned 415:15
  banana skins, sometimes on i. 62:8
  broken i.; Heaven's gates 112:3
  i. is also great 135:11
  I asked for i. 16:6
Ice-cream: emperor of i. 358:11
  just enjoy your i. 402:17
  never . . . lick i. off a hot side walk 339:9
Iceberg: like i.s in the ocean 142:11
Icebox: eaten the plums . . . in the i. 404:28
Iced: i. sugar cakes . . . looked green 125:20
Ichthyosaur: in favour of the i. 397:15
Icicle: eye clear as the bleb of the i. 167:2
Icon: i., a totem, a curio 363:10
Icummen: winter is i. in 302:26
Id: care of the i. by the odd 9:15
  let's put the i. back in yid 325:9
Idea: better to entertain an i. 192:10
  between the i. and the reality 117:18
  from it are our i.s born 141:21
  good i. – son 62:11
  good i. but it won't work 321:15
  i. isn't responsible 251:19

i. of health 377:12
i. that God had 106:10
imprinting an i. on the memory 173:6
in a war of i.s 227:5
in pursuit of an i. 413:2
i.s are born from life 395:2
i.s are of more importance than values 51:23
i.s can be too old 288:10
i.s simply pass through him 49:24
i.s that enter the mind 378:5
i.s that make us optimists 382:5
it would be a good i. 140:23
learn our i.s, or . . . get out 231:1
let the i. die instead of you 233:10
makes people into i.s 413:1
man of many i.s cannot be serious 385:11
music must have an i. or magic 323:15
nothing is more dangerous than an i. 4:14
only country . . . founded on a good i. 156:22
powerful i. communicates . . . its power 307:4
right i. at the wrong time 388:3
second-hand i.s 245:20
two i.s . . . The other one's hats 234:14
when a politician gets an i. 251:16
with i. as with umbrellas 206:7
wonderful i.s books have presented 308:17
you can't massacre an i. 314:1
Idea-bound: race which has become . . . i. 223:4
Ideal: don't worry about his i.s 130:19
i.s of a nation by its advertisements 109:1
shoes with broken high i.s 243:15
we are an i. couple 373:2
Idealism: alcohol, morphine or i. 199:5
i. . . . shocked by its rascality 258:19
Idealist: I'm an i. . . . I'm on my way 334:21
Identified: i. with . . . cheering us all up 37:3
Identify: i. his footmarks 330:2
Identity: associate prejudice with i. 48:6
Ideological: nuance in an i. difference 87:1
Idiot: i. culture 39:22
like the i. or clown 349:12
Idle: somebody for i. hands to do 170:11
Idling: impossible to enjoy i. thoroughly 194:9
Idly: are we i. occupied 412:2
Idol: God . . . would be an i. 46:9
Idolater: who dies for him are alike i.s 344:27
Idologies: all i. are relative 144:6
Idyll: gift of the i. 218:18
Ignoble: doctrine of i. ease 323:5
Ignorance: dead languages to hide his i. 376:18
education costs . . . but then so does i. 272:1
i. bumping its head in the dark 129:19
i. is strength 286:23
i. must necessarily be infinite 301:2
i. of the gods 61:9
inhibition caused by i. 245:15
Ignorant: i. as the dawn 416:1
i., only on different subjects 321:21
if girls aren't i. they're cultured 91:1
Ignore: children . . . with nothing to i. 277:23
clan has a tendency to i. me 409:14

Ike: I Like I. 11:28
Iliad: authorship of the *I.* 183:12
I admire it [*I.*] greatly 164:6
Ill: for what human i. does not dawn 402:15
got i., you were poor, you died 251:1
we are all i. 377:12
Ill-health: cynicism is humour in i. 397:8
Ill-housed: one-third of a nation i. 322:14
Ill-informed: better un-informed than i. 111:1
Illegal: i., immoral, or fattening 413:5
President does it . . . it is not i. 281:3
Illegitimate: no i. children 415:2
Illiterate: i.s can read and write 269:1
Illness: i. is the most heeded of doctors 308:9
i. is the night-side of life 353:8
i. . . . what the world has done 259:16
no i. which it cannot counterfeit 307:21
special i. of the ear 18:12
Illnesses: episode between i. 201:14
Illumination: for support rather than i. 220:11
Illusion: by manifold i. 417:22
Great I. 8:16
i. . . . what is not written 64:8
indulging in i.s 242:17
just one i. about them 94:20
life's i.s I recall 265:25
one i. – France 206:11
Illustrious: i. without any strain 308:1
Image: bind you to an i. and a posture 319:13
blotted out man's i. 417:21
delivering the i. from its prison 280:8
nation that can see beyond its own i. 205:7
so very like their own i. of him 293:13
society after their own i. 377:22
wronging your i. 416:23
Imaged: O man-projected figure, of late i. 162:16
Imagery: i. is part of a continuous body 208:4
Imaginary: belongs entirely to the i. 318:15
happiness is an i. condition 364:4
Imagination: i. . . . content with argument 417:24
i. of the living 38:6
i. reacted 189:22
lived largely in the i. 304:11
no i. there is no horror 110:8
skill without i. 360:1
strip our pleasures of i. 307:12
travel is for people without i. 317:3
Imaginative: language of an i. race 52:2
Imagine: they i. the past 277:5
where nobody i.s living 152:19
Imitate: art does not i. life 53:11
free . . . they . . . i. each other 176:1
immature poets i. 119:6
Imitating: worry about not i. them 395:14
Imitation: invention that begins as an i. 294:7
man . . . is an i. of something 288:11
Imitator: advantage of having i.s 47:6
Immaculate: I. Conception was spontaneous
combustion 292:7
i. contraceptives for the populace 197:11
Immanent: i. will that stirs and urges 162:10

Indecision: nothing is habitual but i. 191:16
Indemnity: i. is instantaneous 91:19
Indented: not so much born as i. for 140:14
Independence: i. in the wrong place 75:16
Independent: end of Britain as an i. state 138:11
    I have an i. mind 239:22
    never promises to make them i. 186:12
    something about an I. Labour Party 393:10
Indescribable: describe the i. 75:20
Indestructible: is love eternal, i. 107:23
Indeterminate: only an i. sentence 180:24
Index: true i. of a man's character 88:25
India: I. is a geographical term 79:8
    introduced bottled water into I. 69:13
    one voyage to I. is enough 80:26
    own to the possession of money in I. 214:9
    pink is the navy blue of I. 388:15
Indian: I. in an overcoat 368:13
    last wild I. of America 301:1
    world of Gary Coopers you are the I. 23:4
Indicative: first person, present i. 408:2
Indifference: benign i. of the universe 65:25
    fern-dark i. of . . . Australia 223:11
    my belief in God's i. 189:16
    total i. to public notice 361:4
Indifferent: i. . . . . essence of inhumanity 343:4
    universe is i. 176:15
Indigestion: bore . . . with your i. 156:14
Indignation: mists of righteous i. 272:15
    righteous i. into the wrong things 78:4
Indignity: all this i. . . . on thee 162:9
Indispensable: full of i. men 141:14
    i. when you don't want to do anything 139:6
    i.s . . . get on . . . without them 182:26
Indistinguishable: i. from magic 83:14
Individual: cult of the i. 207:13
    i. has become increasingly gregarious 27:4
    i.s do not vitally concern me 224:18
Individualism: American system of rugged i. 177:4
    bits of insane i. 75:16
Individualistic: science must be i. 77:18
Individuality: just let his i. develop 110:15
    paradise of i. 335:10
Indivisible: peace is i. 235:5
Indoors: 'er i. 155:12
    God having given us i. and out-of-doors 241:3
Induction: someone not prepared to use i. 70:5
Industrial: i. relations are like sexual 123:9
    i. worker would sooner have a £5 note 44:17
    military-i. complex 116:14
Industrialization: i. . . . . lead the snail 227:11
Industry: being a captain of i. again 410:7
    chief i. . . . is getting by 234:3
    when . . . i. can't take you 382:11
Inefficient: efficient and the i. 343:22
Ineligible: i. for the struggle of life 88:11
Inequality: i. . . . . to eliminate poverty 197:5
Inevitable: i. gradualness 394:5
    we resist only what is i. 262:5
Inexactitude: terminological i. 78:18
Inexhaustible: i. bodies . . . not dead 365:8

Inexperience: had to confess inexperience 48:4
Inexperienced: young and i. house 194:12
Inexterminable: i. – like flies 136:9
Infancy: hell lay about him in his i. 153:10
Infant: i. child is not aware he has been eaten 178:15
    I wish I'd been a mixed i. 31:7
    small terrors i.s go through 110:12
    unkillable i.s of the very poor 303:21
Infantile: nationalism is an i. disease 115:16
Infantry: rag-time i. 12:19
Infection: i. of the common sky 151:24
Inference: apart from difficult i.s 114:9
Inferior: feel i. without your consent 322:7
    i., like a man who has paid for a woman 153:15
    titles . . . are disgraced by the i. 344:31
    where does she find them [i.s] 292:21
Inferiority: fortunate i. 76:3
    i. complex about other people 407:13
    imperialism with an i. complex 166:9
    they'll say he has an i. complex 333:16
    to the point of dispelling that i. 308:5
Infernal: after we cross the i. ripples 303:12
Inferno: i. of his passions 199:3
Infidelity: accused him [Adam] of i. 42:6
Infinite: Health is i. 331:1
    ignorance must necessarily be i. 301:2
Infinities: our place among the i. 135:20
Infinitive: when I split an i. 72:13
Infinity: i. is a dreadfully poor place 199:21
Inflammatory: word for brother. It's i. 404:8
Inflated: i. style is . . . euphemism 287:13
Inflection: beauty of i.s 358:18
Influence: always prefer i. to power 252:8
    aspired to power instead of i. 366:1
    bad philosophers may have a certain i. 328:20
    how to win friends and i. people 68:3
    politics . . . can be settled by i. 127:27
    [religion] attempted to i. his life 130:22
    spread out his i. thin over millions 252:1
    what have I got? I. 240:4
Influenza: my aunt died of i. 345:19
    no i. in my young days 37:2
Informed: better i. 43:3
Inhale: as though she would i. them 125:24
Inherited: takes away . . . what we have i. 51:25
Inheriting: i. is culture 249:24
Inhibition: cultivate a few i.s 237:11
    i. caused by ignorance 245:15
Inhumanity: essence of i. 343:4
Iniquity: mammon of i. 167:4
    quite an air of i. 136:21
Initiation: gives us our first i. 319:18
Injustice: i. between the setting . . . sun 19:23
Ink: crossword puzzles in i. 129:1
Inn: gin in the lowest kind of i. 74:22
    go to i.s to dine 75:2
    i.s are not residences 268:17
    when you have lost your i.s 33:17
Innisfree: arise now . . . and go to I. 416:18
Innocence: ceremony of i. is drowned 417:12
    i. is on at such a rakish angle 136:21

insanity is a kind of i. 154:9
spurious i. 34:4
wept for the end of i. 146:9
Innocent: i. children and devils 83:11
i. of mathematics 320:15
Innuendo: murmur or i. causes panic 73:14
Innuendoes: beauty of i. 358:18
Inoculation: degree was kind of i. 36:8
Inquisition: i. fulminating 395:4
Insane: when dealing with the i. 171:13
Insanity: i. is a kind of innocence 154:9
prelude to i. 392:10
Insect: transformed . . . into a . . . i. 200:10
Inseparable: i. my nose and thumb 291:3
Inside: i., it is . . . his nursery 239:1
i. my tent pissing out 195:20
short back and i.s 243:17
whenever I look i. myself 194:19
Insight: added judgement to i. 130:21
flashes of i. beyond meanings 400:21
Insignificance: of the utmost i. 98:9
Insincerity: enemy of . . . language is i. 287:13
Get Well Card with a hint of i. 338:4
Insolence: lazy i. of a shoe salesman 295:7
Insoluble: critical questions that are i. 201:3
political ones are i. 109:4
Insomnia: amor vincit i. 136:27
no wonder you've got i. 105:2
Inspiration: genius is one per cent i. 115:2
no more i. . . . than . . . muffins 344:11
Instability: i. of evil 401:11
Instalment: last i. missing 95:23
one more i. and Baby will be ours 309:1
Instant: i. sex will never supersede 95:24
Instantaneous: i. photograph of a Derby 241:10
Instead: not before or after, but i. 10:2
Instinct: all healthy i. for it 61:24
i.s already catered for 36:3
of i. rather than of practice 314:13
reasons for what we believe upon i. 49:22
Instinctive: appealed to the i. bigamist 183:11
Institute: gas was on in the I. 40:17
Institution: i. . . . the lowest common denominator 192:14
not so dominant an i. as ours 68:4
see an i. without hitting it 96:5
Instruction: no i. book came with it 137:12
Instrument: i. to measure Spring with 97:23
jazz . . . having all the best i.s 150:16
most sensitive i. known to man 29:21
Insulation: i. in the particular 71:7
Insulted: i. where the average negro 101:2
Insurance: poisoning . . . for their i. 110:5
stick out your tongue at the i. doctor 251:5
Insured: his neighbour's house is not i. 231:16
i. for the accidents most likely 91:19
Insurrection: feminism is an i. 29:12
i. is an art 378:1
i. stands in . . . relation 378:4
Integrity: i. was not enough 18:12
kind of i. 360:21

Intellect: halitosis of the i. 185:4
higher the voice the smaller the i. 279:7
i. deteriorates after every surrender 27:8
not to make the i. our God 115:20
very incarnation of i. 345:33
Intellection: i. is to skip an hour's TV 8:5
Intellectual: formative i. matrices 155:19
i. – one educated beyond the bounds 9:8
i. . . . a man who's untrue to his wife 18:7
i. attitude . . . political 249:25
i. disgrace 17:17
i. elbow-room 190:10
i. hatred is the worst 417:5
i. is someone whose mind watches itself 65:22
I too wanted to become an i. 339:18
i.s . . . ideas are of more importance 51:23
i.s . . . opening an umbrella 248:8
i.'s problem is . . . commitment 155:18
i.s should suffer . . . persecution 329:1
most sinister phenomena in i. history 66:5
tears may be i 33:24
treason of the i.s 35:10
Intelligence: arresting the human i. 225:14
down with i.! 261:3
i. is almost useless 68:7
key of i. 335:5
man carries the terrible burden of i. 92:13
military i. is a contradiction in terms 253:18
organ through which our i. is revealed 308:12
sole entrant in an i. contest 239:14
thoroughbred i. 413:2
three kinds of i. 315:10
Intelligent: cannot be both honest and i. 287:15
i. but not . . . quite i. enough 183:9
old and i. enough to come home again 49:7
won't eat anything that has i. life 123:18
Intelligentsia: intelligent are to the i. 23:12
Intelligible: best to aim at being i. 177:9
Intended: I i. an ode 107:12
Intensity: full of passionate i. 417:12
Intent: i. on one thing 318:5
Intention: hell is paved with good i.s 345:4
Intercourse: arising from . . . human i. 106:11
i. began in nineteen-sixty-three 221:3
Interest: benefit of i. in all the moneys 303:9
best i.s of the nation 281:1
seldom against their i.s 317:2
worry is the i. paid on trouble 186:18
Interesting: exciting but not i. 273:1
interesting, but tough 379:17
some not i. even then 366:10
that a proposition be i. 401:1
very i. . . . but stupid 195:9, 325:15
Interlude: strange dark i.s 285:4
International: cause of i. conflict 394:11
Interpenetrate: men and sea i. 89:12
Interplay: i. between nature and ouselves 168:4
Interpret: to i. it [justice] 140:12
Interpretation: i. is a free walk 338:13
machine for generating i.s 114:7
Interpreter: i. can do no more with it 29:15

Interrupt: i. me when I'm interupting 63:18
Interval: enjoy the i. 335:14
  i. without an opera 279:5
Interview: i.s are funny things 361:19
Interviewing: i. a faded female in a damp basement
    162:1
  i. people who can't read 420:7
Interviewing 72:18
Intestine: tapeworm in an i. 146:8
Intimacy: common-sense to baulk i. 246:8
  i. and solitude have lost their value 27:4
Intimate: small circle of i.s 252:1
Intimidated: i. by reality 389:1
Intolerable: i. wrestle with words 116:28
Intolerance: i. by the sea 31:12
Intoxication: like hangover without i. 108:1
Introduce: i. you to the last king 115:5
Introduced: when I'm i. to one 311:9
  without ever having been i. 95:10
Introduction: buy back my i. to you 253:6
Introspection: i. . . . in the Five Towns 30:2
Invasion: waiting for the promised i. 79:20
Invent: certainty, order, all that? Then i. it 25:3
  rest he i.s 324:7
Invented: everything that had to be i. 360:4
  i. . . . for . . . becoming extinct 98:3
  only lies are i. 50:17
  we i. the Revolution 394:14
Invention: great and blessed i. 342:22
  i. of recent date 131:13
  i. that begins as an imitation 294:7
  i.s that are not made . . . rarely missed 138:16
  marriage is a wondeful i. 87:12
  no great i. . . . not hailed as an insult 159:1
  one i. still lacking 66:16
  woman's virtue is man's greatest i. 349:19
Invest: never i. in anything that eats 323:20
  never i. in anything that sleeps 300:3
Investment: no finer i. for a country 80:3
Inviolable: most i. thing to occur 66:22
Invisible: best clothes are i. 160:18
  Campland, an i. country 352:22
  freedom is an i. word 405:4
  letting off i. fireworks 393:18
  no i. means of support 57:14
  text written in i. ink 216:11
Invite: i. with gilded edges 18:24
Invited: going where you haven't been i. 114:5
Inviting: i. trouble; it . . . accepts 248:4
Involuntary: i.. They sank my boat 205:10
Involved: chicken is i. 278:14
Invulnerable: i. . . . perish 366:14
  i. retrograde Masoch 317:14
Inwards: wit never turns i. 100:8
Ionic: enormous fluted I. columns 246:6
Ireland 381:5
  brought up in I. 380:23
  called I. for short 198:24
  great Gaels of I. 74:10
  I. is . . .full of genius 230:16
  I. is the old sow that eats her farrow 198:7

I would have liked to go to I. 403:12
  in I. there is a precedent 208:3
  romantic I.'s dead and gone 417:17
Irish: alike . . . I. more so 112:1
  being a woman is like being I. 274:8
  glass of water . . . 'I. or Scotch?' 159:9
  guess the answer to the I. question 341:8
  I. . . . devotion to higher arts 139:1
  I. don't know what they want 10:10
  I. . . . have a psychosis 31:11
  liver, . . . assaulted by the I. 341:12
  we I. had the right word 56:2
  yer I. . . . they've got sounds 354:10
Irishman: I. is . . . harmless as a powder magazine
    112:2
  Irishman thinks afterward 285:1
  Jesus must have been an I. 87:3
Iron: behind the i. curtain 352:4
  depth of i. 278:19
  i. curtain has descended 80:7
  i. curtain would at once descend 145:17
  i. girder in a house of cards 255:18
  i. has entered his soul 236:8
  i. lady of the Western World 367:15
  I. Maiden 306:10
  whim of i. 171:4
Ironies: life's little i. 163:26
Irregular: Baker Street I.s 110:7
  one of those i. verbs 239:22
Irregularity: i. . . . a crime 240:2
Irresolute: resolved to be i. 79:10
Irresponsible: i. and right 80:12
Irving, Sir Henry: H. would have loved it 367:14
Ishmaelite: better sort of I.s 393:3
Islam: I. . . . came with a sword 326:10
Island: favourite i.s 17:6
  glory came to the I. people 81:9
  i. in the North Sea governed 156:7
  i. . . . of coal and surrounded by fish 41:9
  look stranger at this i. now 17:23
Isle: colonized the I. of Wight 32:5
  ship, an i., a sickle moon 128:18
  ships and stars and i.s 128:7
Isle of Man: Kelly from the I. 274:14
Isms: passion and death than . . . these i. 223:7
Isness: i. of things 29:13
Isolated: i. way of having a bad time 73:19
  stands i. in Europe 131:11
Isolation: intense i. 55:15
Israel: challenging I. to peace 13:5
  [I.] . . . four million prime ministers 289:1
  in I. it's enough to live 325:3
Issue: contrived corridors and i.s 117:13
  moral i. . . . more than a real i. 257:13
  personal i. of adipose tissue 93:15
It: it's just I. 214:25
Italian: baseball in I. 259:13
  Heaven is where the lovers are I. 9:23
  I. . . . people say what they mean 270:21
  I.s will laugh at me 275:11
  one well-kept I. hand 191:5

translated into I. 399:11
Italy: Creator made I. 380:4
  in I. . . . under the Borgias 395:12
Itch: i. to talk about themselves 256:20
  Seven Year I. 19:25
Itchez: when ah i., ah scratchez 278:2
Ivory: new moon hangs like an i. bugle 370:13
  peacocks, apes and i. 212:4
Ivy: it was agony, I. 313:8
  just like the i. I'll cling to you 264:4
Ivy-covered: archaic i. ruins 306:8
Ivy League: not impressed by the I. establishments
  105:13

J

Jack: damn you, J. – I'm all right 45:18
Jack Frost: J. dancing bespangled 80:17
Jack-knife: just a j. has Macheath 51:20
Jackinabox: j. and knocked his daddy down 181:11
Jacky Tar: J., the son of of a gun 198:19
Jacob: J. is a German shepherd 92:8
Jahweh: J. . . . [tries] to ruin 258:16
Jail: I write to get out of j. 361:17
  j.s called schools 382:11
Jake: everything is simply j. 108:5
Jam: all humanity is j. to you 222:13
  rush-hour j. in the subway 82:24
Jamais: j. triste archy j. triste 251:14
James, Saint: ladies of J.'s 107:11
James I: [J.] . . . an omniscient umpire 377:11
James, Henry 49:2, 373:3
  J. . . . divisible 156:6
  poor H.. he's spending eternity 256:9
James: home, J. and don't spare the horses 172:6
  J. J. Morrison Morrison 264:7
Jane: I'd call 'em all J. 396:17
  J., J., tall as a crane 348:18
  me Tarzan, you J. 394:16
Japan: means the defeat of J. 323:3
  next week in J. 368:12
Japanese: J. have perfected good manners 368:11
  reconcile J. action with prudence 79:24
Jar: folk out in front that I j. 121:7
Jarvis, Jonah: I'm J., come to a bad end 369:22
Jaw-jaw: j. is always better than war-war 80:15
  j. is better than war-war 245:9
Jazz: j. . . . all the best instruments 150:16
  J. Age 126:11
  way j. is performed 305:8
Jealous: house is j. of its nastiness 151:13
  j. because of his *amour propre* 154:19
  j. . . . for being shot 418:7
  never dream of being j. of *her* 188:10
Jealousies: j., each . . . is ephemeral 306:19
Jealousy: all j. to the bride 26:13
  j. is no more than feeling alone 48:8
Jeans: just something in my j. 44:4
Jeeves: like Wodehouse dropping J. 393:24

Jefferson, Thomas: way J. did [study] Montesquieu
  387:4
  when J. dined alone 204:21
Jehovah: J. complex 168:5
  J. of the Thunders 210:30
  two solemn little J.s 132:14
Jehovah's Witnesses: J., awaiting the Last Day
  231:16
Jellicoe, Admiral, Earl: J. . . . could lose the war in
  an afternoon 82:2
Jelly: feed a grub on royal j. 82:8
  from the way he eats j. beans 313:15
Jellyfish: as little uproar as a j. 410:2
  who wants my j.? 277:17
Jem: J. is joky for Jacob 197:16
Jerusalem: New J. based on the . . . Ideal Home
  Exhibition 208:5
Jester: designated court j.s 299:19
  humour is like a j.'s bladder 271:19
Jesus Christ 46:10, 148:19, 225:6
  allow C. to have died on the Cross 106:7
  C. of his gentleness 151:15
  C. would . . . have been arrested 101:22
  came C. the tiger 117:12
  cold C. and tangled trinities 212:10
  despised C. . . . the son of a carpenter 153:18
  I thought I saw J. on a tram 263:6
  if J. returned today 164:7
  it's hard to see C. for priests 265:18
  J. died for somebody's sins 351:9
  J. . . . first rate political economist 342:12
  J. loves you more than you will know 347:20
  J. must have been an Irishman 87:3
  J. never travelled 317:3
  J. saves but he couldn't on my wages 149:19
  J. was a typical man 149:20
  leaders of the stature of J. 383:15
  people ask why I killed J. 57:4
  record that C. laughed or played 130:11
  thing J. *really* would have liked 333:17
  to the right of . . . J. 382:14
  told the truth about his father was J. 36:13
  we're more popular than J. 229:9
  when J. came to Birmingham 363:3
  who dreamed that C. had died in vain 349:1
Jew 33:19, 202:7
  American . . . a J. or an anti-Semite 335:24
  came for the J.s and I didn't speak up 280:5
  coloured, one-eyed j. 101:3
  half of Christendom worships a J. 9:6
  hated . . . as if I were a J. 418:13
  I decide who is a J. 239:3
  J.s bring the unlike 420:4
  J.s find themselves numbered 312:15
  J.s . . . have a psychosis 31:11
  J.s have made a contribution 383:15
  like J.s or Germans or films 187:8
  like other J.s, only less so 312:20
  liver, chopped up . . . by the J.s 341:12
  look at them [J.s] in the . . . carriage 130:25
  luxury that a J. never can allow himself 258:7

no J. was ever fool enough 420:1
not really a J.; just J.-ish 262:10
noticed that J.s shout 325:3
to choose the J.s 121:17
two J.s there are three opinions 27:15
what one J. copies from another 239:2
where a J. feels even slightly uneasy 196:6
Jewellery: don't ever wear artistic j. 86:5
experienced pain and bought j. 326:8
I always recognize the j. 144:17
rattle your j. 229:13
remember to hang on to her j. 237:8
Jewish: because I'm J. . . . people ask 57:4
behind . . . America . . . a J. financier 317:10
Hitlerism is . . . of J. origin 78:2
J. man with parents alive 325:10
J. National Home 47:11
J. or of an ancient English family 153:20
J. porno film 319:20
national home for the Jewish people 23:19
peopling Palestine with J. immigrants 186:19
riveted by J. abnormality 325:4
since my daughter is only half-J. 253:21
total solution of the J. question 146:3
Jewry: instrument of [world] J. 375:5
Jigsaw: j. puzzle under house arrest 247:1
piece in a j. puzzle – a missing piece 249:12
Jim: boy whose name was J. 32:14
Lucky J. 7:12
poor J. Jay got stuck fast 103:10
Jinete: el j. se acercaba tocando el tambor 140:8
Jingoes: against the j. at its close 81:2
Joan of Arc, St 299:4
who was Noah's wife? J. 166:4
Job: he's doing a grand j. 134:22
in a way, he's got no j. 366:19
look for a new j. afterward 106:6
only j. . . . a woman can beat a man 170:4
thou has a good j.. Don't blow it 6:11
tricky j. being Home Secretary 102:12
we have finished the j. 158:7
we will finish the j. 79:21
you are not up to the j. 371:1
your neighbour loses his j. 378:17
Jock: yer J.s . . . they've got sounds 354:10
Joffre, General Joseph 178:2
Jogging: j. . . . I could hear heavy breathing 45:8
j. is very beneficial 339:10
John-Sebastian-like: little more J. 182:18
John Thomas: J. marryin' Lady Jane 223:17
Johnny Head-in-Air: not despair for J. 308:20
Johnson, President Lyndon B.: hey, hey, L.B.J.
149:10
Johnson, Samuel 87:22
Joined: if they were not j. on right 38:5
Joke: aim of a j. 287:11
as if a j. were a charity auction 243:19
I don't make j.s 321:26
if we live inside a bad j. 311:2
j. with a double meaning 25:12
Krishna's j.s may be vapid 130:11

last to get the j. 85:16
my little j.s on Thee 135:7
no more j.s in music-halls 337:1
Normans don't j. . . . about food 339:17
subtleties of the American j. 380:3
woman who can't tell a j. and 154:23
worst j. God can play 48:10
Joker: said the j. to the thief 113:5
Joking: way of j. is to tell the truth 343:19
Jolly: j. D.! 178:3
three j. farmers once bet a pound 103:17
Jolly-rodgered: j. sea 369:21
Jones: shouldn't know J. 92:12
Joneses: cheaper to drag the J. down 95:11
keeping up with the J. 268:21
Jordan: do not take a bath in J. 348:23
shaped the J. near my home 368:20
Joseph, Keith: J.? . . . Rasputin and Tommy Cooper
166:15
Josephine: not tonight, J. 98:8
Joss-sticks: odour of j. 50:10
Jour: tous les j.s, à tous points de vue 93:9
Journal: you can read it in the J. 351:17
Journalese: j. is any old words 374:8
Journalism 64:12
j. . . . an extension of conversation 334:5
j. . . . like turning one's enemies 56:8
j. . . . saying 'Lord Jones dead' 77:20
j. . . . will be grasped at once 87:18
j. . . . will interest less tomorrow 143:19
patron saint of bad j. 387:12
rock j. 420:7
why j.? 24:1
Journalist 241:11
bribe . . . the British j. 411:11
diplomats tell lies to j.s 217:4
j.s . . . have nothing to say 217:14
j.s say a thing 37:9
Journey: is your j. really necessary? 3:16
it [education] should be a j. 36:8
j. guided by . . . hierarchical authority 53:24
long day's j. into night 285:3
prepare [for a j.] as though for death 250:6
wandering j. from the East 273:8
worst time of year for a j. 117:20
Journeyed: j. to the centre of dialogue 189:2
Journeying: seat sat the j. boy 163:7
Jowled: j. or hawk-like foreign faces 246:6
Joy: man's greatest source of j. 139:5
no j. . . . greater 125:30
no j. in pouring out one's sins 125:32
O j. of the gnat 318:16
politics of j. 181:17
rent spontaneous j. 416:6
strength through j. 233:20
their j. or their pain 370:20
Joyce, James 225:7, 412:24
could not write the words Mr J. used 346:3
J. was a synthesizer 29:9
Joyful: tears are j. 360:12
Judaism: religious, like J. itself 411:14

k. you a different way 321:18
meet interesting people and k. them 12:2
men are prepared to k. one another 343:32
my k. shall be thy k. 214:3
novel . . . for the ladies to k. time 112:13
ordeal which will not actually k. him 40:6
to k. a man is to merit a woman 144:15
waste remains and k.s 120:21
why k. time when you can k. yourself? 161:7
will not die even if they k. me 156:2
Killed: animal is k. and yet mourned 134:8
  I don't mind your being k. 215:6
  not people k. in battle 337:8
Killing: all for k. animals 411:21
  k. is the ultimate simplification 242:18
  k. [killin'] meself workin' 284:1
  k. Kruger with your mouth 209:12
  k. time – there's nothing else 238:7
  k. time is the essence 382:4
  k. time . . . the multifarious ways 349:6
  living unless I'm k. myself 174:12
  never of k. for their country 329:10
  older than the art of k. 388:13
Kilt: beautiful day for putting on a k. 107:18
  k. is an unrivalled garment 254:22
  worn a k. in the . . . Highland manner 59:10
Kin: one's own k. and kith were more fun 277:13
Kind: k. of people do they think we are 79:24
  k. people have a wonderful dream 270:9
  man she had was k. and clean 291:13
  one that is ever k. 416:8
  too k. – too k. 280:6
Kind: wer zeigt ein K., so wie es steht? 318:6
Kinder: make k. the face of the nation 60:13
Kindle: k. a light in the darkness 199:4
Kindliness: cool k. of sheets 54:12
Kindly-meant: like a k. lie 44:12
Kindness: k. of strangers 404:22
  k. of the poor to the rich 76:18
  k. of wooed and wooer 288:20
  to k. and wisdom we make promises 308:9
King: as a prince, as a k., as a man 90:3
  captains and the k.s depart 212:15
  discharge my duties as k. 115:7
  he who slays a k. 344:27
  honour has come back, as a k. 54:11
  in search of mythical k.s 305:9
  K. asked the Queen 264:10
  k. is a thing men have made 10:15
  k. over all the children of pride 212:12
  K.s and governments may err 170:26
  K.'s First Minister 80:1
  k.s is mostly rapscallions 379:18
  k.s of the earth are old 319:14
  last k. of England 115:5
  musing upon the k. 118:12
  never . . . sit down unless you're a k. 181:14
  old k. to the sparrow 103:19
  only seeing the K. and a few friends 16:1
  son of a thousand k.s 209:14
  soon be only five k.s left 122:12

swinging his axe to fell k.s 58:12
tradition of k.s wearing heads 162:2
walk with k.s 210:33
when I'm already k. 107:4
your K. and country need you 124:8
Kingdom: k. of the well and . . . the sick 353:8
Kingfish: I'm the K. 237:2
Kinquering: k. congs their titles take 355:14
Kip: celibate kip 381:5
Kipling, Rudyard: sort of gutless K. 287:7
Kipper: load of k.s, two-faced 167:17
Kiss: every Duchess . . . wanting to k. me 243:5
  I will not k. your f.ing flag 97:14
  if you weren't going to k. me 255:4
  k. is just a k. 182:3
  K. K. Bang Bang 200:4
  k. me any time during the evening 126:17
  k. of death 350:2
  k. of the sun for pardon 156:24
  k. without a moustache 71:3
  rough male k. of blankets 54:12
  sisterly k.. Older sister 247:11
  someone might blow you a k. 355:10
  told and did not k. 266:5
Kissed: hasn't been k. for forty years 325:19
  k. . . . who didn't wax his moustache 214:18
  k. her once by the pigsty 369:24
  k. her way into society 376:19
  k. the lovely grass 54:14
  known that their cheeks could be k. 307:9
Kissing: I wasn't k. her, I was whispering 252:13
  I Wonder Who's K. Her Now 2:4
  k. . . . between 'Hi' and fucking 236:17
  k. is . . . getting . . . so close 415:3
  k. Marilyn Monroe was like k. Hitler 98:5
Kissinger, Henry: K. brought peace to Vietnam 168:24
  medium-sized K. 168:25
Kit-bag: troubles in your old k. 14:10
Kitchen: get out of the k. 386:10
  k.-sink-revolutionary look 398:21
  scrub a k. pavement 415:6
  take it into the k. and eat it 327:21
  to live under the k. 281:18
  waiting at the k-k-k-k. door 284:15
Kitchener, Horatio, Earl 15:22
Kite: fit only for k. flying 35:2
Kitten: trouble with a k. 277:18
Klee, Paul: K. . . . dreams with proper awe 66:22
Kleiner: K. Mann, was nun? 122:3
Knave: dumbfounded before a k. 416:12
Kneadable: needless k. flesh 341:22
Knee: gardener's work is done upon his k.s 210:25
  go in the water up to her k.s 253:21
  k.s up, Mother Brown 227:12
  let man's hand stay off my k.s 20:7
  now they are all on their k.s 163:9
  than to live on your k.s 185:1
  there wanders through the world a k. 269:5
  upon what were once k.s 97:14

L

wild ecstatic l. 10:11
Lear, King: imagined behaving to L. 106:9
Learn: anything that he doesn't want to l. 334:7
    l. all we lacked before 55:8
    l. by going where I have to go 321:9
    l. the lines 94:22
    we want to l. 'em 150:15
Learned: l. with little labour 75:15
Learning: beauty and the lust for l. 30:21
    l., earning and yearning 269:14
Learnt: love is not l. 319:6
    remember what I l. 400:13
    what has been l. has been forgotten 349:18
Leave: all things l. me 363:14
    dead men on l. 232:6
    thus we live for ever taking l. 318:17
Leaves: as the l. grow on the tree 416:3
    burning of the l. 42:1
    deck put on its l. again 128:17
    famous harmony of l. 417:21
    home before the l. have fallen 403:10
    lets l. into the grass slip 370:11
    voice of falling leaves 73:14
    where the l. drip with sweet 348:20
Leaving: l. home after living alone 230:6
Leavis, F.R.: L. . . . moral earnestness 232:18
Leben: L. geht hin mit Verwandlung 318:14
    so l. wir 318:17
Lecherous: l. liars 403:7
Lecture: better . . . shop-lifting than to give l.s 52:5
    friend . . . comes to hear your l.s 49:5
    to l. rooms is forced 75:11
Left: being l. fifty thousand pounds 264:20
    more to the l. than you, Mr Stalin 397:14
    support the l., . . . leaning to the right 56:17
    there aren't many l. like him 392:7
    truth is simply what is l. 385:2
    what his other l. hand is doing 324:5
    wonder why they l. 376:16
    you get what's l. 322:18
Left-handed: decisive blows are struck l. 35:13
Leg: between your l.s . . . instrument 29:21
    born with your l.s apart 286:5
    cursed with a right l. 68:10
    four l.s good, two l.s bad 286:9
    men's l.s have a terribly lonely life 107:21
    most meaningless l.s imaginable 56:10
    never trust men with short l.s 94:18
    nowhere unless you use your own l.s 334:9
    open my l.s and think of England 172:7
    pulls the l.s of his dreams 369:25
    run your l.s off 51:17
    short, fat, hairy l.s 269:3
    strongest l.s in Pontefract 40:14
Legend: l. becomes fact 31:22
    l. is an old man with a cane 101:1
    l.s of the green chapels 369:11
    she leaves only a name and a l. 25:10
Leggings: lambs leap with stiff l. 418:17
Legion: ere yet we loose the l.s 210:30
    l. of the lost ones 210:23

Legion of Honour: L. has been conferred 380:16
Legitimacy: defend his nation's l. 122:8
Leica: me no l. 228:9
Leicester Square: farewell L. 403:22
Leiden: nicht sind die L. erkannt 319:6
Leisure: l. is work you volunteer for 320:18
    l. to bother about whether you are happy
      345:11
    reputability to the gentleman of l. 386:15
Leitern: nur aneinander lehnenden L. 318:9
Lemming: thousand l.s can't be wrong 149:29
Lemonade: I cannot drink my l. 175:18
Lenin, Vladimir Ilyich 82:1, 207:12
    L. was an admirable man 45:6
    L. was the first to discover 366:4
    L was literate 53:21
Lent: human flesh uncooked in L. 393:3
Leonardo da Vinci: most significant figure . . . since
    L. 238:3
Leopard: three white l.s sat 116:19
Lergy: dreaded l. 263:17
Lesbian: all women are l.s 196:11
    l.s are mighty fine 12:7
    my mother made me a L. 149:25
Less: can't take anything l. 147:10
    l. is more 260:16
    l. of this than meets the eye 24:7
    l. she wouldn't do 168:11
    more and more about l. and l. 60:8
Lesser: l. breeds without the law 212:16
Lesson: never had a l. in her life 274:18
    satire is a l. 276:10
    we taught them a lesson in 1918 228:2
Lest: l. we forget 212:15
Let: l. down my friends. I l. down my country
    281:2
    l.'s all go down the Strand 70:12
Lethal: Average made l. 342:4
Lethe: if no L. flows beneath 312:5
    small chat to the babbling of L. 28:15
Letter: I would have answered your l. sooner 1:3
    in this you can also write your l.s 66:8
    know a woman until you've had a l. 231:12
    l. for a spy 212:21
    l. of hate 288:8
    l.s that I drive in like nails 84:4
    painter of l.s 145:10
    those l.s to be sincere l.s 168:16
Letter box: two hands to open a l. 261:2
Letting: it's all right l. yourself go 189:5
Lettuce: too much l. is soporific 302:16
Level: love is all 30:28
Levin, Bernard 397:19
Lewd: l. forefathers of the village 356:1
Liar: fighting a l. in the quad 355:17
    fool, or a l. or both 341:17
    I am the club l. 332:10
    l. . . . imagines that his lie rings true 206:3
    lecherous l.s 403:7
    Muse prefers the l.s 418:5
    of easy virtue and a proved l. 158:10

poet is a l. 85:10
quite picturesque l. 380:11
signposts like grim l.s 44:5
they only answered little l. 32:24
Libel: l. . . . impossible to write 39:20
Liberal: especially every British L. 37:5
fallacy of the l. mind 273:2
if God had been a L. 49:20
ineffectual l.'s problem 133:3
l. is a conservative . . . arrested 9:9
l. is a man who uses his legs 322:19
l. . . . too broad-minded 136:16
like an old l. between the wars 300:5
L.s think that goats are just sheep 49:17
you may be the most l. L. Englishman 223:8
Liberate: first . . . l. the children 327:21
Liberation: l., a human phenomenon 133:10
mankind's war of liberation 205:1
Liberté: délivrez-moi de la l. 84:5
Liberties: O freedom, what l. are taken 142:8
taking l., and these l. were once ours 371:6
Liberty: bitter taste of l. 106:15
deliver me from liberty 84:5
if l. means anything at all 287:19
L., Equality, Adultery! 34:9
l. is conforming to the majority 338:3
l. . . . must be rationed 229:8
price of l. is . . . eternal dirt 287:1
shall the voices of l. be mute? 97:26
there can be no effective l. 31:20
they took away my l., not my freedom 203:18
Libidinous: bogeys are l. 52:17
Librarian: l.'s duty to distinguish 361:7
Library: hair done in the l. 375:7
l. is thought in storage 334:11
like a l. on Sundays 14:14
lumber-room of his l. 109:14
replaced the l. pass 236:16
sober me up to sit in a l. 126:14
Libya: travel in groups or bomb L. 209:2
Lice: I've l. in my tunic 18:14
Licence: l. to print money 371:11
sure he didn't get a dog's l. 253:7
Licensed: based upon l. premises 283:7
Lichen: better to l. on a rock 88:18
Licht: let there be l., 242:16
Lick: I know what I l. 133:13
Licorice: l. fields of Pontefract 40:14
Liddell: said L. to Scott 163:5
Lie: believe a l. 328:17
better than a useful l. 249:23
came home, home to a l. 303:16
confess the l.s he tells himself 178:14
couldn't l. if you paid him 212:2
everywhere you go people tell l.s 52:9
evry word she writes is a l. 242:9
good of a l. if it's seen through 153:12
hypocrite . . . l.s with sincerity 143:17
kindly-meant l. 44:12
leader who can l. 96:17
l. about the Democrats 359:1

l. can be half-way round the world 63:12
l. down, young yeomen 179:14
l. even when it is inconvenient 387:9
l. has become . . . a pillar of state 353:1
l. is an abomination 358:20
l. where shades of darkness 103:2
l.s about his wooden horse 128:16
l.s about the Republican Party 104:6
l.s are the mortar that binds 396:25
l.s damned l.s and statistics 379:19
l.s in the shape of false teeth 397:1
l.s of tongue and pen 74:24
live by what they know to be a lie 160:20
Matilda told such dreadful l.s 32:21
misleading impression, not a l. 14:6
more easily fall victims to a big l. 173:7
nothing to hide rather than . . . to l. 65:15
old l. *Dulce et decorum* . . . 288:18
only l.s are invented 50.17
polite by telling l.s 49:12
rather l. on a sofa 89:14
someone who cannot tell a l. 2:19
three kinds of l.s 379:19
Liebe: nicht ist die L. gelernt 319:6
Life: all human l. is there 190:19, 279:10
all l. is six to five against 326:17
and the l. goes on 303:2
at war you think about a better l. 402:19
brief and powerless is man's l. 328:12
constantly to seek the purpose of l. 217:21
do you believe in the l. to come? 28:17
essential quality of l. 134:18
essentially how I feel about l. 5:17
experience of l. drawn from l. itself 30:22
first day of the rest of your l. 102:10
first prize in the lottery of l. 316:2
forever viewing l. 42:25
happiness is the only sanction of l. 335:8
house of l. 372:20
I really don't know l. at all 265:25
ideas are born from l. 395:2
inconveniences of l. 315:11
ineligible for the struggle of l. 88:11
interest in l. does not lie 412:4
isn't l. a terrible thing 369:27
it may be l., but ain't it slow? 170:25
it's art that makes l. 191:9
keen observer of l. 18:7
lay down his friends for his l. 371:12
lay down your l. for his country 156:12
l. and death is cat and dog 136:25
l. becomes fiction, and fiction l. 219:5
l. before death 149:17
l. begins at forty 299:13, 379:11
l. begins on the other side of despair 336:3
l. deceives us so much 308:17
l. enchantments 38:1
l. exists . . . because the carbon atom 193:1
l. . . . exists for its own sake 401:7
l. had prepared Podduyev for living 352:8
l. has different laws in here 352:22

l. in my men 398 4
l. is a cheap *table d'hote* 206:8
l. is a drama and not a progress 273:3
l. is a foreign language 269:15
l. is a gamble, at terrible odds 361:3
l. is a maze 88:20
l. is a predicament 335:16
l. is a process of filling in time 39:21
l. is a tragedy 73:2
l. is all right for the time being 43:7
l. is an abnormal business 187:10
l. is an offensive 400:20
l. is doubt 382:2
l. is . . . drawing . . . conclusions 61:12
l. is just a bowl of cherries 56:14
l. is just a novitiate eternity 93:6
l. is like a sewer 228:3
l. is . . . like a tin of sardines 35:23
l. is not a series of gig lamps 412:5
l. is not having been told 278:9
l. is nothing until it is lived 336:2
l. is one long process of getting tired 61:11
l. is one tenth Here and Now 363:12
l. is what happens 229:16
l. itself. . . was enough 412:16
l. loves the liver of it 8:17
l. makes no absolute statement 223:12
l. of every man is . . . the l. of man 273:9
l. of the mind 306:13
l. . . . one damned thing after another 180:20
l. passes in transformation 318:14
l. persists in the vulnerable 366:14
l. shouldn't be printed on dollar bills 284:11
l. till my work is done 177:1
l. was a funny thing 95:20
l. with the dull bits left out 172:14
l.? There's nothing more terrifying 195:7
l.'s battle is a conquest for the strong 254:13
l.'s little ironies 163:26
l.'s longing for itself 143:5
l.'s troubled bubble broken 103:22
long littleness of l. 93:3
making l. into art 284:18
man who questioned l. 248:7
measured out my l. with coffee spoons 117:24
more to l. than having everything 341:16
my chance with one of the Lords of l. 222:23
my l., in self-surrender, had a goal 160:6
newspapers . . . relationship to l. 217:13
no l. is lived for . . . an obituary 53:12
no more guilty of imitating 'real l.' 276:5
no one owns l. 60:1
one may call l. in general 412:4
one of the worst things about l. 304:7
painting is a way to forget l. 325:13
people say that l. is the thing 350:23
priceless gift of l. 324:6
Raphael is the l. itself 367:12
real l. seems to have no plots 86:21
remember this day for the rest of your l. 141:2

rent everything other than . . . l. 217:1
richness of l. lies in the memories 294:4
right order of l. 365:13
she is mine for l. 354:3
so it is with Time in one's l. 307:2
stand aside from l. 86:19
strive . . . to give our l. its form 307:18
taking l. by the throat 136:5
that was all of Ida's l. 357:10
there was l. – pale and hoar 163:13
they want my l., and that I cannot give 218:3
this car is the motor of l. 242:1
three ingredients in the good l. 269:14
to give l. shape 12:23
too small for l. 74:11
true to the flame of l. 223:10
ultimate simplification of l. 242:18
walls of l.'s exclusive city 222:19
we talked a lot about l. 385:5
what a queer thing L. is! 410:9
what am I, L.? 254:7
youth . . . a little later in l. 15:17
Life-insurance: l. agents . . . argue 225:20
Life-like: Dickens' world is not l. 71:5
Life-sentence: l. in the dungeon of self 88:26
  l. which fate carries in her other hand 225:1
Life-support: poetry . . . on a l. system 165:4
Lifeboat: touchy if you say one word; l. 155:22
Lifemanship: murmured . . . the word 'L'. 302:21
Lifetime: not even perhaps in our l. 204:19
  not see them lit again in our l. 155:8
  wrap up a quarter of a l. 57:20
Lift: education is a sieve as well as a l. 73:3
  London . . . designed in the lift 176:11
Light: art is l. synthesis 217:5
  can't stand a naked l. bulb 404:20
  give me a l. that I may tread safely 165:12
  go very l. on vices 290:3
  it gives a lovely l. 261:6
  l. breaks where no sun shines 369:8
  l. so dim . . . not have chosen a suit 78:10
  l. that failed 214:12
  leaping l. for your delight discovers 17:23
  l.s everywhere except in the minds 313:11
  optics is the geometry of l. 102:8
  thousand points of l. 60:12
  turn up the l.s 170:20
  turning money into l. 46:14
  up with the l. 370:18
  watching his luck was his l. o' love 341:20
Lightbulb: l. . . . cannot switch itself off 91:6
Lightfoot: many a l. lad 180:2
Lightning: attention span of a bolt of l. 314:4
  scratch my head with the l. 380:6
  to keep the l. out 187:16
  writing history with l. 407:3
Like: changed him they don't l. him 106:1
  [human nature] too much l. my own 108:4
  I don't l. it at all 351:3
  I know she l.s me 362:9
  I know what I like 30:27

just l. that! 90:19
l. me more than you don't l. me 103:28
lot of guys l. me 331:12
not a lot . . . but you'll l. it 99:11
nothing says we've got to l. each other 105:3
our business to know what we l. 119:4
seek not to make them l. you 143:5
some of them I don't l. 69:10
somebody up there l.s me 153:3
something you l. about someone 405:11
what we l. is not necessarily good 31:20
you either like 'em or don't 396:23
Liked: he's l., but he's not well l. 261:19
Likely: not bloody l. 345:21
Lilac: breeding l.s out of the dead land 117:37
Lilac-time: go down to Kew in l. 282:3
Lilas: je n'oublierai jamais les l. ni les roses 13:6
Lilies: beauty lives though l. die 128:7
considers the l., the rewards 172:1
Lilliputian: either a poet or a L. 388:14
Lily: it trembles to a l. 107:11
L. O'Grady: L., silly and shady 348:22
Limb: femme fatale l. 68:10
if these poor l.s die 55:4
l.s casually placed 396:4
Lime: you've got to give her l. 211:14
Limelight: pool of l. 283:13
Limestone: what I see is a l. landscape 17:18
Limit: draw a l. to thinking 408:3
Limitation: l. of armaments by . . . appeasement
237:17
range of l.s 153:5
Limited: l. to men who insist on knowing 303:26
vocabulary of Bradshaw is . . . l. 110:10
Limousine: l. and a ticket for the peepshow 246:3
one perfect l. 291:5
Limp: L-I-M-P pronounced l. 263:5
Limpopo: great, grey-green, greasy L. 214:6
Lincoln, Abraham: I am a Ford not a L. 129:15
L. . . . such an artful manipulator 90:2
when L. was shovelled 334:16
Line: draw a l. without blurring it 80:10
l. has been drawn in the sand 60:15
l. will take us hours 415:5
learn the l.s 94:22
party l. is that there is no party l. 107:8
pray to God and say the l.s 100:17
stand in l. to hate him 11:20
walk on the l.s or the squares 264:12
Linen: criminal . . . who dirties the l. 58:2
Linger: melody l.s on 39:13
Lingerie: brevity is the soul of l. 292:14
l. is on the next floor 297:20
Linie: wo sonst die l. 56 hält 202:1
Link: nothing l.s man to man 347:10
Linnet: evening full of the l.'s wings 416:20
Linoleum: photograph me through l. 24:10
Lion: if there must be a l. in the household 2:7
l. and the calf shall lie down together 6:12
l. tamer enter a cage with a book 266:14
l.s led by donkeys 176:4

race . . . that had the l.'s heart 80:16
thought the l. was dead 410:17
Lionized: wasn't spoilt by being l. 376:17
Lip: in the grave with my l.s moving 249:2
just put your l.s together and blow 21:2
l.s . . . which are for kissing 97:23
move their l.s when reading 251:21
read my l.s: no new taxes 60:11
Lipstick: when you've got on too much l. 277:26
Liquid: l. hands tapped on the womb 368:20
l. 'istory 59:21
sex is only the l. centre 90:17
Liquidation: l. of the British Empire 80:1
nation about to go into voluntary l. 243:21
Liquor: l. and love rescue . . . sense 405:1
l. is quicker 278:1
we drank our l. straight 18:16
Lissom: l., clerical, printless toe 54:17
Listen: it's the poet himself who l.s 167:6
l. a lot and talk less 96:15
Listener: are we now the l.s 319:19
good l. is a good talker 401:24
Listening: [actor] ain't l. 145:2
l. and hearing is never repetition 357:18
l. without hearing 348:1
they think they're l. 10:1
Listless: l. form and face 163:7
Literacy: uses of l. 176:7
Literary: first great nonstop l. drinker 371:15
l. man puts together two words 91:10
l. movement: . . . people who hate 329:13
Literature: all that most l. is 392:1
art and l. are left to . . . bums 233:18
Bible is l., not dogma 335:6
edge of the chair of l. 372:20
enfant terrible of l. 61:20
fleas in the double bed of l. 188:14
higher-water mark . . . of Socialist l. 287:7
history to produce a little l. 190:17
if God exists, what's the good of l. 187:13
if we can't stamp out l. 393:8
l. . . . best when it is half a trade 186:14
l. clear and cold . . . and very dead 233:19
l. has no relation with [life] 308:17
l. . . . is a hard row to hoe 75:20
l. is mostly about having sex 236:9
l. is news that stays news 303:24
l. is . . . something . . . read twice 87:18
l. is the one place in any society 327:17
l. . . . language charged with meaning 303:27
modern American l. comes from one book
169:8
remarks are not l. 357:4
what is going to happen to l.? 306:6
why it's L.! 396:8
world could get on . . . without l. 336:12
Litmus: real l. test 196:6
Little: how shall we turn to l. things 143:14
how very l., since things were made 213:9
l. man, what now? 122:3
l. man, you've had a busy day 347:11

l. orphan Annie 152:21
l. she hadn't tried 168:11
l. things are . . . the most important 109:11
licht, . . . and there was a l. 242:16
poor l. rich girl 93:21
Littleness: long l. of life 93:3
Live: America to die – but never . . . to l. 191:7
do you want to l. for ever? 99:10
don't actually l. longer 133:14
flesh perishes, I l. on 162:19
I wouldn't want to l. there 157:3
if I'd known I was going to l. this long 43:14
if you can't l. without me 168:1
if you don't l. it [music] 290:9
it's unwise to l. 346:1
l. .. on the proceeds 350:16
l. backwards from in front 400:17
l. beyond his moral means 376:7
l. now, pay later 361:20
l. on your knees 185:1
l. with proud peacocks 100:12
others merely l. 88:27
people who have had to l. 380:13
sef-willed determination to l. 171:17
something to l. for 160:4
think as if you will l. for ever 275:13
thus we l. for ever taking leave 318:17
to l. is like to love 61:14
to l. is not like walking 293:10
we l. as we dream – alone 89:6
you have to l. with rich people 350:18
you might as well l. 291:8
Lived: had we l., I should have had a tale 340:2
he is l. 51:21
life is nothing until it is l. 336:2
Livelihood: though I must slave for l. 2:2
Liver: French . . . kill their l.s 96:9
l., doted upon by the French 341:12
life loves the l. of it 8:17
Liverpool: folks that live in L. 74:23
Lives: conduct our differing l. 17:15
cracks of other people's l. 399:18
great history and . . . small l. 80:5
l. with the mainspring left out 127:3
live as many more l. . . . as we wish 166:5
moments of other people's l. 299:11
plant ourselves in their l. 235:7
Living: art of l. that your price shall suit 161:11
dead be wiser than the l. 128:11
dead far outnumber the l. 218:17
different l. 354:18
if l. isn't a seeking for the grail 127:21
l. and partly l. 118:22
l. are getting rarer 187:11
l. is made . . . by selling 402:21
l. unless I'm killing myself 174:12
l. well is the best revenge 375:6
lest they . . . earn their l.s 150:12
people live instead of l. yourself 341:25
position of the dead among the l. 413:4
summertime and the l. is easy 142:21

they won't look after the l. 375:17
until we learn the use of l. words 103:25
world . . . does not owe us a l. 296:14
Living room: brutality of war into the l. 245:3
household name in his own l. 99:13
lost in the l.s of America 245:3
Lizard: if men were as much l.s as l.s 19:7
Llama: female l. surprised in her bath 82:13
Lloyd, Selwyn 41:12
Lloyd George, David, Earl 15:19, 15:20, 28:10
L. . . . detected . . . in . . . an argument 37:6
when he [L.] is alone 207:8
Lloyd Webber, Andrew 230:24
Loadsamoney 120:23
Loafed: better to have l. and lost 372:7
Loafing: cricket as organized l. 367:6
Lob: nothing but a l. 327:10
Lobby: go into the L. against us 23:9
Lobcock: dine with Lord L. 18:24
Lobotomy: like paradise, with a l. 347:15
Lobster: world is your l. 155:14
Local: little l. difficulties 245:8
Locally: think globally, act l. 12:8
Lock: fingers at the l.s 368:23
they still l. them up 352:13
Lockjaw: Linda Lovelace with l. 73:10
Locomotion: human l. 108:14
Locust: decade the l.s ate 235:10
famine grew, and l.s came 369:3
years that the l. hath eaten 187:1
Lodestar: wife is the l. of his life 291:11
Lodger: one you're going to be a l. in 292:26
Logic: condition . . . like l. 408:10
in l. process and result 408:8
l. and metaphysics are true 20:6
l. is the art of going wrong 9:12
l. of our times 101:21
l. rather than upon the crime 109:12
Logical: imaginative l. construction 401:10
not conceived by any l. process 83:7
Logically: deduced the rest l. 36:4
Loincloth: l.s and aprons 152:17
Lolita: L. light of my life 276:3
London: crowd flowed over L. Bridge 118:5
dead lies L.'s daughter 369:15
in L. town a man gets mugged 246:14
it's still 1938 in L. 260:13
jumping the L. streets 246:7
L. . . . a lot of soup walking about 174:11
L. belongs to me 86:13
L. . . . clearing-house of the world 71:13
L. . . . designed in the lift 176:11
L. doesn't love the latent 190:7
L. is a teen-ager and urchin 38:15
L. is full of chickens 302:8
L. spread out in the sun 221:18
L.'s noble Fire Brigade 32:22
one road leads to L. 254:9
power station in the middle of L. 73:8
put me on the train to L. Town 264:5
that I love L. so 154:24

this – is L. 275:4
to speak against L. 130:18
Londoner: maybe it's because I'm a L. 154:24
Loneliness: shade and l. and mire 55:9
your l. may spur you 160:4
Lonely: all the l. people 229:20
doesn't explain why I'm l. 331:12
for fear I may be l. 194:20
if one is l. one prefers 153:19
l. and poor of old 54:10
l. crowd 318:3
l. of heart is withered away 416:21
men's legs have a . . . l. life 107:21
no man is l. while eating spaghetti 270:1
Sergeant Pepper's l. hearts club 230:4
'we' . . . makes her feel less l. 209:9
Lonely-hearts: write-to-Miss-L. 398:18
Lonesome: l. blues collide 266:2
Long: in the l. run we are all dead 207:3
it just means you're a l. couple 347:18
l. and the short and the tall 204:10
L. Hot Summer 123:5
there's a l., l. trail a-winding 208:16
Long Island Sound: silent is L. 272:6
Long-shot: life . . . is a . . . comedy in l. 73:2
Long-yarded: l. and great-bellied 151:20
Longer: it just seems longer 133:14
some [parts] are a bit longer 284:21
Longest: l. essay, irrespective of merit 392:5
time is the l. distance 404:17
Longevity: done to achieve l. 269:20
Longing: l. for love 328:1
l.s that can't be fulfilled 304:16
Look: l. again when it's safe 363:11
l. for him rather than themselves 407:16
l. thy last on things lovely 103:3
not possible to l. and listen 24:19
some men never l. at you 290:13
something younger than she l.s 125:29
stop; l.; listen 383:4
that is where to l. 205:16
way people l. and laugh 412:13
Looked: l. not often, but suddenly 366:15
Looking: here's l. at you, kid 44:22
she was l. all the time 369:24
Looking-glass: used as a captive l. 387:5
Looking-glasses: women . . . as l. 412:19
Loophole: l. through which the pervert 54:5
Loose: l. when you begin to fight 139:20
let l. upon the world with £300 26:21
Loose-fitting: see women . . . as l. men 48:20
Loosened: l. like the long hair 319:4
Loot: widen the rift and gather the l. 166:8
Lord: divinity of Our L. 348:3
L. of the Dance 69:11
men no l.s can buy or sell 75:5
my chance with one of the L.s of life 222:23
neither a L., nor a privy, nor a seal 21:13
praise the L. and pass the ammunition 130:1
what . . . th' L. wud do if He knew 111:20
see also House of Lords

Lord Mayor: L. raising his hat 132:9
Lord's Prayer: I could cut the L. 315:4
L. when playing canasta 119:10
Los Angeles 72:9, 234:21, 292:20, 347:15
difference between L. and yogurt 365:12
L. has Hollywood – and hates it 72:10
not in the L. telephone directory 67:12
two modes of transport in L. 227:1
Lose: army l.s if it does not win 214:30
guerrilla wins if he does not l. 214:30
l. him decisively 26:30
l. more of yourself than you redeem 167:3
we don't want to l. you 326:4
whatever we l. 97:21
Loser: all are l.s 71:17
Losing: Napoleon brought peace . . . by l. 168:24
never lost sight of l. you 272:9
two ways of l. oneself 71:7
Loss: suffer the l. they were afraid of 18:22
Lost: everything . . . found is always l. again 174:2
explorers have to be ready to die l. 174:18
l. and waiting for you 210:17
l. generation 357:17
loved and l. than never to have l. at all 62:6
scared to go to the brink, you are l. 111:4
we weren't l. 373:7
Lot: not a l. . . . but you'll like it 99:11
wot a l. I got 3:29
Lottery: first prize in the l. of life 316:22
Lötze, Rudolph H.: L.'s classroom 159:10
Lou: lady known as L. 341:20
Loud: am I too l.? 268:14
Louder: says another, cleverer, l. thing 62:9
Loungin': l. round and sufferin' my son 213:24
Lourdes: compete with those of L. 134:3
Louse: scarce the soul of a l. 213:5
Lousy: l. but loyal 12:4
one fault. It was kind of l. 373:9
unethical and l. 14:7
Lout: our national l. 247:15
Love: a-waggle with l. 222:14
all you need is l. 229:17
always ourselves we l. 22:3
breakfast food of l. 4:7
caution in l. 328:8
constancy of the woman who l.s me 345:13
did not that l. shut his door on me 350:17
easier . . . than to l. one's neighbour 176:2
'Emily, I l. you' on the back 252:19
enough to make him fall in l. 306:15
expressing l. . . . among the undeveloped 34:14
fall half in l. with them 333:11
falling in l. is wonderful 39:4
falling in l. . . . sign of failure 358:9
fell in l. . . . with himself 303:30
help and support of the woman I l. 115:7
hid in the heart of l. 417:4
how did you l. my picture? 147:23
'I l.', 'I hate', 'I suffer' 412:6
I l. or I hate 297:16
I speak the words of my l. 321:7

I wish I could fall in l. 383:21
if l. is the answer 375:10
imagine a faultless l. 17:18
in a dark room with someone you l. 181:16
in l. as in sport, the amateur status 152:10
in l. with making movies 395:14
infinity of successive l.s 306:19
intensity of l. and sex 265:14
interested before they have made l. 145:4
is l. eternal, indestructible 107:23
know all about l. . . . live without it 294:6
lack of l. contaminates 156:19
laughter and the l. of friends 32:27
learn to l. by loving 183:15
let us make l. deathless 377:6
let's fall in l. 301:21
liquor and l. rescue . . . sense 405:1
longing for l. 328:1
looking for . . . perfect l. 395:7
l. and marriage 63:8
l. doesn't know . . . renunciation 187:5
l. each other like dogs 108:10
l. fled 417:28
l. for something else 307:13
l. is a fanclub with only two fans 169:20
l. is a universal migraine 152:2
l. is like the measles 194:10
l. is not learnt 319:6
l. is not the dying moan 295:10
l. is . . . the gift of oneself 12:21
l. . . . is the honest state 224:22
l. levels all 30:28
l. . . . never having to say you're sorry 340:13
l. one another, yes, yes 105:3
l. only others, he cannot l. at all 134:14
l. set you going 299:23
l. song is just a caress 322:6
l. the things we l. for what they are 135:15
l. we swore would last 101:18
make l., not war 12:5
make l. . . . to all the women 203:17
man in l. is incomplete 138:3
marriage without l. 83:4
masturbating and making l. 28:5
mediocrity that makes us let go of l. 187:5
money can't buy me l. 229:19
[money] ranks with l. as . . . joy 139:5
most exclusive l. for a person 307:13
my l. and I did meet 416:3
narrow theme of l. 417:19
never too late to fall in l. 406:14
next to . . . god america I l. you 97:24
no peace of mind in l. 307:6
nobody l.s a fairy when she's forty 169:19
O fat white woman whom nobody l.s 93:4
Oh, when I was in l. with you 179:18
only one duty and that is to l. 65:23
paths of l. are rougher 162:14
perfect fear casteth out l. 89:3
phenomenon that we call l. 307:3
reliance on . . . the forms of l. 206:10

she l.s you, yeh, yeh, yeh 230:5
though l. can initially degrade 107:23
tired of l. 32:30
to l. – . . . reason is against it 61:24
too young to really be in l. 102:11
try thinking of l. or something 136:27
two kinds of l. 86:8
violence masquerading as l. 219:11
war is like l. 51:11
watching his luck was his light o' l. 341:20
we must l. one another or die 18:19
what a mischievous devil L. is 61:23
what will survive of us is l. 221:4
when l. gets to be important 358:9
who l.s finds the door open 365:5
whose l. is given over-well 291:7
why does free l. cost so much? 12:9
wider shores of l. 43:17
will you l. me in December 390:7
with l. and squalor 333:18
with l. from me to you 229:22
women always want to be our last l. 338:18
yet l. survives 151:11
you made me l. you 241:13
your voice falls as . . . l. should 221:8
Love-bird: l. to get above herself 409:5
Loved: feared rather than l. 328:5
l. himself only as much 366:15
l. the pilgrim soul 417:27
never to have loved a tall 209:4
those that l. you best 33:14
what did your l. one pass on from? 392:23
who would be l. 302:9
Lovelace, Linda: useful as L. with lockjaw 73:10
Lovelies: fifty l. in the rude 370:2
Loveliest: l. and best has smiled 32:31
l. of trees, the cherry 179:10
Loveliness: fashioned forth its l. 163:3
woman of so shining l. 417:15
Lovely: everything in the garden's l. 164:21
look thy last on things l. 103:3
two l. black eyes 85:2
when l. woman stoops to folly 118:15
wouldn't it be l. 230:18
Lover: even l.s find their peace 128:8
had three hundred l.s 397:22
Heaven is where the l.s are Italian 9:23
hello, young l.s 160:9
husband is what is left of the l. 325:22
in every l. a feigned l. 386:2
keep half a dozen l.s guessing 325:21
l.s lying two by two 179:16
neither father nor l. 321:7
to lose a l. 399:23
unwearied still, l. by l. 417:29
Lover-like: to abuse a man is a l. thing 69:15
Loving: if we stop l. animals 352:10
Low: l. on whom assurance sits 118:14
Lowbrow: first militant l. 39:14
Lowells: L. talk to the Cabots 47:8
Lower: there is a l. class, I am in it 102:6

Lower-middle class: describes himself as . . . l. 261:1

Lowered: her body has been l. 189:18

Lowest: l. form of life 110:16

Lowness: his l. creeped out first 197:17

Loyal: don't care a damn for your l. service 267:8
easier . . . to be l. to his club 400:4
lousy but l. 12:4

Loyalty: I want . 196:2

Lucid: l. friend to aerial raiders 355:4

Lucifer: fitful, fiery L. 418:16

Luck: bad l. was always as welcome 316:1
self-made man . . . believes in l. 356:14
until one is amazed at one's l. 274:7
watching his l. was his light o' love 341:20
wish me l. as you wave me goodbye 124:18
with a little bit of l. 230:19

Lucky: L. Jim 7:12
you l. people! 377:15

Luftwaffe: give this much to the L. 73:7

Lugged: l. into Family Rows 409:14

Lull: interlude of l. 199:18

Lumbago: L. and the Laxative Islands 341:6

Lumber: stowed away in a Montreal l. room 62:7

Lumber-jack: I'm a l. and I'm OK 268:3

Lumber-room: l. of his library 109:14

Luminous: l., . . . the serpent-haunted sea 128:6

Lump: l. the whole thing 380:4
there are l.s in it 358:4

Luna: l. de cien rostros iguales 140:5

Lunar: modus of l. eclipses 303:12

Lunatic: l. asylum run by l.s 235:20
l. fringe 323:12
l.s and . . . great men of history 328:5
l.s have taken over the asylum 325:21
who believe in themselves are all in l. asylums 76:28

Lunch: no free l. 11:6
she's unable to l. today 302:1
take a cannibal to l. 149:34
whether he has enough money for l. 265:12

Lundy, Lord: L. . . . moved to tears 32:17

Lung: don't keep using your l.s 225:19

Lust: beauty and the l. for learning 30:21
enjoy his l. 302:9
l. for certainty may be a sin 158:27
l. of knowing what should not be known 128:12

Lust: ihre Türme aus L. 318:9

Lustre: crocus l.s of the stars 95:6

Lusty: while I am young and l. 290:11

Luxuries: give me the l. of life 413:11
l. not for him 74:19

Luxury: every l. was lavished on you 286:1
honour is a l. for aristocrats 76:15
l. liner is . . . a bad play 189:15

Lying: diplomacy – l. in state 171:6
l. hardly describes it 344:13
one of you is l. 291:14
that branch of the art of l. 93:2
truth acceptable to l. men 18:13

Lyme: there was an old party of L. 267:9

Lynching: attended a l. every day 351:19

Lyonesse: when I set out for L. 163:18

Lyre: when 'Omer smote 'is bloomin' l. 213:16

M

MCC: hard to tell where M. ends 305:17

MFI: our bed's only M. 411:22

MGM 106:2

Mabel: whatever M.'s been up to 351:18

MacArthur, General 378:20

Macavity: M. wasn't there 117:29

MacDonald, Ramsay 79:7, 79:9, 82:6, 257:12
M. had sufficient conscience to bother him 236:1

McEwan: M's beer as usual 87:11

Macheath: just a jack-knife has M. 51:20

Machine: best m. in the world 61:3
dogma of the ghost in the m. 330:1
I have tested your m. 376:21
if you fall in love with a m. 273:20
man who rides up on a great m. 262:2
m. for generating interpretations 114:7
m. for living in 227:10
m. for turning . . . wine . . . into urine 106:12
m. threatens all achievement 319:11
more a great thought than a great m. 193:2
no m. can do the work 180:22
you're not a man, you're a m. 342:20

Machine-à-habiter: une maison est une m. 227:10

Machine-gun: m. riddling her hostess 182:25

Machinery: immediately you come to m. 386:4

Machismo: m. . . . . man is never quite man 154:22

Macho: m. doesn't prove mucho 138:6

Mackerel: as mute as a m. 351:5

Mackerel-crowded: m. seas 417:9

Macleod, Iain 333:23

Macmillan, Harold, Lord Stockton 41:12, 371:12, 386:20
knew what M. was made of 232:1
M. advancing . . . with a paralysed shuffle 231:19
M. . . . . to embody the national decay 272:17
[M.] exuded a flavour of moth-balls 272:17

Maconides: old M. the blind said it 128:19

Macy's: kiss my ass in M. window 196:2

Mad: as soon as he ceased to be m. 307:19
Englishmen taking m. dogs for walks 263:3
go m. in good company 101:19
m. about the boy 94:15
m. and dead as nails 368:19
m. as the mist and snow 416:24
m. eye of the fourth person singular 124:3
poets do not go m. 76:29
tends the grave of M. Carew 166:6
to be m. is not easy 151:14
we are all born m. 29:7
whom the m. would destroy 232:5

Madame Bovary: I could think of . . . M. 242:6

Maddest: m. of all mankind 211:9

Made: m. it, Ma . . . top of the world 146:5

Madeira: from M., but . . . respectable 345:31

Madeleine: little piece of m. 306:12

Mademoiselle: m. from Armenteers 325:19

Madman: Hugo was a m. 85:7
 m. . . . lost everything except his reason 76:30

Madness: best minds . . . destroyed by m. 144:3
 m. need not be all breakdown 219:13
 near to reality in his madness 317:8
 rest is the m. of art 190:20

Madonna: M. of the Slums 235:18

Madras: M. is hot for ten months 277:7

Maestro: music, m., please 247:3

Magazine: by the butt of the M. Wall 197:10

Maggot: m.'s weak clamour 151:17

Magic: art is full of m. and trickery 274:12
 dead to life is no great m. 152:4
 fooleries of m. and religion 183:9
 have to do m. on television 395:15
 m. and delicious power 412:19
 m. realism, then 228:11
 music must have an idea or m. 323:15
 technology is . . . m. 83:14
 that old black m. 260:1
 what was once a M. Flute 9:26

Magical: purely m. object 27:2
 submission to m. forces 301:4

Magistrate: strength of weak m.s 144:12

Magnanimity: in victory: m. 81:4

Magnanimous: m. and the rest 306:16

Magnificent: more than m. – it's mediocre 147:22

Magnificently: m. unprepared 93:3

Magnifying-glass: splinter . . . the best m. 2:18

Magnitude: single room . . . has no . . . m. 225:15

Magpie: life of a guinea-pig or a m. 190:18
 swollen m. in a fitful sun 303:10

Mai: *M. qui fut sans nuage* 13:6

Maid: alas, no m. shall get him 305:10
 call women ladies . . . treat them as m.s 255:3
 m. and her wight come whispering by 163:1
 old m. among novelists 398:23
 old m. is like death by drowning 124:2
 way of a man with a m. 211:24

Maida Vale: in the mists of M. 300:7

Maiden: Iron M. 306:10
 marrying left your m. name disused 221:9
 voyaging after m.s 197:22

Maidenform: Cleopatra in my M. bra 3:14

Mail: *Daily M.* is read by the wives 3:31

Mail order: m. city 72:10

Mailer, Norman 387:14

Main: m. road of procreation 392:12

Maine: or you live in the State of M. 129:14

Mainspring: lives with the m. left out 127:3

Majesty: if Her M. stood for Parliament 354:11

Major, John 44:13, 129:13, 166:16

Major: live with scarlet M.s at the base 336:29
 m., whether they choke or not 400:3

Majorism: M. is Toryism with regrets 209:11

Majorities: politics does not reflect m. 159:19

Majority: enable the m. to have their way 21:14
 great silent m. 280:15
 liberty is conforming to the m. 338:3
 one with the law is a m. 90:7
 substituted m. for power 171:15

Maker: primal simplicity in every m. 389:10

Making: reporting something and m. it up 133:2

Maladies: m. we must not seek to cure 307:19

Malaise: Wembley . . . a vague m. 194:6

Malaysia: in M. [it was] 1937 368:12

Male: dream of the American m. 400:6
 especially the m. of the species 222:20
 m. . . . doesn't even take off his hat 373:3
 m. sex . . . obstinate vested interest 237:3
 no reason for the . . . m. sex 399:1
 seldom female in a world of m.s 299:14

Malice: m. is like a game of poker 355:8

Malicious: God is subtle . . . not m. 115:11

Malignant: part of Randolph . . . not m. 393:17

Malingering: genius for m. 307:21

Malleable: in a highly m. condition 213:26

Malpractice: economy or m.? 285:22
 m. . . . a crime and you can prove it 240:2

Malt: m. does more than Milton can 180:3

Malvern: prefer Perrier or M. water 36:23

Mama: I encountered the m. of dada 122:1

Mammon: m. of iniquity 167:4

Man: ain't a fit night for m. or beast 125:11
 ascent of m. 54:1
 before you can call him a m. 113:7
 best m. in England 313:17
 bias in favour of m. 397:15
 Christianity is a m.'s religion 395:4
 everything depended on m. 354:15
 get along even better without m. 336:12
 give a m. a free hand 398:5
 go to pieces like a m. 372:26
 hand that holds dominion over M. 369:3
 if you want a speech . . . ask a m. 367:19
 looked from pig to m. 286:13
 M. as nature's last word 409:2
 m. at twice its natural size 412:19
 m. be my metaphor 369:7
 m. by . . . a sheep on its hind legs 30:23
 m. dies when he wants 12:25
 m. for others 46:10
 M. . . . grows beyond his work 357:20
 m. has every season 129:8
 m. in the house is worth two 397:21
 m. is a useless passion 335:25
 m. is . . . a wild animal 100:3
 m. is an invention of recent date 131:13
 m. is an ungrateful beast 33:9
 m. is as he is 288:11
 m. is condemned to be free 336:1
 m. is dead 134:21
 m. is jealous because of his *amour propre* 19
 m. is m., woman woman, and tree tree 246:11
 m. is made out of mud 376:15
 m. is more complex 385:20

m. is neither the oldest . . . problem 131:12
m. is never quite m. enough 154:22
m. is only m. at the surface 386:4
m. . . . not locked into his environment 54:1
m. wants a great deal 372:8
m. will go down the pit 23:17
m.'s novel with no women in it 17:2
m.'s ultimate love for m. 223:14
miracle of m. 13:10
no other m. seems quite good enough 91:2
one small step for [a] m. 14:5
only real danger that exists is m. 199:13
quite be the m. he once was 372:9
reflecting the figure of m. 412:19
simple to keep a m. 159:15
stand by your m. 414:1
[Thatcher] . . . the best m. among them 70:10
what is m., . . . asks the biochemist 341:14
willing . . . to make a m. of . . . you 407:9
woman without a m. 357:22
wonderful new m. 6:5
you'll be a m., my son 211:1
you're not a m., you're a machine 342:20
Man-cub: m. is a m. and he must learn 213:30
Man-in-the-street: m. . . . . observer of life 18:7
Man-of-war: every Spaniard is like a m. 52:6
Man-projected: O m. figure, of late imaged 162:16
Management: not under the same m. 174:4
Manager: demanding to see the m. 346:17
m.s in fancy dress 239:21
prerogative of the . . . m. 401:19
Mandalay: on the road to M. 211:29
Mandarin: christen this style the M. 87:16
m. with absolute power 373:14
m.s who 'appreciate' beauty 297:16
Mandatory: both carry a m. life sentence 270:12
Mandela, Nelson 57:20
Mandelstam, Osip 4:11
Manderley: I dreamt I went to M. 111:7
Manet, Edouard 136:28
Manhattan: middle-management of M. 8:2
Manifestation: m.s . . . from his nature 156:23
Manifesto: first powerful m. 354:19
Manifold: take the m.s out of my larynx 12:16
Manipulator: artful m. of the good 90:2
Mankind: believed in for all m. 411:14
education . . . is not natural to m. 80:22
giant leap for m. 14:5
lost m. dreading to find its father 17:13
m. is a club 77:23
M. *versus* Ironmongery 397:6
m. won 207:19
one disillusion – m. 206:11
possible to sacrifice half m. 250:16
prospect and outlook of m. 80:11
there is no history of m. 301:7
Mann, Thomas: M., forever viewing life 42:25
Manner: English m.s are . . . frightening 192:5
good m.s . . . indistinguishable 368:11
good prose is an affair of good m.s 256:19
if it weren't for his good m.s 144:7

m.s are . . . the need of the plain 393:21
restraint and good m.s are necessary 52:6
shoddy table m.s . . . have broken up 86:4
Mannish: m. manner of mind and face 69:14
Manufacturer: to see who the m. was 263:7
Manure: m. of the next [epoch] 88:23
throws a heap of m. all over us 11:15
Many: done because we are too m. [menny]
163:25
was so much owed by so m. to so few 79:19
Many-minded: m. Homer 416:24
Mao Zedong 232:5
as for M., he even wrote verse 53:21
Map: creating in the mind a m. 354:18
geography is about m.s 37:16
m. is not the territory 216:21
Marble: blessed be death that cuts in m. 261:8
chair . . . glowed on the m. 118:7
March: America that is on the m. 205:6
m. away ere the barncocks say 163:6
m. of the retreating world 288:27
Marched: m. lying down 264:1
Margin: in the m.s we'll find the poems 249:5
Marijuana: is m. addictive? 278:23
Marinading: trousers m. overnight 52:17
Mariner: where m.s had fabled news 238:10
Marital: m. relations have been broken 108:1
Market: don't understand m. relations 207:11
great m. by the sea 128:8
m. for same is sluggish 408:20
m. value of the chemicals 146:18
Marks and Spencers: not through M. 49:19
Marlowe, Christopher: Shakespeare with M.
412:14
Marmalade: m.-downwards-incidence 193:18
tangerine trees and m. skies 230:1
Marmion: [*Iliad*] in the M. class 164:16
men of the M. class 112:14
Marriage 279:9
all m.s are different 346:5
between prostitution and m. 349:20
blessings of m. 344:22
both my m.s were failures 247:7
distrust . . . a definition of m. 49:1
doesn't have to get anywhere in a m. 274:9
every m. is different 38:11
exotic m.s 34:10
in a happy m. . . . the wife . . . provides 51:26
just as humdrum a m. 153:11
known any open m.s 138:5
love and m. 63:8
main purpose of m. 329:14
m. . . . . appoints the other guardian 319:17
m. as a train you simply have to catch 48:9
m. combines the maximum of temptation
344:30
m. has been made in Heaven 333:7
m. is a bribe 403:2
m. is a wonderful invention 87:12
m. is not all bed and breakfast 93:10
m. is to courtship 104:20

M. master, a mistress and two slaves 42:19
m. . . . night owl into a homing pigeon 9:13
m. without love means love without m. 83:4
m.? . . . a matter of taste 331:11
more m.s and more Matisses 192:9
Moses had a mixed m. 47:9
say you are all for m. 401:22
so that is m. 412:20
value of m. is not . . . children 105:10
what is m. but prostitution to one man 69:5
whether the m. is true or false 144:20
Married: aunts who are not m. 75:11
because I've always been m. 138:4
best part of m. life 403:3
climbs into their graves m. 402:16
enter . . . politics . . . unhappily m. 293:7
every night of her m. life 369:23
gifted girls m. impossible men 151:26
how to be happy though m. 162:3
I m. beneath me. All women do 16:9
I'm getting m. in the morning 230:21
m. for his own money 254:19
m. her if she had only one million 231:9
no man is genuinely happy, m. 259:11
pray thee, . . . that I may not be m. 106:13
seven weeks of our m. life 373:2
she m. a numskull 343:16
she makes you think you m. too soon 10:25
Trade Unionism of the m. 344:21
until he has m.. Then he's finished 138:3
unwise to be m. 346:1
wanted me, in a general way, to be m. 189:3
when m. people don't get on 255:20
who is not m. is only half a man 87:22
whose life was m. to it [the sea] 375:12
woman's business to get m. 344:10
writing is like getting m. 274:7
young man m. is a young man marred 212:28
Marrow-bone: go down upon your m.s 415:6
Marry: excited about nothing – and . . . m. him 73:18
I would not m. God 119:14
if men knew . . . they'd never m. 170:9
if only you could persuade him to m. 232:13
m. a swan 121:3
m. for purely selfish reasons 55:11
m. in haste and repeat at leisure 63:2
m. me and you'll be farting through silk 266:7
m. me . . . never look at another horse 252:21
m. your mistress . . . job vacancy 146:20
tried and not been able [to m.] 190:16
Marrying: John Thomas m. Lady Jane 223:17
kept on m. 410:20
m. left your maiden name disused 221:9
Mars: foreign exchange from M. 339:14
M. a day 3:18
next July we collide with M. 302:5
Marshmallow: ten-pound m. 90:20
Martin, Mary 260:4
Martini: dry m. . . . Shaken and not stirred 128:20
slip . . . into a dry M. 402:9

Martyr: m. to music 369:29
m.s do not build churches 65:29
Martyrdom: dreadful m. must run its course 18:2
m. . . . become famous without ability 346:4
m. meaningless 123:15
Marvellous: 's wonderful! 's m. 142:16
Marx, Groucho 149:18
Marx, Karl 49:19, 207:12, 236:22
M. is a case in point 139:3
stature of . . . M. 383:15
teaching of M. 222:1
things that M. did not see 102:4
Marxiste: M., tendance Groucho 149:18
Mary: Hail M., quite contrary 154:5
Marylebone: Elector of M. 52:16
M'as-tu vu: cruel French call *m.* 361:24
Maschine: alles Erworbene bedroht die M. 319:11
Masculine: m. figure created by a woman 258:11
m. principle in its women 400:11
Masefield, John: swear-word . . . to M. 30:6
Maserati: hole in your neighbour's M. 91:19
Mask: m. of the preceding scene 102:3
m. that eats into the face 383:3
Masoch: M., . . . more constant 317:14
Masonry: social m. 396:25
Mass: m. times the speed of light 115:10
Massacre: not as sudden as a m. 379:21
you can't m. an idea 314:1
Masses: brutal empire of the m. 285:15
epoch of the m. 285:15
faces from 'em by calling 'em the m. 305:14
m. are . . . people not . . . qualified 285:14
new world of the m. 306:8
poor huddled m., let's club 'em 314:19
Masseur: at a convention of m.s 382:15
Mast: m. burst open with a rose 128:17
Master: m., a mistress and two slaves 42:19
m.s of little bits of man alive 224:3
M.s Wet, Dim, Drip and Bleak 18:8
we are the m.s at the moment 346:13
Mastered: m. a destiny which broke 173:17
Masterpiece: adventures of his mind among m.s 132:3
nothing is likely about m.s 362:15
Mastodon: like m.s bellowing 409:14
Masturbating: between m. and making love 28:5
Masturbation: don't knock m. 5:21
m. of war 311:4
m.; the primary sexual activity 364:2
Match: burnt m. skating in a urinal 95:2
magazine built over a m. factory 112:2
Matchboxes: substitute out of . . . m. 108:16
Matches: all m. are unwise 346:1
lighted m. between the toes 410:11
with the help of three m. 81:21
Mate: I can't m. in captivity 357:23
very popular among his m.s 121:13
Material: m. served by men 295:15
m. which should have a life of its own 87:20
Materialistic: only really m. people 242:2
Mathematical: tendency to think . . . m. 193:3

Mathematics: avoid pregnancy by a resort to m.
258:14
I don't believe in m. 116:7
I speak it [m.] like a native 263:22
innocent of m. 320:15
laws of m. refer to reality 115:19
m. . . . know what we are talking about 328:14
m. possesses not only truth 328:13
pure m. consists . . . of assertions 328:15
sense of m. greater 153:14
Matilda: come a-waltzing M. 293:14
M. told such dreadful lies 32:21
Mating: only in the m. season 263:14
Matisse, Henri: more marriages and more M.s
192:9
squinting husks provided by M. 233:11
Matrimony: critical period in m. 171:1
m. and murder both carry 270:12
Matter: everything goes and nothing m.s 325:11
it m.s less than they suppose 192:11
m. . . . a convenient formula 328:18
m. as derivative from consciousness 299:18
most of what m.s in your life 327:13
not a thing that m.s 396:23
very few things m. at all 24:2
what can I do that m.s? 355:5
Matthew Passion: M. . . . human authors 182:18
Matthews, Jessie 337:18
Mattress: you don't crack it open on a m. 261:20
Mature: m. poets steal 119:6
mark of the m. man 358:1
Maturing: m. late, or . . . rotted early 277:20
Maturity: m. . . . break in adolescence 123:14
m. is the assimilation of the features 389:7
Matzo: other part of a m. you can eat? 267:15
Maugham, W. Somerset 94:20
Mauling: all m. and muttering 103:29
Maupassant, Guy de: then I beat Mr M. 169:13
Mausoleum: designing m.s for his enemies 234:12
Maximum: m. of temptation 344:30
Maxwell, Robert 10:12
Maxwell: M.'s silver hammer 230:2
May: M. month flaps its glad green leaves 162:5
M. will be fine next year 178:18
M. without cloud 13:6
season was the airiest M. 151:24
sweet and bitter scent of the m. 44:12
there's an end of M. 178:17
Maybe: definite m. 147:20
Mayer, Louis B. 10:22
Mayflower: there to meet the boat [M.] 322:2
Mayor: town tart who . . . married the m. 27:14
what did the m. do? 152:6
why should I run for m. 107:4
Maze: life is a m. 88:20
m. not a mortuary 106:16
watches rats in m.s 114:9
McCarthyism: M. is Americanism 241:14
McGregor: don't go into Mr M.'s garden 302:15
Me: m., the m. that is seen, is m. 223:22
m., what's that after all? 174:13

my thought is m. 336:9
where's the rest of M.? 314:2
Meadow: poinsettia m.s of her tides 95:6
Meagre: leaving something . . . more m. 127:25
Mealtime: m.s more than the meals 354:2
never see me again, except at m.s 187:7
Mean: down these m. streets a man 72:11
I m. every word you say 168:16
it all depends what you m. by . . . 194:17
Meaning: language charged with m. 303:27
m.s stabilized in etymology 400:21
real m. lies underneath 68:;1
tend to lose the m. of the play 102:3
wrestle with words and m.s 116:28
Meanness: m. . . . in Scotland translated 371:9
Means: always work . . . below your m. 297:9
as a m. the business man is tolerable 206:17
in the mercy of his m. 369:1
Private M. is dead 331:16
Meant: it's what I m. 386:12
Measles: love is like the m. 194:10
stars like m. fade at last 175:15
Measure: unceasing the m. 303:7
Measured: fine time when they m. by me 269:6
m. out my life with coffee spoons 117:24
Measurement: what are your m.s 59:17
Meat: buys its opinions as it buys its m. 61:25
I can't abide his m. 103:9
one man's m. is another woman's Sunday 64:2
very new cheese of very old m. 347:16
Meatier: always given the m. rolls 181:18
Meatloaf: frequently mistaken for a m. 215:12
Mecca: some to M. turn to pray 128:9
Mechanical: appropriate to a m. creation 58:19
Mechanism: m. of the Universe 400:20
Medal: nothing to do with m.s and ribbons 34:3
they stuck a m. on it 66:20
Medallion: dumb as old m.s to the thumb 244:10
Mede: one man's M. 202:6
Media: daily m. add to this by cutting off 38:17
m. . . . convention of spiritualists 360:14
Medical: advance of . . . m. thought 409:16
Medici: Miniver loved the M. 320:14
Mediocre: gilded tomb of a m. talent 350:20
make you an artist but only a m. artist 48:10
more than magnificent – it's m. 147:22
some men are born m. 168:12
titles distinguish the m. 344:31
Mediocrity: it isn't evil . . . but m. 323:16
m. knows nothing higher 110:11
m. of the apparatus 378:6
m. that makes us let go of love 187:5
Meditation: m. . . . the means and the end 217:23
m. upon the dewdrop 143:11
Mediterranean: ever taken from the M. 342:3
set out again immediately for the M. 341:3
Medium: call it a m. because nothing's well done
1:2
hot m. . . . extends 245:1
m. is the message 244:18
m. . . . neither rare nor well done 217:2

Medium-sized: m. Kissinger 168:25
Meek: m. shall inherit 142:23
Meet: m. me in St Louis 358:7
   m. with triumph and disaster 210:32
   two people m. . . . six people present 191:22
   we'll m. again 59:18
   why do I often m. your visage here 95:3
   you'll m. them on the way down 266:20
Meeting: m.s are indispensable 139:6
   m.s that do not come off 48:7
   pleasure of m. myself 337:15
Megalomania: illness of the U S is m. 17:4
Megalomaniac: m. . . . from the narcissist 328:5
Meistersinger: M., . . . breath in steel 94:29
Melancholy: m. sexual perversion 182:7
Mellifluous: old Corndrinking M. 169:14
Mellow: not old, but m., like good wine 297:3
Melodies: m. are not too sublime 257:4
Melody: m. imposes continuity 259:17
   m. lingers on 39:13
Melting: great m. pot 420:3
Member: acquainted with the other m.s 400:4
   club that will accept me as a m. 253:11
   when she saw the sign 'M.s only' 263:11
Memo pad: that m. you call your mind 311:6
Memoirs: m. . . . can never be wholly true 304:5
Memorability: m. has been bought 383:7
Memorable: finding . . . that he was not m. 341:5
Memorably: all it [poem] has to say m. 152:11
Memorandum: m. is written . . . to protect 1:9
Memories: m. are card-indexes 88:28
   m. are hunting-horns 13:2
   m. of men are too frail 359:13
   m. we have forgotten 294:4
   nostalgic m. of it [history] 290:8
   only with beauty wake wild m. 103:1
   so young they have no m. 200:3
   where these m. grow 365:8
Memory: amnesia, my m.'s very good 12:24
   camera relieves us of the burden of m. 38:12
   footfalls echo in the m. 116:24
   idea on the m. of the crowd 173:6
   m. ceases to be necessary 38:12
   m. is a present that never stops 294:8
   m. is what is left 46:11
   thanks for the m. 320:11
   wrong m. at the wrong place or time 153:19
Memsahib: plus c'est la m. 278:10
Men: all its young m. slain 17:19
   all men are rapists 133:11
   American women like quiet m. 10:1
   created by m. with women in mind 376:12
   I don't hate men 407:17
   I like m. to behave like m. 331:10
   if m. could get pregnant 204:9
   life in my m. 398:4
   m. and sea interpenetrate 89:12
   m. are as chancy as children 214:8
   m. are born makers 389:10
   m. are so honest 230:22
   m. are unwise and curiously planned 128:14

m. come of age at sixty 358:5
m. have never been good 26:28
m. in a world of m. 210:13
m. like war 120:8
m. see objects 131:18
m. were made for war 119:16
m. were the answer 25:18
m. wouldn't get . . . a glance 385:4
m.are *so* romantic 395:7
so many kinds of awful m. 91:7
thought m. were a phallusy 150:4
together with and not against m. 411:10
when a lot of m. get together 55:20
Menace: avoid being a public m. 59:3
Mendacity: ecstasy of m. 344:13
Menservant: in the m.s' lavatory 393:9
Menstruate: men m. by shedding 120:8
Mental: m. reflection is . . . interesting 299:7
   tactful decorations for a m. home 233:11
Mention: just m. my name 126:17
Menu: national dish of America is m.s 321:3
Menuhin, Yehudi 67:13
Mercenary: followed their m. calling 179:5
Merchant: not least of your m. princes 212:3
   rich m. in Stambouli 303:4
Mercy: die together, we do not want m. 71:4
   in the m. of his means 369:1
Mère: la m. fait du tricot 305:6
Meredith, George: M. . . . daintily dressed 77:14
Meredith: we're in M., we're in 215:5
Merger: m. between Heaven and Hell 397:16
Meridian: m.s and parallels of latitude 380:6
Merit: longest essay, irrespective of m. 392:5
Meritocracy: rise of m. 419:1
Mermaid: m. in your lap 369:31
   Millie, a messy old m. 62:13
Merrily: m. answered staid drinkers 370:14
Merry: always m. and bright 407:5
Merrygoround: it's no go on the m. 246:3
Mess: another nice m. 162:4
   it was in a thorough m. 396:6
Mess-maker: pioneers . . . are . . . m.s 299:8
Message: he will be given m.s 262:2
   medium is the m. 244:18
   pot of m. 10:9
Messenger: I am a m. 262:2
   its [mind's] function of m. 223:13
Messiah: self-appointed prophets and m.s 289:1
Messing: m. about in boats 150:13
Métamorphoses: mois des m. 13:6
Metaphor: all slang is m. 76:5
   man be my m. 369:7
   m.s of speed 65:2
   plays work through m. 361:18
   quarter-pound of mixed m.s 92:11
   sculptures are plastic m.s 297:19
Metaphysical: m. brothel for emotions 216:6
Metaphysician: scientist must be a m. 342:21
Metaphysics: cheating on my m. final 5:19
   fortune-tellers to m. 217:13
   m. is the finding of bad reasons 49:22

principles of logic and m. are true 20:6
Metempsychosis: m. . . . drunk when sober 170:10
Meter: lovely Rita. m. maid 229:26
Method: you know my m. 109:8
  you know my m.s, Watson 109:22
Methodist: seeing he was a M. 21:16
Metre: bird . . . when I think of m. 224:14
  m. [follows] the ring of the anvil 389:8
Metro-Goldwyn-Mayer: born . . . on a M. lot 141:1
  M. production of *The School for Scandal* 220:3
Mexico: down M. way 204:13
  in M. the gods ruled 87:1
  M. . . . where men despise sex 224:7
  to be a gringo in M. 137:8
Mice: cats the way most people have m. 372:25
  even the m. eat next door 340:5
  even the m. were bow-legged 254:20
Michelangelo 273:19
  Italy from designs by M 380:4
  talking of M. 117:22
  they produced M. 395:12
Michelin: any M. guide would . . . condemn 263:4
Microwave: old age stuck in a m. 312:2
  stop the sky turning into a m. oven 73:9
Midday: burning the m. oil 313:19
  out in the m. sun 94:13
Middle: eliminated the m. man 123:13
  here I am, in the m. way 117:2
  people who stay in the m. of the road 41:16
  right wing of the m. of the road 35:16
Middle age: m. is the best time 186:17
  m. snuffs out ten times more talent 181:6
  temptation came to him, in m. 333:3
Middle-aged: m. celebrate the decade of their youth 387:26
  m. couples with failing marriages 371:7
  m. is merry, and I love to lead it 277:24
Middle class 192:21
  clever m. to govern 96:8
  describes himself as . . . lower-m. 261:1
  healthy type that was essentially m. 127:19
  into the hands of m. morality 345:22
  m. . . . considered beauty 336:14
  m. education . . . training of servants 404:3
  m., middle-aged maiden lady 313:3
  m. weapon to keep children good 54:9
  we of the sinking m. 287:10
  what fools m. girls are 110:14
  what goes on in a m. family 119:9
  worst thing about being a m. woman 239:4
Middle classes: comfort . . . with the m. 31:19
Middle-management: m. of Manhattan 8:2
Middlemarch: M., the magnificent book 412:7
Midget: as a m. is good at being short 189:17
Midland: M., bound for Cricklewood 40:15
Midlands: M. that are sodden and unkind 33:10
Midnight: alone on a hill during a clear m. 163:22
  drunk in a m. choir 85:12
  stroke of m. ceases 179:9
Mieux: *je vais de m. en m.* 93:9
Might: m. be; but I don't know 9:22

we Britons use 'm'. 393:6
Mightn't: when you think that you m. 211:10
Migraine: love is a universal m. 152:2
  their smell brings on my m. 50:21
Mile: m.s to go before I sleep 136:4
Militancy: Ursula Andress of m. 378:12
Militant: m.s are like cleaning women 378:12
  optimist, unrepentant and m. 383:12
Militant Tendency: M. childbirth 68:9
Militarism: hatred of war and m. 53:26
Military: intelligence of the m. 315:10
  m.- industrial complex 116:14
  m. intelligence is a contradiction 253:18
  m. justice is to justice 9:14
  m. mind in their grip 379:8
  not susceptible to a m. solution 205:8
  prefer our m. past 383:18
Milk: adult form of m. 86:25
  between the m. and the yoghurt 270:19
  gin was mother's m. to her 345:20
  like a cow in a m. bar 216:15
  m. is more likely to be watered 61:25
  m. of human kindness 156:5
  one end is moo, the other m. 277:12
  putting m. into babies 80:3
Milked: waited their turn to be milked 143:1
Mill: water under a ruined m. 64:17
Millennium: if m. is not created 406:25
Miller, Arthur 386:9
Miller, Henry: M. is . . . a non-stop talker 52:3
Millie: I'm M., a messy old mermaid 62:13
Million: first ten m. years were the worst 1:16
  here's a m. dollars. Don't lose it 280:10
  m. dollars . . . in well-used notes 69:9
  multitude of one m. divided by one m. 216:7
  proud to be of 200 m. Americans 129:15
  spread out his influence thin over m. 252:1
  think in m.s – other people's m.s 37:4
  with a m. stars you pin it 122:10
  worth a m. statues 97:9
Millionaire: all m.s have baked apple 125:28
  even a m. is only a customer 201:15
  frock-coated . . . type of m. 127:12
  I am a m.. That is my religion 343:26
  m.s and bums taste about alike 251:7
  old-fashioned m. 215:7
  silk hat on a Bradford m. 118:14
  who wants to be a m.? 302:6
Mills, Ogden 350:2
Milton, John: Chinese Wall of M. 118:29
  malt does more than M. can 180:3
  pneumatic sterility of Milton 119:17
  what M. saw when he went blind 251:20
Mime: too many conductors who m. 108:7
Mince: I don't m. my words 118:11
Mind: agitation of the m. 171:11
  attracted to me by what I don't m. 227:15
  beauty is momentary in the m. 358:17
  best m.s of my generation 144:3
  beyond the power of any single m. 412:14
  body and m. entire 412:3

sexual pull towards m.s 86:22
Slough in your rear view m. 149:8
standin' up into m. 334:1
they both fight for the m. 315:18
write something on a steamed m. 111:12
Mirth: m. that has no bitter springs 210:2
Prime Minister of M. 320:5
song of the birds for m. 156:24
Mischief: m. . . . with the cooking sherry 371:15
Misconception: compound of m.s 375:14
Miserable: never happy unless he is m. 9:16
secret of being m. 345:11
Miserly: m. drunkards 403:7
Misery: difficulty of avoiding the m. 283:2
man hands on m. to man 221:16
that at least was a glorious m. 298:22
world . . . saved an infinity of m. 397:3
Misfortune: m. to ourselves 42:10
preserve . . . for its taste of m. 249:4
Misguided: guided missiles and m. men 208:14
Mislead: another to m. the Cabinet 15:16
Misleading: least m. thing we have 61:15
Mispronounce: all men m. it 269:15
Misrepresentation: to escape m. 226:9
Miss: m. mine by just a few days 203:23
Miss T.: whatever M. eats turns into M. 103:14
Missed: he [Hitler] m. the bus 72:2
inventions . . . not made . . . rarely m. 138:16
m. the bus 173:18
Missile: guided m.s and misguided men 208:14
m. . . . called the civil servant 390:9
Upper Volta, but with m.s 11:12
Missing: forty-eight hours before you're m. 347:17
m. link . . . is ourselves 237:16
m. so much and so much 93:4
wants to be at the party he's m. 123:10
Missionaries: m. first came to Africa 379:14
Missionary: slum m. saving young virgins 12:13
Mist: grey m. on the sea's face 254:10
in the m.s of Maida Vale 300:7
mad as the m. and snow 416:24
Mistah Kurtz: M. – he dead 89:9
Mistake: always made a new m. instead 91:7
Europe . . . a conglomeration of m.s 121:2
God was a m. 66:18
hippopotamus as an enormous m. 76:3
I'd make all the same m.s 24:9
if I make m.s 205:23
keep a promise by m. 407:19
learned from the m. of the past 366:7
make the same m. once 28:4
makes m.s according to the rules 385:14
man who has made all the m.s 45:3
m.s of the eternal builder 348:16
two people make a m. 102:15
when women want to make m.s 202:3
worse than immoral, it's a m. 1:9
worst m.s in his subject 168:3
Mistaken: m. signal 101:20
Mister: solitary m. 369:4
Mistress: finding a husband for one's m. 91:2

m. in my own [house] 212:8
marry your m. you create a job vacancy 146:20
money differs from . . . a m. 139:5
Mistresses: English actresses are m. 161:8
Mistrust: m. of the . . . upper classes 270:18
Misunderstanding: hullabaloo of m.s 372:24
no m. when I go home 283:11
Misunderstood: m. by . . . sisters of uncharity
251:10
those who long to be m. 386:16
Mithridates: M., he died old 180:5
Mitty, Walter: made M. . . . unimaginative 166:12
Mix: m. what they believe 383:2
Mixed: I wish I'd been a m. infant 31:7
Mnetha: brother to M.'s daughter 368:20
Moan: dying m. of a distant violin 295:10
Mob: m. cannot shout down a telephone 77:18
mostly they're a decent m., the dead 265:17
Moby Dick: is M. the whale or the man? 324:16
Mock: m. ye not 180:16
reeks a m. rose 103:5
Mockingbird: it's a sin to kill a m. 227:16
Model 1910 m. 127:12
New York is the perfect m. of a city 274:2
Moderation: carry m. unto excess 216:17
m. in the pursuit of justice 147:2
Modern: Historic Exhibitions of M. Art 111:15
m. child will answer you back 296:1
sentence will suffice for m. man 65:8
skill without imagination . . . m. art 360:1
Modest: m. about my not knowing all 276:4
m. little man with much to be m. about 82:6
most m. of animals 337:16
right to be m. and a duty to be vain 217:7
Modesty: all m. is false 36:12
time to cultivate m. 349:4
Modulation: m. correctly executed 362:12
Moi-même: plus m. que moi 84:6
Mois: m. des floraisons 13:6
Moist: no more . . . than your m. hand 358:19
Mole: m. busy 101:15
Molehill: look after the m.s 296:7
Mollusc: soft urban m. 292:25
Molotov, V.M. 81:6
Mom: never eat at any place called M.'s 5:9
Moment: any m. may be the next 112:4
does not seem a m.'s thought 415:5
m.s of other people's lives 299:11
no more distressing m. 379:9
total of such m.s is my life 88:6
Momentariness: take your delight in m. 151:25
Momentary: beauty is m. in the mind 358:17
Momma: last of the red-hot m.s 379:10
ma m. done tol' me 259:20
Mon Dieu: m.s [Mong Jews] 213:25
Monarchy: believe in God than . . . m. 196:9
M. along with feeding the pigeons 160:3
m. . . . has too much power 77:24
m. is . . . labour-intensive 406:8
Monday: I don't like M.s 141:20
on M. I'm taken by a tar 407:8

on M. when the sun is hot 265:7
Monet, Claude: M.'s pictures . . . draughty 102:14
Monetarism: doing for m. 166:11
Monetarist: she was a monetarist 245:16
Money: all power and m. and fine robes 395:4
American people take half my m. 125:12
anyone listening to whom I owe m. 129:3
bring a specimen of your money 253:9
by God, how the m. rolls in 12:13
chief value of m. 259:14
divided up their m. 356:16
don't give your son m. 80:23
education costs m. 272:1
fool and his m. 128:25
for m. makes it any more moral 296:18
give him the m., Barney 298:11
give . . . m. and don't worry 130:19
Good Samaritan . . . had m. as well 367:22
her voice is full of m. 126:19
Hollywood m. isn't m. 292:9
if you can actually count your m. 142:22
importance of m. 206:19
licence to print m. 371:11
long enough to get m. from it 225:14
love of m. for its own sake 368:2
man of m. [is ruined] by m. 171:14
married for his own m. 254:19
m. [can buy] a better class of enemy 263:12
m. can't buy me love 229:19
m. doesn't talk, it swears 113:13
m. falls apart in your hands 402:13
m. gives me pleasure all the time 32:30
m. has something to do with life 221:10
m. is a singular thing 139:5
m. is a wonderful thick hedge 201:15
m. is better than poverty 6:14
m. is good for bribing yourself 315:11
m. is like a sixth sense 256:18
m. is the sixth sense 248:13
m. is used to pay bills 390:16
m. like that and not swell out 396:20
m. lords . . . who control 272:4
m. through times of no dope 346:21
m. to help her pass it 313:3
m. to last . . . unless I buy something 254:16
m.s which it, the bank, creates 303:9
neither is there poetry in m. 152:12
nice feet and plenty of m. 15:10
nobody lends him [a kidder] money 261:25
only country with any m. left 285:12
only interested in m. 346:9
own to the possession of m. in India 214:9
reputation, . . . but no m. 380:19
rhetoric, so long as it doesn't cost m. 280:13
rich . . . have more m. 127:11
rich man without m. 383:10
size of sums of m. appears to vary 183:21
so bad that you lose all your m. 242:14
they hired the m., didn't they? 90:10
this West stuffed with m. 327:12
try to rub up against m. 326:15

turning m. into light 46:14
turning one's enemies into m. 56:8
want of money is [root of all evil] 61:8
way the banks will give you m. 105:13
what . . . God thinks of m. 25:7
what is the root of m.? 312:1
when you don't have any m. 108:5
whether he has enough m. for lunch 265:12
with m. they had not got 161:20
woman must have m. and a room 412:18
young without m. 404:14
Monk: I said to this m. 298:16
Monkey: make a m. of a man . . . quote him 35:1
m.s and cats – all human life is there 190:19
no reason to attack the m. 41:12
strong as a m.'s tail 113:1
Monnet, Jean 267:10
Monocle: in pursuit of his m. 307:10
Monogamous: polygamous but emotionally m.
52:14
Monogamy: looking for m. . . . marry a swan
121:3
m. is [having one husband too many] 9:1
who seek to find m. 291:9
Monograph: m. on . . . tobacco 109:9, 110:3
Monopolies: only one M. Commission 149:11
Monopoly: m. stage of capitalism 228:12
oppressors do not perceive their m. 133:9
Monotomy: chord of m. is stretched 76:26
Monroe, Marilyn 386:9
kissing M. was like kissing Hitler 98:5
[M] was good at playing abstract confusion
189:17
mouth of M. 266:18
she [M.] won't be there 262:4
Mons Veneris: m. as . . . Mount Everest 182:19
Monsoon: then the m.s came 263:28
Monster: Effie M. was a m. 227:18
states are frigid m.s 141:12
Monstre: états sont les m.s froids 141:12
Monstrous: all that is m. under the sun 146:13
m. anger of the guns 288:14
m. head and sickening cry 74:14
m. mother would be tragic 383:5
Montesquieu, Charles: the way Jefferson did [study]
M. 387:4
Montezuma: America [denies] M. still 222:16
M.'s revenge 10:16
Montgomery, Field-Marshal 24:20, 82:16
Month: for m.s and m.s and m.s 365:3
old man in a dry m. 117:11
Montparnasse: mugged on M. 105:1
Montreal: O God! O M. 62:7
Monument: only m. the asphalt road 118:25
smashing m.s: save the pedestals 227:4
society wants to vote a m. [monyment] 111:18
Moo: one end is m., the other milk 277:12
you silly m. 354:8
Mookse: M. and the Gripes 197:14
Moon: brilliant pilot m. 355:4
buckle it with the m. 122:10

don't lets ask for the m. 100:22
he astride the m. 363:16
like the poet woo the m. 65:2
m. . . . circumambulatory aphrodisiac 136:24
m. in the breast of man is cold 40:2
m. of a hundred identical faces 140:5
m. plucked at my rein 416:11
m. shone bright on Mrs Porter 118:13
m.'s a balloon 97:3
m.s not hers lie mirrored on her sea 175:9
new m. hangs like an ivory bugle 370:13
only a paper m. 161:17
only you beneath the m. 302:3
part of the m. was falling down 135:8
ritual observance of the m. 370:4
sad as a gypsy serenading the m. 259:23
saw the ruddy m. lean over a hedge 181:15
sheriff sun and rustler m. 260:12
shine on, harvest m. 281:21
ship, an isle, a sickle m. 128:18
silver apples of the m. 417:20
slowly, silently, now the m. 103:18
walk on the m. and look at the earth 120:24
what do you think of it, m. 163:15
Moon-daisies: tall m. alight 101:15
Moon-washed: m. apples of wonder 110:19
Moonbeam: carry m.s home in a jar 59:16
Mooning: m. upon bare hills 303:2
Moonless: m. night in the small town 369:20
Moonlight: get no more from the m. 358:19
Moonlit: knocking on the m. door 103:11
Moonshine: talking m. 329:17
Moore, George 124:10
Mope: only housemaids m. 90:12
Mopser: has anyone seen my M.? 102:22
Moral: basing m.s on myth 334:8
  can't afford them [m.s], Governor 345:17
  for money makes it any more m. 296:18
  Leavis demands m. earnestness 232:18
  live beyond his m. means 376:7
  m. as soon as one is unhappy 307:7
  m. climate of America 322:15
  m. flabbiness born . . . Success 191:20
  m. issue . . . more than a real issue 257:13
  m. leadership . . . it's much overrated 327:19
  m. of the work 81:4
  m. order of the world 401:11
  m. when he is only uncomfortable 344:17
  more moved by economics than by m.s 297:2
  personal m. liability was crucial 371:8
  preach a high m. lesson 362:3
  providence . . . for their m. 418:6
  quality of m. behaviour varies 182:21
  Social Revolution will be m. 294:19
  story with a bad m. 164:3
  take the m. law 358:12
  this story has no m. 333:5
Morality: law and m. are . . . brothers-in-law
    204:2
  m. . . . is an unmitigated evil 223:2
  m. loses the foundation 334:8

middle class m. 345:22
  no m. can be founded on authority 20:5
  so-called new m. 346:14
Moralized: it m. them 154:18
More: less is m. 260:16
  like everyone else, only m. so 126:2
  m. and m. about less and less 60:18
  m. will mean worse 7:20
  some m. than others 93:14
Morning: and in the m. 43:2
  each m. you open your eyes 376:13
  if they take you in the m. 23:3
  it's nice to get up in the m. 222:7
  m. has broken 122:9
  m. of which it was bereaved 374:16
  m. prayers in a workhouse 191:14
  not to have somewhere to go in the m.s 60:8
  Oh, how I hate to get up in the m. 39:12
  Oh, what a beautiful m. 160:11
  pitiful appendage to life's m. 199:15
  see me any m. in the park 117:32
  voluptuaries of the m. after 167:1
Morning Star: M. is read by people 3:31
Morocco: M. bound 96:16
Moron: genius with the IQ of a m. 387:25
  protons and m.s in the atom 194:2
Morris, William: M. . . . all-round man 31:1
Mort: il n'y a de m.s 247:2
Mortal: every m. sin on my conscience 405:8
Mortality: religion was m. and appearance 119:15
Mortar: if you are m. 98:12
  m., or the alibi 65:29
  m. that binds the savage 396:25
Mortuary: maze not a m. 106:16
Mosaic: m. swimming-pool age 84:17
Moscow 207:11
  M. was our Rome 68:8
  made twelve trips to M. 413:16
Moses: face shining like M. 377:2
  instead of M., he had dictated 281:12
  M. had a mixed marriage 47:9
  saw his role as being that of M. 192:23
  since M. wrote the Ten Commandments 1:4
Moslem: way M.s take off their shoes 297:14
Mosquito: word stung him like a m. 348:20
Mosquitoes: crossing salmon with m. 271:12
Moss: down an alley of green m. 390:1
Most: m. of everything 72:8
Mostes': hostess with the m. 39:7
Moth: unfading m.s 54:13
Moth-ball: exuded a flavour of m.s 272:17
Moth-eaten: vast m. musical brocade 221:5
Mother: and her m. came too 282:2
  artist will let his . . . m. drudge 344:7
  can you hear me, m.? 304:18
  clean-limbed American boys have m.s 9:20
  content to be nothing but a m. 66:4
  country home and m. 97:8
  dark veins of her m. 369:15
  English girl hates more than her m. 344:12
  gin was m.'s milk to her 345:20

Great M. Empire . . . isolated 131:11
his m. would bore right in 400:14
I remember my m., the day that we met 75:12
if a writer has to rob his m. 123:4
men . . . fight to impress their m.s 124:11
monstrous m. would be tragic 383:5
more of your m.'s immoral earnings 288:9
M. always feels the girl is safe 127:18
M. died today or, maybe yesterday 65:24
m. doesn't cook 375:13
m. of battles 182:5
m. of the free 37:14
m. to dozens, and nobody's wife 170:27
m. was frugal in her habits 286:4
m. will be there 170:23
m.s and fathers throughout the land 113:23
my m., drunk or sober 76:6
my m. made me a Lesbian 149:25
my m. was a bus-horse 350:5
no different from all other m.s 189:3
no m.s, only women 345:30
no woman can shake off her m. 345:30
one [language] for your m. 66:8
relationship between m. and child 311:3
so unconscionably rude to his m. 348:3
someone watches over us when we write. M. 8:1
step on the m. 257:19
took great care of his m. 264:7
when he walked with his m. 369:11
you don't have to tell your m. 298:13
you don't sell your m. 418:12
Mother-in-law: m. with only one eye 196:1
Motherhood: deprived m. 120:3
[m.] is a dead-end job 313:9
Motherly: children to the m. 51:1
Motion: between the m. and the act 117:18
Motion picture: I've done my bit for m.s 234:1
Motive: m.s meaner than your own 26:27
suspicion of one's m.s 328:6
Motor: this car is the m. of life 242:1
Motor-car: his m. was poetry 233:17
Motorem: indicat M. Bum 145:14
Motto: I've gotter m. [motter] 407:5
Mottoes: m. on sundials 303:14
Mould: frozen in an out-of-date m. 193:14
Perelman, they broke the m. 292:22
Moulting: m. they're pretty revolting 277:12
Mountain: blue m. barred with snow 128:13
five minutes on even the nicest m. 18:1
if the Swiss had designed these m.s 368:9
into the m.s to lead a revolution 214:35
m. of Mourne sweep down to the sea 133:12
m.s will look after themselves 296:6
paced upon the m.s overhead 417:28
truth about a m. in Africa 106:11
whenever I look at a m. 363:8
Mountaineer: Kremlin m. 248:18
Mountainous: Pam, you great big m. girl 40:16
Mourn: England m.s for her dead 43:2
here is no cause to m. 288:26

one m.s alone 38:11
whatever m.s when many leave 288:21
Mourne: mountains of M. sweep down 133:12
Mourning: don't waste any time m. 172:3
m. figure walks 234:7
m. is a hard business 247:20
m. . . . is not so much grief 249:21
Mouse: always leave room for the m. 332:14
way a m. waltzes 400:10
Moustache: kiss without a m. 71:3
kissed by a man who didn't wax his m. 214:18
man who waxes his m. 316:17
only one that hasn't a m. 63:3
Mouth: citizen to keep his m. open 151:4
feeding the m. that bites you 105:9
m. of Marilyn Monroe 266:18
not quite right about the m. 335:17
open up his m. too wide 130:6
roll it [failure] round my m. 90:16
whispering in her m. 252:13
Mouthfulness: gift horse in the m. 316:12
Mouthpiece: m. of nature 319:9
Move: chessman if it made its own m. 192:7
did thee feel the earth m.? 169:7
ground . . . seems not to m. 307:2
Moveable: Paris is a m. feast 169:9
Movement: almost a palpable m. 163:22
m. and space composition 38:1
m.; not where you are 189:19
she said m.s instead 134:4
whom I detest as a m. 252:2
Movie: adultery and m.-going 53:8
basic appeal of m.s 200:4
harmful for m.-makers to see movies 395:14
how not to write for the m.s 72:14
in love with making m.s 395:14
m.-making is seeing with a child's eye 46:15
m.s . . . beginning, a middle and an end 145:11
Moving: in home-sickness . . . keep m. 356:4
m. yet never leaving anything 232:10
man has stopped m. 367:3
Mower: drone of m.s on suburban lawns 317:15
Mown: may I be m. down at dawn 243:16
Mozart, W.A. 362:22
en famille they [angels] play M. 26:29
Hockney. . . . taken for M. 181:10
sonatas of M. are unique 338:17
when M. was my age 228:4
Mrs Dale's Diary: my favourite . . . is M. 119:9
Much: missing so m. and so m. 93:4
was so m. owed by so many to so few 79:19
Much-loved: m. and elegant friend 73:5
Muck: boating around in m. 153:8
some bony structure under the m. 72:10
Muck-rakes: men with the m.s 323:8
Mücke: o Glück der M. 318:16
Mud: cover the universe with m. 130:10
man is made out of m. 376:15
one sees the m., and one the stars 220:13
waste of water and m. 118:21
Muddied: m. oafs at the goals 211:4

Muddier: diving deeper. . . coming up m. 183:13
Muddle: beginning, a m., and an end 221:21
   transitory and unnecessary m. 206:15
Muddle-headed: gallant if m. girl 299:4
Mudging: fed up with fudging and m. 288:12
Muerte: sólo m. 382:2
Muffin: plateful of m.s 344:11
   room to eat m.s in 395:18
Mug: for m.s a bait 300:7
Mugged: m. on Montparnasse 105:1
   man gets m. every twenty minutes 246:14
Mullah: deadlands of the m.s 294:3
Multiply: be fruitful and m. 6:23, 186:7
Multitude: echo of a m. 42:7
   m. of one million divided by one million 216:7
Mum: ay, m.s the word 103:21
   be like Dad, keep M. 11:22
   they fuck you up, your m. and dad 221:15
Mumbo-Jumbo: M. is dead in the jungle 234:10
Mummy: short of an Egyptian m. 409:15
Mumsy: M. was vague 43:11
Murder: better to be wanted for m. 407:10
   cannot claim them [grounds] for m. 65:27
   matrimony and m. 270:12
   never m. . . . a suicide 406:23
Murderer: I try to be an innocent m. 65:26
Murdoch, Rupert 10:3
   M. has found a gap in the market 3:31
Murmur: m. of underground streams 17:18
   m. or innuendo causes panic 73:14
Murmured: my bride to be m. [murmered] 15:9
Murry, John Middleton 376:7
Muscle: house the m.s working its wings 159:6
   it [the intellect] has powerful m.s 115:20
   made out of m. and blood 376:15
   m.s of a welter-weight 408:15
Muscle-bound: m. from jumping to conclusions
   203:11
Muse: bid the M. go pack 417:24
   M. prefers the liars 418:5
   tenth American m. 54:7
Museum: mind is a m. to be looted 311:7
   ornament to any anthropological m. 109:20
Mushroom: life is too short to stuff a m. 89:13
   like m.s: we're kept in the dark 11:15
   m. of boiling dust 373:15
   supramundane m. 222:10
Music: already writing the m. 334:3
   as military m. is to m. 9:14
   classical m. and jazz 305:8
   dead spots where the m. can't be heard 244:13
   don't know anything about m. 30:27
   dream . . . about m. critics 362:21
   English may not like m. 29:19
   fiction set to . . . lascivious m. 259:5
   fiddled whisper m. 118:16
   film m. . . . same relationship 362:19
   hawks have no m. 389:6
   hills are alive with the sound of m. 160:15
   his m. accepts it [Legion d'Honneur] 337:13
   how potent cheap m. is 94:4

I can't listen to m. too often 229:5
I got m. 142:12
if a child hears m. 363:7
if m. be the breakfast food of love 4:7
I'm a martyr to m. 369:29
in m., the punctuation is . . . strict 316:20
Irving Berlin *is* American m. 205:17
man who can read m. but can't hear it 29:16
marvellous operas but dreadful m. 347:8
massive, often paroxysmal m. 27:4
most civilized m. 383:8
much good m. to be written in C. major 339:1
m. begins to atrophy 303:22
m. . . . . better than it can be performed 338:10
m. . . . . closely structured nonsense 59:12
m. creates order out of chaos 259:17
m. . . . . is an imitation of history 19:10
m. is . . . digesting time 19:14
m. is immediate 19:10
m. is natural law 394:7
m. is the arithmetic of sounds 102:8
m. is the brandy of the damned 344:16
m. is your own experience 290:9
m. isn't right 24:5
m., maestro, please 247:3
m. must have an idea or magic 323:15
m. of the past 141:16
m. *per se* means nothing 29:15
m. says nothing to the reason 59:12
m. teacher came twice a week 2:11
m. that changed a . . . vote 338:12
m. which is fantasy 167:10
my m. is best understood 362:20
O body swayed to m. 415:10
one m. . . . with no beginning, no end 47:14
people who attend chamber m. concerts 19:19
puts together two words about m. 91:10
rightful owner of the m. 293:15
Scarlatti condensed so much m. 58:11
silence is the essence of m. 52:8
spots mean pop m. 120:12
talking about m. 252:10
tall conductors . . . with slow m. 251:22
teaching m. is not my main purpose 363:7
theatre of the absurd set to m. 350:7
Van Gogh's ear for m. 402:14
Wagner is the Puccini of m. 271:20
what m. is more enchanting 350:14
when m. sounds 103:15
your voice is m. 30:27
Music-hall: m. songs provide the dull with wit
   256:25
   no more jokes in m.s 337:1
Musical: foreign m. with no dancing 360:19
   kind of m. Malcolm Sargent 29:18
   M. Banks 61:5
   m. beds 4:17
   m. daggers 406:10
   unquestioned law of the m. world 399:11
Musician: m. . . . . most modest of animals 337:16
   of all m.s flautists . . . know something 194:4

Musicologist: m. . . . can read music 29:16
Musing: m. upon the king 118:12
Musket: Sam, Sam, pick oop tha' m. 176:14
Mussolini, Benito 45:12, 58:5, 132:4, 366:8
  M. was bloody 246:19
Mustard: m.'s no good without roast beef 252:11
Musty: you will be frail and m. 290:11
Mute: as m. as a mackerel 351:5
  poem should be palpable and m. 244:10
  shall the voices of liberty be m.? 97:26
Muttering: all mauling and m. 103:29
Mutton: m. chop, not an Earl 410:19
  yesterday's cold m. 256:4
Myriad: there died a m. 303:17
Myself: anything except m. 361:10
  m. talking to m. 34:18
  more m. than me 84:6
  my real opposition is m. 342:6
  too busy thinking about m. 349:4
Mystery: clouds of self-serving m. 378:12
  for tribal man space was the m. 244:16
  hissed all the m. lectures 355:17
  m. and memory and electricity 341:13
  riddle wrapped in a m. inside an enigma 79:12
  thrust your pure m., unsung 318:10
Mysticism: m . . . to get rid of mystery 137:2
Myth: basing morals on m. 334:8
  explode a m. 329:20
  from being a patriotic m. 378:3
  is it m.s who think us up? 144:9
  m. is a fixed way of looking 46:12
  m. is a type of speech 27:3
  m. is recognized for what it is 334:8
  science must begin with m.s 301:8
  that great bridge, our M. 94:29
  truth and m. are one and the same 336:18
Mythical: in search of m. kings 305:9
Mythology: m. of self 358:10

N

Nageurs: *n. morts* 13:1
Nagging: nothing but his n. gods 206:9
Nail: blind as the . . . n.s upon the Cross 349:2
  Devil he blew upon his n.s 213:4
  four n.s make a cross 294:5
  I used to bite my n.s 291:21
  letters that I drive in like n.s 84:14
  mad and dead as n.s 368:19
  n. those coonskins to the wall 195:18
  stop biting your n.s 322:1
  wood the n.s are banged into 295:1
Nailing: n. his colours . . . to the fence 346:16
Naissons: *nous ne n. pas seuls* 84:7
Naïve: n. domestic Burgundy 372:12
  n. forgive and forget 364:6
  think their children are n. 277:9
Naked: can't stand a n. light bulb 404:20
  in the n. frosty blue 370:13

listen to with the n. eye 354:5
looks n. towards the shires 213:1
more enterprise in walking n. 415:14
n. ape 270:3
n. Civil Servants 95:22
n. into the conference chamber 41:13
n. to study the history of his body 122:8
n. underneath her clothes 132:11
n. . . . without furniture 303:29
president . . . must have to stand n. 113:12
pretty girl n. 97:9
starving hysterical n. 144:3
to be n. is to be oneself 38:19
truth is n. 385:12
Nakedness: n. is a luxury 375:21
  stratagem to cover n. 299:3
Name: child to call you by your first n. 226:19
  confused things with their n.s 336:23
  giving girls n.s like that 396:17
  headstones yield their n.s 365:7
  made you change your n. 365:11
  my n. is a dirty word 288:2
  n. and date split in soft slate 58:9
  n. comes first 374:17
  n.s, faces, and – the third 363:9
  n.s off yesterday's prison walls 313:5
  remembered your n. perfectly 355:15
  somebody else of the same n. 183:12
  thy sons acclaim your glorious n. 97:25
  your n. as if I should recognize it 109:25
Nameless: intolerably n. names 337:7
Naming: n. the parts does not show us 247:9
  today we have n. of parts 314:9
Napkin: same compartment . . . as . . . n.s 119:15
Napoleon Bonaparte 173:17
  N. brought peace to Europe; by losing 168:25
  N. had commanded 286:10
  N. of crime 109:24
Napoleon III 366:7
Narcissist: differs from the n. 328:5
Narrative: in a n. you know 389:12
Narrowing: n. rails slide together 117:7
Narrowness: grave's n. 151:25
Nastier: found anything n. to say 337:19
Nastiness: house is jealous of its n. 151:13
Nasty: how n. the nice people can be 304:7
  something n. in the woodshed 142:24
Nation: America became top n. 341:9
  day of small n.s has long passed away 71:15
  Empire is a Commonwealth of N.s 324:1
  exterminate a n. 355:13
  guide of the n. 141:15
  his castle is the n.'s 140:13
  ideals of a n. by its advertisements 109:1
  life of n.s . . . in the imagination 304:11
  living n.s wait 17:16
  n. cannot tolerate an authority 201:17
  n. is a society united by a delusion 186:20
  n. of amateurs 324:2
  n. of governesses 346:6
  n. President Roosevelt hoped for 195:19

n. shall speak unto n. 315:14
n. talking to itself 262:3
n.s . . . die by . . . degrees 144:23
people behaved in the way n.s do 404:23
perfectly demoralize the n. 40:5
prize amateur n. 406:21
so long to transcend the n. 159:3
National Anthem: endorsed the N. 130:22
Nationalism: n. is an infantile disease 115:16
n. is . . . like class 404:5
Nationalist: n. . . . . hates everybody 235:3
Nationality: other people have a n. 31:11
Native: n. intellectual 122:8
n. . . . who belong somewhere else 357:5
so long as the n.s are waiters 269:18
Nativity: n. in all disordered 151:16
NATO: N. running our armed forces 35:19
Natur: aus beiden Reichen erwuchs seine . . . N.
   319:5
ein Mund der N. 319:9
Natural: advantages . . . spoken of as n. 190:22
living example of n. selection 146:8
music is n. law 394:7
n. science does not simply describe 168:4
none had ever died there a n. death 135:18
Naturally: doin' what comes n. 39:3
Naturalness: n. of the hippopotamus 268:15
Nature: dead n. aims at nothing 401:7
defend us against n. 134:1
fruitful altruisms of N. 308:18
geography of one's own n. 48:11
hit off human n. 170:18
in n. the only end is death 152:20
in n. there are no rewards 385:1
interplay between n. and ourselves 168:4
Man as n.'s last word 409:2
mouthpiece of n. 319:9
n. grew from both realms 319:5
n. is as wasteful of . . . young men 181:6
n. . . . to rise above 170:21
n., which is always true 301:1
n.'s only interest 395:10
n.'s truth is primary 371:2
no individual enjoyment in n. 401:8
no poet ever interpreted n. 144:19
opinion of their position in n. 257:1
order of n. has any greater bias 397:15
relationship between n. and humanity 35:15
representations of our true n. 199:2
stuff that n. replaces it with 404:15
technology is not the master of n. 35:15
Naught: I tell you n. for your comfort 74:9
Nauses: he merd such a n. 198:3
Naval: don't talk . . . about n. tradition 82:20
Nave: from the n. build haunted heaven 358:12
Navel: knee-cap and ended at the n. 233:9
Navies: your nutshell n. came 210:15
Navy: being put in charge of the N. 68:17
dialect that has an army and a n. 394:13
joined the N. to see the world 39:8
the N.'s here 10:19

Nearer: always n. by not keeping still 156:21
Nearly-young: blonde, n. American woman 68:13
Neat: n. ones in your awkward squad 64:13
Necessarily: it ain't n. so 142:20
Necessary: even if it were [n.] 158:9
evil makes democracy n. 280:3
Necessities: do without the n. 413:11
Necessity: charge me with the n. 142:9
Neck: n. God made for other use 179:15
n. seemed to go up the back of his hat 262:16
n. wrung like a chicken 399:10
purpose in equipping us with a n. 216:14
short n. denotes a good mind 353:16
some chicken: some n. 79:25
till someone comes and wrings our n.s 20:8
Need: human n. and unreasonable silence 65:16
n. not greed 219:3
n.s they are unable to satisfy 250:21
nobody n.s at any time 402:21
prove . . . you don't need it 105:13
things that people don't n. 391:2
travels . . . in search of what he n.s 268:10
whether or not you n. to know 239:23
Needle, n. . . . . the eye of a camel 354:14
Nefarious: pity she is so n. 327:1
Negative: Europe is the unfinished n. 242:5
Negligence: winter . . . sacked for n. 243:18
Negotiate: never n. out of fear 204:18
Negrified: the other half half n. 173:20
Négritude: ma n. n'est pas une pierre 71:6
Negro: n. could never hope to get insulted 101:2
one drop – you are a n. 181:5
Neigh: most people expect me to n. 8:19
Neighbour: common hatred of its n. 186:20
death is my n. now 121:9
do not love your n. as yourself 344:25
good fences make good n.s 135:17
hate my next-door n. 75:15
humanity . . . than to love one's n. 176:2
lady of the house was everyone's n. 140:15
n.s asking why 17:21
policy of the good n. 322:11
same goes for the n.'s wife 37:21
Scots . . . kill their n.s 96:9
your n. loses his job 378:17
Nelson, Horatio, Lord: good Lord N. had a swollen
   gland 112:12
N. born in a fortunate hour 377:9
Nemesis: Hubris clobbered by N. 5:4
Neo-Keynesian: she was a n. 245:16
Nephew: n. to a lord 300:5
Nero: N. the ideal man 148:7
not that N. played 323:16
Nerve: after the n. has been extracted 325:22
my n.s are bad tonight 118:10
n. of the national spirit 90:4
nation that gets on its n.s 201:17
Nervous: being attacked by the n. system 174:3
n. about doing something 124:7
Nest: build their n.s in our hair 255:1
Net: n.s of wrong and right 416:16

Nettle: dust on the n.s 370:17
Nettle-rash: one-armed man with the n. 170:3
Network: gladly eat a n. executive 123:18
Neues: im Westen nichts N. 315:13
Neuroses: days of whine and n. 188:3
Neurosis: eager for the n. 169:2
   n. has . . . genius for malingering 307:21
   n. . . . way of avoiding non-being 374:1
Neurotic: blockheads and two cocky n.s 276:7
   great has come from n.s 307:20
   inclinations – n. 325:6
   n. . . . builds a castle in the air 224:25
   n. if he suffers 364:8
Neutralism 111:5
Neutrality: armed n. 406:18
   n., . . . has so often been disregarded 40:8
   n. . . . robs us of . . . tragedy 395:16
   positive n. 217:19
Never: didn't ought n. to have done it 42:1
   I don't know. I'm n. there 293:8
   n. in the field of human conflict 79:19
   second things n. 89:15
   sometimes always, by God, n. 317:12
   you've n. had it so good 245:6
New: just got into the n. wave 403:19
   n. class 107:9
   n. deal for the American people 322:9
   n. roads: n. ruts 78:5
   signs of a N. Age coming 351:13
   sun shone . . . on the nothing n. 28:23
   tells you he has discovered something n. 341:17
New-caught: your n., sullen peoples 213:17
New England: charge . . . against N. 218:4
New South Wales: go out and govern N. 32:20
New Statesman: we were promised a N. 350:9
New Testament: N. . . . commercial success
   153:18
New York 167:14, 170:7
   Andy Warhol N. City Diet 391:1
   anywhere but in little old N. 170:6
   N. . . . centre of American Culture 34:11
   N. is the perfect model of a city 274:2
   N. tolerated hypocrisy 399:13
   N. . . . would make a stone sick 208:2
   N.'s a small place 409:20
   way all N. barbers eventually go 333:20
New Yorker: N. . . . for the old lady 324:17
New Zealand 133:15
Newberry Fruit: great N. of friendship 90:17
Newgate: condemned cells of N. 61:29
Newman, Cardinal John: face like . . . N.'s 69:17
Newman, Paul 314:4
Newness: n., whatever it costs 382:13
News: all the n. that's fit to print 279:13
   foreign stories . . . not *real* n. 393:1
   good n. yet to hear 74:28
   hard n. that catches readers 281:14
   n. is whatever a good editor chooses 243:11
   n. . . . makes a reader say 'Gee whiz' 243:11
   n. of one day 40:5
   n. that stays n. 303:24

n. until he's read it 393:2
niche in the n. 151:14
obvious. It is always n. to somebody 203:1
Newscast: provided the ten o'clock n. 203:20
Newspaper: art of n. paragraphing 251:18
   don't work on a n.: own it 64:10
   drudgery in n. work 372:29
   it's the n.s I can't stand 360:16
   like a n. inside a prison 350:1
   never believe in mirrors or n.s 287:24
   n. . . . form of continuous fiction 41:17
   n. is a nation talking to itself 262:3
   n. with a little paragraph cut out 248:12
   n.s have . . . relationship to life 217:13
   reading someone else's n. 49:8
   Third World never sold a n. 274:13
   time it takes to read n.s 401:17
   why single out n.s? 52:9
Newspaperman: best n. . . . President 56:6
Newspapermen: what I think of n. 167:13
Newspeak: N. was the official language 286:24
Newstatesmanship: mention in N. 302:23
Newton, Isaac: another N. 183:16
Niagara Falls 81:19, 247:5
   spitting in N. 43:9
Nice: all the n. girls love a sailor 264:3
   all the n. people were poor 353:20
   another n. mess you've gotten me into 162:4
   be n. to people on the way up 266:20
   everyone says you're important and n. 274:8
   n. guys finish last 112:10
   n. one, Cyril 12:14
   n. to see you – to see you, n. 131:9
   n. unparticular man 163:23
   n. was a four letter word 357:1
   n. work if you can get it 142:14
   nicer, much nicer in N. 406:12
   such n. things . . . at their funerals 203:23
   things I think are n. 291:3
Nicer: not a n. girl than you are 93:19
Nicest: n. boy who ever committed the sin 354:1
   n. girls I was ever engaged to 410:21
Niche: n. in the news 151:14
Nick-name: nobody ever makes up n.s 321:1
Niece: carrying of n.s 317:16
Nieswurz-Sonate: spielt darauf v. Korfs N. 269:9
Nietzsche: dynamic exhibit who read N. 411:6
Night: come back the next n. 316:19
   every n. of her married life 369:23
   it sounded like n. prayer 127:15
   it's been a hard day's n. 229:25
   it's going to be a bumpy n. 249:13
   long day's journey into n. 285:3
   n. and day you are the one 302:3
   n. hours of an owl 193:6
   n. starvation 279:17
   n. was tailing 374:16
   n. will never stay 122:10
   one n. or the other n. 128:10
   real dark n. of the soul 126:10
   stirred in the condensed n. 313:5

then it's n. once more 29:8
through the shrinking n. 101:17
where the blue of the n. 96:11
why live in n.? 131:17
Night-hung: n. houses 103:23
Night-side: illness is the n. of life 353:8
Night-time: dog did nothing in the n. 109:27
Nightingale, Florence: sake of Miss N. 362:1
Nightingale: n. sang in Berkeley Square 253:25
  n.s are sobbing 18:17
  n.s sing out of tune 190:22
  tales told . . . by Eve's n.s 102:18
  towering dead with their n.s 239:8
Nightmare: n. of the dark 17:16
Nihilist: part-time n. 65:27
Nimble: n. fingers are no more n. 349:7
  n. in the calling of selling houses 233:16
Nine: n. children! 374:10
Nineteenth century: swim a n. dress 341:24
Nineveh: quinquireme. of N. 254:2
Nixon, President Richard: between N. and the
    White House 205:9
  if N. was second-rate 168:23
  N. could not tell the truth 331:14
  N. is a purposeless man 52:10
  Sincerely, N. 334:2
  you won't have N. to kick around 280:10
Nneumann, John von 54:4
No: can't say N. in any of them 292:16
  man who says n. 65:28
No-encouragement: expression of n. 50:9
No-time: happy n. of his sleeping 288:17
Noah: his own health rather than in N.'s Ark
    159:7
  N. . . . said to his wife 75:14
  only one poor N. dare hope to survive 183:16
Nobility: n. of England would have snored 45:5
Nobleness: n. walks in our ways 54:11
Noblest: honest God's the n. work of man 61:27
Nobly: wants to die n. for a cause 358:1
Nobody: in heaven an angel is n. 345:1
  n. else's n. 43:19
  n., not even the rain 97:30
  n. tells me anything 139:16
Nocturnal: as if n. women were beating 412:15
Nod: n. politely, but he won't understand 200:9
  passed with a n. of the head 416:4
Nodded: I did not stop to speak, but n. 181:15
Noggin: preliminary n. is essential 410:16
Noise: argues by increments of n. 62:9
  but they . . . love the n. it makes 29:19
  happy n. to hear 179:20
  hates to be moved to folly by a n. 225:2
  loud n. at one end 216:1
  most sublime n. 130:14
  n.s upon the air 87:20
  reduced it to n. 17:8
Nom de plume: n. de ma tante 155:1
Non-aligned: n. with the United States 239:24
Non-being: way of avoiding n. 374:1
Non-combatant: no fury like a n. 267:17

Non-commissioned: backbone . . . the N. man
    210:12
Non-conformity: all advance comes from n. 366:6
Non-existence: warlike n. 239:17
Non-existent: denying n. facts 111:2
Non-member: for the benefit of n.s 367:8
Non-reading: time to do all this n. 217:9
Non-U: U and N. 324:14
Non-violence: n. is also the last article 140:1
Nonbeing: n. must in some sense be 310:5
Nonconformist: n. like everybody else 182:2
Nonsense: closely structured n. 59:12
  mind oscillates between sense and n. 199:1
  n. does not pass by but into us 27:8
Nonsensical: cover them with n. forms 136:29
Nonstop: n. literary drinker 371:15
Noon: where the Princes ride at n. 102:20
Noose: n.s give 291:8
Nordic: destruction of N. science 375:5
Norfan: I'm a N., both sides 396:16
Norfolk: bear him up the N. sky 40:10
  very flat, N. 94:3
Normal: fortunate settled n. person 191:2
  N. is the good smile in a child's eyes 342:4
Norman, Montagu 85:21
Normans: N. don't joke . . . about food 339:17
North: heart of the N. is dead 224:21
  inhabitant of N. of England 129:14
  this N. that taught us 327:12
North American: N.s have a peculiar bias 245:5
Northcliffe, Lord: [N.] aspired to power 366:1
Northerner: n.s don't live in the north 24:16
Norway: ten [years ago] in N. 368:12
Norwegian: only as rather mad N.s 220:14
Nose: assiduously picking his n. 125:32
  Catalonia is the n. of the earth 99:6
  foot and n. disease 41:7
  he can't see beyond his own n. 29:25
  I've . . . a cold in my n. 18:14
  keep a clean n. 113:20
  little red n. and very little clothes 274:19
  n. . . . stupidity is . . . displayed 308:12
  n. that can see is worth two 187:9
  n.s too far off the ground 124:6
  put on a false n. and be himself 384:1
  tell him that you pick your n.? 64:14
  they haven't got no n.s 75:7
Noselessness: n. of man 75:8
Nostalgia: n. for an imagined past 185:5
  n. isn't what it was 149:27
Nostalgic: we're n. we take pictures 353:11
Notches: three n. on his walking stick 107:19
Nothing: behind them there is n. 336:8
  between grief and n. 123:3
  doing n. with tremendous skill 63:9
  excited about n. – and . . . marry him 73:18
  God made everything out of n. 385:16
  he who believes in n. 324:13
  I got plenty o' n. [nuthin'] 142:19
  man with that Certain N. 83:19
  most of everything and the best of n. 72:8

n. . . . half so much worth doing 150:13
n. for n. 275:7
n. is wasted, n. is in vain 170:28
n. [nothin'] ain't worth n. 218:1
N. scrawled on a five-foot page 75:6
n. to be done 293
n. to say and I am saying it 63:6
people don't resent having n. 86:15
people of whom we know n. 71:19
play in which n. happens – twice 260:3
profoundly optimistic about n. 21:6
spend our lives doing n. 96:12
what it doesn't do n. else but 410:23
when one does n. 335:23
Nothingness: eternal n. 6:9
modern painter begins with n. 324:7
Notice: [clothes] make you notice the person 160:18
give offence by giving n. 360:17
man who used to n. such things 162:5
Noticing: n. . . . puts things in a room 307:8
Nought: n. but vast sorrow was there 103:6
Nourished: n. during his whole life 319:16
Novel: in the n., the particular 413:3
B-grade n.s, ideological fiction 276:12
bad n. tell us the truth 76:17
because a n.'s invented, it isn't true 304:5
can't think of a single Russian n. 257:5
few n.s for grown up people 412:7
finest French n. in the English language 321:6
in the n. are all things given full play 224:4
more interesting than half the n.s 256:21
not a n. to be tossed aside lightly 292:3
n. . . . can subside into an ocean 274:12
[n. is] a machine for generating 114:7
n. is . . . a Protestant form of art 286:18
n. is a static thing 380:26
n. is born 137:10
n. refers to something . . . happened 64:6
n. tells a story 130:9
n. was invented for the ladies 112:13
n. would trade the . . . diamond 224:16
[n.s] relied on the classic formula 221:21
things that the n. does not say 64:8
we can Learn even from N.s 396:18
what is fictitious in a n. 4:15
when a n. comes it's a grace 247:16
woman's n. with no men in it 17:2
write more than five or six [n.s] 59:11
Novel-reading: n. re-enacts the Fall 98:1
Novelist: authors who are not really n.s 131:4
battered old n. 191:8
being a n., I [am] superior 224:3
great 19th-century English novelists 388:4
n. he was almost successful 125:26
n. is . . . at home on the surface 276:14
n. teaches the reader to comprehend 218:16
n. too busy to write 88:9
no . . . n. . . . wishes he were the only one 19:4
only the n. can [get at the truth] 52:7
time was invented to kill the n. 112:13

November: sombre N. 118:21
than these N. skies 133:6
Novitiate: life is just a n. eternity 93:6
Now: n. what? 335:21
right n. would be a good time 53:1
the word 'now' is like a bomb 261:13
time we've reached the 'w' of n. 132:13
Nowhere: if you must go n., step out 233:12
n. but in England 89:12
real n. man 230:3
there, in the n. 238:10
there was n. else to go 347:5
when you've n. to go 100:20
Nuance: n. . . . is a wide chasm 87:1
Nuclear: n. arms race has no . . . purpose 272:12
n. attack it'll look the same 87:7
n. power station in the middle of London 73:8
n. waste fades your genes 149:28
one n. bomb can ruin your whole day 149:21
Nude: bare like n. giant girls 355:3
n. is to be seen naked by others 38:19
Nudge: n., n., wink, wink 268:5
Nudist: at the superior n. camps 152:17
give a nudist on his birthday 124:19
Nudity: n. is a form of dress 38:19
Nuisance: exchange of one n. for another n. 120:4
n. for the few people who grow up 76:25
not composing of it becomes a . . . n. 176:17
together a bloody n. 246:19
Number: I am not a n. – I am a free man 251:2
telephone n.. . . . in the high n.s 207:10
Numinosum: altered by n. 199:8
Nun: n., at best, is only half a woman 258:18
n.s who never take a bath 328:4
Nuremberg trials 82:21
Nurse: always keep a hold of N. 32:16
Nursery: inside, it is . . . his n. 239:1
Nut: N.s! 241:7
squeeze you n.s and open your face 97:18
Nutshell: your n. navies came 210:15
Nuvoletta: N. in her lightdress 197:15
Nymph: half-filled with . . . bathing n.s 183:1

O

OED: volume of the O. in carpet-slippers 167:5
Oak: greater . . . than o. and ash and thorn 213:8
Oat: bread I break was once the o. 369:18
Oates, Captain 16:11
Obedience: be swift in all o. 212:25
Obey: Believe! O.! Fight! 275:10
don't o. no orders 210:11
pain we o. 308:9
Obituary: make the o. column 410:17
no life is lived for . . . an o. 53:12
o. in serial form 95:23
on the east by o. 156:8
Object: over-development of o.s 148:12
relationship between o.s 131:8

Old Glory: let's keep the glow in O. 278:22

Old Kent Road: knocked 'em in the O. 78:8

Older: as I get o. I seem to believe less 193:12
    don't know better as they grow o. 332:13
    I was so much o. then 113:19
    must make way for an o. man 255:15
    o. men declare war 177:7
    o. she gets, the more interested 78:15

O'Leary: with O. in the grave 417:17

Oligarchic: o. character of the modern 76:18

Olive-oil: smell of crude o. 68:15

Olivier, Laurence, Lord 384:1

Olympic Games: important thing in the O. 93:8

Omelette: making eggs out of an o. 22:10
    o. without frying eggs 102:13

Omen: precise meaning of the o. 50:8

Omnibuses: run up the steps of o. 412:13

Omnipotence: final proof of God's o. 105:6

Omniscience: his specialism is o. 109:18

Omniscient: o. umpire 377:11

Oncoming: light of the o. train 238:6

One: at o. with the O. 153:9
    how to be o. up 302:20
    if we knew o., we knew two 114:10
    o. with the law is a majority 90:7
    the o. was me 183:16

One-and-twenty: when I was o. 179:17

One-armed: o. economist 379:3
    o. . . . man in a dark room 410:22
    o. man with the nettle-rash 170:3

One-eyed: coloured, o. jew 101:3
    little o., blinking sort o' place 163:29
    o. son of a bitch 97:23
    sleeping o. 327:5

One-horse: little o. town 380:18

One-parent: royal o. family 296:21

One-third: o. of a nation ill-housed 322:14

Oneself: one owes to o. to be o. 219:14

Onion: carry their own o.s when cycling 92:2
    our sages know their o.s 273:16

Onward: 'O.', the sailors cry 47:20

Oompus-Boompus: Unsafe To Try Any O. 409:19

Ooze: o. of the past 276:14

Open: his mind is so o. 49:24
    o. to all . . . like the Ritz 99:14
    still keeping o. bed 182:8

Open-eyed: when time was o. 238:10

Opening: it's always o. time 369:28

Opera 360:19
    bed . . . is the poor man's o. 182:22
    French o.s sung by Swedish artists 399:11
    interval without an o. 279:5
    kind of o. that starts at six 312:3
    marvellous o.s but dreadful music 347:8
    mind what language an o. is sung in 13:4
    o. ain't over till the fat lady sings 89:19
    o. . . . . imitation of human wilfulness 19:10
    o. in English 259:13
    o. is the theatre of the absurd 350:7
    o. . . . one of the strangest inventions 83:7

Opera-glasses: you could take o. 317:17

Operatic: so romantic, so o. 308:11

Operating: o. by day 91:20

Operation: o.s we can perform 401:5

Operative: o. statement 420:10

Ophir: quinquireme . . . from distant O. 254:2

Opinion: anger of men who have no o.s 76:21
    buys its o.s as it buys its meat 61:25
    difference of o. . . . makes horse races 380:14
    man who wishes to impose his o.s 385:13
    o. . . . . goes unheeded 383:24
    o.s . . . conducive to our own welfare 61:7
    people are responsible for . . . o.s 418:6
    public o. minus his o. 76:13
    study of the history of o. 206:13
    two Jews there are three o.s 27:15
    whole climate of o. 17:15

Opponent: know who your o. is 383:21
    never ascribe to an o. motives 26:27
    o. . . . . honest and intelligent 287:15
    refer to my o.s as Miss Hughes 304:13

Opportunist: rather be an o. and float 23:15

Opportunity: maximum of o. 344:30

Oppose: even if it were we should o. it 158:9
    support whatever the enemy o.s 250:12

Opposite: o. is always a profound truth 45:2
    two o.s that never meet 391:6
    whose o. is also a great truth 249:20

Opposition: my real o. is myself 342:6

Oppressed: admit other women are o. 325:18
    mind of the o. 42:24

Oppressor: o. and the man he oppresses 336:26
    o.s do not perceive their monopoly 133:9

Optics: o. is the geometry of light 102:8

Optimism: o. of the will 150:19
    pessimism . . . as agreeable as o. 37:7

Optimist: ideas that make us o.s 382:5
    only a great cynic would be an o. 218:20
    o. claims . . . best of all possible worlds 63:4
    o. . . . . crossword puzzle in ink 347:6
    o. . . . . has never had much experience 251:8
    o. replies: 'Oh yes they could' 58:3
    o. thought everything good 77:5
    o., unrepentant and militant 383:12
    o. who carries a raincoat 406:11
    pessimism is just a well-informed o. 9:17

Optimistic: profoundly o. about nothing 21:6

Optimo-pessimism: my theory of o. 359:18

Option: free to renew your o. 329:14

Optional: plug . . . an o. extra 120:7

Opulence: private o. and public squalor 138:18

Oral: worst thing about o. sex 235:1

Orang utan: und o. hingen in den zweigen 202:1

Orange: tea and o.s 85:13
    who ever heard of a clockwork o. 58:19

Orator: bigot is a stone-deaf o. 143:8
    o.s . . . do not know what they have said 78:20

Oratorio: too autocratic for o. 370:23

Oratory: if you want real o. 410:16

Orchard: keep cold young o. 135:14
    o.s of our mother 18:17

Orchestra: only recognizable to the o. 108:7

Own: I am my o. man 247:18
  I wouldn't want to o. one 124:20
  no one o.s life 60:1
  you mean apart fom my o.? 138:8
Ownership: liable to a change of o. 206:7
Ox: if your o. kicks a hole 91:19
Oxen: come and see the o. kneel 163:10
  years like great black o. 415:16
Oxford: all put gently back at O. 30:7
  clever men at O. know all 150:14
  nice sort of place, O. 344:9
  secret in the O. sense 132:7
  sends his son to O. 356:15
Oxygen: I take up all the o. 316:5
  o. on which they depend 367:21
Oxymoron 334:2
Oyster: every pearl has its o. 192:13
  open an o. at sixty paces 408:22
  unselfishness of an o. 332:18
  world is an o. but you don't crack it 261:20

P

Pace: p.s about her room again, alone 118:15
Pacifist: against the P.s 81:2
Pack: bid the Muse go p. 417:24
  peasantry its p. animal 377:24
Packaging: throw-away plastic p. 107:23
Padded: comfortably padded . . . asylums 412:8
Paddle: p. in the cold . . . streams 417:29
Paddling: form the p. of life 399:15
Padlock: heavy p. on the door 375:1
Padlocked: rodent-like with p. ears 362:21
Pagan: find the p. – spoiled 420:2
Page: Nothing scrawled on a five-foot p. 75:6
  p. that aches for a word 105:17
Pageant: all part of life's rich p. 252:4
Pagoda: by the old Moulmein P. 211:33
Paid: getting what you haven't p. for 399:20
  I HAVE P., BUT 47:13
  might as well get paid for it 111:14
  ye are not p. to think 211:27
Pain: clenched on a round p. 368:18
  experienced p. and bought jewellery 326:8
  I heard a sudden cry of p. 358:3
  intoxication with p. 54:5
  no gains without p.s 358:21
  p. is produced by . . . pleasure 345:2
  p. we obey 308:9
  p.s in my wallet 63:17
  sympathize with people's p.s 182:23
  their joy or their p. 370:20
Paint: good artist p.s what he is 300:19
  it's a pity he doesn't p. 71:8
  p. the full face of sensuality 370:21
Painted: every p. image of something 38:16
  not so young as they are p. 30:3
  p. to the eyes 107:11
Painter: as p.s, not as surveyors 307:16

p. of letters 145:10
p. should not paint what he sees 385:15
p.s are outside the class system 52:5
p.s no longer live within a tradition 297:11
photographer would like to be a p. 297:12
that's why p.s live so long 297:14
Painting: all p. . . . is abstract 175:6
  cheating checkmate by p. 151:7
  if the p. stands up 71:9
  never make a p. as a work of art 298:5
  p. is a blind man's profession 298:1
  p. is a dramatic action 297:10
  p. is a sign 297:15
  p. is a way to forget life 325:13
  p. is about the presence of absence 38:16
  p. is its own language 21:5
  p. is saying 'Ta' to God 354:16
  p. is self-discovery 300:19
  p. shouldn't be a *trompe l'oeil* 297:19
  whoever devotes himself to p. 255:10
Pairing: specific p. we have postulated 95:8
Palace: mob can shout round a p. 77:18
  shining p. built upon the sand 261:7
Palate: distinguish . . . with his p. 338:21
  our grosser p.s 415:7
Pale: p. Ebenezer thought it wrong 33:1
  p. hands I loved 177:21
  pink pills for p. people 3:6
  very p. owing to the drains 15:3
  whiter shade of p. 55:10
Palestine: establishment in P. of a national home
    23:19
  haven in sunny P. 254:2
  peopling P. with Jewish immigrants 186:19
Palm: p.s before my feet 74:15
  quietly sweating p. to p. 183:17
Palmer, Samuel: sixteen P.s in a weekend 203:14
Palpable: almost a p. movement 163:22
  poem should be p. and mute 244:10
Paltry: aged man is but a p. thing 417:10
Pam: P., you great big mountainous girl 40:16
Pamphleteer: this is not the age of p.s 176:6
Pan: fish that talks in the frying p. 102:16
Pancreas: an adorable p. 205:24
Panic: bachelor's p. 148:4
  don't p. 1:12
  murmur or innuendo causes p. 73:14
  wind of p. 13:7
Panique: vent de p. 13:7
Pantheist: p. not only sees the god 224:9
Panther: sofa upholstered in p. skin 300:8
Pants: p. were so thin 376:8
  secret of life in your p. 97:20
Papal: better send them a P. Bull 98:10
Paper: all reactionaries are p. tigers 250:13
  as blameless as p. 400:14
  fornicated and read the p.s 65:8
  he's got my p.s, this man 298:17
  just for a scrap of p. 40:8
  keep the p. work down 286:3
  no more personality than a p. cup 72:9

Pause: conversation without a single p. 300:6
   eine kleine p. 124:4
   most precious thing in speech are p.s 317:9
   p.s between the notes 338:16
Paved: hell is p. with good intention 345:4
   p. paradise and put up a parking lot 265:24
Pavilion: I am . . . the p. cat 220:10
Pawn: p. the Bechstein grand 94:1
Pawned: as if he's p. his real ones 174:10
Pax: P. Britannia . . . bit of keeping up 70:2
Pax Romana: P. . . . . vulgar . . . civilization 59:4
Pay: bloomin' good p. 212:20
   does not pay to the future 300:16
   justice, but do you want to p. for it? 50:22
   live now, p. later 361:20
   not a penny off the p. 89:18
   pass the hat . . . and p. p. p.! 209:15
   we p. for everything 232:9
   wonders what to p. 179:4
Paycock: sthruttin' about . . . like a p. 284:1
Paying: one of them goes on p. for it 102:15
   p. for what she doesn't get 399:20
P.C. 49 164:16
Pea: ability to sort p.s 177:3
   if p.s were eaten with the knife 311:10
Peace: all her paths are p. 355:20
   be at p. with them [devils] 224:1
   brought p. to Europe; by losing 168:24
   challenging Israel to p. 13:5
   deep, deep p. of the double bed 65:1
   deep p. burnt me alive 254:5
   defence of p. 382:9
   deliberate aim at P. 401:2
   deny you p. but give you glory 382:7
   disciplined by a hard and bitter p. 204:16
   even lovers find their p. 128:8
   give p. a chance 229:24
   grave's narrowness though not its p. 151:25
   half the world is at p. with itself 360:12
   if p. is a chimera 222:11
   in p.: goodwill 81:4
   in the arts of p. Man is a bungler 344:19
   muttering the one word: 'P.' 5:2
   our p. betrayed us; we betrayed our p. 273:5
   p. . . . . a more comfortable one 402:19
   P.: a period of cheating 42:21
   p. comes dropping slow 416:19
   p. for our time 71:19
   p. has broken out 51:13
   p. is indivisible 235:5
   p. offensive 72:3
   p. running wild all over the place 51:6
   p. that is never achieved 326:10
   poetry is an act of p. 278:20
   question of p. . . . . talk to the Devil 171:8
   rarely make a good p. 81:3
   right is more precious than p. 406:20
   under the semblance of p. 417:22
   war is p. 286:23
   war was . . . speeded up p. 312:16
   who will bring white p. 234:8

Peaceful: opposite of p. coexistence 239:17
Peacemaker: cursed are the p.s 175:2
Peacetime: where they're living it's p. 217:3
Peacock: live with proud p.s 100:12
   p.s, apes and ivory 212:4
   who said 'P. Pie'? 103:19
Peak: p. of summer's past 101:18
Peanut: failed in the p. business 123:6
   I cannot chew my p.s 175:18
   more salted p.s consumed 355:11
   price of a cocktail – a salted p. 249:15
   stop after eating one p. 300:18
   tied your p. butter sandwich in a knot 339:7
Pear: change the p. by eating it 250:8
   here we go round the prickly p. 117:17
Pearl: every p. has its oyster 192:13
   false p.s before real swine 115:4
   string of p.s to me 321:12
   string the p.s were strung on 190:14
Pearly: through P. Gates where river flow 9:22
Peasant: how do p.s die? 375:3
   p.s are the most observant class 38:13
   p.'s idea of order 53:10
Peasantry: p. its pack animal 377:24
Pebble: not be worth that p. on the path 217:21
   where does a wise man kick a p.? 76:23
Peck: hide my light under a p. 273:18
Peckham: classes within classes in P. 353:15
Peculiar: funny p. or funny ha-ha? 166:2
Pedalling: p. in the opposite direction 363:5
Peddle: p. gold bricks to each other 167:14
Pedestal: place my wife under a p. 6:15
   when smashing monuments: save the p.s 227:4
Pedestrian: two classes of p..s 105:15
Pee: the colour of children's p. 7:9
Peeing: have them p. on my cheapest rug 167:9
Peel: p. me a grape 398:2
   stuff you had to p. and cook 95:24
Peepshow: ticket for the p. 246:3
Peer: blubber which encases an English p. 88:12
   English p. of the right sort 410:18
   p.s and they are hereditary 235:19
Peerage: I want a p., I will pay for it 281:15
Peering: p. beneath my writing arm 151:23
Peg: p. to hang a Hatton 165:19
Pekingese: P. taking a pill 409:1
Pelican: wonderful bird is the p. 260:7
Pen: far less brilliant p. than mine 30:5
Penal Code: read the P. and the Bible 347:14
Pendulum: p. of the mind 199:1
Penetrate: English will p. 241:2
   seize and clutch and p. 118:19
Penetrated: p. into the ear of man 130:14
Penguin: worse time than an Emperor p. 73:20
Penis: *Homo sapiens* . . . biggest p. 270:4
   my. p. hangs slightly to the left 203:21
   we broke over the concept of p. envy 6:8
Penitence: p. by being remarried 399:16
Pennies: p. from heaven 59:15
   throw down p. 349:10
Penny: not a p. off the pay 89:18

you're some kind of deviated p. 218:8
Pessimism: p. . . . a Jew never can allow 258:7
   p. . . . as agreeable as optimism 37:7
   p. of the spirit 150:19
   p. . . . that makes our ideas 382:5
Pessimist: p. fears this is so 63:4
   p. finds this out anew 383:12
   p. is just a well-informed optimist 9:17
   p. . . . looks both ways 296:2
   p. . . . never happy unless he is miserable 9:16
   p. . . . things couldn't possibly be worse 58:3
   p. thought everything bad 77:5
   real p. 9:7
   scratch a p. 41:22
Pesticide: good laugh is the best p. 276:13
Pestilence: p.s and there are victims 65:26
Pétain, Marshal: P. in petticoats 166:14
Petal: peel all the p.s off 20:3
   p.s on a wet black bough 303:20
Peter Pan: wholly in *P.* 380:24
Peter Principle 296:3
Peter Rabbit: P. . . . McGregor's garden 174:14
Petrified: p. adolescence 41:14
Petrol: p. is more likely than wheat 394:11
Pettiness: something to expiate; a p. 222:23
Petty: suffering . . . makes men p. 256:14
Pew: warm hassock in the numbered p. 371:8
Phagocyte: stimulate the p.s 343:7
Phallusy: thought men were a p. 150:4
Pharisee: now is the time of P.s 293:10
Pharmacopoeia: known to the British p. 79:3
Phenomena: p. as phlegm and tooth-decay 168:14
Phenomenon: p. that we call love 307:3
Philadelphia: I'd rather be in P. 125:6
Philanthropist: necessary for the p. 328:6
Philanthropy: p. and symphony concerts 399:17
Philately: don't know much about p. 133:13
Philistine: Eggheads are terrible P.s 276:12
Philistinism: yawning P. 306:1
Philologic: invoke the p. pen 75:13
Philomel: change of P. 118:8
Philosopher: bad p.s may have a certain influence 328:20
   only five-lettered p. 90:14
   p. like a blind man in dark cellar 191:21
   p., not the protozoon 328:16
   too much of a p. 330:2
Philosophic: defence of p. doubt 23:16
Philosophical: European p. tradition 401:9
   interest in the photocopier was p. 175:15
Philosophies: when all p. shall fail 74:11
Philosophy: ice-cream . . . that's my p. 402:17
   in p. . . . you aren't moving 274:5
   less than p. 341:11
   pale gruel of p. 377:22
   p. is a battle against the bewitchment 332:5
   p. . . . is a fight 408:1
   p. is concerned with two matters 201:13
   p. is 'Critique of language' 408:5
   p. is not a theory 408:6
   p. . . . is the art of concealment 274:10

p. is the product of wonder 401:6
p. ought to be patient 312:12
p. . . . replacement of category-habits 329:18
p. was wrong, and you may meet 312:5
psychiatry's chief contribution to p. 73:11
superstition to enslave a p. 186:11
system of p. to be substantially true 335:15
useful provided it is not called p. 328:21
Phlegm: p. and tooth-decay 168:14
Phoenician: drowned P. sailor 118:4
Phoenix: p. who runs with arsonists 34:6
Phone: ET p. home 255:5
   happy to hear that the p. is for you 226:21
   how pretty you are on the p. 156:15
   p. for the fish-knives 40:12
   you couldn't p. it in 266:16
Phoney: p. war 99:4
Phoniness: p. beyond reasonable doubt 204:1
Phonograph: p.s of Hades in the brain 95:2
   vaccinated with a p. needle 253:1
Photo: p. is a piece of reality 363:10
   p. is a reprieve 363:11
Photocopier: my interest in the p. 175:5
Photograph: all you can do with . . . p.s 175:3
   epic scope of a p. album 151:1
   he takes p.s of it [the god] 224:9
   instantaneous p. of a Derby winner 241:10
   p. is, visually, high definition 245:1
   p. is not only an image 353:10
   you should see his p. 10:18
Photographed: husband had p. her 126:13
   she had a heart. It p. 337:18
Photographer: every p. would like to be a painter 297:12
Photography: p. is a moment of embarrassment 35:21
   p. . . . is always flirting with death 38:14
   p. is truth 145:8
Phrase: what do I mean by a p.? 136:10
Phyllida: P. her colour comes and goes 107:11
Physician: p. can bury his mistakes 413:12
   then they [p.s] get honest 322:5
Physicist: anything from the theoretical p.s 115:17
   p. . . . is a bootstrapper 78:11
   p.s are made of atoms 389:13
   p.s have known sin 285:6
Physics: acting according to the laws of p. 124:5
   forbidden to resort to p. 258:14
   gap between such p. 276:12
   p. and stamp-collecting 329:16
   p. is the study of simple things 101:4
   true p. is . . . German spirit 375:5
Piano: help with moving the p. 399:1
   p. . . . it has not written the concerto 249:14
   p. for twenty years in a brothel 10:4
   p. is the easiest instrument 178:9
   they laughed when I sat down at the p. 67:3
Piano-player: I'm a p. in a brothel 340:15
Piano-playing: p. in my living-room 362:19
Picardy: give me that song of P. 244:7

roses are flowering in P. 394:2

Picasso, Pablo: P. insisted everything was
    miraculous 298:6
    P. is a Communist 99:8
    what a genius, that P. 71:8

Piccadilly: good-bye P. 403:22

Pick: p. up those [ideals] for himself 130:19
    tell him that you p. your nose 64:14

Pick-me-up: Jeeves's p. 409:15

Picking: in the order of their p. 112:19

Pickle: weaned on a p. 237:5

Picnic: tea . . . a p. indoors 390:2
    teddy bears have their p. 204:12

Picture: dead man than a good p. 343:9
    every p. tells a story 3:8
    get me at the end of the p. 100:18
    how did you love my p.? 147:23
    it's no go at the p. palace 246:4
    Monet's p.s are always too draughty 102:14
    obliquely an invented p. starts up 318:15
    one . . . goes to a p. gallery 257:5
    p. papers . . . with . . . bathing nymphs 183:1
    pleasure of cutting all the p.s out 32:26
    p.s got smaller 402:8
    take a p. of it 363:11
    when the earth's last p. is painted 213:14
    you furnish the p.s 167:7

Picturesque: quite p. liar 380:11

Pie: p. in the sky when you die 172:2

Pie-eyed: unless p. you cannot hope 410:16

Piece: always a little p. in the corner 35:24
    go to p.s like a man 372:26

Pier: effusive welcome of the p. 17:6

Piety: fear of life become p. 258:13

Piffle: p. before the wind 15:5

Pig: forced to behave like a p. 119:19
    looked from p. to man 286:13
    p. got up 60:3
    p. is committed 278:14

Pigeon: keep your city clean – eat a p. 149:22
    mate for life like p.s or Catholics 6:3
    Monarchy along with feeding the p.s 160:3
    night owl into a homing p. 9:13
    p. on the grass alas 357:8
    p.s . . . grey, second-hand suits 68:12

Pike: still as the dead the great p. lies 44:9

Pilgrim: land of the p. and so forth 97:24
    loved the p. soul in you 417:27
    we are the p.s, master 128:13

Pilgrimage: strown blisses about my p. 162:17
    with songs beguile your p. 128:7

Pilgrim's Progress: P., . . . man who left his family
    379:17

Pill: pink p.s for pale people 3:6
    Protestant women may take the P. 370:25

Pillar: lie has become . . . a p. of state 353:1
    pylons, those p.s 355:3

Pillow: p. was gone 90:20

Pimpernel: that demmed elusive P. 285:10

Pimple: boff over his p. 327:3
    knew her by the p. . . . on her nose 320:9

p.s on .. the boot-boy 412:24

Pin: p. are a great means of saving life 267:18
    p. back your lug-'oles 128:22
    stand as straight as a pin 70:19

Pine: p.s are gossip p.s 128:4

Ping-pong: some people like p. 229:14

Pink: I like p. 250:1
    p. is the navy blue of India 388:15
    p. sweet filled with snow 102:7

Pint: a p. . . . that's nearly an armful 161:6
    drinka p.a milka day 3:5
    someone who orders p.s in pubs 188:13
    you can get a quart into a p. pot 70:17

Pioneer: p.s . . . are . . . mess-makers 299:8

Pip: squeeze her until the p.s squeak 141:17

Pipe: his p. might fall out 130:6
    walking along with a couple of p.s 169:23

Piss: fiction is p. 55:24
    I can p. the old boy in the snow 234:2
    p. off, he said to me 298:16
    we all p. in the swimming pool 201:11
    your poor I'll p. on them 314:19

Piss-house: can't find anything in a p. 373:12

Pissed: Lazarus – p. every night 59:8

Pisses: it p. God off 390:5

Pissing: inside my tent p. out 195:20
    p. in his shoe keeps no man warm 341:15

Piston: black statement of p.s 354:19
    take . . . the p.s out of my kidneys 12:16

Pit: man will go down the p. 23:17

Pitcher: I am your p. (if I break) 319:15

Pitt-Kethley, Fiona 25:4

Pity: avoid the feeling of p. 86:17
    God in His p. knows 103:5
    I thought it was a pity to get up 256:6
    p. beyond all telling 417:4
    p. of war 288:13
    p. our poor dear queen 296:21
    p. the dead that are dead 222:19
    unbearable p. for the suffering 328:1

Pivotal: storm bears down the p. tree 206:10

Pix: sticks nix hick p. 347:13

Pizzicati: pulse p. of Hosanna 358:16

Placard: stuck with p.s for 'Deathless' 319:2

Place: any p. in particular 326:14
    in p. of strife 70:11
    p. in the sun 403:9
    p. within each of us 320:16
    precisely in the right p. 49:8

Plafond: inscrite dans les lignes du p. 120:16

Plagiarism: if you steal from one author it's p.
    267:1

Plagiarizing: 'real life' is responsible for p. me
    276:5

Plague-germ: carrier of the p. 65:26

Plain: cards . . . as if she were p. 127:23
    criminal: he's in p. clothes 348:12
    manners are . . . the need of the p. 393:21
    this p. she makes a shining bone 355:4
    watch the p. clothes 113:20

Plan: p. for freedom 301:6

Plane: fly a p. with one hand 261:2
  how many p.s joined the raid 161:13
Planet: disgrace to the p. 359:17
  fell on the wrong p. 50:19
  he would love to save the p. 176:10
  loyal to his club than to his p. 400:4
  p. is poorly equipped for delight 257:16
  p. is the territory 403:23
Planetary: democratic p. community 238:1
Planned: unwise and curiously p. 128:14
Planning: rhetoric of p. 84:2
Plant: call a street lamp a minor p. 251:25
  p. ourselves in their lives 235:7
Plash: through the p. his lithe bright vassals 44:9
Plaster: don't grow into p. saints 213:7
Plastic: born with a p. spoon 376:3
  given a big enough p. bag 360:10
  looks from her father . . . p. surgeon 253:20
  my sculptures are p. metaphors 297:19
  throw-away p. packaging 107:23
Plate: changing the p.s before . . . enough 206:8
  you have to clean your p. 324:4
Platinum: bullets made of p. 32:9
  eyebrows made of p. 130:7
Platitude: duckbilled p. 97:13
  stroke a p. until it purrs 251:18
Plato: choose P. and Plotinus 417:24
  footnotes to P. 401:9
  P. . . . five-lettered philosopher 90:14
  P. is there . . . with Aristotle 412:14
  P. was . . . unreliable Platonist 330:2
  P.'s beard: . . . dulling the edge 310:5
Platonic: dislike is purely p. 376:19
Plätze: P., o Platz in Paris 318:8
Plausibility: p. must be invoked 152:9
Play: bad p. surrounded by water 189:15
  but when I started to p.! 67:3
  great thing about writing p.s 299:2
  in the p. we recognize the general 413:3
  knowing what sort of p. you are in 143:20
  nobody asked me to p. 124:16
  p. chooses its audience 37:1
  p. is a dynamic thing 380:26
  p. it Sam 38:20
  p. that would paint the full face 370:21
  p. work through metaphor 361:18
  p.s them back when I'm out 407:21
  p.s which remind the drama 380:25
  profess to write better p.s 345:28
  publishing a p. is reversing 342:2
  rehearsing a p. is making the word flesh 342:2
  sit, wink and p. 27:9
  tend to lose the meaning of the p. 102:3
  that interesting p. 32:23
  you do not p. things as they are 358:13
Playboy: P. of the Western World 363:17
  P. while your wife turns the pages 313:14
Played: p. the way I would have liked to write 202:19
  that he [Nero] p. badly 323:16
Player: changes the props but keeps the p.s 244:6

Playful: when I'm p. 380:6
Playing: work terribly hard at p. 270:15
Playmates: Hello p. 15:12
Plaything: choice of p.s 214:8
Playwright: p. . . . . slamming down his . . . curtain 333:22
  p.s . . . dead for three hundred years 249:16
Pleasant: p. cuckoo, loud and long 100:9
  p. things in life are worth 278:23
  we could not lead a p. life 311:10
Please: always trying to p. us back 390:5
  not p. but thank you 106:5
  things . . . which p. no one but myself 268:15
  we aim to p.. You aim too p. 150:2
Pleasing: honest about pleasing himself 268:20
Pleasure: earnestly pursued p. 42:12
  give p. a bad name 131:7
  I don't feel quite happy about p. 18:9
  if this is p. 94:10
  moments of p. 35:21
  p. . . . . is a safer guide than . . . right 62:3
  p. seeker [is ruined] by p. 171:14
  pain is produced by prolonging . . . p. 345:2
  praise of . . . friends is . . . unmixed p. 252:3
  strip our p.s of imagination 307:12
  understanding will . . . extinguish p. 180:7
Pledge: redeem our p., not wholly 278:18
Pleiads: rainy P. wester 179:9
Plenitude: because of its p., the future 53:5
Plenty: I got p. o' nuthin' 142:19
Plonking: p. tone of voice 302:21
Plot: p. of a thousand acres 365:8
  real life seems to have no p.s 86:21
Plotinus: choose Plato and P. 417:24
Plough: epic follows the p. 389:8
  land you used to p. 179:25
  p. my own furrow alone 324:3
Ploughed: p. fields, like ten full-stops 254:8
Ploughing: is my team p. 179:24
  start p. pertinent wives 4:19
Ploughman: heavy steps of the p. 416:23
Pluck: p. till . . . times are done 417:20
Plug: p. . . . . an optional extra 120:7
Plugging: I just keep p. away 181:16
Plum: eaten the p.s . . . in the icebox 404:28
Plumber: p.'s idea of Cleopatra 125:5
  try getting a p. on weekends 6:10
Plumbing: assembly of portable p. 269:13
Plunging: when the p. hoofs were gone 103:13
Plural: in the p. and they bounce 239:7
Pluto: tom looks like one of p.'s demons 251:11
Plutocracy: in a p. the natural hero 404:24
Plutography: p. . . . . acts of the rich 411:19
Pneumatic: p. sterility of M. 119:17
  promise of p. bliss 118:18
  wonderfully p. 182:11
Pneumonia: never anything small like p. 327:9
Pocket: afraid of having your p.s picked? 84:14
  boy does not put his hand in his p. 26:17
  instrument thrust into someone's p. 42:18
  other [hand] straight into her p. 191:5

p. was the first instinct of humanity 283:8
pound . . . in your p. 406:5
smile I could feel in my p. 72:1
young man feels his p.s 179:4
Pod: open the p. door, Hal 83:16
Poe, Edgar Allan: P. . . . nonstop literary drinker
371:15
Poem: aunt is so deflating to a p. 251:24
bad p.s created during abstinence 315:8
child that knows p.s 319:7
forgotten therefore used up p. 167:19
good p. as one that makes . . . sense 152:11
I knew it wouldn't be much of a p. 91:5
if p.s can teach one anything 311:2
in the margins we'll find the p.s 249:5
known among the stars by our p.s 13:10
majority of p.s one outgrows 118:30
no p. . . . written for its story line 53:12
p. . . . an anxiety meets a technique 112:23
p. every week 59:5
p. is never finished only abandoned 385:17
p. is not made from these letters 84:4
p. lovely as a tree 208:6
p. should be palpable and mute 244:10
p. should not mean but be 244:10
p.s about what he knows 349:15
p.s are made by fools like me 208:7
we all write p.s 131:16
Poet: approached by the statistician or p. 130:16
did not the p. sing it 415:9
for the p. remembers 265:11
greater p. than Porson 180:9
I don't call myself a p. 113:27
I knew myself once more a p. 151:19
if you call La Gallienne a minor p. 251:25
immature p.s imitate 119:6
like the p. woo the moon 65:2
no bad man can be a good p. 293:12
no p. . . . wishes he were the only one 19:4
no wonder p.s sometimes have to seem 135:19
not look at his change is no true p. 75:22
p. engenders . . . advertising men 265:18
p. gives us his essence 412:3
p. himself who listens 167:6
p. in Russia is more than a p. 418:15
p. is a condition 152:14
p. is a liar 85:10
p. is carried away by speech 379:7
p. is the most defenceless of all beings 385:9
p. . . . technical expert 88:3
p. trying to keep his hand in 152:13
p. who has stopped writing 307:22
p.s . . . are outside the class system 52:5
p.s, and they think 119:1
p.s are dead by their late twenties 152:13
p.s do not go mad 76:29
p.s get a quizzical ahem 137:15
p.s who read from their own works 400:3
p.s whose . . . names were Tom or Thomas
188:11
p.s . . . write in words 131:16

role of the p. 306:7
room of the banished p. 4:11
true p. . . . not poetical 85:8
truth . . . for the p. 335:13
you don't have to suffer to be a p. 83:1
you're either a p. or a Lilliputian 388:11
Poetry 44:2
all metaphor is p. 76:5
between p. and belle-litter 361:7
borderline that p. operates on 166:17
by accident . . . not great p. 418:21
cliché is d. poetry 52:2
even when p. has a meaning 180:7
farce as inverted p. 306:3
if a line of p. strays into my memory 180:8
made p. seem word-bound 202:19
'making poetry' is . . . 'to breathe' 320:1
most people ignore most p. 265:19
neither is there p. in money 152:12
nothing to say . . . and that is p. 63:6
p. . . . appreciated. . . by the undevout 180:6
p. begins to atrophy 303:22
p. is a comforting piece of fiction 259:5
p. is an act of peace 278:20
p. is an extra hand 265:20
p. is baroque 256:19
p. is for women 376:12
p. is in the pity 288:13
p. is kept on a life-support system 165:4
p. is never . . . a higher mode 167:19
p. is not the . . . party line 144:5
p. is received in a hostile spirit 320:3
p. is the achievement of the synthesis 335:1
p. is the best words 374:8
p. is . . . the escape from personality 119:7
p. is the supreme fiction 358:12
p. is to prose as dancing is 389:4
p. is what Milton saw 251:20
[p.] . . . means of overcoming chaos 316:16
p. must be human 5:7
p. of history 377:10
P. . . . relation to Prose 19:22
p. reminds him of the richness 205:4
p. should improve your life 14:16
p., surely, is a crisis 333:19
p. . . . taking life by the throat 136:5
p. that will be their own secret 249:1
p. . . . turned to . . . advertising copy 218:2
quarrel with ourselves, p. 418:2
resuscitate the dead art of p. 303:13
Shaw . . . has never written any p. 77:3
sublime art of ruining p. 337:16
unreasonably p. is shaped 202:13
verbal art like p. is reflective 19:9
when power corrupts, p. cleanses 205:4
Poggio's: P. where people go 112:18
Poinsettia: p. meadows of her tides 95:6
Point: observant fellow who p.s 412:23
still p. of the turning world 116:26
up to a p., Lord Copper 392:27
Poise: without pose and full of p. 279:19

Poison: if you were my wife I'd drink it [p.] 16:7
  p. and antidote 329:2
  p. the whole blood stream fills 120:21
  what p. pours she 44:6
Poisoned: crams with cans of p. meat 75:3
  literature . . . p. by its own secretions 52:2
Poisoning: p. . . . children for their insurance
  110:5
Poke: p. in the eye makes him see stars 69:19
Poker: malice is like a game of p. 355:8
  p. exemplifies the worst aspects 255:12
  p. . . . in a house with women 404:21
Poland: idea of P. moving westwards 81:21
  withdraw their troops from P. 72:1
Polar: p. exploration . . . the cleanest 73:19
Polarized: consumption is p. 185:8
Pole: expotition to the North P. 265:8
  latest P. transmit the Preludes 117:31
  P. first, a Pope second 354:7
  virtues which the P.s do not possess 80:6
  wherever there are three P.s 389:14
Police: Heaven is where the p. are British 9:23
  help the p., beat yourself up 149:9
  occupation we encourage among p. officers
  286:3
  only the Thought P. mattered 286:22
  p. stations were like toilets 255:11
  replaced . . . the Throne by the p. 334:14
Policeman: ask a p. 321:10
  park, p. and a pretty girl 72:20
  p. a burglar who has retired 307:22
Policemen: contrary to what . . . p. believe 368:8
  how young the p. look 171:19
  only [problems] with p. 316:10
  p. . . . must be protected 286:2
  p. with smaller feet 105:23
  so many p. to make it work 14:11
Polis: the P. as P., in this city 284:5
Polite: one must avoid p. society 268:13
  p. meaningless words 416:4
  P. Society believed in God 336:20
Politely: I rose p. in the club 74:5
Political: clearly points to a p. career 343:31
  history of p. power 301:7
  intellectual attitude is latently p. 249:25
  our day of p. pride is over 186:15
  p. ones [problems] are insoluble 109:4
  p. power grows out of the barrel 250:10
  p. power wears out 8:15
  p. utopias are a form of nostalgia 185:5
  prejudices . . . called p. philosophy 328:21
  we are not p. whores 275:12
Politician: at home you're just a p. 245:10
  contempt earned by the Utopian p. 258:2
  every p. is emphatically a promising p. 77:12
  far higher plane than any p. 73:1
  forward-looking p.s 265:22
  gladly eat a . . . p. 123:18
  good man fallen among p.s 99:2
  latter-day p.s 406:10
  Outer Mongolia for retired p.s 35:17

path of p. is bestrewn by banana skins 62:8
p. . . . approaches every question 359:10
p. . . . at the service of the nation 300:20
p. . . . dead ten . . . years 378:18
p. is an animal who can sit on a fence 9:18
p. is an arse 97:27
p. no one is afraid of 379:2
p. rises on the backs of his friends 181:7
p. . . . will lay down your life 156:12
p.s are the same all over 207:17
p.s . . . believe . . . you can fool all 2:3
p.s feel a sexual pull towards mirrors 86:22
television has devalued p.s 294:11
too serious . . . to be left to the p.s 141:8
when a p. does get an idea 251:16
Politics: drunk . . . when he talks p. 284:8
  enter local p. . . . unhappily married 293:7
  first rule of p. 239:13
  no matter what we thought about p. 94:8
  no time to fool around with 321:17
  not p. which is the arch enemy 395:16
  p. are not my concern 213:28
  p. are too serious a matter 141:8
  p. . . . can be settled by influence 127:27
  p. does not reflect majorities 159:19
  p. is for the present 116:1
  p. is not the art of the possible 139:7
  p. is the art of preventing people 385:22
  p. is the art of the possible 61:2
  p. is war without bloodshed 250:9
  p. of happiness, . . . p. of joy 181:17
  p. . . . practical and music . . . fantasy 167:10
  p.: who gets what, when, how 222:3
  sex is just p. with the clothes off 49:4
  ultimate p. 144:4
  wanted to get into p. 57:19
  week is a long time in p. 406:4
Polka: see me dance the p. 348:21
Pollen: stars lay like yellow p. 418:18
Polling booth: p. for responsibility 171:15
Pollock, Jackson 324:7
  might have bought a . . . large P. 168:25
Polycentric: p. system 374:13
Polygamous: p. but emotionally monogamous
  52:14
Pond: fall on an indifferent pond 318:4
Ponies: two p. drown under me 402:10
Pontefract: licorice fields of P. 40:14
Pony: there must be a p. 214:29
Poodle: French . . . p.s to the Germans 318:2
  Mr Balfour's p. 235:15
  power that created the p. 373:4
Pool: we all piss in the swimming p. 201:11
Poor: all the nice people were p. 353:20
  can't abide contact with the p. 86:7
  fatally p. and dingy 399:17
  gentleman. I live by robbing the p. 344:14
  how extremely expensive it is to be p. 23:2
  I, being p., have only my dreams 418:1
  I was black once – when I was p. 176:16
  kindness of the p. to the rich 76:18

more p. people 251:1
p. are our equals 377:14
p. get poorer 201:10
p. little rich girl 93:21
p. society cannot be too p. 365:13
p. . . . to put the crumbs back 57:10
she was p. but she was honest 12:17
unkillable infants of the very p. 303:21
very p. They are unthinkable 130:16
you got ill, you were p., you died 251:1
your p. I'll piss on them 314:19
Poorly: so p. and so run down 125:31
Pop: p. art and fine art stand 243:20
p. culture for those with bad memories 200:3
spots mean p. music 120:12
Popcorn: everything else is mere p. 34:3
Pope: anybody can be P. 195:2
no P. here. Lucky P. 149:26
Pole first, a P. second 354:7
P. kissing the tarmac 16:17
P.! How many divisions 356:8
remember I am the P. 195:1
Poppies: in Flanders fields the p. blow 242:11
Poppycock: executive p. 121:5
Popular: very p. among his mates 121:13
Population: male p. . . . will be over 100 92:10
p. explosion 57:7
vast p. able to read 377:7
Porcupine: fucking a p. 267:3
throw two p.s under you 207:20
Pork: on top of last night's p. chops 221:1
Porno: Jewish p. film 319:20
Pornography: p. in yer Sunday papers 354:13
p. is the attempt to insult sex 223:25
p. of war 311:4
p. was the great vice of the Seventies 411:19
Porridge: sand in the p. 94:10
Porson, Richard: seen P. sober 180:9
Port: p., and sleep – and learning 33:4
Portal: fitful tracing of a p. 358:17
Portentous: p. and a thing of state 234:7
Porter: decompose in a barrel of p. 108:6
embraced by the p. 358:19
moon shone bright on Mrs P. 118:13
Oh, mister P., what shall I do? 235:13
Porter, Cole: P. of figurative painting 181:10
Portion: sent me back my missing p. 128:24
Portrait: grow to look like his p. 99:9
man's work . . . is a p. of himself 62:1
paint a p. I lose a friend 335:18
paint his own p. for the Uffizi 30:25
p. of the artist as a young man 198:6
p.s of famous bards 369:32
test of a good p. 297:4
what people in p.s are thinking 235:8
Portray: 'p'. . . . has become synonymous 363:6
Pose: ceased to p. as its prophets 301:5
without p. and full of poise 279:19
Posing: p. in the old back yard 274:19
Position: every p. must be held 158:6
holders of one p. 18:22

p. of the dead amomg the living 413:4
Positive: every p. value has its price 297:13
p. neutrality 217:19
power of p. thinking 294:10
Possessed: much p. by death 118:17
Possibilities: sum-total of out vital p. 285:16
Possible: capacity for good makes democracy p.
280:3
didn't have the p. things 294:14
politics is not the art of the p. 139:7
politics is the art of the p. 61:2
Post-impressionism 44:15, 241:10
Post-Impressionists: Manet and the P. 136:28
Post-modernism: p. has cut off the present 38:17
Post Office: between the Church and the P. 84:3
Postal: desire to take p. courses 48:18
p. districts packed like . . . wheat 221:18
Postcard: French don't even put on p.s 177:15
Poster: he is a great poster 15:22
Posterity: to evoke p. is to weep 152:5
Postern: Present has latched its p. 162:5
Postlots: prize of schillings, p.s free 197:9
Postpone: good time to p. everything 53:1
Posture: bind you to an image and a p. 319:13
Pot: everything else has gone to p. 385:2
Potatoes: curly stuff is p. 353:3
Potent: how p. cheap music is 94:4
Poultry: all p. eaters are psychopaths 302:8
mere chicken feed. A p. matter 252:15
Pound: p. . . . in your pocket 406:5
p. notes as bookmarks 54:8
three jolly farmers once bet a p. 103:17
Poverty: do you call p. a crime? 343:33
from nothing to a state of extreme p. 253:8
inequality in order to eliminate p. 197:5
keep the old man [Gandhi] in p. 272:13
money is better than p. 6:14
our p. . . . signified chiefly 349:10
possible to conquer p. 195:15
undeserving p. is my line 345:18
war on p. 195:13
who has ever struggled with p. 23:2
Powder: as harmless as a p. magazine 112:2
Power: all I want is . . . unlimited p. 53:3
all p. and money and fine robes 395:4
all the p.s of the President 379:1
always prefer influence to p. 252:8
aspired to p. instead of influence 366:1
corridors of p. 351:22
designing or controlling p. 193:3
dying monarchy . . . has too much p. 77:24
God must have loved the people in p. 293:13
lack of p. corrupts absolutely 359:8
man of p. is ruined by p. 171:14
maximal authority and minimal p. 364:3
men who do not read are unfit for p. 129:10
no limit to the p. it can generate 155:9
no p. if the white master gives him none 14:4
one mandarin with absolute p. 373:14
political p. wears out 8:15
p. by riding on the back of a tiger 204:17

p. . . . don't take everything 352:15
p. grows out of the barrel of a gun 250:10
p. is the ultimate aphrodisiac 214:33
p. lying in the street 13:14
p. narrows the area of man's concern 205:4
p. we have been and are no longer 186:15
p. which stands on privilege 32:32
p. without responsibility 23:6, 214:27
prostitute all their p.s 130:8
responsibility without p. 361:12
substituted majority for p. 171:15
super p.s 131:19
Women and Horses and P. and War 209:19
wrong sort . . . are always in p. 414:2
Powerful: p. rather than charming 328:5
Pox: bloody sight more p. than pax 198:20
Practice: different preoccupations and p.s 349:20
my p. is never absorbing 109:16
of instinct rather than of p. 314·13
p. with the hard bits left out 321:4
Practise: prudence never to p. either 380:1
Prague: for the sake of P. 246:1
Praise: all things thou wouldst p. 103:4
countryman must have p. 44:17
criticism, but they only want p. 256:17
give them not p. 353:12
highest p. of God 308:2
let us now p. famous men 212:27
p. the Lord and pass the ammunition 130:1
p. the world to the angel 319:1
Praised: p. for virtues you never had 359:16
Praising: doing one's p. for oneself 62:4
Pram: Mr Schulz went off his p. 209:6
p. in the hall 87:23
Pray: dying p. at the last 106:5
family that p.s together 338:1
one [language] in which you pray 66:8
p. as if everything depended on God 354:15
p. exclusively of others 393:15
p. for us now and at . . . our birth 116:16
p. to have me back 69:2
some to Mecca turn to p. 128:9
wish to p. is a prayer 39:17
work and p., live on hay 172:2
Prayer: believed his work was p. 389:11
[cathedrals] used to be p. factories 112:21
Christopher Robin is saying his p.s 264:13
Coming in on a Wing and a P. 2:6
Conservative party at p. 326:1
family p.s kneeling on the cat 318:1
frame of mind close to that of p. 255:6
it sounded like night p. 127:15
p. . . . had lodged . . . like wax 154:1
p.s about to be said 368:21
p.s are like those appeals of ours 352:20
scientific work is a place of p. 278:17
Praying: if you talk to God you are p. 364:9
Pre-existing: uprising against p. order 285:17
Pre-natal: Russia . . . her p. struggling 223:26
Pre-Whitman: p. . . . not prepossessing 260:9
Preacher: famous bards and p.s 369:32

Precaution: p.s to avoid having parents 95:16
took p. against it [death] 139:15
Precedent: p. for everything 208:3
Preceding: mask of the preceding scene 102:3
Precious: it turned out to be p. 95:9
three unspeakably p. things 380:1
Precipice: chair up close to the . . . p. 127:16
Precise: cannot be p. and still be pure 71:10
Predestination: p. in the stride 211:25
Predicament: life is a p. 335:16
p. is not the difficulty of attaining 283:2
Predict: first-rate theory p.s 215:4
p. things after they have happened 187:12
Prefab: better than a p. 74:1
Pregnancy: Catholic woman to avoid p. 258:14
Pregnant: if men could get p. 204:9
without stopping at p. 232:2
Prejudge: mistake to p. the past 402:1
Prejudice: associate p. with identity 48:6
merely rearranging their p.s 192:1
P. a vagrant opinion 42:22
p.s acquired by age eighteen 116:5
p.s . . . called political philosophy 328:21
suit their p.s 329:3
Prelude: latest Pole transmit the P.s 117:31
p. to insanity 392:10
Premature: would that be p. 101:20
Premeditated: p. . . . not committed 339:19
Premise: insufficient p.s 61:12
Preoccupation: p.s and practices 349:20
Preoccupied: p. with sex than occupied 171:3
Preparation: p. for this hour 81:8
writing was just a p. 394:15
Prepared: Be P. 21:7
world is not yet p. 109:17
Prepossessing: pre-Whitman . . . but not p. 260:9
Prerogative: p. of the Almighty 104:3
p. of the eunuch 361:12
p. of the harlot throughout the ages 214:27
Presbyterian: strict P.s as a carnal sin 371:10
Presence: murmur of voices, of p.s 224:11
not very conscious of His p. 154:13
rushing into his p. uncalled for 104:3
woman's p. . . . defines 38:18
Present: both perhaps p. in time future 116:23
contemporaneous with our p. 102:3
cut off the p. from all futures 38:17
eternal p. of immediate expectation 38:12
everything he knows is always p. to Him 66:23
giving p.s is . . . most possessive 235:7
liberating the p. 374:3
link between the p. and the future 206:19
never more than two persons p. 400:5
nothing about the p. 206:13
on the surface of the p. 276:14
past cannot teach the p. 174:1
p. Mrs Harris 372:2
when the P. has latched its postern 162:5
who controls the p. 286:26
Preservative: [old] need all the p.s 285:9
Preserve: If I do not p. [surroundings] 285:13

Preserving: no notion of p. 75:19
Preside: p. over the liquidation 80:1
Presidency: Teflon-coated p. 339:2
President: all the powers of the P. 379:1
  all the P.'s men 214:32
  anybody could become P. 100:2
  anyone can be P. 129:16
  bank p.s and not revolutionaries 214:35
  being P. of the United States 372:29
  forgotten whose P. you are 382:1
  nobody is strongminded around a P. 315:2
  P. does it . . . it is not illegal 281:3
  P. is never going to eat broccoli 60:10
  p. . . . must have to stand naked 113:12
  P. of the Immortals 164:1
  P.'s answers totter forward 176:9
  P.'s carnation 88:18
  something about being P. 116:12
  three ex-p.s 107:22
  whether or not their P. is a crook 280:17
Press: freedom of the p. 234:4
  I'm with you on the free p. 360:16
  King over all . . . is the P. 212:12
  p. lords who control the old parties 272:4
Pressed: p. into service means p. out of shape
  136:1
Pressure: grace under p. 169:11
Presumption: amused by its p. 372:12
Presumptuous: in a servant it looks p. 360:17
Pretence: p. of wit 416:12
Pretend: we p. to work and they p. to pay 11:14
Pretending: p. he just doesn't see 113:8
  whoever it is you're p. to be 25:19
Pretentious: p.? *Moi?* 84:10
Prettiness: bodies lopped of every p. 97:7
Pretty: as to the p. girls 307:9
  comes along and does it p. 298:2
  filled with pretty people 97:3
  how p. you are on the phone 156:15
  it's p. but is it Art? 210:8
  not so p. anyone would want to ruin her 51:12
  park, policeman and a p. girl 72:20
  p. can get away with anything 393:21
  p. girl naked 97:9
  p. girl who plays her cards 127:23
Prevent: our duty to try to p. it 265:10
Prey: self-possessed . . . p. to doubt 73:15
Price: [fig-leaf] into a p. tag 34:15
  what p. glory? 8:11
Priceless: p. gift of life 324:6
Prick: bring out my p.? 143:21
  hundred p.s against one 267:3
Prickly: here we go round the p. pear 117:17
Pride: Britain has lost its p. 255:16
  our day of political p. is over 186:15
  p. in having given up his p. 333:21
  p. is faith in the idea that God had 106:10
  vanity is other people's p. 156:16
Priest: associate with a lot of p.s 33:18
  Dublin without p.s 31:12
  followed by the p.s and bigots 65:29

it's hard to see Christ for p.s 265:18
p. is only half a man 258:18
p.s interpreted and interposed 87:1
whisky p. 154:7
why he was a p. 407:14
Priestley, J.B. 320:19
Prima donna: p. inter pares 96:7
Primal: p. desert ship 156:13
Primary: nature's truth is p. 371:2
  p. sexual activity 364:2
Prime Minister: best P. we have 60:19
  every p. should have a Willie 368:4
  Leo Amery would have been P. 366:11
  most P.s would not be interesting 366:10
  nearly all of them want to be P. 123:7
  next P. but three 32:19
  position of . . . P. is filled by fluke 304:14
  powers . . . P.s never yet been invested 80:21
  p. before he was thirty 88:11
  P. of Mirth 320:5
  P. . . . what have I got? *Influence* 240:4
  P. who has made twelve trips to Moscow
    413:16
  P. who hasn't got any political ideas 129:13
  25 times as much as it pays its P. 405:19
  uneasy coalition of four million p.s 289:1
  unknown P. 15:18
  when a British P. sneezes 232:3
Primeval: p. disaster in . . . Man 348:24
Prince: as a p., as a king, as a man 90:3
  His Weariness the P. 125:18
  not least of your merchant p.s 212:3
  p.s kept the view 113:6
  some day my p. will come 107:1
  where the P.s ride at noon 102:20
  who's danced with the P. of Wales 122:12
Principalities: guarded by timeless p. 151:19
Principle: death being contrary to their p.s 139:15
  doctrinaires are the vultures of p. 236:3
  [Englishman] does everything on p. 345:8
  my p.s and if you don't like them 11:7
  p. in life with me 345:32
  p. seems the same 81:19
  p.s on which we will build 340:17
  to the bottom with my p.s round my neck 23:15
Print: all the news that's fit to p. 279:13
  eternity of p. 412:10
Printed: leave the p. lawn 179:3
Printemps: ceux que le p. dans ses plis a gardé 13:6
Prison: delivering the image from its p. 280:8
  feel comparatively at home in p. 392:19
  formula for p. 53:9
  home is the girl's p. 345:5
  in p. with only ham and eggs 246:17
  like a newspaper inside a p. 350:1
  names off yesterday's p. walls 313:5
  one . . . in office and the other in p. 58:1
  p. . . . deterrent to those who walk past 16:16
  p. of our mind 383:17
  p.s where decent men and women rotted 14:12
  while there is a soul in p. 102:6

Prisoner: I object to your being taken p. 215:6
  if the p. is happy, why lock him in? 344:22
Privacy: glass bowl for all the p. I got 332:15
  right to share your p. 383:20
  silent in the p. of his head 263:8
Private: at least I thought it was p. 174:15
  essentially p. man 361:4
  get yourself into the p. sector 36:2
  human body is p. property 262:12
  hypocrisy in p. relations 399:13
  keep abreast of p. consumption 138:18
  leave it to p. enterprise 206:18
  leave the whole field to p. industry 168:15
  making the p. world public 144:5
  one of the most p. things 126:6
  p. faces in public places 17:24
  p. life punctuated by . . . public adulation
    193:15
  P. Means is dead 351:16
  p. opulence and public squalor 138:18
  p. school has all the faults 88:7
  p. sector . . . the Government controls 146:19
  public version of a p. darkness 368:14
  should never be allowed out in p. 78:16
Privilege: defender of p. 41:22
  first p. of goodness 396:1
  only extended p. 171:22
  power which stands on p. 32:32
  p. which dehumanizes others 133:9
Privileged: not that the p. are conscious 189:14
Privy: neither a Lord, nor a p. 21:13
Prize: more p.s than it has writers 387:22
  p. of schillings, postlots free 197:9
Problem: Economic P. . . . a frightful muddle
    206:15
  nerve of the . . . p. 90:4
  no one who hates . . . p. plays 351:5
  no p. is insoluble 360:10
  p. are by definition insoluble 60:12
  p. of the colour line 110:24
  p.s which it then fails to solve 204:1
  they can't see the p. 77:11
  those that are p.s 85:15
  three-pipe p. 109:15
  two p.s in my life 109:4
  you're part of the p. 84 8
Proceeds: live . . . on the p. 350:16
Process: p. and result are equivalent 408:8
  p. in the weather of the heart 369:13
Procession: p.s that lack high stilts 416:15
Procrastinated: principle of p. rape 306:4
Procrastination: p. . . . keeping up with yesterday
    251:6
Procreate: interest is in having you p. 395:10
Procreation: main road of p. 392:12
Prodigal: enthusiasm . . . over the p.'s return
    332:27
Producing: consumes without p. 286:8
Profanation: from sale and p. 74:24
Profession: condition rather than a p. 152:14
  hero is . . . the shortest-lived p. 321:25

most ancient p. in the world 214:20
p. has to create grave problems 204:1
p.s are conspiracies 343:8
raise hindsight to the status of a p. 49:18
Professional: only the bad ones who become p.s
  60:7
  prize p. nation 406:21
  p. sympathy 382:15
Professor: culture . . . to manufacture p.s 394:10
  old p.s never die 137:4
  p. . . . talks in someone else's sleep 19:20
Profile: no face, only two p.s 16:3
Profit: he p.s most who serves best 346:18
  making substantial p.s 240:1
Profited: p. them to carry on the imposture
  256:11
Profound: opposite is always a p. truth 45:2
Profoundest: p. thoughts in the simplest way
  116:2
Profumo, John 316:9
Programme: my favourite p. 119:9
  p.s I don't want to see 407:25
Progress: fascinated by the idea of p. 218:15
  ladder of predictable p. 148:14
  life is a drama and not a p. 273:3
  notion of p. in a single line 274:3
  on the side of p.: he had false teeth 36:1
  p. can be good or bad 187:8
  p. . . . depends on retentiveness 335:9
  p. depends on the unreasonable man 345:3
  p. . . . desire to live beyond its income 61:13
  p. . . . exchange of one nuisance 120:4
  p. if a cannibal uses knife and fork 227:3
  p. is a comparative 76:10
  p. would be wonderful 275:6
  this is what p. is 39:15
  we have stopped believing in p. 47:4
Progressive: one of those p. places 22:1
Prohibition: Communism is like p. 321:15
  idea of exclusion and p. 261:15
  p. came too late and stopped too early 8:8
  we used to drink water before P. 221:2
Projected: they stay as they were p. 48:7
Prole: p.s are not human beings 286:28
Proletariat: crimes the P. commits 94:12
  dictatorship of the p. 229:1
Prolonged: war is being deliberately p. 337:10
Promethean: P. as a cash register 200:5
Prometheus: P. stole fire from Heaven 388:1
  P. watching his vulture 411:9
Promisck: home from a breach of p. 197:23
Promiscuity: emotional p. 247:10
  p. in his affections 328:3
Promise: keep a p. by mistake 407:19
  p. of pneumatic bliss 118:18
  to kindness and wisdom we make p.s 308:9
Promised: I never p. you a rose garden 153:7
  we . . . will get to the P. Land 208:12
  woman led him to the p. land 112:12
Promising: every politician is . . . a p. politician
  77:12

hit the trail for that p. land 101:19
nature is as wasteful of p. young men 181:6
they first call p. 87:21
Promoted: p. clown 366:8
Prompt: I meant to be p. 101:8
Promptly: if one is p. found out 206:14
Pronounce: spell better than they p. 380:2
Pronouncement: leave off making p.s 193:4
Proof: America is the p. 242:5
Propaganda: p. has to be confirmation 208:8
p. is . . . the art of lying 93:2
struggle . . . between education and p. 57:12
Propagated: human . . . p. by cutting 159:4
Proper: never does a p. thing 343:30
Property: man of p. 139:18
ridiculous to approve of p. 401:22
Prophecy: p. divines the figuration 389:8
Prophet: ceased to pose as its p.s 301:5
habit with p.s to be unhealthy 53:16
P.'s Cam-u-el that primal desert ship 156:13
p.s were twice stoned 269:16
self-appointed p.s and messiahs 289:1
sole qualification to be a p. 79:6
words of the p. are written 348:2
Proposition: that a p. be interesting 389:8
whether the first p. is really true 328:15
Propped: p. between trees and water 369:4
Props: dramatist changes the p. 244:6
Prose: good p. is the selection 374:8
great p. may occur by accident 418:21
his own remarks as p. 17:5
I can only write p. today 418:9
poetry is to p. as dancing is 389:4
p. books are the show dogs 152:16
p. for God 25:9
p. in our future 53:17
p. is an affair of good manners 256:19
p. takes the mould of the body 412:3
p. that has something wrong with it 192:17
p. without the con 273:17
set in the form of p. 59:5
Prosody: p., . . . simply a repository 53:13
Prosper: to the motherly that they p. 51:1
Prostitute: allowed it to . . . p.s 336:14
doormat or a p. 398:24
p. all their powers 130:18
p. more moral than a wife 296:18
p.s . . . below any standards of dress 188:12
small nations like p.s 218:5
Prostitution 238:16
between p. and marriage 349:20
don't think p. . . . encouraged 405:12
p. . . . keeps her out of trouble 168:17
p. to one man instead of many 69:5
Protect: p. ourselves from ourselves 45:16
Protection: if that p. is taken away 177:6
Protestant: how you P.s can be expected 405:8
I was a P. so I didn't speak up 280:5
novel is . . . a P. form of art 286:18
P. ethic 394:6
P. with a horse 31:3

P. women may take the Pill 370:25
Protestantism: contribution of P. to human
thought 259:1
favourite pastime of extreme P. 220:6
Protestants protesting against P. 224:2
she detested P. 119:17
Protozoon: p. to the philosopher 328:16
Proud: p. of my knowing something 276:4
too p. to fight 406:17
we're gay and we're p. 12:7
Proust, Marcel: anyone who has read P. 26:2
P. about something in particular 353:19
Prove: I could p. everything 298:17
you can't p. a thing 398:15
Providence: I go the way P. dictates 173:11
p. . . . for their morals 418:6
Province: fifth p. is not anywhere 320:16
Provincialism: in adultery than in p. 182:6
Pru: man from the P. 3:17
Prudence: effect of p. on rascality 344:34
p. never to practise either 380:1
reconcile Japanese action with p. 79:24
Prudish: my p. hand would refuse to form 346:3
Prussic: p. acid . . . hands of a . . . boy 108:9
Psalm: with their nightingales and p.s 239:8
Psyche: his p. should be studied 199:13
Psychiatrist: anybody who goes to see a p. 147:17
century of the p.'s couch 244:17
nearly as many p.s 92:15
not being caught by a p. 299:16
p. collects the rent 224:25
p. . . . goes to the Folies-Bergère 359:15
Psychiatry: p. is the care of the id by the odd 9:15
p's chief contribution to philosophy 73:11
Psychoanalysis: in p. nothing is true 2:17
p. . . . in a Vienna of stiff collars 59:10
p. is a permanent fad 104:22
p. . . . regards itself as a therapy 217:15
Psychoanalyst: no p. has knocked 74:4
Psychological: no such thing as p. 336:25
Psychology: [children] have no use for p. 348:17
p. . . . pulling habits out of rats 60:9
popularity and persuasiveness of p. 353:9
Psychopath: all poultry eaters are p.s 302:8
Psychosis: Irish and the Jews have a p. 31:11
Psychotic: p. if he makes others suffer 364:8
p. . . . lives in it 224:25
p. ship's captain 52:13
Pterodactyl: in favour of the . . . p. 397:15
Pub: in all the p.s in Dublin 108:6
there wasn't a p. open in the city 31:9
will someone take me to a p. 74:5
Puberty: all American at p. 393:13
Pubic: hound that caught the P. Hare 31:5
Public: in p. as we do in private 144:4
laughter people laugh at p. events 243:19
life punctuated by . . . p. adualtion 193:15
nor p. men, nor cheering crowds 416:17
not even a p. figure 98:9
private faces in p. places 17:24
p. is entitled to what it wants 72:17

no wonder they call me the Virgin Q. 62:15
old q. measuring a town 416:1
one of the Q.s of England 62:14
pity our poor dear q. 296:21
Q. asked the dairymaid 264:10
Q. . . . is not embarrassed 36:15
q. of air and darkness 178:16
slides like a q. 151:7
Queenly: q. in her own room 399:19
Queer: drink to our q. old Dean 355:16
former beauty q. 229:10
putting my q. shoulder to the wheel 144:2
q. are the ways of a man I know 163:11
we're here because we're q. 31:10
Queerer: q. than we *can* suppose 159:8
Quenching: promoted thirst without q. 382:12
Querelleurs: oiseaux q. 13:8
Questing: Q. Beast ever since 400:16
Question: all q.s are open 31:20
approaches every q. with an open mouth
    359:10
comprehend the world as a q. 218:16
could you rephrase the q. 375:10
don't ask what are q.s 301:9
Great Q. of Life 1:13
'how are you' is a greeting not a q. 156:14
in that case what is the q.? 357:19
make two q.s grow 386:14
never quite reaching the q. 176:9
not a wise q. . . . to answer 114:11
q.s from women about tappets 325:7
q.s that life puts to us 160:5
q.s that no one has asked them 375:2
q.s the distempered part 117:17
radical . . . thinking up new q.s 279:12
they [men] weren't even the q.s 25:18
to ask the hard q. is simple 18:11
we need to ask q.s 53:24
who – or what – put the q. 160:6
who cares if the q. is wrong? 199:20
Questioned: in what name he q. life 248:7
Quiche: real men don't eat q. 123:16
Quick: pedestrians . . . q. and the dead 105:15
turns on the q. and the dead 368:21
you're q., aren't you? 262:14
Quicker: liquor is q. 278:1
Quiet: all q. on the western front 315:13
American women like q. men 10:1
cheerfulness is a q. condition 255:2
from q. homes and first beginning 32:27
Quietly: we mean to live very q. 16:1
Quinquireme: q. of Nineveh 254:2
Quintilian: Q. or Max Beerbohm who said 156:4
Quit: try again. Then q. 125:8
Quite: Hail Mary q. contrary 154:5
Quiver: q. for arrows is one example 283:8
Quixote: original creation . . . Don Q. 256:24
Quotation: q.s beautiful from minds profound
    291:20
uneducated man to read books of q.s 80:25
Quote: he lived by writing things to q. 58:7

I'll kill you if you q. it 59:14
make a monkey of a man . . . q. him 35:1
men who . . . q. aptly 176:6
Quoted: q. dead languages 376:18

R

Rabbit: run, r. 128:2
struck a direct blow by a r. 70:8
tale of four little r.s 302:14
there is a r. in a snare 358:3
world of r.s ruled by stoats 287:9
Rabble: r. of the filthy, sturdy 303:22
Raboo-loose: Frenchman . . . called R. 396:7
Race: difference of opinion . . . horse r.s 380:14
great r. we are and shall remain 186:15
r. between education and catastrophe 397:2
r. between human skill . . . and folly 328:10
r. is not always to the swift 205:16
Racehorse: r.s and the cheaper clarets 332:22
Rachmaninov, Sergei: R.'s . . . scowl 362:14
Racially: not r. pure are mere chaff 173:4
Racing: r. book about . . . the horses 39:20
Racket: it ruins the whole r. 237:13
Rad-Lib: R. philosophy 360:10
Radiator: a man not a r. cap 48:16
Radical: few r.s have good digestions 61:14
I never dared be r. when young 135:22
r. chic 411:17
r.: . . . his other left hand is doing 324:5
r. . . . thinking up new questions 279:12
r. . . . with both feet . . . in the air 322:19
strong r. bias 35:16
Radio: howling r. for our paraclete 246:2
I had the r. on 267:14
r. personality who outlived his prime 393:25
still be eating frozen r. dinners 69:1
thin squeaks of r. static 94:27
Radish: r., red outside, white inside 174:20
Rag-and-bone: r. shop of the heart 415:13
Rag-time: lurching to r. tunes 337:1
Rage: boredom is r. spread thin 374:5
much did I rage when young 418:1
Ragged: pair of r. claws 117:25
r. and gap-toothed as it [theatre] is 164:9
Raid: say how many planes joined the r. 161:13
Raider: lucid friend to aerial r.s 355:4
Rail: narrowing r.s slide together 117:7
Railing: zebra synchronized with the r.s 193:9
Railroad: country of r.s 73:16
Railway: alone in r. carriages 262:11
hands of clocks in r. stations 88:10
r. termini . . . gates to the glorious 130:13
Rain: blows of the r. 368:19
given up like fallen r. 319:4
hard r.'s a-gonna fall 113:9
He comes in the terrible R. 349:1
r. comes pattering out of the sky 18:14
r. is listless 303:2

Renaissance: r. was . . . the green end 131:15
Rendezvous: r. with death 340:10
  r. with destiny 322:12
Renewal: r. is fruitful 362:13
Rent: better than a prefab – no r. 74:1
  I r. everything other than . . . life 217:1
  r. out my room 6:25
Renunciation: love doesn't know . . . r. 187:5
Repainting: anything that . . . needs r. 323:20
Repaired: future – it was being r. 64:3
Repartee: I cannot think of any r. 37:15
Repeat: condemned to r. it [the past] 335:9
  marry in haste and r. at leisure 63:2
  what they hear, they r. 348:20
Repeating: worth endlessly r. 278:23
Repelled: only r. by man 186:10
Repertory: plays many parts . . . in r. 132:15
Repetition: listening and hearing is never r.
  357:18
  only constant r. will finally succeed 173:6
  r. of the wrong way of living 112:20
Rephrase: could you r. the question 375:10
Replay: today is an action r. 32:4
Replete: green r. old age 355:26
Repletion: others [voyages] are merely r. 80:26
Report: r. of my death is exaggerated 380:21
Reporter: r. . . . has renounced everything 274:16
  r.s don't believe in anything 32:7
Reporting: r. something and making it up 133:2
Repository: r. of time within language 53:13
Republic: Love the Beloved R. 131:2
  perfect r.s are perfect nonsense 131:17
  they were called a R. 393:4
Republican: R.s like trees and animals 120:6
  telling lies about the R. Party 104:6
  telling the truth about them [R.s] 359:1
Reputation: r., . . . but no money 380:19
  see your r. die three times 216:19
Requirement: barest r.s of feasibility 243:9
Research: outcome of any serious r. 386:14
  [painting]. It's all research 298:5
  r. is like shooting an arrow 2:12
  r. is the art of the soluble 258:2
  r. is . . . what I don't know I'm doing 50:20
  responsible for their r. . . . morally 67:11
  steal from many [authors] it's r. 267:1
  to do r. . . . attack the facts 153:4
Researches: r. in original sin 300:8
Resembling: has he tried r. anybody? 348:6
Reservation: go back to your r.s 149:31
Reserve: r. is an artificial quality 256:20
Reservoir: r. of good will toward us 405:3
Residence: inns are not r.s 268:17
Resign: to him . . . we all keys must r. 103:7
Resignation: r. is active 127:28
  r. is for beaten people 187:5
Resist: almost nothing to r. at all 222:26
  we r. only what is inevitable 262:5
Resistance: r. of its class enemies 356:5
Resistant: people who were always r. 352:9
Resistentialism: r. . . . things think 193:17

Resolution: in war: r. 81:4
  not to write r.s 356:7
Resolved: r. to be irresolute 79:10
Resonance: r. of his solitude 87:13
Resort: r. to r. getting more tired 294:18
Resource: gorgeous r.s of credit 90:2
Respect: r. and apprehension 52:13
  victims who r. their executioners 335:22
Respectable: aren't r. live beyond other people's
  332:19
  Madeira, but perfectly r. 345:31
  more r. he is 344:5
Respecting: r. anybody who can spell 264:18
Respiration: he said it was artificial r. 59:2
Respond: not clear how to r. to it 49:8
  r.s without getting annoyed 97:14
Respondent: reader who is the r. 400:5
Responsibility: heavy burden of r. 115:7
  no sense of r. at the other 216:1
  polling booth for r. 171:15
  power without r. 23:6, 214:27
  r. without power 361:12
  realize the r. I carry 205:9
Responsible: r., forever, for what you have tamed
  332:4
  r. and wrong 80:12
  r. for everything 335:23
Rest: first day of the r. of your life 102:10
  lie there and r. awhile 114:2
  more r. if one doesn't sleep 392:13
  where good men r. 128:7
  where r.s she now her head 103:20
  where's the r. of Me? 314:2
Restaurant: always going to the nearest r. 25:5
  always went right to a r. 220:16
Restive: victims who begin by being r. 242:19
Restrained: r. in the manifestations 156:23
Restraint: firm r. with which they write 65:3
  r. and good manners are necessary 52:6
Restrictive: no place for r. practices 406:1
Result: one immediately sees the r.s 116:6
  process and r. are equivalent 408:8
Resurrection: if there is to be a r. 148:6
  since the R. it had been religion 91:15
Retainer: play the Old R. 32:18
Retaliation: get your r. in first 189:8
Retentiveness: progress . . . depends on r. 335:9
Retire: put off being young until you r. 221:10
Retirement: there must be no r. 158:6
Retreat: right is in r. 129:5
  territory to r. from 377:17
Retrospect: history is written in r. 394:8
Retrospective: r. is making a will 272:8
Return: alas! we r. 130:13
  I shall r. 241:1
  no r. game between a man and his stars 28:24
Returnable: children [are] not r. 95:12
Revelation: existence is a medium of R. 367:5
  glorious r. of . . . Raboo-loose 396:7
Revenge: living well is the best r. 375:6
  Montezuma's r. 10:16

Reverberation: paucity of the r. 247:12
Reverence: how much r. can you have 168:14
    take off my cycle-clips in awkward r. 221:6
Reverse: how to r. explosions 66:16
Reversible: r. coat – seamy on both sides 170:5
Review: I have your r. before me 315:5
    it won't get the r.s but . . . money 152:23
    so long writing my r. 253:17
Reviewer: r.s . . . fall into two classes 30:12
Revival: history of r.s 61:18
Revivalism: sensuality, rebellion and r. 370:21
Reviving: thought that they need r. 243:12
Revolt: Gothic . . . is all r. and aspiration 52:1
    in the first days of the r. 336:26
    r. of a population injected with needs 250:21
Revolting: hearty, robust and r. 296:10
    moulting they're pretty r. 277:12
Revolution: every r. evaporates 201:5
    first day of the r. 377:20
    go into the mountains to lead a r. 214:35
    Hitler has carried out a r. on our lines 275:19
    in r. he [Kaiser] abdicated 82:14
    r. as instant coffee 114:8
    r. by its very nature 377:17
    r. chooses its enemies 182:4
    r. could not be made with rose-water 129:11
    r. does not choose 377:21
    r. in the r. 102:2
    r. is . . . setting-up of a new order 285:17
    r. only remains victorious 248:5
    r.s are always verbose 377:23
    r.s are the kicking of a rotten door 139:3
    r.s have ended in a reinforcement 66:1
    r.s have never succeeded 383:13
    r.s . . . they are no longer dangerous 47:16
    rotten way to run a r. 142:5
    Russia is a collapse not a r. 223:23
    same relation to r. 378:4
    Social R. will be moral 294:19
    true r. till we know 363:13
    victory of the r. over tsarism 229:1
    we invented the R. 394:14
    we make little r.s 336:28
    white heat of this r. 406:1
Revolutionaries: bank presidents and not r.
    214:35
    r. don't make revolutions 13:14
Revolutionary: feed people with r. slogans 207:21
    fierce and r. in a bathroom 234:15
    kitchen-sink-r. look 398:21
    patriotism . . . is a r. duty 378:8
    r. simpleton is everywhere 233:13
    r. theories advanced by turnips 247:8
    successful r. is a statesman 134:16
    you're either a r. or you're not 361:9
Revolve: worlds r. like ancient women 117:35
Revolver: small r. for killing wasps 349:11
    talk of culture, I reach for my r. 196:12
Reward: he considers the lilies, the r.s 172:1
    no r.s or punishments 385:1
    reap his old r. 213:18

Rewind: tunnels that r. themselves 95:2
Reworded: how time could be r. 389:9
Rewrite: sounds like writing, I r. it 230:13
Rewriting: reading is a sort of r. 335:26
Rhetoric: quarrel with others, r. 418:2
    r. of planning 84:2
    r.: so long as it doesn't cost money 280:13
Rhetorician: r.s . . . only think talking 15:19
Rhine: you think of the R. 23:8
Rhodes, Cecil 379:23
Rhyme: out of us all that make r.s 370:20
    r. is still the most effective drum 144:18
    r.s that please the ear 389:3
    still ore tired of r. 32:30
    wove the thing to a random r. 107:10
Rhythm: all God's chillun got r. 201:9
    I got r. 142:12
    perpetual alternation between two r.s 194:20
    r. imposes unanimity 259:17
    r. is a form cut into TIME 303:25
Rib: complained about his r.s 348:7
Ribbon: r. lost from the robe of . . . summer 170:2
    soldier's r. on a tunic tacked 1:1
    winds endless r.s 318:8
Ribstone Pippin: right as a R. 32:29
Rich: acts of the r. 411:19
    believe me r. is better 150:10
    best of the r. being poor 353:20
    by the rascals, for the r. 357:3
    count your money . . . not a r. man 142:22
    do you sincerely want to be r.? 92:19
    having a r. friend is like drowning 155:22
    if all the r. men 356:16
    if you want to get r. by writing 251:21
    kindness of the poor to the r. 76:18
    knowledge of the r. 86:15
    never be too thin or too r. 407:11
    no substitute for a r. man 172:1
    over the r. dead 54:10
    poor little r. girl 93:21
    r. . . . are different from you and me 127:11
    r. are only defeated when running 189:21
    r. are the scum of the earth 76:7
    r. get richer and the poor get poorer 201:10
    r. . . . have more money 127:11
    r. . . . in the freedom to use them 185:9
    r. is better 233:6
    r. man without money 383:10
    r. society too r. to have need 365:13
    so friendly and so r. 18:6
    very tired r. man 359:9
    wretchedness of being r. 350:18
Richard Gare de Lyon 341:3
Richer: r. dust concealed 55:5
Rickshaw: it's no go on the r. 246:3
Rid: idea of getting r. of it 194:16
    time we got r. of him [God] 22:17
Riddle: make a r. out of a solution 217:6
    r. wrapped in a mystery 79:12
Ride: ticket to r. 230:7
Ridiculous: fine sense of the r. 4:18

Rien: non, je ne regrette r. 297:6
Riff-raff: r. apply to . . . respectable 177:11
Rift: r. in the lute 166:8
Right: customer is always r. 340:18
   damn you Jack, I'm all r. 45:18
   every . . . one – of – them – is – r. 211:2
   gets it more or less r. 49:13
   give my r. hand to be ambidextrous 149:12
   he has a r. . . . to be wrong 364:1
   I am not . . . a man of the r. 272:5
   if you are not bothered about being r. 246:13
   in his place, by r., not grace 213:11
   incoming traffic has the r. of way 230:14
   irresponsible and r. 80:12
   needed to be absolutely r. 45:6
   only make the r. wing strong 338:8
   rather be r. than reasonable 277:15
   r. deed for the wrong reason 118:23
   r. is more precious than peace 406:20
   r. stuff 411:18
   r. when other people are wrong 345:34
   r. wing of the middle of the road 35:16
   r.-wing truths . . . left-wing man taught 336:18
   r. words in the r. order 44:2
   safer guide than r. or duty 62:3
   tell me what's r. 407:1
   thou knowest my r.s 125:14
   to be decorative and to do r. 125:19
   to the right of . . . Jesus Christ 382:14
   very important to be r. 82:9
   whoever says the first word . . . is r. 146:1
   you use both r.s extensively 209:8
Righteous: r. indignation into the wrong things
   78:4
   seen the r. forsaken 44:10
   some lonely and R. man 396:19
   that one r. person 352:19
Righteousness: he made r. readable 45:19
Rightful: r. owner of the music 293:15
Rightly: r. or wrongly, quite wrong 402:3
Rigid: most r. code of immorality 48:19
   r., the skeleton of habit 412:17
Rimbaud, Jean: always chasing R.s 291:19
Rime: r. was on the spray 163:18
Ring: one r. to rule them all 374:15
   r. if [they] didn't leave their receivers off 200:8
   r. of the anvil 389:8
Rio: I'd like to roll to R. 211:5
Rio Grande: old cow-hand from the R. 259:22
Riot: r. . . . language of the unheard 208:13
   R. popular entertainment 42:23
Ripon: when the race is at R. 94:24
Ripple: after we cross the infernal r.s 303:12
Rise: put into this world to r. above 170:21
   r. to his level of incompetence 296:3
Risk: childhood's a r. we all take 181:2
Rita: lovely R., meter maid 229:26
Ritz: children of the R. 94:12
   open to all . . . like the R. 99:14
River: Ol' Man R. 160 13
   r. is a strong brown god 117:5

   r. is within us 117:6
   r. of knowledge . . . has turned back 193:4
   to Oceanus, the ocean r. 69:3
   travel with the r. 108:3
River-wise: carry time looped so r. 152:3
Rivering: r. waters of . . . Night 197:21
Riverrun: r., past Eve and Adam's 197:8
Road: all the r.s lead to France 370:16
   drive the r. 212:25
   he watched the ads, and not the r. 277:19
   how many r.s must a man walk down 113:7
   I love r.s; the goddesses 370:15
   keep right on to the end of the r. 222:6
   laborious r., dry, empty, and white 163:28
   new r.s: new ruts 78:5
   restless r.s of the world 318:8
   r. that . . . cuts off the country 273:7
   rolling English r. 74:27
   softly along the r. of evening 103:16
   we don't need r.s 420:8
   white in the moon the long r. lies 179:30
Roadway: cry of a child by the r. 416:23
Roamin': r. in the gloamin' 222:8
Roar: called upon to give the r. 80:16
Roaring: among the r. dead 290:11
   r. Bill . . . thought it right 33:1
Rob: r.s you on business principles 345:8
   some r. you with a six gun 157:4
Robbed: we was r. 188:5
   when you've r. a man of everything 352:15
Robbing: r. a bank compared to founding 51:19
Robe: from the r. of a careless summer 170:2
Robed: r. in the long friends 369:15
Robert E. Lee: waiting for the *R.* 143:22
Roberts, Earl: red-faced man which is Bobs [R.]
   209:23
Robey, George: who is R.? 43:5
Robinson: here's to you Mrs R. 347:20
Robinson Crusoe: R. existence will pall 300:10
Robot: modern conception of a r. 81:6
   r. may not injure a human being 15:11
Robotics: laws of R. 15:11
Robust: hearty, r. and revolting 296:10
Rock: R. and roll or Christianity 229:9
   r. journalism 420:7
   r.s came home in scramble sort 175:10
   seas roll over, but the r.s remain 170:28
   there are no r.s at Rockaway 272:6
   upon solid r. the ugly houses stand 261:7
Rocking-horse: r. . . . the true horse 241:10
Rococo: r. even spread to England 83:9
Rod: they believe in r., the scourger 198:19
Rode: r. madly off in all directions 226:5
Rogers, Ginger 170:21
Rogue: r. is outlining a . . . plan 132:18
Roll: always given the meatier r.s 181:18
   r. it round my mouth 90:16
   r. of the world eastward 163:22
   r. over Beethoven 39:23
   singing r. or bowl a ball 167:12
Rolled: bottom of my trousers r. 117:28

Rolling: like a r. stone 113:15
  r. English road 74:27
Rolls-Royce 61:3
  lawn-mower . . . brakes of a R. 239:16
  loudest noise in this new R. 284:13
  R. body and a Balham mind 271:4
Roman: before the R. came to Rye 74:27
  Greeks in the R. Empire 245:18
  no R. ever was able to say 30:9
  R. and his trouble are ashes 179:28
  R. Caesar is held down 417:11
  R. Conquest was . . . a *Good Thing* 340:22
  R. Emperor who has sat up 410:10
  R. . . . his cloacal obsession 198:12
  R. road runs straight and bare 163:12
  R.s . . . lasted four hundred years 72:17
Roman Catholic: companionability of a R.
    cathedral 106:8
  50 million R. . . . as many psychiatrists 92:15
  R. . . . taking the *Tablet* 370:25
Roman Catholicism: condensed R. 139:11
Romance: born into r. 76:16
  confound r.! 211:8
Romantic: r. Ireland's dead and gone 417:17
  sunsets, they're so r., so operatic 308:11
Rome: as R. denied Etruria 222:16
  burn with Athens and with R. 65:4
  Moscow was our R. 68:8
  R. is feminine 38:15
  R.'s just a city 59:6
Roo: Kanga and baby R. 265:6
Roof: cat on a hot tin r. 404:12
  so broadened that the r. falls in 338:9
  wind's text blown through the r. 371:2
Roof-wrecked: bower . . . to Tennyson is r. 162:6
Rook-delighting: cold and r. heaven 415:15
Room: across a crowded r. 160:16
  all I want is a r. somewhere 230:18
  always leave r. for the mouse 332:14
  feeling that somebody has left the r. 297:4
  in her own r., with the door shut 399:19
  in the r. the women come and go 117:22
  other voices, other r.s 67:7
  r. at the top 50:7
  r. to eat muffins in 395:18
  r. with a view 94:9
  who's in the next r.? – who? 163:19
  woman must have . . . a r. of her own 412:18
  you took away the oceans and all the r. 249:3
Room-mate: hard to be r.s 333:13
Roöötten: R. Beëëastly, Silly Hole! 396:5
Roosevelt, Eleanor: [R's] glow has warmed 359:6
Roosevelt, President F.D. 56:6, 81:5, 82:17, 90:2,
    145:18
  in R. there died the greatest . . . friend 81:23
  nation R. hoped for 195:19
Roost: birds coming home to r. 395:17
Root: black telephone's off at the r. 299:21
  fail to take r. in others 378:7
  what is the r. of money? 312:1
Roothold: nourishing earth for r.s 334:19

Rope: drowning man both ends of a r. 21:9
  piece of the r. for a keepsake 379:23
  r. stretched across the abyss 338:6
  stretch, and come undone, like a r. 181:9
Rosary: I count them over . . . my r. 321:12
Rose: ash the burnt r.s leave 117:19
  do you call that a r.? 20:3
  English unofficial r. 54:16
  even bein' Gawd ain't a bed of r.s 87:5
  everything's coming up r.s 353:4
  he r. without trace 272:14
  hot the scent is of the summer r. 151:8
  I cut my last winter r. for her 263:7
  I r. in rainy autumn 369:10
  I see his blood upon the r. 300:13
  it wavers to a r. 107:11
  je n'oublierai jamais les lilas ni les r.s 13:6
  mast burst open with a r. 128:17
  mighty lak' a r. 356:13
  most secret and inviolate R. 417:14
  never promised you a r. garden 153:7
  nursery gardener scent his r.s 85:8
  odour of a r. 119:1
  one perfect r. 291:5
  reeks a mock r. 103:5
  r. is a r. is a r. is a r. is a r. 357:13
  r. is beauty 107:10
  R. of all R.s. R. of all the World! 417:6
  r. that blossoms in the deeps 416:23
  r.s are flowering in Picardy 394:2
  roves back the r. 102:17
  swear-words like r.s in their talk 246:8
  tell me it smells like r.s 196:2
  third day he r. again from bed 198:19
  twilight dim with r. 103:16
  whose r.s [rozez] he knowzez 102:23
Rose-garden: door we never opened into the r.
    116:24
Rose-lipt: many a r. maiden 180:2
Rose-water: her blood is nothing but r. 125:31
  revolution could not be made with r. 129:11
Rosin: arctic zones of the eternal r. 172:10
Rossetti, D.G.: do with the Grail . . . R.? 30:30
Roster: r. of Those Who Do Things 291:21
Rotarians: r. in outer space 387:11
Rothermere, Harold Harmsworth, Viscount · 23:6
Rotted: r. for their opinions 14:12
Rotten: r. way to run a revolution 142:5
Rottenness: perfection of r. 192:2
Rottweiler: turn a spaniel into a R. 166:16
Rough: kept me from children who were r. 355:2
  r. male kiss of blankets 54:12
Rougher: r. than thoroughfares of stones 162:14
Round: Memorable R. Table 341:2
  r. peg in a square hole 180:24
Roundabout: what's lost on the r.s 71:12
Rousseau, Jean-Jacques 149:36
  R. was the first militant lowbrow 39:14
Routine: only people free from r. 234:18
Rove: r.s back the rose 102:17
Roved: as when I r. the heather 101:17

Row: r. after rich r. 365:7
   too far for one to r. 161:4
Royal: being r. has many painful drawbacks 15:7
   butter for the r. slice of bread 264:10
   can't be all of the Blood r. 15:4
   feed a grub on r. jelly 82:8
   paid his subjects with a r. wage 54:11
   R. Commission is a broody hen 129:9
   r. one-parent family 296:21
Royalties: fresh air and r. 15:6
   his r. as recording angel 246:12
   r. are nice 227:14
Royalty: only r. America ever had 100:19
Rub: some of it may r. off on you 326:15
Rubbish: make good use of bad r. 38:4
   r. doesn't care about the . . . skip 145:4
   what do you think of the show so far? R. 269:2
Rubble: anything more offensive than r. 73:7
Rudder: like a ship without a r. 215:3
Rude: r. remark or a vulgar action 404:20
   slam *at* you when people are r. 126:21
   so unconscionably r. to His mother 348:3
Rudeness: indistinguishable from r. 368:11
Rudolph: R., the red-nosed reindeer 250:22
Rue: with r. my heart is laden 180:2
Rug-making: r. or wife-swapping 46:2
Rugby Union: second fiddle only to R. 370:21
Ruin: nuclear bomb can r. your whole day 149:21
   pretty anyone would want to r. her 51:12
   r. can become charming 406:13
   r.s that Cromwell knocked about 235:12
Ruined: r. buildings . . . no r. stones 243:1
Ruines: r. du ghetto 120:17
Rule: brought under a r. 417:22
   exception disproves the r. 110:6
   mere r.s of succession 401:8
   not the clear-sighted who r. the world 89:11
   reasons for the r. change 362:17
   there are no golden r.s 344:26
   they that r. in England 74:17
   time . . . to r. openly 411:10
   when you've shouted 'R. Britannia' 209:12
Ruled: r. thirty million people 397:22
Ruler: natural . . . secret r.s 411:10
   oldest and strongest desires of r.s 66:7
Rum: if the sergeant steals your r. 12:12
   r., sodomy and the lash 82:20
   what a R. Go everything is 396:24
Rummy: r. to a degree 410:1
Rumour: *Times* has published no r.s 360:3
Run: he'll r. it all over you 398:5
   lady, lady, better r. 291:11
   they get r. over 41:16
   time for you to r. out of me 388:9
   we don't know how to r. it 394:14
Run-up: trouble with her r. 374:10
Runcie, Dr Robert 346:16
Runcorn: raspberry time in R. 93:22
Running: double up by r. the country 203:15
   rich are only defeated when r. 189:21
Ruped: four r.s, one at each corner 273:10

Rural: sly shade of a R. Dean 54:17
Rush-hour: r. jam in the subway 82:24
Rushdie, Salman 270:20
Rushes: Czar of all the r. 339:4
Ruskin, John: I doubt that art needed R. 361:16
Russell, Bertrand, Lord 36:4, 326:5
   Well, Lord R., what's it all about? 10:23
Russell, Ken 334:3
Russia 53:7, 388:4
   campaign against R. . . . fourteen days 159:12
   going in without the help of R. 236:2
   if R. is winning 378:14
   in R. . . . all my primary training 358:8
   led R. into the enchanted quagmire 82:1
   outlaw R. for ever 313:18
   poet in R. is more than a poet 418:15
   possible for R. to be run by empresses 53:19
   R. . . . a riddle wrapped in a mystery 79:12
   R. is a collapse not a revolution 223:23
   R. is an enormous lunatic asylum 375:1
   R. will certainly inherit the future 223:26
Russian: by this I am a R. 418:13
   R. circus in town 149:32
   R. national interest 79:12
   R. novel where one of the characters 257:5
   R. people . . . an awful reality 378:3
   test the R.s not the bombs 138:9
   we praise the R. army 40:7
Rust: r. in their Volvo 92:15
   r. to the harrow 103:19
Rustic: being a r. after about 1400 7:10
Rustler: sheriff sun and r. moon gamble 260:12
Rusty: better r. than missing 252:18
Rutland: R. blue's got out of passion 197:13
Rye: before the Roman came to R. 74:27

S

SDP: S. childbirth 68:9
Sabbath: holy S., on the peaceful day 348:23
   keep the S. and everything else 323:17
Sabotage: sagacious use of s. 386:13
Sack: back us or s. us 63:14
Sacked: winter . . . s. for negligence 243:18
Sackville-West, Victoria 89:4
Sacrament: abortion would be a s. 204:9
Sacred: books and therefore s. 151:2
Sacredness: s. of mass 123:19
Sacrifice: I have escaped the s. 162:11
   it is possible to s. half mankind 250:16
   still stands thine ancient s. 212:15
   woman . . . can never forgive s.s 256:15
   woman will always s. herself 255:19
Sacrificed: was s., flayed and curried 198:19
Sacrilegious: s. atheist 333:17
Sad: how s. a place the world can be 383:12
   never s. enough to improve the world 66:12
   no laughter is s. 360:12
   s. as a gypsy serenading the moon 259:23

s. person's view of a gay person 96:2
s. woman who buys her own perfume 193:8
saw a s. land 288:23
Sadat, Anwar el 258:8
Saddest: s. tale told on land or sea 119:13
Saddled: s. in the enclosure at Epsom 94:24
Sade, Marquis de: S., the gallant 317:14
Sadism: s. . . . transform a man 134:18
Sadness: birds of s. 255:1
  farewell s. 120:16
  s. of her s. 26:15
Safe: look again when it's safe 363:11
  s. shall be my going 55:4
  s. to be unpopular 359:3
  s. upon solid rock the ugly houses 261:7
  s. with his wound 337:6
  widow to one s. home 261:9
  world . . . s. for democracy 406:19
Safer: s. than a known way 165:12
Safety: concern for one's own s. 168:10
  safe though all s.'s lost 55:4
Safire: diamond and s. bracelet lasts 237:10
Saga: on our eyes the frosty s.s 94:28
Sage: our s.s know their onions 273:16
  s. feels too small for life 74:11
Sagged: s. ominously upon the earth 151:24
Säglichen: hier ist des S. Zeit 318:18
Sahara: man crawling across the S. 36:23
Said: everything that can be s. 408:7
  nobody had s. it before 380:9
Sail: old ships s. like swans asleep 128:15
  red s.s in the sunset 204:11
  s. in an eighteenth century play 341:24
  seawards to the white dipping s.s 254:9
Sailor: all the nice girls love a s. 264:3
  bad s. keeps clear of the engine room 216:2
  drowned Phoenician s. 118:4
  heard the silly s.-folk 211:18
  s. men 'ave their faults 188:7
Saint: before we know he is a s. 154:8
  better class of S.s 215:17
  disillusionments in the lives of . . . s.s 332:22
  don't grow into plaster s.s 213:7
  face of a s. 397:7
  reason s.s wear haloes 24:14
  s., but perhaps not a hero 297:18
  torero, the government, or a s. 314:7
  woman to qualify as a s. 359:14
St Paul's: say I'm designing S. 37:19
Salad: green parrot is also a green s. 298:4
  know chicken shit from chicken s. 195:11
  s. . . . the Lord's Prayer in beetroot 15:25
Sale: from s. and profanation 74:24
Salesman: s. is got to dream 261:26
  s. must have the quality of saying 60:16
Salesmanship: at bottom a form of s. 176:8
Salesmen: s. can fondle her breasts 217:10
  what Boston Strangler did for . . . s. 166;11
Salley: down by the s. gardens 416:3
Sally: S. is gone that was so kindly 33:2
Salmon: between smoked s. and tinned 405:18

cider and tinned s. 392:28
crossing s. with mosquitoes 271:12
s.-falls: s., the mackerel-crowded sea 417:9
thou canst not serve both cod and s. 231:13
two s. this morning, and . . . Exchequer 71:16
Salt: egg without s. 71:3, 214:18
  s. solution in . . . saturation 341:14
Salteena: Mr S. was an elderly man of 42 15:1
Saltier: s. oblivion of the sea 365:10
Salty: admit that the sea is s. 70:5
Saluting: s. strange women 277:25
Salvation: confuse it with the S. Army 14:16
  dumbness is its s. 92:13
  hope of s. . . . surprised by the Other 185:7
  What is the s.? Go shopping 261:27
  wot prawce s. [selvytion] nah? 343:28
Sam: play it, S. 38:20
  S., S., pick oop tha' musket 176:14
Samaritan: Good S. . . . had money 367:22
Samarkand: golden road to S. 128:12
Same: all is yet the same 101:17
  all made the s. 93:14
  just the s. on the other side 84:19
  saying the s. things over and over 111:14
  they all look just the s. 315:19
  two things are always the s. 357:7
Sameness: s. . . . object of his devotion 328:3
Sammlerwert: ganz nett, besäss aber kaum noch S.
  201:19
Samuel, Herbert, Viscount: circumcised S. 236:5
San Salvador: bells off S. 95:6
Sanction: happiness is the only s. 335:8
Sand: gift for mixing s. and water 164:12
  line has been drawn in the s. 60:15
  s. in the porridge 94:10
  shining palace built upon the s. 261:7
Sandal: her massive s. set on stone 261:4
Sandalwood: s., . . . and sweet white wine 254:2
Sanders, George 280:9
Sandham, Alf 320:4
Sandwiches: brown s. and green s. 347:16
  come back as ham s. 374:11
Sandy: welcome as a s. foreskin 316:1
Sane: no s. person would do at eleven 343:29
  pretend to be s. 171:13
  rewards for being s. 7:17
  show me a s. man and I will cure him 199:10
Sang: he s. his didn't 97:19
  s. as one who on a tilting deck sings 101:16
  s. in my chains like the sea 369:1
  where once we s. 162:6
Sanitary: glorified s. engineer 362:2
Sanity: s. . . . caught by a psychiatrist 299:16
  there ain't no S. Clause 252:12
Sank: they s. my boat 205:10
Santa Claus: arrival of death or S. 39:21
Sap: dried the s. out of my veins 416:6
Sarcasm: s. the condition of truth 27:1
Sardines: life is like a tin of s. 35:23
  s., the riches of life therein 35:24
Sargent, Malcolm: kind of musical S. 29:18

Sartre, Jean-Paul 149:36

Sat: last person who s. on him 158:5

Satan: forced S. to . . . live in the pit 119:19

S. . . . is a hard boss to work for 170:11

Satin: black s. at her coming-out ball 399:12

ease a heart like a s. gown 291:10

Satire: British must be gluttons for s. 236:10

s. . . . closes on Saturday night 202:5

s. is a lesson 276:11

s. is dependent on strong beliefs 55:13

s. is simply humour in uniform 194:8

Satirist: s.s should be heard 347:2

Satisfaction: I can't get no s. 189:7

look of deep and complacent s. 270:11

Satisfactory: as an end he is not so s. 206:17

Satisfy: never . . . worth while to s. it 178:12

s. themselves that it is still there 44:20

Saturation: more or less s. 341:14

Saturday: couple of drinks on a S. 137:18

on S. I'm willing 407:9

right to a S. night bath 195:13

S. before you realize it's Thursday 298:12

satire . . . closes on S. night 202:5

Saucer: pieces of blue and white s.s 91:16

white s. like some full moon descends 267:12

Sauntering: s. past a stucco gate 300:7

Sausage: break up the union because of s. 148:3

Sausinges: where's the s.? 263:24

Savage: hairy s.s sitting down for lunch 263:13

if an uneducated s. can do that 90:13

man who has not w. is a s. 335:3

summer talk stopped on that s. coast 17:20

Savaged: s. by a dead sheep 166:10

Save: fight again to s. the party we love 138:10

rushed through life trying to s. 321:20

s. water – dilute it 149:33

whenever you s. 5 shillings 206:16

Savile Row: S. tailor calls four times 271:5

Saviour: not a perfect s. 373:15

Saw: I s. a man this morning 346:15

Sawdust: s. Caesar 340:16

Say: always something more to s. 361:15

as long as they do what I s. 367:16

best writer . . . nothing to say 413:9

how much one has to s. 66:13

it's the way they s. it 357:21

more to s. when I am dead 320:13

never s. anything 226:9

never say the things we should like to 308:7

not to s. what they really do 388:4

not what he s.s, but what he whispers 350:21

nothing to s., only to add 387:6

people who s. nothing 352:11

s. it with flowers 284:16

s. what you have to s. 48:15

those who had little to s. 30:12

those who have something to s. 83:11

till I see what I s. 390:14

Saying: redaction known as the S.s 197:9

Scab: s. on their achievement 362:16

Scaffold: never on the s. 79:1

Scalpel: like operating with a s. 63:10

Scandal: brought down because of a s. 158:10

s., the incredible come-down 30:13

there is only silence or s. 257:10

Scare: anything s.s anyone 357:6

Scarecrow: measure the s.s for new suits 271:5

Scared: s. of dying 160:14

s. to go to the brink 111:4

Scarlatti, Domenico: S. condensed so much music
58:11

Scarlet: his sins were s. 32:33

Scene: mask of the preceding scene 102:3

Scenery: all for s. – yes 191:4

Scent: hot the s. is of the summer rose 151:8

nor does a nursery gardener s. his roses 85:8

Scepticism: s. kept her from being an atheist
336:21

s. of everything 305:1

Schedule: my s. is already full 214:31

Schizophrenia: God talks to you, you have s.
364:9

illness . . . of Canada is paranoid s. 17:4

s. cannot be understood 219:6

Schizophrenic: behaviour that gets labelled s.
219:12

two persons in every one . . . are s. 150:1

Schlief: als ich zurückkam, sah ich s. 202:2

Scholar: film is not the art of s.s 171:11

I am a greater s. than Wordsworth 180:9

last humiliation of an aged s. 86:9

Scholarship: greatest danger to s. 334:6

slender indications of s. 80:18

School: all s.s are hell 90:15

art of getting on at s. 88:9

at s. [nonsense] is all put gently back 30:7

away to s. until they're old 49:7

class s.s into four grades 392:3

depraved until he has been to a good s. 332:7

greatest mind ever to stay in prep s. 247:17

I think I'll not send him to s. 110:15

jails called s.s 382:11

love and the Board s. 30:28

no one can enjoy a public s. 87:17

private s. has . . . faults of a public s. 88:7

s. may [master] the thought 334:6

s.'s out 100:14

s.s [skools] are quite remarkable 403:15

she has been late for s. 369:23

she would set fire to the S. 340:8

some of us have to go to summer s. 105:11

State in order before . . . a State s. 75:17

see also Sunday-school

School for Scandal: M.G.M. production of the *S.*
220:3

Schoolboy: s. is a novelist too busy to write 88:9

s. repeating my words by heart 249:2

s. who wipes his fingers on a slate 44:15

Schooling: twenty years of s. 113:21

Schoolmaster: hobby for embittered s.s 46:2

s.s of ever afterwards 127:17

you'll be becoming a s. 392:2

Science: contribute to s. 51:5
  destruction of Nordic s. 375:5
  enfant terrible of . . . s. 61:20
  essence of s. 54:3
  natural s. does not simply describe 168:4
  religion is far more acute than s. 130:21
  s. can find no aim in Nature 401:8
  s. can only state what is 116:9
  s. fiction is no more . . . for scientists 5:5
  s. is all those things . . . confirmed 148:15
  s. is any discipline in which the fool 145:7
  s. is built of facts 300:14
  s. is divided into two categories 329:16
  s. is really anti-intellectual 259:2
  s. is what one Jew copies from another 239:2
  s. knows only one commandment 51:5
  s. must be individualistic 77:18
  s. must begin with myths 301:8
  s. reassures 50:16
  s. should leave off . . . pronouncements 193:4
  s. which hesitates 401:12
  s. without religion is lame 115:13
Scientific: copyright in s. discoveries 258:4
  s. method . . . 20-20 hindsight 299:10
  s. work is a place of prayer 278:17
Scientist: company of s.s 19:7
  elderly but distinguished s. 83:17
  no s. is admired for failing 258:2
  s. must be . . . a metaphysician 342:21
  s.s are faced with . . . culture 352:3
  s.s are responsible for their research 67:11
Scope: epic s. of a photograph album 151:1
Score: continually changing the s. 316:20
  I never used a s. 266:14
  s.s of lovely, gifted girls 151:26
Scorer: when the One Great S. comes 316:6
Scorning: s. parochial ways 163:8
  talking . . . to s. men 386:8
Scotch: S. by absorption 247:4
  water . . . 'Irish or S.?' 159:9
  working on a case of S. 34:23
Scotland: if Labour is dead in S. 63:13
  in S. translated into . . . 'thrift' 371:9
Scots: S. . . . do not have . . . a government 122:2
  S. drink in bouts 96:9
Scotsman: greatest moral attribute of a S. 26:22
  S. on the make 26:23
  S. with a grievance 408:13
  to a S. something is what it is 243:2
  young s. of your ability 26:21
Scotsmen: island . . . governed by S. 156:7
Scott: said Liddell to S. 163:5
Scott, C.P. 45:19
Scott, Sir Walter: not even S. 346:2
Scottish: he [Knox] split the S. mind 188:1
  shiver ran throught the S. MPs 56:16
Scoundrel: every man over forty is a s. 345:6
Scoutmaster: exaltation of s.s 317:4
Scramble: rocks came home in s. sort 175:10
  s. into my clothes 358:6
Scrambled: cold s. eggs on . . . pork chops 221:1

Scrap: one decent bar s. 396:15
Scratch: s. my head with the lightning 380:6
  s. the Christian 420:2
  sit there and scratch it 29:21
  where is s.? 66:24
Scratchez: when ah itchez, ah s. 278:2
Scream: girls s., boys shout 100:14
  thcream, an' t., an' t. till I'm thick 96:10
Screen: flimsiest of s.s 191:18
Screenwriter: blue and so are the s.s 234:21
Screw: seek the right s. under the sofa 177:3
Screwy: s. visions 34:9
Scribble: stars s. on our eyes 94:28
Scribbled: dominion over man by a s. name 369:3
Scripture: little of the s. did he understand 112:12
  searching the s.s for hints 220:6
Scrotumtightening: s. sea 198:9
Sculptor: I was meant to be a s. 70:1
  s. . . . inventing . . . the curve 280:8
Sculpture: cold and austere like that of s. 328:13
  my s.s are plastic metaphors 297:19
  s. is not for young men 50:11
Sculptured: s. Ann is seventy years 368:18
Scum: now it means you're s. 357:21
  rich are the s. of the earth 76:7
Scuttleful: whole s. of chef douvres 251:4
Scuttling: s. across the floors 117:25
Sea: axe for the frozen s. inside us 201:6
  drink all the water in the s. 70:5
  fed our s. for a thousand years 210:4
  floors of silent s.s 117:25
  gong-tormented s. 415:12
  great markets by the s. 128:8
  he had the s. in his blood 263:1
  He walks again on the S.s of Blood 349:1
  houses are all gone under the s. 116:29
  I am very much at s. 68:17
  I must go down to the s.s again 254:10
  if ye take away the s. 211:16
  jolly-rodgered s. 369:21
  likes to imagine himself at s. 66:6
  mackerel-crowded s.s 417:9
  men and sea interpenetrate 89:12
  mirrors of the s. are strewn 128:18
  never seen the point of the s. 36:14
  ourselves we find in the s. 97:21
  s. in which the guerrilla swims 250:18
  s. is all about us 117:6
  s. rises higher 74:9
  s. was ever loved 375:12
  saltier oblivion of the s. 365:10
  sang in my chains like the s. 369:1
  satisfy twice a day the insatiable s. 88:17
  secret of the s. 143:11
  serpent-haunted s. 128:6
  since the s. had to live 389:11
  snotgreen s. 198:9
  s.s of pity 17:17
  s.s roll over, but the rocks remain 170:28
  that angry or that glimmering s. 128:13
  what did we see? We saw the s. 39:8

where no s. runs 369:8
within a walk of the s. 33:11
Sea-shell: she sells s.s on the sea-shore 363:4
Sea-sick: nobody is ever s. – on land 194:15
Sea sickness: as universal as s. 344:20
Seal: neither a Lord, a privy, nor a s. 21:13
you heard a s. bark 372:1
Seamy: reversible coat – s. on both sides 170:5
Search: in s. of a fairy 102:23
s. for knowledge 328:1
Seaside: I do like to be beside the s. 145:6
people have described a day at the s. 345:10
Seaside: drawback of all s. places 108:14
Season: dry brain in a dry s. 117:14
her changing s.s correct 371:2
man has every s. 129:8
s. was the airiest May 151:24
winter is an abstract s. 53:15
Seat: damps there drip upon sagged s.s 162:6
Seated: President looked wiser when s. 206:12
Seats: bottoms on s.s 159:18
Seawards: my road leads me s. 254:9
Sebastian, St: shin-bone of S. 84:17
Second: first and s. class citizens 405:2
first turning of the s. stair 116:20
I'll be the s. to admit it 205:23
in the wood . . . you get a s. chance 26:4
no s. acts in American lives 127:2
not a s. on the day 89:18
s. night if there is one 82:22
s. things never 89:15
s. thought is never an odd thought 283:9
sixty s.s' worth of distance run 211:1
sound of the s. circle 90:15
Second-hand: buy a s. car from this man? 331:16
even original sin is s. 44:1
history has to use s. timber 181:8
originality in a s. suit 267:20
pigeons . . . in their grey, s. suits 68:12
s. ideas passed on by his advisers 245:20
Second-rate: if Nixon was s. 168:23
so many s. [conductors] of our own 29:20
Secret: Englishman told you he was a s. agent
93:20
giant girls that have no s. 355:3
Official S.s Act is . . . to protect 239:11
poetry that will be their own s. 249:1
publish the s. treaties 378:10
s. by the unmourning water 369:15
s. in the Oxford sense 132:7
s. none can utter 310:3
s. of being miserable 345:11
s. of life in your pants 97:20
whither so s. away? 103:23
Secretary: hit a moving s. with an egg 411:3
lazy to have an affair with your s. 25:5
wife to tell him . . . and a s. to do it 248:11
Secretary General: most powerful S. 377:19
Secretion: poisoned by its own s.s 52:2
Secretly: s., like wrongs hushed up 288:22
Secular: S. City 94:23

Sécurité: *s. collective* 35:11
Security: collective s. 35:11
lovely feeling of s. 73:13
only freedom can make s. secure 301:6
s. without values 215:3
Sedentary: true knowledge is s. 266:15
Sediment: dregs? That's what he s. 149:3
s. of permanent adulation 88:12
Seduction: ethical or social s. 41:10
See: art . . . makes us s. 215:8
come up some time, s. me 398:9
each man as he s.s himself 191:22
I'd rather s. than be one 59:13
nice to s. you – to s. you, nice 131:9
reality is what I s., not what you s. 59:9
wait and s. 15:15
Seeing: s. what everybody has seen 364:10
Seek: all who s. you tempt you 319:13
if he finds what he s.s 217:21
we s. him here, we s. him there 285:10
Seemly: s. that I . . . should be hurled 351:3
Seen: fine things to be s. 74:28
justice should . . . be s. to be done 171:18
pleasure of being s. for what one is 110:13
satirists should be heard and not s. 347:2
things a' didn't wish s., anybody will see 163:27
twice is not s. 265:9
Seer: most s.s are unhealthy 53:16
Seine: parallels of latitude for a s. 380:6
Seize: s. and clutch and penetrate 118:19
Seldom: s. female in a world of males 299:14
Selection: natural s. . . . has no purpose 101:5
Self: dungeon of s. 88:26
mythology of s. 358:10
Self-adjusting: s. card table 372:10
Self-assertion: s. abroad 392:26
Self-assured: not state it in a s. way 260:20
Self-centred: drawbacks to s. passions 328:3
s. army without parade or gesture 225:5
Self-confidence: you lose all your s. 242:14
Self-conscious: race which has become s. 223:4
Self-consciousness: s. at Christmastime 148:5
Self-denial: s. is not a virtue 344:34
Self-discovery: painting is s. 300:19
Self-esteem: s. is the most voluble 85:20
Self-humiliation: readiness to risk s. 104:4
Self-indulgence: favourite form of s. 255:19
Self-indulgent: s. fiction 62:10
Self-interest: s. was bad morals 322:13
Self-love: s. seems so often requited 303:30
Self-made: s. man . . . believes in luck 356:15
s. . . . working with inferior materials 11:9
Self-Pity: ought to be labelled S. 26:1
Self-possessed: like all s. people 73:15
Self-realization: s. . . . supreme principle 328:9
Self-respect: live out in dignity and s. 324:6
only as much as s. required 366:15
Self-serving: clouds of s. mystery 378:12
Self-sufficiency: s. at home 392:26
Self-surrender: my life in s. had a goal 160:6
Selfish: discover a s. motive for anything 246:12

marry for purely s. reason 55:11
s. gene 101:6
Selfridges: by reality I mean . . . S. 225:7
Selling: depends if you're buying or s. 148:17
    writers are always s. somebody out 105:21
Selt: I am a S. you are a sunt 60:6
Selvytion: wot prawce S. nah? 343:28
Selznick, David: S. would hand . . . memo 346:17
Semi-colonial: fullstoppers and s.s 197:14
Semi-human: liberation . . . by s.s 133:10
Senator: s.s burst with laughter 17:11
Send: for God's sake don't s. me 231:3
    s. in the clowns 353:6
Senescence: shadows their s. 240:5
Senile: sign that they now consider him s. 86:9
Sense: distrust of our s.s 64:9
    five s.s within whose pentagon 38:7
    good poem as one that makes s. 152:11
    money is like a sixth sense 256:18
    money is the sixth s. 248:13
    no substitute for s. 118:19
    nothing other than the s. you choose 336:2
    s. to come in out of the rain 313:2
    talk s. to the American people 358:21
Sensibilities: one's own fine s. 169:4
Sensibility: dissociation of s. 119:2
    modified his s. 119:1
    never goes beyong his own s. 297:17
Sensible: s. about social advance 351:15
Sensitiveness: s. . . . of the true artist 30:24
Sensuality: paint the full face of s. 370:21
Sentence: declared meaning of a spoken s. 68:1
    forming a complete s. 400:6
    I write one s.; then I write another 362:6
    not all s.s are statements 310:4
    s. is a sound in itself 136:6
    single s. will suffice for modern man 65:8
    structure of the ordinary British s. 80:19
Sentiment: spheres of s. 335:5
Sentimental: because of s. value 136:20
Sentimentalism: s. is the working off 223:24
Sentimentality: s. is only sentiment 257:6
    s. is the emotional promiscuity 247:10
    s. . . . the sentiment we don't share 154:15
Sentry: wearily the s. moves 5:2
Sentry-box: quadrille in a s. 190:10
Separate: keep them [body and soul] s. 238:16
    Spaniards . . . are a people s. 270:6
Separated: s. by the same language 346:10
Separateness: evil . . . makes for s. 182:17
Separation: s. is a more lasting experience 53:14
    supreme s. 66:2
Serenading: sad as a gypsy s. the moon 259:23
Serengeti National Park: six of them left in the S.
    36:7
Serenity: s. to accept things 280:2
Sergeant: if the s. steals your rum 12:12
Serial: obituary in s. form 95:23
Serious: [football] is much more s. than that 342:9
    his audience takes him s. 321:24
    protect us from others . . . more s. 307:19

s. house on s. earth 221:7
s. man has few ideas 385:11
s. writer may be a hawk or a buzzard 169:15
same thing as s. reading 396:18
too s. . . . to be left to the politicians 141:8
Seriously: s. though, he's doing a grand job
    134:22
    tell the boys . . . to take me s. 191:13
Seriousness: wallowing in low s. 34:12
Sermon: principles of the S. on the Mount 244:9
    snored through the S. on the Mount 45:5
Serpent: not have talked with the s. 397:3
Serpent-haunted: s. sea 128:6
Serpentine: dignify the S. 107:13
Servant: being said by the s. girls 363:15
    equality in the s.'s hall 26:3
    in a s. it looks presumptuous 360:17
    naked Civil S.s 95:22
    obligation to become the s. of a man 343:11
    upper s.s to supervise and direct 404:2
    wife or s. to read this book 155:11
Serve: he profits most who s.s best 346:18
Service: goods and s.s can be paid for 281:8
    s. of my love 355:18
    s.s are voluntary 392:16
Serviette: crumpled the s.s 40:12
    matters like . . . s.s 396:23
Servile: S. State 33:16
Serving-men: six honest s. 211:6
Sesquippledan: s. verboojuice 396:9
Set: she's part of the s. 127:4
Settle: winter evening s.s down 117:34
Seven: next to S.-up 111:11
    S. Historic Exhibitions 111:15
    s. types of ambiguity 120:22
    S. Year Itch 19:25
Seventeenth century: conviction that one died in
    the s. 52:12
    dance as she moves in a s. play 341:24
Seventh: s. degree of concentration 343:14
Severn: or out to S. strode 74:27
    stuff the S. Tunnel 271:16
Sew: go out to s. for the rich 86:7
Sewer: life is like a s. 228:3
    s. in a glass-bottomed boat 267:2
    through a s. in a glass-bottomed boat 390:8
    walk into an open s. and die 55:21
Sex: always wanted to know about s. 315:15
    attempt to insult s. 223:25
    Continental people have s. life 260:18
    fair s. is your department 110:2
    fiction is to make s. exciting 387:21
    food is more dangerous than s. 254:17
    he gave her class and she gave him s. 170:22
    human desire for food and s. 375:15
    if God had meant us to have group s. 49:14
    if I have to cry, I think of my s. life 188:2
    if s. is so personal 375:8
    if s. were all 358:15
    if S-E-X ever rears its ugly head 20:1
    if there was a third s. 385:4

in my day you didn't have s. 411:20
in s. no less than in war 183:13
instant s. will never supersede 95:24
intensity of love and s. 265:14
is s. dirty? 5:16
know nothing about s. 138:4
literature is mostly about having s. 236:9
make s. last . . . twenty minutes 154:16
making up these s. rules 333:10
Mexico . . . where men despise s. 224:7
no reason for the . . . male s. 399:1
one minute of s. 319:20
open mind about s. 355:7
preoccupied with s. than occupied 171:3
s. . . . I . . . don't understand 333:10
s. is good for headaches 402:6
s. is here to stay 302:4
s. is just politics with the clothes off 49:4
s. is one of the nine reasons 262:6
s. is only the liquid centre 90:17
S. Life in Ancient Rome face 7:13
s. like a glass of water 216:20
s. suppressed will go berserk 121:16
s. used to be single-crop farming 34:5
s. with someone I love 5:21
s. without using someone 58:17
s. you can get anywhere in the world 49:3
s.? I'd rather have a cup of tea 142:7
take the s. out of glamour 67:18
when the S. War ended 17:14
when you have money, it's s. 108:5
women are a s. by themselves 30:11
worst thing about oral s. 235:1
Sex-change: teenage s. priest 234:19
Sexes: absurd division into s. 392:20
distinction between s. 131:18
more difference within the s. 86:20
Sexophones: s. . . . like melodious cats 182:12
Sexton: s. to willow 103:21
Sextones: s. with princess effect 197:13
Sexual: as in the s. experience 400:5
industrial . . . are like s. relations 123:9
making s. infatuation a tragic theme 345:26
primary s. activity of mankind 364:2
proper s. intercourse 46:1
s. attraction through . . . my voice 162:1
s. intercourse began in 1963 221:3
s. perversion known as continence 182:7
s. pull towards mirrors 86:22
vital need, especially the s. 315:7
Shabby: how much of a s. animal 223:27
Shade: lie where s.s of darkness 103:2
s. of the old apple tree 403:21
s.s of Arabia 102:20
Shadow: falls the s. 117:18
flits a s. and a sigh 212:26
little s.s come about her eyes 416:8
live in this s. [of history] 290:8
live under the s. of a war 355:5
longer s. as time recedes 93:5
man's s. shortened by the sun 192:14

me and my s. 323:19
s. at morning 118:2
s.s flew as fast 418:19
Shafting: in storm the s. broken 101:20
Shake: persons whom you want . . . to s. 190:13
Shaken: s. and not stirred 128:20
Shakespeare, William 317:4, 345:27
among that billion minus one . . . S. 183:16
BETTER THAN S.? 345:29
despise so entirely as I despise S. 346:2
dig him up and throw stones at him [S.] 346:2
just as Stratford trades on S. 59:6
long runs as S. . . . seems to suggest 132:15
Mother. Teacher. S. 8:1
playing S. is very tiring 181:14
read S. and found him weak in chemistry 397:9
right to criticize S. 345:28
Shake was a dramatist of note 58:7
S. – the nearest thing . . . to . . . God 284:19
S. . . . turned so little knowledge 118:27
S. with Marlowe 412:14
Shakespearean: S. way . . . to take life 305:1
Shaking: s. the beads brings in money 227:14
s. them to make sure 43:6
Shalimar; beside the Shalimar 177:21
Shame: s. to their love pure 288:20
Shammin': generally s. when 'e's dead 210:22
Shape: s. all the singing tomorrows 295:12
s. of things to come 397:4
same s. twisted on the banister 116:20
water's the same s. as the glass 91:11
we tolerate s.s in human beings 186:24
Shaped: unreasonably poetry is s. 202:13
Shapeless: s. as the water 368:20
Shapely: important for a theory to be s. 160:19
Share: take your proper s. man 18:25
Shared: suppose everyone s. enough 57:15
Shark: s. has pretty teeth 51:20
Sharpened: s. by his death 415:7
Shatter: s. the faith of men 382:6
Shave: lies a haircut and a s. 175:19
man who s.s and takes a train 400:2
Shaved: only s. on Saturdays 69:17
Shaw, George Bernard 29:25, 80:17, 82:22,
380:23, 398:25
all S.'s characters are himself 343:10
Mr S. . . . has never written any poetry 77:3
puppets stuck up to spout S. 343:10
S. appearing as S. is sadly miscast 347:2
S., . . . you look as if there were famine 346:11
[S.] is a good man fallen among Fabians 229:7
Shee: want to s. the wheels go wound 158:1
Sheep: don't call the bleeders s. 314:11
dream of electric s. 105:18
look at the s. out of the window 395:8
s. in wolf's clothing 82:7
savaged by a dead s. 166:10
standing a s. on its hind legs 30:23
Sheep-hearding: rest is mere s. 303:26
Sheepdog: called German s.s? 92:8
Sheet: cool kindliness of s.s 54:12

Shelf-life: s. of the modern . . . author 270:19

Shell: that's S., that was 3:23

Shelley, Percy Bysshe: S. and Keats . . . chemical
    knowledge 158:13

    S. had a hyper-thyroid face 355:25

Shem: S. was a sham and a low sham 197:16

Shepherd: old Nod the s. goes 103:6

    what do the Germans call s.s? 92:8

Shepherd's Bush: got this mate in S. 298:15

Sheridan, R.B. 380:23

Sheriff: s. sun and rustler moon gamble 260:12

Sherry: first rate s. 300:6

    I am very fond of brown s. 75:18

    mischief . . . with the cooking s. 371:15

Shift: they put you on the day s. 113:21

Shilling: if you'll only take the s. 407:9

    s. life will give you all the facts 18:28

    s. [shillin'] a day, bloomin' good pay 212:20

Shimmering: in the matter of s. 410:1

Shimmy: put thy s. on Lady Chatterley! 223:19

Shin: multitude of s.s 398:13

Shin-bone: s. of St Sebastian 84:17

Shine: always to s. 257:15

    s. on, harvest moon 281:21

    that's where I s. 35:5

Shining: all her s. keys will be took 163:27

    I see it s. plain 179:32

    s. palace built upon the sand 261:7

    s. space with the grave's narrowness 151:25

    this plain she makes a s. bone 355:4

    woman of so s. loveliness 417:15

Shiny: s. stuff is tomatoes 353:3

Ship: all I ask is a tall s. 254:10

    American s. good grub 237:1

    Argentinians [are descended] from the s.s 294:9

    English s. . . . poor grub 237:1

    like a s. without a rudder 215:3

    old s.s sail like swans asleep 128:15

    s., an isle, a sickle moon 128:18

    s. me somewhere east of Suez 211:33

    s. on the sea 140:9

    s.s and stars and isles 128:7

    s.'s party on a ferry boat 127:14

    s.s shall go abroad 211:18

    so old a s. – who knows 128:17

    something wrong with our bloody s.s 28:3

    teeth like s.s at sea 102:22

    when stately s.s are twirled and spun 175:11

Shipwreck: s. and somnambulation 198:22

Shiraz: red wine of S. into urine 106:12

Shire: calling for them from sad s.s 288:15

    round both the s.s they ring them 179:20

Shirt: dangerous . . . getting into his s. 223:18

    good solid s., with stripes 298:18

    more warmly than the coarse s.s 371:3

    no s. or collar ever comes back twice 226:6

Shit: bird in the hand s.s on your wrist 87:10

    by my green candle, s., madam 192:20

    history is in the s. sense 55:24

    horse s. – there must be a pony 214:29

    I know chicken s. from chicken salad 195:11

    some s. I will not eat 97:15

    treating all men like s. 98:5

    you don't give a s. for nothing 181:3

Shiver: s. ran through the Scottish MPs 56:16

Shock: future s. 374:12

    s. of the new 111:15

Shoe: come back . . . as a s.-cleaning kit 20:2

    lazy insolence of a s. salesman 295:7

    pissing in his s. keeps no man warm 341:15

    s.s described but had never seen any 160:1

    s.s with broken high ideals 243:14

    their s.s are made of python 246:3

    wouldn't have minded being in his s.s 39:19

    you haven't got a pair of s.s 298:16

Shoe-size: s. in earth and bars around it 249:3

Shoeshine: riding on a smile and a s. 261:26

Shoestring: fortune into a s. 413:7

Shone: but a star that once had s. 128:8

Shook: ten days that s. the world 314:18

Shoon: walks the night in her silver s. 103:18

Shoot: they shout and they s. 186:4

    up and s. themselves 54:20

    when we're afraid we s. 353:11

Shooting: war minus the s. 287:17

Shop: men might shun the awful s. 75:2

    then I will close the s. 378:10

Shop-lifter: your readers are my s.s 10:3

Shop-lifting: better . . . to practise s. 52:5

Shopkeeper: among small clerks and s.s 397:10

Shopping: what is the salvation? Go s. 261:27

Shore: more stony than a s. 404:25

    you miss the s. 36:14

Short: life is too s. to stuff a mushroom 89:13

    never trust men with s. legs 94:18

    s. enough . . . to succeed on my own 6:4

    s., fat, hairy legs 269:3

    s. words and vulgar fractions 80:14

Shot: golden s. storms in the freezing tomb 369:13

    jealous . . . for being s. 418:7

    long s., Watson, a very long s. 109:26

    never s. anything 349:9

Shoulder: keep looking over his s. 27:7

    one tapped my s. 17:12

    s. the sky, my lad, and drink your ale 178:20

    their s.s held the sky suspended 179:6

    you gave me the hard s. 169:21

    you reading over my s. 151:23

Shout: noticed that Jews s. 325:3

    rushed in for a quick s. 208:4

    they s. and they shoot 186:4

Shouting: tumult and the s. dies 212:15

Shoveacious: S. Cult 396:11

Shovel: s. them under and let me work 334:18

Show: don't talk at all. S. me 230:20

    s. God ought surely to shut up 163:15

    s. me a hero 127:5

    some to s. themselves 317:1

    think of it [life] as a show 163:15

    what do you think of the s. so far? 269:2

Show business: boxing's just s. with blood 57:8

    no business like s. 39:4

s. is worse than dog eat dog 5:24
unself-conscious adjunct of s. 356:11
what s. is for 391:3
Shower: prove the sweetness of a s. 370:17
walked abroad in a s. 369:10
Showing: her soul is s. 381:4
Shrapnel: defensive hats, and s. 401:13
Shrewd: trying to be fair, not s. 168:18
Shrieking: in the midst of a s. world 272:7
Shrimp: until a s. learns to whistle 207:12
Shrined: bower we s. to Tennyson 162:7
Shrink: I did not s., I did not strive 254:5
Shrinking: through the s. night 101:17
Shrivel: he'd s. up at once 300:9
Shroud: gaiety is a striped s. 370:24
Shrunken: floors are s. 162:6
Shudder: I s. and I sigh to think 416:24
Shut: God ought surely to s. up soon 163:15
it [New Zealand] seemed to be shut 133:15
s. it on something solid 78:3
they s. the road through the woods 213:12
Shuttle: buggered by the s. 258:5
Shyness: s. is just egoism 203:24
Sick: more than a little s. 210:1
s., divided and impossible men 306:2
s. in soul and body both 175:8
s. with inbreeding 371:4
s., you shouldn't take it [exercise] 129:20
Sickle: ship, an isle, a s. moon 128:18
Sickness: universal s. implies 377:12
Sidcup: if only I could get down to S. 298:17
Side: even if there is only one s. 41:4
is he a man of this s.? 319:5
looked at him from both s.s now 265:25
no s. here, but plenty of edge 193:10
s. dish he hadn't ordered 220:17
s. of the hill that grew it 90:16
say she supported both s.s 243:6
when to move over to the other s. 314:13
Side-issue: watchword for s. specialists 296:6
Side-whiskers: acceptable by growing s. 397:7
Sidi Barrani: when I was in S. 178:7
Siegfried Line: washing on the S. 204:14
Sieve: education is a s. 73:3
mind is . . . nothing but an empty s. 351:4
Sigh: flits a shadow and a s. 212:26
he s.s, and the waves are a city 314:6
s. is just a s. 182:3
s. like the wind 409:7
telling this with a s. 135:23
white childhood moving like a s. 18:4
Sighed: Ida never s. 357:10
she even s. offensively 142:9
Sight: dislike before first s. 82:15
hated each other at half s. 64:15
never lost s. of losing you now 272:9
Sightless: blind man on the s. horse 389:15
Signal: mistaken s. 101:20
Signalling: thin one wildly s. 88:24
Signed: hand that s. the treaty 369:3
s. my death warrant 86:12

universe was dictated but not s. 269:17
Significant: s. form 31:14
very s. 362:4
Signpost: s.s like grim liars 44:5
Silence: appalling s. of the good people 208:10
fifteen minutes of s. 199:18
if s. has taught us anything 73:6
in the s. you don't know 29:2
more absolute s. of America 224:11
only s. or scandal 257:10
s. and sleep like fields of amaranth 102:19
s. immediately drew the curtain 191:3
s. is the essence of music 52:9
s. is the real crime against humanity 248:15
s. sounds no worse than cheers 179:19
s. surged softly backward 103:13
s. to recover from the futility of words 199:9
s. went straight from rapt to fraught 232:2
slightly *frappé* s. 410:6
that man's s s. is wonderful to listen to 164:4
thought up out of s. 150:9
unreasonable s. of the world 65:16
Silent: absolutely s. and infinitely bored 215:19
great s. majority 280:15
s. in many languages 161:15
s. in the privacy of his head 263:8
s. is Long Island Sound 272:6
thereof one must be s. 408:9
to be heard when silent 66:13
Silently: slowly, s., now the moon 103:18
Silk: farting through s. 266:7
it wasn't really s. at all 288:7
s. hat on a Bradford millionaire 118:14
s. purse out of your wife's ear 271:14
sheer s., too often hides eczema 65:7
your s. stocking's hanging down 341:4
Silliest: s. woman can manage a clever man
214:14
Silly: s. only if it is absent-minded 54:8
show how s. they [animals] aren't 174:16
to be s. is not to be foolish 36:22
Silver: crown . . . and the thirty pieces of s. 41:15
first of all the Georgian s. goes 245:17
s. lining in the sky-ee 399:7
s. lining through the dark cloud 129:21
s. spoons in his pocket 77:17
s. threads among the gold 315:17
strewn between their s. bars 128:19
walks the night in her s. shoon 103:18
when I'm 91 with s. hair 243:17
wind instruments of plated s. 392:9
Silvy: golded s. 197:13
Simian: some other s. has formerly said 101:12
Simon, Sir John 236:8
Simple: every work of art . . . is simple 76:24
lawlessness of something s. 238:5
show him the s. thing 319:1
s. as all truly great swindles 170:12
s. as possible but not simpler 116:4
s. bird that thinks two notes a song 100:9
teach us to delight in s. things 210:2

those who harm s. people 265:11
to ask the hard question is s. 18:11
went for the S. Life 74:19
Simplest: thoughts in the s. way 116:2
Simpleton: revolutionary s. is everywhere 233:13
Simplicity: bewildered by their s. 85:6
Simplification: ultimate s. of life 242:18
Simplify: s. me when I am dead 108:11
Simplifying: s. something by destroying 75:19
Simultaneously: grow old s. 88:23
Sin: absurd is s. without God 65:18
  all s. tends to be addictive 19:3
  beauty is only s. deep 333:2
  Christ died for our s.s 123:15
  confess your s.s before a parson 64:14
  hear about the s.s of the world 144:11
  his s.s were scarlet 32:33
  lust for certainty may be a s. 158:2
  original thought is like original s. 226:17
  physicists have known s. 285:7
  reheat his s.s for breakfast 105:22
  researches in original s. 300:8
  roots of s. are there 213:5
  s. of whisky 354:1
  s.s are attempts to fill voids 394:9
  s.s which they do not themselves commit 307:5
  wages of s. are increased circulation 13:11
  weighed together with their s.s 200:13
  wore their bodies out with nasty s.s 337:8
  worst s. towards our fellow creatures 343:4
Sinatra, Frank 149:36
Sincere: it is dangerous to be s. 345:7
  too true, too s. 418:5
Sincerely: do you s. want to be rich? 92:19
  S., Nixon 334:2
Sincerity: betray himself by . . . s. 76:22
  hypocrite to see even his s. 76:12
  s. of defection 312:17
  s.. Once you can fake that 284:22
  strength; that is to say their s. 336:17
  too much s. in society 255:18
  true hypocrite . . . lies with s. 143:17
Sing: he didn't s. to me 358:2
  s., and louder s. 417:10
  s. to find your hearts 128:7
  so zestfully canst thou s. 162:9
  till the fat lady s.s 89:19
  Welsh . . . just s. 392:9
  what boy can s. as the thrush s.s? 260:11
  while all the night you s. 267:13
Singapore: cross between S. and Telford 89:23
Singer: s. in the park 266:1
  s.s . . . benefit from . . . treatment 314:17
Singing: as humming is to s. 104:20
  everyone suddenly burst out s. 337:3
  shape all the s. tomorrows 295:12
  in s. not to sing 135:21
  s. bird forgets its cage 265:13
  s. in the rain 133:5
  s. roll or bowl a ball 167:12
  s. sweetly on a tree 358:2

s. will never be done 337:4
  what language was he s. in? 103:"30
Single: as a body everyone is s. 171:16
  s. men in barracks 213:7
  s. room . . . has no parts 225:15
Single-crop: sex used to be s. farming 34:5
Single-handed: won the war s. 50:15
Singly: sweaty feet seldom come s. 51:15
Singularity: s. is . . . invariably a clue 109:7
Sinister: most s. phenomena in . . . history 66:5
  s., princely death 319:16
Sink: go and pour them down the s. 75:9
Sinking: before deciding that a ship was s. 272:2
  s. pool for learning to drown 265:16
Sinned: s. against are not always the best 86:18
  would have s. incessantly 320:14
Sinner: combination s.s 403:7
Sinning: in good shape for more s. 327:2
  nothing so artificial as s. 224:12
Sinus: Sinai . . . the plural for s. 4:9
Sir: Yes s. That's my baby 201:8
Sister: asked . . . if she could bring a s. 6:24
  her elder s. was not gratified 332:24
  I wouldn't want one to bury my s. 266:8
  never praise a s. to a s. 214:13
  s. to the fathering worm 368:20
  she isn't a sister 10:17
  s.s under their skins 211:13
  will the veiled s. pray for children 116:22
Sisterly: she gave me a s. kiss 247:11
Sisyphus: imagine S. happy 65:19
Sit: can't s. on it for long 418:11
  get to s. down unless you're a king 181:14
  nobody can tell you to s. down 116:12
  s., wink and play 27:9
  s. and drink with me 33:11
  s. by and see the blind man 389:15
  s. down, man. You're a bloody tragedy 257:12
  s. not easy when all goes well 75:5
  somewhere left to . . . s. 120:24
  teach us to s. still 116:18
Sitting: are you s. comfortably? 220:12
  he struts s. down 113:2
  most of my work s. down 35:5
Situation: possible you haven't grasped the s. 205:22
  s. excellent 129:4
Sitwell, Sir George 349:11
Sitwells: S. belong to . . . of publicity 226:11
Six: all life is s. to five against 326:17
  for s. days this labour continued 100:6
  s. characters in search of an author 299:5
  some rob you with a s. gun 157:4
Sixpence: for s. he can get drunk 314:7
  so shocked . . . he'll give him s. 51:16
  we could have saved s. 28:14
Sixteen: s. before I knew I was a boy 202:7
Sixth-form: Lower S. we all got . . . religion 46:1
  s. teachers are . . . like firemen 152:22
Sixties: if you can remember the s. 24:15
  nothing happened in the s. 229:15

Sloane Ranger: read Proust is not a S. 26:2
Slogan: coin s.s without betraying ideas 35:14
   s. . . . for which memorability . . . bought 383:7
Slope: s. is always steeper 154:25
Sloppy: at Dirty Dick's and S. Joe's 18:16
Slouches: s. towards Bethlehem 417:13
Slough: come friendly bombs and fall on S. 40:18
   S. in your rear view mirror 149:8
Slow: it may be life, but ain't it s.? 170:25
   s. boat to China 236:19
   s. natural deaths 337:8
   tall conductors . . . with s. music 251:22
Slowly: s., silently, now the moon 103:18
   s. but s. asking his way 229:12
Slowness: s. of a man unable to see 188:9
Sludge: concept of Activated S. 194:2
Sluggish: s. or even non-existent 408:20
Sluicing: excellent browsing and s. 410:5
Slum: if you've seen one city s. 4:8
   Madonna of the S.s 235:18
   swear-word in a rustic s. 30:6
Slumber: s.'s ear 44:6
Slumbering: worm s. at the root 148:11
Slush: pure as the driven s. 24:8
Sly: s. shade of a Rural Dean 54:17
Small: break the big laws . . . you get s. laws
   77:22
   God who looks after s. things 214:24
   great history and . . . s. lives 80:5
   great man who makes every man feel s. 75:24
   s. business in Tory Britain 356:18
   s. is beautiful 339:12
   s. man can be just as exhausted 261:24
   s. of my back is too big 348:13
   s. talk . . . was bigger 104:13
   there are now only s. countries 227:19
Small-pox: died in the house full of s. 127:7
Smaller: higher the voice the s. the intellect 279:7
   pictures got s. 402:8
Smallest: sitting in the s. room 315:5
Smart: s. but not wise 301:1
   s. girl is one who knows how to play 314:5
Smash: great society is going s. 18:29
Smell: I can smell it [failure] 90:16
   s. of steaks in passage ways 117:34
   s. someone just thinking about food 339:8
   sweet s. of success 227:23
   tell me it s.s like roses 196:2
   their s. brings on my migraine 50:21
Smell-organ: Palmström builds himself a s. 269:9
Smile: Cambridge people rarely s. 54:19
   fifty-million-year-old s. 403:23
   his s. is like sunshine on putty 124:10
   my s. falls heavily 117:33
   Normal is the good s. in a child's eyes 342:4
   nothing has changed except the s. 44:13
   riding on a s. and a shoeshine 261:26
   s. at us, pay us, pass us 75:1
   s. I could feel in my pocket 72:7
   s. of the absent cat 115:18
   s. out; but still suffer 162:14

   s. that children could warm their hands 26:6
s.s involve the abandonment 207:12
society protecting itself – with a s. 305:11
stood at the end of s.s 318:13
where the s. dwells a little longer 73:4
Smiling: feeling alone among s. enemies 48:4
   s. and beautiful countryside 109:13
   s. as they run 74:20
   when you're s. the whole world smiles 147:29
   who is the s. stranger 70:18
Smith: chuck it, S. 74:3
Smith, Bessie 197:2
Smith, Reggie 22:6
Smithy: inside the s. the child 140:8
   sparks blown out of a s. 417:16
Smoke: s. gets in your eyes 161:14
   someone will s. in your place 337:12
   taste of misfortune and smoke 249:4
   when I don't s. 174:12
Smoke-filled: s. room 100:4
Smoking: drug that's s. in a girl 369:6
   s. is one of the leading causes 215:14
Smollett, Tobias 306:2
Smooth: many cities had rubbed him s. 153:20
Smoothes: s. . . . . with automatic hand 118:15
Smug: s. suppressions of his face 397:1
Snaffle: used the s. and the bit all right 65:3
Snail: lead the s. back to his shell 227:11
Snake: s. came to my water-trough 222:22
   s. is living yet 33:7
   s.s still walk upright 180:19
Snap: each Sunday s.s us from above 151:1
Snare: there is a rabbit in a s. 358:3
Sneakers: s., guns, dope, or sloth 411:15
Sneer: s. at acne 120:12
Sneeze: it's like having a good s. 224:15
   recognize . . . by the way they sneeze 144:22
   when a British Prime Minister s.s 232:3
Sneeze-wort: plays Korf's s. sonata 269:9
Snicker: hold my coat and s. 117:26
Sniffle: in spite of her s. 278:4
Snigger: between a eunuch and a s. 125:22
Snobbery: if s. died 383:22
Snobbish: said Marx, don't be s. 236:22
Snobbishness: immune from s. 308:313
Snopake: let S. grow on trees 20:7
Snored: s. through the Sermon on the Mount 45:5
Snoring: I had to stop her s. 150:8
Snotgreen: s. sea 198:9
Snow: in the dark over the s. 370:12
   mountain barred with s. 128:13
   pink sweet filled with s. 102:7
   s. and chocolate melt 92:1
   s. blind twilight 369:19
   s.s of yesterday 281:10
   to see the cherry hung with s. 179:12
Snow White: I used to be S. 398:12
Snow-white: little s. feet 416:3
Snub: I never s. anybody accidentally 144:8
Snuffle: some girls with a s. 278:5
Snug: squat pen rests; as s. as a gun 166:19

So long: s.. it's been good to know yuh 157:5
So-so: rest is merely s. 403:3
Soap: mother washed her mouth with s. 291:12
  one foot on a bar of s. 309:2
  s. and education 379:21
  tattoo s. bubbles 56:11
Sob: silver coins s. in the pocket 140:5
Sober: early, s., and alone 383:6
  half drunk when s. 170:10
  men at whiles are s. 178:21
  one sees in Garbo s. 380:27
  s. man may become a drunkard 76:2
  s. me up to sit in a library 126:14
  when s., will not concede 170:16
Sociable: s. worker 31:8
Social: admit their lower s. standing 152:17
  full time work being on s. security 395:6
  knows its s. limits 368:16
  [North Americans] go home to be s. 245:5
  Oh to become sensible about s. advance 351:15
  S. Contract is . . . a vast conspiracy 396:25
  s. masonry 396:25
  S. Revolution will be moral 294:19
Social Democratic Party 99:1
Socialism: education in s. 378:5
  making capitalism out of s. 22:10
  s. by a royal decree 150:18
  S. with a human face 110:21
  S. with a human *head* 177:4
  s. without social justice 296:9
  same sick horror as the thought of S. 396:3
  things . . . for others as s. 391:10
  under s. all will govern in turn 228:17
  worst advertisement for S. 287:4
Socialist: higher-water mark . . . of S. literature
    287:7
  result of this sloppy s. thinking 251:1
  S. mind and a Conservative heart 125:13
  S.s believe in two things 159:13
  thought is a S. temptation 276:16
  typical S. . . . a prim little man 287:5
Society: Affluent S. 138:13
  avenue of assimilation into s. 107:15
  carrying on in s. 290:3
  conformity with the rest of s. 307:11
  dropped by s. he has all his life 88:1
  education is the soul of s. 78:1
  effluent s. 368:7
  great s. is going smash 18:29
  hang around the edges of s. 299:19
  if s. fits you comfortably 136:11
  indispensible to the progress of s. 80:22
  kissed her way into s. 376:19
  looking closely at s. 377:13
  open s. . . . sets free 301:4
  poor s. cannot be too poor 365:13
  regarding s. as something eternal 286:16
  s. after their own image 377:22
  s. is making each other feel better 36:15
  s. moves by . . . parricide 39:15
  s. protecting itself – with a smile 305:11

  s. where it is safe to be unpopular 359:3
  s. which pays a harlot 405:19
  there is no such thing as s. 367:23
  transition from tribal or 'closed s.' 301:4
  upward to the Great S. 195:16
Sock: ankle s.s . . . of the vicar's wife 119:17
  his s.s compelled one's attention 332:20
  s. it to me 325:17
  s..s . . . to make one matching pair 164:18
Socratic: S. manner is not a game 30:26
Soda: wash their feet in s. water 118:13
Sodden: Midlands that are s. and unkind 33:10
Sodomy: comedy, like s. 123:17
  rum, s. and the lash 82:20
Sofa: rather lie on a s. 89:14
  s. upholstered in panther skin 300:8
Softening: at least have s. of the brain 77:4
Softly: s. along the road of evening 103:16
Soil: blood and s. 100:1
Sojers: we should act like s. 257:9
Sol: down went my Uncle S. 97:22
Sold: s. and again s. 334:19
  streets of heaven have all been s. 157:2
Soldan: S. of Byzantium is smiling 74:20
Soldats: s. qui passaient sur l'aile de la peur 13:7
Soldier: ask any s. 144:15
  British s. can stand up to anything 343:5
  chocolate cream s. 342:17
  I never expect a s. to think 343:5
  I'm a Wall s. 18:14
  innocent delight in playing s.s 53:26
  old s.s never die 129:6
  on Sunday I walk out with a s. 407:8
  only living unknown s. 206:1
  s. and sailor too 212:22
  shirts for s.s, Sister Susie sews 399:5
  s.s are citizens of death's grey land 337:2
  s.'s life is terrible hard 264:6
  s.s who passed on the wings of fear 13:7
  we should act like s.s [sojers] 257:9
  when a s. sees a clean face 51:8
Sole meunière: s. comes to you untouched 360:11
Solemn: in s. beauty like slow old tunes 253:27
  s. writer is always a bloody owl 169:15
Solicitor: s.s are lawyers trying to be gentlemen
    265:23
Solid: s. as echo 303:2
  s. for fluidity 79:10
Soliloquy: s. is likely to be affected 234:13
  television is a form of s. 83:10
Solipsist: artist . . . is by nature a s. 256:23
Solitaire: s. . . .demands . . . honesty 400:1
Solitary: even more s. 140:11
  man is not a s. animal 328:9
  s. confinement inside our own skins 404:18
  s. laugh is often a laugh of superiority 154:4
  s. mister 369:4
Solitude: guardian of his s. 319:17
  race which has . . . disturbed its s. 23:17
  resonance of his s. 87:13
  s. is not very likely 218:17

struggles with his own s. in mystery 224:6
toilet is the seat of the s. 73:12
unless s. clap its hands 417:10
where is your s. gone, where? 379:6
while there is a s. in prison 102:6
wonderful mine of s.s 319:3
Sound: articulate sweet s.s together 415:6
music . . . is sheer s. 29:15
s. of music 160:15
s. of my own voice 279:15
's.' finance may be right psychologically 207:6
Soundproofing: s. your m. 324:15
Soup: clear s. was a more important factor 332:8
s. for lunch 316:17
source of his or her kind of s. 174:11
stuff that moves is s. 353:3
Sour: s. grapes and ashes 15:8
Source: s. of his or her kind of soup 174:11
South: bible-ridden white S. 8:13
go s. in the winter 118:1
if you went to the S. Pole 39:18
s. of the border 204:13
South Africa: not force people in S. 47:10
South African: S. Police . . . even terror of their
lives 342:10
Souvenirs: s. sont cors de chasse 13:2
Sovereign: do not aspire to advise my s. 393:20
thick, brassy and wanted to be a s. 308:19
Soviet: four problems with S. agriculture 11:5
patriotism to the S. State 378:8
reply of a S. artist to just criticism 347:7
Soviet Union: S. as a breakaway organization
10:14
twenty years ago in the S. 368:12
Sow: silk purse out of a s.'s ear, but 164:17
Soya: gigantic field of s. beans 360:9
Space: attempt to fill an empty s. 29:11
captured fume of s. 94:27
clears a s. for us 307:8
design is determined S. 303:25
fence with s.s you could look through 269:7
for tribal man s. was the . . . mystery 244:16
from s. the planet is blue 403:23
lack of s. counterbalanced 53:9
more s. where nobody is 357:9
most important s. is between the ears 14:4
one advantage over Time and S. 304:20
range of human societies in . . . s. 232:7
relation of s. to time 308:13
shining s. with the grave's narrowness 151:25
s. composition 38:1
s.s between the houses 124:1
two objects cannot occupy the same s. 261:15
unvanquished s. 94:28
within a s. and a wearywide s. 197:14
Spaceship: passenger on the s., Earth 137:11
Spaghetti: lonely while eating s. 270:1
Spain: in S., the priests ruled 87:1
like slow old tunes of S. 253:27
one has arrived in S. 68:15
Spam: wanted steak and they offered s. 247:21

Span: flung the s. on even wing 94:29
grasped the skies in a s. 74:25
Spaniard: every S. is like a man-of-war 52:6
S.s . . . are a people separate 270:6
Spaniel: turn a s. into a Rottweiler 166:16
Spanish: cradle of S. walnut 299:24
S. five minutes 31:23
S. is seldom spoken 125:15
some are fond of S. wine 254:1
Spare: brother, can you s. a dime? 161:16
home, James and don't s. the horses 172:6
hypocrisy . . . practised at s. moments 256:8
time to s. from company 162:20
Spark: s.s blown out of a smithy 417:16
Spark-gap: s. is mightier than the pen 176:6
Sparkle: eighty-year-old lady with a s. 114:5
Sparkled: s. mineral sphere 106:4
Sparrow: brawling of a s. 417:21
enough . . . to feed the s.s 139:10
old king to the s. 103:19
see a s. fall to the ground 283:4
Speak: s. and proclaim 318:18
s. softly and carry a big stick 323:6
s.-your-weight machine and a whoopee-cushion
232:4
there was no one to s. up 280:5
whereof one cannot s. 408:9
Speaking: Englishman's way of s. 230:17
talking without s. 348:1
Spearmint: does the s. lose its flavour 323:18
Special: still want to be s. 152:18
Specialism: his s. is omniscience 109:18
Specialist: s. – . . . knows more and more 257:20
Speciality: my s. is being right 345:34
Specializing: something has been s. 262:1
Species: female of the s. is more deadly 210:18
one s. I wouldn't mind seeing vanish 36:7
Specific: I should have been more s. 389:2
s. pairing we have postulated 95:8
Specimen: bring a s. of your money 253:9
Spectator: got instead? The S. 350:9
Spectral: art is s. analysis 217:5
s. dance, before the dawn 54:17
Spectre: s. of Communism 366:3
Speech: everybody favours free s. 56:4
freedom of s. and expression 322:23
freedom of s. . . . and prudence 380:1
her face in s. 191:3
I have never delivered a firebrand s. 173:8
if you want a s. made 367:19
monkeys . . . refrain from speech 150:12
most precious things in s. 317:9
poet is carried away by s. 379:7
s. a vain average would make 192:15
s. . . . . stratagem to cover nakedness 299:3
Speeches: from all the easy s. 74:24
have its old s. burnt 352:5
s. two pages too long 366:11
Speechless: s. evil 17:8
Speechlessness: columns to express its s. 78:19
Speed: metaphors of s. 65:2

Station: it isn't that sort of station 312:22
   not the same people who left that s. 117:7
   that would have been above my s. 248:16
Stationmaster: duped – the s. 244:7
   s. on a small country branch line 41:6
Statistically: s. it is not likely 302:10
Statistician: approached by the s. 130:16
   s.s . . . have never kept the score 372:8
Statistics: feed the hungry on s. 235:14
   lies damned lies and s. 379:19
   my facts are just s. 239:19
   one of the leading causes of s. 215:14
   proved by s. . . . cause was just 18:20
   s. show . . . the habit of eating 187:14
   two kind of s. 361:21
   unless s. lie 97:16
   uses s. as a drunken man 220:11
Statue: finest s. of a man 66:21
   no s. . . . put up to a critic 347:9
   s. inside every block of stone 286:14
   S. of Bigotry 314:19
   s., tolerant through . . . weather 40:4
   worth a million s.s 97:9
Stature: advance in the s. of man 80:11
Status quo: restore the s. 355:23
Stay: behind my tremulous s. 162:5
   s., thou unhappy one 103:23
   s. longer in an hour 180:13
   that which s.s give us 319:8
   to s. as they are, . . . to change 220:1
   why did they s. so long? 40:7
Stay-at-home: sweet s. 100:15
Stayed: number two [wife] s. 247:7
Steady: S. the Buffs 214:19
Steak: s. and they offered spam 247:21
   smell of s.s in passage ways 117:34
   when you've got s. at home 279:19
Steal: each year more than he s.s 279:14
   good composer . . . s.s 362:18
   mature poets s. 119:6
   s. from many it's research 267:1
   s. milk through the fence 48:21
Stealing: for de big s. 285:2
Stealthily: s. like a parson's damn 163:24
Steam: sing the Song o' Steam 211:28
Steam-roller: gallant sailors on a s. 350:5
Steamer: all you big s. 209:22
   daily the s.s slide 17:6
   s.s made an excursion to hell 305:15
Steed: arm-chair for my s. 65:2
Steel: thou set breath in s. 94:29
   wounded surgeon plies the s. 117:1
Steeper: always s. . . . going up 154:25
Steeple: s.s far and near 179:20
Steerage: s. passengers report 83:12
Steered: s. into haven 198:19
Stein: I don't like the family S. 9:24
Stencilled: directly s. off the real 353:10
Stendhal: fought two draws with Mr S. 169:13
Step: one s. forward; two s.s back 228:14
   one small s. for [a] man 14:5

Sterbe: *was wirst du tun, Gott, wenn ich s.?* 319:15
Stereoscopic: s. view of a character 393:22
Sterility: pneumatic s. of Milton 119:17
Sterilize: power to s. 99:5
Stern: s. is sinking 83:12
Stewart, Jimmy: S. for governor 391:9
Stewed: get s., books are . . . crap 221:13
Sthruttin': s. . . . like a paycock 284:1
Stick: don't let it s. out 284:14
   he meant us to s. it out 216:14
   my little s. of Blackpool rock 130:4
   nothing s.s to him 339:2
   on wid the s. 151:6
   speak softly and carry a big s. 323:6
   s.s nix hick pix 347:13
Stiff-necked: s. Glasgow beggar 212:2
Stifle: ways which don't s. the spirit 255:9
Stigma: any s. . . . will serve 156:3
Still: always nearer by not keeping s. 156:21
   s. point of the turning world 116:26
Stilt: processions that lack high s.s 416:15
Stimulate: s. the phagocytes 343:7
Stimulated: looks down on airships when s.
   170:10
Stimulus: truth, . . . is only a s. 335:13
Stipple: s. leaves with sun 331:6
Stir: immanent will that s.s and urges 162:10
Stirred: down in the forest something s. 348:4
   shaken and not s. 128:20
Stirring: s. suddenly from long hibernation 151:19
   s. up complacency 402:2
Stirrup-pump: s. can extinguish hell 314:8
Stitching: s. . . . has been naught 415:5
Stoat: world of rabbits ruled by s.s 287:9
Stockings: her last good pair of s. 72:5
Stockpile: s.s enough socks 164:18
Stoic: self-pitying s. 104:18
Stole: s. everything but the cameras 311:5
Stolen: s. his wits away 102:21
Stolid: He looked s. He said little 81:1
Stomach: armies used to march on their s.s 341:7
   encounter on an empty s. 409:11
   healthy s. is . . . conservative 61:14
   her s. thinks her throat is cut 326:13
   man is not . . . a kind of walking s. 287:8
   worship . . . on an empty s. 406:16
Stone: bed beneath this s. 383:6
   break s.s like an old pauper 415:6
   give them s.s 398:19
   hand of s. on your white breastbone 70:19
   I asked for bread and was given s. 95:9
   seventy years of s. 368:18
   shrivel up at once and turn to s. 300:9
   stained s.s kissed by the English dead 288:20
   statue inside every block of s. 286:14
   s. from s. and wash them 118:24
   threw words like s.s 355:2
   throw s.s at him [Shakespeare] 346:2
   turns you like them to s. 365:9
Stone Age: bomb them back into the S. 228:10
Stone-deaf: bigot is a s. orator 143:8

Stone-like: naked and s. 133:7
Stoned: prophets were twice s. 269:16
Stony: more s. than a shore 404:25
Stood: I should of s. [have stayed] in bed 188:4
  only s. up to sleep 264:1
Stop: as soon as one approaches your s. 91:3
  s.; look; listen 383:4
  s. me and buy one 3:22
  s. the world. I want to get off 279:3
  s.s like an electric clock 373:6
Stopped: I s., I looked and I listened 320:8
Stopping: I'm not s. 300:2
Storage: thought in s. 334:11
Store: divided like a hundredfold s. 319:4
  owe my soul to the company s. 376:15
Storesmen: created them to be s. 140:14
Storey: one s. higher 223:9
Stories: all good s. have a coarse touch 164:3
  all s. . . . begin with the end 38:10
  man . . . lives surrounded by his s. 336:6
  only in s. or pictures 379:6
Stork: figuration of s.s 389:8
  kept the s. 398:16
  reads s.s instead of stocks 134:5
  throwing rocks at the s. 253.5
Storm: before the s.s 17:20
  in s. the shafting broken 101:20
Story: ere their s. die 163:1
  every picture tells a s. 3:8
  it's an old s. – f's for s's 152:7
  most interesting thing about any s. 360:13
  no poem is ever written for its s. line 53:12
  novel tells a s. 130:9
  place where a s. ended 117:9
  Short S. Conference with God 1:4
  s. follows 374:17
  s. is like the wind 386:7
  s. line accepted on Monday 234:21
  s. that owns us and directs us 1:6
  s. . . . the world is not yet prepared 109:17
  s. with a bad moral 164:3
Stove-lid: reddened like s.s 167:4
Straight: how s. he can stand 373:5
  Roman road runs s. and bare 163:12
  stand as s. as a pin 70:19
Straightener: s.s, managers and cashiers 61:5
Straightfaced: s. in his cunning sleep 369:25
Straightforward: simple s. minds 50:21
Strait laced: s. prune faced bunch 251:10
Straitjacket: all be put in s.s 404:23
Strand: I walk down the S. with my gloves 164:14
  let's all go down the S. 70:12
Strange: stranger in a s. land 168:2
Stranger: express themselves to s.s 49:6
  I, a s. and afraid 178:22
  kindness of s.s 404:22
  less danger from the wiles of the s. 277:13
  look, s., at this island now 17:23
  never fight fair with a s. 261:21
  no right to cry in s.s' houses 250:4
  s. across a crowded room 160:16

s. in a strange land 168:2
  tell whether a s. is your friend 130:24
  who is the smiling s. 70:18
Strangling: s. in a string 179:15
Strapping: on of those s. florid girls 332:11
Stratagem: constant s. to cover nakedness 299:3
Strategist: position to be s.s 38:13
Strategy: million [hostages] it's s. 341:21
  s. is nothing but tactics 196:16
Stratford-on-Avon: S. trades on Shakespeare 59:6
Strauss, Franz-Josef 14:13
Strauss, Richard 29:14
  for S. the composer 375:20
Stravinsky, Igor: S.'s music used to be original
  279:4
Straw: bricks with ephemeral s. 64:12
  s. vote . . . which way the hot air 170:17
  you'll sleep on s. 73:17
Strawberries: wild boys innocent as s. 369:5
Strawberry: roughly that of s. mousse 67:16
  teach you how to make s. jam 266:4
Stream: dark-lit s. has drowned the Future 370:8
  murmur of underground s.s 17:18
  only dead fish swim with the s. 272:19
Streamline: Tangerine Flake S. Baby 411:16
Street: all s.s are theatres 44:21
  call a s. lamp a minor plant 251:25
  finest women who ever walked the s.s 398:17
  inability to cross the s. 412:21
  power lying in the s. 13:14
  s.s are so clean 6:18
  s.s full of water 35:3
  s.s of heaven have all been sold 157:2
  sunny side of the s. 124:14
  talking at s. corners to scorning men 386:8
  we shall fight in the s.s 79:15
  worth two in the s. 397:21
Streetcar: s. named desire 404:19
Strength: feeling of s. in reserve 297:9
  full of the s. of five 40:16
  ignorance is s. 286:23
  my s. and my weakness 290:10
  necessary s. and no defences 146:12
  s. through joy 233:20
Strenuous: doctrine of the s. life 323:5
Stress: reality is the leading cause of s. 389:1
  s. on not changing his mind 256:16
Stretch: s. out our arms further 126:20
Stretched: things which he s. 379:16
Stretcher: greatest s. in the world 110:16
Stride: s. in the twentieth century 341:24
Striding: shadow . . . s. behind you 118:2
Strife: in place of s. 70:11
Strike: s. against the public safety 90:6
  s. it [a child] in anger 344:32
String: chewing little bits of s. 32:12
  I'll s. along with you 110:22
  s. the pearls were strung on 190:14
  whisper music on those s.s 118:16
Stringed: s. instruments' fingerboard 172:10
Striped: gaiety is a s. shroud 370:24

Strive: I did not shrink, I did not s. 254:5
Stroke: at a s. . . . reduce unemployment 89:17
   none so fast as s. 85:17
   s. its back and it turns vicious 187:3
   s. the heads of people 229:5
Stroking: s. a cat . . . a carnal sin 371:10
Stroll: s.s emitting minute grins 97:5
   who s.s so late 300:7
Strong: errors of those who think they are s. 42:5
   excellence of the s. man 46:8
   only the s. shall thrive 341:19
   s. and shadeless days 212:30
   s. as a monkey's tail 113:1
   s. enough to win a war 195:14
   still going s. 3:3
   you realize how s. she is 313:12
Stronger: young get s. 270:7
Strongminded: s. around a President 315:2
Strop: mind's a razor on the body's s. 273:14
Struck: collected . . . its strength and s. 179:1
   s. a direct blow by a rabbit 70:8
   s. regularly, like gongs 94:5
Structuralism: theme defeats s. 146:10
Structure: s. of the . . . British sentence 80:19
Struggle: after you cease to s. 124:2
   not the triumph but the s. 93:8
   s. against death 171:17
   s. . . . between education and propaganda 57:12
Strumpet: half some sturdy s. 163:4
Strut: he s.s sitting down 113:2
Stucco: sauntering past a s. gate 300:7
Student: notice the existence of s.s 276:6
Stuff: right s. 411:18
   s. of life to knit me 179:19
Stuffed: we are the s. men 117:16
Stumbling-block: s.s in a girl's education 86:4
Stupid: not equally s. in all directions 34:7
   s. enough to want it [money] 77:19
   s. man doing something he is ashamed of
     342:25
   s. neither forgive nor forget 364:6
   sincere unless you are also s. 345:7
   very interesting . . . but s. 195:9, 325:15
   you can stay s. in a village 386:17
Stupidest: undoubtedly the stupidest 19:16
Stupidity: organ in which s. is 308:12
Stupor: dozed off into a s. 34:18
Sturdy: s. legs were flannel-slacked 40:14
Stuttering: s. rifles' rapid rattle 288:14
Style: alpha and omega of s. 344:3
   compression is the first grace of s. 268:18
   he [God] has no real s. 297:8
   made habitable by s. 311:2
   s. is just the outside of content 145:9
   s. is knowing what sort of play 143:20
   s. of most artists and all humbugs 87:16
   s. slaps you in the face 83:20
   s. . . . too often hides eczema 65:7
Su-superior: sucked in by the s. 222:17
Subject: my s. is war 288:13
   odd thought on some great s. 195:5

three most perennially popular s.s 91:18
   who brought the subject up first? 353:5
Sublimated: s. . . . into sexual activity 48:18
   s. spiritualism 353:9
Sublime: most s. noise 130:14
   one vulgar and the other s. 335:5
   s. in the old sense 303:13
Sublimity: his style touches s. 118:26
Submarine: we all live in a yellow s. 230:10
Subscription: club to which we owe our s. 77:23
Subservience: man [is ruined] by s. 171:14
Subsidized: divinely s. to provoke 136:24
Substantive: s.s from the adjectives 246:19
Substitute: no s. for a rich man 172:1
   no s. for sense 118:19
   no s. . . . for the force 191:9
Subtle: God is s. but he is not malicious 115:11
   s. in the Australian character 400:11
Subtleties: s. of the American joke 380:3
Subtopia 277:4
Suburb: s.s in search of a city 292:20
Suburban: drone of mowers on s. lawns 317:15
   protective . . . shell of . . . s. man 245:3
Suburbia: I come from s. 312:10
Subway: Baghdad-on-the-S. 170:7
   into the s. without using anybody's name
     291:17
   on the s. walls and tenement halls 348:2
   one look at the rush-hour jam in the s. 82:24
   perspective of a s. tunnel 375:14
Succeed: not enough to s. 387:19
   relish . . . for anything that doesn't s. 262:13
   you don't s., try again. Then quit 125:8
Success: as difficult to overcome s. 390:17
   bitch-goddess S. 191:20
   black the boots of s. 97:8
   New Testament . . . howling commercial s.
     153:18
   no s. like failure 113:16
   nothing succeeds like the appearance of s.
     221:24
   owed his lack of s. to nobody 168:6
   place where s. comes before work 337:11
   s. is paralysing only to those 402:20
   s. or failure in competitive activities 287:12
   sweet smell of s. 227:23
   their s. is the first to go 87:15
   when s. happens to an English writer 8:6
   worst part of having s. 260:15
   yours [religion] is S. 26:19
Successful: as a novelist he was almost s. 125:26
   s. but it fell on the wrong planet 50:19
Succession: mere rules of s. 401:8
Such: s. as she was, s. has she become 135:13
Suck: writers started to s. up to them 393:23
Sucker: good enough for them, the s.s 152:7
   hello, s. 156:10
   never give a s. an even break 125:1
Sudden: this is so s. 15:9
Sudetenland: [S.] is the last . . . claim 173:13
Sued: publish and be s. 186:26

Suez: S. Canal . . . through my drawing room
    115:1
  ship me somewhere east of S. 211:33
Suffer: artist cannot s. alone 204:3
  'I love', 'I hate', 'I s.' 412:6
  man who s.s and the mind which creates 119:5
  psychotic if he makes others s. 364:8
  s. what is insufferable 172:11
  smile out; but still s. 162:14
  to s. in one's whole self 224:20
  you don't have to s. to be a poet 83:1
Suffered: s. under rump and dozen 198:19
Sufferer: s.s suffer at the same rate 33:26
Suffering: about s. they were never wrong 18:2
  adolescence is enough s. 83:1
  eighteen is a good time for s. 146:12
  pity for the s. of mankind 328:1
  s. . . . makes men petty and vindictive 256:14
  Sole meunière. . . . untouched by s. 360:11
  you can't avoid s. 91:1
Suffice: s.s us for God 151:10
Suffolk: S. used to worship Sunday 44:18
Suffrage: universal s. . . . leads to . . . bribery 186:3
Suffragette: s.s were triumphant 50:4
Sugar: blood, dirt and sucked s. stick 418:4
Suggestion: would have been ten s.s 49:20
Suicide: hearing of the latest s. 114:5
  I want to commit s. 359:9
  if one denies there are grounds for s. 65:27
  I've thought about s. 6:29
  never murder . . . a s. 406:23
  s. kills two people 261:14
  s. remains the courageous act 153:14
  s. to be abroad 28:13
  s. twenty-five years after his death 28:9
  s. was invading the prerogative 104:3
  without the possibility of s. 83:2
Suit: it was the wrong s. 69:4
  would not have chosen a s. by it 78:10
  your price shall s. everybody 161:11
Suitcase: a damn whose s.s are better 333:13
  s. full of clothes and underwear 173:3
Sullen: your new-caught s. peoples 213:17
Sulphur: puffed its s. to the sunset 40:15
Sum: inverse proportion to the s. involved 293:5
  saved the s. of things for pay 179:6
Sum-total: s. of our vital possibilities 285:16
Sumatra: giant rat of S. 109:17
Summer: hot the scent is of the s. rose 151:8
  I drank s. like a sweet wine 13:9
  it's all right in the s. time 274:19
  Long Hot S. 123:5
  lost from the robe of a careless s. 170:2
  now the peak of s.'s past 101:18
  oldest griefs of s. 317:15
  some of us have to go to s. school 105:11
  s. afternoon . . . most beautiful words 191:10
  s. all the year round 286:15
  s. talk stopped 17:20
  stood there then in the s. noon 369:12
  winter's big with s. in her womb 331:7

your English s.'s done 211:21
Summertime: in s. on Bredon 179:20
  s. and the living is easy 142:21
Sumo: s. wrestlers, plush with . . . flesh 341:22
Sun: at the going down of the s. 43:2
  black s. has appeared 413:17
  born of the s. 355:1
  break in the s. till the s. breaks 368:19
  glory of the s. will be dimmed 23:17
  golden apples of the s. 417:20
  how do you find the s., ladies 97:11
  I will sing of the s. 303:11
  kiss of the s. for pardon 156:24
  laughed in the s. 54:14
  left the s. on all day 243:18
  light breaks where no s. shines 369:8
  move him into the s. 288:19
  never loved the frenzy of the s. 206:19
  only you . . . under the s. 302:3
  out in the midday s. 94:13
  people who carry their own s. 137:7
  place in the s. 403:9
  sheriff s. and rustler moon gamble 260:12
  so punctual, you could regulate the s. 136:26
  S. – . . . a gap in the market 3:31
  s. moves always west 179:14
  s. never sets on Government House 94:14
  s. shone, having no alternative 28:23
  s. was laughing sweetly 416:11
  s. . . . is not a ball of flaming gas 224:24
  s.'s gonna shine in my back do' 196:15
  thank heavens, the s. has gone in 351:2
  that shall cut off the s. 101:16
  that s.'s hot 262:19
  unregulated s. 54:16
  we are old and the s. is going down 351:13
  why the s. isn't shining any more 288:5
Sundae: first mouthful of hot fudge s. 265:14
Sunday: another woman's S. gone 64:2
  bugger S. 44:18
  calm S. that goes on and on 128:8
  each S. snaps us from above 151:1
  feeling of S. 316:4
  God made Boston on a wet S. 72:19
  here of a S. morning 179:21
  like a library on S.s 14:14
  nothing but S.s for weeks on end 174:6
  on S. I walk out with a soldier 407:8
  [S. evening trains] are full 281:6
  S. paper . . . for kite flying 35:2
  Suffolk used to worship S. 44:18
  took you off the streets on a S. morning 31:9
  untidy S, throng 40:4
  what to do . . . on a rainy S. 121:4
Sunday-school: at S. I was always in demand
    181:18
  not s. words 380:17
  nowt'll replace . . . well run S. 155:19
Sundial: mottoes on s.s 303:14
Sung: I have s. women in three cities 303:11
Sunk: we're all s. 359:5

Sunlight: paint s. on the side of a house 178:1
  she's somewhere in the s. strong 227:21
Sunlit: I saw the s. vale 44:12
Sunny: s. side of the street 124:14
  they called him S. Jim 161:9
  we'll meet again some s. day 59:18
Sunrise: had seen their s. pass 74:8
  submerged s. of wonder 75:23
Sunset: Autumn s.s exquisitely dying 183:18
  puffed its sulphur to the s. 40:15
  red sails in the s. 204:11
  s. mistaken for a dawn 102:9
  s.s, they're so romantic, so operatic 308:11
Sunshine: artist's job to create s. 322:4
  smile is like s. on putty 124:10
Super: s. powers 131:19
Super-Mac: introducing S. 387:2
Supercalifragilisticexpialidocious 106:17
Superhuman: between beast and s. 338:6
Superior: s. people never make long visits 268:16
  s. persons can remain s. 286:30
  s. to that upon which he depends 53:22
  titles . . . embarrass the s. 344:31
Superiority: laugh of s. 154:4
Superlative: not settled the s. 76:10
Supernatural: nothing to the s. sense 356:2
Superstar: s.s . . . more famous than God 312:19
Superstition: democracy a s. and a fetish 186:1
  s. to enslave a philosophy 186:11
Supplementary: s. person 307:3
Support: for s. rather than illumination 220:11
  help and s. of the woman I love 115:7
  s. whatever the enemy opposes 250:12
Supporter: victim and a s. of the system 283:14
Suppose: s. that we . . . came to an end 101:20
Supposing: s. I had gone to the country 23:10
Suppressed: sex s. will go berserk 121:16
Suppressing: s. the resistance 356:5
Suppression: accuracy of s. 33:20
  smug s.s of his face 397:1
Supramundane: s. mushroom 222:10
Supreme: reverence . . . for a S. Being 168:14
Surdité: sa s. ruée contre la clameur du jour 71:6
Sure: what nobody is s. about 33:6
Surged: silence s. softly backward 103:13
Surgeon: wounded s. plies the steel 117:1
Surprise: learn to receive further s.s 185:7
  s. even those who have seen furthest 174:19
  you're sure of a big s. 204:12
Surprised: lady, if s. by melancholy 360:15
Surrealist: theatre of the s. body 37:20
Surrender: we shall never s. 79:15
Surround: universe and all that s.s it 89:22
Surrounded: s. by . . . his fellows 375:21
Surrounding: I am I plus my s.s 285:13
Surveyor: as painters, not as s.s 307:16
  we have no need of a Land S. 200:6
Survival: mathematics is greater than . . . s.
  153:14
  without victory there is no s. 79:14
Survive: Lord s. the rainbow of His will 238:11

s. in cracks . . . that's us 136:9
  what will s. of us is love 221:4
  yet love s.s 151:11
Susceptible: everything is s. 247:8
Susie: shirts for soldiers Sister S. sews 399:5
Suspect: always worse than most people s. 280:4
  s.s himself of . . . cardinal virtues 126:15
Suspected: s. of stealing an umbrella 130:15
Suspended: dust in the air s. 117:9
Suspension: act of s., a charm 363:11
Suspicion: democracy is the recurrent s. 400:8
  people under s. are better moving 200:13
  s. of one's motives 328:6
  usually has his s.s 267:4
Suspicious: s. of guilt in myself 169:4
Sussex: S. by the sea 213:2
Sustain: both s.s and kills – like a God 342:4
Suzanne: S. takes you down to her place 85:13
Swagman: once a jolly s. camped 293:11
Swallow: believes in giraffes would s. anything
  265:15
  just don't s. it 340:10
  s.s twisting here and there 418:19
Swallowing: by not s. the [pins] 267:18
Swamp: why you decided to drain the s. 196:4
Swan: marry a s. 121:3
  old ships sail like s.s asleep 128:15
Swayed: O body s. to music 115:10
  s. by their own passions 377:10
Swear: by the time you s. you're his 291:14
  I s. before the dawn 416:7
  money doesn't talk, it s.s 113:13
Swear-word: foreign s. . . . is inoffensive 368:16
  interpolate s.s like roses 246:8
  s. in a rustic slum 30:6
Swearing: s. properly in any language 120:9
Sweat: blood, toil, tears and s. 79:13
  s. of their browbeating 182:1
  weak with s.s of death 288:23
Sweating: quietly s. palm to palm 183:17
Sweaty: s. feet seldom come singly 51:15
Sweep: lie on a sofa than s. beneath it 89:14
Sweet: pink s. filled with snow 102:7
  so s. and so cold 404:28
  s. smell of success 227:23
  s. stay-at-home, s. well-content 100:15
  where the leaves drip with s. 348:20
Sweet-smelling: s. virgins close to them 358:14
Sweetes': s li'l' feller 356:13
Sweetness: prove the s. of a shower 370:17
Swell: money like that and not s. out 396:20
  what a s. party this is 302:5
Swerve: from s. of shore to bend of bay 197:8
Swift-terror: s. on the dark 133:7
Swim: because I cannot s. 103:31
  only dead fish s. with the stream 272:19
  s. in a nineteenth century dress 341:24
Swimming: writing is s. under water 127:24
Swimming-pool: I really don't deserve a s. 315:9
  mosaic s. age 84:17
  we all piss in the s. 201:11

Swindle: simple as all truly great s.s 170:12
Swindling: succeeded . . . in s. themselves 139:8
Swine: false pearls before real s. 115:4
   s. to show you where the truffles are 5:1
Swing: s. me suddenly into the shade 55:9
   we pulls up on the s.s 71:12
   would you like to s. on a star 59:16
Swinger: s. of the birches 135:6
Swinging: s. door which allows us 320:16
Swiss: if the S. had designed these mountains
    368:9
   like the way a S. waiter talks 72:13
   S. . . . are not so much a people 123:1
   S. have sublimated their sense of time 195:8
   S. managed to build a lovely country 260:17
   somebody else's S. cheese 126:7
   where the administrators are S. 9:23
Switch: lightbulb that cannot s. itself off 91:6
   shame more people don't s. over 299:7
Switzerland 92:1, 361:5
   Austria is S., speaking pure German 270:2
   in S. they had brotherly love 395:12
   no one who hates . . . S. 351:5
S. . . . where very few things begin 127:6
Swoon: wearied band s.s to a waltz 183:17
Sword: bank was mightier than the s. 300:5
   believed he had a s. upstairs 415:9
   honour and the s. 74:24
   Islam . . . came with a s. 326:10
   s. into assorted villains 152:23
   wit is like a s. 271:19
Sword-light: s. in the sky flashed 133:7
Sword-pen: against this I raise my s. 58:19
Swore: love we s. would last 101:18
Syllable: s.s all over 'em 91:17
Syllogism: conclusion of your s. 283:7
Symbol: we need s.s to protect us 45:16
Sympathies: cosmopolitan s. 324:9
   personalize your s. 186:8
Sympathy: failed to inspire s. in men 30:20
   machine-gun riddling . . . with s. 182:25
   no need of your God-damned s. 413:6
   tea and s. 8:12
Symphony: a s. must be like the world 247:6
   philanthropy and s. concerts 399:17
Synagogue: s. of the ear of corn 369:14
Synapses: upon whose s. the termites 173:2
Synthesis: arrives at a s. of both views 132:18
   s. of hyacinths and biscuits 335:1
Synthesiser: Joyce was a s. 29:9
System: polycentric s. 374:13
   what chance has man got against a s.?
    174:3

T

TTFN 203:9
TV 177:16
   feeling fom a T. set 141:19

from . . . Terrible Vaudeville 1:2
   intellection is to skip an hour's T. 8:5
   so much more interesting than T. 299:7
   they're imitating T. 200:3
   [TV] a medium because nothing's well done 1:2
   see also Television
Ta: painting is saying 'T.' to God 354:16
Ta-ra-ra-boom-de-ay! 337:20
Table: etherized upon a t. 117:21
   how's that for a t. lamp? 107:18
   never put on the t. of Demos 281:16
   not at t. if you please 301:10
   put his feet on the t. 119:19
Tablet: must keep taking the T. 370:25
Taboo: religious or semi-religious t.s 152:9
Tack: when you come to brass t.s 117:36
Tact: essential t. in daring 85:4
Tactics: strategy is nothing but t. 196:16
Tactile: t. values 38:1
Taft, President William H. 220:17
Tail: such a little t. behind 32:8
   thy t. hangs down behind 212:19
Tailing: t. against the morning 374:16
Take: I wanted to t. the little place 403:12
   t. it from me – he's got the goods 170:19
Talcum: a bit of t. is always walcum 277:8
   heavy fall of t. 295:6
Tale: man is always a teller of t.s 336:6
   most tremendous t. of all 40:9
   saddest t. told on land or sea 119:13
   t.s, marvellous t.s 128:7
   t.s told in dim Eden 102:18
Talent: Frenchmen to exhibit t. 95:25
   full of genius but . . . no t. 230:16
   genius without t. is *nothing* 385:8
   gilded tomb of a mediocre t. 350:20
   is there no beginning to your t.s? 8:9
   most extraordinary collection of t. 204:21
   our t.s and our expectations 46:13
   she's OK if you like t. 260:4
   t. instantly recognizes genius 110:11
   t. is what man possesses 11:3
   t. to amuse 93:12
   t. which does what it can 25:6
   very few who have a t. for it 358:9
   worm slumbering at the root of his t. 148:11
Talented: don't tell me how t. you are 326:6
Talk: careless t. costs lives 11:24
   elbow-room, with freedom of t. 190:10
   English t. is a quadrille 190:10
   fatigue makes women t. more 232:16
   fish that t.s in the frying pan 102:16
   I have to t. to myself 132:5
   I want to t. like a lady 345:16
   if you can t. with crowds 210:33
   kind of guy that wouldn't t. 333:12
   money doesn't t., it swears 113:13
   no healthy male ever . . . t.s 259:10
   nothing else to t. about 385:5
   small t. . . . was bigger 104:13
   so much more to t. about 399:21

t. brought down communism 175:5
t. is indistinguishable from magic 83:14
t. is not the mastery of nature 35:15
t. . . . knack of arranging the world 134:12
Tedium: bounded . . . on the west by t. 156:8
t. of the unrequiting 360:20
Teenage: t. sex-change priest 234:19
Teenager: London is a t. 38:15
t. . . . happy to hear . . . the phone 226:21
Teeth: blow in the t. of a wrong 254:6
born with natural false t. 321:2
dialectics, a kind of false t. 66:26
have three or four of my t. out 173:16
I wish I'd looked after me t. 20:10
lies in the shape of false t. 397:1
shark has pretty t. 51:20
t. like ships at sea 102:22
t. like splinters 70:20
t. like the Ten Commandments 377:2
take the bull between the t. 147:26
to lose one's t. is a catastrophe 399:23
women are like t. 367:11
Teetotaller: not a champagne t. 343:3
secret t. 287:5
t., arter four or five whiskies 188:6
Teflon-coated: T. presidency 339:2
Teich: fallen ein auf teilnahmslosen T. 318:4
Teléfono: contesta Tú el t. 67:12
Telegraph: T. is read by people who remember
3:31
t. one of my paintings to New York 297:15
Telephone: answer Thou the t. 67:12
black t.'s off at the root 299:21
mob cannot shout down a t. 77:18
no private rooms or t.s 39:11
t. directory is . . . a work of art 148:13
t. exchange without enough subscribers 399:4
t. is a cool medium 245:1
t. number. . . . in the high numbers 207:10
Telescope: spent the proceeds on a t. 135:20
Television 219:5
all the garbage is on t. 6:18
brought the brutality of war 245:3
creating . . . a closed-circuit t. 132:14
have to do magic on t. 395:15
it's t. . . . if you're not on 180:18
nearer a real grief than the t. news 202:18
Philo T. Farnsworth, inventor of t. 69:1
stay at home and see bad t. 147:7
[t.] a medium so called 217:2
t. . . . entertained in your living room 135:3
t. . . . half Greek and half Latin 340:1
t. has devalued politicians 294:11
t. is a form of soliloquy 83:10
t. is for appearing on 94:16
t. is more interesting than people 92:14
t. . . . stops . . . anything useful 341:25
t., the key to all minds 87:2
see also TV
Telford: cross between Singapore and T. 89:23
Tell: how could they t.? 292:4

t. them I came 103:12
wants to t. us about it 392:1
will inadvertently t. one much more 44:19
you never can t. 345:32
Tellable: time of the t. 318:18
Tellurian: indubitably t. 97:5
Temp: if . . . dictated them to a t. 281:12
Temper: truth that has lost its t. 143:9
Temperament: t. and not of income 350:12
Temperance: 'T. Hotel'.! . . . celibate kip 381:5
Temperature: air is blood t. 111:13
beauty at low t.s 53:15
Tempered: t. by war 204:16
Temple, Shirley: T. through gauze 24:10
Temple, Archbishop William 242:13
Temple: for the t.-bells are ringing 211:33
out of which they build t.s 217:24
Tempo: difference of t. 303:28
Temporary: I still feel – kind of t. 261:22
[suicide] . . . only a t. solution 6:29
Tempt: all who seek you t. you 319:13
do not t. us to invoke design 101:4
t. my Lady Poltagrue 32:34
things that are bad for me do not t. 342:15
though women t. you more than plenty 175:16
Temptation: I never resist t. 342:15
last t. is the greatest treason 118:23
maximum of t. 344:30
pride in being exempt from t. 232:17
t. came to him, in middle age 333:3
t. from the tree of knowledge 98:30
Ten: [songs] are about t. minutes long 113:25
they are only t. 281:17
Ten-pound: t. marshmallow 90:20
1066: 1066 and All That 340:21
Tenant: t.s of the house 117:14
Tender-minded: 't'. and 'tough-minded' 191:15
Tenement: subway walls and t. halls 348:2
Tennis: conversation is like playing t. 236:15
malice is like a game of . . . t. 355:8
not just involved in t. but committed 278:14
t. with the net down 136:7
Tennyson, Alfred, Lord: bower we shrined to T.
162:7
T. and Browning are poets 119:1
T. goes without saying 61:21
[T.] had the finest ear 19:16
Tent: inside my t. pissing out 195:20
Teppichfresser: T.! Animal that chews 11:4
Terminological: t. inexactitude 78:18
Terminus: or who will arrive at any t. 117:7
Termite: synapses the t.s have dined 173:2
Terra firma: t. – the more firma, the less terra
202:10
Terrace: stand on the white t. and confer 156:20
t.s of sound 267:13
Terrain: t. fit only for barbarians 137:14
Terre: nous resterons sur la t. 305:7
Terrible: t. to be bad 132:16
t. with raisins in it 291:22
Terrifying: life? There's nothing more t. 195:7

Territorial: last t. claim 173:13
Territory: it comes with the t. 261:26
  map is not the t. 216:21
  t. to retreat from 377:17
  t. where no one possesses the truth 218:10
Terror: even t. of their lives 342:10
  flame of incandescent t. 117:10
  from all that t. teaches 74:24
  life points only towards the t. 174:14
  no t. in a bang 172:15
  shot through with t. 407:2
  t. and panic you feel inside yourself 133:4
  t. celibans 148:4
  t. of St Trinians 340:6
  towns in t. 17:19
Terrorism: ten hostages is t. 341:21
Terrorist: starve the t. 367:21
  t.s end up . . . at the Dorchester 138:12
Test: t, the Russians not the bombs 138:9
Testament: we discussed the New T. 6:24
Texas: deep in the heart of T. 171:10
Text: listen instead to the wind's t. 371:2
  t. for sorrow 101:20
  thundering t. 151:21
Texte: il n'y a pas dehors texte 104:7
Textual: what if I am a t. deviant 37:23
Texture: t. of one's existence 216:11
Thais: T. . . . nicest people money can buy 153:2
Thames: every drop of the T. is liquid 'istory 59:21
  hunts south of the T. 316:17
  unmourning water of the riding T. 369:15
Thamesfontein: look after me in the T. 212:17
Thank: ay t. [thang] you 15:13
  no one to t. 390:19
  not please but t. you 106:5
Thanksgiving: with proud t. 43:1
That: and t. (said John) is t. 264:9
  goodbye to all t. 152:8
Thatcher, Margaret [later Lady] 4:9, 7:22, 14:17,
    44:13, 66:28, 70:10, 89:23, 96:5, 96:7,
    133:16, 144:23, 164:10, 166:14, 180:12,
    306:10, 398:21
  at least Mrs T. has got guts 209:5
  I like T.; she knows my own mind 64:1
  if T. is the answer . . . silly question 149:14
  one day Mrs T. comes to me 266:17
  [pound] should . . . be called the T. 308:19
  [T.] has the mouth of Marilyn Monroe 266:18
  T. is doing for monetarism 166:11
  [T.] is the best man in England 313:17
  T. may be a woman but she isn't a sister 10:17
  'we' . . . makes her [T.] feel less lonely 209:9
Thatcherism: T. . . . seeks to create a New
    Jerusalem 208:5
  T. was Toryism without regrets 209:11
Thaw: The T. 115:9
Thcream: t., an' t. till I'm thick 96:10
Theatre: all streets are t.s 44:21
  cinema has become . . . like the t. 103:29
  entry before the t. is built 47:7
  farce is the essential t. 94:25

go to the t. to be entertained 89:20
goes to the t. unless . . . bronchitis 4:5
in t. you are really jumping 274:12
in the t., the director is God 295:18
it [cricket] belongs with t. 189:20
resented . . . filing out of the t. 333:22
t. is like operating with a scalpel 63:10
t. is the best way of showing the gap 164:9
t. of his time 381:1
t. of the absurd set to music 350:7
t. . . . to take its audiences seriously 25:11
unable to pass a t. 189:4
Theatrical: t. whore 159:17
Theft: armed hot dog t.s 375:15
Them: we think them 304:20
Theme: infatuation a tragic t. 345:26
  narrow t. of love 417:19
  speaks on a t. that is timeless 105:17
  to leave great t.s unfinished 241:8
Themselves: demanding something for t. 352:9
  such good terms with t. 78:14
  take t. along 305:2
Theogony: God of some oriental t. 307:14
Theologian: put together by t.s 92:17
Theology: keep history and t. apart 397:5
  t. finds the cat 191:21
  t. is the act of concealment 274:10
Theory: experiment to the birth of a t. 116:8
  important for a t. to be shapely 160:19
  not a t. but an activity 408:6
  t. is often just practice 321:4
  third-rate t. explains after the event 215:4
Therapy: psychoanalysis . . . as a t. 217:15
  t. has become the tenth American muse 54:7
There: because it's t. 248:3
Thesis: commit no t. 215:13
They: everyone else is T. 213:13
  where t. leave off I begin 174:13
Thick: lay it on so t. 62:4
Thicker: history gets t. 366:2
Thief: said the joker to the t. 113:5
Thieves: one of the t. was saved 28:21, 360:12
Thievish: little picking t. hands 214:2
Thimble: t. lies cold and tarnished 349:7
Thin: enclosing every t. man 392:25
  never be too t. or too rich 407:11
  outside every t. woman 401:20
  so t. . . . recognized her skeleton 192:8
  t. man inside every fat man 286:14
  t. one wildly signalling 88:24
Thing: Graduated Hostility of T.s 193:18
  I do not believe in t.s 50:18
  the real t. 190:21
  transform a man into a t. 134:18
  t.s as they are are changed 358:13
  t.s could be otherwise 132:12
  what t.s think about men 193:17
Thingish: seemed very t. inside you 264:19
Think: do not t. what you want to t. 96:19
  easier to act than to t. 13:13
  fellows whom it hurts to t. 180:4

he can't t. without his hat 29:5
how can I know what I think 390:14
I exist by what I t. 336:9
I had to t. 320:15
I t. continually of those 354:21
improvise what I t. I t. I t. 361:19
inclined to t.. I should do so 110:9
inquire into what men t. 14:1
Irishman t.s afterward 285:1
it's what you t. you are 391:3
learn to t. imperially 71:14
man able to t. isn't defeated 218:19
man must t. o' things 211:26
never expect a soldier to t. 343:5
not so t. as you drunk I am 355:24
only t. talking 15:19
open my legs and t. of England 172:7
people who t. too much 352:7
something else with them besides t. 237:6
sometimes I t. and sometimes I *am* 385:21
sooner die than t. 329:5
t. by fits and starts 178:21
t. . . . exclusively of others 393:15
t. we t. 42:9
tendency to t. . . . mathematical 193:3
what the Bandar-log t. now 214:1
writing plays . . . you don't t. 299:2
ye are not paid to t. 211:27
Thinker: t.s . . . re-think 386:3
Thinking: Churchill liked t. aloud 46:3
draw a limit to t. 408:3
everything except our way of t. 115:15
excuse for t. hard 279:19
false t. brings wrong conduct 183:22
I can't prevent myself from t. 336:9
many people think they are t. 192:1
only happy when it was t. 264:21
only t. lays lads underground 180:1
perform without t. 401:5
power of positive t. 294:10
recording, not t. 187:15
says what everybody is t. 323:14
smell someone just t. about food 339:8
t. . . . by a very small number 203:15
t. their own thoughts 377:10
t. what nobody has thought 364:10
t. what you really think 144:5
think that by t. about t. 371:1
too much t. . . . is not becoming 276:16
war . . . was bound to start you t. 286:16
way of not t. 169:4
what people in portraits are t. 235:8
Third: close encounters of the t. kind 355:9
golf, cats, and the T. Reich 91:18
if there was a t. sex 385:4
sole entrant . . . he'd come t. 239:14
t. world 22:14
T. World never sold a newspaper 274:13
Third-class: in the t. seat sat the journeying boy
163:7
Third-rate: what in the world is t. 168:23

Thirst: an' a man can raise a t. 211:33
no wine so wonderful as t. 261:5
promoted t. without quenching 382:12
yet drinks the t. from pot lips 303:2
Thirsting: t. and hungering 151:15
Thirteen: when I was but t. or so 379:13
Thirtieth: my t. year to heaven 369:12
Thirty: and the next t. years 126:18
This: t. [tombstone] is on me 292:11
Thistle: sooner sleep in t.s 399:5
Thomas, St: T., . . . writing of incest 198:15
Thorn: oak and ash and t. 213:8
Thoroughbred: t. intelligence 413:2
Thoroughfare: rougher than t.s of stones 162:14
Thou: I and T. 57:11
Thought: archaeology of our t. 131:13
by which t. develops into action 4:15
censor one's own t.s 389:15
dark alleys of t. 276:15
does not seem a moment's t. 415:5
his t.s, few that they were 263:8
history of t. 86:10
hundred schools of t. contend 250:15
man whose second t.s are good 26:25
more a great t. than a great machine 193:2
more complex . . . than his t.s 385:20
my t. is me 336:9
only the T. Police mattered 286:22
original t. is like original sin 226:17
profoundest t.s in the simplest way 116:2
religion is the frozen t. of men 217:24
second t. is never an odd t. 283:9
smallest amount of t. 79:9
t. . . . conceived in an enormous room 83:6
t. in storage 334:11
t. is a man in his wholeness 222:25
t. is a Socialist temptation 276:16
t. is only a flash 300:15
t. it out with both hands 337:19
t. . . . leads to its own starting point 331:2
t.s as still as the water 64:17
t.s by England given 55:6
t.s of a dry brain 117:14
true t.s . . . do not understand themselves 2:20
walk through Reagan's deepest t.s 11:19
what must still be t. 167:17
who think what was t. before 386:3
Thousand: end of a t. years of history 138:11
Maconides . . . three t. years ago 128:19
t. lost golf balls 118:25
t. points of light 60:12
[women] are born three t. years old 103:27
Thread-paper: undone and worn to a t. 302:13
Three: although he was only t. 264:7
always t. o'clock in the morning 126:10
next Prime Minister but t. 32:19
other t. [feet] in the cash box 403:4
t. o'clock is always too late 336:5
t.-pipe problem 109:15
t. wise men – are you serious 149:35
though you're only t. 56:13

with Major Major it had been all t. 168:12
Threescore: now of my t. years and ten 179:11
Thresh: t. of the deep-sea rain 211:22
Threshold: t. of your own mind 143:4
Thrift: virtue called 't'. 371:9
  wealth decays, whatever T. may be doing 207:4
Thriller: t. is . . . twentieth-century form 56:3
Thriving: happy the great ones are t. 243:12
Throat: comes . . . to the cutting of t.s 397:10
  if your t. is hard to slit 208:17
  look out it doesn't cut your throat 295:9
  taking life by the t. 136:5
Throb: t. in witching chords 358:16
Throne: replaced the Altar and the T. 334:14
  t. from bayonets 418:11
  t. of bayonets 186:13
Through: best way out is always t. 136:2
Throw: you t. up every morning? 201:7
Throw-away: t. plastic packaging 107:23
Thrush: t.'s song in the thick bush 371:2
  what boy can sing as the t. sings? 260:11
Thrushes: t.' ancestors as sweetly sung 370:19
Thrust: mediocrity t. upon them 168:12
  rolls under the long t. of his heel 181:13
  t. ivrybody, but cut the ca-ards 111:21
Thumb: between my finger and my t. 166:19
  fingerprint . . . under someone's t. 25:1
  if you have any strength in your t. 314:10
  t. is born knowing 71:11
Thump: gods be said to t. the clouds 369:16
Thunder: clouds are cursed by t. 369:16
  purr myself to sleep with the t. 380:6
Thunderbolt: when struck by a t. 50:8
Thunderstorm: t. in my right ear 87:11
Thurber, James 167:8
  T. is the greatest unlistener 324:19
  T. wrote the way a child skips 400:10
Thursday: I do not love you T. 261:10
Thus: it were ever t. 128:14
Tiananmen Square, Beijing 413:17
Tiber: River T. foaming with much blood 304:12
Tick: bomb through the window, and it t.s 261:13
  not only t.s, he also chimes 373:6
  on t. – the t. of a time bomb 84:1
Ticket: donating kidneys to get t.s 360:19
  t. at Victoria Station 42:2
  t. to ride 230:7
  they don't sell t.s to the past 352:16
Ticking: I am the very t. 137:15
Tickled: how t. I am 107:17
  t. to death to go 399:7
Ticky-tacky: all made out of t. 315:19
Tidal wave: longed for t. of justice 166:18
Tiddely pom: nobody knows (T.) 264:15
Tide: blood-dimmed t. is loosed 417:12
  call of the running t. 254:11
  drew these t.s of men into my hands 225:3
  water of the heart push in their t.s 369:8
Tideless: t. waves struggled 68:13
Tie: see if your t. is straight 409:12
  struggle with . . . evening t. 40:20

t. that only death can sever 255:20
  when he buys his t.s he has to ask 127:10
Tier: das T., das es nicht gibt 319:10
Tiers: t. monde 22:14
Tiger: all reactionaries are paper t.s 250:13
  came Christ the t. 117:12
  defenceless against t.s 376:5
  put a t. in your tank 3:21
  riding on the back of a t. 204:17
  their halls arc lined with t. rugs 246:3
  vegetarian t. 217:19
Tigger: T.s don't like honey 264:16
Tight: old and terrified and t. 41:1
  played it in t.s 30:10
Tightrope: walk a t. safely 329:6
Tile: not even red brick, but white t. 288:3
Tim: poor tired T. 103:24
Timber: house with love for t. 261:9
  rising cost of t. 31:24
Timbuktu: recordings are for . . . T. 91:9
Time: as t. goes by 182:3
  bleeding to death of t. 151:9
  book to kill t. 241:5
  born at the wrong end of t. 400:17
  ever-flowing stream of t. 69:3
  fill the t. available 293:2
  find something to do with the t. 321:20
  gardener, t. 107:10
  haven't had t. to work in weeks 205:19
  He's right on time 10:7
  how t. could be reworded 389:9
  I . . . may be some t. 283:3
  if you want to know the t. 321:10
  in the city t. becomes visible 274:4
  [instant dislike] because it saves t. 230:24
  it means your t. is done 313:4
  killing t. – there's nothing else 238:7
  logic of our t.s 101:21
  new direction of t. 222:24
  no dividend from t.'s tomorrows 337:2
  notions of t. are vaguer than yours 305:18
  one advantage over T. and Space 304:20
  peace for our t. 71:19
  range of human societies in t. 232:7
  redeem the t. 116:21
  relation of space to t. 308:13
  rhythm is a form cut into T. 303:25
  same old druid t. as ever 324:8
  so conscious he how short t. was 260:10
  so it is with T. in one's life 307:2
  so little t. to do so much 322:24
  surplus of t. 53:9
  takes his t. before . . . anything else 170:8
  teaches the t. that we are living in 375:11
  that passed the t. 29:6
  throw t. into tins 313:5
  till t. and t.s are done 417:20
  t., you old gipsy man 175:13
  t. and motion clock 20:9
  t. can but make her beauty 416:9
  t. changing the plates 206:8

t. drops in decay 417:2
t. for a little something 265:5
t. for you to run out of me 388:12
t. forgets and never heals 354:20
t. future contained in t. past 116:23
t. held me green and dying 369:1
t. is the longest distance 404:17
t. looped so river-wise 152:3
t. mirrors in itself 401:10
t. of the tellable 318:18
t. . . . prevents everything 85:14
t. spent on any item of the agenda 293:5
t. to stand and stare 100:13
t. walks by your side 136:17
t. was away and somewhere else 246:10
t. was invented to kill the novelist 112:13
t. would pass 189:19
t. wounds all heels 253:22
t.'s deer is slain 273:7
T.'s most lethal weapon 349:8
t.'s winged chariot changing gear 234:16
to the gardener that t. is a friend 279:14
trains run to t. 11:8
use t. as a tool not as a couch 205:11
waiting t. . . . is the hardest t. 108:8
ways by which T. kills us 349:6
we haven't the t. to take our t. 187:4
when t. was open-eyed 238:10
who's got t. to keep up with the t.s? 113:26
Time-honoured: t. bread-sauce 191:6
Time-table: I would sooner read a t. 256:21
Timeless: speaks on a theme that is t. 105:17
t. home of the mind 331:2
Times: Financial T. is read 3:31
letters to *T.* about . . . the Corn Laws 30:29
T has published no rumours 360:3
T. is read 3:31
T. is speechless 78:19
Timid: I'm really a t. person 6:6
Tin: French cook, we open t.s 139:22
little t. gods on wheels 212:13
millions of t. cans clanking 246:7
only a t. full of people 262:18
throw time into t.s 313:5
Tinker: they don't matter a t.'s cuss 347:4
Tinkling: chime of words t. in the mind 351:7
t. silence thrills 212:30
Tinned: I'd have it t.. With vinegar 405:18
Tinsel: below the glitter, it's solid t. 147:18
laid on the t. in splotches 190:15
phoney t. off .. find the real t. 231:6
Tinted: in all his t. Orders 125:18
Tiomkin, Dimitri 334:3
Tip-and-run: watch him play t. 125:25
Tipperary: long way to T. 403:22
Tipple: French t. all the time 96:9
Tipster: t. . . . reached Hitler's level 366:5
Tiptoe: t. through the tulips 110:22
why did you keep me on t. so long 255:4
Tiptoed: we t. round each other 205:18
Tired: I'm t., send one of them home 398:11

one long process of getting t. 61:11
people like you make me feel so t. 270:9
poor t. Tim 103:24
pursuing, the busy, and the t. 126:16
t. of living, and scared of dying 160:14
too t. to yawn 103:24
walking round him has always t. me 31:1
your t. your poor I'll piss on them 314:19
Tisane: dipping it first in her . . . t. 306:12
Tissue: personal issue of adipose t. 93:15
Tit: audience . . . but a vast t.? 259:19
if you've got t.s 36:2
Titanic: furniture on the deck of the T. 271:21
T. seamanship 236:4
Title: friends could only read the t. 412:12
I love the t. 91:5
t.s distinguish the mediocre 344:31
Titled: allowed it [beauty] to t. women 336:14
Tito, Marshal: T. is always using the car 55:19
Toad: for the eye of t. or adder to catch 273:4
intelligent Mr T. 150 14
t. beneath the harrow knows 212:9
why should I let the t. work 221:17
Toast: t. and marmalade were made 193:18
Toasting: bird-cage played with t. forks 29:22
hold on to our t. forks 148:6
Toastmaster: bad-tempered t. 411:1
Tobacco: monograph on . . . tobacco 109:9, 110:3
Tod: den ganzen T. . . . zu enthalten 318:7
was im T. uns entfernt 319:6
Today: doubts of t. 323:4
I didn't get where I am t. 281:5
language, literature are always t. 53:20
they think about . . . another t. 336:10
Todd, Sir Garfield 374:11
Toddle: a trull before she could t. 351:20
Todlos: des 'T'., jenes bitteren Biers 319:2
Toe: warring country between his t.s 122:7
Together: how they got t. in the first place 128:25
in this t. by ourselves 375:9
state like that to hold t. 173:20
t. for ever and ever 369:30
Togetherness: spaces in your t. 143:6
Toil: blood, t., tears and sweat 79:13
Toilet: can't tear the t. paper 402:13
cheeks like . . . pink t. paper 398:20
police stations were like t.s 255:11
t. is the seat of the soul 73:11
Ulysses . . . read in the t. 262:7
you're like a pay t. 181:3
Toilet-flush: t. . . . finishes before you 57:3
Told: t. and did not kiss 266:5
Tolerable: means the business man is t. 206:17
Tolerance: forget . . . t. 406:24
Tolerant: t. through years of weather 40:4
Tolstoy, Leo 11:18
advised them not to read T.'s novels 352:17
get in any ring with Mr T. 169:13
Tom: names were T. or Thomas 188:11
t. looks like one of pluto's demons 251:11
Tomatoes: shiny stuff is t. 353:3

Tomb: in the cool t.s 334:16
  shot storms in the freezing t. 369:13
  this side of the t. 100:10
Tombstone: end of the fight is a t. white 212:7
  like my t. to be blank 390:20
  you may carve it on his t. 212:28
Tommy: it's T. this, an' T. that 213:6
Tommyguns: gangsters with hamfisted t. 243:17
Tomorrow: [ethics] may even constitute t. 53:20
  if I died t. 375:18
  it [poetry] might start t. 112:22
  less t. than it does today 143:19
  no dividend from time's t.s 337:2
  realization of t. 323:4
  shan't know till I get it t. 320:7
  shape all the singing t.s 295:12
  start again t. 112:20
  t. . . . is usually the same day 360:18
  t., more's the pity, away 179:8
  t. we will run faster 126:20
  they think about T. 336:10
  won't happen until t. 57:7
  word for doing things t. 342:22
  yesterday's cold mutton into t.'s lamb 256:4
Tongue: begin by cutting out his own t. 255:10
  does not always pay to have a golden t. 196:7
  give a little more t. to your cheek 312:14
  my t. is always in it [cheek] 284:10
  now with flattering t. 418:1
  sharp t. in your head 295:9
  your t. at the insurance doctor 251:5
Tonight: no more t. than a dream 370:8
  not t., Josephine 98:8
  t. shall find no dying 368:21
Took: 'e went an' t. – the same as me 213:16
Tool: give us the t.s 79:21
  use time as a t. not as a couch 205:11
  what shall we do with the t.s? 158:7
Tooth-decay: such phenomena as phlegm and t.
  168:14
Tooth-point: exactly where each t. goes 212:9
Toothache: fine young man with a bad t. 191:1
  for the sake of their t.s 106:7
  t.. Kind of dull and general 160:22
Toothbrush: could not purchase a t. 376:11
  t. which played 'Annie Laurie' 349:11
Toothpaste: below the t. 95:3
  t. out of the tube 159:11
Toothsome: t. amalgam of Americanisms 213:27
Top: by looking at the men at the t. 85:19
  it isn't important to come out on t. 51:3
  room at the t. 50:7
  started at the t. and worked . . . down 395:13
  you're the t.! 302:7
Toppling: nigh this t. reed 44:9
Torch: t. . . . to a new generation 204:16
Torero: t., the government, or a saint 314:7
Tories: T. are not always wrong 46:5
  T. . . . would win every election 354:11
Torment: t. men inflict on each other 144:6
Tormented: something to say are . . . t. 83:11

Tortoise: what it's like to be a t. 391:13
Tortoise-shell: the tap of her t. 190:2
Torture: behaviourism works. So does t. 18:31
  t.s called education 382:11
Tory: every Briton is at heart a T. 37:5
  small business in T. Britain 356:18
  T. childbirth 68:9
Toryism: thinking . . . not becoming to T. 276:16
  T. with regrets 209:11
Tosh: never have I read such t. 412:24
Total: t. solution of the Jewish question 146:3
Totem: t.-animal . . . substitute for the father 134:9
Totem: icon, a t., a curio 363:10
Toten: nah ist der Held . . . den jugendlich T. 318:11
Totter: President's answers t. forward 176:9
Touch: gently its t. awoke him once 288:19
  how anyone can say he is out of t. 109:5
  lose the t. of flowers and women's hands 66:2
  t. him when he doesn't want to be 25.20
  well, you shouldn't t. it 262:19
Toucher: ingratiating wheedle of the t. 231:19
Tough: when the going gets t. 205:3
Tough-minded: tender-minded and t. 191:15
Toujours: t. gai t. gai 251:3
  T. Lautrec 147:14
Tour: ni une t. ni une cathédrale 71:6
Tourism: political t. 53:24
  t. is their religion 326:9
Tourist: British t. is always happy abroad 269:18
  to give t.s something solid 92:1
Tower: their t.s of pleasure 318:9
Towering: compete with the t. dead 239:8
Town: little one-horse town 380:18
  never go down to the end of the t. 264:8
  old queen measuring a t. 416:1
  seven men . . . back to t. again 209:16
  this was the good t. once 273:5
  t.s have only one day 336:10
  white faces like t. children 181:15
Town-land: riding to the t. 416:11
Toy: attic of forgotten toys 284:20
Trace: he rose without t. 272:14
  O endless t. 319:9
  projecting time and t. 162:19
Tracing: fitful t. of a portal 358:17
Track: bright t.s where I have been 157:1
  t.s leading from somewhere to nowhere 4:10
Trade: best of all t.s 33:15
  half a t. and half an art 186:14
  how is your t., Aquarius 152:1
  things have altered in the building t. 213:9
Trade-English: he spoke and wrote t. 213:27
Trade Unionism: the T. of the married 344:21
Trade unionist: [Nazis] came for the t.s 280:5
Tradesmen: not counting t. 409:21
Tradition: European philosophical t. 401:9
  hand in hand with t. 362:13
  naval t. . . . rum, sodomy and the lash 82:20
  painters no longer live within a t. 297:11
  t. . . . is the democracy of the dead 77:27
  t. it'll squeak if you touch it 294:1

Traditional: forget everything t. 374:4
    t. scientific method 299:10
Traffic: t. runs you over 386:17
Tragedies: more true . . . than . . . t.s 270:10
    t. of antiquity 360:22
    t. of life bear no relation 85:6
    that is why we like t. 152:20
    there are two t.s in life 344:23
Tragedy: comedy is t. interrupted 20:4
    core of t. and comedy 156:1
    farce brutalized becomes t. 94:25
    fate wrote her a most tremendous t. 30:10
    food a t. 304:1
    hero and I will write you a t. 127:5
    life is a t. when seen in close-up 73:2
    robs us of the sense of t. 395:16
    sense of both comedy and t. 373:4
    t. is if I cut my finger 55:21
    we participate in a t. 182:14
    you're a bloody t. 257:12
Tragic: monstrous mother would be t. 383:5
    sexual infatuation a t. theme 345:26
Trahison: t. des clercs 35:10
Trail: long, long t. a-winding 208:16
Train: light of the oncoming t. 238:6
    man who shaves and takes a t. 400:2
    marriage as a t. 48:9
    next t.'s gone 251:23
    one to leave on the t. 105:20
    she never, never missed the t. 313:6
    stop t.s 40:5
    t. needs . . . its passengers to shove 361:16
    t.s run to time 11:8
    where is the London t. [twain]? 48:14
Training: reaction against one's t. 38:2
Trainset: biggest t. a boy ever had 395:11
Trait: death is an acquired t. 6:27
    projecting t. and trace 162:19
Tram: I'm not even a bus, I'm a tram 164:13
    know her again if we met in a t. 75:12
Tramcar: man's opinion on t. matters 76:9
Tramp: that's why the lady is a t. 165:6
Trample: learnt to t. on the past 276:17
Tranced: each tree stood like a t. woman 133:7
Tranquillity: chaos remembered in t. 373:1
    t. remembered in emotion 291:23
Transcend: never heals far less t.s 354:20
    so long to t. the nation 159:3
Transcendent: hope so t. 225:5
Transcendental: t. hotel 270:17
Transform: t. and yet not destroy 232:8
Transformation: our life passes in t. 318:14
Transition: not clear when t. takes place 249:18
    we live in an age of t. 185:13
Translation: inferior t. 21:5
    left out of verse . . . in t. 136:12
    t.s (like wives) are seldom faithful 65:6
Translator: whether t.s are heroes 194:7
Transmigration: if there is t. of souls 201:4
Transport and General Workers' Union: breakaway
    . . . from the T. 10:14

Transporting: device for t. itself 320:2
Transsexual: aspiring male t.s 226:15
Trap: trapped like a t. in a t. 291:25
Trappist: decent diplomat is a dead T. 227:6
    only T.s avoid the trap 312:18
Travel: despair . . . does not t. 258:3
    he t.s the fastest who t.s alone 213:23
    I t. light as light 136:20
    t. . . . contracts the mind 368:10
    t. with the river 108:3
    unanticipated invitations to t. 388:11
    why, oh why, do the wrong people t. 94:6
    writing about t.s is . . . tedious 273:1
    you want to t. blind 85:13113
Travelled: I've never t. 125:17
    one less t. by 135:23
Traveller: 'anybody there?' said the t. 103:11
    trouble with many t.s 305:2
Travelling: t. introduces . . . encapsulation 368:10
    t. . . . like war 273:1
    t. . . . narrows the mind 317:3
Treachery: patriotism . . . is t. 378:8
Treacle: allow an author to smell t. 323:17
Tread: heavy is the t. of the living 370:16
    t. softly . . . you t. on my dreams 416.14
Treadmill: set you on the t. 365:11
Treason: never committed even low t. 98:2
    t. of the intellectuals 35:10
    temptation is the greatest t. 118:23
Treasure: t., the figure in the carpet 190:14
Treasury: T. are never happy 171:2
    T. operates like . . . howitzers 165:18
    T. to fill old bottles with banknotes 206:18
    Vatican, the T. and the miners 23:13
Treaties: publish the secret t. 378:10
    t. whatever they may be worth 13:10
Treaty: hand that signed the t. 369:3
Tree: billboard lovely as a t. 278:6
    birds of the winged t.s 369:9
    each t. stood like a tranced woman 133:7
    finds that the t. continues to be 215:16
    lowest branch of the ecclesiastical t. 195:5
    man is man, woman woman, and t. t. 246:11
    O dreamy, gloomy, friendly t.s 377:5
    O t.s of life, when will it be winter 318:4
    of all the t.s that grow so fair 213:8
    only God can make a t. 208:7
    poem lovely as a t. 208:6
    propped between t.s and water 369:4
    t. continues to be 9:21
    t. explodes every spring 303:28
    temptation from the t. of knowledge 98:1
Treeless: t. jungle 165:2
Trees: filled the t.s and flapped 175:10
Tremble: it t.s to a lily 107:11
    some t. and never fall 367:11
Trembled: t. through his happy . . . air 162:12
Trembling: every t. hand 358:15
Tremulous: its postern behind my t. stay 162:5
Trenches: t. and trying on gas-masks 71:18
    this isn't time to dig t. 253:2

Trendy: t. is emulating your children 154:17
Trent Bridge: at T. . . . four o'clock 67:14
Tress: little stolen t. 417:15
Trial: t. if I recognize it as such 200:11
Triangle: eternal t. 10:6
Tribal: for t. man space 244:16
　transition from t. . . . society 301:4
Trick: asked me to do a t. 395:15
　such affected t.s 32:11
　t. that everyone abhors 32:25
　thought is not a t. 222:25
　when the long t.'s over 254:12
Tricked: they will be t. and sold 334:19
Trickery: art is full of magic and t. 274:12
Trickle: t. down theory 139:10
Tricky: t. job being Home Secretary 102:12
Tried: pick the one I never t. before 398:6
Trifle: observance of t.s 109:8
Trigger: whose finger on the t.? 99:2
Trim: t. as the daughters of the people 398:21
Trinians, St: terror of St T. 340:6
Trinities: cold Christ and tangled T. 212:10
Trinket: ye returned to your t.s 211:4
Trip: t. through a sewer in a . . . boat 267:2
Triple: just a tiny t. 14:9
　t. ways to take 211:24
Triste: jamais t. archy jamais t. 251:14
Tristesse: *bonjour* t. 120:16
Trite: t., . . . truss-advertisement 221:12
Triumph: meet with t. and disaster 210:32
　not the t. but the struggle 93:8
　t. confirms us in our habits 189:12
Trivial: let's hope it's nothing trivial 84:18
　soluble questions that are t. 201:13
Triviality: Law of T. 293:5
Trompe l'oeil: t. but a trompe l'esprit 297:19
Tropical: t. night . . . companionability 106:8
Trot: I don't trot it about yet 86:2
Trotsky, Leon: T. couldn't hit 411:3
Trouble: aged by t. 408:14
　air of one who had seen t. 396:16
　house that has got over all its t.s 194:12
　inviting t., it generally accepts 248:4
　pack up your t.s 14:10
　time of t. when it is not our t. 251:15
　t. was new to him 191:1
　t. . . . which had never happened 81:12
　t.s of our proud and angry dust 178:20
　whose t.s are worse than your own 5:9
　worry is the interest paid on t. 186:18
Trouble-maker: if there had been no t.s 366:6
Troubled: life's t. bubble broken 103:22
　like a bridge over t. water 347:19
Trousers: before the human race had t. 283:8
　in the dark in your t. all day 107:21
　may have to buy a new pair of t. 298:14
　no t. as such 290:6
　they have asked for my t. 218:3
　t. marinading overnight 52:17
　wear the bottom of my t. rolled 117:28
Troy: another T. for her to burn 417:3

Truck: Englishman aplogises to the t. 254:18
Trucking: keep on t. 12:3
Trudeau, Pierre Elliott 225:10
Trudge: weary t. home 10:11
True: and is it t.? 40:9
　because a novel's invented, it isn't t. 304:5
　believe himself that it is really t. 317:6
　philosophy to be substantially t. 335:15
　too t., too sincere 418:5
　saying it long enough it will be t. 37:9
　t. to the flame of life 223:10
　t. to you, darlin', in my fashion 301:12
　what people say of us is t. 350:11
Truer: t. than if they really happened 169:12
Truffle: might . . . be called t. hunters 230:25
　swine to show you where the t.s are 5:1
Trull: a t. before she could toddle 351:20
Truman, President H.S.: nation . . . T. worked for 195:19
Trumpet: dreads the final t. 163:4
Trunk: so large a t. before 32:8
Truss-advertisement: t. truth 221:12
Trust: best t. the happy moments 253:28
　I don't t. him. We're friends 51:7
　kinds of man you must never t. 316:17
　never t. men with short legs 94:18
　never t.s anyone that one has deceived 239:18
　t. an Englishman in the dark 353:13
　t. your editor . . . sleep on straw 73:17
Truth: all this stuff about the t. 52:9
　all t.s are half-truths 401:4
　aphorism never coincides with the t. 217:12
　[art] makes us realize the t. 298:3
　as freely as a lawyer interprets t. 144:19
　before the t. has got its boots on 63:2
　behold this is the t. 412:22
　boasts that he . . . tells the t. 259:8
　build a home for the t. 72:16
　can't get at the t. by writing history 52:7
　committing ourselves to the t. 280:12
　count t.s like lovers 234:20
　earth's moving nearer to t. 248:17
　economical with the t. 14:6
　exactitude is not t. 255:7
　faith has need of the whole t. 367:1
　first casualty . . . is t. 195:10
　good art speaks t., indeed is t. 274:6
　great t.s begin as blasphemies 342:13
　half-t. or one-and-a-half t.s 217:12
　harder to make him confess the t. 178:14
　harmful t. is better than a useful lie 249:23
　however improbable . . . the t. 109:6
　Hume . . . wanted to get at the t. 329:3
　kill a man who . . . has found the t. 58:15
　let's tell them the t. 358:21
　liar who always speaks the t. 85:10
　loyalty to the t. 209:1
　mainly he told the t. 379:16
　man can embody t. 418:8
　mistook disenchantment for t. 336:22
　Nixon could not tell the t. 331:14

novel tells us the t. about its author 76:17
polite by telling the t. 49:12
sarcasm the condition of t. 27:1
she took to telling the t. 332:24
strict regard for t. 32:21
telling the t. about [Republicans] 359:1
there are no new t.s 242:7
they worship T. 54:20
three fundamental t.s 31:20
till t. obeyed his call 415:4
to forsake this t. is to pay too high 324:6
told the t. about his father 36:13
truss-advertisement t. 221:12
trusted to speak the t. 23:18
t. . . . a compound of two half-truths 361:15
t. about the Democrats 104:6
t. acceptable to lying men 18:13
t. and myth are one and the same 336:18
t. . . . as phoney as a glass eye 167:14
t. being . . . a current which flows 308:14
t. even if it didn't happen 206:5
t. . . . everyone can be shown to know 242:7
t. exists 50:17
t., . . . for the poet 335:13
t. . . . from . . . human intercourse 106:11
t. . . . funniest joke in the world 343:19
t. hears him and runs away 34:1
t. is a pathless land 217:25
t. is an odd number 283:10
t. is discovered by someone else 352:21
t. is naked 385:12
t. is not victorious 385:2
t. is . . . something to be cherished 259:8
t. is the most valuable thing 379:22
t. . . . let us economize it 379:22
t. that has lost its temper 143:9
t. twenty-four times a second 145:8
t. which men prefer not to hear 4:2
t. whose opposite is also a great t. 249:20
t.s that become old 288:10
two sorts of t. 45:2
victor . . . whether he told the t. 173:9
what they believe . . . to be the t. 160:20
when they told the t. on me 119:13
where no one possesses the t. 218:10
writers . . . speak the t. 19:18
Truthful: t. when you are alone 106:11
Try: t. again. Fail again. 29:1
t. him afterward 380:5
t. to tell us we're too young 102:11
we t. harder 3:25
you can get it – if you t. 142:14
Trying: just goes on t. other things 297:18
Tryst: made a t. with destiny 278:18
Tsarism: victory of the revolution over t. 229:1
Tube: as the t. doors were closing 403:19
t.s are twisted and dried 213:14
Tuesday: anybody who can spell T. 264:18
T. . . . with a baby Boy Scout 407:8
Tulip: apart from cheese and t.s 92:4
here t.s bloom as they are told 54:16

tiptoe through the t.s 110:22
Tumblerful: liberal t. 410:15
Tumour: I'm 73 & in constant good t. 243:16
Tumult: t. and the shouting dies 212:15
t. in the clouds 416:17
Tumultuous: t. body now denies 55:8
Tune: like slow old t.s of Spain 253:27
like sorrow or a t. 122:10
many a good t. played on an old fiddle 62:5
nightingales sing out of t. 190:22
turn on, t. in, and drop out 226:7
Tunnel: down some profound dull t. 288:24
order more t. 310:17
t.s that rewind themselves 95:2
Tupperware: rhetoric of the t. party 208:5
Turd: break up like a baked t. 294:1
Turgenev, I.S.: I beat Mr T. 169:13
Turkey: in T. it was always 1952 368:12
Turn: because I do not hope to t. again 116:17
I t. and the world t.s 193:16
left a t. unstoned 407:6
t. on, tune in, and drop out 226:7
Turned: t. down . . . like a bedspread 410:14
Turning: first t. of the second stair 116:20
lady's not for t. 367:17
still point of the t. world 116:26
t. in the widening gyre 417:12
Turret: ears in the t.s hear 368:23
Turtle: t. lives twixt plated decks 278:7
Turtledove: as nearly like a t. 411:1
Tutelage: t. of governesses 173:15
Twain, Mark: from one book by T. 169:8
Twain: never the t. shall meet 209:19
where is the London t.? 48:14
Twang: something t.s and breaks 246:9
triumphant t. of a bedspring 295:10
Twelve-winded: yon t. sky 179:29
Twenties: man in his t. in love 38:15
poets are dead by their late t. 152:13
Twentieth century: all . . . the t. wants to know 56:3
is the nineteenth 156:9
stride in the t. 341:24
Twenty: hindsight is always t.-t. 402:12
say what you have to say in t. minutes 48:15
tell me I had t. years left 58:13
t. t. hindsight 299:10
t. will not come again 179:11
t. years largely wasted 117:2
t. years of schoolin' 113:21
t. years seems like a reasonable term 329:14
you're t. minutes 402:7
Twenty-four: but then we shall all be t. 178:18
t. hour day has come to stay 30:1
Twice: play in which nothing happens – t. 260:3
something read twice 87:18
thinks once before he speaks t. 34:25
t. is not seen 265:9
t Wagner, t. 360:15
you'll have to see this picture t. 200:1
Twice-over: t. cannot be 163:13

Undersold: never knowingly u. 233:7
Understand: contempt for anything he didn't u. 413:8
   don't criticize what you can't u. 113:23
   even I do not u. it 91:16
   language I don't u. 13:4
   men who u. 54:18
   telling them stories they can u. 25:11
   what we . . . u. we can do 404:3
Understanding: piece of cod passes all u. 239:6
   too much u. 146:13
   u. will . . . extinguish pleasure 180:7
Understood: right to be u. 218:10
   she u. as women often do 68:1
   those who long to be u. 386:16
   u. only by him and me 151:12
Undertaker: corpse would give an u. 23:14
   nothing against u.s personally 266:8
   overtakers keep the u.s busy 299:17
   u. cleans his sign 93:22
Undertaking: no such u. has been received 72:1
Underwear: addiction to silk u. 65:7
   bringing a change of u. 6:17
Undeservedly: some books are u. forgotten 19:4
Undeserving: u. poverty is my line 345:18
Undeveloped: among the u. countries 34:14
Undevout: appreciated . . . by the undevout 180:6
Undisciplined: u. squads of emotion 117:3
Undiscovered: u. ends 32:27
Undone: save the u. years 288:26
   u. and worn to a thread-paper 302:13
Uneasy: Jew feels even slightly u. 196:6
Uneducated: government by the badly e. 77:25
   if an u. savage can do that 90:13
   u. man to read books of quotations 80:25
Unemployment: at a stroke . . . reduce u. 89:17
   there need be no more u. 206:18
Unendurable: endure the u. 172:11
   reality . . . is u. 88:22
Unethical: conduct u. and lousy 14:7
Unexpected: most u. of all the things 377:18
Unexplored: u. . . . fingerboard 172:10
   u. side of the park 300:10
Uneyes: u. safely ensconced 97:12
Unfinished: Europe is the u. negative 242:5
   to leave great themes u. 241:8
Unforgiveness: alp of u. 300:4
Unforgiving: fill the u. minute 211:1
Ungentlemanly: hesitate to do an u. thing 256:1
   u. to write more than five or six 59:11
Ungifted: supreme virtue of the u. 204:4
Ungrateful: man is an u. beast 33:9
Ungrudgingly: so u. of his discovery 333:8
Unguarded: pinch of unseen, u. dust 163:14
Unhappen: does not completely u. 46:11
Unhappily: bad end u. 361:2
Unhappiness: u. is the difference 46:13
Unhappy: as u. as the next braggart's 104:11
   instinct for being u. highly developed 332:17
   making one another u. 258:16
   moral as soon as one is u. 307:7

relatives in Kansas City to be u. 253:12
stay, thou u. one 103:23
today you're u.? 261:27
u. about a person . . . worth his while 306:17
u. the land that is in need of heroes 51:4
Unhealthy: habit with prophets to be u. 53:16
Unheard: language of the u. 208:13
Unhearing: u. aid 43:8
Unheeded: opinion . . . goes u. 383:24
Unholy: refrain from u. pleasure 32:26
Unhoped: u. serene, that men call age 54:10
Unicorn: rarer than the u. 197:1
   u. among the cedars 18:4
Unicycle: easier on tandem than u. 363:5
Uniform: satire is simply humour in u. 194:8
   u. 'e wore was nothing much before 210:27
Unimportant: think what they hear is u. 299:7
Uninteresting: no . . . u. subject 76:11
Uninvited: happiness comes u. 217:20
Union: break up the u. because of sausage 148:3
Unitary: u., orthodox language 137:10
United: no more a u. nation than the equator 79:8
United Nations: U. side 340:14
United States 23:1, 68:4, 392:21
   best immediate defence of the U. 322:21
   best newspaperman . . . President of the U. 56:6
   best prose writer in the U. 19:21
   come to the U. till . . . ten months 358:8
   God bless the U., so large 18:6
   in the U., Englishmen are . . . pets 96:1
   national mental illness of the U. 17:4
   non-aligned with the U. 239:24
   president of the U. . . . naked 113:12
   something new in the U. 34:2
   U. is like a gigantic boiler 155:9
   U. of Europe 80:8
   U. . . . . six hours behind 174:22
Unity: good . . . makes for u. 182:17
   illusion of u. 306:19
   u. of a nation . . . single paranoic 66:15
Universal: Aunt Edna is u. 313:3
   dilution in the u. 71:17
   relationship between particular and u. 38:9
   u. sickness implies 377:12
   u. suffrage . . . leads to . . . bribery 186:3
   unless freedom is u. 171:22
Universally: I'm so u. liked 105:12
Universe: benign indifference of the u. 65:25
   corner of the u. . . . . improving 183:14
   cover the u. with mud 130:10
   do not pretend to understand the u. 361:13
   feeling comfortable in the u. 64:9
   God, who created the u. 258:20
   hell of a good u. next door 97:28
   I accept the u. 183:8
   organic or inorganic in the u. 357:20
   repetitious mechanism of the U. 400:20
   this U. must not fail 236:18
   U. and all that surrounds it 89:22
   U. as One Thing 194:3
   u. is expanding 105:4

v. was a special illness of the ear 18:12
Verse-factory 40 and have a little v. 202:4
Versfabrik: habe eine kleine v. 202:4
Version: one religion . . . hundred v.s 345:14
Versuchen: alle die dich suchen, v. dich 319:13
Vertical: v. man 17:10
Verwandlung: Leben geht hin mit V. 318:14
Verweilende: das V. erst weiht uns ein 319:8
Vested: males sex . . . v. interest 237:3
Vet: if a v. can't catch his patient 171:9
Vexing: husband or two can be v. 399:23
Vibration: sympathetic v.s 259:18
Vicar: hairy calves of the v.'s wife 119:17
    hundred v.s down the lawn 54:17
    v. coming in twice a week 22:1
Vice: dishonour the v.s 403:7
    dwelling on their v.s 343:15
    extremism . . . is no v. 147:2
    full many a v. is born to blush 355:26
    v. . . . is a creature of heejus mien 111:22
    v. pays homage to virtue 62:2
    v.s of his ancestors 122:14
    v.s such as carrying on in society 290:3
Vichy: something V. about the French 282:1
Vicious: stroke its back and it turns v. 187:3
Victim: biographers pick a v. 296:11
    every reformation must have its v.s 332:27
    pestilences and there are v.s 65:26
    v. and a supporter of the system 283:14
    v.s who begin by being restive 242:19
    v.s who respect their executioners 335:22
    what the v. has done with his world 259:16
Victoire: v, c'est la volonté 129:5
Victor: dance at the Golf Club, my v. and I 40:20
    side may call itself the v. 71:17
Victoria: less expensive than . . . v. 326:14
Victoria, Queen 362:5, 403:12
    V. had the makings of a cricketer 374:9
Victoria Station: buy a ticket at V. 42:2
Victorian: antagonistic to the V. age 405:13
    as the V.s were Christians 244:9
    barmaid of the V. soul 194:18
    [V.s] were lame giants 77:26
    whiskers . . . of V. bushiness 410:21
Victorious: truth is not v. 385:2
Victory: aboard the V., V. O 112:12
    attribute of a v. 81:10
    before Alamein we never had a v. 81:17
    dig for v. 351:10
    in v., magnanimity 81:4
    not right that matters, but v. 173:9
    v. at all costs 79:14
    v. finds a hundred fathers 82:23
    V for V. 231:8
    'v.!' he concluded 174:8
    war . . . to produce v. parades 174:21
    without v. there is no survival 79:14
Victuals: tumble v. in 311:11
Vicus: commodious v. of recirculation 197:8
Vida: la v. es duda 382:2
Video: v. recorder records 407:21

Vienna: I set out for V. 173:3
    V. of stiff collars 59:10
Viennese: different from . . . the new V. school
    198:15
    loathed the V. quack [Freud] 276:15
Vietnam 196:1, 228:10
    best play about V. 361:18
    Kissinger brought peace to V. 168:24
    to win in V. 355:13
    V. was lost in the living rooms 245:3
View: extreme v.s weakly held 366:9
    princes kept the v. 113:6
    room with a v. 94:9
    we had seen the v. from elsewhere 327:12
    whenever you accept our v.s 101:14
    worm's eye v. 165:15
    worst thing about oral sex. The v. 235:1
Vikings: wars were girly after the V. 120:13
Vile: what of v. dust? 74 26
Villa, Pancho 321:28
Villa: v.s . . . where I learned 75:15
Village: global 244:15
    lewd forefathers of the v. 356:1
    v. atheist brooding and blaspheming 77:14
    v. explainer 357:15
    v. which men call Tyre 128:15
    you can stay stupid v. 386:17
    you know it is a bad v. 375:17
Villager: black, the v.s 222:18
    problem of two thousand million v.s 339:13
Villain: if a man is going to be a v. 367:4
    sword into assorted v.s 152:23
    v. still pursued her 281:7
    what more could a v. want? 50:3
Villainous: you v. demi-tasses 350:4
Vin: j'ai bu l'été comme un v. doux 13:9
Vinci: spell it V. and pronounce it Vinchy 380:2
Vindictive: suffering . . . makes men . . . v. 256:14
Vinegar: I'd have it tinned. With v. 405:18
    some turn to v. 194:23
Vines: architect can only . . . plant v. 413;12
Vintage: I can tell you the v. 90:16
Violence: keep v. in the mind 5:6
    source of all v. 336:13
    unending v. of US and THEM 165:3
    v. is American as apple pie 56:9
    v. is man re-creating himself 122:6
    v. masquerading as love 219:11
    v. of men who charge into a vacuum 139:3
    v. punctuated by committee meetings 403:14
    v. shapes and obsesses our society 45:15
    v. to the *ultima ratio* 285:18
Violet: bats . . . in the v. light 118:16
    raining v.s 238:2
Violin: dying moan of a distant v. 295:10
    v. is like holding a young bird 259:18
Virgil: V. was no good 61:21
Virgin: Doris Day before she was a v. 253:14
    God to arrange a v. birth 193:11
    no wonder they call me the V. Queen 62:15
    saving young v.s from sin 12:13

sweet-smelling v.s close to them 358:14
v. territory for whorehouses 67:5
Virginia: while we ate V. hams 40:25
Virginity: just a little more v. 377:4
lost your v. in Cork 42:28
v. might possibly be quite nice 201:19
Virtue: ape-like v.s 87:17
few v.s which the Poles do not possess 80:6
form of every v. at the testing point 232:19
make v.s of their weaknesses 258:13
measured the v.s of other writers 47:2
moderation . . . is no v. 147:2
my v. is still far too small 86:2
no v. now in blind reliance on place 206:10
other crimes are v.s beside it 343:33
praised for v.s you never had 359:16
prejudice in favour of v. 183:3
self-denial is not a v. 344:34
seven deadly v.s 255:21
suspects . . . one of the cardinal v.s 126:15
v. more difficult to portray 305:21
v. of the bored 393:14
v. . . . Trade Unionism of the married 344:21
v. uniquely among v.s 360:6
v. . . . weakness of strong generals 144:12
woman of easy v. and a proved liar 158:10
woman's v. is man's greatest invention 349:19
your life . . . discovering his v.s 240:6
Virtuous: v.. It's our national pastime 137:9
Visa: give you a v. even if you haven't 285:11
Visage: why do I often meet your v. here 95:3
Visible: in the city time becomes v. 274:4
Vision: awakens devils to contest his v. 247:13
bright stain on the v. 152:2
not with his eyes but with his v. 331:6
screwy v.s 34:9
whom he assumes to have perfect v. 215:2
Visit: nice place to v. 157:3
superior people never make long v.s 268:16
Visiting: I'm only v. 149:16
Visitor: v.s who . . . remain inconspicuous 227:1
Visual: identifying . . . with the v. image 223:22
Vital: some kind of record seemed v. 91:5
Vitality: v. in a woman 344:6
Vitamin: hatred is like v.s 388:7
Vive: V. l'Interieur 341:7
Vivid: left the v. air 355:1
Vocabulary: v. needs . . . fertilizing 393:16
v. of Bradshaw is . . . limited 110:10
Vocal: vasectomy of the v. cords 7:4
Vocational: all education is . . . v. 279:11
Vodka: medium v. dry martini 128:20
Vogue: he'd be working for *V.* 383:23
Voice: good v. but too autocratic 370:23
her v. is full of money 126:19
higher the v. the smaller the intellect 279:7
I like my v. when I sing 413:14
on me your v. falls 221:8
other v.s, other rooms 67:7
sexual attraction through . . . my v. 162:1
shall the v.s of liberty be mute? 97:26

songs that v.s never shared 348:1
sound of my own v. 279:15
v. like beer trickling 408:23
v. . . . never had once to raise itself 191:2
v. . . . of . . . confidence-tricksters 231:19
v. of falling leaves 73:14
v. that used to shake the ferryboats 251:12
v. . . . to defrost her refrigerator 361:22
v. without a face 18:20
v.s just can't worm through 299:21
v.s of young people 350:14
v.s talking about everything 327:17
v.s . . . to sing with 97:23
your v. is music 30:27
Void: sins are attempts to fill v.s 394:9
v. where confused signals buzz about 73:14
Volcano: expect it to turn into a v. 363:8
Vole: passes the questing v. 392:29
Volonté: victoire, c'est la v. 129:5
Volta: Upper V., but with missiles 11:12
Voltaire 361:11
Bible . . . next to V. 329:2
Voluble: most v. of the emotions 85:20
Volume: come unequipped with v. knobs 341:22
Voluntary: services are v. 392:16
Volunteer: leisure is work you v. for 320:18
Voluptuaries: v. of the morning after 167:1
Volvo: rust in their V. 92:15
V.s like to pick a dentist 320:21
Vorrat: ausgeteilt wie hundertfacher V. 319:4
Vorsprung: V. durch Technik 3:24
Vote: assassination . . . used as the v. 184:1
don't buy a single v. 205:12
music that changed a . . . v. 338:12
straw v. . . . hot air blows 170:17
v. . . . means nothing to women 283:6
Voting: not the voting that's democracy 360:8
Vow: I v. to thee, my country 355:18
Voyage: *make v.s † Attempt them!* 404:10
one v. to India is enough 80:26
Voyager: fare forward, v.s 117:8
Voyaging: v. after maidens 197:22
Vulgar: he's v., . . . He has a v. mind 232:14
I like short words and v. fractions 80:14
one v. and the other sublime 335:5
rather be called wicked than v. 233:1
rude remark or a v. action 404:20
v. . . . mistakes the exceptional 186:9
Vulgarities: they may have other v. 169:3
Vulgarizing: haven't succeeded in . . . v. 182:20
Vulnerability: dependence entails v. 53:22
Vulnerable: life persists in the v. 366:14
Vulture: v. dropping in for lunch 411:9
v.s of principle 236:3

W

Wag: every time it w.s its tail 376:4
Wage: Jesus saves but he couldn't on my w.s 149:19

paid his subjects with a royal w. 54:11
took their w.s and are dead 179:5
work for which they draw the w. 213:11
w.s of gin is breadth 171:7
w.s of sin are increased circulation 13:11
Wagner, Richard: W. is the Puccini of music
   271:20
   W. writhes 61:17
Waif: land of w.s and strays 392:22
Waist: hero from the w. up 263:10
   Lady Chatterley above the w. 89:4
Waistcoat: w. swelled like the sail 409:8
Wait: someone w.s for me 96:11
   very well, I can w. 338:23
   w. and see 15:15
Waiter 202:11
   guy who orders the w. 37:12
   myself and a dam' good head w. 156:17
   so long as the natives are w.s 269:18
Waiting: greater our capacity for w. 366:16
   people w. for you 144:16
   w. at the church 228:5
   'W. for Godot' is a dramatic vacuum 380:25
   w. for the end, boys 120:20
   w. for the *Robert E. Lee* 143:22
   w. time, my brothers 108:8
   we're w. for Godot 29:4
Waitresses: w. . . . . disgustingly rude 300:21
Wake: it used to w. you up 248:1
   only with beauty w. wild memories 103:1
   part that w.s up 409:20
   w. up, England 142:1
Wakefulness: wear . . . out with our w. 91:6
Wakey-wakey 93:7
Waking: imagine w. up in the morning 112:9
   take my w. slow 321:9
   w. consciousness 191:19
   w. up . . . always as the same person 351:6
Walcum: a bit of talcum is always w. 277:8
Waldheim, Kurt 10:21
Wales, Prince of: W. feels extra sympathy 366:19
   who's danced with the P. 122:11
Wales: apple wood . . . all the way to W. 74:13
   bleeds upon the road to W. 179:27
   influence of W. 392:8
   one road runs to W. 254:9
   position of the artists of W. 370:3
   W. . . . . concession to gaiety 370:24
Walk: anything that can w. by itself 113:24
   before we have learnt to w. 88:20
   Englishmen taking mad dogs for w.s 263:3
   harrowing clods in a slow silent w. 162:22
   he w.s again on the Seas of Blood 349:1
   I don't like going for w.s 320:17
   somewhere left to w. 120:24
   tho' I w.s wth fifty 'ousemaids 211:32
   w. for a w.'s sake 215:9
   w. on the lines or the squares 264:12
   w. over a man once 28:12
   w.s the night in her silver shoon 103:18
   within a w. of the sea 33:11

Walked: w. abroad in a shower 369:10
   w. eye-deep in hell 303:16
   w. other men and women 377:10
   when he w. with his mother 369:11
   who ever w. the streets 398:17
Walker: w. in the rain 266:1
Walking: all w. in one kind of wilderness 161:12
   always w. on his hands 385:9
   as dancing is to w. 389:4
   as if supported by a w. frame 176:9
   companion for a w. tour 411:7
   devil's w. parody 74:14
   he disappears w. 262:2
   kind of w. stomach 287:8
   let it keep on w. 372:24
   like w. through a field 293:10
   more enterprise in w. naked 415:14
   religion is a way of w. 186:23
   three notches on his w. stick 107:19
   trick of w. into himself 372:28
   w. my baby back home 379:12
   w. the earth like brothers 208:15
   w. with destiny 81:8
Wall: apprehension that w.s have ears 234:13
   Chinese W. of Milton 118:29
   father was the Great Wall of China 390:10
   graffiti lower on the w.s 373:13
   I'm a W. soldier 18:14
   noticed how many w.s the room had 72:18
   picked up with stones to build a w. 136:3
   something . . . that doesn't love a w. 135:16
   there are no w.s 375:1
   thick w.s and running comment 34:16
   walks through a w. 247:22
   watch the w., my darling 212:21
   we are the writing on your w. 150:3
Wall-paper: one-armed . . . pasting on w. 170:3
Walled: vain citadels that are not w. 288:27
Wallet: more will than w. 60:14
   pains in my w. 63:17
Wallowing: w. in low seriousness 34:12
Walnut: cradle of Spanish w. 299:24
   w. tree with two dun cows 333:4
Walpole, Robert: W. . . . . gamekeeper's letters
   377:8
Walrus: W. and Carpenter divided up the Sixties
   232:1
Walter: W.! W.! Lead me to the altar 124:17
Waltz: wearied band swoons to a w. 183:17
Waltzes: way a mouse w. 400:10
Waltzing: you'll come a-w., Matilda 293:14
Wampum: blow incredible w. 97:6
Wandering: or but a w. voice 376:1
Want: freedom from w. 322:23
   get what you w. . . . . enjoy it 350:10
   God can't w. that 158:3
   makes death a long-felt w. 376:21
   making things he does not w. 177:12
   man dies when he w.s 12:25
   w. of money is [root of all evil] 61:8
   w. something you probably won't w. 177:8

what more do you w.? 192:20
without some of the things you w. 328:7
w.s the way other people have toothache
    160:22
w.s what he is supposed to w. 134:17
Wanted: better to be w. for murder 407:10
put his hand on the one that's w. 174:7
what you would have w. had you known
    203:22
War: aftermath of w. 177:7
all of you . . . who served in the w. 357:17
all their w.s are merry 74:10
and the w. goes on 40:2
as drama the W. is . . . disappointing 155:10
at w. you think about a better life 402:19
beating of w. drums 216:12
before the w. . . . it was summer 286:15
began this w. by snatching glory 305:15
bungled, unwise w. 300:4
capitalism 'caused' the First World W. 366:4
cold w. 27:5
dance and w. are . . . the same 357:7
day w. broke out 407:4
defeat without a w. 79:11
done well out of the w. 23:5
enable it to make w. 394:11
everything . . . wrong since the w. 7:11
except the casualty list of the World W. 67:4
Fascism means w. 361:25
fight in here. This is the W. Room 218:7
films make more money than the w. lost 388:2
give a w., and nobody will come 334:20
government get out of w. 168:15
Great Britain is going to make w. 40:8
guarantee success in w. 81:13
how pretty w. is 12:26
if we lose this w., I'll start another 101:13
I'll furnish the w. 167:7
in a civil w., a general must know 314:13
in every w. they kill you 321:18
in sex no less than in w. 183:13
in the w. and he was very drunk 392:15
in . . . w. it is not right that matters 173:9
in w., resolution 81:4
jaw-jaw is better than w.-w. 80:15, 245:9
like a couple between the w.s 300:6
like w. and fornication 273:1
live under the shadow of a w. 355:5
lose the w. in an afternoon 82:2
lost a battle . . . not the w. 141:7
make love, not w. 12:5
mankind's w. of liberation 205:1
many deeds of w. 135:13
men get together it's called a w. 55:20
men like w. 120:8
men were made for w. 119:16
my subject is w. 288:13
my w.s were global from the start 314:12
never understood this liking for w. 36:3
no discharge in the w. 209:24
not be sent into any foreign w. 322:20

not just getting them killed in w.s 181:6
old liberal between the w.s 300:5
older men declare w. 177:7
once lead this people into w. 406:24
one of the main effects of w. 388:8
people taut for w. 371:3
phoney w. 99:4
pornography of w. 311:4
profound hatred of w. and militarism 53:26
quickest way of ending a w. 287:16
son is fighting the w. 305:6
start bloody w.s they can't afford 354:9
state of w. would exist between us 72:1
strong enough to win a w. 195:14
take care not to lose the next w. 82:21
tempered by w. 204:16
there ain't gonna be no w. 245:7
they could do with . . . a good w. 51:6
think that w. . . . is not a crime 169:17
this country is at w. with Germany 72:1
to the old w.s; Arise 370:18
too old in any case to go to w. 351:17
Unnecessary W. 81:5
w. abhorrent to all real women 131:18
w. between men and women 372:18
w. brings out the best in a man 238:4
w. can only be abolished through w. 250:11
w. . . . does not escape the laws 308:16
w. hath no fury like a non-combatant 267:17
w. into the living room 245:3
w. is being deliberately prolonged 337:10
w. is capitalism with the gloves off 361:6
w. is like love 51:11
w. is much too important 84:11
w. is peace 286:23
w. is politics with bloodshed 250:9
w. is . . . the universal perversion 311:4
w. knows no power 55:4
w. . . . lost without him [Joffre] 178:2
w. minus the shooting 287:17
w. more evil, ere all w.s cease 75:4
w. of ideas . . . people who get killed 227:5
w. of the peoples 78:17
w. on poverty 195:13
w. . . . perpetual becoming 308:16
w. to end w. 397:13
w. . . . to produce victory parades 174:21
w. . . . was bound to start you thinking 286:16
w. was . . . speeded up peace 312:16
w. wasn't fought that way 324:21
w. we . . . face next time 407:2
w. will never cease 258:17
w.'s annals will cloud into night 163:1
w.s are fought by children 235:6
w.s are not won by evacuations 81:10
w.s begin in the minds 382:9
w.s that cause armaments 246:16
w.s were girly after the Vikings 120:13
way to win an atomic w. 50:2
we are not at w. with Egypt 114:13
we have all lost the w.. All Europe 223:15

we're living through war 217:3
what, then, was w.? 151:24
what did you do in the Great W., daddy 3:26
what w. is about only when it is over 50:6
when w. of giants is over 81:22
win a w. well 81:3
with material . . . that one makes w. 295:15
Women and Horses and Power and W. 209:19
won the w. single-handed 50:15
wrong w., at the wrong place 50:1
years between the w.s 117:2
War Office: anything except the . . . W. 343:5
Warehouse: best w. I ever saw 397:18
Wares: if you want to buy my w. 301:22
   w. are so much harder to get rid of 135:19
Warfare: aerial w. was . . . indecisive 397:11
Warhol, Andy 387:23
   W. New York City Diet 391:1
Warily: as w. as Antarctica was circled 116.10
Warlike: w. non-existence 239:17
Warm: no dying but alive and w. 368:21
Warmly: more w. than the coarse shirts 371:3
   w. surrounded by the multitude 375:21
Warmonger: drawn into conflicts by w.s 356:6
Warmth: cold was cursing the w. 374:16
Warner Bros: working for W. is like fucking 267:3
Warning: my w.s had been so numerous 81:8
Warped: much that's w. and cracked 95:5
Warrant: signed my death w. 86:12
Warring: w. country between his toes 122:7
Warrior: this is the happy w. 313:10
Warty: gay and w. lads 418:5
Wary: lot to be w. about 391:11
Wash: w. me in the water 12:18
   w. that man right out of my hair 160:17
   w. the wind 118:24
   w. their feet in soda water 118:13
Washed: w. the eyes of the stars 370:18
Washing: only w.. And babies 369:26
   w. on the Siegfried Line 204:14
Washington, George: W. could not tell a lie
   331:14
Wasp: sitting in a cloud of w.s 11:2
   small revolver for killing w.s 349:11
Waste: [God] w.s nothing 316:18
   I don't particularly mind w. 54:8
   land laid w. with . . . young men slain 17:19
   w. of water and mud 118:21
   w. remains and kills 120:21
Waste Land: W. is . . . wastepaper 248:10
Wasted: if you're gonna get w., get w. 316:11
   w. years of my life 306:20
Wastepaper: The Waste Land is . . . w. 248:10
   work of art compared to the w. basket 148:13
Watch: has a w. and chain, of course 321:10
   he's dead, or my w. has stopped 252:17
   like a fat gold w. 299:23
   look at your w. and it says 6.20 312:3
   repair a w. with his gloves on 371:17
   some people wear a w. 203:19
   tell you how the w. was made 413:19

w. each other w. each other 112:18
w. the wall, my darling 212:21
w. them filing out 87:14
why not carry a w.? 376:20
Watch-chain: soul dangles from his w. 97:8
Watched: ally has to be w. 378:11
Watches: people looking at their watches 43:6
   someone whose mind w. itself 65:22
Watching: before I tire of w. you 55:9
   Big Brother is w. you 286:21
   for appearing on, not w. 94:16
   second thoughts are good is worth w. 26:25
Watchmaker: blind w. 101:5
   I should have become a w. 115:14
Watchtower: all along the w. 113:6
Water: bad play surrounded by w. 189:15
   best contraceptive is a glass of cold w. 10:2
   biggest waste of w. 296:16
   blood . . . than w. like Pilate 153:17
   bridge over troubled w. 347:19
   Charley, do not go upon the w. 351:12
   chittering w.s of 197:19
   covered by useless w. 108:14
   cup w. in our hands 177:3
   drank rapidly a glass of w. 97:26
   drink a glass of dirty w.? 216:20
   flash of w. 278:19
   flower that one w.s but does not cut 385:13
   gift for mixing sand and w. 164:12
   glass of w. . . . . 'Irish or Scotch?' 159:9
   he's fallen in the w. 263:19
   I don't care where the w. goes 75:14
   icy w. is turning blacker 248:17
   invented by w. 320:2
   it's not the taste of w. I object to 215:3
   make one's ears w. 326:3
   nothing but food and w. 125:10
   on w. I am a coward 173:21
   once a Magic Flute is now a W. Carrier 9:26
   our future is on the w. 403:9
   propped between trees and w. 369:4
   refusing to walk on w. 346:20
   save w. – dilute it 149:33
   shapeless as the w. 368:20
   streets full of w. 35:3
   thoughts as still as the w. 64:17
   wash me in the w. 12:18
   waste of w. and mud 118:21
   w. polo? . . . dangerous? 402:10
   w. still keeps falling over 81:19
   w.s of the heart push in 369:8
   w.'s the same shape as the glass 91:11
   we have all passed a lot of w. 147:12
   we used to drink w. before Prohibition 221:2
   when I makes w. I makes w. 198:10
Water-bird: birthday began with the w.s 369:9
Water-closet: let us construct a w. 198:12
   whole island is a w. 244:4
Water-trough: snake came to my w. 222:22
Waterer: valley to the w.s 51:1
Watergate 420:10

W. are all actors 60:7
W. . . . just sing 392:9
Welt: Preise dem Engel die W. 319:1
Welter-weight: muscles of a w. 408:15
Wembley: 'I feel a bit w. this morning' 194:6
Wenceslas: adviser to King W. 192:20
Wept: Grand Central Station I sat down and w.
349:21
   w. for the end of innocence 146:9
   young man who has not w. 335:3
Werk: zwar ein W., wie allerwärts 269:10
Wesker, Arnold: W. is not as wonderful 397:19
West, Mae 125:5, 162:1, 311:5
West: applause of the W. 382:1
   God planted another one down in the w. 47:19
   in the high w. there burns 358:14
   in this W. stuffed with money 327:12
   w. of these out to sea 128:5
   w. wind, wanton wind 345:23
   where the W. begins 73:4
West Bromwich: make straight for W. 305:20
Westen: im W. nichts Neues 315:13
Wester: rainy Pleiads w. 179:9
Western: all quiet on the w. front 315:13
   Playboy of the W. World 363:17
   seen one W. 401:15
Westward: land vaguely realizing w. 135:13
Westwards: idea of Poland moving w. 81:21
Wet: touch it when you're w. 141:19
   w. crabs in a basket 112:15
Wetsments: one can smell off his w. 197:23
Weygand, General Max 79:16
Whale: drag the Atlantic Ocean for w.s 380:6
   dwarfs trying to grill a w. 305:13
   not of humans, but of the w. 403:23
Whale-backed: bow-headed, w. Downs 212:29
What: now w.? 335:21
   w. is which and which is w. 265:7
   w.'s up Doc? 58:8
What ho! 408:15
Wheat: petrol is more likely than w. 394:11
Wheedle: ingratiating w. of the toucher 231:19
Wheel: do not let the w.s show 129:7
   little tin gods on w.s 212:13
   sound of your own w.s drive you crazy 112:5
   telling one how he makes a w. 44:19
   w. to shee the w.s go wound 158:1
   when ladies . . . rolled along on w.s 183:5
   w.'s kick and the wind's song 254:10
Wheelbarrow: red w. glazed with rain 404:27
When: forgotten to say 'W'. 411:5
Where: w. am I. I don't know 29:2
   w. are they all [all sorts] 342:7
Whereabouts: addresses . . . conceal w. 332:9
Wherefore: w. does he why? 230:11
Whetted: wind's like a w. knife 254:12
Which: impossible to say w. was w. 286:13
   what is w. and w. is what 265:7
Whim: every conviction begins as a w. 56:5
   tempted by a private w. 32:34
   w. of iron 171:4

Whimper: not with a bang but a w. 117:19
Whimpering: go husk this w. thief 213:4
   w. to and fro 210:14
Whin: three w. bushes 202:14
Whine: days of w. and neuroses 188:3
Whip: he brings down the w. 231:2
Whipper-snapper: w. of criticism 376:18
Whipping: ships . . . twirled like w. tops 175:11
Whisker: can't speak above a w. 249:7
   old gentleman with iron-grey w.s 30:29
   w.s . . . of Victorian bushiness 410:24
Whiskies: below par . . . extent of two w. 267:19
Whisky: education and w. being the price it is
392:7
   little nips of w. 9:27
   practical electrician but fond of w. 397:9
   sin of w. 354:1
   w. on their breath 383:1
   w. priest 154:7
Whisper: breathe not a w. 103:23
   fiddled w. music 118:16
   not what he says, but what he w.s 350:21
   there's a w. down in the field 211:21
   w. who dares 264:13
Whispered: w. into your brain 365:11
Whispering: maid and her wight come w. by
163:1
   w. in her mouth 252:13
Whistle: joy or their pain to w. through 370:20
   transcribed it for a penny w. 141:16
   until a shrimp learns to w. 207:12
   w. a happy tune 160:8
   w. while you work 107:2
   you know how to whistle, don't you 21:2
Whistled: bats . . . w. 118:16
Whistling: blackbird w. 358:18
White: America means w. 270:8
   anything that is w. is sweet 353:3
   blacks and w.s working together 350:8
   enough w. lies to ice a cake 15:24
   Gardener in w. 128:10
   God was w. and a man 390:4
   hair as w. as gin 70:18
   he wouldn't have w. servants 291:15
   I wish they were like the W. Rhino 36:7
   lower classes had such w. skins 98:11
   not even red brick, but w. tile 288:3
   O fat w. woman whom nobody loves 93:4
   paradise of crisp w. cities 180:19
   take up the w. man's burden 213:18
   their w. it stays for ever 107:11
   they'll 'elp you a lot with the W. 211:10
   though w. is not my favourite colour 221:14
   whether a w. man likes him 244:1
   w., clear w. inside 210:28
   w. candle in a holy place 64:16
   w. childhood 18:4
   w. cliffs of Dover 60:5
   w. faces like town children 181:15
   w. founts falling in the courts 74:20
   w. heat of this revolution 406:1

W. Horse of the W. Horse Vale 74:8
w. in the moon the long road lies 179:30
w. man . . . looks into the eyes 231:2
w. man's brother, not his brother-in-law 208:9
w. race does not think they belong 357:5
w. which remains on the paper 84:4
whiter than w. 3:27
who will bring w. peace 234:8
you can take W. Horse anywhere 3:30
White House: between Nixon and the W. 205:9
funny thing . . . on the way to the W. 359:4
no whitewash at the W. 280:16
Whited: Is the w. monster 238:10
Whitehall 61:3
Whitelaw, William [later Lord] 368:4
Whiteness: fleeing from himself into w. 14:3
Whiter: w. shade of pale 55:10
Whitest: w. man I know 166:7, 198:23
Whitewash: be strengthened by w. 135:4
no w. at the White House 280:16
whiter than the w. on the wall 12:18
Whither: w. is he withering 230:11
w. so secret away? 103:23
Whitman, Walt: beautiful aged W. 140:6
daintily dressed W. 77:14
viejo hermoso W. 140:6
W. . . . laid end to end 236:11
Whizz-bang: hush! Here comes a w. 399:7
Whizzing: w. them over the net 40:16
Who: w. were you with last night? 145:13
w., whom? We or they? 229:6
w.'s for you and w.'s against you 196:5
Whole: till man made up the w. 417:25
upon the w. . . . much as you said 162:18
who needs a w. girl 53:18
Wholeness: in his w. wholly attending 222:25
Wholesome: it provides . . . w. exercise 168:17
Whoop: devil w.s as he whooped of old 210:7
Whoopee-cushion: speak-your-weight machine
and a w. 232:4
Whore: more like a w.'s than a man's 212:1
second-rate w.s 300:6
theatrical w. of the first quality 159:17
there's one more w. in the world 51:8
we are not political w.s 275:12
w. in the bedroom 159:15
w.s as little as possible 405:12
you can lead a w. to culture 292:10
Whorehouse: virgin territory for w.s 67:5
Why: not to enquire the w. or whither 402:17
w., oh w., do the wrong people travel 94:6
w. did you do that? 134:7
Whyness: w. that makes life worth living 29:13
Wicked: boys are dreaming w. 369:21
mine is being w. 372:27
rather be called w. than vulgar 233:1
w. man in the bathroom cupboard 121:15
w. pack of cards 118:3
Wickedness: w. of the world is so great 51:17
Wide: everything . . . is on w. screen 95:10
so fearfully w. of the mark 300:10

w. screen . . . a bad film twice as bad 147:8
Wide-mouthed: w., long-yarded 151:20
Wider: w. still and w. 37:14
Widow: college w. stood for . . . plenty 253:4
families naturally prefer w.s 336:15
hands of the sons of the W. 213:20
this is the Black W., death 238:9
W. at Windsor 213:19
w. to one safe home 261:9
Wife: and the w. smiles 26:26
didn't want me . . . to have a w. 189:3
don't take your w. into a brothel 149:2
explaining how you sleep with your w. 221:22
health of his w. 88:25
his wife . . . edited him 55:25
like sleeping with someone else's w. 49:8
look in the same manner at your w. 195:6
man who mistook his w. for a hat 331:3
man who's untrue to his w. 18:7
more constant than a w. 317:14
mother to dozens, and nobody's w. 170:27
my w. was immature 6:30
my w. won't let me 228:5
place my w. under a pedestal 6:15
prostitute more moral than a w. 296:18
riding to and from his w. 400:2
start another in my w.'s name 101:13
that's my first w. 372:2
there's my w.; look well at her 355:21
think you've quarrelled with your w. 7:1
through his w.'s belly 4:19
true artist will let his w. starve 344:7
want [your w.] back in a hurry 248:12
why . . . should I get a w. 233:4
w. got the house 6:31
w. is beautiful and his children smart 258:12
w. loves him and [tries] to turn him 77:6
w. or servant to read this book 155:11
w. to tell him what to do 248:11
Wife-swapping: weekend occupation as . . . w.
46:2
Wight: maid and her w. come whispering by
163:1
Wild: I went hunting w. 288:26
last w. Indian of America 301:1
man is a w. animal 100:3
only with beauty wake w. memories 103:1
through what w. centuries 102:17
w. boys innocent as strawberries 369:5
Wilde, Oscar 231:14, 291:6, 380:23
Wilder, Thornton 84:16
Wilder: w. shores of love 43:17
Wilderness: all walking in one kind of w. 161:12
Christ . . . walked in the w. 151:15
left over from the Edwardian W. 288:5
Wilfulness: imitation of human w. 19:11
Wilhelm, Kaiser: *see* Kaiser
Will: immobilize the most resilient w. 40:5
indomitable w. in my heart 173:3
Lord survives the rainbow of His w. 238:11
more w. than wallet 60:14

optimism of the w. 150:19
retrospective is making a w. 272:8
w. is simply the engine in the car 70:5
wrote my w. across the sky in stars 225:3
Will-o'-the-wisp: strange as a w. 259:23
Williams, Kenneth: W. suffers fools 160:24
Williams, Shirley 398:21
compassionate hair . . . go to W. 7:22
Willie: prime minister should have a W. 368:4
Willing: only w. when you compel them 144:14
w. . . . to make a man of . . . you 407:9
Willis, Norman 294:12
Willow: sexton to w. 103:21
Wilmington: Long Man of W. 213:1
Wilson, Harold [later Lord] 58:6, 96:17, 166:12,
186:27
fourteenth Mr W. 109:3
W. . . . twentieth-century citizen 231:19
W. was made of the same stuff 232:1
Wilson, President Woodrow: [W.] looked wiser
when seated 206:12
Win: anybody can w. 2:10
how to w. friends and influence people 68:3
it is his [a general's] job to w. 24:20
leaving all that here can w. us 163:6
nobody w.s unless everybody w.s 355:22
not to w. but to take part 93:8
[writers] w. in the end 299:19
Wind: and the stormy w.s do blow 274:19
answer, my friend, is blowin in the w. 113:8
as the w.s use a crack 370:20
bellies and drags in the w. 415:11
bind it with the blowing w. 122:10
blow down w. instruments 392:9
fine w. is blowing the new direction 222:24
how the w. doth ramm 302:26
it's a warm w., the west w. 254:14
know which way the w. blows 113:20
learned how the w. would sound 370:10
listen instead to the w.'s text 371:2
piffle before the w. 15:5
she calls me in the w.'s soft song 227:21
stand upright in the w.s 45:4
story is like the w. 386:7
wash the w. 118:24
west w., wanton w., wilful w. 345:23
where the w.'s like a whetted knife 254:12
w. blows over the lonely 416:21
w. of change is blowing 245:11
w. of the heavens dance between you 143:6
w. was on the lea 358:2
w.s carry no passports 147:28
w.s of the world, give answer 210:14
Winden: so drängen wir uns plötzlich W. auf 318:4
Window: all those w.s 403:15
don't stand too close to the w. 355:10
face in speech was like a lighted w. 191:3
house of fiction has many w.s 49:2
life as before some full shop w. 190:2
we love the w.s bright 215:17
when I'm cleaning w.s 130:3

Windowpane: rubs its back upon the w.s 117:23
Windsor: Widow at W. 213:19
Windy: we flung us on the w. hill 54:14
Wine: air is like a draught of w. 93:22
beer and w. remain 5:15
days of w. and roses 259:21
drink from the whole w. 415:7
grow excited with w. 416:2
if it [water] doesn't get into the w. 75:14
leave an inch or so of good w. 305:19
make the most lovely home-made w. 164:17
men are like w. 194:23
no w. so wonderful as thirst 261:5
not old, but mellow, like good w. 297:3
red sweet w. of youth 54:10
small people talk about w. 226:18
some are fond of Spanish w. 254:1
too late over the Falernian w. 410:10
turning the red w. of Shiraz into urine 106:12
w. experts are of two classes 244:5
w. just like we used to drink water 221:2
w. they drink in Paradise 74:12
w. upon a foreign tree 369:18
w. was a farce 304:1
Wine-breath: drink from the w. 415:7
Wing: Coming in on a W. and a Prayer 2:6
Creative Endeavour lost her w.s 393:7
flung the span on even w. 94:29
house the muscles working its w.s 159:6
nor knowest'ou w. from tail 303:10
on bent and battered w.s 305:9
only make the right w. strong 338:8
this gives us w.s 177:3
w.s of birds coming home to roost 395:17
Winged: birds of the w. trees 369:9
Wink: sit, w. and play 27:9
Winner: knowing a real w. when I see one 281:5
there are no w.s 71:17
Winning: art of w. without actually cheating
302:19
wear of w. 32:27
Winston: W. [Churchill] is back 81:7
Winter: behind you, like the w. 319:12
civilization's hardest w.s 131:15
do we believe in w.? 325:8
forget not bees in w. 331:7
go south in the w. 118:1
in the wood the furious w., blowing 312:6
it is a w.'s tale 369:19
kill w. with your cannon 5:2
many . . . say that they enjoy the w. 2:5
wie der W. der eben geht 319:12
w. evening settles down 117:34
w. has been sacked for negligence 243:18
w. is an abstract season 53:15
w. is for women 299:24
w. is icummen in 302:26
w.'s big with summer in her womb 331:7
Wire: bite the w. nettin' 20:9
like a bird on a w. 85:12
Wisdom: beginning in w., dying in doubt 238:12

wrecks a w.'s reputation 86:5
Womanhood: became aware of her own w. 223:3
Womanist: w. is to feminist 390:6
Womanly: shall there be w. times 243:10
Womb: alive in the unmeasurable w. 202:13
    free-range w. 56:1
    from the w., remember 354:21
    liquid hands tapped on the w. 368:20
    stepped out of my mother's w. 95:12
    winter's big with summer in her w. 331:7
    w. is all! 318:16
Women: admit other w. are oppressed 325:18
    all fat w. look the same 17:1
    all w. are lesbians 196:11
    and w. even more 372:8
    certain w. should be struck regularly 94:5
    created by men with w. in mind 376:12
    fatigue makes w. talk more 232:16
    female impersonators are w. 35:22
    fisher of men and of w. 108:17
    free half of the human race, the w. 290:5
    Freud felt it should be limited to w. 6:8
    gets off with w. . . . can't get on 227:24
    getting under the feet of w. 119:16
    give w. the vote . . . tax on bachelors 344:2
    I always liked big w. 70:1
    I do not avoid w. 218:6
    I have sung w. in three cities 303:11
    I learned about w. from 'er 211:11
    I married beneath me. All w. do 16:9
    if men knew how w. pass the time 170:9
    in the room the w. come and go 117:22
    keeps getting in bed with w. 324:21
    kill more w. and children more quickly 23:7
    looked on a lot of w. with lust 69:9
    masculine principle in its w. 400:11
    most w. set out to change a man 106:1
    not much in it for w. 395:4
    of all those young w. 303:12
    only fourteen types of w. 242:14
    other w. as though she would inhale 125:24
    poker . . . in a house with w. 404:21
    see w. . . . as loose fitting men 48:20
    she understood as w. often do 68:1
    there should be no mothers, only w. 345:30
    though w. tempt you more than plenty 175:16
    three . . . matter, and all of them are w. 66:28
    touch of flowers and w.'s hands 66:2
    vote . . . means nothing to w. 283:6
    war abhorrent to all real w. 131:19
    why don't w. like me? 130:5
    winter is for w. 299:24
    W., and Champagne, and Bridge 32:32
    w. always want to be our last love 338:18
    W. and Horses and Power and War 209:19
    w. are a sex by themselves 30:11
    w. are brighter than men 237:13
    w. are . . . disgusted with themselves 154:21
    w. are in furious secret rebellion 343:11
    w. are like teeth 367:11
    w. are not so completely enslaved 343:12

w. are not so young as they are painted 30:3
w. . . . as looking-glasses 412:19
w. . . . believe that men were the answer 25:18
w. [come of age] at fifteen 358:5
w. demand both [money and life] 61:28
w. get all excited about nothing 73:18
w. . . . guardians of wisdom 411:10
w. . . . like gentlemen 244:3
w. . . . little idea of how much men hate 154:20
w. more interested . . . after . . . love 145:4
w. never have young minds 103:27
w. see the relationship between objects 131:18
w. weeping, and its towns in terror 17:19
w. who love the same man 30:19
w. who wear ankle socks 36:16
w. would rather be right 277:15
worlds revolve like ancient w. 117:35
young w. should stop being raped 356:3
Won: he marks not that you w. or lost 316:6
Wonder: Boneless W. 79:7
    continual flight from w. 116:3
    moon-washed apples of w. 110:19
    only w. at so grotesque a blunder 37:18
    philosophy is the product of w. 401:6
    submerged sunrise of w. 75:23
    w.s out of natural . . . relationships 193:11
Wonderful: *exactly* as w. as you think 397:19
    falling in love is w. 39:4
    's w.! 's marvellous 142:16
    w. all things considered 242:14
    you've the w. way wid you 151:5
Wonderfulness: blameless w. of God 119:19
Wondering: desert-folk that listened w. 151:15
Woo: like the poet w. the moon 65:2
Wood: culture is no better than its w.s 18:29
    flee the w. and the springs 13:8
    for the w.s against the world 44:7
    if you go down to the w.s today 204:12
    people who love chopping w. 116:6
    they shut the road through the w.s 213:12
    two roads diverged in a w. 135:23
    w. the nails are banged into 295:1
    when these old w.s were young 370:19
    w.s are lovely, dark and deep 136:4
Woodcock: well-shot w. 40:10
Wooden: I wouldn't leave my little w. hut 258:10
    lies about his w. horse 128:16
    open-eyed, w. and childish 238:10
Woodlands: about the w. I will go 179:12
Woodlouse: w. or the maggot's . . . clamour
    151:17
Woodshed: something nasty in the w. 142:24
Woodwork: crawled out of the w. 365:11
Woodworm: w. obligingly held hands 111:8
Woofle: stricken w. like a bull-dog 411:4
Wool: all fur and w. 369:32
Woolf, Virginia 221:25
    W.. 'a beautiful little knitter' 349:3
    Who's Afraid of V.? 4:16
Woolworths: the other [foot] in W. 177:19
Word: all I want is a . . . kind w. 53:3

any old w.s in any old order 374:8

be as a page that aches for a w. 105:17

beautiful w. for doing things tomorrow 342:22

best w.s in the b. order 374:8

beware of . . . 'in other w.s' 269:19

chime of w.s tinkling in the mind 351:7

don't listen to their w.s 115:17

Greeks had a w. for it 4:13

harder to turn w. in to deed 148:8

his w.s like measures of weight 248:18

I don't like the w. [poet] 113:27

I speak the w.s of my love 321:7

largest amount of w.s 79:9

let the w. go forth 204:16

not a w. to Bessie about this 178:6

not Sunday-school w.s 380:17

poets write in w.s 131:16

polite meaningless w.s 416:4

put the w.s down and push them 393:26

recover from the futility of w.s 199:9

schoolboy repeating my w.s by heart 249:2

selection of the best w.s 374:8

short w. and vulgar fractions 80:14

some of them w.s 91:17

sound called w.s may be strung 136:6

tell them . . . that I kept my w. 103:12

ten thousand w.s arousing enthusiasm 60:16

this w. alone shall fit 74:11

threw w.s like stones 355:2

trains of thought from a single w. 200:9

two possible w.s . . . choose the lesser 385:18

until we learn the use of living w.s 103:25

use w.s as they are used 86:19

we need w.s to keep us human 185:6

wished-for w.s 358:15

w. carved on the sill 151:11

w. of a common man 74:25

w. stung him like a mosquito 348:20

w.s are . . . the most powerful drug 214:26

w.s never seen in each other's company 236:11

w.s of the prophet are written 348:2

w.s that open our eyes 201:16

worst thing one can do with w.s 287:14

wrestle with w.s and meanings 116:28

Word-bound: he made poetry seem w. 202:19

Wordless: song was w. 337:4

Wordsworth, William: Cambridge . . . has seen W.
  drunk 180:9

famous for a book on W. 88:15

what daffodils were for W. 221:17

Wore: w. their bodies out with . . . sins 337:8

Work: believed his w. was prayer 389:11

doesn't w. and can't be fired 390:9

extra w. I had when I was a god 172:12

go to w. on an egg 3:11

hard w. never hurt 313:20

haven't had time to w. in weeks 205:19

how can I take an interest in my w. 21:4

humanity is just w. in progress 404:11

I ain't gonna w. on Maggie's Farm 113:17

I like w.: it fascinates me 194:16

idling . . . unless one has plenty of w. 194:9

leisure is w. you volunteer for 320:18

life till my w. is done 177:1

Man . . . grows beyond his w. 357:20

man's w. . . . is a portrait of himself 62:1

Mars a day helps you w. rest and play 3:18

men who simply do the w. 213:11

more people worry than w. 136:15

nice w. if you can get it 142:14

on his bike and looked for w. 366:18

put a man out of w. for a day 206:16

seven make so much w. for each other 293:4

spits on its hands and goes to w. 335:2

tell me how hard you w. 326:6

their w. continueth 212:27

thought my w. was in front of me 28:8

to w. harder than all these 415:6

we pretend to w. and they pretend to pay 11:14

where success comes before w. 337:11

whistle while you w. 107:2

whole day's w. ahead of me 142:18

wonderful change from wives and w. 121:16

w. and pray, live on hay 172:2

w. as if everything depended upon man 354:15

w. expands so as to fill the time 293:2

w. is accomplished by those employees 296:4

w. is much more fun than fun 94:19

w. parallels your life 91:11

w. was like cats were supposed to be 7.18

w. your hands from day to day 246:5

world's w. . . . is done by men 139:2

you're in the wrong line of w. 196:5

Worker: organized w.s . . . are our friends 347:3

sociable w. 31:8

spiritually speaking there are no w.s 23:1

weapon with a w. at each end 11:21

Workhouse: Christmas Day in the w. 348:15

home is the . . . woman's w. 345:5

like morning prayers in a w. 191:14

Working: Heaven will protect the w. girl 350:4

w. on a case of Scotch 34:23

Working-class: best elements of the w. 356:10

deferential w. vote 96:8

inherent in w. life 286:31

into the w. where we belong 287:10

Working classes: wrote about the w. 393:23

Workmanship: art is thoughtful w. 231:5

World: afraid in w. I never made 178:22

America . . . resolved to buy it [the w.] 249:22

anarchy is loosed upon the w. 417:12

artist . . . sits on the edge of the w. 349:12

attachment to the things of this w. 249:19

being by the w. oppressed 418:1

better the w. should perish 328:17

comprehend the w. as a question 218:16

earth is one, but the w. is not 57:6

elevated into the history of the w. 301:7

English-speaking race against the w. 145:12

enquired the cause of the w. 303:12

enthusiasm moves the w. 23:18

ethics does not treat of the w. 408:10

fixed way of looking at the w. 46:12
for the woods against the w. 44:7
frontier . . . as large as the w. 420:4
greatest week in the history of the w. 280:14
hammer to shape the w. 257:17
her glow has warmed the w. 359:7
how sad a place the w. can be 383:12
I carry the w. within me 277:1
I turn and the w. turns 193:16
interesting discovery about the w. 49:9
joined the Navy to see the w. 39:8
laid the w. away 54:10
lie can be half way round the w. 63:12
made it, Ma . . . top of the w. 146:5
many a crime the w. does not discuss 355:26
moral order of the w. 401:11
move out into the open w. 57:20
never sad enough to improve the w. 66:12
no city can stand. Nor the w. 352:19
not a woman of the w. 8:3
one man and his guitar against the w. 83:3
only saved the w. 32:28
our present w. 106:4
reasonable man adapts himself to the w. 345:3
reduce the w. to . . . a chessboard 287:6
reduce the w. to itself 331:1
renounced everything . . . but the w. 274:16
rest of the w. goes on out there 217:3
roll of the w. eastward 163:22
seldom female in a w. of males 299:14
so utterly out of the w.! 300:10
some say the w. will end in fire 135:11
still point of the turning w. 116:26
stop the w.. I want to get off 279:3
symphony must be like the w. 247:6
ten days that shook the w. 314:18
their w. gives way and dies 246:9
third w. 22:14
this is the w., look around you 25:3
way the w. ends 117:19
we knew the w. would not be the same 285:6
what of the w.'s bane? 416:11
whole w. a vast house of assignation 95:17
whole w.s [worl's] in a state of chassis 284:3
wickedness of the w. is so great 51:17
words that open our eyes to the w. 201:16
w. . . . a long way away to Americans 327:18
w. as a moral gymnasium 344:8
w. can only be grasped by action 54:2
w. . . . does not owe us a living 296:14
w. ended yesterday 32:4
w. exists only for [the artist] 256:23
w. has wasted a great deal of time 174:1
w. into which his reader may enter 72:15
w. is a global campus 236:16
w. is a nice place to visit 157:3
w. is disgracefully managed 125:27
w. is divided into two groups 111:6
w. is everything 408:4
w. is half the devil's 369:6
w. is more godless 46:7

w. is . . . more like black and grey 154:12
w. is the sum-total 285:16
w. is your lobster 155:14
w. must be made safe 81:20
w. outside your head 403:5
w. rolls under the long thrust of his heel 181:13
w. . . . safe for democracy 406:19
w. safe for hypocrisy 411:13
w. . . . saved an infinity of misery 397:3
w. would be a . . . field of soya beans 360:19
w.s of reputation 380:19
w.s revolve like ancient women 117:35
years like . . . oxen tread the w. 415:16
World-famous: w. . . . all over Canada 317:11
World-saver: one w. at a time is enough 90:1
Worm: against the w. of death 151:19
I was one of the w.s 28:6
most exclusive w.s 290:12
sister to the fathering w. 368:20
started a w. farm 97:22
tasted two whole w.s 355:17
ten thick w.s his fingers 248:19
voices just can't w. through 299:21
why should a w. turn 84:19
w. slumbering at the root 148:11
w. that never dies 54:13
w.'s eye view 165:15
Worm-eaten: corpses w. in the shade 175:18
Worn: w. to a ravelling 302:12
Worried: to be w. and not to be w. 131:6
Worry: cakes . . . looked green with w. 125:20
more people w. than work 136:15
w. is the interest paid on trouble 186:18
Worrying: what's the use of w.? 14:10
w. the carcase of an old song 371:4
Worse: defend the bad against the w. 101:21
each party is w. than the other 321:27
everything wrong and expects . . . w. 139:4
for fear of finding something w. 32:16
more will mean w. 7:20
Worship: roots lie in ancestor w. 349:16
small w. area at one end 105:5
w. God in his own way 322:23
Worst: constantly prepared for the w. 195:14
do your w. 79:23
exacts a full look at the w. 162:21
expects the w., but makes the w. of it 14:2
like to be told the w. 79:22
so much good in the w. of us 175:1
w. are full of . . . intensity 417:12
w. is yet to come 196:8
Worth: overpaying him but he's w. it 147:25
w. doing it is w. doing badly 77:15
Worthington: daughter on the stage Mrs W. 93:18
Worthless: essentially w. 146:15
Worthwhile: w. setting out 320:17
Wot: w. a lot I got 3:29
Wotthehell: but w. w. oh I should worry 251:3
Would: he w. wouldn't he? 316:8
sorrow for where you . . . w. be 103:1

Wound: as raw as w.s 354:20
   most writers need a w. 8:8
   safe with his w. 337:6
   time w.s all heels 253:22
   world's worst w. 337:7
Wounded: w. surgeon plies the steel 117:1
Wounded Knee: bury my heart at W. 35:12
Wove: w. the thing to a random rhyme 107:10
Wrangling: be silent w. birds 13:8
   good men made evil w. with the evil 273:5
Wrapper: she'd eat the w. 346:19
Wrapping: Christmas through its w. 400:7
Wreck: my brother's w. 118:12
   w.s will surface over the sea 121:14
Wren: little brown w. 100:18
   poor w.s, who simply squawk away 195:5
Wren, Sir Christopher: W. said 37:19
Wrestle: w. with words and meanings 116:28
Wrestled: w. with a . . . card table 372:10
Wretchedness: w. of being rich 350:18
Wrinkled: w. with age and drenched 103:16
Wrist: bird in the hand shits on your w. 87:10
Write: better to w. for yourself 89:1
   do not w. on both sides .. at once 341:10
   I like to w. when I feel spiteful 224:15
   I w. to get out of jail 361:17
   people read because they want to w. 335:26
   played the way I would have liked to w. 202:19
   w. . . . exclusively of others 393:15
   w. for children . . . as for adults 148:9
   w. it, damn you w. it 198:4
   you'd never w. another 395:2
Writer: best prose w. in the US 19:21
   best w. in America 413:9
   dead w. can at least be illustrious 308:1
   expect their w. to redeem humanity 348:17
   function of a w. 88:16
   good reader is rarer than a good w. 47:5
   good w. does not write a large number 49:13
   great w. creates a world of his own 87:14
   great w.s . . . make our fingers burn 388:5
   greatest w. cannot see 19:6
   health of a w. should not be too good 88:4
   if a w. has to rob his mother 123:4
   I'm a w. not a genre 137:6
   it is easy . . . not to be a w. 25:16
   liking a w. and then meeting the w. 216:16
   love being a w. 105:14
   moment when I am no longer a w. 66:3
   more prizes than it has w.s 387:20
   most w.s need a wound 8:8
   no regime has ever loved great w.s 352:18
   one must read all w.s twice 217:8
   only half a w. 87:22
   risk of being spoilt by the w. 308:17
   self-esteem of the quality w. 92:9
   serious w. is not to be confounded 169:15
   soul of the w. flopping 368:16
   successful w. . . . indistinguishable 233:19
   those big-shot w.s 355:11
   true w.s encounter their characters 66:17

when all my good w.s are in jail 147:15
virtues of other w.s 47:2
w. honest about pleasing himself 268:19
w. . . . taken up very late 88:1
w. who interrupts his work 308:18
w. who is the impregnator 400:5
w.s are always selling somebody out 105:21
w.s are the engineers 356:9
w.s aren't exactly people 127:1
w.s could live in their own minds 48:17
w.s don't give prescriptions 1:7
w.s . . . speak the truth 19:18
w.s tend to hang around the edges 299:19
w.s want to be not good but great 387:8
w.s were really people 192:6
Writhe: two parts w. in public 70:6
Writing: end by w. so as not to die 137:5
   God is love but get it in w. 227:13
   great thing about w. plays 299:2
   historians left blanks in their w.s 303:5
   I don't put anything in w. 28:2
   if it sounds like w., I rewrite it 230:13
   if you want to get rich by w. 251:21
   in w. what one accumulates 53:8
   obstacle to professional w. 34:21
   peering beneath my w. arm 151:23
   spend every morning of your life w. 304:10
   thought nothing of her w. 349:3
   we are the w. on your wall 150:3
   what they do . . . isn't w. 67:6
   what's the point of w.? 187:13
   w. about travels is . . . tedious 273:1
   w. always means hiding something 64:7
   w. . . . exposes . . . a yearning 368:15
   w. is . . . a guided dream 46:21
   w. is a sheer paring away 127:25
   w. is like getting married 274:7
   w. is swimming under water 127:24
   w. . . . like running through a field 362:6
   w. songs that voices never shared 348:1
   w. to myself 320:7
   w. was just a preparation 394:15
Written: bathroom walls . . . not been w. 113:4
   history is w. in retrospect 394:8
   look at the w. words 64:5
   w. on the subway walls 348:2
Wrong: about suffering they were never w. 18:2
   anxious to do the w. thing correctly 332:28
   authors could not endure being w. 65:9
   being right when other people are w. 345:34
   blow in the teeth of a w. 254:6
   can't see anything w. 415:3
   climbed the ladder of success w. by w. 398:1
   different kinds of w. 86:18
   eating people is w. 128:3
   everything w. and expects . . . worse 139:4
   fifty million Frenchmen can be w. 156:11
   going w. with confidence 9:12
   he has a right . . . to be w. 364:1
   hundred thousand lemmings can't be w.
     149:29

I know when I'm doing w. 405:8
I want it most when you think I am w. 267:8
if anything can go w. it will 274:15
if I called the w. number 372:15
let the w. cry out 354:20
nets of w. and right 416:16
never find an Englishman in the w. 345:8
no harm in being sometimes w. 206:14
one of them will be w. 91:10
only for telling a man he was w. 85:2
orthodoxy means being w. 76:8
responsible and w. 80:12
right deed for the w. reason 118:23
rightly or wrongly, quite w. 402:3
secretly, like w.s hushed up 288:22
totally and catastrophically w. 132:17
two w.s . . . make a good excuse 364:7
why, oh why, do the w. people travel 94:6
w. at the right moment 46:5
w. from the start 303:13, 371:2
w. place at the right time 391:4
w. sort . . . are always in power 414:2
w. war, at the w. place 50:1
Wronged: not to be w. is to forgo 396:1
Wronging: w. your image 416:23
Wrote: hour with the man who w. it 406:15
w. with action in mind 394:15
Wrung: neck w. like a chicken 399:10

X

X-ray: x. pince-nez 24:12
Xerox: X. makes everybody a publisher 245:4

Y

Y-shaped: to the grave in a Y. coffin 286:5
Yacht: had to sink my y. 127:13
Yale: Y. is terrific 411:15
Yard: last y.s are run alone 266:16
y. . . . 3.37 inches longer 92:2
Yarn: all I ask is a merry y. 254:12
Yawn: even the grave y.s for him 377:3
ten words causing people to y. 60:16
too tired to y. 103:24
when a book is boring, they y. openly 348:17
Year: anything . . . happening that y. 403:18
in the juvescence of the y. 117:12
man who stood at the gate of the y. 165:12
nor the y.s condemn 43:2
sung in the old y.s 370:19
thousand light y.s from the Vatican 83:15
undone y.s 288:26
worst time of the y. for a journey 117:20
wrong for y.s 18:22
y.s like great black oxen 415:16
y.s of l'entre deux guerres 117:2

y.s teach us patience 366:16
y.s that the locust hath eaten 187:1
you wait for about a y. 91:3
Yearning: all writing . . . exposes . . . a y. 368:15
learning, earning and y. 269:14
while your hearts are y. 129:21
Yeats, William Butler: he thinks he's Y. 121:13
Y., . . . brother of the more famous Jack 376:9
Yell: y. if you like 43:8
Yelled: y. like bloody hell 198:19
Yellow: how y. everything looks 192:16
one-eyed y. idol to the north 166:6
paved with y. brick 27:11
under great y. flags and banners 348:24
we all live in a y. submarine 230:10
y. fog that rubs its back 117:23
Yellow-eyed: y. hawk of the mind 416:12
Yellow River: diverted the Y. 305:16
Yeoman: lie down young y. 179:14
Yes: answer y. without having asked 65:10
don't say y. until I've finished 420:5
expecting the answer 'Y., but –' 226:12
I did answer Yes to someone 160:6
if an ambassador says y. 290:4
like an enormous y. 221:8
y. Minister 96:18
y., we have no bananas 347:12
Yesterday: art of keeping up with y. 251:6
better y. 99:1
ethics . . . are always y. 53:20
got stuck fast in y. 103:10
have not yet got home y. 10:24
Mother died today. Or, maybe, y. 65:24
y.'s cold mutton into tomorrow's lamb 256:4
y.'s men 219:2
Yid: let's put the id back in y. 325:9
Yoghurt: between the milk and the y. 270:19
difference between Los Angeles and y. 365:12
York, Duke and Duchess of 296:21
Young: ale from the Country of the Y. 416:13
angry y. man 123:8, 293:16
as a y. man you knock him down 377:1
as y. as ever I did 35:6
good sense to banish y. 311:3
I, being y. and foolish 416:3
I have been y. 44:10
I'll die y. 57:5
much did I rage when y. 418:1
Oh as I was y. and easy 369:1
only the y. die good 171:5
put off being y. until you retire 221:10
sculpture is not for y. men 50:11
so y., and already so unknown 293:17
stay y. inside 85:9
they try to tell us we're too y. 102:11
very y. at a very old time 337:14
voices of y. people 350:14
when these woods were y. 370:19
while I am y. and lusty 290:11
women are not so y. as they are painted 30:3
women never have y. minds 103:27

y. and inexperienced house 194:12
y., I had not given a penny 415:9
y. fogey 294 21
y. get stronger 270:7
y. have aspirations 332:21
y. in one another's arms 417:9
y. man married is a y. man marred 212:28
y. man who has not wept 335:3
y. men read chronicles 76:20
you can be y. without money 404:14
Younger: almost never had been y. 357:11
y. people than me at his disposal 308:6
y. than that now 113:19
Youngman: let me die a y.'s death 243:15
Yourself: if you are on good terms with y. 344:25
Youth: anything to do with y. clubs 353:15
caught our y. 55:2
forties are the old age of y. 173:22
in this way I spent y. 221:12
laugh uproariously in their y. 54:20
red sweet wine of y. 54:10
strong disposition in y. 304:4

y. must inherit the tribulation 177:7
y. of his own generation 127:17
y. would be an ideal state 15:17
Yucatan: I had an aunt in Y. 33:7
Yukon: Law of the Y. 341:19

Z

Zebra: z. synchronized with the railings 193:9
z. without stripes 407:19
Zero-rated: enabling the pin to be z. 92:17
Zestfully: so z. canst thou sing 162:9
Zion: in Z. at their ease 213:22
round Z. of the water bead 369:14
Zipless: z. fuck is the purest thing 197:1
Zipper: forget to pull your z. down 324:12
Zoo: human z. 270:5
Zugvögel: sind nicht wie die Z. verständigt 318:4
Zürich: I learned three things in Z. 361:9
little gnomes of Z. 405:16